CASES AND MATERIALS ON
EMPLOYMENT DISCRIMINATION AND EMPLOYMENT LAW
Third Edition

By

Samuel Estreicher
Dwight D. Opperman Professor of Law
New York University

Michael C. Harper
Barreca Labor Relations Scholar and Professor of Law
Boston University

AMERICAN CASEBOOK SERIES®

THOMSON
WEST

Mat #40698237

American Casebook Series and West Group are trademarks
registered in the U.S. Patent and Trademark Office.

© West, a Thomson business, 2000, 2004
© 2008 Thomson/West
  610 Opperman Drive
  St. Paul, MN 55123
  1–800–313–9378

Printed in the United States of America

ISBN: 978–0–314–18975–2

 *TEXT IS PRINTED ON 10% POST
CONSUMER RECYCLED PAPER*

To my little wing and our life together...

SE

To Marvis, silver to gold

MH

*

Preface

This text is the third edition of a work that grew out of our initial text, Cases and Materials on the Law Governing the Employment Relationship. We retain and update all of the chapters from the second edition including the chapters on the Fair Labor Standards Act (FLSA), the Employment Retirement Income Security Act (ERISA), and post-termination restraints on employees, that we added in the second edition.

We are also publishing this year two shorter books drawn from this larger text. One of these focuses on employment discrimination law, while the other covers employment law. We recognize that many instructors desire leaner texts that separate the civil rights orientation of traditional employment discrimination courses from the employee benefits and contractual orientation of employment law offerings.

We continue to believe that the traditional subject matter of the employment discrimination course is best integrated into the employment and labor curriculum if presented as part of a broader set of legal restraints that have been placed on employers' basic personnel decisions. We therefore offer instructors the option of designing a broader course out of the materials included in this larger text.

We understand that this book cannot be taught from cover to cover in one three-hour semester course. The book remains modular and supportive of several different kinds of courses. First, an instructor might use the book as a basis for two three-hour courses: a first semester course on employment discrimination law, drawn primarily from Part Two and with some supplementation for the treatment of procedural issues in Part Six; and a second semester course on Employment Law that focuses on the other state and federal wrongful termination (and post-termination) law covered in Parts Three and Four as well as the minimum terms legislation treated in Part Five. The second semester's study would be enhanced by the perspectives gained during the first semester, but the instructor need not make the first semester a prerequisite for the second course.

The text can also serve as the basis for a one-semester course. Such a course, taught for most of two decades by one of us, can cover most (though possibly not all) of the discrimination chapters, as well as a selection of chapters from other sections of the book. To offer one of many possible combinations, an instructor might treat chapters two (the race paradigm), five (sex), six (age), seven (disability), and ten (anti-retaliation), to provide a comprehensive perspective on status discrimination regulation, and then offer comparisons to other forms of statutory and common law regulation by coverage of chapters eleven (public policy and whistleblower protections), and twelve (contractual, wrongful discharge law). The course might conclude with a selection of procedural issues in Part Six, including preemption and the trend toward arbitration.

The notes and questions that follow the principal readings are designed to expose the student to the emerging cutting-edge issues in the particular area. The note material is intended primarily as a teaching tool rather than as a vehicle for expressing our particular viewpoints. In this text, as well as in earlier editions, we have not tried to reach complete consensus concerning the wording and the balance of each of our notes. Although we both engaged in close and extensive editing of all chapters, each chapter in this book was the primary responsibility of only one of us, and that author had the final authority to determine its contents.

In order to avoid excessive use of asterisks in our editing of cases and secondary material, we indicate ellipses only when our excerpt deletes substantive material from the original text. We do not typically indicate the fact that the excerpt we use may come from the middle of an opinion, or that its ending does not correspond with the end of the opinion. Although we have preserved case citations where appropriate, so that students can check the court's authorities on their own, we have not included references to prior lower court opinions in the same case or to trial or appellate records and briefs or internal references to majority or dissenting opinions. We also often do not include subheadings. These omissions, made in the interest of readability, are not always indicated in our excerpts. For Supreme Court decisions in which a majority of the Justices have not joined a single opinion, we include both the plurality and important concurring opinions. As a general matter, however, we do not indicate the position taken by every single member of the Court.

We wish to again express our debt to our spouses, Aleta G. Estreicher and Marvis Ann Knospe, and to our children, Michael Simon Estreicher, Jessica Aronson, Hannah Rose Estreicher, and Oliver Louis and Nicholas Skelly Harper. We appreciate the research assistance of many students, especially Michelle L. Booth (B.U.), Jon Bourgault (N.Y.U.), Sandra K. Davis (B.U.), Chris Garafalo (N.Y.U.), Celinda Gebhardt (B.U.), Lauryn Gouldin (N.Y.U.), Megan Lewis (N.Y.U.), Ryan McCarthy (B.U.), Luke McLaughlin (N.Y.U.), Terence P. Noonan (B.U.), Mark Seidel (N.Y.U.), and Murshed M. Zaheed (B.U.); and the secretarial assistance of Rosetta Abraham (N.Y.U.). Finally, we note that this test benefitted from the comments of students and instructors who used our predecessor texts.

We thank the copyright holders identified below for permission to reprint excerpts from the following material:

Jay M. Feinman, The Development of the Employment At Will Rule, 20 Am.J.Legal Hist. 118 (1976), copyright © 1976 by the American Journal of Legal History.

Richard Epstein, In Defense of the Contract at Will, 51 U.Chi.L.Rev. 947 (1984), copyright © 1984 by the University of Chicago Law Review.

Paul C. Weiler, Governing the Workplace: The Future of Labor and Employment Law, copyright © 1990 by the Harvard University Press.

Samuel Estreicher, Unjust Dismissal Laws: Some Cautionary Notes, 33 Am.J.Comp.L. 310 (1985), copyright © 1985 by the American Journal of Comparative Law.

Alfred W. Brumrosen, The Binding Effect of Affirmative Action Guidelines, 1 The Lab.Lawy. 261 (1985), copyright © 1985 by the American Bar Association.

John T. Addison and Barry T. Hirsch, The Economic Effects of Employment Regulation: What Are the Limits?, in Government Regulation of the Employment Relationship (Bruce E. Kaufman ed., 1997), copyright © 1997 by Industrial Relations Research Association.

Samuel Estreicher and Stewart J. Schwab, Foundations of Labor and Employment Law, copyright © 2000 by Foundation Press.

*

Summary of Contents

Table of Contents

———————

PART THREE. PROTECTING SOCIALLY VALUED ACTIVITY

*

Table of Cases

The principal cases are in bold type. Cases cited or discussed in the text are roman type. References are to pages. Cases cited in principal cases and within other quoted materials are not included.

*

Table of Authorities

Bold type indicates principal selections

CASES AND MATERIALS ON
EMPLOYMENT DISCRIMINATION AND EMPLOYMENT LAW

Third Edition

*

INTRODUCTION

Frank Tannenbaum opened his 1951 work, A Philosophy of Labor, with the observation: "We have become a nation of employees" increasingly dependent on the job as the critical resource of our lives. The continuing contraction of American farming and other self-employment makes this even truer today. For most members of modern society, no public relationship is more important than their relation to the entity for which they work or would like to work. This book is an introductory exploration of the role of law in regulating the employment relationship.

Organization of the Book

The exploration focuses on the legal rules governing the commencement, development and termination of employment relationships. It does so by considering how American law affects decisions to hire, promote, compensate, otherwise reward, discipline, and fire employees. The opening chapter (Part I) considers the threshold coverage question whether the individual seeking the protection of the employment laws is an employee warranting that protection, and the related issue of whether claims may be asserted against not only the immediate employer but other firms that have an effective influence over employment terms and conditions. Part II discusses laws designed to protect individuals from employment decisions that affect them unfairly because of an immutable status (such as race, sex, age and disability) apparently irrelevant to their productivity as employees. Part III considers the extent to which the law prevents employers from discouraging activity that our society for one reason or another highly values or seeks to protect, perhaps because unrestrained employer authority may entail adverse effects on third-party interests. Part IV explores our society's regulatory efforts, both public and private, to eliminate or curb employment decisions that seem unfair, arbitrary or intrusive. This part of the book looks at evolving legal developments in the legislatures and courts to move away from the "at will" premise of U.S. employment contracts: that absent an express contract for a definite term, the employment relationship can be terminated by either part at any time, with or without a nondiscriminatory cause. In Part V, we consider a form of employment regulation that, while prominent in continental Europe, has played only a limited role in this country: the enactment of "minimum terms" laws to establish regulatory floors for the private negotiation of employment contracts. The final chapters of the book (Part VI) take up the procedural design of regulatory systems for employment relationships and questions of coordination of multiple systems.

Identifying the Purposes of Regulation

Some might suppose that the project of this book should primarily consist of determining how the force of law can be best employed to most

1

quickly and effectively eliminate undesirable employer decisionmaking. Questions of regulatory efficacy are certainly an important part of this book. However, they do not exhaust the range of issues that careful students of the law in this area must confront.

We need, initially, to go beyond a statement of generally laudatory goals to define as precisely as possible the purposes of employment laws. Precise definition can illuminate critical regulatory choices. Social advancement of unfairly treated status groups, for instance, may require more than the elimination of employment decisions motivated by hostility or even lack of equal regard for members of the groups. Are all employment decisions that are not directly related to firm productivity and that have an unequal effect on particular groups to be prohibited? Similarly, the regulation of employer decisions affecting socially valued activity requires a consideration of the kinds of activity that should be protected, and why. For instance, should the law's protection be confined to employee speech on matters of public interest or are there circumstances in which speech on matters of private interest also should be insulated from employer power? A similar elaboration is required for regulations that seek to curb arbitrary and intrusive decisionmaking by employers. Is the purpose of such rules to protect longevity of service, to check supervisory judgments, or to displace private judgments entirely with a regulated system akin to the civil service laws governing public employment? "Minimum terms" laws also must be evaluated in terms of their underlying purpose to avoid undesirable over-and under-regulation.

Assessing the Justifications for Regulation

Thorough analysis of our society's regulation of the employment relationship does not end with a determination of how precisely defined goals can be most effectively achieved through regulation. We also must confront the more fundamental question of whether such goals should or need to be achieved through particular forms of legal intervention rather than through passive reliance on market forces to curb undesirable behavior.

1. *Traditional Economic Model of Labor Markets*. To provide a basis for assessing this question, economists employ a model of individual decisionmaking that assumes that human beings, and the economic entities that they control, are rational actors who know their true preferences and generally act to further those preferences, never trading something that is more valuable to them for something less valuable. This model, as conventionally formulated, also weighs equally everyone's preferences, regardless of their content, and defines social welfare as the aggregation of individual welfare decisions. It is then argued that, given any particular distribution of wealth, human satisfaction can be maximized by permitting unregulated free trading. Free trading is said to ensure that any good, including rights to engage in or be protected from particular activity, will be allocated to those parties who value it most highly, and hence will make most productive use of that good. Regulation is thus said to be presumptively undesirable: it will tend to prevent

trades from being made that would further the preferences of the contracting parties, or otherwise distort the outcomes that would be reached by private bargaining.

Applied to the employment context, this theory argues for allowing an employer to purchase, say, the right to be free of restrictions in personnel decisionmaking by giving its employees some good in exchange which is more valuable to them than a right to be treated fairly, but is less valuable to the employer than the right to act with complete discretion. Such exchanges, because they reflect actual preferences, will presumably make both the employer and the employees better off than arrangements that prevent the parties from acting on their preferences. Regulation that seeks to curb arbitrary treatment of employees can only prevent such mutually beneficial exchanges from occurring in labor markets and thus can only detract from social welfare.

The same analysis follows for any form of status or protected activity discrimination. For example, Gary Becker of the University of Chicago and other economists have posited that some employers may have a "taste for discrimination," either because the employers personally hold such preferences or because they defer to the preferences of their existing employees or customers. If all preferences are to be considered equally worthy, the argument goes, the satisfaction of even such "tastes" should be part of a welfare calculus.

Economists also may argue that competitive market forces adequately check preferences that are irrational in the sense that they obstruct maximization of profit. For instance, a discriminatory firm artificially limits the available supply of workers bidding for jobs and hence pays a premium for the workers it does employ. Nondiscriminatory competitor firms will then emerge to take advantage of the potentially lower labor costs and to offer the same product or service more cheaply. Similarly, a firm intent on treating its employees arbitrarily will be vulnerable to competition from other firms that fairly reward productive employee behavior and fairly penalize unproductive behavior. The economic argument concludes that firms that do not discriminate or treat their employees arbitrarily will earn higher profits and be able to raise more capital for expansion. Firms that persist in engaging in unfair practices in the long run will be driven from the market.

2. *Questioning the Premises of the Model.* One form of counterargument is to question whether the assumptions underlying this economic model are applicable to the employment relationship. Several conditions are assumed: (1) employment decisions are made in the context of competitive markets, where there are many firms bidding for workers and many workers bidding for jobs; (2) such decisions are based on perfect knowledge, in that the parties know their preferences, can accurately value the various goods being exchanged, and are fully aware of alternative opportunities; (3) the parties to the relationship are mobile, in that if either party is dissatisfied with the proposed bargain, it can readily terminate the relationship and seek more advantageous

terms elsewhere; and (4) there are no significant transaction costs to the making of beneficial trades.

   a. *The Market for Human Capital.* It may be argued that the market for human labor does not always satisfy these conditions. First, in some settings employers may enjoy a measure of monopoly (or monopsony) power, where they are relatively insulated from product market competition or they function in somewhat isolated labor markets free of any real competition for the services of their employees. "Internal labor market" considerations often may be more important to employers and employees than external market forces; where both parties have made investments in firm-specific training, the employment relationship may be better viewed as a "bilateral monopoly." Second, trades may be distorted when one or both parties have less than perfect information about what they are trading. Employees may not, for instance, understand what it means to have no contractual protection against arbitrary discharge, because they make erroneous assumptions about what employers lawfully may do or fail accurately to assess the probability that they may be terminated unjustifiably. Third, mobility in labor markets may be questionable. Individuals often find it difficult to uproot their families in order to take advantage of better opportunities elsewhere. Moreover, a variety of forces, including investments in firm-specific training, bonuses for outstanding past services, and pension and other fringe-benefit policies, may bind the employee to the job. Firms often pay workers more than would be required by supply and demand forces because they want to attract and retain workers willing to compete to work more productively to avoid the risk of losing especially attractive employment. Finally, while the transactions costs of contract-making are, on one level, relatively low in the employment setting, the parties at the outset of a relationship may find it difficult to talk about and bargain for certain terms, such as job-security provisions governing the termination of the relationship. These aspects of the real economic world all suggest that there may be situations where private bargains between employers and employees do not in fact reflect a mutually advantageous exchange.

   b. *"Agency Costs" of Firms.* Aspects of the real economic world also suggest that market forces might not be as effective in checking employer practices that have an adverse effect on firm productivity as a simple economic model might posit. Thus, while some discriminatory or arbitrary treatment of employees by agents of a firm may detract from firm profits, the costs to the firm in lost productivity may be lower than the costs entailed in identifying and eliminating such treatment. It may be a long time before firms see a pattern of terminations which may create a basis for questioning the judgments of particular supervisors. Hence, economically rational owners of the firm who otherwise would be inclined to minimize unfair practices do not in fact do so because of the costs of controlling prejudiced or arbitrary agents.

   c. *Attenuated Product Market Competition.* Moreover, given the many market imperfections in the real world, the short run in which inefficient employment practices persist can become quite a long period for many employers and their employees. Any employer with a monopolistic position in its product market, for instance, would only detract from its monopoly profits by continuing inefficient discrimination; it would not be threatened with extinction. Market imperfections created by other government regulations, often in place perhaps for good independent justifications, might also serve to perpetuate inefficient discrimination. Minimum wage legislation, for example, may make it more difficult for nondiscriminatory employers to reduce their relative labor costs by hiring the disfavored and thereby undercutting the prices of discriminatory employers. Similarly, "prevailing wage" requirements for federal construction projects may affirmatively erect barriers to entry by new firms. Also, because of the tendency of firms to adopt the personnel practices of other firms, product market competition may have to be quite vigorous before its influence filters down to the personnel department. Regulation might therefore be justified as a means of accelerating the elimination of persistent, albeit inefficient, employment practices.

d. *Do All Preferences Count Equally?* Other arguments against the economic model question whether social welfare should be computed by an aggregation of individual welfare decisions. Society collectively may be quite willing to overcome scruples about judging some human preferences less worthy than others. We may, for instance, wish to exclude the satisfaction of human "tastes" for at least some forms of discrimination from the welfare calculus. Indeed, one role of law might be to reshape the preferences of even a majority of citizens in accord with deeper (or at least higher) social values. The purpose of regulation might also be avowedly redistributive, in contrast with an economic argument that accepts the existing distribution of wealth and bargaining power as a given. Regulation might be premised either on a society's judgments that the marginal satisfaction of the desires of some of its less fortunate members is worth more than the marginal satisfaction of some of its more fortunate, or on a recognition that employers often can afford to bid more for what is actually worth more to workers. Also, the simplified economic model presented above ignores the effects of trades on third parties such as the general community. To the extent the parties to an agreement do not bear fully the costs of their activity, there may be a need for the law's intervention. Thus, some regulation of employment decisionmaking may be justified by the benefits it ultimately provides to society, rather than to the parties directly affected.

Such arguments suggest that society might wish to eliminate some discriminatory or arbitrary preferences even when they contribute to firm productivity. First, some discriminatory employment practices may be consistent with profitability only because of the prejudice of employees or customers. Members of socially favored groups may find it distasteful to work alongside, or especially under the supervision, of members of socially disfavored groups. If so, the socially favored groups might demand a wage premium which could increase a nondiscriminating employer's labor costs and reduce its profits. Potential customers also might find certain goods or services less valuable if they are dispensed by members of disfavored social groups. If so, the customers will be willing to pay less and profits could be reduced. Our society, however, may no more wish to include the discriminatory tastes of employees and customers in its welfare calculus than when similar tastes are indulged in by employers. As suggested, even if a prejudice pervades the culture, we may wish to attempt to transform that culture by forcing ourselves to live up to our higher values.

Second, we may wish to prohibit reliance on some generalizations or stereotypes that are sufficiently accurate to be efficient, because their use is nonetheless unfair to many individuals or will have a cumulative deleterious social impact. An employer, for instance, might rationally conclude that membership in a particular social group or engagement in a particular activity is a good predictor of a job applicant's potential productivity and indeed may be less costly than other means of assessing qualifications. Our society might insist, however, that such a screening device not be used because it penalizes even individuals who would be productive, and either aggravates the social disabilities of all members of the excluded group or discourages the activity even more than is warranted by productivity concerns.

More generally, as suggested above, we might wish to regulate the employment relationship either to reduce third-party effects or to redistribute wealth to employees. Profit maximization may serve neither of these goals. An employer who threatens to discharge an employee for disclosing the firm's price-fixing activity to public authorities in violation of the antitrust laws may be acting as a rational profit-maximizer; society may, however, wish to encourage such disclosure to avert harmful impact on the community. Similarly, from the standpoint of the individual firm, it may be quite rational to discharge older workers who, because of seniority-based compensation policies, are paid at a level higher than the value they currently contribute to the firm; society may, however, wish to bolster the economic position of older workers because of the difficulties they confront in securing alternative employment. Even the intentional arbitrary discharge of easily replaced unskilled workers may be efficient for firms that wish to maintain unquestioned control of their workplace; but society may want to prevent such practices to provide a minimum level of dignity to all its workers.

Assessing the Costs of the Regulation

Analysis cannot stop, however, with a determination that some form of regulation to address a particular undesirable employment practice is warranted. The student must also consider the appropriateness of the particular systems of regulation that have been adopted, which in turn requires consideration of the costs of these systems as well as their benefits.

Administrative, Litigation and Error Costs. The costs of regulation include the administrative, litigation and error costs of enforcement.

This book should enable the reader to assess the efficacy of alternative systems of implementation. The sixth and final part of the text is devoted to a consideration of the processes by which the substantive regulations are to be achieved. Moreover, a consideration of the costs of enforcement and the merits of alternative schemes is a necessary part of the analysis of each area of substantive law treated below.

Over-Enforcement? Other costs of regulation also need to be treated, however. One important set are the costs of over-enforcement. Legal presumptions provide a good example. The most effective way to eliminate a particular practice may be to reduce the difficulty of proving that practice has occurred by establishing such presumptions. For instance, as a means of facilitating challenges to employment decisions motivated by prejudice against a particular status group, the law might erect a conclusive presumption that employment practices having a significant adverse effect on members of that group are tainted by prejudice. Such a presumption may effectively extirpate prejudicial decisionmaking; but it may also encourage other kinds of inefficient decisionmaking, such as absolute preferences for less qualified members of the particular status group, that we may not wish to encourage. Even rules precisely tailored to cover only that which we want to proscribe may have some over-enforcement costs, as employers attempt to insure against costly litigation by compromising otherwise efficient practices.

"Backlash" Costs? Two other kinds of costs of regulation ought also to be noted in this introduction. Both might be described as backlash costs. Political backlash can occur when those who are not included in groups directly benefited by the regulation, and who may even be adversely affected by it, react against not only the regulation, but also its beneficiaries. Economic backlash can occur when employers forced to provide benefits to certain groups of workers respond by denying other benefits or even employment. For example, employers faced with costly litigation or regulatory oversight when they have members of a statutorily protected group on their payroll may seek to avoid those difficulties by not hiring members of the group, confident that lawsuits are not likely to be brought. Employers may even move work sites to towns or regions of the country where they are less likely to have job applications from members of a group more likely to generate litigation. Such a reaction may be economically rational, and depending on the nature of the labor market and the content and enforcement of other laws, a predictable response to regulation.

Part One

THE EMPLOYMENT RELATIONSHIP

The laws dealt with in this book involve regulations of the employment relationship. With a few notable exceptions like 42 U.S.C. § 1981 (which bars racial and certain forms of national origin discrimination in the making of any contract), these laws protect individuals only if they are employees of an employer. Customers or vendors of the employer are not regulated. Nor are independent contractors who may provide services for the employer that resemble services provided by undisputed employees. Defining the employment relationship, moreover, has become increasingly important with the growth of temporary agencies, manpower services companies and telecommuting. Our first chapter thus deals with the threshold questions of whether the individual seeking the law's protection is in an employment relationship, and if so, with which employers.

Chapter One

DEFINING EMPLOYEE STATUS

A. EMPLOYEES OR INDEPENDENT CONTRACTORS?

NATIONWIDE MUTUAL INSURANCE COMPANY v. DARDEN
Supreme Court of the United States, 1992.
503 U.S. 318, 112 S.Ct. 1344, 117 L.Ed.2d 581.

JUSTICE SOUTER delivered the opinion of the Court.

In this case we construe the term "employee" as it appears in § 3(6) of the Employee Retirement Income Security Act of 1974 (ERISA), 88 Stat. 834, 29 U.S.C. § 1002(6), and read it to incorporate traditional agency law criteria for identifying master-servant relationships.

I

From 1962 through 1980, respondent Robert Darden operated an insurance agency according to the terms of several contracts he signed with petitioners Nationwide Mutual Insurance Co. et al. Darden promised to sell only Nationwide insurance policies, and, in exchange, Nationwide agreed to pay him commissions on his sales and enroll him in a company retirement scheme called the "Agent's Security Compensation Plan" (Plan). The Plan consisted of two different programs: the "Deferred Compensation Incentive Credit Plan," under which Nationwide annually credited an agent's retirement account with a sum based on his business performance, and the "Extended Earnings Plan," under which Nationwide paid an agent, upon retirement or termination, a sum equal to the total of his policy renewal fees for the previous 12 months.

Such were the contractual terms, however, that Darden would forfeit his entitlement to the Plan's benefits if, within a year of his termination and 25 miles of his prior business location, he sold insurance for Nationwide's competitors. The contracts also disqualified him from receiving those benefits if, after he stopped representing Nationwide, he ever induced a Nationwide policyholder to cancel one of its policies.

9

In November 1980, Nationwide exercised its contractual right to end its relationship with Darden. A month later, Darden became an independent insurance agent and, doing business from his old office, sold insurance policies for several of Nationwide's competitors. The company reacted with the charge that his new business activities disqualified him from receiving the Plan benefits to which he would have been entitled otherwise. Darden then sued for the benefits, which he claimed were nonforfeitable because already vested under the terms of ERISA. 29 U.S.C. § 1053(a). Darden brought his action under 29 U.S.C. § 1132(a), which enables a benefit plan "participant" to enforce the substantive provisions of ERISA. The Act elsewhere defines "participant" as "any employee or former employee of an employer ... who is or may become eligible to receive a benefit of any type from an employee benefit plan...." § 1002(7). Thus, Darden's ERISA claim can succeed only if he was Nationwide's "employee," a term the Act defines as "any individual employed by an employer." § 1002(6).

* * *

II

We have often been asked to construe the meaning of "employee" where the statute containing the term does not helpfully define it. Most recently we confronted this problem in *Community for Creative Non-Violence v. Reid*, 490 U.S. 730, 104 L. Ed. 2d 811, 109 S. Ct. 2166 (1989), a case in which a sculptor and a nonprofit group each claimed copyright ownership in a statue the group had commissioned from the artist. The dispute ultimately turned on whether, by the terms of § 101 of the Copyright Act of 1976, 17 U.S.C. § 101, the statue had been "prepared by an employee within the scope of his or her employment." Because the Copyright Act nowhere defined the term "employee," we unanimously applied the "well established" principle that

> "where Congress uses terms that have accumulated settled meaning under ... the common law, a court must infer, unless the statute otherwise dictates, that Congress means to incorporate the established meaning of these terms.... In the past, when Congress has used the term 'employee' without defining it, we have concluded that Congress intended to describe the conventional master-servant relationship as understood by common-law agency doctrine. * * *"

While we supported this reading of the Copyright Act with other observations, the general rule stood as independent authority for the decision. So too should it stand here. ERISA's nominal definition of "employee" as "any individual employed by an employer," 29 U.S.C. § 1002(6), is completely circular and explains nothing. As for the rest of the Act, Darden does not cite, and we do not find, any provision either giving specific guidance on the term's meaning or suggesting that construing it to incorporate traditional agency law principles would thwart the congressional design or lead to absurd results. Thus, we adopt a common-law test for determining who qualifies as an "employee" under ERISA, a test we most recently summarized in *Reid*:

> "In determining whether a hired party is an employee under the general common law of agency, we consider the hiring party's right to control the manner and means by which the product is accomplished. Among the other factors relevant to this inquiry are the skill required; the source of the instrumentalities and tools; the location of the work; the duration of the relationship between the parties; whether the hiring party has the right to assign additional projects to the hired party; the extent of the hired party's discretion over when and how long to work; the method of payment; the hired party's role in hiring and paying assistants; whether the work is part of the regular business of the hiring party; whether the hiring party is in business; the provision of employee benefits; and the tax treatment of the hired party." 490 U.S. at 751–752 (footnotes omitted)."

Cf. Restatement (Second) of Agency § 220(2) (1958) (listing nonexhaustive criteria for identifying master-servant relationship); Rev. Rul. 87–41, 1987–1 Cum. Bull. 296, 298–299 (setting forth 20 factors as guides in determining whether an individual qualifies as a common-law "employee" in various tax law contexts). Since the common-law test contains "no shorthand formula or magic phrase that can be applied to find the answer, ... all of the incidents of the relationship must be assessed and weighed with no one factor being decisive." *NLRB v. United Ins. Co. of America*, 390 U.S. at 258.

In taking its different tack, the Court of Appeals cited *NLRB v. Hearst Publications, Inc.*, 322 U.S. [111,] 120–129 [(1944)], and *United States v. Silk*, 331 U.S. [704,] 713 [(1947)], for the proposition that "the content of the term 'employee' in the context of a particular federal statute is 'to be construed "in the light of the mischief to be corrected and the end to be attained." ' " *Darden*, 796 F.2d at 706, quoting *Silk*, *supra*, at 713, in turn quoting *Hearst*, *supra*, at 124. But *Hearst* and *Silk*, which interpreted "employee" for purposes of the National Labor Relations Act and Social Security Act, respectively, are feeble precedents for unmooring the term from the common law. In each case, the Court read "employee," which neither statute helpfully defined,[4] to imply something broader than the common-law definition; after each opinion, Congress amended the statute so construed to demonstrate that the usual common-law principles were the keys to meaning. * * *

* * * At oral argument, Darden tried to subordinate *Reid* to *Rutherford Food Corp. v. McComb*, 331 U.S. 722, 91 L. Ed. 1772, 67 S. Ct. 1473 (1947), which adopted a broad reading of "employee" under the Fair Labor Standards Act (FLSA). And amicus United States, while rejecting

---

4. The National Labor Relations Act simply defined "employee" to mean (in relevant part) "any employee." 49 Stat. 450 (1935). The Social Security Act defined the term to "include," among other, unspecified occupations, "an officer of a corporation." 49 Stat. 647.

Darden's position, also relied on *Rutherford Food* for the proposition that, when enacting ERISA, Congress must have intended a modified common-law definition of "employee" that would advance, in a way not defined, the Act's "remedial purposes." * * * But *Rutherfood Food* supports neither position. The definition of "employee" in the FLSA evidently derives from the child labor statutes, see *Rutherford Food, supra,* at 728, and, on its face, goes beyond its ERISA counterpart. While the FLSA, like ERISA, defines an "employee" to include "any individual employed by an employer," it defines the verb "employ" expansively to mean "suffer or permit to work." 52 Stat. 1060, § 3, codified at 29 U.S.C. §§ 203(e),(g). This latter definition, whose striking breadth we have previously noted, *Rutherford Food, supra,* at 728, stretches the meaning of "employee" to cover some parties who might not qualify as such under a strict application of traditional agency law principles. ERISA lacks any such provision, however, and the textual asymmetry between the two statutes precludes reliance on FLSA cases when construing ERISA's concept of "employee." * * *

III

While the Court of Appeals noted that "Darden most probably would not qualify as an employee" under traditional agency law principles, *Darden, supra,* at 705, it did not actually decide that issue. We therefore reverse the judgment and remand the case to that court for proceedings consistent with this opinion.

SECRETARY OF LABOR v. LAURITZEN

U.S. Court of Appeals, Seventh Circuit, 1987.
835 F.2d 1529.

WOOD, JR., J.

This, as unlikely as it may at first seem, is a federal pickle case. The issue is whether the migrant workers who harvest the pickle crop of defendant Lauritzen Farms, in effect defendant Michael Lauritzen, are employees for purposes of the Fair Labor Standards Act of 1938 ("FLSA"), or are instead independent contractors not subject to the requirements of the Act. The Secretary, alleging that the migrant harvesters are employees, not independent contractors, brought this action seeking to enjoin the defendants from violating the minimum wage requirements and to enforce the record-keeping and child labor provisions of the Act.

* * * The district court granted the Secretary partial summary judgment, determining the migrants to be employees, not independent contractors. * * *

On a yearly basis the defendants plant between 100 to 330 acres of pickles on land they either own or lease. The harvested crop is sold to various processors in the area. The pickles are handpicked, usually from July through September, by migrant families from out of state. Sometimes the children, some under twelve years of age, work in some capacity in the fields alongside their parents. Many of the migrant families return each harvest season by arrangement with the defendants, but, each year, other migrant families often come for the first time from Florida, Texas and elsewhere looking for work. The defendants would inform the families, either orally or sometimes in writing, of the amount of compensation they were to receive. Compensation is set by the defendants at one-half of the proceeds the defendants realize on the sale of the pickles that the migrants harvest on a family basis. Toward the end of the harvest season, when the crop is less abundant and, therefore, less profitable, the defendants offer the migrants a bonus to encourage them to stay to complete the harvest, but some leave anyway.

Wisconsin law requires a form "Migrant Work Agreement" to be signed, and it was used in this case. It provides for the same pay scale as is paid by the defendants except the minimum wage is guaranteed. The Wisconsin Migrant Law invalidates agreements that endeavor to convert migrant workers from employees to independent contractors. Wis. Stat. Ann. § 103.90 –.97 (West 1987); 71 Op. Att'y Gen. Wis. 92 (1982). Accompanying the work agreement is a pickle price list purporting to set forth what the processors will pay the defendants for pickles of various grades. This price list is the basis of the migrant workers' compensation. The workers are not parties to the determination of prices agreed upon between the defendants and the processors.

All matters relating to planting, fertilizing, insecticide spraying, and irrigation of the crop are within the defendants' direction, and performed by workers other than the migrant workers here involved. Occasionally a migrant who has worked for the defendant previously and knows the harvesting will suggest the need for irrigation. In order to conduct their pickle-raising business, the defendants have made a considerable investment in land, buildings, equipment, and supplies. The defendants provide the migrants free housing which the defendants assign, but with regard for any preference the migrant families may have. The defendants also supply migrants with the equipment they need for their work. The migrants need supply only work gloves for themselves.

The harvest area is subdivided into migrant family plots. The defendants make the allocation after the migrant families inform them how much acreage the family can harvest. Much depends on which areas are ready to harvest, and when a particular migrant family may arrive ready to work. The family, not the defendants, determines which family members will pick the pickles. If a family arrives before the harvest begins, the defendants may, nevertheless, provide them with housing. A few may be given some interim duties or be permitted to work temporarily for other farmers. When the pickles are ready to pick, however, the migrant family's attention must be devoted only to their particular pickle plot.

The pickles that are ready to harvest must be picked regularly and completely before they grow too large and lose value when classified. The defendants give the workers pails in which to put the picked pickles. When the pails are filled by the pickers the pails are dumped into the defendants' sacks. At the end of the harvest day a family member will use one of the defendants' trucks to haul the day's pick to one of defendants' grading stations or sorting sheds. After the pickles are graded the defendants give the migrant family member a receipt showing pickle grade and weight. The income of the individual families is not always equal. That is due, to some extent, to the ability of the migrant family to judge the pickles' size, color, and freshness so as to achieve pickles of better grade and higher value.

* * *

It is well recognized that under the FLSA the statutory definitions regarding employment[5] are broad and comprehensive in order to accomplish the remedial purposes of the Act. See, e.g., *United States v. Rosenwasser*, 323 U.S. 360, 362–63, 89 L. Ed. 301, 65 S. Ct. 295 (1945); *Real v. Driscoll Strawberry Associates, Inc.*, 603 F.2d 748, 754 (9th Cir.1979). Courts, therefore, have not considered the common law concepts of "employee" and "independent contractor" to define the limits of the Act's coverage. We are seeking, instead, to determine "economic reality." *Brock v. Mr. W Fireworks, Inc.*, 814 F.2d 1042, 1043 (5th Cir.1987); *Karr v. Strong Detective Agency, Inc.*, 787 F.2d 1205, 1207 (7th Cir.1986). For purposes of social welfare legislation, such as the FLSA, " 'employees are those who as a matter of economic reality are dependent upon the business to which they render service.' " *Mednick v. Albert Enterprises, Inc.*, 508 F.2d 297, 299 (5th Cir.1975) (quoting *Bartels v. Birmingham*, 332 U.S. 126, 130, 91 L. Ed. 1947, 67 S. Ct. 1547 (1947)).

In seeking to determine the economic reality of the nature of the working relationship, courts do not look to a particular isolated factor but to all the circumstances of the work activity. *Rutherford Food Corp. v. McComb*, 331 U.S. 722, 730, 91 L. Ed. 1772, 67 S. Ct. 1473 (1947). Certain criteria have been developed to assist in determining the true nature of the relationship, but no criterion is by itself, or by its absence, dispositive or controlling.

Among the criteria courts have considered are the following six:

1) the nature and degree of the alleged employer's control as to the manner in which the work is to be performed;

2) the alleged employee's opportunity for profit or loss depending upon his managerial skill;

3) the alleged employee's investment in equipment or materials required for his task, or his employment of workers;

---

5. The Act defines an employee simply as "any individual employed by an employer." 29 U.S.C. § 203(e)(1). An "employer" is defined to include "any person acting directly or indirectly in the interest of an employer in relation to an employee." 29 U.S.C. § 203(d). To "employ includes to suffer or permit to work." 29 U.S.C. § 203(g).

4) whether the service rendered requires a special skill;

5) the degree of permanency and duration of the working relationship;

6) the extent to which the service rendered is an integral part of the alleged employer's business.

* * *

A. Control

* * *

* * * In this case, the defendants did occasionally visit the families in the fields. The workers sometimes referred to Michael Lauritzen as the "boss," and some of them expressed a belief that he had the right to fire them. Moreover, * * * we believe that the defendants' right to control applies to the entire pickle-farming operation, not just the details of harvesting. The defendants exercise pervasive control over the operation as a whole. We therefore agree with the district court that the defendants did not effectively relinquish control of the harvesting to the migrants.

B. Profit and Loss

* * * Although the profit opportunity may depend in part on how good a pickle picker is, there is no corresponding possibility for migrant worker loss. [A] reduction in money earned by the migrants is not a loss sufficient to satisfy the criteria for independent contractor status. * * * The migrants have invested nothing except for the cost of their work gloves, and therefore have no investment to lose. Any reduction in earnings due to a poor pickle crop is a loss of wages, and not of an investment.

C. Capital Investment

The capital investment factor is interrelated to the profit and loss consideration. * * * The workers here are responsible only for providing their own gloves. Gloves do not constitute a capital investment. * * * [W]e believe that the migrant workers' disproportionately small stake in the pickle-farming operation is an indication that their work is not independent of the defendants.

D. Degree of Skill Required

Although a worker must develop some specialized skill in order to recognize which pickles to pick when, this development of occupational skills is no different from what any good employee in any line of work must do. Skills are not the monopoly of independent contractors. * * *

E. Permanency

Another factor in the employment analysis is permanency and duration of the relationship. * * * Many seasonal businesses necessarily hire only seasonal employees, but that fact alone does not convert seasonal employees into seasonal independent contractors. * * * [H]owever temporary the relationship may be it is permanent and exclusive for the duration of that harvest season. * * * One indication of permanency in this case is the fact that it is not uncommon for the migrant families to return year after year.

F. Harvesting as an Integral Part of Defendants' Business

* * * It does not take much of a record to demonstrate that picking the pickles is a necessary and integral part of the pickle business * * *.

G. Dependence of Migrant Workers

Our final task is to consider the degree to which the migrant families depend on the defendants. Economic dependence is more than just another factor. It is instead the focus of all the other considerations. * * * If the migrant families are pickle pickers, then they need pickles to pick in order to survive economically. The migrants clearly are dependent on the pickle business, and the defendants, for their continued employment and livelihood. * * * That is why many of them return year after year. The defendants contend that skilled migrant families are in demand in the area and do not need the defendants. Were it not for the defendants the migrant families would have to find some other pickle grower who would hire them. Until they found another grower, they would be unemployed. It is not necessary to show that workers are unable to find work with any other employer to find that the workers are employees rather than contractors.

We cannot say that the migrants are not employees, but, instead, are in business for themselves and sufficiently independent to lie beyond the broad reach of the FLSA. They depend on the defendants' land, crops, agricultural expertise, equipment, and marketing skills. They are the defendants' employees. * * *

EASTERBROOK, J., concurring.

People are entitled to know the legal rules before they act, and only the most compelling reason should lead a court to announce an approach under which no one can know where he stands until litigation has been completed. * * *

Consider the problems with the balancing test. These are not the factors the Restatement (Second) of Agency § 2(3) (1958) suggests for identifying "independent contractors." The Restatement takes the view that the right to control the physical performance of the job is the central element of status as an independent contractor. My colleagues, joining many other courts, say that this approach is inapplicable because we should "accomplish the remedial purposes of the Act":

> Courts, therefore, have not considered the common law concepts of "employee" and "independent contractor" to define the limits of the Act's coverage. We are seeking, instead, to determine "economic reality."

This implies that the definition of "independent contractor" used in tort cases is inconsistent with "economic reality" but that the seven factors applied in FLSA cases capture that "reality." In which way did "economic reality" elude the American Law Institute and the courts of 50 states? What kind of differences between FLSA and tort cases are justified? * * *

* * *

We should abandon [the court's] unfocused "factors" and start again. The language of the statute is the place to start. Section 3(g), 29 U.S.C. § 203(g), defines "employ" as including "to suffer or permit to work". This is "the broadest definition ' ... ever included in any one act.' "*United States v. Rosenwasser*, 323 U.S.360, 363 n. 3, 89 L. Ed. 301, 65 S. Ct. 295, 297 n. 3 (1945), quoting from Sen. Hugo Black, the Act's sponsor, 81 Cong.Rec. 7657 (1937). No wonder the common law definition of "independent contractor" does not govern. * * *

Unfortunately there is no useful discussion in the legislative debates about the application of the FLSA to agricultural workers. This drives us back to more general purposes—those of the FLSA in general, and those of the common law definition of the independent contractor. Section 2 of the FLSA, 29 U.S.C. § 202, supplies part of the need. Courts are "to correct and as rapidly as practical eliminate", § 2(b), the "labor conditions detrimental to the maintenance of the minimum standard of living necessary to health, efficiency, and general well-being of workers", § 2(a) * * *.

The purposes Congress identified * * * strongly suggest that the FLSA applies to migrant farm workers. [T]he statute was designed to protect workers without substantial human capital, who therefore earn the lowest wages. No one doubts that migrant farm workers are short on human capital; an occupation that can be learned quickly does not pay great rewards.

The functions of the FLSA call for coverage. How about the functions of the independent contractor doctrine? This is a branch of tort law, designed to identify who is answerable for a wrong (and therefore, indirectly, to determine who must take care to prevent injuries). To say "X is an independent contractor" is to say that the chain of vicarious liability runs from X's employees to X but stops there. This concentrates on X the full incentive to take care. It is the right allocation when X is in the best position to determine what care is appropriate, to take that care, or to spread the risk of loss. See *Anderson v. Marathon Petroleum Co.*, 801 F.2d 936, 938–39 (7th Cir.1986); Alan O. Sykes, The Economics of Vicarious Liability, 93 Yale L.J. 1231 (1984). This usually follows the right to control the work. Someone who surrenders control of the details of the work—often to take advantage of the expertise (human capital) of someone else—cannot determine what precautions are appropriate; his ignorance may have been the principal reason for hiring the independent contractor. Such a person or firm specifies the outputs (design the building; paint the fence) rather than the inputs. Imposing liability on the person who does not control the execution of the work might induce pointless monitoring. All the details of the common law independent contractor doctrine having to do with the right to control the work are addressed to identifying the best monitor and precaution-taker.

The reasons for blocking vicarious liability at a particular point have nothing to do with the functions of the FLSA. * * *

The migrant workers are selling nothing but their labor. They have no physical capital and little human capital to vend. This does not belittle their skills. Willingness to work hard, dedication to a job, honesty, and good health, are valuable traits and all too scarce. Those who possess these traits will find employment; those who do not cannot work (for long) even at the minimum wage in the private sector. But those to whom the FLSA applies must include workers who possess only dedication, honesty, and good health. So the baby-sitter is an "employee" even though working but a few hours a week, and the writer of novels is not an "employee" of the publisher even though renting only human capital. The migrant workers labor on the farmer's premises, doing repetitive tasks. Payment on a piecework rate (e.g., 1 cents per pound of cucumbers) would not take these workers out of the Act, any more than payment of the sales staff at a department store on commission avoids the statute. The link of the migrants' compensation to the market price of pickles is not fundamentally different from piecework compensation. Just as the piecework rate may be adjusted in response to the market (e.g., to 1 cents per 1.1 pounds, if the market falls 10%), imposing the market risk on piecework laborers, so the migrants' percentage share may be adjusted in response to the market (e.g., rising to 55% of the gross if the market should fall 10%) in order to relieve them of market risk. Through such adjustments Lauritzen may end up bearing the whole market risk, and in the long run must do so to attract workers.

There are hard cases under the approach I have limned, but this is not one of them. Migrant farm hands are "employees" under the FLSA—without regard to the crop and the contract in each case.

Notes and Questions

1. *"Right to Control" Test.* Is the holding in *Darden* that in the absence of some indication to the contrary, as in the case of ERISA (treated in chapter 16), Congress is deemed to be employing "common-law agency principles" in defining covered employees? The common-law definition, as the Court's quotation from its prior decision in *Reid* indicates, looks to "the hiring party's right to control the manner and means by which the [work] is accomplished". However, the Court also notes that several other factors (including nine listed in the second part of § 220 of the Restatement (Second) of Agency) are "relevant to this inquiry * * * ." Is there some other ultimate consideration to which all these factors are relevant? Are multi-factor tests like this inherently malleable and hence unpredictable? Are they nonetheless necessary here?

As Judge Easterbrook points out in his concurrence in *Lauritzen*, common law courts originally developed the "right to control" test for the purpose of determining when it is appropriate to impose respondeat superior (i.e., strict) liability on a principal, as a "master", for the torts of an agent, as a "servant." See also Marc Linder, The Employment Relationship in Anglo–American Law: A Historical Perspective 133–70 (1989); Richard R. Carlson, Why the Law Still Can't Tell an Employee When It Sees One and How It Ought to Stop Trying, 22 Berk. J. of Emp. & Lab. L. 295, 302–06 (2001). The test clearly makes sense in this context; only a principal that controls the details of an agent's work should be given the incentive of potential liability to monitor that work. Consider in the course of reading this text whether the test serves equally well the purposes of antidiscrimination and employment laws.

2.   *"Economic Realities" or "Economic Dependence" Test.* As stated in *Darden*, the FLSA (considered in detail in chapter 15) contains a definition of "employ" upon which courts have based a somewhat differently formulated test for employment status than the common law's "right to control" test. In *Rutherford Food Corp. v. McComb,* the seminal Supreme Court decision cited in both *Darden* and *Lauritzen*, the Court found that skilled boners were employees of a slaughterhouse for purposes of the FLSA based on the "circumstances of the whole activity":

> Viewed in this way, the workers did a specialty job on the production line. The responsibility under the boning contracts without material changes passed from one boner to another. The premises and equipment of Kaiser were used for the work. The group had no business organization that could or did shift as a unit from one slaughterhouse to another. The managing official of the plant kept close touch on the operation. While profits to the boners depended upon the efficiency of their work, it was more like piecework than an enterprise that actually depended for success upon the initiative, judgment or foresight of the typical independent contractor.

331 U.S. at 730.

As illustrated by *Lauritzen*, the courts since *Rutherford* have claimed to consider the total "economic reality" when determining the existence of an employment relationship under the FLSA. Is Judge Easterbrook correct that as formulated by the majority in *Lauritzen* the test is "unfocused"? Does the majority explain the relevance of its first six factors, and provide focus and guidance, by stressing "economic dependence"?

How, if at all, does the "economic reality" test differ in practice from the common law test? Would application of the "economic reality" factors listed in *Laurtizen* produce a different result in a case like *Darden*? Would application of the factors mentioned in the quote from *Reid* in *Darden* produce a different result in a case like *Lauritzen*? Might both sets of factors be based on the same ultimate consideration? Consider the next note.

3.   *"Entrepreneurial Control" Test.* The Reporters for the Restatement (Third) of Employment Law have proposed the following test for whether a service provider is an "independent business person" or an employee:

An individual renders services as an "independent business person" rather than as an employee if the individual has entrepreneurial control of the manner and means by which the services are performed such that the individual can seek to increase personal economic returns through, for example, the scheduling of the performance, the hiring of assistants, or the use of capital in place of labor.

How does this test differ, if at all, from the common law test? From the "economic realities" test? For decisions expressly focusing on entrepreneurial control, see, e.g., NLRB v. Friendly Cab Co., 512 F.3d 1090 (9th Cir. 2008) (placing "particular significance on [employer's] requirement that its drivers may not engage in any entrepreneurial opportunities"); Corporate Express Delivery Sys. v. NLRB, 292 F.3d 777 (D.C. Cir. 2002) (finding employee status because of the absence of "entrepreneurial opportunity"); Desimone v. Allstate Insurance Co., 2000 WL 1811385 (N.D. Cal. 2000) (finding independent contractor status); Estrada v. FedEx Ground Package System, Inc., 154 Cal.App.4th 1, 64 Cal.Rptr.3d 327 (2007) (drivers who lacked a "true entrepreneurial opportunity" were employees). Cf. also Michael C. Harper, Defining the Economic Relationship Appropriate for Collective Bargaining, 38 B.C.L. Rev. 329 (1998).

4. *Some Difficult Cases.* How should the following economic relationships be treated under the various tests suggested in the cases and the above notes? What additional facts would be relevant?

a. taxicab drivers who rent their cabs from fleet owners and charge fares as regulated by government, but are free to adopt any route they wish or work on any shift they wish;

b. owner-drivers of trucks that service a single customer, say, the area's single large department store;

c. registered nurses who perform home health care services for elderly patients, but are not actively supervised by a referring organization;

d. lawyers who "telecommute" at home drafting briefs and papers for a number of law firms, although 80% of their work is done for one major law firm;

e. freelance musicians who as "regular players" for local orchestras must accept the majority of work offered, see Lerohl v. Friends of Minn. Sinfonia, 322 F.3d 486 (8th Cir. 2003).

5. *Relevance of the Parties' Formal Description of the Economic Relationship?* To what extent should the parties' own characterization of their relationship control? Should a formal denomination carry any independent weight? See, e.g., *Rutherford*, supra, 331 U.S. at 729 ("Where the work done, in its essence, follows the usual path of an employee, putting on an "independent contractor" label does not take the worker from the protection of the Act."); Treas. Reg. § 31.31221(d)–1(a)(3) ("it is of no consequence that the employee is designated as a partner, coadventurer, agent, independent contractor, or the like"). Cf. Vizcaino v. Microsoft Corp., 120 F.3d 1006 (9th Cir. 1997) (en banc), excerpted at p. 1001 infra.

6. *Are Volunteers Employees?* Agents under the full control of their principals are treated as employees by the common law for purposes of

vicarious liability, regardless of whether they perform their work without compensation. See § 7.07(3)(b) of the Restatement (Third) of Agency. The courts have held, however, that those who work voluntarily without compensation are not employees for purposes of various employment laws. See, e.g., York v. Ass'n of the Bar of the City of N.Y., 286 F.3d 122 (2d Cir. 2002) (prospect of future employment through networking in volunteer position not sufficient for employee status under Title VII); Mendoza v. Town of Ross, 128 Cal.App.4th 625, 27 Cal.Rptr.3d 402 (2005) (case under California Fair Employment and Housing Act, Cal. Gov. §§ 12900 et seq.): see generally Mitchell H. Rubinstein, Our Nation's Forgotten Workers: The Unprotected Volunteers, 9 U. Pa. J. Lab. & Emp. L. 147 (2006). The exclusion of volunteers extends to the FLSA, notwithstanding its broad definition of "employ" as "to suffer or permit to work." See Walling v. Portland Terminal Co., 330 U.S. 148, 152, 67 S.Ct. 639, 91 L.Ed. 809 (1947) (brakemen not employees while in training and not compensated). What is the justification for not treating volunteers as employees under the FLSA? Under antidiscrimination laws?

7. *Comparative Note: Coverage for Some Independent Contractors.* Some other developed countries have posited an intermediate category of workers, falling between the employee and independent contractor poles. German law, for instance, extends some labor and antidiscrimination protections to "employee-like persons" ("Arbeitnehmerahnliche Personem") who may be technically self-employed, but are nonetheless economically dependent on the users of their services; unjust dismissal law protection, however, is not offered to this group. See Wolfgang Daubler, Working People in Germany, 21 Comp. Lab. L. & Pol. J. 77, 94–95 (1999). See also Brian A. Langille & Guy Davidov, Beyond Employees and Independent Contractors: A View from Canada, 21 Comp. Lab. L. & Pol. J. 7 (1999); Taco van Peijpe, Independent Contractors and Protected Workers in Dutch Law, 21 Comp. Lab. L. & Pol. J. 127 (1999); Ronnie Eklund, A Look At Contract Labor in the Nordic Countries, 18 Comp. Lab. L.J. 229 (1997). For a survey of the British approach, see Harry Hutchison, Subordinate or Independent, Status or Contract, Clarity or Circularity: British Employment Law, American Implications, 28 Ga. J. Intl. & Comp. L. 55 (1999).

B.   EMPLOYEES OR EMPLOYERS?

CLACKAMAS GASTROENTEROLOGY ASSOCIATES, P. C. v. WELLS
Supreme Court of the United States, 2003.
538 U.S. 440, 123 S.Ct. 1673, 155 L.Ed.2d 615 .

JUSTICE STEVENS delivered the opinion of the Court.

The Americans with Disabilities Act of 1990 (ADA or Act), 104 Stat. 327, as amended, 42 U.S.C. § 12101 et seq., like other federal antidiscrimination legislation, is inapplicable to very small businesses. Under the ADA an "employer" is not covered unless its workforce includes "15 or more employees for each working day in each of 20 or more calendar weeks in the current or preceding calendar year." § 12111(5). The question in this case is whether four physicians actively engaged in medical practice as shareholders and directors of a professional corporation should be counted as "employees."

I

Petitioner, Clackamas Gastroenterology Associates, P. C., is a medical clinic in Oregon. It employed respondent, Deborah Wells, as a bookkeeper from 1986 until 1997. After her termination, she brought this action against the clinic alleging unlawful discrimination on the basis of disability under Title I of the ADA. Petitioner denied that it was covered by the Act and moved for summary judgment, asserting that it did not have 15 or more employees for the 20 weeks required by the statute. It is undisputed that the accuracy of that assertion depends on whether the four physician-shareholders who own the professional corporation and constitute its board of directors are counted as employees.

The District Court, adopting the Magistrate Judge's findings and recommendation, granted the motion. Relying on an "economic realities" test adopted by the Seventh Circuit in *EEOC v. Dowd & Dowd, Ltd.*, 736 F.2d 1177, 1178 (1984), the District Court concluded that the four doctors were "more analogous to partners in a partnership than to shareholders in a general corporation" and therefore were "not employees for purposes of the federal antidiscrimination laws."

A divided panel of the Court of Appeals for the Ninth Circuit reversed. Noting that the Second Circuit had rejected the realities approach, the majority held that the use of any corporation, including a professional corporation, " 'precludes any examination designed to determine whether the entity is in fact a partnership.' " * * *

II

"We have often been asked to construe the meaning of 'employee' where the statute containing the term does not helpfully define it." *Nationwide Mut. Ins. Co. v. Darden*, 503 U.S. 318, 322, 117 L.Ed. 2d 581, 112 S.Ct. 1344 (1992). The definition of the term in the ADA simply states that an "employee" is "an individual employed by an employer." 42 U.S.C. § 12111(4). * * *

In *Darden* * * * we adopted a common-law test for determining who qualifies as an "employee" under ERISA.[5] * * * We explained that " 'when Congress has used the term 'employee' without defining it, we have concluded that Congress intended to describe the conventional master-servant relationship as understood by common-law agency doctrine.' " *Darden*, 503 U.S., at 322–323.

Rather than looking to the common law, petitioner argues that courts should determine whether a shareholder-director of a professional

---

5. [The] particular factors [cited in *Darden*] are not directly applicable to this case because we are not faced with drawing a line between independent contractors and employees. Rather, our inquiry is whether a shareholder-director is an employee or, alternatively, the kind of person that the common law would consider an employer.

corporation is an "employee" by asking whether the shareholder-director is, in reality, a "partner." The question whether a shareholder-director is an employee, however, cannot be answered by asking whether the shareholder-director appears to be the functional equivalent of a partner. Today there are partnerships that include hundreds of members, some of whom may well qualify as "employees" because control is concentrated in a small number of managing partners. Cf. *Hishon v. King & Spalding*, 467 U.S. 69, 80, n. 2, 81 L.Ed. 2d 59, 104 S.Ct. 2229 (1984) (Powell, J., concurring) ("An employer may not evade the strictures of Title VII simply by labeling its employees as 'partners' "); *EEOC v. Sidley Austin Brown & Wood*, 315 F.3d 696, 709 (CA7 2002) (Easterbrook, concurring in part and concurring in judgment); *Strother v. Southern California Permanente Medical Group*, 79 F.3d 859 (CA9 1996). Thus, asking whether shareholder-directors are partners—rather than asking whether they are employees—simply begs the question.

Nor does the approach adopted by the Court of Appeals in this case fare any better. The majority's approach, which paid particular attention to "the broad purpose of the ADA," 271 F.3d at 905, is consistent with the statutory purpose of ridding the Nation of the evil of discrimination. See 42 U.S.C. § 12101(b).[6] Nevertheless, two countervailing considerations must be weighed in the balance. First, as the dissenting judge noted below, the congressional decision to limit the coverage of the legislation to firms with 15 or more employees has its own justification that must be respected—namely, easing entry into the market and preserving the competitive position of smaller firms. See 271 F.3d at 908 (opinion of Graber, J.) ("Congress decided 'to spare very small firms from the potentially crushing expense of mastering the intricacies of the antidiscrimination laws, establishing procedures to assure compliance, and defending against suits when efforts at compliance fail' " (quoting Papa v. Katy Industries, Inc., 166 F.3d 937, 940 (CA7 1999))). Second, as *Darden* reminds us, congressional silence often reflects an expectation that courts will look to the common law to fill gaps in statutory text, particularly when an undefined term has a settled meaning at common law. Congress has overridden judicial decisions that went beyond the common law in an effort to correct "the mischief" at which a statute was aimed. See *Darden*, 503 U.S., at 324–325.

Perhaps the Court of Appeals' and the parties' failure to look to the common law for guidance in this case stems from the fact that we are dealing with a new type of business entity that has no exact precedent in the common law. State statutes now permit incorporation for the pur-

---

6. The meaning of the term "employee" comes into play when determining whether an individual is an "employee" who may invoke the ADA's protections against discrimination in "hiring, advancement, or discharge," 42 U.S.C. § 12112(a), as well as when determining whether an individual is an "employee" for purposes of the 15–employee threshold. [citations omitted] Consequently, a broad reading of the term "employee" would—consistent with the statutory purpose of ridding the Nation of discrimination—tend to expand the coverage of the ADA by enlarging the number of employees entitled to protection and by reducing the number of firms entitled to exemption.

pose of practicing a profession, but in the past "the so-called learned professions were not permitted to organize as corporate entities." 1A W. Fletcher, Cyclopedia of the Law of Private Corporations § 112.10 (rev. ed. 1997–2002). Thus, professional corporations are relatively young participants in the market, and their features vary from State to State. See generally 1 B. Bittker & J. Eustice, Federal Income Taxation of Corporations and Shareholders ¶ 2.06 (7th ed. 2002) (explaining that States began to authorize the creation of professional corporations in the late 1950's and that the momentum to form professional corporations grew in the 1970's).

Nonetheless, the common law's definition of the master-servant relationship does provide helpful guidance. At common law the relevant factors defining the master-servant relationship focus on the master's control over the servant. The general definition of the term "servant" in the Restatement (Second) of Agency § 2(2) (1958), for example, refers to a person whose work is "controlled or is subject to the right to control by the master." * * * In addition, the Restatement's more specific definition of the term "servant" lists factors to be considered when distinguishing between servants and independent contractors, the first of which is "the extent of control" that one may exercise over the details of the work of the other. Id., § 220(2)(a). We think that the common-law element of control is the principal guidepost that should be followed in this case.

This is the position that is advocated by the Equal Employment Opportunity Commission (EEOC), the agency that has special enforcement responsibilities under the ADA and other federal statutes containing similar threshold issues for determining coverage. It argues that a court should examine "whether shareholder-directors operate independently and manage the business or instead are subject to the firm's control." According to the EEOC's view, "if the shareholder-directors operate independently and manage the business, they are proprietors and not employees; if they are subject to the firm's control, they are employees."

Specific EEOC guidelines discuss both the broad question of who is an "employee" and the narrower question of when partners, officers, members of boards of directors, and major shareholders qualify as employees. See 2 Equal Employment Opportunity Commission, Compliance Manual §§ 605:0008–605:00010 (2000) (hereinafter EEOC Compliance Manual). With respect to the broad question, the guidelines list 16 factors—taken from *Darden*, 503 U.S., at 323–324—that may be relevant to "whether the employer controls the means and manner of the worker's work performance." EEOC Compliance Manual § 605:0008, and n. 71. The guidelines list six factors to be considered in answering the narrower question, which they frame as "whether the individual acts independently and participates in managing the organization, or whether the individual is subject to the organization's control." Id., § 605:0009.

We are persuaded by the EEOC's focus on the common-law touch-stone of control, see *Skidmore v. Swift & Co.*, 323 U.S. 134, 140, 89 L.Ed. 124, 65 S.Ct. 161 (1944), and specifically by its submission that each of the following six factors is relevant to the inquiry whether a shareholder-director is an employee:

"Whether the organization can hire or fire the individual or set the rules and regulations of the individual's work

"Whether and, if so, to what extent the organization supervises the individual's work

"Whether the individual reports to someone higher in the organization

"Whether and, if so, to what extent the individual is able to influence the organization

"Whether the parties intended that the individual be an employee, as expressed in written agreements or contracts

"Whether the individual shares in the profits, losses, and liabilities of the organization." EEOC Compliance Manual § 605:0009.[10]

As the EEOC's standard reflects, an employer is the person, or group of persons, who owns and manages the enterprise. The employer can hire and fire employees, can assign tasks to employees and supervise their performance, and can decide how the profits and losses of the business are to be distributed. The mere fact that a person has a particular title—such as partner, director, or vice president—should not necessarily be used to determine whether he or she is an employee or a proprietor. See *ibid.* ("An individual's title ... does not determine whether the individual is a partner, officer, member of a board of directors, or major shareholder, as opposed to an employee"). Nor should the mere existence of a document styled "employment agreement" lead inexorably to the conclusion that either party is an employee. See *ibid.* (looking to whether "the parties intended that the individual be an employee, as expressed in written agreements or contracts"). Rather, as was true in applying common law rules to the independent-contractor-versus-employee issue confronted in *Darden*, the answer to whether a shareholder-director is an employee depends on " 'all of the incidents of the relationship ... with no one factor being decisive.' " 503 U.S., at 324 (quoting *NLRB v. United Ins. Co. of America*, 390 U.S. 254, 258, 19 L.Ed. 2d 1083, 88 S.Ct. 988 (1968)).

III

Some of the District Court's findings—when considered in light of the EEOC's standard—appear to weigh in favor of a conclusion that the

---

10. The EEOC asserts that these six factors need not necessarily be treated as "exhaustive." We agree. The answer to whether a shareholder-director is an employee or an employer cannot be decided in every case by a " 'shorthand formula or magic phrase.' " Nationwide Mut. Ins. Co. v. Darden, 503 U.S. 318, 324, 117 L.Ed. 2d 581, 112 S.Ct. 1344 (1992) (quoting NLRB v. United Ins. Co. of America, 390 U.S. 254, 258, 19 L.Ed. 2d 1083, 88 S.Ct. 988 (1968)).

four director-shareholder physicians in this case are not employees of the clinic. For example, they apparently control the operation of their clinic, they share the profits, and they are personally liable for malpractice claims. There may, however, be evidence in the record that would contradict those findings or support a contrary conclusion under the EEOC's standard that we endorse today.[11] Accordingly, as we did in *Darden*, we reverse the judgment of the Court of Appeals and remand the case to that court for further proceedings consistent with this opinion.

JUSTICE GINSBURG, with whom JUSTICE BREYER joins, dissenting.

"There is nothing inherently inconsistent between the coexistence of a proprietary and an employment relationship." Goldberg v. Whitaker House Cooperative, Inc., 366 U.S. 28, 32, 6 L.Ed.2d 100, 81 S.Ct. 933 (1961). As doctors performing the everyday work of petitioner Clackamas Gastroenterology Associates, P.C., the physician-shareholders function in several respects as common-law employees, a designation they embrace for various purposes under federal and state law. Classifying as employees all doctors daily engaged as caregivers on Clackamas' premises, moreover, serves the animating purpose of the Americans With Disabilities Act of 1990 (ADA or Act). Seeing no cause to shelter Clackamas from the governance of the ADA, I would affirm the judgment of the Court of Appeals. * * *

Are the physician-shareholders "servants" of Clackamas for the purpose relevant here? The Restatement defines "servant" to mean "an agent employed by a master to perform service in his affairs whose physical conduct in the performance of the service is controlled or is subject to the right to control by the master." Restatement (Second) of Agency § 2(2) (1958) (hereinafter Restatement). When acting as clinic doctors, the physician-shareholders appear to fit the Restatement definition. The doctors provide services on behalf of the corporation, in whose name the practice is conducted. See Ore. Rev. Stat. Ann. § 58.185(1)(a) (1998 Supp.) (shareholders of a professional corporation "render the specified professional services of the corporation" (emphasis added)). The doctors have employment contracts with Clackamas, under which they receive salaries and yearly bonuses, and they work at facilities owned or leased by the corporation. In performing their duties, the doctors must "comply with ... standards [the organization has] established." See Restatement, ch. 7, tit. B, Introductory Note, p. 479 ("Fully employed but highly placed employees of a corporation ... are no less servants because they are not controlled in their day-to-day work by other human beings. Their physical activities are controlled by their sense of obligation to devote their time and energies to the interests of the enterprise.").

---

11. For example, the record indicates that the four director-shareholders receive salaries, that they must comply with the standards established by the clinic, and that they report to a personnel manager.

The physician-shareholders, it bears emphasis, invite the designation "employee" for various purposes under federal and state law. The Employee Retirement Income Security Act of 1974 (ERISA), much like the ADA, defines "employee" as "any individual employed by an employer." 29 U.S.C. § 1002(6). Clackamas readily acknowledges that the physician-shareholders are "employees" for ERISA purposes. Indeed, gaining qualification as "employees" under ERISA was the prime reason the physician-shareholders chose the corporate form instead of a partnership. Further, Clackamas agrees, the physician-shareholders are covered by Oregon's workers' compensation law, a statute applicable to "persons . . . who . . . furnish services for a remuneration, subject to the direction and control of an employer," Ore. Rev. Stat. Ann. § 656.005(30) (1996 Supp.). Finally, by electing to organize their practice as a corporation, the physician-shareholders created an entity separate and distinct from themselves, one that would afford them limited liability for the debts of the enterprise. §§ 58.185(4), (5), (10), (11) (1998 Supp.). I see no reason to allow the doctors to escape from their choice of corporate form when the question becomes whether they are employees for purposes of federal antidiscrimination statutes.

Notes and Questions

1. *Holding?* How would you frame the test that the lower court is to apply on remand? Does the Court's reference to the EEOC's "standard" mean that the EEOC's Compliance Manual is controlling law? Do the six factors listed in this Manual, and quoted by the Court, yield a clear standard? A workable test?

2. *A Common Law Test?* Do the *Clackamus* decision and the EEOC Compliance Manual reformulate the common law for purposes of employment statutes like the ADA? As explained above, the common law definition of employee served the function of setting boundaries on an enterprise's vicarious liability for the torts of its agents. Under the common law, enterprises are liable for the torts of servants who are in positions of control. As Justice Ginsburg notes, under the common law as formulated in the Restatement (Second) of Agency in 1958, "highly placed employees of a corporation, such as presidents and general managers, are not less servants because they are not controlled in their day-to-day work by other human beings. Their physical activities are controlled by their sense of obligation to devote their time and energies to the interests of the enterprise." Restatement ch. 7, topic 2, title B, introductory note, p. 479. Furthermore, under the Restatement working partners also can be employees: "When one of the partners is in active management of the business or is otherwise regularly employed in the business, he is a servant of the partnership." Restatement § 14 A, comment a, p. 62. Can the EEOC's position be reconciled with that of the Restatement? Are there good reasons to assume that employment laws were not intended to cover some managing owners or partners who would be treated as employees for purposes of assigning vicarious liability?

3. *Control through Ownership?* Does the Court's analysis in *Clackamus* indicate that those who serve an enterprise that they control are not its

employees, regardless of their ownership interest in that enterprise? Or must the control derive from ownership? For instance, how would the Court treat a corporation's chief executive officer who does not own a controlling block of shares in the corporation, but who faces a friendly Board of Directors and widely dispersed shareholders? The Reporters for the Restatement (Third) of Employment Law have proposed black letter providing, for purposes of employment law, that "an individual who, through an ownership interest, controls all or a significant part of an enterprise for which the individual provides services is not an employee of the enterprise."

4. *Partners as Employees?* After *Clackamus*, are all partners in large law or accounting firms employees for purposes of an employment law like the ADA, regardless of their status under state partnership law? Might partners who control their own cases and matters be excluded, even though their compensation is set by a managing group of partners? Are all those on a firm's managing committee excluded from employee status, or must their position on the committee derive from a dominant ownership share in the partnership, rather than from other managerial qualifications? Before *Clackamus*, the Courts of Appeals were split as to whether de jure partners in a formal partnership can ever be treated as employees under the antidiscrimination laws. Compare, Simpson v. Ernst & Young, 100 F.3d 436 (6th Cir. 1996) (treating individual denominated as a partner and with full liability for firm losses, as employee under federal antidiscrimination and employment laws), with Wheeler v. Hurdman, 825 F.2d 257 (10th Cir. 1987) (rejecting EEOC test and holding bona fide general partners to not be employees under antidiscrimination laws). See also EEOC v. Sidley Austin Brown & Wood, 315 F.3d 696 (7th Cir. 2002) (majority opinion by Judge Posner and partial concurrence by Judge Easterbrook). Currently, many large law and accounting firms require partners to retire at age 65. Presumably, such requirements violate the federal Age Discrimination in Employment Act (ADEA) only if the partner is treated as an "employee" for ADEA purposes.

The partnership consideration process is covered by the antidiscrimination laws, even if once admitted into the partnership the plaintiff would then be excluded from the laws' reach. See Hishon v. King & Spalding, 467 U.S. 69, 104 S.Ct. 2229, 81 L.Ed.2d 59 (1984); Price Waterhouse v. Hopkins, 490 U.S. 228, 109 S.Ct. 1775, 104 L.Ed.2d 268 (1989). In the *Price Waterhouse* litigation, a Title VII violation was found and the court ordered that the plaintiff be admitted to the partnership. See Hopkins v. Price Waterhouse, 920 F.2d 967 (D.C.Cir.), affirming 737 F.Supp. 1202 (D.D.C.1990).

5. *Fifteen-Employee Threshold and Relationship Between Employer and Affiliates.* In determining whether the 15–employee threshold for Title VII coverage has been met, may the courts count the number of individuals employed by affiliated firms? The National Labor Relations Board's "integrated enterprise" or "single employer" doctrine focuses on four factors: "(1) interrelation of operations, (2) common management, (3) centralized control of labor relations, and (4) common ownership or financial control." NLRB v. Browning–Ferris Indus. of Pa., 691 F.2d 1117, 1122 (3d Cir. 1982). This approach has been used by some Title VII courts. See, e.g., Anderson v. Pacific Maritime Assn., 336 F.3d 924, 929 (9th Cir. 2003). Other courts have found the test unhelpful in the antidiscrimination context. See, e.g., Nesbit v. Gears Unlimited, Inc., 347 F.3d 72, 86–87 (3d Cir. 2003) (single employer

status will be found where (1) company is split into two or more parts to evade Title VII, (2) the parent has directed the subsidiary to commit the allegedly discriminatory act, or (3) the affiliate companies exhibit a "degree of operational entanglement" that warrant their consolidation for bankruptcy purposes). As the next case illustrates, similar issues arise in determining whether individuals can be deemed jointly employed by two or more firms engaged in an interdependent operation.

C. JOINT EMPLOYERS

ZHENG v. LIBERTY APPAREL COMPANY INC.

U.S. Court of Appeals, Second Circuit, 2003.
355 F.3d 61.

JOSE A. CABRANES, *Circuit Judge*:

This case asks us to decide whether garment manufacturers who hired contractors to stitch and finish pieces of clothing were "joint employers" within the meaning of the *Fair Labor Standards Act of 1938 ("FLSA"), 29 U.S.C. § 201 et seq.*, and New York law. Plaintiffs, garment workers in New York City who were directly employed by the contractors, claim that the manufacturers were their joint employers because they worked predominantly on the manufacturers' garments, they performed a line-job that was integral to the production of the manufacturer's product, and their work was frequently and directly supervised by the manufacturers' agents. The manufacturers respond that the contractors, who, among other things, hired and paid plaintiffs to assemble clothing for numerous manufacturers, were plaintiffs' sole employers. Both plaintiffs and the manufacturers moved for summary judgment on the issue of joint employment.

The United States District Court for the Southern District of New York * * *, applying the four-factor test set forth in *Carter v. Dutchess Community College, 735 F.2d 8 (2d Cir. 1984)*, granted the manufacturers' motion, and held that the manufacturers could not be held liable for violations of the *FLSA* or its New York statutory analogues. The District Court also declined to exercise supplemental jurisdiction over a surviving New York claim.

* * *

Plaintiffs-Appellants are 26 non-English-speaking adult garment workers who worked in a factory at 103 Broadway in New York's Chinatown. They brought this action against both (1) their immediate employers, six contractors doing business at 103 Broadway ("Contractor Corporations") and their principals (collectively, "Contractor Defendants"), and (2) Liberty Apparel Company, Inc. ("Liberty") and its principals, Albert Nigri and Hagai Laniado (collectively, "Liberty Defendants"). Because the Contractor Defendants either could not be located or have ceased doing business, plaintiffs have voluntarily dismissed their claims against those defendants with prejudice. Accordingly, plaintiffs now seek damages only from the Liberty Defendants.

Liberty, a "jobber" in the parlance of the garment industry, is a manufacturing company that contracts out the last phase of its production process. That process, in broad terms, worked as follows: First, Liberty employees developed a pattern for a garment, cut a sample from the pattern, and sent the sample to a customer for approval. Once the customer approved the pattern, Liberty purchased the necessary fabric from a vendor, and the vendor delivered the fabric to Liberty's warehouse. There, the fabric was graded and marked, spread out on tables, and, finally, cut by Liberty employees.

After the fabric was cut, Liberty did not complete the production process on its own premises. Instead, Liberty delivered the cut fabric, along with other essential materials, to various contractors for assembly. The assemblers, in turn, employed workers to stitch and finish the pieces, a process that included sewing the fabrics, buttons, and labels into the garments, cuffing and hemming the garments, and, finally, hanging the garments. The workers, including plaintiffs, were paid at a piece rate for their labor.

From March 1997 through April 1999, Liberty entered into agreements with the Contractor Corporations under which the Contractor Corporations would assemble garments to meet Liberty's specifications. During that time period, Liberty utilized as many as thirty to forty assemblers, including the Contractor Corporations. Liberty did not seek out assemblers; instead, assemblers came to Liberty's warehouse looking for assembly work. In order to obtain such work, a prospective assembler was required by Liberty to sign a form agreement.

Plaintiffs claim that approximately 70–75% of their work during the time period at issue was for Liberty. They explain that they knew they were working for Liberty based on both the labels that were sown into the garments and the specific lot numbers that came with the garments. Liberty's co-owner, Albert Nigri, asserts that the percentage of the Contractor Corporations' work performed for Liberty was closer to 10–15%. He derives that figure from individual plaintiffs' handwritten notes and records.

The parties do not dispute that Liberty employed people to monitor Liberty's garments while they were being assembled. However, the parties dispute the extent to which Liberty oversaw the assembly process. Various plaintiffs presented affidavits to the District Court stating that two Liberty representatives—a man named Ah Sen and "a Taiwanese woman"—visited the factory approximately two to four times a week for up to three hours a day, and exhorted the plaintiffs to work harder and faster. In their affidavits, these plaintiffs claim further that, when they finished working on garments, Liberty representatives—as opposed to employees of the Contractor Corporations—inspected their work and gave instructions directly to the workers if corrections needed to be made. One of the plaintiffs also asserts that she informed the

"Taiwanese woman" that the workers were not being paid for their work at the factory.

* * *

In previous cases, we have applied * * * different tests to determine whether an employment relationship exists in light of the Supreme Court's admonition that "economic reality" govern our application of the *FLSA*. In *Carter v. Dutchess Community College, 735 F.2d 8 (2d Cir. 1984)*, we held that an inmate conducting tutorial classes in a program managed by a community college had raised genuine issues of material fact as to whether the college was an employer under the *FLSA*, where, among other things, the college sent compensation directly to the inmate and set the inmate's tutoring schedule. *See Carter, 735 F.2d at 13–15.* To reach that conclusion, we evaluated whether the college

> (1)had the power to hire and fire the employees, (2) supervised and controlled employee work schedules or conditions of employment, (3) determined the rate and method of payment, and (4) maintained employment records.

See Carter, 735 F.2d at 12 (borrowing factors from *Bonnette v. California Health & Welfare Agency, 704 F.2d 1465, 1470 (9th Cir. 1983)*).

* * *

Despite [the] distinction between joint employment cases and independent contractor cases, [however,] we have never suggested that, in analyzing joint employment, the four *Carter* factors alone are relevant, and that other factors that bear on the relationship between workers and potential joint employers should be ignored. Thus, in *Lopez v. Silverman, 14 F. Supp. 2d 405 (S. D.N.Y. 1998)*, [drawing on] the Supreme Court's decision in *Rutherford Food Corp. v. McComb, 331 U.S. 722, 91 L. Ed. 1772, 67 S. Ct. 1473 (1947)*, Judge Cote concluded that the following *seven* factors should be considered in determining whether garment workers are jointly employed by a "jobber":

> (1) the extent to which the workers perform a discrete line-job forming an integral part of the putative joint employer's integrated process of production or overall business objective;
>
> (2) whether the putative joint employer's premises and equipment were used for the work;
>
> (3) the extent of the putative employees' work for the putative joint employer;
>
> (4) the permanence or duration of the working relationship between the workers and the putative joint employer;
>
> (5) the degree of control exercised by the putative joint employer over the workers;
>
> (6) whether responsibility under the contract with the putative joint employer passed "without material changes" from one group of potential joint employees to another; and

(7)   whether the workers had a "business organization" that could or did shift as a unit from one putative joint employer to another.

* * *

We conclude, for the reasons set forth below, that the District Court erred when, based *exclusively* on the four factors mentioned in *Carter*, it determined that the Liberty Defendants were not, as a matter of law, joint employers under the *FLSA*. In our view, the broad language of the *FLSA*, as interpreted by the Supreme Court in *Rutherford*, demands that a district court look beyond an entity's formal right to control the physical performance of another's work before declaring that the entity is not an employer under the *FLSA*. * * *

* * *

Rutherford confirmed that the definition of "employ" in the *FLSA* cannot be reduced to formal control over the physical performance of another's work. In *Rutherford*, the Supreme Court held that a slaughterhouse jointly employed workers who de-boned meat on its premises, despite the fact that a boning supervisor—with whom the slaughterhouse had entered into a contract—directly controlled the terms and conditions of the meat boners' employment. Specifically, the supervisor, *rather than the slaughterhouse*, (i) hired and fired the boners, (ii) set their hours, and, (iii) after being paid a set amount by the slaughterhouse for each one hundred pounds of de-boned meat, paid the boners for their work. *Rutherford, 331 U.S. at 726, 730.*

In determining that the meat boners were employees of the slaughterhouse notwithstanding the role played by the boning supervisor, the Court examined the "circumstances of the whole activity," *id. at 730*, but also isolated specific relevant factors that help distinguish a legitimate contractor from an entity that "suffers or permits" its subcontractor's employees to work. First, the Court noted that the boners "did a specialty job on the production line"; that is, their work was "a part of the integrated unit of production" at the slaughterhouse. *Id. at 729–30.* The Court noted also that responsibility under the boning contracts passed from one boning supervisor to another "without material changes" in the work performed at the slaughterhouse; that the slaughterhouse's premises and equipment were used for the boners' work; that the group of boners "had no business organization that could or did shift as a unit from one slaughterhouse to another"; and that the managing official of the slaughterhouse, in addition to the boners' purported employer, closely monitored the boners' performance and productivity. *Id.* Based on its analysis of these factors, the Court imposed *FLSA* liability on the slaughterhouse.

Like the case at bar, *Rutherford* was a joint employment case, as it is apparent from the Supreme Court's opinion that the boners were, first and foremost, employed by the boning supervisor who had entered into a contract with the slaughterhouse. *See id. at 724–25* (explaining that the boning supervisor exercised the prerogatives of an employer, including hiring workers, managing their work, and paying them). *Rutherford* thus held that, in certain circumstances, an entity can be a joint employer under the *FLSA* even when it does not hire and fire its joint employees, directly dictate their hours, or pay them.

* * *

The factors we find pertinent in these circumstances, listed in no particular order, are (1) whether Liberty's premises and equipment were used for the plaintiffs' work; (2) whether the Contractor Corporations had a business that could or did shift as a unit from one putative joint employer to another; (3) the extent to which plaintiffs performed a discrete line-job that was integral to Liberty's process of production; (4) whether responsibility under the contracts could pass from one subcontractor to another without material changes; (5) the degree to which the Liberty Defendants or their agents supervised plaintiffs' work; and (6) whether plaintiffs worked exclusively or predominantly for the Liberty Defendants. *See Rutherford, 331 U.S. at 724–25, 730; see also Lopez, 14 F. Supp. 2d at 416–18* (summarizing the factors considered in *Rutherford*).

These particular factors are relevant because, when they weigh in plaintiffs' favor, they indicate that an entity has functional control over workers even in the absence of the formal control measured by the *Carter* factors. Thus, in *Rutherford*, by looking beyond the boning supervisor's formal prerogatives, the Supreme Court determined, based principally on the factors listed above, that the slaughterhouse dictated the terms and conditions of the boners' employment. First, although it did not literally pay the workers, the slaughterhouse *de facto* set the workers' wages, because the boners did no meat boning for any other firm and shared equally in the funds paid to the boning supervisor. See *Rutherford, 331 U.S. at 726, 730.* The slaughterhouse also controlled employee work schedules, both because the boners' hours were dependent on the number of cattle slaughtered, and also because the slaughterhouse manager was constantly "after" the boners about their work. *See Rutherford, 331 U.S. at 726.* Finally, the slaughterhouse effectively "controlled the [boners'] . . . conditions of employment," *Carter, 735 F.2d at 12*, because the boners worked for the slaughterhouse as an in-house boning unit on the slaughterhouse's premises, see *id. at 730.* In sum, the relationship between the slaughterhouse and the successive boning supervisors who managed the boners had no substantial, independent economic purpose; instead, it was most likely a subterfuge meant to evade the *FLSA* or other labor laws.

The first two factors derived from *Rutherford* require minimal discussion. The first factor—namely, whether a putative joint employer's premises and equipment are used by its putative joint employees—is relevant because the shared use of premises and equipment may support the inference that a putative joint employer has functional control over the plaintiffs' work. Similarly, the second factor—namely, whether the putative joint employees are part of a business organization that shifts as a unit from one putative joint employer to another—is relevant because a subcontractor that seeks business from a variety of contractors is less likely to be part of a subterfuge arrangement than a subcontractor that serves a single client. Although neither shared premises nor the absence of a broad client base is anything close to a perfect proxy for joint employment (because they are both perfectly consistent with a legitimate subcontracting relationship), the factfinder can use these readily verifiable facts as a starting point in uncovering the economic realities of a business relationship.

The other factors we have pointed out are less straightforward. *Rutherford* considered the extent to which plaintiffs performed a line-job that is integral to the putative joint employer's process of production. Interpreted broadly, this factor could be said to be implicated in *every* subcontracting relationship, because all subcontractors perform a function that a general contractor deems "integral" to a product or a service. However, we do not interpret the factor quite so broadly. The factor is derived from the *Rutherford* Court's statement that the boners at the slaughterhouse should be considered joint employees because, *inter alia*, "[they] did a specialty job on the production line." *Rutherford, 331 U.S. at 730*. Based on this statement in *Rutherford*, . . . we construe *Rutherford* to mean that work on a production line occupies a special status under the *FLSA*, at least when it lies on "the usual path of an employee," *id. at 729*.

Rutherford, however, offers no firm guidance as to how to distinguish work that "in its essence, follows the usual path of an employee," *id.*, from work that can be outsourced without attracting increased scrutiny under the *FLSA*. In our view, there is no bright-line distinction between these two categories of work. On one end of the spectrum lies the type of work performed by the boners in *Rutherford*—*i.e.*, piecework on a producer's premises that requires minimal training or equipment, and which constitutes an essential step in the producer's integrated manufacturing process. On the other end of the spectrum lies work that is not part of an integrated production unit, that is not performed on a predictable schedule, and that requires specialized skills or expensive technology. In classifying business relationships that fall in between these two poles, we are mindful of the substantial and valuable place that outsourcing, along with the subcontracting relationships that follow from outsourcing, have come to occupy in the American economy. * * * Accordingly, we resist the temptation to say that any work on a so-called production line—no matter what product is being manufactured—should attract heightened scrutiny. Instead, in determining the weight and degree of factor (3), we believe that both industry custom and historical practice should be consulted. Industry custom may be relevant because, insofar as the practice of using subcontractors to complete a particular task is widespread, it is unlikely to be a mere subterfuge to avoid complying with labor laws. At the same time, historical practice may also be relevant, because, if plaintiffs can prove that, as a historical matter, a contracting device has developed in response to and as a means to avoid applicable labor laws, the prevalence of that device may, in particular circumstances, be attributable to widespread evasion of labor laws. Ultimately, this factor, like the other factors derived from *Rutherford* is not independently determinative of a defendant's status, because the mere fact that a manufacturing job is not typically outsourced does not necessarily mean that there is no substantial economic reason to outsource it in a particular case. However, as *Rutherford* indicates, the type of work performed by plaintiffs can bear on the overall determination as to whether a defendant may be held liable for an FLSA violation.

The fourth factor the Court considered in *Rutherford* is whether responsibility under the contracts could pass from one subcontractor to another without material changes. That factor is derived from the *Rutherford* Court's observation that "the responsibility under the boning contracts without material changes passed from one boner to another." *Rutherford, 331 U.S. at 730*. In the quoted passage, the Supreme Court was referring to the fact that, even when the boning supervisor abandoned his position and another supervisor took his place (as occurred several times, *see id. at 725)*, the *same* employees would continue to do the *same* work in the *same* place. Under *Rutherford*, therefore, this factor weighs in favor of a determination of joint employment when employees are tied to an entity such as the slaughterhouse rather than to an ostensible direct employer such as the boning supervisor. In such circumstances, it is difficult *not* to draw the inference that a subterfuge arrangement exists. Where, on the other hand, employees work for an entity (the purported joint employer) only to the extent that their direct employer is hired by that entity, this factor does not in any way support the determination that a joint employment relationship exists.

The fifth factor listed above—namely, the degree to which the defendants supervise the plaintiffs' work—also requires some comment, as it too can be misinterpreted to encompass run-of-the-mill subcontracting relationships. Although *Rutherford* indicates that a defendant's extensive supervision of a plaintiff's work is indicative of an employment relationship, *see Rutherford, 331 U.S. at 730* (noting that "the managing official of the plant kept close touch on the operation"), *Rutherford* indicates also that such extensive supervision weighs in favor of joint employment only if it demonstrates effective control of the terms and conditions of the plaintiff's employment, *see Rutherford, 331 U.S. at 726* (suggesting the slaughterhouse owner's close scrutiny of the boners' work played a role in setting the boners' schedule); * * * By contrast, supervision with respect to contractual warranties of quality and time of delivery has no bearing on the joint employment inquiry, as such supervision is perfectly consistent with a typical, legitimate subcontracting arrangement. *See Moreau v. Air France, 343 F.3d 1179, 1188 (9th Cir. 2003)* (supervision of workers not indicative of joint employment where principal merely gave "specific instructions to a service provider" concerning performance under a service contract); *cf.* James Brian Quinn and Frederick G. Hilmer, *Strategic Outsourcing*, Sloan Mgmt. Rev., Summer 1994, at 43, 53 (explaining that "the most successful outsourcers find it absolutely essential to have both close personal contact and rapport at the floor level and political clout and understanding with the supplier's top management'').

Finally, the *Rutherford* Court considered whether the purported joint employees worked exclusively or predominantly for the putative joint employer. In describing that factor, we use the words ''exclusively or predominantly'' on purpose. * * * In those situations, the joint employer may *de facto* become responsible, among other things, for the amount workers are paid and for their schedules, which are traditional indicia of employment. On the other hand, where a subcontractor performs merely a majority of its work for a single customer, there is no sound basis on which to infer that the customer has assumed the prerogatives of an employer.

* * *

Although summary judgment might also be granted to plaintiffs even when isolated factors point against imposing joint liability, * * * the District Court's conclusion that, in the present circumstances, the record cannot support summary judgment in plaintiffs' favor, remains undisturbed. This case is quite different from *Rutherford*, in which the Supreme Court concluded that the slaughterhouse was a joint employer as a matter of law. In *Rutherford*, unlike in this case, *every* relevant factor described above weighed in favor of a joint employment relationship, and the record as a whole compelled the conclusion that the slaughterhouse exercised functional control over the boners. *See Rutherford, 331 U.S. at 730.* Should the District Court, on remand, deny summary judgment in favor of defendants, it will be incumbent upon the Court to conduct a trial.

[*Eds.* The court's discussion of the state law claims is omitted.]

Notes and Questions

1. *A Predictable and Coherent Test?* Consider again Judge Easterbrook's criticism of the majority's ''economic reality'' test in *Lauritzen*. Does the *Zheng* court's multi-factor test provide a predictable and coherent guidepost for potential employers? On what ultimate standard does the court intend the determination of joint employer status to depend?

Does the court help clarify the test for determining whether an employee has an employment relationship with a second employer by distinguishing it from the test for determining whether a worker has such a relationship with one employer? Should there be a difference between the two tests? The Reporters for the Restatement (Third) of Employment Law propose that a service provider should be treated as an employee of any employer that meets the conditions of an employment relationship, including having sufficient control over the manner and means of the service provider's performance of the services.

2. *''Joint Employers'' Need Not Be a ''Single Enterprise''.* Does a manufacturer's status as a joint employer necessarily mean that it and its

contractors are a "single enterprise" under common control? While common ownership and control of integrated enterprises is sufficient to make each enterprise a joint employer, see, e.g., Chao v. A–One Medical Servs., Inc., 346 F.3d 908 (9th Cir. 2003), as the *Zheng* decision illustrates, it is not necessary for joint employer status under the FLSA. Rather the courts apply factors like those used by the *Zheng* court to determine whether putative joint employers share in the actual or functional control of the work or the compensation of the employees. Similar analysis is applied under other employment laws. See, e.g., NLRB v. Browning–Ferris Indus. of Penn., 691 F.2d 1117 (3d Cir. 1982 (operator of refuse site and brokers were joint employers under National Labor Relations Act (NLRA) though not a single enterprise); McMullin v. Ashcroft, 337 F.Supp.2d 1281 (2004) (§ 501 of Rehabilitation Act applicable because separate federal employer shared control over working conditions of employees supplied by contractor); cf. Moreau v. Air France, 343 F.3d 1179 (9th Cir. 2003) (as discussed in *Zheng*, under Family and Medical Leave Act, airline not a joint employer of employees of catering service). Thus, temporary employment agencies and their clients may be joint employers of employees supplied by the agencies, if, for instance, the agencies set and pay wages while the clients control the details of the work. See, e.g., NLRB v. Western Temporary Serv., 821 F.2d 1258 (7th Cir. 1987) (temporary agency and client joint employers under NLRA); Ansoumana v. Gristede's Operating Corp., 255 F.Supp.2d 184 (S.D. N.Y. 2004) (drug store was joint employer under FLSA of delivery workers provided by contractors); Amarnare v. Merrill Lynch, 611 F.Supp. 344 (S.D.N.Y. 1984) (temporary employment agency and client both employers under Title VII).

3. *The "Sweatshop" Problem.* The fact pattern treated in *Zheng* is not aberrant. In the garment industry, workers often are employed by small, thinly capitalized firms that are difficult to monitor and, even when caught violating the employment laws, may be judgment-proof as a practical matter. As one response to this problem, the New York legislature amended the state labor law, inter alia, to make manufacturers and contractors jointly liable for unpaid wages owed contractors' employees. See New York Labor Law §§ 340–45 & 348. Note also that the FLSA prohibits anyone from transporting or selling "hot goods," i.e., goods which are produced in violation of the minimum wage and overtime provisions of the law. 29 U.S.C. § 215. See Herman v. Fashion Headquarters, Inc., 992 F.Supp. 677 (S.D.N.Y.1998) (discussing Secretary of Labor's authority to require manufacturer to monitor compliance by contractors with FLSA requirements). See generally Andrew Elmore, State Joint Employer Liability Laws and Pro Se Back Wage Claims in the Garment Industry: A Federalist Approach to a National Crisis, 49 U.C.L.A. L. Rev. 395 (2001).

4. *Joint Employers of Farmworkers.* Agriculture is another economic sector that has posed frequent questions of joint employment status. Farm operator-growers often use labor contractors to recruit and supervise farm laborers. These contractors, like the contractors in the garment industry, may be thinly capitalized and judgment proof. Applying factors like those applied in *Zheng*, courts have found farm operators to be joint employers where they share in the supervision of the laborers' work and the contractors provide only workers and no substantial capital equipment and housing.

See, e.g., Reyes v. Remington Hybrid Seed Co., 495 F.3d 403 (7th Cir. 2007) (Easterbrook, J.); Charles v. Burton, 169 F.3d 1322 (11th Cir. 1999); Torres-Lopez v. May, 111 F.3d 633 (9th Cir. 1997); Antenor v. D & S Farms, 88 F.3d 925 (11th Cir. 1996). But see Aimable v. Long & Scott Farms, 20 F.3d 434 (11th Cir. 1994) (farm operator not an employer of workers provided by a contractor who also provided housing and transportation and had sole supervisory control); Gonzalez-Sanchez v. International Paper Co., 346 F.3d 1017 (11th Cir. 2003) (laborers who hand-planted seedlings in forests owned by International Paper were not IP's employees where only contractors supervised and supplied housing, equipment and transportation). Should it matter in the latter case that the regeneration of forests was not "integral" to IP's total operations or even its paper manufacturing, which relied on the purchase of wood from other companies?

5. *"Joint Employer" Doctrine and Discrimination Laws.* In the view of the EEOC:

> A client of a temporary agency typically qualifies as an employer of the temporary worker during the job assignment, along with the agency. This is because the client usually exercises significant supervisory responsibility over the worker. . . . On the other hand, the client would not qualify as an employer if the staffing firm furnishes the job equipment and has the exclusive right, through on-site managers, to control the details of the work, to make or change assignments, and to terminate the workers.

"Enforcement Guidance: Application of EEO Laws to Contingent Workers Placed by Temporary Employment Agencies and Other Staffing Firms." (12/03/1997) Having the status of a joint employer would not necessarily make a client firm liable for discrimination by the staffing firm, however. For instance, the EEOC does not suggest that a client firm would be responsible for the discriminatory assignment of employees by the staffing firm if it did not know and had no reason to know of the staffing firm's discrimination. Conversely, without knowledge or constructive knowledge, the staffing firm would not be liable for a client firm's discriminatory treatment of referred employees. See, e.g., Caldwell v. ServiceMaster, 966 F.Supp. 33 (D.D.C.1997). If a staffing firm does have knowledge of a client's firm's discriminatory conduct, what exactly should be its responsibility?

6. *Discrimination Claims in the Absence of a Direct Employment Relationship.* Some antidiscrimination laws like 42 U.S.C. § 1981 (discussed further at pp. 201–203 infra) reach all contractual dealings, and hence do not require the existence of an employment relationship. See, e.g., Danco, Inc. v. Wal–Mart Stores, Inc., 178 F.3d 8 (1st Cir.1999). In addition, an enterprise that fits the statutory definition of employer may not need to have an employment relationship with a particular employee to be liable for discriminatory conduct against that employee. A statutory employer has been held to violate Title VII, for instance, by using its position of power and control to interfere for discriminatory reasons with a plaintiff's employment relationship with a third party. The lead case is Sibley Memorial Hosp. v. Wilson, 488 F.2d 1338 (D.C.Cir.1973), involving a suit by a male nurse alleging that the hospital discriminated on the basis of sex by refusing to refer male nurses to female patients. The *Sibley* court observed:

Control over access to the job market may reside * * * in a labor organization, an employment agency, or an employer as defined in Title VII; and it would appear that Congress has determined to prohibit each of these from exerting any power it may have to foreclose, on invidious grounds, access by any individual to employment opportunities otherwise available to him. To permit a covered employer to exploit circumstances peculiarly affording it the capability of discriminatorily interfering with an individual's employment opportunities with another employer, while it could not do so with respect to employment in its own service, would be to condone continued use of the very criteria that Congress has prohibited.

Id. at 1341. But see Gulino v. New York State Educ. Dept., 460 F.3d 361, 374 (2d Cir. 2006) (questioning whether the *Sibley* court's reasoning has support in the language of Title VII).

In order to receive the protection of the modern employment discrimination laws, in any event, the victim of the discrimination will have to be an employee rather than an independent contractor. See, e.g., Aberman v. J. Abouchar & Sons, Inc., 160 F.3d 1148 (7th Cir.1998) (independent contractor not protected by ADA). Should these laws be so limited?

Part Two

PROTECTING EMPLOYEES
FROM STATUS
DISCRIMINATION

This major Part of the book examines American employment law framed to protect individuals from disadvantage because of membership in particular social groups. Its first and longest chapter considers the basic doctrines through which that law (especially Title VII of the 1964 Civil Rights Act) attempts to control several types of status discrimination in employment, including race discrimination. The reach of Title VII's antidiscrimination principle is the subject of the next two chapters, which explore, first, that statute's solicitude for seniority systems, and, second, efforts to give special treatment to members of historically disadvantaged groups. The final three chapters in Part II consider special issues that arise in connection with the regulation of discrimination against members of groups defined by three special types of status: sex, age, and disability.

Part II begins by asking why a society might wish to pass laws regulating status discrimination. Such laws might be directed at one or both of two kinds of practices. First, such laws might seek to purify employer decisionmaking by penalizing decisions that are significantly influenced by consideration of the presumptively irrelevant characteristic of group membership. Alternatively, or in addition, these laws could prohibit employment decisions that, even in the absence of discriminatory intent, significantly disadvantage members of particular social groups without adequate justification.

There are reasons to condemn employment decisions influenced by consideration of a particular status, even when those decisions are not animated by hostility toward anyone and perhaps are economically efficient. Stereotypes or generalizations about a protected class may be sufficiently accurate to move an efficiency-minded decision-maker to use them rather than a more refined, but expensive test. But even such efficient generalizations can inflict on their objects significant cumulative psychological and economic harm. This harm could fuel a vicious cycle that enhances the accuracy and hence the efficiency of the generalizations. The victims of such discrimination may, in time, even come to embrace their assigned roles, hence aggravating the continuing inequality.

The importance and difficulty of breaking vicious cycles may also provide a basis for adopting the second kind of regulation of status discrimination—prohibiting all employment decisions that significantly disadvantage members of particular social groups without adequate compensatory justification. Many of the reasons that employers may be influenced by status categories such as race and sex are affected by the disproportionate allocation of roles in the society. Prohibiting employment decisions that, without some significant justification, aggravate this disproportionate allocation is a means of loosening the linkage between role and membership in particular groups, and hence counteracting the salience of group membership to employment decisionmaking.

This future-oriented justification for the second kind of regulation of status discrimination may be complemented by justifications resting on recognition of present and past unfair treatment. Discrimination in other arenas, such as in education and housing, may also make it more difficult for some individuals to satisfy certain ostensibly neutral employment qualifications. Society therefore may be concerned that even decisions untainted by prejudice may compound other unfair treatment of particular social groups.

Indeed, society also may wish to remove unnecessary barriers to the employment of individuals whose disadvantage was not caused by present or past unfair treatment. This seems especially plausible if the disadvantage is of a type for which the society does not want to hold the individual responsible. We will consider disability discrimination regulation as a possible example. This rationale also seems especially plausible if the disadvantage results from some service the individual has given society or some of its members in the past. The regulation of discrimination against veterans may be an example; age discrimination regulation may be another.

The two forms of status discrimination regulation may impose different costs. Prohibition of discriminatory motivation works a limited intrusion into the sphere of employer discretion, for it need not entail second-guessing by regulatory authorities of the reasonableness of firm requirements. However, a rule invalidating practices having an unjustified adverse impact on a particular group authorizes government directly to question the need for practices that the firm has put in place for nondiscriminatory business reasons. The incidence of error or other costs of over-compliance thus may be greater with respect to this second type of regulation.

This overview of possible justifications for the two principal forms of status discrimination regulation cannot pretend to be fully comprehensive. It should, however, present the reader with some questions to ask in considering the materials in this first part of the book. What kind of status discrimination regulation does a particular legal doctrine express? What might justify that form of regulation for the particular group in question? Is that justification adequate given the costs and incidental effects of the regulation?

Chapter Two

PRINCIPLES FOR RACE AND OTHER STATUS DISCRIMINATION REGULATION

A. INTRODUCTION

Note on the Economic Status of African–Americans

Title VII of the 1964 Civil Rights Act prohibits discrimination on account of religion, national origin and sex as well as race and color. However, the primary impetus for the statute was the post-World War II movement for racial equality in America. The statute reflects Congress's concern with the problem of racism in American labor markets, and with the failure of the descendants of those brought to America as slaves to achieve economic equality. Although this chapter considers legal doctrine that applies to other forms of status discrimination, inasmuch as American status discrimination law was first developed principally to modify our society's treatment of its black citizens, it begins by highlighting the contemporary economic position of these citizens.

The economically adverse position of blacks in contemporary American society remains a stubborn reality even after almost four decades since the passage of Title VII. The median income of black families is less than two thirds that of white families. See Council of Economic Advisors, Economic Report of the President, Table B–33 (2008). Moreover, in 2000, the median net worth of households maintained by whites was more than ten times that of households maintained by blacks. Shawna Orzechowski & Peter Sepielli, U.S. Census Bureau, Current Population Reports, Household Economic Studies: Net Worth and Asset Ownership of Households, 12–13 (2003). Since 1972 the unemployment rate for blacks or African Americans has ranged from a high of 19.5% in 1983 to a low of 7.6% in 2000. See Economic Report of the President, supra, at Table B–43. Throughout this period the unemployment rate for blacks has been more than twice that for whites. Id.

Black men's wages rose relative to those of white males until the middle to late 1970s, but their relative pay declined over the next decade, and the record to the mid–1990s showed no further clear improvement in relative pay until the economic expansion of the late 1990s seemed to push their income to about three fourths that of white males. Council of Economic Advisors, Changing America: Indicators of Social Well–Being by Race and Hispanic Origin, 23, 28 (1998). This ratio has been maintained in this decade. See Economic Report of the President, supra, at Table B–33 (data through 2006). Black women have fared better relative to white women, with full-time black female workers actually almost achieving parity with their white counterparts in weekly wages in the mid 1970s; yet black women failed to keep full pace with the increases in the income of white women over the next three decades. Id.; Changing America, supra, at 23, 31.

Nevertheless, there has been substantial improvement in the economic status of a significant portion of American blacks. The officially reported poverty rate for black families was reported to be the lowest in 2000, at 19.3%, since original publication of the data in 1982. Economic Report of the President, supra, at Table B–33 (also noting a rate of 21.5% in 2006). The poverty rate continues to be much higher for black families, but it has dipped below a multiple of three times the rate for white families. Although most of the improvement occurred before 1970, since 1994 the poverty rate for blacks has been below thirty percent. Id. Moreover, by 1995 almost one in two black families had incomes at least double that of the poverty line, compared to three of four white families. See Stephen Thernstrom & Abigal Thernstrom, America in Black and White, 196 (1998). Also by 1995 the upper two fifths of African–American households had average incomes of over $36,700; the top fifth earned an average of almost $77,000. These figures compare favorably with averages of about $27,500 and $53,000 for 1967 (expressed in 1995 dollars). See Orlando Patterson, The Ordeal of Integration, 22 (1997). In 2001 the median family income for black households headed by a married couple was eighty four percent of that of comparable white families. U.S. Census Reports, Tables F–7A and F–7B (Sept. 30, 2002). This is a significant improvement over 1967, when the median income of black families headed by a married couple was only sixty eight percent of that of their white counterparts. See Patterson, supra, at 27. Black poverty has been increasingly concentrated in female headed households. See Thernstrom & Thernstrom, supra, at 232–245. In the mid–1990s ninety four percent of poor African–American children were in such families. See Patterson, supra, at 29.

These statistics seem to suggest a picture of two black Americas—one that is on the path that has been open to other ethnic groups in America, and one that continues to face significant barriers to any advance. What explains the persistence of the second part of the picture? Part of the explanation must be the continued disproportionate assignment of blacks to less desirable, remunerative, and stable jobs. See, e.g., Alfred W. Blumrosen & Ruth G. Blumrosen, Chapter 11, Discrimination Against Blacks, in The Reality of Intentional Job Discrimination in Metropolitan America—1999, 111 (2002), available at http://law.newark.rutgers.edu/blumrosen-eeo.html (study concluding that in 1999 over one-fourth of establishments studied did not hire roughly proportionate numbers of blacks in at least one occupational category). This continued job segregation may in part derive from what economists call "supply" factors—the cumulative effects of broken families, inferior school systems, lack of training and dashed expectations that reflect a failure of national will during reconstruction, a century of governmentally sanctioned segregation and continued resistance to integration, and perhaps perverse incentives embedded in welfare regulations and a culture of poverty. Together these "supply" factors may create what the economist Glenn Loury has termed a "development bias", an unequal opportunity to acquire productivity that disadvantages African Americans in the United States. See Glenn Loury, The Anatomy of Racial Inequality 93 (2002).

Discriminatory bias against African–Americans remains a serious problem, however, suggesting that a part of the explanation for the economic subordination of some black Americans may also continue to lie on the "demand" side, the discriminatory preferences of employers and incumbent white employees. For a theoretical account of the role of racial discrimination in labor markets, consider the reading that follows, by Kenneth Arrow, a Nobel laureate for economics.

KENNETH J. ARROW, MODELS OF JOB DISCRIMINATION*

The most natural starting point for analysis is to look at the proximate determinant of the demand for labor, the employer's decisions. If we assume away productivity differences between black and white employees, the simplest explanation of the existence of wage differences is the taste of the employer. Formally, we might suppose that the employer acts so as to maximize a utility function that depends not only on profits but also on the numbers of white and black employees * * *. Presumably, other variables being held constant, the employer has a negative marginal utility for black labor. A positive marginal utility for white labor might also be expected, if only in some sense to offset and dilute the black labor. A specific version of this hypothesis would be that the employer's utility depends only on the ratio of black to white workers and is independent of the scale of operations of the firm.

Under these circumstances, the employer will hire white workers up to a point somewhat beyond where their marginal productivity equals their wage, since he is also rewarded through their positive marginal utility. Similarly, he will stop hiring black laborers at a point somewhat before the point that equates their marginal productivity to their wage. Under the assumption that the two kinds of workers are perfect substitutes in production, the marginal productivities of the two kinds of workers are equal. Their common value depends only on the total number of workers of both races hired. It follows, then, that equilibrium is possible only when the wages of white workers are above the marginal product of labor and the wages of black workers below. To be precise, white wages will exceed marginal product by the marginal rate of substitution between white workers and profits, the rate being computed at the white-black ratio in the labor force. A similar statement holds for black wages.

* From Racial Discrimination in Economic Life, ch. 2, pp. 83–102 (A.H. Pascal, ed., 1972).

Under this model, it is clear that black workers incur a definite loss, as compared with the competitive level in the absence of discrimination. On the other hand, white workers are likely gainers relative to the nondiscriminatory level * * *.

[*Eds.* Arrow then proceeds to apply a similar utility analysis for the possibly discriminatory preferences of unions, coworkers and customers.]

At a certain level, then, we have a coherent and by no means implausible account of the economic implications of racial discrimination. In the grossest sense, it accounts for the known facts. For example, the fact that discrimination against blacks increases with the level of education implies that the rate of return to the investment in human capital is lower for blacks than for whites, explaining in turn why the proportion of blacks in college is lower than that of whites.

* * *

A model in which white employers and employees were motivated by a dislike of association with blacks as well as more narrowly economic motives would give a satisfactory qualitative account of observed racial discrimination in wages but, at least as far as employers are concerned, it is hard to understand how discriminatory behavior could persist in the long run in the face of competitive pressures. Several assumptions have been made, implicitly or explicitly, and perhaps should be restated here: constant returns to scale in the long run, a sufficiently wide spectrum of tastes toward discrimination and in particular a sufficient number of actual or potential nondiscriminating employers, and an adequate freedom of entry. The last condition, let me stress, is consistent with a certain amount of imperfect competition. If there is enough entry by nondiscriminating entrepreneurs to absorb the entire black labor force and some more, then wages would be equalized, but the surviving discriminating firms would now be completely segregated. Obviously, the degree of freedom of entry necessary to eliminate racial wage differentials depends upon the proportion of blacks in the labor force. But, in the United States, the black workers constitute some fifteen percent of the labor force; if employer discrimination were the sole cause of wage differences, it is hard to believe that competitive forces are inadequate to eliminate racial wage differentials.

* * *

We thus see that the structure of tastes that seems adequate to give a short-period explanation does not seem to resist the operations of competitive pressures in the long run. One might search for other and more stable explanatory structures, but I know of none that have been proposed or that seem at all credible. Instead, I propose that we look more closely at the long-run adjustment processes. * * * We have only to assume that the employer makes an investment, let us call it a personnel investment, every time a worker is hired. He makes this investment with the expectation of making a competitive return on it; if he himself has no racial feelings, the wage rate in full equilibrium will equal the marginal product of labor less the return on the personnel investment. Let us consider the simplest of the above models, that of discrimination by fellow employees who are perfect substitutes. If the firm starts with an all-white labor force, it will not find it profitable to fire that force, in which its personnel capital has already been sunk, and hire an all-black force in which a new investment has to be made simply because black wages are now slightly less than white wages. Of course, if the wage difference is large enough, it does pay to make the shift.

* * * The typical firm may remain segregated white though possibly adding more white workers, it may switch entirely to a segregated black state, or it may find it best to keep its present white working force while adding black workers. In the last case, of course, it will have to increase the wages of the white workers to compensate for their feelings of dislike, but it may still find it profitable to do so because replacing the existing white workers by blacks means a personnel investment. If we stick closely to the model with all of its artificial conditions, we note that only the all-white firms are absorbing the additional supply of white workers, so there must be some of those in the new equilibrium situation. On the other hand, there must be some firms that are all black or else some integrated firms whose new workers are black in order to absorb the new black workers. It can be concluded in either case, however, that a wage difference between black and white workers will always remain in this model. Furthermore, there will be some segregated white firms. Whether the remaining firms will be segregated black or integrated will depend on the degree of discriminatory feeling by white workers against mixing with blacks.

* * *

This concludes what may be thought of as the central model. I cannot help but feel that still other factors exist. I have two suggestions to make, both of a very tentative nature. The first is that what I have referred to as the discriminator tastes of the employer might in fact be better described as a problem in perception * * *. That is, employers discriminate against blacks because they believe them to be inferior workers. Notice that in this view the physical prominence of skin color is highly significant. As an employer, I might have all sorts of views about the relative productivities of different kinds of workers. Determining what kind of a worker he is may be a costly operation in information gathering; even if I hold my beliefs strongly, it may not, in many circumstances, be worthwhile in my calculations to screen employees according to them. Skin color is a cheap source of information, however, and may therefore be used. In the United States today, I believe it fair to say that school diplomas are being widely used by employers for exactly that reason; it is believed that schooling has something to do with productivity, and asking for a diploma is an inexpensive operation.

* * *

The second assumption is that the qualities of the individual are not known to the employer beforehand. The most interesting case of that kind is one in which the worker must make some investment in himself but one which the employer can never be sure of. I am thinking here not of the conventional types of education or experience, which are easily observable, but more subtle types the employer cannot observe directly: the habits of action and thought that favor good performance in skilled jobs, steadiness, punctuality, responsiveness, and initiative. A worker who has made the requisite investment will be said to be *qualified*.

* * *

Since personnel investments are greater at higher levels, this model of personnel investment and uncertainty about qualifications also helps to explain the increasing discrimination against blacks in higher-level jobs. * * * Without going into detailed discussion of the somewhat variant viewpoints, the common view is that blacks are largely, though not exclusively, confined to marginal jobs marked by low wages, low promotion possibilities, and instability of employment. The instability, incidentally, is in large part voluntary; it is interpreted as a rational response to limited opportunity, which both increases the value and decreases the cost of search.

Notes and Questions

1. *Does Arrow Explain the Long–Run Persistence of Racial Discrimination?* Arrow suggests that competitive forces will not necessarily result in the elimination of job segregation and wage discrimination because of the role of personnel investment and perception. How do these factors, according to Arrow, tend to discourage employers from taking advantage of the availability of a pool of ostensibly qualified workers bidding for the same jobs at lower wages, and hence undercut the competitive dynamic that, in theory, should make discriminatory preferences unprofitable?

2. *A Vicious Cycle?* Although Arrow begins his analysis by stating that his focus is on the demand rather than the supply side of the labor market, by the end of his essay is he suggesting that supply and demand factors combine to fuel a vicious cycle that continues to assign blacks disproportionately to less remunerative and stable jobs? Such outcomes may be the result of what another Nobel laureate Edmund Phelps first called "statistical discrimination," see Phelps, The Statistical Theory of Racism and Sexism, 62 Am.Econ.Rev. 659 (1972)—drawing inferences about an entire status group because of average characteristics of members of that group. Such discrimination cannot be dismissed as irrational decisionmaking. Employers, trying to determine which workers are more likely to respond dependably to the responsibilities of higher paying and more secure jobs, rationally look for easily observed, if rough, predictive factors. Disproportionately large numbers of blacks, raised in poverty and conscious of an American history of racial barriers, may rationally decide to invest less in the development of those personal attributes, including but certainly not limited to educational achievement, that are important to success in those higher paying jobs.

Employers may determine that it is efficient to consider race, or perhaps characteristics closely associated with race, when predicting which prospective employees are likely to repay the costs of training. However, the consideration of race and closely associated characteristics will screen out many blacks who might have responded to the challenges of higher paying jobs by making the necessary human capital investments. The continuation of job segregation makes the rejection of such investments seem rational for more young blacks, and the cycle continues. For another description of a cycle of "self-confirming stereotypes", see Loury, supra, at 26–33.

3. *Relaxing Some Assumptions of Traditional Economic Theory.* Labor economists have developed models—other than the variant on the traditional neoclassical model employed by Arrow—that may be useful to understanding racial discrimination and its persistence in at least some parts of our economy. Institutional economists, for instance, have set aside the neoclassical assumptions about labor markets discussed in the introduction of this book. They have suggested that in industries where the acquisition of skills useful only for the particular employer is important, the focus of employers is primarily on the internal labor market, on encouraging workers to make investments in firm-specific training, to make long-term commitments to the firm, and to cooperate in the training of newly hired workers. Other "secondary labor markets" are characterized by unstable jobs involving relatively low wages, little training, small chance of advancement and tolerance of poor work habits. See, e.g., Peter Doeringer & Michael Piore, Internal Labor Markets and Manpower Analysis (1971). To the extent that a segregated, poverty-afflicted subclass of blacks continues to be caught within a vicious cycle in secondary markets, they are less likely to develop the skills and attitudes necessary to compete effectively in the primary markets. See id. at 34–38; Michael Piore, Jobs and Training, in The State and the Poor (Samuel H. Beer & Richard E. Barringer, eds. 1970).

Other economists have attempted to develop "efficiency wage" or "tournament" models of labor markets by using the tools of the neoclassical economists while modifying some of their assumptions. See, e.g., Andrew Weiss, Efficiency Wages: Models of Unemployment, Layoffs, and Wage Dispersion (1990); Paul L. Milgrom & John Roberts, Economics, Organization, and Management (1992). These economists, like their institutional colleagues, have recognized that the assumptions of the traditional model, including that of market-clearing wages set at the level necessary to eliminate unemployment of qualified workers, do not describe the reality of most American labor markets. The "efficiency wage" and "tournament" models of labor markets, also like the institutional models, incorporate the reality of complex internal incentives and hierarchies within most large firms. They do so, however, in a way that may provide further insight into the persistence of race and other forms of discrimination in at least some American labor markets. Consider, for instance, the efforts of two American law professors to use this economic modeling to explain discrimination in "high-level" jobs:

DAVID CHARNY & G. MITU GULATI, EFFICIENCY WAGES, TOURNAMENTS, AND DISCRIMINATION*

* * * [F]irms that we describe either pay higher-than-market wages to ward off shirking, or offer tournament bonuses to induce extra effort. So long as the extra benefit in terms of inducing effort or attracting high ability workers is greater than the extra wages, this is a rational profit-maximizing strategy, and firms will continue to use it. Wages far above the hypothetical market-clearing wage lead to considerable involuntary unemployment. For example, at the wages paid by elite law firms, many unemployed lawyers, as well as lawyers consigned to non-elite firms, are willing and able to do elite firm work. Yet the elite firms choose not to lower their wages. The factors we have enumerated—difficulty in detecting quality, inflexible efficiency/tournament wages, and a resulting pool of unemployed qualified workers—set the stage, as the next section explains, for a substantial degree of self-perpetuating discrimination in hiring and promotion.

* * *

Will firms discriminate when choosing among job applicants? Consider a firm that faces an applicant pool including "typical" and minority applicants. Minority applicants are members of a group that has historically suffered from discrimination in education and job opportunities. In analyzing the firms' decisions, we take the existence of past societal discrimination as given. Past discrimination establishes a baseline level of statistical discrimination—a level which reflects the influence of societal discrimination on the human capital of applicants. Paradoxically, the discrimination we describe will prove stable, once in place, even if the background societal discrimination is eliminated. Alternatively, we might assume that firms discriminate on the basis of taste—i.e., dislike of some groups—or high costs of integration of minority groups into the workplace. In our model, this discrimination, like statistical discrimination, would persist and cause an insufficient investment in human capital by minority workers.

Our analysis here proceeds in two stages. At the first stage, we identify the fundamental features of discrimination in an efficiency-wage or tournament setting. These differ in three important respects from discrimination in a market where "wage equals marginal product." First, it does not hurt the firm economically to indulge a taste for discrimination, so long as this taste is exercised in choosing between identical candidates. Firms that engage in taste-based discrimination do not disappear, * * *. Second, even absent a taste for discrimination, the rational firm will use minority group status as a signal if the mean achievement level of minority group members is less than that of the "typical" group. Third, minorities end up with reduced total compensation because as a group they are valued less than the "typical" workers.

* 33 Harv. Civ.Rts–Civ.Lib. L.Rev. 57 (1998).

Having explained these basic claims, we then turn to a more detailed and inevitably more speculative analysis of minority workers' responses to this discriminatory dynamic. In particular, we shall stipulate that workers choose among various career "strategies," and argue that minority workers radically alter their choice of strategies in response to the discrimination that we describe. Our model of strategic choices points to further consequences of discrimination in the efficiency-wage and tournament settings. Most importantly, and perhaps most counterintuitively, individuals from minority groups are less likely to get hired, even if their mean achievement level is the same as the mean achievement level of the "typical" group. This result occurs because of the self-reinforcing interactions between the strategies workers adopt in the face of discrimination, the reliability of the signals they generate as a result, and the mechanisms that the firms use to respond to the relative unreliability of minority applicants' signals. This in turn exacerbates the effects of the statistical discrimination, which occurs when the mean achievement level of the minority group is less than that of the "typical" group. Once minorities' strategic choices are taken into account, it appears even more strongly, then, that firms engaging in discrimination are robust against market competition.

* * * Minority applicants have lower incentives to invest in signals that would place them on par with "typical" applicants because minority applicants know that if a choice between workers is made, they will lose out. In aggregate, minority applicants choose strategies that are likely to produce either "superstar" or "low-achiever" signals. This change in distribution of signals in turn affects the evaluation of minority applicants. Even if the average level of achievement for minority applicants is the same, the difference in distribution, and correspondingly, in noisiness of signals, indicates the perpetuation of statistical discrimination.

* * * The skewed strategy is in the self-interest of the individual minority who is unlikely to get a job if she correctly signals herself as average, but has a better chance if she falsely signals herself as a "superstar." Across the economy, however, firms now are even more likely to discriminate because correlating achievement signals of minorities to their true abilities has become harder to do than it is for "typicals." Achievement signals are now distributed so that members of minority groups, who are producing a large number of noisy and false signals, are more likely to fall at the extremes than are "typicals," most of whom correctly signal themselves as average. This distribution is likely to occur when individuals' investment in credentials is affected by discrimination.

Notes and Questions

1. *Descriptive of Reality?* Note that Charney and Gulati describe how supply and demand may interact to limit the achievement of even those minorities who have broken out of a cycle of poverty. The reading thus may suggest why certain forms of employment discrimination may be particularly

resilient in some labor markets. The authors only suggest a plausible theory, however; they do not offer empirical proof that the theory explains reality. What sort of evidence would you consider relevant?

2. *An Explanation for High Level Jobs Only?* The subtitle of the Charney–Gulati essay is: "A Theory of Employment Discrimination for 'High–Level' Jobs." Might the theory help explain the "ceilings" that allegedly limit the advancement of black, and female, professionals and managers? Does the theory help explain the persistence of a poverty-afflicted subclass of blacks during a period of advancement for a substantial number of African Americans? For the view that social policy must move beyond the demand-side focus of antidiscrimination law to address the supply-side problems of the "truly disadvantaged", including those caused by the deindustrialization of major American cities, see, e.g., William J. Wilson, When Work Disappears: the World of the New Urban Poor (1996), and The Truly Disadvantaged: The Inner City, the Underclass, and Public Policy (1987).

3. *Correctable by Antidiscrimination Law?* As you study in this chapter the antidiscrimination doctrine applied under Title VII, consider whether that law is able to control the processes that Charney and Gulati describe. The authors argue that it cannot, in part because Title VII doctrine makes the proof of covert discrimination too difficult, especially where applicants from within and without a protected class have roughly equal qualifications.

Note on Title VII of the 1964 Civil Rights Act and Other Federal Initiatives Against Race Discrimination in Employment

The federal government did not begin to take seriously the problem of racial discrimination until the 1960s. Eighty years before, a modest legislative effort to challenge certain barriers was rebuffed by the Supreme Court in the In re Civil Rights Cases, 109 U.S. 3, 3 S.Ct. 18, 27 L.Ed. 835 (1883), which adopted a very narrow view of Congress's authority to enforce the antidiscrimination commands of the Thirteenth and Fourteenth Amendments. During the Second World War, President Roosevelt created the Fair Employment Practices Committee, which investigated discriminatory practices and attempted to pressure federal contractors and others to hire black workers. The Court, too, began during this period to enforce more aggressively equal protection principles against segregationist political parties, labor unions and land-use regulations. However, it was not until the Court's 1954 decision in Brown v. Board of Education, 347 U.S. 483, 74 S.Ct. 686, 98 L.Ed. 873 (1954), and the ensuing decade of resistance to integration and the emergence of a national civil rights movement, that federal involvement began in earnest. In 1962, President Kennedy issued an executive order that authorized enforcement mechanisms to give effect to the ban on discrimination by federal contractors put in place by his predecessors. Three years later, President Johnson issued Executive Order 11246, which remains in force to this day. As elaborated below at pp. 298–301, the Executive Order extends beyond antidiscrimination commands to require all federal contractors to ensure the utilization of qualified minority group workers. Furthermore, in the 1970s the Supreme Court held that a reconstruction-era civil rights law, 42 U.S.C. § 1981, proscribes racial discrimination by private sector employers.

The most important federal initiative, however, was Title VII of the Civil Rights Act of 1964, 42 U.S.C. 2000e et seq. Passed over considerable opposition by representatives from the Southern states, Title VII extended antidiscrimination commands to private employment, and sought to promote the economic integration of blacks into the mainstream of American society. President Johnson and the Congress witnessed the civil rights movement's hard-fought, successful attack on the most blatant legacy of slavery, the de jure system of segregation and discrimination in public facilities in the South. They recognized, however, that blacks in the North as well as the South confronted other discriminatory barriers in private as well as public employment. See discussion in United Steelworkers of America v. Weber, 443 U.S. 193, 202, 99 S.Ct. 2721, 2727, 61 L.Ed.2d 480 (1979).

After amendments in 1972, Title VII covers not only all private employers affecting interstate commerce with fifteen or more employees, but also all governmental employers—federal, state and local—as well.

The central prohibition of Title VII provides:

Sec. 703. (a) It shall be an unlawful employment practice for an employer—

(1) to fail or refuse to hire or to discharge any individual, or otherwise to discriminate against any individual with respect to his compensations, terms, conditions, or privileges of employment, because of such individual's race, color, religion, sex, or national origin; or

(2) to limit, segregate, or classify his employees or applicants for employment in any way which would deprive or tend to deprive any individual of employment opportunities, or otherwise adversely affect his status as an employee, because of such individual's race, color, religion, sex, or national origin.

Title VII also proscribes discriminatory practices by labor organizations and employment agencies.

Title VII establishes an executive agency, the Equal Employment Opportunity Commission (EEOC). The EEOC investigates complaints by or on behalf of persons claiming to be aggrieved by a violation of the Act as well as any charges of discrimination lodged by one of its members. If the EEOC determines that there is good cause to believe that the complaint is well-founded, it attempts to remedy the problem through informal conciliation with the party charged. If it cannot do so satisfactorily, the agency has the authority to bring a court action against that party. The EEOC has no authority to issue enforcement orders itself; it must obtain relief from courts, which are granted power to enjoin illegal practices and to provide "any other equitable relief as the court deems appropriate * * *."

Aggrieved individuals have a private right of action under the statute. Since passage of the Civil Rights Act of 1991, they may seek limited legal damages, as well as equitable relief, to compensate for intentional discrimination. However, complainants cannot exercise their Title VII right of action until they first give the EEOC an opportunity to conciliate and to bring its own public suit. Moreover, aggrieved individuals must also give state and local agencies possessing antidiscrimination authority an opportunity to remedy the problem before proceeding to court. This system was framed as a compromise to encourage conciliation and to allay the concerns of certain members of Congress that "zealous" federal regulators would unduly disrupt private decisionmaking.

The next sections of this chapter focus on the three most important approaches to establishing violations of Title VII that have been developed by judicial interpretations of the statute. Following the language of the courts, the book denominates these approaches individual disparate treatment, systemic disparate treatment, and disparate impact.

B. PROVING INDIVIDUAL DISPARATE TREAT-MENT

McDONNELL DOUGLAS CORP. v. GREEN
Supreme Court of the United States, 1973.
411 U.S. 792, 93 S.Ct. 1817, 36 L.Ed.2d 668.

JUSTICE POWELL delivered the opinion of the Court.

Petitioner, McDonnell Douglas Corp., is an aerospace and aircraft manufacturer headquartered in St. Louis, Missouri, where it employs over 30,000 people. Respondent, a black citizen of St. Louis, worked for petitioner as a mechanic and laboratory technician from 1956 until August 28, 1964 when he was laid off in the course of a general reduction in petitioner's work force.

Respondent, a long-time activist in the civil rights movement, protested vigorously that his discharge and the general hiring practices of petitioner were racially motivated. As part of this protest, respondent and other members of the Congress on Racial Equality illegally stalled their cars on the main roads leading to petitioner's plant for the purpose of blocking access to it at the time of the morning shift change. The District Judge described the plan for, and respondent's participation in, the "stall-in" as follows:

* * *

"Acting under the 'stall in' plan, plaintiff [respondent in the present action] drove his car onto Brown Road, a McDonnell access road, at approximately 7:00 a.m., at the start of the morning rush hour. Plaintiff was aware of the traffic problems that would result. He stopped his car with the intent to block traffic. The police arrived shortly and requested plaintiff to move his car. He refused to move his car voluntarily. Plaintiff's car was towed away by the police, and he was arrested for obstructing traffic. Plaintiff pleaded guilty to the charge of obstructing traffic and was fined."

On July 2, 1965, a "lock-in" took place wherein a chain and padlock were placed on the front door of a building to prevent the occupants, certain of petitioner's employees, from leaving. Though respondent apparently knew beforehand of the "lock-in," the full extent of his involvement remains uncertain.

Some three weeks following the "lock-in," on July 25, 1965, petitioner publicly advertised for qualified mechanics, respondent's trade, and respondent promptly applied for re-employment. Petitioner turned down respondent, basing its rejection on respondent's participation in the "stall-in" and "lock-in." Shortly thereafter, respondent filed a formal complaint with the Equal Employment Opportunity Commission, claiming that petitioner had refused to rehire him because of his race and persistent involvement in the civil rights movement, in violation of §§ 703(a)(1) and 704(a) of the Civil Rights Act of 1964, 42 U.S.C. §§ 2000e–2(a)(1) and 2000e–3(a). The former section generally prohibits racial discrimination in any employment decision while the latter forbids discrimination against applicants or employees for attempting to protest or correct allegedly discriminatory conditions of employment.

The Commission made no finding on respondent's allegation of racial bias under § 703(a)(1), but it did find reasonable cause to believe petitioner had violated § 704(a) by refusing to rehire respondent because of his civil rights activity. After the Commission unsuccessfully attempted to conciliate the dispute, it advised respondent in March 1968, of his right to institute a civil action in federal court within 30 days.

[*Eds.* The Court reported that the District Court, with the affirmance of the Court of Appeals, found that the plaintiff's participation in illegal demonstrations was not protected by § 704(a), and that plaintiff did not seek further review of this issue. Justice Powell also noted that the District Court had dismissed plaintiff's § 703(a) claim because the EEOC had failed to make a determination of reasonable cause to believe that a violation of that section had been committed. The Supreme Court, however, agreed with the Court of Appeals that an EEOC "cause" finding was not required. The Court stressed that Title VII "does not restrict a complainant's right to sue to those charges as to which the Commission has made findings of reasonable cause * * *." It was thus necessary to remand the case for trial of plaintiff's § 703(a) discrimination claim, and the Court offered the following instructions to guide the trial on remand:]

The complainant in a Title VII trial must carry the initial burden under the statute of establishing a prima facie case of racial discrimination. This may be done by showing (i) that he belongs to a racial minority; (ii) that he applied and was qualified for a job for which the employer was seeking applicants; (iii) that, despite his qualifications, he was rejected; and (iv) that, after his rejection, the position remained open and the employer continued to seek applicants from persons of complainant's qualifications.[13] In the instant case, we agree with the Court of Appeals that respondent proved a prima facie case. Petitioner

---

13. The facts necessarily will vary in Title VII cases, and the specification above of the prima facie proof required from re-spondent is not necessarily applicable in every respect to differing factual situations.

sought mechanics, respondent's trade, and continued to do so after respondent's rejection. Petitioner, moreover, does not dispute respondent's qualifications and acknowledges that his past work performance in petitioner's employ was "satisfactory."

The burden then must shift to the employer to articulate some legitimate, nondiscriminatory reason for the employee's rejection. We need not attempt in the instant case to detail every matter which fairly could be recognized as a reasonable basis for a refusal to hire. Here petitioner has assigned respondent's participation in unlawful conduct against it as the cause for his rejection. We think that this suffices to discharge petitioner's burden of proof at this stage and to meet respondent's prima facie case of discrimination.

The Court of Appeals intimated, however, that petitioner's stated reason for refusing to rehire respondent was a "subjective" rather than objective criterion which "carr[ies] little weight in rebutting charges of discrimination". This was among the statements which caused the dissenting judge to read the opinion as taking "the position that such unlawful acts as Green committed against McDonnell would not legally entitle McDonnell to refuse to hire him, even though no racial motivation was involved * * *." Regardless of whether this was the intended import of the opinion, we think the court below seriously underestimated the rebuttal weight to which petitioner's reasons were entitled. Respondent admittedly had taken part in a carefully planned "stall-in," designed to tie up access to and egress from petitioner's plant at a peak traffic hour. Nothing in Title VII compels an employer to absolve and rehire one who has engaged in such deliberate, unlawful activity against it.[17]

* * *

Petitioner's reason for rejection thus suffices to meet the prima facie case, but the inquiry must not end here. While Title VII does not, without more, compel rehiring of respondent, neither does it permit petitioner to use respondent's conduct as a pretext for the sort of discrimination prohibited by § 703(a)(1). On remand, respondent must, as the Court of Appeals recognized, be afforded a fair opportunity to show that petitioner's stated reason for respondent's rejection was in fact pretext. Especially relevant to such a showing would be evidence that white employees involved in acts against petitioner of comparable seriousness to the "stall-in" were nevertheless retained or rehired. Petitioner may justifiably refuse to rehire one who was engaged in unlawful, disruptive acts against it, but only if this criterion is applied alike to members of all races.

Other evidence that may be relevant to any showing of pretext includes facts as to the petitioner's treatment of respondent during his

17. The unlawful activity in this case was directed specifically against petitioner. We need not consider or decide here whether, or under what circumstances, unlawful activity not directed against the particular employer may be a legitimate justification for refusing to hire.

prior term of employment; petitioner's reaction, if any, to respondent's legitimate civil rights activities; and petitioner's general policy and practice with respect to minority employment. On the latter point, statistics as to petitioner's employment policy and practice may be helpful to a determination of whether petitioner's refusal to rehire respondent in this case conformed to a general pattern of discrimination against blacks. *Jones v. Lee Way Motor Freight, Inc.*, 431 F.2d 245 (C.A.10 1970); Blumrosen, Strangers in Paradise: Griggs v. Duke Power Co., and the Concept of Employment Discrimination, 71 Mich.L.Rev. 59, 91–94 (1972).[19] In short, on the retrial respondent must be given a full and fair opportunity to demonstrate by competent evidence that the presumptively valid reasons for his rejection were in fact a coverup for a racially discriminatory decision.

TEXAS DEPT. OF COMMUNITY AFFAIRS v. BURDINE

Supreme Court of the United States, 1981.
450 U.S. 248, 101 S.Ct. 1089, 67 L.Ed.2d 207.

JUSTICE POWELL delivered the opinion of the Court.

I

Petitioner, the Texas Department of Community Affairs (TDCA), hired respondent, a female, in January 1972, for the position of accounting clerk in the Public Service Careers Division (PSC). PSC provided training and employment opportunities in the public sector for unskilled workers. When hired, respondent possessed several years' experience in employment training. She was promoted to Field Services Coordinator in July 1972. Her supervisor resigned in November of that year, and respondent was assigned additional duties. Although she applied for the supervisor's position of Project Director, the position remained vacant for six months.

PSC was funded completely by the United States Department of Labor. The Department was seriously concerned about inefficiencies at PSC. In February 1973, the Department notified the Executive Director of TDCA, B.R. Fuller, that it would terminate PSC the following month. TDCA officials, assisted by respondent, persuaded the Department to continue funding the program, conditioned upon PSC's reforming its operations. Among the agreed conditions were the appointment of a permanent Project Director and a complete reorganization of the PSC staff.

---

19. The District Court may, for example, determine, after reasonable discovery that "the [racial] composition of defendant's labor force is itself reflective of restrictive or exclusionary practices." See Blumrosen, *supra*, at 92. We caution that such general determinations, while helpful, may not be in and of themselves controlling as to an individualized hiring decision, particularly in the presence of an otherwise justifiable reason for refusing to rehire. See generally *United States v. Bethlehem Steel Corp.*, 312 F.Supp. 977, 992 (W.D.N.Y. 1970), order modified, 446 F.2d 652 (C.A.2 1971); Blumrosen, *supra*, n. 19, at 93.

After consulting with personnel within TDCA, Fuller hired a male from another division of the agency as Project Director. In reducing the PSC staff, he fired respondent along with two other employees, and retained another male, Walz, as the only professional employee in the division. It is undisputed that respondent had maintained her application for the position of Project Director and had requested to remain with TDCA. Respondent soon was rehired by TDCA and assigned to another division of the agency. She received the exact salary paid to the Project Director at PSC, and the subsequent promotions she has received have kept her salary and responsibility commensurate with what she would have received had she been appointed Project Director.

Respondent filed this suit in the United States District Court for the Western District of Texas. She alleged that the failure to promote and the subsequent decision to terminate her had been predicated on gender discrimination in violation of Title VII. After a bench trial, the District Court held that neither decision was based on gender discrimination. The court relied on the testimony of Fuller that the employment decisions necessitated by the commands of the Department of Labor were based on consultation among trusted advisors and a nondiscriminatory evaluation of the relative qualifications of the individuals involved. * * *

The Court of Appeals, however, reversed the District Court's finding that Fuller's testimony sufficiently had rebutted respondent's prima facie case of gender discrimination in the decision to terminate her employment at PSC. The court reaffirmed its previously announced views that the defendant in a Title VII case bears the burden of proving by a preponderance of the evidence the existence of legitimate nondiscriminatory reasons for the employment action and that the defendant also must prove by objective evidence that those hired or promoted were better qualified than the plaintiff. The court found that Fuller's testimony did not carry either of these evidentiary burdens.

II

In *McDonnell Douglas Corp. v. Green,* 411 U.S. 792, 93 S.Ct. 1817, 36 L.Ed.2d 668 (1973), we set forth the basic allocation of burdens and order of presentation of proof in a Title VII case alleging discriminatory treatment. * * *

The nature of the burden that shifts to the defendant should be understood in light of the plaintiff's ultimate and intermediate burdens. The ultimate burden of persuading the trier of fact that the defendant intentionally discriminated against the plaintiff remains at all times with the plaintiff. See *Board of Trustees of Keene State College v. Sweeney,* 439 U.S. 24, 25, n. 2, 99 S.Ct. 295, 296, n. 2, 58 L.Ed.2d 216 (1978); *id.,* at 29, 99 S.Ct., at 297 (STEVENS, J., dissenting). See generally 9 J. Wigmore, Evidence § 2489 (3d ed. 1940) (the burden of persuasion "never shifts"). The *McDonnell Douglas* division of intermediate evidentiary burdens serves to bring the litigants and the court expeditiously and fairly to this ultimate question.

The burden of establishing a prima facie case of disparate treatment is not onerous. The plaintiff must prove by a preponderance of the evidence that she applied for an available position for which she was qualified, but was rejected under circumstances which give rise to an inference of unlawful discrimination.[6] The prima facie case serves an important function in the litigation: it eliminates the most common nondiscriminatory reasons for the plaintiff's rejection. See *Teamsters v. United States,* 431 U.S. 324, 358, and n. 44, 97 S.Ct. 1843, 1866, n. 44, 52 L.Ed.2d 396 (1977). As the Court explained in *Furnco Construction Corp. v. Waters,* 438 U.S. 567, 577, 98 S.Ct. 2943, 2949, 57 L.Ed.2d 957 (1978), the prima facie case "raises an inference of discrimination only because we presume these acts, if otherwise unexplained, are more likely than not based on the consideration of impermissible factors." Establishment of the prima facie case in effect creates a presumption that the employer unlawfully discriminated against the employee. If the trier of fact believes the plaintiff's evidence, and if the employer is silent in the face of the presumption, the court must enter judgment for the plaintiff because no issue of fact remains in the case.[7]

The burden that shifts to the defendant, therefore, is to rebut the presumption of discrimination by producing evidence that the plaintiff was rejected, or someone else was preferred, for a legitimate, nondiscriminatory reason. The defendant need not persuade the court that it was actually motivated by the proffered reasons. See *Sweeney, supra,* at 25, 99 S.Ct., at 296. It is sufficient if the defendant's evidence raises a genuine issue of fact as to whether it discriminated against the plaintiff.[8] To accomplish this, the defendant must clearly set forth, through the introduction of admissible evidence, the reasons for the plaintiff's rejection. The explanation provided must be legally sufficient to justify a judgment for the defendant. If the defendant carries this burden of

---

6. * * *

In the instant case, it is not seriously contested that respondent has proved a prima facie case. She showed that she was a qualified woman who sought an available position, but the position was left open for several months before she finally was rejected in favor of a male, Walz, who had been under her supervision.

7. The phrase "prima facie case" not only may denote the establishment of a legally mandatory, rebuttable presumption, but also may be used by courts to describe the plaintiff's burden of producing enough evidence to permit the trier of fact to infer the fact at issue. 9 J. Wigmore, Evidence § 2494 (3d ed. 1940). *McDonnell Douglas* should have made it apparent that in the Title VII context we use "prima facie case" in the former sense.

8. This evidentiary relationship between the presumption created by a prima facie case and the consequential burden of pro-

duction placed on the defendant is a traditional feature of the common law. "The word 'presumption' properly used refers only to a device for allocating the production burden." F. James & G. Hazard, Civil Procedure § 7.9, p. 255 (2d ed. 1977) (footnote omitted). See Fed.Rule Evid. 301. See generally 9 J. Wigmore, Evidence § 2491 (3d ed. 1940). Cf. J. Maguire, Evidence, Common Sense and Common Law 185–186 (1947). Usually, assessing the burden of production helps the judge determine whether the litigants have created an issue of fact to be decided by the jury. In a Title VII case, the allocation of burdens and the creation of a presumption by the establishment of a prima facie case is intended progressively to sharpen the inquiry into the elusive factual question of intentional discrimination.

production, the presumption raised by the prima facie case is rebutted,[10] and the factual inquiry proceeds to a new level of specificity. Placing this burden of production on the defendant thus serves simultaneously to meet the plaintiff's prima facie case by presenting a legitimate reason for the action and to frame the factual issue with sufficient clarity so that the plaintiff will have a full and fair opportunity to demonstrate pretext. The sufficiency of the defendant's evidence should be evaluated by the extent to which it fulfills these functions.

The plaintiff retains the burden of persuasion. She now must have the opportunity to demonstrate that the proffered reason was not the true reason for the employment decision. This burden now merges with the ultimate burden of persuading the court that she has been the victim of intentional discrimination. She may succeed in this either directly by persuading the court that a discriminatory reason more likely motivated the employer or indirectly by showing that the employer's proffered explanation is unworthy of credence.

* * *

III

The Court of Appeals has misconstrued the nature of the burden that *McDonnell Douglas* and its progeny place on the defendant. We stated in *Sweeney* that "the employer's burden is satisfied if he simply 'explains what he has done' or 'produc[es] evidence of legitimate nondiscriminatory reasons.' " 439 U.S., at 25, n. 2, 99 S.Ct., at 296 n. 2, quoting *id.,* at 28, 29, 99 S.Ct., at 297–298 (STEVENS, J., dissenting). It is plain that the Court of Appeals required much more: it placed on the defendant the burden of persuading the court that it had convincing, objective reasons for preferring the chosen applicant above the plaintiff.[11]

10. See generally J. Thayer, Preliminary Treatise on Evidence 346 (1898). In saying that the presumption drops from the case, we do not imply that the trier of fact no longer may consider evidence previously introduced by the plaintiff to establish a prima facie case. A satisfactory explanation by the defendant destroys the legally mandatory inference of discrimination arising from the plaintiff's initial evidence. Nonetheless, this evidence and inferences properly drawn therefrom may be considered by the trier of fact on the issue of whether the defendant's explanation is pretextual. Indeed, there may be some cases where the plaintiff's initial evidence, combined with effective cross-examination of the defendant, will suffice to discredit the defendant's explanation.

11. The court reviewed the defendant's evidence and explained its deficiency:

"Defendant failed to introduce comparative factual data concerning Burdine and Walz. Fuller merely testified that he discharged and retained personnel in the spring shakeup at TDCA primarily on the recommendations of subordinates and that he considered Walz qualified for the position he was retained to do. Fuller failed to specify any objective criteria on which he based the decision to discharge Burdine and retain Walz. He stated only that the action was in the best interest of the program and that there had been some friction within the department that might be alleviated by Burdine's discharge. Nothing in the record indicates whether he examined Walz' ability to work well with others. This court [previously has] found such unsubstantiated assertions of 'qualification' and 'prior work record' insufficient absent data that will allow a true *comparison* of the individuals hired and rejected."

* * * We have stated consistently that the employee's prima facie case of discrimination will be rebutted if the employer articulates lawful reasons for the action; that is, to satisfy this intermediate burden, the employer need only produce admissible evidence which would allow the trier of fact rationally to conclude that the employment decision had not been motivated by discriminatory animus. The Court of Appeals would require the defendant to introduce evidence which, in the absence of any evidence of pretext, would *persuade* the trier of fact that the employment action was lawful. This exceeds what properly can be demanded to satisfy a burden of production.

The court placed the burden of persuasion on the defendant apparently because it feared that "[i]f an employer need only *articulate*—not prove—a legitimate, nondiscriminatory reason for his action, he may compose fictitious, but legitimate, reasons for his actions." *Turner v. Texas Instruments, Inc.,* [555 F.2d 1251, 1255 (C.A.5 1977)] (emphasis in original). We do not believe, however, that limiting the defendant's evidentiary obligation to a burden of production will unduly hinder the plaintiff. First, as noted above, the defendant's explanation of its legitimate reasons must be clear and reasonably specific. See *Loeb v. Textron, Inc.,* 600 F.2d 1003, 1011–1012, n. 5 (C.A.1 1979). This obligation arises both from the necessity of rebutting the inference of discrimination arising from the prima facie case and from the requirement that the plaintiff be afforded "a full and fair opportunity" to demonstrate pretext. Second, although the defendant does not bear a formal burden of persuasion, the defendant nevertheless retains an incentive to persuade the trier of fact that the employment decision was lawful. Thus, the defendant normally will attempt to prove the factual basis for its explanation. Third, the liberal discovery rules applicable to any civil suit in federal court are supplemented in a Title VII suit by the plaintiff's access to the Equal Employment Opportunity Commission's investigatory files concerning her complaint. See *EEOC v. Associated Dry Goods Corp.,* 449 U.S. 590, 101 S.Ct. 817, 66 L.Ed.2d 762 (1981). Given these factors, we are unpersuaded that the plaintiff will find it particularly difficult to prove that a proffered explanation lacking a factual basis is a pretext. We remain confident that the *McDonnell Douglas* framework permits the plaintiff meriting relief to demonstrate intentional discrimination.

The Court of Appeals also erred in requiring the defendant to prove by objective evidence that the person hired or promoted was more qualified than the plaintiff. *McDonnell Douglas* teaches that it is the plaintiff's task to demonstrate that similarly situated employees were not treated equally. 411 U.S., at 804, 93 S.Ct., at 1825. The Court of Appeals' rule would require the employer to show that the plaintiff's objective qualifications were inferior to those of the person selected. If it cannot, a court would, in effect, conclude that it has discriminated.

The court's procedural rule harbors a substantive error. Title VII prohibits all discrimination in employment based upon race, sex, and national origin. "The broad, overriding interest, shared by employer, employee, and consumer, is efficient and trustworthy workmanship assured through fair and * * * neutral employment and personnel decisions." *McDonnell Douglas, supra,* at 801, 93 S.Ct., at 1823. Title VII, however, does not demand that an employer give preferential treatment to minorities or women. 42 U.S.C. § 2000e–2(j). See *Steelworkers v. Weber,* 443 U.S. 193, 205–206, 99 S.Ct. 2721, 2728–2729, 61 L.Ed.2d 480 (1979). The statute was not intended to "diminish traditional management prerogatives." *Id.,* at 207, 99 S.Ct., at 2729. It does not require the employer to restructure his employment practices to maximize the number of minorities and women hired. *Furnco Construction Corp. v. Waters,* 438 U.S. 567, 577–578, 98 S.Ct. 2943, 2949–2950, 57 L.Ed.2d 957 (1978).

The views of the Court of Appeals can be read, we think, as requiring the employer to hire the minority or female applicant whenever that person's objective qualifications were equal to those of a white male applicant. But Title VII does not obligate an employer to accord this preference. Rather, the employer has discretion to choose among equally qualified candidates, provided the decision is not based upon unlawful criteria. The fact that a court may think that the employer misjudged the qualifications of the applicants does not in itself expose him to Title VII liability, although this may be probative of whether the employer's reasons are pretexts for discrimination. *Loeb v. Textron, Inc., supra,* at 1012, n. 6; see *Lieberman v. Gant,* 630 F.2d 60, 65 (C.A.2 1980).

Notes and Questions

1. *What Kind of Discrimination Is Reached by These Decisions?* At page 40 the introduction suggests that employment laws might be framed to eliminate one or both of two kinds of practices. Do the above decisions interpret Title VII to prohibit one or both? Do the decisions require that animus toward a protected class be an element of illegal discrimination?

2. *Purposes of* McDonnell Douglas *Burden Shifting.* What is the purpose of the *McDonnell Douglas* prima facie case and burden shifting? The Supreme Court has confirmed that a complaint need not allege a prima facie *McDonnell Douglas* case in order to survive a motion to dismiss. Swierkiewicz v. Sorema, 534 U.S. 506, 122 S.Ct. 992, 152 L.Ed.2d 1 (2002). It is also difficult to understand the 1970s-fashioned prima facie case and burden shifting as jury control devices. Prior to the Civil Rights Act of 1991, Title VII actions were bench-tried. Moreover, the Court has made clear in a series of cases, including *Swierkiewicz,* that Title VII plaintiffs "may prevail without proving all the elements of a prima facie case" if they have direct evidence of discrimination. Id. at 511. See also, e.g., United States Postal Service Board v. Aikens, 460 U.S. 711, 715, 103 S.Ct. 1478, 75 L.Ed.2d 403 (1983) ("[w]here the defendant [by articulating a legitimate reason for its decision] has done everything that would be required of him if the plaintiff had properly made out a prima facie case, whether the plaintiff really did so is no longer relevant" to plaintiff's success). Conversely, plaintiffs do not guarantee a jury trial by presenting an adequate prima facie case. See, e.g.,

Wallis v. J.R. Simplot Co., 26 F.3d 885 (9th Cir.1994) (plaintiff can present a prima facie case and still lose on motion for summary judgment).

What, then, is the purpose of enabling plaintiffs to shift a burden of production on to defendants by making the relatively easy *McDonnell Douglas* prima facie case? Given the comparable ease with which defendants can meet their burden of production, and the consequent likelihood of plaintiffs in most cases having to prove discrimination without the aid of any presumption, how does *McDonnell Douglas* help plaintiffs? Do you understand why some direct proof of intentional discrimination is not required to establish a prima facie showing?

The Court makes clear that Title VII plaintiffs do not have to establish the four *McDonnell Douglas* factors in every hiring or promotion case. Are there situations where an employer might have discriminated in violation of Title VII where one of the *McDonnell Douglas* factors is not present? If so, how might a plaintiff prove the existence of discrimination in such a case?

3. *Can Whites Use the* McDonnell Douglas *Mode of Proof?* In McDonald v. Santa Fe Trail Transp. Co., 427 U.S. 273, 96 S.Ct. 2574, 49 L.Ed.2d 493 (1976), the Court held that white employees can challenge adverse treatment on account of their race under Title VII as well as 42 U.S.C. § 1981. Does this mean that the first *McDonnell Douglas* factor, belonging to a racial minority, can be ignored? Does *McDonnell Douglas* assume that belonging to a racial minority is relevant to creating a suspicion of discrimination? In what situations might suspicion of discrimination against a white be equally appropriate? See Harding v. Gray, 9 F.3d 150, 153 (D.C.Cir.1993) (plaintiff established a prima facie case because he proved "background circumstances [that] support the suspicion that the defendant is that unusual employer who discriminates against the majority"), quoting Parker v. Baltimore & O.R.R., 652 F.2d 1012, 1017 (D.C.Cir.1981). See also, e.g., Notari v. Denver Water Dept., 971 F.2d 585 (10th Cir.1992) (reverse discrimination plaintiff cannot use *McDonnell Douglas* presumption unless there is reason for suspicion of discrimination); Murray v. Thistledown Racing Club, Inc., 770 F.2d 63 (6th Cir.1985) (accord); cf. Walker v. Secretary of Treasury, I.R.S., 713 F.Supp. 403 (N.D.Ga.1989) (light-skinned black stated cause of action by alleging discrimination on the basis of color by darker-skinned supervisor). For discussion of affirmative action, see chapter 4 infra.

4. *Adaptation for Discharge or Working–Conditions Case.* The four *McDonnell Douglas* factors seem framed for a hiring or promotion case. How would the factors have to be reformulated for a discharge or on-the-job treatment case? See, e.g., Kendrick v. Penske Transp. Services, 220 F.3d 1220 (10th Cir.2000) (in discharge case must only show as fourth factor that job was not eliminated).

5. *Applicable to All Employment Decisions?* Are there some kinds of employment decisions, such as lateral transfers, to which the *McDonnell Douglas* framework is not applicable? If so, is this because Title VII does not reach all kinds of employer actions? Consider the language of § 703(a). In Burlington Northern & Santa Fe Ry. v. White, 548 U.S. 53, 126 S.Ct. 2405, 165 L.Ed.2d 345 (2006), included at pp. 647–654 infra, the Court held that § 704, the anti-retaliatory provision of Title VII, protects employees from employer actions that are "materially adverse", stressing the importance of

separating "significant from trivial harms" under Title VII. The *Burlington* Court's indication that some employment actions do not entail sufficiently "materially adverse" consequences to be actionable accords with the approach the lower courts have taken under § 703. See, e.g., Mitchell v. Vanderbilt Univ., 389 F.3d 177 (6th Cir. 2004) (reduction of laboratory space and not being selected for desired lateral transfer not materially adverse where medical professor retained salary and tenured employment status); Herrnreiter v. Chicago Housing Authority, 315 F.3d 742, 744 (7th Cir.2002) (§ 703(a) does not reach "*any* action that displeases the employee", but only those that reduce either the employee's financial terms or his "career prospects by preventing him from using the skills in which he is trained and experienced", or that subject "him to a humiliating, degrading, unsafe, unhealthful, or otherwise significantly negative alteration in his working environment"); Davis v. Town of Lake Park, Fla., 245 F.3d 1232 (11th Cir.2001) (negative evaluations not actionable simply because they could potentially influence future decisions). For an argument that § 703(a) should be read to cover all discriminatory job-related actions, see Rebecca Hanner White, De Minimis Discrimination, 47 Emory L.J. 1121 (1998). For treatment of workplace harassment as discrimination, see pp. 349–378 infra.

6. *What Constitutes Being "Qualified"?* In both *McDonnell Douglas* and *Burdine,* there were strong independent reasons for presuming that the plaintiffs were qualified for the position in question. What is required for a similar presumption in the typical failure to hire or failure to promote case? What about in a discharge case, where the employer's stated reason for termination is poor performance or that the employee's skills had not kept up with evolving job requirements? Should plaintiffs have to prove as part of their prima facie case their ability to meet employers' subjectively applied hiring standards, such as sincerity or integrity, as well as objective standards such as experience or education? Compare Hill v. Seaboard Coast Line Railroad Co., 885 F.2d 804 (11th Cir.1989), with Lynn v. Regents of the University of California, 656 F.2d 1337 (9th Cir.1981).

7. *Must Plaintiff Prove Relative Qualification?* The *McDonnell Douglas* formulation of the prima facie showing assumes that the position that plaintiff sought remained open after the plaintiff was rejected. If another individual has been hired, is the plaintiff required, as part of a prima facie proof, to show that he or she was more qualified than the other individual? See Walker v. Mortham, 158 F.3d 1177 (11th Cir.1998) (not part of prima facie case). See also Note, Relative Qualifications and the Prima Facie Case in Title VII Litigation, 82 Colum.L.Rev. 553 (1982). Should the plaintiff have to prove this if the employer articulates relative qualifications as a reason for its refusal to hire or promote the plaintiff? See Young v. Lehman, 748 F.2d 194 (4th Cir.1984) (yes). See also Ash v. Tyson Foods, Inc., 546 U.S. 454, 126 S.Ct. 1195, 163 L.Ed.2d 1053 (2006) ("qualification evidence may suffice, at least in some circumstances, to show pretext").

8. *Must Anyone Hired or Promoted in Plaintiff's Place Be Outside of Plaintiff's Protected Class?* Should a disappointed black job applicant be able to sue an employer for maintaining a higher qualification threshold for employing blacks, or for penalizing certain personality traits only when found in blacks, even when the person ultimately selected is a particularly well qualified black? If so, should a plaintiff be permitted to use *McDonnell*

Douglas to attempt to prove disparate treatment because of race only if the individual hired was of a different race? Most courts of appeals have held in discharge cases that plaintiffs are not "precluded from meeting the prima facie burden by an inability to demonstrate that the replacement employee does not share her protected attribute." Perry v. Woodward, 199 F.3d 1126, 1138 (10th Cir.1999). See also, e.g., Stella v. Mineta, 284 F.3d 135 (D.C.Cir. 2002); Pivirotto v. Innovative Systems, Inc., 191 F.3d 344 (3d Cir.1999); Carson v. Bethlehem Steel Corp., 82 F.3d 157 (7th Cir.1996). But see Miles v. Dell, Inc., 429 F.3d 480 (4th Cir. 2005) (requiring that replacement be outside protected class except in special circumstances). Should courts require the proof of special circumstances to raise an inference of discrimination to establish a *McDonnell Douglas* prima facie case where a job *applicant* lost out to another member of his protected class?

9. *Legal Consequences of An Employer's Articulation* Vel Non. If the employer fails to "articulate some legitimate, nondiscriminatory reason," must the court find for the plaintiff upon the four-factor *McDonnell Douglas* showing, or does it retain discretion to find for the defendant? On the other hand, if the employer succeeds in such an articulation, must the court find for the defendant unless the plaintiff enters additional evidence? Can the court at least consider the plaintiff's prima facie case as having some probative value?

10. *Nature of Employer's Burden of Articulation.* Does "articulate" require more than a statement of an employer's agent on the witness stand? Does it require more than an averment of a general consideration, such as "we want high qualifications," without any specific application to plaintiff's individual case? See, e.g., IMPACT v. Firestone, 893 F.2d 1189, 1193–94 (11th Cir.1990) (averment of general practice of hiring the more qualified not sufficient). Does it require a showing sufficient to overcome the inference of racial motivation drawn from the prima facie showing? If the plaintiff presents a prima facie case that extends beyond the *McDonnell Douglas* factors to include some direct evidence of illegitimate motive, does the employer have a correspondingly greater rebuttal burden?

11. *A "Legitimate, Nondiscriminatory Reason".* What kind of reason must an employer advance to negate a plaintiff's prima facie case? Does "legitimate" mean more than credible? Does it mean not illegal on other grounds? Does it mean business-related? Reasonable? Compelling? Could an employer answer a prima facie case by demonstrating that its harsh and arbitrary treatment of a black plaintiff was consistent with its treatment of whites?

12. *Should the Burden of Persuasion Shift?* What are the justifications for *Burdine's* holding that the persuasion burden remains with the plaintiff even after establishing a prima facie case? Which party is in a better position to establish motivation? Are there other reasons that Congress might want the burden of persuasion as to discriminatory motive to remain on plaintiffs?

13. *Plaintiff's Ultimate Burden After Rebuttal of the Prima Facie Case.* *Burdine* states that a plaintiff may sustain its ultimate persuasion burden "either directly by persuading the court that a discriminatory reason more likely motivated the employer or indirectly by showing that the employer's offered explanation is unworthy of credence." What is the difference between

these two types of proof? What are examples of each? In what category do statistics concerning the employer's general treatment of other applicants or employees in the plaintiff's class fit?

Should general statistics be sufficient alone to establish or defeat an individual discrimination case? See, e.g., Deloach v. Delchamps, Inc., 897 F.2d 815, 820 (5th Cir.1990) (plaintiff cannot prove pretext with statistical evidence alone); Cross v. United States Postal Service, 639 F.2d 409 (8th Cir.1981) (defendant's statistics demonstrating hiring of member's class not an absolute defense). Should plaintiffs be able to introduce evidence of other individual instances of discrimination against members of plaintiff's class by the same decisionmaker? By others in the same place of work? Compare Spulak v. K Mart Corp., 894 F.2d 1150, 1156 (10th Cir.1990) (admissible), with Schrand v. Federal Pac. Elec. Co., 851 F.2d 152, 156 (6th Cir.1988) (reversible error to admit comments by non-decisionmakers). Should evidence of discrimination by other supervisors ever be treated as relevant? See Cummings v. Standard Register Co., 265 F.3d 56, 63 (1st Cir.2001) (evidence of "discriminatory atmosphere" may be admissible).

14. *"Same Decisionmaker" Defense.* Should employers be able to defeat a plaintiff's claim that she was a victim of post-hiring discrimination merely by proving that the decisionmaker who made the decision to hire the alleged victim is the same decisionmaker whom she charges with post-hiring discrimination? Might some decisionmakers accept blacks or women in entry-level positions, but not want to promote them or give them equal working conditions? Might they also impose tougher standards on them when considering discipline or discharge? While all courts find "same decisionmaker" evidence relevant, the courts of appeals differ on the amount of weight that it should be given. Compare, e.g., Wexler v. White's Fine Furniture, Inc., 317 F.3d 564, 573 (6th Cir.2003) (rejecting "the idea that a mandatory inference must be applied * * * whenever the claimant has been hired and fired by the same individual"), with Proud v. Stone, 945 F.2d 796, 797 (4th Cir.1991) ("where the hirer and firer are the same individual and the termination of employment occurs within a relatively short time span following the hiring, a strong inference exists that discrimination was not a determining factor"). See also Linda Hamilton Krieger & Susan T. Fiske, Behavioral Realism in Employment Discrimination Law: Implicit Bias and Disparate Treatment, 94 Cal. L. Rev. 997, 1046 (2006) (contending that unconscious bias may explain discrimination by same decisionmaker since "an employer might be unaware of his own stereotypical view . . . at the time of hiring", quoting Johnson v. Zema Sys. Corp., 170 F.3d 734, 745 (7th Cir. 1999).

15. *Imputing the Discriminatory Bias of a Non-Decisionmaker.* When might the discriminatory bias of a supervisor or evaluator provide the basis for a Title VII violation even when the challenged employment decision is made by another unbiased decisionmaker? When the decision is based on good faith consideration of biased evaluations, recommendations, or reports? What if a supervisor's bias led to an employer's investigation and discovery of an employee's dereliction of duty that in turn prompted the employee's dismissal? When can it be said that the biased supervisor did not "cause" the challenged decision? See, e.g., EEOC v. BCI Coca-Cola Bottling Co. of L.A., 450 F.3d 476 (10th Cir. 2006), cert. dismissed, __ U.S. __, 127 S.Ct. 1931, 167 L.Ed.2d 583 (2007) (employer liability turns on "whether the

biased subordinate's discriminatory reports, recommendations, or other actions caused the adverse employment action"; an employer can avoid liability
and cut the "causal link" "by conducting an independent investigation of
the allegations"); Poland v. Chertoff, 494 F.3d 1174 (9th Cir. 2007) (an
investigation prompted by biased supervisor's allegations may establish
legitimate cause for discharge only if biased supervisor does not influence
the process or result of investigation); Byrd v. Illinois Dept. of Public Health,
423 F.3d 696 (7th Cir. 2005) (employee need not prove employer knew or
should have known of bias, but no liability where ultimate decision is based
on independent and legally permissible basis). But see Hill v. Lockheed
Martin Logistics Mgmt., Inc., 354 F.3d 277, 288–89 (4th Cir. 2004) (en banc)
(biased subordinate must be "principally responsible" and "actual decisionmaker"). For the standard for employer liability for punitive damages, see
pp. 378–387 infra.

16. *Is Proof of "Pretext" Necessarily Sufficient?* Does the second proof
alternative offered by the *Burdine* decision—showing that the employer's
stated motivation is "unworthy of credence"—necessarily establish the existence of a discriminatory motive? Can the employer still argue that irrespective of the credibility of its stated reasons, the plaintiff has not produced
sufficient proof that a discriminatory motive was more likely than not to
have affected the disputed decision? Consider the following case.

REEVES v. SANDERSON PLUMBING PRODUCTS, INC.

Supreme Court of the United States, 2000.
530 U.S. 133, 120 S.Ct. 2097, 147 L.Ed.2d 105.

JUSTICE O'CONNOR delivered the opinion of the Court.

* * *

In October 1995, petitioner Roger Reeves was 57 years old and had
spent 40 years in the employ of respondent, Sanderson Plumbing Products, Inc., a manufacturer of toilet seats and covers. Petitioner worked in
a department known as the "Hinge Room," where he supervised the
"regular line." Joe Oswalt, in his mid-thirties, supervised the Hinge
Room's "special line," and Russell Caldwell, the manager of the Hinge
Room and age 45, supervised both petitioner and Oswalt. Petitioner's
responsibilities included recording the attendance and hours of those
under his supervision, and reviewing a weekly report that listed the
hours worked by each employee.

In the summer of 1995, Caldwell informed Powe Chesnut, the
director of manufacturing and the husband of company president Sandra
Sanderson, that "production was down" in the Hinge Room because
employees were often absent and were "coming in late and leaving
early." Because the monthly attendance reports did not indicate a
problem, Chesnut ordered an audit of the Hinge Room's timesheets for
July, August, and September of that year. According to Chesnut's
testimony, that investigation revealed "numerous timekeeping errors
and misrepresentations on the part of Caldwell, Reeves, and Oswalt."

Following the audit, Chesnut, along with Dana Jester, vice president of human resources, and Tom Whitaker, vice president of operations, recommended to company president Sanderson that petitioner and Caldwell be fired. In October 1995, Sanderson followed the recommendation and discharged both petitioner and Caldwell.

In June 1996, petitioner filed suit in the United States District Court for the Northern District of Mississippi, contending that he had been fired because of his age in violation of the Age Discrimination in Employment Act of 1967 (ADEA), 81 Stat. 602, as amended, 29 U. S. C. § 621 *et seq.* At trial, respondent contended that it had fired petitioner due to his failure to maintain accurate attendance records, while petitioner attempted to demonstrate that respondent's explanation was pretext for age discrimination. Petitioner introduced evidence that he had accurately recorded the attendance and hours of the employees under his supervision, and that Chesnut, whom Oswalt described as wielding "absolute power" within the company, had demonstrated age-based animus in his dealings with petitioner. During the trial, the District Court twice denied oral motions by respondent for judgment as a matter of law under Rule 50 of the Federal Rules of Civil Procedure, and the case went to the jury. The court instructed the jury that "[i]f the plaintiff fails to prove age was a determinative or motivating factor in the decision to terminate him, then your verdict shall be for the defendant." So charged, the jury returned a verdict in favor of petitioner * * *.

The Court of Appeals for the Fifth Circuit reversed, holding that petitioner had not introduced sufficient evidence to sustain the jury's finding of unlawful discrimination. * * *

We granted certiorari to resolve a conflict among the Courts of Appeals as to whether a plaintiff's prima facie case of discrimination (as defined in *McDonnell Douglas Corp.* v. *Green,* 411 U. S. 792, 802 (1973)), combined with sufficient evidence for a reasonable factfinder to reject the employer's nondiscriminatory explanation for its decision, is adequate to sustain a finding of liability for intentional discrimination.

* * *

II

* * *

In this case, the evidence supporting respondent's explanation for petitioner's discharge consisted primarily of testimony by Chesnut and Sanderson and documentation of petitioner's alleged "shoddy record keeping." Chesnut testified that a 1993 audit of Hinge Room operations revealed "a very lax assembly line" where employees were not adhering to general work rules. As a result of that audit, petitioner was placed on 90 days' probation for unsatisfactory performance. In 1995, Chesnut ordered another investigation of the Hinge Room, which, according to his testimony, revealed that petitioner was not correctly recording the absences and hours of employees. Respondent introduced summaries of that investigation documenting several attendance violations by 12 employees under petitioner's supervision, and noting that each should have been disciplined in some manner. Chesnut testified that this failure to discipline absent and late employees is "extremely important when you are dealing with a union" because uneven enforcement across departments would keep the company "in grievance and arbitration cases, which are costly, all the time." He and Sanderson also stated that petitioner's errors, by failing to adjust for hours not worked, cost the company overpaid wages. Sanderson testified that she accepted the recommendation to discharge petitioner because he had "intentionally falsif[ied] company pay records."

Petitioner, however, made a substantial showing that respondent's explanation was false. First, petitioner offered evidence that he had properly maintained the attendance records. Most of the timekeeping errors cited by respondent involved employees who were not marked late but who were recorded as having arrived at the plant at 7 a.m. for the 7 a.m. shift. Respondent contended that employees arriving at 7 a.m. could not have been at their workstations by 7 a.m., and therefore must have been late. But both petitioner and Oswalt testified that the company's automated timeclock often failed to scan employees' timecards, so that the timesheets would not record any time of arrival. On these occasions, petitioner and Oswalt would visually check the workstations and record whether the employees were present at the start of the shift. They stated that if an employee arrived promptly but the timesheet contained no time of arrival, they would reconcile the two by marking "7 a.m." as the employee's arrival time, even if the employee actually arrived at the plant earlier. On cross-examination, Chesnut acknowledged that the timeclock sometimes malfunctioned, and that if "people were there at their work station[s]" at the start of the shift, the supervisor "would write in seven o'clock." Petitioner also testified that when employees arrived before or stayed after their shifts, he would assign them additional work so they would not be overpaid.

Petitioner similarly cast doubt on whether he was responsible for any failure to discipline late and absent employees. Petitioner testified that his job only included reviewing the daily and weekly attendance reports, and that disciplinary writeups were based on the monthly reports, which were reviewed by Caldwell. Sanderson admitted that Caldwell, and not petitioner, was responsible for citing employees for violations of the company's attendance policy. Further, Chesnut conceded that there had never been a union grievance or employee complaint arising from petitioner's recordkeeping, and that the company had never calculated the amount of overpayments allegedly attributable to petitioner's errors. Petitioner also testified that, on the day he was fired, Chesnut said that his discharge was due to his failure to report as absent one employee, Gina Mae Coley, on two days in September 1995. But petitioner explained that he had spent those days in the hospital, and that Caldwell was therefore responsible for any overpayment of Coley. Finally, petitioner stated that on previous occasions that employees were paid for hours they had not worked, the company had simply adjusted those employees' next paychecks to correct the errors.

Based on this evidence, the Court of Appeals concluded that petitioner "very well may be correct" that "a reasonable jury could have found that [respondent's] explanation for its employment decision was pretextual." Nonetheless, the court held that this showing, standing alone, was insufficient to sustain the jury's finding of liability: "We must, as an essential final step, determine whether Reeves presented sufficient evidence that his age motivated [respondent's] employment decision." And in making this determination, the Court of Appeals ignored the evidence supporting petitioner's prima facie case and challenging respondent's explanation for its decision. The court confined its review of evidence favoring petitioner to that evidence showing that Chesnut had directed derogatory, age-based comments at petitioner, and that Chesnut had singled out petitioner for harsher treatment than younger employees. It is therefore apparent that the court believed that only this additional evidence of discrimination was relevant to whether the jury's verdict should stand. That is, the Court of Appeals proceeded from the assumption that a prima facie case of discrimination, combined with sufficient evidence for the trier of fact to disbelieve the defendant's legitimate, nondiscriminatory reason for its decision, is insufficient as a matter of law to sustain a jury's finding of intentional discrimination.

In so reasoning, the Court of Appeals misconceived the evidentiary burden borne by plaintiffs who attempt to prove intentional discrimination through indirect evidence. This much is evident from our decision in *St. Mary's Honor Center* [*v. Hicks*, 509 U.S. 502 (1993)]. There we held that the factfinder's rejection of the employer's legitimate, nondiscriminatory reason for its action does not *compel* judgment for the plaintiff. 509 U. S., at 511. The ultimate question is whether the employer intentionally discriminated, and proof that "the employer's proffered reason is unpersuasive, or even obviously contrived, does not necessarily establish that the plaintiff's proffered reason ... is correct." *Id.*, at 524. In other words, "[i]t is not enough * * * to *dis*believe the employer; the factfinder must *believe* the plaintiff's explanation of intentional discrimination." *Id.*, at 519.

In reaching this conclusion, however, we reasoned that it is *permissible* for the trier of fact to infer the ultimate fact of discrimination from the falsity of the employer's explanation. Specifically, we stated:

> "The factfinder's disbelief of the reasons put forward by the defendant (particularly if disbelief is accompanied by a suspicion of mendacity) may, together with the elements of the prima facie case, suffice to show intentional discrimination. Thus, rejection of the defendant's proffered reasons will *permit* the trier of fact to infer the ultimate fact of intentional discrimination." *Id.*, at 511.

Proof that the defendant's explanation is unworthy of credence is simply one form of circumstantial evidence that is probative of intentional discrimination, and it may be quite persuasive. See *id.*, at 517

("[P]roving the employer's reason false becomes part of (and often considerably assists) the greater enterprise of proving that the real reason was intentional discrimination"). In appropriate circumstances, the trier of fact can reasonably infer from the falsity of the explanation that the employer is dissembling to cover up a discriminatory purpose. * * * Once the employer's justification has been eliminated, discrimination may well be the most likely alternative explanation, especially since the employer is in the best position to put forth the actual reason for its decision. * * * Thus, a plaintiff's prima facie case, combined with sufficient evidence to find that the employer's asserted justification is false, may permit the trier of fact to conclude that the employer unlawfully discriminated.

This is not to say that such a showing by the plaintiff will *always* be adequate to sustain a jury's finding of liability. Certainly there will be instances where, although the plaintiff has established a prima facie case and set forth sufficient evidence to reject the defendant's explanation, no rational factfinder could conclude that the action was discriminatory. For instance, an employer would be entitled to judgment as a matter of law if the record conclusively revealed some other, nondiscriminatory reason for the employer's decision, or if the plaintiff created only a weak issue of fact as to whether the employer's reason was untrue and there was abundant and uncontroverted independent evidence that no discrimination had occurred. See *Aka* v. *Washington Hospital Center*, 156 F. 3d 1284, 1291–1292 (D.C.Cir.1998) see also *Fisher* v. *Vassar College*, 114 F.3d, 1332, 1338 (2d Cir.1997) ("[I]f the circumstances show that the defendant gave the false explanation to conceal something other than discrimination, the inference of discrimination will be weak or nonexistent"). To hold otherwise would be effectively to insulate an entire category of employment discrimination cases from review under Rule 50, and we have reiterated that trial courts should not " 'treat discrimination differently from other ultimate questions of fact.' " *St. Mary's Honor Center, supra*, at 524 (quoting *Aikens*, 460 U. S., at 716).

Whether judgment as a matter of law is appropriate in any particular case will depend on a number of factors. Those include the strength of the plaintiff's prima facie case, the probative value of the proof that the employer's explanation is false, and any other evidence that supports the employer's case and that properly may be considered on a motion for judgment as a matter of law. For purposes of this case, we need not–and could not—resolve all of the circumstances in which such factors would entitle an employer to judgment as a matter of law. It suffices to say that, because a prima facie case and sufficient evidence to reject the employer's explanation may permit a finding of liability, the Court of Appeals erred in proceeding from the premise that a plaintiff must always introduce additional, independent evidence of discrimination.

III

The remaining question is whether, despite the Court of Appeals' misconception of petitioner's evidentiary burden, respondent was nonetheless entitled to judgment as a matter of law. Under Rule 50, a court should render judgment as a matter of law when "a party has been fully heard on an issue and there is no legally sufficient evidentiary basis for a reasonable jury to find for that party on that issue." Fed. Rule Civ. Proc. 50(a); * * *.

* * * [T]he standard for granting summary judgment "mirrors" the standard for judgment as a matter of law, such that "the inquiry under each is the same." *Anderson* v. *Liberty Lobby, Inc.,* 477 U. S. 242, 250–251 (1986); see also *Celotex Corp.* v. *Catrett,* 477 U. S. 317, 323 (1986). It therefore follows that, in entertaining a motion for judgment as a matter of law, the court should review all of the evidence in the record. In doing so, however, the court must draw all reasonable inferences in favor of the nonmoving party, and it may not make credibility determinations or weigh the evidence. * * * Thus, although the court should review the record as a whole, it must disregard all evidence favorable to the moving party that the jury is not required to believe. That is, the court should give credence to the evidence favoring the nonmovant as well as that "evidence supporting the moving party that is uncontradicted and unimpeached, at least to the extent that that evidence comes from disinterested witnesses."

Applying this standard here, it is apparent that respondent was not entitled to judgment as a matter of law. In this case, in addition to establishing a prima facie case of discrimination and creating a jury issue as to the falsity of the employer's explanation, petitioner introduced additional evidence that Chesnut was motivated by age-based animus and was principally responsible for petitioner's firing. Petitioner testified that Chesnut had told him that he "was so old [he] must have come over on the Mayflower" and, on one occasion when petitioner was having difficulty starting a machine, that he "was too damn old to do [his] job." * * *

Further, petitioner introduced evidence that Chesnut was the actual decisionmaker behind his firing. Chesnut was married to Sanderson, who made the formal decision to discharge petitioner. * * *

In holding that the record contained insufficient evidence to sustain the jury's verdict, the Court of Appeals misapplied the standard of review dictated by Rule 50. Again, the court disregarded critical evidence favorable to petitioner-namely, the evidence supporting petitioner's prima facie case and undermining respondent's nondiscriminatory explanation. The court also failed to draw all reasonable inferences in favor of petitioner. For instance, while acknowledging "the potentially damning nature" of Chesnut's age-related comments, the court discounted them on the ground that they "were not made in the direct context of Reeves's termination." And the court discredited petitioner's evidence that Chesnut was the actual decisionmaker by giving weight to the fact that there was "no evidence to suggest that any of the other decision makers were motivated by age." Moreover, the other evidence on which the court relied—that Caldwell and Oswalt were also cited for poor recordkeeping, and that respondent employed many managers over age 50—although relevant, is certainly not dispositive. * * *

Notes and Questions

1. St. Mary's: *Where Trier of Fact Finds Pretext But Not Discrimination*. Note the *St. Mary's Honor Center v. Hicks* decision, discussed in *Reeves*. In *St. Mary's* the trial judge as the trier of fact concluded that the defendant employer had provided a false reason for its demotion and later discharge of Hicks, but that Hicks nonetheless could not prevail because he had failed to prove that the real reason for his adverse treatment was racial rather than personal animus. The Court of Appeals set this determination aside, holding that a plaintiff who proves all of a defendant's "proffered reasons for the adverse employment actions to be pretextual" is "entitled to judgment as a matter of law." The Supreme Court in *St. Mary's* disagreed. It held that since "the *McDonnell Douglas* framework—with its presumptions and burdens—is no longer relevant" after the defendant carries its burden of production by proffering some legitimate reason for its actions, the plaintiff's proof of the defendant's pretext does not compel the trier of fact to find illegal discriminatory intent. 509 U.S. at 510. The trier of fact must determine whether the plaintiff has proven such intent based on all the evidence, both inculpatory and exculpatory.

2. Reeves: *Where Trier of Fact Finds Discrimination on the Basis of Pretext*. In a dissenting opinion in *St. Mary's* Justice Souter asserted that it was not clear from the majority opinion whether the trier of fact as a matter of law is not *permitted* to rule for a plaintiff who has only offered evidence of the employer's pretext in addition to proving a prima facie case, or that the trier of fact simply is not *compelled* to find for a plaintiff who has proven pretext in addition to a prima facie case. How does the *Reeves* decision resolve the question?

3. *Pretext Instructions After* Reeves? In an appropriate case, must a trial judge instruct a jury that they may find discrimination if they find the employer-defendant's proffered explanations to be pretextual? Can a judge after *Reeves* avoid any reference to the complicated *McDonnell Douglas* framework in the usual case where the judge can determine that the defendant has at least carried its burden of production to rebut any prima facie case? Where a plaintiff claims not being hired because of intentional race discrimination, for instance, should the following simple instruction normally suffice?: "You must determine whether plaintiff has demonstrated by a preponderance of the evidence that race was a motivating factor in the defendant employer's decision not to employ the plaintiff." Compare, e.g., Townsend v. Lumbermens Mutual Casualty Co., 294 F.3d 1232, 1241 (10th Cir.2002) (pretext instruction mandatory), with Conroy v. Abraham Chevrolet–Tampa, Inc., 375 F.3d 1228, 1233 (11th Cir.2004) (not reversible error to refuse pretext instruction).

4. *What Is the Purpose of the* McDonnell Douglas *Framework After* St. Mary's *and* Reeves? In his dissenting opinion in *St. Mary's* Justice Souter charged that the majority in that case had rendered pointless the imposition of the *McDonnell Douglas* production burden on defendants because plain-

tiffs could not be assured of being able to prove discrimination by proving pretext. In light of *Reeves* do you agree that *McDonnell Douglas* is now pointless? Do plaintiffs reap no benefits from defendants being forced to articulate legitimate explanations? In most cases, will factfinders (especially juries) be more likely to find discrimination after being convinced that a defendant's explanation is pretextual? For commentary before *Reeves*, see Deborah C. Malamud, The Last Minuet: Disparate Treatment After *Hicks*, 93 Michigan Law Review, 2229 (1995) (arguing that the *McDonnell Douglas* structure should be abandoned because it complicates litigation without assisting plaintiffs); William R. Corbett, Of Babies, Bathwater, and Throwing Out Proof Structures: It Is Not Time to Jettison *McDonnell Douglas*, 2 Emp. Rts. & Emp. Pol.J. 361 (1998) (contesting Malamud's claims).

5. *When Might Judgment As a Matter of Law Be Appropriate Against a Plaintiff Who Has Proven Pretext?* The *Reeves* Court expressly states that "judgment as a matter of law" may be appropriate in some cases against plaintiffs who offer adequate proof of pretext along with their prima facie case. What kinds of exculpatory evidence might support an employer's summary judgment or Rule 50 motion in the face of a plaintiff's adequate proof of pretext? Statistics indicating a substantial employment of members of plaintiff's minority group? The employer's key decisionmaker(s) belonging to the same minority group as the plaintiff?

For a defendant employer to overcome a plaintiff's adequate proof of pretext must the employer present some strong exculpatory evidence other than that supporting the credibility of its proffered explanations? See, e.g., Laxton v. Gap Inc., 333 F.3d 572 (5th Cir.2003) (finding evidence in support of proffered explanation insufficient to fit one of exceptions noted in *Reeves);* EEOC v. Sears Roebuck and Co., 243 F.3d 846 (4th Cir.2001) (reversing grant of summary judgment because employer failed to present other uncontradicted exculpatory evidence). Most courts upholding grants of summary judgment to defendants without primary reliance on further exculpatory evidence have emphasized plaintiffs' failure to raise an inference of discrimination in a prima facie case or to offer adequate proof of pretext. See, e.g., Holland v. Washington Homes, Inc., 487 F.3d 208 (4th Cir. 2007); Tysinger v. Police Dept. of City of Zanesville, 463 F.3d 569 (6th Cir. 2006); Waterhouse v. District of Columbia, 298 F.3d 989 (D.C. Cir.2002).

6. *Can Title VII Uncover the Subconscious Use of Stereotypes?* Drawing on studies by cognitive and social psychologists, Professor Krieger has argued that discrimination often results from the subconscious use of stereotypes:

> Social cognition theory provides a fundamentally different explanation of how stereotypes cause discrimination. Stereotypes are viewed as social schemas or person prototypes. They operate as implicit expectancies that influence how incoming information is interpreted, the causes to which events are attributed, and how events are encoded into, retained in, and retrieved from memory. In other words, stereotypes cause discrimination by biasing how we process information about other people.

Linda H. Krieger, The Content of Our Categories: A Cognitive Bias Approach to Discrimination and Equal Employment Opportunity, 47 Stan.

L.Rev. 1161 (1995). Cf. Thomas v. Eastman Kodak Co., 183 F.3d 38, 59–61 (1st Cir.1999) ("[s]tereotypes or cognitive bias" leading to disparate treatment constitute violation of Act). Does the *McDonnell Douglas* framework, as clarified in *St. Mary's* and *Reeves*, enable plaintiffs to uncover subconscious bias? Krieger thinks that Title VII doctrine must be developed further to deal with this type of case. Could it be? Should it be? Compare Amy Wax, Discrimination as Accident, 74 Ind. L.J. 1129 (1999), with Michael Selmi, Discrimination as Accident: Old Whine, New Bottle, 74 Ind. L.J. 1234 (1999). See also, e.g., Symposium on Behavioral Realism, 94 Calif. L. Rev. 945 (2006); Melissa Hart, Subjective Decisionmaking and Unconscious Discrimination, 56 Ala. L. Rev. 741 (2005); cf. Charles R. Lawrence III, The Id, the Ego, and Equal Protection: Reckoning with Unconscious Racism,. 39 Stan. L.Rev. 317, 328–344 (1987).

DESERT PALACE, INC. v. COSTA

Supreme Court of the United States, 2003.
539 U.S. 90, 123 S.Ct. 2148, 156 L.Ed.2d 84.

Justice Thomas delivered the opinion of the Court.

The question before us in this case is whether a plaintiff must present direct evidence of discrimination in order to obtain a mixed-motive instruction under Title VII of the Civil Rights Act of 1964, as amended by the Civil Rights Act of 1991 (1991 Act). We hold that direct evidence is not required.

I

A

Since 1964, Title VII has made it an "unlawful employment practice for an employer ... to discriminate against any individual ..., because of such individual's race, color, religion, sex, or national origin." 78 Stat. 255, 42 U.S.C. § 2000e–2(a)(1) (emphasis added). In *Price Waterhouse v. Hopkins*, 490 U.S. 228, 104 L. Ed. 2d 268, 109 S. Ct. 1775 (1989), the Court considered whether an employment decision is made "because of" sex in a "mixed-motive" case, i.e., where both legitimate and illegitimate reasons motivated the decision. The Court concluded that, under § 2000e–2(a)(1), an employer could "avoid a finding of liability ... by proving that it would have made the same decision even if it had not allowed gender to play such a role." Id., at 244; see id., at 261, n. (White, J., concurring in judgment); id., at 261 (O'Connor, J., concurring in judgment). The Court was divided, however, over the predicate question of when the burden of proof may be shifted to an employer to prove the affirmative defense.

Justice Brennan, writing for a plurality of four Justices, would have held that "when a plaintiff ... proves that her gender played a motivating part in an employment decision, the defendant may avoid a finding of liability only by proving by a preponderance of the evidence that it would have made the same decision even if it had not taken the plaintiff's gender into account." Id., at 258 (emphasis added). The plurality did not, however, "suggest a limitation on the possible ways of proving that [gender] stereotyping played a motivating role in an employment decision." Id., at 251–252.

Justice White and Justice O'Connor both concurred in the judgment. Justice White would have held that the case was governed by *Mt. Healthy City Bd. of Ed. v. Doyle*, 429 U.S. 274, 50 L. Ed. 2d 471, 97 S. Ct. 568 (1977), and would have shifted the burden to the employer only when a plaintiff "showed that the unlawful motive was a substantial factor in the adverse employment action." *Price Waterhouse, supra*, at 259. Justice O'Connor, like Justice White, would have required the plaintiff to show that an illegitimate consideration was a "substantial factor" in the employment decision. 490 U.S., at 276. But, under Justice O'Connor's view, "the burden on the issue of causation" would shift to the employer only where "a disparate treatment plaintiff [could] show by direct evidence that an illegitimate criterion was a substantial factor in the decision." *Ibid.* (emphasis added).

Two years after *Price Waterhouse*, Congress passed the 1991 Act "in large part [as] a response to a series of decisions of this Court interpreting the Civil Rights Acts of 1866 and 1964." *Landgraf v. USI Film Products*, 511 U.S. 244, 250, 128 L. Ed. 2d 229, 114 S. Ct. 1483 (1994). In particular, § 107 of the 1991 Act, which is at issue in this case, "responded" to *Price Waterhouse* by "setting forth standards applicable in 'mixed motive' cases" in two new statutory provisions.[1] 511 U.S., at 251. The first establishes an alternative for proving that an "unlawful employment practice" has occurred:

> " 'Except as otherwise provided in this subchapter, an unlawful employment practice is established when the complaining party demonstrates that race, color, religion, sex, or national origin was a motivating factor for any employment practice, even though other factors also motivated the practice.' " 42 U.S.C. § 2000e–2(m).

The second provides that, with respect to " 'a claim in which an individual proves a violation under section 2000e–2(m),' " the employer has a limited affirmative defense that does not absolve it of liability, but restricts the remedies available to a plaintiff. The available remedies include only declaratory relief, certain types of injunctive relief, and attorney's fees and costs. 42 U.S.C. § 2000e–5(g)(2)(B). In order to avail itself of the affirmative defense, the employer must "demonstrate that [it] would have taken the same action in the absence of the impermissible motivating factor." *Ibid.*

Since the passage of the 1991 Act, the Courts of Appeals have divided over whether a plaintiff must prove by direct evidence that an impermissible consideration was a "motivating factor" in an adverse employment action. See 42 U.S.C. § 2000e–2(m). Relying primarily on Justice O'Connor's concurrence in *Price Waterhouse*, a number of courts

---

1. This case does not require us to decide when, if ever, § 107 applies outside of the mixed-motive context.

have held that direct evidence is required to establish liability under § 2000e–2(m). (citations omitted) In the decision below, however, the Ninth Circuit concluded otherwise.

B

Petitioner Desert Palace, Inc., dba Caesar's Palace Hotel & Casino of Las Vegas, Nevada, employed respondent Catharina Costa as a warehouse worker and heavy equipment operator. Respondent was the only woman in this job and in her local Teamsters bargaining unit.

Respondent experienced a number of problems with management and her co-workers that led to an escalating series of disciplinary sanctions, including informal rebukes, a denial of privileges, and suspension. Petitioner finally terminated respondent after she was involved in a physical altercation in a warehouse elevator with fellow Teamsters member Herbert Gerber. Petitioner disciplined both employees because the facts surrounding the incident were in dispute, but Gerber, who had a clean disciplinary record, received only a 5–day suspension.

Respondent subsequently filed this lawsuit against petitioner in the United States District Court for the District of Nevada, asserting claims of sex discrimination and sexual harassment under Title VII. The District Court dismissed the sexual harassment claim, but allowed the claim for sex discrimination to go to the jury. At trial, respondent presented evidence that (1) she was singled out for "intense 'stalking'" by one of her supervisors, (2) she received harsher discipline than men for the same conduct, (3) she was treated less favorably than men in the assignment of overtime, and (4) supervisors repeatedly "stacked" her disciplinary record and "frequently used or tolerated" sex-based slurs against her.

Based on this evidence, the District Court denied petitioner's motion for judgment as a matter of law, and submitted the case to the jury with instructions, two of which are relevant here. First, without objection from petitioner, the District Court instructed the jury that " 'the plaintiff has the burden of proving ... by a preponderance of the evidence that she "suffered adverse work conditions" and that her sex "was a motivating factor in any such work conditions imposed upon her." ' "

Second, the District Court gave the jury the following mixed-motive instruction:

> " 'You have heard evidence that the defendant's treatment of the plaintiff was motivated by the plaintiff's sex and also by other lawful reasons. If you find that the plaintiff's sex was a motivating factor in the defendant's treatment of the plaintiff, the plaintiff is entitled to your verdict, even if you find that the defendant's conduct was also motivated by a lawful reason.

> " 'However, if you find that the defendant's treatment of the plaintiff was motivated by both gender and lawful reasons, you must decide whether the plaintiff is entitled to damages. The plaintiff is entitled to damages unless the defendant proves by a preponderance

of the evidence that the defendant would have treated plaintiff similarly even if the plaintiff's gender had played no role in the employment decision.' ''

Petitioner unsuccessfully objected to this instruction, claiming that respondent had failed to adduce "direct evidence" that sex was a motivating factor in her dismissal or in any of the other adverse employment actions taken against her. The jury rendered a verdict for respondent, awarding backpay, compensatory damages, and punitive damages. The District Court denied petitioner's renewed motion for judgment as a matter of law.

* * *

The Court of Appeals reinstated the District Court's judgment after rehearing the case en banc. The en banc court saw no need to decide whether Justice O'Connor's concurrence in Price Waterhouse controlled because it concluded that Justice O'Connor's references to "direct evidence" had been "wholly abrogated" by the 1991 Act. And, turning "to the language" of § 2000e–2(m), the court observed that the statute "imposes no special [evidentiary] requirement and does not reference 'direct evidence.' '' Accordingly, the court concluded that a "plaintiff ... may establish a violation through a preponderance of evidence (whether direct or circumstantial) that a protected characteristic played 'a motivating factor.' '' Based on that standard, the Court of Appeals held that respondent's evidence was sufficient to warrant a mixed-motive instruction and that a reasonable jury could have found that respondent's sex was a "motivating factor in her treatment." Four judges of the en banc panel dissented, * * *.

II

* * *

Our precedents make clear that the starting point for our analysis is the statutory text. And where, as here, the words of the statute are unambiguous, the " 'judicial inquiry is complete.' '' Section 2000e–2(m) unambiguously states that a plaintiff need only "demonstrate" that an employer used a forbidden consideration with respect to "any employment practice." On its face, the statute does not mention, much less require, that a plaintiff make a heightened showing through direct evidence. Indeed, petitioner concedes as much.

Moreover, Congress explicitly defined the term "demonstrates" in the 1991 Act, leaving little doubt that no special evidentiary showing is required. Title VII defines the term " 'demonstrates' '' as to "meet the burdens of production and persuasion." § 2000e(m). If Congress intended the term " 'demonstrates' '' to require that the "burdens of production and persuasion" be met by direct evidence or some other heightened showing, it could have made that intent clear by including language to that effect in § 2000e(m). Its failure to do so is significant, for Congress has been unequivocal when imposing heightened proof requirements in other circumstances, including in other provisions of Title 42. * * *

In addition, Title VII's silence with respect to the type of evidence required in mixed-motive cases also suggests that we should not depart from the "conventional rule of civil litigation [that] generally applies in Title VII cases." Ibid. That rule requires a plaintiff to prove his case "by a preponderance of the evidence," ibid. using "direct or circumstantial evidence," *Postal Service Bd. of Governors v. Aikens*, 460 U.S. 711, 714, n. 3, 75 L. Ed. 2d 403, 103 S. Ct. 1478 (1983). We have often acknowledged the utility of circumstantial evidence in discrimination cases. For instance, in *Reeves v. Sanderson Plumbing Products, Inc.*, 530 U.S. 133, 147 L. Ed. 2d 105, 120 S. Ct. 2097 (2000), we recognized that evidence that a defendant's explanation for an employment practice is "unworthy of credence" is "one form of circumstantial evidence that is probative of intentional discrimination." Id., at 147 (emphasis added). The reason for treating circumstantial and direct evidence alike is both clear and deep-rooted: "Circumstantial evidence is not only sufficient, but may also be more certain, satisfying and persuasive than direct evidence." *Rogers v. Missouri Pacific R. Co.*, 352 U.S. 500, 508, n. 17, 1 L. Ed. 2d 493, 77 S. Ct. 443 (1957).

The adequacy of circumstantial evidence also extends beyond civil cases; we have never questioned the sufficiency of circumstantial evidence in support of a criminal conviction, even though proof beyond a reasonable doubt is required. And juries are routinely instructed that "the law makes no distinction between the weight or value to be given to either direct or circumstantial evidence." 1A K. O'Malley, J. Grenig, & W. Lee, Federal Jury Practice and Instructions, Criminal § 12.04 (5th ed. 2000); see also 4 L. Sand, J. Siffert, W. Loughlin, S. Reiss, & N. Batterman, Modern Federal Jury Instructions P74.01 (2002) (model instruction 74–2). * * *

Finally, the use of the term "demonstrates" in other provisions of Title VII tends to show further that § 2000e-2(m) does not incorporate a direct evidence requirement. See, e.g., 42 U.S.C. §§ 2000e-2(k)(1)(A)(i), 2000e–5(g)(2)(B). For instance, § 2000e–5(g)(2)(B) requires an employer to "demonstrate that [it] would have taken the same action in the absence of the impermissible motivating factor" in order to take advantage of the partial affirmative defense. Due to the similarity in structure between that provision and § 2000e–2(m), it would be logical to assume that the term "demonstrates" would carry the same meaning with respect to both provisions. But when pressed at oral argument about whether direct evidence is required before the partial affirmative defense can be invoked, petitioner did not "agree that . . . the defendant or the employer has any heightened standard" to satisfy. Absent some congressional indication to the contrary, we decline to give the same term in the same Act a different meaning depending on whether the rights of the plaintiff or the defendant are at issue.

For the reasons stated above, we agree with the Court of Appeals that no heightened showing is required under § 2000e–2(m).

In order to obtain an instruction under § 2000e–2(m), a plaintiff need only present sufficient evidence for a reasonable jury to conclude, by a preponderance of the evidence, that "race, color, religion, sex, or national origin was a motivating factor for any employment practice." Because direct evidence of discrimination is not required in mixed-motive cases, the Court of Appeals correctly concluded that the District Court did not abuse its discretion in giving a mixed-motive instruction to the jury. Accordingly, the judgment of the Court of Appeals is affirmed.

Notes and Questions

1. *Availability of "Motivating Factor" Instruction?* Does the *Desert Palace* decision mean that plaintiffs always can establish a violation of Title VII by proving, through the use of any relevant direct or circumstantial evidence, that one of the forbidden categories was a "motivating factor" for an adverse employment action, absent some statutory defense? Does such a conclusion follow from a straightforward reading of § 107?

Should plaintiffs in all future Title VII cases then be able to obtain the kind of jury instruction to which Desert Palace objected? If not, in which kinds of cases would such an instruction be inappropriate? Why do you suppose that Desert Palace objected only to the second jury instruction, which noted its affirmative defense under § 107, without objecting to the first instruction, which also asserted the "motivating factor" causation standard?

2. *Meaning of Footnote 1?* What did the *Desert Palace* Court in footnote 1 mean by suggesting that § 107 may not apply "outside of the mixed-motive context"? How is a trial court to determine that its case is "outside" such a context? Unless the evidence in a particular case should not even be presented to a jury because it cannot support the existence of a proscribed motive, how can a court determine that a decision did not have a "mixed-motive" without allowing the jury to decide whether there was a good motive, a bad motive, or both? See William R. Corbett, McDonnell Douglas, 1973–2003: May You Rest in Peace, 6 Univ. of Pa. J. of Lab. & Emp. L. 199 (2003). Does footnote one allow defendants to argue for the continued bifurcation of disparate treatment cases, to deny § 107 jury instructions to plaintiffs who apart from evidence of pretext do not have adequate proof of a discriminatory motive? For lower court interpretations of *Desert Palace*, see, e.g., Fogg v. Gonzales, 492 F.3d 447 (D.C. Cir. 2007) (§ 703(a)(1) and § 703(m) offer alternative standards for liability to be analyzed separately; no affirmative defense to pretext, single motive proof); Wright v. Murray Guard, Inc., 455 F.3d 702 (6th Cir. 2006) (applying *Desert Palace* to summary judgment motions, but separating analysis of pretext and mixed-motive claims); Griffith v. City of Des Moines, 387 F.3d 733 (8th Cir. 2004) (*Desert Palace* applies only to post-trial motions; pretext cases still distinguishable from mixed-motive cases for purposes of summary judgment motions); Rachid v. Jack in the Box, Inc., 376 F.3d 305 (5th Cir. 2004) (*Desert Palace* applies to all cases and thus requires a merging of *McDonnell Douglas* and *Price Waterhouse* so that plaintiff need only prove discrimination was "motivating factor" to shift burden to employer).

3. *Rationale of § 107 of the 1991 Act.* What social policies underlying the regulation of status discrimination are served by making it illegal to consider an impermissible status when making a personnel decision if such consideration would not have changed the decision? Are there reasons that our society might want to condemn employer consideration of certain status categories even when such consideration in fact does not influence a decision?

Consider, however, the relief that § 107 permits a court to grant after a defendant proves that it would have taken the same action in the absence of the impermissible motivating factor. This relief does not include "damages or * * * an order requiring any admission, reinstatement, hiring, promotion" or back pay. A court may grant only "declaratory relief, injunctive relief * * *, and attorney's fees and costs." Is finding a violation of Title VII and granting such relief likely to serve, rather than disserve, Title VII policies? Will this depend on plaintiffs at least being able to obtain attorney's fees in all cases where discrimination is found? Does the wording of § 107 suggest that such fees always should be rewarded even in cases where the plaintiffs cannot obtain any meaningful declaratory relief? See Canup v. Chipman–Union, Inc., 123 F.3d 1440 (11th Cir.1997) (holding that trial court has discretion not to award fees where plaintiff does not obtain any other meaningful relief because of defendant's "same-decision" defense). See also discussion at p. 1119, note 10 infra.

4. *"Same Decision" Proof.* How might a defendant prove that it would have taken the same action in the absence of the impermissible motivating factor? Should comparative evidence (similar treatment of individuals outside plaintiff's class) be most probative? Should the courts accept credible testimony by an employer as sufficient evidence?

Price Waterhouse involved a multimember decisionmaking body where there was evidence that an impermissible motive animated some of the members, but there was uncertainty as to whether the motive determined the group's decision. Should it be more difficult for an employer to prove that it would have taken the same action in a case, like *Desert Palace*, where most of the challenged decisions seemed to have been rendered by a single individual? Should a decisionmaker be able to defend a decision that in fact has been tainted by impermissible motive by asserting, without convincing comparative evidence, that despite the tainted motive it would have taken the same action?

Note on Relief Available to Individual Victims of Title VII Violations

Section 706(g) governs judicial remedial authority in Title VII cases. Some major remedial issues raised by this section, such as the availability of class-based affirmative relief and the impact of seniority systems on remedial orders, will be discussed in later chapters. However, some basic Title VII remedial doctrine, especially that governing the monetary relief obtainable by successful plaintiffs in individual disparate treatment cases, should be presented at this point.

In an early Title VII case, Albemarle Paper Co. v. Moody, 422 U.S. 405, 421, 95 S.Ct. 2362, 2373, 45 L.Ed.2d 280 (1975), the Supreme Court held that trial courts should grant back pay in most cases for any wages that were lost because of the defendant's illegal actions: "[B]ack pay should be denied only for reasons which, if applied generally, would not frustrate the central statutory purposes of eradicating discrimination throughout the economy and making persons whole for injuries suffered through past discrimination." The Court suggested that laches might be one such reason by remanding for a determination of whether the employer had been prejudiced by plaintiff's delay in asserting a back pay claim.

The *Albemarle* Court also held that an employer's good faith was not a sufficient reason to deny back pay inasmuch as Title VII remedies were primarily compensatory, rather than penal. Section 713(b) of the Act, however, does provide that no person shall be subject to any liability for good faith reliance "on any written interpretation or opinion" of the EEOC. This can include opinion letters, matter published in the Federal Register and designated as a written interpretation of the Commission, and a Commission interpretation of "no reasonable cause" when such determination states that it is a written interpretation of the Commission. In subsequent decisions concerned with widely used discriminatory pension practices, the Court denied retroactive, back pay relief out of a concern that such relief could bankrupt some pension funds and thereby harm many innocent employees. Florida v. Long, 487 U.S. 223, 108 S.Ct. 2354, 101 L.Ed.2d 206 (1988); Arizona Governing Committee v. Norris, 463 U.S. 1073, 103 S.Ct. 3492, 77 L.Ed.2d 1236 (1983); City of Los Angeles, Dept. of Water & Power v. Manhart, 435 U.S. 702, 98 S.Ct. 1370, 55 L.Ed.2d 657 (1978). These cases are further discussed in chapter 5.

Section 706(g) requires plaintiffs to mitigate their damages: "Interim earnings or amounts earnable with reasonable diligence by the person or persons discriminated against shall operate to reduce the back pay otherwise allowable." In Ford Motor Co. v. EEOC, 458 U.S. 219, 102 S.Ct. 3057, 73 L.Ed.2d 721 (1982), the Court stated that although this mitigation requirement does not demand that an unemployed claimant "go into another line of work, accept a demotion, or take a demeaning position, he forfeits his right to backpay if he refuses a job substantially equivalent to the one he was denied." Id. at 231. The lower courts generally have held that employers have the burden of showing that the plaintiff could have obtained comparable employment in the same commuting area, although some courts have held that it is sufficient for the employer to prove that the plaintiff made no reasonable efforts to seek such employment. See, e.g., Greenway v. Buffalo Hilton Hotel, 143 F.3d 47 (2d Cir.1998). Most courts require backpay claimants who have suffered discrimination short of discharge to remain in their jobs unless they can claim "constructive discharge"—that is the discrimination would force a "reasonable person" to feel compelled to resign. See generally Mark S. Kende, Deconstructing Constructive Discharge: The Misapplication of Constructive Discharge Standards in Employment Discrimination Remedies, 71 Notre.D.L.Rev. 39 (1995).

Back pay for periods in which the plaintiff was not able to work because of sickness or disability has been denied. The courts are divided over whether back pay awards should be reduced by funds plaintiffs have received from collateral governmental sources, such as social security, welfare, or unemployment compensation. Supreme Court precedent under the National

Labor Relations Act (NLRA) suggests that such collateral income may be disregarded. See NLRB v. Gullett Gin Co., 340 U.S. 361, 71 S.Ct. 337, 95 L.Ed. 337 (1951). The 1972 amendments to § 706(g) state that "back pay liability shall not accrue from a date more than two years prior to the filing of a charge" with the EEOC. The back pay period normally terminates when the plaintiff is unconditionally offered, either through judicial decree or unilateral employer action, the disputed position or whatever else has been denied. Under Ford Motor Co. v. EEOC, supra, a reinstatement offer terminates the back pay period even though it does not itself include back pay or retroactive seniority. The back pay period also ends when and if the plaintiff becomes ineligible for, or becomes otherwise unable to fill, the disputed position.

In addition to back pay, courts normally have offered successful plaintiffs instatement or reinstatement in jobs from which they have wrongfully been denied, or in lieu thereof "front pay" in cases where the work environment would be too hostile for plaintiffs to return. See, e.g., Griffith v. State of Colo., Div. of Youth Services, 17 F.3d 1323, 1330 (10th Cir.1994). Courts also have offered plaintiffs promotions that they were wrongfully denied. For instance, on remand in the *Price Waterhouse* case, Hopkins was granted the partnership that the court found she had been denied because of her sex. Hopkins v. Price Waterhouse, 920 F.2d 967 (D.C.Cir.1990), affirming 737 F.Supp. 1202 (D.D.C.1990). The Court of Appeals stressed the broad "make whole" remedial reach of § 706(g), and the Supreme Court's holding in Hishon v. King & Spalding, 467 U.S. 69, 104 S.Ct. 2229, 81 L.Ed.2d 59 (1984), that the discriminatory denial of partnership can constitute a violation of Title VII. The court concluded that the "mere fact that elevation to partnership may place the beneficiary beyond Title VII's reach in no way proves that Title VII is powerless to elevate a victim of discrimination to that position in the first place." Id. at 978. See also Ezold v. Wolf, Block, Schorr and Solis–Cohen, 758 F.Supp. 303 (E.D.Pa.1991), reversed on other grounds, 983 F.2d 509 (3d Cir.1992) (even if discriminatory denial of partnership status in law firm does not constitute constructive discharge, award of partnership or front pay may be appropriate relief); Brown v. Trustees of Boston Univ., 891 F.2d 337 (1st Cir.1989) (tenure may be ordered if its discriminatory denial was "obviously" or "manifestly" unsupported).

Section 706(g) authorizes only equitable relief. Before the Civil Rights Act of 1991 compensatory and punitive damages were not available to successful plaintiffs, and Title VII litigants had no right to a jury trial. Plaintiffs who alleged race or certain ancestry discrimination could sue for legal damages and obtain a jury trial by proceeding under 42 U.S.C. § 1981, the reconstruction-era civil rights statute that had been interpreted in the 1970s to condemn race discrimination by private employers. But those who complained of other forms of discrimination condemned by Title VII, including sex discrimination, could not obtain damages or a jury trial under federal law.

Section 102 of the 1991 Act, however, provides that Title VII complainants may recover compensatory damages for "unlawful intentional discrimination". Section 102 contemplates compensatory damages for "future pecuniary losses, emotional pain, suffering, inconvenience, mental anguish, loss of enjoyment of life, and other nonpecuniary losses". 42 U.S.C. § 1981a(b)(3). Section 102 also allows punitive damages for intentional discrimination engaged in by a private employer "with malice or with reckless indifference to the federally protected rights of an aggrieved individual". 42 U.S.C. § 1981a(b)(1). Legal damages, however, are only made available to Title VII complainants who "cannot recover" under § 1981; and the sum of compensatory and punitive damages is capped at levels ranging from $50,000 to $300,000, depending on the number of employees employed by a defendant employer. Section 102 also provides that if a complaining party seeks legal damages, "any party may demand a trial by jury". 42 U.S.C. § 1981a(c)(1).

The allowance of compensatory and punitive damages only for Title VII complainants who cannot recover under § 1981 creates several interpretive issues. It is clear that this provision was intended to allow damage suits by Title VII complainants whose claims are not covered by § 1981. The terms of the provision, however, also might be read to allow Title VII damage suits by race discrimination complainants who can no longer recover under § 1981 for some procedural reason, such as the running of the § 1981 statute of limitations or an effective waiver. It is also not clear whether the EEOC can seek damages for a victim of racial discrimination. The EEOC has asserted that it can because it does not have jurisdiction to sue under § 1981. See Enforcement Guidance: Compensatory and Punitive Damages Available Under § 102 of the Civil Rights act of 1991, EEOC Policy Document N915.002 (July 14, 1992).

The capping of compensatory and punitive damages also presents numerous issues. In Pollard v. E.I. du Pont de Nemours & Co., 532 U.S. 843, 121 S.Ct. 1946, 150 L.Ed.2d 62 (2001), the Court unanimously held that front pay, like back pay, is not an element of compensatory damages and therefore is not subject to the damages cap. The lower courts have held that the cap covers all Title VII claims made in a single lawsuit or arising out of the same factual dispute; plaintiffs cannot, for instance, recover the cap once for a race discrimination claim and a second time for a retaliation claim. See, e.g., Hudson, supra; Baty v. Willamette Industries, Inc., 985 F.Supp. 987 (D.Kan.1997). When there are multiple plaintiffs in an individual suit, however, each plaintiff presumably should be able to recover the full cap amount. The EEOC also has asserted a separate cap should be applied to each individual for whom it brings suit. See EEOC v. W.&O., Inc., 213 F.3d 600 (11th Cir.2000) (agreeing with EEOC). See also Guidance: Compensatory and Punitive Damages Available Under § 102 of the Civil Rights Act of 1991, supra; Donald R. Livingston, The Civil Rights Act of 1991 and EEOC Enforcement, 23 Stet.L.Rev. 53 (1993). Where there are multiple defendants, a plaintiff probably cannot recover more in total than the cap amount. See EEOC v. AIC Security Investigations, Ltd., 823 F.Supp. 571 (N.D.Ill.1993), reversed on other grounds, 55 F.3d 1276 (7th Cir.1995) (plaintiff limited to one damage cap.) For further discussion of remedial issues under the 1991 Act, see p. 1058 infra.

McKENNON v. NASHVILLE BANNER
PUBLISHING COMPANY
Supreme Court of the United States, 1995.
513 U.S. 352, 115 S.Ct. 879, 130 L.Ed.2d 852.

JUSTICE KENNEDY delivered the opinion of the Court.

The question before us is whether an employee discharged in violation of the Age Discrimination in Employment Act of 1967 is barred from all relief when, after her discharge, the employer discovers evidence of wrongdoing that, in any event, would have led to the employee's termination on lawful and legitimate grounds.

I

For some 30 years, petitioner Christine McKennon worked for respondent Nashville Banner Publishing Company. She was discharged, the Banner claimed, as part of a work force reduction plan necessitated by cost considerations. McKennon, who was 62 years old when she lost her job, thought another reason explained her dismissal: her age. She filed suit in the United States District Court for the Middle District of Tennessee, alleging that her discharge violated the Age Discrimination in Employment Act of 1967 (ADEA). * * * McKennon sought a variety of legal and equitable remedies available under the ADEA, including backpay.

In preparation of the case, the Banner took McKennon's deposition. She testified that, during her final year of employment, she had copied several confidential documents bearing upon the company's financial condition. She had access to these records as secretary to the Banner's comptroller. McKennon took the copies home and showed them to her husband. Her motivation, she averred, was an apprehension she was about to be fired because of her age. When she became concerned about her job, she removed and copied the documents for "insurance" and "protection." A few days after these deposition disclosures, the Banner sent McKennon a letter declaring that removal and copying of the records was in violation of her job responsibilities and advising her (again) that she was terminated. The Banner's letter also recited that had it known of McKennon's misconduct it would have discharged her at once for that reason.

For purposes of summary judgment, the Banner conceded its discrimination against McKennon. The District Court granted summary judgment for the Banner, holding that McKennon's misconduct was grounds for her termination and that neither backpay nor any other remedy was available to her under the ADEA. The United States Court of Appeals for the Sixth Circuit affirmed on the same rationale.* * *

II

We shall assume, as summary judgment procedures require us to assume, that the sole reason for McKennon's initial discharge was her age, a discharge violative of the ADEA. Our further premise is that the misconduct revealed by the deposition was so grave that McKennon's immediate discharge would have followed its disclosure in any event. The District Court and the Court of Appeals found no basis for contesting that proposition, and for purposes of our review we need not question it here. We do question the legal conclusion reached by those courts that after-acquired evidence of wrongdoing which would have resulted in discharge bars employees from any relief under the ADEA. That ruling is incorrect.

The Court of Appeals considered McKennon's misconduct, in effect, to be supervening grounds for termination. That may be so, but it does not follow, as the Court of Appeals said in citing one of its own earlier cases, that the misconduct renders it " 'irrelevant whether or not [McKennon] was discriminated against.' " We conclude that a violation of the ADEA cannot be so altogether disregarded. * * *

The ADEA and Title VII share common substantive features and also a common purpose: "the elimination of discrimination in the workplace." *Oscar Mayer & Co. v. Evans*, 441 U.S. 750, 756, 60 L. Ed. 2d 609, 99 S. Ct. 2066 (1979). Congress designed the remedial measures in these statutes to serve as a "spur or catalyst" to cause employers "to self-examine and to self-evaluate their employment practices and to endeavor to eliminate, so far as possible, the last vestiges" of discrimination. *Albemarle Paper Co. v. Moody*, 422 U.S. 405, 417–418, 45 L. Ed. 2d 280, 95 S. Ct. 2362 (1975) (internal quotation marks and citation omitted); see also *Franks v. Bowman Transportation Co.*, 424 U.S. 747, 763, 47 L. Ed. 2d 444, 96 S. Ct. 1251 (1976). Deterrence is one object of these statutes. Compensation for injuries caused by the prohibited discrimination is another. *Albemarle Paper Co. v. Moody, supra*, at 418; *Franks v. Bowman Transportation Co.*, supra, at 763–764. The ADEA, in keeping with these purposes, contains a vital element found in both Title VII and the Fair Labor Standards Act [the statute that provides the model for ADEA's procedural provisions]: it grants an injured employee a right of action to obtain the authorized relief. 29 U.S.C. § 626(c). The private litigant who seeks redress for his or her injuries vindicates both the deterrence and the compensation objectives of the ADEA. * * * It would not accord with this scheme if after-acquired evidence of wrongdoing that would have resulted in termination operates, in every instance, to bar all relief for an earlier violation of the Act.

The objectives of the ADEA are furthered when even a single employee establishes that an employer has discriminated against him or her. The disclosure through litigation of incidents or practices which violate national policies respecting nondiscrimination in the work force is itself important, for the occurrence of violations may disclose patterns of noncompliance resulting from a misappreciation of the Act's operation or entrenched resistance to its commands, either of which can be of industry-wide significance. * * *

* * *

* * * [T]he case comes to us on the express assumption that an unlawful motive was the sole basis for the firing. McKennon's misconduct was not discovered until after she had been fired. The employer could not have been motivated by knowledge it did not have and it cannot now claim that the employee was fired for the nondiscriminatory reason. Mixed motive cases are inapposite here, except to the important extent they underscore the necessity of determining the employer's motives in ordering the discharge, an essential element in determining whether the employer violated the federal antidiscrimination law. * * *

Our inquiry is not at an end, however, for even though the employer has violated the Act, we must consider how the after-acquired evidence of the employee's wrongdoing bears on the specific remedy to be ordered. Equity's maxim that a suitor who engaged in his own reprehensible conduct in the course of the transaction at issue must be denied equitable relief because of unclean hands, a rule which in conventional formulation operated in limine to bar the suitor from invoking the aid of the equity court, 2 S. Symons, Pomeroy's Equity Jurisprudence § 397, pp. 90–92 (5th ed. 1941), has not been applied where Congress authorizes broad equitable relief to serve important national policies. We have rejected the unclean hands defense "where a private suit serves important public purposes." *Perma Life Mufflers, Inc. v. International Parts Corp.*, 392 U.S. 134, 138, 20 L. Ed. 2d 982, 88 S. Ct. 1981 (1968) (Sherman and Clayton Antitrust Acts). That does not mean, however, the employee's own misconduct is irrelevant to all the remedies otherwise available under the statute. The statute controlling this case provides that "the court shall have jurisdiction to grant such legal or equitable relief as may be appropriate to effectuate the purposes of this chapter, including without limitation judgments compelling employment, reinstatement or promotion, or enforcing the liability for [amounts owing to a person as a result of a violation of this chapter]." 29 U.S.C. § 626(b); see also § 216(b). In giving effect to the ADEA, we must recognize the duality between the legitimate interests of the employer and the important claims of the employee who invokes the national employment policy mandated by the Act. The employee's wrongdoing must be taken into account, we conclude, lest the employer's legitimate concerns be ignored. The ADEA, like Title VII, is not a general regulation of the workplace but a law which prohibits discrimination. The statute does not constrain employers from exercising significant other prerogatives and discretions in the course of the hiring, promoting, and discharging of their employees. * * * In determining appropriate remedial action, the employee's wrongdoing becomes relevant not to punish the employee, or out of concern "for the relative moral worth of the parties," but to take due account of the lawful prerogatives of the employer in the usual course of its business and the corresponding equities that it has arising from the employee's wrongdoing.

The proper boundaries of remedial relief in the general class of cases where, after termination, it is discovered that the employee has engaged in wrongdoing must be addressed by the judicial system in the ordinary course of further decisions, for the factual permutations and the equitable considerations they raise will vary from case to case. We do conclude that here, and as a general rule in cases of this type, neither reinstatement nor front pay is an appropriate remedy. It would be both inequitable and pointless to order the reinstatement of someone the employer would have terminated, and will terminate, in any event and upon lawful grounds.

The proper measure of backpay presents a more difficult problem. Resolution of this question must give proper recognition to the fact that an ADEA violation has occurred which must be deterred and compensated without undue infringement upon the employer's rights and prerogatives. The object of compensation is to restore the employee to the position he or she would have been in absent the discrimination, *Franks v. Bowman Transportation Co.*, 424 U.S. at 764, but that principle is difficult to apply with precision where there is after-acquired evidence of wrongdoing that would have led to termination on legitimate grounds had the employer known about it. Once an employer learns about employee wrongdoing that would lead to a legitimate discharge, we cannot require the employer to ignore the information, even if it is acquired during the course of discovery in a suit against the employer and even if the information might have gone undiscovered absent the suit. The beginning point in the trial court's formulation of a remedy should be calculation of backpay from the date of the unlawful discharge to the date the new information was discovered. In determining the appropriate order for relief, the court can consider taking into further account extraordinary equitable circumstances that affect the legitimate interests of either party. An absolute rule barring any recovery of backpay, however, would undermine the ADEA's objective of forcing employers to consider and examine their motivations, and of penalizing them for employment decisions that spring from age discrimination.

Where an employer seeks to rely upon after-acquired evidence of wrongdoing, it must first establish that the wrongdoing was of such severity that the employee in fact would have been terminated on those grounds alone if the employer had known of it at the time of the discharge. The concern that employers might as a routine matter undertake extensive discovery into an employee's background or performance on the job to resist claims under the Act is not an insubstantial one, but we think the authority of the courts to award attorney's fees, mandated under the statute, 29 U.S.C. §§ 216(b), 626(b), and in appropriate cases to invoke the provisions of Rule 11 of the Federal Rules of Civil Procedure will deter most abuses.

Notes and Questions

1. *Applicable to Title VII?* Is there any doubt that the holding of *McKennon* is applicable to Title VII as well as to the ADEA? The lower courts have so ruled. See, e.g., Wallace v. Dunn Const. Co., 62 F.3d 374 (11th Cir.1995); Wehr v. Ryan's Family Steak Houses, Inc. 49 F.3d 1150 (6th Cir.1995).

2. *Undermining Title VII Goals?* In those cases in which the employer would not have obtained knowledge of the plaintiff's misconduct in the absence of Title VII litigation, will the remedies contemplated by the *McKennon* Court place the victims of discrimination in after-acquired evidence cases in the position they would have been in absent discrimination? If not, will these remedies fully serve the compensation objectives of the antidiscrimination laws? The deterrent objectives of these laws? Do practical limits on effective regulation and respect for employers' control of their businesses nonetheless provide sufficient justification for the limitations on normal remedies contemplated by the Court in after-acquired evidence cases?

3. *Other Approaches?* Could the Court have approved an award of full back pay up until the date of the Title VII judgment without also approving reinstatement or front pay? Back pay up until the date the employee's wrongdoing would have been discovered absent litigation? Would it be practical to assign such a hypothetical date?

4. *Does* McKennon *Encourage Retaliatory Investigations?* Justice Kennedy for the Court acknowledges the not "insubstantial" concern that employers as a routine matter might undertake extensive discovery of the files and background of any employee who claims discriminatory treatment. Should this response be a concern under the antidiscrimination laws? Note Title VII's prohibition in § 704 of retaliation against discrimination complainants (treated in chapter 10 infra). Will the attorney's fees mandate or Rule 11 of the Federal Rules of Civil Procedure adequately curb retaliatory investigations?

5. *Compensatory Damages?* Does *McKennon* suggest that plaintiffs subject to an after-acquired evidence defense should be allowed, in at least some cases, to recover compensatory damages? See Crapp v. City of Miami Beach, 242 F.3d 1017 (11th Cir.2001) (proper to deny backpay and reinstatement, but allow compensatory damages). Recovery for what type of harm might be consistent with *McKennon*? See also note 6 infra.

6. *The EEOC's Position.* The EEOC has issued an Enforcement Guidance on the *McKennon* decision, EEOC Notice No. 915.002 (Dec. 14, 1995), which is applicable to Title VII, the Americans with Disabilities Act, and the Equal Pay Act, as well as the ADEA. It states that if an employer fails to prove that it would have taken the challenged disciplinary action on the basis of after-acquired evidence of misconduct, relief may not be limited by such evidence. The memorandum directs EEOC investigators to analyze how the employer has treated other instances of similar misconduct in the past, whether the misconduct was criminal in nature, and whether the misconduct compromised the integrity of the employer or otherwise would have made the challenged discipline reasonable and justifiable. The Commission interprets *McKennon* to allow an award of backpay until the date a charge or complaint is resolved where the evidence of misconduct by the charging party is uncovered during a "retaliatory investigation, i.e., one initiated in response to a complaint of discrimination in an attempt to uncover derogatory information about the complaining party or discourage other charges or opposition", rather than in the normal course of investigating the charge.

The EEOC memorandum also states that a charging party may recover as compensatory damages out-of-pocket costs incurred only from the date of an unlawful adverse action until the date such new information is discovered. However, the memorandum instructs agency personnel to seek relief for emotional harm caused by discriminatory conduct even to the extent that harm continues after a legitimate reason for the adverse action has been discovered. Also, the agency's view is that punitive damages are not barred by after-acquired evidence when the charged party has been shown to have acted initially with malice or reckless indifference to the charging party's rights.

Is the EEOC's Enforcement Guidance consistent with *McKennon*? How might courts distinguish between "retaliatory investigations" and ones undertaken "in the normal course" of probing and defending against a discrimination charge?

7. *Relevant to Post–Termination Misconduct?* Does *McKennon* have relevance for a case in which the employer-defendant discovers that the plaintiff *after* a discriminatory termination has engaged in conduct that independently would warrant termination? See Sellers v. Mineta, 358 F.3d 1058 (8th Cir. 2004) (post-termination conduct may limit recovery of front pay). See generally Christine Neylon O'Brien, The Law of After–Acquired Evidence in Employment Discrimination Cases: Clarification of the Employer's Burden, Remedial Guidance, and the Enigma of Post–Termination Misconduct, 65 UMKC L. Rev. 159 (1996). Should it matter if the conduct occurs during proceedings occasioned by the discriminatory termination? See Medlock v. Ortho Biotech, Inc., 164 F.3d 545 (10th Cir.1999) (misconduct at a hearing concerning termination properly treated as not relevant to damages).

C.   PROVING SYSTEMIC DISPARATE TREATMENT

INTERNATIONAL BROTH. OF TEAMSTERS v. UNITED STATES

Supreme Court of the United States, 1977.

431 U.S. 324, 97 S.Ct. 1843, 52 L.Ed.2d 396.

Mr. Justice Stewart delivered the opinion of the Court.

The central claim in [the] lawsuits was that the company had engaged in a pattern or practice of discriminating against minorities in hiring so-called line drivers.[3] Those Negroes and Spanish-surnamed persons who had been hired, the Government alleged, were given lower paying, less desirable jobs as servicemen or local city drivers, and were

---

3. *Line drivers,* also known as over-the-road drivers, engage in long-distance hauling between company terminals. They compose a separate bargaining unit at the company. Other distinct bargaining units include *servicemen,* who service trucks, unhook tractors and trailers, and perform similar tasks; and *city operations,* composed of dockmen, hostlers, and city drivers who pick up and deliver freight within the immediate area of a particular terminal. All of these employees were represented by the petitioner union.

thereafter discriminated against with respect to promotions and transfers.

* * *

Consideration of the question whether the company engaged in a pattern or practice of discriminatory hiring practices involves controlling legal principles that are relatively clear. The Government's theory of discrimination was simply that the company, in violation of § 703(a) of Title VII, regularly and purposefully treated Negroes and Spanish-surnamed Americans less favorably than white persons. The disparity in treatment allegedly involved the refusal to recruit, hire, transfer, or promote minority group members on an equal basis with white people, particularly with respect to line-driving positions. The ultimate factual issues are thus simply whether there was a pattern or practice of such disparate treatment and, if so, whether the differences were "racially premised." *McDonnell Douglas Corp. v. Green,* 411 U.S. 792, 805 n. 18, 93 S.Ct. 1817, 1825, 36 L.Ed.2d 668.

As the plaintiff, the Government bore the initial burden of making out a prima facie case of discrimination. *Albemarle Paper Co. v. Moody,* 422 U.S. 405, 425, 95 S.Ct. 2362, 2375, 45 L.Ed.2d 280; *McDonnell Douglas Corp. v. Green, supra,* 411 U.S., at 802, 93 S.Ct., at 1824. And, because it alleged a systemwide pattern or practice of resistance to the full enjoyment of Title VII rights, the Government ultimately had to prove more than the mere occurrence of isolated or "accidental" or sporadic discriminatory acts. It had to establish by a preponderance of the evidence that racial discrimination was the company's standard operating procedure—the regular rather than the unusual practice.[16]

We agree with the District Court and the Court of Appeals that the Government carried its burden of proof. As of March 31, 1971, shortly after the Government filed its complaint alleging systemwide discrimination, the company had 6,472 employees. Of these, 314 (5%) were Negroes and 257 (4%) were Spanish-surnamed Americans. Of the 1,828 line drivers, however, there were only 8 (0.4%) Negroes and 5 (0.3%) Spanish-surnamed persons, and all of the Negroes had been hired after the litigation had commenced. With one exception—a man who worked as a line driver at the Chicago terminal from 1950 to 1959—the company and its predecessors *did not employ a Negro on a regular basis as a line*

---

16. The "pattern or practice" language in § 707(a) of Title VII was not intended as a term of art, and the words reflect only their usual meaning. Senator Humphrey explained:

"[A] pattern or practice would be present only where the denial of rights consists of something more than an isolated, sporadic incident, but is repeated, routine, or of a generalized nature. There would be a pattern or practice if, for example, a number of companies or persons in the same industry or line of business discrim-

inated, if a chain of motels or restaurants practiced racial discrimination throughout all or a significant part of its system, or if a company repeatedly and regularly engaged in acts prohibited by the statute.

* * *

"The point is that single, insignificant, isolated acts of discrimination by a single business would not justify a finding of a pattern or practice * * *." 110 Cong.Rec. 14270 (1964).

driver until 1969. And, as the Government showed, even in 1971 there were terminals in areas of substantial Negro population where all of the company's line drivers were white.[17] A great majority of the Negroes (83%) and Spanish-surnamed Americans (78%) who did work for the company held the lower paying city operations and serviceman jobs,[18] whereas only 39% of the nonminority employees held jobs in those categories.

The Government bolstered its statistical evidence with the testimony of individuals who recounted over 40 specific instances of discrimination. Upon the basis of this testimony the District Court found that "[n]umerous qualified black and Spanish-surnamed American applicants who sought line driving jobs at the company over the years, either had their requests ignored, were given false or misleading information about requirements, opportunities, and application procedures, or were not considered and hired on the same basis that whites were considered and hired." Minority employees who wanted to transfer to line-driver jobs met with similar difficulties.[19]

The company's principal response to this evidence is that statistics can never in and of themselves prove the existence of a pattern or practice of discrimination, or even establish a prima facie case shifting to the employer the burden of rebutting the inference raised by the figures. But, as even our brief summary of the evidence shows, this was not a case in which the Government relied on "statistics alone." The individuals who testified about their personal experiences with the company brought the cold numbers convincingly to life.

17. In Atlanta, for instance, Negroes composed 22.35% of the population in the surrounding metropolitan area and 51.31% of the population in the city proper. The company's Atlanta terminal employed 57 line drivers. All were white. In Los Angeles, 10.84% of the greater metropolitan population and 17.88% of the city population were Negro. But at the company's two Los Angeles terminals there was not a single Negro among the 374 line drivers. The proof showed similar disparities in San Francisco, Denver, Nashville, Chicago, Dallas, and at several other terminals.

18. Although line-driver jobs pay more than other jobs, and the District Court found them to be "considered the most desirable of the driving jobs," it is by no means clear that all employees, even driver employees, would prefer to be line drivers. Of course, Title VII provides for equal opportunity to compete for *any* job, whether it is thought better or worse than another. See, *e.g., United States v. Hayes Int'l Corp.,* 456 F.2d 112, 118 (CA5); *United States v. National Lead Co.,* 438 F.2d 935, 939 (CA8).

19. Two examples are illustrative:

George Taylor, a Negro, worked for the company as a city driver in Los Angeles, beginning late in 1966. In 1968, after hearing that a white city driver had transferred to a line-driver job, he told the terminal manager that he also would like to consider line driving. The manager replied that there would be "a lot of problems on the road * * * with different people, Caucasian, et cetera," and stated: "I don't feel that the company is ready for this right now. * * * Give us a little time. It will come around, you know." Mr. Taylor made similar requests some months later and got similar responses. He was never offered a line-driving job or an application.

Feliberto Trujillo worked as a dockman at the company's Denver terminal. When he applied for a line-driver job in 1967, he was told by a personnel officer that he had one strike against him. He asked what that was and was told: "You're a Chicano, and as far as we know, there isn't a Chicano driver in the system."

In any event, our cases make it unmistakably clear that "[s]tatistical analyses have served and will continue to serve an important role" in cases in which the existence of discrimination is a disputed issue. *Mayor of Philadelphia v. Educational Equality League,* 415 U.S. 605, 620, 94 S.Ct. 1323, 1333, 39 L.Ed.2d 630. See also *McDonnell Douglas Corp. v. Green,* 411 U.S., at 805, 93 S.Ct., at 1825. Cf. *Washington v. Davis,* 426 U.S. 229, 241–242, 96 S.Ct. 2040, 2048–2049, 48 L.Ed.2d 597. We have repeatedly approved the use of statistical proof, where it reached proportions comparable to those in this case, to establish a prima facie case of racial discrimination in jury selection cases, see, *e.g., Turner v. Fouche,* 396 U.S. 346, 90 S.Ct. 532, 24 L.Ed.2d 567; *Hernandez v. Texas,* 347 U.S. 475, 74 S.Ct. 667, 98 L.Ed. 866; *Norris v. Alabama,* 294 U.S. 587, 55 S.Ct. 579, 79 L.Ed. 1074. Statistics are equally competent in proving employment discrimination.[20] We caution only that statistics are not irrefutable; they come in infinite variety and, like any other kind of evidence, they may be rebutted. In short, their usefulness depends on all of the surrounding facts and circumstances. See, *e.g., Hester v. Southern R. Co.,* 497 F.2d 1374, 1379–1381 (CA5).

In addition to its general protest against the use of statistics in Title VII cases, the company claims that in this case the statistics revealing racial imbalance are misleading because they fail to take into account the company's particular business situation as of the effective date of Title VII. The company concedes that its line drivers were virtually all white in July 1965, but it claims that thereafter business conditions were such that its work force dropped. Its argument is that low personnel turnover, rather than post-Act discrimination, accounts for more recent statistical disparities. It points to substantial minority hiring in later years, especially after 1971, as showing that any pre-Act patterns of discrimination were broken.

The argument would be a forceful one if this were an employer who, at the time of suit, had done virtually no new hiring since the effective date of Title VII. But it is not. Although the company's total number of

---

20. Petitioners argue that statistics, at least those comparing the racial composition of an employer's work force to the composition of the population at large, should never be given decisive weight in a Title VII case because to do so would conflict with § 703(j) of the Act, 42 U.S.C. § 2000e–2(j). * * *

The argument fails in this case because the statistical evidence was not offered or used to support an erroneous theory that Title VII requires an employer's work force to be racially balanced. Statistics showing racial or ethnic imbalance are probative in a case such as this one only because such imbalance is often a telltale sign of purposeful discrimination; absent explanation, it is ordinarily to be expected that nondiscriminatory hiring practices will in time result in a work force more or less representative of

the racial and ethnic composition of the population in the community from which employees are hired. Evidence of longlasting and gross disparity between the composition of a work force and that of the general population thus may be significant even though § 703(j) makes clear that Title VII imposes no requirement that a work force mirror the general population. See, *e.g., United States v. Sheet Metal Workers Local 36,* 416 F.2d 123, 127 n. 7 (CA8). Considerations such as small sample size may, of course, detract from the value of such evidence, see, *e.g., Mayor of Philadelphia v. Educational Equality League,* 415 U.S. 605, 620–621, 94 S.Ct. 1323, 1333, 39 L.Ed.2d 630, and evidence showing that the figures for the general population might not accurately reflect the pool of qualified job applicants would also be relevant. *Ibid.* * * *

employees apparently dropped somewhat during the late 1960's, the record shows that many line drivers continued to be hired throughout this period, and that almost all of them were white.[21] To be sure, there were improvements in the company's hiring practices. The Court of Appeals commented that "T.I.M.E.—D.C.'s recent minority hiring progress stands as a laudable good faith effort to eradicate the effects of past discrimination in the area of hiring and initial assignment."[22] But the District Court and the Court of Appeals found upon substantial evidence that the company had engaged in a course of discrimination that continued well after the effective date of Title VII. The company's later changes in its hiring and promotion policies could be of little comfort to the victims of the earlier post-Act discrimination, and could not erase its previous illegal conduct or its obligation to afford relief to those who suffered because of it. Cf. *Albemarle Paper Co. v. Moody,* 422 U.S., at 413–423, 95 S.Ct., at 2369–2374.[23]

The District Court and the Court of Appeals, on the basis of substantial evidence, held that the Government had proved a prima facie case of systematic and purposeful employment discrimination, continuing well beyond the effective date of Title VII. The company's attempts to rebut that conclusion were * * * inadequate.[24]

---

21. Between July 2, 1965, and January 1, 1969, hundreds of line drivers were hired systemwide, either from the outside or from the ranks of employees filling other jobs within the company. None was a Negro.

22. For example, in 1971 the company hired 116 new line drivers, of whom 16 were Negro or Spanish-surnamed Americans. Minority employees composed 7.1% of the company's systemwide work force in 1967 and 10.5% in 1972. Minority hiring increased greatly in 1972 and 1973, presumably due at least in part to the existence of the consent decree.

23. The company's narrower attacks upon the statistical evidence—that there was no precise delineation of the areas referred to in the general population statistics, that the Government did not demonstrate that minority populations were located close to terminals or that transportation was available, that the statistics failed to show what portion of the minority population was suited by age, health, or other qualifications to hold trucking jobs, etc.—are equally lacking in force. At best, these attacks go only to the accuracy of the comparison between the composition of the company's work force at various terminals and the general population of the surrounding communities. They detract little from the Government's further showing that Negroes and Spanish-surnamed Americans who were hired were overwhelmingly excluded from line-driver jobs. Such employees were willing to

work, had access to the terminal, were healthy and of working age, and often were at least sufficiently qualified to hold city-driver jobs. Yet they became line drivers with far less frequency than whites. See, *e.g.,* Pretrial Stipulation 14 (of 2,919 whites who held driving jobs in 1971, 1,802 (62%) were line drivers and 1,117 (38%) were city drivers; of 180 Negroes and Spanish-surnamed Americans who held driving jobs, 13 (7%) were line drivers and 167 (93%) were city drivers).

In any event, fine tuning of the statistics could not have obscured the glaring absence of minority line drivers. As the Court of Appeals remarked, the company's inability to rebut the inference of discrimination came not from a misuse of statistics but from "the inexorable zero."

24. * * * The company also attempted to show that all of the witnesses who testified to specific instances of discrimination either were not discriminated against or suffered no injury. The Court of Appeals correctly ruled that the trial judge was not bound to accept this testimony and that it committed no error by relying instead on the other overpowering evidence in the case. The Court of Appeals was also correct in the view that individual proof concerning each class member's specific injury was appropriately left to proceedings to determine individual relief. In a suit brought by the Government under § 707(a) of the Act the District Court's initial concern is in decid-

HAZELWOOD SCHOOL DISTRICT
v. UNITED STATES
Supreme Court of the United States, 1977.
433 U.S. 299, 97 S.Ct. 2736, 53 L.Ed.2d 768.

JUSTICE STEWART delivered the opinion of the Court.

The petitioner Hazelwood School District covers 78 square miles in the northern part of St. Louis County, Mo. In 1973 the Attorney General brought this lawsuit against Hazelwood and various of its officials, alleging that they were engaged in a "pattern or practice" of employment discrimination in violation of Title VII of the Civil Rights Act of 1964.

* * *

From the beginning, Hazelwood followed relatively unstructured procedures in hiring its teachers. Every person requesting an application for a teaching position was sent one, and completed applications were submitted to a central personnel office, where they were kept on file.[2] During the early 1960's the personnel office notified all applicants whenever a teaching position became available, but as the number of applications on file increased in the late 1960's and early 1970's, this practice was no longer considered feasible. The personnel office thus began the practice of selecting anywhere from 3 to 10 applicants for interviews at the school where the vacancy existed. * * *

Interviews were conducted by a department chairman, program coordinator, or the principal at the school where the teaching vacancy existed. Although those conducting the interviews did fill out forms rating the applicants in a number of respects, it is undisputed that each school principal possessed virtually unlimited discretion in hiring teachers for his school. * * *

In the early 1960's Hazelwood found it necessary to recruit new teachers, and for that purpose members of its staff visited a number of colleges and universities in Missouri and bordering States. All the institutions visited were predominantly white, and Hazelwood did not seriously recruit at either of the two predominantly Negro four-year colleges in Missouri.[4] As a buyer's market began to develop for public school teachers, Hazelwood curtailed its recruiting efforts. For the 1971–1972 school year, 3,127 persons applied for only 234 teaching vacancies; for the 1972–1973 school year, there were 2,373 applications for 282 vacancies. A number of the applicants who were not hired were Ne-

---

ing whether the Government has proved that the defendant has engaged in a pattern or practice of discriminatory conduct.

2. Before 1954 Hazelwood's application forms required designation of race, and those forms were in use as late as the 1962–1963 school year.

4. One of those two schools was never visited even though it was located in nearby St. Louis. The second was briefly visited on one occasion, but no potential applicant was interviewed.

groes.[5]

Hazelwood hired its first Negro teacher in 1969. The number of Negro faculty members gradually increased in successive years: 6 of 957 in the 1970 school year; 16 of 1,107 by the end of the 1972 school year; 22 of 1,231 in the 1973 school year. By comparison, according to 1970 census figures, of more than 19,000 teachers employed in that year in the St. Louis area, 15.4% were Negro. That percentage figure included the St. Louis City School District, which in recent years has followed a policy of attempting to maintain a 50% Negro teaching staff. Apart from that school district, 5.7% of the teachers in the county were Negro in 1970.

* * *

The District Court ruled that the Government had failed to establish a pattern or practice of discrimination. * * *

The Court of Appeals for the Eighth Circuit reversed. After suggesting that the District Court had assigned inadequate weight to evidence of discriminatory conduct on the part of Hazelwood before the effective date of Title VII,[7] the Court of Appeals rejected the trial court's analysis of the statistical data as resting on an irrelevant comparison of Negro teachers to Negro pupils in Hazelwood. The proper comparison, in the appellate court's view, was one between Negro teachers in Hazelwood and Negro teachers in the relevant labor market area. Selecting St. Louis County and St. Louis City as the relevant area,[8] the Court of Appeals compared the 1970 census figures, showing that 15.4% of teachers in that area were Negro, to the racial composition of Hazelwood's teaching staff. In the 1972–1973 and 1973–1974 school years, only 1.4% and 1.8%, respectively, of Hazelwood's teachers were Negroes. This statistical disparity, particularly when viewed against the background of the teacher-hiring procedures that Hazelwood had followed, was held to constitute a prima facie case of a pattern or practice of racial discrimination.

In addition, the Court of Appeals reasoned that the trial court had erred in failing to measure the 55 instances in which Negro applicants were denied jobs against the four-part standard for establishing a prima facie case of individual discrimination set out in this Court's opinion in *McDonnell Douglas Corp. v. Green,* 411 U.S. 792, 802, 93 S.Ct. 1817, 1824, 36 L.Ed.2d 668. Applying that standard, the appellate court found 16 cases of individual discrimination, which "buttressed" the statistical proof. Because Hazelwood had not rebutted the Government's prima facie case of a pattern or practice of racial discrimination, the Court of

---

5. The parties disagree whether it is possible to determine from the present record exactly how many of the job applicants in each of the school years were Negroes.

7. * * * The evidence of pre-Act discrimination relied upon by the Court of Appeals included the failure to hire any Negro teachers until 1969, the failure to recruit at predominantly Negro colleges in Missouri, and somewhat inconclusive evidence that Hazelwood was responsible for a 1962 Mississippi newspaper advertisement for teacher applicants that specified "white only."

8. The city of St. Louis is surrounded by, but not included in, St. Louis County. Mo.Ann.Stat. § 46.145 (1966).

Appeals directed judgment for the Government and prescribed the remedial order to be entered.

* * *

There can be no doubt, in light of the *Teamsters* case, that the District Court's comparison of Hazelwood's teacher work force to its student population fundamentally misconceived the role of statistics in employment discrimination cases. The Court of Appeals was correct in the view that a proper comparison was between the racial composition of Hazelwood's teaching staff and the racial composition of the qualified public school teacher population in the relevant labor market.[13] See *Teamsters, supra,* at 337–338, and n. 17, 97 S.Ct., at 1855, and n. 17. The percentage of Negroes on Hazelwood's teaching staff in 1972–1973 was 1.4% and in 1973–1974 it was 1.8%. By contrast, the percentage of qualified Negro teachers in the area was, according to the 1970 census, at least 5.7%.[14] Although these differences were on their face substantial, the Court of Appeals erred in substituting its judgment for that of the

13. In *Teamsters,* the comparison between the percentage of Negroes on the employer's work force and the percentage in the general area-wide population was highly probative, because the job skill there involved—the ability to drive a truck—is one that many persons possess or can fairly readily acquire. When special qualifications are required to fill particular jobs, comparisons to the general population (rather than to the smaller group of individuals who possess the necessary qualifications) may have little probative value. The comparative statistics introduced by the Government in the District Court, however, were properly limited to public school teachers, and therefore this is not a case like *Mayor v. Educational Equality League,* 415 U.S. 605, 94 S.Ct. 1323, 39 L.Ed.2d 630, in which the racial-composition comparisons failed to take into account special qualifications for the position in question. *Id.,* at 620–621, 94 S.Ct., at 1333–1334.

Although the petitioners concede as a general matter the probative force of the comparative work-force statistics, they object to the Court of Appeals' heavy reliance on these data on the ground that applicant-flow data, showing the actual percentage of white and Negro applicants for teaching positions at Hazelwood, would be firmer proof. As we have noted, see n. 5, *supra,* there was no clear evidence of such statistics. We leave it to the District Court on remand to determine whether competent proof of those data can be adduced. If so, it would, of course, be very relevant. Cf. *Dothard v. Rawlinson,* 433 U.S., 321, 330, 97 S.Ct. 2720, 2727, 53 L.Ed.2d 786.

14. As is discussed below, the Government contends that a comparative figure of 15.4%, rather than 5.7%, is the appropriate one. But even assuming, *arguendo,* that the 5.7% figure urged by the petitioners is correct, the disparity between that figure and the percentage of Negroes on Hazelwood's teaching staff would be more than fourfold for the 1972–1973 school year, and threefold for the 1973–1974 school year. A precise method of measuring the significance of such statistical disparities was explained in *Castaneda v. Partida,* 430 U.S. 482, 496–497, n. 17, 97 S.Ct. 1272, 1281, n. 17, 51 L.Ed.2d 498, n. 17. It involves calculation of the "standard deviation" as a measure of predicted fluctuations from the expected value of a sample. Using the 5.7% figure as the basis for calculating the expected value, the expected number of Negroes on the Hazelwood teaching staff would be roughly 63 in 1972–1973 and 70 in 1973–1974. The observed number in those years was 16 and 22, respectively. The difference between the observed and expected values was more than six standard deviations in 1972–1973 and more than five standard deviations in 1973–1974. The Court in *Castaneda* noted that "[a]s a general rule for such large samples, if the difference between the expected value and the observed number is greater than two or three standard deviations," then the hypothesis that teachers were hired without regard to race would be suspect. 430 U.S., at 497 n. 17, 97 S.Ct., at 1281 n. 17.

District Court and holding that the Government had conclusively proved its "pattern or practice" lawsuit.

The Court of Appeals totally disregarded the possibility that this prima facie statistical proof in the record might at the trial court level be rebutted by statistics dealing with Hazelwood's hiring after it became subject to Title VII. Racial discrimination by public employers was not made illegal under Title VII until March 24, 1972. A public employer who from that date forward made all its employment decisions in a wholly nondiscriminatory way would not violate Title VII even if it had formerly maintained an all-white work force by purposefully excluding Negroes.[15] For this reason, the Court cautioned in the *Teamsters* opinion that once a prima facie case has been established by statistical work-force disparities, the employer must be given an opportunity to show that "the claimed discriminatory pattern is a product of pre-Act hiring rather than unlawful post-Act discrimination." 431 U.S., at 360, 97 S.Ct., at 1867.

The record in this case showed that for the 1972–1973 school year, Hazelwood hired 282 new teachers, 10 of whom (3.5%) were Negroes; for the following school year it hired 123 new teachers, 5 of whom (4.1%) were Negroes. Over the two-year period, Negroes constituted a total of 15 of the 405 new teachers hired (3.7%). Although the Court of Appeals briefly mentioned these data in reciting the facts, it wholly ignored them in discussing whether the Government had shown a pattern or practice of discrimination. And it gave no consideration at all to the possibility that post–Act data as to the number of Negroes hired compared to the total number of Negro applicants might tell a totally different story.

What the hiring figures prove obviously depends upon the figures to which they are compared. The Court of Appeals accepted the Government's argument that the relevant comparison was to the labor market area of St. Louis County and the city of St. Louis, in which, according to the 1970 census, 15.4% of all teachers were Negro. The propriety of that comparison was vigorously disputed by the petitioners, who urged that because the city of St. Louis has made special attempts to maintain a 50% Negro teaching staff, inclusion of that school district in the relevant market area distorts the comparison. Were that argument accepted, the percentage of Negro teachers in the relevant labor market area (St. Louis County alone) as shown in the 1970 census would be 5.7% rather than 15.4%.

---

15. This is not to say that evidence of pre–Act discrimination can never have any probative force. Proof that an employer engaged in racial discrimination prior to the effective date of Title VII might in some circumstances support the inference that such discrimination continued, particularly where relevant aspects of the decisionmaking process had undergone little change. Cf. Fed.Rule Evid. 406; *Village of Arlington* *Heights v. Metropolitan Housing Development Corp.,* 429 U.S., 252, 267, 97 S.Ct. 555, 564, 50 L.Ed.2d 450; 1 J. Wigmore, Evidence § 92 (3d ed. 1940); 2 *id.,* 302–305, 371, 375. And, of course, a public employer even before the extension of Title VII in 1972 was subject to the command of the Fourteenth Amendment not to engage in purposeful racial discrimination.

The difference between these figures may well be important; the disparity between 3.7% (the percentage of Negro teachers hired by Hazelwood in 1972–1973 and 1973–1974) and 5.7% may be sufficiently small to weaken the Government's other proof, while the disparity between 3.7% and 15.4% may be sufficiently large to reinforce it.[17] In determining which of the two figures—or, very possibly, what intermediate figure—provides the most accurate basis for comparison to the hiring figures at Hazelwood, it will be necessary to evaluate such considerations as (i) whether the racially based hiring policies of the St. Louis City School District were in effect as far back as 1970, the year in which the census figures were taken; (ii) to what extent those policies have changed the racial composition of that district's teaching staff from what it would otherwise have been; (iii) to what extent St. Louis' recruitment policies have diverted to the city, teachers who might otherwise have applied to Hazelwood; (iv) to what extent Negro teachers employed by the city would prefer employment in other districts such as Hazelwood; and (v) what the experience in other school districts in St. Louis County indicates about the validity of excluding the City School District from the relevant labor market.

It is thus clear that a determination of the appropriate comparative figures in this case will depend upon further evaluation by the trial court. As this Court admonished in *Teamsters*: "[S]tatistics * * * come in infinite variety * * *. [T]heir usefulness depends on all of the surrounding facts and circumstances." 431 U.S., at 340, 97 S.Ct., at 1856–1857. Only the trial court is in a position to make the appropriate determination after further findings. And only after such a determination is made can a foundation be established for deciding whether or not

17. Indeed, under the statistical methodology explained in *Castaneda v. Partida, supra,* 430 U.S., at 496–497, n. 17, 97 S.Ct. 1272, at 1281, n. 17, 51 L.Ed.2d 498 n. 17, involving the calculation of the standard deviation as a measure of predicted fluctuations, the difference between using 15.4% and 5.7% as the areawide figure would be significant. If the 15.4% figure is taken as the basis for comparison, the expected number of Negro teachers hired by Hazelwood in 1972–1973 would be 43 (rather than the actual figure of 10) of a total of 282, a difference of more than five standard deviations; the expected number of 1973–1974 would be 19 (rather than the actual figure 5) of a total of 123, a difference of more than three standard deviations. For the two years combined, the difference between the observed number of 15 Negro teachers hired (of a total of 405) would vary from the expected number of 62 by more than six standard deviations. Because a fluctuation of more than two or three standard deviations would undercut the hypothesis that decisions were being made randomly with respect to race, 430 U.S., at 497 n. 17, 97 S.Ct., at 1281 n. 17, each of these statistical comparisons would reinforce rather than rebut the Government's other proof. If, however, the 5.7% areawide figure is used, the expected number of Negro teachers hired in 1972–1973 would be roughly 16, less than two standard deviations from the observed number of 10; for 1973–1974, the expected value would be roughly seven, less than one standard deviation from the observed value of 5; and for the two years combined, the expected value of 23 would be less than two standard deviations from the observed total of 15. A more precise method of analyzing these statistics confirms the results of the standard deviation analysis. See F. Mosteller, R. Rourke, & G. Thomas, Probability with Statistical Applications 494 (2d ed. 1970).

These observations are not intended to suggest that precise calculations of statistical significance are necessary in employing statistical proof, but merely to highlight the importance of the choice of the relevant labor market area.

Hazelwood engaged in a pattern or practice of racial discrimination in its employment practices in violation of the law.[21]

JUSTICE BRENNAN, concurring.

* * * It is my understanding, as apparently it is Mr. Justice Stevens', that the statistical inquiry mentioned by the Court, and accompanying text, can be of no help to the Hazelwood School Board in rebutting the Government's evidence of discrimination. Indeed, even if the relative comparison market is found to be 5.7% rather than 15.4% black, the applicable statistical analysis at most will not serve to bolster the Government's case. This obviously is of no aid to Hazelwood in meeting *its* burden of proof. Nonetheless I think that the remand directed by the Court is appropriate and will allow the parties to address these figures and calculations with greater care and precision. I also agree that given the misapplication of governing legal principles by the District Court, Hazelwood reasonably should be given the opportunity to come forward with more focused and specific applicant-flow data in the hope of answering the Government's prima facie case. If, as presently seems likely, reliable applicant data are found to be lacking, the conclusion reached by my Brother Stevens will inevitably be forthcoming.

JUSTICE STEVENS, dissenting.

* * * In this case, since neither party complains that any relevant evidence was excluded, our task is to decide (1) whether the Government's evidence established a prima facie case; and (2), if so, whether the remaining evidence is sufficient to carry Hazelwood's burden of rebutting that prima facie case.

I

The first question is clearly answered by the Government's statistical evidence, its historical evidence, and its evidence relating to specific acts of discrimination.

One-third of the teachers hired by Hazelwood resided in the city of St. Louis at the time of their initial employment. As Mr. Justice Clark explained in his opinion for the Court of Appeals, it was therefore appropriate to treat the city, as well as the county, as part of the relevant labor market. In that market, 15% of the teachers were black. In the Hazelwood District at the time of trial less than 2% of the teachers were black. An even more telling statistic is that after Title VII became applicable to it, only 3.7% of the new teachers hired by Hazelwood were black. Proof of these gross disparities was in itself sufficient to make out a prima facie case of discrimination. See *International Brotherhood of Teamsters v. United States,* 431 U.S. 324, 339, 97 S.Ct. 1843, 1856, 52 L.Ed.2d 396 (1977); *Castaneda v. Partida,* 430 U.S. 482, 494–498, 97 S.Ct. 1272, 1280–1282, 51 L.Ed.2d 498.

21. It will also be open to the District Court on remand to determine whether sufficiently reliable applicant-flow data are available to permit consideration of the petitioners' argument that those data may undercut a statistical analysis dependent upon hirings alone.

As a matter of history, Hazelwood employed no black teachers until 1969. Both before and after the 1972 amendment making the statute applicable to public school districts, petitioner used a standardless and largely subjective hiring procedure. Since "relevant aspects of the decisionmaking process had undergone little change," it is proper to infer that the pre-Act policy of preferring white teachers continued to influence Hazelwood's hiring practices.[3]

The inference of discrimination was corroborated by post-Act evidence that Hazelwood had refused to hire 16 qualified black applicants for racial reasons. Taking the Government's evidence as a whole, there can be no doubt about the sufficiency of its prima facie case.

II

* * *

The petitioners offered no evidence concerning wage differentials, commuting problems, or the relative advantages of teaching in an inner-city school as opposed to a suburban school. Without any such evidence in the record, it is difficult to understand why the simple fact that the city was the source of a third of Hazelwood's faculty should not be sufficient to demonstrate that it is a part of the relevant market. The city's policy of attempting to maintain a 50/50 ratio clearly does not undermine that conclusion, particularly when the record reveals no shortage of qualified black applicants in either Hazelwood or other suburban school districts.[4] Surely not *all* of the 2,000 black teachers employed by the city were unavailable for employment in Hazelwood at the time of their initial hire.

But even if it were proper to exclude the city of St. Louis from the market, the statistical evidence would still tend to prove discrimination. With the city excluded, 5.7% of the teachers in the remaining market were black. On the basis of a random selection, one would therefore expect 5.7% of the 405 teachers hired by Hazelwood in the 1972–1973 and 1973–1974 school years to have been black. But instead of 23 black teachers, Hazelwood hired only 15, less than two-thirds of the expected number. Without the benefit of expert testimony, I would hesitate to infer that the disparity between 23 and 15 is great enough, in itself, to

3. Proof that an employer engaged in racial discrimination prior to the effective date of the Act creates the inference that such discrimination continued "particularly where relevant aspects of the decisionmaking process [have] undergone little change". Cf. Fed.Rule Evid. 406; *Village of Arlington Heights v. Metropolitan Housing Development Corp.*, 429 U.S. 252, 267, 97 S.Ct. 555, 50 L.Ed.2d 450; 1 J. Wigmore, Evidence § 92 (3d ed. 1940); 2 *id.*, §§ 302–305, 371, 375. And, of course, a public employer even before the extension of Title VII in 1972 was subject to the command of the Fourteenth Amendment not to engage in purposeful racial discrimination.

Since Hazelwood's hiring before 1972 was so clearly discriminatory, there is some irony in its claim that "Hazelwood continued [after 1972] to select its teachers on the same careful basis that it had relied on before in staffing its growing system."

4. "Had there been evidence obtainable to contradict and disprove the testimony offered by [the Government], it cannot be assumed that the State would have refrained from introducing it." *Pierre v. Louisiana*, 306 U.S. 354, 361–362, 59 S.Ct. 536, 540, 83 L.Ed. 757.

prove discrimination.[5] It is perfectly clear, however, that whatever probative force this disparity has, it tends to prove discrimination and does absolutely nothing in the way of carrying Hazelwood's burden of overcoming the Government's prima facie case.

Absolute precision in the analysis of market data is too much to expect. We may fairly assume that a nondiscriminatory selection process would have resulted in the hiring of somewhere between the 15% suggested by the Government and the 5.7% suggested by petitioners, or perhaps 30 or 40 black teachers, instead of the 15 actually hired.[6] On that assumption, the Court of Appeals' determination that there were 16 individual cases of discriminatory refusal to hire black applicants in the post–1972 period seems remarkably accurate.

Note on Title VII Pattern or Practice Litigation

The United States was a party in both *Teamsters* and *Hazelwood* for a simple reason: before the 1972 amendments to Title VII, § 707 empowered the Attorney General to file suit directly against any employer that it reasonably believed had been engaging in a "pattern or practice" of denying rights secured by the Title. The 1972 amendments, at § 707(c) and (d), transferred this authority (as against private employers) to the EEOC. These amendments also required the EEOC to attempt conciliation before initiating a pattern or practice suit. The procedures governing EEOC suits are further explored in chapter 17.

The 1972 amendments also extended Title VII coverage to state and local government employers. This extension was accommodated in § 706(f) by specifying that the Attorney General is to bring civil actions to remedy individual actions of discrimination by governmental employers. However, Congress neglected, apparently unintentionally, to reserve in § 707 the Attorney General's authority over pattern and practice litigation against state and local governments. In 1978, utilizing his authority to transfer functions from one executive agency to another, President Carter shifted the EEOC's "pattern or practice" litigation authority over state and local governments to the Attorney General. Exec. Order No. 12068, 43 Fed.Reg. 28971. Courts have accepted this assignment of responsibility. See, e.g., United States v. Fresno Unified School District, 592 F.2d 1088, 1095 (9th Cir.1979).

Proof of a pattern or practice of discrimination enables the EEOC or the Attorney General to obtain much broader remedies than would be available in an individual disparate treatment case. An entire system of discrimination can be enjoined. Under certain conditions, as explored in chapter 4, the employer may be required to hire or promote a minimum percentage of

5. After I had drafted this opinion, one of my law clerks advised me that, given the size of the two-year sample, there is only about a 5% likelihood that a disparity this large would be produced by a random selection from the labor pool. If his calculation (which was made using the method described in H. Blalock, Social Statistics 151–

173 (1972)) is correct, it is easy to understand why Hazelwood offered no expert testimony.

6. Some of the other school districts in the county have a 10% ratio of blacks on their faculties.

members of the class subjected to past discrimination. Moreover, as further discussed in chapter 3, the Supreme Court has held that when plaintiffs prove the existence of a discriminatory pattern or practice, the defendant employer bears the burden of proving that any member of the disadvantaged class that was subject to the employer's decisionmaking was also not subject to the proven discriminatory policy. See Franks v. Bowman Transportation Co., 424 U.S. 747, 96 S.Ct. 1251, 47 L.Ed.2d 444 (1976), p. 209 infra. This presumption of individual discrimination upon proof of a general practice of discrimination eases the recovery of back pay for individual victims. Does it also enable the government to now secure compensatory and punitive damages for individuals, even though § 102 of the 1991 Act does not expressly modify the relief which the government has the authority to seek in § 707 litigation?

As illustrated by *Franks* as well as a later case which consolidated government and private systemic litigation, Bazemore v. Friday, 478 U.S. 385, 106 S.Ct. 3000, 92 L.Ed.2d 315 (1986), private plaintiffs may also claim that their treatment was part of a pattern or practice of discrimination. Pattern or practice claims have usually been presented only in class action suits because it is more difficult to prove the existence of a discriminatory system than to prove an individual instance of discrimination. Such class actions conceivably could threaten sufficient liability to provide significant incentives to large firms to institute tight controls over any discriminatory practices. One study, however, found that firms' "shareholder value is not typically affected by either the filing or the settlement" of Title VII class action law suits. See Michael Selmi, The Price of Discrimination: The Nature of Class Action Employment Discrimination Litigation and Its Effects, 81 Tex. L. Rev. 1249, 1315 (2003). Furthermore, one circuit court has held that claims for compensatory and punitive damages under the Civil Rights Act of 1991 render Title VII cases unsuitable for class certification, Allison v. Citgo Petroleum Corp., 151 F.3d 402 (5th Cir.1998), excerpted at p. 1095 infra, while another circuit court has held that private plaintiffs cannot advance a pattern or practice claim without class certification, Lowery v. Circuit City Stores, Inc., 158 F.3d 742 (4th Cir.1998). Title VII class actions are considered in chapter 17.

Note on Statistical Analysis of Discrimination

Teamsters and *Hazelwood* highlight the importance of statistical analysis in systemic disparate treatment cases. Both cases utilize the "binomial distribution" technique, which attempts to draw inferences from a comparison between minority-group selection rates actually observed and the rates one would predict on the basis of that group's representation in the work force, applicant pool, or local population, or some other source of availability data. In Bazemore v. Friday, supra, the Court approved a somewhat distinct statistical approach, termed "multiple regression analysis." The Court's three decisions, viewed jointly, broadly endorse the use of statistics, subject to the caveat stated in *Teamsters:* they "are not irrefutable; they come in infinite variety and like, any other kind of evidence, they may be rebutted. In short, their usefulness depends on all of the surrounding facts and circumstances." Compare the rather different reception accorded statistical analysis in death penalty litigation. See McCleskey v. Kemp, 481 U.S. 279, 107 S.Ct. 1756, 95 L.Ed.2d 262 (1987).

Although statistical analysis is best undertaken with the aid of experts, lawyers do need to have some familiarity with basic concepts. For good general references, see Michael O. Finkelstein & Bruce A. Levin, Statistics for Lawyers (2001); Ramona L. Paetzold & Steven L. Willborn, The Statistics of Discrimination (1994 & 2002 supp.); Walter B. Connolly, Jr. & David W. Peterson, Use of Statistics in Equal Employment Opportunity Litigation (1980).

Drawing Inferences From Statistical Disparity

1. *Types of Comparisons.* Since the binomial method involves a comparison between observed outcomes and predicted outcomes, it must first be determined what is an appropriate basis for comparison. *Teamsters* in footnote 17 compared the percentage of minority line drivers in the employer's work force to the percentage of minorities in the local population (disputed position/general local population comparison); the Court also at least implicitly compared the percentage of minority line drivers to the percentage of minorities in the employer's work force (disputed position/work force comparison). *Hazelwood* involved a comparison between the percentage of minority group teachers in the Hazelwood system with the percentage of minority group teachers in the local labor market (disputed position/qualified local population comparison).

A threshold question is why the Court in both cases did not insist on comparisons to the minority composition of those who actually applied for the disputed positions (disputed position/actual applicant flow comparison). Can a court really determine whether an employer discriminated against minority-group members in its hiring decisions without looking at the universe of individuals who in fact applied? Using proxies for applicant flow data, whether comparisons to general population or local labor market figures, does not replicate the employer's actual decisionmaking process, and may not present a good approximation of the pool of individuals qualified for and interested in the particular position. Consider the following observation from Paetzold & Willborn, supra, § 4.10, at 29, 30:

> If actual applicant data are available and reliable, then selection rates for the groups (e.g., male/female, black/white) should be compared. If actual applicant data are either unavailable or there are questions about the fairness of the process through which applicants are obtained (i.e., recruitment) then an alternative proxy labor pool must be used to estimate the theoretical applicant pool that would have been obtained, absent discrimination.

Paetzold and Willborn thus suggest a general presumption in favor of applicant flow data, subject to the qualification that there may be circumstances where adjustments or proxies may be needed in the face of distortions in actual labor supply. Does footnote 13 of *Hazelwood* support such a presumption, or does it only indicate that comparisons based on applicant flow data could help rebut a prima facie case based on other data? Consider also Wards Cove Packing Co. v. Atonio, p. 139 infra.

There are several possible sources of distortion in applicant flow data. First, the employer may not have compiled reliable data. Neither § 709(c) of Title VII nor EEOC regulations, 29 C.F.R. § 1602.1 et seq., require the maintenance of applicant-flow data; the one exception is where the firm utilizes a selection procedure having an adverse impact on a minority group, see Uniform Guidelines on Employee Selection Procedures (UGESP), 29 C.F.R. § 1607.15. A second difficulty is that even if reliable data have been maintained, there may have been too few hiring (or promotion) decisions during a particular period to permit statistically useful comparisons. There may also have been a large rate of selection from the applicant pool, which would disturb technical requirements for binomial analysis (a point developed below). Finally, there may be reasons to believe that actual applicants are not representative of the pool of individuals who would apply under normal labor supply conditions. The actual applicant flow may underrepresent minority-group availability because of the "chilling effect" of the employer's reputation as a discriminator, as is suggested by the facts in *Teamsters*, or because the employer's eligibility requirements in dispute are generally known and nearly automatically disqualify a particular group—a factor present in Dothard v. Rawlinson, considered later in this chapter. See also UGESP, Supplem. Information, Part II & n. 11, 43 Fed.Reg. 38290, 38291 (Aug. 25, 1978). Does the presence of such factors always justify resort to proxies? See Paetzold & Willborn, supra, § 4.03, at 8–9: "If a problem with the use of the applicant data exists, an alternative proxy population must then be used. * * * A search for the most reliable proxy should be conducted; automatic discarding of the actual applicant data in preference for the labor market or general population data should be avoided."

2. *Binomial Distribution.* Once the appropriate basis for comparison has been determined and selection rates—both observed and expected—have been derived, the question arises whether the differences between these percentage comparisons are attributable to chance. We know from coin-tossing experiments that even though the probability of drawing a head on each coin toss is 50%, there is no guarantee even with a flawless coin that any given pair of tosses will yield one head, or that a string of tails is precluded. If, however, after a 1000 coin tosses (or "trials") you ended up with 200 heads and 800 tails, you might suspect that the coin was "rigged" in some fashion. The binomial model provides a statistical means for determining whether the observed outcomes are likely to be the product of chance (the "null hypothesis"). This technique can be applied to any series of events in which there are (i) two possible outcomes for each trial,(ii) fixed, known probabilities for each outcome, and (iii) independence among the trials (the results of one trial will not affect the probability of the event's occurrence in subsequent trials).

Given a sufficiently large number of trials, the results of a binomial experiment should fall into a pattern called a "normal distribution," which may be graphically depicted as a bell-shaped curve. The curve will reach its highest point at the mean or expected value of the distribution (determined by multiplying the number of trials by the probability of the event's occurrence) and will decline symmetrically on either side. The characteristics of the curve are such that outcomes closest to expected value are more probable than those further down on the curve; outcomes equidistant from the expected value on either side have the same probability of occurrence; and probabilities decline faster for outcomes lying past the point on either side where the curve concaves upward.

A measure of the extent to which the actual outcomes are likely to diverge from the expected value is called the "standard deviation"; the larger the number of standard deviations an observed result is from the expected result, the lower the probability of that event's occurrence. In a normal distribution, 68% of all outcomes are plotted between + 1 and − 1 standard deviations from expected value; 5% of the outcomes lie beyond + 1.96 and − 1.96 standard deviations from the expected value; and only 2% of the outcomes lie beyond + 2 and − 2 standard deviations. As a matter of convention, a result is considered to be "statistically significant" if it will occur as a matter of chance in five or fewer tries out of a hundred. Because outcomes more than two standard deviations from the expected value should occur in two or fewer tries out of a hundred, such a result plainly satisfies the .05 significance test. Thus, the Court observed in Castaneda v. Partida, 430 U.S. 482, 497 n. 17, 97 S.Ct. 1272, 1281 n. 17, 51 L.Ed.2d 498 (1977), "if the difference between the expected value and the observed number is greater than two or three standard deviations," the null hypothesis—that the observed results are attributable to chance—"would be suspect to a social scientist" and presumably may be rejected. The Supreme Court did not bother to calculate standard deviations in *Teamsters* because of the virtually complete exclusion of minorities (13 out of 1828) from line driver positions. It did offer the results of such an analysis in *Hazelwood,* see 433 U.S. at 311 n. 17, 97 S.Ct. 2744 n. 17.

3. *Selected Issues.* a. *The Process of Logical Inference.* Even a score of two or more standard deviations from the expected value does not prove discrimination. The most that such an analysis can provide is a basis for excluding the role of chance, but of course no employer would make hiring or promotion decisions as a matter of random distribution. The Court stated in footnote 20 of *Teamsters*:

> Statistics showing racial or ethnic imbalance are probative in a case such as this one because such imbalance is often a telltale sign of purposeful discrimination; absent explanation, it is ordinarily to be expected that nondiscriminatory hiring practices will in time result in a work force more or less representative of the racial and ethnic composition of the population from which employees are hired.

Whether such evidence of statistical disparity properly supports an inference of discriminatory intent will depend on the extent to which expected outcomes—against which observed outcomes are measured—reflect an available, qualified supply of minority-group workers similar in all relevant respects to the white workers actually hired or promoted. Professor Laycock observes:

> The Court explicitly assumes that but for discrimination, the employer's work force would in the long run mirror the racial composition of the labor force from which it was hired. That conclusion requires the further implicit assumption that the black and white populations are substantially the same in all relevant ways, so that any differences in result are attributable to discrimination.

Some variation of that assumption is critical to all statistical evidence of disparate treatment. It is a powerful and *implausible* assumption: the two populations are assumed to be substantially the same in their distribution of skills, aptitudes, and job preferences. Two hundred and fifty years of slavery, nearly a century of Jim Crow, and a generation of less virulent discrimination are assumed to have had no effect * * *.

Douglas Laycock, Statistical Proof and Theories of Discrimination, 49 L. & Contemp.Probl. 97, 98 (1986) (emphasis added). See also Daniel Rubinfeld, Econometrics in the Courtroom, 85 Colum.L.Rev. 1048, 1057 n. 29 (1985); Louis J. Braun, Statistics and the Law: Hypothesis Testing and its Application to Title VII Cases, 32 Hastings L.J. 59 (1980); Paul Meier, Jerome Sacks & Sandy L. Zabell, What Happened in *Hazelwood*: Statistics, Employment Discrimination, and the 80% Rule, 1984 Am.B.Found.Res.J. 139.

   b. *"Practical Significance."* Although a finding of statistical significance will often depend on the size of the disparity between the results for the two affected groups, statistical significance should not be equated with practical or legal significance. First, with large samples a relatively small difference in percentage points will be statistically significant yet may be viewed as *de minimis* by the courts. *See* Paetzold & Willborn, supra, § 4.09, at 22–28. Conversely, large disparities may not pass conventional significance tests because of a small sample size, yet may still be considered probative evidence. Second, practical or legal significance depends on substantive law considerations. The *Castaneda* rule of thumb and the .05 significance test are conventions which arguably may be varied in appropriate circumstances:

Why apply a five percent significance test before the burden of production can be shifted from the plaintiff to the defendant, particularly where the only possible alternative hypotheses involve discrimination? * * *

The selection of a significance level should include consideration of broader social issues that go beyond the narrow question of whether an individual defendant should be held liable. For example, the level of significance should be lower in situations where there are higher costs to concluding mistakenly that there is discrimination.

Rubinfeld, supra, at 1062–63. See also D.H. Kaye, Is Proof of Statistical Significance Relevant?, 61 Wash.L.Rev. 1333 (1986).

   Note also that the .05 (or 1.96 standard deviations) significance test is known as a "two-tailed" test. With a normal distribution, approximately 2.5% of the distribution lies in each tail of the bell-shaped curve—the area on either side of the expected value before the curve concaves upward. If one uses a "one-tailed" test, which tests only for discrimination *against* the particular group, a disparity of only 1.65 standard deviations will be statistically significant. See Rubinfeld, supra, at 1057 n. 32. The D.C. Circuit in a 1987 opinion, however, announced a preference for the two-tailed test: "After all, the hypothesis to be tested in any disparate treatment claim should generally be that the selection process treated men and women equally, *not* that the selection process treated women at least as well as or better than men. Two-tailed tests are used where the hypothesis to be rejected is that certain proportions are equal and not that one proportion is equal to or greater than the other proportion." Palmer v. Shultz, 815 F.2d 84, 95 (D.C.Cir.1987). Do you agree with this reasoning? *See also* EEOC v. Federal Reserve Bank of Richmond, 698 F.2d 633, 654–60 (4th Cir.1983) (two-tailed test should be used absent independent evidence of discrimination of the type challenged), reversed on other grounds sub nom. Cooper v. Federal Reserve Bank of Richmond, 467 U.S. 867, 104 S.Ct. 2794, 81 L.Ed.2d 718 (1984).

c. *Limits of the Binomial Model.* The binomial model provides a limited tool. First, the binomial technique is inappropriate for small sample sizes because "the binomial distribution approximates the normal distribution well only for sample sizes of sufficient magnitude." Thomas J. Sugrue & William B. Fairley, A Case of Unexamined Assumptions: The Use and Misuse of the Statistical Analysis of *Castaneda/Hazelwood* in Discrimination Litigation, 24 Bost.Coll.L.Rev. 925, 958 (1983). Second, this technique may not be used where its requirements—two possible outcomes for each trial, fixed probabilities associated with each outcome, and independence among the trials—are not satisfied. Hence, it may be used only for selection processes which produce dichotomous results, not for cases involving continuous or interval variables, such as salary discrimination. See id. at 936 n. 49. Moreover, in cases where the number to be selected is a substantial percentage of the eligible pool, the fixed-probability and independence requirements are not met. Use of the binomial technique in such circumstances will "understate the statistical significance of the racial disparities observed": "[I]f blacks, for example, are selected at a disproportionately low rate, the percentage of blacks remaining in the eligible pool will tend to increase as selections are made." Id. at 938.

4. *Other Techniques for Assessing Statistical Disparity.* a. *EEOC's 80% or Four–Fifths Rule.* In disparate-impact challenges, to be considered shortly, the federal enforcement authorities will regard a selection rate for a minority group that is less than 80% of the selection rate for the group with the highest pass rate as evidence of adverse impact. See UGESP, 29 C.F.R. § 1607.4D. This rule of thumb has been much criticized. See, e.g., Elaine Shoben, Differential Pass–Fail Rates in Employment Testing: Statistical Proof Under Title VII, 91 Harv.L.Rev. 793, 805–06 ff., 810–11 (1978) (four-fifths rule fails to detect statistically significant disparities in large sample sizes, fails to consider magnitude of difference in pass rates, and may yield different results when comparing fail rates); Anthony E. Boardman, Another Analysis of the EEOC "Four–Fifths" Rule, 25 Mgmt.Sci. 770, 773 (1979) (same).

b. *Testing the Difference Between Independent Proportions and "Chi-Square" Test.* Whereas the binomial method compares the number of those selected from a given group with an expected number of selections from that group, it is possible to analyze the same data by comparing the selection percentages for each group from among its own eligible population. Thus, if the selection procedure operates independently of race, the proportion of eligible blacks selected should be nearly the same as the proportion of eligible whites selected. A Z-score may be obtained by taking the pass-rate difference between whites and blacks and dividing that difference by the "standard error," which is a uniform measure of the variance or range of scores in a sample. Like the binomial method, this technique requires that there be only two groups, only two possible outcomes for each group, and that selections be independent of one another. However, unlike the binomial technique, it may be used where selections constitute a large proportion of the eligible pool, and is more sensitive to sample-size differences than the four-fifths rule. See Shoben, supra, at 799 ff.; Sugrue & Fairley, supra, at 939–41.

The "chi-square" test is an equivalent test for assessing the statistical significance of an observed difference between two or more proportions. It has received some judicial acceptance. See, e.g., Chance v. Board of Examiners, 330 F.Supp. 203 (S.D.N.Y.1971), affirmed, 458 F.2d 1167 (2d Cir.1972).

Multiple Regression Analysis

Multiple regression analysis is a powerful tool for assessing the relationship between a set of independent or predictor variables and a dependent or outcome variable. The binomial and other methods discussed above are useful for determining whether observed differences in results for two groups are likely to be due to chance, but they are based on a debatable, often readily rebuttable assumption that the characteristics of the two groups are the same in all other relevant respects save group status. Regression analysis provides a means for controlling for important explanatory factors that are likely sources of differences, and thus generating a measure of the explanatory power of the group status variable. See generally Paetzold & Willborn, supra, ch. 6; David E. Bloom & Mark E. Killingsworth, Pay Discrimination Research and Litigation: The Use of Regression, 21 Ind.Rels. 318 (1982); Michael D. Finkelstein, The Judicial Reception of Multiple Regression Studies in Race and Sex Discrimination Cases, 80 Colum.L.Rev. 737 (1980); Franklin M. Fisher, Multiple Regression in Legal Proceedings, 80 Colum.L.Rev. 702 (1980).

Linear multiple regression analysis is normally used for continuous dependent variables such as salary, and has played a very important role in pay discrimination litigation such as Bazemore v. Friday, supra. It is possible in some cases to convert selection processes involving dichotomous outcomes, such as promotions, into a continuous variable by developing a ranking of positions based on, say, the salaries associated with those positions.

Typically, there is no single determinant of salary, and a multivariate analysis considering the impact of several predictor variables is necessary. A model of an employer's wage determination policy positing that wage is a function of experience, age and gender could be expressed in the following regression equation. (This example and some of the discussion that follows is paraphrased from Rubinfeld, supra, at 1066–68.)

$$W = B1 + B2(E) + B3(A) + B4(S) + e, \text{ where}$$

W is hourly wage rate; B1 is a constant reflecting base wage; B2 is the coefficient associated with years of education; B3 is the coefficient associated with age; B4 is the coefficient associated with gender; S is the predictor variable for gender and is equal to one if the worker is female and zero if a male; and e is a random error term which captures all omitted determinants of wage rate. It is critical, however, that there be no correlation between the omitted variables in the error term and explanatory variables of interest. See Fisher, supra, at 708–11, for a good discussion of the technical requirements for the standard error term. The coefficients describe the slope of the multi-dimensional line which relates differences in wage rate to differences in experience, age and gender. This equation permits evaluation of the wage differences for men and women of equal age and salary. Theoretically, if gender plays no rule, the B4 coefficient should approximate zero and the B4(S) term should drop out of the equation.

A least-squares estimate of the data in a particular case might appear as follows:

$$W = \underset{(.50)}{1.50} + \underset{(.05)}{.25E} + \underset{(.01)}{.02A} - \underset{(.25)}{.75S} + e \; R^2 = .30$$

The coefficient of .25 for the education variable indicates that the average hourly wage of employees in the sample increases by 25 cents for each year of education. The $-.75$ coefficient for gender suggests that the average wage of women is 75 cents lower than for men, after controlling for age and education. The standard errors of the coefficients are given in the parentheticals. A hypothesis-testing approach similar to the binomial method is employed to determine the statistical significance of the coefficients obtained. If the null hypothesis of no discrimination were correct, we would expect a B4 coefficient of zero. The standard error tells us that we should expect as a matter of random distribution variability in the B4 coefficient of $+.25$ or $-.25$ but not as large as .75. A t-statistic, defined as the estimated coefficient divided by its standard error, is sometimes also used; in large samples a t-statistic of approximately 2.0 is considered significant at the .05 level, and a t-statistic of approximately 2.5 is significant at the .01 level. See Fisher, supra, at 717; Rubinfeld, supra, at 1067.

The R-squared (R^2) statistic tells us how much of the variance in the dependent variable, here wages, is explained by the independent variables in the equation. Because this statistic can be manipulated upwards by, among other things, increasing the number of explanatory variables to observations in the sample, some courts have questioned its utility. See, e.g., Vuyanich v. Republic Nat'l Bank of Dallas, 505 F.Supp. 224, 287 n. 87 (N.D.Tex.1980), vacated & remanded, 723 F.2d 1195 (5th Cir.1984). The *Vuyanich* decision is criticized in Thomas Campbell, Regression Analysis in Title VII Cases: Minimum Standards, Comparable Worth, and Other Issues Where Law and Statistics Meet, 36 Stan.L.Rev. 1299, 1310–11 & nn. 37–38 (1984) (adjusted R-squared statistic can minimize manipulability; courts should be leery if the adjusted R-squared is 10% or less, for less than 10% of the variance in the observed data will be explained by the regression equation).

Typically, a defendant will attempt to impeach a regression study by suggesting that critical explanatory variables which happen to be correlated with gender were omitted from the equation. In the above example, an experience variable such as years on the job and a performance measure such as rating scores were omitted. In *Bazemore,* the plaintiffs' regressions included the variables race, education, experience and tenure, but were faulted by the Court of Appeals for not considering other important variables, notably county-by-county pay differences. Although the United States had presented evidence tending to negate the saliency of county-by-county variations, Justice Brennan's concurrence for a unanimous Court plainly states that a plaintiff's *prima facie* case may include less than "all measurable variables" as long as the "major factors" are accounted for:

> While the omission of variables from a regression analysis may render the analysis less probative than it otherwise might be, it can hardly be said, absent some other infirmity, that an analysis which accounts for the major factors 'must be considered unacceptable as evidence of discrimination' * * *. Normally, failure to include variables will affect the analysis' probativeness, not its admissibility.

478 U.S. at 400, 106 S.Ct. at 3009.

One reason for the Court's seeming leniency may be that the addition of too many variables to a regression equation carries with it certain costs. First, as a general matter, "the more variables in the equation, the larger the population must be," Laycock, supra, at 100, in order to produce statistically significant results. Second, to the extent the added variables are correlated with the group status variable (B4 in the above example), the standard error of the group status coefficient may be inflated, and thus "provides little basis for inference." Paetzold & Willborn, § 6.15, at 40–41. Finally, inclusion of too many variables, or overfitting, can produce multicollinearity, which in turn can affect statistical and legal inferences. It can also alter the overall fit of the model to render it less reliable and can tend to produce nonsignificant coefficients for key predictor variables. Id. at 41, fn. 10.

Aside from these technical problems, defendants may have a difficult time insisting on the addition of particular variables which, despite their important explanatory role, may not be recognized because they depend on subjective judgments, such as job evaluation scores, or are too subject to employer control, such as grade level. See, e.g., James v. Stockham Valves & Fittings Co., 559 F.2d 310, 332 (5th Cir.1977) (subjective merit ratings by white supervisors might conceal supervisory bias); Craik v. Minnesota State University Board, 731 F.2d 465, 475–78 (8th Cir.1984) (evidence of discrimination in rank assignment precluded consideration of rank variable). The question arises whether such variables may be deemed "tainted" simply because of subjectivity or extent of employer control even without proof of actual discrimination. See, e.g., Presseisen v. Swarthmore College, 442 F.Supp. 593, 612–13 (E.D.Pa.1977), affirmed mem., 582 F.2d 1275 (3d Cir.1978) (plaintiff's expert should have included academic rank despite fact women on the average took longer to achieve a given rank than men because the court had denied claim of discrimination in promotions), criticized in Finkelstein, supra, at 741–42. It has been argued that before requiring consideration of such problematic variables, the defendant should have the burden of persuading the trier of fact of their business necessity. See Barbara A. Norris, Multiple Regression Analysis in Title VII Cases: A Structural Approach to Attacks of "Missing Factors" and "Pre–Act Discrimination," 49 L. & Contemp.Probl. 63, 73, 79–81 (1986). Professor Laycock counters that excluding consideration of subjective performance measures ignores differences between the two relevant groups and overstates the explanatory power of the group status variable:

> In disparate treatment cases, proof of differences between the two populations must be admissible. Once admitted, such evidence must not

be subjected to a level of scrutiny that makes it futile. Subjective evaluations must be given reasonable weight and, if necessary, reviewed on an individual basis. For large employers, the court might review a random sample of subjective evaluations to see if they were being used to hide discrimination.

Laycock, supra, at 104.

Notes and Questions

1. *Can Statistics Alone Establish Systemic Disparate Treatment?* How did the Court in *Teamsters* respond to the company's argument that statistics cannot "in and of themselves" establish a prima facie case of discrimination? Does footnote 24 also contain an implicit response? Should statistical proof alone ever be enough to prove a discriminatory pattern or practice? Some lower courts have answered affirmatively. See, e.g., Segar v. Smith, 738 F.2d 1249, 1278 (D.C.Cir.1984) ("when a plaintiff's statistical methodology focuses on the appropriate labor pool and generates evidence of discrimination at a statistically significant level, no sound reason exists for subjecting the plaintiff to the additional requirement of * * * proving anecdotal evidence"). Other courts, however, have held that there must be convincing evidence of individual acts of discrimination where there are weaknesses in the statistical proof. See, e.g., EEOC v. Sears, Roebuck & Co., 839 F.2d 302 (7th Cir.1988).

2. *Relevant Labor Pool?* For purposes of statistical analysis, to what labor pool should the hirees for disputed jobs be compared? Note that the Court in *Hazelwood*, but not in *Teamsters*, requires a comparison to the qualified labor market. What explains the difference? Can an employer always defend against a systemic challenge by asserting that there are no or few members of the plaintiff class in the qualified labor market? Cf. Scoggins v. Board of Educ. of Nashville, 853 F.2d 1472, 1478 (8th Cir.1988) (school district with monopoly in area cannot rely on labor market statistics that its discriminatory conduct has created). Should a defendant ever be able to challenge plaintiffs' statistics because the pool compared included workers too qualified to be interested? Cf. EEOC v. Chicago Miniature Lamp Works, 947 F.2d 292, 305 (7th Cir.1991) (government should have considered English fluency requirement for disputed jobs as explanation of low levels of hiring and applications of blacks relative to Hispanics and Asian–Americans in labor market).

Why did the Court not require a comparison to those who actually applied for the disputed positions in both *Teamsters* and *Hazelwood*? Why did Hazelwood fail at trial to introduce an analysis of applicant flow data? Was the majority right in permitting such evidence on remand? Are there reasons to believe that black applications were deterred by Hazelwood's history as a pre-Act discriminator?

Should the proportion of the protected class in other less desirable jobs with a defendant employer ever be relevant? Might such an internal labor market comparison rebut certain employer explanations, such as geographical isolation of the employment site, for low numbers of the protected class in disputed jobs? See footnote 23 in *Teamsters*. See also pp. 140–142 infra.

3. *Geographical Limits on the Labor Pool.* How demanding should the courts be of plaintiffs' geographical definition of the labor pool from which a defendant employer hires? Some jobs may be filled through national searches, but others may be almost exclusively filled from a surrounding region, metropolitan area, or even town. Should plaintiffs at least be permitted to include qualified workers who live within commuting distance of the disputed jobs, rather than accept an employer's claim that it only hires within a limited radius for jobs located in the midst of effectively segregated housing? Compare *Chicago Miniature Lamp Works*, supra, (government should have used relative commuting distance as part of statistical analysis), with Abron v. Black & Decker Manufacturing Co., 439 F.Supp. 1095 (D.Md. 1977) (boundaries of labor force should be defined by reasonable expectation of commuting).

Was the Court right to conclude that it would be unfair to Hazelwood to compare its recent hiring of blacks with the percentage of blacks in both the county and city of St. Louis if the affirmative action hiring policies of the St. Louis City School District "changed the racial composition of that district's teaching staff from what it would otherwise have been"? Decades of discrimination against blacks also may have changed the racial composition of the qualified teacher work force in the county and city of St. Louis. Why should the reason for the relative availability of black workers, rather than their availability *per se*, be pertinent? Does Justice Stevens have the better of the argument by suggesting that inasmuch as a third of the Hazelwood teachers resided in St. Louis when hired, residents of that city must be counted within the qualified labor pool? Who should have the burden of showing the relevance of the city of St. Louis's recruitment of black teachers to the statistical performance of the Hazelwood school district?

4. *Nonstatistical Proof of Systemic Discrimination.* What other kinds of proof do *Teamsters* and *Hazelwood* suggest are relevant to proving a pattern or practice of discrimination? Should evidence of individual instances of discrimination be weighed more heavily if it suggests the involvement of central personnel officers or senior management? The government in *Hazelwood* relied in part on "a history of alleged racially discriminatory practices" and "standardless and largely subjective hiring procedures." How were these factors relevant to the question of the existence of a policy of post-Act discrimination in hiring?

To what extent can nonstatistical proof compensate for deficiencies in plaintiffs' statistical case? See Pitre v. Western Electric Co., 843 F.2d 1262, 1269 (10th Cir.1988) (trial court may base finding of discrimination on a "showing of discriminatory acts and attitudes" even considering "statistics that a social scientist would find insignificant"). Had the Government in *Hazelwood*, as suggested in footnote 17 in the majority opinion, only shown a disparity falling short of two standard deviations between blacks in the qualified county work force and recent hiring by Hazelwood, would its overall showing have been sufficient to establish a pattern or practice of discrimination? Recall the discussion in the Note on Statistical Analysis, supra, suggesting that the two standard deviation test is a convention, as well as the analysis in note 6 below.

5. *Weight Given to Prima Facie Case.* It is clear that the government's prima facie case in *Teamsters* carries much more probative force than the plaintiff's prima facie showing in *McDonnell Douglas,* but how much more? If a pattern or practice prima facie case is not rebutted by the employer, should it mandate a finding for the plaintiff? Can it be rebutted by the mere articulation of a legitimate explanation for the disparate results?

6. *Rebuttal of Prima Facie Case.* To the extent that a prima facie case is based on a statistical disparity, how may it be rebutted? In *Teamsters* the Court stated that an employer may attempt to show that the plaintiffs' proof is "inaccurate or insignificant" or that there is a "nondiscriminatory explanation for the apparently discriminatory result", such as the plaintiffs' failure to control for relevant differences in qualifications. Some courts, relying on *Bazemore v. Friday*, supra, have held that defendants cannot rebut a statistically based inference of discrimination by merely pointing out flaws in the statistical proof without showing how the flaws explain the disparities highlighted by that proof. See, e.g., Hemmings v. Tidyman's Inc., 285 F.3d 1174 (9th Cir.2002); Sobel v. Yeshiva Univ., 839 F.2d 18 (2d Cir.1988).

In what ways, other than showing its inability to compete against the St. Louis City School District, might Hazelwood have attempted to rebut the government's prima facie case?

7. *Relevance of Proof of Differential Interest?* May a defendant rebut a prima facie showing of statistical disparity by demonstrating that members of the plaintiffs' class are not interested in the disputed positions to the same extent as those outside the class? Even in the absence of corroborative applicant flow data? Is it relevant whether any differential interests are at least in part shaped by a history of employment discrimination throughout the economy? Are individual employers held responsible under Title VII for that history? What if the differential interests are shown to derive in part from a work culture created by the employer? See EEOC v. Sears, Roebuck & Co., supra (employer adequately explained disproportionate employment of female salespersons in lower paying but more secure noncommission positions by testimony of managers on differential female interest as confirmed by general social scientific research). Is this differential interest defense likely to be available in a race discrimination case? See generally Vicki Schultz, Telling Stories About Women and Work: Judicial Interpretation of Sex Segregation in the Workplace in Title VII Cases Raising the Lack of Interest Argument, 103 Harv.L.Rev. 1750 (1990).

8. *Application.* A cleaning service employing about 100 cleaners is owned by a Korean–American immigrant. Over the past two years 81% of his employees also have been Korean–Americans. Korean–Americans are only 1% of the general population and only 3% of the workforce engaged in cleaning in the metropolitan area in which the service operates. The owner has records showing that 71% of applicants for employment with the service are also Korean–Americans. The owner testifies that this results from the location of the service's offices in a heavily Korean–American neighborhood and from his reliance on word-of-mouth recruiting. He claims this is the cheapest way to fill his jobs and that he does not need to advertise or recruit. Should the service be found to be in violation of Title VII? What more

information would you like to have? What if the trier of fact believes that the owner prefers hiring Korean–Americans, but would use word-of-mouth recruiting to save costs even if it did not result in a predominantly Korean–American workforce? Compare EEOC v. Consolidated Service Systems, 989 F.2d 233 (7th Cir.1993), with EEOC v. Metal Service Co. 892 F.2d 341, 350–51 (3d Cir.1990).

D. PROVING UNJUSTIFIED DISPARATE IMPACT

1. *Basic Theory and Method of Proof*

GRIGGS v. DUKE POWER CO.
Supreme Court of United States, 1971.
401 U.S. 424, 91 S.Ct. 849, 28 L.Ed.2d 158.

CHIEF JUSTICE BURGER delivered the opinion of the Court.

The District Court found that prior to July 2, 1965, the effective date of the Civil Rights Act of 1964, the Company openly discriminated on the basis of race in the hiring and assigning of employees at its Dan River plant. The plant was organized into five operating departments: (1) Labor, (2) Coal Handling, (3) Operations, (4) Maintenance, and (5) Laboratory and Test. Negroes were employed only in the Labor Department where the highest paying jobs paid less than the lowest paying jobs in the other four "operating" departments in which only whites were employed. Promotions were normally made within each department on the basis of job seniority. Transferees into a department usually began in the lowest position.

In 1955 the Company instituted a policy of requiring a high school education for initial assignment to any department except Labor, and for transfer from the Coal Handling to any "inside" department (Operations, Maintenance, or Laboratory). When the Company abandoned its policy of restricting Negroes to the Labor Department in 1965, completion of high school also was made a prerequisite to transfer from Labor to any other department. From the time the high school requirement was instituted to the time of trial, however, white employees hired before the time of the high school education requirement continued to perform satisfactorily and achieve promotions in the "operating" departments. Findings on this score are not challenged.

The Company added a further requirement for new employees on July 2, 1965, the date on which Title VII became effective. To qualify for placement in any but the Labor Department it became necessary to register satisfactory scores on two professionally prepared aptitude tests, as well as to have a high school education. Completion of high school alone continued to render employees eligible for transfer to the four desirable departments from which Negroes had been excluded if the incumbent had been employed prior to the time of the new requirement. In September 1965 the Company began to permit incumbent employees who lacked a high school education to qualify for transfer from Labor or

Coal Handling to an "inside" job by passing two tests—the Wonderlic Personnel Test, which purports to measure general intelligence, and the Bennett Mechanical Comprehension Test. Neither was directed or intended to measure the ability to learn to perform a particular job or category of jobs. The requisite scores used for both initial hiring and transfer approximated the national median for high school graduates.[3]

The District Court had found that while the Company previously followed a policy of overt racial discrimination in a period prior to the Act, such conduct had ceased. The District Court also concluded that Title VII was intended to be prospective only and, consequently, the impact of prior inequities was beyond the reach of corrective action authorized by the Act.

* * *

The Court of Appeals reversed the District Court in part, rejecting the holding that residual discrimination arising from prior employment practices was insulated from remedial action.[4] The Court of Appeals noted, however, that the District Court was correct in its conclusion that there was no showing of a racial purpose or invidious intent in the adoption of the high school diploma requirement or general intelligence test and that these standards had been applied fairly to whites and Negroes alike. It held that, in the absence of a discriminatory purpose, use of such requirements was permitted by the Act.

* * *

The objective of Congress in the enactment of Title VII is plain from the language of the statute. It was to achieve equality of employment opportunities and remove barriers that have operated in the past to favor an identifiable group of white employees over other employees. Under the Act, practices, procedures, or tests neutral on their face, and even neutral in terms of intent, cannot be maintained if they operate to "freeze" the status quo of prior discriminatory employment practices.

The Court of Appeals' opinion, and the partial dissent, agreed that, on the record in the present case, "whites register far better on the Company's alternative requirements" than Negroes.[6] This consequence

---

3. The test standards are thus more stringent than the high school requirement, since they would screen out approximately half of all high school graduates.

4. The Court of Appeals ruled that Negroes employed in the Labor Department at a time when there was no high school or test requirement for entrance into the higher paying departments could not now be made subject to those requirements, since whites hired contemporaneously into those departments were never subject to them. The Court of Appeals also required that the seniority rights of those Negroes be measured on a plantwide, rather than a depart-

mental, basis. However, the Court of Appeals denied relief to the Negro employees without a high school education or its equivalent who were hired into the Labor Department after institution of the educational requirement.

6. In North Carolina, 1960 census statistics show that, while 34% of white males had completed high school, only 12% of Negro males had done so. U.S. Bureau of the Census, U.S. Census of Population: 1960, Vol. 1, Characteristics of the Population, pt. 35, Table 47.

Similarly, with respect to standardized tests, the EEOC in one case found that use

would appear to be directly traceable to race. Basic intelligence must have the means of articulation to manifest itself fairly in a testing process. Because they are Negroes, petitioners have long received inferior education in segregated schools and this Court expressly recognized these differences in *Gaston County v. United States*, 395 U.S. 285, 89 S.Ct. 1720, 23 L.Ed.2d 309 (1969). There, because of the inferior education received by Negroes in North Carolina, this Court barred the institution of a literacy test for voter registration on the ground that the test would abridge the right to vote indirectly on account of race. Congress did not intend by Title VII, however, to guarantee a job to every person regardless of qualifications. In short, the Act does not command that any person be hired simply because he was formerly the subject of discrimination, or because he is a member of a minority group. Discriminatory preference for any group, minority or majority, is precisely and only what Congress has proscribed. What is required by Congress is the removal of artificial, arbitrary, and unnecessary barriers to employment when the barriers operate invidiously to discriminate on the basis of racial or other impermissible classification.

Congress has now provided that tests or criteria for employment or promotion may not provide equality of opportunity merely in the sense of the fabled offer of milk to the stork and the fox. On the contrary, Congress has now required that the posture and condition of the job-seeker be taken into account. It has—to resort again to the fable—provided that the vessel in which the milk is proffered be one all seekers can use. The Act proscribes not only overt discrimination but also practices that are fair in form, but discriminatory in operation. The touchstone is business necessity. If an employment practice which operates to exclude Negroes cannot be shown to be related to job performance, the practice is prohibited.

On the record before us, neither the high school completion requirement nor the general intelligence test is shown to bear a demonstrable relationship to successful performance of the jobs for which it was used. Both were adopted, as the Court of Appeals noted, without meaningful study of their relationship to job-performance ability. Rather, a vice president of the Company testified, the requirements were instituted on the Company's judgment that they generally would improve the overall quality of the work force.

The evidence, however, shows that employees who have not completed high school or taken the tests have continued to perform satisfactorily and make progress in departments for which the high school and test criteria are now used.[7] The promotion record of present employees who

of a battery of tests, including the Wonderlic and Bennett tests used by the Company in the instant case, resulted in 58% of whites passing the tests, as compared with only 6% of the blacks. Decision of EEOC, CCH Empl.Prac.Guide, ¶ 17,304.53 (Dec. 2, 1966). See also Decision of EEOC 70–552,

CCH Empl.Prac.Guide, ¶ 6139 (Feb. 19, 1970).

7. For example, between July 2, 1965, and November 14, 1966, the percentage of white employees who were promoted but who were not high school graduates was

would not be able to meet the new criteria thus suggests the possibility that the requirements may not be needed even for the limited purpose of preserving the avowed policy of advancement within the Company. In the context of this case, it is unnecessary to reach the question whether testing requirements that take into account capability for the next succeeding position or related future promotion might be utilized upon a showing that such long-range requirements fulfill a genuine business need. In the present case the Company has made no such showing.

The Court of Appeals held that the Company had adopted the diploma and test requirements without any "intention to discriminate against Negro employees." We do not suggest that either the District Court or the Court of Appeals erred in examining the employer's intent; but good intent or absence of discriminatory intent does not redeem employment procedures or testing mechanisms that operate as "built-in headwinds" for minority groups and are unrelated to measuring job capability.

The Company's lack of discriminatory intent is suggested by special efforts to help the undereducated employees through Company financing of two-thirds the cost of tuition for high school training. But Congress directed the thrust of the Act to the *consequences* of employment practices, not simply the motivation. More than that, Congress has placed on the employer the burden of showing that any given requirement must have a manifest relationship to the employment in question. The facts of this case demonstrate the inadequacy of broad and general testing devices as well as the infirmity of using diplomas or degrees as fixed measures of capability. History is filled with examples of men and women who rendered highly effective performance without the conventional badges of accomplishment in terms of certificates, diplomas, or degrees. Diplomas and tests are useful servants, but Congress has mandated the commonsense proposition that they are not to become masters of reality. The Company contends that its general intelligence tests are specifically permitted by § 703(h) of the Act.[8] That section authorizes the use of "any professionally developed ability test" that is not "designed, intended *or used* to discriminate because of race * * *." (Emphasis added.)

The Equal Employment Opportunity Commission, having enforcement responsibility, has issued guidelines interpreting § 703(h) to permit only the use of job-related tests.[9] The administrative interpretation

nearly identical to the percentage of non-graduates in the entire white work force.

8. Section 703(h) applies only to tests. It has no applicability to the high school diploma requirement.

9. EEOC Guidelines on Employment Testing Procedures, issued August 24, 1966, provide:

"The Commission accordingly interprets 'professionally developed ability test' to mean a test which fairly measures the knowledge or skills required by the particular job or class of jobs which the applicant seeks, or which fairly affords the employer a chance to measure the applicant's ability to perform a particular job or class of jobs. The fact that a test was prepared by an individual or organization claiming expertise in test preparation does not, without more, justify its use within the meaning of Title VII."

of the Act by the enforcing agency is entitled to great deference. See, *e.g., United States v. City of Chicago*, 400 U.S. 8, 91 S.Ct. 18, 27 L.Ed.2d 9 (1970); *Udall v. Tallman*, 380 U.S. 1, 85 S.Ct. 792, 13 L.Ed.2d 616 (1965); *Power Reactor Development Co. v. Electricians*, 367 U.S. 396, 81 S.Ct. 1529, 6 L.Ed.2d 924 (1961). Since the Act and its legislative history support the Commission's construction, this affords good reason to treat the guidelines as expressing the will of Congress.

CONNECTICUT v. TEAL

Supreme Court of the United States, 1982.
457 U.S. 440, 102 S.Ct. 2525, 73 L.Ed.2d 130.

JUSTICE BRENNAN delivered the opinion of the Court.

I

Four of the respondents, Winnie Teal, Rose Walker, Edith Latney, and Grace Clark, are black employees of the Department of Income Maintenance of the State of Connecticut. Each was promoted provisionally to the position of Welfare Eligibility Supervisor and served in that capacity for almost two years. To attain permanent status as supervisors, however, respondents had to participate in a selection process that required, as the first step, a passing score on a written examination. This written test was administered on December 2, 1978, to 329 candidates. Of these candidates, 48 identified themselves as black and 259 identified themselves as white. The results of the examination were announced in March 1979. With the passing score set at 65,[3] 54.17 percent of the identified black candidates passed. This was approximately 68 percent of the passing rate for the identified white candidates.[4] The four respondents were among the blacks who failed the examination, and they were thus excluded from further consideration for permanent supervisory positions. * * *

The EEOC position has been elaborated in the new Guidelines on Employee Selection Procedures, 29 CFR § 1607, 35 Fed. Reg. 12333 (Aug. 1, 1970). These guidelines demand that employers using tests have available "data demonstrating that the test is predictive of or significantly correlated with important elements of work behavior which comprise or are relevant to the job or jobs for which candidates are being evaluated." *Id.*, at § 1607.4(c).

3. The mean score on the examination was 70.4 percent. However, because the black candidates had a mean score 6.7 percentage points lower than the white candidates, the passing score was set at 65, apparently in an attempt to lessen the disparate impact of the examination.

4. The following table shows the passing rates of various candidate groups:

Candidate Group	Number	No. Receiving Passing Score	Passing Rate (%)
Black	48	26	54.17
Hispanic	4	3	75.00
Indian	3	2	66.67
White	259	206	79.54
Unidentified	15	9	60.00
Total	329	246	74.77

Petitioners do not contest the District Court's implicit finding that the examination itself resulted in disparate impact under the "eighty percent rule" of the Uniform Guidelines on Employee Selection Procedures adopted by the Equal Employment Opportunity Commission. Those guidelines provide that a selection rate that "is less than [80 percent] of the rate for the group with the highest rate will generally be regarded * * * as evidence of adverse impact." 29 CFR § 1607.4D (1981).

More than a year after this action was instituted, and approximately one month before trial, petitioners made promotions from the eligibility list generated by the written examination. In choosing persons from that list, petitioners considered past work performance, recommendations of the candidates' supervisors and, to a lesser extent, seniority. Petitioners then applied what the Court of Appeals characterized as an affirmative-action program in order to ensure a significant number of minority supervisors. Forty-six persons were promoted to permanent supervisory positions, 11 of whom were black and 35 of whom were white. The overall result of the selection process was that, of the 48 identified black candidates who participated in the selection process, 22.9 percent were promoted and of the 259 identified white candidates, 13.5 percent were promoted.[6] It is this "bottom-line" result, more favorable to blacks than to whites, that petitioners urge should be adjudged to be a complete defense to respondents' suit.

* * *

II

* * *

Petitioners' examination, which barred promotion and had a discriminatory impact on black employees, clearly falls within the literal language of § 703(a)(2), as interpreted by *Griggs*. The statute speaks, not in terms of jobs and promotions, but in terms of *limitations* and *classifications* that would deprive any individual of employment *opportunities*. A disparate-impact claim reflects the language of § 703(a)(2) and Congress' basic objectives in enacting that statute: "to achieve equality of employment *opportunities* and remove barriers that have operated in the past to favor an identifiable group of white employees over other employees." 401 U.S., at 429–430, 91 S.Ct., at 852–853 (emphasis added). When an employer uses a nonjob-related barrier in order to deny a minority or woman applicant employment or promotion, and that barrier has a significant adverse effect on minorities or women, then the applicant has been deprived of an employment *opportunity* "because of * * * race, color, religion, sex, or national origin." In other words, § 703(a)(2) prohibits discriminatory "artificial, arbitrary, and unnecessary barriers to employment," 401 U.S., at 431, 91 S.Ct., at 853, that "limit * * * or classify * * * applicants for employment * * * in any way which would deprive or tend to deprive any individual of employment *opportunities*." (Emphasis added.)

* * *

The [United States] Government [as amicus curiae] argues that the test administered by the petitioners was not "used to discriminate" [within the meaning of § 703(h)] because it did not actually deprive

---

6. The actual promotion rate of blacks was thus close to 170 percent that of the   actual promotion rate of whites.

disproportionate numbers of blacks of promotions. But the Government's reliance on § 703(h) as offering the employer some special haven for discriminatory tests is misplaced. * * * A nonjob-related test that has a disparate racial impact, and is used to "limit" or "classify" employees, is "used to discriminate" within the meaning of Title VII, whether or not it was "designed or intended" to have this effect and despite an employer's efforts to compensate for its discriminatory effect. See *Griggs,* 401 U.S., at 433, 91 S.Ct., at 854.

In sum, respondents' claim of disparate impact from the examination, a pass-fail barrier to employment opportunity, states a prima facie case of employment discrimination under § 703(a)(2), despite their employer's nondiscriminatory "bottom line," and that "bottom line" is no defense to this prima facie case under § 703(h).

* * *

Having determined that respondents' claim comes within the terms of Title VII, we must address the suggestion of petitioners and some *amici curiae* that we recognize an exception, either in the nature of an additional burden on plaintiffs seeking to establish a prima facie case or in the nature of an affirmative defense, for cases in which an employer has compensated for a discriminatory pass-fail barrier by hiring or promoting a sufficient number of black employees to reach a nondiscriminatory "bottom line." We reject this suggestion, which is in essence nothing more than a request that we redefine the protections guaranteed by Title VII.[12]

* * *

In suggesting that the "bottom line" may be a defense to a claim of discrimination against an individual employee, petitioners and *amici* appear to confuse unlawful discrimination with discriminatory intent. The Court has stated that a nondiscriminatory "bottom line" and an employer's good-faith efforts to achieve a nondiscriminatory work force, might in some cases assist an employer in rebutting the inference that particular action had been intentionally discriminatory: "Proof that [a] work force was racially balanced or that it contained a disproportionately

---

12. Petitioners suggest that we should defer to the EEOC Guidelines in this regard. But there is nothing in the Guidelines to which we might defer that would aid petitioners in this case. The most support petitioners could conceivably muster from the Uniform Guidelines on Employee Selection Procedures, 29 CFR pt. 1607 (1981) (now issued jointly by the EEOC, the Office of Personnel Management, the Department of Labor, and the Department of Justice, see 29 CFR § 1607.1A (1981)), is *neutrality* on the question whether a discriminatory barrier that does not result in a discriminatory overall result constitutes a violation of Title VII. Section 1607.4C of the Guidelines, relied upon by petitioners, states that as a matter of "*administrative and prosecutorial discretion, in usual circumstances,*" the agencies will not take enforcement action based upon the disparate impact of any component of a selection process if the total selection process results in no adverse impact. (Emphasis added.) The agencies made clear that the "guidelines do not address the underlying question of law," and that an individual "who is denied the job because of a particular component in a procedure which otherwise meets the 'bottom line' standard * * * retains the right to proceed through the appropriate agencies, and into Federal court." 43 Fed.Reg. 38291 (1978). See 29 CFR § 1607.16I (1981). * * *

high percentage of minority employees is not wholly irrelevant on the issue of intent when that issue is yet to be decided." *Furnco Construction Corp. v. Waters,* 438 U.S. 567, 580, 98 S.Ct. 2943, 2951, 57 L.Ed.2d 957 (1978). See also *Teamsters v. United States,* 431 U.S. 324, 340, n. 20, 97 S.Ct. 1843, 1856–1857, n. 20, 52 L.Ed.2d 396 (1977). But resolution of the factual question of intent is not what is at issue in this case. Rather, petitioners seek simply to justify discrimination against respondents on the basis of their favorable treatment of other members of respondents' racial group.

* * *

It is clear that Congress never intended to give an employer license to discriminate against some employees on the basis of race or sex merely because he favorably treats other members of the employees' group.

JUSTICE POWELL, with whom THE CHIEF JUSTICE, JUSTICE REHNQUIST, and JUSTICE O'CONNOR join, dissenting.

Today's decision takes a long and unhappy step in the direction of confusion. Title VII does not require that employers adopt merit hiring or the procedures most likely to permit the greatest number of minority members to be considered for or to qualify for jobs and promotions. See *Texas Dept. of Community Affairs v. Burdine,* 450 U.S. 248, 258–259, 101 S.Ct. 1089, 1096–1097, 67 L.Ed.2d 207 (1981); *Furnco,* 438 U.S., at 578, 98 S.Ct., at 2950. Employers need not develop tests that accurately reflect the skills of every individual candidate; there are few if any tests that do so. Yet the Court seems unaware of this practical reality, and perhaps oblivious to the likely consequences of its decision. By its holding today, the Court may force employers either to eliminate tests or rely on expensive, job-related, testing procedures, the validity of which may or may not be sustained if challenged. For state and local governmental employers with limited funds, the practical effect of today's decision may well be the adoption of simple quota hiring.[8] This arbitrary method of employment is itself unfair to individual applicants, whether or not they are members of minority groups. And it is not likely to produce a competent work force. Moreover, the Court's decision actually may result in employers employing *fewer* minority members.

Notes and Questions

1. *Discrimination Without Intent?* Chief Justice Burger's opinion in *Griggs* authorizes a Title VII challenge based on the disparate impact of

---

8. Another possibility is that employers may integrate consideration of test results into one overall hiring decision based on that "factor" *and* additional factors. Such a process would not, even under the Court's reasoning, result in a finding of discrimination on the basis of disparate impact unless the actual hiring decisions had a disparate impact on the minority group. But if employers integrate test results into a single-step decision, they will be free to select *only* the number of minority candidates proportional to their representation in the work force. If petitioners had used this approach, they would have been able to hire substantially fewer blacks without liability on the basis of disparate impact. The Court hardly could have intended to encourage this.

employment practices that are "neutral on their face, and even neutral in terms of intent." Can *Griggs* nonetheless be explained as a judicial response to the difficulty of proving intent to discriminate—as a presumption that an employer intends to disadvantage a protected class if it significantly impairs the opportunities of that class without a clear business justification? Is it likely that the Duke Power Company's high school diploma and aptitude test criteria were utilized after Title VII's effective date precisely because of their exclusionary impact on blacks? When did Duke first institute its diploma requirement?

2. *Discriminatory Intent in* Teal*?* Would the Court's decision in *Teal* have come out differently if the disparate impact method of proof was authorized only as a short cut to proof of discriminatory intent? Do "bottom line" statistics that are favorable to plaintiff's group substantially negative any inference of discriminatory intent against that group? Is it likely that Connecticut administered its challenged written examination for discriminatory reasons?

3. *"Perpetuation" Theory?* What reasons does the Supreme Court give for its decision to prohibit employment decisions because of their effects, rather than because of their intent? Can *Griggs* be understood as a case subjecting an employer's post–1965 ostensibly neutral selection procedures to judicial scrutiny because those practices have the effect of perpetuating the employer's pre-Title VII discrimination? Because diploma requirements, scored tests and similar proxies for more individualized consideration may have the effect of perpetuating general educational and cultural disadvantages of certain minority groups? Consider the compromise ruling of the Court of Appeals set forth in footnote 4 of *Griggs*. How did the Court's decision differ from the Court of Appeals' approach? Can the Court's decision be explained by an even broader rational based on concerns about aggravating social and economic inequalities?

The literature on the disparate impact methodology and its justifications is copious. See, e.g., Samuel Estreicher, The Story of Griggs v. Duke Power Co., ch. 5 in Employment Discrimination Stories (Joel Wm. Friedman ed. 2006); Pamela Perry, Two Faces of Disparate Impact Discrimination, 59 Ford. L.Rev. 523 (1991); George Rutherglen, Disparate Impact Under Title VII: An Objective Theory of Discrimination, 73 Va.L.Rev. 1297 (1987); Paulette Caldwell, Reaffirming the Disproportionate Effects Standard of Liability in Title VII Litigation, 46 U. Pitt. L.Rev. (1985); Steven Willborn, The Disparate Impact Model of Discrimination: Theory and Limits, 34 Am. U. L.Rev. 799 (1985).

4. *Should Generally Advantaged Groups Be Able to Use Disparate Impact Proof?* Would any of the possible justifications for the disparate impact model apply to selection criteria that disproportionately impede white males? Cf. Livingston v. Roadway Express, Inc., 802 F.2d 1250 (10th Cir. 1986) (male challenge to height limitation).

5. *Statutory Basis for Griggs.* Congress did not expressly authorize the disparate impact methodology of proof until its passage of the Civil Rights Act of 1991. See § 105 of that Act, discussed in detail below at pp. 147–150. Does the language of § 703(a), which was not amended by the 1991 Act, itself support the disparate impact method of proof? Before the 1991 Act,

some argued that the statements of the legislators who enacted Title VII indicate that Congress was exclusively concerned with intentional discrimination. See, e.g., Michael Gold, *Griggs'* Folly: An Essay on the Theory, Problems, and Origin of the Adverse Impact Definition of Employment Discrimination and a Recommendation for Reform, 7 Indus.Rel.L.J. 429 (1985). Should statements of legislators completely control the process of statutory interpretation, or should the Court make the best sense of § 703(a)'s broad language in light of the overall statutory objective of promoting the economic integration of previously disadvantaged status groups?

When Congress amended Title VII in 1972, the *Griggs* theory of discrimination had just been established. The 1972 legislative history suggests that *Griggs* was not regarded as controversial; however, no amendment or resolution was passed formally approving the disparate impact theory. Should acquiescence by Congress be sufficient to codify a judicial decision? For responses to Gold, see Katherine Thomson, The Disparate Impact Theory: Congressional Intent in 1972, 8 Indus.Rel.L.J. 105 (1986); Alfred Blumrosen, *Griggs* Was Correctly Decided, 8 Indus.Rel.L.J. 443 (1986).

6. *Proving Disparate Impact.* How did the Court in *Griggs* determine whether the high school diploma requirement and intelligence tests had an adverse impact on blacks? Was adverse impact shown in a different manner in *Teal?*

Should plaintiffs claiming the disparate impact on their class of a criterion for promotion always be required to demonstrate the impact on an internal labor pool of incumbent workers seeking promotion? See Johnson v. Uncle Ben's, Inc., 965 F.2d 1363 (5th Cir.1992) (rejecting national statistics and requiring statistics on employees seeking promotion to determine the disparate impact of educational requirements). Is such a requirement consistent with *Griggs?* What if the employer fills the higher position with workers from the external labor market and the plaintiffs are challenging the practice of not promoting from within? See Wards Cove Packing Co. v. Atonio, 490 U.S. 642, 109 S.Ct. 2115, 104 L.Ed.2d 733 (1989), infra at p. 139. What if applicant data are deficient for some of the reasons discussed at p. 104 supra?

Should the likely impact of the challenged employment practice influence how demanding courts should be of the plaintiffs' statistics? For instance, can a court find that an employer's policy of hiring through nepotism and incumbent employee references disparately impacted blacks and maintained a completely white workforce even if hiring was at too low a rate to provide a statistically significant sample? See EEOC v. Steamship Clerks Union, Local 1066, 48 F.3d 594, 604 (1st Cir.1995) (even small samples may be acceptable in a compelling factual context).

7. *Use of Disparate Impact Proof to Challenge Discriminatory Working Conditions?* Should the disparate impact approach be limited to challenges to criteria for hiring and promotions? Or can it be applied in challenges to compensation standards or other working conditions? Does § 105 of the 1991 Act help provide an answer? Both before and after the 1991 Act, some courts have applied *Griggs* to compensation and other working conditions. See, e.g., Maldonado v. City of Altus, 433 F.3d 1294 (10th Cir. 2006)

(considering challenge to "English only" rule by Hispanic employees); Davey v. City of Omaha, 107 F.3d 587 (8th Cir.1997) (considering challenge to salary classifications); Fitzpatrick v. City of Atlanta, 2 F.3d 1112 (11th Cir.1993) (considering challenge to "no-beard" rule because of disparate impact on blacks); Lynch v. Freeman, 817 F.2d 380 (6th Cir.1987) (considering female plaintiffs' challenge to employer's failure to maintain clean toilets). But see, e.g., Garcia v. Spun Steak Co., 998 F.2d 1480 (9th Cir.1993) (finding impact of "English only" rule on Hispanic employees not sufficient to state Title VII claim). See also discussion of the difficulties of the use of the disparate impact approach to challenge pay disparities between men and women, at pp. 410–411 infra.

8. *Likely Effects of* Teal? Should the propriety of the "bottom line" defense turn on whether it is likely to encourage employers to select members of disadvantaged minority groups who otherwise would not be selected? Would such an inquiry be more consistent with the objectives of the disparate impact model than the individualist approach of the *Teal* majority? See Alfred Blumrosen, The Group Interest Concept, Employment Discrimination, and Legislative Intent: The Fallacy of Connecticut v. Teal, 20 Harv.J. on Legis. 99 (1983). On the other hand, is it clear which approach—the majority's or the dissent's—is more likely to promote minority-group job advancement? On what basis does Justice Powell predict that *Teal* will lead to either (i) decreased use of economically efficient tests and increased use of economically inefficient quotas, or (ii) the employment of fewer minority members? Can it be argued that *Teal* helps the most disadvantaged minorities find jobs?

9. *A "Bottom Line" Defense for Multicomponent Decisionmaking?* Some lower courts followed footnote 8 in Justice Powell's opinion by confining *Teal* to tests that completely screen out applicants as pass-fail barriers, rather than simply forming one part of a multicomponent decision. See, e.g., Carroll v. Sears, Roebuck & Co., 708 F.2d 183, 189 (5th Cir.1983). Can these decisions be reconciled with the rationale of the *Teal* majority?

Section 105 of the 1991 Act provides that a plaintiff must "demonstrate that each particular challenged employment practice causes a disparate impact", except that where the plaintiff can demonstrate "that the elements of a respondent's decisionmaking process are not capable of separation for analysis, the decisionmaking process may be analyzed as one employment practice." Does this indicate that where a plaintiff can separate out the disparate impact of certain elements of a multicomponent process, it is sufficient to do so, regardless of any aggregate statistics that an employer can present to show a "good" bottom line? Reconsider after reading Wards Cove Packing Co. v. Atonio, infra.

10. *Can the EEOC and the Courts Ever Consider the "Bottom Line"?* Does the rejection of the "bottom line" defense by the majority in *Teal* mean that an employer's aggregate employment statistics cannot be considered by the EEOC when deciding whether to bring suit? By a trial court when fashioning relief?

11. *Would Connecticut Have Violated the 1991 Act?* Section 106 of the 1991 Act adds a new subsection (1) to § 703 of Title VII, making it an unlawful employment practice "to adjust the scores of, use different cutoff

scores for, or otherwise alter the results of, employment related tests on the basis of race, color, religion, sex, or national origin." Does this new provision reach Connecticut's adjustment of the passing score on its test for all candidates in order "to lessen the disparate impact of the examination"? See footnote 3 in the majority opinion in *Teal*. If Connecticut had found that the scores of blacks on the examination on the average somewhat underpredicted their success as supervisors, while the scores of whites on the average somewhat overpredicted their success, could the state have compensated by setting different, but equally predictive, scores for white and black candidates?

DOTHARD v. RAWLINSON

Supreme Court of the United States, 1977.
433 U.S. 321, 97 S.Ct. 2720, 53 L.Ed.2d 786.

JUSTICE STEWART delivered the opinion of the Court.

I

Appellee Dianne Rawlinson sought employment with the Alabama Board of Corrections as a prison guard, called in Alabama a "correctional counselor." * * *

At the time she applied for a position as correctional counselor trainee, Rawlinson was a 22–year–old college graduate whose major course of study had been correctional psychology. She was refused employment because she failed to meet the minimum 120–pound weight requirement established by an Alabama statute. The statute also establishes a height minimum of 5 feet 2 inches.[2]

* * *

II

* * *

A

The gist of the claim that the statutory height and weight requirements discriminate against women does not involve an assertion of purposeful discriminatory motive. It is asserted, rather, that these facially neutral qualification standards work in fact disproportionately to exclude women from eligibility for employment by the Alabama Board of Corrections. We dealt in *Griggs v. Duke Power Co., supra* and *Albemarle Paper Co. v. Moody,* 422 U.S. 405, 95 S.Ct. 2362, 45 L.Ed.2d 280, with

2. The statute establishes minimum physical standards for all law enforcement officers. In pertinent part, it provides:

"(d) *Physical qualifications.*—The applicant shall be not less than five feet two inches nor more than six feet ten inches in height, shall weigh not less than 120 pounds nor more than 300 pounds and shall be certified by a licensed physician designated as satisfactory by the appointing authority as in good health and physically fit for the performance of his duties as a law-enforcement officer. The commission may for good cause shown permit variances from the physical qualifications prescribed in this subdivision." Ala.Code, Tit. 55, § 373(109) (Supp.1973).

similar allegations that facially neutral employment standards disproportionately excluded Negroes from employment, and those cases guide our approach here.

Those cases make clear that to establish a prima facie case of discrimination, a plaintiff need only show that the facially neutral standards in question select applicants for hire in a significantly discriminatory pattern. Once it is thus shown that the employment standards are discriminatory in effect, the employer must meet "the burden of showing that any given requirement [has] * * * a manifest relationship to the employment in question." *Griggs v. Duke Power Co., supra,* at 432, 91 S.Ct., at 854. If the employer proves that the challenged requirements are job related, the plaintiff may then show that other selection devices without a similar discriminatory effect would also "serve the employer's legitimate interest in 'efficient and trustworthy workmanship.' " *Albemarle Paper Co. v. Moody, supra,* at 425, 95 S.Ct., at 2375, quoting *McDonnell Douglas Corp. v. Green,* 411 U.S. 792, 801, 93 S.Ct. 1817, 1823, 36 L.Ed.2d 668.

Although women 14 years of age or older compose 52.75% of the Alabama population and 36.89% of its total labor force, they hold only 12.9% of its correctional counselor positions. In considering the effect of the minimum height and weight standards on this disparity in rate of hiring between the sexes, the District Court found that the 5' 2"-requirement would operate to exclude 33.29% of the women in the United States between the ages of 18–79, while excluding only 1.28% of men between the same ages. The 120–pound weight restriction would exclude 22.29% of the women and 2.35% of the men in this age group. * * * Accordingly, the District Court found that Rawlinson had made out a prima facie case of unlawful sex discrimination.

The appellants argue that a showing of disproportionate impact on women based on generalized national statistics should not suffice to establish a prima facie case. They point in particular to Rawlinson's failure to adduce comparative statistics concerning actual applicants for correctional counselor positions in Alabama. There is no requirement, however, that a statistical showing of disproportionate impact must always be based on analysis of the characteristics of actual applicants. See *Griggs v. Duke Power Co., supra,* 401 U.S., at 430, 91 S.Ct., at 853. The application process might itself not adequately reflect the actual potential applicant pool, since otherwise qualified people might be discouraged from applying because of a self-recognized inability to meet the very standards challenged as being discriminatory. See *International Brotherhood of Teamsters v. United States,* 431 U.S. 324, 365–367, 97 S.Ct. 1843, 1869–1871, 52 L.Ed.2d 396. A potential applicant could easily determine her height and weight and conclude that to make an application would be futile. Moreover, reliance on general population demographic data was not misplaced where there was no reason to suppose that physical height and weight characteristics of Alabama men and women differ markedly from those of the national population.

For these reasons, we cannot say that the District Court was wrong in holding that the statutory height and weight standards had a discriminatory impact on women applicants. The plaintiffs in a case such as this are not required to exhaust every possible source of evidence, if the evidence actually presented on its face conspicuously demonstrates a job requirement's grossly discriminatory impact. If the employer discerns fallacies or deficiencies in the data offered by the plaintiff, he is free to adduce countervailing evidence of his own. In this case no such effort was made.

B

We turn, therefore, to the appellants' argument that they have rebutted the prima facie case of discrimination by showing that the height and weight requirements are job related. These requirements, they say, have a relationship to strength, a sufficient but unspecified amount of which is essential to effective job performance as a correctional counselor. In the District Court, however, the appellants produced no evidence correlating the height and weight requirements with the requisite amount of strength thought essential to good job performance. Indeed, they failed to offer evidence of any kind in specific justification of the statutory standards.

If the job-related quality that the appellants identify is bona fide, their purpose could be achieved by adopting and validating a test for applicants that measures strength directly. Such a test, fairly administered, would fully satisfy the standards of Title VII because it would be one that "measure[s] the person for the job and not the person in the abstract." *Griggs v. Duke Power Co.,* 401 U.S., at 436, 91 S.Ct., at 856. But nothing in the present record even approaches such a measurement.

MR. JUSTICE REHNQUIST, with whom THE CHIEF JUSTICE and MR. JUSTICE BLACKMUN join, concurring in the result and concurring in part.

Appellants, in order to rebut the prima facie case under the statute, had the burden placed on them to advance job-related reasons for the qualification. *McDonnell Douglas Corp. v. Green,* 411 U.S. 792, 802, 93 S.Ct. 1817, 1824, 36 L.Ed.2d 668 (1973). This burden could be shouldered by offering evidence or by making legal arguments not dependent on any new evidence. The District Court was confronted, however, with only one suggested job-related reason for the qualification—that of strength. Appellants argued only the job-relatedness of actual physical strength; they did not urge that an equally job-related qualification for prison guards is the *appearance* of strength. As the Court notes, the primary job of correctional counselor in Alabama prisons "is to maintain security and control of the inmates * * *," a function that I at least would imagine is aided by the psychological impact on prisoners of the presence of tall and heavy guards. If the appearance of strength had been urged upon the District Court here as a reason for the height and weight minima, I think that the District Court would surely have been entitled to reach a different result than it did. For, even if not perfectly correlated, I would think that Title VII would not preclude a State from saying that anyone under 52 or 120 pounds, no matter how strong in fact, does not have a sufficient appearance of strength to be a prison guard.

NEW YORK CITY TRANSIT AUTHORITY v. BEAZER

Supreme Court of the United States, 1979.
440 U.S. 568, 99 S.Ct. 1355, 59 L.Ed.2d 587.

JUSTICE STEVENS delivered the opinion of the Court.

I

The Transit Authority (TA) operates the subway system and certain bus lines in New York City. It employs about 47,000 persons, of whom many—perhaps most—are employed in positions that involve danger to themselves or to the public. For example, some 12,300 are subway motormen, towermen, conductors, or bus operators. The District Court found that these jobs are attended by unusual hazards and must be performed by "persons of maximum alertness and competence." Certain other jobs, such as operating cranes and handling high-voltage equipment, are also considered "critical" or "safety sensitive," while still others, though classified as "noncritical," have a potentially important impact on the overall operation of the transportation system.

TA enforces a general policy against employing persons who use narcotic drugs. The policy is reflected in Rule 11(b) of TA's Rules and Regulations.

> "Employees must not use, or have in their possession, narcotics, tranquilizers, drugs of the Amphetamine group or barbiturate derivatives or paraphernalia used to administer narcotics or barbiturate derivatives, except with the written permission of the Medical Director—Chief Surgeon of the System."

Methadone is regarded as a narcotic within the meaning of Rule 11(b). No written permission has ever been given by TA's medical director for the employment of a person using methadone.

The District Court found that methadone is a synthetic narcotic and a central nervous system depressant. If injected into the bloodstream with a needle, it produces essentially the same effects as heroin. Methadone has been used legitimately in at least three ways—as a pain killer, in "detoxification units" of hospitals as an immediate means of taking addicts off of heroin, and in long-range "methadone maintenance programs" as part of an intended cure for heroin addiction. See 21 CFR § 310.304(b) (1978). In such programs the methadone is taken orally in regular doses for a prolonged period. As so administered, it does not produce euphoria or any pleasurable effects associated with heroin; on the contrary, it prevents users from experiencing those effects when they inject heroin, and also alleviates the severe and prolonged discomfort otherwise associated with an addict's discontinuance of the use of heroin.

About 40,000 persons receive methadone maintenance treatment in New York City, of whom about 26,000 participate in the five major public or semipublic programs, and 14,000 are involved in about 25 private programs. The sole purpose of all these programs is to treat the addiction of persons who have been using heroin for at least two years.

* * *

The evidence indicates that methadone is an effective cure for the physical aspects of heroin addiction. But the District Court also found "that many persons attempting to overcome heroin addiction have psychological or life-style problems which reach beyond what can be cured by the physical taking of doses of methadone." The crucial indicator of successful methadone maintenance is the patient's abstinence from the illegal or excessive use of drugs and alcohol. The District Court found that the risk of reversion to drug or alcohol abuse declines dramatically after the first few months of treatment. Indeed, "the strong majority" of patients who have been on methadone maintenance for at least a year are free from illicit drug use. But a significant number are not. On this critical point, the evidence relied upon by the District Court reveals that even among participants with more than 12 months' tenure in methadone maintenance programs, the incidence of drug and alcohol abuse may often approach and even exceed 25%.

* * *

The District Court enjoined TA from denying employment to any person solely because of participation in a methadone maintenance program. Recognizing, however, the special responsibility for public safety borne by certain TA employees and the correlation between longevity in a methadone maintenance program and performance capability, the injunction authorized TA to exclude methadone users from specific categories of safety-sensitive positions and also to condition eligibility on satisfactory performance in a methadone program for at least a year. In other words, the court held that TA could lawfully adopt general rules excluding all methadone users from some jobs and a large number of methadone users from all jobs.

* * *

II

The District Court's findings do not support its conclusion that TA's regulation prohibiting the use of narcotics, or its interpretation of that regulation to encompass users of methadone, violated Title VII of the Civil Rights Act.

A prima facie violation of the Act may be established by statistical evidence showing that an employment practice has the effect of denying the members of one race equal access to employment opportunities. Even assuming that respondents have crossed this threshold, when the entire record is examined it is clear that the two statistics on which they and the District Court relied do not prove a violation of Title VII.

First, the District Court noted that 81% of the employees referred to TA's medical director for suspected violation of its narcotics rule were either black or Hispanic. But respondents have only challenged the rule to the extent that it is construed to apply to methadone users, and that statistic tells us nothing about the racial composition of the employees suspected of using methadone. Nor does the record give us any information about the number of black, Hispanic, or white persons who were dismissed for using methadone.

Second, the District Court noted that about 63% of the persons in New York City receiving methadone maintenance in *public* programs— *i.e.,* 63% of the 65% of all New York City methadone users who are in such programs—are black or Hispanic. We do not know, however, how many of these persons ever worked or sought to work for TA. This statistic therefore reveals little if anything about the racial composition of the class of TA job applicants and employees receiving methadone treatment. More particularly, it tells us nothing about the class of otherwise-qualified applicants and employees who have participated in methadone maintenance programs for over a year—the only class improperly excluded by TA's policy under the District Court's analysis. The record demonstrates, in fact, that the figure is virtually irrelevant because a substantial portion of the persons included in it are either unqualified for other reasons—such as the illicit use of drugs and alcohol—or have received successful assistance in finding jobs with employers other than TA.[29] Finally, we have absolutely no data on the 14,000 methadone users in the *private* programs, leaving open the possibility that the percentage of blacks and Hispanics in the class of methadone users is not significantly greater than the percentage of those minorities in the general population of New York City.[30]

At best, respondents' statistical showing is weak; even if it is capable of establishing a prima facie case of discrimination, it is assuredly rebutted by TA's demonstration that its narcotics rule (and the rule's application to methadone users) is "job related."[31] The District Court's

29. Although "a statistical showing of disproportionate impact [need not] always be based on an analysis of the characteristics of actual applicants," *Dothard v. Rawlinson,* 433 U.S. 321, 330, 97 S.Ct. 2720, 2727, 53 L.Ed.2d 786, "evidence showing that the figures for the general population might not accurately reflect the pool of qualified job applicants" undermines the significance of such figures. *Teamsters v. United States, supra,* 431 U.S., at 340 n. 20, 97 S.Ct., at 1857 n. 20.

30. If all of the participants in private clinics are white, for example, then only about 40% of all methadone users would be black or Hispanic—compared to the 36.3% of the total population of New York City that was black or Hispanic as of the 1970 census. Assuming instead that the percent-

age of those minorities in the private programs duplicates their percentage in the population of New York City, the figures would still only show that 50% of all methadone users are black or Hispanic compared to 36.3% of the population in the metropolitan area. (The 20% figure relied upon by the dissent refers to blacks and Hispanics in the work force, rather than in the total population of the New York City metropolitan area. The reason the total-population figure is the appropriate one is because the 63% figure relied upon by respondents refers to methadone users in the population generally and not just those in the work force.)

31. Respondents recognize, and the findings of the District Court establish, that TA's legitimate employment goals of safety

express finding that the rule was not motivated by racial animus forecloses any claim in rebuttal that it was merely a pretext for intentional discrimination. We conclude that respondents failed to prove a violation of Title VII.

[*Eds.* Justice White argued in dissent that plaintiffs had established a prima facie impact case by showing that about 63% of methadone users in the New York City area are black or Hispanic, whereas such groups comprise only 20% of the population. Hence, "blacks and Hispanics suffer three times as much from the operation of the challenged rule excluding methadone users as one would expect from a neutral practice." He rejected the majority's seeming insistence on applicant data because defendants had refused to allow discovery of the makeup of the applicant pool. In any case, methadone users do apply for jobs with the Transit Authority and 5% of all applicants are rejected because of the challenged rule. Justice White thus maintained that in the absence of a convincing showing by defendants, there was no reason to adopt the inference that black or Hispanic methadone users would apply with less frequency, or would be less likely to succeed on methadone, than methadone users generally. Disputing the majority's assertion, the dissent contended that the studies relied upon by the District Court did include public as well as private methadone clinics. Finally, Justice White argued that defendants had failed to demonstrate business necessity:

> "Petitioners had the burden of showing job relatedness. They did not show that the rule results in a higher quality labor force, that such a labor force is necessary, or that the cost of making individual decisions about those on methadone was prohibitive. * * * I think it insufficient that the rule as a whole has some relationship to employment so long as a readily identifiable and severable part of it does not."

440 U.S. at 602.]

Notes and Questions

1. *Rationale for Disparate Impact Proof in* Dothard? Does the Court's acceptance of a disparate impact challenge in *Dothard* tell us anything about the justifications for the disparate impact model of proof? Does the average relative size of women reflect past or present societal discrimination? Does *Dothard* therefore suggest that disparate impact analysis may reach barriers to employment even where they do not derive from discrimination?

and efficiency require the exclusion of all users of illegal narcotics, barbiturates, and amphetamines, and of a majority of all methadone users. The District Court also held that those goals require the exclusion of all methadone users from the 25% of its positions that are "safety sensitive." Finally, the District Court noted that those goals are significantly served by—even if they do not require—TA's rule as it applies to all methadone users including those who are seeking employment in nonsafety-sensitive positions. The record thus demonstrates that TA's rule bears a "manifest relationship to the employment in question." *Griggs v. Duke Power Co.*, 401 U.S. 424, 432, 91 S.Ct. 849, 854, 28 L.Ed.2d 158. See *Albemarle Paper Co. v. Moody*, 422 U.S. 405, 425, 95 S.Ct. 2362, 2375, 45 L.Ed.2d 280. Whether or not respondents' weak showing was sufficient to establish a prima facie case, it clearly failed to carry respondents' ultimate burden of proving a violation of Title VII.

2. *Relevant Labor Pool in Disparate Impact Cases?* The *Dothard* Court permits plaintiffs to demonstrate the disparate impact of Alabama's height and weight requirements on the basis of general population statistics. It does not require evidence of a disparate impact on women who actually applied for jobs as Alabama prison guards. Why? Cf. Pumphrey v. City of Coeur D'Alene, 17 F.3d 395 (9th Cir.1994) (finding that police force's requirement that officers use a large-gripped standard duty weapon "could be expected to have a disparate impact on women because of an identifiable physical difference"). On the other hand, is it likely that the average woman who wants to be a prison guard, or police officer, is bigger than the average woman in the labor market?

In *Beazer,* by contrast, the Court discounts plaintiffs' showing that a disproportionately high percentage of individuals in methadone treatment in the New York metropolitan area are black or Hispanic. Is there a principled basis for reconciling the Court's different treatment of general population comparisons in the two cases? Which, if any, of the *Beazer* Court's justifications for discounting plaintiff's evidence do you find persuasive? Should there generally be as strong a presumption in favor of the use of applicant flow data in disparate impact cases as in disparate treatment cases? Presumably, where the employer's intent is the critical issue, the statistical showing generally should attempt to approximate the actual pool of applicants from which the employer made its employment decisions. Is the same premise applicable in disparate impact cases?

If general population statistics are adequate in some cases to establish disparate impact, from what population should the statistics be drawn? In *Griggs* the Court considered the impact of Duke Power's high school diploma requirement on black and white males in the North Carolina labor market. In *Dothard* the Court considered the impact of Alabama's size requirements on women and men in the entire United States population. Would it be appropriate to use national population statistics in all cases? Statewide statistics? Should the *Griggs* Court have considered that Duke Power's Dan River plant was in a rural area near the Virginia border? If a plaintiff challenges an employer's practice of recruiting from only one ethnically homogenous locality, from what labor pool should statistics demonstrating an impact be drawn? Compare Newark Branch, NAACP v. Town of Harrison, 940 F.2d 792 (3d Cir.1991) (approving use of four county area from which employer recruited for other positions), with EEOC v. Chicago Miniature Lamp Works, 947 F.2d 292 (7th Cir.1991) (assuming commuting distance will discourage workers from seeking unskilled, low pay jobs). Under what circumstances must disparate impact be demonstrated by reference to the *qualified* labor market? See Wards Cove Packing Co. v. Atonio, 490 U.S. 642, 109 S.Ct. 2115, 104 L.Ed.2d 733 (1989), infra at p. 139.

3. *How Disproportionate Must the Adverse Impact Be?* Whether applicant flow, qualified labor market, or more general population data are used, how disparate must the impact on a minority group be to force the employer to justify a challenged employment practice? The *Teal* Court in footnote four cites an EEOC guideline providing that a "selection rate * * * which is less than four fifths * * * of the rate for the group with the highest rate will generally be regarded * * * as evidence of adverse impact." 29 C.F.R. § 1607.4D. This guideline on its face only guides the EEOC in determining

whether to initiate enforcement actions. Should it also influence the courts? See Isabel v. City of Memphis, 404 F.3d 404 (6th Cir. 2005) (actionable disparate impact may be demonstrated by alternative statistical analysis even when test complies with four-fifths rule). As noted at p. 108 supra, the EEOC's four-fifths rule of thumb has been criticized on several grounds.

Should the courts be fairly lenient in judging whether there has been a disparate impact, but adjust the employer's burden of justification in accordance with the strength of the disparate impact showing? See Rutherglen, supra, 73 Va.L.Rev. at 1320. Does *Beazer* support such an approach? Is a "sliding scale" workable? Does it fairly take into account the employer's need to determine in advance whether its selection procedures will be subject to challenge?

4. Beazer *Under the 1991 Act*. Section 105 of the Civil Rights Act of 1991 adds a new provision, § 703(k)(3), to Title VII which limits the use of disparate impact analysis in challenges to bars to the employment of drug users. How would this provision apply to the challenge in *Beazer*?

5. *Appearance of Strength as a Potential Defense in* Dothard? Justice Rehnquist, in his dissent in *Dothard,* suggests that a prison system might justify minimum size requirements by showing that regardless of their actual strength, small guards are not perceived by many prisoners as strong. Should the subjective perceptions of "patrons" or customers ever be an acceptable business related defense to a disparate impact claim? Does it make a difference that the subjective stereotype that Rehnquist posits is, at least ostensibly, about small size rather than about women per se? Does it make a difference that the "patrons" in this case are confined to maximum-security institutions and presumably do not act or respond as typical market participants? Defenses to disparate impact showings are further discussed in several notes at pp. 168–182 infra.

WATSON v. FORT WORTH BANK AND TRUST

Supreme Court of the United States, 1988.
487 U.S. 977, 108 S.Ct. 2777, 101 L.Ed.2d 827.

JUSTICE O'CONNOR delivered the judgment of the Court and the opinion of the Court as to [the part reprinted below:]

This case requires us to decide what evidentiary standards should be applied under Title VII of the Civil Rights Act of 1964, 78 Stat. 253, as amended, 42 U.S.C. § 2000e *et seq.,* in determining whether an employer's practice of committing promotion decisions to the subjective discretion of supervisory employees has led to illegal discrimination.

Petitioner Clara Watson, who is black, was hired by respondent Fort Worth Bank and Trust (the Bank) as a proof operator in August 1973. In January 1976, Watson was promoted to a position as teller in the Bank's drive-in facility. In February 1980, she sought to become supervisor of the tellers in the main lobby; a white male, however, was selected for this job. Watson then sought a position as supervisor of the drive-in bank, but this position was given to a white female. In February 1981, after Watson had served for about a year as a commercial teller in the

Bank's main lobby, and informally as assistant to the supervisor of tellers, the man holding that position was promoted. Watson applied for the vacancy, but the white female who was the supervisor of the drive-in bank was selected instead. Watson then applied for the vacancy created at the drive-in; a white male was selected for that job. The Bank, which has about 80 employees, had not developed precise and formal criteria for evaluating candidates for the positions for which Watson unsuccessfully applied. It relied instead on the subjective judgment of supervisors who were acquainted with the candidates and with the nature of the jobs to be filled. All the supervisors involved in denying Watson the four promotions at issue were white.

* * *

The District Court addressed Watson's individual claims under the evidentiary standards that apply in a discriminatory treatment case. See *McDonnell Douglas Corp. v. Green,* 411 U.S. 792, 93 S.Ct. 1817, 36 L.Ed.2d 668 (1973), and *Texas Department of Community Affairs v. Burdine,* 450 U.S. 248, 101 S.Ct. 1089, 67 L.Ed.2d 207 (1981). It concluded, on the evidence presented at trial, that Watson had established a prima facie case of employment discrimination, but that the Bank had met its rebuttal burden by presenting legitimate and nondiscriminatory reasons for each of the challenged promotion decisions. The court also concluded that Watson had failed to show that these reasons were pretexts for racial discrimination. Accordingly, the action was dismissed.

* * *

Watson argued that the District Court had erred in failing to apply "disparate impact" analysis to her claims of discrimination in promotion. Relying on Fifth Circuit precedent, the majority of the Court of Appeals panel held that "a Title VII challenge to an allegedly discretionary promotion system is properly analyzed under the disparate treatment model rather than the disparate impact model." Other Courts of Appeals have held that disparate impact analysis may be applied to hiring or promotion systems that involve the use of "discretionary" or "subjective" criteria.

* * *

We are persuaded that our decisions in *Griggs* and succeeding cases could largely be nullified if disparate impact analysis were applied only to standardized selection practices. However one might distinguish "subjective" from "objective" criteria, it is apparent that selection systems that combine both types would generally have to be considered subjective in nature. Thus, for example, if the employer in *Griggs* had consistently preferred applicants who had a high school diploma and who passed the company's general aptitude test, its selection system could nonetheless have been considered "subjective" if it also included brief interviews with the candidates. So long as an employer refrained from making standardized criteria absolutely determinative, it would remain free to give such tests almost as much weight as it chose without risking a disparate impact challenge. If we announced a rule that allowed employers so easily to insulate themselves from liability under *Griggs*, disparate impact analysis might effectively be abolished.

We are also persuaded that disparate impact analysis is in principle no less applicable to subjective employment criteria than to objective or standardized tests. In either case, a facially neutral practice, adopted without discriminatory intent, may have effects that are indistinguishable from intentionally discriminatory practices. It is true, to be sure, that an employer's policy of leaving promotion decisions to the unchecked discretion of lower level supervisors should itself raise no inference of discriminatory conduct. Especially in relatively small businesses like respondent's, it may be customary and quite reasonable simply to delegate employment decisions to those employees who are most familiar with the jobs to be filled and with the candidates for those jobs. It does not follow, however, that the particular supervisors to whom this discretion is delegated always act without discriminatory intent. Furthermore, even if one assumed that any such discrimination can be adequately policed through disparate treatment analysis, the problem of subconscious stereotypes and prejudices would remain. In this case, for example, petitioner was apparently told at one point that the teller position was a big responsibility with "a lot of money * * * for blacks to have to count." Such remarks may not prove discriminatory intent, but they do suggest a lingering form of the problem that Title VII was enacted to combat. If an employer's undisciplined system of subjective decisionmaking has precisely the same effects as a system pervaded by impermissible intentional discrimination, it is difficult to see why Title VII's proscription against discriminatory actions should not apply. In both circumstances, the employer's practices may be said to "adversely affect [an individual's] status as an employee, because of such individual's race, color, religion, sex, or national origin." 42 U.S.C. § 2000e–2(a)(2). We conclude, accordingly, that subjective or discretionary employment practices may be analyzed under the disparate impact approach in appropriate cases.

[*Eds.* That part of Justice O'Connor's opinion that was joined in by only a plurality of the Court, as well as the separate concurring opinions of Justices Blackmun and Stevens are omitted.]

Notes and Questions

1. *Subjective vs. Objective Employment Practices.* The Court in *Watson* holds that "subjective or discretionary employment practices" may be challenged under Title VII using the disparate impact approach. What distinguishes such practices from "objective" standards like those challenged in the disparate impact cases previously decided by the Court? Is it that objective criteria are applied the same regardless of the decisionmaker while the effect of subjective criteria depends on who applies them? Does this distinction fully capture the employment practice that was challenged in

Watson, however? Wasn't Watson challenging the process of delegating promotion decisions to the discretion of supervisors, rather than the particular subjective criteria that the supervisors were to use in that process? See generally Paul N. Cox, The Future of the Disparate Impact Theory of Employment Discrimination After Watson v. Fort Worth Bank, 1988 B.Y.U. L.Rev. 753.

2. *Should the Disparate Impact Approach Be Available to Challenge Subjective Processes?* Could *Griggs* and *Teal* be read as decisions creating barriers to the use of "objective" proxies that by embodying the effects of past societal discrimination or economic disadvantage operate as "built-in headwinds" against minorities and perpetuate the cycle of disadvantage and occupational segregation? Under this reading, where employers avoid use of such proxies, should they be able to avoid liability unless their processes reveal intentional discrimination (even if circumstantially proved through statistics)? Does *Watson* decisively reject this rationale for the *Griggs* approach?

3. *How Can the Disparate Impact of Subjective or Discretionary Employment Practices Be Proven?* How might a plaintiff develop a statistical proof that particular aspects of a subjective selection process disproportionately affect his or her protected class? Would a plaintiff in such a case ever be able to find probative general labor market data, like that used in *Griggs*, *Dothard*, and *Beazer*? Cf. EEOC v. Joe's Stone Crab, Inc., 220 F.3d 1263, 1279 (11th Cir.2000) (EEOC failed to demonstrate that any subjective criteria either disproportionately affected actual applicants or discouraged qualified applicants). Must plaintiffs rely on the discovery of data kept by an employer on how its application of the disputed criteria and process have affected the employment opportunities of an actual applicant pool? Cf. Thornton v. Mercantile Stores Co., 180 F.R.D. 437 (M.D.Ala.1998) (authorizing broad discovery).

In a challenge to an employer's system for selecting employees for promotion on the basis of senior officers' subjective evaluations, might plaintiffs prove disparate impact by comparing the average number of years it took members of their minority group to be promoted with the average number of years taken by employees not in their group? See Scales v. J.C. Bradford and Co., 925 F.2d 901, 908 (6th Cir.1991) (approving such proof in a sex discrimination case).

4. *Does Disparate Impact Analysis Help Uncover "Subconscious Stereotypes" in Subjective Selection Processes?* Do you agree that "the problem of subconscious stereotypes and prejudices" cannot be "adequately policed through disparate treatment analysis"? If so, does *Watson* help address the problem? If a subjective selection process produces significant, unexplained statistical disparities, based on unguided supervisory assessments of ostensibly neutral personality criteria, is a pattern of or practice of intentional discrimination not demonstrated under *Teamsters* and *Hazelwood*? Should it not be easier in most cases to justify the delegation of decisionmaking authority as a business practice than to dispel the statistics-created inference of a discriminatory use of that authority?

For instance, in EEOC v. Joe's Stone Crab, Inc., supra, the court of appeals vacated the trial court's finding that the employer-restaurant's undirected delegation of hiring authority had an unjustified disparate impact on women, but remanded for reconsideration of whether the trial court's findings concerning the manner of implementation of the delegated authority warranted a finding of disparate treatment. The appeals court indicated that if the discretionary hiring policy was in fact tainted by sex-based stereotypes, it should be treated as intentionally discriminatory. See also EEOC v. Joe's Stone Crab, Inc., 136 F.Supp.2d 1311 (S.D. Fla.2001), affirmed in relevant part, 296 F.3d 1265 (11th Cir.2002) (finding on remand intentional exclusion of women by subordinates to whom hiring authority was delegated).

5. *Are Disparate Impact Challenges to Subjective Processes Necessary to Prevent the Evasion of* Griggs? Is the Court in *Watson* correct in stating that its decisions in *"Griggs* and succeeding cases could largely be nullified if disparate impact analysis were applied only to standardized selection practices"? Without disparate impact methodology, how would plaintiffs challenge an employer's transformation of a standardized selection criterion, such as a high school diploma, into a subjective standard, such as a personnel officer's judgment that the employment candidate has the generally developed verbal skills of a high school graduate?

6. *Challenge to "Word of Mouth" and Other Informal Hiring Processes.* Does *Watson* mean that any aspect of an employer's processes for hiring (or promoting or firing) is potentially open to disparate impact challenge if a plaintiff can establish that a protected class is disproportionately disadvantaged? In Furnco Construction Corp. v. Waters, 438 U.S. 567, 98 S.Ct. 2943, 57 L.Ed.2d 957 (1978), "fully qualified" black bricklayers challenged the process by which the defendant had rejected their employment applications. The defendant had delegated hiring responsibilities to a job superintendent who did not accept any job site applications, but instead hired primarily bricklayers who had worked for him previously. The Supreme Court maintained that the case was properly analyzed as a disparate treatment rather than disparate impact challenge, noting in a footnote that it did not involve "employment tests" or other "particularized requirements." However, the Court did not explain why the employer's use of "word of mouth" recruiting in *Furnco* was not a "particularized requirement"? Is *Furnco* still good law?

In EEOC v. Chicago Miniature Lamp Works, 947 F.2d 292, 305 (7th Cir.1991), the court held that the EEOC could not use disparate impact analysis to challenge an employer's reliance on unsolicited employment applications, apparently generated by word-of-mouth publication of employment opportunities by the predominantly nonblack workforce. The court stressed that the employer had simply been passive and had not actively encouraged its incumbent employees to find other workers. Cf. Gaines v. Boston Herald, Inc., 998 F.Supp. 91 (D.Mass.1998) (distinguishing active nepotism from *Chicago Lamp* and *Furnco*). Is there any reason, in light of *Watson*, to insulate from disparate impact challenge an employer's "passive" acceptance of employee recruitment efforts? Could the employer in *Chicago Lamp* have provided a cost-based business justification for its passivity, in any event? See note 8, supra, p. 114.

WARDS COVE PACKING CO., INC. v. ATONIO

Supreme Court of the United States, 1989.
490 U.S. 642, 109 S.Ct. 2115, 104 L.Ed.2d 733.

JUSTICE WHITE delivered the opinion of the Court.

I

The claims before us are disparate-impact claims, involving the employment practices of petitioners, two companies that operate salmon canneries in remote and widely separated areas of Alaska. The canneries operate only during the salmon runs in the summer months. They are inoperative and vacant for the rest of the year. * * *

The length and size of salmon runs vary from year to year and hence the number of employees needed at each cannery also varies. Estimates are made as early in the winter as possible; the necessary employees are hired, and when the time comes, they are transported to the canneries. Salmon must be processed soon after they are caught, and the work during the canning season is therefore intense. For this reason, and because the canneries are located in remote regions, all workers are housed at the canneries and have their meals in company-owned mess halls.

Jobs at the canneries are of two general types: "cannery jobs" on the cannery line, which are unskilled positions; and "noncannery jobs," which fall into a variety of classifications. Most noncannery jobs are classified as skilled positions.[3] Cannery jobs are filled predominantly by nonwhites, Filipinos and Alaska Natives. The Filipinos are hired through and dispatched by Local 37 of the International Longshoremen Workers Union pursuant to a hiring hall agreement with the Local. The Alaska Natives primarily reside in villages near the remote cannery locations. Noncannery jobs are filled with predominantly white workers, who are hired during the winter months from the companies' offices in Washington and Oregon. Virtually all of the noncannery jobs pay more than cannery positions. The predominantly white noncannery workers and the predominantly nonwhite cannery employees live in separate dormitories and eat in separate mess halls.

In 1974, respondents, a class of nonwhite cannery workers who were (or had been) employed at the canneries, brought this Title VII action against petitioners. Respondents alleged that a variety of petitioners' hiring/promotion practices—*e.g.*, nepotism, a rehire preference, a lack of objective hiring criteria, separate hiring channels, a practice of not promoting from within—were responsible for the racial stratification of

---

3. The noncannery jobs were described as follows by the Court of Appeals: "Machinists and engineers are hired to maintain the smooth and continuous operation of the canning equipment. Quality control personnel conduct the FDA-required inspections and recordkeeping. Tenders are staffed with a crew necessary to operate the vessel. A variety of support personnel are employed to operate the entire cannery community, including, for example, cooks, carpenters, store-keepers, bookkeepers, beach gangs for dock yard labor and construction, etc."

the work force, and had denied them and other nonwhites employment as noncannery workers on the basis of race. Respondents also complained of petitioners' racially segregated housing and dining facilities. All of respondents' claims were advanced under both the disparate-treatment and disparate-impact theories of Title VII liability.

The District Court held a bench trial, after which it entered 172 findings of fact. It then rejected all of respondents' disparate-treatment claims. It also rejected the disparate-impact challenges involving the subjective employment criteria used by petitioners to fill these noncannery positions, on the ground that those criteria were not subject to attack under a disparate-impact theory. Petitioner's "objective" employment practices (*e.g.*, an English language requirement, alleged nepotism in hiring, failure to post noncannery openings, the rehire preference, etc.) were found to be subject to challenge under the disparate-impact theory, but these claims were rejected for failure of proof. Judgment was entered for petitioners.

On appeal, a panel of the Ninth Circuit affirmed, but that decision was vacated when the Court of Appeals agreed to hear the case en banc. * * *

On remand, the panel applied the en banc ruling to the facts of this case. It held that respondents had made out a prima facie case of disparate-impact in hiring for both skilled and unskilled noncannery positions. The panel remanded the case for further proceedings, instructing the District Court that it was the employer's burden to prove that any disparate impact caused by its hiring and employment practices was justified by business necessity. Neither the en banc court nor the panel disturbed the District Court's rejection of the disparate-treatment claims.

* * *

In holding that respondents had made out a prima facie case of disparate impact, the court of appeals relied solely on respondents' statistics showing a high percentage of nonwhite workers in the cannery jobs and a low percentage of such workers in the noncannery positions. Although statistical proof can alone make out a prima facie case, see *Teamsters v. United States*, 431 U.S. 324, 339, 97 S.Ct. 1843, 1856, 52 L.Ed.2d 396 (1977); *Hazelwood School Dist. v. United States*, 433 U.S. 299, 307–308, 97 S.Ct. 2736, 2741–2742, 53 L.Ed.2d 768 (1977), the Court of Appeals' ruling here misapprehends our precedents and the purposes of Title VII, and we therefore reverse.

"There can be no doubt," as there was when a similar mistaken analysis had been undertaken by the courts below in *Hazelwood, supra,* at 308, 97 S.Ct., at 2741, "that the * * * comparison * * * fundamentally misconceived the role of statistics in employment discrimination cases." The "proper comparison [is] between the racial composition of [the at-issue jobs] and the racial composition of the qualified * * * population in the relevant labor market." *Ibid.* It is such a comparison—

between the racial composition of the qualified persons in the labor market and the persons holding at-issue jobs—that generally forms the proper basis for the initial inquiry in a disparate impact case. Alternatively, in cases where such labor market statistics will be difficult if not impossible to ascertain, we have recognized that certain other statistics—such as measures indicating the racial composition of "otherwise-qualified applicants" for at-issue jobs—are equally probative for this purpose. See, *e.g., New York City Transit Authority v. Beazer,* 440 U.S. 568, 585, 99 S.Ct. 1355, 1366, 59 L.Ed.2d 587 (1979).[6]

It is clear to us that the Court of Appeals' acceptance of the comparison between the racial composition of the cannery work force and that of the noncannery work force, as probative of a prima facie case of disparate impact in the selection of the latter group of workers, was flawed for several reasons. Most obviously, with respect to the skilled noncannery jobs at issue here, the cannery work force in no way reflected "the pool of *qualified* job applicants" or the "*qualified* population in the labor force." Measuring alleged discrimination in the selection of accountants, managers, boat captains, electricians, doctors, and engineers—and the long list of other "skilled" noncannery positions found to exist by the District Court—by comparing the number of nonwhites occupying these jobs to the number of nonwhites filling cannery worker positions is nonsensical. If the absence of minorities holding such skilled positions is due to a dearth of qualified nonwhite applicants (for reasons that are not petitioners' fault),[7] petitioners' selection methods or employment practices cannot be said to have had a "disparate impact" on nonwhites.

* * *

* * * The Court of Appeals' theory, at the very least, would mean that any employer who had a segment of his work force that was—for some reason—racially imbalanced, could be haled into court and forced to engage in the expensive and time-consuming task of defending the "business necessity" of the methods used to select the other members of his work force. The only practicable option for many employers will be to adopt racial quotas, insuring that no portion of his [sic] work force deviates in racial composition from the other portions thereof; this is a result that Congress expressly rejected in drafting Title VII. See 42 U.S.C. § 2000e–2(j). * * *

6. In fact, where "figures for the general population might * * * accurately reflect the pool of qualified job applicants," cf. *Teamsters v. United States,* 431 U.S. 324, 340, n. 20, 97 S.Ct. 1843, 1856 n. 20, 52 L.Ed.2d 396 (1977), we have even permitted plaintiffs to rest their prima facie cases on such statistics as well. See, *e.g., Dothard v. Rawlinson,* 433 U.S. 321, 329–330, 97 S.Ct. 2720, 2726, 53 L.Ed.2d 786 (1977).

7. Obviously, the analysis would be different if it were found that the dearth of qualified nonwhite applicants was due to practices on petitioner's part which—expressly or implicitly—deterred minority group members from applying for noncannery positions. See, *e.g., Teamsters v. United States, supra,* 431 U.S., at 365, 97 S.Ct., at 1869.

The Court of Appeals also erred with respect to the unskilled noncannery positions. Racial imbalance in one segment of an employer's work force does not, without more, establish a prima facie case of disparate impact with respect to the selection of workers for the employer's other positions, even where workers for the different positions may have somewhat fungible skills (as is arguably the case for cannery and unskilled noncannery workers). As long as there are no barriers or practices deterring qualified nonwhites from applying for noncannery positions, if the percentage of selected applicants who are nonwhite is not significantly less than the percentage of qualified applicants who are nonwhite, the employer's selection mechanism probably does not operate with a disparate impact on minorities.[8] Where this is the case, the percentage of nonwhite workers found in other positions in the employer's labor force is irrelevant to the question of a prima facie statistical case of disparate impact. As noted above, a contrary ruling on this point would almost inexorably lead to the use of numerical quotas in the workplace, a result that Congress and this Court have rejected repeatedly in the past.

* * *

The peculiar facts of this case further illustrate why a comparison between the percentage of nonwhite cannery workers and nonwhite noncannery workers is an improper basis for making out a claim of disparate impact. Here, the District Court found that nonwhites were "overrepresent[ed]" among cannery workers because petitioners had contracted with a predominantly nonwhite union (Local 37) to fill these positions. As a result, if petitioners (for some permissible reason) ceased using Local 37 as its hiring channel for cannery positions, it appears (according to the District Court's findings) that the racial stratification between the cannery and noncannery workers might diminish to statistical insignificance. Under the Court of Appeals' approach, therefore, it is possible that *with no change whatsoever* in their hiring practices for noncannery workers—the jobs at-issue in this lawsuit—petitioners could make respondents' prima facie case of disparate impact "disappear."

* * *

III

Since the statistical disparity relied on by the Court of Appeals did not suffice to make out a prima facie case, any inquiry by us into whether the specific challenged employment practices of petitioners

---

8. We qualify this conclusion—observing that it is only "probable" that there has been no disparate impact on minorities in such circumstances—because bottom-line racial balance is not a defense under Title VII. See *Connecticut v. Teal,* 457 U.S. 440, 102 S.Ct. 2525, 73 L.Ed.2d 130 (1982). Thus, even if petitioners could show that the percentage of selected applicants who are nonwhite is not significantly less than the percentage of qualified applicants who are nonwhite, respondents would still have a case under Title VII, if they could prove that some particular hiring practice has a disparate impact on minorities, notwithstanding the bottom-line racial balance in petitioners' workforce. See *Teal, supra,* at 450, 102 S.Ct., at 2532 * * *.

caused that disparity is pretermitted, as is any inquiry into whether the disparate impact that any employment practice may have had was justified by business considerations. Because we remand for further proceedings, however, on whether a prima facie case of disparate impact has been made in defensible fashion in this case, we address two other challenges petitioners have made to the decision of the Court of Appeals.

A

First is the question of causation in a disparate-impact case. The law in this respect was correctly stated by Justice O'Connor's opinion (for a plurality of the Court) last Term in *Watson v. Fort Worth Bank & Trust,* 487 U.S., at 994, 108 S.Ct., at 2788:

> "[W]e note that the plaintiff's burden in establishing a prima facie case goes beyond the need to show that there are statistical disparities in the employer's work force. The plaintiff must begin by identifying the specific employment practice that is challenged * * *. Especially in cases where an employer combines subjective criteria with the use of more rigid standardized rules or tests, the plaintiff is in our view responsible for isolating and identifying the specific employment practices that are allegedly responsible for any observed statistical disparities."

* * *

Our disparate-impact cases have always focused on the impact of *particular* hiring practices on employment opportunities for minorities. Just as an employer cannot escape liability under Title VII by demonstrating that, "at the bottom line," his work force is racially balanced (where particular hiring practices may operate to deprive minorities of employment opportunities), see *Connecticut v. Teal,* 457 U.S., at 450, 102 S.Ct., at 2532, a Title VII plaintiff does not make out a case of disparate impact simply by showing that, "at the bottom line," there is racial *imbalance* in the work force. As a general matter, a plaintiff must demonstrate that it is the application of a specific or particular employment practice that has created the disparate impact under attack. Such a showing is an integral part of the plaintiff's prima facie case in a disparate-impact suit under Title VII.

Here, respondents have alleged that several "objective" employment practices (*e.g.,* nepotism, separate hiring channels, rehire preferences), as well as the use of "subjective decision making" to select noncannery workers, have had a disparate impact on nonwhites. Respondents base this claim on statistics that allegedly show a disproportionately low percentage of nonwhites in the at-issue positions. However, even if on remand respondents can show that nonwhites are underrepresented in the at-issue jobs in a manner that is acceptable under the standards set forth in Part II, *supra,* this alone will *not* suffice to make out a prima facie case of disparate impact. Respondents will also have to demonstrate that the disparity they complain of is the result of one or more of the employment practices that they are attacking here, specifically showing that each challenged practice has a significantly disparate impact on employment opportunities for whites and nonwhites. To hold otherwise would result in employers being potentially liable for "the myriad of innocent causes that may lead to statistical imbalances in the composition of their work forces." *Watson v. Fort Worth Bank & Trust, supra,* 487 U.S., at 992, 108 S.Ct., at 2787 (plurality opinion).

Some will complain that this specific causation requirement is unduly burdensome on Title VII plaintiffs. But liberal civil discovery rules give plaintiffs broad access to employers' records in an effort to document their claims. Also, employers falling within the scope of the Uniform Guidelines on Employee Selection Procedures, 29 CFR § 1607.1 *et seq.* (1988), are required to "maintain * * * records or other information which will disclose the impact which its tests and other selection procedures have upon employment opportunities of persons by identifiable race, sex, or ethnic group[s.]" See § 1607.4(A). This includes records concerning "the individual components of the selection process" where there is a significant disparity in the selection rates of whites and nonwhites. See § 1607.4(C). Plaintiffs as a general matter will have the benefit of these tools to meet their burden of showing a causal link between challenged employment practices and racial imbalances in the work force; respondents presumably took full advantage of these opportunities to build their case before the trial in the District Court was held.[10]

* * *

B

If, on remand, respondents meet the proof burdens outlined above, and establish a prima facie case of disparate impact with respect to any of petitioners' employment practices, the case will shift to any business justification petitioners offer for their use of these practices. This phase of the disparate-impact case contains two components: first, a consideration of the justifications an employer offers for his use of these practices; and second, the availability of alternate practices to achieve the same business ends, with less racial impact. See, *e.g., Albemarle Paper Co. v. Moody,* 422 U.S., [405], 425, 95 S.Ct., [2362,] 2375 [(1975)]. We consider these two components in turn.

(1)

Though we have phrased the query differently in different cases, it is generally well-established that at the justification stage of such a disparate impact case, the dispositive issue is whether a challenged practice serves, in a significant way, the legitimate employment goals of the employer. See, *e.g., Watson v. Fort Worth Bank & Trust Co.,* 487 U.S., at 997, 108 S.Ct., at 2790; *New York Transit Authority v. Beazer,* 440 U.S., at 587, n. 31, 99 S.Ct., at 1366, n. 31; *Griggs v. Duke Power*

---

10. Of course, petitioners' obligation to collect or retain any of these data may be limited by the Guidelines themselves. See 29 CFR § 1602.14(b) (1988) (exempting "seasonal" jobs from certain record-keeping requirements).

Co., 401 U.S., at 432, 91 S.Ct., at 854. The touchstone of this inquiry is a reasoned review of the employer's justification for his use of the challenged practice. A mere insubstantial justification in this regard will not suffice, because such a low standard of review would permit discrimination to be practiced through the use of spurious, seemingly neutral employment practices. At the same time, though, there is no requirement that the challenged practice be "essential" or "indispensable" to the employer's business for it to pass muster: this degree of scrutiny would be almost impossible for most employers to meet, and would result in a host of evils we have identified above.

In this phase, the employer carries the burden of producing evidence of a business justification for his employment practice. The burden of persuasion, however, remains with the disparate-impact plaintiff. * * * This rule conforms with the usual method for allocating persuasion and production burdens in the federal courts, see Fed. Rule Evid. 301, and more specifically, it conforms to the rule in disparate-treatment cases that the plaintiff bears the burden of disproving an employer's assertion that the adverse employment action or practice was based solely on a legitimate neutral consideration. See *Texas Dept. of Community Affairs v. Burdine,* 450 U.S. 248, 256–258, 101 S.Ct. 1089, 1095–1096, 67 L.Ed.2d 207 (1981). We acknowledge that some of our earlier decisions can be read as suggesting otherwise. See *Watson, supra,* 487 U.S., at 1001, 108 S.Ct., at 2794 (BLACKMUN, J., concurring). But to the extent that those cases speak of an employers' "burden of proof" with respect to a legitimate business justification defense, see, *e.g., Dothard v. Rawlinson,* 433 U.S. 321, 329, 97 S.Ct. 2720, 2726, 53 L.Ed.2d 786 (1977), they should have been understood to mean an employer's production—but not persuasion—burden. Cf., *e.g., NLRB v. Transportation Management Corp.,* 462 U.S. 393, 404, n. 7, 103 S.Ct. 2469, 2475, n. 7, 76 L.Ed.2d 667 (1983). The persuasion burden here must remain with the plaintiff, for it is he who must prove that it was "because of such individual's race, color," etc., that he was denied a desired employment opportunity. See 42 U.S.C. § 2000e–2(a).

(2)

Finally, if on remand the case reaches this point, and respondents cannot persuade the trier of fact on the question of petitioners' business necessity defense, respondents may still be able to prevail. To do so, respondents will have to persuade the factfinder that "other tests or selection devices, without a similarly undesirable racial effect, would also serve the employer's legitimate [hiring] interest[s]"; by so demonstrating, respondents would prove that "[petitioners were] using [their] tests merely as a 'pretext' for discrimination." *Albemarle Paper Co., supra,* 422 U.S., at 425, 95 S.Ct., at 2375; see also *Watson,* 487 U.S., at 998, 108 S.Ct., at 2779 (O'Connor, J.); *id.,* at 1003, 108 S.Ct., at 2781 (Blackmun, J.). If respondents, having established a prima facie case, come forward with alternatives to petitioners' hiring practices that reduce the racially-disparate impact of practices currently being used, and petitioners refuse to adopt these alternatives, such a refusal would belie a claim by petitioners that their incumbent practices are being employed for non-discriminatory reasons.

Of course, any alternative practices which respondents offer up in this respect must be equally effective as petitioners' chosen hiring procedures in achieving petitioners' legitimate employment goals. Moreover, "[f]actors such as the cost or other burdens of proposed alternative selection devices are relevant in determining whether they would be equally as effective as the challenged practice in serving the employer's legitimate business goals." *Watson, supra,* at 998, 108 S.Ct., at 2790 (O'Connor, J.). "Courts are generally less competent than employers to restructure business practices," *Furnco Construction Corp. v. Waters,* 438 U.S. 567, 578, 98 S.Ct. 2943, 2950, 57 L.Ed.2d 957 (1978); consequently, the judiciary should proceed with care before mandating that an employer must adopt a plaintiff's alternate selection or hiring practice in response to a Title VII suit.

JUSTICE STEVENS, with whom JUSTICE BRENNAN, JUSTICE MARSHALL, and JUSTICE BLACKMUN join, dissenting.

* * * [T]he Court announces that our frequent statements that the employer shoulders the burden of proof respecting business necessity "should have been understood to mean an employer's production—but not persuasion—burden." Our opinions always have emphasized that in a disparate impact case the employer's burden is weighty. "The touchstone," the Court said in *Griggs,* "is business necessity." 401 U.S., at 431, 91 S.Ct., at 853. Later, we held that prison administrators had failed to "rebu[t] the prima facie case of discrimination by showing that the height and weight requirements are * * * essential to effective job performance," *Dothard v. Rawlinson,* 433 U.S. 321, 331, 97 S.Ct. 2720, 2727, 53 L.Ed.2d 786 (1977). I am thus astonished to read that the "touchstone of this inquiry is a reasoned review of the employer's justification for his use of the challenged practice * * *. [T]here is no requirement that the challenged practice be * * * 'essential.'" * * *

* * *

Petitioners contend that the relevant labor market in this case is the general population of the " 'external' labor market for the jobs at issue." While they would rely on the District Court's findings in this regard, those findings are ambiguous. At one point the District Court specifies "Alaska, the Pacific Northwest, and California" as "the geographical region from which [petitioners] draw their employees," but its next finding refers to "this relevant geographical area for cannery worker, laborer, and other nonskilled jobs." There is no express finding of the relevant labor market for noncannery jobs.

Even assuming that the District Court properly defined the relevant geographical area, its apparent assumption that the population in that area constituted the "available labor supply," is not adequately founded. An undisputed requirement for employment either as a cannery or noncannery worker is availability for seasonal employment in the far reaches of Alaska. Many noncannery workers, furthermore, must be available for preseason work. Yet the record does not identify the portion of the general population in Alaska, California, and the Pacific Northwest that would accept this type of employment. This deficiency respecting a crucial job qualification diminishes the usefulness of petitioners' statistical evidence. In contrast, respondents' evidence, comparing racial compositions within the work force, identifies a pool of workers willing to work during the relevant times and familiar with the workings of the industry. Surely this is more probative than the untailored general population statistics on which petitioners focus. Cf. *Hazelwood,* 433 U.S., at 308, n. 13, 97 S.Ct., at 2742, n. 13; *Teamsters,* 431 U.S., at 339–340, n. 20, 97 S.Ct., at 1856, n. 20.

Evidence that virtually all the employees in the major categories of at-issue jobs were white, whereas about two-thirds of the cannery workers were nonwhite, may not by itself suffice to establish a prima facie case of discrimination. But such evidence of racial stratification puts the specific employment practices challenged by respondents into perspective. Petitioners recruit employees for at-issue jobs from outside the work force rather than from lower-paying, overwhelmingly nonwhite, cannery worker positions. Information about availability of at-issue positions is conducted by word of mouth; therefore, the maintenance of housing and mess halls that separate the largely white noncannery work force from the cannery workers, coupled with the tendency toward nepotistic hiring, are obvious barriers to employment opportunities for nonwhites. Putting to one side the issue of business justifications, it would be quite wrong to conclude that these practices have no discriminatory consequence. Thus I agree with the Court of Appeals, that when the District Court makes the additional findings prescribed today, it should treat the evidence of racial stratification in the work force as a significant element of respondents' prima facie case.

Notes and Questions

1. *Congressional Reaction to* Wards Cove. Congressional dissatisfaction with the *Wards Cove* decision was one of the major reasons for passage of the Civil Rights Act of 1991. Section 105 of that Act rejects some, though not all, of the analysis of *Wards Cove.* First, Congress repudiated the *Wards Cove* Court's assignment to plaintiffs of the burden of persuasion at the justification stage of a disparate impact case. Section 105 adds to § 703 of Title VII a new subsection (k) which states that an unlawful employment practice is established if a complaining party demonstrates a disparate impact "and the respondent fails to demonstrate that the challenged practice is job related for the position in question and consistent with business necessity". Section 104 of the 1991 Act defines "demonstrates" to mean "meets the burdens of production and persuasion".

Second, the "job related" and "business necessity" standards of justification required by § 105 are similar to standards first articulated in *Griggs*

and recited in subsequent Supreme Court and lower court cases before
Wards Cove. Furthermore, § 105(b) of the 1991 Act takes the extraordinary
step of directing courts to use as legislative history for purposes of "construing or applying, any provision of this Act that relates to Wards Cove",
including "(b)usiness necessity", only one interpretive memorandum appear-
ing at 137 Cong.Rec. S 15276 (daily ed. Oct. 25, 1991). This memorandum
states the "terms 'business necessity' and 'job related' are intended to reflect
the concepts enunciated by the Supreme Court in *Griggs* * * * and in the
other Supreme Court decisions prior to *Wards Cove*".

2. *The Policy Debate on* Wards Cove. The debate within the Court over
the allocation of the burden of persuasion at the justification stage of a
disparate impact case and over the appropriate standards for justification
was mirrored in a debate between the Democratic leadership in Congress
and President Bush and his advisors over the 1991 Act. Before finally
agreeing to the 1991 Act's rejection of the approach of the *Wards Cove*
majority to these issues, President Bush claimed that the *Wards Cove*
approach was necessary to avoid encouraging employers to adopt "quota"
hiring policies to escape disparate impact suits. Did the President overstate
his case?

Was the debate over disparate impact after *Wards Cove* something of a
"tempest in a teapot"? Even before that decision relatively few disparate
impact cases were being brought. An American Bar Foundation study found
that disparate impact cases comprised only 1.84% of all employment-related
civil rights cases in the federal courts between 1985 and 1987. See John J.
Donohue III & Peter Siegelman, The Changing Nature of Employment
Discrimination Litigation, 43 Stan. L. Rev. 983, 998 n. 57 (1991). There has
been no marked increase in disparate impact litigation since the 1991 Act.

3. *Preserving the Alternative Employment Practice Option.* New
§§ 703(k)(1)(A)(ii) and (k)(1)(C) provide that a plaintiff can also establish an
unlawful practice by making a demonstration with respect to an "alternative
employment practice" "in accordance with the law as it existed on June 4,
1989", the day before *Wards Cove*, if the "respondent refuses to adopt such
alternative employment practice." This somewhat cryptic language is not
explained in the interpretive memorandum, under § 105(b), which the 1991
Act provides shall be the only relevant legislative history for construing or
applying the Act as it relates to an "alternative business practice". However,
as explained in the *Wards Cove* decision, prior Supreme Court decisions,
including *Dothard,* contemplated a third stage in a disparate impact case in
which plaintiffs could respond to a defendant's demonstration of business
necessity by demonstrating that an alternative employment practice could
also effectively serve the defendant's legitimate business interests without a
similarly undesirable racial effect. See Julia Lamber, Alternatives to Challenged Employee Selection Criteria, 1985 Wisc. L.Rev. 1. The 1991 Act's
provisions on "alternative employment practices" seem to endorse this law,
while rejecting any possible modification wrought by the *Wards Cove* decision.

4. *Timing of an Employer's Refusal of an Alternative Practice?* Note
that the 1991 Act authorizes a finding of illegality based on the existence of
a less discriminatory alternative practice only if the defendant refuses to

adopt the practice. The wording of the Act raises a number of problems, however. Do plaintiffs have the burden of proving a refusal? What constitutes a refusal? Must the employer know not only of the alternative practice but also of its validity before taking the challenged employment actions? See Adams v. City of Chicago, 469 F.3d 609 (7th Cir. 2006) (defendant must have had an opportunity to adopt the alternative practice and must be aware of its validity at the time of making the challenged decisions).

5. *Proving   Causation   in   Disparate   Impact   Cases.*   New § 703(k)(1)(B)(i), as added by § 105 of the 1991 Act, provides that the plaintiff in a Title VII disparate impact case must demonstrate that a "particular" employment practice causes a disparate impact, "except that if the complaining party can demonstrate to the court that the elements of a respondent's decisionmaking process are not capable of separation for analysis, the decisionmaking process may be analyzed as one employment practice." Section 703(k)(1)(B)(ii) further provides that if "the respondent demonstrates that a specific employment practice does not cause the disparate impact, the respondent shall not be required to demonstrate that such practice is required by business necessity."

Do these provisions modify the approach of the *Wards Cove* majority to the issue of causation in disparate impact cases? If so, how? Under *Wards Cove* would plaintiffs be able to use disparate impact methodology to challenge bottom-line results of evaluation systems that use several subjective processes or criteria if the employer did not keep data evidencing how each process or criterion was applied? Does the 1991 Act contemplate that in such a case the criteria "are not capable of separation", even though they theoretically could have been separated had the employer kept sufficient data? Is the 1991 Act's approach consistent with the earlier disparate impact decisions that you have read? Does the 1991 Act settle the issue raised in footnote 8 in Justice Powell's dissent in *Teal*? See note 9, supra p. 125.

Note that the *Wards Cove* majority affirms *Teal* in Part III A and footnote 8, and thus does not require proof that any challenged practice resulted in disproportionately low hiring of the plaintiffs' class. It instead demands a "showing that each challenged practice has a significantly disparate impact on employment opportunities for whites and nonwhites." Does this mean that if Wards Cove's elimination of one practice, such as nepotism, that was proven to screen out minorities, would not lead to the hiring of more minorities because of some other practice, such as not promoting from within, that also screened them out, the first as well as the second practice could be enjoined as discriminatory? See Ramona L. Paetzold & Steven L. Willborn, Deconstructing Disparate Impact: A View of the Model Through New Lenses, 74 N.C. L.Rev. 326 (1996) (taking this position). Compare United States v. City of Warren, 138 F.3d 1083, 1093 (6th Cir.1998) (if residency requirement and recruiting practices both disproportionately affect opportunities, it is no defense that each alone would be sufficient cause of hiring disparity), with Newark Branch, NAACP v. City of Bayonne, 134 F.3d 113, 123–24 (3d Cir.1998) (residency requirement not shown to have disparate impact on ultimate hiring notwithstanding relative proportions of minorities in surrounding area).

6. *Record Keeping On Adverse Impact.* Should the EEOC require all employers to maintain data on the impact of all of their employment practices? Is such a requirement in place? Consider UGESP, 29 C.F.R. § 1607.15(a) ("[u]sers of selection procedures * * * should maintain and have available for each job information on adverse impact of the selection process for that job"). Will § 703(k) encourage employers to maintain information that separates the impact of each element of their selection processes?

7. *"Functionally–Integrated" Practices.* Section 105(b) of the 1991 Act states that the interpretive memorandum cited above shall be the only legislative history for construing or applying "any provision of this Act that relates to * * * cumulation". The word "cumulation" is not otherwise used in § 105, or elsewhere in the 1991 Act. This apparently is a reference back to new § 703(k)(1)(B)'s allowance of disparate impact challenges to the cumulative effects of entire employment practices where the effects of elements of such practices cannot be separated. However, the interpretive memorandum states that:

> When a decision-making process includes particular, functionally-integrated practices which are components of the same criterion, standard, method of administration, or test, such as the height and weight requirements designed to measure strength in *Dothard* * * *, the particular, functionally-integrated practices may be analyzed as one employment practice.

Could the effects of the height requirement employed in *Dothard* be relatively easily separated from the effects of the weight requirement? Were they "functionally-integrated practices"? Does the interpretive memorandum suggest that courts should combine the effects of "functionally-integrated" employment standards to determine whether the aggregate effect is sufficient to constitute a disparate impact that requires justification, under the EEOC's four-fifths rule or some other standard? Would such aggregation make a difference in some cases where the effect of each of several elements may not be significant, but the aggregation of several effects would be? Is this sensible only when employees are given a cumulative score on a battery of answers to various questions or on a series of evaluations? Or should this kind of aggregation be allowed in all cases? See Paetzold and Willborn, supra. To what extent does the text of § 105 support aggregation? Exactly what effect does the interpretive memorandum have? Is it part of the law, or can it only be used to interpret ambiguous provisions in the text of the 1991 Act?

8. *Combining Systemic Disparate Treatment and Disparate Impact Approaches?* Under the 1991 Act might plaintiffs use statistics in a systemic disparate treatment claim to force an employer to justify using criteria that the plaintiff has not proven caused the suspicious statistics? Assume that a plaintiff establishes a strong systemic disparate treatment case primarily by demonstrating a statistically significant disparity that the plaintiff contends is inexplicable except by an assumption of race-influenced decisionmaking. The defendant might then defend against this case by proving that the statistics reflect the impact of employment practices that are facially neutral with regard to race. Does the assertion of such a defense also establish for

the plaintiff a prima facie disparate impact claim against the employer-identified neutral employment practices, triggering an inquiry into business necessity for the particular practices? See Segar v. Smith, 738 F.2d 1249, 1270 (D.C.Cir.1984). See also, e.g., Anderson v. Zubieta, 180 F.3d 329 (D.C.Cir.1999) (plaintiffs established a prima facie case of both disparate treatment and disparate impact, where reasonable factfinder could believe that challenged pay policy had no business justification and was also pretextual).

9. *Defining the Relevant Labor Market for Comparison.* The 1991 Act does not disturb part II of the majority opinion in *Wards Cove.* It is not difficult to understand why the Court rejected the plaintiffs' comparison of the percentage of nonwhite workers in the cannery jobs with the much lower percentage of nonwhite workers in the relatively skilled noncannery positions. The Court's insistence that the plaintiffs use a pool of only workers who have the special qualifications needed for the various skilled noncannery positions is consistent with *Hazelwood.* But why does the Court also state that the cannery workforce does not provide an appropriate labor pool to determine the relative impact on nonwhites of the employer's methods for filling the unskilled noncannery positions?

How should the labor market be defined on remand in *Wards Cove?* Should it include all qualified workers in the Pacific coast states, or would this distort the pool of workers who would actually be willing to work in seasonal jobs in remote areas of Alaska? Should the labor market instead include just those qualified workers who applied for a noncannery position, or would this pool be tainted by some of the challenged employment practices, such as word-of-mouth and nepotistic recruitment, and the failure to post job openings? Should the pool used for cannery positions be added to the actual applicants for unskilled noncannery positions to define the relevant labor market?

The Court of Appeals ultimately affirmed the trial court's finding, following a bench trial, that the plaintiffs did not prove any of their disparate impact claims. Atonio v. Wards Cove Packing Company, Inc., 275 F.3d 797 (9th Cir. 2001). The Court of Appeals had earlier approved the trial court's acceptance of the defendant's proffered census data (indicating a labor pool approximately 10% nonwhite), and rejection of the plaintiffs' alternative proposals of either the total salmon canning industry work force (48% nonwhite) or those applicants who identified their ethnicity on Wards Cove's application forms (26% nonwhite), to define the relevant labor market. See 10 F.3d 1485 (9th Cir.1993). For another decision discussing the holding of *Wards Cove* on defining the relevant labor market in a disparate impact case, see Malave v. Potter, 320 F.3d 321 (2d Cir.2003).

2. *Establishing Business Necessity*

ALBEMARLE PAPER CO. v. MOODY
Supreme Court of the United States, 1975.
422 U.S. 405, 95 S.Ct. 2362, 45 L.Ed.2d 280.

JUSTICE STEWART delivered the opinion of the Court.

Like the employer in *Griggs* [*v. Duke Power Co.*, 401 U.S. 424, 91 S.Ct. 849, 28 L.Ed.2d 158 (1971)], Albemarle uses two general ability tests, the Beta Examination, to test nonverbal intelligence, and the Wonderlic Test (Forms A and B), the purported measure of general verbal facility which was also involved in the *Griggs* case. Applicants for hire into various skilled lines of progression at the plant are required to score 100 on the Beta Exam and 18 on one of the Wonderlic Test's two alternative forms.

The question of job relatedness must be viewed in the context of the plant's operation and the history of the testing program. The plant, which now employs about 650 persons, converts raw wood into paper products. It is organized into a number of functional departments, each with one or more distinct lines of progression, the theory being that workers can move up the line as they acquire the necessary skills. The number and structure of the lines have varied greatly over time. For many years, certain lines were themselves more skilled and paid higher wages than others, and until 1964 these skilled lines were expressly reserved for white workers. In 1968, many of the unskilled "Negro" lines were "end-tailed" onto skilled "white" lines, but it apparently remains true that at least the top jobs in certain lines require greater skills than the top jobs in other lines. In this sense, at least, it is still possible to speak of relatively skilled and relatively unskilled lines.

In the 1950's while the plant was being modernized with new and more sophisticated equipment, the Company introduced a high school diploma requirement for entry into the skilled lines. Though the Company soon concluded that this requirement did not improve the quality of the labor force, the requirement was continued until the District Court enjoined its use. In the late 1950's, the Company began using the Beta Examination and the Bennett Mechanical Comprehension Test (also involved in the *Griggs* case) to screen applicants for entry into the skilled lines. The Bennett Test was dropped several years later, but use of the Beta Test continued.[23]

The Company added the Wonderlic Tests in 1963, for the skilled lines, on the theory that a certain verbal intelligence was called for by the increasing sophistication of the plant's operations. The Company made no attempt to validate the test for job relatedness,[24] and simply

23. While the Company contends that the Bennett and Beta Tests were "locally validated" when they were introduced, no record of this validation was made. Plant officials could recall only the barest outlines of the alleged validation. Job relatedness cannot be proved through vague and unsubstantiated hearsay.

24. As explained by the responsible plant official, the Wonderlic Test was chosen in rather casual fashion:

"I had had experience with using the Wonderlic before, which is a short form Verbal Intelligence Test, and knew that it had, uh, probably more validation studies behind it than any other short form Ver-

bal Intelligence Test. So, after consultation we decided to institute the Wonderlic, in addition to the Beta, in view of the fact that the mill had changed quite a bit and it had become exceedingly more complex in operation * * *. [W]e did not, uh, validate it, uh, locally, primarily, because of the, the expense of conducting such a validation, and there were some other considerations, such as, uh, we didn't know whether we would get the co-operation of the employees that we'd need to validate it against [sic] in taking the test, and we certainly have to have that, so, we used National Norms and on my suggestion after study of the Wonderlic and Norms had been established nationally adopted the national "norm" score of 18 as a cut-off point for new job applicants. After 1964, when it discontinued overt segregation in the lines of progression, the Company allowed Negro workers to transfer to the skilled lines if they could pass the Beta and Wonderlic Tests, but few succeeded in doing so. Incumbents in the skilled lines, some of whom had been hired before adoption of the tests, were not required to pass them to retain their jobs or their promotion rights. The record shows that a number of white incumbents in high-ranking job groups could not pass the tests.[25]

* * *

Four months before this case went to trial, Albemarle engaged an expert in industrial psychology to "validate" the job relatedness of its testing program. He spent a half day at the plant and devised a "concurrent validation" study, which was conducted by plant officials, without his supervision. The expert then subjected the results to statistical analysis. The study dealt with 10 job groupings, selected from near the top of nine of the lines of progression. Jobs were grouped together solely by their proximity in the line of progression; no attempt was made to analyze jobs in terms of the particular skills they might require. All, or nearly all, employees in the selected groups participated in the study—105 employees in all, but only four Negroes. Within each job grouping the study compared the test scores of each employee with an independent "ranking" of the employee, relative to each of his coworkers, made by two of the employee's supervisors. The supervisors, who did not know the test scores, were asked to

> "determine which ones they felt irrespective of the job that they were actually doing, but in their respective jobs, did a better job than the person they were rating against * * *."

For each job grouping, the expert computed the "Phi coefficient" of statistical correlation between the test scores and an average of the two supervisorial rankings. Consonant with professional conventions, the expert regarded as "statistically significant" any correlation that could have occurred by chance only five times, or fewer, in 100 trials. On the basis of these results, the District Court found that "[t]he personnel test administered at the plant have undergone validation studies and have been proven to be job related." Like the Court of Appeals, we are constrained to disagree.

The EEOC has issued "Guidelines" for employers seeking to determine, through professional validation studies, whether their employment

for skilled jobs, we developed a, uh, cut-off score of eighteen (18)."

25. In the course of a 1971 validation effort, test scores were accumulated for 105 incumbent employees (101 of whom were white) working in relatively high-ranking jobs. Some of these employees apparently took the tests for the first time as part of this study. The Company's expert testified that the test cut-off scores originally used to screen these incumbents for employment or promotion "couldn't have been * * * very high scores because some of these guys tested very low, as low as 8 in the Wonderlic test, and as low as 95 in the Beta. They couldn't have been using very high cut-off scores or they wouldn't have these low testing employees."

tests are job related. 29 CFR Part 1607. These Guidelines draw upon and make reference to professional standards of test validation established by the American Psychological Association. The EEOC Guidelines are not administrative "regulations" promulgated pursuant to formal procedures established by the Congress. But, as this Court has heretofore noted, they do constitute "[t]he administrative interpretation of the Act by the enforcing agency," and consequently they are "entitled to great deference." *Griggs v. Duke Power Co.*, 401 U.S., at 433–434, 91 S.Ct., at 854. See also *Espinoza v. Farah Mfg. Co.*, 414 U.S. 86, 94, 94 S.Ct. 334, 339, 38 L.Ed.2d 287 (1973).

The message of these Guidelines is the same as that of the *Griggs* case—that discriminatory tests are impermissible unless shown, by professionally acceptable methods, to be "predictive of or significantly correlated with important elements of work behavior which comprise or are relevant to the job or jobs for which candidates are being evaluated." 29 CFR § 1607.4(c).

Measured against the Guidelines, Albemarle's validation study is materially defective in several respects:

(1) Even if it had been otherwise adequate, the study would not have "validated" the Beta and Wonderlic test battery for all of the skilled lines of progression for which the two tests are, apparently, now required. The study showed significant correlations for the Beta Exam in only three of the eight lines. Though the Wonderlic Test's Form A and Form B are in theory identical and interchangeable measures of verbal facility, significant correlations for one form but not for the other were obtained in four job groupings. In two job groupings neither form showed a significant correlation. Within some of the lines of progression, one form was found acceptable for some job groupings but not for others. Even if the study were otherwise reliable, this odd patchwork of results would not entitle Albemarle to impose its testing program under the Guidelines. A test may be used in jobs other than those for which it has been professionally validated only if there are "no significant differences" between the studied and unstudied jobs. 29 CFR § 1607.4(c)(2). The study in this case involved no analysis of the attributes of, or the particular skills needed in, the studied job groups. There is accordingly no basis for concluding that "no significant differences" exist among the lines of progression, or among distinct job groupings within the studied lines of progression. Indeed, the study's checkered results appear to compel the opposite conclusion.

(2) The study compared test scores with subjective supervisorial rankings. While they allow the use of supervisorial rankings in test validation, the Guidelines quite plainly contemplate that the rankings will be elicited with far more care than was demonstrated here.[30]

---

30. The Guidelines provide, at 29 CFR §§ 1607.5(b)(3) and (4):

"(3) The work behaviors or other criteria of employee adequacy which the test is intended to predict or identify must be fully described; and, additionally, in the case of rating techniques, the appraisal form(s) and instructions to the rater(s)

Albemarle's supervisors were asked to rank employees by a "standard" that was extremely vague and fatally open to divergent interpretations. As previously noted, each "job grouping" contained a number of different jobs, and the supervisors were asked, in each grouping to

> "determine which ones [employees] they felt irrespective of the job that they were actually doing, but in their respective jobs, did a better job than the person they were rating against * * *."

There is no way of knowing precisely what criteria of job performance the supervisors were considering, whether each of the supervisors was considering the same criteria or whether, indeed, any of the supervisors actually applied a focused and stable body of criteria of any kind.[32] There is, in short, simply no way to determine whether the criteria *actually* considered were sufficiently related to the Company's legitimate interest in job-specific ability to justify a testing system with a racially discriminatory impact.

(3) The Company's study focused, in most cases, on job groups near the top of the various lines of progression. In *Griggs v. Duke Power Co., supra,* the Court left open "the question whether testing requirements that take into account capability for the next succeeding position or related future promotion might be utilized upon a showing that such long-range requirements fulfill a genuine business need." 401 U.S., at 432, 91 S.Ct., at 854. The Guidelines take a sensible approach to this issue, and we now endorse it:

> "If job progression structures and seniority provisions are so established that new employees will probably, within a reasonable period of time and in a great majority of cases, progress to a higher level, it may be considered that candidates are being evaluated for jobs at that higher level. However, where job progression is not so nearly automatic, or the time span is such that higher level jobs or employees' potential may be expected to change in significant ways, it shall be considered that candidates are being evaluated for a job at or near the entry level." 29 CFR § 1607.4(c)(1).

The fact that the best of those employees working near the top of a line of progression score well on a test does not necessarily mean that that

---

must be included as a part of the validation evidence. Such criteria may include measures other than actual work proficiency, such as training time, supervisory ratings, regularity of attendance and tenure. Whatever criteria are used they must represent major or critical work behaviors as revealed by careful job analyses.

"(4) In view of the possibility of bias inherent in subjective evaluations, supervisory rating techniques should be carefully developed, and the ratings should be closely examined for evidence of bias. In addition, minorities might obtain unfairly low performance criterion scores for rea-

sons other than supervisor's prejudice, as when, as new employees, they have had less opportunity to learn job skills. The general point is that all criteria need to be examined to insure freedom from factors which would unfairly depress the scores of minority groups."

32. It cannot escape notice that Albemarle's study was conducted by plant-officials, without neutral, on-the-scene oversight, at a time when this litigation was about to come to trial. Studies so closely controlled by an interested party in litigation must be examined with great care.

test, or some particular cutoff score on the test, is a permissible measure of the minimal qualifications of new workers entering lower level jobs. In drawing any such conclusion, detailed consideration must be given to the normal speed of promotion, to the efficacy of on-the-job training in the scheme of promotion, and to the possible use of testing as a promotion device, rather than as a screen for entry into low-level jobs. The District Court made no findings on these issues. The issues take on special importance in a case, such as this one, where incumbent employees are permitted to work at even high-level jobs without passing the company's test battery. See 29 CFR § 1607.11.

(4) Albemarle's validation study dealt only with job-experienced, white workers; but the tests themselves are given to new job applicants, who are younger, largely inexperienced, and in many instances non-white. The APA Standards state that it is "essential" that

> "[t]he validity of a test should be determined on subjects who are at the age or in the same educational or vocational situation as the persons for whom the test is recommended in practice."

The EEOC Guidelines likewise provide that "[d]ata must be generated and results separately reported for minority and nonminority groups wherever technically feasible." 29 CFR § 1607.5(b)(5). In the present case, such "differential validation" as to racial groups was very likely not "feasible," because years of discrimination at the plant have insured that nearly all of the upper level employees are white. But there has been no clear showing that differential validation was not feasible for lower level jobs.

* * *

For all these reasons, we agree with the Court of Appeals that the District Court erred in concluding that Albemarle had proved the job relatedness of its testing program and that the respondents were consequently not entitled to equitable relief.

Notes and Questions

1. *Discriminatory Intent in* Albemarle? Would you conclude from the facts presented by the Court that the Albemarle Paper Company adopted its challenged tests for discriminatory purposes? Does the Court's analysis indicate that the company's intent was relevant in any way?

2. *Congressional Confirmation?* Recall that § 105 of the Civil Rights Act of 1991 amends Title VII to endorse the "business necessity" and "job related" standards for the justification of disparate impact, and that § 105(b) of the 1991 Act provides that interpretations of these standards are to be governed by an interpretive memorandum in the Congressional Record which states that these terms are intended to reflect Supreme Court decisions prior to *Wards Cove.* Does § 105 thus confirm the holdings of *Albemarle,* the leading Supreme Court case on establishing the "business necessity" of scored tests?

3. *Can Nonvalidated Tests Be Used for Other Jobs?* Does *Albemarle* stand for the proposition that the tests in question may not be utilized by other employers? By Albemarle Paper in its other facilities? Is it relevant that these tests may have survived challenge in other cases? See, e.g., Cormier v. P.P.G. Industries, Inc., 519 F.Supp. 211, 258 (W.D.La.1981), affirmed per. curiam, 702 F.2d 567 (5th Cir.1983) (Bennett Mechanical).

4. *Flawed Psychological Premise for General Aptitude Tests?* The tests used were scored psychological instruments, which seek to measure an individual's traits or skills—in this case, verbal and mechanical intelligence and problem-solving abilities. They are based on a psychological theory that individuals have certain stable personality traits and skills which are not modified by workplace environment. Is this an adequate model of human personality and behavior? Some psychologists have suggested that personality characteristics and innate skills are not as good predictors of subsequent behavior as changes in immediate situational conditions. See, e.g., W. Mischel, Personality and Assessment (1968); Susan T. Fiske, The Limits for the Conventional Science of Personality, 42 J. Personality 1 (1974). For the view that alternative models of behavior cast doubt on the validity of scored personality tests, see Craig Haney, Employment Tests and Employment Discrimination: A Dissenting Psychological Opinion, 5 Indus.Rel.L.J. 1, 48 ff. (1982).

5. *Criterion Validation. Albemarle* involved a particular mode of establishing business necessity for job testing—criterion-related validation. This was the preferred method under the EEOC Guidelines in effect at the time. Under this approach, a test is "valid" if it can predict successful job performance. Usually measures of job performance or criteria obtained from supervisory ratings of a sample of incumbent employees are compared to test scores achieved by these workers. If there is a sufficient correlation between the performance scores and test scores (termed the "correlation coefficient") and the results satisfy conventions of statistical significance (normally, a five-percent or less probability that the results are the product of chance), the test is considered to have sufficient predictive power to be used notwithstanding its adverse impact on minorities.

6. *Promotability As a Criterion.* Promotability to higher-level jobs is a criterion previously encountered in *Griggs*. Why has this criterion encountered sharp judicial scrutiny? Are there circumstances where employers should be able to restrict entry-level positions to individuals who are likely to be promoted to higher levels in the organization? The Uniform Guidelines on Employee Selection Procedures (1978), which were promulgated after *Albemarle,* would permit testing for promotability where "job progression structures are so stabilized that employees will probably, within a reasonable period of time and in a majority of cases, progress to a higher level," but would not permit such testing where "there is a reason to doubt that the higher level job will continue to require essentially similar skills during the progression period," or where the skills required are expected to develop from training or on-the-job experience. 29 C.F.R. § 1607.5(I). Does this provision impose significant costs on some employers?

7. *Supervisor Ratings As a Criterion.* What was wrong with the supervisors' ratings of job performance? Objective measures such as performance

rate and error rate might be preferable, but not all jobs can be reduced to quantifiable, readily observable measures. In the absence of such measures, what purports to be an objective, empirical assessment of test validity will boil down to a comparison of test scores against subjective supervisor ratings. Are there reasons for concern apart from the possibility that the supervisors may be prone to intentional racial or gender bias? What steps would you propose for cabining the subjectivity of supervisor ratings? For further discussion, see Note on Uniform Guidelines and Employment Testing Litigation, at p. 168 infra.

8. *Differential Validation.* Albemarle's validation study failed to provide evidence of "differential validity": proof that tests, which may be valid for the tested population overall, are also good predictors of job performance for particular minority subgroups. Are there good reasons for requiring such validation? The concept has been much criticized in the psychological literature. See, e.g., Virginia R. Boehm, Differential Prediction: A Methodological Artifact?, 62 J. of Applied Psych. 146 (1977); Frank Schmidt, John G. Berner & John E. Hunter, Racial Differences in Validity of Employment Tests: Reality or Illusion?, 58 J. of Applied Psych. 5 (1973). The Uniform Guidelines "generally" require a differential study only where it is "technically feasible," i.e., where the minority composition of the workforce is large enough to permit separate assessment of validity with respect to that group. 29 C.F.R. § 1607.14(B)(8).

The EEOC's test for differential validity requires that a test predict minority performance on the job as well as it predicts nonminority performance. Is this sufficiently demanding to avoid unjustifiable disparate impacts on blacks? Mark Kelman has argued that if a much higher proportion of blacks than whites do not achieve a passing score on a test that is imperfectly correlated with success on the job, a much higher proportion of blacks than of whites who could have been successful on the job will be eliminated by the test, even if the test is equally valid under the EEOC's approach for both races. See Kelman, Concepts of Discrimination in "General Ability" Job Testing, 104 Harv.L.Rev. 1157, 1222–27 (1991). See also p. 173 infra.

WASHINGTON v. DAVIS
Supreme Court of the United States, 1976.
426 U.S. 229, 96 S.Ct. 2040, 48 L.Ed.2d 597.

Justice White delivered the opinion of the Court.

This case involves the validity of a qualifying test administered to applicants for positions as police officers in the District of Columbia Metropolitan Police Department. The test was sustained by the District Court but invalidated by the Court of Appeals. We are in agreement with the District Court and hence reverse the judgment of the Court of Appeals.

I

* * *

According to the findings and conclusions of the District Court, to be accepted by the Department and to enter an intensive 17–week training program, the police recruit was required to satisfy certain physical and character standards, to be a high school graduate or its equivalent, and to receive a grade of at least 40 out of 80 on "Test 21," which is "an examination that is used generally throughout the federal service," which "was developed by the Civil Service Commission, not the Police Department," and which was "designed to test verbal ability, vocabulary, reading and comprehension."

* * *

III

* * *

The submission of the defendants in the District Court was that Test 21 complied with all applicable statutory as well as constitutional requirements; and they appear not to have disputed that under the statutes and regulations governing their conduct standards similar to those obtaining under Title VII had to be satisfied. The District Court also assumed that Title VII standards were to control the case, identified the determinative issue as whether Test 21 was sufficiently job related and proceeded to uphold use of the test because it was "directly related to a determination of whether the applicant possesses sufficient skills requisite to the demands of the curriculum a recruit must master at the police academy." The Court of Appeals reversed because the relationship between Test 21 and training school success, if demonstrated at all, did not satisfy what it deemed to be the crucial requirement of a direct relationship between performance on Test 21 and performance on the policeman's job.

We agree with petitioners and the federal parties that this was error. The advisability of the police recruit training course informing the recruit about his upcoming job, acquainting him with its demands, and attempting to impart a modicum of required skills seems conceded. It is also apparent to us, as it was to the District Judge, that some minimum verbal and communicative skill would be very useful, if not essential, to satisfactory progress in the training regimen. Based on the evidence before him, the District Judge concluded that Test 21 was directly related to the requirements of the police training program and that a positive relationship between the test and training-course performance was sufficient to validate the former, wholly aside from its possible relationship to actual performance as a police officer. This conclusion of the District Judge that training-program validation may itself be sufficient is supported by regulations of the Civil Service Commission, by the opinion evidence placed before the District Judge, and by the current views of the Civil Service Commissioners who were parties to the case.[16]

16. See n. 17, *infra*. Current instructions of the Civil Service Commission on "Examining, Testing, Standards, and Employment Practices" provide in pertinent part:

"S2–2—Use of applicant appraisal procedures

"a. *Policy*. The Commission's staff develops and uses applicant appraisal procedures to assess the knowledges, skills,

Nor is the conclusion foreclosed by either *Griggs* or *Albemarle Paper Co. v. Moody,* 422 U.S. 405, 95 S.Ct. 2362, 45 L.Ed.2d 280 (1975); and it seems to us the much more sensible construction of the job-relatedness requirement.

The District Court's accompanying conclusion that Test 21 was in fact directly related to the requirements of the police training program was supported by a validation study, as well as by other evidence of record;[17] and we are not convinced that this conclusion was erroneous.

JUSTICE STEVENS, concurring.

The Court's specific holding on the job-relatedness question contains, I believe, two components. First, as a matter of law, it is permissible for the police department to use a test for the purpose of predicting ability to master a training program even if the test does not otherwise predict ability to perform on the job. I regard this as a reasonable proposition and not inconsistent with the Court's prior holdings, although some of its prior language obviously did not contemplate this precise problem. Second, as a matter of fact, the District Court's finding that there was a correlation between success on the test and success in the training program has sufficient evidentiary support to withstand attack under the "clearly erroneous" standard mandated by Fed.Rule Civ.Proc. 52(a). Whether or not we would have made the same finding of fact, the opinion evidence identified in n. 17 of the Court's opinion—and indeed the assumption made by the Court of Appeals quoted therein—is surely adequate to support the finding under the proper standard of appellate review.

JUSTICE BRENNAN, with whom JUSTICE MARSHALL joins, dissenting.

The [Civil Service Commission (CSC)'s] standards * * * recognize that Test 21 can be validated by a correlation between Test 21 scores

and abilities of persons for jobs and not persons in the abstract.

"(1) Appraisal procedures are designed to reflect real, reasonable, and necessary qualifications for effective job behavior.

"(2) An appraisal procedure must, among other requirements, have a demonstrable and rational relationship to important job-related performance objectives identified by management, such as:

"(a) Effective job performance;

"(b) Capability;

"(c) Success in training;

"(d) Reduced turnover; or

"(e) Job satisfaction."

37 Fed.Reg. 21557 (1972). See also Equal Employment Opportunity Commission Guidelines on Employee Selection Procedures, 29 CFR § 1607.5(b)(3) (1975), discussed in *Albemarle Paper Co. v. Moody,* 422 U.S., at 430–435, 95 S.Ct. 2362, 2378–2380, 45 L.Ed.2d 280, 304–307.

17. The record includes a validation study of Test 21's relationship to performance in the recruit training program. The study was made by D.L. Futransky of the Standards Division, Bureau of Policies and Standards, United States Civil Service Commission. Findings of the study included data "support[ing] the conclusion that T[est] 21 is effective in selecting trainees who can learn the material that is taught at the Recruit School." Opinion evidence, submitted by qualified experts examining the Futransky study and/or conducting their own research, affirmed the correlation between scores on Test 21 and success in the training program. * * *

The Court of Appeals was "willing to assume for purposes of this appeal that appellees have shown that Test 21 is predictive of further progress in Recruit School."

and recruits' averages on training examinations only if (1) the training averages predict job performance or (2) the averages are proved to measure performance in job-related training. There is no proof that the recruits' average is correlated with job performance after completion of training. And although a positive relationship to the recruits' average might be sufficient to validate Test 21 if the average were proved to reflect mastery of material on the training curriculum that was in turn demonstrated to be relevant to job performance, the record is devoid of proof in this regard. First, there is no demonstration by petitioners that the training-course examinations measure comprehension of the training curriculum; indeed, these examinations do not even appear in the record. Furthermore, the Futransky study simply designated an average of 85 on the examination as a "good" performance and assumed that a recruit with such an average learned the material taught in the training course.[7] Without any further proof of the significance of a score of 85, and there is none in the record, I cannot agree that Test 21 is predictive of "success in training."

The EEOC regulations require that the validity of a job qualification test be proved by "empirical data demonstrating that the test is predictive of or significantly correlated with important elements of work behavior which comprise or are relevant to the job or jobs for which candidates are being evaluated." 29 CFR § 1607.4(c) (1975). This construction of Title VII was approved in *Albemarle,* where we quoted this provision and remarked that "[t]he message of these Guidelines is the same as that of the *Griggs* case." 422 U.S., at 431, 95 S.Ct., at 2378, 45 L.Ed.2d, at 304. The regulations also set forth minimum standards for validation and delineate the criteria that may be used for this purpose.

> "The work behaviors or other criteria of employee adequacy which the test is intended to predict or identify must be fully described; and, additionally, in the case of rating techniques, the appraisal form(s) and instructions to the rater(s) must be included as a part of the validation evidence. Such criteria may include measures other than actual work proficiency, such as training time, supervisory ratings, regularity of attendance and tenure. Whatever criteria are used they must represent major or critical work behaviors as revealed by careful job analyses." 29 CFR § 1607.5(b)(3) (1975).

This provision was also approved in *Albemarle,* 422 U.S., at 432, 95 S.Ct., at 2379, 45 L.Ed.2d, at 304, and n. 30.

If we measure the validity of Test 21 by this standard, which I submit we are bound to do, petitioners' proof is deficient in a number of ways similar to those noted above. First, the criterion of final training

---

7. The finding in the Futransky study on which the Court relies, was that Test 21 "is effective in selecting trainees who can learn the material that is taught at the Recruit School," because it predicts averages over 85. On its face, this would appear to be an important finding, but the fact is that *everyone* learns the material included in the training course. The study noted that all recruits pass the training examinations; if a particular recruit has any difficulty, he is given assistance until he passes.

examination averages does not appear to be "fully described." Although the record contains some general discussion of the training curriculum, the examinations are not in the record, and there is no other evidence completely elucidating the subject matter tested by the training examinations. Without this required description we cannot determine whether the correlation with training examination averages is sufficiently related to petitioners' need to ascertain "job-specific ability." See *Albemarle*, 422 U.S., at 433, 95 S.Ct., at 2379, 45 L.Ed.2d, at 305. Second, the EEOC regulations do not expressly permit validation by correlation to training performance, unlike the CSC instructions. Among the specified criteria the closest to training performance is "training time." All recruits to the Metropolitan Police Department, however, go through the same training course in the same amount of time, including those who experience some difficulty. See n. 7, *supra.* Third, the final requirement of § 1607.5(b)(3) has not been met. There has been no job analysis establishing the significance of scores on training examinations, nor is there any other type of evidence showing that these scores are of "major or critical" importance.

* * *

* * * Sound policy considerations support the view that, at a minimum, petitioners should have been required to prove that the police training examinations either measure job-related skills or predict job performance. Where employers try to validate written qualification tests by proving a correlation with written examinations in a training course, there is a substantial danger that people who have good verbal skills will achieve high scores on both tests due to verbal ability, rather than "job-specific ability." As a result, employers could validate any entrance examination that measures only verbal ability by giving another written test that measures verbal ability at the end of a training course. Any contention that the resulting correlation between examination scores would be evidence that the initial test is "job related" is plainly erroneous. It seems to me, however, that the Court's holding in this case can be read as endorsing this dubious proposition. Today's result will prove particularly unfortunate if it is extended to govern Title VII cases.

UNITED STATES v. STATE OF SOUTH CAROLINA

United States District Court, District of South Carolina, 1977.
445 F.Supp. 1094.

Before HAYNSWORTH and RUSSELL, CIRCUIT JUDGES and SIMONS, DISTRICT JUDGE.

For over thirty years [defendants] have used scores on the [National Teachers' Examinations (NTE)] to make decisions with respect to the certification of teachers and the amount of state aid payable to local school districts. Local school boards within the State use scores on the NTE for selection and compensation of teachers. From 1969 to 1976, a minimum score of 975 was required by the State for its certification and state aid decisions. In June, 1976, after an exhaustive validation study by Educational Testing Service (ETS), and, after a critical review and evaluation of this study by the Board of Education's Committee on Teacher Recruitment, Training and Compensation and the Department Staff, the State established new certification requirements involving different minimum scores in various areas of teaching specialization that range from 940 to 1198.

* * *

Plaintiffs have proved that the use of NTE scores by the State in its certification decisions disqualifies substantially disproportionate numbers of blacks. The burden of proof was thereby shifted to the defendants, and in an effort to meet this burden the State commissioned an extensive validity study by ETS. The design of this study is novel, but consistent with the basic requirements enunciated by the Supreme Court, and we accordingly hold such study sufficient to meet the burden placed on defendants under Title VII.

The study seeks to demonstrate content validity by measuring the degree to which the content of the tests matches the content of the teacher training programs in South Carolina. It also seeks to establish a minimum score requirement by estimating the amount of knowledge (measured by the ability to answer correctly test questions that have been content validated) that a minimally qualified teacher candidate in South Carolina would have.

To conduct the study, all 25 of the teacher training institutions in South Carolina were canvassed for experienced teacher educators in the various specialty fields tested in the NTE program. A group of 456 persons with the requisite professional credentials was assembled including representative numbers from each institution and both races. All were volunteers nominated by the colleges themselves. These 456 participants were divided into two general groups. One group was assigned the task of assessing the content validity of the NTE as compared to the curriculum in South Carolina institutions. The other was assigned the task of establishing the minimum score requirement. The two large groups were then each subdivided into panels of about 10 participants assigned to each test in the Common Examinations and each of the Area Examinations. The panelists were given the questions and answers on two current forms of the NTE and asked to record certain judgments about the tests.

Each content review panel member was asked to decide whether each question on the tests involved subject matter that was a part of the curriculum at his or her teacher training institution, and therefore could be judged to be appropriate for use in South Carolina. Each minimum score panel member was asked to look at each of the questions on the test and estimate the percentage of minimally qualified students in teacher education programs in South Carolina who would know the correct answer. Each test was evaluated by teacher educators specializing in the field or one of the major fields covered by the test. Art education teachers evaluated the test in Art Education; French teachers evaluated the test in French, and so on.

The content review panels determined that from 63% to 98% of the questions on the various tests were content valid for use in South Carolina. The panel members' overview of the tests as a whole also found the NTE to be sufficiently closely related to the curriculum in South Carolina to be an appropriate measure of achievement with respect to that curriculum.

The estimates made by the minimum score panel members (as to the percentage of minimally qualified students who would answer the question correctly) were combined statistically and analyzed to generate scaled scores that reflected, for each test, the level that would be achieved by the minimally knowledgeable candidate. Only test questions that had been determined by a majority of the content review panel members to be content appropriate for use in South Carolina were used in making the minimum score estimates.

* * *

The design of the validity study is adequate for Title VII purposes. The Supreme Court made clear once again in *Washington v. Davis* that a content validity study that satisfies professional standards also satisfies Title VII. 426 U.S. at 247, n. 13, 96 S.Ct. 2040. The defendants called as an expert witness Dr. Robert M. Guion, the principal author of *Standards for Educational and Psychological Tests* published by the American Psychological Association and a nationally recognized authority in the field of testing and measurement who testified in an unqualified fashion that in his expert opinion the ETS study design met all of the requirements of the APA Standards, the Division 14 Principles, and the EEOC Guidelines. Two other experts testified similarly, and ETS sought and obtained favorable opinions on the study design, before its implementation, from another two independent experts. The ETS decision to validate against the academic training program rather than job performance is specifically endorsed in principle in *Davis, supra* * * *.

NATIONAL EDUCATION ASS'N
v. SOUTH CAROLINA
Supreme Court of the United States, 1978.
434 U.S. 1026, 98 S.Ct. 756, 54 L.Ed.2d 775.

JUSTICE WHITE, with whom JUSTICE BRENNAN joins, dissenting [from the Court's summary affirmance on appeal].

For many years, South Carolina has used the National Teachers' Examinations (NTE) in hiring and classifying teachers despite the advice of its authors that it should not be used as the State uses it and despite the fact that it serves to disqualify a greater proportion of black applicants than white and to place a greater percentage of black teachers in lower paying classifications. For example, the new test score requirements contained in the 1976 revision of the State's plan will disqualify 83% of black applicants, but only 17.5% of white applicants; and 96% of the newly certified candidates permitted to teach will be white teachers.

This litigation began when the United States brought suit challenging the use of the NTE under both the Constitution and Title VII of the Civil Rights Act of 1964. The District Court upheld the State's use of the test and rejected both claims. Not only had plaintiffs failed to prove a racially discriminatory purpose in the State's uses of the NTE but, in the view of the District Court, the State had carried its burden of justifying the test despite its disparate racial impact.

The State's evidence in this regard consisted of a validation study prepared by the authors of the test at the request of the State. The District Court deemed the study sufficient to validate the NTE, even though the validation was not in relation to job performance and showed at best that the test measured the familiarity of the candidate with the content of certain teacher training courses.

Washington v. Davis, 426 U.S. 229, 96 S.Ct. 2040, 48 L.Ed.2d 597 (1976), was thought by the District Court to have warranted validating the test in terms of the applicant's training rather than against job requirements; but *Washington v. Davis,* in this respect, held only that the test there involved, which sought to ascertain whether the applicant had the minimum communication skills necessary to understand the offerings in a police training course, could be used to measure eligibility to enter that program. The case did not hold that a training course, the completion of which is required for employment, need not itself be validated in terms of job relatedness. Nor did it hold that a test that a job applicant must pass and that is designed to indicate his mastery of the materials or skills taught in the training course can be validated without reference to the job. Tests supposedly measuring an applicant's qualifications for employment, if they have differential racial impact, must bear some "manifest relationship to the employment in question," *Griggs v. Duke Power Co.,* 401 U.S. 424, 432, 91 S.Ct. 849, 854, 28 L.Ed.2d 158 (1971), and it is insufficient for the employer "to demonstrate some rational basis for the challenged practices." *Washington v. Davis, supra,* at 247, 96 S.Ct., at 2051.

The District Court here held that no other measures would satisfy the State's interest in obtaining qualified teachers and paying them fairly. But only two other States use the NTE for initial certification and South Carolina is the *only* State which uses the NTE in determining pay. Furthermore, the authors of the test themselves advise against using it for determining the pay for experienced teachers and believe that the NTE should not be the sole criterion for initial certification.

The question here is not merely whether the District Court, applying correct legal standards, reached the correct conclusion on the record before it, but whether the court was legally correct in holding that the NTE need not be validated against job performance and that the validation requirement was satisfied by a study which demonstrated only that a trained person could pass the test.

I therefore dissent from the Court's summary affirmance and would set the case for oral argument.

Notes and Questions

1.   Davis*'s Precedential Effect? Davis* reflects a considerably less deferential treatment of the EEOC Guidelines than that given by the Court in *Albemarle.* Is Justice Brennan right that the EEOC Guidelines require that before success on a training examination may be used as the criterion for validating an entrance test, the training test itself must be empirically shown to be related to the job? This is also the approach taken by the Uniform Guidelines, 29 C.F.R. § 1607.14(B)(3). Is it possible to dismiss the *Davis* Court's reference to Title VII as dicta since the events giving rise to the *Davis* litigation antedated the 1972 Amendments which made Title VII applicable to the Federal Government, the litigation had proceeded under § 1981, the D.C.Code and the Constitution, rather than under Title VII, and plaintiffs conceded in oral argument that Title VII filing requirements had not been complied with? See 426 U.S. at 238 n. 10, 96 S.Ct. at 2047 n. 10. The courts of appeals have tended to read *Davis* narrowly. See, e.g., Guardians Ass'n of the New York City Police Dep't v. Civil Service Comm'n, 633 F.2d 232, 247 (2d Cir.1980) (test seeking to do more than screen for minimal requirements for a training program must be job-related); Craig v. County of Los Angeles, 626 F.2d 659, 663 (9th Cir.1980). But cf. Commonwealth of Pennsylvania v. Flaherty, 983 F.2d 1267, 1273–74 (3d Cir.1993) (accepting correlation between scores on challenged pre-training written test and performance in police academy that taught skills "critical" for police work as proof of no discriminatory intent).

Can both *Davis* and *South Carolina* be further qualified by the fact that they preceded the promulgation in 1978 of the Uniform Guidelines on Employee Selection Procedures (UGESP)? The UGESP were jointly endorsed by the four federal agencies with EEO responsibilities—the EEOC, the U.S. Civil Service Commission (now Office of Personnel Management), and the Departments of Justice and Labor, and represented the culmination of an extensive reexamination of testing principles in consultation with industrial psychologists' Division 14 of the American Psychological Association.

2.   *Is Training Program Success a Valid Criterion?* When should it be permissible for an employer to predicate a test's validity on its capacity for predicting training program success without a further demonstration that such success is a good predictor of job performance or that what goes on in the training program closely mirrors the content of the job? Is it legitimate to take into account the cost of training to the employer? How do you assess the argument that the inability to demonstrate a statistically significant relationship between training performance and subsequent job performance may occur for reasons unrelated to the test's validity? Consider the following:

Employees who pass the training course have demonstrated a certain minimal competence and have obtained a certain level of knowledge and skill necessary to the job. Subsequent differences in job performance among these employees are, therefore, likely to reflect other characteristics—such as individual motivation in the job environment, dependability, or other personality traits—which are not incorporated in the training nor necessarily reflected in training performance. Individual differences, however, do not denigrate the importance of the trained knowledge or skill to successful job performance.

Dean Booth & James L. Mackay, Legal Constraints on Employment Testing and Evolving Trends in the Law, 29 Emory L.J. 121, 137 n. 78 (1980). If the training program does impart knowledge and skills necessary to the job, as assumed by Booth and Mackay, might content validation (see note 4 below) be possible even if criterion validation is not? Cf. *Guardians Ass'n of the New York City Police Dep't v. Civil Service Comm'n,* 630 F.2d 79 (2d Cir.1980), discussed at p. 174 infra (finding a multiple choice test for police officer jobs to be content valid, though rejecting particular cutoff score and rank ordering).

3. *Was* South Carolina *Distinguishable from* Davis? Even in light of *Davis,* was it appropriate for South Carolina, in the absence of a showing of job-relatedness, to use the NTE examination as it did? Did Justice White, who authored the *Davis* opinion, have a legitimate basis for distinguishing *Davis* in his dissent from the affirmance in *South Carolina?* Note that South Carolina began administering the NTE after a Fourth Circuit ruling invalidating a race-based dual pay system in Virginia similar to its own, and that the initial administration of the test resulted in 90% of the white teachers qualifying for the two highest pay categories while 73% of the black teachers fell within the two lowest pay categories. See United States v. South Carolina, 445 F.Supp. 1094, 1102 (D.S.C.1977), affirmed, 434 U.S. 1026, 98 S.Ct. 756, 54 L.Ed.2d 775 (1978).

4. *Content Validation. South Carolina* involved a second mode of test validation—content-based validation. Content validity is based not on a statistical correlation of success on the test with some criterion of job performance, but rather on the extent to which the test is correlated with the content of a job, by assessing a representative sample of important areas of job knowledge or skills required for success. Content validation, like criterion validation, thus must be related to the particular jobs at issue. Compare Williams v. Ford Motor Co., 187 F.3d 533 (6th Cir.1999) (upholding content-validation study for unskilled workers based on analysis of multiple job classifications through which workers could be expected to rotate), with Walston v. County School Bd., 492 F.2d 919 (4th Cir.1974) (National Teacher Examinations valid for some teaching positions may not be valid for others).

In the *South Carolina* case the state sought to show that the test was correlated not with the content of the job of teaching but rather with the content of teacher training programs. Was such an approach justifiable? Could the Court assume that the knowledge transmitted in teachers' colleges is representative of the body of knowledge teachers will need on the job? Should it be relevant that there was great variation of job content in the numerous institutions making up the state system? See Booth & Mackay, supra, at 139 n. 90.

Note on Uniform Guidelines and Employment Testing Litigation

The UGESP, while a considerably more flexible set of principles than the earlier, superseded EEOC Guidelines, nevertheless contemplate a fairly formal, empirical approach to the validation of scored tests. This formality generally has been accepted by testing professionals and courts since the promulgation of the UGESP. Justice O'Connor's plurality opinion for four Justices in *Watson* did state, in dicta, that "employers are not required, even when defending standardized or objective tests, to introduce formal 'validation studies' showing that particular criteria predict actual on-the-job performance." However, as noted above, § 105(b) of the Civil Rights Act of 1991 alludes to legislative history confirming pre-*Wards Cove* decisional law on establishing "business necessity", and as we have seen, that law had endorsed the kind of formal validation required by the UGESP for at least scored selection criteria. Moreover, in 1993, nine years after promising a review and possible revisions, the EEOC announced that it no longer anticipated changes in the Guidelines. 58 Fed. Reg. 25,902 (1993). The Guidelines thus are likely to continue to be influential in employment testing litigation, and should be reviewed.

The Disparate Impact Predicate

The Uniform Guidelines do not require test users to develop evidence of validity unless their selection procedures work a disparate impact on a statutorily protected group. However, because such evidence is gathered in any event for the purpose of assessing the usefulness of the testing program and because of the widespread perception that certain minorities do not perform as well as their white counterparts on standardized aptitude tests, see Haney, supra, 5 Indus.Rel.L.J. at 27 n. 131 (collecting authorities), large employers may undertake a validation effort pursuant to the UGESP in advance of any threat of litigation.

Local Validation

Under the UGESP and the case law, the general rule is one of local validation for the jobs tested at the particular site for which the test is being administered. The Uniform Guidelines offer some flexibility here. Interim use of a selection procedure is permitted provided "[t]he user has available substantial evidence of validity" and, where technically feasible, has a study in progress "which is designed to produce the additional evidence required by these guidelines within a reasonable time." 29 C.F.R. § 1607.5(J). Evidence for a particular unit covered by a multiunit study is not required "unless there are variables which are likely to affect validity significantly." Id. § 1607.7(C). Most importantly, users may rely on validity studies conducted by other test users or test publishers, provided that the evidence from these satisfies the guidelines and the jobs for which the user wishes to test are "substantially the same" as the jobs for which the validity studies were undertaken. Id. § 1607.7(B). This job-similarity requirement for "transportability" limits its practical utility; typically, both the professional literature and test manuals report the results of other validity studies without replicating or otherwise making accessible the job analyses underlying those studies. See American Society for Personnel Administration, A Professional and Legal Analysis of the Uniform Guidelines on Employee Selection Procedures 127 (1981).

Some professional opinion holds that job similarity data are not necessary where a large body of research has accumulated demonstrating the validity of particular cognitive measures for broadly formulated occupational categories. See, e.g., John E. Hunter, Frank Schmidt & Greg B. Jackson, Meta–Analysis: Cumulating Research Findings Across Studies (1982); Frank Schmidt, Kenneth Pearlman, John E. Hunter & Hannah Rothstein Hirsh, Forty Questions About Validity Generalization and Meta–Analysis, 38 Personnel Psych. 697 (1985). This approach, called "validity generalization," has been utilized by several offices of the United States Employment Service (USES), enjoys considerable professional endorsement, see Society for Industrial and Organizational Psychology, Principles for the Validation and Use of Personnel Selection Procedures: 26–27 (3d ed. 1987); Anne Anastasi, Psychological Testing 437 (5th ed. 1982); and some judicial recognition, see Pegues v. Mississippi State Employment Service, 488 F.Supp. 239, 254 (N.D.Miss. 1980), affirmed in part, 699 F.2d 760 (5th Cir.1983) (no adverse impact found); EEOC v. Atlas Paper Box Co., 680 F.Supp. 1184, 1189 (E.D.Tenn. 1987) (workforce too small for local validation), reversed, 868 F.2d 1487 (6th Cir.1989). It is doubtful, however, that validity generalization comports with the situation-specific validity premise of the Uniform Guidelines. See Vanguard Justice Society, Inc. v. Hughes, 471 F.Supp. 670, 731 (D.Md.1979); Dickerson v. United States Steel Corp., 472 F.Supp. 1304, 1338–40 (E.D.Pa. 1978), vacated sub nom. Worthy v. United States Steel Corp., 616 F.2d 698 (3d Cir.1980). In 1989, a government panel reviewed the reliability of validity generalization and issued a qualified endorsement of the approach with some criticism of its application to the test battery used by the USES. See Fairness in Employment Testing: Validity Generalization, Minority Issues, and the General Aptitude Test Battery, chs. 6–7 (John Hartigan & Alexandra K. Wigdor, eds. 1989).

Modes of Establishing Test Validity

The Uniform Guidelines contemplate three methods for establishing the validity of a scored selection procedure. The two principal approaches—criterion validation and content validation—were presented in the above cases. The third, construct validation, is used for tests which measure psychological "constructs," such as intelligence, verbal fluency, mechanical comprehension, and motivation. Test users are required through a job analysis to identify the construct or constructs necessary to successful job performance, and then to demonstrate that the test reliably measures that construct. The UGESP caution that this is "a relatively new and developing procedure in the employment field, and there is at present a lack of substantial literature extending the concept to employment practices." The UGESP hence require back-up criterion studies to demonstrate "[t]he relationship between the construct as measured by the selection procedure and the related work behavior(s) * * *." 29 C.F.R. § 1607.14(D)(3). Not surprisingly, construct validation has not been extensively utilized in the employment setting.

Although the EEOC Guidelines stated a preference for criterion studies, the UGESP adopt a neutral stance as between criterion and content approaches. Practical considerations are likely to influence which course is taken. Although criterion validation establishes a test's predictive capacity, the necessary empirical effort requires large test samples in order to produce useful correlations, and is therefore quite expensive to undertake. In contrast, the content validation effort is confined to an analysis of the job and the development of an appropriate test instrument.

Selected Issues in Criterion Validation

1. *Job Analysis.* Both criterion and content studies require a thorough analysis of the jobs for which tests are being administered (although the job analysis is likely to loom larger in significance in content studies). For criterion studies, the critical knowledge, skills and abilities (KSAs) identified in the job analysis will govern the range of test instruments considered appropriate, and more importantly will dictate the criterion measures that may be utilized. Only certain objective criteria, such as production rate, error rate, tardiness, length of service, etc., may be used without a full-scale job analysis. Otherwise, "[w]hatever criteria are used should represent important or critical work behavior(s) or work outcomes." 29 C.F.R. § 1607.14(B)(3). For example, as both *Griggs* and *Albemarle* illustrate, if promotability is a criterion, the job analysis should confirm that a majority of employees in the tested categories will progress to higher-level positions within a reasonable time.

2. *Selection of the Sample.* *Albemarle* involved what is called the "concurrent" variant of criterion validation. In that case, the tests were administered to incumbents who had been hired without testing and whose job performance scores may have been significantly influenced by on-the-job training and other workplace factors. The theoretically preferred approach—"predictive" criterion validation—would have been to control for these workplace factors by hiring a group of applicants irrespective of test scores, and then comparing subsequent performance against test scores. Practical considerations—such as the size of the group hired for a particular job, the unwillingness of employers to hire individuals deemed unqualified because of their test scores and the difficulties inherent in discharging low-test scorers once the "experiment" is concluded—explain the professional and judicial acceptance of the "concurrent" approach. But see Guardians Ass'n v. Civil Service Commission, 431 F.Supp. 526, 546 (S.D.N.Y.), vacated and remanded mem., 562 F.2d 38 (2d Cir.1977); Vulcan Society v. Civil Service Comm'n, 360 F.Supp. 1265, 1274 n. 28 (S.D.N.Y.1973), modified, 490 F.2d 387 (2d Cir.1973).

The widespread use of the "concurrent" approach, however, raises questions about the results of such studies. The range of scores is likely to be restricted because incumbents tend to be relatively homogenous in their abilities, and this drives down the correlation coefficients that can be expected. Such studies also may confuse the flow of causation—performance scores may be a function of on-the-job experience rather than the innate traits or skills measured by the test. They may also present "false negative" errors, for conceivably individuals denied employment might have performed as well as the incumbents. Finally, again as illustrated by *Albemarle,* the sample of incumbents may not be representative of the minority composition of the applicant pool; such representativeness is required "insofar as feasible" by the UGESP, 29 C.F.R. § 1607.14(B)(4).

3. *The Criterion Measure.* The criterion selected must represent important or critical work behaviors or outcomes, as reflected in the job analysis. A test may be deemed criterion valid even if it is found to be a good predictor only of a single criterion. But resting validity on only one criterion is a hazardous course because of the generally low correlation coefficients one is likely to obtain.

As *Albemarle* illustrates, to the extent the criterion is based on supervisor evaluations, steps must be taken to eliminate excessive subjectivity in performance ratings. The courts generally have insisted that supervisors make a focused evaluation of the employees in terms of the specific skills or work functions identified in the work analysis, rather than generalized assessments of overall job performance. In addition to *Albemarle,* see Watkins v. Scott Paper Co., 530 F.2d 1159, 1189 (5th Cir.1976); Brito v. Zia Co., 478 F.2d 1200, 1206 (10th Cir.1973); Rowe v. General Motors Corp., 457 F.2d 348, 358 (5th Cir.1972); Allen v. Isaac, 39 FEP Cas. 1142, 1147, 1154, 1157 (N.D.Ill.1986), vacated on other grounds, 881 f.2d 375 (7th cir. 1989). For successful use of supervisor ratings, see, e.g., Thompson v. McDonnell Douglas Corp., 416 F.Supp. 972, 982 (E.D.Mo.1976), affirmed, 552 F.2d 220 (8th Cir.1977); Arnold v. Ballard, 390 F.Supp. 723, 732 (N.D.Ohio 1975).

One concern here is, of course, the danger that the discriminatory preferences of supervisors will taint their performance ratings. The psychological literature suggests that a "halo" effect may cause even well-intentioned supervisors to rate particular employees positively on overall job performance because of subjective predispositions, whether based on physical appearance, irrelevant personal skills or other non-job related factors. *See* Patricia Cain Smith & L.M. Kendall, Retranslation of Expectations: An Approach to the Construction of Unambiguous Anchors for Rating Scales, 47 J. of Applied Psych. 149–55 (1963); Richard Campbell, Marvin D. Dunnette, Richard D. Arvey & Lowell V. Hellervik, The Development and Evaluation of Behaviorally Based Rating Scales, 57 J. of Applied Psych. 15–22 (1973).

The Uniform Guidelines are remarkably ambiguous on this point. On the one hand, test users are urged to develop carefully rating techniques and rater instructions because of "the possibility of bias in subjective evaluations," 29 C.F.R. § 1607.14(B)(2), and are admonished that "[w]hatever criteria are used should represent important or critical work behavior(s) or work outcomes," id. § 1607.14(B)(3). Yet, on the other hand, the UGESP permit use of "[a] standardized rating of overall work performance * * * where a study of the job shows that it is an important criterion." Id. Perhaps what is envisioned is evidence either that global assessments correlate closely with some hard objective performance measure, or of high correlations between one group of raters evaluating employees in terms of the KSAs identified in the job analysis and another group utilizing global ratings.

4. *Practical and Statistical Significance of the Correlations.* Once the test scores and criterion measures have been collected, the next step is to determine whether the correlations between the two sets of scores are strong enough to warrant a conclusion that the former is a good predictor of the latter. A perfect correlation between test scores and criterion measures is termed a 1.00 correlation coefficient, and would indicate that the test is a virtually flawless predictor of successful job performance. In the real world of job testing, such perfect correlations never occur. The size of the correlation coefficient will be a function of sample size and the range of differences in the tested group. The smaller the sample and the more homogenous the group, the greater the restriction on the range of scores obtainable. Because of practical considerations limiting sample size and prompting reliance on concurrent validity studies, relatively low correlations are sanctioned by the professional literature. One leading text suggests that "[u]nder certain circumstances, even validities as low as .20 and .30 may justify inclusion in a selection program," Anastasi, supra, at 160; and the American Psychological Association has stated that "most personnel research workers are usually pleased with a correlation of .30." Br. for the Exec. Comm. of the Div. of Industrial and Organizational Psychology, American Psychological Association as Amicus Curiae, A–3, in *United States v. Georgia Power Co.*, 474 F.2d 906 (5th Cir.1973).

With such low correlations, even "valid" tests offer only modest predictive power for the range of performance scores. By squaring the correlation coefficient, one can determine the "variance" in job performance predicted by the test instrument. Thus, a .30 correlation accounts for only 9 percent of the variance, a .40 correlation (which would be a very strong finding of validity) accounts for only 16 percent of the variance, and so on. The UGESP do not stipulate minimum correlation coefficients, preferring instead to balance the magnitude of the correlations against the degree of adverse impact, the importance and number of the aspects of job performance covered by the criteria, and the availability of other valid selection procedures with less adverse impact. See 29 C.F.R. § 1607.14(B)(6). The courts also have been reluctant to stipulate a minimally acceptable coefficient, although there is some authority that less than a .30 magnitude of correlation will not pass muster. See, e.g., Dickerson v. United States Steel Corp., supra, 20 FEP Cas. at 408; Boston Chapter, NAACP v. Beecher, 371 F.Supp. 507, 516 (D.Mass.), affirmed, 504 F.2d 1017, 1024 n. 13 (1st Cir.1974).

Not only must the magnitude of the correlation be practically useful, but also the results must be "statistically significant," which by convention normally means a .05 level of confidence, i.e., that the correlation relationship found will occur as a matter of chance no more than 5 out of 100 tries. The Uniform Guidelines adopt the .05 level of confidence convention as a "general" benchmark, but without identifying the circumstances which would justify departure from it. See 29 C.F.R. § 1607.14(B)(5). Sample size will determine the correlation coefficient necessary to obtain a .05 level of significance, as evidenced by the following chart, taken from Booth & Mackay, supra, 29 Emory L.J. at 174:

Minimum Number of Persons Tested	Minimum Coefficient
5	.75
25	.38
100	.195
1000	.06

5. *Differential Validity and Cut–Off Scores.* As discussed in the questions following *Albemarle,* the Uniform Guidelines require a study of the "fairness" or possibility of "differential validity" where "technically feasible." 29 C.F.R. § 1607.14(B)(8). "Unfairness" is defined as a situation where a test is found to have a disparate impact on a minority group and the difference in test scores is not related to differences in a measure of job performance. Where members of a minority group are shown by such a study to do better on the performance measure than on test scores, the user may either revise the selection procedure or set different cut-off scores ("continue to use the selection instrument operationally with appropriate revisions in its use to assure compatibility between the probability of successful job performance and the probability of being selected," id. § 1607.14(B)(8)(d)).

Section 106 of the Civil Rights Act of 1991, however, makes legally problematic the setting of lower cut-off scores for a minority group to reflect the differential validity of the test for that group. This section prohibits using "differential cutoff scores" or otherwise altering "the results of employment related tests on the basis of race, color, religion, sex, or national origin." See, e.g., Billish v. City of Chicago, 989 F.2d 890, 895 (7th Cir.1993) (giving extra points on tests on basis of race forbidden by § 106). Does this mean that an employer cannot alter passing scores for particular protected groups where doing so makes the test equally predictive of job success for those who benefit and those who do not benefit from the alteration?

Selected Issues in Content Validation

Content validation is more popular because it avoids the difficulties caused by narrow ranges of scores and small sample sizes in criterion studies. The theory of validity is not the test's predictive power but, rather, its ability to represent the content of the job itself: "A selection procedure can be supported by a content validity strategy to the extent that it is a representative sample of the content of the job." 29 C.F.R. § 1607.14(C)(1). As a leading test theorist has observed, because the test samples the job directly, eventual "performance in the domain [of work samples or work skills] sampled will be reflected in performance on the sample itself." Guion, "Content Validity" in Moderation, 31 Personnel Psych. 205, 209 (1978).

1. *Testing for Knowledge, Skills and Abilities (KSA).* In its simplest, least problematic form, a content-valid test would contain actual work samples from the job. The typing test conventionally given to secretarial candidates is a good example; typing speed, accuracy, and even language skills are tested in a manner replicating on-the-job conditions.

Standardized task-oriented tests that purport to identify higher-level potential also have been developed. One method, the assessment center, involves presenting applicants with a set of tasks, based on an analysis of the higher-level job, which are performed under the observation of a team of raters trained to assess potential for advancement. See D. Bray, R. Campbell & D. Grant, Formative Years in Business: A Long–Term AT & T Study of Managerial Lives (2d ed. 1979); Moses, The Development of an Assessment Center for the Early Identification of Supervisory Potential, 26 Personnel Psych. 569 (1973).

> A unique contribution of assessment centers is the inclusion of situational tests in the assessment battery. The rationale behind using such exercises is that they simulate the type of work to which the candidate will be exposed and allow his performance to be observed under somewhat realistic conditions. Contrary to the aptitude test approach, samples, not signs of behavior, are used for prediction.

Howard, An Assessment of Assessment Centers, 17 Acad.Mgmt.J. 115, 117 (1974).

The Uniform Guidelines also sanction, however, the use of content validity for selection procedures which sample not actual work tasks but the KSA's necessary to successful job performance, provided that the skill or ability being measured is "operationally defined in terms of observable aspects of work behavior of the job." 29 CFR § 1607.14(C)(4). The content strategy may not be used, the UGESP caution, for tests "which purport to measure traits or constructs, such as intelligence, aptitude, personality, common sense, judgment, leadership, and spatial ability," or where the KSA's in question will be expected to be learned on the job. Id. § 1607.14(C)(1). A sliding scale inquiry is envisioned:

> As the content of the selection procedure less resembles a work behavior, or the setting and manner of the administration of the selection procedure less resemble the work situation, or the result less resembles a work product, the less likely the selection procedure is to be content valid, and the greater the need for other evidence of validity.

Id. § 107.14(C)(4).

Despite these disclaimers, with this extension of the content strategy to scored tests which measure skills and abilities rather than work tasks, the UGESP blur the distinctions between content and construct validity and create a risk that employers will be permitted to use selection procedures which closely resemble aptitude tests but without having to demonstrate ability to predict successful job performance.

Witness the Second Circuit's consideration of a test for entry-level policemen in Guardians Ass'n of New York City v. Civil Service Comm'n, 630 F.2d 79, 93–94 (2d Cir.1980):

> [A]bilities, at least those that require any thinking, and constructs are simply different segments along a continuum reflecting a person's capacity to perform various categories of tasks. This continuum starts with precise capacities and extends to increasingly abstract ones—from the capacity for filling out forms to the capacity for exercising judgment.
>
> Recognition that abilities and constructs are not entirely distinct leads to a conclusion that a validation technique for purposes of determining Title VII compliance can be best selected by a functional approach that focuses on the nature of the job. The crucial question under

Title VII is job relatedness—whether or not the abilities being tested for are those that can be determined by direct, verifiable observation to be required or desirable for the job * * *.

* * *

Applying the approach just outlined, we conclude, at least as an initial matter, that content validation may properly be selected as the appropriate technique for assessing Exam No. 8155. The exam tests for three basic abilities (although it purports to test for five): the ability to remember details, the ability to fill out forms, and the ability to apply general principles to specific facts. The third ability is assessed in three contexts: the application of general statements of criminal offenses to the facts of specific events, the application of procedures and standards to the facts of specific policing activities, and the application of procedures and standards to the facts of specific situations involving human relations problems. The three basic abilities are not so abstract, on their face, as to preclude content validation, provided that subsequent consideration of the job analysis does not demonstrate that important and more concrete abilities necessary to the job were needlessly omitted * * *. Though all three abilities involve some inference about mental processes, they are based on observable behaviors and are far less abstract than such traits as intelligence, leadership and judgment * * *. Though all three abilities can be trained to some extent, the test-makers were entitled to select applicants with existing ability so that training would enhance their abilities and prepare them for other tasks requiring similar talents.

See also Gillespie v. Wisconsin, 771 F.2d 1035 (7th Cir.1985) ("abilities to communicate in standard written English, to prepare a written job description, and to place the analysis of a recruiting problem in acceptable form are concrete, observable and quantifiable characteristics" that may be subject to content validation). Cf. also Gulino v. New York State Educ. Dept., 460 F.3d 361 (2d Cir. 2006) (two standardized certification tests for all teachers subject to content validation under *Guardians* standards); Association of Mexican–American Educators v. State of California, 231 F.3d 572 (9th Cir.2000) (finding valid single test for all California teachers, counselors, and school administrators, used to measure reading, writing, and mathematical skills).

But contrast the Eighth Circuit's invalidation of a fire-scene simulation test in which candidates for promotion to fire fighter captain positions were shown slides of a large fire and were asked to respond in writing to questions regarding their observations and what orders they would give:

The fire scene simulation * * * cannot avoid testing the candidate's proficiency in the written exercise of verbal skills which is certainly not a critical or necessary job behavior for a fire captain. The candidates may be very proficient at assessing the scene of a fire and issuing appropriate oral orders but ineffectual in communicating those orders in writing.

Firefighters Institute v. City of St. Louis, 616 F.2d 350, 361 (8th Cir.1980).

2. *Job Analysis and Test Construction.* For content validity, the key stages will be job analysis and test construction. Considerable care must be taken to ensure that the job analysis identifies all the important work behaviors or skills and their relative importance, and that the selection procedure is "representative" of the job, in that it tests for "critical work behavior(s) and/or important work behavior(s) constituting most of the job." 29 C.F.R. § 1607.14(C)(2).

The extent to which the test is representative of key work behaviors and skills will often be the focus of litigation. In the *Guardians Ass'n* suit, the Second Circuit sustained the test for entry-level police officers despite its failure to measure for human relations skills identified by the job analysis as important:

> [T]he [skills the test] did measure—memory, the ability to fill out forms, and the ability to apply rules to factual situations—are all significant aspects of entry-level police work. To be sure, this conclusion would have been easier to reach if the City had spelled out the relationship between the abilities that were tested for and the job behaviors that had been identified. But the relationship is sufficiently apparent to indicate that the City was not seizing on minor aspects of the police officer's job as the basis for selection of candidates. The inadequate assessment of human relations skill lessens the representativeness of the exam and consequently lessens its degree of content validity, but this deficiency is not fatal, especially in light of the difficulty of measuring such an abstract ability.

630 F.2d at 99. Judge Sifton, concurring separately, was more skeptical on this point:

> While I join in rejecting the argument of the United States as *amicus,* that the requirement of representativeness means that *all* the knowledges, skills and abilities needed for police work must be tested, each in its proper proportions, I disagree with the [majority's] conclusion that an exam which contains omissions as extensive as the present exam meets the "representative requirements to an adequate degree."

* * *

> The practical effect of validating a test for New York City police work which does not examine for human relations skills is to leave out of the entry level employment decision an area of qualifications in which minority groups would, one must assume, perform well despite educational and other deprivations.

Id. at 113–14 (emphasis in original).

3. *Scoring.* The reliability of the test scores obtained as a measure of job performance, while also an issue in criterion studies, is particularly important here, because of the absence of empirical evidence of the predictive capacity of the selection procedure. The USESP provide:

> If a user can show, by a job analysis or otherwise, that a higher score on a content valid selection procedure is likely to result in better job performance, the results may be used to rank persons who score above minimum levels. Where a selection procedure supported solely or pri-

marily by content validity is used to rank job candidates, the selection procedure should measure those aspects of performance which differentiate among levels of job performance.

29 C.F.R. § 1607.14(C)(9). Some courts have required additional empirical evidence of the ability of the test to differentiate among levels of performance before it may be used as a basis for rank-ordering of candidates. See, e.g., Guardians Ass'n of New York City v. Civil Service Comm'n, supra, 630 F.2d at 100; Firefighters Institute v. City of St. Louis, supra, 616 F.2d at 358–60; Thomas v. City of Evanston, 610 F.Supp. 422, 431 (N.D.Ill.1985). Such a requirement may reduce the attractiveness of the content strategy for public-sector employers who often are required by state law to make selection decisions on the basis of rank-ordering of examination results.

The Guidelines provide that "[w]here cutoff scores are used, they should normally be set so as to be reasonable and consistent with normal expectations of acceptable proficiency within the work force." 29 C.F.R. § 1607.5(H). Compare Lanning v. Southeastern Pennsylvania Transportation Authority, 181 F.3d 478 (3d Cir.1999) (study showing that factor is "related to the job" is not alone sufficient to validate cutoff), with Lanning v. Southeastern Transportation Authority, 308 F.3d 286, 291 (3d Cir.2002) (finding business necessity for cutoff based on study that those who passed test had 70% to 90% success rate on job standards, while those who did not had only 5% to 20% success rate). In *Guardians Ass'n* the Second Circuit stated that an employer might establish a valid cutoff score "by analyzing the test results to locate a logical 'break-point' in the distribution of scores." 630 F.2d at 105. In Association of Mexican–American Educators v. State of California, supra, 231 F.3d at 590, the Ninth Circuit upheld a cutoff score as "logical" and "reasonable", even though it was slightly above that considered a passing score by a majority of expert readers relied on to validate the test.

The Plaintiff's Rebuttal Case

The Uniform Guidelines require test users to undertake, as part of an adequate validity study, "an investigation of suitable alternative selection procedures and suitable alternative methods of using the selection procedure which have as little adverse impact as possible, to determine the appropriateness of using or validating them in accord with these guidelines." 29 C.F.R. § 1607.3(B). The "Supplementary Information" section which accompanies the UGESP states:

> In conducting a validation study, the employer should consider available alternatives which will achieve its legitimate business purpose with lesser adverse impact. The employer cannot concentrate solely on establishing the validity of the instrument or procedure which it has been using in the past.

43 Fed.Reg. 38290, 38291 (Aug. 25, 1978).

Although some courts followed the UGESP in requiring such a showing from employers, see, e.g., Allen v. City of Mobile, 464 F.Supp. 433, 439–40 (S.D.Ala.1978), this approach now seems inconsistent with *Wards Cove*'s analysis, and with the 1991 Act's placement on plaintiffs of the burden of proof on the existence of an alternative employment practice.

Note on Nonscored, Objective Selection Criteria

We know from cases like *Griggs, Beazer* and *Dothard* that many employment practices other than the use of scored tests can be challenged because of their disparate impact. Disparate impact challenges have been brought against educational, prior-experience, English language proficiency, and residency requirements, height-and-weight restrictions, antinepotism rules, exclusions of former convicts or drug users, and many similar practices.

"Facial Validity"

The Uniform Guidelines, with their insistence on empirical demonstration of validity, purport to apply to all selection procedures: "These guidelines apply to tests and other selection procedures which are used as a basis for any employment decision." 29 C.F.R. § 1607.2(B). However, as *Dothard* and *Beazer* (to the extent its discussion of business justification is not dicta despite the Court's rejection of plaintiffs' prima facie case) illustrate, the courts have allowed a considerably less rigorous, "facial validity" demonstration of the business necessity for nonscored, objective selection requirements. Despite the facts of *Griggs*, "facial validity" review has been routinely applied to educational requirements for positions other than factory workers. Witness, for example, the Fifth Circuit's acceptance of the City of Dallas's requirement that applicants for police officers must have completed 45 semester hours of college credit with at least a C average at an accredited institution of higher education:

> Because of the professional nature of the job, coupled with the risks and public responsibility inherent in the position, we conclude that empirical evidence is not required to validate the job relatedness of the educational requirement. This is not to say, of course, that validation is not required. We simply recognize that the danger the hiring of an unqualified police officer might pose to the public and the impossibility of reducing job characteristics to measurable components separate the position of police officer from jobs considered in cases where validation studies were required.

Davis v. City of Dallas, 777 F.2d 205, 217 (5th Cir.1985). The Seventh Circuit has recognized the presumptive validity of a high school education for corrections officers: "Sometimes the appropriateness of an educational requirement is sufficiently obvious to allow dispensing with empirical validation." Aguilera v. Cook County Police and Corrections Merit Bd., 760 F.2d 844, 847 (7th Cir.1985).

To some extent, these rulings are explainable as instances of judicial reluctance to second-guess employer judgments where the costs of an erroneous selection decision are likely to affect not simply employer profits, but also the safety of the public. An explicit statement of the judicial caution underlying what might be termed a "variable business-necessity" approach can be found in Spurlock v. United Airlines, Inc., 475 F.2d 216, 219 (10th Cir.1972), sustaining United's requirement of a college degree and 500 prior flight hours for employment as an airline flight officer:

When a job requires a small amount of skill and training and the consequences of hiring an unqualified applicant are insignificant, the courts should examine closely any pre-employment standard or criteria which discriminate against minorities * * *. On the other hand, when the job clearly requires a high degree of skill and the economic and human risks involved in hiring an unqualified applicant are great, the employer bears a corresponding lighter burden to show that his employment criteria are job-related * * *. The courts, therefore, should proceed with great caution before requiring an employer to lower his pre-employment standards for such a job.

Cf. El v. Southeastern Pennsylvania Trans. Auth., 479 F.3d 232 (3d Cir. 2007) (no prior conviction qualification for drivers for the disabled shown to be a "business necessity" based on expert testimony on risks to passengers); Lanning v. Southeastern Pennsylvania Transp. Authority, 308 F.3d 286, supra, (maximum time of 12 minutes for 1.5 mile run as requirement for transit patrol shown to measure "minimum" qualification for job); Fitzpatrick v. City of Atlanta, 2 F.3d 1112 (11th Cir.1993) (upholding "no-beard" policy for firefighters notwithstanding disparate impact on blacks); Zamlen v. City of Cleveland, 906 F.2d 209 (6th Cir.1990) (upholding physical test for firefighters notwithstanding disparate impact on women); Porter v. Kansas, 757 F.Supp. 1224 (D.Kan.1991) (upholding lifting test for psychiatric aides notwithstanding impact on women); United States v. City of Wichita Falls, 704 F.Supp. 709 (N.D.Tex.1988) (upholding physical tests for police officers notwithstanding impact on women). But cf. EEOC v. Dial Corp., 469 F.3d 735 (8th Cir. 2006) (strength test for workers in sausage plant not shown to be necessary to reduce injuries); Pietras v. Farmingville Fire Dist., 180 F.3d 468 (2d Cir.1999) (test for ability to drag especially heavy fire hose not job related for firefighters).

Prior-experience requirements have not fared well for blue-collar positions, however, see, e.g., Davis v. Richmond, Fredericksburg and Potomac R.R. Co., 803 F.2d 1322 (4th Cir.1986) (training program for locomotive engineers); Kilgo v. Bowman Transp., Inc., 789 F.2d 859 (11th Cir.1986) (over-the-road truck drivers), or first-level supervisors, see, e.g., Walker v. Jefferson County Home, 726 F.2d 1554 (11th Cir.1984).

Legitimate Business Justifications or Job–Relatedness?

To a considerable extent, the critical force of the *Griggs* challenge has stemmed from its insistence that ostensibly neutral policies having a disparate impact not be allowed unless they are needed for successful job performance. Thus, policies which might pass muster under a more deferential, "rational basis" regime, such as an exclusion of former convicts, see, e.g., Green v. Missouri Pacific R.R., 523 F.2d 1290 (8th Cir.1975), inquiries into arrest records, see, e.g., Gregory v. Litton Systems, Inc., 472 F.2d 631 (9th Cir.1972), use of only English language on the job, see Maldonado v. City of Altus, 433 F.3d 1294 (10th Cir. 2006), and residency requirements, see United States v. Village of Elmwood Park, 43 FEP Cases 995 (N.D.Ill. 1987), have been subject to challenge because of the absence of a demonstrated relationship to the legitimate requirements of the job.

Section 105 of the Civil Rights Act of 1991 requires a showing that an employment practice with a disparate impact be justified as "job related for the position in question and consistent with business necessity." Does this mean that an employer cannot defend practices that further business, though not job-related, goals? Some policies are thought, for example, to promote a desirable, and ultimately more productive, workplace environment even though a direct relationship to job performance is difficult to demonstrate, empirically or otherwise. See, e.g., Roman v. Cornell Univ., 53 F.Supp.2d 223, 237 (N.D.N.Y. 1999) (accepting English language-only rule for "avoiding or lessening interpersonal conflicts, preventing non-foreign language speaking individuals from feeling left out of conversations, and preventing non-foreign language speaking individuals from feeling that they are being talked about in a language they do not understand"). Some courts have sustained antinepotism rules because they "plausibly improve[ ] the work environment" despite the fact that the employer cannot "prove that its rule increases production * * *." Yuhas v. Libbey–Owens–Ford Co., 562 F.2d 496, 499–500 (7th Cir.1977). Moreover, provisions of health and welfare benefit plans are difficult to justify in job-relatedness terms. Consider the Sixth Circuit's rationale for upholding a "head of household" provision of a medical and dental insurance plan which permits an employee to elect coverage for his or her spouse only if the spouse earns less than the employee:

> As found by the district judge, Penney adopted the head of household requirement in order to 'provide the greatest benefits for the people who need the coverage,' 632 F.Supp. 871, 874, workers without a more highly paid spouse, and because the head of household requirement was an administratively efficient proxy to avoid covering those spouses most likely to have coverage from their own employers. This is a legitimate business justification for choosing this method of supplying an insurance coverage benefit. Any employer choosing a comprehensive fringe benefit package faces the challenge of maximizing employee satisfaction while minimizing or controlling cost. Penney could legitimately conclude that insurance would be more likely valuable to the lower-paid spouse, and thus would engender more satisfaction in the employee.

EEOC v. J.C. Penney Co. Inc., 843 F.2d 249, 253 (6th Cir.1988). Is the Sixth Circuit correct that cost-minimization or administrative convenience should justify a policy having a disparate impact on protected groups? Should this justification be limited to benefits policies? Consider the application of such justification to the discharge of employees who have had their wages repeatedly garnished. See, e.g., Johnson v. Pike Corporation of America, 332 F.Supp. 490 (C.D.Cal.1971). See generally, Mark Brodin, Costs, Profits, and Equal Employment Opportunity, 62 Notre D. L.Rev. 318 (1987) (arguing against cost-based defense).

A related question is the extent to which employers may seek to promote external social policies through requirements which work an adverse impact on minority groups. An example is suggested by employer policies of administering urine tests to employees for the purpose of identifying and removing from the workforce present drug users, even though the tests typically used do not measure recency of use or on-the-job impairment. Cf. Chaney v.

Southern Ry. Co., 847 F.2d 718, 725 (11th Cir.1988) (allowing disparate impact challenge).

Note on the Defense of Subjective Evaluation Systems

Many courts have implicitly drawn a distinction between challenges to subjective evaluation systems for blue collar, relatively low responsibility jobs, on the one hand, and challenges to subjective systems for supervisory, managerial and relatively high responsibility positions, on the other. For the former, the courts generally have been suspicious of the delegation of unguided discretion to low-level supervisors, and willing to proscribe such delegations based on statistical disparities, often presented as part of a systemic disparate treatment case. See, e.g., Rowe v. General Motors Corp., 457 F.2d 348 (5th Cir.1972); Brown v. Gaston County Dyeing Mach. Co., 457 F.2d 1377, 1382 (4th Cir.1972); cf., e.g., United States v. City of Chicago, 549 F.2d 415, 432 (7th Cir.1977) (no justification for disparate impact caused by use of vague criteria for background check of police applicants).

By contrast, the courts generally have accepted employers' claims that supervisory, managerial or professional jobs require key attributes measurable only by subjective judgments. See, e.g., Scott v. Parkview Memorial Hospital, 175 F.3d 523 (7th Cir.1999); Ezold v. Wolf, Block, Schorr & Solis–Cohen, 983 F.2d 509, 527–28 (3d Cir.1992); Zahorik v. Cornell University, 729 F.2d 85, 96 (2d Cir.1984). *Zahorik,* cited with apparent approval by the *Watson* plurality, sustained a university's subjective tenure review process as "an historically settled process" using "plainly relevant criteria". The Second Circuit broadly deferred to the university's business judgment as to the degree of subjectivity required for selecting a tenured faculty, and did not require a study showing that Cornell's selection system produced "better" academic departments. But see, e.g., Bennun v. Rutgers State Univ., 941 F.2d 154, 174 (3d Cir.1991) (cautioning that Title VII requires searching review even for promotion and tenure decisions); Sweeney v. Board of Trustees of Keene State College, 569 F.2d 169, 176 (1st Cir.), vacated & remanded on other grounds, 439 U.S. 24, 99 S.Ct. 295, 58 L.Ed.2d 216 (1978) (cautioning against excessive judicial deference).

Even for higher-level positions the courts may be skeptical of vague or attitudinal subjective selection criteria, such as "skill" or "trust" or "ability to get along with people." See, e.g., Stallworth v. Shuler, 777 F.2d 1431 (11th Cir.1985); Crawford v. Western Elec. Co., Inc., 614 F.2d 1300, 1314 (5th Cir.1980). Employers may be required to explain why they cannot guide their decisionmakers with criteria that state more precisely, and with reference to specific knowledge, skills and abilities, what is required for successful job performance. Courts also consider the procedural protections offered those judged by subjective evaluations: Did a candidate for promotion have an opportunity to review and comment upon a written evaluation? See, e.g., Pouncy v. Prudential Ins. Co., 499 F.Supp. 427, 448 (S.D.Tex.1980), affirmed, 668 F.2d 795 (5th Cir.1982). Did the subjective evaluation reflect the judgments of multiple evaluators? See, e.g., Frink v. United States Navy, 16 FEP 67, 69–70 (E.D.Pa.1977), affirmed mem., 609 F.2d 501 (3d Cir.1979), cert. denied, 445 U.S. 930, 100 S.Ct. 1319, 63 L.Ed.2d 763 (1980). Plaintiffs may have difficulty proving that the lack of any particular procedures caused the disparate impact, but courts may be less likely to accept as justifiable a system lacking certain minimum procedures.

It seems doubtful, however, that courts will go beyond requiring reasonable specificity of standards and minimum procedures, to also require formal validation studies. As noted, the *Watson* plurality specifically eschewed formal validation. The plurality further stated:

> In the context of subjective or discretionary employment decisions, the employer will often find it easier than in the case of standardized tests to produce evidence of a "manifest relationship to the employment in question." It is self-evident that many jobs, for example those involving managerial responsibilities, require personal qualities that have never been considered amenable to standardized testing.

487 U.S. at 999, 108 S.Ct. at 2791. See also Andrew C. Spiropoulos, Defining the Business Necessity Defense to the Disparate Impact Cause of Action: Finding the Golden Mean, 74 N.C. L.Rev. 1479 (1996) (arguing that employers should be given more discretion in selecting employees for more complex jobs requiring special skills and qualities that cannot be measured empirically).

Careful job analysis would help insure that particular subjective standards reflected skills and abilities necessary to the jobs in question. However, the validation strategies authorized by the Uniform Guidelines appear to be designed for assessing the validity of proxies for individualized considerations, rather than the validity of the delegation of subjective discretion to engage in such considerations. Most challenges to subjective processes are to the delegation of discretion, not simply the standards used. Moreover, criterion validation ultimately depends on some assessor's subjective evaluation of performance. Subjective performance evaluations (absent any of the pitfalls identified in *Albemarle*) typically provide the criterion against which the predictive capacity of scored tests is measured. This problem cannot be avoided unless objectively measurable standards, independent of those specified by employers, are imposed to define what makes a good professor or physician or manager. This may not be feasible or desirable in all settings.

Might employers be required to use assessment center techniques as an alternative to validation? See pp. 173–74 supra. This approach offers the advantage of testing applicants under simulated conditions of the actual jobs in question. Here too, however, reliance on an assessor's subjective evaluation cannot be avoided. Moreover, one may ask how much of a manager's range of responsibilities can be simulated at tolerable cost levels.

E.   DISCRIMINATION BY UNIONS

Section 703(c) of Title VII proscribes the same five types of status discrimination (race, color, religion, sex, or national origin) by a labor organization that § 703(a) prohibits by employers. "Labor organization" is defined broadly in § 701(d) to include any kind of group or plan that exists in whole or in part to deal with employers in behalf of employees, and that also is "engaged in an industry affecting commerce". Section 701(e) in turn defines when a labor organization is so engaged. It must operate a hiring hall or have at least fifteen members, and also either be certified as a bargaining representative under federal labor laws, be recognized as such a representative by an employer engaged in an industry affecting commerce, or be formally associated with a body that is or seeks to become such a representative. Since an "industry affecting commerce" is defined by § 701(h) to include any governmental industry, unions representing state and local governmental employees are covered by § 703(c). The coverage of federal employee unions seems more problematic because the federal government is excluded from the definition of employer in § 701(b); and § 717 only covers discrimination in federal "personnel actions", not by federal unions. But see Jennings v. American Postal Workers Union, 672 F.2d 712 (8th Cir.1982). Unions with fifteen or more employees of course may be covered as private employers, whether or not their business activity as the representative of the employees of other employers is covered.

Title VII's prohibition of union discrimination in § 703(c) is as comprehensive as its prohibition of employer discrimination in § 703(a). Section 703(c) has been interpreted to proscribe both discrimination in the representation of employees and in the conduct of internal union affairs. Unions thus cannot discriminate in the selection of members, in the dispensation of union benefits and burdens, in helping workers to obtain or retain jobs, or in obtaining and protecting the benefits of employment. See, e.g., Maalik v. Int'l Union of Elevator Constructors, Local 2, 437 F.3d 650 (7th Cir. 2006) (union responsible for a member's discriminatory operation of apprentice program under union's authority). One decision found illegal a union's discriminatory organizational strategies. Gray v. Bartenders, Local 52, No. C 73–838, 1974 WL 10575 (N.D.Cal.1974). Several courts have entertained disparate impact challenges to union membership and apprenticeship requirements. See, e.g., EEOC v. Steamship Clerks Union, Local 1066, 48 F.3d 594 (1st Cir. 1995); United States v. Ironworkers, Local 86, 443 F.2d 544 (9th Cir. 1971). Furthermore, § 703(c)(3) expressly prohibits causing or attempting to cause an employer to discriminate in violation of the Act.

The decision that follows, however, raises the difficult issue of whether § 703 imposes affirmative duties on unions to resist an employer's discriminatory practices. The union defendants in this case were the exclusive representatives of all the firm's employees within units determined to be appropriate for bargaining by the National Labor Relations Board. This bargaining authority and the nature of the collective bargaining agreements that the unions negotiated gave the unions exclusive control over when the negotiated grievance system could be invoked. Absent a breach of the union's duty of fair representation, that grievance procedure provided the exclusive means of enforcing employee claims under the labor contract.

GOODMAN v. LUKENS STEEL CO.

Supreme Court of the United States, 1987.
482 U.S. 656, 107 S.Ct. 2617, 96 L.Ed.2d 572.

JUSTICE WHITE delivered the opinion of the Court.

In 1973, individual employees of Lukens Steel Company (Lukens) brought this suit on behalf of themselves and others, asserting racial discrimination claims under Title VII of the Civil Rights Act of 1964, 78 Stat. 253, as amended, 42 U.S.C. § 2000e *et seq.*, and 42 U.S.C. § 1981 against their employer and their collective-bargaining agents, the United Steelworkers of America and two of its local unions (Unions). * * * On the merits, the District Court found that Lukens had discriminated in certain respects, but that in others plaintiffs had not made out a case. The District Court concluded that the Unions were also guilty of discriminatory practices, specifically in failing to challenge discriminatory discharges of probationary employees, failing and refusing to assert instances of racial discrimination as grievances, and in tolerating and tacitly encouraging racial harassment. The District Court entered separate injunctive orders against Lukens and the Unions, reserving damages issues for further proceedings. [*Eds.* The Court of Appeals affirmed the liability judgment against the Unions.]

The Unions contend that the judgment against them rests on the erroneous legal premise that Title VII and § 1981 are violated if a Union passively sits by and does not affirmatively oppose the employer's racially discriminatory employment practices. It is true that the District Court declared that mere Union passivity in the face of employer discrimination renders the Union liable under Title VII and, if racial animus is properly inferable, under § 1981 as well.[10] We need not discuss this rather abstract observation, for the court went on to say that the evidence proves "far more" than mere passivity.[11] As found by the court, the facts were that since 1965, the collective-bargaining contract con-

---

10. The first part of this statement must have been addressed to disparate impact, for discriminatory motive is required in disparate treatment Title VII cases as it is in § 1981 claims. See *Teamsters v. United States,* 431 U.S. 324, 335–336, n. 15, 97 S.Ct. 1843, 1854–1855, n. 15, 52 L.Ed.2d 396 (1977); *General Building Contractors Ass'n Inc. v. Pennsylvania,* 458 U.S. 375, 391, 102 S.Ct. 3141, 3150, 73 L.Ed.2d 835 (1982). Because the District Court eventually found that in each respect the Unions violated both Title VII and § 1981 in exactly the same way, liability did not rest on a claim under Title VII that did not rest on intentional discrimination.

11. The District Court commented that there was substantial evidence, related to events occurring prior to the statute of limitations period, which "casts serious doubt on the unions' total commitment to racial

equality." The District Court noted that it was the company, not the Unions, which pressed for a nondiscrimination clause in the collective-bargaining agreement. The District Court found that the Unions never took any action over the segregated locker facilities at Lukens and did not complain over other discriminatory practices by the company. The District Court found that when one employee approached the president of one of the local unions to complain about the segregated locker facilities in 1962, the president dissuaded him from complaining to the appropriate state agency. The District Court, however, found "inconclusive" the evidence offered in support of the employees' claim that the Unions discriminated against blacks in their overall handling of grievances under the collective-bargaining agreement.

tained an express clause binding both the employer and the Unions not to discriminate on racial grounds; that the employer was discriminating against blacks in discharging probationary employees, which the Unions were aware of but refused to do anything about by way of filing proffered grievances or otherwise; that the Unions had ignored grievances based on instances of harassment which were indisputably racial in nature; and that the Unions had regularly refused to include assertions of racial discrimination in grievances that also asserted other contract violations.[12]

* * *

The Unions insist that it was error to hold them liable for not including racial discrimination claims in grievances claiming other violations of the contract. The Unions followed this practice, it was urged, because these grievances could be resolved without making racial allegations and because the employer would "get its back up" if racial bias was charged, thereby making it much more difficult to prevail. The trial judge, although initially impressed by this seemingly neutral reason for failing to press race discrimination claims, ultimately found the explanation "unacceptable" because the Unions also ignored grievances which involved racial harassment violating the contract covenant against racial discrimination but which did not also violate another provision. The judge also noted that the Unions had refused to complain about racially based terminations of probationary employees, even though the express undertaking not to discriminate protected this group of employees, as well as others, and even though, as the District Court found, the Unions knew that blacks were being discharged at a disproportionately higher rate than whites. In the judgment of the District Court, the virtual failure by the Unions to file any race-bias grievances until after this lawsuit started, knowing that the employer was practicing what the contract prevented, rendered the Unions' explanation for their conduct unconvincing.

As we understand it, there was no suggestion below that the Unions held any racial animus against or denigrated blacks generally. Rather, it was held that a collective-bargaining agent could not, without violating Title VII and § 1981, follow a policy of refusing to file grievable racial discrimination claims however strong they might be and however sure the agent was that the employer was discriminating against blacks. The Unions, in effect, categorized racial grievances as unworthy of pursuit and, while pursuing thousands of other legitimate grievances, ignored racial discrimination claims on behalf of blacks, knowing that the employer was discriminating in violation of the contract. * * *

The courts below, in our view, properly construed and applied Title VII and § 1981. Those provisions do not permit a union to refuse to file

12. The District Court also found that although the Unions had objected to the company's use of certain tests, they had never done so on racial grounds, even though they "were certainly chargeable with knowledge that many of the tests" had a racially disparate impact.

any and all grievances presented by a black person on the ground that the employer looks with disfavor on and resents such grievances. It is no less violative of these laws for a union to pursue a policy of rejecting disparate treatment grievances presented by blacks solely because the claims assert racial bias and would be very troublesome to process.

JUSTICE POWELL, with whom JUSTICE SCALIA joins, and with whom JUSTICE O'CONNOR joins [in part], concurring in part and dissenting in part.

Close examination of the findings of the District Court is essential to a proper understanding of this case. The plaintiffs, blacks employed by the Lukens Steel Company, sued the United Steelworkers of America and two of its local unions (Unions) for alleged violations of § 1981 and Title VII. The plaintiffs' allegations were directed primarily at the Unions' handling of grievances on behalf of black members. The District Court found that "[t]he steady increase in grievance filings each year has not produced a corresponding increase in the capacity of the grievance-processing system to handle complaints." Consequently, the court found, the Unions gave priority to "[s]erious grievances"—that is, "those involving more than a four-day suspension, and those involving discharges." In an effort to reduce the backlog of grievances, the Unions disposed of many less serious grievances by simply withdrawing them and reserving the right to seek relief in a later grievance proceeding. The District Court found "no hard evidence to support an inference that these inadequacies disadvantage blacks to a greater extent than whites." The incomplete evidence in the record suggests that the percentage of grievances filed on behalf of black employees was proportional to the number of blacks in the work force. Of the relatively few grievances that proceeded all the way to arbitration, the District Court found that the number asserted on behalf of black members was proportional to the number of blacks in the work force. Moreover, black members had a slightly higher rate of success in arbitration than white members.[1]

* * *

The Unions offered a nondiscriminatory reason for their practice of withdrawing grievances that did not involve a discharge or lengthy suspension. According to the Unions, this policy, that is racially neutral on its face, was motivated by the Unions' nondiscriminatory interest in using the inadequate grievance system to assist members who faced the most serious economic harm. The District Court made no finding that the Unions' explanation was a pretext for racial discrimination. The Unions' policy against pursuing grievances on behalf of probationary employees also permitted the Unions to focus their attention on members with the most to lose. Similarly, the Unions' stated purpose for

---

1. The District Court found that black union members "actively participated" in union meetings and affairs. A black member served as chairman of the grievance committee, and other black members served on the committee. The percentage of black shop stewards, the Union's primary representatives in the grievance process, frequently exceeded the percentage of black members in the bargaining unit.

processing racial grievances on nonracial grounds—to obtain the swiftest and most complete relief possible for the claimant—was not racially invidious. The Unions opposed the use of tests that had a disparate impact on black members, although not on that ground. Their explanation was that more complete relief could be obtained by challenging the tests on nonracial grounds. The District Court made no finding that the Unions' decision to base their opposition on nonracial grounds was motivated by racial animus. Absent a finding that the Unions intended to discriminate against black members, the conclusion that the Unions are liable under § 1981 or the disparate treatment theory of Title VII is unjustified.

Although the District Court stated that the plaintiffs raised both disparate treatment and disparate impact claims, it did not make specific findings nor did it conclude that the plaintiffs are entitled to recover under a disparate impact theory. Indeed, the limited amount of statistical evidence discussed by the District Court indicates that the Unions' grievance procedures did not have a disparate impact on black members. Moreover, neither the District Court nor the Court of Appeals considered the validity of potential defenses to disparate impact claims.

* * *

Notes and Questions

1. *Basis for Union Liability?* Note the finding of the lower court (summarized by Justice Powell) that the grievance system was administered, in the aggregate, in a manner which benefitted blacks equally with whites. Note also the majority's acknowledgement that there was no suggestion that the unions "held any racial animus against or denigrated blacks generally." On what basis then were the unions found to have discriminated on the basis of race?

2. *Should Unions Have Affirmative Duties to Resist Employer Discrimination?* What is the justification for the *Goodman* Court's apparent requirement that unions raise race discrimination grievances even where other, less incendiary contractual bases are available to assert claims on behalf of particular black employees? Should liability turn not on whether a union takes the racial character of a grievance into account, but on whether the union had legitimate reasons, consistent with equal regard for its black members, such as giving priority to discharge grievances or to the interests of more senior employees, for not pressing a claim of racial bias?

There would seem no good reason why a union's leaders should be able to justify race conscious policies by the racial prejudice of a majority of the union's membership if an employer cannot justify race conscious policies by the prejudice of its employees or customers. However, are the considerations different when union leaders justify race conscious decisions by the prejudice of the employer with whom they must bargain to obtain benefits for their constituents? Consider that requiring all unions to resist the discriminatory practices of employers will have some overall impact on the other benefits that the unions can obtain for their constituents, including their black members.

3. *Importance of the Antidiscrimination Clause in the Collective Agreement?* Would *Goodman* have been decided differently had the labor agreement not contained an express antidiscrimination clause? Does *Goodman* require unions to take steps to guard against the *potential* for discrimination by pressing in negotiations for clauses prohibiting and remedying race discrimination? To strike to secure such remedies? To resist facially neutral employment policies that have a disparate impact on a racial minority? Can some forms of union "passivity" be distinguished from what was condemned in *Goodman?* But cf. Macklin v. Spector Freight Systems, Inc., 478 F.2d 979, 989 (D.C.Cir.1973) (union may be responsible for resisting at the negotiating table an employer's known extant race discrimination).

4. *Employer Liability for Passive Acceptance of Union Discrimination?* In General Building Contractors Ass'n v. Pennsylvania, 458 U.S. 375, 102 S.Ct. 3141, 73 L.Ed.2d 835 (1982), the Court held that an employer should not be liable under § 1981 for a union's discriminatory operation of a hiring hall that furnished the employer with workers. It stressed that § 1981 is only violated by intentional discrimination and concluded that the employer had no duty to discover and eliminate discrimination at the hiring hall. Is this decision consistent with *Goodman?* Why should an employer not be liable for acquiescing in a union's independent discrimination if a union is liable for acquiescing in an employer's independent discrimination? Can an employer justify discriminatory decisions, such as the appointment of only white supervisors, by a need "to keep peace with the union?" See Grant v. Bethlehem Steel Corp., 635 F.2d 1007 (2d Cir.1980) (no).

5. *Joint and Several Liability for Concerted Discrimination.* The courts generally have made employers and unions jointly and severally liable for all damages caused by discriminatory provisions in collective bargaining agreements and other concerted efforts to discriminate. See, e.g., Russell v. American Tobacco Co., 528 F.2d 357 (4th Cir.1975). In Northwest Airlines, Inc. v. Transport Workers Union, 451 U.S. 77, 101 S.Ct. 1571, 67 L.Ed.2d 750 (1981), the Supreme Court held that if *one* jointly liable party is sued under Title VII and loses, it cannot then bring an *independent* action for contribution from the other party. If both the employer and the union are named as defendants, however, the decision may not foreclose one from making a cross-claim for contribution from the other. Prior to *Northwest Airlines,* some courts exercised discretion in apportioning primary liability based on the relative responsibilities of multiple defendants. See, e.g., Guerra v. Manchester Terminal Corp., 498 F.2d 641 (5th Cir.1974) (employer guilty of Title VII violation, but unions must pay full back pay because they insisted on discriminatory system). In addition, although *Northwest Airlines* does not preclude an employer from filing an independent charge against a union (or vice versa) for having caused the filing party to violate Title VII, no court seems to have recognized such an implied right of action. Cf. Smart v. IBEW, Local 702, 315 F.3d 721, 727 (7th Cir.2002) (employer cannot sue union for discriminating against employer's employee).

6. *Coverage of Employment Agencies.* In addition to proscribing discrimination by unions and employers, Title VII also prohibits the same five

types of status discrimination by an "employment agency"—defined as "any person regularly undertaking * * * to procure employees for an employer or to procure for employees opportunities to work for an employer * * *." See §§ 703(b) and 701(c).

F. OTHER FEDERAL CAUSES OF ACTION AGAINST STATUS DISCRIMINATION

Title VII does not provide the only federal cause of action against status discrimination in employment in general, nor even against race discrimination in particular. The remainder of this chapter presents four additional sources of federal antidiscrimination law—the Constitution, the Reconstruction Era Civil Rights Acts (in particular § 1981), Title VI of the Civil Rights Act of 1964, and the Immigration Control and Reform Act. Subsequent chapters will consider some additional federal status discrimination laws that have raised especially significant and interesting issues.

1. *The Constitutional Promise of Equal Protection: Application to Sexual Orientation Discrimination*

The fourteenth amendment's command that no "state" shall "deny to any person within its jurisdiction the equal protection of the laws" has been held to apply to the federal government through the due process clause of the fifth amendment. Bolling v. Sharpe, 347 U.S. 497, 74 S.Ct. 693, 98 L.Ed. 884 (1954). The constitutional equal protection principle reaches only governmental action; it does not, as a general matter, reach the decisions of private employers.

The Court has interpreted the equal protection clause with sensitivity to its historical origins in the post-Civil War efforts of our society to eradicate the vestiges of slavery. It has presumed that any racial classification reflects a lack of equal respect or regard for black people, and since World War II has demanded that such a classification be narrowly tailored to serve some compelling state interest. In fact, during the post-War period no Supreme Court opinion has found an intentional racial classification that disadvantages blacks to satisfy this demanding test. But see Korematsu v. United States, 323 U.S. 214, 65 S.Ct. 193, 89 L.Ed. 194 (1944) (compelling state interest justifies war-time internment of Japanese–American citizens).

In another part of Washington v. Davis, supra, not reprinted above, the Court held that government actions that are not undertaken for a racially discriminatory motive but have a disproportionate adverse impact on blacks do not trigger the "strict scrutiny" that attends race-based classifications. The Court's refusal to interpret equal protection as embodying a *Griggs*-type analysis stemmed in part from prudential concerns about the implications of such a mode of challenge for governmental programs outside of employment, such as "tax, welfare, public service, regulatory, and licensing * * * that may be more burdensome to the poor and to the average black than to the more affluent white." 426 U.S. at 248, 96 S.Ct. at 2051. *Davis* also seems to reflect the view that the intense suspicion of governmental motives that attends an explicit racial classification is not appropriate when government acts on neutral grounds even if blacks, perhaps because of their relative poverty, are adversely affected.

The *Davis* Court's finding that the District of Columbia government did not administer Test 21 for racially discriminatory reasons did not completely resolve the Equal Protection issue in that case, however. Test 21, though it did not classify along racial lines, nonetheless did classify applicants for employment. Under established equal protection doctrine it was thus necessary for the Court to consider whether the Test at least had some minimal "rational basis". Although the Court had no difficulty finding this rational basis in a desire to upgrade the "communicative abilities" of employees, there may be cases where government programs will have greater difficulty satisfying such scrutiny.

HIGH TECH GAYS v. DEFENSE INDUSTRIAL SECURITY CLEARANCE OFFICE

United States Court of Appeals, Ninth Circuit, 1990.
895 F.2d 563.

BRUNETTI, CIRCUIT JUDGE.

The plaintiffs-appellees challenge whether the Department of Defense's (DoD) policy of subjecting all homosexual applicants for Secret and Top Secret clearances to expanded investigations and mandatory adjudications, and whether the alleged DoD policy and practice of refusing to grant security clearances to known or suspected gay applicants, violates the equal protection component of the Fifth Amendment's Due Process Clause.

* * *

It is apparent that while the Supreme Court has identified that legislative classifications based on race, alienage, or national origin are subject to strict scrutiny and that classifications based upon gender or illegitimacy call for a heightened standard, the Court has never held homosexuality to a heightened standard of review.

To be a "suspect" or "quasi-suspect" class, homosexuals must 1) have suffered a history of discrimination; 2) exhibit obvious, immutable, or distinguishing characteristics that define them as a discrete group; and 3) show that they are a minority or politically powerless, or alternatively show that the statutory classification at issue burdens a fundamental right.

While we do agree that homosexuals have suffered a history of discrimination, we do not believe that they meet the other criteria. Homosexuality is not an immutable characteristic; it is behavioral and hence is fundamentally different from traits such as race, gender, or alienage, which define already existing suspect and quasi-suspect classes.

The behavior or conduct of such already recognized classes is irrelevant to their identification.

Moreover, legislatures have addressed and continue to address the discrimination suffered by homosexuals on account of their sexual orientation through the passage of anti-discrimination legislation. Thus, homosexuals are not without political power; they have the ability to and do "attract the attention of the lawmakers," as evidenced by such legislation.[10] Lastly, as previously noted, homosexual conduct is not a fundamental right.

* * *

Under a rational basis review as promulgated by the Supreme Court * * *, the DoD is not required to conclusively establish that homosexuals have transmitted classified information for its policy of subjecting homosexual applicants to expanded investigations to be constitutional. The DoD need only show a rational basis for its policy and that its policy is rationally related to the legitimate governmental interest of protecting classified material for it to be constitutional.

* * *

The DoD has determined what groups are targeted by hostile intelligence efforts. If an applicant falls within a targeted group—like homosexuals—the DoD subjects the applicant to an expanded investigation. The expanded investigation determines whether the applicant is susceptible to coercion or otherwise vulnerable to hostile intelligence efforts. * * *

Special deference must be given by the court to the Executive Branch when adjudicating matters involving their decisions on protecting classified information. * * *

No one has the "right" to a security clearance. We recognize that "[t]he attempt to define not only the individual's future actions, but those of outside and unknown influences renders the 'grant or denial of security clearance * * * an inexact science at best.' " Inexact science or not the DoD has articulated a rational relationship between their policy of subjecting homosexual applicants to expanded investigations and its compelling interest in national security.[13]

* * *

10. For example: Wisconsin has a comprehensive statute barring employment discrimination on the basis of sexual orientation, Wis.Stat.Ann. §§ 111.31–.395 (West 1988); California has barred violence against persons or property based on sexual orientation, Cal.Civ.Code § 51.7 (West 1984); and Michigan has barred the denial of care in health facilities on the basis of sexual orientation, Mich.Comp.Laws Ann. § 333.20201(2)(a) (West 1984). Executive Orders in other states prohibit such discrimination. See e.g., N.Y.Comp.Codes R. & Regs. tit. 4, § 28 (1983) (barring discrimination in state employment or in the provision of state services and benefits on the basis of sexual orientation.) Many cities and counties have also enacted anti-discrimination regulations, including New York, Los Angeles, Chicago, Washington D.C., Atlanta, Boston, Philadelphia, Seattle, and San Francisco. Developments in the Law, Sexual Orientation and the Law, 102 Harv.L.Rev. 1509, 1667–68, n. 49–51 (citations omitted).

13. The DoD advances other justifications for its policy: a homosexual may be

* * * [T]he plaintiffs rely on a resolution of the American Psychological Association which states that homosexuality "implies no impairment in judgment, stability, reliability or general social or vocational capabilities." According to the plaintiffs, the "KGB's [*Eds.* Soviet Union's intelligence agency] obsolete opinions on homosexual behavior" should be rejected in favor of adopting the position of the American Psychological Association. However, the counterintelligence agencies' reasons for targeting homosexuals—even if based on continuing ignorance or prejudice—are irrelevant.[14] If hostile intelligence efforts are directed at homosexuals, the DoD must be assured that because of the targeting, the individual will not compromise national secrets.

Accordingly, the district court erred in denying the DoD's motion for summary judgment.

HIGH TECH GAYS v. DEFENSE INDUSTRIAL SECURITY CLEARANCE OFFICE

United States Court of Appeals, Ninth Circuit, 1990.
909 F.2d 375.

The panel has voted to deny the petition for rehearing and to reject the suggestion for a rehearing en banc.

CANBY, CIRCUIT JUDGE, joined by CIRCUIT JUDGE NORRIS, dissenting from denial of rehearing en banc.

It is important to understand what this case is not about. The plaintiffs do not contend that the Department of Defense is without power to investigate fully persons seeking a clearance who it has reason to believe may be unstable or unreliable. Nothing in the district court's order, which the panel reversed, precluded the Department from so proceeding on a case-by-case basis. Plaintiffs also do not contend that the Department is improperly denying clearances at the conclusion of its investigations; indeed, the Department grants clearances to most homosexuals. What plaintiffs challenge is the Department's practice of subjecting all homosexuals, automatically and as a class, to expanded and time-consuming security clearance procedures that are required of no other class. Homosexuals are never granted clearance, as many applicants are, after a brief initial investigation; they are always subjected to an expanded investigation, and they are always referred for further review to a separate office charged with adjudicating questionable cases. The district court found that this practice inflicted injury on the plaintiffs, both in the discriminatory treatment itself, and in the loss of

emotionally unstable and homosexual conduct may be criminal. Because we conclude that the targeting of homosexuals by hostile intelligence agencies is a legitimate if not compelling justification for the expanded investigations, we need not address these additional justifications.

14. Despite evidence that attitudes toward homosexual conduct have changed among some groups in society, the Navy could conclude that a substantive number of naval personnel have feelings regarding homosexuality based upon moral precepts recognized by many in our society as legitimate, which would create tensions and hostilities, and might undermine the ability of a homosexual to perform supervisory duties.

employment opportunities because of the excessive delay in obtaining clearances.

The first thing that ought to be clear about the panel's opinion is that it applies the wrong standard of review. The class of "homosexuals" clearly qualifies as a suspect category, triggering strict judicial scrutiny of any governmental discrimination against them. The applicable criteria are properly described but improperly applied by the panel. * * *

The panel agrees that the first criterion is met; homosexuals have suffered a history of discrimination. This point should not be put quickly out of mind, however, for this history of discrimination makes it far more likely that differential treatment is simply a resort to old prejudices. As the district court said, "[l]esbians and gays have been the object of some of the deepest prejudice and hatred in American society." That fact tends to make discrimination against them all too easy. We should be careful not to endorse that tendency.

With regard to the second criterion, the panel's opinion states: "Homosexuality is not an immutable characteristic; it is behavioral and hence is fundamentally different from traits such as race, gender, or alienage, which define already existing suspect and quasi-suspect classes." There are several problems with this conclusion. In the first place, the criterion quoted earlier by the panel required that the class, to be suspect, "exhibit obvious, immutable, or distinguishing characteristics that define them as a discrete group." The Supreme Court has more than once recited the characteristics of a suspect class without mentioning immutability. See, e.g., *City of Cleburne v. Cleburne Living Center,* 473 U.S. 432, 440–41, 105 S.Ct. 3249, 3254–55, 87 L.Ed.2d 313 (1985); *Massachusetts Bd. of Retirement v. Murgia,* 427 U.S. 307, 313, 96 S.Ct. 2562, 2566–67, 49 L.Ed.2d 520 (1976); *San Antonio School Dist. v. Rodriguez,* 411 U.S. 1, at 28, 93 S.Ct. 1278, at 1294, 36 L.Ed.2d 16 (1973). Aliens, for example, constitute a suspect category, but the condition is not immutable. See *Graham v. Richardson,* 403 U.S. 365, 371–72, 91 S.Ct. 1848, 1851–52, 29 L.Ed.2d 534 (1971). The real question is whether discrimination on the basis of the class's distinguishing characteristic amounts to an unfair branding or resort to prejudice, not necessarily whether the characteristic is immutable.

Immutability, of course, does make discrimination more clearly unfair. There is every reason to regard homosexuality as an immutable characteristic for equal protection purposes. It is not enough to say that the category is "behavioral." One can make "behavioral" classes out of persons who go to church on Saturday, persons who speak Spanish, or persons who walk with crutches. The question is, what causes the behavior? Does it arise from the kind of a characteristic that belongs peculiarly to a group that the equal protection clause should specially protect?

Homosexuals are physically attracted to members of their own sex. That is the source of the behavior that we notice about them. Did they choose to be attracted by members of their own sex, rather than by members of the opposite sex? The answer, by the overwhelming weight of respectable authority, is "no." Sexual identity is established at a very early age; it is not a matter of conscious or controllable choice. * * *

The panel's opinion also concludes that homosexuals are not politically powerless. Its support for this proposition is that one state broadly bars employment discrimination against homosexuals, two other states more narrowly bar discrimination against homosexuals[1], and a few cities bar some types of discrimination. That showing is clearly insufficient to deprive homosexuals of the status of a suspect classification. Compare the situation with that of blacks, who clearly constitute a suspect category for equal protection purposes. Blacks are protected by three federal constitutional amendments, major federal Civil Rights Acts of 1866, 1870, 1871, 1875 (ill-fated though it was), 1957, 1960, 1964, 1965, and 1968, as well as by antidiscrimination laws in 48 of the states. By that comparison, and by absolute standards as well, homosexuals are politically powerless. They are so because of their numbers, which most estimates put at around 10 per cent of the population, and by the fact that many of them keep their status secret to avoid discrimination. That secrecy inhibits organization of homosexuals as a pressure group.

* * *

Under a standard equal protection approach, the absence of a fundamental right does not preclude the possibility that a suspect classification demands heightened scrutiny. The Supreme Court has made it clear that there is no fundamental right to education, for equal protection purposes. *San Antonio School Dist.,* 411 U.S. [1] at 33–37, 93 S.Ct. [1278] at 1296–99. Yet racial segregation in federal schools is subject to the same strict scrutiny that applies to state racial segregation. *Bolling v. Sharpe,* 347 U.S. 497, 74 S.Ct. 693, 98 L.Ed. 884 (1954). The suspect category triggers the highest level of scrutiny regardless of whether the government regulation impinges on a fundamental right.

* * *

The panel that decided this case erred fundamentally, then, in not selecting a higher standard of scrutiny. But it also erred in applying the standard of review that it did select. Indeed, the dangers of rational basis review are well illustrated by this decision, for the truth of the matter is that nothing in the record justifies a conclusion that the Defense Department's discrimination is rational. The panel concludes that the Department's discrimination against homosexuals is rationally based because the KGB "targets" homosexuals in attempting to gain access to classified materials. * * *

The most fundamental reason not to accept the "targeting" rationale is that it helps to perpetuate the wrongful discrimination. * * * In other words, if our society treats a group unfairly, then our government

---

1. It says something about the condition of homosexuals in our society that California's law bans violence against persons or property on the basis of sexual orientation. See 10 Cal.Civ.Code § 51.7 (West 1984).

is justified in treating that group even more unfairly because the KGB will seek to exploit the "outcast" feelings of that group. Who is going to break the discriminatory cycle if we don't?

The irrationality of the panel's reasoning is pounded home by its conclusion that it is irrelevant that the KGB's policy itself may be irrational. Thus, even if the KGB's policy never works, gays and lesbians may be subjected to stricter standards of examination for security clearances than other groups, just because the KGB (perhaps indulging in some stereo-typical prejudices of its own) incorrectly assumes homosexuals to be less loyal than other citizens. The Supreme Court has made it clear that bias on the part of our own citizenry cannot justify governmental discrimination. See *Cleburne,* 473 U.S. at 448, 105 S.Ct. at 3258–59 (in zoning against a home for the mentally retarded, a "city may not avoid the strictures of [the Equal Protection] Clause by deferring to the wishes or objections of some fraction of the body politic"); *Palmore v. Sidoti,* 466 U.S. 429, 104 S.Ct. 1879, 80 L.Ed.2d 421 (1984) (existence of prejudice among public not sufficient to justify removing child from custody of white mother who is living with black man). As one of the amici bluntly puts it: "If the government may not adopt the prejudices of its own citizens as a rationale for discrimination, certainly it cannot adopt those of the Soviet Union."

There is every reason to believe that any "targeting" of homosexuals by the KGB is irrational, at least insofar as this record reveals. Over 30 years ago, the Navy's own Crittendon Report concluded that "[n]o factual data exist to support the contention that homosexuals are a greater [security] risk than heterosexuals." Crittendon Report, 1957 (Gibson, 1978). There is no more factual support for the contention now than there was then. * * * For purposes of equal protection, it is not enough to show that a burden imposed on a group serves some governmental purpose. It must be shown that there is some rational basis for treating that group differently from others.

Notes and Questions

1. *Could the Department of Defense's Policy Have Survived Strict Scrutiny?* Do you think the Department of Defense's rationales for subjecting homosexual applicants to expanded security investigations could have survived serious strict scrutiny? Is there reason to think that the officials who developed the policy were influenced by a prejudice against homosexuality, rather than simply by a desire to protect national security?

2. *Does* Lawrence v. Texas *Require Strict Scrutiny?* In Lawrence v. Texas, 539 U.S. 558, 123 S.Ct. 2472, 156 L.Ed.2d 508 (2003), the Supreme Court struck down a state criminal statute's ban on sodomy. The Court held that the statute denied a right of liberty guaranteed by the due process clause of the fourteenth amendment by intruding "into the personal and private life of the individual" without any "legitimate state interest." Does this holding necessarily mean that any state action that discriminates against homosexuals, whether challenged under the equal protection or due

process clause, must survive strict scrutiny, including having a "compelling" justification, because it intrudes on the liberty protected by the due process clause? The *Lawrence* Court relied on Planned Parenthood of Southeastern Pa. v. Casey, 505 U.S. 833, 851, 112 S.Ct. 2791, 120 L.Ed.2d 674 (1992), in which the Court, as stated in *Lawrence*, 539 U.S. at 573–74, "confirmed that our laws and tradition afford constitutional protection to personal decisions relating to marriage, procreation, contraception, family relationships, child rearing and education." Yet the majority of the Court in *Casey* demanded only that the state regulation of abortion which it reviewed not impose an "undue burden" on liberty. In *Lawrence* the Court does not define the level of review it applies.

3. *Could the Department of Defense's Policy Survive Rational Basis Review in the Supreme Court?* As a general matter, the Court has viewed the "rational basis" test as a highly deferential form of review, under which it will tolerate a considerable degree of imprecision between the classification employed and the stated objectives of the challenged measure. It also generally has given great weight to the government's interest in administrative convenience.

However, in another decision involving state action adverse to homosexuals and relied on by the Court in *Lawrence*, Romer v. Evans, 517 U.S. 620, 116 S.Ct. 1620, 134 L.Ed.2d 855 (1996), the Court indicated that governmental classifications sometimes can fail even rational basis review. In *Romer* Colorado voters through a statewide referendum had adopted a state constitutional amendment which precluded all legislative, executive, or judicial action at any level of state or local government designed to protect any person or class of persons on the basis of "homosexual, lesbian or bisexual orientation, conduct, practices or relationships." Though it professed to apply only rational basis review, the Court held that the state constitutional amendment denied homosexuals equal protection of the laws. The Court stressed that the amendment had "the peculiar property of imposing a broad and undifferentiated disability" on one group of citizens to seek aid from the government. Id. at 632. The Court found that this preclusion could not be justified by any interest asserted by Colorado, and thus raised "the inevitable inference that the disadvantage imposed is born of animosity toward the class of persons affected." Id. at 634. Could the Department of Defense practices challenged in *High Tech* have been overturned under this rational basis approach? (The *Lawrence* Court declined an invitation to decide its case on the basis of the equal protection approach of *Romer*, stressing that it wanted to clarify that its holding reached statutes that treated heterosexual and homosexual sodomy equally. 539 U.S. at 575.)

4. *Relevance of Political Power?* What weight should be given to a group's political power in determining whether classifications burdening that group warrant heightened review? Race is accepted as the paradigm suspect classification, despite the recent political successes and general political muscle of African–Americans (made possible in large part by the Voting Rights Act). Does this suggest that political powerlessness is not a necessary criterion for strict scrutiny, at least where strong prejudice against an adversely affected group might provoke a backlash against its assertion of political muscle? Should political weakness nevertheless be a sufficient basis for judicial solicitude under the equal protection clause?

5. *Relevance of Immutability?* Should the immutability of a characteristic defining a class be a necessary precondition for heightened review? Is the ultimate reason for giving closer review to some classifications than to others that there is greater reason to be suspicious of government bias against or lack of equal respect for the adversely affected groups? See John Hart Ely, Democracy and Distrust: A Theory of Judicial Review (1980). The criteria applied by both the *High Tech* panel and Judge Canby's dissent state that there must be "obvious immutable, or distinguishing characteristics that define" a group as discrete. Might this criterion be explained best as highlighting only one aspect of group identification that makes prejudice more likely?

6. *Relevance of Public Attitudes?* If the likelihood of governmental bias or animus against a group best explains the need for strict scrutiny, do classifications burdening homosexuals warrant such review? Regardless of the political successes achieved by homosexuals in certain cities and states, if a substantial number of Americans, and hence their elected representatives, condemn homosexuality as at least deviant, if not immoral, isn't it likely that some governmental classifications of homosexuals will reflect those attitudes? Or does the equal protection guarantee not condemn governmental devaluation of a group that is based on moral judgments about that group's behavior?

Note on Sexual Orientation Discrimination

At least before the Court's decision in *Lawrence* lower courts had not read *Romer* expansively to strike down all governmental classifications that intentionally disadvantage homosexuals. Most prominently, the courts of appeals continued to uphold the military's "don't ask/don't tell" policy under which the armed services do not accept persons who demonstrate a propensity or intent to engage in homosexual acts. See Able v. United States, 155 F.3d 628 (2d Cir.1998); Holmes v. California Army National Guard, 124 F.3d 1126 (9th Cir.1997). See also Richenberg v. Perry, 97 F.3d 256 (8th Cir.1996); Thomasson v. Perry, 80 F.3d 915 (4th Cir.1996) (en banc)). Citing precedent supporting especially deferential review of the military, e.g., Goldman v. Weinberger, 475 U.S. 503, 106 S.Ct. 1310, 89 L.Ed.2d 478 (1986), the courts accepted Congress's reliance on the military's judgment that the policy is necessary to avoid "an unacceptable risk to the high standards of morale, good order and discipline, and unit cohesion that are the essence of military capability." 10 U.S.C. § 654(a)(15).

Outside the context of military and national security, however, are governmental employers likely to be able to convince courts they have acceptable reasons for not granting equal treatment to homosexuals? See, e.g., Quinn v. Nassau County Police Dept., 53 F.Supp.2d 347 (E.D.N.Y.1999) (police officer could not be subjected to harassment because of his sexual orientation); Weaver v. Nebo School Dist., 29 F.Supp.2d 1279 (D.Utah 1998) (finding no rational, job-related reason to not assign lesbian as volleyball coach); Glover v. Williamsburg Local School Dist. Bd. of Educ., 20 F.Supp.2d 1160 (S.D.Ohio 1998) (non-renewal of teaching contract because of sexual orientation held denial of equal protection); Jantz v. Muci, 759 F.Supp. 1543

(D.Kan.1991), reversed on other grounds, 976 F.2d 623 (10th Cir.1992) (teacher could not be rejected merely because of "homosexual tendencies").

The lower courts have ruled consistently that Title VII's prohibition of sex discrimination was intended to cover only discrimination on the basis of gender, not discrimination on the basis of sexual orientation. See, e.g., Dawson v. Bumble & Bumble, 398 F.3d 211 (2d Cir. 2005); Bibby v. Philadelphia Coca–Cola Bottling Co., 260 F.3d 257 (3d Cir. 2001); Higgins v. New Balance Athletic Shoe, Inc., 194 F.3d 252 (1st Cir. 1999); DeSantis v. Pacific Tel. & Tel., 608 F.2d 327 (9th Cir.1979). Can a strong argument be made, however, that discrimination on the basis of sexual orientation is a form of discrimination "on account of sex"? If an employer permits male employees to have sexual relations with females, why is it not discrimination against women to not permit female employees to have sexual relations with other females? Why is such a differential policy any less gender discrimination than a policy permitting male employees, but not female employees, to be married? Can the courts' treatment of sexual orientation discrimination under Title VII be squared with their interpretation of Title VII to condemn discrimination against interracial sexual relationships? See, e.g., Holcomb v. Iona College, 521 F.3d 130 (2d Cir. 2008); Deffenbaugh–Williams v. Wal–Mart Stores, Inc., 156 F.3d 581, 588–89 (5th Cir.1998); Parr v. Woodmen of the World Life Ins. Co., 791 F.2d 888, 891–92 (11th Cir.1986). If requiring female employees to be less aggressive than valued male employees is sex discrimination, is not requiring male employees to have sexual roles or lifestyles not expected of valued female employees also sex discrimination? See Price Waterhouse v. Hopkins, 490 U.S. 228, 109 S.Ct. 1775, 104 L.Ed.2d 268 (1989), and accompanying notes, at pp. 342–348 infra.

Even if Title VII was not intended to proscribe discrimination on the basis of sexual orientation, it could be amended to do so. Is it necessary to determine that homosexuality is a biologically ascribed status, like race or gender, rather than some sort of "voluntary" choice? Should employers be permitted to make decisions on the basis of a characteristic that is not relevant to job performance, even when those decisions may express the morality of a segment of the population? Legislation to extend Title VII's prohibitions to include sexual orientation discrimination has been introduced repeatedly. On November 7, 2007, the House of Representatives passed legislation that would prohibit sexual orientation discrimination in employment pursuant to the same language set forth in § 703(a)(1) and (2), although expressly excluding disparate impact claims. H.R. 3685, 110th Cong., 1st Sess. President Clinton also added sexual orientation to the categories of discrimination forbidden in the federal civilian workforce under Executive Order 11478.

In addition, more and more state and local laws providing protection against sexual orientation discrimination in private as well as public employment are being enacted. See Arthur S. Leonard, Sexual Orientation and the Workplace: A Rapidly Developing Field, 44 Lab.L.J. 574, 576 (1993). At least twenty states (California, Colorado, Connecticut, Hawaii, Illinois, Iowa, Maine, Maryland, Massachusetts, Minnesota, Nevada, New Hampshire, New Jersey, New Mexico, New York, Oregon, Rhode Island, Vermont, Washington, and Wisconsin) as well as the District of Columbia and most major American cities have enacted prohibitions. See generally Todd R. Dickey,

Reorienting the Workplace: Examining California's New Labor Code Section 1102.1 and Other Legal Protections Against Employment Discrimination Based on Sexual Orientation, 66 S.Cal.L.Rev. 2297 (1993).

Might laws prohibiting sex discrimination protect individuals who have undergone sex changes even if the laws do not cover sexual orientation discrimination? The lower courts have held that Title VII does not protect transsexuals, see, e.g., Etsitty v. Utah Transit Auth., 502 F.3d 1215 (10th Cir. 2007); Ulane v. Eastern Airlines, 742 F.2d 1081 (7th Cir.1984). The 2007 legislation passed by the House did not protect transsexuals. Can an argument be made that discrimination against those who have changed their sex fits within a definition of sex discrimination more comfortably than does discrimination on the basis of sexual orientation? See Schroer v. Billington, 424 F.Supp.2d 203 (D.D.C. 2006); Maffei v. Kolaeton Industry, Inc., 164 Misc.2d 547, 626 N.Y.S.2d 391 (1995) (interpreting Administrative Code of City of New York).

Note on the Enforcement of the Equal Protection Command

Section 1983 of Title 42 of the United States Code, originally enacted as § 1 of the Civil Rights Act of 1871, provides both a legal and equitable cause of action for individuals who have been denied a constitutional (or federal statutory) right by a state or local governmental official. Section 1983 authorizes an action for injunctive relief and damages (including punitive damages) against government officials sued in their personal capacity even when the conduct in question also violates state or local law. All government officials, however, even when not fully immune from civil liability as judges, prosecutors, or legislators, "are shielded from liability for civil damages insofar as their conduct does not violate clearly established statutory or constitutional rights of which a reasonable person would have known." Davis v. Scherer, 468 U.S. 183, 190–91, 104 S.Ct. 3012, 82 L.Ed.2d 139 (1984).

Although suit may be brought against the local government entity itself, the Court has interpreted § 1983 to reject the doctrine of respondeat superior. A § 1983 action lies against a local governmental entity only with respect to actions condoned by official policy or custom. See Monell v. Department of Social Services, 436 U.S. 658, 98 S.Ct. 2018, 56 L.Ed.2d 611 (1978); Pembaur v. Cincinnati, 475 U.S. 469, 106 S.Ct. 1292, 89 L.Ed.2d 452 (1986) (municipality may be held liable only for "acts which the municipality has officially sanctioned or ordered" through an officer with "final policy-making authority"); St. Louis v. Praprotnik, 485 U.S. 112, 108 S.Ct. 915, 99 L.Ed.2d 107 (1988) (plurality opinion holding that municipality could not be held liable for retaliatory transfer because mayor and aldermen—the officials with final policymaking authority—had not enacted an ordinance or otherwise indicated that such retaliatory decisions were permissible). Section 1983 actions against governmental entities are treated differently in other respects as well. See City of Newport v. Fact Concerts, Inc., 453 U.S. 247, 101 S.Ct. 2748, 69 L.Ed.2d 616 (1981) (punitive damages are not recoverable); Owen v. City of Independence, 445 U.S. 622, 100 S.Ct. 1398, 63 L.Ed.2d 673 (1980) (no good-faith defense to municipal § 1983 liability).

State governments are insulated from both legal and equitable suits under § 1983 by the doctrine of sovereign immunity as embodied in the eleventh amendment. See Quern v. Jordan, 440 U.S. 332, 99 S.Ct. 1139, 59 L.Ed.2d 358 (1979); Edelman v. Jordan, 415 U.S. 651, 94 S.Ct. 1347, 39 L.Ed.2d 662 (1974). However, even absent a waiver of sovereign immunity, § 1983 may be used to obtain prospective injunctive or declaratory relief and attorney's fees from state officials sued in their official capacities; and also to obtain monetary damages from state (as well as local government) officials sued in their personal capacities, absent an official immunity defense. See Hafer v. Melo, 502 U.S. 21, 112 S.Ct. 358, 116 L.Ed.2d 301 (1991); Scheuer v. Rhodes, 416 U.S. 232, 94 S.Ct. 1683, 40 L.Ed.2d 90 (1974). Section 1983 suits may be brought in state courts where the eleventh amendment does not apply. However, in Will v. Michigan Department of State Police, 491 U.S. 58, 109 S.Ct. 2304, 105 L.Ed.2d 45 (1989), the court insured that the same sovereign immunity limits apply to § 1983 actions in state courts by holding that grievants cannot sue for monetary damages under § 1983 states or state officers in their official capacities.

The Court has held that the eleventh amendment erects no bar to Title VII actions because Congress, pursuant to its enforcement authority under the fourteenth amendment, qualified the states' immunity from Title VII back pay awards. See Fitzpatrick v. Bitzer, 427 U.S. 445, 96 S.Ct. 2666, 49 L.Ed.2d 614 (1976). Query, however, whether the Court's subsequent limitations on Congressional power under the fourteenth amendment, see City of Boerne v. Flores, 521 U.S. 507, 117 S.Ct. 2157, 138 L.Ed.2d 624 (1997), call into question monetary recoveries in disparate impact actions against state governments, given the fourteenth amendment's condemnation of only intentional discrimination. See Okrulik v. University of Arkansas, 255 F.3d 615 (8th Cir. 2001); In re Employment Discrimination Litigation Against the State of Alabama, 198 F.3d 1305 (11th Cir.1999) (both holding disparate impact action can proceed). This question has become more salient in the wake of Board of Trustees of the Univ. of Alabama v. Garrett, 531 U.S. 356, 121 S.Ct. 955, 148 L.Ed.2d 866 (2001) (discussed at p. 558 infra) and Kimel v. Florida Board of Regents, 528 U.S. 62, 120 S.Ct. 631, 145 L.Ed.2d 522 (2000)(discussed at p. 429 infra), which held respectively that sovereign immunity bars private rights of action under the Americans with Disabilities Act (ADA) and the Age Discrimination in Employment Act (ADEA) against state governments. In *Garrett* and *Kimel* the Court stressed that disability and age, unlike race, are not suspect classifications under the equal protection clause.

Section 1983 does not create a right of action for decisions made under the authority of federal law. See Wheeldin v. Wheeler, 373 U.S. 647, 650 n. 2, 83 S.Ct. 1441 n. 2, 10 L.Ed.2d 605 (1963). A grievant seeking relief from a discriminatory employment decision made by a federal official might try to sue directly under the due process clause of the fifth amendment. In Davis v. Passman, 442 U.S. 228, 99 S.Ct. 2264, 60 L.Ed.2d 846 (1979), however, the Court held that such a cause of action is available only if the federal employee is not covered by Title VII. The *Passman* Court referred to its decision in Brown v. GSA, 425 U.S. 820, 96 S.Ct. 1961, 48 L.Ed.2d 402 (1976), holding that Congress intended § 717 of Title VII to provide an exclusive remedy for claims of Title VII-type status discrimination. For further discussion, see chapter 18.

2. Section 1981

Originally part of § 1 of the Civil Rights Act of 1866, and now codified as § 1981 of Title 42 of the United States Code, this provision guarantees all persons the same right "to make and enforce contracts * * * as is enjoyed by white citizens * * *." Unlike § 1983, § 1981 not only protects rights deriving from other legal sources such as the constitution. It is itself a source of a right to engage in a range of economic and political activities free of racial discrimination.

Section 1981 reaches all forms of racial discrimination. In McDonald v. Santa Fe Trail Transportation Co., supra, the Court held that whites complaining of racial discrimination could sue under § 1981. Then in Saint Francis College v. Al–Khazraji, 481 U.S. 604, 107 S.Ct. 2022, 95 L.Ed.2d 582 (1987), and Shaare Tefila Congregation v. Cobb, 481 U.S. 615, 107 S.Ct. 2019, 95 L.Ed.2d 594 (1987), the Court held that the Congress that enacted § 1981 intended to proscribe "ancestry or ethnic" discrimination, which it would have viewed as equivalent to racial discrimination. However, "the same right * * * as is enjoyed by white citizens" language of § 1981 has been read to preclude the statute's extension to discrimination on account of sex, religion or age; and *Saint Francis* clarifies that it does not cover discrimination based on "place or nation of * * * origin." The courts of appeals have disagreed on coverage of alienage (citizenship) discrimination. Compare Anderson v. Conboy, 156 F.3d 167 (2d Cir.1998) (coverage), with Bhandari v. First National Bank of Commerce, 887 F.2d 609 (5th Cir.1989) (en banc) (no coverage).

Section 1981 actions generally cannot be brought against federal employers because of the holding in Brown v. GSA, supra. Moreover, in Jett v. Dallas Independent School District, 491 U.S. 701, 109 S.Ct. 2702, 105 L.Ed.2d 598 (1989), a majority of the Justices concluded that there is no private right of action for damages against state and local government "actors" under § 1981 that is independent of the remedy provided by § 1983. This conclusion is significant because it makes clear that the limitations governing § 1983 actions cannot be avoided by proceeding under § 1981. *Jett* itself, for instance, held that § 1981 could not be invoked to avoid the *Monell* doctrine, which precludes a local government's damages liability for its employees' violations of § 1983 unless the conduct in question constituted the government's official custom or policy. Cf. also Federation of African American Contractors v. Oakland, 96 F.3d 1204, 1214–15 (9th Cir.1996) (although 1991 Civil Rights Act's addition of new § 1981(c) provides an independent cause of action against state actors, principles such as the *Monell* doctrine derived for § 1983 suits apply). *Jett's* rationale also would seem to settle that § 1981 does not constitute a congressional override of the eleventh amendment's sovereign immunity doctrine, see Edelman v. Jordan, 415 U.S. 651, 94 S.Ct. 1347, 39 L.Ed.2d 662 (1974), under which § 1983 plaintiffs are able to obtain damages only from state governmental officials sued as individuals, rather than from the state employer itself. See, e.g., Single-tary v. Missouri Dept. of Corrections, 423 F.3d 886 (8th Cir. 2005) (§ 1981 does not abrogate sovereign immunity).

Section 1981 provides an independent cause of action for damages against private employers. The Court in Jones v. Alfred H. Mayer Co., 392 U.S. 409, 88 S.Ct. 2186, 20 L.Ed.2d 1189 (1968), held that private discrimination was covered by 42 U.S.C. § 1982, a companion provision from the same 1866 statute. Seven years later, the Court intimated that § 1981 also reaches private sector discrimination, see Johnson v. Rail-way Express Agency, Inc., 421 U.S. 454, 95 S.Ct. 1716, 44 L.Ed.2d 295 (1975), and expressly so held the following year in Runyon v. McCrary, 427 U.S. 160, 96 S.Ct. 2586, 49 L.Ed.2d 415 (1976). In *Jett* the Court confirmed that an independent private damage action can be implied directly from § 1981 against private violators. 491 U.S. at 731–32, 109 S.Ct. at 2720. Unlike Title VII claims, the § 1981 cause of action does not require exhaustion of administrative procedures at the EEOC or state agencies.

Section 101 of the Civil Rights Act of 1991, moreover, expressly confirms Congressional intent to reach "nongovernmental discrimination" through § 1981. 42 U.S.C. § 1981(c). This section of the 1991 Act also overturns an attempt by the Supreme Court in 1989, in Patterson v. McLean Credit Union, 491 U.S. 164, 109 S.Ct. 2363, 105 L.Ed.2d 132 (1989), to restrict the reach of § 1981. The *Patterson* Court held that § 1981 prohibits discrimination in the formation of contracts and in the process by which they are enforced, but does not extend to prohibiting discriminatory conduct "after the contract relation has been established, including breach of the terms of the contract or imposition of discriminatory working conditions." Section 101 rejects *Patterson* by expressly including within the reach of § 1981 "the making, performance, modification, and termination of contracts, and the enjoyment of all benefits, privileges, terms, and conditions of the contractual relationship." 42 U.S.C. § 1981(b).

Although a few district courts and the Seventh Circuit have assert-ed, notwithstanding § 101, that an employment-at-will relationship can-not be the basis for a § 1981 claim, see Gonzalez v. Ingersoll Milling Mach. Co., 133 F.3d 1025 (7th Cir.1998), several other Courts of Appeals and a majority of district courts have recognized that a contractual relationship can exist between employers and employees, even when the relationship can be terminated by any party at any time. See, e.g., Turner v. Arkansas Insurance Dept., 297 F.3d 751 (8th Cir.2002) (dismissing *Gonzalez* as dicta and holding, upon review of cases, that it is "clearly established" that § 1981 protects at-will employees); Lauture v. International Business Machines Corp., 216 F.3d 258 (2d Cir.2000); Spriggs v. Diamond Auto Glass, 165 F.3d 1015 (4th Cir.1999); Fadeyi v. Planned Parenthood Ass'n, 160 F.3d 1048 (5th Cir.1998). Cf. Haddle v. Garrison, 525 U.S. 121, 119 S.Ct. 489, 142 L.Ed.2d 502 (1998) ("interference with at-will employment relations alleged here is merely a species of the traditional torts of intentional interference with contractual relations" and constitutes an actionable "injury" under civil rights conspiracy statute, § 1985).

3. Title VI of the Civil Rights Act of 1964 and Title IX of the Education Amendments of 1972

Title VI of the Civil Rights Act of 1964 provides that no person "shall, on the ground of race, color, or national origin, * * * be subjected to discrimination under any program or activity receiving Federal financial assistance." Title IX of the Education Act Amendments of 1972 provides that no person "shall, on the basis of sex, * * * be subjected to discrimination under any education program or activity receiving Federal financial assistance." In the Civil Rights Restoration Act of 1987, 42 U.S.C. § 2000d–4a, Pub.L. 100–259, 102 Stat. 28, Congress overturned a 1984 Supreme Court opinion, Grove City College v. Bell, 465 U.S. 555, 104 S.Ct. 1211, 79 L.Ed.2d 516 (1984), to make clear (with some exceptions) that the Title VI and Title IX antidiscrimination obligations apply to the entire public or private institution accepting federal funds, not simply the specific program or activity to which the funds are allotted. But see Schroeder v. Chicago, 715 F.Supp. 222 (N.D.Ill.1989) (entire municipality not covered, just particular institution like hospital or university receiving funds). (The Restoration Act also amended two other federal statutes modeled after Title VI: § 504 of the Rehabilitation Act of 1964, 29 U.S.C. § 794, proscribing disability discrimination by recipients of federal funds; and the Age Discrimination Act of 1975, 42 U.S.C. § 1607, proscribing age discrimination by recipients of federal financial assistance.)

The Supreme Court has held that Title IX, as well as Title VI, may be enforced through a private right of action. See Cannon v. University of Chicago, 441 U.S. 677, 99 S.Ct. 1946, 60 L.Ed.2d 560 (1979). Under Franklin v. Gwinnett County Public Schools, 503 U.S. 60, 112 S.Ct. 1028, 117 L.Ed.2d 208 (1992), courts may award private plaintiffs damages for at least intentional violations of Title IX, as well as Title VI. This doctrine could be helpful for some victims of employment discrimination because Title VI and Title IX, like § 1981, but unlike Title VII, do not require exhaustion of administrative procedures before suit. However, some lower courts have held that private plaintiffs cannot circumvent the Title VII administrative system by suing for damages under Title IX. See, e.g., Lakoski v. James, 66 F.3d 751 (5th Cir. 1995) (relying on Great American Federal Savings & Loan Assn. v. Novotny, 442 U.S. 366, 99 S.Ct. 2345, 60 L.Ed.2d 957 (1979), page 1126 infra.)

Furthermore, the Court has strictly limited Title VI and Title IX actions. First, in Guardians Ass'n v. Civil Serv. Comm'n, 463 U.S. 582, 103 S.Ct. 3221, 77 L.Ed.2d 866 (1983), a majority of Justices held that unlike Title VII, Title VI of its own force reaches only intentional discrimination. Though a different majority in *Guardians* agreed that agency regulations implementing Title VI could require recipients to avoid practices that are discriminatory in effect as well as purpose, five other Justices in the *Guardians* case maintained that private plaintiffs cannot obtain compensatory or any other retroactive relief, including comparative seniority, without proof of discriminatory intent; and in Alexander v. Sandoval, 532 U.S. 275, 121 S.Ct. 1511, 149 L.Ed.2d 517 (2001), the Court held that the disparate impact regulations cannot be enforced at all through a private action. Second, in Gebser v. Lago Vista Independent School District, 524 U.S. 274, 118 S.Ct. 1989, 141 L.Ed.2d 277 (1998), the Court held that Title IX plaintiffs could not obtain damages for a teacher's sexual harassment of a student without establishing that some school official with corrective authority had actual notice of and was deliberately indifferent to the misconduct. The holding in *Gebser* was limited to its factual context of teacher-student sexual harassment, but the Court's reasoning (based on ensuring that federal funds recipients have adequate notice that they could be liable) could extend the decision's actual knowledge and deliberate indifference standard to at least other Title IX and possibly Title VI employment discrimination cases as well. Cf. Davis v. Monroe County Board of Education, 526 U.S. 629, 119 S.Ct. 1661, 143 L.Ed.2d 839 (1999) (applying *Gebser* to student-student sexual harassment).(*Gebser*'s holding should be contrasted with the more liberal agency doctrine for Title VII cases pronounced by the Court in the same term. See pp. 360–378 infra.) Finally, in Barnes v. Gorman, 536 U.S. 181, 122 S.Ct. 2097, 153 L.Ed.2d 230 (2002), the Court held in a disability discrimination case brought in part under § 504 of the Rehabilitation Act of 1964, that punitive damages are not available in private suits to enforce statutes governing federal fund recipients, such as § 504, Title VI, and Title IX.

4. *The Immigration Reform and Control Act*

Although Title VII prohibits discrimination on account of national origin, it does not bar discrimination on account of alienage or lack of citizenship. See Espinoza v. Farah Mfg. Co., 414 U.S. 86, 94 S.Ct. 334, 38 L.Ed.2d 287 (1973) (permitting challenge only where citizenship requirement has disparate impact on national origin minority). This is especially significant because the immigration laws not only have historically utilized national origin categories to determine entry into this country, but also have directly restricted the employment of noncitizens who have not acquired resident alien status. Congress in Title VII presumably sought to bar only that dimension of anti-foreigner discrimination that is based on national origin rather than citizenship status.

Before 1986 employers did not violate the immigration laws by hiring nonresident aliens even though the individuals hired were themselves working in violation of federal law. However, the Immigration Reform and Control Act of 1986 (IRCA), Pub.L. 99–603, 8 U.S.C. §§ 1324a–1324b, now prohibits the knowing employment, recruitment and referral of "unauthorized aliens," defined as noncitizens who are not resident aliens or otherwise authorized to work in the United States. IRCA also requires employers to obtain documentation of citizenship or authorization to work from all employees, and subjects employers to fines for noncompliance. These provisions raised considerable concern that employers would use the documentation requirement as a device for excluding employees of particular national origins who would be unable to marshal proof of their citizenship or work-authorization.

In part to meet this concern, Congress provided in § 102 of IRCA that it is an "unfair immigration-related employment practice" to discriminate against "any individual (other than an unauthorized alien)" who is an "intending citizen" (either a resident alien or an alien seeking legalization under IRCA's amnesty program or lawfully admitted under the refugee and asylum provisions) because of such individual's national origin or "citizenship status." Expressly excluded from this provision is national origin discrimination covered by Title VII and citizenship requirements required by federal or state law or "which the Attorney General determines to be essential for an employer to do business with" a government agency. An Office of the Special Counsel for Immigration–Related Unfair Unemployment Practices, located within the Justice Department, enforces this provision. In late 1987, the Justice Department issued a ruling that § 102 of IRCA reaches only intentional citizenship status discrimination. See 28 C.F.R. Part 44. The Department thus will investigate employment barriers like English-only rules, residence requirements, or a preference for certain verification documents, only for the presence of intentional bias. IRCA's prohibition of citizenship status discrimination does not, of course, protect aliens who are not lawfully in the United States or within the "intending citizen" category.

Are workers who are "unauthorized aliens" under the IRCA protected by American employment laws? For instance, should an alien who does not receive a promotion because of his national origin be required to show that he can legally work to establish a prima facie case of discrimination under Title VII? Or should his illegal status under the IRCA be treated, under McKennon v. Nashville Banner Publishing Co., supra p. 85, like any other legitimate reason not to hire of which the employer was not aware, and thus relevant only to the remedy that the worker might obtain from the court? See Egbuna v. Time–Life Libraries, Inc., 153 F.3d 184 (4th Cir.1998) (divided en banc decision holding *McKennon* does not control; alien plaintiff must show legal authorization to work in U.S.). If unauthorized aliens are protected by Title VII, notwithstanding the IRCA, does the latter statute restrict the award of backpay or reinstatement as remedies? In Hoffman Plastic Compounds, Inc. v. NLRB, 535 U.S. 137, 122 S.Ct. 1275, 152 L.Ed.2d 271 (2002), the Court held that although an employer may violate the National Labor Relations Act by discharging undocumented aliens for supporting a union, the IRCA precludes the Labor Board from ordering backpay or reinstatement. In Rivera v. NIBCO, Inc., 364 F.3d 1057 (9th Cir. 2004), the court refused to allow an employer to conduct discovery on the immigration status of the employee plaintiffs because of the court's concern with chilling the employees' and the public's interest in enforcing Title VII. The court further opined:

We seriously doubt that *Hoffman* * * * applies in Title VII cases.
* * * First, the NLRA authorizes only certain limited private causes of
action, while Title VII depends principally upon private causes of action
for enforcement. * * * Second, Congress has armed Title VII plaintiffs
with remedies designed to punish employers who engage in unlawful
discriminatory acts, and to deter future discrimination both by the
defendant and by all other employers. Title VII's enforcement regime
includes not only traditional remedies for employment law violations,
such as backpay, frontpay, and reinstatement, but also full compensatory and punitive damages. Third, under the NLRA, the NLRB may award
backpay to workers when it has found that an employer has violated the
Act. Under Title VII, a federal court decides whether a statutory
violation warrants a backpay award. This difference is significant given
that *Hoffman* held that the NLRB possesses only the discretion to
"select and fashion remedies for violations of the NLRA," and that this
discretion, "though broad, is not unlimited." *535 U.S. at 142–43* (citations omitted). The Court held that, given the strong policies underlying
IRCA and the Board's limited power to construe statutes outside of its
authority, the NLRB's construction of the NLRA was impermissible.
This limitation on the Board's authority says nothing regarding a
federal court's power to balance IRCA against *Title VII* if the two
statutes conflict. * * *

We need not decide the *Hoffman* question in this case, however.
Regardless whether *Hoffman* applies in Title VII cases, it is clear that it
does not *require* a district court to allow the discovery sought here. No
backpay award has been authorized in this litigation. Indeed, the plaintiffs have proposed several options for ensuring that, whether or not
Hoffman applies, no award of backpay is given to any undocumented
alien in this proceeding. * * *

Id. at 1067–69. Are you persuaded by the *Rivera* court's distinction of
Hoffman?

Chapter Three

THE STATUS OF SENIORITY SYSTEMS UNDER TITLE VII

A. INTRODUCTION

Seniority rules pervade internal labor markets, providing a basis both for dispensing nonexclusive benefits, such as severance pay and sick leave, and for allocating scarce or exclusive opportunities or protections, such as choice job assignments, promotions and security against layoffs. An influential text termed provisions governing the former "benefit seniority" rules, and provisions governing the latter "competitive status seniority" rules. *See* Sumner H. Slichter, James J. Healy & E. Robert Livernash, The Impact of Collective Bargaining on Management 104–06 (1960). Several reasons explain the widespread use of such rules both in collective bargaining and even in some nonunion settings. First, seniority rules tend to promote long-term commitment to the firm. They encourage workers to acquire job-specific skills, to train newcomers without fear of being replaced, and to continue to work hard to gain deferred benefits. Second, unions traditionally have favored seniority rules because they operate to limit the discretion of management and provide a relatively neutral means of resolving the competing interests of their members. Finally, such rules enjoy legitimacy among many workers because the rules are based on a criterion—length of service—which confirms the worth of past work and which offers greater security to all workers who remain with the firm. There is also a documented, apparent psychological preference in our culture for having greater economic benefits later in life. See, e.g., George Loewenstein & Nachum Sicherman, Do Workers Prefer Increasing Wage Profiles?, J. Lab. & Econ. 67, 77–80 (1989).

Despite these advantages, seniority systems pose a major dilemma for statutes like Title VII that seek to promote the integration of previously disadvantaged groups into the larger economy. Because such systems favor incumbency and length of service over new entrants, they necessarily operate to perpetuate the effects of prior exclusion of particular groups from the workplace. This is most true of "competitive status seniority" rules, especially those governing layoffs and promotions. For instance, to the extent that an employer's average black employee, perhaps because of historical discrimination, was hired more recently than the employer's average white employee, competitive status seniority rules may make the black employee more vulnerable to being laid off in an economic downturn and less able to compete for a promotion when a better position is available. Also, many seniority systems seek to encourage long-term commitment to a particular department of the firm by requiring workers who transfer to new departments to forfeit their competitive status seniority. By discouraging blacks from transferring to more desirable departments from which they previously had been excluded, such arrangements in effect maintain prior discriminatory barriers.

Congress in § 703(h) of Title VII attempted to resolve the conflict between the legitimate interests advanced by seniority rules and the remedial goals of the statute by providing that differentials created by "bona fide" seniority systems are insulated from challenge if they "are not the result of an intention to discriminate because of race, color, religion, sex, or national origin * * *." This attempted resolution left open a number of major questions addressed in this chapter. First, to what extent does the § 703(h) shield operate as a limit on the remedies courts may order for discriminatory conduct that is independent of the operation of the seniority system?

Second, to what extent does the provision protect seniority systems in units from which blacks previously had been excluded? Initially, a number of courts, see, e.g., Local 189, United Papermakers v. United States, 416 F.2d 980 (5th Cir.1969); Quarles v. Philip Morris, Inc., 279 F.Supp. 505 (E.D.Va.1968), and commentators, see, e.g., George Cooper & Richard B. Sobol, Seniority and Testing Under Fair Employment Laws: A General Approach to Objective Criteria of Hiring and Promotion, 82 Harv.L.Rev. 1598 (1969), took the view that § 703(h) does not extend to facially neutral seniority systems that perpetuate the effects of past intentional discrimination. Although this "perpetuation" theory was available to the *Griggs* Court as a ground for invalidating Duke Power's post–1965 high school diploma and testing requirements, the Court opted for a broader disparate impact theory that authorized scrutiny on the basis of effects irrespective of the historical origin of the challenged practice, while permitting employers to provide business justifications.

The disparate impact doctrine fashioned by the *Griggs* Court was not readily transferable to seniority systems. Because such systems are in place for reasons other than the prediction of job performance, there is no easily identifiable objective criterion by which to validate as job-or business-related some, but not all, seniority systems. At the root lies a fundamental policy question—whether the legitimate reasons for adopting seniority rules are sufficient to overcome their frequent disparate impact on minority workers. In most cases, the critical issue for seniority systems is the weight of the nondiscriminatory goals, not whether particular systems serve those goals.

Finally, even if seniority systems are not invalid simply because they perpetuate past discrimination, and conventional disparate impact analysis is not available, are there special circumstances that render systems vulnerable to challenge? In particular, the language of § 703(h) raises questions about how courts should otherwise determine whether a seniority system is "bona fide" and whether it is "not the result of an intention to discriminate" on racial or other invidious grounds.

B. THE IMPACT OF TITLE VII REMEDIES ON SE-NIORITY

FRANKS v. BOWMAN TRANSPORTATION CO.
Supreme Court of the United States, 1976.
424 U.S. 747, 96 S.Ct. 1251, 47 L.Ed.2d 444.

JUSTICE BRENNAN delivered the opinion of the Court.

* * *

II

In affirming the District Court's denial of seniority relief to the class 3 group of discriminatees, the Court of Appeals held that the relief was barred by § 703(h) of Title VII, 42 U.S.C. § 2000e–2(h). We disagree. * * *

* * *

The black applicants for OTR [over-the-road] positions composing [the class 3 group of discriminatees] are limited to those whose applications were put in evidence at the trial. The underlying legal wrong affecting them is not the alleged operation of a racially discriminatory seniority system but of a racially discriminatory hiring system. Petitioners do not ask for modification or elimination of the existing seniority system, but only an award of the seniority status they would have individually enjoyed under the present system but for the illegal discriminatory refusal to hire. It is this context that must shape our determination as to the meaning and effect of § 703(h).

On its face, § 703(h) appears to be only a definitional provision; as with the other provisions of § 703, subsection (h) delineates which employment practices are illegal and thereby prohibited and which are not. Section 703(h) certainly does not expressly purport to qualify or proscribe relief otherwise appropriate under the remedial provisions of Title VII, § 706(g), 42 U.S.C. § 2000e–5(g), in circumstances where an illegal discriminatory act or practice is found. * * * There is no indication in the legislative materials that § 703(h) was intended to modify or restrict relief otherwise appropriate once an illegal discriminatory practice occurring after the effective date of the Act is proved—as in the instant case, a discriminatory refusal to hire. * * * We therefore hold that the Court of Appeals erred in concluding that, as a matter of law, § 703(h) barred the award of seniority relief to the unnamed class 3 members.

III

There remains the question whether an award of seniority relief is appropriate under the remedial provisions of Title VII, specifically, § 706(g).

* * * Last Term's *Albemarle Paper Co. v. Moody,* 422 U.S. 405, 95 S.Ct. 2362, 45 L.Ed.2d 280 (1975), consistently with the congressional plan, held that one of the central purposes of Title VII is "to make persons whole for injuries suffered on account of unlawful employment discrimination." *Id.,* at 418, 95 S.Ct., at 2372, 45 L.Ed.2d, at 297. To effectuate this "make whole" objective, Congress in § 706(g) vested broad equitable discretion in the federal courts to "order such affirmative action as may be appropriate, which may include, but is not limited to, reinstatement or hiring of employees, with or without back pay * * *, or any other equitable relief as the court deems appropriate." The legislative history supporting the 1972 amendments of § 706(g) of Title VII affirms the breadth of this discretion. "The provisions of [§ 706(g)] are intended to give the courts wide discretion exercising their equitable powers to fashion the most complete relief possible. * * * [T]he Act is intended to make the victims of unlawful employment discrimination whole, and * * * the attainment of this objective * * * requires that persons aggrieved by the consequences and effects of the unlawful employment practice be, so far as possible, restored to a position where they would have been were it not for the unlawful discrimination." Section-by-Section Analysis of H.R. 1746, accompanying the Equal Employment Opportunity Act of 1972—Conference Report, 118 Cong.Rec. 7166, 7168 (1972). This is emphatic confirmation that federal courts are empowered to fashion such relief as the particular circumstances of a case may require to effect restitution, making whole insofar as possible the victims of racial discrimination in hiring. Adequate relief may well be denied in the absence of a seniority remedy slotting the victim in that position in the seniority system that would have been his had he been hired at the time of his application. It can hardly be questioned that ordinarily such relief will be necessary to achieve the "make-whole" purposes of the Act.

Seniority systems and the entitlements conferred by credits earned thereunder are of vast and increasing importance in the economic employment system of this Nation. S. Slichter, J. Healy, & E. Livernash, The Impact of Collective Bargaining on Management 104–115 (1960). Seniority principles are increasingly used to allocate entitlements to scarce benefits among competing employees ("competitive status" seniority) and to compute noncompetitive benefits earned under the contract of employment ("benefit" seniority). *Ibid.* We have already said about "competitive status" seniority that it "has become of overriding importance, and one of its major functions is to determine who gets or who keeps an available job." *Humphrey v. Moore,* 375 U.S. 335, 346–347, 84 S.Ct. 363, 370, 11 L.Ed.2d 370, 380 (1964). "More than any other provision of the collective[-bargaining] agreement * * * seniority affects the economic security of the individual employee covered by its terms." Aaron, Reflections on the Legal Nature and Enforceability of Seniority Rights, 75 Harv.L.Rev. 1532, 1535 (1962). "Competitive status" seniority also often plays a broader role in modern employment systems, particularly systems operated under collective agreements:

> "Included among the benefits, options, and safeguards affected by competitive status seniority, are not only promotion and layoff, but also transfer, demotion, rest days, shift assignments, prerogative in scheduling vacation, order of layoff, possibilities of lateral transfer to avoid layoff, 'bumping' possibilities in the face of layoff, order of recall, training opportunities, working conditions, length of layoff endured without reducing seniority, length of layoff recall rights will withstand, overtime opportunities, parking privileges, and, in one plant, a preferred place in the punch-out line." * * *

Seniority standing in employment with respondent Bowman, computed from the departmental date of hire, determines the order of layoff and recall of employees. Further, job assignments for OTR drivers are posted for competitive bidding and seniority is used to determine the highest bidder. As OTR drivers are paid on a per-mile basis, earnings are therefore to some extent a function of seniority. Additionally, seniority computed from the company date of hire determines the length of an employee's vacation and pension benefits. Obviously merely to require Bowman to hire the class 3 victim of discrimination falls far short of a "make whole" remedy.[1] A concomitant award of the seniority credit he presumptively would have earned but for the wrongful treatment would also seem necessary in the absence of justification for denying that relief. Without an award of seniority dating from the time when he was discriminatorily refused employment, an individual who applies for and obtains employment as an OTR driver pursuant to the District Court's order will never obtain his rightful place in the hierarchy of seniority according to which these various employment benefits are distributed. He will perpetually remain subordinate to persons who, but for the illegal discrimination, would have been in respect to entitlement to these benefits his inferiors.

* * *

1. Further, at least in regard to "benefit"-type seniority such as length of vacation leave and pension benefits in the instant case, any general bar to the award of retroactive seniority for victims of illegal hiring discrimination serves to undermine the mutually reinforcing effect of the dual purposes of Title VII; it reduces the restitution required of an employer at such time as he is called upon to account for his discriminatory actions perpetrated in violation of the law. See *Albemarle Paper Co. v. Moody,* 422 U.S. 405, 417–418, 95 S.Ct. 2362, 2371–2372, 45 L.Ed.2d 280, 296–297 (1975).

IV

We are not to be understood as holding that an award of seniority status is requisite in all circumstances. The fashioning of appropriate remedies invokes the sound equitable discretion of the district courts. Respondent Bowman attempts to justify the District Court's denial of seniority relief for petitioners as an exercise of equitable discretion, but the record is its own refutation of the argument.

Albemarle Paper, supra, at 416, 95 S.Ct., at 2371, 45 L.Ed.2d, at 296, made clear that discretion imports not the court's " 'inclination, but * * * its judgment; and its judgment is to be guided by sound legal principles.' " Discretion is vested not for purposes of "limit[ing] appellate review of trial courts, or * * * invit[ing] inconsistency and caprice," but rather to allow the most complete achievement of the objectives of Title VII that is attainable under the facts and circumstances of the specific case. 422 U.S., at 421, 95 S.Ct., at 2373, 45 L.Ed.2d, at 298. Accordingly, the District Court's denial of any form of seniority remedy must be reviewed in terms of its effect on the attainment of the Act's objectives under the circumstances presented by this record. No less than with the denial of the remedy of backpay, the denial of seniority relief to victims of illegal racial discrimination in hiring is permissible "only for reasons which, if applied generally, would not frustrate the central statutory purposes of eradicating discrimination throughout the economy and making persons whole for injuries suffered through past discrimination." *Ibid.*

The District Court stated two reasons for its denial of seniority relief for the unnamed class members. The first was that those individuals had not filed administrative charges under the provisions of Title VII with the Equal Employment Opportunity Commission and therefore class relief of this sort was not appropriate. We rejected this justification for denial of class-based relief in the context of backpay awards in *Albemarle Paper,* and for the same reasons reject it here.

* * *

The second reason stated by the District Court was that such claims "presuppose a vacancy, qualification, and performance by every member. There is no evidence on which to base these multiple conclusions."

* * *

We read the District Court's reference to the lack of evidence regarding a "vacancy, qualification, and performance" for every individual member of the class as an expression of concern that some of the unnamed class members (unhired black applicants whose employment applications were summarized in the record) may not in fact have been actual victims of racial discrimination. That factor will become material however only when those persons reapply for OTR positions pursuant to the hiring relief ordered by the District Court. Generalizations concerning such individually applicable evidence cannot serve as a justification for the denial of relief to the entire class. Rather, at such time as individual class members seek positions as OTR drivers, positions for which they are presumptively entitled to priority hiring consideration under the District Court's order,[31] evidence that particular individuals were not in fact victims of racial discrimination will be material. But petitioners here have carried their burden of demonstrating the existence of a discriminatory hiring pattern and practice by the respondents and, therefore, the burden will be upon respondents to prove that individuals who reapply were not in fact victims of previous hiring discrimination. *Cf. McDonnell Douglas Corp. v. Green,* 411 U.S. 792, 802, 93 S.Ct. 1817, 1824, 36 L.Ed.2d 668, 677 (1973); *Baxter v. Savannah Sugar Rfg. Corp.,* 495 F.2d 437, 443–444 (C.A.5), cert. denied, 419 U.S. 1033, 95 S.Ct. 515, 42 L.Ed.2d 308 (1974).[32] Only if this burden is met may retroactive seniority—if otherwise determined to be an appropriate form of relief under the circumstances of the particular case—be denied individual class members.

Respondent Bowman raises an alternative theory of justification. Bowman argues that an award of retroactive seniority to the class of discriminatees will conflict with the economic interests of other Bowman employees. Accordingly, it is argued, the District Court acted within its discretion in denying this form of relief as an attempt to accommodate the competing interests of the various groups of employees.

We reject this argument for two reasons. First, the District Court made no mention of such considerations in its order denying the seniority relief. As we noted in *Albemarle Paper,* 422 U.S., at 421 n. 14, 95 S.Ct., at 2373, 45 L.Ed.2d, at 299, if the district court declines, due to the peculiar circumstances of the particular case, to award relief generally appropriate under Title VII, "[i]t is necessary * * * that * * * it carefully articulate its reasons" for so doing. Second, and more fundamentally, it is apparent that denial of seniority relief to identifiable victims of racial discrimination on the sole ground that such relief diminishes the expectations of other, arguably innocent, employees would if applied generally frustrate the central "make whole" objective of Title VII. These conflicting interests of other employees will, of course, always be present in instances where some scarce employment benefit is distributed among employees on the basis of their status in the

---

31. The District Court order is silent as to whether applicants for OTR positions who were previously discriminatorily refused employment must be presently qualified for those positions in order to be eligible for priority hiring under that order. The Court of Appeals, however, made it plain that they must be. We agree.

32. Thus, Bowman may attempt to prove that a given individual member of class 3 was not in fact discriminatorily refused employment as an OTR driver in order to defeat the individual's claim to seniority relief as well as any other remedy ordered for the class generally. Evidence of a lack of vacancies in OTR positions at the time the individual application was filed, or evidence indicating the individual's lack of qualification for the OTR positions—under nondiscriminatory standards *actually applied* by Bowman to individuals who were in fact hired—would of course be relevant. It is true, of course, that obtaining the third category of evidence with which the District Court was concerned—what the individual discriminatee's job performance would have been but for the discrimination—presents great difficulty. No reason appears, however, why the victim rather than the perpetrator of the illegal act should bear the burden of proof on this issue.

seniority hierarchy. But, as we have said, there is nothing in the language of Title VII, or in its legislative history, to show that Congress intended generally to bar this form of relief to victims of illegal discrimination, and the experience under its remedial model in the National Labor Relations Act points to the contrary.

* * *

With reference to the problems of fairness or equity respecting the conflicting interests of the various groups of employees, the relief which petitioners seek is only seniority status retroactive to the date of individual application, rather than some form of arguably more complete relief. No claim is asserted that nondiscriminatee employees holding OTR positions they would not have obtained but for the illegal discrimination should be deprived of the seniority status they have earned. It is therefore clear that even if the seniority relief petitioners seek is awarded, most if not all discriminatees who actually obtain OTR jobs under the court order will not truly be restored to the actual seniority that would have existed in the absence of the illegal discrimination. Rather, most discriminatees even under an award of retroactive seniority status will still remain subordinated in the hierarchy to a position inferior to that of a greater total number of employees than would have been the case in the absence of discrimination. Therefore, the relief which petitioners seek, while a more complete form of relief than that which the District Court accorded, in no sense constitutes "complete relief." Rather, the burden of the past discrimination in hiring is with respect to competitive status benefits divided among discriminatee and nondiscriminatee employees under the form of relief sought. The dissent criticizes the Court's result as not sufficiently cognizant that it will "directly implicate the rights and expectations of perfectly innocent employees." We are of the view, however, that the result which we reach today—which, standing alone, establishes that a sharing of the burden of the past discrimination is presumptively necessary—is entirely consistent with any fair characterization of equity jurisdiction, particularly when considered in light of our traditional view that "[a]ttainment of a great national policy * * * must not be confined within narrow canons for equitable relief deemed suitable by chancellors in ordinary private controversies." *Phelps Dodge Corp. v. NLRB,* 313 U.S. [177,] 188, 61 S.Ct. [845,] 850, 85 L.Ed. [1271,] 1280 [(1941)].

Certainly there is no argument that the award of retroactive seniority to the victims of hiring discrimination in any way deprives other employees of indefeasibly vested rights conferred by the employment contract. This Court has long held that employee expectations arising from a seniority system agreement may be modified by statutes furthering a strong public policy interest.

* * *

V

In holding that class-based seniority relief for identifiable victims of illegal hiring discrimination is a form of relief generally appropriate under § 706(g), we do not in any way modify our previously expressed view that the statutory scheme of Title VII "implicitly recognizes that there may be cases calling for one remedy but not another, and—owing to the structure of the federal judiciary—these choices are, of course, left in the first instance to the district courts." *Albemarle Paper,* 422 U.S., at 416, 95 S.Ct., at 2370, 45 L.Ed.2d at 295. Circumstances peculiar to the individual case may, of course, justify the modification or withholding of seniority relief for reasons that would not if applied generally undermine the purposes of Title VII. In the instant case it appears that all new hirees establish seniority only upon completion of a 45-day probationary period, although upon completion seniority is retroactive to the date of hire. Certainly any seniority relief ultimately awarded by the District Court could properly be cognizant of this fact. *Amici* and the respondent union point out that there may be circumstances where an award of full seniority should be deferred until completion of a training or apprentice-ship program, or other preliminaries required of all new hirees. We do not undertake to delineate all such possible circumstances here. Any enumeration must await particular cases and be determined in light of the trial courts' "keener appreciation" of peculiar facts and circum-stances. *Albemarle Paper, supra,* at 421–422, 95 S.Ct., at 2373, 45 L.Ed.2d, at 299.

Mr. Chief Justice Burger, concurring in part and dissenting in part.

* * * I would stress that although retroactive benefit-type seniority relief may sometimes be appropriate and equitable, competitive-type seniority relief at the expense of wholly innocent employees can rarely, if ever, be equitable if that term retains traditional meaning. More equita-ble would be a monetary award to the person suffering the discrimina-tion. An award such as "front pay" could replace the need for competi-tive-type seniority relief. Such monetary relief would serve the dual purpose of deterring wrongdoing by the employer or union—or both—as well as protecting the rights of innocent employees. In every respect an innocent employee is comparable to a "holder-in-due-course" of negotia-ble paper or a bona fide purchaser of property without notice of any defect in the seller's title. In this setting I cannot join in judicial approval of "robbing Peter to pay Paul."

I would stress that the Court today does not foreclose claims of employees who might be injured by this holding from securing equitable relief on their own behalf.

INTERNATIONAL BROTH. OF TEAMSTERS
v. UNITED STATES

Supreme Court of the United States, 1977.
431 U.S. 324, 97 S.Ct. 1843, 52 L.Ed.2d 396.

[*Eds.* For additional excerpts from this decision, see pp. 90–94 supra and pp. 224–228 infra.]

Justice Stewart delivered the opinion of the Court.

III

Our conclusion that the seniority system does not violate Title VII will necessarily affect the remedy granted to individual employees on remand of this litigation to the District Court. Those employees who suffered only pre-Act discrimination are not entitled to relief, and no person may be given retroactive seniority to a date earlier than the effective date of the Act. Several other questions relating to the appropriate measure of individual relief remain, however, for our consideration.

The petitioners argue generally that the trial court did not err in tailoring the remedy to the "degree of injury" suffered by each individual employee, and that the Court of Appeals' "qualification date" formula sweeps with too broad a brush by granting a remedy to employees who were not shown to be actual victims of unlawful discrimination. Specifically, the petitioners assert that no employee should be entitled to relief until the Government demonstrates that he was an actual victim of the company's discriminatory practices; that no employee who did not apply for a line-driver job should be granted retroactive competitive seniority; and that no employee should be elevated to a line-driver job ahead of any current line driver on layoff status. We consider each of these contentions separately.

A

* * *

If an employer fails to rebut the inference that arises from the Government's prima facie case, a trial court may then conclude that a violation has occurred and determine the appropriate remedy. Without any further evidence from the Government, a court's finding of a pattern or practice justifies an award of prospective relief. Such relief might take the form of an injunctive order against continuation of the discriminatory practice, an order that the employer keep records of its future employment decisions and file periodic reports with the court, or any other order "necessary to ensure the full enjoyment of the rights" protected by Title VII.

When the Government seeks individual relief for the victims of the discriminatory practice, a district court must usually conduct additional proceedings after the liability phase of the trial to determine the scope of individual relief. The petitioners' contention in this case is that if the Government has not, in the course of proving a pattern or practice, already brought forth specific evidence that each individual was discriminatorily denied an employment opportunity, it must carry that burden at the second, "remedial" stage of trial. That basic contention was rejected in the *Franks* case. As was true of the particular facts in *Franks,* and as is typical of Title VII pattern-or-practice suits, the question of individual relief does not arise until it has been proved that the employer has followed an employment policy of unlawful discrimination. The force of that proof does not dissipate at the remedial stage of the trial. The employer cannot, therefore, claim that there is no reason to believe that its individual employment decisions were discriminatorily based; it has already been shown to have maintained a policy of discriminatory decisionmaking.

The proof of the pattern or practice supports an inference that any particular employment decision, during the period in which the discriminatory policy was in force, was made in pursuit of that policy. The Government need only show that an alleged individual discriminatee unsuccessfully applied for a job and therefore was a potential victim of the proved discrimination. As in *Franks,* the burden then rests on the employer to demonstrate that the individual applicant was denied an employment opportunity for lawful reasons. See 424 U.S., at 773 n. 32, 96 S.Ct., at 1268.

* * * [W]e have held that the District Court and Court of Appeals were not in error in finding that the Government had proved a system-wide pattern and practice of racial and ethnic discrimination on the part of the company. On remand, therefore, every post-Act minority group applicant[49] for a line-driver position will be presumptively entitled to relief, subject to a showing by the company that its earlier refusal to place the applicant in a line-driver job was not based on its policy of discrimination.[50]

B

* * *

The question whether seniority relief may be awarded to nonapplicants was left open by our decision in *Franks,* since the class at issue in that case was limited to "identifiable applicants who were denied employment * * * after the effective date * * * of Title VII." 424 U.S., at 750, 96 S.Ct., at 1257. We now decide that an incumbent employee's failure to apply for a job is not an inexorable bar to an award of retroactive seniority. Individual nonapplicants must be given an opportunity to undertake their difficult task of proving that they should be treated as applicants and therefore are presumptively entitled to relief accordingly.

* * * The effects of and the injuries suffered from discriminatory employment practices are not always confined to those who were expressly denied a requested employment opportunity. A consistently enforced discriminatory policy can surely deter job applications from those who are aware of it and are unwilling to subject themselves to the humiliation of explicit and certain rejection.

---

49. Employees who initially applied for line-driver jobs and were hired in other jobs before the effective date of the Act, and who did not later apply for transfer to line-driver jobs, are part of the group of nonapplicants discussed *infra.*

50. Any nondiscriminatory justification offered by the company will be subject to

further evidence by the Government that the purported reason for an applicant's rejection was in fact a pretext for unlawful discrimination. *McDonnell Douglas Corp. v. Green,* 411 U.S., at 804–806, 93 S.Ct., at 1825–1826.

If an employer should announce his policy of discrimination by a sign reading "Whites Only" on the hiring-office door, his victims would not be limited to the few who ignored the sign and subjected themselves to personal rebuffs. The same message can be communicated to potential applicants more subtly but just as clearly by an employer's actual practices—by his consistent discriminatory treatment of actual applicants, by the manner in which he publicizes vacancies, his recruitment techniques, his responses to casual or tentative inquiries, and even by the racial or ethnic composition of that part of his work force from which he has discriminatorily excluded members of minority groups. When a person's desire for a job is not translated into a formal application solely because of his unwillingness to engage in a futile gesture he is as much a victim of discrimination as is he who goes through the motions of submitting an application.

* * *

The denial of Title VII relief on the ground that the claimant had not formally applied for the job could exclude from the Act's coverage the victims of the most entrenched forms of discrimination. Victims of gross and pervasive discrimination could be denied relief precisely because the unlawful practices had been so successful as totally to deter job applications from members of minority groups.

* * *

To conclude that a person's failure to submit an application for a job does not inevitably and forever foreclose his entitlement to seniority relief under Title VII is a far cry, however, from holding that nonapplicants are always entitled to such relief. A nonapplicant must show that he was a potential victim of unlawful discrimination. Because he is necessarily claiming that he was deterred from applying for the job by the employer's discriminatory practices, his is the not always easy burden of proving that he would have applied for the job had it not been for those practices. Cf. *Mt. Healthy City Board of Education v. Doyle,* 429 U.S. 274, 97 S.Ct. 568, 50 L.Ed.2d 471. When this burden is met, the nonapplicant is in a position analogous to that of an applicant * * *.

The Government contends that the evidence it presented in this case at the liability stage of the trial identified all nonapplicants as victims of unlawful discrimination "with a fair degree of specificity," and that the Court of Appeals' determination that qualified nonapplicants are presumptively entitled to an award of seniority should accordingly be affirmed. In support of this contention the Government cites its proof of an extended pattern and practice of discrimination as evidence that an application from a minority employee for a line-driver job would have been a vain and useless act. It further argues that since the class of nonapplicant discriminatees is limited to incumbent employees, it is likely that every class member was aware of the futility of seeking a line-driver job and was therefore deterred from filing both an initial and a followup application.[52]

We cannot agree. While the scope and duration of the company's discriminatory policy can leave little doubt that the futility of seeking line-driver jobs was communicated to the company's minority employees, that in itself is insufficient. The known prospect of discriminatory rejection shows only that employees who wanted line-driving jobs may have been deterred from applying for them. It does not show which of the nonapplicants actually wanted such jobs, or which possessed the requisite qualifications.[53] There are differences between city-and line-driving jobs, for example, but the desirability of the latter is not so self-evident as to warrant a conclusion that all employees would prefer to be line drivers if given a free choice.[55] Indeed, a substantial number of white city drivers who were not subjected to the company's discriminatory practices were apparently content to retain their city jobs.

* * * A willingness to accept the job security and bidding power afforded by retroactive seniority says little about what choice an employee would have made had he previously been given the opportunity freely to choose a starting line-driver job. While it may be true that many of the nonapplicant employees desired and would have applied for line-

52. * * * The refused applicants in *Franks* had been denied an opportunity they clearly sought, and the only issue to be resolved was whether the denial was pursuant to a proved discriminatory practice. Resolution of the nonapplicant's claim, however, requires two distinct determinations: that he would have applied but for discrimination and that he would have been discriminatorily rejected had he applied. The mere fact of incumbency does not resolve the first issue, although it may tend to support a nonapplicant's claim to the extent that it shows he was willing and competent to work as a driver, that he was familiar with the tasks of line drivers, etc. An incumbent's claim that he would have applied for a line-driver job would certainly be more superficially plausible than a similar claim by a member of the general public who may never have worked in the trucking industry or heard of the company prior to suit.

53. Inasmuch as the purpose of the nonapplicant's burden of proof will be to establish that his status is similar to that of the applicant, he must bear the burden of coming forward with the basic information about his qualifications that he would have presented in an application. As in *Franks,* * * * the burden then will be on the employer to show that the nonapplicant was nevertheless not a victim of discrimination. For example, the employer might show that there were other, more qualified persons who would have been chosen for a particu-

lar vacancy, or that the nonapplicant's stated qualifications were insufficient. See *Franks,* 424 U.S., at 773 n. 32, 96 S.Ct., at 1268.

55. The company's line drivers generally earned more annually than its city drivers, but the difference varied from under $1,000 to more than $5,000 depending on the terminal and the year. In 1971 city drivers at two California terminals, "LOS" and San Francisco, earned substantially more than the line drivers at those terminals. In addition to earnings, line drivers have the advantage of not being required to load and unload their trucks. City drivers, however, have regular working hours, are not required to spend extended periods away from home and family, and do not face the hazards of long-distance driving at high speeds. As the Government acknowledged at argument, the jobs are in some sense "parallel"—some may prefer one job and some may prefer another.

The District Court found generally that line-driver jobs "are considered the most desirable of the driving jobs." That finding is not challenged here, and we see no reason to disturb it. We observe only that the differences between city and line driving were not such that it can be said with confidence that all minority employees free from the threat of discriminatory treatment would have chosen to give up city for line driving.

driver jobs but for their knowledge of the company's policy of discrimination, the Government must carry its burden of proof, with respect to each specific individual, at the remedial hearings to be conducted by the District Court on remand.[58]

C

The task remaining for the District Court on remand will not be a simple one. Initially, the court will have to make a substantial number of individual determinations in deciding which of the minority employees were actual victims of the company's discriminatory practices. After the victims have been identified, the court must, as nearly as possible, " 'recreate the conditions and relationships that would have been had there been no' " unlawful discrimination. *Franks,* 424 U.S., at 769, 96 S.Ct., at 1266. This process of recreating the past will necessarily involve a degree of approximation and imprecision. Because the class of victims may include some who did not apply for line-driver jobs as well as those who did, and because more than one minority employee may have been denied each line-driver vacancy, the court will be required to balance the equities of each minority employee's situation in allocating the limited number of vacancies that were discriminatorily refused to class members. * * *

After the evidentiary hearings to be conducted on remand, both the size and the composition of the class of minority employees entitled to relief may be altered substantially. Until those hearings have been conducted and both the number of identifiable victims and the consequent extent of necessary relief have been determined, it is not possible to evaluate abstract claims concerning the equitable balance that should be struck between the statutory rights of victims and the contractual rights of nonvictim employees.[61] That determination is best left, in the first instance, to the sound equitable discretion of the trial court.[62]

58. While the most convincing proof would be some overt act such as a pre-Act application for a line-driver job, the District Court may find evidence of an employee's informal inquiry, expression of interest, or even unexpressed desire credible and convincing. The question is a factual one for determination by the trial judge.

61. The petitioners argue that to permit a victim of discrimination to use his rightful-place seniority to bid on a line-driver job before the recall of all employees on layoff would amount to a racial or ethnic preference in violation of § 703(j) of the Act. Section 703(j) provides no support for this argument. It provides only that Title VII does not require an employer to grant preferential treatment to any group in order to rectify an imbalance between the composition of the employer's work force and the makeup of the population at large. To allow

identifiable victims of unlawful discrimination to participate in a layoff recall is not the kind of "preference" prohibited by § 703(j). If a discriminatee is ultimately allowed to secure a position before a laid-off line driver, a question we do not now decide, he will do so because of the bidding power inherent in his rightful-place seniority, and not because of a preference based on race. See *Franks,* 424 U.S., at 792, 96 S.Ct., at 1277 (Powell, J., concurring in part and dissenting in part).

62. Other factors, such as the number of victims, the number of nonvictim employees affected and the alternatives available to them, and the economic circumstances of the industry may also be relevant in the exercise of the District Court's discretion. See *Franks, supra,* at 796 n. 17, 96 S.Ct., at 1362 (Powell, J., concurring in part and dissenting in part).

Notes and Questions

1. *Why Does § 703(h) Not Apply to Title VII Remedies?* The *Franks* Court draws a distinction between (i) direct challenges to the validity of a seniority system (as to which the § 703(h) shield may apply) and (ii) remedies for discriminatory conduct that is independent of the operation of a seniority system (as to which § 703(h) apparently has no application). What is the practical significance of this distinction? Is it consistent with the statutory language? With a coherent explanation of legislative purpose?

2. *Seniority and "Make Whole" Relief Under § 706(g).* Building on *Albemarle,* the Court in *Franks* explains that a court's equitable discretion under § 706(g) is bounded by the "make whole" principle: victims of discrimination should be placed, as nearly as possible, in the position that they would have occupied in the absence of discrimination. Does the *Franks* Court nonetheless seem to permit departures from the "make whole" ideal? Why does the Court stop short of requiring full "rightful place" seniority, even if this means allowing discriminatees to bump incumbent employees? Is there really a difference in principle between bumping laid-off workers on a recall list and bumping them when on the job? Indeed, in cases decided under the National Labor Relations Act (NLRA), incumbents who obtain their jobs because they replaced those who were out on an unfair labor practice (ULP) strike are invariably displaced by reinstated ULP strikers, on the theory that the act of replacing those strikers was void *ab initio.* Is this situation analogous to the race-based hiring or promotion of white workers?

The lower courts generally have ordered the displacement of incumbent employees only in "extraordinary" circumstances "when a careful balancing of the equities" indicates that absent bumping plaintiff's relief will be inadequate. See Walters v. City of Atlanta, 803 F.2d 1135, 1149 (11th Cir.1986) (plaintiff, who was frequent victim of discrimination, sought a unique position, and bumped employee could make lateral move). See also Lander v. Lujan, 888 F.2d 153, 156–58 (D.C.Cir.1989) (employer may be required to displace a high-level employee to open a job where there are no reasonable substitutes for victim of discrimination). Courts, however, generally have required only that victims of discrimination be given priority for future openings. See, e.g., Mims v. Wilson, 514 F.2d 106 (5th Cir.1975) (remanding to district court to consider the feasibility of affirmative recruitment efforts).

3. *When May Retroactive Seniority Relief Be Denied?* In what other ways do *Franks* and *Teamsters* require a Title VII Court to account for incumbent employees' interests when fashioning retroactive seniority? What if there are a large number of "rightful place" claimants relative to the number of positions? Compare Romasanta v. United Air Lines, 717 F.2d 1140 (7th Cir.1983) (award of retroactive seniority would result in discharge of hundreds of incumbents), with EEOC v. Rath Packing, 787 F.2d 318, 335 (8th Cir.1986) (grant of retroactive seniority would defeat expectations, but not result in discharges). Should victims of discrimination be deprived of retroactive seniority, or have such awards delayed, when there are a large number of workers on lay-off status?

4. *Should Incumbent Workers Have to Bear the Burden of Seniority Relief?* Is the "sharing of the burden" compromise fashioned in *Franks* satisfactory? Should white (or male) workers have to "pay" (in terms of greater vulnerability to layoff or lowered chances of obtaining a desired promotion) for an employer's past illegal decisions? Is the *Franks* approach likely to create antagonisms among groups of workers destructive of the larger objective of integration of previously excluded groups in the workplace? Should culpable employers be required to retain both discrimination victims and the incumbent employees who would have been displaced under *Franks*? See Iris D. Burke & Oscar G. Chase, Resolving The Seniority/Minority Layoffs Conflict: An Employer–Targeted Approach, 13 Harv.C.R.–C.L.L. Rev. 81 (1978). Does Chief Justice Burger have the better view in arguing for a presumption in favor of monetary remedies such as "front pay", or are there more serious problems with the "front pay" option? Would it be preferable to provide compensation to the incumbent employees displaced by *Franks* remedial orders? See Note, Compensating Victims of Preferential Employment Discrimination Remedies, 98 Yale L.J. 1479 (1989). See generally Richard Fallon & Paul C. Weiler, Conflicting Models of Racial Justice, 1984 Sup. Ct. Rev. 1, 58.

5. *Burden of Proof on Employer at Remediation Stage.* Both principal cases involve allegations of systemic disparate treatment. The Court indicates that such litigation may be divided into liability and remediation stages. In the first stage, as explained in chapter 2, the plaintiffs have the burden of demonstrating the existence of a pattern or practice of discrimination. Once a discriminatory policy has been found, a shift in the burden of persuasion occurs. All applicants (and some nonapplicants) for the disputed positions are presumed to have been victims of that policy. What precisely is the burden that is imposed on employers at the remedial stage? How might employers carry that burden? Consider footnotes 31 and 32 in *Franks* and footnote 53 in *Teamsters*.

Will employers at this stage of the litigation be required to give back pay and retroactive seniority to more members of a plaintiff class than they would or even could have hired absent discrimination? Compare, e.g., United States v. Lee Way Motor Freight, Inc., 625 F.2d 918, 935–36, (10th Cir.1979) (remedy not limited to the percentage of blacks in the employment area population), with Association Against Discrimination in Employment, Inc. v. City of Bridgeport, 647 F.2d 256, 270, 282 (2d Cir.1981) (order of back pay and instatement priority limited to the number of possible victims reflecting percentage of minorities in the labor force). No court seems to have ordered the instatement of a number of potential victims greater than the number of openings that the employer had available during the period of discrimination.

6. *Nonapplicants: Broadening the Class of Possible Discriminatees.* *Teamsters* expands the class of victims entitled to retroactive seniority to include some individuals who never actually applied for the jobs in question but can prove that they would have applied but for the employer's discriminatory policy. How might nonapplicant plaintiffs go about proving what they might have done in that hypothetical situation?

Does the deterred applicant theory accepted by the Court in *Teamsters* allow all nonapplicant members of a protected class at least to proceed to trial if they can present a prima facie case of a pattern and practice of discrimination, or must nonapplicants to avoid summary judgment allege further facts sufficient to prove their hypothetical intent and the futility of application? See, e.g., Wynn v. National Broadcasting Co., Inc., 234 F.Supp.2d 1067 (C.D.Cal. 2002) (nonapplicant in age discrimination case must allege more than pattern and practice of discrimination to avoid summary judgment). Cf. also Fox v. Baltimore City Police Dept., 201 F.3d 526 (4th Cir.2000) (deterred applicant theory not available under Veterans' Reemployment Rights Act).

7. *Class-Wide Remedies. Teamsters* states that certain equitable remedies can be imposed on a defendant in a pattern-or-practice case before any individuals establish their claims for relief. Are any of the remedies listed by the Court likely to be significant? Are race-based hiring goals permissible even if the beneficiaries are not *Franks*-discriminatees? This is one of the questions addressed in the next chapter.

8. *Who Is Bound By Seniority Relief Orders?* A union need not be found guilty of discrimination in order for it (or its members) to be subject to an order that awards retroactive seniority in derogation of the seniority arrangements established in its collective agreement. See Zipes v. Trans World Airlines, 455 U.S. 385, 399, 102 S.Ct. 1127, 1135, 71 L.Ed.2d 234 (1982). However, under the terms of § 703(n), as added by § 108 of the Civil Rights Act of 1991, employees who are not parties to the litigation leading to the remedial seniority award would not be barred from challenging an order that altered their seniority rights, unless they had "actual notice" and a reasonable opportunity to present objections to the order prior to its entry, or unless their interests were "adequately represented by another person who had previously challenged" the order.

Note on Ford Motor Co. v. EEOC

Under § 706(g), "[i]nterim earnings or amounts earnable with reasonable diligence by the person or persons discriminated against shall operate to reduce the back pay otherwise allocable." To what extent does this mitigation principle operate as a limitation on *Franks*-type seniority relief? It seems clear that if immediately after being rejected for a position by a discriminatory employer, an individual secures a position with another employer at the same salary and benefits and with the same seniority that the individual would have had with the first employer, there can be no back pay or seniority award for that individual. The same would seem to follow if the first employer had second thoughts about a previous decision and offered the discriminatee reinstatement with back pay and seniority from the date of the initial application. However, what if the first employer offers reinstatement only, with back pay and competitive seniority to await the outcome of litigation? Should such an offer, if refused, operate to curtail liability for post-offer back pay and seniority?

In Ford Motor Co. v. EEOC, 458 U.S. 219, 102 S.Ct. 3057, 73 L.Ed.2d 721 (1982), the Supreme Court gave an affirmative answer to the last question. In that case, plaintiffs, having been laid-off by General Motors, applied at a nearby Ford plant for equivalent positions, which were discriminatorily denied to them. The plaintiffs then were recalled to their former positions at General Motors. Ford subsequently offered plaintiffs positions similar to the ones they had previously been denied, but without back pay or competitive seniority. The Supreme Court, in an opinion by Justice O'Connor, held that this offer was sufficient to toll post-offer back pay liability. The Court believed its rule to be consistent with the "make whole" remedial objective of § 706(g): "we conclude that when a claimant rejects the offer of the job he originally sought, as supplemented by a right to full court-ordered compensation, his choice can be taken as establishing that he considers the ongoing injury he has suffered at the hands of the defendant to have been ended by availability of better opportunities elsewhere." Id. at 238.

The *Ford* decision, however, may in part rest on the protection of the seniority expectations of incumbent employees. Justice O'Connor stressed that if tolling did not occur after an offer of reinstatement without seniority, "an employer may cap backpay liability only by forcing his incumbent employees to yield seniority to a person who has not proved, and may never prove, unlawful discrimination." Id. at 239. The dissent by Justice Blackmun in *Ford* argued that the majority was authorizing employers to make "cheap offers" of reinstatement to their discrimination victims that the victims often cannot reasonably accept. Moreover, Justice Blackmun emphasized, if an offer is accepted, a claimant must work for a time at a seniority disadvantage and continue to suffer the effects of the employer's discriminatory conduct.

C.   DIRECT TITLE VII CHALLENGES TO SENIORITY SYSTEMS

INTERNATIONAL BROTH. OF TEAMSTERS v. UNITED STATES

Supreme Court of the United States, 1977.
431 U.S. 324, 97 S.Ct. 1843, 52 L.Ed.2d 396.

[*Eds.* For additional excerpts, see pp. 90–94 and 215–220 supra.]

MR. JUSTICE STEWART delivered the opinion of the Court.

The District Court and the Court of Appeals also found that the seniority system contained in the collective-bargaining agreements between the company and the union operated to violate Title VII of the Act.

For purposes of calculating benefits, such as vacations, pensions, and other fringe benefits, an employee's seniority under this system runs from the date he joins the company, and takes into account his total service in all jobs and bargaining units. For competitive purposes, however, such as determining the order in which employees may bid for particular jobs, are laid off, or are recalled from layoff, it is bargaining-unit seniority that controls. Thus, a line driver's seniority, for purposes of bidding for particular runs and protection against layoff, takes into account only the length of time he has been a line driver at a particular terminal. The practical effect is that a city driver or serviceman who transfers to a line-driver job must forfeit all the competitive seniority he has accumulated in his previous bargaining unit and start at the bottom of the line drivers' "board."

The vice of this arrangement, as found by the District Court and the Court of Appeals, was that it "locked" minority workers into inferior jobs and perpetuated prior discrimination by discouraging transfers to jobs as line drivers. While the disincentive applied to all workers, including whites, it was Negroes and Spanish-surnamed persons who, those courts found, suffered the most because many of them had been denied the equal opportunity to become line drivers when they were initially hired, whereas whites either had not sought or were refused line-driver positions for reasons unrelated to their race or national origin.

* * *

The union, while acknowledging that the seniority system may in some sense perpetuate the effects of prior discrimination, asserts that the system is immunized from a finding of illegality by reason of § 703(h) of Title VII.

* * *

The Government responds that a seniority system that perpetuates the effects of prior discrimination—pre-Act or post-Act—can never be "bona fide" under § 703(h); at a minimum Title VII prohibits those applications of a seniority system that perpetuate the effects on incumbent employees of prior discriminatory job assignments.

* * *

Because the company discriminated both before and after the enactment of Title VII, the seniority system is said to have operated to perpetuate the effects of both pre-and post-Act discrimination. Post–Act discriminatees, however, may obtain full "make whole" relief, including retroactive seniority under *Franks v. Bowman, supra,* without attacking the legality of the seniority system as applied to them. *Franks* made clear and the union acknowledges that retroactive seniority may be awarded as relief from an employer's discriminatory hiring and assignment policies even if the seniority system agreement itself makes no provision for such relief. 424 U.S., at 778–779, 96 S.Ct., at 1271. Here the Government has proved that the company engaged in a post-Act pattern of discriminatory hiring, assignment, transfer and promotion policies. Any Negro or Spanish-surnamed American injured by those policies may receive all appropriate relief as a direct remedy for this discrimination.[30]

30. The legality of the seniority system insofar as it perpetuates post-Act discrimination nonetheless remains at issue in this case, in light of the injunction entered against the union. Our decision today in *United Air Lines, Inc. v. Evans,* 431 U.S.

What remains for review is the judgment that the seniority system unlawfully perpetuated the effects of *pre-Act* discrimination. We must decide, in short, whether § 703(h) validates otherwise bona fide seniority systems that afford no constructive seniority to victims discriminated against prior to the effective date of Title VII, and it is to that issue that we now turn.

* * *

Were it not for § 703(h), the seniority system in this case would seem to fall under the *Griggs* rationale. The heart of the system is its allocation of the choicest jobs, the greatest protection against layoffs, and other advantages to those employees who have been line drivers for the longest time. Where, because of the employer's prior intentional discrimination, the line drivers with the longest tenure are without exception white, the advantages of the seniority system flow disproportionately to them and away from Negro and Spanish-surnamed employees who might by now have enjoyed those advantages had not the employer discriminated before the passage of the Act. This disproportionate distribution of advantages does in a very real sense "operate to 'freeze' the status quo of prior discriminatory employment practices." But both the literal terms of § 703(h) and the legislative history of Title VII demonstrate that Congress considered this very effect of many seniority systems and extended a measure of immunity to them.

Throughout the initial consideration of H.R. 7152, later enacted as the Civil Rights Act of 1964, critics of the bill charged that it would destroy existing seniority rights.[33] The consistent response of Title VII's congressional proponents and of the Justice Department was that seniority rights would not be affected, even where the employer had discriminated prior to the Act. An interpretive memorandum placed in the Congressional Record by Senators Clark and Case stated:

> "Title VII would have no effect on established seniority rights. Its effect is prospective and not retrospective. Thus, for example, *if a business has been discriminating in the past and as a result has an all-white working force, when the title comes into effect the employer's obligation would be simply to fill future vacancies on a non-discriminatory basis.* He would not be obliged—or indeed, permitted—to fire whites in order to hire Negroes or to prefer Negroes for

553, 97 S.Ct. 1885, 52 L.Ed.2d 571, is largely dispositive of this issue. *Evans* holds that the operation of a seniority system is not unlawful under Title VII even though it perpetuates post-Act discrimination that has not been the subject of a timely charge by the discriminatee. Here, of course, the Government has sued to remedy the post-Act discrimination directly, and there is no claim that any relief would be time barred. But this is simply an additional reason not to hold the seniority system unlawful, since such a holding would in no way enlarge the relief to be awarded. See *Franks v. Bow-*

man, Transportation Co., 424 U.S. 747, 778–779, 96 S.Ct. 1251, 1271, 47 L.Ed.2d 444. Section 703(h) on its face immunizes all bona fide seniority systems, and does not distinguish between the perpetuation of pre-and post-Act discrimination.

33. *E.g.*, H.R.Rep. No. 914, 88th Cong., 1st Sess., 65–66, 71 (1963) (minority report); 110 Cong.Rec. 486–488 (1964) (remarks of Sen. Hill); *id.*, at 2726 (remarks of Rep. Dowdy); *id.*, at 7091 (remarks of Sen. Stennis).

future vacancies, or, once Negroes are hired, to give them special seniority rights at the expense of the white workers hired earlier." 110 Cong.Rec. 7213 (1964) (emphasis added).[35]

A Justice Department statement concerning Title VII, placed in the Congressional Record by Senator Clark, voiced the same conclusion:

"Title VII would have no effect on seniority rights existing at the time it takes effect. If, for example, a collective bargaining contract provides that in the event of layoffs, those who were hired last must be laid off first, such a provision would not be affected in the least by title VII. *This would be true even in the case where owing to discrimination prior to the effective date of the title, white workers had more seniority than Negroes." Id.,* at 7207 (emphasis added).

While these statements were made before § 703(h) was added to Title VII, they are authoritative indicators of that section's purpose. Section 703(h) was enacted as part of the Mansfield–Dirksen compromise substitute bill that cleared the way for the passage of Title VII. The drafters of the compromise bill stated that one of its principal goals was to resolve the ambiguities in the House-passed version of H.R. 7152. * * * As the debates indicate, one of those ambiguities concerned Title VII's impact on existing collectively bargained seniority rights.

* * *

To be sure, § 703(h) does not immunize all seniority systems. It refers only to "bona fide" systems, and a proviso requires that any differences in treatment not be "the result of an intention to discriminate because of race * * * or national origin * * *." But our reading of the legislative history compels us to reject the Government's broad argument that no seniority system that tends to perpetuate pre-Act discrimination can be "bona fide." To accept the argument would require us to hold that a seniority system becomes illegal simply because it allows the full exercise of the pre-Act seniority rights of employees of a company that discriminated before Title VII was enacted. It would place an affirmative obligation on the parties to the seniority agreement to subordinate those rights in favor of the claims of pre-Act discriminatees without seniority. The consequence would be a perversion of the congressional purpose. We cannot accept the invitation to disembowel § 703(h) by reading the words "bona fide" as the Government would have us do.[38]

35. Senators Clark and Case were the "bipartisan captains" responsible for Title VII during the Senate debate. Bipartisan captains were selected for each title of the Civil Rights Act by the leading proponents of the Act in both parties. They were responsible for explaining their title in detail, defending it, and leading discussion on it. * * *

38. For the same reason, we reject the contention that the proviso in § 703(h), which bars differences in treatment resulting from "an intention to discriminate,"

applies to any application of a seniority system that may perpetuate past discrimination. In this regard the language of the Justice Department memorandum introduced at the legislative hearings, is especially pertinent: "It is perfectly clear that when a worker is laid off or denied a chance for promotion because under established seniority rules he is 'low man on the totem pole' he is not being discriminated against because of his race. * * * Any differences in treatment based on established seniority rights would not be based on race and

Accordingly, we hold that an otherwise neutral, legitimate seniority system does not become unlawful under Title VII simply because it may perpetuate pre-Act discrimination.

* * *

That conclusion is inescapable even in a case, such as this one, where the pre-Act discriminatees are incumbent employees who accumulated seniority in other bargaining units. Although there seems to be no explicit reference in the legislative history to pre-Act discriminatees already employed in less desirable jobs, there can be no rational basis for distinguishing their claims from those of persons initially denied *any* job but hired later with less seniority than they might have had in the absence of pre-Act discrimination.[41]

The seniority system in this litigation is entirely bona fide. It applies equally to all races and ethnic groups. To the extent that it "locks" employees into non-line-driver jobs, it does so for all. The city drivers and servicemen who are discouraged from transferring to line-driver jobs are not all Negroes or Spanish-surnamed Americans; to the contrary, the overwhelming majority are white. The placing of line drivers in a separate bargaining unit from other employees is rational in accord with the industry practice, and consistent with National Labor Relations Board precedents.[42] It is conceded that the seniority system did not have its genesis in racial discrimination, and that it was negotiated and has been maintained free from any illegal purpose. In these circumstances, the single fact that the system extends no retroactive seniority to pre-Act discriminatees does not make it unlawful.

[*Eds.* The opinion of JUSTICE MARSHALL, with whom JUSTICE BRENNAN joins, concurring in part and dissenting in part, is omitted.]

Notes and Questions

1. *Was the Court's Rejection of the "Perpetuation" Theory Required by § 703(h)?* Does *Teamsters* hold that bona fide seniority systems cannot be

would not be forbidden by the title." 110 Cong.Rec. 7207 (1964).

41. In addition, there is no reason to suppose that Congress intended in 1964 to extend less protection to legitimate departmental seniority systems than to plantwide seniority systems. Then, as now, seniority was measured in a number of ways, including length of time with the employer, in a particular plant, in a department, in a job, or in a line of progression. See Aaron, Reflections on the Legal Nature and Enforceability of Seniority Rights, 75 Harv.L.Rev. 1532, 1534 (1962); Cooper & Sobol, Seniority and Testing under Fair Employment Laws: A General Approach to Objective Criteria of Hiring and Promotion, 82 Harv. L.Rev. 1598, 1602 (1969). The legislative

history contains no suggestion that any one system was preferred.

42. See *Georgia Highway Express,* 150 N.L.R.B. 1649, 1651: "The Board has long held that local drivers and over-the-road drivers constitute separate appropriate units where they are shown to be clearly defined, homogeneous, and functionally distinct groups with separate interests which can effectively be represented separately for bargaining purposes. * * * In view of the different duties and functions, separate supervision, and different bases of payment, it is clear that the over-the-road drivers have divergent interests from those of the employees in the [city operations] unit * * * and should not be included in that unit."

challenged on the ground that they perpetuate the effects of past discrimination? Is this the only reasonable reading that can be given to § 703(h)? Can its language, "provided such differences are not the result of an intention to discriminate," be read to mean "not the result of the perpetuation of intentional discrimination"? See *Quarles,* supra, 279 F.Supp. at 518 ("The Act does not condone present differences that are the result of an intention to discriminate before the effective date of the act"). Would such a reading preserve any role for § 703(h)?

The pre-*Teamsters* decisions in the lower courts drew a distinction between claimants who were incumbent employees challenging the seniority system's perpetuation of pre-Act discrimination in departmental and job assignments, and claimants who never obtained a job because of hiring discrimination. Section 703(h) therefore was read to protect the employment seniority rather than departmental or job seniority of incumbent white employees. See, e.g., *Quarles* and *Papermakers, Local 189*, both cited at p. 208 supra. The distinction between discrimination victims who were not permitted to do any work for an employer and victims who actually did work might be sensible as a political compromise; but can it be supported by the language of § 703(h)?

2. *Disparate Impact Challenges to Seniority Systems After* Teamsters? Does *Teamsters* preclude any role for disparate impact analysis in seniority system challenges? Does the decision effectively interpret § 703(h) to establish an irrebuttable presumption that any bona fide seniority system is justified as business-related and that there are no less restrictive alternatives that must be used in its stead? What is the justification for such a presumption? Would application of the usual disparate impact methodology make any difference in most cases as long as employers could justify any disparate impact in terms of the protection of the expectations of incumbent employees? Would the *Teamsters* case, for instance, have been decided differently under a *Griggs* test if protection of incumbent employee expectations is an adequate justification? Even if protection of seniority expectations would ordinarily suffice, however, are there aspects of seniority systems that might be amenable to a *Griggs*-type challenge because they directly advance neither incumbent employee expectations or job performance? Reconsider this question after reading the *Evans* and *Bryant* decisions later in this chapter.

3. *"Bona Fide" Seniority Systems?* Seniority systems are protected by § 703(h) only if they are "bona fide." Review the Court's discussion of the reasons why the system in that case was bona fide. Within a year of the *Teamsters* decision, the Fifth Circuit read this discussion to focus on four factors critical to judging whether a seniority system is bona fide: (1) whether the seniority system operates to discourage all employees equally from transferring between seniority units; (2) whether the seniority units are in the same or separate bargaining units (if the latter, whether that structure is rational and in conformance with industry practice); (3) whether the seniority system had its genesis in racial discrimination; and (4) whether the system was negotiated and has been maintained free from any illegal purpose. James v. Stockham Valves & Fittings Co., 559 F.2d 310, 352 (5th Cir.1977). See generally Mark Brodin, Role of Fault and Motive in Defining

Discrimination: The Seniority Question Under Title VII, 62 N.C.L.Rev. 943 (1984).

In Pullman–Standard v. Swint, 456 U.S. 273, 102 S.Ct. 1781, 72 L.Ed.2d 66 (1982), the Court implicitly reaffirmed the relevance of these factors, though it cautioned that its *Teamsters* discussion was not meant to present an exhaustive list. More importantly, the *Swint* Court also confirmed that the determination of whether a seniority system is bona fide ultimately must turn on a finding of fact by the trial court—"a finding of actual intent to discriminate on racial grounds on the part of those who negotiated or maintained the system." Although discriminatory impact may be relevant to determination of intent, it would not be appropriate for a lower court to employ a legal presumption that impact proves intent: "Discriminatory intent here means actual motive; it is not a legal presumption to be drawn from a factual showing of something less than actual motive." Id. at 289–90, 102 S.Ct. at 1790–91.

Since *Swint* the lower courts have held that other factors may be relevant to the question of intent, and that legitimate business justifications are determinative only if they were the actual motivation for adoption and application of the system. See, e.g., Harvey v. United Transp. Union, 878 F.2d 1235, 1244, 1250 (10th Cir.1989). Can a departmental seniority system ever be "bona fide" if it was adopted at a time when racial discrimination in departmental and job assignments was openly practiced and its predictable effect was to perpetuate those initially biased decisions? See Gantlin v. Westvaco Corp., 734 F.2d 980 (4th Cir.1984) (system found bona fide).

4. *Burden of Proof as to the Seniority System's Validity.* Who should have the burden of persuasion on the issue of a system's validity under § 703(h)? In Lorance v. AT & T Technologies, 490 U.S. 900, 109 S.Ct. 2261, 104 L.Ed.2d 961 (1989), discussed at p. 1077 infra, the Court made clear that it does not "view § 703(h) as merely providing an affirmative defense." Instead, proof that a system is intentionally discriminatory must be "an element of any Title VII action challenging a seniority system."

5. *Treatment of Seniority Systems Under Other Laws.* Do the principles established in the *Teamsters* decision apply only to Title VII claims? Could a seniority system that is legal under Title VII because of § 703(h) be illegal under § 1981? Most courts have held that validity under Title VII controls the § 1981 claim. See, e.g., NAACP, Detroit Branch v. Detroit Police Officers Assoc., 900 F.2d 903, 911–12 (6th Cir.1990); Pettway v. American Cast Iron Pipe Co., 576 F.2d 1157, 1189 n. 37 (5th Cir.1978); Johnson v. Ryder Truck Lines, Inc., 575 F.2d 471, 474 (4th Cir.1978). But see Bolden v. Pennsylvania State Police, 578 F.2d 912 (3d Cir.1978). Should seniority systems insulated by § 703(h) also be insulated from challenges under Executive Order 11246, which is applicable to contractors with the federal government (see discussion in chapter 4)? The circuits passing on the question have answered in the affirmative. See, e.g., NAACP v. Detroit Police Officers Ass'n, 900 F.2d 903 (6th Cir.1990); United States v. Trucking Management, Inc., 662 F.2d 36 (D.C.Cir.1981).

UNITED AIR LINES v. EVANS

Supreme Court of the United States, 1977.
431 U.S. 553, 97 S.Ct. 1885, 52 L.Ed.2d 571.

JUSTICE STEVENS delivered the opinion of the Court.

Respondent was employed by United Air Lines as a flight attendant from November 1966 to February 1968. She was rehired in February 1972. Assuming, as she alleges, that her separation from employment in 1968 violated Title VII of the Civil Rights Act of 1964, the question now presented is whether the employer is committing a second violation of Title VII by refusing to credit her with seniority for any period prior to February 1972.

* * *

During respondent's initial period of employment, United maintained a policy of refusing to allow its female flight attendants to be married.[2] When she married in 1968, she was therefore forced to resign. Although it was subsequently decided that such a resignation violated Title VII, *Sprogis v. United Air Lines,* 444 F.2d 1194 (C.A.7 1971), cert. denied, 404 U.S. 991, 92 S.Ct. 536, 30 L.Ed.2d 543, respondent was not a party to that case and did not initiate any proceedings of her own in 1968 by filing a charge with the EEOC within 90 days of her separation.[3] A claim based on that discriminatory act is therefore barred.[4]

In November 1968, United entered into a new collective-bargaining agreement which ended the pre-existing "no marriage" rule and provided for the reinstatement of certain flight attendants who had been terminated pursuant to that rule. Respondent was not covered by that agreement. On several occasions she unsuccessfully sought reinstatement; on February 16, 1972, she was hired as a new employee. Although her personnel file carried the same number as it did in 1968, for seniority purposes she has been treated as though she had no prior service with United. She has not alleged that any other rehired employees were given credit for prior service with United, or that United's administration of the seniority system has violated the collective-bargaining agreement covering her employment.

* * *

2. At that time United required that all flight attendants be female, except on flights between the mainland and Hawaii and on overseas military charter flights. See *Sprogis v. United Air Lines,* 444 F.2d 1194, 1203 (C.A.7 1971) (Stevens, J., dissenting), cert. denied, 404 U.S. 991, 92 S.Ct. 536, 30 L.Ed.2d 543.

3. Section 706(d), 78 Stat. 260, 42 U.S.C. § 2000e–5(e), then provided in part: "A charge under subsection (a) shall be filed within ninety days after the alleged unlawful employment practice occurred * * *." The 1972 amendments to Title

VII added a new subsection (a) to § 706. Consequently, subsection (d) was redesignated as subsection (e). At the same time it was amended to enlarge the limitations period to 180 days. See 86 Stat. 105, 42 U.S.C. § 2000e–5(e) (1970 ed., Supp. V).

4. Timely filing is a prerequisite to the maintenance of a Title VII action. *Alexander v. Gardner–Denver Co.,* 415 U.S. 36, 47, 94 S.Ct. 1011, 1019, 39 L.Ed.2d 147. See *Electrical Workers v. Robbins & Myers, Inc.,* 429 U.S. 229, 239–240, 97 S.Ct. 441, 448–449, 50 L.Ed.2d 427.

Respondent recognizes that it is now too late to obtain relief based on an unlawful employment practice which occurred in 1968. She contends, however, that United is guilty of a present, continuing violation of Title VII and therefore that her claim is timely. She advances two reasons for holding that United's seniority system illegally discriminates against her: First, she is treated less favorably than males who were hired after her termination in 1968 and prior to her re-employment in 1972; second, the seniority system gives present effect to the past illegal act and therefore perpetuates the consequences of forbidden discrimination. Neither argument persuades us that United is presently violating the statute.

It is true that some male employees with less total service than respondent have more seniority than she. But this disparity is not a consequence of their sex, or of her sex. For females hired between 1968 and 1972 also acquired the same preference over respondent as males hired during that period. Moreover, both male and female employees who had service prior to February 1968, who resigned or were terminated for a nondiscriminatory reason (or for an unchallenged discriminatory reason), and who were later re-employed, also were treated as new employees receiving no seniority credit for their prior service. Nothing alleged in the complaint indicates that United's seniority system treats existing female employees differently from existing male employees, or that the failure to credit prior service differentiates in any way between prior service by males and prior service by females. Respondent has failed to allege that United's seniority system differentiates between similarly situated males and females on the basis of sex.

Respondent is correct in pointing out that the seniority system gives present effect to a past act of discrimination. But United was entitled to treat that past act as lawful after respondent failed to file a charge of discrimination within the 90 days then allowed by § 706(d). A discriminatory act which is not made the basis for a timely charge is the legal equivalent of a discriminatory act which occurred before the statute was passed. It may constitute relevant background evidence in a proceeding in which the status of a current practice is at issue, but separately considered, it is merely an unfortunate event in history which has no present legal consequences.

* * * Since respondent does not attack the bona fides of United's seniority system, and since she makes no charge that the system is intentionally designed to discriminate because of race, color, religion, sex, or national origin, § 703(h) provides an additional ground for rejecting her claim.

The Court of Appeals read § 703(h) as intended to bar an attack on a seniority system based on the consequences of discriminatory acts which occurred prior to the effective date of Title VII in 1965, but having no application to such attacks based on acts occurring after 1965. This reading of § 703(h) is too narrow. The statute does not foreclose attacks on the current operation of seniority systems which are subject to challenge as discriminatory. But such a challenge to a neutral system may not be predicated on the mere fact that a past event which has no present legal significance has affected the calculation of seniority credit, even if the past event might at one time have justified a valid claim against the employer. A contrary view would substitute a claim for seniority credit for almost every claim which is barred by limitations. Such a result would contravene the mandate of § 703(h).

AMERICAN TOBACCO CO. v. PATTERSON
Supreme Court of the United States, 1982.
456 U.S. 63, 102 S.Ct. 1534, 71 L.Ed.2d 748.

JUSTICE WHITE delivered the opinion of the Court.

* * * Under § 703(h), the fact that a seniority system has a discriminatory impact is not alone sufficient to invalidate the system; actual intent to discriminate must be proved. The Court of Appeals in this case, however, held that § 703(h) does not apply to seniority systems adopted after the effective date of the Civil Rights Act.

* * *

I

Petitioner American Tobacco Co. operates two plants in Richmond, Va., one which manufactures cigarettes and one which manufactures pipe tobacco. Each plant is divided into a prefabrication department, which blends and prepares tobacco for further processing, and a fabrication department, which manufactures the final product. Petitioner Bakery, Confectionery & Tobacco Workers' International Union and its affiliate Local 182 are the exclusive collective-bargaining agents for hourly paid production workers at both plants.

It is uncontested that prior to 1963 the company and the union engaged in overt race discrimination. The union maintained two segregated locals, and black employees were assigned to jobs in the lower paying prefabrication departments. Higher paying jobs in the fabrication departments were largely reserved for white employees. An employee could transfer from one of the predominately black prefabrication departments to one of the predominately white fabrication departments only by forfeiting his seniority.

In 1963, under pressure from Government procurement agencies enforcing the antidiscrimination obligations of Government contractors, the company abolished departmental seniority in favor of plantwide seniority and the black union local was merged into the white local. However, promotions were no longer based solely on seniority but rather on seniority plus certain qualifications, and employees lost accumulated seniority in the event of a transfer between plants. Between 1963 and 1968, when this promotions policy was in force, virtually all vacancies in the fabrication departments were filled by white employees due to the discretion vested in supervisors to determine who was qualified.

In November 1968, the company proposed the establishment of nine lines of progression, six of which are at issue in this case. The union accepted and ratified the lines of progression in 1969. Each line of progression generally consisted of two jobs. An employee was not eligible for the top job in the line until he had worked in a bottom job. Four of the six lines of progression at issue here consisted of nearly all-white top jobs from the fabrication departments linked with nearly all-white bottom jobs from the fabrication departments; the other two consisted of all-black top jobs from the prefabrication departments linked with all-black bottom jobs from the prefabrication departments. The top jobs in the white lines of progression were among the best paying jobs in the plants.

* * *

II

Petitioners argue that the plain language of § 703(h) applies to post-Act as well as pre-Act seniority systems. The respondent employees claim that the provision "provides a narrow exemption—from the ordinary discriminatory impact test—which was specifically designed to protect bona fide seniority systems which were in existence before the effective date of Title VII." Respondent EEOC supports the judgment below, but urges us to interpret § 703(h) so as to protect the post-Act *application* of a bona fide seniority system but not the post-Act *adoption* of a seniority system or an aspect of a seniority system.

* * *

On its face § 703(h) makes no distinction between pre-and post-Act seniority systems, just as it does not distinguish between pre-and post-Act merit systems or pre-and post-Act ability tests. The section does not take the form of a saving clause or a grandfather clause designed to exclude existing practices from the operation of a new rule.

* * *

Furthermore, for the purpose of construing § 703(h), the proposed distinction between application and adoption on its face makes little sense. The adoption of a seniority system which has not been applied would not give rise to a cause of action. A discriminatory effect would arise only when the system is put into operation and the employer "applies" the system. Such application is not infirm under § 703(h) unless it is accompanied by a discriminatory purpose. An adequate remedy for adopting a discriminatory seniority system would very likely include an injunction against the future application of the system and backpay awards for those harmed by its application. Such an injunction, however, would lie only if the requirement of § 703(h)—that such application be intentionally discriminatory—were satisfied.

* * *

A further result of the EEOC's theory would be to discourage unions and employers from modifying pre-Act seniority systems or post-Act systems whose adoption was not timely challenged. Any modification, if timely challenged, would be subject to the *Griggs* standard—even if it benefited persons covered by Title VII—thereby creating an incentive to retain existing systems which enjoy the protection of § 703(h).[5]

* * *

We have not been informed of and have not found a single statement anywhere in the legislative history saying that § 703(h) does not protect seniority systems adopted or modified after the effective date of Title VII. Nor does the legislative history reveal that Congress intended to distinguish between adoption and application of a bona fide seniority system. The most which can be said for the legislative history of § 703(h) is that it is inconclusive with respect to the issue presented in this case.

* * * Congress was well aware in 1964 that the overall purpose of Title VII, to eliminate discrimination in employment, inevitably would, on occasion, conflict with the policy favoring minimal supervision by courts and other governmental agencies over the substantive terms of collective-bargaining agreements. *California Brewers Assn. v. Bryant,* 444 U.S. 598, 608, 100 S.Ct. 814, 820, 63 L.Ed.2d 55 (1980). Section 703(h) represents the balance Congress struck between the two policies, and it is not this Court's function to upset that balance.[17]

JUSTICE BRENNAN, with whom JUSTICE MARSHALL and JUSTICE BLACKMUN join, dissenting.

* * * [Section] 703(h) should not be construed to further objectives beyond those which Congress expressly wished to serve. As demonstrated by the legislative history * * *, Congress' basic purpose in adding the provision was to protect the *expectations* that employees acquire through the continued operation of a seniority system. A timely challenge to the *adoption* of a seniority plan may forestall discrimination *before* such legitimate employee expectations have arisen.

* * *

While [the] legislative history does not contain any explicit reference to the distinction between adoption and application urged by the EEOC, it surely contains no suggestion that Congress intended to treat the decision *to adopt* a seniority plan any differently from the decision *to*

---

5. "Significant freedom must be afforded employers and unions to create differing seniority systems." *California Brewers Assn. v. Bryant,* 444 U.S. 598, 608, 100 S.Ct. 814, 820, 63 L.Ed.2d 55 (1980). Respondents' interpretation of § 703(h) would impinge on that freedom by discouraging modification of existing seniority systems or adoption of new systems.

17. JUSTICE BRENNAN'S dissent makes no mention of the importance which Congress and this Court have accorded to seniority systems and collective bargaining. It reads the legislative history as showing that Congress' basic purpose in enacting § 703(h) was to protect employee expectations. In doing so, it ignores the policy favoring minimal governmental intervention in collective bargaining.

adopt a discriminatory employment practice unrelated to seniority. Rather, the legislative history indicates that Congress was concerned *only* about protecting the good-faith expectations of employees who rely on the continued *application* of established, bona fide seniority systems.

* * *

JUSTICE STEVENS, dissenting.

It is clear to me that a seniority system that is unlawful at the time it is adopted cannot be "bona fide" within the meaning of § 703(h). Thus, a post-Act seniority system cannot be bona fide if it was adopted in violation of Title VII; such a system would not provide an employer with a defense under § 703(h). Section 703(h) itself does not address the question of how to determine whether the adoption of a post-Act merit or seniority system is unlawful. Since the adoption of a seniority system is in my opinion an employment practice subject to the requirements of Title VII, it is reasonable to infer that the same standard that applies to hiring, promotion, discharge, and compensation practices also applies to the adoption of a merit or seniority system.

This inference is confirmed by the fact that § 703(h) does not merely provide an affirmative defense for seniority systems; it also provides a similar defense for merit systems and professionally developed ability tests. * * *

The Court in this case, however, reads the "specific intent" proviso of § 703(h) as though it were intended to define the proper standard for measuring any challenge to a merit or seniority system. This reading of the proviso is entirely unwarranted. The proviso is a limitation on the scope of the affirmative defense. It addresses the problem created by pre-Act seniority systems, which of course were "lawful" because adopted before the Act became effective and therefore presumptively "bona fide" within the meaning of § 703(h). As the legislative history makes clear, Congress sought to protect seniority rights that had accrued before the effective date of the Act, but it did not want to extend that protection to benefits under seniority systems that were the product of deliberate racial discrimination. The obvious purpose of the proviso was to place a limit on the protection given to pre-Act seniority systems. The Court's broad reading of the proviso ignores both its context in § 703(h) and the historical context in which it was enacted.

The Court's strained reading of the statute may be based on an assumption that if the *Griggs* standard were applied to the adoption of a post-Act seniority system, most post-Act systems would be unlawful since it is virtually impossible to establish a seniority system whose classification of employees will not have a disparate impact on members of some race or sex. Under *Griggs,* however, illegality does not follow automatically from a disparate impact. If the initiation of a new seniority system—or the modification of an existing system—is substantially related to a valid business purpose, the system is lawful. "The touchstone is business necessity." *Griggs, supra,* at 431, 91 S.Ct. at 853; cf. *New York*

Transit Authority v. Beazer, 440 U.S. 568, 587, 99 S.Ct. 1355, 1366, 59 L.Ed.2d 587. A reasoned application of *Griggs* would leave ample room for bona fide systems; the adoption of a seniority system often may be justified by the need to induce experienced employees to remain, to establish fair rules for advancement, or to reward continuous, effective service. I can find no provision of Title VII, however, that grants a blanket exemption to the initiation of every seniority system that has not been conceived with a deliberate purpose to discriminate because of race or sex.

Notes and Questions

1. *Did* Teamsters *Turn on the Pre–Title VII Origin of the Perpetuated Discrimination?* Could *Evans* have been distinguished plausibly by reading § 703(h) and congressional purpose to preclude attacks on seniority systems that perpetuate the effects of pre-Title VII discrimination, while permitting challenges to systems that perpetuate post-Act discrimination? Consider the legislative history discussed in *Teamsters.*

2. *Viability of Disparate Impact Challenges to Aspects of Seniority Systems Not Tied to Rewards for Past Service?* Is it clear that *Teamsters'* reading of § 703(h) precludes disparate impact challenges to all aspects of a seniority system, even aspects that are not closely tied to a policy of rewarding past service for the employer? Note that in *Evans,* rewarding past service probably benefitted women as a group because of the historical exclusion of men from flight attendant positions, but the break-in-service rule probably disproportionately disadvantaged women because of their greater likelihood of leaving the work force for family reasons. In this light, do the justifications for *Teamsters'* interpretation of § 703(h) support a refusal to apply disparate impact theory to United Airlines' break-in-service rule?

3. *Was* Patterson *Distinguishable?* How does American Tobacco Co. v. Patterson extend the holdings of *Teamsters* and *Evans*? Consider the position of the EEOC as adopted in Justice Brennan's dissent. Does this position make linguistic sense of § 703(h)? Why would Congress have wanted to shield the unmodified aspects of pre-Act seniority systems but not seniority provisions that either were put in place or modified after Title VII's effective date?

How does Justice White, writing for the majority in *Patterson,* respond to Justice Brennan? Do you find that response compelling? Consider footnote 17 in the majority opinion. Does this footnote suggest that seniority systems that were unilaterally adopted by employers rather than collectively bargained with unions should be treated differently under § 703(h)? Would the language of § 703(h) support such a distinction? Some lower courts have held that *Teamsters* applies to unilateral employer systems. See Williams v. New Orleans S. S. Ass'n, 673 F.2d 742 (5th Cir.1982); EEOC v. E.I. duPont de Nemours & Co., 445 F.Supp. 223, 249 (D.Del.1978).

4. *Justice Stevens's Alternative.* Does Justice Stevens, in his *Patterson* dissent, interpret "bona fide" in the seniority provision of § 703(h) to mean "free of intentional discrimination" when considering pre-Act systems, but

"free of intentional *and* effects discrimination" when considering post-Act systems? Can the provision be reasonably read to carry such a dual meaning? Is there any point in adopting such a reading given Justice Stevens's concession that the disparate impact of post-Act seniority systems could be justified by considerations other than the prediction of job performance, such as the protection of employee expectations based on length of service? Would Stevens's view permit the challenge suggested in note 2 above?

5. *Statute of Limitations for Seniority System Challenges.* In a case determining when Title VII's administrative filing period begins to run, Lorance v. AT & T Technologies, 490 U.S. 900, 109 S.Ct. 2261, 104 L.Ed.2d 961 (1989), discussed below at p. 1077, the Court held that facially neutral seniority systems that allegedly are intended to disadvantage a protected Title VII group can be challenged only within the 180 or 300 day limitation period after their adoption. The Civil Rights Act of 1991 rejected this holding. Section 112 of that Act amended § 706(e) of Title VII to clarify that an "unlawful employment practice occurs" when an intentionally discriminatory seniority system "is adopted, when an individual becomes subject to the seniority system, or when a person aggrieved is injured by the application of the seniority system".

CALIFORNIA BREWERS ASS'N v. BRYANT
Supreme Court of the United States, 1980.
444 U.S. 598, 100 S.Ct. 814, 63 L.Ed.2d 55.

JUSTICE STEWART delivered the opinion of the Court.

The present case concerns the application of § 703(h) to a particular clause in a California brewery industry collective-bargaining agreement. That agreement accords greater benefits to "permanent" than to "temporary" employees, and the clause in question provides that a temporary employee must work at least 45 weeks in a single calendar year before he can become a permanent employee. The Court of Appeals for the Ninth Circuit held that the 45–week requirement was not a "seniority system" or part of a "seniority system" within the meaning of § 703(h).

* * *

The complaint, as amended, alleged that the respondent had been intermittently employed since May 1968 as a temporary employee of one of the defendants, the Falstaff Brewing Corp. It charged that all the defendant employers had discriminated in the past against Negroes, that the unions had acted in concert with the employers in such discrimination, and that the unions had discriminated in referring applicants from hiring halls to the employers. The complaint further asserted that this historical discrimination was being perpetuated by the seniority and referral provisions of the collective-bargaining agreement (Agreement) that governed industrial relations at the plants of the seven defendant employers.

* * *

The Agreement is a multiemployer collective-bargaining agreement negotiated more than 20 years ago, and thereafter updated, by the California Brewers Association (on behalf of the petitioner brewing companies) and the Teamsters Brewery and Soft Drink Workers Joint Board of California (on behalf of the defendant unions). The Agreement establishes several classes of employees and the respective rights of each with respect to hiring and layoffs. Three of these classes are pertinent here: "permanent," "temporary," and "new" employees.

A permanent employee is "any employee * * * who * * * has completed forty-five weeks of employment under this Agreement in one classification[5] in one calendar year as an employee of the brewing industry in [the State of California]." An employee who acquires permanent status retains that status unless he "is not employed under this Agreement for any consecutive period of two (2) years. * * * "[6] A temporary employee under the Agreement is "any person other than a permanent employee * * * who worked under this agreement * * * in the preceding calendar year for at least sixty (60) working days. * * * "A new employee is any employee who is not a permanent or temporary employee.

The rights of employees with respect to hiring and layoffs depend in substantial part on their status as permanent, temporary, or new employees.[7] The Agreement requires that employees at a particular plant be laid off in the following order: new employees in reverse order of their seniority at the plant, temporary employees in reverse order of their plant seniority, and then permanent employees in reverse order of their plant seniority. Once laid off, employees are to be rehired in the reverse order from which they were laid off.

The Agreement also gives permanent employees special "bumping" rights. If a permanent employee is laid off at any plant subject to the Agreement, he may be dispatched by the union hiring hall to any other plant in the same local area with the right to replace the temporary or new employee with the lowest plant seniority at that plant.

Finally, the Agreement provides that each employer shall obtain employees through the local union hiring hall to fill needed vacancies. The hiring hall must dispatch laid-off workers to such an employer in the following order: first, employees of that employer in the order of their seniority with that employer; second, permanent employees registered in the area in order of their industry seniority; third, temporary employees in the order of their seniority in the industry; and fourth, new

---

5. The Agreement classifies employees into brewers, bottlers, drivers, shipping and receiving clerks, and checkers. Under the Agreement, separate seniority lists have to be maintained for each of these classifications of employees. The respondent is a brewer.

6. An employee may also lose permanent status if he "quits the industry" or is discharged for certain specified reasons.

7. In addition, permanent employees are given preference over temporary employees with respect to various other employment matters, such as the right to collect supplemental unemployment benefits upon layoff, wages and vacation pay, and choice of vacation times.

employees in the order of their industry seniority. The employer then "shall have full right of selection among" such employees.

* * *

In the area of labor relations, "seniority" is a term that connotes length of employment. A "seniority system" is a scheme that, alone or in tandem with non-"seniority" criteria,[13] allots to employees ever improving employment rights and benefits as their relative lengths of pertinent employment increase. Unlike other methods of allocating employment benefits and opportunities, such as subjective evaluations or educational requirements, the principal feature of any and every "seniority system" is that preferential treatment is dispensed on the basis of some measure of time served in employment.

Viewed as a whole, most of the relevant provisions of the Agreement before us in this case conform to these core concepts of "seniority." Rights of temporary employees and rights of permanent employees are determined according to length of plant employment in some respects, and according to length of industry employment in other respects. Notwithstanding this fact, the Court of Appeals concluded that the 45–week rule should not be viewed, for purposes of § 703(h), as part of what might otherwise be considered a "seniority system." For the reasons that follow, we hold that this conclusion was incorrect.

First, by legislating with respect to "systems" of seniority in § 703(h), Congress in 1964 quite evidently intended to exempt from the normal operation of Title VII more than simply those components of any particular seniority scheme that, viewed in isolation, embody or effectuate the principle that length of employment will be rewarded. In order for any seniority system to operate at all, it has to contain ancillary rules that accomplish certain necessary functions, but which may not themselves be directly related to length of employment. For instance, every seniority system must include rules that delineate how and when the seniority time clock begins ticking,[17] as well as rules that specify how and when a particular person's seniority may be forfeited.[18] Every seniority system must also have rules that define which passages of time will "count" towards the accrual of seniority and which will not.[19] Every

---

13. A collective-bargaining agreement could, for instance, provide that transfers and promotions are to be determined by a mix of seniority and other factors, such as aptitude tests and height requirements. That the "seniority" aspects of such a scheme of transfer and promotion might be covered by § 703(h) does not mean that the aptitude tests or the height requirements would also be so covered.

17. By way of example, a collective-bargaining agreement could specify that an employee begins to accumulate seniority rights at the time he commences employment with the company, at the time he

commences employment within the industry, at the time he begins performing a particular job function, or only after a probationary period of employment.

18. For example, a collective-bargaining agreement could provide that accumulated seniority rights are permanently forfeited by voluntary resignation, by severance for cause, or by non-employment at a particular plant or in the industry for a certain period.

19. For instance, the time an employee works in the industry or with his current employer might not be counted for the purpose of accumulating seniority rights,

seniority system must, moreover, contain rules that particularize the types of employment conditions that will be governed or influenced by seniority, and those that will not.[20] Rules that serve these necessary purposes do not fall outside § 703(h) simply because they do not, in and of themselves, operate on the basis of some factor involving the passage of time.[21]

Second, Congress passed the Civil Rights Act of 1964 against the backdrop of this Nation's longstanding labor policy of leaving to the chosen representatives of employers and employees the freedom through collective bargaining to establish conditions of employment applicable to a particular business or industrial environment. * * *

What has been said does not mean that § 703(h) is to be given a scope that risks swallowing up Title VII's otherwise broad prohibition of "practices, procedures, or tests" that disproportionately affect members of those groups that the Act protects. Significant freedom must be afforded employers and unions to create differing seniority systems. But that freedom must not be allowed to sweep within the ambit of § 703(h) employment rules that depart fundamentally from commonly accepted notions concerning the acceptable contours of a seniority system, simply because those rules are dubbed "seniority" provisions or have some nexus to an arrangement that concededly operates on the basis of seniority. There can be no doubt, for instance, that a threshold requirement for entering a seniority track that took the form of an educational prerequisite would not be part of a "seniority system" within the intendment of § 703(h).

The application of these principles to the case at hand is straightforward. The Agreement sets out, in relevant part, two parallel seniority ladders. One allocates the benefits due temporary employees; the other identifies the benefits owed permanent employees. The propriety under § 703(h) of such parallel seniority tracks cannot be doubted after the Court's decision in the *Teamsters* case. The collective-bargaining agreement at issue there allotted one set of benefits according to each employee's total service with the company, and another set according to each employee's service in a particular job category. Just as in that case the separation of seniority tracks did not derogate from the identification of the provisions as a "seniority system" under § 703(h), so in the present case the fact that the system created by the Agreement establishes two or more seniority ladders does not prevent it from being a "seniority system" within the meaning of that section.

The 45–week rule, correspondingly, serves the needed function of establishing the threshold requirement for entry into the permanent-

---

whereas the time the employee works in a particular job classification might determine his seniority.

20. By way of example, a collective-bargaining agreement could provide that an employee's seniority will govern his entitlement to vacation time and his job security in the event of layoffs, but will have no influence on promotions or job assignments.

21. The examples in the text of the types of rules necessary to the operation of a seniority system are not intended to and do not comprise an exhaustive list.

employee seniority track. As such, it performs the same function as did the employment rule in *Teamsters* that provided that a line driver began to accrue seniority for certain purposes only when he started to work as a line driver, even though he had previously spent years as a city driver for the same employer. In *Teamsters,* the Court expressed no reservation about the propriety of such a threshold rule for § 703(h) purposes. There is no reason why the 45–week threshold requirement at issue here should be considered any differently.

The 45–week rule does not depart significantly from commonly accepted concepts of "seniority." The rule is not an educational standard, an aptitude or physical test, or a standard that gives effect to subjectivity. Unlike such criteria, but like any "seniority" rule, the 45–week requirement focuses on length of employment.

Moreover, the rule does not distort the operation of the basic system established by the Agreement, which rewards employment longevity with heightened benefits. A temporary employee's chances of achieving permanent status increase inevitably as his industry employment and seniority accumulate. The temporary employees with the most industry seniority have the first choice of new jobs within the industry available for temporary employees. Similarly, the temporary employees with the most plant seniority have the first choice of temporary employee jobs within their plant and enjoy the greatest security against "bumping" by permanent employees from nearby plants. As a general rule, therefore, the more seniority a temporary employee accumulates, the more likely it is that he will be able to satisfy the 45–week requirement. That the correlation between accumulated industry employment and acquisition of permanent employee status is imperfect does not mean that the 45–week requirement is not a component of the Agreement's seniority system. Under any seniority system, contingencies such as illnesses and layoffs may interrupt the accrual of seniority and delay realization of the advantages dependent upon it.[22]

Justice Marshall, with whom Justice Brennan and Justice Blackmun join, dissenting.

The Court concedes * * * that a " 'seniority system' is a scheme that, alone or in tandem with non-'seniority' criteria, allots to employees ever improving employment rights and benefits as their relative lengths of pertinent employment increase." In my view, that concession is dispositive of this case. The principal effect of the 45–week requirement is to ensure that employee rights and benefits in the California brewing industry are not "ever improving" as length of service increases. Indeed, cumulative length of service is only incidentally relevant to the 45–week rule. The likelihood that a temporary employee will attain permanent employee status is largely unpredictable. The 45–week period, which is

---

22. There are indications in the record of this case that a long-term decline in the California brewing industry's demand for labor is a reason why the accrual of seniority as a temporary employee has not led more automatically to the acquisition of permanent status. But surely, what would be part of a "seniority system" in an expanding labor market does not become something else in a declining labor market.

exclusive of vacation, leaves of absence, and time lost because of injury or sickness, represents almost 90% of the calendar year. Even if an employee is relatively senior among temporaries, his ability to work 45 weeks in a year will rest in large part on fortuities over which he has no control. The most obvious reason that employees have been prevented from attaining permanent employee status—a reason barely referred to by the Court—is that the brewing industry is a seasonal one. An employee may also be prevented from becoming permanent because of replacement by permanent employees or an employer's unexpected decision to lay off a particular number of employees during the course of a year.[5]

* * * The mere fact that the 45–week rule is in some sense a measure of "time" does not demonstrate a valid relation to concepts of seniority. Such a conclusion would make the § 703(h) exemption applicable to a rule under which permanent employee status is dependent on number of days served within a week, or hours served within a day.[8]

Notes and Questions

1. *Part of a Scheme of Intentional Discrimination?* Might the forty-five week rule have been adopted and applied to make it easier for industry employers to use minority workers when seasonal demand was high without ever including them within the core (predominantly white) work force when demand was low? Might this have resulted in some "permanent" white workers having priority over many "temporary" black workers with more cumulative time in the industry? Note that the Supreme Court's decision in *California Brewers* reaches only the question of whether the forty-five week rule was part of a "seniority system" covered by § 703(h); it does not address whether evidence of hiring or other intentional discrimination might detract from the "bona fide" status of the system under the *Stockham Valve* test or would otherwise support a remedial order under *Franks*.

2. *Noncumulative Seniority Job Allocation Rules?* Did the forty-five week rule provide an example of a formally neutral rule that does not fit within the basic congressional decision to exempt seniority systems from disparate impact challenges? On the one hand, disparate impact analysis would have facilitated proof of the current manipulation of the rule for the discriminatory purposes suggested in the last note. It also would have enabled plaintiffs to address any general failure of blacks to pass the forty-

5. Indeed, the agreement expressly provides that a permanent employee laid off at one facility will replace (or "bump") the temporary employee with the lowest *plant* seniority, even if that employee has more industry seniority than others. As a result, temporaries who are relatively senior in terms of industry seniority may have less opportunity to work 45 weeks in a calendar year than temporaries with less industry seniority but more plant seniority. Thus, it is simply not true that temporary employees obtain permanent employee status in order of cumulative length of employment, for the requisite 45 weeks is computed on the basis of service in the industry rather than in particular plants.

8. For example, there can be no serious question that a provision making permanent status dependent on 7 days of work per week, or 12 hours per day would not be part of a "seniority system" within the meaning of § 703(h).

five week test that stemmed from their being relatively recent entrants in a declining industry that once intentionally discriminated against their class.

On the other hand, do the justifications for rejecting disparate impact challenges to seniority systems extend to noncumulative classifications like the forty-five week rule at issue in *California Brewers* ? Was it a sufficient justification for the union and employers to have wanted to subordinate the job claims of workers who have chosen not to work full time in the industry? Could this purpose have been adequately served by a rule that tested availability for employment? What if the parties to a collective bargaining agreement in another case sought to protect through a noncumulative seniority rule a preexisting incumbent group that in a key labor negotiation had permitted the employer to introduce job-saving technology in exchange for enhanced job security? Should such justifications be tested in disparate impact adjudication?

3. *Non-Seniority Elements of Job Allocation Rules?* Are all job allocation rules included in a seniority system protected by the seniority provision in § 703(h)? The *California Brewers* opinion suggests, for example, that educational prerequisites to obtaining employment which counts for seniority purposes would not be part of a seniority system protected by § 703(h). What distinguishes the educational prerequisite from other threshold requirements? Is it simply "commonly accepted notions concerning the contours of a seniority system"? Whether the requirement is somehow related to the passage of time? Is Justice Marshall's assumption in footnote 8 open to question? See generally Chambers v. Parco Foods, 935 F.2d 902, 904–05 (7th Cir.1991) (absolute hiring preference for those who had served within same department is an aspect of a protected departmental seniority system); Allen v. Prince George's County, 737 F.2d 1299, 1302 (4th Cir.1984) (policy of filling vacancies from within before hiring new employees is a seniority system).

Does § 703(h) insulate a two-tier wage and pension system under which those hired after a certain date are disfavored? See Prieto v. City of Miami Beach, 190 F.Supp.2d 1340 (S.D.Fla.2002) (treated as a protected seniority system). Does it insulate a pay system that provides for automatic annual increases from a base level set by factors other than length of employment? See Mitchell v. Jefferson County Bd. of Educ., 936 F.2d 539, 545–46 (11th Cir.1991) (not treated as protected seniority system).

Chapter Four

AFFIRMATIVE ACTION

A. INTRODUCTION

Note on the Justifications for Affirmative Action

As the previous chapters make clear, the regulation of status discrimination may induce employers to do more to include previously excluded groups into the workplace than merely purging their employment decisions of any consideration of membership in particular status groups. Under the disparate impact approach, employers are given incentives to avoid practices that have a disproportionate adverse impact on particular groups. Furthermore, the evidentiary weight aggregate employment statistics carry in systemic disparate treatment or disparate impact cases may impel employers wishing to avoid difficult litigation to hire and promote with an eye to avoiding underrepresentation of members of protected classes in their work forces. This chapter, however, considers the extent to which existing law directly requires, permits, or prohibits the affirmative grant of preferences to members of particular disadvantaged groups for the purpose of furthering their employment and advancement in the work place.

There are a variety of potential uses in employment for affirmative action strategies such as status-conscious goals or preferences. They have been most frequently used in Title VII remedial orders. In theory, judicial imposition of affirmative action goals or preferences should not be necessary to achieve the elimination of proven discrimination; a simple cease and desist order should suffice. Soon after Title VII's enactment, however, courts came to recognize that the elimination of discrimination by recalcitrant employers and unions required more aggressive orders. The use of race-conscious goals may be necessary as a means of tracking compliance or eliminating the chilling effect on minority participation that may have been generated by a previously discriminatory environment. See generally Eric Schnapper, The Varieties of Numerical Remedies, 39 Stan.L.Rev. 851 (1987).

Second, affirmative action goals have been used by employers prior to litigation as part of an effort to rectify a disparity between their rate of utilization of a particular group and the availability of qualified workers from that group in their labor market. Employers may make such an effort in response to pressure from enforcement authorities, out of fear of expensive litigation, or simply as a matter of good business practice.

Third, status-conscious goals have been used to attempt to compensate for general disadvantages imposed on particular groups in the past or present due to discrimination in employment, education, housing or other areas. Preferential consideration of members of these groups may be thought critical to efforts to free them from a cycle of poverty or subordination. "Status-blind" employment decisionmaking is deemed inadequate by some because members of certain groups may have been prevented or discouraged by the experience of poverty and discrimination from entering into particular fields or from making necessary investments in education and training. Preferential consideration is thus used to accelerate the undoing of the effects of prior societal discrimination.

Affirmative action goals also may be employed for "forward-looking" reasons not requiring an identification of "victims" or a determination of individual or general societal "fault" for past discrimination. See Kathleen Sullivan, Sins of Discrimination: Last Term's Affirmative Action Cases, 100 Harv.L.Rev. 78 (1986). A diverse work force may be thought to directly further the mission of some employers, including educational institutions and some local police departments. Some have suggested that affirmative action may be used by employers to reduce the likelihood of unconscious bias or stereotyping affecting managerial decisionmaking, see Jerry Kang & Mahzarin R. Banaji, Fair Measures: A Behavioral Realist Revision of "Affirmative Action", 94 Cal. L. Rev. 1063 (2006); Michael J. Yelnosky, The Prevention Justification for Affirmative Action, 64 Ohio St. L.J. 1385 (2003), or to promote integration of particular groups in the larger society, see Cynthia L. Estlund, Working Together: The Workplace, Civil Society, and the Law, 89 Geo. L.J. 1 (2000).

Affirmative action strategies, however, have aroused considerable opposition. For many the formal equality of "status blind" decisionmaking is the only equality that justice should or at least can demand. Disadvantage is a matter of degree and derives from a multiplicity of sources only some of which have anything to do with membership in a particular group. It is impossible for employers to compensate to a proportionate extent for the disadvantages of all applicants. In some cases, individuals benefited by status-conscious preferences may have enjoyed greater material advantages than individuals who belong to no statutorily protected status group.

Moreover, preferential hiring for any purpose is thought to impose certain social costs. First, such hiring may do damage to the acceptance of "status-blind" employment decisionmaking as an ultimate social goal because the use of group preferences may further entrench racial and other status group consciousness. Some believe that affirmative action will lead to societal acceptance of the principle that goods and benefits be distributed in close proportion to the numerical prevalence of groups. A second, related cost may be a backlash of animosity from those who do not benefit from preferences directed at those who do benefit. This danger may be particularly significant because of the predispositions to prejudice that such a backlash can rekindle. Third, preferential decisionmaking potentially can stigmatize those whom it is intended to benefit. The more widespread the social perception that members of historically disadvantaged groups have achieved success because they have been favored, the less likely that this success will change the prejudices that at least in part have maintained the groups' inferior social or economic position. Fourth, to the extent that preferences result in the hiring and promotion of less productive workers, all of society at least in the short run will pay.

Whether these potential costs are sufficiently great to outweigh the potential benefits of a particular type of preferential decisionmaking in a particular case is, of course, to a great extent an empirical question. For policy makers acting upon imperfect information, however, it is also a question of values. The major cases in this chapter demonstrate how various Supreme Court Justices have been rendering these judgments on the basis of the values that they perceive to be expressed in Title VII and the Constitution.

B. JUDICIALLY ORDERED AFFIRMATIVE ACTION

LOCAL 28, SHEET METAL WORKERS v. EEOC
Supreme Court of the United States, 1986.
478 U.S. 421, 106 S.Ct. 3019, 92 L.Ed.2d 344.

JUSTICE BRENNAN announced the judgment of the Court and delivered the opinion of the Court with respect to Parts I, II, III, and VI, and an opinion with respect to Parts IV, V, and VII in which JUSTICE MARSHALL, JUSTICE BLACKMUN, and JUSTICE STEVENS join.

Following a trial in 1975, the District Court concluded that petitioners had violated both Title VII and New York law by discriminating against nonwhite workers in recruitment, selection, training, and admission to the union. Noting that as of July 1, 1974, only 3.19% of the union's total membership, including apprentices and journeymen, was nonwhite, the court found that petitioners had denied qualified nonwhites access to union membership through a variety of discriminatory practices. First, the court found that petitioners had adopted discriminatory procedures and standards for admission into the apprenticeship program. The court examined some of the factors used to select apprentices, including the entrance examination and high-school diploma requirement, and determined that these criteria had an adverse discriminatory impact on nonwhites, and were not related to job performance. The court also observed that petitioners had used union funds to subsidize special training sessions for friends and relatives of union members taking the apprenticeship examination.

Second, the court determined that Local 28 had restricted the size of its membership in order to deny access to nonwhites. The court found that Local 28 had refused to administer yearly journeymen's examinations despite a growing demand for members' services. Rather, to meet this increase in demand, Local 28 recalled pensioners who obtained doctors' certificates that they were able to work, and issued hundreds of

temporary work permits to nonmembers; only one of these permits was
issued to a nonwhite.

* * *

Third, the District Court determined that Local 28 had selectively
organized non-union sheet metal shops with few, if any, minority employees, and admitted to membership only white employees from those
shops. * * *

Finally, the court found that Local 28 had discriminated in favor of
white applicants seeking to transfer from sister locals. * * *

The District Court entered an order and judgment (O & J) enjoining
petitioners from discriminating against nonwhites, and enjoining the
specific practices the court had found to be discriminatory. Recognizing
that "the record in both state and federal court against these defendants
is replete with instances of . . . bad faith attempts to prevent or delay
affirmative action," the court concluded that "the imposition of a
remedial racial goal in conjunction with an admission preference in favor
of non-whites is essential to place the defendants in a position of
compliance with Title VII." The court established a 29% nonwhite
membership goal, based on the percentage of nonwhites in the relevant
labor pool in New York City, for the union to achieve by July 1, 1981.
The parties were ordered to devise and to implement recruitment and
admission procedures designed to achieve this goal under the supervision
of a court-appointed administrator.

* * *

The Court of Appeals for the Second Circuit affirmed the District
Court's determination of liability, finding that petitioners had "consistently and egregiously violated Title VII." The court upheld the 29%
nonwhite membership goal as a temporary remedy, justified by a "long
and persistent pattern of discrimination," and concluded that the appointment of an administrator with broad powers was clearly appropriate, given petitioners' refusal to change their membership practices in
the face of prior state and federal court orders. However, the court
modified the District Court's order to permit the use of a white-nonwhite
ratio for the apprenticeship program only pending implementation of
valid, job-related entrance tests. Local 28 did not seek certiorari in this
Court to review the Court of Appeals' judgment.

On remand, the District Court adopted a Revised Affirmative Action
Program and Order (RAAPO) to incorporate the Court of Appeals'
mandate. RAAPO also modified the original Affirmative Action Program
to accommodate petitioners' claim that economic problems facing the
construction industry had made it difficult for them to comply with the
court's orders. Petitioners were given an additional year to meet the 29%
membership goal. RAAPO also established interim membership goals
designed to "afford the parties and the Administrator with some device
to measure progress so that, if warranted, other provisions of the
program could be modified to reflect change (sic) circumstances." The

Local 28 Joint Apprenticeship Committee (JAC) was directed to indenture at least 36 apprentices by February 1977, and to determine the size of future apprenticeship classes subject to review by the administrator. A divided panel of the Court of Appeals affirmed RAAPO in its entirety, including the 29% nonwhite membership goal. Petitioners again chose not to seek certiorari from this Court to review the Court of Appeals' judgment.

In April 1982, the City and State moved in the District Court for an order holding petitioners in contempt. They alleged that petitioners had not achieved RAAPO's 29% nonwhite membership goal, and that this failure was due to petitioners' numerous violations of the O & J, RAAPO, and orders of the administrator. The District Court, after receiving detailed evidence of how the O & J and RAAPO had operated over the previous six years, held petitioners in civil contempt. The court did not rest its contempt finding on petitioners' failure to meet the 29% membership goal, although nonwhite membership in Local 28 was only 10.8% at the time of the hearing. Instead, the court found that petitioners had "failed to comply with RAAPO * * * almost from its date of entry," identifying six "separate actions or omissions on the part of the defendants [that] have impeded the entry of non-whites into Local 28 in contravention of the prior orders of this court."

* * *

In 1983, the City brought a second contempt proceeding before the administrator, charging petitioners with additional violations of the O & J, RAAPO, and various administrative orders. The administrator found that the JAC had violated RAAPO [with respect to certain reporting and record keeping requirements].

The District Court adopted the administrator's findings and once again adjudicated petitioners guilty of civil contempt. The court ordered petitioners to pay for a computerized recordkeeping system to be maintained by outside consultants, but deferred ruling on additional contempt fines pending submission of the administrator's fund proposal. The court subsequently adopted the administrator's proposed Employment, Training, Education, and Recruitment Fund (Fund) to "be used for the purpose of remedying discrimination." The Fund was used for a variety of purposes. In order to increase the pool of qualified nonwhite applicants for the apprenticeship program, the Fund paid for nonwhite union members to serve as liaisons to vocational and technical schools with sheet metal programs, created part-time and summer sheet metal jobs for qualified nonwhite youths, and extended financial assistance to needy apprentices. The Fund also extended counseling and tutorial services to nonwhite apprentices, giving them the benefits that had traditionally been available to white apprentices from family and friends. Finally, in an effort to maximize employment opportunities for all apprentices, the Fund provided financial support to employers otherwise unable to hire a sufficient number of apprentices, as well as matching funds to attract additional funding for job training programs.[1]

The District Court also entered an Amended Affirmative Action Plan and Order (AAAPO) which modified RAAPO in several respects. AAAPO established a 29.23% minority membership goal to be met by August 31, 1987. The new goal was based on the labor pool in the area covered by the newly expanded union. The court abolished the apprenticeship examination, concluding that "the violations that have occurred in the past have been so egregious that a new approach must be taken to solve the apprentice selection problem." Apprentices were to be selected by a three-member Board, which would select one minority apprentice for each white apprentice indentured. Finally, to prevent petitioners from underutilizing the apprenticeship program, the JAC was required to assign to Local 28 contractors one apprentice for every four journeymen, unless the contractor obtained a written waiver from respondents.

Petitioners appealed the District Court's contempt orders, the Fund order, and the order adopting AAAPO. A panel of the Court of Appeals [largely] affirmed the District Court's contempt findings * * *. * * * The court also affirmed the District Court's contempt remedies, including the Fund order, and affirmed AAAPO with two modifications: it set aside the requirement that one minority apprentice be indentured for every white apprentice,[18] and clarified the District Court's orders to allow petitioners to implement objective, nondiscriminatory apprentice selection procedures.

* * *

IV

Petitioners, joined by the Solicitor General, argue that the membership goal, the Fund order, and other orders which require petitioners to grant membership preferences to nonwhites are expressly prohibited by § 706(g), 42 U.S.C. § 2000e–5(g), which defines the remedies available under Title VII. Petitioners and the Solicitor General maintain that § 706(g) authorizes a district court to award preferential relief only to the actual victims of unlawful discrimination.[25] * * *

1. The Fund was to be financed by the $150,000 fine from the first contempt proceeding, plus an additional payment of $0.02 per hour for each hour worked by a journeyman or apprentice. The Fund would remain in existence until the union achieved its nonwhite membership goal, and the District Court determined that the Fund was no longer necessary.

18. The court recognized that "temporary hiring ratios may be necessary in order to achieve integration of a work force from which minorities have been unlawfully barred," but cautioned that "such race-conscious ratios are extreme remedies that must be used sparingly and 'carefully tai-

lored to fit the violations found.' " Noting that petitioners had voluntarily indentured 45% nonwhites since January of 1981, the court concluded that a strict one-to-one hiring requirement was not needed to insure that a sufficient number of nonwhites were selected for the apprenticeship program.

25. The last sentence of § 706(g) addresses only court orders requiring the "admission or reinstatement of an individual as a member of a union." 42 U.S.C. § 2000e–5(g). Thus, even under petitioners' reading of § 706(g), that provision would not apply to several of the benefits conferred by the Fund, to wit, the tutorial, liaison, counseling, stipend, and loan programs extended to

A

* * *

The last sentence of § 706(g) prohibits a court from ordering a union to admit an individual who was "refused admission * * * for any reason other than discrimination." It does not, as petitioners and the Solicitor General suggest, say that a court may order relief only for the actual victims of past discrimination. The sentence on its face addresses only the situation where a plaintiff demonstrates that a union (or an employer) has engaged in unlawful discrimination, but the union can show that a particular individual would have been refused admission even in the absence of discrimination, for example because that individual was unqualified. In these circumstances, § 706(g) confirms that a court could not order the union to admit the unqualified individual. * * * In this case, neither the membership goal nor the Fund order required petitioners to admit to membership individuals who had been refused admission for reasons unrelated to discrimination. Thus, we do not read § 706(g) to prohibit a court from ordering the kind of affirmative relief the District Court awarded in this case.

B

The availability of race-conscious affirmative relief under § 706(g) as a remedy for a violation of Title VII also furthers the broad purposes underlying the statute. * * *

In most cases, the court need only order the employer or union to cease engaging in discriminatory practices, and award make-whole relief to the individuals victimized by those practices. In some instances, however, it may be necessary to require the employer or union to take affirmative steps to end discrimination effectively to enforce Title VII. Where an employer or union has engaged in particularly longstanding or egregious discrimination, an injunction simply reiterating Title VII's prohibition against discrimination will often prove useless and will only result in endless enforcement litigation. In such cases, requiring recalcitrant employers or unions to hire and to admit qualified minorities roughly in proportion to the number of qualified minorities in the work force may be the only effective way to ensure the full enjoyment of the rights protected by Title VII.

* * *

nonwhites. Moreover, the District Court established the Fund in the exercise of its contempt powers. Thus, even assuming that petitioners correctly read § 706(g) to limit the remedies a court may impose *for a violation of Title VII*, that provision would not necessarily limit the District Court's authority to order petitioners to implement the Fund. The Solicitor General, without citing any authority, maintains that "contempt sanctions imposed to enforce Title VII must not themselves violate the statute's policy of providing relief only to the actual victims of discrimination." We need not decide whether § 706(g) restricts a court's contempt powers, since we reject the proposition that § 706(g) always prohibits a court from ordering affirmative race-conscious relief which might incidentally benefit individuals who were not the actual victims of discrimination.

Further, even where the employer or union formally ceases to engage in discrimination, informal mechanisms may obstruct equal employment opportunities. An employer's reputation for discrimination may discourage minorities from seeking available employment.

* * *

Finally, a district court may find it necessary to order interim hiring or promotional goals pending the development of nondiscriminatory hiring or promotion procedures. In these cases, the use of numerical goals provides a compromise between two unacceptable alternatives: an outright ban on hiring or promotions, or continued use of a discriminatory selection procedure.

C

[*Eds.* The Court's discussion of the legislative history and administrative interpretation is omitted.]

D

* * *

Petitioners claim to find their strongest support in *Firefighters v. Stotts,* 467 U.S. 561, 104 S.Ct. 2576, 81 L.Ed.2d 483 (1984). In *Stotts,* the city of Memphis, Tennessee had entered into a consent decree requiring affirmative steps to increase the proportion of minority employees in its Fire Department. Budgetary cuts subsequently forced the city to lay off employees; under the city's last-hired, first-fired seniority system, many of the black employees who had been hired pursuant to the consent decree would have been laid off first. These employees sought relief, and the District Court, concluding that the proposed layoffs would have a racially discriminatory effect, enjoined the city from applying its seniority policy "insofar as it will decrease the percentage of black[s] that are presently employed." *Id.,* at 567, 104 S.Ct., at 2582. We held that the District Court exceeded its authority.

First, we rejected the claim that the District Court was merely enforcing the terms of the consent decree since the parties had expressed no intention to depart from the existing seniority system in the event of layoffs. Second, we concluded that the District Court's order conflicted with § 703(h) of Title VII, which "permits the routine application of a seniority system absent proof of an intention to discriminate." *Id.,* at 577. Since the District Court had found that the proposed layoffs were not motivated by a discriminatory purpose, we held that the court erred in enjoining the city from applying its seniority system in making the layoffs.

We also rejected the Court of Appeals' suggestion that the District Court's order was justified by the fact that, had plaintiffs prevailed at trial, the court could have entered an order overriding the city's seniority system. Relying on *Teamsters* [*v. United States,* 431 U.S. 324, 97 S.Ct. 1843, 52 L.Ed.2d 396 (1977)], we observed that a court may abridge a bona fide seniority system in fashioning a Title VII remedy only to make victims of intentional discrimination whole, that is, a court may award competitive seniority to individuals who show that they had been discriminated against. However, because none of the firefighters protected by the court's order was a proven victim of illegal discrimination, we reasoned that at trial the District Court would have been without authority to override the city's seniority system, and therefore the court could not enter such an order merely to effectuate the purposes of the consent decree.

While not strictly necessary to the result, we went on to comment that "[o]ur ruling in *Teamsters* that a court can award competitive seniority only when the beneficiary of the award has actually been a victim of illegal discrimination is consistent with the policy behind § 706(g)" which, we noted, "is to provide 'make-whole' relief only to those who have been actual victims of illegal discrimination." *Id.*, at 579–580. Relying on this language, petitioners, joined by the Solicitor General, argue that both the membership goal and the Fund order contravene the policy behind § 706(g) since they extend preferential relief to individuals who were not the actual victims of illegal discrimination. We think this argument both reads *Stotts* too broadly and ignores the important differences between *Stotts* and this case.

Stotts discussed the "policy" behind § 706(g) in order to supplement the holding that the District Court could not have interfered with the city's seniority system in fashioning a Title VII remedy. This "policy" was read to prohibit a court from awarding make-whole relief, such as competitive seniority, back pay, or promotion, to individuals who were denied employment opportunities for reasons unrelated to discrimination. The District Court's injunction was considered to be inconsistent with this "policy" because it was tantamount to an award of make-whole relief (in the form of competitive seniority) to individual black firefighters who had not shown that the proposed layoffs were motivated by racial discrimination.[44] However, this limitation on *individual* make-whole relief does not affect a court's authority to order race-conscious affirmative action. The purpose of affirmative action is not to make identified victims whole, but rather to dismantle prior patterns of employment discrimination and to prevent discrimination in the future. Such relief is provided to the class as a whole rather than to individual members; no individual is entitled to relief, and beneficiaries need not show that they were themselves victims of discrimination. In this case, neither the membership goal nor the Fund order required the petitioners to indenture or train particular individuals, and neither required them to admit to membership individuals who were refused admission for reasons unrelated to discrimination. We decline petitioners' invitation to read *Stotts* to prohibit a court from ordering any kind of race-conscious affirmative relief that might benefit nonvictims. This reading would

44. We note that, consistent with *Stotts,* the District Court in this case properly limited make-whole relief to the actual victims of discrimination. The court awarded back pay, for example, only to those class members who could establish that they were discriminated against.

distort the language of § 706(g), and would deprive the courts of an important means of enforcing Title VII's guarantee of equal employment opportunity.

E

Although we conclude that § 706(g) does not foreclose a district court from instituting some sorts of racial preferences where necessary to remedy past discrimination, we do not mean to suggest that such relief is always proper. While the fashioning of "appropriate" remedies for a particular Title VII violation invokes the "equitable discretion of the district courts," *Franks* [*v. Bowman Transportation Co.*, 424 U.S. 747, 770 96 S.Ct. 1251, 1267, 47 L.Ed.2d 444 (1976),] we emphasize that a court's judgment should be guided by sound legal principles. In particular, the court should exercise its discretion with an eye towards Congress' concern that race-conscious affirmative measures not be invoked simply to create a racially balanced work force. * * * We note * * * that a court should consider whether affirmative action is necessary to remedy past discrimination in a particular case before imposing such measures, and that the court should also take care to tailor its orders to fit the nature of the violation it seeks to correct. In this case, several factors lead us to conclude that the relief ordered by the District Court was proper.

First, both the District Court and the Court of Appeals agreed that the membership goal and Fund order were necessary to remedy petitioners' pervasive and egregious discrimination. * * *

Both the membership goal and Fund order were similarly necessary to combat the lingering effects of past discrimination. In light of the District Court's determination that the union's reputation for discrimination operated to discourage nonwhites from even applying for membership, it is unlikely that an injunction would have been sufficient to extend to nonwhites equal opportunities for employment. Rather, because access to admission, membership, training, and employment in the industry had traditionally been obtained through informal contacts with union members, it was necessary for a substantial number of nonwhite workers to become members of the union in order for the effects of discrimination to cease. The Fund, in particular, was designed to insure that nonwhites would receive the kind of assistance that white apprentices and applicants had traditionally received through informal sources. * * *

Second, the District Court's flexible application of the membership goal gives strong indication that it is not being used simply to achieve and maintain racial balance, but rather as a benchmark against which the court could gauge petitioners' efforts to remedy past discrimination. The court has twice adjusted the deadline for achieving the goal, and has continually approved of changes in the size of the apprenticeship classes to account for the fact that economic conditions prevented petitioners from meeting their membership targets; there is every reason to believe that both the court and the administrator will continue to accommodate *legitimate* explanations for the petitioners' failure to comply with the court's orders. Moreover, the District Court expressly disavowed any reliance on petitioners' failure to meet the goal as a basis for the contempt finding, but instead viewed this failure as symptomatic of petitioners' refusal to comply with various subsidiary provisions of RAAPO. In sum, the District Court has implemented the membership goal as a means by which it can measure petitioners' compliance with its orders, rather than as a strict racial quota.

Third, both the membership goal and the Fund order are temporary measures. Under AAAPO "[p]referential selection of union members [w]ill end as soon as the percentage of [minority union members] approximates the percentage of [minorities] in the local labor force." [*United Steelworkers v. Weber*, 443 U.S. 193, 208–209, 99 S.Ct. 2721, 2730 (1979).] * * * Similarly, the Fund is scheduled to terminate when petitioners achieve the membership goal, and the court determines that it is no longer needed to remedy past discrimination. * * *

Finally, we think it significant that neither the membership goal nor the Fund order "unnecessarily trammel the interests of white employees." *Id.,* 443 U.S., at 208, 99 S.Ct., at 2730; *Teamsters,* 431 U.S., at 352–353, 97 S.Ct., at 1863–1864. Petitioners concede that the District Court's orders did not require any member of the union to be laid off, and did not discriminate against *existing* union members. See *Weber, supra,* 443 U.S., at 208, 99 S.Ct., at 2729–2730. While whites seeking admission into the union may be denied benefits extended to their nonwhite counterparts, the court's orders do not stand as an absolute bar to such individuals; indeed, a majority of new union members have been white. Many provisions of the court's orders are race-neutral (for example, the requirement that the JAC assign one apprentice for every four journeymen workers), and petitioners remain free to adopt the provisions of AAAPO and the Fund Order for the benefit of white members and applicants.

V

Petitioners also allege that the membership goal and Fund order contravene the equal protection component of the Due Process Clause of the Fifth Amendment because they deny benefits to white individuals based on race. We have consistently recognized that government bodies constitutionally may adopt racial classifications as a remedy for past discrimination. See *Wygant v. Jackson Board of Education,* 476 U.S. 267, 106 S.Ct. 1842, 90 L.Ed.2d 260 (1986); *Fullilove v. Klutznick,* 448 U.S. 448, 100 S.Ct. 2758, 65 L.Ed.2d 902 (1980); *University of California Regents v. Bakke,* 438 U.S. 265, 98 S.Ct. 2733, 57 L.Ed.2d 750 (1978); *Swann v. Charlotte–Mecklenburg Board of Education,* 402 U.S. 1, 91 S.Ct. 1267, 28 L.Ed.2d 554 (1971). We have not agreed, however, on the proper test to be applied in analyzing the constitutionality of race-conscious remedial measures. * * * We need not resolve this dispute here, since we conclude that the relief ordered in this case passes even the most rigorous test—it is narrowly tailored to further the Government's compelling interest in remedying past discrimination.

JUSTICE POWELL, concurring in part and concurring in the judgment.

I join Parts I, II, III, and VI of JUSTICE BRENNAN'S opinion. * * * I write separately with respect to the issues raised in parts IV and V to explain why I think the remedy ordered under the circumstances of this case violated neither Title VII nor the Constitution.

* * *

The history of petitioners' contemptuous racial discrimination and their successive attempts to evade all efforts to end that discrimination is well stated in part I of the Court's opinion. Under these circumstances the District Court acted within the remedial authority granted by § 706(g) in establishing the Fund order and numerical goal at issue in this case. * * *

There remains for consideration the question whether the Fund order and membership goal contravene the equal protection component of the Due Process Clause of the Fifth Amendment because they may deny benefits to white individuals based on race. * * *

The finding by the District Court and the Court of Appeals that petitioners have engaged in egregious violations of Title VII establishes, without doubt, a compelling governmental interest sufficient to justify the imposition of a racially classified remedy. It would be difficult to find defendants more determined to discriminate against minorities. My inquiry, therefore, focuses on whether the District Court's remedy is "narrowly tailored" to the goal of eradicating the discrimination engaged in by petitioners. I believe it is.

The Fund order is supported not only by the governmental interest in eradicating petitioners' discriminatory practices, it also is supported by the societal interest in compliance with the judgments of federal courts. Cf. *United States v. Mine Workers,* 330 U.S. 258, 303, 67 S.Ct. 677, 701, 91 L.Ed. 884 (1947). The Fund order was not imposed until *after* petitioners were held in contempt. In requiring the Union to create the Fund, the District Court expressly considered " 'the consequent seriousness of the burden' to the defendants." Moreover, the focus of the Fund order was to give minorities opportunities that for years had been available informally only to nonminorities. The burden this imposes on nonminorities is slight. Under these circumstances, I have little difficulty concluding that the Fund order was carefully structured to vindicate the compelling governmental interests present in this case.

The percentage goal raises a different question. * * *

First, it is doubtful, given petitioners' history in this litigation, that the District Court had available to it any other effective remedy. * * * Second, the goal was not imposed as a permanent requirement, but is of limited duration. Third, the goal is directly related to the percentage of nonwhites in the relevant workforce.

* * *

[Fourth, the] flexible application of the goal requirement in this case demonstrates that it is not a means to achieve racial balance. * * *

It is also important to emphasize that on the record before us, it does not appear that nonminorities will be burdened directly, if at all. * * *

JUSTICE O'CONNOR, concurring in part and dissenting in part.

* * * I would reverse the judgment of the Court of Appeals on statutory grounds insofar as the membership "goal" and the Fund order are concerned, and I would not reach petitioners' constitutional claims. I agree with Justice White, however, that the membership "goal" in this case operates as a rigid racial quota that cannot feasibly be met through good-faith efforts by Local 28. In my view, § 703(j), 42 U.S.C. § 2000e–2(j), and § 706(g), 42 U.S.C. § 2000e–5(g), read together, preclude courts from ordering racial quotas such as this. I therefore dissent from the Court's judgment insofar as it affirms the use of these mandatory quotas.

* * *

To be consistent with § 703(j), a racial hiring or membership goal must be intended to serve merely as a benchmark for measuring compliance with Title VII and eliminating the lingering effects of past discrimination, rather than as a rigid numerical requirement that must unconditionally be met on pain of sanctions. To hold an employer or union to achievement of a particular percentage of minority employment or membership, and to do so regardless of circumstances such as economic conditions or the number of available qualified minority applicants, is to impose an impermissible quota. By contrast, a permissible goal should require only a good faith effort on the employer's or union's part to come within a range demarcated by the goal itself.

* * *

In this case, I agree with Justice White that the membership "goal" established by the District Court's successive orders in this case has been administered and will continue to operate "not just [as] a minority membership goal but also [as] a strict racial quota that the union was required to attain." It is important to realize that the membership "goal" ordered by the District Court goes well beyond a requirement, such as the ones the plurality discusses approvingly, that a union "admit qualified minorities roughly in proportion to the number of qualified minorities in the work force." The "goal" here requires that the racial composition of Local 28's entire membership mirror that of the relevant labor pool by August 31, 1987, without regard to variables such as the number of qualified minority applicants available or the number of new apprentices needed. The District Court plainly stated that "[i]f the goal is not attained by that date, defendants will face fines that will threaten their very existence."

* * * For similar reasons, I believe that the Fund order, which created benefits for minority apprentices that nonminority apprentices were precluded from enjoying, operated as a form of racial quota.

[*Eds.* The dissenting opinions of JUSTICE WHITE and JUSTICE REHN-QUIST, with whom CHIEF JUSTICE BURGER joined, are omitted.]

Note on United States v. Paradise

In United States v. Paradise, 480 U.S. 149, 107 S.Ct. 1053, 94 L.Ed.2d 203 (1987), one term after its decision in *Sheet Metal Workers,* the Supreme Court again addressed a constitutional challenge to a court-imposed race-conscious remedial order. The order included a "one-black-for-one-white promotion requirement to be applied * * * to state trooper promotions in the Alabama Department of Public Safety" to the extent "qualified black candidates were available" and "until the Department implemented an acceptable promotion procedure * * *." Id. at 153, 107 S.Ct. at 1057. Because the order was based on a violation of the equal protection clause, Title VII principles, including those embodied in § 706(g), were not at issue.

By a 5–4 vote, the Court upheld the order. Justice Brennan wrote a plurality opinion representing the views of four Justices. As in *Sheet Metal Workers,* the plurality opinion did not pass on the constitutional standard for review, finding that the promotion goal could survive even strict scrutiny analysis because it was "narrowly tailored" to serve a "compelling [govern-mental] purpose * * *." Id. at 167, 107 S.Ct. at 1065. The primary compelling state interest was the remedying of almost four decades of discrimination by the defendant Department, which "resulted in a departmental hierarchy dominated exclusively by nonminorities * * *." Id. at 168, 107 S.Ct. at 1065. Moreover, because of a history of twelve years of resistance by the defendant to the trial court's previous remedial decrees, the challenged order was "also supported by the societal interest in compliance with the judgments of federal courts." Id. at 170, 107 S.Ct. at 1066.

The remedial order in *Paradise* was also found to be narrowly tailored to serve these two compelling purposes. First, the plurality agreed that the order was necessary in light of the inadequacy of possible alternatives. Given the Department's failure either to develop a nondiscriminatory promotion procedure over the past twelve years or voluntarily to promote any blacks, the district court properly discounted the Department's promise that it would develop such a procedure after it was allowed to make a large number of urgent promotions to the first promotional rank of corporal. The trial court also properly rejected the alternative of imposing heavy fines and fees because such approaches had not worked in the past, and even heavy fines would do nothing to compensate black employees "for the long delays in implementing acceptable promotion procedures." Id. at 175, 107 S.Ct. at 1069.

Second, the Brennan plurality noted that the one-for-one promotion requirement was intended to be a flexible goal rather than a quota. It only applied if the Department determined a need to make promotions and if qualified black candidates were available, and would only last "until the Department comes up with a procedure that does not have a discriminatory impact on blacks * * *." Id. at 178, 107 S.Ct. at 1070.

Third, the promotion requirement was found to be appropriately related to the percentage of blacks in the relevant labor market. Justice Brennan emphasized that the fifty per cent requirement would remain in effect only until blacks were twenty-five percent of the defendant's work force. Thus, "the 50% figure is not itself the goal; rather it represents the speed at which the goal of 25% will be achieved." Id. at 179, 107 S.Ct. at 1071.

Finally, the one-for-one requirement did not impose an "unacceptable burden on innocent third parties." Justice Brennan noted again the flexible, temporary and limited nature of the requirement, and stressed that it did not operate as an "absolute bar" to the promotion of whites or require their layoff or discharge. The challenged requirement "only postpones the promotions of qualified whites," and thus, "like a hiring goal," only imposes a "diffuse" burden. Id. at 182–83, 107 S.Ct. at 1072–73.

Justice Stevens filed a separate concurrence. Although he withheld a fifth vote from the Brennan plurality, his concurrence seems to authorize even more discretion for courts in fashioning affirmative action orders against public employers adjudged guilty of discrimination in violation of the fourteenth amendment. Stevens would grant such courts the same "broad and flexible" discretion granted lower courts to eliminate the effects of racial segregation in public schools by Swann v. Charlotte–Mecklenburg Bd. of Education, 402 U.S. 1, 91 S.Ct. 1267, 28 L.Ed.2d 554 (1971). 480 U.S. at 189–90, 107 S.Ct. at 1076–77. Thus, rather than requiring a lower court's remedial order to be narrowly tailored to achieve a compelling governmental interest, Stevens would require a "party who has been found guilty of repeated and persistent violations of the law" to bear "the burden of demonstrating that the [court's] efforts to fashion effective relief exceed the bounds of 'reasonableness.' " Id. at 193, 107 S.Ct. at 1078.

Justice O'Connor dissented in an opinion joined by Chief Justice Rehnquist and Justice Scalia. She contended that the plurality had not applied stringent equal protection strict scrutiny to the order, and that the order was not narrowly tailored to the remedying of past and present discrimination. She asserted that the promotional requirement should not have been set at a level substantially greater than the representation of black workers in the Department's labor force. She also argued that the trial court could have achieved full compliance with the consent decrees and avoided further discrimination in promotions, either by appointing "a trustee to develop a promotion procedure" or by imposing "stiff fines or other penalties for contempt". Id. at 200, 107 S.Ct. at 1082. Justice White also dissented, cryptically "[a]greeing with much of what Justice O'Connor has written in this case." Id. at 196, 107 S.Ct. at 1080.

Notes and Questions

1. *Acceptable Purposes for Race–Conscious Title VII Remedies?* Has a majority of the Court in *Sheet Metal Workers* (the four-Justice plurality and Justice Powell) endorsed the proposition that in appropriate circumstances

Title VII courts may order race-conscious relief that benefits individuals other than those who have been judged direct victims of a defendant's discrimination? What purposes does at least the plurality opinion suggest such orders may appropriately serve? Which of these purposes, if any, do you think were served by the challenged order in *Sheet Metal Workers*?

2. *Limitations on Acceptable Race–Conscious Relief?* Assuming acceptable purposes, what limitations does the *Sheet Metal Workers* plurality suggest should be placed on orders for race-conscious relief for Title VII violations? What limitations would Justice Powell impose?

3. *Justice O'Connor and the Distinction Between Goals and Quotas.* How do Justice O'Connor's views differ from those of the plurality in *Sheet Metal Workers*? Does she simply have a different view of the trial court's willingness to be flexible in response to changing economic conditions? Or does her distinction of permissible "goals" from impermissible "quotas" have some predictable meaning for future cases? If the latter, what exactly is the distinction?

Consider how Justice O'Connor contrasted quotas and goals seventeen years later in her opinion for the Court in Grutter v. Bollinger, 539 U.S. 306, 123 S.Ct. 2325, 156 L.Ed.2d 304 (2003), upholding the University of Michigan Law School's affirmative action plan for student admissions:

> Properly understood, a quota is a program in which a certain fixed number or proportion of opportunities are reserved exclusively for certain minority groups. Quotas impose a fixed number or percentage which must be attained, or which cannot be exceeded, and insulate the individual from comparison with all other candidates for the available seats. In contrast, a permissible goal requires only a good-faith effort ... to come within a range demarcated by the goal itself, and permits consideration of race as a plus factor in any given case while still ensuring that each candidate competes with all other qualified applicants.... (Citations and quotations omitted.)

539 U.S. at 336. See also Gratz v. Bollinger, 539 U.S. 244, 123 S.Ct. 2411, 156 L.Ed.2d 257 (2003) (stressing the importance of each candidate being given individualized consideration).

4. *Is Race–Conscious Relief Ever Required?* Does the *Sheet Metal Workers* decision require trial courts to order affirmative action relief that may directly benefit non-victims in cases where the standards it posits for permitting such relief are met? May an appellate court order a trial court to grant such relief? See Eldredge v. Carpenters 46 Northern California Counties JATC, 94 F.3d 1366 (9th Cir.1996) (requiring trial court to order union to implement affirmative action plan proposed by the plaintiff class).

5. *The Continuing Relevance of* Stotts? Consider the *Sheet Metal Workers* decision's treatment of Firefighters v. Stotts, 467 U.S. 561, 104 S.Ct. 2576, 81 L.Ed.2d 483 (1984). Why was race-conscious relief held not acceptable in *Stotts*? Was it because the trial court in *Stotts* framed its decree to provide "make-whole relief" to particular laid-off black employees who were not actual direct victims of the defendant's past discrimination, rather than as "forward looking" affirmative action "to dismantle prior patterns of employment discrimination and to prevent discrimination in the future?"

Could the trial court in *Stotts* have justified ordering a suspension of the normal operation of the fire department's bona fide seniority system as necessary to dismantle a system of discrimination? Or would such a justification have been inconsistent with the assumption embodied in § 703(h) that bona fide seniority systems are not discriminatory?

Do *Stotts* and *Sheet Metal Workers* together stand for the proposition that Title VII courts can order race-conscious relief that directly benefits those who have not been subject to the defendant's past discrimination only where that relief is necessary to dismantle a system of illegal discrimination and avoid its continuation? If so, do these decisions prevent the grant to non-victims of any particular relief other than the modification of a bona fide seniority system? How about backpay or compensatory damages?

6. *What Role Does A Defendant's Contumacious Behavior Play?* Can a Title VII court order as a remedy for a defendant employer's contempt back pay to individuals who are not proven victims of discrimination, but who were not hired during a period when the defendant failed to meet a court-imposed affirmative action hiring goal? See EEOC v. Guardian Pools, Inc., 828 F.2d 1507, 1513–16 (11th Cir.1987) (allowing such an order). Consider also footnote 25 in the *Sheet Metal Workers* plurality opinion.

7. *Constitutional vs. Title VII Standards for Race–Conscious Relief.* What standards for judging the constitutionality of affirmative action relief are suggested by the plurality opinions in *Sheet Metal Workers* and *Paradise* and Justice Powell's concurring opinion in *Sheet Metal Workers*? Do these differ from the Title VII standards as applied in *Sheet Metal Workers*? Does the equal protection clause, like Title VII, demand that any relief that directly benefits non-victims be framed to avoid future discrimination, rather than only to compensate for past discrimination?

Should § 706(g) be read to give Title VII courts greater discretion to use race-conscious remedies than does the Constitution? To give them less discretion? Must the constitutional standard be the same in a case like *Sheet Metal Workers,* where a private defendant has been adjudged guilty of violating Title VII, as in a case like *Paradise,* where a public employer has been adjudged guilty of violating the Constitution's equal protection guarantee? Why did Justice Stevens join the plurality opinion in *Sheet Metal Workers,* but write separately in *Paradise*?

8. The Title VII court's authority to approve race-conscious classwide remedies as part of a consent decree is considered in connection with Local No. 93, International Assn. of Firefighters v. Cleveland, at pp. 290–291 infra.

C. VOLUNTARY AFFIRMATIVE ACTION

1. *The Constitutional Standard*

WYGANT v. JACKSON BOARD OF EDUCATION
Supreme Court of the United States, 1986.
476 U.S. 267, 106 S.Ct. 1842, 90 L.Ed.2d 260.

JUSTICE POWELL announced the judgment of the Court and delivered an opinion in which THE CHIEF JUSTICE and JUSTICE REHNQUIST joined, and which JUSTICE O'CONNOR joined in parts I, II, III–A, III–B, and V.

I

In 1972 the Jackson Board of Education, because of racial tension in the community that extended to its schools, considered adding a layoff provision to the Collective Bargaining Agreement (CBA) between the Board and the Jackson Education Association (the Union) that would protect employees who were members of certain minority groups against layoffs.[1] The Board and the Union eventually approved a new provision, Article XII of the CBA, covering layoffs. It stated:

> "In the event that it becomes necessary to reduce the number of teachers through layoff from employment by the Board, teachers with the most seniority in the district shall be retained, except that at no time will there be a greater percentage of minority personnel laid off than the current percentage of minority personnel employed at the time of the layoff. In no event will the number given notice of possible layoff be greater than the number of positions to be eliminated. Each teacher so affected will be called back in reverse order for positions for which he is certificated maintaining the above minority balance."[2]

As a result, during the 1976–1977 and 1981–1982 school years, nonminority teachers were laid off, while minority teachers with less seniority were retained. The displaced nonminority teachers, petitioners here, brought suit in Federal District Court, alleging violations of the Equal Protection Clause, Title VII, 42 U.S.C. § 1983, and other federal and state statutes.

* * *

II

Petitioners' central claim is that they were laid off because of their race in violation of the Equal Protection Clause of the Fourteenth Amendment. * * *

The Court has recognized that the level of scrutiny does not change merely because the challenged classification operates against a group that historically has not been subject to governmental discrimination. * * * "Any preference based on racial or ethnic criteria must necessarily receive a most searching examination to make sure that it does not conflict with constitutional guarantees." *Fullilove v. Klutznick,* 448 U.S. 448, 491, 100 S.Ct. 2758, 2781, 65 L.Ed.2d 902 (1980) (opinion of Burger, C.J.). There are two prongs to this examination. First, any racial classification "must be justified by a compelling governmental interest."

---

1. Prior to bargaining on this subject, the Minority Affairs Office of the Jackson Public Schools sent a questionnaire to all teachers, soliciting their views as to a layoff policy. The questionnaire proposed two alternatives: continuation of the existing straight seniority system, or a freeze of minority layoffs to ensure retention of minority teachers in exact proportion to the minority student population. Ninety-six percent of the teachers who responded to the questionnaire expressed a preference for the straight seniority system.

2. Article VII of the CBA defined "minority group personnel" as "those employees who are Black, American Indian, Oriental, or of Spanish descendancy."

Palmore v. Sidoti, 466 U.S. 429, 432, 104 S.Ct. 1879, 1882, 80 L.Ed.2d 421 (1984). * * * Second, the means chosen by the State to effectuate its purpose must be "narrowly tailored to the achievement of that goal." *Fullilove,* 448 U.S., at 480, 100 S.Ct., at 2776. We must decide whether the layoff provision is supported by a compelling state purpose and whether the means chosen to accomplish that purpose are narrowly tailored.

III

A

The Court of Appeals, relying on the reasoning and language of the District Court's opinion, held that the Board's interest in providing minority role models for its minority students, as an attempt to alleviate the effects of societal discrimination, was sufficiently important to justify the racial classification embodied in the layoff provision. The court discerned a need for more minority faculty role models by finding that the percentage of minority teachers was less than the percentage of minority students.

This Court never has held that societal discrimination alone is sufficient to justify a racial classification. Rather, the Court has insisted upon some showing of prior discrimination by the governmental unit involved before allowing limited use of racial classifications in order to remedy such discrimination. This Court's reasoning in *Hazelwood School District v. United States,* 433 U.S. 299, 97 S.Ct. 2736, 53 L.Ed.2d 768 (1977), illustrates that the relevant analysis in cases involving proof of discrimination by statistical disparity focuses on those disparities that demonstrate such prior governmental discrimination. In *Hazelwood* the Court concluded that, absent employment discrimination by the school board, " 'nondiscriminatory hiring practices will in time result in a work force more or less representative of the racial and ethnic composition of the population in the community from which the employees are hired.' " *Id.,* at 307, 97 S.Ct., at 2741, quoting *Teamsters v. United States,* 431 U.S. 324, 340, n. 20.

* * *

Unlike the analysis in *Hazelwood,* the role model theory employed by the District Court has no logical stopping point. The role model theory allows the Board to engage in discriminatory hiring and layoff practices long past the point required by any legitimate remedial purpose.

* * *

Societal discrimination, without more, is too amorphous a basis for imposing a racially classified remedy. The role model theory announced by the District Court and the resultant holding typify this indefiniteness. There are numerous explanations for a disparity between the percentage of minority students and the percentage of minority faculty, many of them completely unrelated to discrimination of any kind. In fact, there is no apparent connection between the two groups. Nevertheless, the District Court combined irrelevant comparisons between these two groups with an indisputable statement that there has been societal discrimination, and upheld state action predicated upon racial classifications. No one doubts that there has been serious racial discrimination in this country. But as the basis for imposing discriminatory *legal* remedies that work against innocent people, societal discrimination is insufficient and over expansive. In the absence of particularized findings, a court could uphold remedies that are ageless in their reach into the past, and timeless in their ability to affect the future.

B

Respondents also now argue that their purpose in adopting the layoff provision was to remedy prior discrimination against minorities by the Jackson School District in hiring teachers. Public schools, like other public employers, operate under two interrelated constitutional duties. They are under a clear command from this Court, starting with *Brown v. Board of Education,* 349 U.S. 294, 75 S.Ct. 753, 99 L.Ed. 1083 (1955), to eliminate every vestige of racial segregation and discrimination in the schools. Pursuant to that goal, race-conscious remedial action may be necessary. *North Carolina State Board of Education v. Swann,* 402 U.S. 43, 46, 91 S.Ct. 1284, 1286, 28 L.Ed.2d 586 (1971). On the other hand, public employers, including public schools, also must act in accordance with a "core purpose of the Fourteenth Amendment" which is to "do away with all governmentally imposed distinctions based on race." *Palmore v. Sidoti,* 466 U.S., at 432, 104 S.Ct., at 1881–1882. These related constitutional duties are not always harmonious; reconciling them requires public employers to act with extraordinary care. In particular, a public employer like the Board must ensure that, before it embarks on an affirmative action program, it has convincing evidence that remedial action is warranted. That is, it must have sufficient evidence to justify the conclusion that there has been prior discrimination.

Evidentiary support for the conclusion that remedial action is warranted becomes crucial when the remedial program is challenged in court by nonminority employees. In this case, for example, petitioners contended at trial that the remedial program—Article XII—had the purpose and effect of instituting a racial classification that was not justified by a remedial purpose. In such a case, the trial court must make a factual determination that the employer had a strong basis in evidence for its conclusion that remedial action was necessary. The ultimate burden remains with the employees to demonstrate the unconstitutionality of an affirmative action program. But unless such a determination is made, an appellate court reviewing a challenge to remedial action by nonminority employees cannot determine whether the race-based action is justified as a remedy for prior discrimination.

Despite the fact that Article XII has spawned years of litigation and three separate lawsuits, no such determination ever has been made.

Although its litigation position was different, the Board in [two prior suits brought to compel the Board's adherence to its Article XII obligations] denied the existence of prior discriminatory hiring practices. * * * Both courts concluded that any statistical disparities were the result of general societal discrimination, not of prior discrimination by the Board. The Board now contends that, given another opportunity, it could establish the existence of prior discrimination. Although this argument seems belated at this point in the proceedings, we need not consider the question since we conclude below that the layoff provision was not a legally appropriate means of achieving even a compelling purpose.[5]

IV

The Court of Appeals examined the means chosen to accomplish the Board's race-conscious purposes under a test of "reasonableness." That standard has no support in the decisions of this Court. As demonstrated in Part II above, our decisions always have employed a more stringent standard—however articulated—to test the validity of the means chosen by a state to accomplish its race-conscious purposes. See, *e.g., Palmore,* 466 U.S., at 432, 104 S.Ct., at 1882 ("to pass constitutional muster, [racial classifications] must be necessary * * * to the accomplishment of their legitimate purpose") (quoting *McLaughlin v. Florida,* 379 U.S. 184, 196, 85 S.Ct. 283, 290, 13 L.Ed.2d 222 (1964); *Fullilove,* 448 U.S., at 480, 100 S.Ct., at 2775 (opinion of Burger, C.J.) * * *. "Racial classifications are simply too pernicious to permit any but the most exact connection between justification and classification." *Id.,* at 537, 100 S.Ct., at 2805 (Stevens, J., dissenting).

We have recognized, however, that in order to remedy the effects of prior discrimination, it may be necessary to take race into account. As part of this Nation's dedication to eradicating racial discrimination, innocent persons may be called upon to bear some of the burden of the remedy. "When effectuating a limited and properly tailored remedy to cure the effects of prior discrimination, such a 'sharing of the burden' by innocent parties is not impermissible." *Id.,* at 484, 100 S.Ct., at 2778, quoting *Franks v. Bowman Transportation Co.,* 424 U.S. 747.[8]

---

5. * * *

The real dispute * * * is not over the state of the record. It is disagreement as to what constitutes a "legitimate factual predicate." If the necessary factual predicate is *prior discrimination*—that is, that race-based state action is taken to remedy prior discrimination by the governmental unit involved—then the very nature of appellate review requires that a factfinder determine whether the employer was justified in instituting a remedial plan. Nor can the respondent unilaterally insulate itself from this key constitutional question by conceding that it has discriminated in the past, now that it is in its interest to make such a

concession. Contrary to the dissent's assertion, the requirement of such a determination by the trial court is not some arbitrary barrier set up by today's opinion. Rather, it is a necessary result of the requirement that race-based state action be remedial. * * *

8. Of course, when a state implements a race-based plan that requires such a sharing of the burden, it cannot justify the discriminatory effect on some individuals because other individuals had approved the plan. Any "waiver" of the right not to be dealt with by the government on the basis of one's race must be made by those affected. Yet Justice Marshall repeatedly con-

Significantly, none of the cases discussed above involved layoffs. Here, by contrast, the means chosen to achieve the Board's asserted purposes is that of laying off nonminority teachers with greater seniority in order to retain minority teachers with less seniority. We have previously expressed concern over the burden that a preferential layoffs scheme imposes on innocent parties. See *Firefighters v. Stotts,* 467 U.S. 561, 574–576, 578–579, 104 S.Ct. 2576, 81 L.Ed.2d 483 (1984) * * *. In cases involving valid *hiring* goals, the burden to be borne by innocent individuals is diffused to a considerable extent among society generally. Though hiring goals may burden some innocent individuals, they simply do not impose the same kind of injury that layoffs impose. Denial of a future employment opportunity is not as intrusive as loss of an existing job.

* * *

While hiring goals impose a diffuse burden, often foreclosing only one of several opportunities, layoffs impose the entire burden of achieving racial equality on particular individuals, often resulting in serious disruption of their lives. That burden is too intrusive. We therefore hold that, as a means of accomplishing purposes that otherwise may be legitimate, the Board's layoff plan is not sufficiently narrowly tailored. Other, less intrusive means of accomplishing similar purposes—such as the adoption of hiring goals—are available. For these reasons, the Board's selection of layoffs as the means to accomplish even a valid purpose cannot satisfy the demands of the Equal Protection Clause.[13]

JUSTICE O'CONNOR, concurring in part and concurring in the judgment.

tends that the fact that Article XII was approved by a majority vote of the Union somehow validates this plan. He sees this case not in terms of individual constitutional rights, but as an allocation of burdens "between two racial groups." * * * Thus, Article XII becomes a political compromise that "avoided placing the entire burden of layoffs on either the white teachers as a group or the minority teachers as a group." * * * But the petitioners before us today are not "the white teachers as a group." They are Wendy Wygant and other individuals who claim that they were fired from their jobs because of their race. That claim cannot be waived by petitioners' more senior colleagues. In view of the way union seniority works, it is not surprising that while a straight freeze on minority layoffs was overwhelmingly rejected, a "compromise" eventually was reached that placed the entire burden of the compromise on the most junior union members. The more senior union members simply had nothing to lose from such a compromise. * * * ("To petitioners, at the bottom of the seniority scale among white teachers, fell the lot of bearing the white group's proportionate share of layoffs that became necessary in 1982.") The fact that such a painless accommodation was approved by the more senior union members six times since 1972 is irrelevant. The Constitution does not allocate constitutional rights to be distributed like bloc grants within discrete racial groups; and until it does, petitioners' more senior union colleagues cannot vote away petitioners' rights. * * *

13. The Board's definition of minority to include blacks, Orientals, American Indians, and persons of Spanish descent, further illustrates the undifferentiated nature of the plan. There is no explanation of why the Board chose to favor these particular minorities or how in fact members of some of the categories can be identified. Moreover, respondents have never suggested—much less formally found—that they have engaged in prior, purposeful discrimination against members of each of these minority groups.

I agree with the Court that a governmental agency's interest in remedying "societal" discrimination, that is, discrimination not traceable to its own actions, cannot be deemed sufficiently compelling to pass constitutional muster under strict scrutiny. * * * I also concur in the Court's assessment that use by the courts below of a "role model" theory* to justify the conclusion that this plan had a legitimate remedial purpose was in error. * * * Thus, in my view, the District Court and the Court of Appeals clearly erred in relying on these purposes and in failing to give greater attention to the School Board's asserted purpose of rectifying its own apparent discrimination.

* * *

The courts below ruled that a particularized, contemporaneous finding of discrimination was not necessary and upheld the plan as a remedy for "societal" discrimination, apparently on the assumption that in the absence of a specific, contemporaneous finding, any discrimination addressed by an affirmative action plan could only be termed "societal." I believe that this assumption is false and therefore agree with the Court that a contemporaneous or antecedent finding of past discrimination by a court or other competent body is not a constitutional prerequisite to a public employer's voluntary agreement to an affirmative action plan.

* * *

The imposition of a requirement that public employers make findings that they have engaged in illegal discrimination before they engage in affirmative action programs would severely undermine public employers' incentive to meet voluntarily their civil rights obligations. * * * This result would clearly be at odds with this Court's and Congress' consistent emphasis on "the value of voluntary efforts to further the objectives of the law." * * * The value of voluntary compliance is doubly important when it is a public employer that acts, both because of the example its voluntary assumption of responsibility sets and because the remediation of governmental discrimination is of unique importance. See S.Rep. No. 92–415, p. 10 (1971) (accompanying the amendments extending coverage of Title VII to the States) ("Discrimination by government * * * serves a doubly destructive purpose. The exclusion of minorities from effective participation in the bureaucracy not only promotes ignorance of minority problems in that particular community, but also creates mistrust, alienation, and all too often hostility toward the entire process of government"). * * *

---

* The goal of providing "role-models" discussed by the courts below should not be confused with the very different goal of promoting racial diversity among the faculty. Because this latter goal was not urged as such in support of the layoff provision before the District Court and the Court of Appeals, however, I do not believe it necessary to discuss the magnitude of that interest or its applicability in this case. The only governmental interests at issue here are those of remedying "societal" discrimination, providing "role-models," and remedying apparent prior employment discrimination by the School District.

Such results cannot, in my view, be justified by reference to the incremental value a contemporaneous findings requirement would have as an evidentiary safeguard. As is illustrated by this case, public employers are trapped between the competing hazards of liability to minorities if affirmative action *is not* taken to remedy apparent employment discrimination and liability to nonminorities if affirmative action *is* taken. Where these employers, who are presumably fully aware both of their duty under federal law to respect the rights of *all* their employees and of their potential liability for failing to do so, act on the basis of information which gives them a sufficient basis for concluding that remedial action is necessary, a contemporaneous findings requirement should not be necessary.

* * *

There is, however, no need to inquire whether the provision actually had a legitimate remedial purpose based on the record, such as it is, because the judgment is vulnerable on yet another ground: the courts below applied a "reasonableness" test in evaluating the relationship between the ends pursued and the means employed to achieve them that is plainly incorrect under any of the standards articulated by this Court. Nor is it necessary, in my view, to resolve the troubling questions of whether any layoff provision could survive strict scrutiny or whether this particular layoff provision could, when considered without reference to the hiring goal it was intended to further, pass the onerous "narrowly tailored" requirement. Petitioners have met their burden of establishing that this layoff provision is not "narrowly tailored" to achieve its asserted remedial purpose by demonstrating that the provision is keyed to a hiring goal that itself has no relation to the remedying of employment discrimination.

Although the constitutionality of the hiring goal as such is not before us, it is impossible to evaluate the necessity of the layoff provision as a remedy for the apparent prior employment discrimination absent reference to that goal. * * * In this case, the hiring goal that the layoff provision was designed to safeguard was tied to the percentage of minority students in the school district, not to the percentage of qualified minority teachers within the relevant labor pool. The disparity between the percentage of minorities on the teaching staff and the percentage of minorities in the student body is not probative of employment discrimination; it is only when it is established that the availability of minorities in the relevant labor pool substantially exceeded those hired that one may draw an inference of deliberate discrimination in employment. See *Hazelwood School District v. United States,* 433 U.S. 299, 308, 97 S.Ct. 2736, 2741, 53 L.Ed.2d 768 (1977) (Title VII context). Because the layoff provision here acts to maintain levels of minority hiring that have no relation to remedying employment discrimination, it cannot be adjudged "narrowly tailored" to effectuate its asserted remedial purpose.

JUSTICE WHITE, concurring in the judgment.

The school board's policy when layoffs are necessary is to maintain a certain proportion of minority teachers. This policy requires laying off non-minority teachers solely on the basis of their race, including teachers with seniority, and retaining other teachers solely because they are black, even though some of them are in probationary status. None of the interests asserted by the board, singly or together, justify this racially discriminatory layoff policy and save it from the strictures of the Equal Protection Clause. Whatever the legitimacy of hiring goals or quotas may be, the discharge of white teachers to make room for blacks, none of whom has been shown to be a victim of any racial discrimination, is quite a different matter. I cannot believe that in order to integrate a work force, it would be permissible to discharge whites and hire blacks until the latter comprised a suitable percentage of the work force. None of our cases suggest that this would be permissible under the Equal Protection Clause. Indeed, our cases look quite the other way. The layoff policy in this case—laying off whites who would otherwise be retained in order to keep blacks on the job—has the same effect and is equally violative of the Equal Protection Clause. I agree with the plurality that this official policy is unconstitutional and hence concur in the judgment.

JUSTICE MARSHALL, with whom JUSTICE BRENNAN and JUSTICE BLACKMUN join, dissenting.

* * *

The principal state purpose supporting Article XII is the need to preserve the levels of faculty integration achieved through the affirmative hiring policy adopted in the early 1970's. Justification for the hiring policy itself is found in the turbulent history of the effort to integrate the Jackson Public Schools—not even mentioned in the majority opinion—which attests to the bona fides of the Board's current employment practices.

The record and lodgings indicate that the [Michigan Civil Rights] Commission, endowed by the State Constitution with the power to investigate complaints of discrimination and the duty to secure the equal protection of the laws, Mich. Const., Art. V, § 29, prompted and oversaw the remedial steps now under attack. When the Board agreed to take specified remedial action, including the hiring and promotion of minority teachers, the Commission did not pursue its investigation of the apparent violations to the point of rendering formal findings of discrimination.

Instead of subjecting an already volatile school system to the further disruption of formal accusations and trials, it appears that the Board set about achieving the goals articulated in the settlement.

* * *

Testimony of both Union and school officials illustrates that the Board's obligation to integrate its faculty could not have been fulfilled meaningfully as long as layoffs continued to eliminate the last hired. In addition, qualified minority teachers from other States were reluctant to uproot their lives and move to Michigan without any promise of protection from imminent layoff. The testimony suggests that the lack of some layoff protection would have crippled the efforts to recruit minority applicants. Adjustment of the layoff hierarchy under these circumstances was a necessary corollary of an affirmative hiring policy.

Under Justice Powell's approach, the community of Jackson, having painfully watched the hard-won benefits of its integration efforts vanish as a result of massive layoffs, would be informed today, simply, that preferential layoff protection is never permissible because hiring policies serve the same purpose at a lesser cost. * * * As a matter of logic as well as fact, a hiring policy achieves no purpose at all if it is eviscerated by layoffs. Justice Powell's position is untenable.

* * *

The Board's goal of preserving minority proportions could have been achieved, perhaps, in a different way. For example, if layoffs had been determined by lottery, the ultimate effect would have been retention of current racial percentages. A random system, however, would place every teacher in equal jeopardy, working a much greater upheaval of the seniority hierarchy than that occasioned by Article XII; it is not at all a less restrictive means of achieving the Board's goal.

JUSTICE STEVENS, dissenting.

In the context of public education, it is quite obvious that a school board may reasonably conclude that an integrated faculty will be able to provide benefits to the student body that could not be provided by an all white, or nearly all white, faculty. For one of the most important lessons that the American public schools teach is that the diverse ethnic, cultural, and national backgrounds that have been brought together in our famous "melting pot" do not identify essential differences among the human beings that inhabit our land. It is one thing for a white child to be taught by a white teacher that color, like beauty, is only "skin deep"; it is far more convincing to experience that truth on a day to day basis during the routine, ongoing learning process.

* * *

Even if there is a valid purpose to the race consciousness, however, the question that remains is whether that public purpose transcends the harm to the white teachers who are disadvantaged by the special preference the Board has given to its most recently hired minority teachers. In my view, there are two important inquiries in assessing the harm to the disadvantaged teacher. The first is an assessment of the procedures that were used to adopt, and implement, the race-conscious action. The second is an evaluation of the nature of the harm itself.

In this case, there can be no question about either the fairness of the procedures used to adopt the race-conscious provision, or the propriety of its breadth. As Justice Marshall has demonstrated, the procedures for adopting this provision were scrupulously fair. The Union that represents the petitioners negotiated the provision and agreed to it; the agreement was put to a vote of the membership, and overwhelmingly approved. Again, not a shred of evidence in the record suggests *any* procedural unfairness in the adoption of the agreement. Similarly, the provision is specifically designed to achieve its objective—retaining the minority teachers that have been specially recruited to give the Jackson schools, after a period of racial unrest, an integrated faculty. * * *

Finally, we must consider the harm to the petitioners. Every layoff, like every refusal to employ a qualified applicant, is a grave loss to the affected individual. However, the undisputed facts in this case demonstrate that this serious consequence to the petitioners is not based on any lack of respect for their race, or on blind habit and stereotype. Rather, petitioners have been laid off for a combination of two reasons: the economic conditions that have led Jackson to lay off some teachers, and the special contractual protections intended to preserve the newly integrated character of the faculty in the Jackson schools. Thus, the same harm might occur if a number of gifted young teachers had been given special contractual protection because their specialties were in short supply and if the Jackson Board of Education faced a fiscal need for layoffs.[14]

Note on Richmond v. J.A. Croson Co. and the Affirmation of Wygant

Several important positions taken by Justice Powell in his opinion in *Wygant* did not command the explicit concurrence of a majority of the Court. However, a decision rendered a year after Justice Powell's retirement, City of Richmond v. J.A. Croson Co., 488 U.S. 469, 109 S.Ct. 706, 102 L.Ed.2d 854 (1989), indicates that these positions were soon embraced by a majority of the Justices.

In *Croson* the Court struck down a plan of the city of Richmond that required prime contractors awarded construction contracts to subcontract at least 30% of the value of each contract to "minority business enterprises," defined to include any business at least 51% of which is owned by black, Spanish-speaking, Oriental, Indian, Eskimo, or Aleut citizens. The Richmond City Council, a majority of whose members were black, adopted the plan after expressing its view that there had been past discrimination in the local

---

14. The fact that the issue arises in a layoff context, rather than a hiring context, has no bearing on the equal protection question. For if the Board's interest in employing more minority teachers is sufficient to justify providing them with an extra incentive to accept jobs in Jackson, Michigan, it is also sufficient to justify their retention when the number of available jobs is reduced. Justice Powell's suggestion, * * * that there is a distinction of constitutional significance under the Equal Protection Clause between a racial preference at the time of hiring and an identical preference at the time of discharge is thus wholly unper-

suasive. He seems to assume that a teacher who has been working for a few years suffers a greater harm when he is laid off than the harm suffered by an unemployed teacher who is refused a job for which he is qualified. In either event, the adverse decision forecloses "only one of several opportunities" that may be available, * * * to the disappointed teacher. Moreover, the distinction is artificial, for the layoff provision at issue in this case was included as part of the terms of the *hiring* of minority and other teachers under the collective-bargaining agreement.

construction industry and noting that minority businesses received only .67% of contracts from the city while constituting 50% of the city's population.

Writing for four Justices (herself, Rehnquist, White and Kennedy), Justice O'Connor stated that the equal protection clause requires heightened or strict scrutiny of any racial classification, regardless of "the race of those burdened or benefitted * * *." 109 S.Ct. at 721. In a concurring opinion Justice Scalia agreed. Justice O'Connor also cautioned that such scrutiny could not be satisfied by an asserted governmental interest in the remedying of general "societal discrimination." Rather, the government must be attempting to "rectify the effects of identified discrimination within its jurisdiction", with "a strong basis in evidence" that remedial action is necessary. Justice O'Connor stated that only in "the extreme case" might "some form of narrowly tailored racial preference * * * be necessary to break down patterns of deliberate exclusion." Justice Scalia would be even more restrictive of state power, allowing the states to use race to undo the effects of past discrimination only "where that is necessary to eliminate their own maintenance" of a racially discriminatory system. Justices Stevens and Kennedy, in separate concurring opinions, agreed that broad quota plans like that of Richmond's cannot be justified as a remedy for past discrimination.

Notes and Questions

1. *Justification for Strict Scrutiny?* Consider Justice Powell's position for the *Wygant* plurality—endorsed in *Croson*, as well as later decisions, by a majority of the Court—that preferences for racial groups historically subject to discrimination must withstand the same "strict scrutiny" as race-based classifications that disadvantage such groups. This equal protection standard operates as a rule of presumptive invalidity that first emerged because of suspicion about the legitimacy of the government's motives when historically subordinated groups are further disadvantaged. Is such a presumption appropriate in the affirmative action context?

2. *Implications of Political Representation Theory.* Professor John Hart Ely argued that heightened judicial scrutiny is inappropriate in the affirmative action context because the normal majoritarian political process can be counted on to take account of the interests of the burdened or nonbenefitted majority group. See John H. Ely, Democracy and Distrust 170 (1980). Justice O'Connor invoked this political representation theory in support of applying strict scrutiny in *Croson*, noting that blacks comprised a majority of the Richmond City Council—an approach Ely presumably would favor, see Ely, The Constitutionality of Reverse Racial Discrimination, 41 U.Chi.L.Rev. 723, 739 n. 58 (1974). In *Wygant*, Justice Powell's plurality opinion and Justice Marshall's and Justice Stevens's dissents take different views of whether the negotiation of the layoff quota with the union representative of a bargaining unit that included the affected workers provided a sufficient guarantee that the interests of the burdened group were adequately taken into account.

3. *Level of Review for Sex–Based Affirmative Action Plans?* Should affirmative action programs for women be reviewed under a less demanding standard in accordance with the way the Court generally treats gender classifications. See, e.g., Mississippi Univ. for Women v. Hogan, 458 U.S.

718, 102 S.Ct. 3331, 73 L.Ed.2d 1090 (1982) (intermediate scrutiny). Compare Danskine v. Miami Dade Fire Dept, R.D. (11th Cir.2001), with Brunet v. City of Columbus, 1 F.3d 390, 403–04 (6th Cir.1993).

4. *Is Remedying "Societal Discrimination" A Compelling Purpose?* Even if affirmative action plans must be justified by a compelling state interest, why is not the elimination of societal discrimination as compelling a state interest as remedying a particular employer's wrongdoing? Is it because the former objective would support a much more extensive affirmative action program than would the latter purpose? This is presumably what Justice Powell means by "no logical stopping point." But why should the difficulty of drawing lines render void the justification altogether? Also, why should other forward-looking justifications, such as a public school's interest in providing affirmative role models for school children, not be acceptable? See Sullivan, Sins of Discrimination, supra, 100 Harv.L.Rev. 78.

5. *Is Remedying Past Discrimination A Sufficient Justification?* Note again that the *Sheet Metal Workers* Court requires that racial preferences in judicial remedial orders be necessary to the avoidance of future discrimination, not simply to compensate for past discrimination. Are public employers' voluntarily adopted plans being treated differently? Should the *Sheet Metal Workers* standard apply to voluntary plans? Would many employers voluntarily adopt affirmative action plans designed to avoid further discrimination if they had to demonstrate that such plans were necessary for this purpose? Some lower courts seem to require the voluntary plans of public employers to meet the more demanding *Sheet Metal Workers* standard. See, e.g., Dallas Fire Fighters Ass'n v. Dallas, 150 F.3d 438, 441 (5th Cir. 1998) (striking down plan where record was "devoid of proof of a history of egregious and pervasive discrimination or resistance to affirmative action that has warranted more serious measures in other cases", and citing *Sheet Metal Workers* and *Paradise*.) But see City of Dallas v. Dallas Fire Fighters Assn., 526 U.S. 1046, 119 S.Ct. 1349, 143 L.Ed.2d 511 (1999) (Breyer, J., dissenting from denial of certiorari).

6. *Burden of Proof.* On which party does the *Wygant* plurality (and Justice O'Connor) place the ultimate burden of proof on the constitutionality of an affirmative action program? Does an employer defending such a program nonetheless have a burden of producing "the strong basis in evidence for its conclusion that remedial action was necessary"? See, e.g., Rothe Development Corp. v. United States Dept. Of Defense, 262 F.3d 1306, 1317 (Fed.Cir.2001) (yes). Accord Cotter v. City of Boston, 323 F.3d 160 (1st Cir.2003); Concrete Works of Colorado, Inc. v. City and County of Denver, 321 F.3d 950 (10th Cir.2003). Cf. Bass v. Board of County Commissioners, 256 F.3d 1095 (11th Cir.2001) (interpreting *Croson* to place burden of persuasion on employer).

7. *What Evidence of Past Discrimination Must an Employer Have?* What exactly does the *Wygant* plurality demand of a public employer who claims that its affirmative action plan is justified by the need to remedy its own past discrimination? Does the plurality demand that the employer, contemporaneous with its adoption of the plan, have factual findings of past discrimination? Does Justice O'Connor? How are employers to demonstrate that there is a need to remedy past discrimination absent either a contempo-

raneous or antecedent determination of such discrimination by some appropriate authority? Must employers at least have evidence sufficient to support a prima facie case of systemic disparate treatment? See Maryland Troopers Ass'n, Inc. v. Evans, 993 F.2d 1072, 1074 (4th Cir.1993)(applying this standard). In Cotter v. City of Boston, supra, at 169–170, the court held sufficient "evidence approaching a prima facie case of a constitutional or statutory violation", including "a statistical disparity between the racial composition of the workforce and the relevant, qualified employment pool."

8. *Are Layoff Preferences Ever Acceptable?* Justice Powell's plurality opinion in *Wygant* draws a distinction between race-conscious hiring goals and layoff plans. In times of economic retrenchment, can there be meaningful hiring goals without some complementary layoff protection? Should the question of justification be directed, as Justice O'Connor suggests, to the initial hiring goals rather than the layoff provisions? See also Crumpton v. Bridgeport Educ. Ass'n, 993 F.2d 1023, 1030–31 (2d Cir.1993) (dicta asserting that layoff plan protecting minorities proportionally in workforce could be acceptable if contemplated by collective bargaining agreement and necessary to maintain progress in hiring).

Are layoff preferences problematic for the *Wygant* plurality and Justice White because they harm particular individuals who do not share in the employer's culpability? Is this also the effect of giving competitive seniority to *Franks* victims? Do laid-off employees care whether they were chosen for layoff because of their junior status or because of the operation of an affirmative action plan? Note also that neither the Constitution nor other federal law requires public employers to adhere to seniority principles in selecting employees for layoff. If a public employer can lawfully burden innocent senior employees when departing from seniority principles for no strong reason, why should it not be able to depart from such principles for the purpose of preserving the integrity of its hiring goals? For the purpose of encouraging participation by certain groups in occupations in which they are sparsely represented?

Note on Grutter v. Bollinger and Diversity As a Compelling Justification

The Supreme Court's closely divided 2003 decision upholding from equal protection challenge the University of Michigan Law School's race conscious admissions system, Grutter v. Bollinger, 539 U.S. 306, 123 S.Ct. 2325, 156 L.Ed.2d 304 (2003), qualifies one principle suggested by the *Wygant* and *Croson* decisions—"that remedying past discrimination is the only permissible justification for race-based governmental action", 123 S.Ct. at 2338. The *Grutter* Court's acceptance of the Law School's plan was premised on its holding that the Law School "has a compelling interest in attaining a diverse student body." The Court deferred to the "Law School's educational judgment[s] that such diversity is essential to its educational mission," and that the "educational benefits that diversity is designed to produce" require the presence of a "critical mass" of minority students. Id. at 2339. Justice O'Connor, writing for the five-Justice majority, asserted:

> These benefits are substantial. As the District Court emphasized, the Law School's admissions policy promotes "cross-racial understand-

ing," helps to break down racial stereotypes, and "enables [students] to better understand persons of different races." These benefits are "important and laudable," because "classroom discussion is livelier, more spirited, and simply more enlightening and interesting" when the students have "the greatest possible variety of backgrounds." * * *

The Law School does not premise its need for critical mass on "any belief that minority students always (or even consistently) express some characteristic minority viewpoint on any issue." To the contrary, diminishing the force of such stereotypes is both a crucial part of the Law School's mission, and one that it cannot accomplish with only token numbers of minority students.

Id. at 2339–41.

The Court's opinion in *Grutter* does not purport to address affirmative action plans for employment. Moreover, the opinion is tailored to underscore "education as pivotal to 'sustaining our political and cultural heritage' with a fundamental role in maintaining the fabric of society." Although nothing in *Grutter* suggests that the Court would afford any public employers the same deference given the Law School's administrators, its acceptance of the goal of diversity as compelling for admissions programs in higher education nonetheless would seem to leave the door ajar for arguments that a similar goal could be compelling for certain public sector jobs. Might a police force, for instance, concerned about understanding the needs of all of it constituents, use diversity to justify a narrow plan for race conscious hiring and promotion? Or might a school system justify limited race conscious hiring as facilitating achievement of the same goals of class room diversity accepted by the Court in *Grutter*? Note that Justice O'Connor in a footnote in her concurring opinion in *Wygant* distinguished the rejected "role-models" justification from "the very different goal of promoting racial diversity among the faculty", which was not advanced by the employer there and thus was not "necessary to discuss". Compare Lomack v. City of Newark, 463 F.3d 303 (3d Cir. 2006) (diversity not a compelling justification for use of race in assigning firefighters), with Petit v. City of Chicago, 352 F.3d 1111, 1114 (7th Cir. 2003) (diversity provides a compelling justification for consideration of race in promotions in large urban police department). Cf. also Lutheran Church–Missouri Synod v. Federal Communications Commission, 141 F.3d 344 (D.C.Cir. 1998) (doubting that broadcast program diversity can provide a compelling justification for race-conscious hiring goals); Taxman v. Board of Education of Township of Piscataway, 91 F.3d 1547 (3d Cir. 1996) (holding that achieving racial "diversity" in teaching staff is not an objective that warrants departure from Title VII's prohibition of race-conscious employment decisions).

Justice O'Connor's broad interpretation of the concept of "diversity" in *Grutter* also suggests a somewhat different kind of argument to justify affirmative action plans for some jobs and employment training programs. In addition to accepting the Law School's arguments about how diversity provides a richer educational experience for students, Justice O'Connor stressed that

universities, and in particular, law schools, represent the training ground for a large number of our Nation's leaders. * * * The pattern is even more striking when it comes to highly selective law schools. A handful of these schools accounts for 25 of the 100 United States Senators, 74 United States courts of appeals judges, and nearly 200 of the more than 600 United States District Court judges.

In order to cultivate a set of leaders with legitimacy in the eyes of the citizenry, it is necessary that the path to leadership be visibly open to talented and qualified individuals of every race and ethnicity. All members of our heterogeneous society must have confidence in the openness and integrity of the educational institutions that provide this training.

123 S.Ct. at 2341.

How does Justice O'Connor's concept of "diversity" as "legitimacy" differ from the "role models" theory she rejected in *Wygant*? Does "legitimacy" provide a justification for limited affirmative action in management training and promotion programs? For all hiring by urban police forces? Is it further relevant to these questions that Justice O'Connor endorsed assertions in an amicus brief filed by retired military officers that the military "must be selective in admissions for training and education for the officer corps, *and* it must train and educate a highly qualified, racially diverse officer corps in a racially diverse setting"? But cf. Christian v. United States, 46 Fed.Cl. 793 (2000) (flexible race-conscious goals in Army layoff plan cannot be justified by purpose of insuring "perception of equal opportunity").

2. The Title VII Standard

PAUL E. JOHNSON v. TRANSPORTATION AGENCY, SANTA CLARA COUNTY

Supreme Court of the United States, 1987.
480 U.S. 616, 107 S.Ct. 1442, 94 L.Ed.2d 615.

JUSTICE BRENNAN delivered the opinion of the Court.

I

A

In December 1978, the Santa Clara County Transit District Board of Supervisors adopted an Affirmative Action Plan (Plan) for the County Transportation Agency. The Plan implemented a County Affirmative Action Plan, which had been adopted, declared the County, because "mere prohibition of discriminatory practices is not enough to remedy the effects of past practices and to permit attainment of an equitable representation of minorities, women and handicapped persons." Relevant to this case, the Agency Plan provides that, in making promotions to positions within a traditionally segregated job classification in which women have been significantly underrepresented, the Agency is authorized to consider as one factor the sex of a qualified applicant.

In reviewing the composition of its work force, the Agency noted in its Plan that women were represented in numbers far less than their proportion of the county labor force in both the Agency as a whole and in five of seven job categories. Specifically, while women constituted 36.4% of the area labor market, they composed only 22.4% of Agency employees. Furthermore, women working at the Agency were concentrated largely in EEOC job categories traditionally held by women: women made up 76% of Office and Clerical Workers, but only 7.1% of Agency Officials and Administrators, 8.6% of Professionals, 9.7% of Technicians, and 22% of Service and Maintenance workers. As for the job classification relevant to this case, none of the 238 Skilled Craft Worker positions was held by a woman. The Plan noted that this underrepresentation of women in part reflected the fact that women had not traditionally been employed in these positions, and that they had not been strongly motivated to seek training or employment in them "because of the limited opportunities that have existed in the past for them to work in such classifications." The Plan also observed that, while the proportion of ethnic minorities in the Agency as a whole exceeded the proportion of such minorities in the county work force, a smaller percentage of minority employees held management, professional, and technical positions.

The Agency stated that its Plan was intended to achieve "a statistically measurable yearly improvement in hiring, training and promotion of minorities and women throughout the Agency in all major job classifications where they are underrepresented." As a benchmark by which to evaluate progress, the Agency stated that its long-term goal was to attain a work force whose composition reflected the proportion of minorities and women in the area labor force. Thus, for the Skilled Craft category in which the road dispatcher position at issue here was classified, the Agency's aspiration was that eventually about 36% of the jobs would be occupied by women.

The Plan acknowledged that a number of factors might make it unrealistic to rely on the Agency's long-term goals in evaluating the Agency's progress in expanding job opportunities for minorities and women. Among the factors identified were low turnover rates in some classifications, the fact that some jobs involved heavy labor, the small number of positions within some job categories, the limited number of entry positions leading to the Technical and Skilled Craft classifications, and the limited number of minorities and women qualified for positions requiring specialized training and experience. As a result, the Plan counselled that short-range goals be established and annually adjusted to serve as the most realistic guide for actual employment decisions.

* * *

The Agency's Plan thus set aside no specific number of positions for minorities or women, but authorized the consideration of ethnicity or sex as a factor when evaluating qualified candidates for jobs in which members of such groups were poorly represented. One such job was the road dispatcher position that is the subject of the dispute in this case.[2]

B

On December 12, 1979, the Agency announced a vacancy for the promotional position of road dispatcher in the Agency's Roads Division. Dispatchers assign road crews, equipment, and materials, and maintain records pertaining to road maintenance jobs. The position requires at minimum four years of dispatch or road maintenance work experience for Santa Clara County. The EEOC job classification scheme designates a road dispatcher as a Skilled Craft worker.

Twelve County employees applied for the promotion, including Joyce and Johnson. Joyce had worked for the County since 1970, serving as an account clerk until 1975. She had applied for a road dispatcher position in 1974, but was deemed ineligible because she had not served as a road maintenance worker. In 1975, Joyce transferred from a senior account clerk position to a road maintenance worker position, becoming the first woman to fill such a job. During her four years in that position, she occasionally worked out of class as a road dispatcher.

* * *

Nine of the applicants, including Joyce and Johnson, were deemed qualified for the job, and were interviewed by a two-person board. Seven of the applicants scored above 70 on this interview, which meant that they were certified as eligible for selection by the appointing authority. The scores awarded ranged from 70 to 80. Johnson was tied for second with a score of 75, while Joyce ranked next with a score of 73. A second interview was conducted by three Agency supervisors, who ultimately recommended that Johnson be promoted. Prior to the second interview, Joyce had contacted the County's Affirmative Action Office because she feared that her application might not receive disinterested review.[5] The

---

2. No constitutional issue was either raised or addressed in the litigation below. We therefore decide in this case only the issue of the prohibitory scope of Title VII. Of course, where the issue is properly raised, public employers must justify the adoption and implementation of a voluntary affirmative action plan under the Equal Protection Clause. See *Wygant v. Jackson Board of Education*, 476 U.S. 267, 106 S.Ct. 1842, 90 L.Ed.2d 260 (1986).

5. Joyce testified that she had had disagreements with two of the three members of the second interview panel. One had been her first supervisor when she began work as a road maintenance worker. In performing arduous work in this job, she had not been issued coveralls, although her male co-workers had received them. After ruining her pants, she complained to her supervisor, to no avail. After three other similar incidents, ruining clothes on each occasion, she filed a grievance, and was

issued four pair of coveralls the next day. Joyce had dealt with a second member of the panel for a year and a half in her capacity as chair of the Roads Operations Safety Committee, where she and he "had several differences of opinion on how safety should be implemented." In addition, Joyce testified that she had informed the person responsible for arranging her second interview that she had a disaster preparedness class on a certain day the following week. By this time about ten days had passed since she had notified this person of her availability, and no date had yet been set for the interview. Within a day or two after this conversation, however, she received a notice setting her interview at a time directly in the middle of her disaster preparedness class. This same panel member had earlier described Joyce as a "rebel-rousing, skirt-wearing person."

Office in turn contacted the Agency's Affirmative Action Coordinator, whom the Agency's Plan makes responsible for, *inter alia,* keeping the Director informed of opportunities for the Agency to accomplish its objectives under the Plan. At the time, the Agency employed no women in any Skilled Craft position, and had never employed a woman as a road dispatcher. The Coordinator recommended to the Director of the Agency, James Graebner, that Joyce be promoted.

Graebner, authorized to choose any of the seven persons deemed eligible, thus had the benefit of suggestions by the second interview panel and by the Agency Coordinator in arriving at his decision. After deliberation, Graebner concluded that the promotion should be given to Joyce. As he testified: "I tried to look at the whole picture, the combination of her qualifications and Mr. Johnson's qualifications, their test scores, their expertise, their background, affirmative action matters, things like that * * * I believe it was a combination of all those."

The certification form naming Joyce as the person promoted to the dispatcher position stated that both she and Johnson were rated as well-qualified for the job.

* * *

II

As a preliminary matter, we note that petitioner bears the burden of establishing the invalidity of the Agency's Plan. Only last term in *Wygant v. Jackson Board of Education,* 476 U.S. 267, 277–78, 106 S.Ct. 1842, 1849, 90 L.Ed.2d 260 (1986), we held that "[t]he ultimate burden remains with the employees to demonstrate the unconstitutionality of an affirmative-action program," and we see no basis for a different rule regarding a plan's alleged violation of Title VII. This case also fits readily within the analytical framework set forth in *McDonnell Douglas Corp. v. Green,* 411 U.S. 792, 93 S.Ct. 1817, 36 L.Ed.2d 668 (1973). Once a plaintiff establishes a prima facie case that race or sex has been taken into account in an employer's employment decision, the burden shifts to the employer to articulate a nondiscriminatory rationale for its decision. The existence of an affirmative action plan provides such a rationale. If such a plan is articulated as the basis for the employer's decision, the burden shifts to the plaintiff to prove that the employer's justification is pretextual and the plan is invalid. As a practical matter, of course, an employer will generally seek to avoid a charge of pretext by presenting evidence in support of its plan. That does not mean, however, as petitioner suggests, that reliance on an affirmative action plan is to be treated as an affirmative defense requiring the employer to carry the burden of proving the validity of the plan. The burden of proving its invalidity remains on the plaintiff.

The assessment of the legality of the Agency Plan must be guided by our decision in [*United Steelworkers v. Weber,* 443 U.S. 193, 99 S.Ct. 2721, 61 L.Ed.2d 480 (1979)]. In that case, the Court addressed the question whether the employer violated Title VII by adopting a voluntary affirmative action plan designed to "eliminate manifest racial imbalances in traditionally segregated job categories." *Id.*, at 197, 99 S.Ct., at 2724. The respondent employee in that case challenged the employer's denial of his application for a position in a newly established craft training program, contending that the employer's selection process impermissibly took into account the race of the applicants. The selection process was guided by an affirmative action plan, which provided that 50% of the new trainees were to be black until the percentage of black skilled craftworkers in the employer's plant approximated the percentage of blacks in the local labor force. Adoption of the plan had been prompted by the fact that only 5 of 273, or 1.83%, of skilled craftworkers at the plant were black, even though the work force in the area was approximately 39% black. Because of the historical exclusion of blacks from craft positions, the employer regarded its former policy of hiring trained outsiders as inadequate to redress the imbalance in its work force.

We upheld the employer's decision to select less senior black applicants over the white respondent, for we found that taking race into account was consistent with Title VII's objective of "break[ing] down old patterns of racial segregation and hierarchy." *Id.*, at 208, 99 S.Ct., at 2730.

* * *

We noted that the plan did not "unnecessarily trammel the interests of the white employees," since it did not require "the discharge of white workers and their replacement with new black hirees." *Ibid.* Nor did the plan create "an absolute bar to the advancement of white employees," since half of those trained in the new program were to be white. *Ibid.* Finally, we observed that the plan was a temporary measure, not designed to maintain racial balance, but to "eliminate a manifest racial imbalance." *Ibid.* As Justice Blackmun's concurrence made clear, *Weber* held that an employer seeking to justify the adoption of a plan need not point to its own prior discriminatory practices, nor even to evidence of an "arguable violation" on its part. *Id.*, at 212, 99 S.Ct., at 2731. Rather, it need point only to a "conspicuous * * * imbalance in traditionally segregated job categories." *Id.*, at 209, 99 S.Ct., at 2730. Our decision was grounded in the recognition that voluntary employer action can play a crucial role in furthering Title VII's purpose of eliminating the effects of discrimination in the workplace, and that Title VII should not be read to thwart such efforts. *Id.*, at 204, 99 S.Ct., at 2727–28.[8]

---

8. * * * The dissent's suggestion that an affirmative action program may be adopted only to redress an employer's past discrimination was rejected in *Steelworkers v. Weber,* 443 U.S. 193, 99 S.Ct. 2721, 61 L.Ed.2d 480 (1979), because the prospect of liability created by such an admission would create a significant disincentive for voluntary action. As JUSTICE BLACKMUN's concur- rence in that case pointed out, such a standard would "plac[e] voluntary compliance with Title VII in profound jeopardy. The only way for the employer and the union to keep their footing on the 'tightrope' it creates would be to eschew all forms of voluntary affirmative action." 443 U.S., at 210, 99 S.Ct., at 2731. Similarly, JUSTICE O'CONNOR has observed in the constitutional con-

In reviewing the employment decision at issue in this case, we must first examine whether that decision was made pursuant to a plan prompted by concerns similar to those of the employer in *Weber.* Next, we must determine whether the effect of the plan on males and non-minorities is comparable to the effect of the plan in that case.

The first issue is therefore whether consideration of the sex of applicants for skilled craft jobs was justified by the existence of a "manifest imbalance" that reflected underrepresentation of women in "traditionally segregated job categories." *Id.,* at 197, 99 S.Ct., at 2724. In determining whether an imbalance exists that would justify taking sex or race into account, a comparison of the percentage of minorities or women in the employer's work force with the percentage in the area labor market or general population is appropriate in analyzing jobs that require no special expertise, see *Teamsters v. United States,* 431 U.S. 324, 97 S.Ct. 1843, 52 L.Ed.2d 396 (1977). * * * Where a job requires special training, however, the comparison should be with those in the labor force who possess the relevant qualifications. See *Hazelwood School District v. United States,* 433 U.S. 299, 97 S.Ct. 2736, 53 L.Ed.2d 768 (1977). * * * The requirement that the "manifest imbalance" relate to a "traditionally segregated job category" provides assurance both that sex or race will be taken into account in a manner consistent with Title VII's purpose of eliminating the effects of employment discrimination, and that the interests of those employees not benefitting from the plan will not be unduly infringed.

A manifest imbalance need not be such that it would support a prima facie case against the employer, as suggested in Justice O'Connor's concurrence, since we do not regard as identical the constraints of Title VII and the federal constitution on voluntarily adopted affirmative action plans. Application of the "prima facie" standard in Title VII cases would be inconsistent with *Weber*'s focus on statistical imbalance,[9] and

text that "[t]he imposition of a requirement that public employers make findings that they have engaged in illegal discrimination before they engage in affirmative action programs would severely undermine public employers' incentive to meet voluntarily their civil rights obligations." *Wygant, supra,* at 290, 106 S.Ct., at 1855 (O'Connor, J., concurring in part and concurring in the judgment).

9. The difference between the "manifest imbalance" and "prima facie" standards is illuminated by *Weber.* Had the Court in that case been concerned with past discrimination by the employer, it would have focused on discrimination in hiring skilled, not unskilled, workers, since only the scarcity of the former in Kaiser's work force would have made it vulnerable to a Title VII suit. In order to make out a prima facie case on such a claim, a plaintiff would be required to compare the percentage of black skilled workers in the Kaiser work force with the percentage of black skilled craft workers in the area labor market.

Weber obviously did not make such a comparison. Instead, it focused on the disparity between the percentage of black skilled craft workers in Kaiser's ranks and the percentage of blacks in the area labor force. 443 U.S., at 198–199, 99 S.Ct., at 2724–2725. Such an approach reflected a recognition that the proportion of black craft workers in the local labor force was likely [to be] as miniscule as the proportion in Kaiser's work force. The Court realized that the lack of imbalance between these figures would mean that employers in precisely those industries in which discrimination has been most effective would be precluded from adopting training programs to increase the percentage of qualified minorities. Thus, in cases such as *Weber,* where the employment decision at issue involves

could inappropriately create a significant disincentive for employers to adopt an affirmative action plan. See *Weber, supra,* 443 U.S., at 204, 99 S.Ct., at 2727–28 (Title VII intended as a "catalyst" for employer efforts to eliminate vestiges of discrimination). A corporation concerned with maximizing return on investment, for instance, is hardly likely to adopt a plan if in order to do so it must compile evidence that could be used to subject it to a colorable Title VII suit.

It is clear that the decision to hire Joyce was made pursuant to an Agency plan that directed that sex or race be taken into account for the purpose of remedying underrepresentation.

* * *

As an initial matter, the Agency adopted as a benchmark for measuring progress in eliminating underrepresentation the long-term goal of a work force that mirrored in its major job classifications the percentage of women in the area labor market. Even as it did so, however, the Agency acknowledged that such a figure could not by itself necessarily justify taking into account the sex of applicants for positions in all job categories. For positions requiring specialized training and experience, the Plan observed that the number of minorities and women "who possess the qualifications required for entry into such job classifications is limited." The Plan therefore directed that annual short-term goals be formulated that would provide a more realistic indication of the degree to which sex should be taken into account in filling particular positions.

* * *

As the Agency Plan recognized, women were most egregiously underrepresented in the Skilled Craft job category, since *none* of the 238 positions was occupied by a woman. In mid–1980, when Joyce was selected for the road dispatcher position, the Agency was still in the process of refining its short-term goals for Skilled Craft Workers in accordance with the directive of the Plan. This process did not reach fruition until 1982, when the Agency established a short-term goal for that year of three women for the 55 expected openings in that job category—a modest goal of about 6% for that category.

* * *

We reject petitioner's argument that, since only the long-term goal was in place for Skilled Craft positions at the time of Joyce's promotion, it was inappropriate for the Director to take into account affirmative action considerations in filling the road dispatcher position. The Agency's Plan emphasized that the long-term goals were not to be taken as guides for actual hiring decisions, but that supervisors were to consider a

the selection of unskilled persons for a training program, the "manifest imbalance" standard permits comparison with the general labor force. By contrast, the "prima facie" standard would require comparison with the percentage of minorities or women qualified for the job for which the trainees are being trained, a standard that would have invalidated the plan in *Weber* itself.

host of practical factors in seeking to meet affirmative action objectives, including the fact that in some job categories women were not qualified in numbers comparable to their representation in the labor force.

By contrast, had the Plan simply calculated imbalances in all categories according to the proportion of women in the area labor pool, and then directed that hiring be governed solely by those figures, its validity fairly could be called into question. This is because analysis of a more specialized labor pool normally is necessary in determining underrepresentation in some positions. If a plan failed to take distinctions in qualifications into account in providing guidance for actual employment decisions, it would dictate mere blind hiring by the numbers, for it would hold supervisors to "achievement of a particular percentage of minority employment or membership * * * regardless of circumstances such as economic conditions or the number of qualified minority applicants * * *," *Sheet Metal Workers v. EEOC,* 478 U.S. 421, 106 S.Ct. 3019, 92 L.Ed.2d 344 (1986) (O'CONNOR, J., concurring in part and dissenting in part).

The Agency's Plan emphatically did *not* authorize such blind hiring. It expressly directed that numerous factors be taken into account in making hiring decisions, including specifically the qualifications of female applicants for particular jobs. Thus, despite the fact that no precise short-term goal was yet in place for the Skilled Craft category in mid–1980, the Agency's management nevertheless had been clearly instructed that they were not to hire solely by reference to statistics. The fact that only the long-term goal had been established for this category posed no danger that personnel decisions would be made by reflexive adherence to a numerical standard.

* * *

We next consider whether the Agency Plan unnecessarily trammeled the rights of male employees or created an absolute bar to their advancement. In contrast to the plan in *Weber,* which provided that 50% of the positions in the craft training program were exclusively for blacks, and to the consent decree upheld last term in *Firefighters v. Cleveland,* 478 U.S. 501, 106 S.Ct. 3063, 92 L.Ed.2d 405 (1986), which required the promotion of specific numbers of minorities, the Plan sets aside no positions for women. The Plan expressly states that "[t]he 'goals' established for each Division should not be construed as 'quotas' that must be met." Rather, the Plan merely authorizes that consideration be given to affirmative action concerns when evaluating qualified applicants. As the Agency Director testified, the sex of Joyce was but one of numerous factors he took into account in arriving at his decision. The Plan thus resembles the "Harvard Plan" approvingly noted by Justice Powell in *University of California Regents v. Bakke,* 438 U.S. 265, 316–319, 98 S.Ct. 2733, 2761–63, 57 L.Ed.2d 750 (1978), which considers race along with other criteria in determining admission to the college.

* * *

In addition, petitioner had no absolute entitlement to the road dispatcher position. Seven of the applicants were classified as qualified and eligible, and the Agency Director was authorized to promote any of the seven. Thus, denial of the promotion unsettled no legitimate firmly rooted expectation on the part of the petitioner. Furthermore, while the petitioner in this case was denied a promotion, he retained his employment with the Agency, at the same salary and with the same seniority, and remained eligible for other promotions.

Finally, the Agency's Plan was intended to *attain* a balanced work force, not to maintain one. The Plan contains ten references to the Agency's desire to "attain" such a balance, but no reference whatsoever to a goal of maintaining it. The Director testified that, while the "broader goal" of affirmative action, defined as "the desire to hire, to promote, to give opportunity and training on an equitable, non-discriminatory basis," is something that is "a permanent part" of "the Agency's operating philosophy," that broader goal "is divorced, if you will, from specific numbers or percentages."

The Agency acknowledged the difficulties that it would confront in remedying the imbalance in its work force, and it anticipated only gradual increases in the representation of minorities and women. It is thus unsurprising that the Plan contains no explicit end date, for the Agency's flexible, case-by-case approach was not expected to yield success in a brief period of time. * * *

JUSTICE STEVENS, concurring.

The logic of antidiscrimination legislation requires that judicial constructions of Title VII leave "breathing room" for employer initiatives to benefit members of minority groups. If Title VII had never been enacted, a private employer would be free to hire members of minority groups for any reason that might seem sensible from a business or a social point of view. The Court's opinion in *Weber* reflects the same approach; the opinion relied heavily on legislative history indicating that Congress intended that traditional management prerogatives be left undisturbed to the greatest extent possible. See 443 U.S., at 206–207, 99 S.Ct., at 2728–2729.

JUSTICE O'CONNOR, concurring in the judgment.

In my view, the proper initial inquiry in evaluating the legality of an affirmative action plan by a public employer under Title VII is no different from that required by the Equal Protection Clause. In either case, consistent with the congressional intent to provide some measure of protection to the interests of the employer's nonminority employees, the employer must have had a firm basis for believing that remedial action was required. An employer would have such a firm basis if it can point to a statistical disparity sufficient to support a prima facie claim under Title VII by the employee beneficiaries of the affirmative action plan of a pattern or practice claim of discrimination.

* * *

While employers must have a firm basis for concluding that remedial action is necessary, neither *Wygant* nor *Weber* places a burden on employers to prove that they actually discriminated against women or minorities. Employers are "trapped between the competing hazards of liability to minorities if affirmative action is *not* taken to remedy apparent employment discrimination and liability to nonminorities if affirmative action *is* taken." *Wygant v. Jackson Board of Education,* 476 U.S., at 291, 106 S.Ct., at 1856 (O'CONNOR, J., concurring in part and concurring in judgment). Moreover, this Court has long emphasized the importance of voluntary efforts to eliminate discrimination. *Id.,* at 290, 106 S.Ct., at 1855. Thus, I concluded in *Wygant* that a contemporaneous finding of discrimination should not be required because it would discourage voluntary efforts to remedy apparent discrimination. A requirement that an employer actually prove that it had discriminated in the past would also unduly discourage voluntary efforts to remedy apparent discrimination.

* * *

In this case, I am also satisfied that the respondent had a firm basis for adopting an affirmative action program. Although the District Court found no discrimination against women in fact, at the time the affirmative action plan was adopted, there were *no* women in its skilled craft positions. The petitioner concedes that women constituted approximately 5% of the local labor pool of skilled craft workers in 1970. Thus, when compared to the percentage of women in the qualified work force, the statistical disparity would have been sufficient for a prima facie Title VII case brought by unsuccessful women job applicants.

JUSTICE WHITE, dissenting.

* * * My understanding of *Weber* was, and is, that the employer's plan did not violate Title VII because it was designed to remedy intentional and systematic exclusion of blacks by the employer and the unions from certain job categories. That is how I understood the phrase "traditionally segregated jobs" we used in that case. The Court now interprets it to mean nothing more than a manifest imbalance between one identifiable group and another in an employer's labor force. As so interpreted, that case, as well as today's decision, as Justice Scalia so well demonstrates, is a perversion of Title VII. I would overrule *Weber* and reverse the judgment below.

JUSTICE SCALIA, with whom THE CHIEF JUSTICE joins, and with whom JUSTICE WHITE joins in Parts I and II, dissenting.

* * * today's decision goes well beyond merely allowing racial or sexual discrimination in order to eliminate the effects of prior societal *discrimination*. The majority opinion often uses the phrase "traditionally segregated job category" to describe the evil against which the plan is legitimately (according to the majority) directed. As originally used in *Steelworkers v. Weber,* 443 U.S. 193, 99 S.Ct. 2721, 61 L.Ed.2d 480 (1979), that phrase described skilled jobs from which employers and unions had systematically and intentionally excluded black workers—traditionally segregated jobs, that is, in the sense of conscious, exclusionary discrimination. See *id.,* at 197–198, 99 S.Ct., at 2724–2725. But that is assuredly not the sense in which the phrase is used here. It is absurd to think that the nationwide failure of road maintenance crews, for example, to achieve the Agency's ambition of 36.4% female representation is attributable primarily, if even substantially, to systematic exclusion of women eager to shoulder pick and shovel. It is a "traditionally segregated job category" *not* in the *Weber* sense, but in the sense that, because of longstanding social attitudes, it has not been regarded *by women themselves* as desirable work. * * * There are, of course, those who believe that the social attitudes which cause women themselves to avoid certain jobs and to favor others are as nefarious as conscious, exclusionary discrimination. Whether or not that is so (and there is assuredly no consensus on the point equivalent to our national consensus against intentional discrimination), the two phenomena are certainly distinct. And it is the alteration of social attitudes, rather than the elimination of discrimination, which today's decision approves as justification for state-enforced discrimination. This is an enormous expansion, undertaken without the slightest justification or analysis.

Notes and Questions

1. *Different Standards for Voluntary Plans Under Title VII and the Constitution?* Compare the constitutional standard adopted by the plurality opinion in *Wygant* with the Title VII standard adopted in *Johnson.* In what ways do these standards differ? Specifically, does the Title VII standard, like the *Wygant* plurality's constitutional standard, require the employer to show that its purpose in adopting the challenged plan was to remedy its own past discrimination? Note that while the *Johnson* case involved a public employer, no constitutional issue was raised in that litigation.

Does the *Johnson* majority's "conspicuous * * * imbalance in traditionally segregated job categories" test also differ from Justice O'Connor's standard for both Title VII and the constitution—a prima facie showing of systemic disparate treatment? Would these tests produce different results in either *Johnson* or *Weber?* Consider the justifications for the long-term goals of the Santa Clara County's plan and footnote 9 in the majority opinion in *Johnson.* Note also Justice White's criticism that the "conspicuous imbalance" test was extended in *Johnson* to reach mere underrepresentation of women in particular job categories. But cf. Schurr v. Resorts International Hotel, Inc., 196 F.3d 486 (3d Cir. 1999) (interpreting "traditionally segregated" to mean caused by past discrimination in the industry).

What might justify the use of different standards for Title VII and the equal protection clause? Are there reasons why Congress might have wanted the Title VII standard to be more tolerant of race-conscious preferences for statutory groups than the applicable constitutional standard for government? To be more restrictive?

2. *Different Title VII Standards for Voluntary and for Court–Ordered Relief?* Compare the standards for judging the appropriateness of affirmative

action relief under § 706(g) of Title VII suggested by the opinions in *Sheet Metal Workers* with the standards for judging voluntary affirmative action plans under § 703 set forth in *Johnson*. Does *Johnson* require voluntary plans to be "necessary" to prevent further discrimination? What might be justifications for permitting a voluntary affirmative action plan in circumstances that would not support a judicial order of a similar plan? Might Congress, on the other hand, have intended to permit affirmative action relief of the sort approved in *Sheet Metal Workers*, while eschewing race-conscious preferences not mandated by a court order?

3. *What Predicate Showing for Affirmative Action?* Both the conspicuous imbalance and prima facie tests may present statistical issues similar to those that have been salient in Title VII pattern and practice litigation. Should principles developed in the latter context, such as preferences for applicant flow data and qualified labor force statistics in the employer's area of recruitment, apply with the same force to the question of whether a sufficient predicate showing has been made for voluntary affirmative action? Should this depend on which test is used? See, e.g., Janowiak v. South Bend, 836 F.2d 1034 (7th Cir.1987) (imbalance must be between relevant qualified area labor pool and employer's work force); Hammon v. Barry, 826 F.2d 73 (D.C.Cir.1987) (imbalance must be shown in the area of recruitment).

4. *Narrow Tailoring of Voluntary Plans.* Consider the standards employed by the Court in *Johnson* for judging the particular terms of an affirmative action plan, including the question of whether the plan "unnecessarily trammeled the rights" of majority group workers. Could a plan, like that in *Wygant*, that departed from seniority standards for layoffs in order to maintain existing minority hiring levels survive scrutiny under *Johnson?*

How important to the result in *Johnson* was the fact that the challenged plan set flexible goals rather than definite quotas for the promotion of women? See Hammon v. Barry, supra. Note that in *Weber* the challenged selection process for the training program set a definite quota of 50% black trainees. Should promotion quotas raise greater problems than quotas in training programs? But cf. Grutter v. Bollinger, supra, ("universities cannot establish quotas for members of certain racial groups or put members of those groups on separate admission tracks"). Note also that the plan in *Weber* had a bounded duration. Why did the Court not require the plan in *Johnson* to be similarly bounded?

5. *Allocation of Burden of Proof.* Who bears the burden of proving the validity, or invalidity, of an affirmative action plan: the nonminority plaintiff or the defendant employer? Is it appropriate to squeeze affirmative action cases into the *McDonnell Douglas* framework as did the *Johnson* Court? Note that the *McDonnell Douglas* approach is intended to determine whether the defendant was motivated by considerations of race or sex, while the issue in affirmative action cases is the very different one of whether such considerations are justified. Note also that McDonald v. Santa Fe Trail Transp. Co., discussed at p. 63 supra, indicates that any race-conscious plan would violate § 703 absent sufficient affirmative action justifications. Does this mean that the validity of an affirmative action plan is in the nature of an affirmative defense that the defendant should have to prove?

6. *Social Channeling vs. Social Discrimination?* In his dissent in *Johnson,* Justice Scalia contends that the majority opinion effectively approves affirmative action plans designed simply to facilitate the "alteration of social attitudes" shared by most women concerning what jobs are most appropriate for them. He asserts that it is "absurd" to conclude that the absence of females in many traditionally male jobs "is attributable primarily, if even substantially, to systematic exclusion of women * * *."

Can a sharp distinction really be drawn between choices derived from "social attitudes" and choices caused by discrimination? Are the occupational preferences of women, whether independently derived or filtered through family or school influences, significantly shaped by expectations of whether the marketplace would be receptive to female entry into certain occupations? Furthermore, should Title VII be read to prevent an employer from attempting to increase its long-run productivity by expanding the supply of labor for particular occupations by changing social attitudes?

In Justice Powell's terms, is there "a logical stopping point" to this justification for affirmative action? Would its acceptance mean that the law must allow employers to allocate employment opportunities to groups in proportion to their relative population?

7. *Voluntary Employer Alteration of Objective Test Scores.* In light of § 703(*l*) of Title VII, as added by § 106 of the Civil Rights Act of 1991, may an employer dissatisfied with the pass rate of minority applicants on an employment test, as part of an affirmative action plan, now rescore the examination results so as to reduce adverse impact on blacks and women? See Dean v. City of Shreveport, 438 F.3d 448 (5th Cir. 2006) (no). How might the employer use the results of the test differently in order to avoid the adverse impact?

8. *Relevance of the Civil Rights Act of 1991.* Section 116 of the 1991 Act provides that "[n]othing in the amendments made by this title shall be construed to affect court-ordered remedies, affirmative action, or conciliation agreements, that are in accordance with the law." What effect does this disclaimer have on the legality of affirmative action plans under Title VII?

Might § 107 of the 1991 Act, which prohibits using race or other protected categories as "a motivating factor for any employment practice" (see pp. 75–81 supra), be read to further restrict affirmative action plans? See Officers for Justice v. Civil Service Commission, 979 F.2d 721, 725 (9th Cir.1992) (holding that § 116 prevents construing the 1991 Act, including § 107, to affect the legality of affirmative action plans).

Note on *Gratz v. Bollinger* and the Requirement of *Individualized Consideration*

On the same day that it upheld the University of Michigan Law School's admissions system from a constitutional challenge in *Grutter v. Bollinger,* supra,, the Supreme Court held in Gratz v. Bollinger, 539 U.S. 244, 123 S.Ct. 2411, 156 L.Ed.2d 257 (2003), that the University's use of racial preferences in undergraduate admissions violated the equal protection clause. The *Gratz* Court concluded that the undergraduate admissions system was not "narrowly tailored to achieve the interest in educational diversity" that the

University claimed as a justification. The Court rested this conclusion on its finding that the undergraduate system did not consider "each particular applicant as an individual, assessing all of the qualities that individual possesses, and in turn, evaluating that individual ability's to contribute to the unique setting of higher education." Rather than provide this "individualized consideration" to each applicant, the undergraduate admissions plan "automatically" distributed 20 extra points on an 150 point scale to every single applicant from an "underrepresented minority" group, as defined by the University. Justice Rehnquist, writing for the Court, stressed that these 20 points had "the effect of making 'the factor of race * * * decisive' for virtually every minimally qualified underrepresented minority applicant."

Justice O'Connor, by joining in the Court's *Gratz* opinion as well as through a separate concurring opinion in *Gratz* and her majority opinion in *Grutter*, made clear her agreement that individualized consideration of each applicant is necessary to insure that an affirmative action program for admissions to higher education is narrowly tailored to achieve an acceptable goal of diversity. In her concurring opinion in *Gratz*, she contrasted with the undergraduate admissions system the law school's admissions system upheld in *Grutter*; the latter "enables admissions officers to make nuanced judgments with respect to the contributions each applicant is likely to make to the diversity of the incoming class." 539 U.S. at 279. In *Grutter* she stressed that "the Law School engages in a highly individualized, holistic review of each applicant's file, giving serious consideration to all the ways an applicant might contribute to a diverse educational environment." 539 U.S. at 338.

The Supreme Court stressed the importance of "individualized" review to the "narrow tailoring" prong of strict scrutiny again in its decision finding unconstitutional two school districts' use of race in assigning children to particular schools. See Parents Involved in Community Schools v. Seattle School District No. 1, __ U.S. __, 127 S.Ct. 2738, 168 L.Ed.2d 508 (2007). In a part of his opinion supported by a majority of the Court, Chief Justice Roberts acknowledged the Court's recognition as "compelling" justifications for racial classifications "in the school context" not only "remedying the effects of past intentional discrimination", but also an "interest in diversity in higher education". Without deciding that the latter justification could extend to the government's consideration of race in other contexts, including less advanced education, the majority held that the school districts had used race as the University of Michigan had for its undergraduate admissions, not as "one factor weighed with others" "to achieve exposure to widely diverse people, culture, ideas and viewpoints", but rather as "*the* factor" "decisive by itself", in a "nonindividualized, mechanical" manner. 127 S.Ct. at 2753–54. See Samuel Estreicher, The Non-Preferment Principle, 2006–07 Cato Sup.Ct.Rev. 239.

Does the requirement of individualized consideration also apply to all affirmative action plans for employment? Does it apply to private employers under Title VII as well as public employers through equal protection review? Does it apply even where an employer to justify its plan relies not on a diversity goal, but rather on strong evidence of the lingering effects of its prior discrimination? Consider, for instance, an employer that scored applicants based on the evaluations of prior experience, quality of recommendations, interview assessments, and perhaps some job-related aptitude test.

Could that employer add points for all applicants from a minority group which was under represented in its work force because of its prior discrimination? How might such an employer provide adequate "individualized consideration"? Were Joyce and Johnson given such consideration by the Santa Clara County Transportation Agency?

Note on Title VII Consent Orders: Local No. 93, International Association of Firefighters v. Cleveland

The Court's construction of § 703 in *Johnson* and *Weber* indicates that employers and unions can voluntarily adopt affirmative action plans in circumstances that would not support a judicial remedial order under § 706(g) of Title VII. This raises the question of whether affirmative action plans in the formal injunction provision of court-approved settlement agreements—consent decrees—should be judged under § 706(g) or only under § 703 standards. The question arises because consent decrees involve aspects of both voluntary agreements and the exercise of judicial authority.

In Firefighters Local 1784 v. Stotts, 467 U.S. 561, 104 S.Ct. 2576, 81 L.Ed.2d 483 (1984), discussed at pp. 252 and 254 supra, the Court hinted that consent decrees would have to meet § 706(g) standards. That case involved a court's unilateral modification of a consent decree, against the wishes of the defendant municipal fire department and its union, to provide that impending layoffs not reduce the percentage of black employees who had been hired pursuant to the terms of the initial decree. Justice White's opinion for the Court questioned whether the consent decree could have required layoff quotas benefitting nonvictims when a Title VII court would not have been able to order such quotas as a remedy under § 706(g). The dissent, authored by Justice Blackmun, noted that the purpose of consent decrees is to avoid litigation, and that at the time such decrees are normally entered, plaintiffs have not had an opportunity to prove the defendant's past discrimination or to establish the identities of individual victims who would be entitled to relief under *Franks*.

Two years later in Local No. 93, International Association of Firefighters v. Cleveland, 478 U.S. 501, 106 S.Ct. 3063, 92 L.Ed.2d 405 (1986), a case decided the same day as *Sheet Metal Workers,* the Court rejected the implications of some of Justice White's language in *Stotts* and held that consent decrees are to be judged only under § 703 and not § 706(g) standards. In an opinion for six Justices, Justice Brennan explained that the congressional preference for voluntary compliance in Title VII required that consent decrees not be evaluated in the same terms as judicially mandated action under § 706(g). Justice Brennan discounted the fact that consent decrees, unlike other voluntary agreements, can be enforced through judicial contempt proceedings: "For the choice of an enforcement scheme—whether to rely on contractual remedies or to have an agreement entered as a consent decree—is itself made voluntarily by the parties." Id. at 523, 106 S.Ct. at 3076.

The *Cleveland* decision did not purport to overrule *Stotts,* noting that "the court's *exercise* of the power to modify the decree over the objection of a party to the decree does implicate section 706(g)." Id. at 523 n. 12, 106 S.Ct. at 3076 n. 12. In *Cleveland* there was no such modification. The Court also made clear that where the employer is a public entity, an affirmative action plan contained in a consent decree can be challenged under the constitutional standards articulated in *Wygant,* as well as under § 703; it simply cannot be challenged under § 706(g).

The union intervenor in *Cleveland* had argued that the consent decree was invalid because it was reached without the union's consent. The Court rejected that contention, reasoning that any two parties to a litigation can settle their differences without the consent of other parties as long as the objections of the other parties are given a fair hearing, and the settlement imposes no obligations on the objecting parties. Here, Justice Brennan explained, the decree did not bind the union to do or not do anything and did not purport to resolve any claims the union might have under the fourteenth amendment or § 703 of Title VII, or as a matter of contract; these substantive objections were for the district court to decide in the first instance. For criticism of the *Cleveland* Court's treatment of the intervening union's objections, see Douglas Laycock, Consent Decrees Without Consent: The Rights of Nonconsenting Third Parties, 1987 U.Chi.Legal F. 103; Larry Kramer, Consent Decrees and the Rights of Third Parties, 87 Mich.L.Rev. 321 (1988).

In Martin v. Wilks, 490 U.S. 755, 109 S.Ct. 2180, 104 L.Ed.2d 835 (1989), the Court held that white employees who were disadvantaged by an affirmative action consent decree established in litigation in which they did not intervene, but of which they had notice, could challenge under Title VII decisions made pursuant to that decree. However, the *Wilks* decision was substantially modified by § 108 of the Civil Rights Act of 1991. This section added a new § 703(n) to Title VII, which provides that a litigated or consent judgment that resolves federal claims of employment discrimination cannot be challenged "in a claim under the Constitution or Federal civil rights laws", either by persons with actual notice of the judgment and with an opportunity to present objections prior to the judgment's entry, or by persons "whose interests were adequately represented by another person who had previously challenged the judgment or order on the same legal grounds and with a similar factual situation, unless there has been an intervening change in law or fact."

D.   EXECUTIVE OR CONGRESSIONALLY ORDERED AFFIRMATIVE ACTION

Thus far, this chapter has considered standards for judging affirmative action plans developed free of external governmental coercion (whether or not prompted by an administrative agency investigation) and affirmative action plans required by judicial orders. Such plans also may be mandated by the nonjudicial branches of the federal government. Most importantly, the President through Executive Order 11246 has required all government contractors to analyze the extent to which they utilize available minority and women workers and, if there is underutilization, to develop an appropriate affirmative action plan, subject to oversight by the Office of Federal Contract Compliance Programs (OFCCP) in the Department of Labor. Are the standards for judging affirmative action programs either voluntarily adopted by state or local government employers, or ordered by the judiciary, appropriate for judging affirmative action compelled by comprehensive federal executive or legislative action? Consider the following decision.

ADARAND CONSTRUCTORS, INC. v. FEDERICO PENA

Supreme Court of the United States, 1995.
515 U.S. 200, 115 S.Ct. 2097, 132 L.Ed.2d 158.

JUSTICE O'CONNOR announced the judgment of the Court and delivered an opinion with respect to Parts I, II, III–A, III–B, III–D, and IV, which was for the Court except insofar as it might be inconsistent with the views expressed in JUSTICE SCALIA's concurrence, and an opinion with respect to Part III–C in which JUSTICE KENNEDY joins.

I

* * *

The contract giving rise to the dispute in this case came about as a result of the Surface Transportation and Uniform Relocation Assistance Act of 1987, Pub. L. 100–17, 101 Stat. 132 (STURAA), a DOT appropriations measure. Section 106(c)(1) of STURAA provides that "not less than 10 percent" of the appropriated funds "shall be expended with small business concerns owned and controlled by socially and economically disadvantaged individuals." 101 Stat. 145. STURAA adopts the Small Business Act's definition of "socially and economically disadvantaged individual," including the applicable race-based presumptions, and adds that "women shall be presumed to be socially and economically disadvantaged individuals for purposes of this subsection." § 106(c)(2)(B), 101 Stat. 146. STURAA also requires the Secretary of Transportation to establish "minimum uniform criteria for State governments to use in certifying whether a concern qualifies for purposes of this subsection." § 106(c)(4), 101 Stat. 146. The Secretary has done so in 49 CFR pt. 23, subpt. D (1994). Those regulations say that the certifying authority should presume both social and economic disadvantage (i. e., eligibility to participate) if the applicant belongs to certain racial groups, or is a woman. 49 CFR § 23.62 (1994); 49 CFR pt. 23, subpt. D, App. C (1994). As with the SBA programs, third parties may come forward with evidence in an effort to rebut the presumption of disadvantage for a particular business. 49 CFR § 23.69 (1994).

The operative clause in the contract in this case reads as follows:

"Subcontracting. This subsection is supplemented to include a Disadvantaged Business Enterprise (DBE) Development and Subcontracting Provision as follows:

"Monetary compensation is offered for awarding subcontracts to small business concerns owned and controlled by socially and economically disadvantaged individuals. * * *

"A small business concern will be considered a DBE after it has been certified as such by the U.S. Small Business Administration or any State Highway Agency. Certification by other Government agencies, counties, or cities may be acceptable on an individual basis provided the Contracting Officer has determined the certifying agency has an acceptable and viable DBE certification program. If the Contractor requests payment under this provision, the Contractor shall furnish the engineer with acceptable evidence of the subcontractor(s) DBE certification and shall furnish one certified copy of the executed subcontract(s). * * *

"The Contractor will be paid an amount computed as follows:

"1. If a subcontract is awarded to one DBE, 10 percent of the final amount of the approved DBE subcontract, not to exceed 1.5 percent of the original contract amount.

"2. If subcontracts are awarded to two or more DBEs, 10 percent of the final amount of the approved DBE subcontracts, not to exceed 2 percent of the original contract amount."

To benefit from this clause, Mountain Gravel had to hire a subcontractor who had been certified as a small disadvantaged business by the SBA, a state highway agency, or some other certifying authority acceptable to the Contracting Officer. Any of the three routes to such certification described above—SBA's 8(a) or 8(d) program, or certification by a State under the DOT regulations—would meet that requirement. The record does not reveal how Gonzales obtained its certification as a small disadvantaged business.

After losing the guardrail subcontract to Gonzales, Adarand filed suit against various federal officials in the United States District Court for the District of Colorado, claiming that the race-based presumptions involved in the use of subcontracting compensation clauses violate Adarand's right to equal protection. The District Court granted the Government's motion for summary judgment. The Court of Appeals for the Tenth Circuit affirmed. It understood our decision in *Fullilove v. Klutznick*, 448 U.S. 448, 65 L. Ed. 2d 902, 100 S. Ct. 2758 (1980), to have adopted "a lenient standard, resembling intermediate scrutiny, in assessing" the constitutionality of federal race-based action. Applying that "lenient standard," as further developed in *Metro Broadcasting, Inc. v. FCC*, 497 U.S. 547, 111 L. Ed. 2d 445, 110 S. Ct. 2997 (1990), the Court of Appeals upheld the use of subcontractor compensation clauses. * * *

III

* * *

Adarand's claim arises under the Fifth Amendment to the Constitution, which provides that "No person shall * * * be deprived of life, liberty, or property, without due process of law." Although this Court has always understood that Clause to provide some measure of protection against arbitrary treatment by the Federal Government, it is not as explicit a guarantee of equal treatment as the Fourteenth Amendment, which provides that "No State shall deny to any person within its jurisdiction the equal protection of the laws" * * *. Our cases have accorded varying degrees of significance to the difference in the language of those two Clauses. * * *

Despite lingering uncertainty in the details, however, the Court's cases through [*Richmond v. J.A.*] *Croson* [*Co.*, 488 U.S. 469 (1989),] had established three general propositions with respect to governmental racial classifications. First, skepticism: " 'any preference based on racial or ethnic criteria must necessarily receive a most searching examination,' " *Wygant*, 476 U.S. at 273 (plurality opinion of Powell, J.); *Fullilove*, 448 U.S. at 491 (opinion of Burger, C. J.); see also id., at 523 (Stewart, J., dissenting) ("Any official action that treats a person differently on account of his race or ethnic origin is inherently suspect") [further citations omitted]. Second, consistency: "the standard of review under the Equal Protection Clause is not dependent on the race of those burdened or benefitted by a particular classification," *Croson*, 488 U.S. at 494 (plurality opinion); id., at 520 (Scalia, J., concurring in judgment); i.e., all racial classifications reviewable under the Equal Protection Clause must be strictly scrutinized. And third, congruence: "equal protection analysis in the Fifth Amendment area is the same as that under the Fourteenth Amendment," *Buckley v. Valeo*, 424 U.S. [1,] at 93 [(1976)] [further citations omitted]. Taken together, these three propositions lead to the conclusion that any person, of whatever race, has the right to demand that any governmental actor subject to the Constitution justify any racial classification subjecting that person to unequal treatment under the strictest judicial scrutiny. * * *

* * *

Perhaps it is not the standard of strict scrutiny itself, but our use of the concepts of "consistency" and "congruence" in conjunction with it, that leads JUSTICE STEVENS to dissent. According to JUSTICE STEVENS, our view of consistency "equates remedial preferences with invidious discrimination," and ignores the difference between "an engine of oppression" and an effort "to foster equality in society," or, more colorfully, "between a 'No Trespassing' sign and a welcome mat." It does nothing of the kind. The principle of consistency simply means that whenever the government treats any person unequally because of his or her race, that person has suffered an injury that falls squarely within the language and spirit of the Constitution's guarantee of equal protection. It says nothing about the ultimate validity of any particular law; that determination is the job of the court applying strict scrutiny. The principle of consistency explains the circumstances in which the injury requiring strict scrutiny occurs. The application of strict scrutiny, in turn, determines whether a compelling governmental interest justifies the infliction of that injury. * * *

D

* * *

[W]e wish to dispel the notion that strict scrutiny is "strict in theory, but fatal in fact." *Fullilove*, supra, at 519 (Marshall, J., concurring in judgment). The unhappy persistence of both the practice and the lingering effects of racial discrimination against minority groups in this country is an unfortunate reality, and government is not disqualified from acting in response to it. As recently as 1987, for example, every Justice of this Court agreed that the Alabama Department of Public Safety's "pervasive, systematic, and obstinate discriminatory conduct" justified a narrowly tailored race-based remedy. See *United States v. Paradise*, 480 U.S. at 167 (plurality opinion of Brennan, J.); id., at 190 (Stevens, J., concurring in judgment); id., at 196 (O'Connor, J., dissenting). When race-based action is necessary to further a compelling interest, such action is within constitutional constraints if it satisfies the "narrow tailoring" test this Court has set out in previous cases.

IV

Because our decision today alters the playing field in some important respects, we think it best to remand the case to the lower courts for further consideration in light of the principles we have announced. The Court of Appeals, following *Metro Broadcasting* and *Fullilove*, analyzed the case in terms of intermediate scrutiny. It upheld the challenged statutes and regulations because it found them to be "narrowly tailored to achieve [their] significant governmental purpose of providing subcontracting opportunities for small disadvantaged business enterprises." The Court of Appeals did not decide the question whether the interests served by the use of subcontractor compensation clauses are properly described as "compelling." It also did not address the question of narrow tailoring in terms of our strict scrutiny cases, by asking, for example, whether there was "any consideration of the use of race-neutral means to increase minority business participation" in government contracting, *Croson*, supra, at 507, or whether the program was appropriately limited such that it "will not last longer than the discriminatory effects it is designed to eliminate," *Fullilove*, supra, at 513 (Powell, J., concurring).

[*Eds*. The concurring opinions of JUSTICES SCALIA and THOMAS and the dissenting opinion of JUSTICE SOUTER are omitted.]

JUSTICE STEVENS, with whom JUSTICE GINSBURG joins, dissenting.

The Court's concept of "consistency" assumes that there is no significant difference between a decision by the majority to impose a special burden on the members of a minority race and a decision by the majority to provide a benefit to certain members of that minority notwithstanding its incidental burden on some members of the majority. In my opinion that assumption is untenable. There is no moral or constitutional equivalence between a policy that is designed to perpetuate a caste system and one that seeks to eradicate racial subordination. Invidious discrimination is an engine of oppression, subjugating a disfavored group to enhance or maintain the power of the majority. Remedial race-based preferences reflect the opposite impulse: a desire to foster equality in society. No sensible conception of the Government's constitutional obligation to "govern impartially," *Hampton v. Mow Sun Wong*, 426 U.S. 88, 100, 48 L. Ed. 2d 495, 96 S. Ct. 1895 (1976), should ignore this distinction. * * *

* * *

The Court's concept of "congruence" assumes that there is no significant difference between a decision by the Congress of the United States to adopt an affirmative-action program and such a decision by a State or a municipality. In my opinion that assumption is untenable. It ignores important practical and legal differences between federal and state or local decisionmakers. * * *

* * * In his separate opinion in *Richmond v. J. A. Croson Co.*, 488 U.S. 469, 520–524, 102 L. Ed. 2d 854, 109 S. Ct. 706 (1989), JUSTICE SCALIA discussed the basis for this distinction. He observed that "it is one thing to permit racially based conduct by the Federal Government—whose legislative powers concerning matters of race were explicitly enhanced by the Fourteenth Amendment, see U.S. Const., Amdt. 14, § 5—and quite another to permit it by the precise entities against whose conduct in matters of race that Amendment was specifically directed, see Amdt. 14, § 1." Id., at 521–522. Continuing, JUSTICE SCALIA explained why a "sound distinction between federal and state (or local) action based on race rests not only upon the substance of the Civil War Amendments, but upon social reality and governmental theory." Id., at 522.

"What the record shows, in other words, is that racial discrimination against any group finds a more ready expression at the state and local than at the federal level. To the children of the Founding Fathers, this should come as no surprise. An acute awareness of the heightened danger of oppression from political factions in small, rather than large, political units dates to the very beginning of our national history. See G. Wood, The Creation of the American Republic, 1776–1787, pp. 499–506 (1969). * * *." Id., at 523. * * *

An additional reason for giving greater deference to the National Legislature than to a local law-making body is that federal affirmative-action programs represent the will of our entire Nation's elected representatives, whereas a state or local program may have an impact on nonresident entities who played no part in the decision to enact it. Thus, in the state or local context, individuals who were unable to vote for the local representatives who enacted a race-conscious program may nonetheless feel the effects of that program. * * *

JUSTICE GINSBURG, with whom JUSTICE BREYER joins, dissenting.

The lead opinion uses one term, "strict scrutiny," to describe the standard of judicial review for all governmental classifications by race. But that opinion's elaboration strongly suggests that the strict standard announced is indeed "fatal" for classifications burdening groups that have suffered discrimination in our society. * * *

For a classification made to hasten the day when "we are just one race," (Scalia, J., concurring in part and concurring in judgment), however, the lead opinion has dispelled the notion that "strict scrutiny" is " 'fatal in fact.' " (quoting *Fullilove v. Klutznick*, 448 U.S. 448, 519, 65 L.Ed. 2d 902, 100 S.Ct. 2758 (1980) (Marshall, J., concurring in judgment)). * * *

While I would not disturb the programs challenged in this case, and would leave their improvement to the political branches, I see today's decision as one that allows our precedent to evolve, still to be informed by and responsive to changing conditions.

Notes and Questions

1. *Should the Standard of Review for Federally Mandated Affirmative Action Programs Be the Same as That for State and Local Government Programs?* Do you agree with the Court in *Adarand* that review under the equal protection clause of federal affirmative action programs must be "congruent" with the review of state or local government programs? Is section five of the fourteenth amendment relevant? Are the broader political constituencies served by the federal government? The different political stature of coordinate branches of this government? Or does the incorporation of the equal protection clause into the fifth amendment require the congruency asserted by the Court?

2. *Strict but not Fatal?* Justice O'Connor for the Court in *Adarand* states that the same strict scrutiny review should be given to race-conscious government programs that benefit a disadvantaged minority as to those that continue historic discrimination against a minority group. Does Justice Ginsburg nonetheless correctly conclude that the majority opinion, including its remand to the lower courts, means that the strict review it adopts is only "fatal" for "classifications burdening groups that have suffered discrimination in our society?" Consider also Justice O'Connor's opinion for the Court in *Grutter v. Bollinger*, discussed *supra* pp. 274–276. But see Parents Involved in Community Schools v. Seattle School District No. 1, ___ U.S. ___, 127 S.Ct. 2738, 168 L.Ed.2d 508 (2007).

3. *Use of Race as Part of Rebuttable Presumption of Disadvantage?* Why did the *Adarand* Court remand in part for further consideration of whether the challenged program was narrowly tailored to benefit just economically disadvantaged minorities? Under *Wygant* and *Croson* would it be sufficient to show that all beneficiaries were economically disadvantaged, or would the government adopting the affirmative action plan have to show that the disadvantage was caused by its own discrimination or at least by the discrimination of the particular government-funded private entities? Does *Grutter* suggest that the government could have compelling justifications other than the elimination of discrimination? Could the government conceivably have used diversity as a compelling justification for the programs challenged in *Adarand*? Might the government have justified the use of race to establish a rebuttable presumption of economic disadvantage as an

efficient means to enlarge its pool of contractors? See generally Ian Ayres & Frederick E. Vars, When Does Private Discrimination Justify Public Affirmative Action?, 98 Col. L.Rev. 1577 (1998).

4. *Subsequent History of* Adarand. On remand, the trial court in *Adarand* found that Congress enacted the challenged statutes pursuant to the compelling governmental interest of eliminating "discriminatory barriers" that it had "sufficient evidence" to determine "existed in federal contracting." The court did not require that Congress have evidence that the federal government was responsible for the "barriers". See Adarand Constructors, Inc. v. Pena, 965 F.Supp. 1556, 1576–77 (D.Colo.1997). The court also found, however, that the challenged statutes and implementing regulations were not narrowly tailored to achieve this interest, because they presumed both that all members of the named minority groups are disadvantaged and also that all those not in these minority groups are not. Id. at 1580.

The Court of Appeals dismissed the District Court's decision after the Colorado Department of Transportation both eliminated any presumption that minorities or women were socially disadvantaged and also granted Adarand disadvantaged business status. Adarand Constructors, Inc. v. Slater, 169 F.3d 1292 (10th Cir.1999). However, the Supreme Court in a *per curiam* decision again reversed and remanded, noting that federal officials might not accept Adarand's status. Adarand Constructors, Inc. v. Slater, 528 U.S. 216, 120 S.Ct. 722, 145 L.Ed.2d 650 (2000). On remand, the Court of Appeals held that while the federal program was unconstitutional as administered in 1997 and earlier, the program for state and local highway projects as operated under new regulations could survive strict scrutiny analysis. Adarand Constructors, Inc. v. Slater, 228 F.3d 1147 (10th Cir.2000). Although the Supreme Court again granted review, it dismissed this grant as improvidently granted after understanding that Adarand was challenging only the system for direct procurement of Department of Transportation funds, which the Court of Appeals did not consider. Adarand Constructors, Inc. v. Mineta, 534 U.S. 103, 122 S.Ct. 511, 151 L.Ed.2d 489 (2001).

5. *Implications for Title VII Challenges to Private Employer Plans?* Does the *Adarand* Court's stress on "congruence" between the treatment of federal and state affirmative action initiatives (along with Justice O'Connor's concurring opinion in *Johnson*) suggest that the Court would apply the *Wygant* standard to Title VII challenges to private employers' affirmative action plans as well? Or should the Court's Title VII precedent, and Congressional acceptance in the 1991 Act, prevent a judicial merging of the statutory standard?

Note on Executive Order 11246

What are the implications of *Adarand* for the affirmative action obligations of federal contractors pursuant to Executive Order 11246? Consider the following.

Beginning in 1941 during President Roosevelt's tenure and through the two Eisenhower administrations, executive orders were promulgated barring discrimination on account of race, religion, creed or national origin by firms performing procurement contracts for the federal government. Then in 1961, President Kennedy imposed an "affirmative action" obligation on such contractors through Executive Order 10925. In 1963, Executive Order 11114 extended these obligations to federal construction contractors. Finally, in 1965, President Johnson promulgated Executive Order 11246—in effect to this day—which carried forward the expanded obligations of the Kennedy administration orders and transferred enforcement authority from what had been the President's Committee on Equal Employment Opportunity to the Secretary of Labor.

Executive Order 11246 requires "all Government contracting agencies" to include "in every Government contract," except where exempted by regulation, provisions pledging the contractor to not discriminate and to "take affirmative action to ensure that applicants are employed, and that employees are treated during employment, without regard to their race, color, religion, sex or national origin." Contractors are required to include similar pledges in their contracts with subcontractors and vendors. The Order assigns responsibility for its enforcement and administration to the Secretary of Labor. Pursuant to the Secretary's authority, the OFCCP has promulgated extensive regulations. These regulations include some narrow exemptions. For instance, most contractors and subcontractors whose contracts with the federal government totalled $10,000 or less over a 12–month period are altogether exempt from the Order. 41 C.F.R. § 60–1.5(a)(1).

The regulations to implement the Order for nonconstruction contractors or subcontractors were revised in 2000 for the first time in thirty years. These regulations now require any such contractor or subcontractor that employs more than 50 workers and has a contract for at least $50,000 to analyze its utilization of minorities and women workers, and "[w]hen the percentage of minorities or women employed in a particular job group is less than would reasonably be expected given their availability percentage in [a] particular job group," to establish a "a percentage annual placement goal at least equal to the availability figure derived for women or minorities, as appropriate, for that job group." Id. § 60–2.15(b), 2.16(c). "In determining availability, the contractor must consider at least * * * [t]he percentage of minorities and women with requisite skills in the reasonable recruitment area [and] [t]he percentage of minorities or women among those promotable, transferable, and trainable within the contractor's organization." Id. § 60–2.14(c). "Placement goals serve as objectives or targets reasonably attainable by means of applying every good faith effort to make all aspects of the entire affirmative action program work." Id. § 60–2.16(a). Thus, the basis for affirmative action obligations under the Executive Order is not a finding of intentional or adverse impact discrimination, but rather a finding that the contractor has failed to utilize an available minority or female workforce.

The current regulations, however, attempt to protect the program from any equal protection challenge. "Placement goals may not be rigid and inflexible quotas, which must be met, nor are they to be considered as either a ceiling or a floor for the employment of particular groups. Quotas are expressly forbidden." Id. § 2.16(e)(1). Furthermore, "[p]lacement goals do not provide the contractor with a justification to extend a preference to any individual, select an individual, or adversely affect an individual's employment status, on the basis of that person's race, color, religion, sex, or national origin." Id.§ 2.16(e)(2). And "[p]lacement goals do not create set-asides for specific group, nor are they intended to achieve proportional representation or equal results." Id. § 2.16(e)(3). In addition, "[n]o contractor's compliance status shall be judged alone by whether or not it reaches its goals." Rather, OFCCP will review "the nature and extent of the contractor's good faith affirmative action activities * * * and the appropriateness of those activities to identified equal employment opportunity problems." Id. § 60–2.35.

Construction contractors, whether dealing directly with the federal government or receiving federal monies through state, local or private agencies, are covered by a different set of regulations which also impose specific affirmative obligations. These obligations include the validation of selection criteria and the development of on-the-job training and apprenticeship programs that can benefit minorities and women. Id. § 60–4.3. Construction contractors do not develop their own goals and timetables. The OFCCP periodically issues goals and timetables for minority employment in specific geographical areas. Id. § 60–4.6. The agency has also approved several cooperative or "Hometown Plan" agreements among local construction contractors, unions, and minority groups, that set goals and timetables for a particular metropolitan area. Id. §§ 60–4.4 to–4.5.

Initially, the OFCCP attempts to respond to problems uncovered by compliance reviews or meritorious complaints of discrimination by informal conciliation and persuasion of the contractor. If such efforts are unsuccessful, the OFCCP will issue a notice to the contractor to show cause why it should not be subject to enforcement proceedings. It may then refer the case to the Labor Department's Solicitor to initiate administrative enforcement proceedings. The Department of Justice, on its own initiative or after a request from the OFCCP, and without waiting for the completion of any administrative action, may also investigate and bring judicial proceedings against a delinquent contractor. 41 C.F.R. § 60–1.26. If administrative or judicial proceedings result in a finding that the Executive Order has been violated, the violator may not only be placed under a prospective compliance order, but also may have its contract cancelled, or even be placed on a list of employers debarred from eligibility for future contracts, § 209, Exec. Order No. 11246. A debarred contractor must demonstrate its full compliance with the Order in order to achieve reinstatement. In addition, the OFCCP or the Department of Justice may seek compensation for victims of discrimination through an order for back pay or other equitable relief. 41 C.F.R. § 60–1.26(a)(2), (d).

Does the decision by the Court in *Adarand* to apply strict scrutiny to federally mandated affirmative action programs pose a serious challenge to the constitutionality of the Executive Order and its implementing regulations? Or would such a challenge necessarily fail because of the flexibility and reasonableness of the goals that contractors must establish to address "underutilization" of minorities? Must not any race-or sex-conscious goals, no matter how reasonable, have a compelling justification? See Lutheran Church–Missouri Synod v. Federal Communications Commission, 141 F.3d 344 (D.C.Cir. 1998) (holding that any technique that "induces an employer to hire with an eye toward meeting the numerical target" must "serve a compelling state interest"). Is a finding of underutilization adequate under

Wygant as a factual predicate for the remedying of past discrimination? If not, are there other possible compelling justifications for the Executive Order and accompanying regulations? Is the goal of diversity, as recognized in *Grutter*, relevant to most jobs covered by the Order? Can the Order and accompanying regulations be justified as helping to insure that the federal government does not support future discrimination? Or as an encouragement of an efficient enlargement of the utilized labor market? Cf. United States v. New Orleans Public Service, Inc., 553 F.2d 459, 466 (5th Cir.1977), vacated and remanded on other grounds, 436 U.S. 942, 98 S.Ct. 2841, 56 L.Ed.2d 783 (1978); Rossetti Contracting Co. v. Brennan, 508 F.2d 1039, 1045 n. 18 (7th Cir.1974) (finding Presidential power to issue Executive Order delegated from Congress by the Federal Property and Administrative Services Act, 40 U.S.C. § 471 et seq., which empowers the President to provide an "economical and efficient system" for the procurement of services by the federal government).

In a pre-*Grutter* decision potentially relevant to the Executive Order, one court held unconstitutional an FCC rule framed to encourage regulated broadcasters to expand their applicant pool for jobs beyond that which resulted from traditional "word-of-mouth" recruiting. District of Columbia MD/DC/DE Broadcasters Assn. v. Federal Communications Commission, 236 F.3d 13 (D.C.Cir. 2001). The court focused on one of the options afforded to broadcasters, which required reporting on the race, sex, and source of referral of each applicant and a modification of recruitment practices if "the data collected does [sic] not confirm that notifications are reaching the entire community". Recognizing that the rule treated recruitment into an applicant pool rather than actual hiring, the court nonetheless found this option was subject to strict scrutiny because it created "pressure" "to recruit minorities" and the probable nonrecruitment of "some prospective nonminority applicants who [otherwise] would have learned of job opportunities". The court further found that this option was not narrowly tailored to further any compelling governmental interest, because it placed "pressure upon each broadcaster to recruit minorities without a predicate finding that the particular broadcaster discriminated in the past or reasonably could be expected to do so in the future." Id. at 22. Would the decision in *MC/DC/DE* be upheld by the Supreme Court?

Chapter Five

SOME SPECIAL ISSUES ASSO-
CIATED WITH SEX DIS-
CRIMINATION

A. INTRODUCTION

To a large extent a common body of doctrine governs the regulation
of sex (or gender) discrimination and race discrimination. However,
there are several reasons why some of the regulatory choices and
resulting rules may be different in the sex discrimination context. Many
of these derive at least partially from the fact that women and men are
physically different from each other in ways that whites and blacks are
not. Most obviously, men are not able to gestate children, and thus are
always free of the physical and other burdens that may be placed on
pregnant women. Second, there is a difference in average longevity,
whether due to biology or different occupational roles or other life-style
decisions. This has implications for the structuring of benefit programs
that are based on actuarial assumptions about group longevity. Third, on
the average men are larger and, at least in their upper bodies, stronger
than women. These average size and strength differences may have
spawned distorting presumptions and stereotypes about the physical
capabilities of all women. They may also have facilitated male domination of females within the family, as well as in the workplace, and thus
may have helped to determine female assumption of subordinate economic roles.

The occurrence of sex discrimination in employment decisionmaking
may be more impervious to correction by market forces than race
discrimination because of the organization of the modern heterosexual
family. On the one hand, the sharing of economic resources and the
rearing of male and female children in the same family generally has
ensured that girls receive roughly the same early economic and educational advantages as their brothers. On the other hand, however, the
fact that the family unit shares economic resources and assumes the
burden of child care responsibilities has, at least for some spouses,
encouraged keeping one adult out of the external job market for a period

of years. Furthermore, the family has tended to serve as a socializing agent to channel girls and their mothers into different social roles than boys and their fathers.

In addition, the division of home and marketplace responsibilities made possible by the family may compound any external discrimination that women confront in the job market. This is true even for male-female couples who decide which partner will stay home with young children (or whether to relocate for a job opportunity) free of any prior assumptions about whose career is more important. For if a discriminatory job market makes a women's potential earnings somewhat less than her husband's, it may be economically rational for them to subordinate her career to his. Moreover, whether because of family-conditioned or other social expectations or because of overt discriminatory barriers, women seem to have been drawn disproportionately to certain careers irrespective of relative compensation. This results, in the view of some, in a particular kind of labor market failure—a systematic undervaluing of the jobs predominantly filled by women considering the level of training and skills they require.

For these and other reasons, the problem of sex discrimination in the workplace raises a distinct set of challenges for a regulatory regime.

B.   SEX–BASED PENSION FUNDING: THE PROBLEM OF RATIONAL DISCRIMINATORY PREDICTION

ARIZONA GOVERNING COMMITTEE v. NORRIS
Supreme Court of the United States, 1983.
463 U.S. 1073, 103 S.Ct. 3492, 77 L.Ed.2d 1236.

JUSTICE MARSHALL, with whom JUSTICE BRENNAN, JUSTICE WHITE, and JUSTICE STEVENS join, and with whom JUSTICE O'CONNOR joins as to Parts I, II, and III, concurring in the judgment in part.

I

Since 1974 the State of Arizona has offered its employees the opportunity to enroll in a deferred compensation plan administered by the Arizona Governing Committee for Tax Deferred Annuity and Deferred Compensation Plans (Governing Committee). Ariz.Rev.Stat.Ann. § 38–871 *et seq.* (1974 and Supp.1982–1983); Ariz.Regs. 2–9–01 *et seq.* (1975). Employees who participate in the plan may thereby postpone the receipt of a portion of their wages until retirement. By doing so, they postpone paying federal income tax on the amounts deferred until after retirement, when they receive those amounts and any earnings thereon.

After inviting private companies to submit bids outlining the investment opportunities that they were willing to offer state employees, the State selected several companies to participate in its deferred compensation plan. Many of the companies selected offer three basic retirement options: (1) a single lump-sum payment upon retirement, (2) periodic payments of a fixed sum for a fixed period of time, and (3) monthly annuity payments for the remainder of the employee's life. When an employee decides to take part in the deferred compensation plan, he must designate the company in which he wishes to invest his deferred wages. Employees must choose one of the companies selected by the State to participate in the plan; they are not free to invest their deferred compensation in any other way. At the time an employee enrolls in the plan, he may also select one of the payout options offered by the company that he has chosen, but when he reaches retirement age he is free to switch to one of the company's other options. If at retirement the employee decides to receive a lump-sum payment, he may also purchase any of the options then being offered by the other companies participating in the plan. Many employees find an annuity contract to be the most attractive option, since receipt of a lump sum upon retirement requires payment of taxes on the entire sum in one year, and the choice of a fixed sum for a fixed period requires an employee to speculate as to how long he will live.

Once an employee chooses the company in which he wishes to invest and decides the amount of compensation to be deferred each month, the State is responsible for withholding the appropriate sums from the employee's wages and channelling those sums to the company designated by the employee. The State bears the cost of making the necessary payroll deductions and of giving employees time off to attend group meetings to learn about the plan, but it does not contribute any moneys to supplement the employees' deferred wages.

For an employee who elects to receive a monthly annuity following retirement, the amount of the employee's monthly benefits depends upon the amount of compensation that the employee deferred (and any earnings thereon), the employee's age at retirement, and the employee's sex. All of the companies selected by the State to participate in the plan use sex-based mortality tables to calculate monthly retirement benefits. Under these tables a man receives larger monthly payments than a woman who deferred the same amount of compensation and retired at the same age, because the tables classify annuitants on the basis of sex and women on average live longer than men.[1] Sex is the only factor that the tables use to classify individuals of the same age; the tables do not incorporate other factors correlating with longevity such as smoking habits, alcohol consumption, weight, medical history, or family history.

* * *

1. Different insurance companies participating in the plan use different means of classifying individuals on the basis of sex. Several companies use separate tables for men and women. Another company uses a single actuarial table based on male mortality rates, but calculates the annuities to be paid to women by using a 6–year "setback," *i.e.*, by treating a woman as if she were a man six years younger and had the life expectancy of a man that age.

II

We consider first whether petitioners would have violated Title VII if they had run the entire deferred compensation plan themselves, without the participation of any insurance companies. Title VII makes it an unlawful employment practice "to discriminate against any individual with respect to his compensation, terms, conditions, or privileges of employment, because of such individual's race, color, religion, sex or national origin." 42 U.S.C. § 2000e–2(a)(1). There is no question that the opportunity to participate in a deferred compensation plan constitutes a "conditio[n] or privileg[e] of employment," and that retirement benefits constitute a form of "compensation." The issue we must decide is whether it is discrimination "because of * * * sex" to pay a retired woman lower monthly benefits than a man who deferred the same amount of compensation.

In *Los Angeles Dept. of Water & Power v. Manhart,* 435 U.S. 702, 98 S.Ct. 1370, 55 L.Ed.2d 657 (1978), we held that an employer had violated Title VII by requiring its female employees to make larger contributions to a pension fund than male employees in order to obtain the same monthly benefits upon retirement. Noting that Title VII's "focus on the individual is unambiguous," *id.,* at 708, 98 S.Ct., at 1375, we emphasized that the statute prohibits an employer from treating some employees less favorably than others because of their race, religion, sex, or national origin. *Id.,* at 708–709, 98 S.Ct., at 1375–1376. While women as a class live longer than men, *id.,* at 704, 98 S.Ct., at 1373, we rejected the argument that the exaction of greater contributions from women was based on a "factor other than sex"—*i.e.,* longevity—and was therefore permissible under the Equal Pay Act[.][8] * * * We concluded that a plan requiring women to make greater contributions than men discriminates "because of * * * sex" for the simple reason that it treats each woman " 'in a manner which but for [her] sex would [have been] different.' " 435 U.S., at 711, 98 S.Ct., at 1377, * * *.

We have no hesitation in holding, as have all but one of the lower courts that have considered the question, that the classification of employees on the basis of sex is no more permissible at the pay-out stage of a retirement plan than at the pay-in stage.[10] We reject petitioners'

8. Section 703(h) of Title VII, the so-called Bennett Amendment, provides that Title VII does not prohibit an employer from "differentiat[ing] upon the basis of sex in determining the amount of the wages or compensation paid or to be paid to employees of such employer if such differentiation is authorized by [the Equal Pay Act]." 78 Stat. 257, 42 U.S.C. § 2000e–2(h). As in *Manhart, supra,* at 712, n. 23, 98 S.Ct., at 1377, n. 23, we need not decide whether retirement benefits constitute "wages" under the Equal Pay Act, because the Bennett Amendment extends the four exceptions recognized in the Act to all forms of "compensation" covered by Title VII.

10. It is irrelevant that female employees in *Manhart* were required to participate in the pension plan, whereas participation in the Arizona deferred compensation plan is voluntary. Title VII forbids all discrimination concerning "compensation, terms, conditions, or privileges of employment," not just discrimination concerning those aspects of the employment relationship as to which the employee has no choice. It is likewise irrelevant that the Arizona plan includes two options—the lump-sum option and the fixed-sum-for-a-fixed-period op-

contention that the Arizona plan does not discriminate on the basis of sex because a woman and a man who defer the same amount of compensation will obtain upon retirement annuity policies having approximately the same present actuarial value. Arizona has simply offered its employees a choice among different levels of annuity benefits, any one of which, if offered alone, would be equivalent to the plan at issue in *Manhart,* where the employer determined both the monthly contributions employees were required to make and the level of benefits that they were paid. If a woman participating in the Arizona plan wishes to obtain monthly benefits equal to those obtained by a man, she must make greater monthly contributions than he, just as the female employees in *Manhart* had to make greater contributions to obtain equal benefits. For any particular level of benefits that a woman might wish to receive, she will have to make greater monthly contributions to obtain that level of benefits than a man would have to make. The fact that Arizona has offered a range of discriminatory benefit levels, rather than only one such level, obviously provides no basis whatsoever for distinguishing *Manhart.*

* * *

[The] underlying assumption—that sex may properly be used to predict longevity—is flatly inconsistent with the basic teaching of *Manhart:* that Title VII requires employers to treat their employees as *individuals,* not "as simply components of a racial, religious, sexual, or national class." 435 U.S., at 708, 98 S.Ct., at 1375. *Manhart* squarely rejected the notion that, because women as a class live longer than men, an employer may adopt a retirement plan that treats every individual woman less favorably than every individual man. *Id.,* at 716–717, 98 S.Ct., at 1379–1380.

As we observed in *Manhart,* "[a]ctuarial studies could unquestionably identify differences in life expectancy based on race or national origin, as well as sex." *Id.,* at 709, 98 S.Ct., at 1376 (footnote omitted). If petitioners' interpretation of the statute were correct, such studies could be used as a justification for paying employees of one race lower monthly benefits than employees of another race. We continue to believe that "a statute that was designed to make race irrelevant in the employment market," *ibid.,* citing *Griggs v. Duke Power Co.,* 401 U.S. 424, 436, 91 S.Ct. 849, 856, 28 L.Ed.2d 158 (1971), could not reasonably be construed to permit such a racial classification. And if it would be unlawful to use race-based actuarial tables, it must also be unlawful to use sex-based tables, for under Title VII a distinction based on sex stands on the same footing as a distinction based on race unless it falls within one of a few narrow exceptions that are plainly inapplicable here.[13]

tion—that are provided on equal terms to men and women. An employer that offers one fringe benefit on a discriminatory basis cannot escape liability because he also offers other benefits on a nondiscriminatory basis. Cf. *Mississippi University for Women v. Hogan,* 458 U.S. 718, 723–724, n. 8, 102 S.Ct. 3331, 3336, n. 8, 73 L.Ed.2d 1090 (1982).

13. The exception for bona fide occupational qualifications, 42 U.S.C. § 2000e–2(e), is inapplicable since the terms of a

What we said in *Manhart* bears repeating: "Congress has decided that classifications based on sex, like those based on national origin or race, are unlawful." 435 U.S., at 709, 98 S.Ct., at 1376. The use of sex-segregated actuarial tables to calculate retirement benefits violates Title VII whether or not the tables reflect an accurate prediction of the longevity of women as a class, for under the statute "[e]ven a true generalization about [a] class" cannot justify class-based treatment. *Id.*, at 708, 98 S.Ct., at 1375. An individual woman may not be paid lower monthly benefits simply because women as a class live longer than men.[15] Cf. *Connecticut v. Teal,* 457 U.S. 440, 102 S.Ct. 2525, 73 L.Ed.2d 130 (1982) (an individual may object that an employment test used in making promotion decisions has a discriminatory impact even if the class of which he is a member has not been disproportionately denied promotion).

We conclude that it is just as much discrimination "because of * * * sex" to pay a woman lower benefits when she has made the same contributions as a man as it is to make her pay larger contributions to obtain the same benefits.

III

Since petitioners plainly would have violated Title VII if they had run the entire deferred compensation plan themselves, the only remaining question as to liability is whether their conduct is beyond the reach of the statute because it is the companies chosen by petitioners to participate in the plan that calculate and pay the retirement benefits. * * * [T]he State provided the opportunity to obtain an annuity as part of its own deferred compensation plan. It invited insurance companies to

---

retirement plan have nothing to do with occupational qualifications. The only possible relevant exception recognized in the Bennett Amendment, see n. 8, *supra,* is inapplicable in this case for the same reason it was inapplicable in *Manhart:* a scheme that uses sex to predict longevity is based on sex; it is not based on "any other factor other than sex." See 435 U.S., at 712, 98 S.Ct., at 1377 ("any individual's life expectancy is based on any number of factors, of which sex is only one").

15. As we noted in *Manhart,* "insurance is concerned with events that are individually unpredictable, but that is characteristic of many employment decisions" and has never been deemed a justification for "resort to classifications proscribed by Title VII." 435 U.S., at 710, 98 S.Ct., at 1376. It is true that properly designed tests can identify many job qualifications before employment, whereas it cannot be determined in advance when a particular employee will die. See *id.,* 435 U.S., at 724, 98 S.Ct., at 1383 (Blackmun, J., concurring in part and concurring in the judgment). For some jobs, however, there may be relevant skills that

cannot be identified by testing. Yet Title VII clearly would not permit use of race, national origin, sex, or religion as a proxy for such an employment qualification, regardless of whether a statistical correlation could be established.

There is no support in either logic or experience for the view, referred to by Justice Powell, that an annuity plan must classify on the basis of sex to be actuarially sound. Neither Title VII nor the Equal Pay Act "makes it unlawful to determine the funding requirements for an establishment's benefit plan by considering the [sexual] composition of the entire force," *Manhart,* 435 U.S., at 718, n. 34, 98 S.Ct., at 1380, n. 34, and it is simply not necessary either to exact greater contributions from women than from men or to pay women lower benefits than men. For example, the Minnesota Mutual Life Insurance Co. and the Northwestern National Life Insurance Co. have offered an annuity plan that treats men and women equally. See The Chronicle of Higher Education, Vol. 25, No. 7, Oct. 13, 1982, pp. 25–26.

submit bids outlining the terms on which they would supply retirement benefits and selected the companies that were permitted to participate in the plan. Once the State selected these companies, it entered into contracts with them governing the terms on which benefits were to be provided to employees. Employees enrolling in the plan could obtain retirement benefits only from one of those companies, and no employee could be contacted by a company except as permitted by the State. Ariz.Regs. 2–9–06.A, 2–9–20.A (1975).

Under these circumstances there can be no serious question that petitioners are legally responsible for the discriminatory terms on which annuities are offered by the companies chosen to participate in the plan. Having created a plan whereby employees can obtain the advantages of using deferred compensation to purchase an annuity only if they invest in one of the companies specifically selected by the State, the State cannot disclaim responsibility for the discriminatory features of the insurers' options. * * * It would be inconsistent with the broad remedial purposes of Title VII to hold that an employer who adopts a discriminatory fringe-benefit plan can avoid liability on the ground that he could not find a third party willing to treat his employees on a nondiscriminatory basis. An employer who confronts such a situation must either supply the fringe benefit himself, without the assistance of any third party, or not provide it at all.

Justice Powell, with whom The Chief Justice, Justice Blackmun, and Justice Rehnquist join, dissenting in part and concurring in part.

[T]he consequences of the Court's holding are unlikely to be beneficial. If the cost to employers of offering unisex annuities is prohibitive or if insurance carriers choose not to write such annuities, employees will be denied the opportunity to purchase life annuities—concededly the most advantageous pension plan—at lower cost.[4] If, alternatively, insurance carriers and employers choose to offer these annuities, the heavy cost burden of equalizing benefits probably will be passed on to current employees. There is no evidence that Congress intended Title VII to work such a change. Nor does *Manhart* support such a sweeping reading of this statute. That case expressly recognized the limited reach of its holding—a limitation grounded in the legislative history of Title VII and the inapplicability of Title VII's policies to the insurance industry.

* * *

The accuracy with which an insurance company predicts the rate of mortality depends on its ability to identify groups with similar mortality rates. The writing of annuities thus requires that an insurance company

---

4. This is precisely what has happened in this case. Faced with the liability resulting from the Court of Appeals' judgment, the State of Arizona discontinued making life annuities available to its employees. Any employee who now wishes to have the security provided by a life annuity must withdraw his or her accrued retirement savings from the state pension plan, pay federal income tax on the amount withdrawn, and then use the remainder to purchase an annuity on the open market—which most likely will be sex-based. The adverse effect of today's holding apparently will fall primarily on the State's employees.

group individuals according to attributes that have a significant correlation with mortality. The most accurate classification system would be to identify all attributes that have some verifiable correlation with mortality and divide people into groups accordingly, but the administrative cost of such an undertaking would be prohibitive. Instead of identifying all relevant attributes, most insurance companies classify individuals according to criteria that provide both an accurate and efficient measure of longevity, including a person's age and sex. These particular criteria are readily identifiable, stable, and easily verifiable. See Benston, The Economics of Gender Discrimination in Employee Fringe Benefits: *Manhart* Revisited, 49 U.Chi.L.Rev. 489, 499–501 (1982).

It is this practice—the use of a sex-based group classification—that the majority ultimately condemns. * * * The policies underlying Title VII, rather than supporting the majority's decision, strongly suggest—at least for me—the opposite conclusion. This remedial statute was enacted to eradicate the types of discrimination in employment that then were pervasive in our society. The entire thrust of Title VII is directed against *discrimination*—disparate treatment on the basis of race or sex that intentionally or arbitrarily affects an individual. But as Justice Blackmun has stated, life expectancy is a "nonstigmatizing factor that demonstrably differentiates females from males and that is not measurable on an individual basis * * *. [T]here is nothing arbitrary, irrational, or 'discriminatory' about recognizing the objective and accepted * * * disparity in female-male life expectancies in computing rates for retirement plans." *Manhart,* 435 U.S., at 724, 98 S.Ct., at 1383 (concurring in part and concurring in judgment). Explicit sexual classifications, to be sure, require close examination, but they are not automatically invalid. Sex-based mortality tables reflect objective actuarial experience. Because their use does not entail discrimination in any normal understanding of that term,[9] a court should hesitate to invalidate this long-approved practice on the basis of its own policy judgment.

Notes and Questions

1. *Effects of Using Sex–Based vs. Unisex Actuarial Tables.* On the assumption that sex-based actuarial tables on the mortality of men and women are accurate, does the use of such tables mean that women as a group will receive lower annuity benefits proportionate to their contributions than will men? Will more individual women than individual men receive less back than they contributed? On the other hand, does the use of unisex actuarial tables mean that men as a group will receive lower annuity benefits proportionate to their contributions than will women? Will more individual men than individual women receive less back than they contributed?

2. *Rationale for Proscribing Sex–Based Tables?* Why would rational policy makers want to proscribe reliance on sex-based actuarial tables in the

---

9. Indeed, if employers and insurance carriers offer annuities based on unisex mortality tables, men as a class will receive less aggregate benefits than similarly situated women.

calculation of annuities? Do such tables express a lack of equal regard or respect for women, or otherwise stigmatize women? Are such tables part of the institutional system that impedes women from achieving economic equality in our society? Is there a risk that insurers would continue to use sex-based tables even if social and demographic changes led to a convergence of male and female longevity? Or is it simply always wrong for employers to make sex-conscious employment decisions? See generally Lea Brilmayer, Richard W. Hekeler, Douglas Laycock & Teresa Sullivan, Sex Discrimination in Employer–Sponsored Insurance Plans: A Legal and Demographic Analysis, 47 U.Chi.L.Rev. 505, 530, 539–59 (1980); George J. Benston, The Economics of Gender Discrimination in Employee Fringe Benefits; *Manhart* Revisited, 49 U.Chi.L.Rev. 489 (1982); Mayer G. Freed & Daniel D. Polsby, Privacy, Efficiency and the Equality of Men and Women: A Revisionist View of Sex Discrimination in Employment, 1981 Am.B.Found.Res.J. 583; Spencer L. Kimball, Reverse Sex Discrimination: *Manhart,* 1979 Am.B.Found.Res.J. 83.

3. *Do Sex–Based Actuarial Tables Undermine True Sexual Equality?* Note that *Norris* helps ensure that women do not need to save more to have the same expectations as men of a given post-retirement living standard over a longer life span. Might *Norris* thus be best explained by the view that true equality for female workers requires the removal of any extra earnings burden imposed by the greater average longevity of their sex? Should women have to bear an extra burden because of greater average longevity?

4. *Was* Manhart *an Easier Case?* Can *Norris* be persuasively distinguished from *Manhart?* Even if sex-based actuarial tables are not necessarily discriminatory, is there a difference between giving female retirees lower monthly benefits based on average longevity calculations and requiring female employees to make larger contributions in order to save more for their retirement years than men must for their's? Did *Manhart* present a kind of sex-based paternalism not present in *Norris?*

5. *Did the Language of Title VII Compel* Norris? Would the language of Title VII support a holding contrary to that reached in *Norris?* Note the Court's narrowing construction of the bona fide occupational qualification (BFOQ) defense in footnote 13. Would it have been reasonable to read this defense as applicable to a benefit such as a retirement plan? Note also the Court's rejection of the "any other factor than sex" defense in the same footnote. This defense is incorporated into Title VII from the Equal Pay Act by the last sentence in section 703(h), the Bennett Amendment. (For further discussion of the Bennett Amendment, see pp. 403–405 infra.)

6. *Would Accepting Sex–Based Tables Require Accepting All Rational "Statistical Discrimination"?* Would a contrary holding in *Norris,* however reached, have been capable of being confined to the use of actuarial assumptions in retirement benefits? Or would it have led to general acceptance of the use of sex as a proxy for individualized assessment in every case where sex was a rational predictor of performance or some other relevant attribute? Consider an employer that attempted to justify its refusal to hire any women for certain jobs by offering evidence that women are more likely to withdraw from the labor market after a few years before the recoupment of training costs, and that there is no cost-effective way to determine which women are

exceptions to the average profile. Can this argument be distinguished from the claim rejected in *Norris?* Would accepting this argument for the all or nothing hiring decision involved in the hypothetical mean that women would receive fewer employment benefits than their average or aggregate career paths would warrant?

7. *Application to Race Discrimination?* Blacks on the average do not live as long as whites. Could *Norris* have been decided differently without also permitting race-based actuarial calculations to differentiate the pensions of whites from those of blacks?

8. *Practical Effect of* Norris. The insurance industry adjusted to *Norris* by offering unisex annuity options. See Mary Gray and Sana F. Shtasel, Insurers Are Surviving Without Sex, 71 A.B.A.Journal 89–90 (Feb. 1985) (Arizona itself reinstated the annuity option after the *Norris* decision). Is there any reason why insurers cannot derive the same profits from unisex as from sex-based annuities without imposing extra costs on employers? Does anything in *Norris* prohibit insurers from adjusting their annuity pay outs to reflect the proportion of women in their annuity pool? Such an adjustment may result in the reduction of annuities for men as well as the raising of annuities for women, but need it result in employers having any incentive not to hire women? The insurance industry also argued that few men will take a life annuity option from their employer if they know they can receive higher sex-based pay outs by taking a lump sum benefit and purchasing their own annuity on the open market. If this is true, actuaries will calculate employer-connected annuities on the basis of female mortality, and women's annuities will not increase. Is it clear, however, that most men will take lump sum payments, in view of the adverse tax consequences? If they do, should Congress withhold favorable tax treatment from retirement plans that permit employees to purchase annuities on the open market?

C. PREGNANCY AND FERTILITY

GENERAL ELECTRIC CO. v. GILBERT
Supreme Court of the United States, 1976.
429 U.S. 125, 97 S.Ct. 401, 50 L.Ed.2d 343.

MR. JUSTICE REHNQUIST delivered the opinion of the Court.

Petitioner, General Electric Co., provides for all of its employees a disability plan which pays weekly nonoccupational sickness and accident benefits. Excluded from the plan's coverage, however, are disabilities arising from pregnancy.

* * *

Following trial, the District Court made findings of fact and conclusions of law, and entered an order in which it determined that General Electric, by excluding pregnancy disabilities from the coverage of the Plan, had engaged in sex discrimination in violation of § 703(a)(1) of Title VII.

* * *

Between the date on which the District Court's judgment was rendered and the time this case was decided by the Court of Appeals, we decided *Geduldig v. Aiello,* 417 U.S. 484, 94 S.Ct. 2485, 41 L.Ed.2d 256 (1974), where we rejected a claim that a very similar disability program established under California law violated the Equal Protection Clause of the Fourteenth Amendment because that plan's exclusion of pregnancy disabilities represented sex discrimination.

* * *

There is no more showing in this case than there was in *Geduldig* that the exclusion of pregnancy benefits is a mere "pretex[t] designed to effect an invidious discrimination against the members of one sex or the other." The Court of Appeals expressed the view that the decision in *Geduldig* had actually turned on whether or not a conceded discrimination was "invidious" but we think that in so doing it misread the quoted language from our opinion. As we noted in that opinion, a distinction which on its face is not sex related might nonetheless violate the Equal Protection Clause if it were in fact a subterfuge to accomplish a forbidden discrimination. But we have here no question of excluding a disease or disability comparable in all other respects to covered diseases or disabilities and yet confined to the members of one race or sex. Pregnancy is, of course, confined to women, but it is in other ways significantly different from the typical covered disease or disability. The District Court found that it is not a "disease" at all, and is often a voluntarily undertaken and desired condition. We do not therefore infer that the exclusion of pregnancy disability benefits from petitioner's plan is a simple pretext for discriminating against women. * * *

The instant suit was grounded on Title VII rather than the Equal Protection Clause, and our cases recognize that a prima facie violation of Title VII can be established in some circumstances upon proof that the *effect* of an otherwise facially neutral plan or classification is to discriminate against members of one class or another. See *Washington v. Davis,* 426 U.S. 229, 246–248, 96 S.Ct. 2040, 2051, 48 L.Ed.2d 597 (1976). For example, in the context of a challenge, under the provisions of § 703(a)(2), to a facially neutral employment test, this Court held that a prima facie case of discrimination would be established if, even absent proof of intent, the consequences of the test were "invidiously to discriminate on the basis of racial or other impermissible classification," *Griggs v. Duke Power Co.,* 401 U.S. 424, 431, 91 S.Ct. 849, 853, 28 L.Ed.2d 158 (1971). Even assuming that it is not necessary in this case to prove intent to establish a prima facie violation of § 703(a)(1), but cf. *McDonnell Douglas Corp. v. Green,* 411 U.S. 792, 802–806, 93 S.Ct. 1817, 1824–1826, 36 L.Ed.2d 668 (1973), the respondents have not made the requisite showing of gender-based effect.

As in *Geduldig,* respondents have not attempted to meet the burden of demonstrating a gender-based discriminatory effect resulting from the exclusion of pregnancy-related disabilities from coverage. Whatever the ultimate probative value of the evidence introduced before the District

Court on this subject in the instant case, at the very least it tended to illustrate that the selection of risks covered by the Plan did not operate, in fact, to discriminate against women. As in *Geduldig,* we start from the indisputable baseline that "[t]he fiscal and actuarial benefits of the program * * * accrue to members of both sexes," 417 U.S., at 497 n. 20, 94 S.Ct., at 2492 n. 20. We need not disturb the findings of the District Court to note that neither is there a finding, nor was there any evidence which would support a finding, that the financial benefits of the Plan "worked to discriminate against any definable group or class in terms of the aggregate risk protection derived by that group or class from the program," *id.,* at 496, 94 S.Ct., at 2492. The Plan, in effect (and for all that appears), is nothing more than an insurance package, which covers some risks, but excludes others, see *id.,* at 494, 496–497, 94 S.Ct., at 2491–2492. The "package" going to relevant identifiable groups we are presently concerned with—General Electric's male and female employees—covers exactly the same categories of risk, and is facially nondiscriminatory in the sense that "[t]here is no risk from which men are protected and women are not. Likewise, there is no risk from which women are protected and men are not." *Id.,* at 496–497, 94 S.Ct., at 2492. As there is no proof that the package is in fact worth more to men than to women, it is impossible to find any gender-based discriminatory effect in this scheme simply because women disabled as a result of pregnancy do not receive benefits; that is to say, gender-based discrimination does not result simply because an employer's disability-benefits plan is less than all-inclusive.[17] For all that appears, pregnancy-related disabilities constitute an *additional* risk, unique to women, and the failure to compensate them for this risk does not destroy the presumed parity of the benefits, accruing to men and women alike, which results from the facially evenhanded *inclusion* of risks. To hold otherwise would endanger the commonsense notion that an employer who has no disability benefits program at all does not violate Title VII even though the "underinclusion" of risks impacts, as a result of pregnancy-related disabilities, more heavily upon one gender than upon the other.

NASHVILLE GAS CO. v. SATTY

Supreme Court of the United States, 1977.
434 U.S. 136, 98 S.Ct. 347, 54 L.Ed.2d 356.

MR. JUSTICE REHNQUIST delivered the opinion of the Court.

Two separate policies are at issue in this case. The first is petitioner's practice of giving sick pay to employees disabled by reason of

---

17. Absent proof of different values, the cost to "insure" against the risks is, in essence, nothing more than extra compensation to the employees, in the form of fringe benefits. If the employer were to remove the insurance fringe benefits and, instead, increase wages by an amount equal to the cost of the "insurance," there would clearly be no gender-based discrimination, even though a female employee who wished to purchase disability insurance that covered all risks would have to pay more than would a male employee who purchased identical disability insurance, due to the fact that her insurance had to cover the "extra" disabilities due to pregnancy. * * *

nonoccupational sickness or injury but not to those disabled by pregnancy. The second is petitioner's practice of denying accumulated seniority to female employees returning to work following disability caused by childbirth. We shall discuss them in reversed order.

I

Petitioner requires an employee who is about to give birth to take a pregnancy leave of indeterminate length. Such an employee does not accumulate seniority while absent, but instead actually loses any job seniority accrued before the leave commenced. Petitioner will not hold the employee's job open for her awaiting her return from pregnancy leave. An employee who wishes to return to work from such leave will be placed in any open position for which she is qualified and for which no individual currently employed is bidding; before such time as a permanent position becomes available, the company attempts to find temporary work for the employee. If and when the employee acquires a permanent position, she regains previously accumulated seniority for purposes of pension, vacation, and the like, but does not regain it for the purpose of bidding on future job openings.

* * *

We conclude that petitioner's policy of denying accumulated seniority to female employees returning from pregnancy leave violates § 703(a)(2) of Title VII.

* * *

On its face, petitioner's seniority policy appears to be neutral in its treatment of male and female employees. If an employee is forced to take a leave of absence from his or her job because of disease or any disability other than pregnancy, the employee, whether male or female, retains accumulated seniority and, indeed, continues to accrue seniority while on leave. If the employee takes a leave of absence for any other reason, including pregnancy, accumulated seniority is divested. Petitioner's decision not to treat pregnancy as a disease or disability for purposes of seniority retention is not on its face a discriminatory policy. "Pregnancy is, of course, confined to women, but it is in other ways significantly different from the typical covered disease or disability." *Gilbert,* 429 U.S., at 136, 97 S.Ct., at 408.

We have recognized, however, that both intentional discrimination and policies neutral on their face but having a discriminatory effect may run afoul of § 703(a)(2). *Griggs v. Duke Power Co.,* 401 U.S. 424, 431, 91 S.Ct. 849, 854, 28 L.Ed.2d 158 (1971). It is beyond dispute that petitioner's policy of depriving employees returning from pregnancy leave of their accumulated seniority acts both to deprive them "of employment opportunities" and to "adversely affect [their] status as an employee." It is apparent from the previous recitation of the events which occurred following respondent's return from pregnancy leave that petitioner's policy denied her specific employment opportunities that she otherwise would have obtained. Even if she had ultimately been able to regain a permanent position with petitioner, she would have felt the effects of a lower seniority level, with its attendant relegation to less desirable and lower paying jobs, for the remainder of her career with petitioner.

In *Gilbert, supra,* there was no showing that General Electric's policy of compensating for all non-job-related disabilities except pregnancy favored men over women. No evidence was produced to suggest that men received more benefits from General Electric's disability insurance fund than did women; both men and women were subject generally to the disabilities covered and presumably drew similar amounts from the insurance fund.

* * *

Here, by comparison, petitioner has not merely refused to extend to women a benefit that men cannot and do not receive, but has imposed on women a substantial burden that men need not suffer. The distinction between benefits and burdens is more than one of semantics. We held in *Gilbert* that § 703(a)(1) did not require that greater economic benefits be paid to one sex or the other "because of their differing roles in 'the scheme of human existence,'" 429 U.S., at 139 n. 17, 97 S.Ct., at 410 n. 17. But that holding does not allow us to read § 703(a)(2) to permit an employer to burden female employees in such a way as to deprive them of employment opportunities because of their different role.

Recognition that petitioner's facially neutral seniority system does deprive women of employment opportunities because of their sex does not end the inquiry under § 703(a)(2) of Title VII. * * * But we agree with the District Court in this case that since there was no proof of any business necessity adduced with respect to the policies in question, that court was entitled to "assume no justification exists."[5]

II

On the basis of the evidence presented to the District Court, petitioner's policy of not awarding sick-leave pay to pregnant employees is legally indistinguishable from the disability-insurance program upheld in *Gilbert*. As in *Gilbert*, petitioner compensates employees for limited periods of time during which the employee must miss work because of a non-job-related illness or disability. As in *Gilbert*, the compensation is not extended to pregnancy-related absences.

* * *

5. Indeed, petitioner's policy of denying accumulated seniority to employees returning from pregnancy leave might easily conflict with its own economic and efficiency interests. In particular, as a result of petitioner's policy, inexperienced employees are favored over experienced employees; employees who have spent lengthy periods with petitioner and might be expected to be more loyal to the company are displaced by relatively new employees. Female employees may also be less motivated to perform efficiently in their jobs because of the greater difficulty of advancing through the firm.

We again need not decide whether, when confronted by a facially neutral plan, it is necessary to prove intent to establish a prima facie violation of § 703(a)(1).

MR. JUSTICE STEVENS, concurring in the judgment.

The general problem is to decide when a company policy which attaches a special burden to the risk of absenteeism caused by pregnancy is a prima facie violation of the statutory prohibition against sex discrimination. The answer "always," which I had thought quite plainly correct, is foreclosed by the Court's holding in *Gilbert*. The answer "never" would seem to be dictated by the Court's view that a discrimination against pregnancy is "not a gender-based discrimination at all." The Court has, however, made it clear that the correct answer is "sometimes." Even though a plan which frankly and unambiguously discriminates against pregnancy is "facially neutral," the Court will find it unlawful if it has a "discriminatory effect." The question, then, is how to identify this discriminatory effect.

Two possible answers are suggested by the Court. The Court seems to rely on (a) the difference between a benefit and a burden, and (b) the difference between § 703(a)(2) and § 703(a)(1). In my judgment, both of these differences are illusory.[4] I agree with the Court that the effect of the respondent's seniority plan is significantly different from that of the General Electric disability plan in *Gilbert*, but I suggest that the difference may be described in this way: Although the *Gilbert* Court was unwilling to hold that discrimination against pregnancy—as compared with other physical disabilities—is discrimination on account of sex, it may nevertheless be true that discrimination against pregnant or formerly pregnant employees—as compared with other employees—does constitute sex discrimination. This distinction may be pragmatically expressed in terms of whether the employer has a policy which adversely affects a woman beyond the term of her pregnancy leave.

Note on the Pregnancy Discrimination Act of 1978

In 1978 Congress rejected at least the specific holding of *Gilbert* by passing the Pregnancy Discrimination Act (PDA), which added a new definitional section to Title VII. This section, 701(k), provides:

4. Differences between benefits and burdens cannot provide a meaningful test of discrimination since, by hypothesis, the favored class is always benefited and the disfavored class is equally burdened. The grant of seniority is a benefit which is not shared by the burdened class; conversely, the denial of sick pay is a burden which the benefited class need not bear.

The Court's second apparent ground of distinction is equally unsatisfactory. The Court suggests that its analysis of the seniority plan is different because that plan was attacked under § 703(a)(2) of Title VII not § 703(a)(1). Again, I must confess that I do not understand the relevance of this distinction. It is true that § 703(a)(1) refers to "discrimination" and § 703(a)(2) does not. But the Court itself recognizes that this is not significant since a violation of § 703(a)(2) occurs when a facially neutral policy has a *"discriminatory effect."* The Court also suggests that § 703(a)(1) may contain a requirement of intent not present in § 703(a)(2). Whatever the merits of that suggestion, it is apparent that it does not form the basis for any differentiation between the two subparagraphs of § 703 in this case, since the Court expressly refuses to decide the issue.

The terms "because of sex" or "on the basis of sex" include, but are not limited to, because of or on the basis of pregnancy, childbirth, or related medical conditions; and women affected by pregnancy, childbirth, or related medical conditions shall be treated the same for all employment-related purposes, including receipt of benefits under fringe benefit programs, as other persons not so affected but similar in their ability or inability to work, and nothing in section 703(h) of this title shall be interpreted to permit otherwise * * *.

The Supreme Court has had two occasions to interpret the legislative policy expressed in this provision. First, in Newport News Shipbuilding and Dry Dock Co. v. EEOC, 462 U.S. 669, 103 S.Ct. 2622, 77 L.Ed.2d 89 (1983), the Court held that § 701(k) prohibited an employer from providing less health insurance coverage for the pregnancy-related medical expenses of the spouses of its male employees than it provided for either the pregnancy-related expenses of its female employees or for nonpregnancy-related medical expenses of its employees' spouses. The Court took pains to make clear that employers are under no Title VII obligation to provide dependent benefits, and would not violate § 701(k) by providing benefits only for employees and not their spouses.

In its second interpretation of the PDA, California Federal Savings & Loan Association v. Guerra, 479 U.S. 272, 107 S.Ct. 683, 93 L.Ed.2d 613 (1987), the Court confirmed that the purpose of the PDA was to ensure the fair treatment of pregnancy by employers, rather than some formal conception of equal treatment of male and female employees. In that case, excerpted below in chapter 18, the Court held that the PDA does not preempt a California law that requires "employers to provide leave and reinstatement to employees disabled by pregnancy" regardless of the employer's provision of other disability benefits. Even though the PDA does not *require* coverage of pregnancy benefits when other disability benefits are not granted, the states are not barred from giving special protection to disability due to pregnancy because "Congress [intended the PDA to be] a 'floor beneath which pregnancy disability benefits may not drop—not a ceiling above which they may not rise.' " Id. at 280, 107 S.Ct. at 689. The Court further noted that the California statute was "narrowly drawn to cover only the period of *actual physical disability*," and thus "does not reflect archaic or stereotypical notions about pregnancy and the abilities of pregnant workers." Id. at 290, 107 S.Ct. at 694 (emphasis in original).

Justice Stevens concurred on the ground that since the Court in *United Steelworkers v. Weber*, 443 U.S. 193, 99 S.Ct. 2721, 61 L.Ed.2d 480 (1979), had rejected reading § 703 to require status-blind decisionmaking in all cases, there could be no principled opposition to treating female employees more favorably than male employees. Is it appropriate to view *Guerra's* allowance of special treatment for pregnancy as a departure from the antidiscrimination principle of Title VII? Or, rather, does true equality require the lifting of the biological burdens uniquely borne by women? Compare the defense of the *Norris* decision in note 3 on page 310.

Notes and Questions

1. Gilbert *and Disparate Treatment: Absence of Male Comparator.* Could General Electric's exclusion of pregnancy from its disability plan have

been held to constitute disparate treatment of women even before the PDA? In Phillips v. Martin Marietta, 400 U.S. 542, 91 S.Ct. 496, 27 L.Ed.2d 613 (1971), the Court had ruled that an employer discriminates on the basis of sex by implementing an employment policy that discriminates against a subset of all women, such as in that case all women with preschool children. Why did *Phillips* not control the result in *Gilbert*? Did it make a difference that there are men with preschool age children who were treated more favorably in the *Phillips* case, while there are no pregnant men to serve as standards of comparison in a case like *Gilbert*?

Does *Gilbert* suggest that when there are no individuals outside a Title VII-protected class that share the characteristic that defines the disadvantaged subset of that class, we cannot assume that discrimination is based on the protected status, rather than on the further defining characteristic? In such cases must a Title VII court ask how the discriminator treats the most comparable characteristics of individuals outside the protected status group? Justice Brennan in a dissenting opinion in *Gilbert* (not reproduced above) argued that General Electric discriminated on account of sex because it provided coverage for all male single-sex disabilities while excluding pregnancy. Is this an appropriate comparison if pregnancy disability occurs with much greater frequency, and thus imposes much greater cost, than the male single-sex disabilities?

2. Gilbert *and Proof of Disparate Impact: Aggregate Group Benefit Analysis.* Were not only female employees harmed by the exclusion of pregnancy from the General Electric disability plan? Why then did the Court assert that the *Gilbert* plaintiffs "have not made the requisite showing of gender-based effect?" Is Justice Rehnquist's analysis illuminated by his different treatment in *Satty* of the Nashville Gas Company's exclusion of pregnancy from its policy of providing continuing seniority status to those returning from disability leaves? Would this exclusion be likely to have a much greater negative impact on the economic position of women than would the exclusion of pregnancy from disability plans? What is the relevance of Justice Rehnquist's distinction between (i) disability payments as a "benefit" and (ii) the divestment of accumulated seniority as a "burden"? Would Justice Rehnquist permit an employer to give special bonuses to employees on the basis of some criterion, such as a high school diploma, that it could not use to screen employment applicants? Would Justice Rehnquist treat the bonus "benefit" in the last hypothetical differently than he treated the denial of disability benefits for pregnancy because the bonus would have enabled employees outside the protected class to obtain greater aggregate benefits? Would *Gilbert* have been decided differently had the female plaintiffs been able to show that men in fact received coverage of greater value from General Electric's disability plan than did women? Is Justice Rehnquist's benefit versus burden distinction thus only the first of two steps in an analysis that also requires consideration of whether a challenged practice disproportionately provides fewer aggregate benefits to a protected group?

Why did Justice Rehnquist take this aggregation of benefits approach in *Gilbert* and *Satty*? Might he have been concerned that protected classes with special needs could use anti-discrimination law to demand extra support from employers? Does the PDA in part reflect a judgment by Congress that pregnant women should be granted such support in order to achieve workplace equality? Cf. DeClue v. Central Ill. Light Co., 223 F.3d 434 (7th Cir. 2000) (dicta stating that an employer's failure to provide restroom facilities for either sex might be challenged for its disparate impact on women). Does Justice Rehnquist's approach for the Court still have implications for compensation cases not involving pregnancy even after the PDA (and the Civil Rights Act of 1991), however? Consider, for instance, an employer's adoption of a health insurance plan that excluded coverage of the costs of treating AIDS, a disease that has disproportionately afflicted males, blacks, and other Title VII-protected classes. (Consider also the treatment of such an exclusion under the Americans with Disabilities Act, see pp. 580–583.)

3. *Relevancy of Whether Women Would Have to Pay More in the Open Market?* Consider footnote 17 in *Gilbert*. Is the *Gilbert* Court suggesting that one way of testing whether a benefit exclusion is discriminatory is to ask whether in the absence of a disability plan women would have to pay more than men in the open market for the disability coverage they seek? Is this argument any different from the one the Court later rejected in *Manhart* and *Norris*? Or is this discussion in *Gilbert* limited to facially neutral exclusions that are argued to have a disparate impact on a group?

4. Satty *and § 703(h)*. Recall the Court's insulation of break-in-service rules in seniority plans from disparate impact challenges in United Airlines v. Evans, supra p. 231, decided the same year as *Satty*. Why did the Court not grant the same insulation under § 703(h) to the seniority rule challenged in *Satty*?

5. *Applications of* Gilbert *and* Satty *to PDA Litigation?*

a. A school district provides teachers with three different types of leave: (i) paid sick leave, with continuing unpaid illness leave, (ii) unpaid maternity or paternity leave, and (iii) an unpaid leave of absence. The district bars employees from combining any of these leaves. Hence, a pregnant teacher can use her accumulated paid sick leave for the period of her disability, but must return to work when her disability ends. She may not combine paid sick leave with an unpaid maternity leave. Has the school district violated the PDA, even though pregnancy is not treated differently from other disabilities under this plan? If, as most courts have held, disparate impact analysis is available under the PDA, can the employer defend by using Justice Rehnquist's aggregation of benefits analysis? See Scherr v. Woodland School Community Consolidated District No. 50, 867 F.2d 974 (7th Cir.1988).

b. Can an employer fire or refuse to hire a woman because she became pregnant without being married? After the PDA, is there an argument based on *Gilbert* that this does not constitute sex or pregnancy discrimination? What if the employer cited a formal policy against employing any parents of children conceived out of wedlock? Would such a policy have an illegal disparate impact? (Might the BFOQ defense be available, in any event, for a policy against employing single mothers as counselors in a girls' school? See Chambers v. Omaha Girls Club, 834 F.2d 697 (8th Cir.1987).)

6. *Accommodating Pregnancy Disability*. The PDA does not require employers to offer accommodations to pregnant employees not offered to other employees "similar in their ability or inability to work." See, e.g., Stout v. Baxter Healthcare Corp., 282 F.3d 856 (5th Cir.2002) (upholding

employer's policy of granting no leave to probationary employees); Troupe v. May Department Stores Co., 20 F.3d 734 (7th Cir.1994); Marafino v. St. Louis County Circuit Court, 707 F.2d 1005 (8th Cir.1983). Can an employer that offers temporarily disabled employees "light duty" assignments, however, deny the same accommodation to pregnant women who are temporarily unable to perform their regular work? Should it matter whether the employer only offers the "light duty" assignments to employees whose disabilities derive from on-the-job injuries, or because it is under compulsion from the Americans with Disabilities Act (ADA)? Compare Urbano v. Continental Airlines, 138 F.3d 204 (5th Cir.1998), with Ensley–Gaines v. Runyon, 100 F.3d 1220 (6th Cir.1996). The ADA is treated in chapter 7 below.

A number of commentators have argued that the PDA should be amended, or reinterpreted, to require special accommodation of pregnancy-related disability. See Judith G. Greenberg, The Pregnancy Discrimination Act: Legitimating Discrimination Against Pregnant Women in the Workforce, 50 Me. L. Rev. 225 (1998); Deborah A. Calloway, Accommodating Pregnancy in the Workplace, 25 Stetson L. Rev. 1 (1995); Ann C. McGinley & Jeffrey W. Stempel, Condescending Contradictions: Richard Posner's Pragmatism and Pregnancy Discrimination, 46 Fla. L. Rev. 193, 242 (1994); Samuel Issacharoff & Elyse Rosenblum, Women and the Workplace: Accommodating the Demands of Pregnancy, 94 Colum. L. Rev. 2154 (1994); Laura Schlictmann, Accommodation of Pregnancy–Related Disabilities on the Job, 15 Berkeley J. Emp. & Lab. L. 335 (1994).

7. *Infertility.* Does an employer's denial of health insurance coverage for fertility treatments violate the PDA? Title VII generally? Are *Satty* and *Gilbert* relevant? See Krauel v. Iowa Methodist Medical Center, 95 F.3d 674 (8th Cir.1996) (infertility not a "related medical condition" and no showing of a disparate impact on women). What if an employer's plan includes coverage for most infertility treatments, but excludes coverage for surgical impregnation procedures, which of course would only be performed on women? See Saks v. Franklin Covey Co., 316 F.3d 337, 346–47 (2d Cir.2003) (assuming that infertile male employees otherwise would be able to have coverage for surgical impregnation of their spouses, exclusion equally disadvantages male and female employees). For treatment of this issue under the ADA, see p. 504 infra.

8. *Contraception.* Can an employer exclude coverage of prescription contraceptive drugs (which are available only to women) from its employee health plan while covering other preventive drugs and devices? What if the plan covers surgical sterilization for both men and women? See Standridge v. Union Pacific R.R. Co., 479 F.3d 936 (8th Cir. 2007) (not providing health insurance coverage for contraception prescriptions does not violate PDA because contraception prevents and thus is not "related to" pregnancy).

9. *The PDA and Abortion Funding.* The last sentence in § 701(k) provides:

> This subsection shall not require an employer to pay for health insurance benefits for abortion, except where the life of the mother would be endangered if the fetus were carried to term, or except where medical complications have arisen from an abortion: Provided, That nothing

herein shall preclude an employer from providing abortion benefits or otherwise affect bargaining agreements in regard to abortion.

What is the effect of this sentence? Does § 701(k) prevent an employer from discharging a woman because she had an elective or optional abortion? Does it permit employers to exclude the costs of such abortions from their health insurance coverage? Does it permit employers who pay sick leave benefits generally to not pay such benefits for elective abortions? See EEOC, Questions and Answers on Pregnancy Discrimination, 29 C.F.R. § 1604, App. Q–A 34–36.

10. *Pregnancy Disability vs. Maternity Leave.* Can an employer grant maternity leave beyond the period of a new mother's physical disability without also granting comparable paternity leave? See Schafer v. Board of Public Educ. of School Dist. of Pittsburgh, 903 F.2d 243 (3d Cir.1990) (holding that equal leave must be granted to both sexes notwithstanding PDA); but cf. Johnson v. University of Iowa, 431 F.3d 325 (8th Cir. 2005) (university may establish "a period of presumptive disability" for pregnancy). The EEOC's position is in accord with that of the *Schafer* court. See EEOC Policy Guide on Parental Leave (BNA) FEP Man. 405:6885 (1990). See also the discussion of the Family Medical Leave Act at pp. 419–422 below.

11. *Protection of Pregnant Employees from Discharge and Mandatory Leave.* Does the PDA mean that employers can never require pregnant employees to take leaves during the term of their pregnancy? How could such a policy be defended? See Harriss v. Pan American World Airways, Inc., 649 F.2d 670 (9th Cir.1980) (upholding mandatory pregnancy leave for flight attendants). Could such a defense ever justify the discharge of pregnant employees? Consider footnote 5 in the majority opinion in *Satty,* and the International Union, UAW v. Johnson Controls decision below.

D. THE BONA FIDE OCCUPATIONAL QUALIFICATION DEFENSE

INTERNATIONAL UNION, UAW v. JOHNSON CONTROLS, INC.
Supreme Court of the United States, 1991.
499 U.S. 187, 111 S.Ct. 1196, 113 L.Ed.2d 158.

Justice Blackmun delivered the opinion of the Court.

In this case we are concerned with an employer's gender-based fetal-protection policy. May an employer exclude a fertile female employee from certain jobs because of its concern for the health of the fetus the woman might conceive?

* * *

Respondent Johnson Controls, Inc., manufactures batteries. In the manufacturing process, the element lead is a primary ingredient. Occupational exposure to lead entails health risks, including the risk of harm to any fetus carried by a female employee.

Before the Civil Rights Act of 1964 became law, Johnson Controls did not employ any woman in a battery-manufacturing job. In June

1977, however, it announced its first official policy concerning its employment of women in lead-exposure work:

> "[P]rotection of the health of the unborn child is the immediate and direct responsibility of the prospective parents. While the medical profession and the company can support them in the exercise of this responsibility, it cannot assume it for them without simultaneously infringing their rights as persons.

* * *

> " * * * Since not all women who can become mothers wish to become mothers (or will become mothers), it would appear to be illegal discrimination to treat all who are capable of pregnancy as though they will become pregnant."

Consistent with that view, Johnson Controls "stopped short of excluding women capable of bearing children from lead exposure," but emphasized that a woman who expected to have a child should not choose a job in which she would have such exposure. The company also required a woman who wished to be considered for employment to sign a statement that she had been advised of the risk of having a child while she was exposed to lead. The statement informed the woman that although there was evidence "that women exposed to lead have a higher rate of abortion," this evidence was "not as clear * * * as the relationship between cigarette smoking and cancer," but that it was, "medically speaking, just good sense not to run that risk if you want children and do not want to expose the unborn child to risk, however small. * * * "

Five years later, in 1982, Johnson Controls shifted from a policy of warning to a policy of exclusion. Between 1979 and 1983, eight employees became pregnant while maintaining blood lead levels in excess of 30 micrograms per deciliter. This appeared to be the critical level noted by the Occupational Health and Safety Administration (OSHA) for a worker who was planning to have a family. See 29 CFR § 1910.1025 (1989). The company responded by announcing a broad exclusion of women from jobs that exposed them to lead:

> " * * * [I]t is [Johnson Controls'] policy that women who are pregnant or who are capable of bearing children will not be placed into jobs involving lead exposure or which could expose them to lead through the exercise of job bidding, bumping, transfer or promotion rights."

The policy defined "women * * * capable of bearing children" as "[a]ll women except those whose inability to bear children is medically documented." It further stated that an unacceptable work station was one where, "over the past year," an employee had recorded a blood lead level of more than 30 micrograms per deciliter or the work site had yielded an air sample containing a lead level in excess of 30 micrograms per cubic meter.

* * *

The bias in Johnson Controls' policy is obvious. Fertile men, but not fertile women, are given a choice as to whether they wish to risk their reproductive health for a particular job. Section 703(a) of the Civil Rights Act of 1964, prohibits sex-based classifications in terms and conditions of employment, in hiring and discharging decisions, and in other employment decisions that adversely affect an employee's status. Respondent's fetal-protection policy explicitly discriminates against women on the basis of their sex. The policy excludes women with childbearing capacity from lead-exposed jobs and so creates a facial classification based on gender.

* * *

* * * Johnson Controls' policy classifies on the basis of gender and childbearing capacity, rather than fertility alone. Respondent does not seek to protect the unconceived children of all its employees. Despite evidence in the record about the debilitating effect of lead exposure on the male reproductive system, Johnson Controls is concerned only with the harms that may befall the unborn offspring of its female employees. * * * This Court faced a conceptually similar situation in *Phillips v. Martin Marietta Corp.,* 400 U.S. 542, 91 S.Ct. 496, 27 L.Ed.2d 613 (1971), and found sex discrimination because the policy established "one hiring policy for women and another for men—each having pre-school-age children." Id., at 544, 91 S.Ct., at 498. Johnson Controls' policy is facially discriminatory because it requires only a female employee to produce proof that she is not capable of reproducing.

Our conclusion is bolstered by the Pregnancy Discrimination Act of 1978 (PDA), in which Congress explicitly provided that, for purposes of Title VII, discrimination "on the basis of sex" includes discrimination "because of or on the basis of pregnancy, childbirth, or related medical conditions." "The Pregnancy Discrimination Act has now made clear that, for all Title VII purposes, discrimination based on a woman's pregnancy is, on its face, discrimination because of her sex." *Newport News Shipbuilding & Dry Dock Co. v. EEOC,* 462 U.S. 669, 684, 103 S.Ct. 2622, 2631, 77 L.Ed.2d 89 (1983). In its use of the words "capable of bearing children" in the 1982 policy statement as the criterion for exclusion, Johnson Controls explicitly classifies on the basis of potential for pregnancy. Under the PDA, such a classification must be regarded, for Title VII purposes, in the same light as explicit sex discrimination. Respondent has chosen to treat all its female employees as potentially pregnant; that choice evinces discrimination on the basis of sex.

* * * [T]he absence of a malevolent motive does not convert a facially discriminatory policy into a neutral policy with a discriminatory effect. Whether an employment practice involves disparate treatment through explicit facial discrimination does not depend on why the employer discriminates but rather on the explicit terms of the discrimination. * * * The beneficence of an employer's purpose does not undermine the conclusion that an explicit gender-based policy is sex discrimination under § 703(a) and thus may be defended only as a BFOQ.

* * *

The BFOQ defense is written narrowly, and this Court has read it narrowly. See, e.g., *Dothard v. Rawlinson,* 433 U.S. 321, 332–337, 97 S.Ct. 2720, 2728–2731, 53 L.Ed.2d 786 (1977); *Trans World Airlines, Inc. v. Thurston,* 469 U.S. 111, 122–125, 105 S.Ct. 613, 622–624, 83 L.Ed.2d 523 (1985). We have read the BFOQ language of § 4(f) of the Age Discrimination in Employment Act of 1967 (ADEA), as amended, which tracks the BFOQ provision in Title VII just as narrowly. See *Western Air Lines, Inc. v. Criswell,* 472 U.S. 400, 105 S.Ct. 2743, 86 L.Ed.2d 321 (1985). Our emphasis on the restrictive scope of the BFOQ defense is grounded on both the language and the legislative history of § 703.

The wording of the BFOQ defense contains several terms of restriction that indicate that the exception reaches only special situations. The statute thus limits the situations in which discrimination is permissible to "certain instances" where sex discrimination is "reasonably necessary" to the "normal operation" of the "particular" business. Each one of these terms—certain, normal, particular—prevents the use of general subjective standards and favors an objective, verifiable requirement. But the most telling term is "occupational"; this indicates that these objective, verifiable requirements must concern job-related skills and aptitudes.

The concurrence defines "occupational" as meaning related to a job. According to the concurrence, any discriminatory requirement imposed by an employer is "job-related" simply because the employer has chosen to make the requirement a condition of employment. In effect, the concurrence argues that sterility may be an occupational qualification for women because Johnson Controls has chosen to require it. This reading of "occupational" renders the word mere surplusage. "Qualification" by itself would encompass an employer's idiosyncratic requirements. By modifying "qualification" with "occupational," Congress narrowed the term to qualifications that affect an employee's ability to do the job.

Johnson Controls argues that its fetal-protection policy falls within the so-called safety exception to the BFOQ. Our cases have stressed that discrimination on the basis of sex because of safety concerns is allowed only in narrow circumstances. In *Dothard v. Rawlinson,* this Court indicated that danger to a woman herself does not justify discrimination. 433 U.S., at 335, 97 S.Ct., at 2729–2730. We there allowed the employer to hire only male guards in contact areas of maximum-security male penitentiaries only because more was at stake than the "individual woman's decision to weigh and accept the risks of employment." Ibid. We found sex to be a BFOQ inasmuch as the employment of a female guard would create real risks of safety to others if violence broke out because the guard was a woman. Sex discrimination was tolerated because sex was related to the guard's ability to do the job—maintaining prison security. We also required in *Dothard* a high correlation between sex and ability to perform job functions and refused to allow employers to use sex as a proxy for strength although it might be a fairly accurate one.

Similarly, some courts have approved airlines' layoffs of pregnant flight attendants at different points during the first five months of pregnancy on the ground that the employer's policy was necessary to ensure the safety of passengers. See *Harriss v. Pan American World Airways, Inc.,* 649 F.2d 670 (C.A.9 1980); *Burwell v. Eastern Air Lines, Inc.,* 633 F.2d 361 (C.A.4 1980), cert. denied, 450 U.S. 965, 101 S.Ct. 1480, 67 L.Ed.2d 613 (1981); *Condit v. United Air Lines, Inc.,* 558 F.2d 1176 (C.A.4 1977), cert. denied, 435 U.S. 934, 98 S.Ct. 1510, 55 L.Ed.2d 531 (1978); *In re National Airlines, Inc.,* 434 F.Supp. 249 (S.D.Fla.1977). In two of these cases, the courts pointedly indicated that fetal, as opposed to passenger, safety was best left to the mother. *Burwell,* 633 F.2d, at 371; *National Airlines,* 434 F.Supp., at 259.

We considered safety to third parties in *Western Airlines, Inc. v. Criswell,* supra, in the context of the ADEA. We focused upon "the nature of the flight engineer's tasks," and the "actual capabilities of persons over age 60" in relation to those tasks. 472 U.S., at 406, 105 S.Ct., at 2747. Our safety concerns were not independent of the individual's ability to perform the assigned tasks, but rather involved the possibility that, because of age-connected debility, a flight engineer might not properly assist the pilot, and might thereby cause a safety emergency. Furthermore, although we considered the safety of third parties in *Dothard* and *Criswell,* those third parties were indispensable to the particular business at issue. In *Dothard,* the third parties were the inmates; in *Criswell,* the third parties were the passengers on the plane. We stressed that in order to qualify as a BFOQ, a job qualification must relate to the "essence," *Dothard,* 433 U.S., at 333, 97 S.Ct., at 2751, or to the "central mission of the employer's business," *Criswell,* 472 U.S., at 413, 105 S.Ct., at 2751.

The concurrence ignores the "essence of the business" test and so concludes that "the safety to fetuses in carrying out the duties of battery manufacturing is as much a legitimate concern as is safety to third parties in guarding prisons (*Dothard*) or flying airplanes (*Criswell*)." * * * Third-party safety considerations properly entered into the BFOQ analysis in *Dothard* and *Criswell* because they went to the core of the employee's job performance. Moreover, that performance involved the central purpose of the enterprise. *Dothard,* 433 U.S., at 335, 97 S.Ct., at 2729–2730 ("The essence of a correctional counselor's job is to maintain prison security"); *Criswell,* 472 U.S., at 413, 105 S.Ct., at 2751 (the central mission of the airline's business was the safe transportation of its passengers). The concurrence attempts to transform this case into one of customer safety. The unconceived fetuses of Johnson Controls' female employees, however, are neither customers nor third parties whose safety is essential to the business of battery manufacturing. No one can disregard the possibility of injury to future children; the BFOQ, however, is not so broad that it transforms this deep social concern into an essential aspect of batterymaking.

Our case law, therefore, makes clear that the safety exception is limited to instances in which sex or pregnancy actually interferes with the employee's ability to perform the job. * * * [4]

* * *

We have no difficulty concluding that Johnson Controls cannot establish a BFOQ. Fertile women, as far as appears in the record, participate in the manufacture of batteries as efficiently as anyone else. Johnson Controls' professed moral and ethical concerns about the welfare of the next generation do not suffice to establish a BFOQ of female sterility. Decisions about the welfare of future children must be left to the parents who conceive, bear, support, and raise them rather than to the employers who hire those parents.

* * *

Johnson Controls argues that it must exclude all fertile women because it is impossible to tell which women will become pregnant while working with lead. This argument is somewhat academic in light of our conclusion that the company may not exclude fertile women at all; it perhaps is worth noting, however, that Johnson Controls has shown no "factual basis for believing that all or substantially all women would be unable to perform safely and efficiently the duties of the job involved." *Weeks v. Southern Bell Tel. & Tel. Co.,* 408 F.2d 228, 235 (C.A.5 1969), quoted with approval in *Dothard,* 433 U.S., at 333, 97 S.Ct., at 2751. Even on this sparse record, it is apparent that Johnson Controls is concerned about only a small minority of women. Of eight pregnancies reported among the female employees, it has not been shown that any of the babies have birth defects or other abnormalities. The record does not reveal the birth rate for Johnson Controls' female workers but national statistics show that approximately nine percent of all fertile women become pregnant each year. The birthrate drops to two percent for blue collar workers over age 30. * * * Johnson Controls' fear of prenatal injury, no matter how sincere, does not begin to show that substantially all of its fertile women employees are incapable of doing their jobs.

* * *

A word about tort liability and the increased cost of fertile women in the workplace is perhaps necessary. One of the dissenting judges in this

---

4. The concurrence predicts that our reaffirmation of the narrowness of the BFOQ defense will preclude considerations of privacy as a basis for sex-based discrimination. We have never addressed privacy-based sex discrimination and shall not do so here because the sex-based discrimination at issue today does not involve the privacy interests of Johnson Controls' customers. Nothing in our discussion of the "essence of the business test," however, suggests that sex could not constitute a BFOQ when privacy interests are implicated. See, e.g., Backus v. Baptist Medical Center, 510 F.Supp. 1191 (E.D.Ark.1981), vacated as moot, 671 F.2d 1100 (C.A.8 1982) (essence of obstetrics nurse's business is to provide sensitive care for patient's intimate and private concerns).

case expressed concern about an employer's tort liability and concluded that liability for a potential injury to a fetus is a social cost that Title VII does not require a company to ignore. It is correct to say that Title VII does not prevent the employer from having a conscience. The statute, however, does prevent sex-specific fetal-protection policies. These two aspects of Title VII do not conflict.

More than 40 States currently recognize a right to recover for a prenatal injury based either on negligence or on wrongful death. See, e.g., *Wolfe v. Isbell,* 291 Ala. 327, 333–334, 280 So.2d 758, 763 (1973); *Simon v. Mullin,* 34 Conn.Sup. 139, 147, 380 A.2d 1353, 1357 (1977). See also Note, 22 Suffolk U.L.Rev. 747, 754–756, and nn. 54, 57, and 58 (1988) (listing cases). According to Johnson Controls, however, the company complies with the lead standard developed by OSHA and warns its female employees about the damaging effects of lead. It is worth noting that OSHA gave the problem of lead lengthy consideration and concluded that "there is no basis whatsoever for the claim that women of childbearing age should be excluded from the workplace in order to protect the fetus or the course of pregnancy." 43 Fed.Reg. 52952, 52966 (1978). See also *id.,* at 54354, 54398. Instead, OSHA established a series of mandatory protections which, taken together, "should effectively minimize any risk to the fetus and newborn child." *Id.,* at 52966. See 29 CFR § 1910.125(k)(ii) (1989). Without negligence, it would be difficult for a court to find liability on the part of the employer. If, under general tort principles, Title VII bans sex-specific fetal-protection policies, the employer fully informs the woman of the risk, and the employer has not acted negligently, the basis for holding an employer liable seems remote at best.

Although the issue is not before us, the concurrence observes that "it is far from clear that compliance with Title VII will preempt state tort liability." The cases relied upon by the concurrence to support its prediction, however, are inapposite. For example, in *California Federal S. & L. Ass'n. v. Guerra,* 479 U.S. 272, 107 S.Ct. 683, 93 L.Ed.2d 613 (1987), we considered a California statute that expanded upon the requirements of the PDA and concluded that the statute was not pre-empted by Title VII because it was not inconsistent with the purposes of the federal statute and did not require an act that was unlawful under Title VII. Id., at 291–292, 107 S.Ct., at 694–695. Here, in contrast, the tort liability that the concurrence fears will punish employers for complying with Title VII's clear command. When it is impossible for an employer to comply with both state and federal requirements, this Court has ruled that federal law pre-empts that of the States. See, e.g., *Florida Lime & Avocado Growers, Inc. v. Paul,* 373 U.S. 132, 142–143, 83 S.Ct. 1210, 1217–1218, 10 L.Ed.2d 248 (1963).

* * *

If state tort law furthers discrimination in the workplace and prevents employers from hiring women who are capable of manufacturing the product as efficiently as men, then it will impede the accomplishment of Congress' goals in enacting Title VII. Because Johnson Controls has not argued that it faces any costs from tort liability, not to mention crippling ones, the pre-emption question is not before us. We therefore say no more than that the concurrence's speculation appears unfounded as well as premature.

* * * [T]he spectre of an award of damages reflects a fear that hiring fertile women will cost more. The extra cost of employing members of one sex, however, does not provide an affirmative Title VII defense for a discriminatory refusal to hire members of that gender. See *Manhart,* 435 U.S., at 716–718, and n. 32, 98 S.Ct., at 1379–1380, and n. 32. Indeed, in passing the PDA, Congress considered at length the considerable cost of providing equal treatment of pregnancy and related conditions, but made the "decision to forbid special treatment of pregnancy despite the social costs associated therewith." *Arizona Governing Committee v. Norris,* 463 U.S. 1073, 1084, n. 14, 103 S.Ct. 3492, 3499, n. 14, 77 L.Ed.2d 1236 (1983) (opinion of Marshall, J.).

We, of course, are not presented with, nor do we decide, a case in which costs would be so prohibitive as to threaten the survival of the employer's business. We merely reiterate our prior holdings that the incremental cost of hiring women cannot justify discriminating against them.

JUSTICE WHITE, with whom THE CHIEF JUSTICE and JUSTICE KENNEDY join, concurring in part and concurring in the judgment.

* * * For the fetal protection policy involved in this case to be a BFOQ, the policy must be "reasonably necessary" to the "normal operation" of making batteries, which is Johnson Controls' "particular business." Although that is a difficult standard to satisfy, nothing in the statute's language indicates that it could never support a sex-specific fetal protection policy.[1]

On the contrary, a fetal protection policy would be justified under the terms of the statute if, for example, an employer could show that exclusion of women from certain jobs was reasonably necessary to avoid substantial tort liability. Common sense tells us that it is part of the normal operation of business concerns to avoid causing injury to third parties, as well as to employees, if for no other reason than to avoid tort liability and its substantial costs. This possibility of tort liability is not hypothetical; every State currently allows children born alive to recover in tort for prenatal injuries caused by third parties, see W. Keeton, D. Dobbs, R. Keeton, & D. Owen, Prosser and Keeton on Law of Torts § 55,

---

1. The Court's heavy reliance on the word "occupational" in the BFOQ statute, is unpersuasive. Any requirement for employment can be said to be an occupational qualification, since "occupational" merely means related to a job. See Webster's Third New International Dictionary 1560 (1976). Thus, Johnson Controls' requirement that employees engaged in battery manufactur- ing be either male or non-fertile clearly is an "occupational qualification." The issue, of course, is whether that qualification is "reasonably necessary to the normal operation" of Johnson Controls' business. It is telling that the Court offers no case support, either from this Court or the lower Federal Courts, for its interpretation of the word "occupational."

p. 368 (5th ed. 1984), and an increasing number of courts have recognized a right to recover even for prenatal injuries caused by torts committed prior to conception, see 3 F. Harper, F. James, & O. Gray, Law of Torts § 18.3, pp. 677–678, n. 15 (2d ed. 1986).

The Court dismisses the possibility of tort liability by no more than speculating that if "Title VII bans sex-specific fetal-protection policies, the employer fully informs the woman of the risk, and the employer has not acted negligently, the basis for holding an employer liable seems remote at best." Such speculation will be small comfort to employers. First, it is far from clear that compliance with Title VII will pre-empt state tort liability, and the Court offers no support for that proposition. Second, although warnings may preclude claims by injured employees, they will not preclude claims by injured children because the general rule is that parents cannot waive causes of action on behalf of their children, and the parents' negligence will not be imputed to the children. Finally, although state tort liability for prenatal injuries generally requires negligence, it will be difficult for employers to determine in advance what will constitute negligence. Compliance with OSHA standards, for example, has been held not to be a defense to state tort or criminal liability. See *National Solid Wastes Management Assn. v. Killian*, 918 F.2d 671, 680, n. 9 (C.A.7 1990) (collecting cases); see also 29 U.S.C. § 653(b)(4). Moreover, it is possible that employers will be held strictly liable, if, for example, their manufacturing process is considered "abnormally dangerous." See Restatement (Second) of Torts § 869, comment b (1979).

* * *

Dothard and *Criswell* make clear that avoidance of substantial safety risks to third parties is inherently part of both an employee's ability to perform a job and an employer's "normal operation" of its business. Indeed, in both cases, the Court approved the statement in *Weeks v. Southern Bell Telephone & Telegraph Co.,* 408 F.2d 228 (C.A.5 1969), that an employer could establish a BFOQ defense by showing that "all or substantially all women would be unable to perform safely and efficiently the duties of the job involved." Id., at 235 (emphasis added). See *Criswell*, 472 U.S., at 414, 105 S.Ct., at 2751–52; *Dothard,* supra, 433 U.S., at 333, 97 S.Ct., at 2728–29. The Court's statement in this case that "the safety exception is limited to instances in which sex or pregnancy actually interferes with the employee's ability to perform the job," therefore adds no support to its conclusion that a fetal protection policy could never be justified as a BFOQ. On the facts of this case, for example, protecting fetal safety while carrying out the duties of battery manufacturing is as much a legitimate concern as is safety to third parties in guarding prisons (*Dothard*) or flying airplanes (*Criswell*).[5]

5. I do not, as the Court asserts, reject the "essence of the business" test. Rather, I merely reaffirm the obvious—that safety to third parties is part of the "essence" of most if not all businesses. * * *

Dothard and *Criswell* also confirm that costs are relevant in determining whether a discriminatory policy is reasonably necessary for the normal operation of a business. In *Dothard,* the safety problem that justified exclusion of women from the prison guard positions was largely a result of inadequate staff and facilities. See 433 U.S., at 335, 97 S.Ct., at 2729–30. If the cost of employing women could not be considered, the employer there should have been required to hire more staff and restructure the prison environment rather than exclude women. Similarly, in *Criswell* the airline could have been required to hire more pilots and install expensive monitoring devices rather than discriminate against older employees. The BFOQ statute, however, reflects "Congress' unwillingness to require employers to change the very nature of their operations." *Price Waterhouse v. Hopkins,* 490 U.S. 228, 242, 109 S.Ct. 1775, 1786, 104 L.Ed.2d 268 (1989) (plurality opinion).

* * *

Despite my disagreement with the Court concerning the scope of the BFOQ defense, I concur in reversing the Court of Appeals because that court erred in affirming the District Court's grant of summary judgment in favor of Johnson Controls. First, the Court of Appeals erred in failing to consider the level of risk-avoidance that was part of Johnson Controls' "normal operation." * * * If the fetal protection policy insists on a risk-avoidance level substantially higher than other risk levels tolerated by Johnson Controls such as risks to employees and consumers, the policy should not constitute a BFOQ.

Second, even without more information about the normal level of risk at Johnson Controls, the fetal protection policy at issue here reaches too far. This is evident both in its presumption that, absent medical documentation to the contrary, all women are fertile regardless of their age, and in its exclusion of presumptively fertile women from positions that might result in a promotion to a position involving high lead exposure. There has been no showing that either of those aspects of the policy is reasonably necessary to ensure safe and efficient operation of Johnson Controls' battery-manufacturing business. Of course, these infirmities in the company's policy do not warrant invalidating the entire fetal protection program.

Third, it should be recalled that until 1982 Johnson Controls operated without an exclusionary policy, and it has not identified any grounds for believing that its current policy is reasonably necessary to its normal operations. Although it is now more aware of some of the dangers of lead exposure, it has not shown that the risks of fetal harm or the costs associated with it have substantially increased.

Finally, the Court of Appeals failed to consider properly petitioners evidence of harm to offspring caused by lead exposure in males. The court considered that evidence only in its discussion of the business necessity standard, in which it focused on whether petitioners had met their burden of proof. The burden of proving that a discriminatory qualification is a BFOQ, however, rests with the employer. Thus, the court should have analyzed whether the evidence was sufficient for petitioners to survive summary judgment in light of respondent's burden of proof to establish a BFOQ. * * *

JUSTICE SCALIA, concurring in the judgment.

* * * I am willing to assume, as the Court intimates, that any action required by Title VII cannot give rise to liability under state tort law. That assumption, however, does not answer the question whether an action is required by Title VII (including the BFOQ provision) even if it is subject to liability under state tort law. It is perfectly reasonable to believe that Title VII has accommodated state tort law through the BFOQ exception. However, all that need be said in the present case is that Johnson has not demonstrated a substantial risk of tort liability— which is alone enough to defeat a tort-based assertion of the BFOQ exception.

[T]he Court [also] goes far afield, it seems to me, in suggesting that increased cost alone—short of "costs * * * so prohibitive as to threaten survival of the employer's business"—cannot support a BFOQ defense. I agree with Justice White's concurrence that nothing in our prior cases suggests this, and in my view it is wrong. I think, for example, that a shipping company may refuse to hire pregnant women as crew members on long voyages because the on-board facilities for foreseeable emergencies, though quite feasible, would be inordinately expensive. In the present case, however, Johnson has not asserted a cost-based BFOQ.

Notes and Questions

1. *Absence of Race–BFOQ.* Why did Congress provide that sex but not race may be shown to be a bona fide occupational qualification (BFOQ)? Are there any jobs for which race or skin color ought to be a qualification? Certain dramatic roles? Certain police undercover work? Given the absence of an explicit BFOQ provision, how should a Title VII court deal with such special cases? Cf. Wittmer v. Peters, 87 F.3d 916 (7th Cir.1996) (law enforcement and correctional institutions provide settings where "departures from racial neutrality are permissible" under constitution). Has the Court found the absence of a race-BFOQ to be relevant to its treatment of affirmative action programs under Title VII? Is it relevant? See generally Michael J. Frank, Justifiable Discrimination in the News and Entertainment Industries: Does Title VII Need a Race or Color BFOQ?, 35 S. F. L.Rev. 473 (2001).

2. *Why Facial Discrimination?* Note the *Johnson Controls* Court's statement that the absence of a "malevolent motive does not convert a facially discriminatory policy into a neutral policy with a discriminatory effect." Was this position compelled by prior cases, including *Norris* and *Manhart?* Does *Johnson Controls* mean that discrimination against a woman on the basis of the likelihood of her becoming pregnant is intentional discrimination under the PDA? See, e.g., Kocak v. Community Health Partners of Ohio, Inc., 400 F.3d 466 (6th Cir. 2005) (yes).

3. *Could There Be a Sex–Neutral Fetal Protection Policy?* What if an employer expressed equal concern about the harms that might "befall the unborn offspring" of its male employees through a policy that excluded any fertile worker from a job that posed a significant threat to his or her unborn children? Would the *Johnson Controls* majority allow such a policy to be challenged only for any disparate impact on women? What if the employer applied this policy to jobs that in fact threatened only the offspring of female workers, perhaps because the jobs required contact with abortifacient or teratogenic, but not mutagenic agents? (Abortifacient or teratogenic agents can harm children only through their effect on a pregnant woman. Mutagenic agents can harm children through damaging the genetic materials of either parent.) Would it matter whether the employer also applied the policy to other jobs that might threaten the offspring of some men as well as some women, perhaps all those testing abnormally high for some mutagenic agent in their blood stream? What if the standards for certain jobs were more stringent for women because, given current scientific research, more is known about the risks to fetal health transmitted through the mother than those transmitted through the father or by means of mutagenic agents affecting the genetic material of both parents?

For arguments that employers can frame effective fetal protection policies without discriminating against women, see Mary Becker, From *Muller v. Oregon* to Fetal Vulnerability Policies, 53 Univ. of Chi.L.Rev. 1219, 1236–37 (1986); Wendy Williams, Firing the Woman to Protect the Fetus: The Reconciliation of Fetal Protection with Employment Opportunity Goals Under Title VII, 69 Geo.L.J. 641, 657–59 (1981). See also U.S. Office of Technology Assessment, Reproductive Health Hazards in the Workplace (1985). See also European Council Directive 92/85, 1992 O.J. (L 348) 1 (EC) (where there is a risk to "pregnancy or breastfeeding", employer must adjust working conditions, move worker to another job, or grant leave).

4. *Relevance of OSHA Regulation?* The federal agency principally responsible for regulating occupational safety and health is the Occupational Safety and Health Administration of the Department of Labor, which promulgates and enforces standards under the Occupational Safety and Health Act (OSHA) of 1974. If an OSHA standard for allowing exposure to certain chemicals set different exposure levels for men and women, could it justify an employer's excluding women from particular jobs exceeding the levels? *Cf.* Neal Smith & Michael Baram, The Nuclear Regulatory Commission's Regulation of Radiation Hazards in the Workplace: Present Problems and New Approaches to Reproductive Health, 13 Ecol.L.Q. 879 (1987) (discussing differential standards for radiation exposure set by the NRC). What if the OSHA standard was facially neutral, but was more difficult for women to meet? See generally Gary Z. Nothstein & Ian Ayres, Sex–Based Considerations of Differentiation in the Workplace: Exploring the Biomedical Interface Between OSHA and Title VII, 26 Vill.L.Rev. 239 (1981).

5. *Worker Safety and the "Business Essence" Test.* The *Johnson Controls* Court claims to apply the "holdings in *Criswell* and *Dothard* that an employer must direct its concerns about a woman's ability to perform her job safely and efficiently to those aspects of the woman's job-related activities that fall within the 'essence' of the particular business." Is *Johnson Controls* consistent with those earlier decisions? Why did the Court conclude that

maintaining a safe workplace is not "reasonably necessary" to the normal operation of all businesses? Was this conclusion required to give meaning to the word "occupational" in the BFOQ provision? Does *Johnson Controls* mean that the safety of employees alone, rather than that of customers or maintaining public order generally, is not a factor or consideration "reasonably necessary to the normal operation" of any business for purposes of the BFOQ defense? If so, is this sensible policy? Should employers be forced to place some employees at risk? Are there any jobs for which sex-based hiring would be necessary to protect the safety of other employees? See also note 4 at p. 444 infra.

6. *The* Weeks *"All or Substantially All" Test.* Note that the Court in *Johnson Controls*, after defining the "essence" of the business to exclude the protection of workers' unborn children, also relies on *Dothard* to stress that "Johnson Controls has shown no 'factual basis for believing that all or substantially all women would be unable to perform safely and efficiently the duties of the job involved.' " The *Dothard* Court drew this "all or substantially all" test from Weeks v. Southern Bell Tel. & Tel. Co., 408 F.2d 228 (5th Cir.1969). In *Criswell*, a post-*Dothard* ruling interpreting a similar BFOQ defense available under the ADEA, included at pp. 438–443 infra, the Supreme Court supplemented the "business essence" test with a reformulation of the "all or substantially all" test as set forth in Usery v. Tamiami Trail Tours, Inc., 531 F.2d 224, 235 (5th Cir.1976), a case treating a challenge to a company's maximum age restrictions on bus drivers. The *Tamiami* court suggested that an employer could satisfy the *Weeks* test in one of two ways. First, the employer could show that it " 'had reasonable cause to believe, that is, a factual basis for believing, that all or substantially all [persons over the age qualification] would be unable to perform safely and efficiently the duties of the job involved.' " Second, in the alternative, the employer could establish that age was a legitimate proxy for safety-related qualifications by proving that it is " 'impossible or highly impractical' " to make individualized assessments of the qualification of the older worker:

> One method by which the employer can carry this burden is to establish that some members of the discriminated against class possess a trait precluding safe and efficient job performance that cannot be ascertained by means other than knowledge of the applicant's membership in the class.

Is the *Johnson Controls* Court's treatment of the "all or substantially all" BFOQ test consistent with the analytic scheme adopted in *Criswell*? Is the Court suggesting that an employer asserting the BFOQ defense must prove that almost all women cannot perform the essence of a job even in those cases when the employer has no way to determine which particular women are safety risks? Could Johnson Controls be certain which fertile women in its workforce would be the few that became pregnant during a particular time period? Is the Court suggesting that the BFOQ defense should be treated differently in sex than in age discrimination cases? Or is the Court's suggestion simply that where the likelihood of any particular woman not being a safe worker is low, an employer's inability to predict which women will be unsafe does not justify excluding all women of child-bearing age?

7. *Increased Costs as a BFOQ Defense?* The *Johnson Controls* Court concludes that "the extra costs of employing members of one sex" cannot justify refusing to hire that sex, unless perhaps the costs would "threaten the survival of the employer's business". Was this conclusion required or supported by *Norris* and *Manhart?* If the BFOQ defense does not allow consideration of costs generally, how can it be interpreted to allow consideration of costs that threaten a firm's survival in its market? Consider Justice White's description of the *Dothard* and *Criswell* cases as ultimately turning on costs. How might the majority have answered this argument?

8. *Preemption of State Tort Actions?* Can employers now feel reasonably secure that any state law tort action against them for injuries to an unborn offspring that could have been prevented by the exclusion of the mother from a toxic workplace will be preempted by Title VII? Does the Court offer a definitive ruling on this question? Will the availability of federal preemption turn on the reasons why state law might attach liability? Should it matter if the state law is founded in strict liability rather than negligence? What if the liability event was the employer's negligence in not providing a safer workplace for workers of both sexes? What if it was the employer's failure to give clearer warnings of the dangers of becoming pregnant after working at its plant?

How does Justice Scalia respond to the majority's "intimation" that exposure to state tort law should not be the basis for a BFOQ defense because such law should not punish employers for complying with Title VII's commands? To what extent might Congress have wanted to "accommodate" state tort law if it did not wish to permit employers to exclude women from particular jobs to protect potential offspring? See Hannah A. Furnish, Prenatal Exposure to Fetally Toxic Work Environments: The Dilemma of the 1978 Pregnancy Amendment to Title VII of the Civil Rights Act of 1964, 66 Iowa L.Rev. 63 (1980); Becker, supra, at 1244.

WILSON v. SOUTHWEST AIRLINES CO.

United States District Court, Northern District of Texas, 1981.
517 F.Supp. 292.

PATRICK E. HIGGINBOTHAM, District Judge.

This case presents the important question whether femininity, or more accurately female sex appeal, is a bona fide occupational qualification ("BFOQ") for the jobs of flight attendant and ticket agent with Southwest Airlines. Plaintiff Gregory Wilson and the class of over 100 male job applicants he represents have challenged Southwest's open refusal to hire males as a violation of Title VII of the Civil Rights Act of 1964, *as amended,* 42 U.S.C. § 2000e *et seq.*

* * *

Barely intact, Southwest, in early 1971, called upon a Dallas advertising agency, the Bloom Agency, to develop a winning marketing strategy. Planning to initiate service quickly, Southwest needed instant recognition and a "catchy" image to distinguish it from its competitors.

The Bloom Agency evaluated both the images of the incumbent competitor airlines as well as the characteristics of passengers to be served by a commuter airline. Bloom determined that the other carriers serving the Texas market tended to project an image of conservatism. The agency also determined that the relatively short haul commuter market which Southwest hoped to serve was comprised of predominantly male businessmen. Based on these factors, Bloom suggested that Southwest break away from the conservative image of other airlines and project to the traveling public an airline personification of feminine youth and vitality. A specific female personality description was recommended and adopted by Southwest for its corporate image:

> This lady is young and vital * * * she is charming and goes through life with great flair and exuberance * * * you notice first her exciting smile, friendly air, her wit * * * yet she is quite efficient and approaches all her tasks with care and attention * * *.

From the personality description suggested by The Bloom Agency, Southwest developed its now famous "Love" personality. Southwest projects an image of feminine spirit, fun and sex appeal. Its ads promise to provide "tender loving care" to its predominantly male, business passengers. The first advertisements run by the airline featured the slogan, "AT LAST THERE IS SOMEBODY ELSE UP THERE WHO LOVES YOU." Variations on this theme have continued through newspaper, billboard, magazine and television advertisements during the past ten years.

* * *

As an integral part of its youthful, feminine image, Southwest has employed only females in the high customer contact positions of ticket agent and flight attendant. From the start, Southwest's attractive personnel, dressed in high boots and hot-pants, generated public interest and "free ink." Their sex appeal has been used to attract male customers to the airline. Southwest's flight attendants, and to a lesser degree its ticket agents, have been featured in newspaper, magazine, billboard and television advertisements during the past ten years. * * * The airline also encourages its attendants to entertain the passengers and maintain an atmosphere of informality and "fun" during flights. According to Southwest, its female flight attendants have come to "personify" Southwest's public image.

Southwest has enjoyed enormous success in recent years. This is in no small part due to its marketing image.

* * *

Less certain, however, is Southwest's assertion that its females-only hiring policy is necessary for the continued success of its image and its business. Based on two onboard surveys, one conducted in October, 1979, before this suit was filed, and another in August, 1980, when the suit was pending, Southwest contends its attractive flight attendants are the "largest single component" of its success. In the 1979 survey, however, of the attributes considered most important by passengers, the category "courteous and attentive hostesses" ranked fifth in importance behind (1) on time departures, (2) frequently scheduled departures, (3) friendly and helpful reservations and ground personnel, and (4) convenient departure times. Apparently, one of the remaining eight alternative categories, "attractive hostesses," was not selected with sufficient frequency to warrant being included in the reported survey results.

* * *

The 1980 survey proves nothing more. Indeed, rather than Southwest's female personnel being the "sole factor" distinguishing the airline from its competitors, as Defendant contends, the 1980 survey lists Southwest's "personnel" as only one among five characteristics contributing to Southwest's public image. Accordingly, there is no persuasive proof that Southwest's passengers prefer female over male flight attendants and ticket agents, or, of greater importance, that they would be less likely to fly Southwest if males were hired.

In evaluating Southwest's BFOQ defense, therefore, the Court proceeds on the basis that "love," while important, is not everything in the relationship between Defendant and its passengers. Still, it is proper to infer from the airline's competitive successes that Southwest's overall "love image" has enhanced its ability to attract passengers. To the extent the airline has successfully feminized its image and made attractive females an integral part of its public face, it also follows that femininity and sex appeal are qualities related to successful job performance by Southwest's flight attendants and ticket agents. The strength of this relationship has not been proved. It is with this factual orientation that the Court turns to examine Southwest's BFOQ defense.

* * *

Congress provided sparse evidence of its intent when enacting the BFOQ exception to Title VII.[12] The only relevant remarks from the floor of the House were those of Representative Goodell of New York who proposed adding "sex" as a BFOQ category after sex was designated a prohibited classification under Title VII. [He] stated:

> There are so many instances where the matter of sex is a bona fide occupational qualification. For instance, I think of an elderly woman who wants a female nurse. There are many things of this nature which are bona fide occupational qualifications, and it seems to me they would be properly considered here as an exception.

110 Cong.Rec. 2718 (1964).

---

12. Because sex was added as a prohibited classification in a last minute attempt by opponents to block passage of the Civil Rights Bill, House consideration of the BFOQ exception for sex was limited to the final day for House debate on the Bill. *See* 110 Cong.Rec. 2577 (remarks of Rep. Smith), 2581–82 (remarks of Rep. Green) (1964). *See also Barnes v. Costle,* 561 F.2d 983, 987 (D.C.Cir.1977); Sirota, "Sex Discrimination Title VII and the Bona Fide Occupational Qualification," 55 Tex.L.Rev. 1025, 1027 (1977).

Most often relied upon as a source of legislative intent is the Interpretative Memorandum of Title VII submitted by the Senate Floor Managers of the Civil Rights Bill. 110 Cong.Rec. 7212 (1964). The Memorandum referred to the BFOQ as a "limited exception" to the Act's prohibition against discrimination, conferring upon employers a "limited right to discriminate on the basis of religion, sex, or national origin where the reason for the discrimination is a bona fide occupational qualification." *Id.* at 7213. As examples of "legitimate discrimination," the memorandum cited "the preference of a French restaurant for a French cook, the preference of a professional baseball team for male players, and the preference of a business which seeks the patronage of members of particular religious groups for a salesman of that religion * * *." *Id.* In *Dothard v. Rawlinson,* 433 U.S [321, 334, 97 S.Ct. 2720, 2729 53 L.Ed.2d 786], the Court cited the Memorandum in support of its conclusion that Congress intended the BFOQ as an "extremely narrow exception" to Title VII's prohibition against sex discrimination, ignoring Representative Goodell's broader construction.

* * *

[As the Fifth Circuit stated:]

[T]he use of the word "necessary" in Section 703(e) requires that we apply a business *necessity* test, not a business *convenience* test. That is to say, discrimination based on sex is valid only when the *essence* of the business operation would be undermined by not hiring members of one sex exclusively.

[*Diaz v. Pan American World Airways,* 442 F.2d 385, 388 (5th Cir.1971), cert. denied, 404 U.S. 950, 92 S.Ct. 275, 30 L.Ed.2d 267 (1971) (original emphasis)].

Southwest concedes with respect to the test [of *Weeks v. Southern Bell Tel. & Tel. Co.,* 408 F.2d 228 (5th Cir.1969),] that males are able to perform safely and efficiently all the basic, mechanical functions required of flight attendants and ticket agents. * * *

A similar, though not identical, argument [to Southwest's] that females could better perform certain non-mechanical functions required of flight attendants was rejected in *Diaz.* There, the airline argued and the trial court found that being female was a BFOQ because women were superior in "providing reassurance to anxious passengers, giving courteous personalized service and, in general, making flights as pleasurable as possible within the limitations imposed by aircraft operations." Although it accepted the trial court findings, the Court of Appeals reversed, holding that femininity was not a BFOQ, because catering to passengers psychological needs was only "tangential" to what was "reasonably *necessary*" for the business involved (original emphasis). [442 F.2d] at 388.

* * *

Diaz and its progeny establish that to recognize a BFOQ for jobs requiring multiple abilities, some sex-linked and some sex-neutral, the sex-linked aspects of the job must predominate. Only then will an employer have satisfied *Weeks'* requirement that sex be so essential to successful job performance that a member of the opposite sex could not perform the job. An illustration of such dominance in sex cases is the exception recognized by the EEOC for authenticity and genuineness. * * * In the example given in [the EEOC Guidelines] § 1604.2(a)(2), that of an actor or actress, the primary function of the position, its essence, is to fulfill the audience's expectation and desire for a particular role, characterized by particular physical or emotional traits. Generally, a male could not supply the authenticity required to perform a female role. Similarly, in jobs where sex or vicarious sexual recreation is the primary service provided, *e.g.* a social escort or topless dancer, the job automatically calls for one sex exclusively; the employee's sex and the service provided are inseparable. Thus, being female has been deemed a BFOQ for the position of a Playboy Bunny, female sexuality being reasonably necessary to perform the dominant purpose of the job which is forthrightly to titillate and entice male customers. *See St. Cross v. Playboy Club,* Appeal No. 773, Case No. CFS 22618–70 (New York Human Rights Appeal Board, 1971) (dicta); *Weber v. Playboy Club,* Appeal No. 774, Case No. CFS 22619–70 (New York Human Rights Appeal Board, 1971) (dicta). One court has also suggested, without holding, that the authenticity exception would give rise to a BFOQ for Chinese nationality where necessary to maintain the authentic atmosphere of an ethnic Chinese restaurant, *Utility Workers v. Southern California Edison,* 320 F.Supp. 1262, 1265 (C.D.Cal.1970). Consistent with the language of *Diaz,* customer preference for one sex only in such a case would logically be so strong that the employer's ability to perform the primary function or service offered would be undermined by not hiring members of the authentic sex or group exclusively.

The Court is aware of only one decision where sex was held to be a BFOQ for an occupation not providing primarily sex oriented services. In *Fernandez v. Wynn Oil Co.,* 20 FEP Cases 1162 (C.D.Cal.1979), the court approved restricting to males the job of international marketing director for a company with extensive overseas operations. The position involved primarily attracting and transacting business with Latin American and Southeast Asian customers who would not feel comfortable doing business with a woman. The court found that the customers' attitudes, customs, and mores relating to the proper business roles of the sexes created formidable obstacles to successful job performance by a woman. South American distributors and customers, for example, would have been offended by a woman conducting business meetings in her hotel room. Applying the *Diaz* test, the court concluded that hiring a female as international marketing director "would have totally subverted any business [defendant] hoped to accomplish in those areas of the world." *Id.* at 1165. Because hiring a male was *necessary* to the Defendant's ability to continue its foreign operations, sex was deemed a BFOQ for the marketing position.

* * *

While possession of female allure and sex appeal have been made qualifications for Southwest's contact personnel by virtue of the "love" campaign, the functions served by employee sexuality in Southwest's operations are not dominant ones. According to Southwest, female sex appeal serves two purposes: (1) attracting and entertaining male passengers and (2) fulfilling customer expectations for female service engendered by Southwest's advertising which features female personnel. As in *Diaz,* these non-mechanical, sex-linked job functions are only "tangential" to the essence of the occupations and business involved. Southwest is not a business where vicarious sex entertainment is the primary service provided. Accordingly, the ability of the airline to perform its primary business function, the transportation of passengers, would not be jeopardized by hiring males.

* * *

It is also relevant that Southwest's female image was adopted at its discretion, to promote a business unrelated to sex. Contrary to the unyielding South American preference for males encountered by the Defendant company in *Fernandez,* Southwest exploited, indeed nurtured, the very customer preference for females it now cites to justify discriminating against males. Moreover, the fact that a vibrant marketing campaign was necessary to distinguish Southwest in its early years does not lead to the conclusion that sex discrimination was then, or is now, a business *necessity.* Southwest's claim that its female image will be tarnished by hiring males is, in any case, speculative at best.

* * *

* * * Similarly, a potential loss of profits or possible loss of competitive advantage following a shift to non-discriminatory hiring does not establish business necessity under *Diaz.* To hold otherwise would permit employers within the same industry to establish different hiring standards based on the financial condition of their respective businesses. A rule prohibiting only financially successful enterprises from discriminating under Title VII, while allowing their less successful competitors to ignore the law, has no merit.

Notes and Questions

1. *Use of the "Business Essence" Test to Restrict Marketing Techniques?* As suggested by the *Wilson* decision, the "business essence" test was first formulated in the Fifth Circuit's *Diaz* decision, which also concerned an airline's preference for female flight attendants. What is the justification for its use in *Diaz* and *Wilson* to restrict how an employer defines the product or products that it offers for sale? To second-guess an employer's good-faith business judgment that certain marketing strategies may contribute to

profits at a particular point in the firm's development? Why should an employer be barred from selling psychological comfort (*Diaz*) or, more candidly, even sexual flirtation (*Wilson*) along with basic transportation services? Would *Wilson* have been decided differently if the airline's marketing research had demonstrated that female flight attendants continued to be very important to the company's success?

2. *Does Title VII Proscribe the Selling of Sex?* Can *Wilson*, and perhaps implicitly *Diaz*, be best understood as prohibiting the sale of sexual flirtation in certain businesses? Should Title VII be read to effect such a prohibition? Do you agree with the following argument: "While the selling of sex in our society ostensibly may offer more exclusive employment opportunities to women, such practices nevertheless further entrench sexual stereotypes that contribute substantially, though indirectly, to the inferior economic position of women."? If so, was the litigation challenging the female-only table attendant policy of the Hooters restaurant chain meritorious? See, e.g., Latuga v. Hooters, 64 EPD ¶ 43,094 (N.D.Ill.1994). Might there be some industries or firms more legitimately concerned with projecting a sexually tinged "image" than others, even if that image is not the only or even dominant "product" being sold? See Kimberly A. Yuracko, Private Nurses and Playboy Bunnies: Explaining Permissible Sex Discrimination, 92 Cal. L. Rev. 147 (2004).

3. *National Origin vs. Sex–BFOQ.* Note that the BFOQ defense is also available for national origin-based discrimination. Should a Chinese restaurant be able to employ as waiters only those of Chinese descent to preserve an "authentic atmosphere"? If so, should an employer be able to replace female waitresses with male waiters in order to "upgrade" its reputation? Are these two cases distinguishable? What if the second restaurant claims that it wants to effect the authentic atmosphere of an expensive Parisian eatery where all the table attendants are male? See Levendos v. Stern Entertainment, Inc., 723 F.Supp. 1104, 1107 (W.D.Pa.1989), reversed on other grounds, 909 F.2d 747 (3d Cir.1990) (sex is not a BFOQ for server at high-class restaurant). See also EEOC v. Joe's Stone Crab, Inc., 136 F.Supp.2d 1311 (S.D. Fla.2001), affirmed in relevant part, 296 F.3d 1265 (11th Cir. 2002) (Title VII violated by restaurant's preference for male table attendants to effect a European style).

Consider also the Fernandez v. Wynn Oil decision discussed in the *Wilson* opinion. Is that holding consistent with *Diaz* and *Wilson?* Could the *Fernandez* ruling be confined to the international marketing context? Is this a principled line to draw given the clarification in § 109 of the Civil Rights Act of 1991 that Title VII covers citizens employed by American corporations abroad? *Fernandez* was reversed on appeal, 653 F.2d 1273 (9th Cir.1981). See also Ward v. Westland Plastics, Inc., 651 F.2d 1266 (9th Cir.1980).

4. *Privacy BFOQ?* The courts have accepted in limited settings customer preferences based on privacy concerns as justifications for sex-based hiring or job assignments. See, e.g., Everson v. Michigan Dept. of Corrections, 391 F.3d 737 (6th Cir. 2004) (the privacy and security of female inmates justifies hiring only female guards for prison housing units); Jennings v. New York State Office of Mental Health, 786 F.Supp. 376, 380 (S.D.N.Y.1992) (sex-based staffing assignments to protect privacy of patients

in a mental hospital); Brooks v. ACF Industries, Inc., 537 F.Supp. 1122 (S.D.W.Va.1982) (sex-based hiring of attendants in bath and changing rooms); but cf. EEOC v. Sedita, 816 F.Supp. 1291 (N.D.Ill.1993) (requiring trial on question of whether exclusively female workforce was essential to female health club's business). Notwithstanding the courts' sympathy to privacy concerns, however, the EEOC guidelines, without addressing privacy, continue to provide that the preferences of clients or customers never establish a BFOQ, except for the purpose of authenticity, such as for actors and actresses. See 29 C.F.R. § 1604.2(a)(1)(iii).

5. *Documented Customer Preferences as Grounds for a BFOQ Defense?* Even if a marketing survey demonstrating the importance of female flight attendants to Southwest's predominantly male passengers could not have justified its hiring policy, might market research provide justification in other cases? Consider, for instance, a ratings-conscious television station's decision to replace with a younger woman an older female coanchor while retaining its equally old male coanchor. Ostensibly, this seems to be both sex-plus and age-plus discrimination because the station seems to have treated the incumbent male coanchor differently on the basis of sex and the new female coanchor differently on the basis of age. Could the station nonetheless justify its decision by market research that demonstrated the unpopularity of the discharged older female? Cf. Craft v. Metromedia, 766 F.2d 1205 (8th Cir.1985) (partial reliance on market survey to find no discrimination). What if that research indicated that she was unpopular precisely because the public wanted to see a younger woman with the older male coanchor? If the research indicated only that the public generally prefers that women serving as television news anchors be relatively young, without also indicating that the particular discharged older woman was unpopular or responsible for reduced ratings? Can stations justify on the basis of market research hiring one member of each sex to be coanchors?

6. *Psychological Needs or Problems of Customers as Grounds for a BFOQ Defense?* If customer preferences based on sex-based stereotypes or even sexual drives normally cannot provide a basis for a BFOQ defense, can sexually charged psychological problems? For instance, should a psychiatric hospital housing emotionally disturbed patients, some of whom had been sexually abused, be able to make shift assignments on the basis of gender in order to provide both male and female "role models" and confidants for patients of both sexes? See Healey v. Southwood Psychiatric Hospital, 78 F.3d 128 (3d Cir.1996) (accepting BFOQ defense). Should a maximum security women's prison be able to hire only female correctional officers because of expert opinion that the power relationship between male guards and female prisoners could hamper the rehabilitation of prisoners who have suffered unhealthy domination by males? See Torres v. Wisconsin Dept. of Health & Social Services, 859 F.2d 1523 (7th Cir.1988) (en banc) (accepting BFOQ defense).

Do these cases represent an acceptance of customers' sex-based prejudices as a justification for discrimination? Were the decisions supported by the Supreme Court's 1977 ruling in *Dothard* to allow Alabama, based on safety concerns, to hire only male guards for maximum security prisons housing sex offenders who were thought to be more likely to attack females? Does *Dothard* itself represent an acceptance of prison "customer" prejudices and stereotypes as a justification for discrimination? Does allowance of a sex-BFOQ in these limited settings, where the "customers" are patients or prisoners rather than market participants, undermine Title VII goals?

E. SEX–BASED STEREOTYPING

PRICE WATERHOUSE v. HOPKINS
Supreme Court of the United States, 1989.
490 U.S. 228, 109 S.Ct. 1775, 104 L.Ed.2d 268.

JUSTICE BRENNAN announced the judgment of the Court and delivered an opinion, in which JUSTICE MARSHALL, JUSTICE BLACKMUN, and JUSTICE STEVENS join.

* * *

Ann Hopkins had worked at Price Waterhouse's Office of Government Services in Washington, D.C., for five years when the partners in that office proposed her as a candidate for partnership. Of the 662 partners at the firm at that time, 7 were women. Of the 88 persons proposed for partnership that year, only 1—Hopkins—was a woman. Forty-seven of these candidates were admitted to the partnership, 21 were rejected, and 20—including Hopkins—were "held" for reconsideration the following year. Thirteen of the 32 partners who had submitted comments on Hopkins supported her bid for partnership. Three partners recommended that her candidacy be placed on hold, eight stated that they did not have an informed opinion about her, and eight recommended that she be denied partnership.

In a jointly prepared statement supporting her candidacy, the partners in Hopkins' office showcased her successful 2–year effort to secure a $25 million contract with the Department of State, labeling it "an outstanding performance" and one that Hopkins carried out "virtually at the partner level." Despite Price Waterhouse's attempt at trial to minimize her contribution to this project, Judge Gesell specifically found that Hopkins had "played a key role in Price Waterhouse's successful effort to win a multi-million dollar contract with the Department of State." Indeed, he went on, "[n]one of the other partnership candidates at Price Waterhouse that year had a comparable record in terms of successfully securing major contracts for the partnership."

The partners in Hopkins' office praised her character as well as her accomplishments, describing her in their joint statement as "an outstanding professional" who had a "deft touch," a "strong character, independence and integrity." Clients appear to have agreed with these assessments. At trial, one official from the State Department described her as "extremely competent, intelligent," "strong and forthright, very productive, energetic and creative." Another high-ranking official praised Hopkins' decisiveness, broadmindedness, and "intellectual clarity"; she was, in his words, "a stimulating conversationalist." Evaluations such as these led Judge Gesell to conclude that Hopkins "had no difficulty dealing with clients and her clients appear to have been very pleased with her work" and that she "was generally viewed as a highly competent project leader who worked long hours, pushed vigorously to meet deadlines and demanded much from the multidisciplinary staffs with which she worked."

On too many occasions, however, Hopkins' aggressiveness apparently spilled over into abrasiveness. Staff members seem to have borne the brunt of Hopkins' brusqueness. Long before her bid for partnership, partners evaluating her work had counseled her to improve her relations with staff members. Although later evaluations indicate an improvement, Hopkins' perceived shortcomings in this important area eventually doomed her bid for partnership. Virtually all of the partners' negative remarks about Hopkins—even those of partners supporting her—had to do with her "interpersonal skills." Both "[s]upporters and opponents of her candidacy," stressed Judge Gesell, "indicated that she was sometimes overly aggressive, unduly harsh, difficult to work with and impatient with staff."

There were clear signs, though, that some of the partners reacted negatively to Hopkins' personality because she was a woman. One partner described her as "macho"; another suggested that she "overcompensated for being a woman"; a third advised her to take "a course at charm school." Several partners criticized her use of profanity; in response, one partner suggested that those partners objected to her swearing only "because it[']s a lady using foul language." Another supporter explained that Hopkins "ha[d] matured from a tough-talking somewhat masculine hardnosed mgr to an authoritative, formidable, but much more appealing lady ptr candidate." But it was the man who, as Judge Gesell found, bore responsibility for explaining to Hopkins the reasons for the Policy Board's decision to place her candidacy on hold who delivered the *coup de grace:* in order to improve her chances for partnership, Thomas Beyer advised, Hopkins should "walk more femininely, talk more femininely, dress more femininely, wear make-up, have her hair styled, and wear jewelry."

* * *

Judge Gesell found that Price Waterhouse legitimately emphasized interpersonal skills in its partnership decisions, and also found that the firm had not fabricated its complaints about Hopkins' interpersonal skills as a pretext for discrimination. Moreover, he concluded, the firm did not give decisive emphasis to such traits only because Hopkins was a woman; although there were male candidates who lacked these skills but who were admitted to partnership, the judge found that these candidates possessed other, positive traits that Hopkins lacked.

The judge went on to decide, however, that some of the partners' remarks about Hopkins stemmed from an impermissibly cabined view of the proper behavior of women, and that Price Waterhouse had done nothing to disavow reliance on such comments. He held that Price Waterhouse had unlawfully discriminated against Hopkins on the basis of sex by consciously giving credence and effect to partners' comments that resulted from sex stereotyping. Noting that Price Waterhouse could avoid equitable relief by proving by clear and convincing evidence that it would have placed Hopkins' candidacy on hold even absent this discrimination, the judge decided that the firm had not carried this heavy burden.

The Court of Appeals affirmed the District Court's ultimate conclusion, but departed from its analysis in one particular: it held that even if a plaintiff proves that discrimination played a role in an employment decision, the defendant will not be found liable if it proves, by clear and convincing evidence, that it would have made the same decision in the absence of discrimination. * * *

[*Eds.* The plurality's treatment of the causation issue, see Desert Palace, Inc. v. Costa, 539 U.S. 90, 123 S.Ct. 2148, 156 L.Ed.2d 84 (2003), pp. 75–80 supra, is omitted.]

In saying that gender played a motivating part in an employment decision, we mean that, if we asked the employer at the moment of the decision what its reasons were and if we received a truthful response, one of those reasons would be that the applicant or employee was a woman. In the specific context of sex stereotyping, an employer who acts on the basis of a belief that a woman cannot be aggressive, or that she must not be, has acted on the basis of gender. * * * An employer who objects to aggressiveness in women but whose positions require this trait places women in an intolerable and impermissible Catch–22: out of a job if they behave aggressively and out of a job if they don't. Title VII lifts women out of this bind.

Remarks at work that are based on sex stereotypes do not inevitably prove that gender played a part in a particular employment decision. The plaintiff must show that the employer actually relied on her gender in making its decision. In making this showing, stereotyped remarks can certainly be *evidence* that gender played a part. In any event, the stereotyping in this case did not simply consist of stray remarks. On the contrary, Hopkins proved that Price Waterhouse invited partners to submit comments; that some of the comments stemmed from sex stereotypes; that an important part of the Policy Board's decision on Hopkins was an assessment of the submitted comments; and that Price Waterhouse in no way disclaimed reliance on the sex-linked evaluation. This is not, as Price Waterhouse suggests, "discrimination in the air"; rather, it is, as Hopkins puts it, "discrimination brought to ground and visited upon" an employee. By focusing on Hopkins' specific proof, however, we do not suggest a limitation on the possible ways of proving that stereotyping played a motivating role in an employment decision, and we refrain from deciding here which specific facts, "standing alone," would or would not establish a plaintiff's case, since such a decision is unnecessary in this case. * * *

The District Court found that sex stereotyping "was permitted to play a part" in the evaluation of Hopkins as a candidate for partnership.

Price Waterhouse disputes both that stereotyping occurred and that it played any part in the decision to place Hopkins' candidacy on hold. In the firm's view, in other words, the District Court's factual conclusions are clearly erroneous. We do not agree. * * * It takes no special training to discern sex stereotyping in a description of an aggressive female employee as requiring "a course at charm school." Nor, turning to Thomas Beyer's memorable advice to Hopkins, does it require expertise in psychology to know that, if an employee's flawed "interpersonal skills" can be corrected by a soft-hued suit or a new shade of lipstick, perhaps it is the employee's sex and not her interpersonal skills that has drawn the criticism.

* * *

Nor is the finding that sex stereotyping played a part in the Policy Board's decision undermined by the fact that many of the suspect comments were made by supporters rather than detractors of Hopkins. A negative comment, even when made in the context of a generally favorable review, nevertheless may influence the decisionmaker to think less highly of the candidate; the Policy Board, in fact, did not simply tally the "yes's" and "no's" regarding a candidate, but carefully reviewed the content of the submitted comments. The additional suggestion that the comments were made by "persons outside the decisionmaking chain"— and therefore could not have harmed Hopkins—simply ignores the critical role that partners' comments played in the Policy Board's partnership decisions.

* * * It is not our job to review the evidence and decide that the negative reactions to Hopkins were based on reality; our perception of Hopkins' character is irrelevant. We sit not to determine whether Ms. Hopkins is nice, but to decide whether the partners reacted negatively to her personality because she is a woman.

[*Eds.* The concurring opinions of Justice White and Justice O'Connor are omitted here. For Justice O'Connor's opinion, see p. 435 infra.]

JUSTICE KENNEDY, with whom the CHIEF JUSTICE and JUSTICE SCALIA join, dissenting.

Although the District Court's version of Title VII liability is improper under any of today's opinions, I think it important to stress that Title VII creates no independent cause of action for sex stereotyping. Evidence of use by decisionmakers of sex stereotypes is, of course, quite relevant to the question of discriminatory intent. The ultimate question, however, is whether discrimination caused the plaintiff's harm. Our cases do not support the suggestion that failure to "disclaim reliance" on stereotypical comments itself violates Title VII. Neither do they support creation of a "duty to sensitize." As the dissenting judge in the Court of Appeals observed, acceptance of such theories would turn Title VII "from a prohibition of discriminatory conduct into an engine for rooting out sexist thoughts."

Notes and Questions

1. *Two Kinds of Stereotypes.* Justice Brennan in his plurality opinion states that "an employer who acts on the basis of a belief that a woman *cannot* be aggressive, or that she *must not* be, has acted on the basis of gender" (emphasis added). Is there any difference between stereotypes that express an actor's belief about the reality of what women *can* do and stereotypes that express an actor's normative values about what women *should* do? What type of stereotype did the trial judge find to have influenced the Price Waterhouse partners? Are employment decisions influenced by either of these two types of stereotypes always illegal, at least in the absence of a BFOQ defense?

a. *Descriptive Stereotypes.* Employment decisionmakers' beliefs about the capabilities of women, or of minority groups protected by Title VII, may be difficult to prove. It may be even more difficult to prove that any such beliefs actually influenced a particular employment decision. If such proof can be made, however, is there any good argument against finding Title VII liability, at least in the absence of a BFOQ defense? Even if the stereotype has some rough basis in reality? Would liability not exist in all cases where racial descriptive stereotypes were shown to have influenced an adverse employment decision? Does Justice Kennedy have a different view, or does he want to emphasize only that a stereotype must be proven to have caused an adverse decision?

b. *Normative Stereotypes.* Are all normative sex-based stereotypes condemned by the holding in *Price Waterhouse,* concurred in by Justices White and O'Connor as well as the plurality, that denying Hopkins a partnership because of her failure to act "more femininely" would violate Title VII? Was there anything distinctive about the normative stereotyping of women by the Price Waterhouse partners that denied women equal opportunities for advancement? Presumably any adverse employment decision influenced by any normative race-based stereotypes is prohibited by Title VII. Is there any reason to treat sex-based stereotypes differently? Consider also the following notes.

2. *Grooming Codes.* Many employers either expressly or in practice require employees to conform to different standards of grooming for men and women. Most of the standards, such as hair length for men and dresses for women, conform to general social standards for male and female appearance. Individuals who do not conform to such social expectations may alienate others, including any customers with whom they have contact and fellow employees. Do such codes constitute a form of normative sexual stereotyping? The courts have held after *Price Waterhouse* that general grooming codes do not violate Title VII as long as they impose roughly the same aggregate burden on women and men. See, e.g., Jespersen v. Harrah's Operating Co., 444 F.3d 1104 (9th Cir. 2006) (en banc) (requiring only female bartenders to wear makeup not actionable where plaintiff did not present evidence that policy was "more burdensome for women than for men" or required her "to conform to a stereotypical image that would objectively impede her ability to perform her job"); Frank v. United Airlines, Inc., 216 F.3d 845 (9th Cir. 2000); Harper v. Blockbuster Entertainment

Corp., 139 F.3d 1385 (11th Cir. 1998); Tavora v. New York Mercantile Exchange, 101 F.3d 907, 908 (2d Cir.1996). Are these decisions consistent with *Price Waterhouse*? Can one argue that even grooming standards that are equally burdensome on men and women perpetuate stereotypes that may impede the economic advancement of women? See Karl E. Klare, Power/Dressing: Regulation of Employee Appearance, 26 New Eng. L. Rev. 1395 (1992). Are the courts reading some sort of de minimis defense into Title VII?

Even if most general grooming standards do not constitute illegal sex discrimination, how far may an employer go in requiring different grooming standards for men and women? Should an employer be able to require women to wear uniforms, while permitting men to wear generally accepted business attire of their choice? See Carroll v. Talman Federal Sav. & Loan Ass'n of Chicago, 604 F.2d 1028 (7th Cir.1979). What if the uniforms are revealing and prompt sexual harassment from customers and coworkers? See EEOC v. Sage Realty Corp., 507 F.Supp. 599 (S.D.N.Y.1981). Finally, might some sex-neutral grooming requirements be illegal because they have a disparate impact on one sex? For instance, should an employer necessarily be able to impose hair length requirements on both sexes? See generally Marc Linder, Smart Women, Stupid Shoes, and Cynical Employers: The Unlawfulness and Adverse Health Consequences of Sexually Discriminatory Workplace Footwear Requirements for Female Employees, 22 J.Corp.L. 295 (1997); Katharine T. Bartlett, Only Girls Wear Barrettes: Dress and Appearance Standards, Community Norms, and Workplace Equality, 92 Mich. L.Rev. 2541 (1994).

3. *Variant Weight or Height Standards*. Dothard v. Rawlinson, supra page 126, held that an employer cannot impose the same height and weight requirements on men and women if those requirements cannot be justified as a job-related, business necessity under disparate impact analysis. Can an employer, such as an airline hiring flight attendants, impose variant size standards on women and men if the standards proportionately affect members of each sex? Do such variant standards express a normative stereotype about the appropriate size of men and women? Do such standards present a more difficult case than typical grooming standards because they exclude individuals for failing to conform to a standard which they cannot volitionally meet? What business justification could an employer have for having different size standards for men and women? In Frank v. United Airlines, Inc., 216 F.3d 845, 855 (9th Cir.2000), the court held that an airline "may not impose different *and more burdensome* weight standards" on female flight attendants "without justifying those standards as BFOQs." (Emphasis in original) United had chosen weight maximums for women that generally corresponded to the medium frame category in life insurance tables, while choosing maximums for men that corresponded with the large frame category. The court did not decide whether United could have used large frame standards for both men and women. See also Gerdom v. Continental Airlines, 692 F.2d 602 (9th Cir.1982) (illegal to have weight requirement only for women); Laffey v. Northwest Airlines, Inc., 567 F.2d 429 (D.C.Cir.1976) (upholding injunction against discriminatory weight differential).

4. *Sexual Orientation Discrimination*. Does *Price Waterhouse* mean that discrimination on the basis of sexual orientation should be condemned

as illegal sexual stereotyping under Title VII? Does an employer who discriminates on the basis of sexual orientation demand that members of each sex conform to a different normative stereotype of appropriate conduct or character, as males must be sexually oriented toward females, while females must be oriented toward men? Or is this normative stereotype acceptable because it is equally burdensome for each sex?

Although the lower courts have not read *Price Waterhouse* to condemn sexual orientation discrimination under Title VII, see, e.g., Vickers v. Fairfield Med. Ctr., 453 F.3d 757 (6th Cir. 2006) and cases cited on p. 199 supra, several courts of appeals have read the decision to proscribe discrimination against employees because their general behavior is perceived to more closely fit stereotypes of homosexuals rather than that of heterosexuals of their sex. See, e.g, Bibby v. Philadelphia Coca Cola Bottling Co., 260 F.3d 257 (3d Cir.2001); Nichols v. Azteca Restaurant Enterprises, Inc., 256 F.3d 864 (9th Cir.2001); Schmedding v. Tnemec Co., 187 F.3d 862 (8th Cir.1999). Furthermore, in Smith v. Salem, 378 F.3d 566 (6th Cir. 2004), the court held that a fire department discriminated against a male employee with a female sexual identity, a transsexual, because of the employee's feminine appearance and mannerisms:

> After *Price Waterhouse*, an employer who discriminates against women because, for instance, they do not wear dresses or makeup, is engaging in sex discrimination because the discrimination would not occur but for the victim's sex. It follows that employers who discriminate against men because they *do* wear dresses and makeup, or otherwise act femininely, are also engaging in sex discrimination, because the discrimination would not occur but for the victim's sex. . . . [D]iscrimination against a plaintiff who is a transsexual—and therefore fails to act and/or identify with his or her gender—is no different from the discrimination directed against Ann Hopkins in *Price Waterhouse*, who, in sex-stereotypical terms, did not act like a woman. Sex stereotyping based on a person's gender non-conforming behavior is impermissible discrimination, irrespective of the cause of that behavior; a label, such as "transsexual," is not fatal to a sex discrimination claim where the victim has suffered discrimination because of his or her gender non-conformity.

Id. at 574–75. Accord Barnes v. City of Cincinnati, 401 F.3d 729 (6th Cir. 2005). See also Etsitty v. Utah Transit Auth., 502 F.3d 1215 (10th Cir. 2007) (sexual identity is not a status protected by Title VII, but sexual stereotyping may be the basis for cause of action).

Is the distinction embraced by these courts between sexual orientation and sexual identity as non-protected status categories, on the one hand, and impermissable stereotyping, on the other, sensible? Compare Hamm v. Weyauwega Milk Products, Inc., 332 F.3d 1058, 1066 (7th Cir.2003) (Posner, J., concurring, arguing that law has gotten "off the tracks", with Kimberly A. Yuracko, Trait Discrimination as Sex Discrimination: An Argument Against Neutrality, 83 Tex. L. Rev. 167, 235 (2004) (discrimination against effeminate men like discrimination against aggressive women reinforces gender hierarchy in workplace). As these cases involve aspects of sexual harassment, you should consider them further as you read the following section.

F. SEXUAL HARASSMENT

HARRIS v. FORKLIFT SYSTEMS, INC.
Supreme Court of the United States, 1993.
510 U.S. 17, 114 S.Ct. 367, 126 L.Ed.2d 295.

JUSTICE O'CONNOR delivered the opinion of the Court.

In this case we consider the definition of a discriminatorily "abusive work environment" (also known as a "hostile work environment") under Title VII of the Civil Rights Act of 1964.

I

Teresa Harris worked as a manager at Forklift Systems, Inc., an equipment rental company, from April 1985 until October 1987. Charles Hardy was Forklift's president.

The Magistrate found that, throughout Harris' time at Forklift, Hardy often insulted her because of her gender and often made her the target of unwanted sexual innuendos. Hardy told Harris on several occasions, in the presence of other employees, "You're a woman, what do you know" and "We need a man as the rental manager"; at least once, he told her she was "a dumb ass woman." Again in front of others, he suggested that the two of them "go to the Holiday Inn to negotiate [Harris'] raise." Hardy occasionally asked Harris and other female employees to get coins from his front pants pocket. He threw objects on the ground in front of Harris and other women, and asked them to pick the objects up. He made sexual innuendos about Harris' and other women's clothing.

In mid-August 1987, Harris complained to Hardy about his conduct. Hardy said he was surprised that Harris was offended, claimed he was only joking, and apologized. He also promised he would stop, and based on this assurance Harris stayed on the job. Ibid. But in early September, Hardy began anew: While Harris was arranging a deal with one of Forklift's customers, he asked her, again in front of other employees, "What did you do, promise the guy * * * some [sex] Saturday night?" On October 1, Harris collected her paycheck and quit.

Harris then sued Forklift, claiming that Hardy's conduct had created an abusive work environment for her because of her gender. The United States District Court for the Middle District of Tennessee, adopting the report and recommendation of the Magistrate, found this to be "a close case," but held that Hardy's conduct did not create an abusive environment. The court found that some of Hardy's comments "offended [Harris], and would offend the reasonable woman," but that they were not "so severe as to be expected to seriously affect [Harris'] psychological well-being." A reasonable woman manager under like circumstances would have been offended by Hardy, but his conduct would not have risen to the level of interfering with that person's work performance. "Neither do I believe that [Harris] was subjectively so offended that she suffered injury * * *. Although Hardy may at times have genuinely offended [Harris], I do not believe that he created a working environment so poisoned as to be intimidating or abusive to [Harris]."

In focusing on the employee's psychological well-being, the District Court was following Circuit precedent. See *Rabidue v. Osceola Refining Co.*, 805 F.2d 611, 620 (C.A.6 1986), cert. denied, 481 U.S. 1041, 107 S.Ct. 1983, 95 L.Ed.2d 823 (1987). The United States Court of Appeals for the Sixth Circuit affirmed.

* * *

II

Title VII of the Civil Rights Act of 1964 makes it "an unlawful employment practice for an employer * * * to discriminate against any individual with respect to his compensation, terms, conditions, or privileges of employment, because of such individual's race, color, religion, sex, or national origin." 42 U.S.C. § 2000e–2(a)(1). As we made clear in *Meritor Savings Bank v. Vinson,* 477 U.S. 57 (1986), this language "is not limited to 'economic' or 'tangible' discrimination. The phrase 'terms, conditions, or privileges of employment' evinces a congressional intent 'to strike at the entire spectrum of disparate treatment of men and women' in employment," which includes requiring people to work in a discriminatorily hostile or abusive environment. *Id.,* at 64. When the workplace is permeated with "discriminatory intimidation, ridicule, and insult," 477 U.S., at 65, that is "sufficiently severe or pervasive to alter the conditions of the victim's employment and create an abusive working environment," *id.,* at 67, Title VII is violated.

This standard, which we reaffirm today, takes a middle path between making actionable any conduct that is merely offensive and requiring the conduct to cause a tangible psychological injury. As we pointed out in *Meritor*, "mere utterance of an * * * epithet which engenders offensive feelings in a employee" * * * does not sufficiently affect the conditions of employment to implicate Title VII. Conduct that is not severe or pervasive enough to create an objectively hostile or abusive work environment—an environment that a reasonable person would find hostile or abusive—is beyond Title VII's purview. Likewise, if the victim does not subjectively perceive the environment to be abusive, the conduct has not actually altered the conditions of the victim's employment, and there is no Title VII violation.

But Title VII comes into play before the harassing conduct leads to a nervous breakdown. A discriminatorily abusive work environment, even one that does not seriously affect employees' psychological well-being, can and often will detract from employees' job performance, discourage employees from remaining on the job, or keep them from advancing in their careers. Moreover, even without regard to these tangible effects, the very fact that the discriminatory conduct was so severe or pervasive that it created a work environment abusive to employees because of their race, gender, religion, or national origin offends Title VII's broad rule of workplace equality. The appalling conduct alleged in *Meritor*, and the reference in that case to environments " 'so heavily polluted with discrimination as to destroy completely the emotional and psychological stability of minority group workers,' " *supra*, at 66, merely present some especially egregious examples of harassment. They do not mark the boundary of what is actionable.

We therefore believe the District Court erred in relying on whether the conduct "seriously affect[ed] plaintiff's psychological well-being" or led her to "suffe[r] injury." Such an inquiry may needlessly focus the factfinder's attention on concrete psychological harm, an element Title VII does not require. Certainly Title VII bars conduct that would seriously affect a reasonable person's psychological well-being, but the statute is not limited to such conduct. So long as the environment would reasonably be perceived, and is perceived, as hostile or abusive, *Meritor*, supra, 477 U.S., at 67, there is no need for it also to be psychologically injurious.

This is not, and by its nature cannot be, a mathematically precise test. We need not answer today all the potential questions it raises, nor specifically address the EEOC's new regulations on this subject, see 58 Fed.Reg. 51266 (1993) (proposed 29 CFR §§ 1609.1, 1609.2); see also 29 CFR § 1604.11 (1993). But we can say that whether an environment is "hostile" or "abusive" can be determined only by looking at all the circumstances. These may include the frequency of the discriminatory conduct; its severity; whether it is physically threatening or humiliating, or a mere offensive utterance; and whether it unreasonably interferes with an employee's work performance. The effect on the employee's psychological well-being is, of course, relevant to determining whether the plaintiff actually found the environment abusive. But while psychological harm, like any other relevant factor, may be taken into account, no single factor is required.

III

Forklift, while conceding that a requirement that the conduct seriously affect psychological well-being is unfounded, argues that the District Court nonetheless correctly applied the *Meritor* standard. We disagree. Though the District Court did conclude that the work environment was not "intimidating or abusive to [Harris]," it did so only after finding that the conduct was not "so severe as to be expected to seriously affect plaintiff's psychological well-being," and that Harris was not "subjectively so offended that she suffered injury." The District Court's application of these incorrect standards may well have influenced its ultimate conclusion, especially given that the court found this to be a "close case."

We therefore reverse the judgment of the Court of Appeals, and remand the case for further proceedings consistent with this opinion.

JUSTICE SCALIA, concurring. [omitted]

JUSTICE GINSBURG, concurring.

The critical issue, Title VII's text indicates, is whether members of one sex are exposed to disadvantageous terms or conditions of employment to which members of the other sex are not exposed. * * * [T]he adjudicator's inquiry should center, dominantly, on whether the discriminatory conduct has unreasonably interfered with the plaintiff's work performance. To show such interference, "the plaintiff need not prove that his or her tangible productivity has declined as a result of the harassment." *Davis v. Monsanto Chemical Co.*, 858 F.2d 345, 349 (C.A.6 1988). It suffices to prove that a reasonable person subjected to the discriminatory conduct would find, as the plaintiff did, that the harassment so altered working conditions as to "make it more difficult to do the job." See *ibid.*

ONCALE v. SUNDOWNER OFFSHORE SERVICES, INC.

Supreme Court of the United States, 1998.
523 U.S. 75, 118 S.Ct. 998, 140 L.Ed.2d 201.

JUSTICE SCALIA delivered the opinion of the Court.

This case presents the question whether workplace harassment can violate Title VII's prohibition against "discriminat[ion] * * * because of * * * sex," 42 U.S.C. § 2000e–2(a)(1), when the harasser and the harassed employee are of the same sex.

I

The District Court having granted summary judgment for respondent, we must assume the facts to be as alleged by petitioner Joseph Oncale. The precise details are irrelevant to the legal point we must decide, and in the interest of both brevity and dignity we shall describe them only generally. In late October 1991, Oncale was working for respondent Sundowner Offshore Services on a Chevron U. S. A., Inc., oil platform in the Gulf of Mexico. He was employed as a roustabout on an eight-man crew which included respondents John Lyons, Danny Pippen, and Brandon Johnson. Lyons, the crane operator, and Pippen, the driller, had supervisory authority. On several occasions, Oncale was forcibly subjected to sex-related, humiliating actions against him by Lyons, Pippen and Johnson in the presence of the rest of the crew. Pippen and Lyons also physically assaulted Oncale in a sexual manner, and Lyons threatened him with rape.

Oncale's complaints to supervisory personnel produced no remedial action; in fact, the company's Safety Compliance Clerk, Valent Hohen, told Oncale that Lyons and Pippen "picked [on] him all the time too," and called him a name suggesting homosexuality. Oncale eventually quit—asking that his pink slip reflect that he "voluntarily left due to sexual harassment and verbal abuse." When asked at his deposition why he left Sundowner, Oncale stated "I felt that if I didn't leave my job, that I would be raped or forced to have sex."

Oncale filed a complaint against Sundowner in the United States District Court for the Eastern District of Louisiana, alleging that he was discriminated against in his employment because of his sex. Relying on the Fifth Circuit's decision in *Garcia v. Elf Atochem North America*, 28 F.3d 446, 451–452 (C.A.5 1994), the district court held that "Mr. Oncale, a male, has no cause of action under Title VII for harassment by male co-workers." On appeal, a panel of the Fifth Circuit concluded that Garcia was binding Circuit precedent, and affirmed. We granted certiorari.

II

* * *

Title VII's prohibition of discrimination "because of * * * sex" protects men as well as women, *Newport News Shipbuilding & Dry Dock Co. v. EEOC*, 462 U.S. 669, 682, 103 S.Ct. 2622, 2630, 77 L.Ed.2d 89 (1983), and in the related context of racial discrimination in the workplace we have rejected any conclusive presumption that an employer will not discriminate against members of his own race. "Because of the many facets of human motivation, it would be unwise to presume as a matter of law that human beings of one definable group will not discriminate against other members of that group." *Castaneda v. Partida*, 430 U.S. 482, 499, 97 S.Ct. 1272, 1282, 51 L.Ed.2d 498 (1977). * * * In *Johnson v. Transportation Agency, Santa Clara Cty.*, 480 U.S. 616, 107 S.Ct. 1442, 94 L.Ed.2d 615 (1987), a male employee claimed that his employer discriminated against him because of his sex when it preferred a female employee for promotion. Although we ultimately rejected the claim on other grounds, we did not consider it significant that the supervisor who made that decision was also a man. See *id.*, at 624–625, 107 S.Ct., at 1447–1448. If our precedents leave any doubt on the question, we hold today that nothing in Title VII necessarily bars a claim of discrimination "because of * * * sex" merely because the plaintiff and the defendant (or the person charged with acting on behalf of the defendant) are of the same sex.

* * *

We see no justification in the statutory language or our precedents for a categorical rule excluding same-sex harassment claims from the coverage of Title VII. As some courts have observed, male-on-male sexual harassment in the workplace was assuredly not the principal evil Congress was concerned with when it enacted Title VII. But statutory prohibitions often go beyond the principal evil to cover reasonably comparable evils, and it is ultimately the provisions of our laws rather than the principal concerns of our legislators by which we are governed. Title VII prohibits "discriminat[ion] * * * because of * * * sex" in the "terms" or "conditions" of employment. Our holding that this includes sexual harassment must extend to sexual harassment of any kind that meets the statutory requirements.

Respondents and their amici contend that recognizing liability for same-sex harassment will transform Title VII into a general civility code for the American workplace. But that risk is no greater for same-sex than for opposite-sex harassment, and is adequately met by careful attention to the requirements of the statute. Title VII does not prohibit all verbal or physical harassment in the workplace; it is directed only at "discriminat[ion] * * * because of * * * sex." We have never held that workplace harassment, even harassment between men and women, is automatically discrimination because of sex merely because the words used have sexual content or connotations. "The critical issue, Title VII's text indicates, is whether members of one sex are exposed to disadvantageous terms or conditions of employment to which members of the other sex are not exposed." *Harris*, supra, at 25, 114 S.Ct., at 372 (Ginsburg, J., concurring).

Courts and juries have found the inference of discrimination easy to draw in most male-female sexual harassment situations, because the challenged conduct typically involves explicit or implicit proposals of sexual activity; it is reasonable to assume those proposals would not have been made to someone of the same sex. The same chain of inference would be available to a plaintiff alleging same-sex harassment, if there were credible evidence that the harasser was homosexual. But harassing conduct need not be motivated by sexual desire to support an inference of discrimination on the basis of sex. A trier of fact might reasonably find such discrimination, for example, if a female victim is harassed in such sex-specific and derogatory terms by another woman as to make it clear that the harasser is motivated by general hostility to the presence of women in the workplace. A same-sex harassment plaintiff may also, of course, offer direct comparative evidence about how the alleged harasser treated members of both sexes in a mixed-sex workplace. Whatever evidentiary route the plaintiff chooses to follow, he or she must always prove that the conduct at issue was not merely tinged with offensive sexual connotations, but actually constituted "discrimina[tion] * * * because of * * * sex."

And there is another requirement that prevents Title VII from expanding into a general civility code: As we emphasized in *Meritor* and *Harris*, the statute does not reach genuine but innocuous differences in the ways men and women routinely interact with members of the same sex and of the opposite sex. The prohibition of harassment on the basis of sex requires neither asexuality nor androgyny in the workplace; it forbids only behavior so objectively offensive as to alter the "conditions" of the victim's employment. "Conduct that is not severe or pervasive enough to create an objectively hostile or abusive work environment—an environment that a reasonable person would find hostile or abusive—is beyond Title VII's purview." *Harris*, 510 U.S., at 21, 114 S.Ct., at 370, citing *Meritor*, 477 U.S., at 67, 106 S.Ct., at 2405–2406. We have always regarded that requirement as crucial, and as sufficient to ensure that courts and juries do not mistake ordinary socializing in the workplace—

such as male-on-male horseplay or intersexual flirtation—for discriminatory "conditions of employment."

We have emphasized, moreover, that the objective severity of harassment should be judged from the perspective of a reasonable person in the plaintiff's position, considering "all the circumstances." *Harris*, supra, at 23, 114 S.Ct., at 371. In same-sex (as in all) harassment cases, that inquiry requires careful consideration of the social context in which particular behavior occurs and is experienced by its target. A professional football player's working environment is not severely or pervasively abusive, for example, if the coach smacks him on the buttocks as he heads onto the field—even if the same behavior would reasonably be experienced as abusive by the coach's secretary (male or female) back at the office. The real social impact of workplace behavior often depends on a constellation of surrounding circumstances, expectations, and relationships which are not fully captured by a simple recitation of the words used or the physical acts performed. Common sense, and an appropriate sensitivity to social context, will enable courts and juries to distinguish between simple teasing or roughhousing among members of the same sex, and conduct which a reasonable person in the plaintiff's position would find severely hostile or abusive.

Notes and Questions

1. *A Sufficiently Clear Standard?* Note the Court's confirmation in both *Harris* and *Oncale* of its decision in *Meritor* to interpret § 703(a)(1) as "not limited to 'economic' or 'tangible' discrimination", but to "evince[] a congressional intent 'to strike at the entire spectrum of disparate treatment of men and women' in employment." Given this interpretation, can the Court sensibly delineate any bright lines around the kinds of employment discrimination that are actionable under Title VII? Does *Harris* do so? Is Justice Ginsburg's concurring statement clarifying? Given the purposes and language of the statute, could the Court do better? Or must the standard inevitably be vague? If so, is this cause for concern? Does the standard grant too much discretion to juries where they are the finders of fact? Or is significant jury discretion here appropriate? See Theresa M. Beiner, Let the Jury Decide: The Gap Between What Judges and Reasonable People Believe Is Sexually Harassing, 75 S.Cal. L.Rev. 791 (2002) (arguing that judges have exerted excessive control over juries and have a more restrictive view of what is offensive than do most workers).

2. *Application to Racial, Religious and National Origin Harassment.* *Harris* and *Oncale* are both sex discrimination cases, as is *Meritor* on which they relied. *Meritor*, however, itself relies on lower court decisions involving national origin and racial harassment, and suggests that the approach of these cases should be applied to sexual harassment. Does the Court in *Harris* intend its elaboration of the *Meritor* standard to apply to other forms of actionable discrimination under Title VII? Given the language of § 703(a)(1), could the Court appropriately articulate a different standard for other types of discrimination? The lower courts continue to apply harassment law as defined by the Supreme Court to all forms of actionable discriminatory

harassment. See, e.g., Kang v. U. Lim America, Inc., 296 F.3d 810 (9th Cir.2002) (Korean employer's abusive treatment of Korean employee actionable national origin discrimination because employer demanded more of Korean workers); Whidbee v. Garzarelli Food Specialties, Inc., 223 F.3d 62 (2d Cir.2000) (§ 1981 racial harassment claim). See also Pat K. Chew & Robert E. Kelley, Unwrapping Racial Harassment Law, 27 Berk. J. of Emp. & Lab. L. 49 (2006).

3. *"Reasonable Person" vs. "Reasonable Woman" Standard? Harris* states that to be actionable conduct must be "severe or pervasive enough to create * * * an environment that a reasonable person would find hostile or abusive." What is a "reasonable person" in this context: an average person or a model person? Does *Oncale* suggest that what is "reasonable" might vary depending on the working environment? See Conner v. Schrader–Bridgeport Int'l, Inc., 227 F.3d 179 (4th Cir.2000) (work atmosphere relevant to whether plaintiff was treated differently, but there is no "inhospitable environment" exception to discrimination prohibition). Does the *Harris* standard allow courts to take into account, in a sexual harassment case, that the sensibilities of the average woman may vary from those of the average man, or in a racial harassment case, that the sensibilities of an average black may differ from those of an average white? Before *Harris* the EEOC proposed guidelines (since withdrawn) that embraced a "reasonable person" standard, but stated that this standard includes "consideration of the perspective of persons of the alleged victim's race, color, religion, gender, national origin, age, or disability." 58 Fed. Reg. 51266 (Oct. 1, 1993). See also Burns v. McGregor Elec. Indus., 989 F.2d 959, 965 (8th Cir.1993); Ellison v. Brady, 924 F.2d 872, 879 (9th Cir.1991). See generally Gillian K. Hadfield, Rational Women: A Test for Sex–Based Harassment, 83 Calif.L.Rev. 1151 (1995); Jane L. Dolkart, Hostile Environment Harassment: Equality, Objectivity, and the Shaping of Legal Standards, 43 Emory L.J. 151 (1994); Nancy Ehrenreich, Pluralist Myths and Powerless Men: The Ideology of Reasonableness in Sexual Harassment Law, 99 Yale L.J. 1177, 1207–08 (1990); Kathryn Abrams, Gender Discrimination and the Transformation of Workplace Norms, 42 Vand.L.Rev. 1183, 1209–10 (1989).

4. *"Severe or Pervasive"*. Does this phrase mean that some conduct that would be actionable if engaged in repeatedly is not actionable if only represented in isolated incidents? See, e.g., Clark County Sch. Dist. v. Breeden, 532 U.S. 268, 121 S.Ct. 1508, 149 L.Ed.2d 509 (2001) (plaintiff could not reasonably believe that isolated joke at a group meeting could be actionable harassment); Chamberlin v. 101 Realty, Inc., 915 F.2d 777 (1st Cir.1990) (individual sexual proposition not actionable). On the other hand, does the use of the disjunctive word "or" in this phrase indicate that some conduct is sufficiently hostile that only one or two incidents may create an actionable work environment? See, e.g., Little v. Windermere Relocation, Inc., 301 F.3d 958 (9th Cir.2002) (single incident of rape sufficient); Howley v. Town of Stratford, 217 F.3d 141 (2d Cir.2000) (single verbal sexual harassment could be sufficiently severe); Vance v. Southern Bell Tel. & Tel. Co., 863 F.2d 1503 (11th Cir.1989) (noose hung twice over plaintiff's work station may have created racially hostile work environment). But cf. Ann Juliano & Stewart J. Schwab, The Sweep of Sexual Harassment Cases, 86

Corn. L.Rev. 548 (2001) (empirical study finding only 4% of cases involving a single incident).

5. *The Plaintiff's Subjective Perception. Harris* holds that to be actionable the work environment not only must be "objectively hostile or abusive", but also must be "subjectively" so perceived by the plaintiff. On what evidence might a defendant rely to contest a plaintiff's claim that she perceived conduct around her to be hostile, when such a perception would have been objectively "reasonable"? Should it be relevant that the plaintiff participated in the activity or speech that she claims to find offensive? What if the plaintiff engaged in sexual flirtation and banter, but objects to a more extreme and sexually demeaning or misogynist turn taken by some of her coworkers? Compare Carr v. Allison Gas Turbine Div., General Motors Corp., 32 F.3d 1007, 1010 (7th Cir.1994), with Reed v. Shepard, 939 F.2d 484, 490–91 (7th Cir.1991). Should proof of the plaintiff's sexual activity away from the workplace with people other than her alleged harasser be relevant? See Susan Estrich, Sex at Work, 43 Stan. L.Rev. 813, 848–49 (1991). See also Rule 412 of the Federal Rules of Evidence (making inadmissible in trials relating to sexual misconduct "evidence offered to prove that any alleged victim engaged in other sexual behavior * * * [or] * * * to prove any alleged victim's sexual predisposition * * * [unless] its probative value substantially outweighs the danger of harm to any victim and of unfair prejudice").

In *Meritor* a bank employee alleged that she was pressured to engage in sexual relations with her supervisor, a branch office manager. The Court held that the plaintiff's "voluntary" participation in sexual activity would not insulate that activity from being actionable if the plaintiff nonetheless could demonstrate that the activity was "unwelcome." What is the difference between "voluntary" and "welcome" participation? Is a voluntary act simply one that is not physically coerced? The *Meritor* Court stated that "a complainant's sexually provocative speech or dress" is relevant "in determining whether he or she found particular sexual advances unwelcome." Do you agree? Should a woman who dresses in a certain fashion and talks openly about her sexual desires have to say "No" more often and more forcefully to establish that particular sexual advances are unwelcome? See also Swentek v. USAIR, Inc., 830 F.2d 552, 557 (4th Cir.1987) (plaintiff's use of foul language and sexual innuendo to individuals other than aggressor does not make "welcome" aggressor's sexual advances). See generally Henry L. Chambers, Jr., (Un)Welcome Conduct and the Sexually Hostile Environment, 53 Ala. L.Rev. 733 (2002).

6. *The Requirement of "Discrimination".* The *Oncale* Court stresses that to be actionable under Title VII workplace harassment also must be "discrimination because of sex", or because of some other protected status category. Does this mean that if Oncale's sister had worked with him on the oil platform and also had been subjected to sexual taunts, threats, and assaults, neither would have a cause of action under Title VII? Does it mean that a bisexual employer who sexually coerces employees of both sexes does not thereby violate Title VII? See Holman v. Indiana, 211 F.3d 399 (7th Cir. 2000) (sexual harassment of both husband and wife not actionable because not discriminatory). Is there some theory of discrimination that could reach these cases? Or does the *Oncale* Court reject the suggestion, made in Doe v.

Belleville, 119 F.3d 563 (7th Cir.1997), "that workplace harassment that is sexual in content is always actionable, regardless of the harasser's sex, sexual orientation, or motivations"? Cf. Pedroza v. Cintas Corp. No. 2, 397 F.3d 1063 (8th Cir. 2005) (sexual propositioning of female employee by female coworker not actionable discrimination in absence of proof of harasser's homosexuality); EEOC v. Harbert–Yeargin, Inc., 266 F.3d 498 (6th Cir.2001) (refusing to find workplace "goosing" of only male employees actionable where not done to initiate sex or to discourage employment of class or sub class of males). But see Rene v. MGM Grand Hotel, Inc., 305 F.3d 1061 (9th Cir.2002) (plurality of *en banc* panel holds that under *Oncale* it is enough to show "physical conduct of a sexual nature" and discrimination in comparison to others of the plaintiff's own sex); David S. Schwartz, When Is Sex Because of Sex? The Causation Problem in Sexual Harassment Law, 150 Penn. L.Rev. 1697 (2002) (arguing for a per se causation rule when sexual contact is involved).

How does the Court suggest that Oncale might prove discrimination on remand? Do you think that many employees subjected to "same sex" harassment by heterosexual supervisors or coworkers are able to prove discrimination?

7. *Harassment Discrimination as Sex–Plus Discrimination.* Note that Oncale's potential claim is not defeated by other males not being subject to harassment. His claim must be that while being male was not a sufficient cause for being harassed, it was at least a contributing cause. This is consistent with the claim in the more usual harassment case where only selected women are subject to unwelcome advances. It is also in accord with the Court's recognition of actionable discrimination against a subset of women or other protected group, see Phillips v. Martin Marietta, note 1, p. 318 supra, and with the statute's condemnation of employment decisions that are only partly motivated by consideration of a protected category, see § 703(m). Does this mean that Oncale could win his case by proving that Sundowner allowed its employees to treat harshly men with his personality traits, or could Sundowner successfully defend by demanding some demonstration that its employees did not treat women with similar personality traits equally harshly? Could Sundowner also demand proof that its employees would not as egregiously haze any woman who did not conform to a particular accepted "female" personality as any man who did not conform to a particular traditional "male" personality?

8. *Non-Sexual Sexual Harassment.* Neither *Oncale* or *Harris* requires plaintiffs to prove that the hostile work environment that they suffer because of their sex is hostile because of some sexual attraction or sex-related actions. For instance, had Hardy, without referring to sex, repeatedly and viciously berated or slapped Harris for mistakes for which he only mildly reproved male employees, he would be as guilty of sex discrimination as he was in the actual case. See, e.g., Boumehdi v. Plastag Holdings, LLC, 489 F.3d 781 (7th Cir. 2007); EEOC v. National Educ. Ass'n, 422 F.3d 840 (9th Cir. 2005). See generally Vicki Schultz, Reconceptualizing Sexual Harassment, 107 Yale L.J. 1683 (1998).

9. *Relevance of "Sexualized" Common Workplace Environment.* By allowing the open display of sexually oriented pictures or paraphernalia, or

by permitting male and female workers to engage openly in sexual horseplay or affairs, do employers subject female employees to a discriminatory hostile environment without actually treating the females differently than male coworkers? Consider, for instance, an auto repair garage where the open display of pictures of nude women has been indulged by an employer for years while no women were employed. Can a recently employed woman press a Title VII claim? See, e.g., Petrosino v. Bell Atlantic, 385 F.3d 210 (2d Cir. 2004) (sexually offensive material may be actionable because "disproportionately demeaning" of women); Robinson v. Jacksonville Shipyards, Inc., 760 F.Supp. 1486 (M.D.Fla.1991) (finding disparate impact based on expert testimony that "sexualize[d] work environment" disadvantaged female employees). But cf. Lyle v. Warner Bros. Television Productions, 38 Cal.4th 264, 42 Cal.Rptr.3d 2, 132 P.3d 211 (Cal. S.Ct. 2006) (sexually vulgar language not harassment because part of comedy writers' common workplace). If a "sexualized" environment is actionable only under disparate impact theory, are compensatory or punitive damages available under Title VII? See generally, Tristin K. Green, Work Culture and Discrimination, 93 Cal. L. Rev. 623 (2005); Kelly Cahill Timmons, Sexual Harassment and Disparate Impact: Should Non–Targeted Workplace Sexual Conduct Be Actionable Under Title VII?, 81 Neb. L.Rev. 1152 (2003). See also Juliano & Schwab, supra, at 549 (finding "claims involving differential but nonsexual conduct and conduct demeaning to women in general are far less successful" than cases involving "sexualized conduct directed at individual victims").

10. *Harassment Discrimination and Free Speech.* Does the first amendment allow Title VII regulation of expression, like that described in the last note, that is not targeted at particular individuals for purposes of harassment? See *Robinson*, supra (allowing an injunction requiring employer to "curtail the free expression in the workplace of some employees in order to remedy the demonstrated harm inflicted on other employees" who are a captive audience). Should the courts use the same standards to protect potentially offensive speech at the workplace that they use to protect potentially offensive speech in public forums? For differing views, see, e.g., Cynthia L. Estlund, Freedom of Expression in the Workplace and the Problem of Discriminatory Harassment, 75 Tex.L.Rev. 687 (1997); Eugene Volokh, Thinking Ahead About Freedom of Speech and Hostile Work Environment Harassment, 17 Berkeley J.Emp. & Lab.L. 305 (1996); Deborah Epstein, Can a "Dumb Ass Woman" Achieve Equality in the Workplace? Running the Gauntlet of Hostile Environment Harassing Speech, 84 Geo. L.J. 399 (1996); Kingsley R. Browne, Title VII as Censorship: Hostile–Environment Harassment and the First Amendment, 52 Ohio St.L.J. 481 (1991).

11. *Discriminatory Conditions for Employment Benefits.* In addition to the hostile work environment discrimination treated in *Harris* and *Oncale*, as well as *Meritor*, the courts have recognized as a form of sex discrimination an employer's denial of some economic benefit of employment because of an employee's refusal to submit to the advances of a fellow employee, usually one of her supervisors. This form of actionable sexual discrimination, which was first described as "quid pro quo" harassment, usually is also an example of "sex plus" discrimination, as some targeted women are asked to do more than similarly situated men to achieve some employment benefit. Is Title VII

violated where a bisexual supervisor denied promotions both to a female and a male subordinate who refused to accept his sexual propositions? What if a supervisor told a subordinate that he would grant her a pay increase that she did not deserve if she accepted his sexual advances, and then did not grant her the increase when she resisted? Could the subordinate at least claim hostile environment harassment?

12. *Favoritism Toward Lovers.* The courts generally hold that a supervisor's favoritism toward a subordinate with whom he has a consensual romantic relationship does not violate Title VII. See, e.g., Womack v. Runyon, 147 F.3d 1298 (11th Cir.1998); DeCintio v. Westchester County Medical Ctr., 807 F.2d 304 (2d Cir.1986). The EEOC, however, takes the position that where an employee is granted a promotion because she submits to a superior's sexual *coercion*, the employee who deserved the promotion has a cause of action because he or she has been injured by actionable discrimination. See EEOC Policy Guidance on Employer Liability Under Title VII for Sexual Favoritism ((Feb. 15, 1990). The EEOC also holds that "widespread sexual favoritism" at a workplace may create an actionable "demeaning" hostile work environment. Id. Are these positions consistent with judicial decisions finding favoritism toward consensual lovers generally not actionable? See also Tenge v. Phillips Modern Ag Co., 446 F.3d 903 (8th Cir. 2006) (accepting EEOC's distinctions in dicta, but finding disparate treatment based on past consensual affair not actionable); Miller v. Department of Corrections, 36 Cal.4th 446, 30 Cal.Rptr.3d 797, 115 P.3d 77 (2005) (adopting EEOC's view on "widespread" favoritism).

13. *Off-Duty Harassment.* Can discriminatory harassment that occurs during non-working hours be actionable under Title VII? Does this depend on whether the employee-victim is expected to engage in social activity after normal working hours, see, e.g., Little v. Windermere Relocation, Inc., supra, note 4, (socializing with client)? What if the employer could anticipate the likelihood of its employees socializing after hours together in isolated work places? See Ferris v. Delta Air Lines, Inc., 277 F.3d 128 (2d Cir.2001) (hotel room could be part of "work environment" because airline should expect its employees to socialize together during brief layovers in foreign countries). Might an employer also have a duty to separate two employees to avoid the lingering effects of harassment that has no connection to the employer's work? Would failing to do so be discriminatory? Consider this further after reading the following principal case and accompanying notes.

14. *Harassment by Customers or Other Nonemployees.* Employers may also violate Title VII by requiring their female employees to be subject to the sexual attacks or advances of customers or other nonemployees. See, e.g., Little v. Windermere Relocation, Inc., supra; Rodriguez–Hernandez v. Miranda–Velez, 132 F.3d 848 (1st Cir.1998); Crist v. Focus Homes, Inc., 122 F.3d 1107 (8th Cir.1997). What if the victims' managers or supervisors are not aware of the customer attacks, however? Consider the following decision.

FARAGHER v. CITY OF BOCA RATON
Supreme Court of the United States, 1998.
524 U.S. 775, 118 S.Ct. 2275, 141 L.Ed.2d 662.

JUSTICE SOUTER delivered the opinion of the Court.

This case calls for identification of the circumstances under which an employer may be held liable under Title VII of the Civil Rights Act of 1964, 78 Stat. 253, as amended, 42 U.S.C. § 2000e et seq., for the acts of a supervisory employee whose sexual harassment of subordinates has created a hostile work environment amounting to employment discrimination. We hold that an employer is vicariously liable for actionable discrimination caused by a supervisor, but subject to an affirmative defense looking to the reasonableness of the employer's conduct as well as that of a plaintiff victim.

I

Between 1985 and 1990, while attending college, petitioner Beth Ann Faragher worked part time and during the summers as an ocean lifeguard for the Marine Safety Section of the Parks and Recreation Department of respondent, the City of Boca Raton, Florida (City). During this period, Faragher's immediate supervisors were Bill Terry, David Silverman, and Robert Gordon. In June 1990, Faragher resigned.

In 1992, Faragher brought an action against Terry, Silverman, and the City, asserting claims under Title VII, 42 U.S.C. § 1983, and Florida law. So far as it concerns the Title VII claim, the complaint alleged that Terry and Silverman created a "sexually hostile atmosphere" at the beach by repeatedly subjecting Faragher and other female lifeguards to "uninvited and offensive touching," by making lewd remarks, and by speaking of women in offensive terms. The complaint contained specific allegations that Terry once said that he would never promote a woman to the rank of lieutenant, and that Silverman had said to Faragher, "Date me or clean the toilets for a year." Asserting that Terry and Silverman were agents of the City, and that their conduct amounted to discrimination in the "terms, conditions, and privileges" of her employment, 42 U.S.C. § 2000e–2(a)(1), Faragher sought a judgment against the City for nominal damages, costs, and attorney's fees.

Following a bench trial, the United States District Court for the Southern District of Florida found that throughout Faragher's employment with the City, Terry served as Chief of the Marine Safety Division, with authority to hire new lifeguards (subject to the approval of higher management), to supervise all aspects of the lifeguards' work assignments, to engage in counseling, to deliver oral reprimands, and to make a record of any such discipline. Silverman was a Marine Safety lieutenant from 1985 until June 1989, when he became a captain. Gordon began the employment period as a lieutenant and at some point was promoted to the position of training captain. In these positions, Silverman and Gordon were responsible for making the lifeguards' daily assignments, and for supervising their work and fitness training.

The lifeguards and supervisors were stationed at the city beach and worked out of the Marine Safety Headquarters, a small one-story building containing an office, a meeting room, and a single, unisex locker room with a shower. Their work routine was structured in a "paramilitary configuration," with a clear chain of command. Lifeguards reported to lieutenants and captains, who reported to Terry. He was supervised by the Recreation Superintendent, who in turn reported to a Director of Parks and Recreation, answerable to the City Manager. The lifeguards had no significant contact with higher city officials like the Recreation Superintendent.

In February 1986, the City adopted a sexual harassment policy, which it stated in a memorandum from the City Manager addressed to all employees. In May 1990, the City revised the policy and reissued a statement of it. Although the City may actually have circulated the memos and statements to some employees, it completely failed to disseminate its policy among employees of the Marine Safety Section, with the result that Terry, Silverman, Gordon, and many lifeguards were unaware of it.

From time to time over the course of Faragher's tenure at the Marine Safety Section, between 4 and 6 of the 40 to 50 lifeguards were women. During that 5–year period, Terry repeatedly touched the bodies of female employees without invitation, would put his arm around Faragher, with his hand on her buttocks, and once made contact with another female lifeguard in a motion of sexual simulation. He made crudely demeaning references to women generally, and once commented disparagingly on Faragher's shape. During a job interview with a woman he hired as a lifeguard, Terry said that the female lifeguards had sex with their male counterparts and asked whether she would do the same.

Silverman behaved in similar ways. He once tackled Faragher and remarked that, but for a physical characteristic he found unattractive, he would readily have had sexual relations with her. Another time, he pantomimed an act of oral sex. Within earshot of the female lifeguards, Silverman made frequent, vulgar references to women and sexual matters, commented on the bodies of female lifeguards and beachgoers, and at least twice told female lifeguards that he would like to engage in sex with them.

Faragher did not complain to higher management about Terry or Silverman. Although she spoke of their behavior to Gordon, she did not regard these discussions as formal complaints to a supervisor but as conversations with a person she held in high esteem. Other female lifeguards had similarly informal talks with Gordon, but because Gordon did not feel that it was his place to do so, he did not report these complaints to Terry, his own supervisor, or to any other city official. Gordon responded to the complaints of one lifeguard by saying that "the City just [doesn't] care."

In April 1990, however, two months before Faragher's resignation, Nancy Ewanchew, a former lifeguard, wrote to Richard Bender, the City's Personnel Director, complaining that Terry and Silverman had harassed her and other female lifeguards. Following investigation of this complaint, the City found that Terry and Silverman had behaved improperly, reprimanded them, and required them to choose between a suspension without pay or the forfeiture of annual leave.

On the basis of these findings, the District Court concluded that the conduct of Terry and Silverman was discriminatory harassment sufficiently serious to alter the conditions of Faragher's employment and constitute an abusive working environment. The District Court then ruled that there were three justifications for holding the City liable for the harassment of its supervisory employees. First, the court noted that the harassment was pervasive enough to support an inference that the City had "knowledge, or constructive knowledge" of it. Next, it ruled that the City was liable under traditional agency principles because Terry and Silverman were acting as its agents when they committed the harassing acts. Finally, the court observed that Gordon's knowledge of the harassment, combined with his inaction, "provides a further basis for imputing liability on [sic] the City." The District Court then awarded Faragher one dollar in nominal damages on her Title VII claim.

A panel of the Court of Appeals for the Eleventh Circuit reversed the judgment against the City. Although the panel had "no trouble concluding that Terry's and Silverman's conduct * * * was severe and pervasive enough to create an objectively abusive work environment," it overturned the District Court's conclusion that the City was liable. The panel ruled that Terry and Silverman were not acting within the scope of their employment when they engaged in the harassment, that they were not aided in their actions by the agency relationship, and that the City had no constructive knowledge of the harassment by virtue of its pervasiveness or Gordon's actual knowledge.

In a 7–to–5 decision, the full Court of Appeals, sitting en banc, adopted the panel's conclusion. * * *

II

A

* * *

While indicating the substantive contours of the hostile environments forbidden by Title VII, our cases have established few definite rules for determining when an employer will be liable for a discriminatory environment that is otherwise actionably abusive. Given the circumstances of many of the litigated cases, including some that have come to us, it is not surprising that in many of them, the issue has been joined over the sufficiency of the abusive conditions, not the standards for determining an employer's liability for them. * * *

[T]here is also nothing remarkable in the fact that claims against employers for discriminatory employment actions with tangible results, like hiring, firing, promotion, compensation, and work assignment, have resulted in employer liability once the discrimination was shown. See *Meritor* [*Savings Bank, FSB v. Vinson,* 477 U.S. 57, 70–71, 106 S.Ct. 2399, 2407–2408, 91 L.Ed.2d 49] (noting that "courts have consistently held employers liable for the discriminatory discharges of employees by supervisory personnel, whether or not the employer knew, should have known, or approved of the supervisor's actions"); *id.,* at 75, 106 S.Ct., at

2409–2410 (Marshall, J., concurring in judgment) ("[W]hen a supervisor discriminatorily fires or refuses to promote a black employee, that act is, without more, considered the act of the employer"); see also *Anderson v. Methodist Evangelical Hospital, Inc.*, 464 F.2d 723, 725 (C.A.6 1972) (imposing liability on employer for racially motivated discharge by low-level supervisor, although the "record clearly shows that [its] record in race relations * * * is exemplary").

* * *

The soundness of the results in these cases (and their continuing vitality), in light of basic agency principles, was confirmed by this Court's only discussion to date of standards of employer liability, in *Meritor, supra*, which involved a claim of discrimination by a supervisor's sexual harassment of a subordinate over an extended period. In affirming the Court of Appeals's holding that a hostile atmosphere resulting from sex discrimination is actionable under Title VII, we also anticipated proceedings on remand by holding agency principles relevant in assigning employer liability and by rejecting three per se rules of liability or immunity. 477 U.S., at 70–72, 106 S.Ct., at 2407–2408. We observed that the very definition of employer in Title VII, as including an "agent," id., at 72, 106 S.Ct., at 2408, expressed Congress's intent that courts look to traditional principles of the law of agency in devising standards of employer liability in those instances where liability for the actions of a supervisory employee was not otherwise obvious, ibid., and although we cautioned that "common-law principles may not be transferable in all their particulars to Title VII," we cited the Restatement [(Second) of Torts] §§ 219–237, with general approval. *Ibid.*

We then proceeded to reject two limitations on employer liability, while establishing the rule that some limitation was intended. We held that neither the existence of a company grievance procedure nor the absence of actual notice of the harassment on the part of upper management would be dispositive of such a claim; while either might be relevant to the liability, neither would result automatically in employer immunity. *Ibid.* Conversely, we held that Title VII placed some limit on employer responsibility for the creation of a discriminatory environment by a supervisor, and we held that Title VII does not make employers "always automatically liable for sexual harassment by their supervisors," ibid., contrary to the view of the Court of Appeals, which had held that "an employer is strictly liable for a hostile environment created by a supervisor's sexual advances, even though the employer neither knew nor reasonably could have known of the alleged misconduct," *id.*, at 69–70, 106 S.Ct., at 2406–2407.

Meritor's statement of the law is the foundation on which we build today. Neither party before us has urged us to depart from our customary adherence to stare decisis in statutory interpretation, * * *.

B

* * *

1

A "master is subject to liability for the torts of his servants committed while acting in the scope of their employment." Restatement § 219(1). This doctrine has traditionally defined the "scope of employment" as including conduct "of the kind [a servant] is employed to perform," occurring "substantially within the authorized time and space limits," and "actuated, at least in part, by a purpose to serve the master," but as excluding an intentional use of force "unexpectable by the master." *Id.,* § 228(1).

Courts of Appeals have typically held, or assumed, that conduct similar to the subject of this complaint falls outside the scope of employment. [citations omitted] In so doing, the courts have emphasized that harassment consisting of unwelcome remarks and touching is motivated solely by individual desires and serves no purpose of the employer. For this reason, courts have likened hostile environment sexual harassment to the classic "frolic and detour" for which an employer has no vicarious liability.

These cases ostensibly stand in some tension with others arising outside Title VII, where the scope of employment has been defined broadly enough to hold employers vicariously liable for intentional torts that were in no sense inspired by any purpose to serve the employer. In *Ira S. Bushey & Sons, Inc. v. United States,* 398 F.2d 167 (C.A.2 1968), for example, the Second Circuit charged the Government with vicarious liability for the depredation of a drunken sailor returning to his ship after a night's carouse, who inexplicably opened valves that flooded a drydock, damaging both the drydock and the ship. Judge Friendly acknowledged that the sailor's conduct was not remotely motivated by a purpose to serve his employer, but relied on the "deeply rooted sentiment that a business enterprise cannot justly disclaim responsibility for accidents which may fairly be said to be characteristic of its activities," and imposed vicarious liability on the ground that the sailor's conduct "was not so 'unforeseeable' as to make it unfair to charge the Government with responsibility." *Id.,* at 171. Other examples of an expansive sense of scope of employment are readily found, see, e.g., *Leonbruno v. Champlain Silk Mills,* 229 N.Y. 470, 128 N.E. 711 (1920) (opinion of Cardozo, J.) (employer was liable under worker's compensation statute for eye injury sustained when employee threw an apple at another; the accident arose "in the course of employment" because such horseplay should be expected); *Carr v. Wm. C. Crowell Co.,* 28 Cal.2d 652, 171 P.2d 5 (1946) (employer liable for actions of carpenter who attacked a coemployee with a hammer). Courts, in fact, have treated scope of employment generously enough to include sexual assaults. See, e.g., *Primeaux v. United States,* 102 F.3d 1458, 1462–1463 (C.A.8 1996) (federal police officer on limited duty sexually assaulted stranded motorist); *Mary M. v. Los Angeles,* 54 Cal.3d 202, 216–221, 285 Cal.Rptr. 99, 107–111, 814 P.2d 1341, 1349–1352 (1991) (en banc) (police officer raped motorist after placing her under arrest); *Doe v. Samaritan Counseling Ctr.,* 791 P.2d 344, 348–349 (Alaska 1990) (therapist had sexual relations with patient);

Turner v. State, 494 So.2d 1292, 1296 (La.App.1986) (National Guard recruiting officer committed sexual battery during sham physical examinations); *Lyon v. Carey*, 533 F.2d 649, 655 (C.A.D.C.1976) (furniture deliveryman raped recipient of furniture); *Samuels v. Southern Baptist Hospital*, 594 So.2d 571, 574 (La.App.1992) (nursing assistant raped patient). The rationales for these decisions have varied, with some courts echoing *Bushey* in explaining that the employees' acts were foreseeable and that the employer should in fairness bear the resulting costs of doing business, see, e.g., *Mary M., supra*, at 218, 285 Cal.Rptr., at 108, 814 P.2d., at 1350, and others finding that the employee's sexual misconduct arose from or was in some way related to the employee's essential duties. *See, e.g., Samuels, supra*, at 574 (tortious conduct was "reasonably incidental" to the performance of the nursing assistant's duties in caring for a "helpless" patient in a "locked environment").

An assignment to reconcile the run of the Title VII cases with those just cited would be a taxing one. Here it is enough to recognize that their disparate results do not necessarily reflect wildly varying terms of the particular employment contracts involved, but represent differing judgments about the desirability of holding an employer liable for his subordinates' wayward behavior. * * *

The proper analysis * * * calls not for a mechanical application of indefinite and malleable factors set forth in the Restatement, see, e.g., §§ 219, 228, 229, but rather an inquiry into the reasons that would support a conclusion that harassing behavior ought to be held within the scope of a supervisor's employment, and the reasons for the opposite view. The Restatement itself points to such an approach, as in the commentary that the "ultimate question" in determining the scope of employment is "whether or not it is just that the loss resulting from the servant's acts should be considered as one of the normal risks to be borne by the business in which the servant is employed." Id., § 229, Comment a. See generally *Taber v. Maine*, 67 F.3d 1029, 1037 (C.A.2 1995) ("As the leading Torts treatise has put it, 'the integrating principle' of respondeat superior is 'that the employer should be liable for those faults that may be fairly regarded as risks of his business, whether they are committed in furthering it or not' ") (quoting 5 F. Harper, F. James & O. Gray, Law of Torts § 26.8, pp. 40–41 (2d ed.1986))

In the case before us, a justification for holding the offensive behavior within the scope of Terry's and Silverman's employment was well put in Judge Barkett's dissent: "[A] pervasively hostile work environment of sexual harassment is never (one would hope) authorized, but the supervisor is clearly charged with maintaining a productive, safe work environment. The supervisor directs and controls the conduct of the employees, and the manner of doing so may inure to the employer's benefit or detriment, including subjecting the employer to Title VII liability." It is by now well recognized that hostile environment sexual harassment by supervisors (and, for that matter, co-employees) is a persistent problem in the workplace [citations omitted]. An employer can, in a general sense, reasonably anticipate the possibility of such conduct occurring in its workplace, and one might justify the assignment of the burden of the untoward behavior to the employer as one of the costs of doing business, to be charged to the enterprise rather than the victim. * * *

Two things counsel us to draw the contrary conclusion. First, there is no reason to suppose that Congress wished courts to ignore the traditional distinction between acts falling within the scope and acts amounting to what the older law called frolics or detours from the course of employment. * * *

The second reason goes to an even broader unanimity of views among the holdings of District Courts and Courts of Appeals thus far. Those courts have held not only that the sort of harassment at issue here was outside the scope of supervisors' authority, but, by uniformly judging employer liability for co-worker harassment under a negligence standard, they have also implicitly treated such harassment as outside the scope of common employees' duties as well [citations omitted]; see also 29 CFR § 1604.11(d) (1997) (employer is liable for co-worker harassment if it "knows or should have known of the conduct, unless it can show that it took immediate and appropriate corrective action"); 3 L. Larson & A. Larson, Employment Discrimination § 46.07[4][a], p. 46–101 (2d ed.1998) (courts "uniformly" apply EEOC rule; "[i]t is not a controversial area"). If, indeed, the cases did not rest, at least implicitly, on the notion that such harassment falls outside the scope of employment, their liability issues would have turned simply on the application of the scope-of-employment rule. Cf. *Hunter v. Allis–Chalmers, Corp.*, 797 F.2d 1417, 1422 (C.A.7 1986) (noting that employer will not usually be liable under respondeat superior for employee's racial harassment because it "would be the rare case where racial harassment * * * could be thought by the author of the harassment to help the employer's business").

It is quite unlikely that these cases would escape efforts to render them obsolete if we were to hold that supervisors who engage in discriminatory harassment are necessarily acting within the scope of their employment. The rationale for placing harassment within the scope of supervisory authority would be the fairness of requiring the employer to bear the burden of foreseeable social behavior, and the same rationale would apply when the behavior was that of co-employees. The employer generally benefits just as obviously from the work of common employees as from the work of supervisors; they simply have different jobs to do, all aimed at the success of the enterprise. As between an innocent employer and an innocent employee, if we use scope of employment reasoning to require the employer to bear the cost of an actionably hostile workplace created by one class of employees (i.e., supervisors), it could appear just as appropriate to do the same when the environment was created by another class (i.e., co-workers).

* * *

2

* * *

We * * * agree with Faragher that in implementing Title VII it makes sense to hold an employer vicariously liable for some tortious conduct of a supervisor made possible by abuse of his supervisory authority, * * *. Several courts, indeed, have noted what Faragher has argued, that there is a sense in which a harassing supervisor is always assisted in his misconduct by the supervisory relationship. [citations omitted] The agency relationship affords contact with an employee subjected to a supervisor's sexual harassment, and the victim may well be reluctant to accept the risks of blowing the whistle on a superior. When a person with supervisory authority discriminates in the terms and conditions of subordinates' employment, his actions necessarily draw upon his superior position over the people who report to him, or those under them, whereas an employee generally cannot check a supervisor's abusive conduct the same way that she might deal with abuse from a co-worker. When a fellow employee harasses, the victim can walk away or tell the offender where to go, but it may be difficult to offer such responses to a supervisor, whose "power to supervise—[which may be] to hire and fire, and to set work schedules and pay rates—does not disappear * * * when he chooses to harass through insults and offensive gestures rather than directly with threats of firing or promises of promotion." Estrich, Sex at Work, 43 Stan. L.Rev. 813, 854 (1991). Recognition of employer liability when discriminatory misuse of supervisory authority alters the terms and conditions of a victim's employment is underscored by the fact that the employer has a greater opportunity to guard against misconduct by supervisors than by common workers; employers have greater opportunity and incentive to screen them, train them, and monitor their performance.

In sum, there are good reasons for vicarious liability for misuse of supervisory authority. That rationale must, however, satisfy one more condition. We are not entitled to recognize this theory under Title VII unless we can square it with *Meritor*'s holding that an employer is not "automatically" liable for harassment by a supervisor who creates the requisite degree of discrimination, and there is obviously some tension between that holding and the position that a supervisor's misconduct aided by supervisory authority subjects the employer to liability vicariously; if the "aid" may be the unspoken suggestion of retaliation by misuse of supervisory authority, the risk of automatic liability is high. To counter it, we think there are two basic alternatives, one being to require proof of some affirmative invocation of that authority by the harassing supervisor, the other to recognize an affirmative defense to liability in some circumstances, even when a supervisor has created the actionable environment.

There is certainly some authority for requiring active or affirmative, as distinct from passive or implicit, misuse of supervisory authority before liability may be imputed. * * *

But neat examples illustrating the line between the affirmative and merely implicit uses of power are not easy to come by in considering management behavior. Supervisors do not make speeches threatening sanctions whenever they make requests in the legitimate exercise of managerial authority, and yet every subordinate employee knows the sanctions exist; this is the reason that courts have consistently held that acts of supervisors have greater power to alter the environment than acts of co-employees generally. How far from the course of ostensible supervisory behavior would a company officer have to step before his orders would not reasonably be seen as actively using authority? Judgment calls would often be close, the results would often seem disparate even if not demonstrably contradictory, and the temptation to litigate would be hard to resist. We think plaintiffs and defendants alike would be poorly served by an active-use rule.

The other basic alternative to automatic liability would avoid this particular temptation to litigate, but allow an employer to show as an affirmative defense to liability that the employer had exercised reasonable care to avoid harassment and to eliminate it when it might occur, and that the complaining employee had failed to act with like reasonable care to take advantage of the employer's safeguards and otherwise to prevent harm that could have been avoided. This composite defense would, we think, implement the statute sensibly, for reasons that are not hard to fathom.

* * *

The requirement to show that the employee has failed in a coordinate duty to avoid or mitigate harm reflects an equally obvious policy imported from the general theory of damages, that a victim has a duty "to use such means as are reasonable under the circumstances to avoid or minimize the damages" that result from violations of the statute. *Ford Motor Co. v. EEOC*, 458 U.S. 219, 231, n. 15, 102 S.Ct. 3057, 3065, n. 15, 73 L.Ed.2d 721 (1982) (quoting C. McCormick, Law of Damages 127 (1935) (internal quotation marks omitted)). An employer may, for example, have provided a proven, effective mechanism for reporting and resolving complaints of sexual harassment, available to the employee without undue risk or expense. If the plaintiff unreasonably failed to avail herself of the employer's preventive or remedial apparatus, she should not recover damages that could have been avoided if she had done so. If the victim could have avoided harm, no liability should be found against the employer who had taken reasonable care, and if damages could reasonably have been mitigated no award against a liable employer should reward a plaintiff for what her own efforts could have avoided.

In order to accommodate the principle of vicarious liability for harm caused by misuse of supervisory authority, as well as Title VII's equally basic policies of encouraging forethought by employers and saving action by objecting employees, we adopt the following holding in this case and in *Burlington Industries, Inc. v. Ellerth*, [524 U.S. 742, 118 S.Ct. 2257,] also decided today. An employer is subject to vicarious liability to a victimized employee for an actionable hostile environment created by a supervisor with immediate (or successively higher) authority over the employee. When no tangible employment action is taken, a defending employer may raise an affirmative defense to liability or damages, subject to proof by a preponderance of the evidence, see Fed. Rule. Civ. Proc. 8(c). The defense comprises two necessary elements: (a) that the employer exercised reasonable care to prevent and correct promptly any sexually harassing behavior, and (b) that the plaintiff employee unreasonably failed to take advantage of any preventive or corrective opportunities provided by the employer or to avoid harm otherwise. While proof that an employer had promulgated an antiharassment policy with complaint procedure is not necessary in every instance as a matter of law, the need for a stated policy suitable to the employment circumstances may appropriately be addressed in any case when litigating the first element of the defense. And while proof that an employee failed to fulfill the corresponding obligation of reasonable care to avoid harm is not limited to showing an unreasonable failure to use any complaint procedure provided by the employer, a demonstration of such failure will normally suffice to satisfy the employer's burden under the second element of the defense. No affirmative defense is available, however, when the supervisor's harassment culminates in a tangible employment action, such as discharge, demotion, or undesirable reassignment.

Applying these rules here, we believe that the judgment of the Court of Appeals must be reversed. The District Court found that the degree of hostility in the work environment rose to the actionable level and was attributable to Silverman and Terry. It is undisputed that these supervisors "were granted virtually unchecked authority" over their subordinates, "directly controll[ing] and supervis[ing] all aspects of [Faragher's] day-to-day activities." It is also clear that Faragher and her colleagues were "completely isolated from the City's higher management." The City did not seek review of these findings.

While the City would have an opportunity to raise an affirmative defense if there were any serious prospect of its presenting one, it appears from the record that any such avenue is closed. The District Court found that the City had entirely failed to disseminate its policy against sexual harassment among the beach employees and that its officials made no attempt to keep track of the conduct of supervisors like Terry and Silverman. The record also makes clear that the City's policy did not include any assurance that the harassing supervisors could be bypassed in registering complaints. Under such circumstances, we hold as a matter of law that the City could not be found to have exercised reasonable care to prevent the supervisors' harassing conduct. Unlike the employer of a small workforce, who might expect that sufficient care to prevent tortious behavior could be exercised informally, those responsible for city operations could not reasonably have thought that precautions against hostile environments in any one of many departments in far-flung locations could be effective without communicating some formal policy against harassment, with a sensible complaint procedure.

* * *

The City points to nothing that might justify a conclusion by the District Court on remand that the City had exercised reasonable care. Nor is there any reason to remand for consideration of Faragher's efforts to mitigate her own damages, since the award to her was solely nominal.

3

The Court of Appeals also rejected the possibility that it could hold the City liable for the reason that it knew of the harassment vicariously through the knowledge of its supervisors. We have no occasion to consider whether this was error, however. We are satisfied that liability on the ground of vicarious knowledge could not be determined without further factfinding on remand, whereas the reversal necessary on the theory of supervisory harassment renders any remand for consideration of imputed knowledge entirely unjustifiable (as would be any consideration of negligence as an alternative to a theory of vicarious liability here).

JUSTICE THOMAS, with whom JUSTICE SCALIA joins, dissenting.

* * *

Petitioner suffered no adverse employment consequence; thus the Court of Appeals was correct to hold that the City is not vicariously liable for the conduct of Chief Terry and Lieutenant Silverman. Because the Court reverses this judgment, I dissent.

As for petitioner's negligence claim, the District Court made no finding as to the City's negligence, and the Court of Appeals did not directly consider the issue. I would therefore remand the case to the District Court for further proceedings on this question alone. I disagree with the Court's conclusion that merely because the City did not disseminate its sexual harassment policy, it should be liable as a matter of law. The City should be allowed to show either that: (1) there was a reasonably available avenue through which petitioner could have complained to a City official who supervised both Chief Terry and Lieutenant Silverman, or (2) it would not have learned of the harassment even if the policy had been distributed. Petitioner, as the plaintiff, would of course bear the burden of proving the City's negligence.

Notes and Questions

1. *Burlington Industries, Inc. v. Ellerth.* In a separate decision issued the same day as that in *Faragher*, the Court in *Ellerth*, through a similar, but somewhat different analysis provided by Justice Kennedy, articulated the exact same standard as that provided in *Faragher* for qualified vicarious employer liability in Title VII cases where supervisors have created an actionable hostile work environment. *Ellerth* affirmed the reversal of a

summary judgment against the plaintiff. Unlike *Faragher*, it involved alleged threats by a supervisor to take "tangible employment action" against the target of his sexual aggression, but inasmuch as the threats were never carried out, the Court's *Faragher-Ellerth* standard allowed the employer to assert and attempt to prove before the trial court the two-pronged affirmative defense of (i) employer reasonable care and (ii) plaintiff's unreasonable failure to take advantage of preventive or corrective opportunities. Justice Kennedy's opinion was joined by five other Justices, including Justice Souter, but not Justice Ginsburg. The latter concurred in the *Ellerth* judgment, but did not explain her decision to concur only in Justice Souter's opinion in *Faragher*. Justice Thomas, joined by Justice Scalia, also dissented in *Ellerth*.

2. *Seek Recovery from the Harassing Supervisor?* In evaluating the *Faragher-Ellerth* standard for vicarious employer liability, you should consider that Title VII does not authorize victims of sexual harassment, or of other forms of illegal discrimination, to recover damages from the supervisor or other employer agent who actually perpetrates the discrimination. Most courts interpret Congress's use of the word "agent" in the definition of employer in the Act, see § 701(b), to incorporate vicarious liability principles, but not to provide a direct action against the offending supervisor. See, e.g., Wathen v. General Elec. Co., 115 F.3d 400 (6th Cir.1997); Williams v. Banning, 72 F.3d 552 (7th Cir.1995); Tomka v. Seiler Corp., 66 F.3d 1295 (2d Cir.1995). Is congressional intent not to subject individual employees to liability made more clear by the capping of damages provision in the 1991 Act (which refers to size of the workforce of employers)?

Victims of some forms of discrimination, including sexual harassment, however, may be able to recover against responsible individual employees, as well as their employer, under state or local civil rights statutes or through state common law tort actions (such as intentional infliction of emotional distress, assault and battery, or negligent supervision), or if public employees, § 1983. See, e.g., Badia v. City of Miami, 133 F.3d 1443 (11th Cir.1998) (city employee's § 1983 action not barred by supervisor's official immunity because right to be free of sexual harassment is clearly established). In addition, the lower courts have held that racial harassment claims may be brought under § 1981. See, e.g., Whidbee v. Garzarelli Food Specialties, Inc., supra; Allen v. Denver Pub. Sch. Bd., 928 F.2d 978, 983 (10th Cir.1991) (both finding individual liability where there is "some affirmative link to causally connect the actor with the discriminatory action").

3. *Is the* Faragher–Ellerth *Affirmative Defense Justified?* As noted above, the Court's standard for vicarious liability under Title VII permits employers to escape liability by proving a two-part affirmative defense in cases where "no tangible employment action is taken." Are you convinced by the *Faragher* Court's explanations of why such an affirmative defense is appropriate? Justice Souter acknowledges that the common law of vicarious liability ultimately rests on legal policy judgments and that "there is a sense in which a harassing supervisor is always assisted in his misconduct by the supervisory relationship." Was the affirmative defense nonetheless required by the Court's earlier treatment of the issue in *Meritor*? By the desirability of providing incentives for employers to take reasonable preventive and

corrective measures and for victims to use reasonable means to avoid or minimize harassment?

In considering the last question, note that imposing unqualified vicarious liability on employers could create even greater incentives to take preventive measures to avoid liability, while insulating from liability employers whose senior management do not know of some isolated discriminatory "tangible" employment action could create even greater incentives for victims to report suspected discrimination. Professor, now Judge, Calabresi argued that where general deterrence is the primary goal, liability for an accident should be placed on that party who would have been the accident's "cheapest cost avoider". See Guido Calabresi & Jon T. Hirschoff, Toward a Test for Strict Liability in Torts, 81 Yale L.J. 1055 (1972); Guido Calabresi, The Costs of Accidents, (1970), esp. chs. 7 and 10. Does this theory help explain the *Faragher-Ellerth* compromise? Are employers normally likely to be able to prevent at lower costs than victims discriminatory overt, tangible employment actions, while victims have a lower-cost-avoidance step to take in reporting surreptitious, informal workplace harassment where employers have offered a low cost and credible reporting system and an effective corrective policy? For applications of Calabresi's theory to this problem, see Michael C. Harper, Employer Liability for Harassment Under Title VII: A Functional Rationale for *Faragher* and *Ellerth*, 6 San Diego L. Rev. 101 (1999), and J. Hoult Verkerke, Notice Liability in Employment Discrimination Law, 81 Va. L. Rev. 273 (1995); see also chapters by Professors Harper and Verkerke in Sexual Harassment in the Workplace, supra, at 283–329, 345–360.

4. *Elements of an Effective Anti–Harassment Policy.* What would you advise employers to include in their anti-harassment policies? Consider, in particular, how an employer could provide effective assurances to potential victims that they would not be retaliated against for reporting on their superiors, regardless of their relative rank and importance in the firm. Would your advice be the same for all employers, regardless of their size and the scope of their operation?

5. *Effect of Request for Confidentiality.* Victims of sexual harassment may complain to responsible officials, but request that the officials not divulge the complaints to others. Should such requests for confidentiality necessarily establish that the victim unreasonably failed to take advantage of preventive opportunities? See, e.g., Hardage v. CBS Broadcasting, Inc., 427 F.3d 1177 (9th Cir. 2005) (employer not liable where victim stated he wanted to handle harassment himself); Torres v. Pisano, 116 F.3d 625 (2d Cir.1997) (employer generally can honor confidentiality pledge, but employer may have to act to remedy severe or multiple-victim harassment despite complainant's confidentiality request). How would you advise employers to deal with complaints combined with requests for confidentiality?

6. *Qualified Vicarious Liability vs. Negligence?* Prior to *Faragher* and *Ellerth* most courts of appeals had held employers liable for their supervisors' creation of a discriminatory hostile work environment, without the discriminatory denial of some formal job benefit, only under a negligence theory: where superiors of the supervisors knew or should have known of the harassment and failed to take prompt effective remedial action. How is the

Court's qualified vicarious liability standard more favorable to plaintiffs? Is the shifting of the burden of proof to employers significant? Does the adoption of a vicarious liability theory make clear that the harassing supervisor's discriminatory intent can be imputed to the employer for the purposes of allowing compensatory damages, while a negligence theory leaves open the possibility that the employer only unintentionally caused a disparate impact?

Does the Court's vicarious liability standard also free plaintiffs from having to prove that the employer's failure to take reasonable preventive or corrective action caused the continuation of the harassment? Note the different treatment in the majority and dissenting opinions in *Faragher* of the City of Boca Raton's failure to distribute its anti-harassment policy.

7. *Employer Liability Despite Reasonable Corrective System?*

a. *Meaning of Second Prong?* Does the inclusion of the second prong of the *Faragher-Ellerth* affirmative defense mean that where both the employer and the victim exercise reasonable care to prevent and correct harassment, the employer is liable? If both the employer and victim act promptly, "severe or pervasive" actionable harassment often can be avoided. Cf. Indest v. Freeman Decorating, Inc., 164 F.3d 258, 265–66 (5th Cir.1999) (no employer liability if "swift and appropriate remedial response"). Some severe harassment, however, might occur without either party being unreasonable. For instance, if an employee is suddenly raped by her supervisor at a business conference, reports the rape, and then learns that the employer has fired the rapist after a timely investigation, can she sue the employer for damages caused by psychological stress from the rape? Compare Greene v. Dalton, 164 F.3d 671 (D.C.Cir.1999) (employer may be liable for rape, even though not reported for a month, as second prong concerns only victim's mitigation of damages), with Watkins v. Professional Security Bureau, Ltd., 201 F.3d 439 (4th Cir.1999) (not only did failure to report rape promptly satisfy second prong, but also satisfaction of first prong should be sufficient to negate liability). The EEOC's Enforcement Guidance: Vicarious Employer Liability for Unlawful Harassment By Supervisors, June 18, 1999, holds that the employer should be liable in a case of sudden severe harassment.

b. *Justifications for not Using the System.* When an employer has a generally reasonable preventive and corrective system, can it still be vicariously liable when a victim has a good reason not to use the system? For instance, might a temporary filing clerk reasonably fear invoking a well-promulgated and implemented anti-harassment policy to report to the company president that the president's best friend and most productive salesman has been harassing her? Compare Johnson v. West, 218 F.3d 725 (7th Cir.2000) (reasonable employer may still be liable if employee reasonably did not take advantage of corrective system because of intimidation and threats from harasser), with Montero v. AGCO Corp., 192 F.3d 856 (9th Cir.1999) (failure to report not excused by plaintiff claiming to be nonconfrontational or by her working in geographically isolated regional office). Can an employer include any special elements in its policy to make the second prong of its affirmative defense stronger?

8. *Relevance of Pre–Complaint Harassment?* Assume that a supervisor subjects one of his assistants to a continuing assortment of sexist comments. Assume further that the assistant, not wanting to project weakness or to

"make waves", suffers the comments for a year. After she finally decides to complain through the channels specified in the employer's anti-harassment policy, a prompt investigation results in the reprimand and "retraining" of the supervisor and a cessation of the comments. The assistant, however, feels uncomfortable with the supervisor and socially ostracized by her coworkers, and decides to quit. If she then sues the employer for the supervisor's harassment, should the court accept as an adequate affirmative defense the employer's anti-harassment policy and the assistant's failure to complain earlier about the sexist comments?

Since *Faragher* and *Ellerth* lower court decisions indicate that recovery for later harassment should be denied if the victim's failure to report earlier harassment was "unreasonable". See, e.g., Baldwin v. Blue Cross/Blue Shield of Ala., 480 F.3d 1287 (11th Cir. 2007); Jackson v. County of Racine, 474 F.3d 493 (7th Cir. 2007); Phillips v. Taco Bell Corp., 156 F.3d 884 (8th Cir.1998). Is this view compelled by *Faragher* and *Ellerth* or might the courts deny employer liability only for any earlier harassment that was not reported reasonably promptly? Does the denial of liability for not only earlier "unreasonably" unreported, but also for later reported harassment, encourage a proliferation of potentially polarizing and premature complaints based on fears of possible future escalated harassment? Is it relevant that the Supreme Court has held that an employee is not protected by Title VII from retaliation for complaining about supervisory conduct that she could not reasonably believe was sufficiently serious to constitute actionable harassment? See Clark County School District v. Breeden, 532 U.S. 268, 121 S.Ct. 1508, 149 L.Ed.2d 509 (2001). Should the courts at least not preclude recovery for the failure to report any treatment that is itself not clearly severe or pervasive enough to be actionable under Title VII?

The Court's decision in National R.R. Passenger Corp. v. Morgan, 536 U.S. 101, 118, 122 S.Ct. 2061, 153 L.Ed.2d 106 (2002), may also be relevant to the questions posed in the last paragraph. In this case the Court held that "since the incidents comprising a hostile work environment are part of one unlawful employment practice, the employer may be liable for all acts that are part of this single claim", including acts that fall outside the period defined by Title VII's filing deadline, as long as one act occurred within this period. Does this decision's conception of hostile environment harassment as a single employment practice also indicate that courts should deny liability for earlier unreported harassment only if they deem it appropriate under *Farragher* and *Ellerth* to deny liability for later harassment, within the filing period, that is part of the same continuing behavior? See also pp. 1068–1072 infra.

9. *Employer Liability for Nature of Remedial Response After Reasonable Investigation?* Assume, in the hypothetical in the last note, that the supervisor denied making any of the comments attributed to him by the assistant and that after a serious investigation the employer found no basis for believing or disbelieving the allegations. If the employer took no action to separate the supervisor and the assistant, could the assistant in a Title VII action collect damages from the employer for the impact of any actionable comments or harassment from the supervisor? Could she recover damages for post-complaint harassment? Would she first have to complain about this further harassment? Alternatively, what if the employer after its serious, but

inconclusive investigation, transferred the assistant to another position under different supervision? Might the assistant have a claim for retaliation under § 704(a) of the Act if the new position were somehow less attractive to her? Cf. Hostetler v. Quality Dining, 218 F.3d 798 (7th Cir.2000) (transferring victim of harassment to position with longer commute may subject employer to liability for damages). See chapter 10 infra. How would you advise employers to respond when their investigations of alleged surreptitious discriminatory harassment are inconclusive? See *Baldwin*, supra note 8, at 1305 (warning and counseling adequate response to unsubstantial allegations). Consider also the potential for a wrongful discharge action, or a grievance under a collective bargaining agreement, from a falsely accused supervisor. But cf. Cotran v. Rollins Hudig Hall Int'l, Inc., 17 Cal.4th 93, 69 Cal.Rptr.2d 900, 948 P.2d 412 (Cal. 1998) (to deflect implied contractual claims, employer need only act in good faith after an appropriate investigation with reasonable grounds for believing manager engaged in misconduct).

10. *What Is Adequate Corrective Action?* Employers also must decide how to respond after determining that an employee has engaged in illegal harassment. Does Title VII demand punishment commensurate with the degree of harassment, or only a response sufficient to avoid a reoccurrence? See, e.g., Tutman v. WBBM–TV, 209 F.3d 1044 (7th Cir.2000) (question is not which response is sufficiently punitive, but which will prevent reoccurrence, as long as victim is not disadvantaged).

Do rational employers, in any event, have an interest in terminating proven harassers? What if they are especially valuable employees?

11. *What Constitutes a "Tangible Employment Action"?* Does *Faragher* make clear which employment actions should be classified as "tangible" and thus subject to unqualified employer liability under Title VII if discriminatory? Should all work assignments be covered even if not reported or recorded for potential review by the superiors of the discriminating supervisor? Assume, for instance, that Terry regularly assigned Faragher to a dangerous, isolated posting because of her refusal to play along with his sexual games. Should it matter whether these assignments were reported or at least recorded for review? If the harassment is sufficiently severe or "significant" to warrant a finding of constructive discharge, is it necessarily "tangible", even if not recorded or reported?

In Pennsylvania State Police v. Suders, 542 U.S. 129, 124 S.Ct. 2342, 159 L.Ed.2d 204 (2004), the Court held both that Title VII plaintiffs may recover post-resignation damages under the doctrine of constructive discharge, and that the *Faragher-Ellerth* affirmative defense could be available in some cases even where a supervisor's misconduct warranted resignation. A finding of constructive discharge turns on the degree of severity of the harassment, a showing of working conditions so intolerable that a reasonable person would have felt compelled to resign. The availability of the affirmative defense, by contrast, turns not on the degree of severity of the harassment, but on whether the harassment constituted a tangible employment action, or as the *Suders* Court stated, quoting from *Ellerth* (524 U.S. at 762), "an official act of the enterprise, a company act":

Unlike injuries that could equally be inflicted by a co-worker, * * * tangible employment actions "fall within the special province of the supervisor," who "has been empowered by the company as ... [an] agent to make economic decisions affecting other employees under his or her control." ... Often, the supervisor will "use [the company's] internal processes" and thereby "obtain the imprimatur of the enterprise." Ordinarily, the tangible employment decision is documented in official company records, and may be subject to review by higher level supervisors.

Id. at 144–45. The Court concluded that harassment so intolerable as to cause a resignation may be effected through co-worker conduct, unofficial supervisory conduct, or official company acts. Unlike an actual termination, which is always effected through an official act of the company, a constructive discharge need not be. The Court provided as an example of a constructive discharge with no official conduct, for which the affirmative defense would be available, a supervisor's repeated sexual comments and an incident in which he sexually assaulted her. See Reed v. MBNA Marketing Systems, Inc., 333 F.3d 27 (1st Cir. 2003). As an example of a constructive discharge based on official conduct, for which the affirmative defense would not be available, the Court noted a case involving the transfer of a harassment victim to a less desirable position. See Robinson v. Sappington, 351 F.3d 317 (7th Cir. 2003). The Court also noted that while most of the discriminatory behavior alleged by Suders involved conduct that was unofficial, the failure of her supervisors to forward her computer-skill exams for grading and their false reports to her of her failures on these exams, were less obviously unofficial.

12. *Who Is a Supervisor?* Does the Court make clear for which agents of an employer its standard applies? The EEOC's Enforcement Guidance, note 7 supra, states that an individual qualifies as a "supervisor" for purposes of the standard if: "the individual has authority to undertake or recommend tangible employment decisions affecting the employee: or [ ] the individual has authority to direct the employee's daily work activities." The Enforcement Guidance also states that the standard may apply where a supervisor does not have such authority if the harassed employee "reasonably believed that the harasser had such power." Are these positions consistent with *Faragher*? See also Mack v. Otis Elevator Co., 326 F.3d 116, 125 (2d Cir.2003) (supervisory status found where alleged harasser had authority over victim that "materially augmented his ability, to impose a hostile work environment"); Mikels v. City of Durham, 183 F.3d 323 (4th Cir.1999) (supervisory status turns on whether the harasser is "aided by agency relationship" because his position of authority makes him a "continuing threat" to victim).

13. *Standard for Coworker and Customer Harassment?.* Does the *Faragher* opinion make clear that the lower courts should continue to apply a negligence standard to test an employer's liability under Title VII for the discriminatory harassment of one or more of its employees by coworkers who are not their supervisors? How should employer liability for harassment by customers or other nonemployees be treated? See, e.g., Freitag v. Ayers, 463 F.3d 838 (9th Cir. 2006) (prison liable for failure "to take prompt and effective remedial action to address" sexual harassment of female guards by prisoners); Dunn v. Washington County Hosp., 429 F.3d 689 (7th Cir. 2005) (employer may be directly liable for harassment by independent contractor

because of failure to take "reasonable care" to provide nondiscriminatory work environment).

Is the distinction between coworker and supervisory hostile work environment discrimination sustainable? Do employers create, and benefit from, working environments that require coworkers to work closely together and thus give each the opportunity to harass the others? Can employees in fact always easily walk away from harassing coworkers? Of what relevance is it that the costs of screening, training, and monitoring all workers are greater than the costs of these processes for only supervisors? If an employer does not have an adequate reporting system that protects victims from retaliation, is the victim or the employer likely to be the lower-cost-avoider of further coworker harassment? In many cases employees need not fear retaliation from reporting on their coworkers, but where the coworker is much more important to the firm (even though not a supervisor), where the harassers are many and the victim isolated, or where the harassment is physically threatening, is fear of some form of retaliation as reasonable as where the harasser is a supervisor? For further views on this issue, see Harper, supra note 4; Alan Q. Sykes, The Boundaries of Vicarious Liability: An Economic Analysis of the Scope of Employment Rule and Related Legal Doctrines, 101 Harv. L. Rev. 563, 608 (1988).

14. *"Pattern or Practice" of Sexual Harassment.* How should a private class action or an EEOC-initiated suit alleging a pattern or practice of discriminatory harassment be structured? Can the *Franks-Teamsters* two stage model be utilized? If the class representative was able to prove a discriminatory and objectively hostile working environment either caused or known of by supervisors in the first stage, how would individual employees show that they are eligible to recover in the second stage? Would the employer then be able to defend against paying damages to particular individual employees by proving that these employees did not subjectively perceive the environment as hostile or could have taken steps to mitigate their damages? See generally EEOC v. Dial Corp., 156 F.Supp.2d 926 (N.D.Ill 2001); EEOC v. Mitsubishi Motor Manufacturing of America, Inc., 990 F.Supp. 1059 (C.D.Ill.1998) (both allowing EEOC to pursue pattern or practice claim against sexual harassment).

KOLSTAD v. AMERICAN DENTAL ASSOCIATION
Supreme Court of the United States, 1999.
527 U.S. 526, 119 S.Ct. 2118, 144 L.Ed.2d 494.

JUSTICE O'CONNOR delivered the opinion of the Court.

* * *

I

A

In September 1992, Jack O'Donnell announced that he would be retiring as the Director of Legislation and Legislative Policy and Director of the Council on Government Affairs and Federal Dental Services for respondent, American Dental Association (respondent or Association).

Petitioner, Carole Kolstad, was employed with O'Donnell in respondent's Washington, D.C., office, where she was serving as respondent's Director of Federal Agency Relations. When she learned of O'Donnell's retirement, she expressed an interest in filling his position. Also interested in replacing O'Donnell was Tom Spangler, another employee in respondent's Washington office. At this time, Spangler was serving as the Association's Legislative Counsel, a position that involved him in respondent's legislative lobbying efforts. Both petitioner and Spangler had worked directly with O'Donnell, and both had received "distinguished" performance ratings by the acting head of the Washington office, Leonard Wheat.

Both petitioner and Spangler formally applied for O'Donnell's position, and Wheat requested that Dr. William Allen, then serving as respondent's Executive Director in the Association's Chicago office, make the ultimate promotion decision. After interviewing both petitioner and Spangler, Wheat recommended that Allen select Spangler for O'Donnell's post. Allen notified petitioner in December 1992 that he had, in fact, selected Spangler to serve as O'Donnell's replacement. Petitioner's challenge to this employment decision forms the basis of the instant action.

B

The District Court denied petitioner's request for a jury instruction on punitive damages. The jury concluded that respondent had discriminated against petitioner on the basis of sex and awarded her backpay totaling $52,718. Although the District Court subsequently denied respondent's motion for judgment as a matter of law on the issue of liability, the court made clear that it had not been persuaded that respondent had selected Spangler over petitioner on the basis of sex, and the court denied petitioner's requests for reinstatement and for attorney's fees.

Petitioner appealed from the District Court's decisions denying her requested jury instruction on punitive damages and her request for reinstatement and attorney's fees. Respondent cross-appealed from the denial of its motion for judgment as a matter of law. In a split decision, a panel of the Court of Appeals for the District of Columbia Circuit reversed the District Court's decision denying petitioner's request for an instruction on punitive damages. In so doing, the court rejected respondent's claim that punitive damages are available under Title VII only in " 'extraordinarily egregious cases.' " * * *

The Court of Appeals subsequently agreed to rehear the case en banc, limited to the punitive damages question. In a divided opinion, the court affirmed the decision of the District Court. The en banc majority concluded that, "before the question of punitive damages can go to the jury, the evidence of the defendant's culpability must exceed what is needed to show intentional discrimination." Based on the 1991 Act's structure and legislative history, the court determined, specifically, that a defendant must be shown to have engaged in some "egregious"

misconduct before the jury is permitted to consider a request for punitive damages. Although the court declined to set out the "egregiousness"
requirement in any detail, it concluded that petitioner failed to make the
requisite showing in the instant case. * * *

II

A

Prior to 1991, only equitable relief, primarily backpay, was available
to prevailing Title VII plaintiffs; the statute provided no authority for an
award of punitive or compensatory damages. See *Landgraf v. USI Film
Products*, 511 U.S. 244, 252–253, 128 L. Ed. 2d 229, 114 S. Ct. 1483
(1994). With the passage of the 1991 Act, Congress provided for additional remedies, including punitive damages, for certain classes of Title VII
and ADA violations.

The 1991 Act limits compensatory and punitive damages awards,
however, to cases of "intentional discrimination"—that is, cases that do
not rely on the "disparate impact" theory of discrimination. 42 U.S.C.
§ 1981a(a)(1). Section 1981a(b)(1) further qualifies the availability of
punitive awards:

> "A complaining party may recover punitive damages under this
> section against a respondent (other than a government, government
> agency or political subdivision) if the complaining party demon-
> strates that the respondent engaged in a discriminatory practice or
> discriminatory practices with malice or with reckless indifference to
> the federally protected rights of an aggrieved individual." (Emphasis
> added.)

The very structure of § 1981a suggests a congressional intent to
authorize punitive awards in only a subset of cases involving intentional
discrimination. Section 1981a(a)(1) limits compensatory and punitive
awards to instances of intentional discrimination, while § 1981a(b)(1)
requires plaintiffs to make an additional "demonstration" of their eligibility for punitive damages. Congress plainly sought to impose two
standards of liability—one for establishing a right to compensatory
damages and another, higher standard that a plaintiff must satisfy to
qualify for a punitive award.

The Court of Appeals sought to give life to this two-tiered structure
by limiting punitive awards to cases involving intentional discrimination
of an "egregious" nature. We credit the en banc majority's effort to
effectuate congressional intent, but, in the end, we reject its conclusion
that eligibility for punitive damages can only be described in terms of an
employer's "egregious" misconduct. The terms "malice" and "reckless"
ultimately focus on the actor's state of mind. See, e.g., Black's Law
Dictionary 956–957, 1270 (6th ed. 1990); see also W. Keeton, D. Dobbs,
R. Keeton, & D. Owen, Prosser and Keeton, Law of Torts 212–214 (5th
ed. 1984) (defining "willful," "wanton," and "reckless"). While egregious misconduct is evidence of the requisite mental state, * * * § 1981a
does not limit plaintiffs to this form of evidence, and the section does not

require a showing of egregious or outrageous discrimination independent of the employer's state of mind. * * * The employer must act with "malice or with reckless indifference to [the plaintiff's] federally protected rights." § 1981a(b)(1) (emphasis added). The terms "malice" or "reckless indifference" pertain to the employer's knowledge that it may be acting in violation of federal law, not its awareness that it is engaging in discrimination.

* * *

There will be circumstances where intentional discrimination does not give rise to punitive damages liability under this standard. In some instances, the employer may simply be unaware of the relevant federal prohibition. There will be cases, moreover, in which the employer discriminates with the distinct belief that its discrimination is lawful. The underlying theory of discrimination may be novel or otherwise poorly recognized, or an employer may reasonably believe that its discrimination satisfies a bona fide occupational qualification defense or other statutory exception to liability. See, e.g., 42 U.S.C. § 2000e–2(e)(1) (setting out Title VII defense "where religion, sex, or national origin is a bona fide occupational qualification"); see also § 12113 (setting out defenses under ADA). In *Hazen Paper Co. v. Biggins*, 507 U.S. 604, 616, 123 L. Ed. 2d 338, 113 S. Ct. 1701 (1993), we thus observed that, in light of statutory defenses and other exceptions permitting age-based decision-making, an employer may knowingly rely on age to make employment decisions without recklessly violating the Age Discrimination in Employment Act of 1967 (ADEA). Accordingly, we determined that limiting liquidated damages under the ADEA to cases where the employer "knew or showed reckless disregard for the matter of whether its conduct was prohibited by the statute," without an additional showing of outrageous conduct, was sufficient to give effect to the ADEA's two-tiered liability scheme. 507 U.S. at 616, 617.

* * *

Egregious misconduct is often associated with the award of punitive damages, but the reprehensible character of the conduct is not generally considered apart from the requisite state of mind. * * * [U]nder § 1981a(b)(1), pointing to evidence of an employer's egregious behavior would provide one means of satisfying the plaintiff's burden to "demonstrate" that the employer acted with the requisite "malice or * * * reckless indifference." See 42 U.S.C. § 1981a(b)(1); see, e.g., 3 BNA EEOC Compliance Manual N:6085–N6084 (1992) (Enforcement Guidance: Compensatory and Punitive Damages Available Under § 102 of the Civil Rights Act of 1991) (listing "the degree of egregiousness and nature of the respondent's conduct" among evidence tending to show malice or reckless disregard). Again, however, respondent has not shown that the terms "reckless indifference" and "malice," in the punitive damages context, have taken on a consistent definition including an independent, "egregiousness" requirement * * *.

B

The inquiry does not end with a showing of the requisite "malice or * * * reckless indifference" on the part of certain individuals, however. * * * The plaintiff must impute liability for punitive damages to respondent. The en banc dissent recognized that agency principles place limits on vicarious liability for punitive damages. Likewise, the Solicitor General as amicus acknowledged during argument that common law limitations on a principal's liability in punitive awards for the acts of its agents apply in the Title VII context. * * * While we decline to engage in any definitive application of the agency standards to the facts of this case, * * * it is important that we address the proper legal standards for imputing liability to an employer in the punitive damages context. * * *

* * *

The common law has long recognized that agency principles limit vicarious liability for punitive awards. * * *

We have observed that, "in express terms, Congress has directed federal courts to interpret Title VII based on agency principles." *Burlington Industries, Inc. v. Ellerth*, 524 U.S. 742, 754, 141 L. Ed. 2d 633, 118 S. Ct. 2257 (1998); see also *Meritor Savings Bank, FSB v. Vinson*, 477 U.S. 57, 72, 91 L. Ed. 2d 49, 106 S. Ct. 2399 (1986) * * *.

* * * [O]ur interpretation of Title VII is informed by "the general common law of agency, rather than * * * the law of any particular State." *Burlington Industries, Inc.*, supra, at 754 (internal quotation marks omitted). The common law as codified in the Restatement (Second) of Agency (1957), provides a useful starting point for defining this general common law. * * * The Restatement of Agency places strict limits on the extent to which an agent's misconduct may be imputed to the principal for purposes of awarding punitive damages:

"Punitive damages can properly be awarded against a master or other principal because of an act by an agent if, but only if:

"(a) the principal authorized the doing and the manner of the act, or

"(b) the agent was unfit and the principal was reckless in employing him, or

"(c) the agent was employed in a managerial capacity and was acting in the scope of employment, or

"(d) the principal or a managerial agent of the principal ratified or approved the act." Restatement (Second) of Agency, supra, § 217 C.

See also Restatement (Second) of Torts § 909 (same).

The Restatement, for example, provides that the principal may be liable for punitive damages if it authorizes or ratifies the agent's tortious act, or if it acts recklessly in employing the malfeasing agent. The Restatement also contemplates liability for punitive awards where an employee serving in a "managerial capacity" committed the wrong while "acting in the scope of employment." Restatement (Second) of Agency, supra, § 217 C; see also Restatement (Second) of Torts, *supra*, § 909 (same). "Unfortunately, no good definition of what constitutes a 'managerial capacity' has been found," 2 J. Ghiardi [& J. Kircher, Punitive Damages: Law and Practice], § 24.05, at 14 [(1998)], and determining whether an employee meets this description requires a fact-intensive inquiry. * * * Suffice it to say here that the examples provided in the Restatement of Torts suggest that an employee must be "important," but perhaps need not be the employer's "top management, officers, or directors," to be acting "in a managerial capacity." *Ibid.*; see also 2 Ghiardi, *supra*, § 24.05, at 14; Restatement (Second) of Torts, § 909, at 468, Comment b and Illus. 3.

Additional questions arise from the meaning of the "scope of employment" requirement. The Restatement of Agency provides that even intentional torts are within the scope of an agent's employment if the conduct is "the kind [the employee] is employed to perform," "occurs substantially within the authorized time and space limits," and "is actuated, at least in part, by a purpose to serve the" employer. Restatement (Second) of Agency, *supra*, § 228(1), at 504. According to the Restatement, so long as these rules are satisfied, an employee may be said to act within the scope of employment even if the employee engages in acts "specifically forbidden" by the employer and uses "forbidden means of accomplishing results." Id. § 230, at 511, Comment b; see also *Burlington Industries, Inc.*, supra, at 756. * * * On this view, even an employer who makes every effort to comply with Title VII would be held liable for the discriminatory acts of agents acting in a "managerial capacity."

Holding employers liable for punitive damages when they engage in good faith efforts to comply with Title VII, however, is in some tension with the very principles underlying common law limitations on vicarious liability for punitive damages—that it is "improper ordinarily to award punitive damages against one who himself is personally innocent and therefore liable only vicariously." Restatement (Second) of Torts, supra, § 909, at 468, Comment b. Where an employer has undertaken such good faith efforts at Title VII compliance, it "demonstrates that it never acted in reckless disregard of federally protected rights." * * *; see also *Harris*, 132 F.3d at 983, 984 (observing that, "in some cases, the existence of a written policy instituted in good faith has operated as a total bar to employer liability for punitive damages" and concluding that "the institution of a written sexual harassment policy goes a long way towards dispelling any claim about the employer's 'reckless' or 'malicious' state of mind").

Applying the Restatement of Agency's "scope of employment" rule in the Title VII punitive damages context, moreover, would reduce the incentive for employers to implement antidiscrimination programs. In fact, such a rule would likely exacerbate concerns among employers that § 1981a's "malice" and "reckless indifference" standard penalizes those employers who educate themselves and their employees on Title VII's prohibitions. * * * Dissuading employers from implementing programs or policies to prevent discrimination in the workplace is directly contrary to the purposes underlying Title VII. The statute's "primary objective" is "a prophylactic one," *Albemarle Paper Co. v. Moody*, 422 U.S. 405, 417, 45 L. Ed. 2d 280, 95 S. Ct. 2362 (1975); it aims, chiefly, "not to provide redress but to avoid harm," *Faragher*, 524 U.S. at 806. With regard to sexual harassment, "for example, Title VII is designed to encourage the creation of antiharassment policies and effective grievance mechanisms." *Burlington Industries, Inc.*, 524 U.S. at 764. The purposes underlying Title VII are similarly advanced where employers are encouraged to adopt antidiscrimination policies and to educate their personnel on Title VII's prohibitions.

In light of the perverse incentives that the Restatement's "scope of employment" rules create, we are compelled to modify these principles to avoid undermining the objectives underlying Title VII. See generally ibid. See also *Faragher, supra*, at 802, n. 3 (noting that Court must "adapt agency concepts to the practical objectives of Title VII"); *Meritor Savings Bank, FSB*, 477 U.S. at 72 ("Common-law principles may not be transferable in all their particulars to Title VII"). Recognizing Title VII as an effort to promote prevention as well as remediation, and observing the very principles underlying the Restatements' strict limits on vicarious liability for punitive damages, we agree that, in the punitive damages context, an employer may not be vicariously liable for the discriminatory employment decisions of managerial agents where these decisions are contrary to the employer's "good-faith efforts to comply with Title VII." * * *

We have concluded that an employer's conduct need not be independently "egregious" to satisfy § 1981a's requirements for a punitive damages award, although evidence of egregious misconduct may be used to meet the plaintiff's burden of proof. We leave for remand the question whether petitioner can identify facts sufficient to support an inference that the requisite mental state can be imputed to respondent. The parties have not yet had an opportunity to marshal the record evidence in support of their views on the application of agency principles in the instant case, and the en banc majority had no reason to resolve the issue because it concluded that petitioner had failed to demonstrate the requisite "egregious" misconduct. Although trial testimony established that Allen made the ultimate decision to promote Spangler while serving as petitioner's interim executive director, respondent's highest position, * * * it remains to be seen whether petitioner can make a sufficient showing that Allen acted with malice or reckless indifference to petitioner's Title VII rights. Even if it could be established that Wheat effectively selected O'Donnell's replacement, moreover, several questions would remain, e.g., whether Wheat was serving in a "managerial capacity" and whether he behaved with malice or reckless indifference to petitioner's rights. It may also be necessary to determine whether the Association had been making good faith efforts to enforce an antidiscrimination policy. We leave these issues for resolution on remand.

CHIEF JUSTICE REHNQUIST, with whom JUSTICE THOMAS joins, concurring in part and dissenting in part.

* * * I would hold that Congress' two-tiered scheme of Title VII monetary liability implies that there is an egregiousness requirement that reserves punitive damages only for the worst cases of intentional discrimination. Since the Court has determined otherwise, however, I join that portion of Part II–B of the Court's opinion holding that principles of agency law place a significant limitation, and in many foreseeable cases a complete bar, on employer liability for punitive damages.

JUSTICE STEVENS, with whom JUSTICE SOUTER, JUSTICE GINSBURG, and JUSTICE BREYER join, concurring in part and dissenting in part.

The Court properly rejects the Court of Appeals' holding that defendants in Title VII actions must engage in "egregious" misconduct before a jury may be permitted to consider a request for punitive damages. Accordingly, I join Parts I and II–A of its opinion. I write separately, however, because I strongly disagree with the Court's decision to volunteer commentary on an issue that the parties have not briefed and that the facts of this case do not present. I would simply remand for a trial on punitive damages.

Notes and Questions

1. *Plaintiff Victory?* On balance, is *Kolstad* a plaintiff victory (because the Court rejects an "egregiousness" standard, hence limiting occasions for court review of punitive awards by juries) or a defense victory (because agency principles may insulate the employer from liability)?

2. *When May Liability Be Imputed?* Do you understand the Court's teaching on when employers may be liable for the "malice or reckless indifference" of their agents? To what extent does the Court adopt the principles in the Restatement (Second) of Agency that it cites? The Court expressly qualifies condition (c) of Restatement (Second) of Agency § 217C, by providing the employer with a "good-faith" defense. Would that defense help insulate employers under conditions (a) and (d) or would authorization or ratification per se negate good-faith? Would the defense apply to condition (b), an employer's reckless hiring of an unfit agent? Do all the conditions clearly apply to Title VII actions for punitive damages? For purposes of ratification or approval under condition (d), would any supervisor of or officer superior to a "reckless" discriminator constitute a "managerial agent"?

3. *"Managerial Capacity"*. Condition (c), which the Court qualifies in *Kolstad*, applies only to an agent "employed in a managerial capacity" and "acting in the scope of employment." Does this encompass all supervisors covered by the *Faragher-Ellerth* rule or only a more limited class of senior managers? Why was the Court uncertain whether Leonard Wheat, the acting head of the Washington office, was acting in a managerial capacity, even if

he "effectively selected O'Donnell's replacement"? Does the *Kolstad* decision suggest that employers normally will not be exposed to punitive damages for illegal discriminatory tangible employment decisions under Title VII unless a very senior official is shown to have the requisite malice or reckless indifference? Cf. Lowery v. Circuit City Stores, 206 F.3d 431 (4th Cir.2000) (punitive damages may be appropriate despite formal anti-discrimination policy where evidence of "top" executives' bias). Or might the requisite involvement of a senior executive be established by the absence of an adequate "good-faith", antidiscrimination policy? See, e.g., Tisdale v. Federal Express Corp., 415 F.3d 516 (6th Cir. 2005) ("non-senior management employees can serve in a managerial capacity" for purposes of punitive damages in absence of "good-faith" company efforts; EEOC v. Wal–Mart Stores, 187 F.3d 1241 (10th Cir.1999) (punitive damages for violation of Americans with Disabilities Act appropriate under *Kolstad* where discriminating store managers acted within scope of employment and company failed to disseminate or provide training on its antidiscrimination policy). What if senior executives disregard evidence of a pattern of disadvantagement of a protected class by lower level managers to whom discretion has been delegated, as alleged in Dukes v. Wal–Mart Stores, Inc., 222 F.R.D. 137 (N.D. Cal. 2004), aff'd, 509 F.3d 1168 (9th Cir. 2007).

4. *Punitive Damages for Discriminatory Harassment.* As suggested by *Faragher* and *Oncale,* actionable discriminatory harassment that does not result in a "tangible" employment decision typically is committed by agents who are not acting in a managerial capacity within the scope of their employment. What do plaintiffs have to prove in the usual Title VII hostile work environment harassment case to collect punitive damages? Does an inadequate anti-harassment policy constitute employer "authorization"? Does deficient implementation of a formally adequate policy constitute employer "ratification" or "approval"? See Kimbrough v. Loma Linda Development, 183 F.3d 782 (8th Cir.1999) (finding ratification in manager's approval of harassment). Do deficiencies in the formulation or implementation of an anti-harassment policy establish any requisite lack of "good faith"? Could punitive damages be secured in the following cases?

a. Employer delayed discharging employee for repeated lewd harassment of female coworkers because of employee's protection under collection bargaining agreement. See EEOC v. Indiana Bell Tel. Co., 256 F.3d 516 (7th Cir. 2001).

b. Employer was aware of harassment prior to plaintiff's complaint, and plaintiff was in a position of continued contact with alleged harasser. See Knowlton v. Teltrust Phones, Inc., 189 F.3d 1177, 1186 (10th Cir.1999).

c. Employer did not respond promptly to employee's complaints, but ultimately did respond and try to remedy the problem. See Cush–Crawford v. Adchem Corp., 271 F.3d 352 (2d Cir. 2001).

5. *Punitive Award in the Absence of a Compensatory Damages Award?* In previous rulings, the Supreme Court has held that the constitutionality of a punitive damages award, under the due process clause, depends in substan-

tial part on its proportionate relationship to the compensable harm caused by the wrongdoer. See BMW of North America v. Gore, 517 U.S. 559, 116 S.Ct. 1589, 134 L.Ed.2d 809 (1996). Does this mean that a Title VII court cannot approve the award of punitive damages in a case where the jury declines to award compensatory damages? Even in the absence of an award of backpay? For cases holding that a punitive award is permissible in these circumstances, see, e.g., Abner v. Kansas City Southern Railroad Co., 513 F.3d 154 (5th Cir. 2008) ("combination of the statutory cap and high threshhold of culpability for any award confines the amount of the award to a level tolerable by due process"); Cush–Crawford v. Adchem Corp., supra; Timm v. Progressive Steel Treating, Inc., 137 F.3d 1008 (7th Cir.1998); but see Kerr–Selgas v. American Airlines, Inc., 69 F.3d 1205, 1214 (1st Cir.1995) (Title VII award of compensatory or nominal damages is required, discounting damages allocated to claims under Puerto Rico law).

6. *Punitive Damages Under State Law.* Some state civil rights law permit recovery of punitive damages, see, e.g., Rush v. Scott Specialty Gases, Inc., 914 F.Supp. 104 (E.D.Pa.1996) (43 Pa. Cons. Stat. Ann. §§ 951–63); Arthur Young & Co. v. Sutherland, 631 A.2d 354 (D.C.App.1993) (D.C. Human Rights Law), while others do not, see, e.g., Thoreson v. Penthouse Int'l, 179 A.D.2d 29, 583 N.Y.S.2d 213 (1992) (N.Y. Human Rights Law).

In Cavuoti v. New Jersey Transit Corp., 161 N.J. 107, 735 A.2d 548 (1999), the New Jersey high court clarified its holding in Lehmann v. Toys 'R' Us, Inc., 132 N.J. 587, 626 A.2d 445 (1993), that a plaintiff must show "actual participation in or willful indifference to the wrongful conduct on the part of upper management" and "proof that the offending conduct [is] especially egregious." The *Cavuoti* court purported to adopt a "functional assignment[ ]" approach to the "upper management" category to avoid insulating large corporate employers "simply because of [their] size and corporate structure":

> [U]pper management would consist of those responsible to formulate the organization's anti-discrimination policies, provide compliance programs and insist on performance (its governing body, its executive officers), and to whom the organization has delegated the responsibility to execute its policies in the workplace, who set the atmosphere or control the day-to-day operations of the unit (such as heads of departments, regional managers, or compliance officers).

161 N.J. at 128, 735 A.2d at 561. In addition, for a lower-tier of management

> to be considered a member of "upper management," the employee should have either (1) broad supervisory powers over the involved employees, including the power to hire, fire, promote, and discipline, or (2) the delegated responsibility to execute the employer's policies to ensure a safe, productive and discrimination-free workplace.

Id. at 129, 735 A.2d at 561. Is this approach different from the Supreme Court's in *Kolstad*? If so, is it preferable? Will every case go to the jury because of the fact-specific character of the "functional assignment[ ]" inquiry?

G. COMPENSATION DISPARITIES

1. *The Equal Pay Act*

CORNING GLASS WORKS v. BRENNAN

Supreme Court of the United States, 1974.
417 U.S. 188, 94 S.Ct. 2223, 41 L.Ed.2d 1.

JUSTICE MARSHALL delivered the opinion of the Court.

I

Prior to 1925, Corning operated its plants in Wellsboro and Corning only during the day, and all inspection work was performed by women. Between 1925 and 1930, the company began to introduce automatic production equipment which made it desirable to institute a night shift. During this period, however, both New York and Pennsylvania law prohibited women from working at night. As a result, in order to fill inspector positions on the new night shift, the company had to recruit male employees from among its male dayworkers. The male employees so transferred demanded and received wages substantially higher than those paid to women inspectors engaged on the two day shifts.[3] During this same period, however, no plant-wide shift differential existed and male employees working at night, other than inspectors, received the same wages as their day shift counterparts. Thus a situation developed where the night inspectors were all male,[4] the day inspectors all female, and the male inspectors received significantly higher wages.

In 1944, Corning plants at both locations were organized by a labor union and a collective-bargaining agreement was negotiated for all production and maintenance employees. This agreement for the first time established a plant-wide shift differential, but this change did not eliminate the higher base wage paid to male night inspectors. Rather, the shift differential was superimposed on the existing difference in base wages between male night inspectors and female day inspectors.

Prior to June 11, 1964, the effective date of the Equal Pay Act, the law in both Pennsylvania and New York was amended to permit women to work at night. It was not until some time after the effective date of the Act, however, that Corning initiated efforts to eliminate the differen-

---

3. Higher wages were demanded in part because the men had been earning more money on their day shift jobs than women were paid for inspection work. Thus, at the time of the creation of the new night shift, female day shift inspectors received wages ranging from 20 to 30 cents per hour. Most of the men designated to fill the newly created night shift positions had been working in the blowing room where the lowest wage rate was 48 cents per hour and where additional incentive pay could be earned. As night shift inspectors these men received 53 cents per hour. There is also some evidence in the record that additional compensation was necessary because the men viewed inspection jobs as "demeaning" and as "women's work."

4. A temporary exception was made during World War II when manpower shortages caused Corning to be permitted to employ women on the steady night shift inspection jobs at both locations. It appears that women night inspectors during this period were paid the same higher night shift wages earned by the men.

tial rates for male and female inspectors. Beginning in June 1966, Corning started to open up jobs on the night shift to women. Previously separate male and female seniority lists were consolidated and women became eligible to exercise their seniority, on the same basis as men, to bid for the higher paid night inspection jobs as vacancies occurred.

On January 20, 1969, a new collective-bargaining agreement went into effect, establishing a new "job evaluation" system for setting wage rates. The new agreement abolished for the future the separate base wages for day and night shift inspectors and imposed a uniform base wage for inspectors exceeding the wage rate for the night shift previously in effect. All inspectors hired after January 20, 1969, were to receive the same base wage, whatever their sex or shift. The collective-bargaining agreement further provided, however, for a higher "red circle" rate for employees hired prior to January 20, 1969, when working as inspectors on the night shift. This "red circle" rate served essentially to perpetuate the differential in base wages between day and night inspectors.

The Secretary of Labor brought these cases to enjoin Corning from violating the Equal Pay Act and to collect back wages allegedly due female employees because of past violations. Three distinct questions are presented: (1) Did Corning ever violate the Equal Pay Act by paying male night shift inspectors more than female day shift inspectors? (2) If so, did Corning cure its violation of the Act in 1966 by permitting women to work as night shift inspectors? (3) Finally, if the violation was not remedied in 1966, did Corning cure its violation in 1969 by equalizing day and night inspector wage rates but establishing higher "red circle" rates for existing employees working on the night shift?

II

Congress' purpose in enacting the Equal Pay Act was to remedy what was perceived to be a serious and endemic problem of employment discrimination in private industry—the fact that the wage structure of "many segments of American industry has been based on an ancient but outmoded belief that a man, because of his role in society, should be paid more than a woman even though his duties are the same." S.Rep. No. 176, 88th Cong., 1st Sess., 1 (1963). The solution adopted was quite simple in principle: to require that "equal work will be rewarded by equal wages." *Ibid.*

The Act's basic structure and operation are similarly straightforward. In order to make out a case under the Act, the Secretary must show that an employer pays different wages to employees of opposite sexes "for equal work on jobs the performance of which requires equal skill, effort, and responsibility, and which are performed under similar working conditions." Although the Act is silent on this point, its legislative history makes plain that the Secretary has the burden of proof on this issue, as both of the courts below recognized.

The Act also establishes four exceptions—three specific and one a general catchall provision—where different payment to employees of opposite sexes "is made pursuant to (i) a seniority system; (ii) a merit system; (iii) a system which measures earnings by quantity or quality of production; or (iv) a differential based on any other factor other than sex." Again, while the Act is silent on this question, its structure and history also suggest that once the Secretary has carried his burden of showing that the employer pays workers of one sex more than workers of the opposite sex for equal work, the burden shifts to the employer to show that the differential is justified under one of the Act's four exceptions. All of the many lower courts that have considered this question have so held, and this view is consistent with the general rule that the application of an exemption under the Fair Labor Standards Act is a matter of affirmative defense on which the employer has the burden of proof.

The contentions of the parties in this case reflect the Act's underlying framework. Corning argues that the Secretary has failed to prove that Corning ever violated the Act because day shift work is not "performed under similar working conditions" as night shift work. The Secretary maintains that day shift and night shift work are performed under "similar working conditions" within the meaning of the Act.[13] Although the Secretary recognizes that higher wages may be paid for night shift work, the Secretary contends that such a shift differential would be based upon a "factor other than sex" within the catch-all exception to the Act and that Corning has failed to carry its burden of proof that its higher base wage for male night inspectors was in fact based on any factor other than sex.

* * *

The most notable feature of the history of the Equal Pay Act is that Congress recognized early in the legislative process that the concept of equal pay for equal work was more readily stated in principle than reduced to statutory language which would be meaningful to employers and workable across the broad range of industries covered by the Act. As originally introduced, the Equal Pay bill required equal pay for "equal work on jobs the performance of which requires equal skills." There were only two exceptions—for differentials "made pursuant to a seniority or merit increase system which does not discriminate on the basis of sex. * * *"

In both the House and Senate committee hearings, witnesses were highly critical of the Act's definition of equal work and of its exemptions.

---

13. The Secretary also advances an argument that even if night and day inspection work is assumed not to be performed under similar working conditions, the differential in base wages is nevertheless unlawful under the Act. The additional burden of working at night, the argument goes, was already fully reflected in the plant-wide shift differential, and the shifts were made "similar" by payment of the shift differential. This argument does not appear to have been presented to either [of] the [courts below], as the opinions in both cases reflect an assumption on the part of all concerned that the Secretary's case would fail unless night and day inspection work was found to be performed under similar working conditions. For this reason, and in view of our resolution of the "working condition" issue, we have no occasion to consider and intimate no views on this aspect of the Secretary's argument.

Many noted that most of American industry used formal, systematic job evaluation plans to establish equitable wage structures in their plants. Such systems, as explained coincidentally by a representative of Corning Glass Works who testified at both hearings, took into consideration four separate factors in determining job value—skill, effort, responsibility and working conditions—and each of these four components was further systematically divided into various subcomponents. Under a job evaluation plan, point values are assigned to each of the subcomponents of a given job, resulting in a total point figure representing a relatively objective measure of the job's value.

* * *

Indeed, the most telling evidence of congressional intent is the fact that the Act's amended definition of equal work incorporated the specific language of the job evaluation plan described at the hearings by Corning's own representative—that is, the concepts of "skill," "effort," "responsibility," and "working conditions."

* * *

While a layman might well assume that time of day worked reflects one aspect of a job's "working conditions," the term has a different and much more specific meaning in the language of industrial relations. As Corning's own representative testified at the hearings, the element of working conditions encompasses two subfactors: "surroundings" and "hazards." "Surroundings" measures the elements, such as toxic chemicals or fumes, regularly encountered by a worker, their intensity, and their frequency. "Hazards" takes into account the physical hazards regularly encountered, their frequency, and the severity of injury they can cause. This definition of "working conditions" is not only manifested in Corning's own job evaluation plans but is also well accepted across a wide range of American industry.

Nowhere in any of these definitions is time of day worked mentioned as a relevant criterion. The fact of the matter is that the concept of "working conditions," as used in the specialized language of job evaluation systems, simply does not encompass shift differentials. Indeed, while Corning now argues that night inspection work is not equal to day inspection work, all of its own job evaluation plans, including the one now in effect, have consistently treated them as equal in all respects, including working conditions.

* * *

This does not mean, of course, that there is no room in the Equal Pay Act for nondiscriminatory shift differentials. Work on a steady night shift no doubt has psychological and physiological impacts making it less attractive than work on a day shift. The Act contemplates that a male night worker may receive a higher wage than a female day worker, just as it contemplates that a male employee with 20 years' seniority can receive a higher wage than a woman with two years' seniority. Factors such as these play a role under the Act's * * * exceptions—the seniority differential under the specific seniority exception, the shift differential under the catch-all exception for differentials "based on any other factor other than sex."

The question remains, however, whether Corning carried its burden of proving that the higher rate paid for night inspection work, until 1966 performed solely by men, was in fact intended to serve as compensation for night work, or rather constituted an added payment based upon sex. We agree that the record amply supports the District Court's conclusion that Corning had not sustained its burden of proof. As its history revealed, "the higher night rate was in large part the product of the generally higher wage level of male workers and the need to compensate them for performing what were regarded as demeaning tasks." The differential in base wages originated at a time when no other night employees received higher pay than corresponding day workers, and it was maintained long after the company instituted a separate plant-wide shift differential which was thought to compensate adequately for the additional burdens of night work. The differential arose simply because men would not work at the low rates paid women inspectors, and it reflected a job market in which Corning could pay women less than men for the same work. That the company took advantage of such a situation may be understandable as a matter of economics, but its differential nevertheless became illegal once Congress enacted into law the principle of equal pay for equal work.

* * *

We now must consider whether Corning continued to remain in violation of the Act after 1966 when, without changing the base wage rates for day and night inspectors, it began to permit women to bid for jobs on the night shift as vacancies occurred. It is evident that this was more than a token gesture to end discrimination, as turnover in the night shift inspection jobs was rapid. The record * * * shows * * * that during the two-year period after June 1, 1966, the date women were first permitted to bid for night inspection jobs, women took 152 of the 278 openings, and women with very little seniority were able to obtain positions on the night shift. Relying on these facts, the company argues that it ceased discriminating against women in 1966, and was no longer in violation of the Equal Pay Act.

But the issue before us is not whether the company, in some abstract sense, can be said to have treated men the same as women after 1966. Rather, the question is whether the company remedied the specific violation of the Act which the Secretary proved. We agree with the Second Circuit, as well as with all other circuits that have had occasion to consider this issue, that the company could not cure its violation except by equalizing the base wages of female day inspectors with the higher rates paid the night inspectors. This result is implicit in the Act's language, its statement of purpose, and its legislative history.

KOUBA v. ALLSTATE INS. CO.

United States Court of Appeals, Ninth Circuit, 1982.
691 F.2d 873.

Choy, Circuit Judge.

Allstate Insurance Co. computes the minimum salary guaranteed to a new sales agent on the basis of ability, education, experience, and prior salary. During an 8–to–13 week training period, the agent receives only the minimum. Afterwards, Allstate pays the greater of the minimum and the commissions earned from sales. A result of this practice is that, on the average, female agents make less than their male counterparts.

Lola Kouba, representing a class of all female agents, argued below that the use of prior salary caused the wage differential and thus constitutes unlawful sex discrimination. Allstate responded that prior salary is a "factor other than sex" within the meaning of the statutory exception. The district court entered summary judgment against Allstate, reasoning that (1) because so many employers paid discriminatory salaries in the past, the court would presume that a female agent's prior salary was based on her gender unless Allstate presented evidence to rebut that presumption, and (2) absent such a showing (which Allstate did not attempt to make), prior salary is not a factor other than sex.

* * *

Because Kouba brought her claim under Title VII rather than directly under the Equal Pay Act, Allstate contends that the standard Title VII rules govern the allocation of evidentiary burdens. It cites *Texas Department of Community Affairs v. Burdine,* 450 U.S. 248, 253, 101 S.Ct. 1089, 1091, 67 L.Ed.2d 207 (1981), for the proposition that under Title VII an employee alleging sex discrimination bears the burden of persuasion at all times as to all issues, and concludes that Kouba failed to carry the burden of showing that the wage differential did not result from a factor other than sex.

Allstate misallocates the burden. In *County of Washington v. Gunther,* 452 U.S. 161, 170–71, 101 S.Ct. 2242, 2248–49, 68 L.Ed.2d 751 (1981), the Supreme Court recognized that very different principles govern the standard structure of Title VII litigation, including burdens of proof, and the structure of Title VII litigation implicating the "factor other than sex" exception to an equal-pay claim (though the Court reserved judgment on specifically how to structure an equal-pay claim under Title VII). Accordingly, we have held that even under Title VII, the employer bears the burden of showing that the wage differential resulted from a factor other than sex. *Piva v. Xerox Corp.,* 654 F.2d 591, 598–601 (9th Cir.1981); *Gunther v. County of Washington,* 623 F.2d 1303, 1319 (9th Cir.1980) (supplemental opinion denying rehearing), *aff'd,* 452 U.S. 161, 101 S.Ct. 2242, 68 L.Ed.2d 751 (1981). Nothing in *Burdine* converts this affirmative defense, which the employer must plead and prove under *Corning Glass,* into an element of the cause of action, which the employee must show does not exist.

In an effort to carry its burden, Allstate asserts that if its use of prior salary caused the wage differential, prior salary constitutes a factor other than sex. An obstacle to evaluating Allstate's contention is the ambiguous statutory language. The parties proffer a variety of possible interpretations of the term "factor other than sex."

We can discard at the outset three interpretations manifestly incompatible with the Equal Pay Act. At one extreme are two that would tolerate all but the most blatant discrimination. Kouba asserts that Allstate wrongly reads "factor other than sex" to mean any factor that either does not refer on its face to an employee's gender or does not result in all women having lower salaries than all men. Since an employer could easily manipulate factors having a close correlation to gender as a guise to pay female employees discriminatorily low salaries, it would contravene the Act to allow their use simply because they also are facially neutral or do not produce complete segregation. Not surprisingly, Allstate denies relying on either reading of the exception.

At the other extreme is an interpretation that would deny employers the opportunity to use clearly acceptable factors. Kouba insists that in order to give the Act its full remedial force, employers cannot use any factor that perpetuates historic sex discrimination. The court below adopted a variation of this interpretation: the employer must demonstrate that it made a reasonable attempt to satisfy itself that the factor causing the wage differential was not the product of sex discrimination. But while Congress fashioned the Equal Pay Act to help cure long-standing societal ills, it also intended to exempt factors such as training and experience that may reflect opportunities denied to women in the past. H.R.Rep. No. 309, 88th Cong., 1st Sess. 3, *reprinted in* 1963 U.S.Code Cong. & Ad.News 687, 689.

* * *

All three interpretations miss the mark in large part because they do not focus on the reason for the employer's use of the factor. The Equal Pay Act concerns business practices. It would be nonsensical to sanction the use of a factor that rests on some consideration unrelated to business. An employer thus cannot use a factor which causes a wage differential between male and female employees absent an acceptable business reason. Conversely, a factor used to effectuate some business policy is not prohibited simply because a wage differential results.

* * *

Relying on recent Supreme Court precedent, Kouba would limit the category of business reasons acceptable under the exception to those that measure the value of an employee's job performance to his or her employer.

* * *

In drafting the Act, however, Congress did not limit the exception to job-evaluation systems. Instead, it excepted "any other factor other than sex" and thus created a "broad general exception." H.R.Rep. No. 309, 88th Cong., 1st Sess. 3, *reprinted in* 1963 U.S. Code Cong. & Ad. News 687, 689. While a concern about job-evaluation systems served as the impetus for creating the exception, Congress did not limit the exception to that concern.

Other language in the Act supports this conclusion. The statutory definition of equal work incorporates the four factors listed in *Corning Glass* as the standard components in job-evaluation systems. (The Act refers to "equal work on jobs the performance of which requires equal skill, effort, and responsibility, and which are performed under similar working conditions.") It would render the "factor other than sex" exception surplusage to limit the exception to the same four factors. And while we might be able to distinguish other factors that also reflect job value, the scope of the exception would be exceedingly narrow if limited to other apparently uncommon factors. The broad language of the exception belies such limitation.

Accordingly, no court or other authority has inferred a job-evaluation requirement. We, too, reject that limitation on the "factor other than sex" exception.

Allstate provides two business reasons for its use of prior salary that the district court must evaluate on remand.[7] We will discuss each explanation in turn without attempting to establish a comprehensive framework for its evaluation. The district court should mold its inquiry to the particular facts that unfold at trial.

Allstate asserts that it ties the guaranteed monthly minimum to prior salary as part of a sales-incentive program. If the monthly minimum far exceeds the amount that the agent earned previously, the agent might become complacent and not fulfill his or her selling potential. By limiting the monthly minimum according to prior salary, Allstate hopes to motivate the agent to make sales, earn commissions, and thus improve his or her financial position. Presumably, Allstate cannot set a uniform monthly minimum so low that it motivates all sales agents, because then prospective agents with substantially higher prior salaries might not risk taking a job with Allstate.

This reasoning does not explain Allstate's use of prior salary during the initial training period. Because the agents cannot earn commissions at that time, there is no potential reward to motivate them to make sales.

7. A third reason given by Allstate is that an individual with a higher prior salary can demand more in the marketplace. Courts disagree whether market demand can ever justify a wage differential. [citations omitted.] We need not rule whether Congress intended to prohibit the use of market demand. Because Allstate did not present any evidence to support its use of prior salary in response to market demand, the district court properly disposed of that reason on summary judgment.

When commissions become available, we wonder whether Allstate adjusts the guaranteed minimum regularly and whether most agents earn commission-based salaries. On remand, the district court should inquire into these and other issues that relate to the reasonableness of the use of prior salary in the incentive program.

Reasoning that salary corresponds roughly to an employee's ability, Allstate also claims that it uses prior salary to predict a new employee's performance as a sales agent. Relevant considerations in evaluating the reasonableness of this practice include (1) whether the employer also uses other available predictors of the new employee's performance, (2) whether the employer attributes less significance to prior salary once the employee has proven himself or herself on the job, and (3) whether the employer relies more heavily on salary when the prior job resembles the job of sales agent.

Notes and Questions

1. *Why Regulate Pay Discrimination Once Hiring Discrimination Is Proscribed?* Why should anyone concerned about sex discrimination ultimately care about wage disparities between equal jobs as long as women and men have equal access to all jobs? Does ensuring equal access necessarily prevent an employer paying a woman less for doing the same job as a man? Does it at least prevent an employer from dividing workers by sex into two job classifications with the same duties but unequal pay?

2. *"Similar Working Conditions."* Consider the Court's interpretation in *Corning Glass* of the important Equal Pay Act (EPA) phrase "similar working conditions." Does it mean that if Corning Glass had always paid its night shift more than its day shift and had always employed women at night as well as the day, Corning still would be compelled to justify paying a female day worker less than a male night worker? In view of the defenses available to an employer, does this present a significant problem? See also note 7 infra.

Does the Court's reading of "similar working conditions" also mean that if Corning historically had excluded all females from certain especially hazardous jobs, which it compensated at a higher level in part because only males filled them, there would be no EPA cause of action? Is there any way to read the Act to provide a cause of action in such a case? Is one suggested in footnote 13? Can the statutory language be read to support this suggestion?

3. *"Equal Skill, Effort, and Responsibility".* The Court in *Corning Glass* noted in a footnote that the lower courts have not required Equal Pay Act plaintiffs to show that the jobs filled by females are absolutely identical to more highly compensated jobs filled by males. It is sufficient to show that the jobs are "substantially equal." See, e.g., Beck–Wilson v. Principi, 441 F.3d 353 (6th Cir. 2006); Tomka v. Seiler Corp., 66 F.3d 1295, 1312 (2d Cir.1995); Mulhall v. Advance Security, Inc., 19 F.3d 586, 592 (11th Cir. 1994); Thompson v. Sawyer, 678 F.2d 257, 271–72 (D.C.Cir.1982). See generally Mayer Freed & Daniel Polsby, Comparable Worth in the Equal Pay Act, 51 U.Chi.L.Rev. 1078 (1984) and Mary Becker, Comparable Worth In

Antidiscrimination Legislation: A Reply to Freed and Polsby, 51 U.Chi. L.Rev. 1112 (1984).

Nonetheless, plaintiffs must take seriously the requirements of equality in skill, effort, and responsibility, like that of similarity in working conditions, in order to establish a prima facie case under the Equal Pay Act. See, e.g., Wheatley v. Wicomico County, 390 F.3d 328 (4th Cir. 2004) (departmental supervisors have same general duties, but perform different day-to-day functions); Spaulding v. University of Washington, 740 F.2d 686 (9th Cir. 1984) (teaching positions in different academic disciplines carry different responsibilities); EEOC v. Kenosha Unified Sch. Dist. No. 1, 620 F.2d 1220, 1225 (7th Cir.1980) (male custodians' duties differed somewhat from those of female cleaners).

4. *Reliance on "Market Rate" or Prior Salary as a "Factor Other Than Sex"?* How does the *Corning* Court treat the argument that paying men more than women because men will not work for as low a wage as will women is basing pay on a neutral factor other than sex—payment of the wage necessary to secure the available labor? Does the Court hold that an employer's reliance on labor market factors can never constitute reliance on a "factor other than sex"? Does the *Corning* Court effectively reject the "market rate" defense reserved in footnote 7 in *Kouba?* Or did Allstate's reliance on market factors differ from Corning's in a significant way?

Is it likely that an employer normally will be able to secure the best available employees if it does not have a facially neutral policy of matching prior salary or matching a competitor's salary offer? Should an employer have to prove that a high prior salary of a male applicant was not due to discriminatory forces in the labor market? Should an employer have to extend the same starting salary to all female applicants later selected for the same work? For other treatments of a prior salary or matching offer defense under the EPA, see, e.g., Wernsing v. Department of Human Services, 427 F.3d 466 (7th Cir. 2005) (prior salary is factor other than sex for calculating starting salary); Taylor v. White, 321 F.3d 710 (8th Cir.2003) (employer may rely on "salary retention" policy unless used for purpose of taking advantage of women's "market" position as in *Corning*); Glenn v. General Motors Corp., 841 F.2d 1567 (11th Cir.1988) (prior salary cannot justify pay disparity).

5. *Perpetuation of Prior Discrimination?* Could Corning have justified its post-June 1966 day and night shift wage disparities as simply an instance of giving effect to the settled salary expectations of its workforce—a kind of "grandfathering" measure? Given the fact that Corning then provided women equal access to the night shift inspection jobs, why should this justification not be considered a "factor other than sex"?

6. *Allocation of Burden of Proof.* Why did *Corning* assign the burden of persuasion to the employer to show it relied on a "factor other than sex"? Is this consistent with the way the Court has allocated burdens in intentional discrimination litigation under Title VII? Or does the "factor other than sex" provision establish an affirmative defense, like that of the BFOQ?

7. *Must All Substantially Equal Jobs Be Compared?* The lower courts have held that an EPA plaintiff can compare her wages to those paid to male predecessors in her position. See, e.g., Brinkley–Obu v. Hughes Training,

Inc., 36 F.3d 336, 343 (4th Cir.1994); Clymore v. Far–Mar–Co., 709 F.2d 499, 502–03 (8th Cir.1983). Must she also compare her wages to all incumbent male workers in substantially equal jobs, however? Should she have to demonstrate that her wages are below the average wage paid in those jobs in order to establish a prima facie Equal Pay Act case? See Hein v. Oregon College of Education, 718 F.2d 910 (9th Cir.1983) (taking this position).

8. *Disparate Impact Claims Under the EPA?* Does the *Kouba* court's reading of the "factor other than sex" defense equate that provision with Title VII's business necessity defense? Does the court hold that the EPA defense is available whenever the employer uses a neutral standard in subjective good faith, rather than as a pretext for paying women less; or does the court want employers to justify the impact of a facially neutral standard on women's relative compensation by proving that it is actually necessary to the employer's business? Compare EEOC v. J.C.Penney Co., 843 F.2d 249 (6th Cir.1988) (must have "legitimate" business reason), with Behm v. United States, 68 Fed. Cl. 395 (2005) (business reason not required, pay plan need only be neutral and bona fide). Reconsider this issue after reading the Supreme Court's decision in County of Washington v. Gunther infra.

9. *Coverage of Workload Discrimination?* Does the EPA proscribe requiring a woman to work longer hours than a man to earn the same salary in an otherwise substantially equal job? Consider carefully the language of the Act, 29 U.S.C. § 206(d)(1), reprinted in the statutory supplement. Can an EPA court consider an imputed hourly rate of pay for salaried jobs? Or can the court at least take into account whether the man's lighter workload permits him more easily to supplement his income through another job? See Berry v. Board of Supervisors of L.S.U., 715 F.2d 971 (5th Cir.1983) (recognizing the claim of a female professor required to teach at least twice as many hours as her male peers).

10. *Setting the Wage Rate for Substantially Equal Jobs.* The problem of imputing a wage rate as a standard of comparison between substantially equal jobs can arise in other contexts as well. Although the Supreme Court has not addressed the issue, see, e.g., footnote 8 in the *Norris* decision at p. 305 supra, the lower courts generally have considered employees' total compensation, including that in the form of bonuses and fringe benefits, in calculating wages. See, e.g., EEOC v. J.C. Penney Co., 843 F.2d 249, 252 (6th Cir.1988) (differential in group health coverage can state a prima facie case); Gallagher v. Kleinwort Benson Gov't Sec., Inc., 698 F.Supp. 1401, 1404–05 (N.D.Ill.1988) (must consider bonuses as part of total compensation). Consider complications posed by the following two cases:

a. A department store bases the salary of each of its sales personnel in part on the gross markup of that individual's total sales. Because of the appreciably greater markup on most men's clothing, this policy results in the men selling men's clothing making substantially more on average for each hour of work than the women assigned to selling women's clothing. Are the women being paid at a lower rate than the men? Would the women be paid at a lower rate if their average hourly wages were equal to those of the men because the greater volume of sales of women's clothing compensated for the higher markups on men's clothing? Even if the women do earn less, does the employer have a defense to any Equal Pay Act claim? Assume no discriminatory job assignments, but that men gravitated to the men's clothing department, and females gravitated to the women's clothing department. If the job assignments were discriminatory, would any pay disparity be better addressed through a Title VII challenge to the employer's sex-based assignment of sales personnel to men's and women's clothing. Does the employer have a BFOQ defense to such a challenge? Cf. Hodgson v. Robert Hall Clothes, Inc., 473 F.2d 589 (3d Cir.1973), criticized in Paul N. Cox, Equal Work, Comparable Worth and Disparate Treatment: An Argument for Narrowly Construing *County of Washington v. Gunther,* 22 Duq.L.Rev. 65, 77–78 (1983).

b. A chain of unisex health clubs bases the salary of its managers on the number of new memberships they sell. It assigns female managers to manage female clubs and male managers to manage male clubs. The chain has determined that six new female memberships can be sold with the same effort and in the same time that it takes to sell four new male memberships. The chain therefore gives male managers fifty percent more credit for the sale of a male membership than it gives female managers for the sale of a female membership. This has resulted in the average earnings of male and female managers being equal. Can the female managers present a prima facie EPA case? If so, does the employer have an adequate defense? Would the employer also have an adequate BFOQ defense to any Title VII challenge to its sex-based assignment of club managers? Cf. Bence v. Detroit Health Corp., 712 F.2d 1024 (6th Cir.1983).

Note on the Equal Pay Act of 1963

The EPA was to some extent eclipsed by the passage of Title VII only a year later. The latter statute is, of course, much broader in scope. Unlike Title VII, the EPA is limited to sex discrimination and only reaches compensation. Furthermore, the EPA proscribes only discrimination within an "establishment." This makes difficult a company-wide challenge or a challenge requiring comparisons among different plants in the same area owned by the same employer. But see Brennan v. Goose Creek Consol. Ind. Sch. Dist., 519 F.2d 53 (5th Cir.1975) (attack on common hiring and compensation plan for school system).

An understanding of the EPA nonetheless remains important for the employment discrimination lawyer for several reasons. First, as suggested by the *Kouba* case and as will be explored more fully below, the special EPA defenses have been incorporated into Title VII.

Second, the employer and employees covered by the two Acts are not identical; and some employment decisions reached by the EPA are not reached by Title VII. The former Act was passed as an amendment to the Fair Labor Standards Act (FLSA), which also regulates minimum wages, overtime pay, and child labor. If a firm does not fall within one of the EPA exemptions, it is subject to the EPA even if it has less than 15 employees (and hence would not be subject to Title VII). See generally Mack Player, Enterprise Coverage under the Fair Labor Standards Act: An Assessment of the First Generation, 28 Vand.L.Rev. 283 (1975).

Third, plaintiffs may prefer to invoke the EPA for wage discrimination claims because it provides a different procedural-remedial scheme than that of Title VII. The EPA is enforced through the FLSA procedural scheme. Unlike Title VII, this scheme permits aggrieved employees to proceed directly to state or federal court without filing an administrative complaint or waiting for an administrative investigation or mediation. The private right of action afforded by § 16(b) of the FLSA is terminated if the Labor Department (now the EEOC) first brings a suit on the same complaint, but an employee need not wait any minimum period before filing a private suit. Since 1979, the EEOC has been authorized to bring actions under the EPA. A discussion of the relationship between private and EEOC suits under the EPA and the Age Discrimination in Employment Act (ADEA), the two antidiscrimination laws incorporating FLSA procedures, can be found in chapter 17.

The EPA remedial scheme differs from Title VII's in other respects. First, although general compensatory and punitive damages appear to be unavailable, the EPA offers the possibility of "liquidated damages", set at doubled back pay. However, § 11 of the Portal to Portal Act—formally an amendment to the FLSA—provides that if the employer shows that its violation was "in good faith" and it "had reasonable grounds" for believing it was not in violation of the EPA, the trial court has the discretion to award less than full or even no liquidated damages. Second, the FLSA's two-year statute of limitations (three years if a "willful" violation) imposes different time constraints than those for the filing periods under Title VII. See Holt v. KMI–Continental, Inc., 95 F.3d 123, 131–32 (2d Cir.1996) (EPA's statute of limitations do not apply to Title VII.)

A final possible advantage of the Equal Pay Act's remedial scheme may be reflected in the proviso to that Act's basic prohibition of wage discrimination. This proviso requires an employer who is paying unlawfully discriminatory wages to equalize them only by "topping up" the compensation of the lower paid group to the level of the higher paid group. By contrast, Title VII does not include a no-wage reduction clause.

2. Title VII and Comparable Worth

According to the Bureau of Labor Statistics, in the last quarter of 2007 women who usually worked full time had median weekly earnings of about 80% of the median weekly earnings of men. This percentage nonetheless is a substantial improvement from the 61% ratio that existed 30 years earlier. Most of the improvement occurred during the 1980s and early 1990s when there was an appreciable decline in the real wages of men. One study indicates that the real wages of women increased during this period relative to those of men as a result of factors such as increased female experience and education, a decline in unionization for males, and perhaps a decline in statistical discrimination as women became more committed to the labor market. Another factor making a significant contribution to the relative improvement for women was a shift of occupational categories; for instance, managers and professionals were more likely to be women, while clerical and service workers were somewhat less likely to be female. See Francine D. Blau and Lawrence M. Kahn, Gender Differences in Pay, 14 J. of Econ. Persp. 75 (2000); Francine D. Blau, M. Ferber, and Anne E. Winkler, The Economics of Women, Men, and Work 237–39 (3d ed. 1998); Francine D. Blau and Lawrence M. Kahn, Swimming Upstream: Trends in the Gender Wage Differential in the 1980s, 15 J. of Lab. Econ. 1, 30–32 (1997). See also Michael Selmi, Family Leave and the Gender Wage Gap, 78 N.C. L.Rev. 707 (2000).

The EPA cannot be used to address lower pay in predominantly female occupational categories no matter how defined because the law proscribes pay discrimination only between jobs that are equal in skill, effort, and responsibility. Does Title VII provide tools, beyond those of the EPA? The answer in part depends on the reasons for gender-based job segregation. To the extent that women are concentrated in certain occupations because of illegal discriminatory barriers to employment in male occupations, enforcement of Title VII against those barriers should eliminate the disparities. As labor economists have long suggested, barriers to entry into some occupations will lead to an overcrowding of labor in other occupations. The result will be an inflation of the wage rate in the sheltered occupations where labor is artificially scarce and a deflation of the wage rate in the remaining occupations where labor is artificially plentiful. If the barriers are eliminated, the wage rates in all occupations ideally should in the long run stabilize at levels that reflect the relative contributions of all types of workers to their firms' productivity.

Nevertheless, except perhaps in the long run, the utilization of Title VII to attack discriminatory barriers to female employment in male-dominated occupations may not be able to eliminate much of the earnings disparity between men and women that derives from occupational segregation. First, Title VII can only very gradually remove all these barriers. Title VII enforcement is of course imperfect, and there may be numerous subtle barriers to female advancement in at least some male-dominated occupations that the law cannot effectively reach.

Second, the removal of discriminatory barriers may not eliminate earnings disparities between male and female workers that derive from the occupational choices of male and female workers. Occupational choices may themselves be influenced by the knowledge that discriminatory barriers to certain jobs exist. See Gary Becker, Human Capital, Effort, and the Sexual Division of Labor, 3 J. of Lab. Econ. S33 (1985). Legal attacks on these barriers thus will cause workers and prospective workers to reevaluate their educational and training decisions. But the law and the labor markets are not the only socializing agents in our society. Families, the media, the schools, and other cultural institutions may continue to direct women disproportionally into certain occupations regardless of access to higher paying traditional male occupations. There thus may continue to be some overcrowding and a deflation of wage rates in some traditional female occupations.

Those concerned with earnings disparities between female and male workers, however, formulated another way that Title VII might be utilized to reduce these disparities to the extent that they derive from occupational segregation. Title VII plaintiffs directly challenged employers' decisions to provide higher pay for jobs predominantly filled with males than for jobs of "comparable worth" predominantly filled with females, even though the two jobs could not be considered "equal" under EPA standards. These challenges have confronted significant legal hurdles.

COUNTY OF WASHINGTON v. GUNTHER
Supreme Court of the United States, 1981.
452 U.S. 161, 101 S.Ct. 2242, 68 L.Ed.2d 751.

JUSTICE BRENNAN delivered the opinion of the Court.

The question presented is whether § 703(h) of Title VII of the Civil Rights Act of 1964, 78 Stat. 257, 42 U.S.C. § 2000e–2(h), restricts Title VII's prohibition of sex-based wage discrimination to claims of equal pay for equal work.

I

This case arises over the payment by petitioner, County of Washington, Ore., of substantially lower wages to female guards in the female section of the county jail than it paid to male guards in the male section of the jail.[1] Respondents are four women who were employed to guard female prisoners and to carry out certain other functions in the jail.[2] In January 1974, the county eliminated the female section of the jail, transferred the female prisoners to the jail of a nearby county, and discharged respondents.

Respondents filed suit against petitioners in Federal District Court under Title VII, 42 U.S.C. § 2000e *et seq.,* seeking backpay and other relief.[3] They alleged that they were paid unequal wages for work substantially equal to that performed by male guards, and in the alternative, that part of the pay differential was attributable to intentional sex discrimination. The latter allegation was based on a claim that, because of intentional discrimination, the county set the pay scale for female

1. Prior to February 1, 1973, the female guards were paid between $476 and $606 per month, while the male guards were paid between $668 and $853. Effective February 1, 1973, the female guards were paid between $525 and $668, while salaries for male guards ranged from $701 to $940.

2. Oregon requires that female inmates be guarded solely by women, Or.Rev.Stat. §§ 137.350, 137.360 (1979), and the District Court opinion indicates that women had not been employed to guard male prisoners. For purposes of this litigation, respondents concede that gender is a bona fide occupa-

tional qualification for some of the female guard positions. See 42 U.S.C. § 2000e–2(e)(1); *Dothard v. Rawlinson,* 433 U.S. 321, 97 S.Ct. 2720, 53 L.Ed.2d 786 (1977).

3. Respondents could not sue under the Equal Pay Act because the Equal Pay Act did not apply to municipal employees until passage of the Fair Labor Standards Amendments of 1974, 88 Stat. 55, 58–62. Title VII has applied to such employees since passage of the Equal Employment Opportunity Act of 1972, § 2(1), 86 Stat. 103.

guards, but not for male guards, at a level lower than that warranted by its own survey of outside markets and the worth of the jobs.

* * *

We emphasize at the outset the narrowness of the question before us in this case. Respondents' claim is not based on the controversial concept of "comparable worth," under which plaintiffs might claim increased compensation on the basis of a comparison of the intrinsic worth or difficulty of their job with that of other jobs in the same organization or community. Rather, respondents seek to prove, by direct evidence, that their wages were depressed because of intentional sex discrimination, consisting of setting the wage scale for female guards, but not for male guards, at a level lower than its own survey of outside markets and the worth of the jobs warranted. The narrow question in this case is whether such a claim is precluded by the last sentence of § 703(h) of Title VII, called the "Bennett Amendment."

II

* * * The Bennett Amendment to Title VII, however, provides:

"It shall not be an unlawful employment practice under this subchapter for any employer to differentiate upon the basis of sex in determining the amount of the wages or compensation paid or to be paid to employees of such employer if such differentiation is authorized by the provisions of section 206(d) of title 29." 42 U.S.C. § 2000e–2(h).

To discover what practices are exempted from Title VII's prohibitions by the Bennett Amendment, we must turn to § 206(d)—the Equal Pay Act—which provides in relevant part:

"No employer having employees subject to any provisions of this section shall discriminate, within any establishment in which such employees are employed, between employees on the basis of sex by paying wages to employees in such establishment at a rate less than the rate at which he pays wages to employees of the opposite sex in such establishment for equal work on jobs the performance of which requires equal skill, effort, and responsibility, and which are performed under similar working conditions, except where such payment is made pursuant to (i) a seniority system; (ii) a merit system; (iii) a system which measures earnings by quantity or quality of production; or (iv) a differential based on any other factor other than sex." 77 Stat. 56, 29 U.S.C. § 206(d)(1).

On its face, the Equal Pay Act contains three restrictions pertinent to this case. First, its coverage is limited to those employers subject to the Fair Labor Standards Act. S.Rep. No. 176, 88th Cong., 1st Sess., 2 (1963). Thus, the Act does not apply, for example, to certain businesses engaged in retail sales, fishing, agriculture, and newspaper publishing. See 29 U.S.C. §§ 203(s), 213(a) (1976 ed. and Supp. III). Second, the Act is restricted to cases involving "equal work on jobs the performance of which requires equal skill, effort, and responsibility, and which are performed under similar working conditions." 29 U.S.C. § 206(d)(1). Third, the Act's four affirmative defenses exempt any wage differentials attributable to seniority, merit, quantity or quality of production, or "any other factor other than sex." *Ibid.*

* * *

The language of the Bennett Amendment suggests an intention to incorporate only the affirmative defenses of the Equal Pay Act into Title VII. The Amendment bars sex-based wage discrimination claims under Title VII where the pay differential is "authorized" by the Equal Pay Act. Although the word "authorize" sometimes means simply "to permit," it ordinarily denotes affirmative enabling action. Black's Law Dictionary 122 (5th ed. 1979) defines "authorize" as "[t]o empower; to give a right or authority to act." Cf. 18 U.S.C. § 1905 (prohibiting the release by federal employees of certain information "to any extent not authorized by law"); 28 U.S.C. § 1343 (1976 ed., Supp. III) (granting district courts jurisdiction over "any civil action authorized by law"). The question, then, is what wage practices have been affirmatively authorized by the Equal Pay Act.

The Equal Pay Act is divided into two parts: a definition of the violation, followed by four affirmative defenses. The first part can hardly be said to "authorize" anything at all: it is purely prohibitory. The second part, however, in essence "authorizes" employers to differentiate in pay on the basis of seniority, merit, quantity or quality of production, or any other factor other than sex, even though such differentiation might otherwise violate the Act. It is to these provisions, therefore, that the Bennett Amendment must refer.

Petitioners argue that this construction of the Bennett Amendment would render it superfluous. Petitioners claim that the first three affirmative defenses are simply redundant of the provisions elsewhere in § 703(h) of Title VII that already exempt bona fide seniority and merit systems and systems measuring earnings by quantity or quality of production, and that the fourth defense—"any other factor other than sex"—is implicit in Title VII's general prohibition of sex-based discrimination.

We cannot agree. The Bennett Amendment was offered as a "technical amendment" designed to resolve any potential conflicts between Title VII and the Equal Pay Act. Thus, with respect to the first three defenses, the Bennett Amendment has the effect of guaranteeing that courts and administrative agencies adopt a consistent interpretation of like provisions in both statutes. Otherwise, they might develop inconsistent bodies of case law interpreting two sets of nearly identical language.

More importantly, incorporation of the fourth affirmative defense could have significant consequences for Title VII litigation. Title VII's prohibition of discriminatory employment practices was intended to be broadly inclusive, proscribing "not only overt discrimination but also practices that are fair in form, but discriminatory in operation." *Griggs v. Duke Power Co.,* 401 U.S. 424, 431, 91 S.Ct. 849, 853, 28 L.Ed.2d 158 (1971). The structure of Title VII litigation, including presumptions, burdens of proof, and defenses, has been designed to reflect this approach. The fourth affirmative defense of the Equal Pay Act, however, was designed differently, to confine the application of the Act to wage differentials attributable to sex discrimination. H.R.Rep. No. 309, 88th Cong., 1st Sess. 3 (1963), U.S.Code Cong. & Admin.News 1963, p. 687. Equal Pay Act litigation, therefore, has been structured to permit employers to defend against charges of discrimination where their pay differentials are based on a bona fide use of "other factors other than sex." Under the Equal Pay Act, the courts and administrative agencies are not permitted to "substitute their judgment for the judgment of the employer * * * who [has] established and applied a bona fide job rating system," so long as it does not discriminate on the basis of sex. 109 Cong.Rec. 9209 (1963) (statement of Rep. Goodell, principal exponent of the Act). Although we do not decide in this case how sex-based wage discrimination litigation under Title VII should be structured to accommodate the fourth affirmative defense of the Equal Pay Act, we consider it clear that the Bennett Amendment, under this interpretation, is not rendered superfluous.

* * *

Under petitioners' reading of the Bennett Amendment, only those sex-based wage discrimination claims that satisfy the "equal work" standard of the Equal Pay Act could be brought under Title VII. In practical terms, this means that a woman who is discriminatorily underpaid could obtain no relief—no matter how egregious the discrimination might be—unless her employer also employed a man in an equal job in the same establishment, at a higher rate of pay. Thus, if an employer hired a woman for a unique position in the company and then admitted that her salary would have been higher had she been male, the woman would be unable to obtain legal redress under petitioners' interpretation. Similarly, if an employer used a transparently sex-biased system for wage determination, women holding jobs not equal to those held by men would be denied the right to prove that the system is a pretext for discrimination. Moreover, to cite an example arising from a recent case, *Los Angeles, Dept. of Water & Power v. Manhart,* 435 U.S. 702, 98 S.Ct. 1370, 55 L.Ed.2d 657 (1978), if the employer required its female workers to pay more into its pension program than male workers were required to pay, the only women who could bring a Title VII action under petitioners' interpretation would be those who could establish that a man performed equal work: a female auditor thus might have a cause of action while a female secretary might not. Congress surely did not intend the Bennett Amendment to insulate such blatantly discriminatory practices from judicial redress under Title VII.[19]

19. The dissent attempts to minimize the significance of the Title VII remedy in these cases on the ground that the Equal Pay Act already provides an action for sex-

Moreover, petitioners' interpretation would have other far-reaching consequences. Since it rests on the proposition that any wage differentials not prohibited by the Equal Pay Act are "authorized" by it, petitioners' interpretation would lead to the conclusion that discriminatory compensation by employers not covered by the Fair Labor Standards Act is "authorized"—since not prohibited—by the Equal Pay Act. Thus it would deny Title VII protection against sex-based wage discrimination by those employers not subject to the Fair Labor Standards Act but covered by Title VII. There is no persuasive evidence that Congress intended such a result, and the EEOC has rejected it since at least 1965. See 29 CFR § 1604.7.

* * *

III

Petitioners argue strenuously that the approach of the Court of Appeals places "the pay structure of virtually every employer and the entire economy * * * at risk and subject to scrutiny by the federal courts." They raise the specter that "Title VII plaintiffs could draw any type of comparison imaginable concerning job duties and pay between any job predominantly performed by women and any job predominantly performed by men." But whatever the merit of petitioners' arguments in other contexts, they are inapplicable here, for claims based on the type of job comparisons petitioners describe are manifestly different from respondents' claim. Respondents contend that the County of Washington evaluated the worth of their jobs; that the county determined that they should be paid approximately 95% as much as the male correctional officers; that it paid them only about 70% as much, while paying the male officers the full evaluated worth of their jobs; and that the failure of the county to pay respondents the full evaluated worth of their jobs can be proved to be attributable to intentional sex discrimination. Thus, respondents' suit does not require a court to make its own subjective assessment of the value of the male and female guard jobs, or to attempt by statistical technique or other method to quantify the effect of sex discrimination on the wage rates.

We do not decide in this case the precise contours of lawsuits challenging sex discrimination in compensation under Title VII. It is sufficient to note that respondents' claims of discriminatory undercompensation are not barred by § 703(h) of Title VII merely because respondents do not perform work equal to that of male jail guards. The judgment of the Court of Appeals is therefore affirmed.

JUSTICE REHNQUIST, with whom THE CHIEF JUSTICE, JUSTICE STEWART, and JUSTICE POWELL join, dissenting. [omitted]

biased wage discrimination by women who hold jobs not *currently* held by men. But the dissent's position would still leave remediless all victims of discrimination who hold jobs *never* held by men.

AMERICAN FEDERATION OF STATE, COUNTY, AND MUNICIPAL EMPLOYEES, AFL–CIO v. STATE OF WASHINGTON

United States Court of Appeals, Ninth Circuit, 1985.
770 F.2d 1401.

KENNEDY, CIRCUIT JUDGE.

In this class action affecting approximately 15,500 of its employees, the State of Washington was sued in the United States District Court for the Western District of Washington. The class comprises state employees who have worked or do work in job categories that are or have been at least seventy percent female. The action was commenced for the class members by two unions, the American Federation of State, County, and Municipal Employees (AFSCME) and the Washington Federation of State Employees (WFSE). In all of the proceedings to date and in the opinion that follows, the plaintiffs are referred to as AFSCME. The district court found the State discriminated on the basis of sex in violation of Title VII of the Civil Rights Act of 1964, 42 U.S.C. § 2000e–2(a) (1982), by compensating employees in jobs where females predominate at lower rates than employees in jobs where males predominate, if these jobs, though dissimilar, were identified by certain studies to be of comparable worth. The State appeals. We conclude a violation of Title VII was not established here, and we reverse.

* * *

In 1974 the State commissioned a study by management consultant Norman Willis to determine whether a wage disparity existed between employees in jobs held predominantly by women and jobs held predominantly by men. The study examined sixty-two classifications in which at least seventy percent of the employees were women, and fifty-nine job classifications in which at least seventy percent of the employees were men. It found a wage disparity of about twenty percent, to the disadvantage of employees in jobs held mostly by women, for jobs considered of comparable worth. Comparable worth was calculated by evaluating jobs under four criteria: knowledge and skills, mental demands, accountability, and working conditions. A maximum number of points was allotted to each category: 280 for knowledge and skills, 140 for mental demands, 160 for accountability, and 20 for working conditions. Every job was assigned a numerical value under each of the four criteria. The State of Washington conducted similar studies in 1976 and 1980, and in 1983 the State enacted legislation providing for a compensation scheme based on comparable worth. The scheme is to take effect over a ten-year period. Act of June 15, 1983, ch. 75, 1983 Wash.Laws 1st Ex.Sess. 2071.

* * *

AFSCME alleges sex-based wage discrimination throughout the state system, but its explanation and proof of the violation is, in essence, Washington's failure as early as 1979 to adopt and implement at once a comparable worth compensation program. The trial court adopted this theory as well. The comparable worth theory, as developed in the case before us, postulates that sex-based wage discrimination exists if employees in job classifications occupied primarily by women are paid less than employees in job classifications filled primarily by men, if the jobs are of equal value to the employer, though otherwise dissimilar. We must determine whether comparable worth, as presented in this case, affords AFSCME a basis for recovery under Title VII.

* * *

The trial court erred in ruling that liability was established under a disparate impact analysis. The precedents do not permit the case to proceed upon that premise. AFSCME's disparate impact argument is based on the contention that the State of Washington's practice of taking prevailing market rates into account in setting wages has an adverse impact on women, who, historically, have received lower wages than men in the labor market. Disparate impact analysis is confined to cases that challenge a specific, clearly delineated employment practice applied at a single point in the job selection process. *Atonio v. Wards Cove Packing Co.,* 768 F.2d 1120, 1130 (9th Cir.1985); * * *. The instant case does not involve an employment practice that yields to disparate impact analysis. [T]he decision to base compensation on the competitive market, rather than on a theory of comparable worth, involves the assessment of a number of complex factors not easily ascertainable, an assessment too multifaceted to be appropriate for disparate impact analysis. In the case before us, the compensation system in question resulted from surveys, agency hearings, administrative recommendations, budget proposals, executive actions, and legislative enactments. A compensation system that is responsive to supply and demand and other market forces * * * does not constitute a single practice that suffices to support a claim under disparate impact theory. *See* * * * *Pouncy v. Prudential Insurance Co.,* 668 F.2d 795, 800–01 (5th Cir.1982) (disparate impact model is ill-suited for application to wide-ranging challenges to general compensation policies). Such cases are controlled by disparate treatment analysis. Under these principles and precedents, we must reverse the district court's determination of liability under the disparate impact theory of discrimination.

We consider next the allegations of disparate treatment. Under the disparate treatment theory, AFSCME was required to prove a prima facie case of sex discrimination by a preponderance of the evidence. * * * Our review of the record, however, indicates failure by AFSCME to establish the requisite element of intent by either circumstantial or direct evidence.

AFSCME contends discriminatory motive may be inferred from the Willis study, which finds the State's practice of setting salaries in reliance on market rates creates a sex-based wage disparity for jobs deemed of comparable worth. AFSCME argues from the study that the market reflects a historical pattern of lower wages to employees in positions staffed predominantly by women; and it contends the State of Washington perpetuates that disparity, in violation of Title VII, by using market rates in the compensation system. The inference of discriminatory motive which AFSCME seeks to draw from the State's participation in the market system fails, as the State did not create the market disparity and has not been shown to have been motivated by impermissible sex-based considerations in setting salaries.

The requirement of intent is linked at least in part to culpability, *see Spaulding* [*v. University of Washington*, 740 F.2d 686, 708 (9th Cir. 1984)]; *Contreras v. City of Los Angeles*, 656 F.2d 1267, 1275 n. 5 (9th Cir.1981), *cert. denied*, 455 U.S. 1021, 102 S.Ct. 1719, 72 L.Ed.2d 140 (1982). That concept would be undermined if we were to hold that payment of wages according to prevailing rates in the public and private sectors is an act that, in itself, supports the inference of a purpose to discriminate. Neither law nor logic deems the free market system a suspect enterprise. Economic reality is that the value of a particular job to an employer is but one factor influencing the rate of compensation for that job. Other considerations may include the availability of workers willing to do the job and the effectiveness of collective bargaining in a particular industry. *Christensen v. Iowa*, 563 F.2d 353, 356 (8th Cir. 1977). We recognized in *Spaulding* that employers may be constrained by market forces to set salaries under prevailing wage rates for different job classifications, 740 F.2d at 708. We find nothing in the language of Title VII or its legislative history to indicate Congress intended to abrogate fundamental economic principles such as the laws of supply and demand or to prevent employers from competing in the labor market. *See Lemons v. Denver*, 620 F.2d 228, 229 (10th Cir.), *cert. denied*, 449 U.S. 888, 101 S.Ct. 244, 66 L.Ed.2d 114 (1980); *Christensen*, 563 F.2d at 356.

While the Washington legislature may have the discretion to enact a comparable worth plan if it chooses to do so, Title VII does not obligate it to eliminate an economic inequality that it did not create. * * * Title VII was enacted to ensure equal opportunity in employment to covered individuals, and the State of Washington is not charged here with barring access to particular job classifications on the basis of sex. *See Lemons*, 620 F.2d at 230; *Christensen*, 563 F.2d at 356.

* * *

We * * * reject AFSCME's contention that, having commissioned the Willis study, the State of Washington was committed to implement a new system of compensation based on comparable worth as defined by the study. Whether comparable worth is a feasible approach to employee compensation is a matter of debate. * * * Assuming, however, that like other job evaluation studies it may be useful as a diagnostic tool, we reject a rule that would penalize rather than commend employers for their effort and innovation in undertaking such a study. * * * The results of comparable worth studies will vary depending on the number and types of factors measured and the maximum number of points allotted to each factor. A study that indicates a particular wage structure might be more equitable should not categorically bind the employer who commissioned it. The employer should also be able to take into account market conditions, bargaining demands, and the possibility that another study will yield different results. * * *

Notes and Questions

1. *An EPA Claim in* Gunther*?* Would the plaintiffs in *Gunther* have had a viable EPA claim had their case arisen after the effective date of the amendments covering state and local governments? The district court found that male guards supervised more than ten times as many prisoners as did the female guards, but that the female guards performed clerical duties that the male guards did not.

2. *Is Disparate Impact Available for Sex–Based Compensation Discrimination Claims?* In attempting to rebut the argument that the Bennett Amendment is superfluous if it incorporates only the EPA affirmative defenses, has the *Gunther* Court suggested that for Title VII, as well as for the EPA, sex-based discrimination in compensation claims cannot be brought under a disparate impact theory? If so, are you persuaded by the Court's reasoning? Is it likely that concern over disparate impact claims led Congress to include a special provision in Title VII that did nothing more than incorporate the EPA defenses?

Is there an alternative explanation for the "factor other than sex" defense that is consistent with the availability of disparate impact analysis for EPA and related Title VII cases? Might this defense provide only a somewhat broader range of justifications for pay disparities than would be available in a traditional *Griggs* case? Review the *Kouba* decision, supra. Consider also the Court's decision in Smith v. City of Jackson, infra p. 462.

3. *"Head of Household" Benefits Provisions.* Reading the "factor other than sex" defense to preclude the use of disparate impact analysis for pay discrimination cases under the EPA and Title VII has implications for cases outside of the comparable worth context. Does an employer, for instance, violate either statute by maintaining a "head-of-household" rule denying medical and dental insurance coverage to an employee's spouse if the spouse earns more than the employee? Even if the spouse has less favorable or no medical and dental coverage of his or her own? Is this policy reachable, if at all, only under a disparate impact analysis? Would the narrower interpretation of the "factor other than sex" defense suggested in the second paragraph of the preceding note expose such a policy to legal attack? See 29 C.F.R. § 1620.21 (1987); EEOC v. J.C. Penney Co., Inc., 843 F.2d 249 (6th Cir.1988); Colby v. J.C. Penney Co., Inc., 811 F.2d 1119 (7th Cir.1987); see also Wambheim v. J.C. Penney Co., Inc., 705 F.2d 1492 (9th Cir.1983) (not reaching EPA claim).

4. *Would Disparate Impact Make "Comparable Worth" Claims Viable?* Why did the *AFSCME* court reject the disparate impact claim in that case? Is its reasoning persuasive? Why wasn't Washington's decision not to use the Willis study to set its wage rates a "specific, clearly delineated" employment practice? In any event, given § 703(k)(1)(B)(i) as added by the Civil Rights Act of 1991, should comparable worth plaintiffs be frustrated by an inability to isolate the effects of a particular employment practice? On the other hand,

would allowing disparate impact proof lead to the success of comparable worth claims? Would not defendants be able to show that reliance on prevailing market wages was justified by business necessity? See Craik v. Minnesota State University Board, 731 F.2d 465 (8th Cir.1984).

5. *Was Reliance on Market Forces Consistent with* Corning*?* Was the *AFSCME* court's acceptance of Washington's reliance on prevailing labor market rates as proof of the absence of discriminatory intent consistent with the discussion in *Corning* that taking advantage of discriminatory labor markets to reduce labor costs is not legally acceptable? Did the Ninth Circuit hold that there was a failure of proof on this point, or that plaintiffs were not permitted to show that the prevailing wages for jobs dominated by females were lower because the market undervalued women's work? Does it make a difference that Corning Glass used external labor market rates to pay women less to do the same job as men, whereas Washington paid less to the holders of certain jobs that were theoretically open to both men and women? See also International Union UAW v. Michigan, 886 F.2d 766 (6th Cir.1989) (following the labor market disproves discriminatory intent necessary to sustain comparable worth claim).

6. *What Proof of Discriminatory Intent Is Adequate in Job Comparison Cases?* How could plaintiffs in a case like *Gunther* go about proving that intentional sex discrimination was at work in a pay structure? Absent a facially discriminatory policy or inculpating admission, would plaintiffs have to depend on some form of comparable worth analysis, some demonstration that the male employees received additional compensation not warranted by the value of the additional duties they performed, or that females were not compensated appropriately for the additional duties they performed? Should such analysis be sufficient? See also EEOC v. Sears, Roebuck & Co., 839 F.2d 302, 342–43 (7th Cir.1988) (questioning whether "indirect statistical evidence of discriminatory intent would be sufficient under *Gunther*").

Gunther involved a case where the jobs compared shared a substantial common core of duties. In such cases, some lower courts have adapted the *McDonnell Douglas–Burdine* methodology to accept a prima facie case based on unequal pay in "substantially similar" jobs and pretext proof directed at the employer's proffered explanation. See, e.g., Conti v. Universal Enterprises, Inc., 50 Fed.Appx. 690 (6th Cir.2002) (plaintiff may prove discriminatory intent through employer's effective admission or through proof of pretext under *McDonnell Douglas* framework); Mulhall v. Advance Sec., Inc., 19 F.3d 586, 597–98 (11th Cir.1994) (also explaining that the "substantially similar" standard is somewhat more relaxed than the equality standard under the EPA). Proof of pretext under the *McDonnell Douglas* framework presumably would not be available in cases dependent on comparisons of entirely dissimilar jobs, however.

7. *Burden of Proof in Title VII Pay Discrimination Cases. Corning* indicates that a plaintiff can establish an EPA prima facie case without showing discriminatory intent. The persuasion burden then shifts to the defendant to prove any of the EPA affirmative defenses. Does *Gunther* suggest that the normal Title VII principle assigning to plaintiffs the burden of proving discriminatory intent does not apply in sex compensation discrimination cases? The *Kouba* court thought so, and the EEOC agrees, see 29

C.F.R. § 1620.27. See also Korte v. Diemer, 909 F.2d 954, 959 (6th Cir. 1990); McKee v. Bi–State Dev. Agency, 801 F.2d 1014, 1019 (8th Cir.1986) (both agreeing with EEOC that EPA liability necessarily entails Title VII liability). Other circuits, however, have held that plaintiffs must prove discriminatory intent to establish a Title VII case and thus can lose such a case even while being successful on a cognate EPA claim on which the defendant employer has not demonstrated an affirmative defense. See, e.g., Brinkley–Obu v. Hughes Training, Inc., 36 F.3d 336, 343–344 & n. 17 (4th Cir.1994); Meeks v. Computer Assocs. Intl., 15 F.3d 1013 (11th Cir.1994); Fallon v. Illinois, 882 F.2d 1206, 1217 (7th Cir.1989). How should courts treat this issue?

8. *Proposed "Comparable Worth" Legislation.* In response to the barriers to comparable worth litigation under current law, some members of Congress have introduced legislation to amend the Fair Labor Standards Act to facilitate such litigation. For instance, the Fair Pay Act of 2007, S. 1087 and H.R. 2019, 110th Cong. 1st Sess., would prohibit FLSA-covered employers "paying wages * * * in a job that is dominated by employees of a particular sex, race, or national origin at a rate less than the rate at which the employer pays wages to employees * * * in another job [in the same establishment] that is dominated by employees of the opposite sex or of a different race or national origin, respectively, for work on equivalent jobs." Equivalent jobs are defined to mean "jobs that may be dissimilar, but whose requirements are equivalent when viewed as a composite of skill, effort, responsibility, and working conditions." Would such legislation provide for effective comparable worth litigation? Would it have desirable overall economic effects? Consider the following further discussion.

Further Note on the Feasibility and Promise of Comparable Worth Litigation or Legislation

PAUL C. WEILER, THE WAGES OF SEX: THE USES AND LIMITS OF COMPARABLE WORTH*

However scientific job evaluation might seem in its precise numerical ranking of jobs, these numbers ultimately rest on value judgments. As it turns out, conventional job evaluation derives these numbers from, rather than imposes them upon, the labor market. An evaluator customarily begins with a small number of key, benchmark jobs within the firm. These jobs may involve relatively standardized skills for which there is a visible external market (for example, electrician or legal secretary), or they may serve as a "port of entry" into the firm for people with relatively little skill who are hired into low-level classifications (for example, laborer or clerk) where they will be trained and from which they may progress up the job ladder. The assumption underlying job evaluation is that the firm must remain competitive in its pay for these jobs at whatever position it has chosen to occupy in the community's pay spectrum. Thus, these jobs are first broken down into their constituent elements and ranked in terms of the factors considered important in

* 99 Harv.L.Rev. 1728 (1986).

determining job worth. The existing market wage relationships for these jobs are then used as the peg from which to derive the implicit value for each. * * * The evaluation scheme thus serves to establish a decent level of coherence and equity within the internal labor market of the firm while at the same time respecting the real cost and recruiting constraints imposed by the external labor market. * * *

This difficulty does not mean that judges would inevitably have to take the responsibility of making their own "value judgments" about "criteria of pay equity," or even worse, delegate that role to "some group of experts or pseudo experts." Suppose that one selected as benchmark jobs only those that were either integrated or distinctively male in their composition, on the assumption that wages for these jobs were unlikely to have been tainted by sex discrimination. Using statistical analysis, one would try to derive the implicit value to the firm of the relevant job factors. * * * Whatever reward structure one found beneath the entire array of male or integrated jobs could then be used to determine whether the employer was paying the same price for these same factors when they were displayed in identifiably female positions such as secretary or nurse. Indeed, this approach actually would track quite closely the basic theme of the Equal Pay Act itself.

* * * Contrary to the contentions of its detractors, comparable worth need not entail a search for the "just price" of labor. It need only require that the implicit evaluation a firm places on those factors for which it actually rewards its employees working in male jobs should also be applied uniformly and fairly in setting wages for women's work as well.

* * *

[*Editors' Note:* Notwithstanding his view that it could be feasible for courts to evaluate employers' pay scales for the effects of sex discrimination in the labor market, for two sets of reasons, Professor Weiler remains unenthusiastic about comparable worth as a strategy for achieving pay equity for women. First, Weiler contends that the highly decentralized character of the litigation process will place "those employers who were targeted early * * * at a considerable competitive disadvantage vis-a-vis those not yet reached by the law." 99 Harv.L.Rev. at 1776. He notes that, as a practical matter, successful litigation against particular employers will not result in lowering the wages of male-dominated jobs because those probably are set as low as the market permits. A good example of this occurred in Christensen v. Iowa, 563 F.2d 353 (8th Cir.1977), a decision cited in *Gunther*. In that case, the public employer reduced starting wages for the workers in the all-male physical plant department because a job evaluation indicated that their wages were set above their evaluated worth. Unable to recruit qualified workers for the physical plant department at the evaluated wage rates, the employer reverted to what was in effect the prior wage rates; the alternative of raising wages in the female-dominated jobs was rejected because this would increase labor costs beyond what was necessary to attract qualified workers. The employer was then sued (unsuccessfully) by workers in the all-female clerical department who maintained that, given the point scores on the job evaluation, they should have received a corresponding boost in their wages.

Weiler thus suggests that the comparable worth strategy may require coordinated regulation of all employers competing in the same labor market. For example, in 1987 Ontario passed pay equity legislation applicable to all public sector employers and all private companies with more than ten employees in that province. See Solomon, Pay Equity Gets a Tryout in Canada—And U.S. Firms Are Watching Closely, Wall St.J., Dec. 28, 1988, B1, col. 3. But Weiler states that even such legislation is not costless. Australia in the early 1970s mandated a twenty-five percent increase in female pay. As Weiler observes:

> But when the government so raised the price of female labor, it correspondingly reduced the demand. There was an immediate but fairly small increase in female unemployment and a one-third reduction in the expected rate of growth in female employment for the remainder of the decade. The great bulk of these employment effects were felt in the private manufacturing industries * * *. And as expected, the wage gains for women came almost entirely at the expense of men's wages in these manufacturing industries.

99 Harv.L.Rev. at 1776–77, citing R.G. Gregory and R.C. Duncan, Segmented Labor Market Theories and the Australian Experience of Equal Pay for Women, 3 J. Post–Keynesian Econ. 403, 424–27 (1981); R.G. Gregory, P. McMahon & B. Whittingham, Women in the Australian Labor Force: Trends, Causes, and Consequences, 3 J.Lab.Econ. S293 (1985).

Weiler's second ground for skepticism is that statistical studies indicate that only a small proportion of the gender wage gap could be eliminated by a completely successful implementation of the comparable worth strategy. Weiler considers the wage gap from two final perspectives—the "marriage gap" and the "occupational gap"—to determine whether either is likely to be addressed by the comparable worth strategy.]

* * *

1. *The Marriage Gap.*—A quick look at the basic statistics discloses that almost all the wage gap obtains between men and women who are or have been married. Among those never married, women historically have earned nearly as much, if not more, than their male counterparts. By contrast, married women with a spouse present, even if they work full-time, year-round, actually have earned less than forty percent of what married men earn. It is possible, of course, that these crude figures might disguise the fact that single women tend to possess greater "human capital" than single men. When one controls for the standard

variables, however, the adjusted gender wage gap for married workers is still more than three times that for single, never-married workers.

* * *

Simple notions of discrimination in employment on account of sex will not readily explain this pattern in the gender wage gap: why should the impact of such invidious employer motives and practices be borne almost entirely by women who are married, especially by those with children? The answer is that the institution of marriage itself plays a major role as it intersects with the operation of the labor market. Participation in the work force is highest for married men, lowest for married women, with single men and single women at roughly the same point somewhere between. In addition, women are likely to have substantial interruptions in their employment during their child-bearing years. These patterns correlate closely with what we know about the wage gap.

Nor can one ignore the other side of the equation. Recall that marriage produces a sizeable earnings premium for men. Some of this is due to the division of labor and responsibility in the home. Married men have traditionally been relieved of a considerable part of the burden of looking after their domestic needs. At the same time, unlike single men, they have been motivated to work longer and harder to support a family. Conversely, the fact that the primary responsibility for child-rearing and the household typically has devolved upon the wife has meant that marriage tended to reduce her career earnings prospects as compared with those of single women.

I do not mean to imply that these phenomena are the product only of sex-neutral free choice. * * * My point is simply that, to the extent that the interaction between marriage and the labor market is the source of the bulk of the gender wage gap, one cannot thereby infer that the jobs predominantly filled by women are inherently undervalued and underpaid. The policy implication of this alternative diagnosis is that, rather than pursue a comparable worth strategy of altering the relative wages paid in male and female jobs (many of the occupants of the latter being either *single* women or men), society should tackle the problem of the impact of marriage upon work prospects directly. For example, available funds could be expended upon such strategies as better day care facilities or more flexible work schedules.

2. *The Occupational Gap.*—* * * Modern econometric analysis enables us to test the actual importance of female representation in influencing the wages paid for a particular job relative to other jobs. We now have a considerable body of research addressing this issue. On the surface it appears that the proportion of female incumbents has a significant depressing effect upon the wages paid for a job and that this factor explains a considerable share of the wage gap. * * * It is nonetheless misleading to consider this factor in isolation, because it is likely [to be] associated with other factors that affect wage determination, especially those related specifically to sex, such as differences in the experi-

ence of the employees and in the environmental conditions of the job. More sophisticated research studies have controlled for these other relevant factors and have found that much of the significance of the "percent female" variable evaporates, leaving it to explain only a small fraction of the wage gap. * * *

Why does the effect of occupational segregation upon female pay turn out to be so much less than is commonly supposed in the recent debate about this issue? The reason is that empirical research has now turned up another form of sex segregation at work that has an even more powerful depressing effect upon women's wages. Men and women are segregated not only in the jobs they perform but also in the industries and the firms in which they work, regardless of the jobs they occupy. This latter form of segregation is correlated powerfully with disparities in earnings. On brief examination, the relevant statistics reveal that industries such as textile production, retail clothing stores, and banking or nonbanking credit services rank at or near the top in the female composition of their workforce, but near the bottom in their average wage scales. On the other hand, the very highest paying industries, such as mining and construction, have the smallest proportion of women in their employ. When one controls in these crude ratios for human capital variables, segregation by industry and by firm does explain far more of the gap in earnings than does segregation by type of occupation. The policy of "comparable worth," at least when viewed as a legal attack upon wage discrimination, is able at most to deal with the disparity in wages paid for different jobs within the same firm, but not with the disparity in levels of pay across different firms and different industries. Thus, quite a different strategy would be needed to make a major dent in the latter, more significant factor in the overall earnings gap.

Notes and Questions

1. *A Continuing Discrimination Gap?* Some research may suggest that in addition to the factors discussed by Weiler, discrimination by some employers helps explain some of the remaining gap between male and female wages. Some of the studies have examined wage differences among graduate school or college classes and have found an unexplained gender gap of between 10 and 15 percent. See, e.g., Robert G. Wood, Mary E. Corcoran & Paul N. Courant, Pay Differences Among the Highly Paid: The Male–Female Earnings Gap in Lawyers' Salaries, 11 J.Lab.Econ. 417 (1993) (Michigan law school graduates 15 years after graduation). Another project discovered continuing discrimination through the use of a hiring "audit" in which males and females with similar resumes applied to wait on tables at a number of restaurants in Philadelphia. See David Neumark, Sex Discrimination in Restaurant Hiring: An Audit Study, 111 Q.J. Econ. 915 (1996).And yet another study found that the initiation of blind auditions by the top American symphony orchestras explained between a fourth and a half of the significant increase in the percentage of female musicians hired. See Claudia Goldin & Cecilia Rouse, Orchestrating Impartiality: The Impact of "Blind"

Auditions on Female Musicians, 90 Am. Econ. Rev. 715 (2000). These studies, inter alia, are discussed in both Blau and Kahn, supra, at 83, and Christine Jolls, Is There a Glass Ceiling?, 25 Harv. Women's L.J. 1 (2002).

2. *Must a "Comparable Worth" Regime Unfairly Disadvantage Defendant Employers?* Is the highly decentralized character of our legal enforcement system a problem for the implementation of Title VII generally? Does a typical successful systemic disparate treatment or disparate impact case against an employer impose significant additional labor costs and thus make it less able to compete against firms that have not yet been sued? Is it possible to devise legislation that provides for an enforcement scheme that would significantly reduce the costs of uneven enforcement of a comparable worth mandate?

3. *Do "Comparable Worth" Initiatives Affect Female Labor Market Participation Decisions?* Might the potential impact of comparable worth initiatives on the gender wage gap be greater than acknowledged by Weiler because of their influence on labor market decisions by women, such as whether to invest more in human capital and to work more hours, that also help explain the gap? See Stephen Willborn, A Secretary and A Cook: Challenging Women's Wages in the Courts of the United States and Great Britain 142–43 (1989). On the other hand, might increasing the compensation for traditional female jobs simply encourage women to remain in these jobs rather than attempting to break down the barriers to jobs traditionally dominated by males? Cf. Shulamit Kahn, The Economic Implications of Public–Sector Comparable Worth: The Case of San Jose, California, 31 Industrial Relations 270–91 (1992) (finding that the proportion of female employment increased in San Jose city jobs granted upward pay adjustment as a result of union's comparable worth negotiations).

4. *Who Pays For the Gains of "Comparable Worth" Initiatives?* After conducting job evaluation studies, at least twenty states have attempted to implement comparable worth policies in setting compensation for state government jobs. Studies of such initiatives in Minnesota, Washington, and Iowa, found that they were successful in reducing the gender wage gap by several percentage points. See Sarah M. Evans and Barbara J. Nelson, The Impact of Pay Equity on Public Employees, Pay Equity: Empirical Inquiries, eds. R.T. Michael, H.I. Hartmann, and B. O'Farrell 200–221 (1989); Peter F. Orazem and J. Peter Mattila, The Implementation Process of Comparable Worth, 98 J. Pol. Econ. 134–152; June O'Neill, Michael Brien, and James Cunningham, Effects of Comparable Worth Policy, Amer. Econ. Rev. 305–09 (1989). Some studies of comparable worth initiatives also suggest a reduction in employment in the traditional female jobs whose pay is increased, however. See Mark Killingsworth, The Economics of Comparable Worth 135, 212–213 (1990). Does this mean that women who have been unsuccessful in finding employment in traditional jobs in the public sector have been disadvantaged? Have employees in the traditionally higher paying, male dominated jobs probably lost pay increases? But see Heidi Hartmann and Stephanie Aaronson, Pay Equity and Women's Wage Increases: Success in the States, A Model for the Nation, 1 Duke J. Gender L. & Pol'y 69 (1994) (study of state initiatives concluding that well-designed, gradual programs can close wage gap without increasing unemployment or reducing wages of other workers).

Note that Weiler's bottom-line appraisal of the Australian experience is that it improved the conditions of Australian women on the whole and that its distributional effects were justified: "To the extent that the government's policy was designed to eliminate sex discrimination in the pay structure * * *, the distributional consequences of the policy arose simply from the fact that the law had now removed the subsidy that women previously had given to employers through the artificially depressed price of their labor." 99 Harv.L.Rev. at 1777. See also Samuel Estreicher & Miriam Cherry, Global Issues in Employment Law 162–69 (2007).

5. *"Comparable Worth" Across Industries and Firms?* Would it be possible in this country to devise comparable worth legislation that addressed pay disparities among industries and firms? What standards would such legislation use to determine "just" wages? How radical a departure would such legislation be from traditional economic arrangements?

3. *Family Responsibilities and Compensation Disparities*

Consider further Professor Weiler's discussion of what he calls the "marriage gap": the differential earnings of married men and married women. More recent research seems to confirm the impact of being married and having children on women's wages. See, e.g., Jane Waldfogel, Understanding the "Family Gap" in Pay for Women with Children, 12 J. Econ. Persp., Winter 1998. Some commentators have cited research that indicates that family "choices," rather than employer discrimination, explain most of the wage gap between men and women as evidence that this wage gap does not constitute a social problem about which our society needs to be concerned. See, e.g., Lindsay & Shanor, supra, 1 Sup.Ct.Econ.Rev. at 217–21; Daniel Fischel & Edward Lazear, Comparable Worth and Discrimination in Labor Markets, 53 U. of Chi.L.Rev. 891 (1986). There are, however, several reasons why the lessons of this research might be viewed differently.

First, family choice might in part be influenced by labor market, as well as intrafamily, discrimination against women. A husband and wife might decide that since he has a marginal comparative advantage in a somewhat discriminatory labor market, it is more efficient for her to work outside the home only intermittently or part time and use her remaining energies to raise the children and manage the house and their social life. Economically rational family choice thus can compound marginal employment discrimination. This analysis may not recommend a comparable worth strategy. It may support, however, a more vigorous enforcement of the antidiscrimination principle and, possibly, *Johnson*-type affirmative action to open up new employment horizons for married women and thus alter the typical family calculus about the marginal employment prospects of women.

Second, the marriage gap may be explainable at least in part by a form of "statistical discrimination" against married women, and especially women with children. Employers may perceive that some women lose their willingness to expend extra effort on the job after starting a family, while some men seem to work even harder after "settling down" in married life. The employers then make the assumption that most women and men will react similarly and that male workers should therefore be preferred for many jobs. Inasmuch as it is difficult to predict exactly which women will withdraw some of their energies from their jobs after starting a family, the employers' response may be economically rational. However, such assumptions could constitute a significant barrier to the economic advancement of all married women, and could exacerbate the marginal commitment to the labor market caused by the economically rational family choices described above. The result is to confine married women to a cycle of economic inequality in the market place. This analysis argues for clear prohibitions of any discrimination, whether intentional or in effect, against women on account of family status.

Third, the marriage gap research may justify heightened scrutiny under anti-discrimination law of employment policies that unnecessarily aggravate the effects of temporary absences from the work force on workers' careers. Such policies probably have a significant disparate impact on women because of the greater likelihood that they will temporarily leave the workforce to care for young children. See Jane Waldfogel, Working Mothers Then and Now: A Cross–Cohort Analysis of the Effects of Maternity Leave on Women's Pay, in Gender and Family Issues in the Workplace 133 (F. Blau & R.G. Ehrenberg eds., 1997) (finding that women covered by a formal maternity leave policy and who returned to their original employers after their most recent birth have higher pay). The *Satty* decision held illegal a policy causing employees on pregnancy leave to forfeit accumulated seniority when employees on other disability leaves were not so burdened. Should an employment policy that eliminated accumulated seniority whenever an employee returned from a leave of any kind be illegal because of its disparate impact on women? Consider again the *Evans* case in chapter 3 and footnote 5 in the majority opinion in *Satty*. Does § 703(h) insulate such an employment policy from a disparate impact challenge?

Fourth, the marriage gap research may support a range of legislation to remove barriers to career advancement by women who choose to have families. Such legislation, like the Family and Medical Leave Act of 1993 (FMLA), may be framed to require employers to accommodate the discharge of family responsibilities by their male as well as their female employees.

Note on the Family Medical Leave Act and Its Alternatives

The FMLA requires covered employers (including a public agency and an entity employing 50 or more employees for each working day during each of 20 or more calendar weeks in the current or preceding calendar year) to grant eligible employees (those who have worked for the employer for at least twelve months and for at least 1,250 hours during the previous year and who are employed at a worksite where their employer employs at least 50 employees within a 75-mile radius) a total of twelve workweeks of unpaid or paid leave during any twelve month period for one or more of the following reasons: (a) to care for a child born within the last year; (b) to care for a child who has been adopted or placed in foster care with the employee during the past year; (c) to care for a spouse, child, or parent with a serious health condition; or (d) a serious health condition that makes the employee unable to perform the functions of his or her position. 29 U.S.C. § 2612(a). The FMLA also requires employers to reinstate any employee who takes such a leave to the position of employment held by the employee when the leave commenced, or to an equivalent position with equivalent pay, benefits, and other terms and conditions of employment. Id. at § 2614(a). (Reinstatement of employees in the top 10% of the payroll may be denied, however, after giving notice of an opportunity to return, where "necessary to prevent substantial and grievous economic injury to the operations of the business." Id. at § 2614(b).) Furthermore, employers must continue to provide health insurance coverage during FMLA leave, id. at § 2614(c), and may not deny employees who return from taking an FMLA leave any employment benefit, such as accumulated seniority, accrued prior to the date on which the leave commenced, id. at § 2614(a)(2). An employer may not "interfere with, restrain, or deny the exercise of or the attempt to exercise" any of these employee rights. Id. at § 2615(a).

The Supreme Court has upheld the application of the FMLA to state governments as an exercise of Congressional power under § 5 of the fourteenth amendment to "enact so-called prophylactic legislation that proscribes facially constitutional conduct, in order to prevent and deter unconstitutional conduct." Nevada Dept. of Human Resources v. Hibbs, 538 U.S. 721, 727, 123 S.Ct. 1972, 1977, 155 L.Ed.2d 953 (2003). Chief Justice Rehnquist reasoned for the Court:

> By creating an across-the-board, routine employment benefit for all eligible employees, Congress sought to ensure that family-care leave would no longer be stigmatized as an inordinate drain on the workplace caused by female employees, and that employers could not evade leave obligations simply by hiring men. By setting a minimum standard of family leave for all eligible employees, irrespective of gender, the FMLA attacks the formerly state-sanctioned stereotype that only women are responsible for family caregiving, thereby reducing employers' incentives to engage in discrimination by basing hiring and promotion decisions on stereotypes.

Id. at 737.

The FMLA requires employees requesting leave to give their employer 30 days' notice if the need for leave is foreseeable, based on "expected birth or placement" or "planned medical treatment", or at least such notice "as is practicable." 29 U.S.C. § 2612(e). In addition, an employer may request that employees provide the "certification" of a health care provider as a condition of requesting leave based on the serious health condition of a family member or of their own. Notice requirements also are imposed on employers. Id. at § 2613. The statute requires employers to give employees notice of their FMLA rights "in conspicuous places on the premises of the employer". Id. at § 2619. Moreover, the Department of Labor, pursuant to regulations promulgated under its authority to implement the FMLA, requires employers to give notice of employee FMLA rights in employee handbooks or other such written material, and also to give employees notice of their rights and responsibilities under the FMLA when they request leave. The regulations specifically require employers to designate leave as FMLA leave and to notify affected employees of this designation and any responsibility to provide medical certification.

In Ragsdale v. Wolverine World Wide, Inc., 535 U.S. 81, 122 S.Ct. 1155, 152 L.Ed.2d 167 (2002), the Court held that the Department's regulation requiring an employer to designate leave as FMLA leave was invalid in so far as it mandated the tolling of the running of the twelve week period until the employee was advised of the designation. The *Ragsdale* Court found that the regulation was inconsistent with the FMLA because the statute requires employees to prove that an employer's actions or lapses caused "real impairment of their rights and resulting prejudice." Id. at 90. Since *Ragsdale* courts have found that an employer's failure to give notice of rights or responsibilities could cause such prejudice in some cases, however. See, e.g., Lubke v. City of Arlington, 455 F.3d 489 (5th Cir. 2006) (employer's failure to notify employee of responsibility of providing medical certification was prejudicial because employee could have avoided discharge by providing doctors' reports earlier); Conoshenti v. Public Service Electric & Gas Co., 364 F.3d 135 (3d Cir. 2004) (employer's failure to advise employee of his rights to only twelve weeks of FMLA leave may have prejudiced employee who might have postponed surgery to return to work).

The degree to which the FMLA has contributed to achieving greater gender equality at the workplace is not clear. It seems that it has not led to a significantly greater sharing of family responsibilities. FMLA leave has been most often taken by employees because of their own medical condition; and women are much more likely to take FMLA leave to discharge family responsibilities leave than are men. See David Cantor, Balancing the Needs of Families and Employers: Family and Medical Leave Surveys 2000 Update 4–15 (2000). Indeed, in litigated FMLA cases involving births and adoptions, almost all plaintiffs are women. See Rafael Gely & Timothy Chandler, Maternity Leave Under the FMLA: An Analysis of the Litigation Experience, 15 Wash. U. J.L. & Pol'y 143 (2004). The availability of FMLA leave might help some women keep jobs and stay on a career path, however. While any impact of the FMLA on the wages of and employment of women has not been demonstrated, see Steven K. Wisensale, Family Leave Policy: The Political Economy of Work and Family in America 158 (2001), one set of data suggests that comparable earlier state laws mandating leave at least helped eliminate the wage gap for mothers. See Jean Kimmel & Catalina Amuedo-Dorantes, The Effects of Family Leave on Wages, Employment and the Family Wage Gap: Distributorial Implications, 15 Wash. U. J. L. & Pol'y 115 (2004).

The FMLA does not require employers to continue paying workers while they are on leave. Some advocates of stronger family leave legislation have argued that mandating paid leave would more effectively advance gender equality by inducing more men to share in family responsibilities. See, e.g., Nancy E. Dowd, Race, Gender, and Work/Family Policy, 15 Wash. U. J.L. & Pol'y 219 (2004); Michael Selmi, Family Leave and the Gender Wage Gap, 78 N.C.L.Rev. 707 (2000). The FMLA does not preempt state laws that require employers to grant more generous leave and some states have considered laws that would fund such leave through some form of public insurance. In 2002 California became the first state to require employers to provide paid family leave. Cal. Unemp. Ins. Code § 984(a)(2)(B). The California law establishes a disability insurance program to provide up to six weeks of replacement benefits for employees who are caring for a seriously ill child, spouse, parent, or domestic partner, or bonding with a new child. Eligible employees are to be paid 55% of their salary up to a maximum initially set at $728 per week. The benefit will be financed through payroll deductions. Western European nations and Canada also have required employers to provide more generous benefits to employees out on family leave. Most require some degree of wage replacement as well as more extended periods during which leave is allowed. See, e.g., Richard N. Block, Work-Family Legislation in the United States, Canada, and Western Europe: A Quantitative Comparison, 34 Pepp. L. Rev. 333 (2007); Annie Pelletier, The Family Medical Leave Act of 1993—Why Does Parental Leave in the United States Fall So Far Behind Europe?, 42 Gonz. L. Rev. 547 (2007); Dorothea Alewell and Kerstin Pull, An International Comparison and Assessment of Maternity Legislation, 22 Comp. Lab.L. & Po. J. 297 (2001). See also Estreicher and Cherry, supra, at 173–81.

Some commentators have argued that employers should be required to accommodate not only serious medical crises and bonding with new children, but also the routine, day-to-day child care responsibilities that often conflict with work obligations. See, e.g., Katherine B. Silbaugh, Is the Work-Family Conflict Pathological or Normal Under the FMLA? The Potential of the FMLA to Cover Ordinary Work-Family Conflicts, 15 Wash. U. J.L. & Pol'y 193 (2004); Jody Heymann, The Widening Gap (2000); Peggie R. Smith, Accommodating Routine Parental Obligations in an Era of Work-Family Conflict: Lessons from Religious Accommodations, 2001 Wisc. L.Rev. 1443. Further legislative proposals include amending the Fair Labor Standards Act to reduce the length of the work week and promote work sharing, and modifying unemployment insurance, the FMLA, and the Employee Retirement Security Act to benefit part time workers. See, e.g., Joan Williams, Unbending Gender: Why Family and Work Conflict and What to Do About It (2000); Vicki Schultz, Life's Work, 100 Colum. L.Rev. 1881, 1957 (2000).

All proposals that would require employers to subsidize child care directly, or indirectly through a payroll tax, not only would impose a further regulatory burden on the economy, but also would provide an incentive for employers to not employ individuals, perhaps especially single women with children, who are most likely to need accommodation. Cf., e.g., C. Ruhm and J. Teague, Parental Leave Policies in Europe and North America, in Blau & Ehrenberg supra (analysis of nine European countries finding that parental leave mandates result in small wage reductions for female employees). Policy analysts thus must determine whether the enactment of a new mandated benefit for child care ultimately would improve the aggregate economic status of women. Cf. id. (also finding that the overall effect of parental leave in the European countries was an increase in female labor market participation). See also Christine Jolls, Accommodation Mandates, 53 Stan. L. Rev. 223, 292

(2000) (theorizing that where there is "substantial occupational segregation by sex", there need only be a wage and not an employment effect on women). Would proscribing discrimination in employment on the basis of parental status help avoid an employer backlash against one parent families? Would expanded public subsidization of preschool and after school child care be a more effective option, at least for low income families? See generally Sheila B. Kamerman and Alfred J. Kahn, Child Care, Family Benefits and Working Parents (1981).

Employers also can adopt voluntary policies to facilitate the exit and reentry of primary parents, such as parenting leaves and day care benefits. Are there any reasons why employers should not permit flexible periods of consideration for key promotional decisions such as selection to partnership or a tenured faculty position? See generally Kathy Abrams, Gender Discrimination and the Transformation of Workplace Norms, 42 Vand.L.Rev. 1184, 1233–46 (1989); Nancy Dowd, Work and Family: The Gender Paradox and the Limitations of Discrimination Analysis in Restructuring the Workplace, 24 Harv.Civ.Rts.—Civ. Libs.L.Rev. 79 (1989). Should employers formalize a two-track system, one track for "career-primary women" (and men) and another for "career-and-family women" (and men) for whom flexible work arrangements and family supports are provided? See Felice N. Schwartz, Management Women and the New Facts of Life, Harv.Bus.Rev., Jan.–Feb. 1989, at 65 ff. What might be the costs of such a policy?

Chapter Six

AGE DISCRIMINATION

A. INTRODUCTION

This chapter treats an additional type of status discrimination proscribed by a separate federal statute, the Age Discrimination in Employment Act of 1967 (ADEA), 29 U.S.C. §§ 621–34, as well as similar state laws. During consideration of Title VII of the 1964 Civil Rights Act, Congress decided to defer enactment of a federal measure to bar age bias. It directed the Secretary of Labor to investigate the problem and report on whether legislation was needed. Labor Secretary Wirtz's investigation resulted in The Older American Worker—Age Discrimination in Employment, Report of the Secretary of Labor to Congress Under Section 715 of the Civil Rights Act of 1964 (June 1965), reprinted in EEOC, Legislative History of the Age Discrimination in Employment Act (1981). This report ultimately led to the passage of ADEA.

What are the justifications for regulating age discrimination? The reasons, while similar, are certainly not identical to those that may explain regulation of race and sex discrimination. Like race and sex, age is a status over which individuals have no control. As a general proposition, the age of a worker seems to have little bearing on an employer's legitimate business needs. However, unlike race and sex, age is a changing status. Most youths hope to achieve middle and old age. Most also have close members of their families who have achieved that status. It therefore seems less likely that older workers will be the object of antagonistic social prejudice. Furthermore, the profile of the older worker is different from the typical Title VII claimant. At least up to some point in middle age, average earnings increase rather than decline with age; and white, male older workers largely comprise the managerial and supervisory ranks of American firms. It is not clear that older Americans as a class share the economically disadvantaged status of many blacks or confront the same occupational barriers as female workers.

1. *Prejudice.* Despite these differences, there may be strong justifications for age discrimination regulation. First, the anticipation of aging and close association with the elderly does not exclude the possibility of some prejudice against older workers. Prejudice is a complicated phenomenon and need not be dependent on lack of contact, as attested by the presence of sex-based prejudice despite the close intrafamily associa-

tion of men and women. Both the high value placed on novelty and youth in our culture and the force of intergenerational conflict may engender age bias.

2. *Statistical Discrimination.* More important than any form of antagonistic prejudice, however, may be the use of stereotyping presumptions about the capabilities of older workers. Secretary Wirtz's report indeed "found no evidence of prejudice based on dislike or intolerance of the older worker. The issue of discrimination revolves around the nature of the work and its rewards, in relation to the ability or presumed ability of people at various ages, rather than around the people as such." The report concluded that the prevalence of maximum age limitations had a negative effect on the employability of older workers, and that legislation was necessary in part because such limitations often were "established without any determination of their actual relevance to job requirements" and persisted simply because of unfounded assumptions linking declining ability with increasing age. Similar observations can be found in § 2 of ADEA, 29 U.S.C. § 621 ("Congressional Statement of Findings and Purpose").

Maximum age limitations need not be viewed as based solely on stereotypical assumptions. Mandatory retirement, for instance, enables employers to structure compensation to encourage job commitment and productivity by promising workers enhanced compensation in later years and a limited number of senior years at high compensation free of ultimate invidious judgments about performance. This type of justification has also been asserted for university tenure systems and by firms operated as partnerships. Cf. Edward P. Lazear, Why is There Mandatory Retirement?, 87 J. of Pol. Econ. 1261 (Dec. 1979).

Nevertheless, age stereotyping may help explain much of the prevalence and persistence of age limitations in employment. Why might such stereotypes endure in a competitive economy that generally penalizes economically irrational behavior? Why, in other words, might government intervention be necessary? One answer may be that the stereotypes are so widely accepted that most older workers simply withdraw from the labor market after they are terminated. If so, there may not be a large enough pool of workers to attract nondiscriminatory employers in adequate numbers to inflict competitive disadvantage on the discriminatory sector.

The role of employee and customer prejudice in reinforcing the use of age stereotypes by employers is probably less significant than for race and sex stereotyping. There will certainly be situations where employers accede to the associational preferences of coworkers or customers to deal with younger people, but it is questionable whether this is more than a marginal phenomenon.

More likely, the use of age stereotypes may be efficient for reasons not traceable to, and not sustained by, social prejudice, and hence likely to persist in the absence of regulation. In many settings, age may be a relatively good proxy for difficult predictive judgments and cheaper to use than any direct individualized test of present or future capabilities. A rational employer may find it irrelevant that many older workers can efficiently perform a particular job if these capable workers cannot be cheaply segregated from the greater number of less efficient older workers. The probability of such "statistical discrimination" against older workers seems especially strong when those workers apply for a new job. An employer sifting through new job applications must make difficult decisions on the basis of imperfect and indirect information. The employer also might have to train any worker it hires for a period during which the worker may have to be paid more than his or her productivity. All in all, age might well help personnel officers to make predictions about which applicants will end up being the most productive for the longest period. See Robert M. Hutchens, Delayed Payment Contracts and a Firm's Propensity to Hire Older Workers, 4 J.Lab.Econ. 439 (1986) (firms which employ older workers also tend not to hire new older workers).

ADEA's regulations extend, of course, beyond the hiring stage to reach, in a manner akin to Title VII, all personnel decisions affecting the terms and conditions of employment. Are there reasons to suspect that employers engage in statistical discrimination against older incumbent workers as well? Two arguments should be considered. First, incumbent workers applying for a promotion may be only in a slightly better position than external applicants. An employer does have direct knowledge of the general skills of incumbents, but the sought-for position may require additional skills and a training period, and therefore may necessitate the employer making difficult predictive judgments. Second, incumbent older workers may be vulnerable to being bumped out of jobs in which they are performing satisfactorily. An employer may decide that if it does not open up an older employee's space, it risks losing a younger employee whose future contributions to the firm are predicted to be greater simply because of relative age. An employer may also decide to layoff older rather than younger workers during a business contraction because of the employer's age-based predictions of future productivity.

The fact that these forms of statistical discrimination are efficient for individual employers, however, need not make them acceptable to our society. We may be concerned about many individual older workers losing jobs for which they are capable both because we want to extend the opportunity for dignified work to as many citizens as possible, and because of the social costs of supporting potentially productive older workers assigned to an unproductive status. These kinds of concerns seem to be the basis of a European Union Directive to member states to enact laws proscribing age discrimination in employment. Council Directive 2000/78/EC. See Age As An Equality Issue 1, 71 (Sandra Fredman & Sarah Spencer eds. 2003). Research suggests that older workers suffer a decline in average earnings because of the loss of firm-specific human capital associated with job switching, see Stephen McConnell, Age Discrimination in Employment, in Policy Issues in Work and Retirement (H. Parnes ed. 1983); David Shapiro & Steven H. Sandell, Age

Discrimination in Wages and Displaced Older Men, 52 So.Econ.J. 90–102 (July 1985); and face significant difficulty in securing re-employment, see Robert M. Hutchens, Do Job Opportunities Decline With Age?, 42 Ind. & Lab.Rel.Rev. 89 (1988); see generally Work and Retirement: A Longitudinal Study of Men (H. Parnes ed. 1981).

For reasons such as these, an age discrimination statute even might be framed to protect older workers whose pay exceeds their productivity. Cf. Lawrence Friedman, Your Time Will Come: The Law of Age Discrimination and Mandatory Retirement 113 (1984) (ADEA reflects both "civil rights" and "tenure" principles). Under this view, ADEA could be as much a redistributive, job security guarantee as an antidiscrimination measure.

3. *Employer Opportunism.* Another possible justification for using an age discrimination statute to protect the job security of even those older workers whose pay exceeds their productivity might be the avoidance of what some economists call "opportunistic" behavior on the part of employers against older employees. It has been suggested that employers often are able to pay junior employees less than their marginal product because they implicitly promise the employees that they will be paid more than their marginal product as their productivity declines towards the twilight of their careers. See, e.g., Edward P. Lazear, Agency, Earning Profiles, Productivity and Hours Restrictions, 71 Am. Econ.Rev. 606 (1981); Robert M. Hutchens, Delayed Payment Contracts and a Firm's Propensity to Hire Older Workers, supra; Michael L. Wachter & George Cohen, The Law and Economics of Collective Bargaining: An Introduction and Application to the Problems of Subcontracting, Partial Closure, and Relocation, 136 U.Pa.L.Rev. 1349, 1362–64 (1988); but cf. Peter Kuhn, Wages, Effort, and Incentive Compatibility in Life–Cycle Employment Contracts, 4 J.Lab.Econ. 28 (1986) (questioning whether wage payments rise faster than marginal productivity throughout an entire employment relationship). Such arrangements help promote job commitment, which, in turn, yields benefits to the society as a whole. Presumably, these arrangements work without any formal contractual remedy to enforce the implicit promise because younger employees see their employer paying older employees in accord with the promise. However, certain situations such as business contractions, when new employees are not being hired or a firm is withdrawing from a particular line of business, may provide opportunities for employers to take advantage of current older employees without demoralizing new employees. Conceivably, age discrimination laws like ADEA help compel compliance with these implicit relational contracts. But see Richard A. Epstein, Forbidden Grounds: The Case Against Employment Discrimination Laws 448–50 (1992).

Whatever its justifications, ADEA is one of the most significant areas of federal employment law, accounting for a significant portion of the charges filed with the EEOC. Studies of profiles of ADEA claimants suggest a predominantly white, relatively well-educated, professional or middle-management plaintiff class. See Michael Schuster & Christopher

S. Miller, An Empirical Assessment of the Age Discrimination in Employment Act, 38 Ind. & Lab.Rel.Rev. 64 (1984). Except in states where the courts have recognized major departures from the American rule of "at will" employment, ADEA provides the principal means for white male nonunion private employees to challenge termination from employment.

Note on the ADEA Statutory Scheme

ADEA applies to all employers engaged in an industry affecting commerce having twenty or more employees for each working day in each of twenty or more weeks in the current or preceding calendar year. Like Title VII, ADEA also covers labor organizations and employment agencies. The ADEA protected class now includes all individuals over the age of 40 no matter how old. (Under some state laws protection may extend to even earlier ages. See, e.g., Bergen Commercial Bank v. Sisler, 157 N.J. 188, 723 A.2d 944 (1999).)

Congress created in ADEA a hybrid: borrowing the substantive law from Title VII, while incorporating the remedial provisions of the Fair Labor Standards Act of 1938 (FLSA), 29 U.S.C. §§ 211, 216–17, 255, 259. ADEA was administered by the Secretary of Labor until the 1977 Reorganization Act, pursuant to which President Carter transferred authority to the EEOC. Congress did not initially consider utilizing the EEOC because of perceptions that age claims were sufficiently different from race or sex bias claims to require an agency with an independent perspective, and that, in any event, the EEOC had difficulty managing its existing responsibilities. Rather, the choice was between a new public agency, modeled after the National Labor Relations Board, which would have exclusive enforcement authority, and the Department of Labor's existing machinery for enforcing FLSA coupled with a prominent role for the private lawsuit and "voluntary compliance." See S.Rep. No. 723, 90th Cong., 1st Sess. 5 (1967). With Senator Javits's prodding, Congress ultimately chose the latter course, believing that utilization of an existing bureaucracy would ensure expeditious resolution of age bias disputes. See 113 Cong.Rec. 7076 (1967) (remarks of Sen. Javits).

Generally, an ADEA court has the same range of remedial authority as a Title VII court. Under § 7(c)(1), 29 U.S.C. § 626(c)(1), "[a]ny person aggrieved may bring a civil action * * * for such legal or equitable relief as will effectuate" the statute. Moreover, a right to a jury trial "of any issue of fact * * * for recovery of amounts owing as a result of a violation of this Act" is guaranteed by § 7(c)(2), a result of the 1978 amendments. Where the court, in its equitable discretion, declines to award reinstatement, the decisions uniformly authorize an award of "front pay" relief—a development which has carried over to Title VII cases. See, e.g., Graefenhain v. Pabst Brewing Co., 870 F.2d 1198 (7th Cir.1989). See pp. 1056–1057 infra.

Because ADEA incorporates certain FLSA remedial provisions, plaintiffs can also seek to recover an amount equal to their damages as "liquidated damages." However, ADEA permits recovery of such extra damages "only in cases of willful violations." ADEA § 7(b), 29 U.S.C. § 626(b). In Trans World Airlines, Inc. v. Thurston, 469 U.S. 111, 105 S.Ct. 613, 83 L.Ed.2d 523

(1985), the Supreme Court rejected the view that as long as the employer knew ADEA was "in the picture," its acts of intentional discrimination must always be deemed "willful" violations. *Thurston* states that a "willful" violation requires proof that the defendant acted in knowing or "reckless disregard" of ADEA requirements. Presumably, an employer's good-faith effort to conform its conduct with the law would defeat a liquidated-damages claim. See p. 1058 infra.

In Kimel v. Florida Board of Regents, 528 U.S. 62, 120 S.Ct. 631, 145 L.Ed.2d 522 (2000), the Court held that the sovereign immunity principle embodied in the Eleventh Amendment disabled Congress from providing for private damage actions under the ADEA against state government employers. The Court had earlier upheld Congress' authority to enact the ADEA under its article I power to regulate interstate commerce, EEOC v. Wyoming, 460 U.S. 226, 103 S.Ct. 1054, 75 L.Ed.2d 18 (1983), but article I does not provide authority to abrogate state sovereign immunity. Section 5 of the fourteenth amendment does provide such authority, but the Court in *Kimel* held that "the ADEA is not "appropriate legislation" under § 5 of the Fourteenth Amendment" because "the substantive requirements the ADEA imposes on state and local governments are disproportionate to any unconstitutional conduct that conceivably could be targeted by the Act." The EEOC can seek monetary damages from state as well as local governments and private employers, but private plaintiffs are limited to prospective injunctions against state officials, in addition to any rights of action that they have under state age discrimination laws. See, e.g., State Police for Automatic Retirement Ass'n v. DiFava, 317 F.3d 6 (1st Cir.2003) (allowing private ADEA action against state official for prospective injunction).

For a discussion of the relationship between ADEA suits by the EEOC and private rights of action and other procedural design questions, see chapter 17.

B.   DISPARATE TREATMENT

1. *Applicability of Title VII Standards of Proof*

O'CONNOR v. CONSOLIDATED COIN CATERERS CORP.

Supreme Court of the United States, 1996.
517 U.S. 308, 116 S.Ct. 1307, 134 L.Ed.2d 433.

JUSTICE SCALIA delivered the opinion of the Court.

This case presents the question whether a plaintiff alleging that he was discharged in violation of the Age Discrimination in Employment Act of 1967 (ADEA), 81 Stat. 602, as amended, 29 U.S.C. § 621 et seq., must show that he was replaced by someone outside the age group protected by the ADEA to make out a prima facie case under the framework established by *McDonnell Douglas Corp.* v. *Green*, 411 U.S. 792, 36 L. Ed. 2d 668, 93 S. Ct. 1817 (1973).

Petitioner James O'Connor was employed by respondent Consolidated Coin Caterers Corporation from 1978 until August 10, 1990, when, at age 56, he was fired. Claiming that he had been dismissed because of his age in violation of the ADEA, petitioner brought suit in the United States District Court for the Western District of North Carolina. After discovery, the District Court granted respondent's motion for summary judgment, and petitioner appealed. The Court of Appeals for the Fourth Circuit stated that petitioner could establish a prima facie case under *McDonnell Douglas* only if he could prove that (1) he was in the age group protected by the ADEA; (2) he was discharged or demoted; (3) at the time of his discharge or demotion, he was performing his job at a level that met his employer's legitimate expectations; and (4) following his discharge or demotion, he was replaced by someone of comparable qualifications outside the protected class. Since petitioner's replacement was 40 years old, the Court of Appeals concluded that the last element of the prima facie case had not been made out. Finding that petitioner's claim could not survive a motion for summary judgment without benefit of the *McDonnell Douglas* presumption (i.e., "under the ordinary standards of proof used in civil cases,") the Court of Appeals affirmed the judgment of dismissal. * * *

In assessing claims of age discrimination brought under the ADEA, the Fourth Circuit, like others, has applied some variant of the basic evidentiary framework set forth in *McDonnell Douglas*. We have never had occasion to decide whether that application of the Title VII rule to the ADEA context is correct, but since the parties do not contest that point, we shall assume it. On that assumption, the question presented for our determination is what elements must be shown in an ADEA case to establish the prima facie case that triggers the employer's burden of production.

As the very name "prima facie case" suggests, there must be at least a logical connection between each element of the prima facie case and the illegal discrimination for which it establishes a "legally mandatory, rebuttable presumption," [*Texas Dept. of Community Affairs v. Burdine*, 450 U.S. 248, 254 n. 7, 67 L. Ed. 2d 207, 101 S. Ct. 1089 (1981).] The element of replacement by someone under 40 fails this requirement. The discrimination prohibited by the ADEA is discrimination "because of [an] individual's age," 29 U.S.C. § 623(a)(1), though the prohibition is "limited to individuals who are at least 40 years of age," § 631(a). This language does not ban discrimination against employees because they are aged 40 or older; it bans discrimination against employees because of their age, but limits the protected class to those who are 40 or older. The fact that one person in the protected class has lost out to another person in the protected class is thus irrelevant, so long as he has lost out because of his age. Or to put the point more concretely, there can be no greater inference of age discrimination (as opposed to "40 or over" discrimination) when a 40 year-old is replaced by a 39 year-old than when a 56 year-old is replaced by a 40 year-old. Because it lacks probative value, the fact that an ADEA plaintiff was replaced by someone outside the protected class is not a proper element of the *McDonnell Douglas* prima facie case.

Perhaps some courts have been induced to adopt the principle urged by respondent in order to avoid creating a prima facie case on the basis of very thin evidence—for example, the replacement of a 68 year-old by a 65 year-old. While the respondent's principle theoretically permits such thin evidence (consider the example above of a 40 year-old replaced by a 39 year-old), as a practical matter it will rarely do so, since the vast majority of age-discrimination claims come from older employees. In our view, however, the proper solution to the problem lies not in making an utterly irrelevant factor an element of the prima facie case, but rather in recognizing that the prima facie case requires "evidence adequate to create an inference that an employment decision was based on an [illegal] discriminatory criterion. * * * " *Teamsters v. United States*, 431 U.S. 324, 358, 52 L. Ed. 2d 396, 97 S. Ct. 1843 (1977). In the age-discrimination context, such an inference can not be drawn from the replacement of one worker with another worker insignificantly younger. Because the ADEA prohibits discrimination on the basis of age and not class membership, the fact that a replacement is substantially younger than the plaintiff is a far more reliable indicator of age discrimination than is the fact that the plaintiff was replaced by someone outside the protected class. The judgment of the Fourth Circuit is reversed, and the case is remanded for proceedings consistent with this opinion.

Notes and Questions

1. *ADEA and the* McDonnell Douglas *Framework.* Does the Court's analysis in *O'Connor* indicate that the methodology for proving discrimination first set forth for Title VII cases in *McDonnell Douglas* also can be applied in most ADEA cases? Given the similarity of wording in the discrimination prohibitions of the two statutes, is there any reason that *McDonnell Douglas* doctrine should not apply to ADEA? Consider the rationales for the *McDonnell Douglas–Burdine* proof structure addressed in chapter 2 as well as the justifications for age discrimination legislation presented in the introduction to this chapter. Should an older worker's proof of qualifications for an open job for which he was rejected raise suspicions of age-based animus? Do we have reason to have the same suspicion of pervasive age-based animus in our economy as we might have of race-based or sex-based animus? Note that those making the employment decision are not only likely to have close contact with older people, but also are much more likely to be older than forty than they are to be black or female. On the other hand, do we have reason to believe that employers often make age-based hiring, promotion, and discharge decisions for reasons other than animus toward older workers? Is animus a necessary element of a Title VII or ADEA case?

2. *Discrimination Along a Continuum.* Note that the *O'Connor* Court asserts that while the protections of the ADEA extend only to those over the age of 40, the statute prohibits discrimination along the continuum of age rather than on the basis of "class membership." Does this distinguish the ADEA from the prohibitions in Title VII, or should discrimination on the basis of "color", one of the Title VII-prohibited classifications, also be treated along a continuum like age discrimination under the ADEA?

Why did the Court state that ADEA plaintiffs should present proof that their replacements are significantly or substantially younger? Should courts establish some minimum age disparity as an element of a prima facie case under the *McDonnell Douglas* framework? Compare Grosjean v. First Energy Corp., 349 F.3d 332, 340 (6th Cir. 2003) ("an age difference of six years or less between an employee and a replacement is not significant"); Cianci v. Pettibone Corp., 152 F.3d 723, 728 (7th Cir. 1998) ("age disparity of less than ten years is presumptively insubstantial"), with Whittington v. Nordam Group Inc., 429 F.3d 986, 996 (10th Cir. 2005) (rejecting a requirement of direct evidence based on any age-disparity "firm rule outside context of the case"). Could an ADEA plaintiff prevail with strong direct proof of an age-based decision, even if she was immediately replaced by someone who was only a year younger, or even a year older? See, e.g., Greene v. Safeway Stores, Inc., 98 F.3d 554 (10th Cir.1996) (being replaced by older worker does not necessarily defeat age discrimination claim).

3. *An Asymmetrical Prohibition.* Does the ADEA prohibit discrimination against a worker who is forty or older based on that worker being too young for a particular position? What if an employer, for instance, on the basis of age prefers a fifty-five year old to a forty-five year old? In General Dynamics Land Systems, Inc. v. Cline, 540 U.S. 581, 124 S.Ct. 1236, 157 L.Ed.2d 1094 (2004), the Court held that the ADEA does not prohibit favoring older over younger workers. Justice Souter, for a six-Justice majority, found the legislative record

> devoid of any evidence that younger workers were suffering at the expense of their elders, let alone that a social problem required a federal statute to place a younger worker in parity with an older one. Common experience is to the contrary, and the testimony, reports, and congressional findings simply confirm that Congress used the phrase "discrimination ... because of [an] individual's age" the same way that ordinary people in common usage might speak of age discrimination any day of the week. ...
>
> This same idiomatic sense of the statutory phrase is confirmed by the statute's restriction of the protected class to those 40 and above. If Congress had been worrying about protecting the younger against the older, it would not likely have ignored everyone under 40. The youthful deficiencies of inexperience and unsteadiness invite stereotypical and discriminatory thinking about those a lot younger than 40, and prejudice suffered by a 40-year old is not typically owing to youth, as 40-year-olds sadly tend to find out. ... Thus, the 40-year threshold makes sense as identifying a class requiring protection against preference for their juniors, not as defining a class that might be threatened by favoritism toward seniors.

Id. at 591–92.

Some state anti-age discrimination laws proscribe discrimination against younger workers. See, e.g., Ace Electrical Contractors, Inc. v. International Brotherhood of Electrical Workers, 414 F.3d 896 (8th Cir. 2005) (interpreting § 363A.03 of the Minnesota Human Rights Act).

4. *When Decisionmaker Is Same Age or Older than the Plaintiff.* Should an ADEA plaintiff be able to establish a prima facie case without

direct evidence of age bias when the alleged discriminator is older than the plaintiff? A number of courts have considered the older age of the decision-maker to be a weighty factor against an ADEA plaintiff. See, e.g., Elrod v. Sears, Roebuck & Co., 939 F.2d 1466 (11th Cir.1991) (reversing jury verdict for plaintiff because all the decisionmakers were within ADEA-protected class). Consider, however, the following dicta from Judge Posner in Kadas v. MCI Systemhouse Corp., 255 F.3d 359, 361–362 (7th Cir.2001):

> [I]t is altogether common and natural for older people, first, to exempt themselves from what they believe to be the characteristic decline of energy and ability with age; second, to want to surround themselves with younger people; third, to want to protect their own jobs by making sure the workforce is not too old, which might, if "ageist" prejudice is rampant, lead to [workforce reductions] of which they themselves might be the victims; and fourth, to be oblivious to the prejudices they hold, especially perhaps prejudices against the group to which they belong. We emphatically rejected the "same-actor inference" in the race-discrimination setting in Johnson v. Zema Systems Corp., 170 F.3d 734, 745 (7th Cir. 1999), and our conclusion there applies with equal force to proof of age discrimination.

See also Wexler v. White's Fine Furniture, Inc., 317 F.3d 564 (6th Cir.2003) (en banc) (holding in agreement with *Kadas* dicta).

5. *"Same Actor" Defense.* What weight should be given to the fact that the same company officer who hired an alleged victim of discriminatory discharge made the decision to fire? Should the time lapse between hiring and discharge make a difference? Compare Brown v. CSC Logic, Inc., 82 F.3d 651 (5th Cir.1996) (applying the "same actor" defense to the dismissal of a 58 year-old man who was hired four years earlier by the same man who fired him); Proud v. Stone, 945 F.2d 796, 798 (4th Cir.1991) (endorsing defense), with Wexler v. White's Fine Furniture, Inc., supra, (rejecting defense); Haun v. Ideal Industries, Inc., 81 F.3d 541 (5th Cir.1996) ("we decline to establish a rule that no inference of discrimination would arise" where hirer and firer are same individual). Cf. Kadas v. MCI Systemhouse Corp., supra, at 361–62 ("it is eminently reasonable to doubt that, as in this case, a worker hired * * * and terminated *within months*, that is , before he is appreciably older, was a victim of age discrimination").

6. *Prima Facie Proof in Reduction-in-Force Cases.* Age discrimination often has been alleged in cases where the employer does not fill the position from which the alleged victim is laid off or discharged, either because the job function has been entirely eliminated or because aspects of the function have been distributed among several incumbent employees. Should it be sufficient to satisfy the fourth prong of the *McDonnell Douglas* prima facie case in such cases to show that the average age of employees retained in similar positions is lower than that of the plaintiff or plaintiffs? How should the "prima facie" case be framed for reduction-in-force cases?

Consider the Fourth Circuit's position in Blistein v. St. John's College, 74 F.3d 1459, 1470 (1996):

> A plaintiff in such circumstances [cannot point to a replacement] but can establish this element of his prima facie case "either by showing that (comparably qualified) persons outside the protected class were

retained in the same position *or* by producing some other evidence indicating that the employer did not treat age neutrally (in deciding to dismiss the plaintiff)."

Where relative qualification is asserted as the basis of selection for the force reduction, the *Blistein* court would require proof that "the plaintiff was performing at a level substantially equivalent to the lowest level of those retained" and that "the process of selection produced a residual work force with some unprotected persons who were performing at a level lower than that at which the plaintiff was performing." Id. at 1470–1471 n.13. Is this approach consistent with *O'Connor*? For another approach, see Radue v. Kimberly–Clark Corp., 219 F.3d 612, 617 (7th Cir.2000) (plaintiff may show as fourth prong of prima facie case that "other similarly situated employees who were substantially younger than him were treated more favorably"). On the difficulty of proving discrimination in reduction in force cases, see Daniel B. Kohrman and Mark Stewart Hayes, Employers Who Cry "RIF" and the Courts That Believe Them, 23 Hof. L. & Emp.L.J. 153 (2005).

7. *Employer Practices in Reduction-in-Force Cases.* Should what the courts ask of plaintiffs in reduction-in-force cases depend in part on how the defendant employer has treated laid-off workers in the past? Consider, for instance, a case where the employer previously has allowed laid-off workers to bump less senior workers out of jobs for which the more senior laid-off workers are qualified. Should plaintiffs denied such seniority privileges be able to establish a prima facie case of age discrimination by comparing their age to that of the employees they were not allowed to displace? See Ayala v. Mayfair Molded Products Corp., 831 F.2d 1314 (7th Cir.1987) (violation found where bumping on the basis of interdepartmental seniority had been permitted in the past). See also Ridenour v. Lawson Co., 791 F.2d 52 (6th Cir.1986); Foster v. Arcata Associates, Inc., 772 F.2d 1453 (9th Cir.1985). On the other hand, should an employer's consistently applied practice necessarily insulate it from a charge of age discrimination if such a practice has been adopted in part to remove older workers? See Taggart v. Time Inc., 924 F.2d 43 (2d Cir.1991) (refusing to transfer older worker to jobs for which he is "overqualified" treated as possible "euphemism" for age bias).

8. *Age-Based Harassment.* Given the similarity in the language of the two anti-discrimination statutes, is there any reason that Title VII harassment law should not apply to the ADEA? Should subjecting an older worker to abusive working conditions because of her age be treated any differently under discrimination law than subjecting a worker to abusive working conditions because of her sex? See, e.g., Crawford v. Medina General Hospital, 96 F.3d 830 (6th Cir.1996) (applying Title VII hostile work environment doctrine).

Note on Causation Under the ADEA

The Supreme Court's analysis of causation in Price Waterhouse v. Hopkins, 490 U.S. 228, 109 S.Ct. 1775, 104 L.Ed.2d 268 (1989), a Title VII case, has proved more influential for ADEA litigation. Section 107 of the 1991 Act, which modified *Price Waterhouse* and which was interpreted expansively in Desert Palace, Inc. v. Costa, pp. 75–80 supra, by its terms amends only Title VII. The lower courts thus have treated *Price Waterhouse*, and the concurring opinion of Justice O'Connor rejected for Title VII cases in *Desert Palace,* as controlling precedent. See, e.g., Sandstad v. CB Richard Ellis, Inc., 309 F.3d 893 (5th Cir.2002); Febres v. Challenger Caribbean Corp., 214 F.3d 57 (1st Cir.2000); Slathar v. Sather Trucking Corp., 78 F.3d 415, 418–19 (8th Cir.1996). But see, e.g., Fast v. Southern Union Co., 149 F.3d 885, 889 (8th Cir.1998); Gonzagowski v. Widnall, 115 F.3d 744 (10th Cir.1997) (both assuming without analysis that § 107 may be applicable to mixed motive ADEA cases).

Justice Brennan's plurality opinion for four Justices in *Price Waterhouse* interpreted Title VII, before the 1991 Act, to require plaintiffs to prove only that consideration of one of the five proscribed categories was a "motivating" factor; but this opinion also read into the statute a complete affirmative defense for employers who could prove that they would have made the same decision but for the proscribed consideration. Justice O'Connor's views as expressed in her concurring opinion differed somewhat. She read the statute to require proof of "but-for" causation, but she also thought it appropriate to afford plaintiffs the benefit of a rebuttable presumption of such causation in certain cases:

> Where an individual disparate treatment plaintiff has shown by a preponderance of the evidence that an illegitimate criterion was a *substantial* factor in an adverse employment decision, the deterrent purpose of the statute has clearly been triggered. More importantly, as an evidentiary matter, a reasonable factfinder could conclude that absent further explanation, the employer's discriminatory motivation "caused" the employment decision. The employer has not yet been shown to be a violator, but neither is it entitled to the same presumption of good faith concerning its employment decisions which is accorded employers facing only circumstantial evidence of discrimination. Both the policies behind the statute, and the evidentiary principles developed in the analogous area of causation in the law of torts, suggest that at this point the employer may be required to convince the factfinder that, despite the smoke, there is no fire. * * *

> In my view, in order to justify shifting the burden on the issue of causation to the defendant, a disparate treatment plaintiff must show by direct evidence that an illegitimate criterion was a substantial factor in the decision. * * *

> Thus, stray remarks in the workplace * * * cannot justify requiring the employer to prove that its hiring or promotion decisions were based on legitimate criteria. Nor can statements by nondecisionmakers, or statements by decisionmakers unrelated to the decisional process itself suffice to satisfy the plaintiff's burden in this regard. * * * Race and gender always "play a role" in an employment decision in the benign sense that these are human characteristics of which decisionmakers are aware and may comment on in a perfectly neutral and nondiscriminatory fashion. For example, in the context of this case, a mere reference to "a lady candidate" might show that gender "played a role" in the decision, but by no means could support a rational factfinder's inference

that the decision was made "because of" sex. What is required is what Ann Hopkins showed here: direct evidence that decisionmakers placed substantial negative reliance on an illegitimate criterion in reaching their decision. * * *

* * * I would retain but supplement the framework we established in *McDonnell Douglas* and subsequent cases. * * * Once all the evidence has been received, the court should determine whether the *McDonnell Douglas* or *Price Waterhouse* framework properly applies to the evidence before it. If the plaintiff has failed to satisfy the *Price Waterhouse* threshold, the case should be decided under the principles enunciated in *McDonnell Douglas* and *Burdine*, with the plaintiff bearing the burden of persuasion on the ultimate issue whether the employment action was taken because of discrimination. * * *

490 U.S. at 265–279.

Justice White also concurred in *Price Waterhouse*, but his opinion declined to enter what he termed the "semantic discussions" between the plurality and Justice O'Connor and has not been influential. The lower courts instead, assuming—at least before *Desert Palace*—that Justice O'Connor's opinion constitutes the law, have accepted her bifurcation of disparate treatment cases. In ADEA cases, the lower courts cite Hazen Paper Company v. Biggins, 507 U.S. 604, 113 S.Ct. 1701, 123 L.Ed.2d 338 (1993), infra pp. 457–462, for confirming that a "disparate treatment claim cannot succeed" unless the employee's age "had a *determinative* influence on the outcome." (Emphasis supplied). ADEA disparate treatment plaintiffs either must carry the full burden of persuasion in proving this "determinative" influence, or they must have adequate "direct" evidence that age was a substantially motivating cause to shift the burden of persuasion to the employer under Justice O'Connor's *Price Waterhouse* approach.

The lower courts do not fully agree on what might constitute "direct evidence" relevant to shifting the burden of persuasion on to employers. The courts generally have stressed Justice O'Connor's *Price Waterhouse* concurrence's rejection, as sufficiently "direct", of "stray remarks in the work place" and "statements by nondecisionmakers, or statements by decisionmakers unrelated to the decisional process itself". See, e.g., Fakete v. Aetna, Inc., 308 F.3d 335 (3d Cir.2002). Some courts have accepted statements made by decisionmakers close in time to the decision, even where not directly related to the decision, and statements by those who may have influenced or known about the basis for the ultimate decision, even if not the decisionmaker themselves. See, e.g., Rose v. New York City Board of Educ., 257 F.3d 156, 162 (2d Cir.2001) (statements close to time of decision by "immediate supervisor who had enormous influence in the decision-making process"); EEOC v. Liberal R–II School District, 314 F.3d 920, 924 (8th Cir.2002) (statement about decision from "a nondecisionmaker who was closely involved in the decisionmaking process")

Notes and Questions

1. *Should the Courts Apply Justice O'Connor's* Price Waterhouse *Concurrence in ADEA Cases?* In light of the Court's language in *Hazen Paper*

and the restriction of § 107 to Title VII, the lower courts presumably will continue to apply a determinative, rather than motivating, causation standard in ADEA cases. But does the Court's opinion in *Desert Palace* suggest that the lower courts should reconsider their special treatment of "direct" evidence in ADEA cases as well as in Title VII cases? On the one hand, *Desert Palace* relies primarily on § 107 and Congress's silence on the ADEA in this section might be interpreted to express an intent that age cases be governed by *Price Waterhouse*. See Howard Eglit, The Age Discrimination in Employment Act, Title VII, and the Civil Rights Act of 1991: Three Acts and a Dog That Didn't Bark, 39 Wayne L. Rev. 1093, 1158–72 (1993). On the other hand, in *Desert Palace* the Court also stressed that where there is "Congressional silence" the courts "should not depart from the 'conventional rule of civil litigation' ", as well as that of criminal trials, "which makes no distinction between the weight or value to be given to either direct or circumstantial evidence." 539 U.S. at 99–100. Are ADEA courts bound by Justice O'Connor's opinion in *Price Waterhouse*? Was that opinion necessary to form a majority in that case? A number of lower courts have held that *Desert Palace*'s rejection of any special treatment of direct evidence also governs ADEA litigation. See, e.g., Rachid v. Jack in the Box, Inc., 376 F.3d 305 (5th Cir. 2004); Estades-Negroni v. Associates Corp. of N. Am., 345 F.3d 25 (1st Cir. 2003). Under the approach of these courts, plaintiffs gain the benefit of *PriceWaterhouse* burden shifting through any type of proof sufficient to establish age as a motivating factor for the defendant's challenged decision. The defendant's proof that it would have made the same decision absent consideration of age, however, would eliminate any liability, rather than just restrict remedies, given the absence of any legislative response to *Price Waterhouse* applicable to the ADEA. But cf. Warch v. Ohio Casualty Insurance Co., 435 F.3d 510 (4th Cir. 2006) (reserving question of whether *Desert Palace* applies to the ADEA, but finding circumstantial evidence of discriminatory motive inadequate after separate treatment of pretext evidence). See generally Michael J. Zimmer, Chaos or Coherence: Individual Disparate Treatment Discirimination and the ADEA, 51 Mercer L.Rev. 693 (2000); Michael C. Harper, ADEA Doctrinal Impediments to the Fulfillment of the Wirtz Report, 31 Univ. Rich.L. Rev. 757, 773–77 (1997).

2. *Case of Two Controlling Illegitimate Causes?* Consider an employer who refuses to hire either older workers or female workers. Should such an employer be able to assert a "same decision" defense both to an ADEA and to a Title VII hiring discrimination claim by an older female because the employer would have rejected both a younger female and an older male? Should such an employer escape liability under ADEA or remedies under Title VII simply because neither age-bias or sex-bias was a but-for cause of the plaintiff's rejection? Would your analysis be any different if the two controlling causes were race-and sex-bias, both prohibited under the same statute? If one of the controlling causes was only unacceptable under state common law?

2. *Age as a Bona Fide Occupational Qualification*

WESTERN AIR LINES v. CRISWELL
Supreme Court of the United States, 1985.
472 U.S. 400, 105 S.Ct. 2743, 86 L.Ed.2d 321.

JUSTICE STEVENS delivered the opinion of the Court.

I

In its commercial airline operations, Western operates a variety of aircraft, including the Boeing 727 and the McDonnell–Douglas DC–10. These aircraft require three crew members in the cockpit: a captain, a first officer, and a flight engineer. "The 'captain' is the pilot and controls the aircraft. He is responsible for all phases of its operation. The 'first officer' is the copilot and assists the captain. The 'flight engineer' usually monitors a side-facing instrument panel. He does not operate the flight controls unless the captain and the first officer become incapacitated." *Trans World Airlines, Inc. v. Thurston,* 469 U.S. 111, 114, 105 S.Ct. 613, 618, 83 L.Ed.2d 523 (1985).

A regulation of the Federal Aviation Administration prohibits any person from serving as a pilot or first officer on a commercial flight "if that person has reached his 60th birthday." 14 CFR § 121.383(c) (1985). The FAA has justified the retention of mandatory retirement for pilots on the theory that "incapacitating medical events" and "adverse psychological, emotional, and physical changes" occur as a consequence of aging. "The inability to detect or predict with precision an individual's risk of sudden or subtle incapacitation, in the face of known age-related risks, counsels against relaxation of the rule." 49 Fed.Reg. 14695 (1984). See also 24 Fed.Reg. 9776 (1959).

At the same time, the FAA has refused to establish a mandatory retirement age for flight engineers. "While a flight engineer has important duties which contribute to the safe operation of the airplane, he or she may not assume the responsibilities of the pilot in command." 49 Fed.Reg., at 14694. Moreover, available statistics establish that flight engineers have rarely been a contributing cause or factor in commercial aircraft "accidents" or "incidents." *Ibid.*

In 1978, respondents Criswell and Starley were Captains operating DC–10s for Western. Both men celebrated their 60th birthdays in July 1978. Under the collective-bargaining agreement in effect between Western and the union, cockpit crew members could obtain open positions by bidding in order of seniority. In order to avoid mandatory retirement under the FAA's under–age–60 rule for pilots, Criswell and Starley applied for reassignment as flight engineers. Western denied both requests, ostensibly on the ground that both employees were members of the company's retirement plan which required all crew members to retire at age 60.[1] For the same reason, respondent Ron, a career flight engineer, was also retired in 1978 after his 60th birthday.

---

1. The Western official who was responsible for the decision to retire the plaintiffs   conceded that "the sole basis" for the denial of the applications of Criswell, Starley

Mandatory retirement provisions similar to those contained in Western's pension plan had previously been upheld under the ADEA. *United Air Lines, Inc. v. McMann,* 434 U.S. 192, 98 S.Ct. 444, 54 L.Ed.2d 402 (1977). As originally enacted in 1967, the Act provided an exception to its general proscription of age discrimination for any actions undertaken "to observe the terms of a * * * bona fide employee benefit plan such as a retirement, pension, or insurance plan, which is not a subterfuge to evade the purposes of this Act." In April 1978, however, Congress amended the statute to prohibit employee benefit plans from requiring the involuntary retirement of any employee because of age.

* * *

As the District Court summarized, the evidence at trial established that the flight engineer's "normal duties are less critical to the safety of flight than those of a pilot." The flight engineer, however, does have critical functions in emergency situations and, of course, might cause considerable disruption in the event of his own medical emergency.

The actual capabilities of persons over age 60, and the ability to detect disease or a precipitous decline in their faculties, were the subject of conflicting medical testimony. Western's expert witness, a former FAA Deputy Federal Air Surgeon, was especially concerned about the possibility of a "cardiovascular event" such as a heart attack. He testified that "with advancing age the likelihood of onset of disease increases and that in persons over age 60 it could not be predicted whether and when such diseases would occur."

The plaintiffs' experts, on the other hand, testified that physiological deterioration is caused by disease, not aging, and that "it was feasible to determine on the basis of individual medical examinations whether flight deck crew members, including those over age 60, were physically qualified to continue to fly." These conclusions were corroborated by the nonmedical evidence:

> "The record also reveals that both the FAA and the airlines have been able to deal with the health problems of pilots on an individualized basis. Pilots who have been grounded because of alcoholism or cardiovascular disease have been recertified by the FAA and allowed to resume flying. Pilots who were unable to pass the necessary examination to maintain their FAA first class medical certificates, but who continued to qualify for second class medical certificates were allowed to 'down-grade' from pilot to [flight engineer]. There is nothing in the record to indicate that these flight deck crew members are physically better able to perform their duties than flight engineers over age 60 who have not experienced such events or that they are less likely to become incapacitated."

and Ron was the same: "the provision in the pension plan regarding retirement at age 60." In addition, he admitted that he had "no personal knowledge" of any safety rationale for the under–age–60 rule for flight engineers, nor had it played any significant role in his decision to retire them.

Moreover, several large commercial airlines have flight engineers over age 60 "flying the line" without any reduction in their safety record.

The jury was instructed that the "BFOQ defense is available only if it is reasonably necessary to the normal operation or essence of defendant's business." The jury was informed that "the essence of Western's business is the safe transportation of their passengers." * * * The jury rendered a verdict for the plaintiffs, and awarded damages. After trial, the District Court granted equitable relief, explaining in a written opinion why he found no merit in Western's BFOQ defense to the mandatory retirement rule.

On appeal, Western made various arguments attacking the verdict and judgment below, but the Court of Appeals affirmed in all respects.

* * *

II

Throughout the legislative history of the ADEA, one empirical fact is repeatedly emphasized: the process of psychological and physiological degeneration caused by aging varies with each individual. "The basic research in the field of aging has established that there is a wide range of individual physical ability regardless of age." As a result, many older American workers perform at levels equal or superior to their younger colleagues.

* * *

III

In *Usery v. Tamiami Trail Tours, Inc.*, 531 F.2d 224 (1976), the Court of Appeals for the Fifth Circuit was called upon to evaluate the merits of a BFOQ defense to a claim of age discrimination. Tamiami Trail Tours, Inc. had a policy of refusing to hire persons over age 40 as intercity bus drivers. At trial, the bus company introduced testimony supporting its theory that the hiring policy was a BFOQ based upon safety considerations—the need to employ persons who have a low risk of accidents. In evaluating this contention, the Court of Appeals drew on its Title VII precedents, and concluded that two inquiries were relevant.

First, the court recognized that some job qualifications may be so peripheral to the central mission of the employer's business that *no* age discrimination can be "reasonably *necessary* to the normal operation of the particular business." 29 U.S.C. § 623(f)(1). The bus company justified the age qualification for hiring its drivers on safety considerations, but the court concluded that this claim was to be evaluated under an objective standard:

"[T]he job qualifications which the employer invokes to justify his discrimination must be *reasonably necessary* to the essence of his business—here, the *safe* transportation of bus passengers from one point to another. The greater the safety factor, measured by the likelihood of harm and the probable severity of that harm in case of an accident, the more stringent may be the job qualifications designed to insure safe driving." 531 F.2d, at 236.

This inquiry "adjusts to the safety factor" by ensuring that the employer's restrictive job qualifications are "reasonably necessary" to further the overriding interest in public safety. *Ibid.* In *Tamiami,* the court noted that no one had seriously challenged the bus company's safety justification for hiring drivers with a low risk of having accidents.

Second, the court recognized that the ADEA requires that age qualifications be something more than "convenient" or "reasonable"; they must be "reasonably necessary * * * to the particular business," and this is only so when the employer is compelled to rely on age as a proxy for the safety-related job qualifications validated in the first inquiry. This showing could be made in two ways. The employer could establish that it " 'had reasonable cause to believe, that is, a factual basis for believing, that all or substantially all (persons over the age qualifications) would be unable to perform safely and efficiently the duties of the job involved.' " In *Tamiami,* the employer did not seek to justify its hiring qualification under this standard.

Alternatively, the employer could establish that age was a legitimate proxy for the safety-related job qualifications by proving that it is " 'impossible or highly impractical' " to deal with the older employees on an individualized basis. "One method by which the employer can carry this burden is to establish that some members of the discriminated-against class possess a trait precluding safe and efficient job performance that cannot be ascertained by means other than knowledge of the applicant's membership in the class." *Id.,* at 235. In *Tamiami,* the medical evidence on this point was conflicting, but the District Court had found that individual examinations could not determine which individuals over the age of 40 would be unable to operate the buses safely. The Court of Appeals found that this finding of fact was not "clearly erroneous," and affirmed the District Court's judgment for the bus company on the BFOQ defense. *Id.,* at 238.

* * *

Every Court of Appeals that has confronted a BFOQ defense based on safety considerations has analyzed the problem consistently with the *Tamiami* standard. An EEOC regulation embraces the same criteria. Considering the narrow language of the BFOQ exception, the parallel treatment of such questions under Title VII, and the uniform application of the standard by the federal courts, the EEOC and Congress, we conclude that this two-part inquiry properly identifies the relevant considerations for resolving a BFOQ defense to an age-based qualification purportedly justified by considerations of safety.

IV

* * *

On a more specific level, Western argues that flight engineers must meet the same stringent qualifications as pilots, and that it was therefore quite logical to extend to flight engineers the FAA's age–60 retirement rule for pilots. Although the FAA's rule for pilots, adopted for safety reasons, is relevant evidence in the airline's BFOQ defense, it is not to be accorded conclusive weight. *Johnson v. Mayor and City Council of Baltimore,* 472 U.S. 353, 105 S.Ct. 2717, 86 L.Ed.2d 286. The extent to which the rule is probative varies with the weight of the evidence supporting its safety rationale and "the congruity between the * * * occupations at issue." In this case, the evidence clearly established that the FAA, Western, and other airlines all recognized that the qualifications for a flight engineer were less rigorous than those required for a pilot.[28]

In the absence of persuasive evidence supporting its position, Western nevertheless argues that the jury should have been instructed to defer to "Western's selection of job qualifications for the position of [flight engineer] that are reasonable in light of the safety risks." This proposal is plainly at odds with Congress' decision, in adopting the ADEA, to subject such management decisions to a test of objective justification in a court of law. The BFOQ standard adopted in the statute is one of "reasonable necessity," not reasonableness.

In adopting that standard, Congress did not ignore the public interest in safety. That interest is adequately reflected in instructions that track the language of the statute. When an employer establishes that a job qualification has been carefully formulated to respond to documented concerns for public safety, it will not be overly burdensome to persuade a trier of fact that the qualification is "reasonably necessary" to safe operation of the business. The uncertainty implicit in the concept of managing safety risks always makes it "reasonably necessary" to err on the side of caution in a close case. The employer cannot be expected to establish the risk of an airline accident "to a certainty, for certainty would require running the risk until a tragic accident would prove that the judgment was sound." *Usery v. Tamiami Trail Tours, Inc.,* 531 F.2d, at 238. When the employer's argument has a credible basis in the record, it is difficult to believe that a jury of lay persons— many of whom no doubt have flown or could expect to fly on commercial air carriers—would not defer in a close case to the airline's judgment. Since the instructions in this case would not have prevented the airline from raising this contention to the jury in closing argument, we are satisfied that the verdict is a consequence of a defect in Western's proof rather than a defect in the trial court's instructions.

* * *

28. As the Court of Appeals noted, the "jury heard testimony that Western itself allows a captain under the age of sixty who cannot, for health reasons, continue to fly as a captain or co-pilot to downbid to a position as second officer. (In addition,) half the pilots flying in the United States are flying for major airlines which do not require second officers to retire at the age of sixty, and * * * there are over 200 such second officers currently flying on wide-bodied aircraft."

* * * It might well be "rational" to require mandatory retirement at *any* age less than 70, but that result would not comply with Congress' direction that employers must justify the rationale for the age chosen. Unless an employer can establish a substantial basis for believing that all or nearly all employees above an age lack the qualifications required for the position, the age selected for mandatory retirement less than 70 must be an age at which it is highly impractical for the employer to insure by individual testing that its employees will have the necessary qualifications for the job.

* * *

When an employee covered by the Act is able to point to reputable businesses in the same industry that choose to eschew reliance on mandatory retirement earlier than age 70, when the employer itself relies on individualized testing in similar circumstances, and when the administrative agency with primary responsibility for maintaining airline safety has determined that individualized testing is not impractical for the relevant position, the employer's attempt to justify its decision on the basis of the contrary opinion of experts—solicited for the purposes of litigation—is hardly convincing on any objective standard short of complete deference. Even in cases involving public safety, the ADEA plainly does not permit the trier of fact to give complete deference to the employer's decision.

Notes and Questions

1. *Should Safety Standards Be Set by Agencies or by Courts? Criswell* may be a relatively easy case, given the evidence that flight engineers rarely figure in accidents, the FAA's separate treatment of pilots, and the contrary practices of other airlines (footnote 28). In other cases, however, there may be stronger evidence that the employment of older workers in public transportation positions does pose some additional risk. Do you share the Supreme Court's confidence that lay juries will weigh appropriately safety arguments which have "a credible basis in the record," when faced with real-life plaintiffs who have no documented medical problems and are armed with their own expert witnesses? Should these judgments be made in case-by-case adjudication or should the EEOC (or the Federal Aviation Administration) engage in rulemaking on the issue, so that available data can be dispassionately assessed and generic, across-the-board determinations can be made for particular industries?

On December 13, 2007, President Bush signed legislation that allows United States commercial pilots to fly until age 65. P.L. 110–135. Congress acted in response to the FAA's announcement that it would begin a rulemaking procedure to raise the mandatory retirement age to 65.

2. *Permissible Statistical Discrimination to Permit Safety Risks?* As noted in the last chapter, the *Criswell* Court's adoption of the *Tamiami* modification of the two-prong *Diaz* and *Weeks* BFOQ test would seem to permit some degree of statistical discrimination, at least where necessary to protect public safety. The predicate showing required of employers, however,

is a demonstration that it is "impossible or highly impractical" to assess risk on an individualized basis. Is such showing more readily made in age discrimination than in sex discrimination cases?

Might *Criswell* and *Tamiami* be read to permit employers in some cases to use an age cut-off for *hiring* that is many years short of the average age at which motor coordination skills, attention span, and other characteristics related to safe operation of vehicles begin to decline? In Hodgson v. Greyhound Lines, Inc., 499 F.2d 859 (7th Cir.1974), for instance, the employer defended a 35 year age cut-off for hiring drivers with evidence that average safety records improved with 15 to 20 years of experience, but started to decline on the average at age 55. The employer contended that it could not get the benefit of driver experience if it hired post–40 year old drivers and waited until they reached 55 to determine which of them might be exceptions to the average. Is there any reason why this justification, if supported by adequate evidence, should not be sufficient under the *Criswell–Tamiami* standard? On the other hand, is this a form of statistical discrimination based on average group characteristics that is any different from the maximum age limitations criticized in Secretary Wirtz's report?

3. *Use of Age to Predict Future Productivity?* Should the *Tamiami* modification of the *Weeks-Diaz* BFOQ test apply to cases where an employer makes predictions of future average productivity rather than safety? Does the BFOQ defense enable employers overtly to prefer hiring younger workers because on the average they will have more years of high productivity after an initial training period? Is this justification for an age-based hiring preference different from an employer's argument that it prefers male employees because female employees are less likely to stay with the firm long enough to recoup training investments?

4. *Risks to Older Workers as BFOQ?* Should employers be able to justify age cut-offs as a means of protecting the health or safety of older workers and of reducing the risk of employer liability to such workers? See Olivia S. Mitchell, The Relation of Age to Workplace Injuries, Monthly Lab. Rev. (July 1988), at 8 ff. (job risk patterns do not vary with age for temporary disabilities, but workers over age 65 are more likely to suffer permanent disabilities). Consider the treatment of similar justifications in International Union, UAW v. Johnson Controls, pp. 321–331 supra, and for disability discrimination, note 5 at p. 575 infra.

5. *Subjective Component to BFOQ?* Does the *Criswell–Tamiami* test require that the employer adopt its age-based safety standard because of a safety risk it subjectively and in good faith believes? Consider, for instance, a case where the plaintiff shows that the employer discharges all workers above a certain age from a physically demanding and safety-sensitive job, but does not as a general matter test employees for conformity to health, fitness or physical stamina standards? Compare EEOC v. Kentucky State Police Department, 860 F.2d 665 (6th Cir.1988); EEOC v. Pennsylvania, 829 F.2d 392, 395 (3d Cir.1987), with EEOC v. City of East Providence, 798 F.2d 524, 529 (1st Cir.1986); EEOC v. Missouri State Highway Patrol, 748 F.2d 447, 454 (8th Cir.1984).

6. *Exception for Firefighters and Law Enforcement Officers.* The cases cited in the last note would now be addressed under a provision in the ADEA

that under certain limited conditions permits states or local subdivisions to engage in age-based hiring or mandatory retirement of firefighters and law enforcement officers pursuant to bona fide plans. The hiring or retirement action must be based on a state or local law in effect on March 3, 1983 (the date that the Supreme Court upheld application of the ADEA to state governments), or on an age cut-off set by applicable state or local law if that law was enacted after September 30, 1996 (the date of enactment of the ADEA amendments of 1996). If the action is a retirement under a law enacted after September 30, 1996, the terminated individual also must be at least 55. See 29 U.S.C. § 623(j).

7. *Appearance/Customer Preference BFOQ—The Case of Broadcasting.* Assume that a broadcasting station's market research shows that local viewers prefer younger sportscasters. Could the station use this research to justify replacing an older sportscaster? Cf. Craft v. Metromedia, Inc., 766 F.2d 1205 (8th Cir.1985); Wilson v. Southwest Airlines Co., pp. 334–339 supra. What if the research showed that a particular older sportscaster was not as popular as his younger rival on another station? Should the reason for his relative popularity matter? Cf. Ryther v. KARE 11, 108 F.3d 832 (8th Cir.1997) (en banc) (market research found to be pretext for age-based termination).

8. *Seniority and ADEA.* Section 4(f)(2) of ADEA also provides a defense for employers who "observe the terms of a bona fide seniority system." Because seniority systems generally favor older workers, ADEA issues in this context rarely arise. The 1978 amendments add the proviso that such systems may not "require or permit" involuntary retirement on account of age.

In Trans World Airlines, Inc. v. Thurston, supra, the Court held that the carrier's rule preventing pilots over the age of 60 from bumping less senior flight engineers was an age-based classification and not protected by § 4(f)(2). EEOC regulations require that to be bona fide, a seniority system must treat length of service as "the primary criterion for the equitable allocation of available employment opportunities and prerogatives." 29 C.F.R. § 1625.8 (1986).

3. *Systemic Disparate Treatment and Statistical Proof*

MISTRETTA v. SANDIA CORP.

United States District Court, District of New Mexico, 1977.
15 EPD ¶ 7902, affirmed, 639 F.2d 600 (10th Cir.1980).

Mechem, District Judge.

What is presently Sandia Corporation began as an engineering support division of Los Alamos Scientific Laboratory in 1946. In response to a request by the United States Government, Sandia was incorporated as a Delaware corporation in 1949 by Western Electric Company, Incorporated, and its wholly owned subsidiary. Sandia is a prime contractor to the Atomic Energy Commission (AEC), now Energy Research and Development Administration (ERDA).

AEC, and its successor ERDA, review the personnel policies and practices of Sandia, including salary administration, for the purpose of ascertaining compliance with applicable Federal statutes, regulations and executive orders. Sandia's personnel policies are derived from Bell system personnel policies.

The contract between Western Electric and ERDA specifies that there shall be no fee or profit for Western Electric or Sandia, and that all costs incurred under the contract are reimbursable and are funded by the Federal Government. Sandia is a "level of effort" laboratory. It is the responsibility of Sandia's management to staff to the level necessary within its overall budget to accomplish the tasks assigned to it by ERDA.

* * *

Since the early 1950's defendant's scientists and engineers involved in the laboratory's primary research and development activities have been classified as Members of Technical Staff (MTS). Since 1960 other employees involved primarily in various technical and non-technical support activities have been employed under defendant's Position Evaluation Plan (PEP). Prior to April, 1973, PEP employees involved in either technical staff or laboratory staff functions were in the following employee classifications:

1) Technical

(a) *Technical Staff Associate* (TSA)—Professional level, non-degree employees who work with MTS, level obtained by experience or technical school background.

(b) *Staff Assistant Technical* (SAT)—Employees who through experience or education have obtained Technical Institute degree level. They work either in direct assistance to MTS and TSA or work independently in testing, maintenance and assembly operations.

2) Administrative

(a) *Member Laboratory Staff* (MLS)—Professional level administrative employees, non–MTS supervisors and professional level technical employees performing non–MTS functions such as plant engineering.

(b) *Laboratory Staff Associate* (LSA)—Professional level employees who work with administrative MLS. They obtained their level by experience in administrative work.

(c) *Staff Assistant Laboratory* (SAL)—Employees who either provide assistance to MLS in administrative work, provide drafting and routine design work for MTS, or are high level clerical employees.

* * *

Sandia admits that it concentrates on college recruiting to assure continuity and gradual turnover. [Sandia's officials] do not actively recruit in the protected age group because older applicants, they say, are not available in significant numbers. Sandia also considers recent academic training to provide broader knowledge than field experience.

Sandia does not close the door in an older applicant's face. An older or experienced applicant would normally come to Sandia to fill a specific vacancy rather than being hired at the bottom to be trained into a position.

* * *

There is nothing inherently suspicious about on-campus recruiting programs. The available labor market for Sandia technical staff would be expected to come from recent graduates at all degree levels, in addition to the most recent exposure to advanced education, new techniques and new discoveries in the fields of science, this group would be job hunting while those in the protected age group normally would be established in more permanent positions and advanced to positions attributable to their age and experience. Age discrimination cannot be inferred from facts which show that 90% of new hires are younger than the protected age group. This pattern does not show a significant disparity from what would normally be expected in the market place. No evidence was presented to show whether applicants in the protected age group had less success in finding employment at Sandia than applicants generally. Considering all this evidence together, I hold that plaintiffs have not established by a preponderance of the evidence that Sandia has discriminated against individuals from forty to sixty-five years of age in recruiting and hiring policies and practices.

The next area of inquiry, promotions and educational opportunity, is presented only for its evidentiary value. The Secretary of Labor presents this in support of his contention that age discrimination is present in all major areas of Sandia.

* * *

Plaintiff's expert, Dr. Spalding, divided individuals promoted into MTS and PEP categories by year from 1964 to 1974. He compared the mean age of those on [the] roll to the mean age of those promoted and then tested to determine whether it was improbable that the difference could occur by chance. One of the few things plaintiffs' and defendants' experts agreed upon was that the probability of a chance occurrence had to be less than 5% before it could be considered statistically significant.

Dr. Spalding found no statistical significance in the PEP classification, but he did find statistically significant differences in the MTS category in seven of the eleven years analyzed. Once again, however, all Dr. Spalding was saying was that something was causing the difference, but he could not testify as to the cause on the basis of his tests.

If I read Dr. Spalding's summary of MTS promotions, plaintiff's exhibit 89, vertically rather than horizontally, it shows a trend. The mean age of those on [the] roll increased from 36.1 in 1964 to a mean age of 41.4 in 1974. The mean age of those promoted decreases from 36.3 in 1965 to 34.9 in 1974 with a low of 32.1 in 1971.

Defendant criticizes this study as distorted because it assumes that all MTS were eligible for promotion to a supervisory position. It is true that there are considerable restrictions to mobility between divisions or departments and Dr. Spalding did not analyze the positions being filled and those who might be eligible. This evidence, however, was not intended to present a full blown promotion policy case, but was merely intended to show that there was some age bias in the promotion area. There are approximately 250 MTS division supervisors. The evidence is sufficient to cause a reasonable suspicion that age is a factor in MTS promotion to the first level of supervision.

* * *

As noted before, Sandia's budget is determined by the size of the federal government's appropriation to AEC/ERDA. Sandia's growth period ended in 1968. Sandia entered a period of monetary restrictions and reductions with no change in its general mission or scope of operations beginning with Fiscal Year 1971. These restrictions resulted in voluntary and involuntary reductions in force (R.I.F.) in calendar years 1970 and 1971, amounting to 12 percent of the staff. Sandia's population declined from 8,182 on January 31, 1970 to 7,177 as of December, 1972.

The criteria used as the basis for the selection of employees for involuntary termination in 1970 were "contribution to the mission of the laboratory" and "job elimination". Following the reduction in force in 1970, for a period of one week, a compliance officer of the Department of Labor reviewed the layoff for possible age discrimination. No action was taken against Sandia because the compliance officer's report was favorable to defendant.

* * *

The defendant identified some individuals for involuntary layoff by determining which jobs could be eliminated. Actually, many cases of job elimination were cases of reassigning duties of the individual to others. Other candidates were selected by identifying what Sandia termed "least contributors to the mission of the Company." This was determined by an individual's performance rating and a job importance evaluation.

* * *

Following the close of the voluntary termination option on March 2, 1973. Sandia realized it had under-estimated the number of volunteers. Sandia offered forty-one of the employees on the involuntary list a chance to remain on the [roll] and 39 accepted the offer. All but one were in the protected age group. In the Sandian dialect, these individuals are referred to as "Saved by the Sunday exercise".

* * *

[*Eds.* The court proceeded to describe the study conducted by the Secretary's expert, Dr. Spalding.] The variable in the study was age on an ordinal scale of 18 to 64. Dr. Spalding made an assumption called a "null hypothesis", which is a conjecture that any differences in the expected and observed data are due to random sampling chance or, in other words, "that selection for layoff was independent of age". Also included in the null hypothesis is the assumption that all other factors are equal. This analysis was portrayed on a * * * chart which displays graphically the cumulative frequencies of the expected and observed groups.

The next step in the analysis is to measure the difference between the observed and expected frequencies and then use statistical tables to make a statement of the probability that the difference occurs by chance. Statisticians on this case agree that when the probability of a distribution happening by random chance is less than 5%, the result is statistically significant. When the probability of a chance occurrence is less than 5%, the statistician rejects his null hypothesis or conjecture. Dr. Spalding rejected his null hypothesis in 34 of his 36 studies.

* * *

I will not discuss Dr. Spalding's various combination studies in detail. His analysis of all PEP and MTS, supervisors included, is the Lab-wide study (graded employees excluded). It helps normalize or generalize some of this data and shows 33% of those terminated involuntarily were between the ages of 54 and 64, while only 15% of the Lab population falls into this age group.

The Secretary introduced numerous exhibits showing that Sandia's management and lower line supervision tended toward stereotyping older non-supervisory employees as unproductive and becoming technically obsolete. Management also believed that the future of the Lab depended upon "new blood", that is, young Ph'd's. There is a factual explanation for this belief in the rapid changes in technology taking place at that time. The end result was an arbitrary generalization that older employees did not have the ability to keep pace with new developments. This "attitude" evidence corroborates the statistical evidence and supports an inference that age was a factor in selection for layoff.

Sandia contends Dr. Spalding's layoff analysis is misleading and insignificant because he assumed all factors other than age were equal and he cannot testify that any individual was laid off because of his age, i.e., a causal relationship between age and layoff. The latter criticism is misplaced because *Teamsters* [*v. United States,* 431 U.S. 324, 97 S.Ct. 1843, 52 L.Ed.2d 396 (1977),] does not require direct proof of discrimination. The assumption in Dr. Spalding's study that all other factors were equal does not significantly undermine the weight. The strength of Dr. Spalding's analysis does not lie in his methods, probability statements, or rejection of a null hypothesis. The value of his testimony lies in the presentation of the data which I have analyzed by a simple numerical and percentage method.

Although it may be technically improper to discuss defendant's evidence before determining whether plaintiff has proved a prima facie case, it is more convenient to discuss Dr. Prairie's statistical tests at this time.

To rebut Dr. Spalding's testimony, defendant's expert, Dr. Prairie, testified that performance was the most significant factor in selection for layoff. The first step in Dr. Prairie's analysis was to prepare contingency tables by job classification and age. The purpose of a contingency analysis is to determine whether two percentages or proportion[s] can be considered statistically equal. * * * He found a significant age-layoff correlation only in the MLS and SAT classifications. Finding a significant correlation in this analysis does not provide evidence of causality. It indicates that further tests must be performed.

Dr. Prairie then divided MTS and non-supervisory MTS into three sub-groups; low performers, middle performers, and high performers. This * * * analysis formed the basis of his opinion that: 1) age was not a factor in determining whether a low performer was to be laid off; 2) among middle performers the impact was on individuals less than age 40; 3) there were no layoffs among high performers.

Dr. Prairie found a significant correlation between performance and age, i.e., those under 40 tended to get higher ratings. He divided the MTS population into two groups; high education (Master's degree level or above), low education (less than a Master's degree), to determine whether education might explain the difference. Dr. Prairie concludes that education level explains a substantial part of the performance-age relationship in the MTS category with supervisors included. But, with supervision excluded, the explanation is weakened. Dr. Prairie finds that the relationship between education and performance is strong and that the under 40 age group tends to account for a greater percentage of those with high education level.

The next analysis is called a discriminant analysis, the purpose of which, according to Dr. Prairie, is "to determine which of the factors or combination of factors * * * is important in properly assigning * * * people to layoff or non-layoff category." This analysis uses actual ages and a numerical value for education that Sandia uses in the personnel area. The layoff group of 123 MTS's was compared against a random sample of 123 employees not laid off to determine whether the selected factors were valuable in predicting who would be laid off. Dr. Prairie concludes that performance is the key factor in predicting who would be laid off.

* * *

Dr. Prairie's discriminant factors analysis leads to his overall opinion that performance was the decisive factor in the 1973 layoff. This explanation will fail if performance ratings contain age bias. In fact, the discriminant analysis depends on the purity of the performance factor as an appropriate classification.

* * *

An age discrimination case is different from a Title VII case. When Title VII type discrimination is present, it is normally a clear cut pattern or practice against a protected group as a whole. Here the pattern and practice has not been shown to affect the whole protected age group. The evidence establishes a prima facie case that at age 52, age is beginning to appear as a factor in layoff decisions. After age 55, the inference that age was a factor in [the] selection process becomes stronger and this trend continues up to about age 58, and then it appears to remain at the same strength up to age 64. * * * This comes as no surprise because a large number of layoff decisions were made by supervisors who were in the lower half of the protected age group. They did not consider themselves or their peers to be "over the hill".

After examining Dr. Prairie's analysis, I find it insufficient to defeat plaintiff's prima facie showing that individuals aged 52 to 64 were adversely affected by layoff decisions in a pattern significantly different from other employees.

Sandia must shoulder the burden of going forward with evidence of its defense. Defendant's evidence can be designed to defeat plaintiff's prima facie case or to show a non-discriminatory reason for its actions.

* * *

The theme of Sandia's defense is that performance ratings were the main ingredient in layoff decisions. The rating system has been described in a preceding section of this opinion. The system is extremely subjective and has never been validated. Supervisors were not told to consider specific criteria in their ratings. Like the system criticized in *Brito v. Zia Co.*, 478 F.2d 1200, 1206 [(10th Cir.1973)], the evaluations were based on [the] best judgment and opinion of the evaluators, but were not based on any definite identifiable criteria based on quality or quantity of work or specific performances that were supported by some kind of record. Courts have condemned subjective standards as fostering discrimination. Thus, they have declined to give much weight to testimony when a company's justification of its decision or policy is based on subjective criteria. *Muller v. U.S. Steel* [*Corp.*, 509 F.2d 923, 929 (10th Cir.), cert. denied, 423 U.S. 825, 96 S.Ct. 39, 46 L.Ed.2d 41 (1975)]; *Rich v. Martin–Marietta* [*Corp.*], 522 F.2d [333, 350 (10th Cir.1975)] * * *.

[Defendant's experts testified that it would] be very difficult to define goals, (and to) develop objective criteria for evaluating engineers and scientists engaged in research. [They] agree that the value of a person is affected by the importance of his assignments and they observe a tendency in other companies to give more challenging assignments to the young Ph'd's. Defendant's experts * * * see a performance level being identified in about ten years and remaining constant for the rest of an individual's career. It would appear, however, that the problems of stating specific objective rating criteria applies [sic] only to a portion of Sandia's work force—those scientists or engineers engaged in research. It would appear to be a relatively simple task to define objective rating criteria for draftsmen, machinists, computer operators and administrative personnel. * * *

Management's concern about the increasing age of its staff, reduced hiring, new technical developments, and emphasis on recruiting and advancing young Ph'd's might not violate ADEA in themselves, but these policies and attitudes could easily be reflected in subjective performance ratings.

* * * Sandia's experts agree that challenging job assignments at other companies go to younger Ph'd's. In this case there were employees who were laid off because they had been in one line of research too long and were considered less versatile than younger employees. The evidence presented is not sufficient to prove or disprove the contention that at Sandia performance declines with age, but there is sufficient circumstantial evidence to indicate that age bias and age based policies appear throughout the performance rating process to the detriment of the protected age group. This constitutes sufficient reason to reject Dr. Prairie's analyses.

Considering all of defendant's evidence, Sandia's defense does not show: that its actions are nondiscriminatory; that its policies are necessary to the safe and efficient operation of its business; or that its subjective rating system is necessary throughout all of its employee classifications. Sandia has failed to rebut the plaintiff's prima facie case.

I hold that the plaintiffs have established by a preponderance of the evidence that individuals in the 52 to 64 age range were selected for layoff in a pattern which proves that Sandia has engaged in discriminatory conduct.

W. CONNOLLY & D. PETERSON, USE OF STATISTICS IN EQUAL EMPLOYMENT OPPORTUNITY LITIGATION § 10.05 (1985)

There are [several] ways in which age discrimination measurement differs from that for race or sex discrimination. Two of them, described below, are consequences of the natural association between an employee's length of service with an employer, and the employee's age. While it is true that employees with little seniority can be any of a wide range of ages, it is also true that employees with many years of seniority are of necessity relatively old. Seniority, in turn, is a quality of an employee that in many organizations may be benignly predictive of his or her pay or status in the organization.

[a]—The "Peter Principle." In an organization consisting of many job levels, each the main source of candidates for filling vacancies in the next higher level, there may be a tendency for individuals to rise in the organization to a level at which they are barely able to perform. Limited in promotional opportunities by lackluster job performance, such people may witness the promotion from their job level of people more qualified but less senior than themselves. Thus, at any point in time, a given job

level may consist of two types of people: those who have risen as far as is practical, and those who are apparently on their way to greater heights. Because those employees who are stuck in the level continue to accrue seniority, while those just passing through are continually replaced by people with generally less seniority, it is not unreasonable to expect that the more senior employees within a job level tend to be those whose careers have peaked. To the extent that age and seniority are correlated, it is also not unreasonable to expect that within a job level, the older employees will tend to be the less able performers.

In an organization with such a structure, it seems clear that the people promoted from a given level during the course of a year may generally be younger than the people in that level who are not promoted. If the organization is required by legitimate business considerations to reduce the number of employees in a given level by discharging those who perform least satisfactorily, it is likely that the employees discharged from a given level will tend to be older than those who are not.

[b]—The Age–Wage Curve. At a given instant, the relationship between average pay and employee age in an organization may be similar to that shown in Figure [7.1], a curve that rises with increasing age, but progressively less steeply. In such an organization the average amount by which the pay of, for example, thirty-five-year-olds exceeds that of thirty-year-olds is greater than the amount by which the average pay of sixty-year-olds exceeds that of fifty-five-year-olds. A pattern of this type could occur if an employer tended to give more substantial pay increases to younger employees than to older, according to some process unfair to older employees. However, this pattern could also arise as a result of practices that are quite benign, and hence, the existence of that pattern in an employer's labor force need not be probative of age-discriminatory practice.

Figure [7.1] A Possible Relationship Between Employees' Average Pay and their Ages

One mechanism by which such a curve could arise is the following. Suppose an organization consists of some fixed number of job levels, each successively better paying, [with] all persons at the same level being paid at the same rate. Suppose further that experience working at a job in any one level prepares an employee for a job in the next higher-paying level, so that typical career paths involve passage through successive levels. Suppose now that nearly all hiring is done for vacancies at the lowest-paying level and that nearly all other vacancies are filled by promotion from within. Finally, as an extreme case, suppose there are as many employees in one level as there are in any other level.

Consider now the experience of a typical employee hired at the bottom level. The departure of any employee in any level above her will create, by chain reaction, a vacancy at the next level above hers, for which she is in competition with others in her level. She is likely to have, therefore, many more opportunities for advancement than is someone at a higher level, who is competing with the same number of people as she, but whose advancement is contingent on the departure of one of the relatively small[2] number of people in levels above her. Hence, promotions are likely to come more frequently to persons at lower levels in this organization than to those at higher levels.

The longer an employee stays with this organization, the greater is the likelihood he or she will advance to the higher paying levels. However, in some average sense, this progress must slow as one nears the top level, because of the relatively small number of vacancies created by departures. Because no one can advance beyond the top level, the pay accorded persons in that level is an absolute upper limit on pay, that cannot be exceeded by employees of any seniority.

Notes and Questions

1. *Statistical Proof in ADEA Cases. Mistretta* is a relatively rare instance of a private ADEA suit in which statistical proof is made of a pattern and practice of discrimination. See also Barnes v. GenCorp Inc., 896 F.2d 1457 (6th Cir.1990); Mangold v. California Public Utilities Commission, 67 F.3d 1470 (9th Cir.1995).

In *Mistretta* the finding of a "prima facie" case of systemic age bias did not rely on statistics alone; the court also found that evidence of the age-conscious "attitude" of Sandia's management and lower line supervision "corroborates the statistical evidence." Should statistical evidence of age discrimination carry as much weight in an ADEA case as comparable evidence of race or sex discrimination in a Title VII case? Should such evidence ever be sufficient to establish a rebuttable presumption—similar to what *Franks* and *Teamsters* hold appropriate for Title VII litigation, see pp. 209–220 supra—that every laid-off older worker was a victim of a general policy of age discrimination? Should the type of statistical showing in *Mistretta*, perhaps coupled with evidence of reliance on subjective performance appraisals, be enough to establish such a presumption? Is it relevant to

---

2. There are obviously more people in levels above the entry level than there are people above some higher level. *Every* departure above entry level creates an opening, by chain reaction, at the entry level; but only departures at the topmost levels create openings at the upper levels.

answering these questions that most employers are now quite sensitive to ADEA's implications and therefore less likely to leave behind "smoking gun" evidence?

2. *Proving Company-Wide Discrimination in an Individual Disparate Treatment Case?* Under what conditions should an employee claiming that he was adversely affected by an age-based personnel decision be allowed to introduce evidence of age bias from supervisors other than the one making the decision? Consider, for instance, an employee claiming that he was selected by a supervisor on the basis of his age for being laid off in a reduction-in-force. Should the introduction of evidence of age bias by other supervisors be dependent upon the employee introducing statistical or other evidence of a company-wide policy connecting the age bias of various supervisors? See Mendelsohn v. Sprint/United Management Co., 466 F.3d 1223 (10th Cir. 2006), rev'd on other grounds, ___ U.S. ___, 128 S.Ct. 1140, 170 L.Ed.2d 1 (2008).

3. *Special Benign Explanations for Age–Correlated Statistics?* Does the "Peter Principle," as described by Connolly and Peterson, perhaps provide a benign explanation for the suspicious promotion statistics noted by the *Mistretta* court? Does the authors' "Age–Wage Curve" also help provide such an explanation? How might a statistical analysis of possible age bias in promotions control for these two phenomena? Consider again the materials on regression analysis at pp. 109–112 supra.

Might the "Peter Principle" also offer a benign explanation for the correlation of older age with those involuntarily laid off by Sandia? Note that Sandia presumably did not have any legal responsibility to demote rather than layoff relatively unproductive workers. Would a similar correlation with race or sex provide a stronger basis for suspecting a biased selection process?

4. *Special Problems of Statistical Proof in ADEA Hiring Cases.* The *Mistretta* court asserts that the hiring of a very high proportion (90%) of new employees from outside the protected ADEA class does not suggest age bias in hiring absent evidence about the relative numbers of members of the protected class in the qualified applicant pool. Would age-based hiring be suggested by proof that individuals over the age of 40 constituted significantly more than 10% of the pool of qualified workers in the external labor market? Would such statistics be as probative of discrimination as comparable race or sex statistics?

The fact that older workers are less likely than younger workers to seek employment actively in external labor markets may create problems for plaintiffs wishing to mount a systemic disparate treatment challenge to an employer's hiring policies. Such problems seem especially troublesome because any stereotypical assumptions about older workers are likely to be more influential in hiring decisions. Should ADEA plaintiffs thus be able to use statistics reflecting the entire set of qualified workers in a relevant geographical area regardless of whether those workers are actively seeking new employment? Cf. Hazelwood School District v. United States, at pp. 95–102 supra. Should ADEA plaintiffs be able to challenge either an employer's failure to permit lateral hiring from other firms, or its recruitment, like Sandia's, primarily from colleges?

5. *Age-Correlated Declines in Research Productivity.* Sandia was not able to counter the government's correlation of older age with involuntary layoff by proving that it selected individuals on the basis of their relative productivity. However, a correlation between age and declining productivity of those engaged in research seems especially plausible for at least two reasons: (i) the increasing obsolescence of any scientific education and (ii) the risks of increasing specialization in particular research. If such explanations were adequately proven, how might a plaintiff respond? What if the plaintiff could establish that the employer never counseled relatively low performers that they needed to improve their technological knowledge or research skills? Never provided support for continuing education?

6. *Subjective Assessment of Scientific Performance.* Sandia's 1973 performance appraisal was considered inadequate by the court because of its failure to require the supervisors to assess performance in terms of "definite identifiable criteria based on the quality or quantity of work or specific performances that were supported by some kind of record." Cf. Albemarle Paper Co. v. Moody, 151 supra. The court did not necessarily reject, however, Sandia's contention that it could not develop meaningful objective criteria for scientists and engineers engaged in research, where results are often the product of serendipity as much as effort. Should subjective assessments of scientific personnel ever be subject to an age discrimination challenge based solely on statistics? To race or sex discrimination challenges based solely on statistics? See Note on Defense of Subjective Evaluation Systems, at pp. 181–182 supra.

7. *Relevance of Intraclass Statistics.* Note that the *Mistretta* court assumes that age discrimination, unlike race and sex discrimination, may present issues of intraclass discrimination. Is this assumption confirmed by the Supreme Court's later decision in *O'Connor*? See also Mangold v. California Public Utilities Commission, supra. The *Mistretta* court stressed that the plaintiff's evidence suggested an age bias against those in the protected class between the ages of 52 and 64, but not those between the ages of 40 and 52. The court also criticized the defendant's expert for analyzing the impact of involuntary layoffs on those over age 40 as compared with those under age 40, thus possibly "obscur[ing] an impact somewhere inside the protected age group." What if the evidence had shown that individuals between the ages of 52 and 58 comprised 30% of the laid-off group and only 10% of the relevant workforce, but that individuals between the ages of and 65 comprised only 5% of the laid-off group and 10% of the relevant workforce? Would such a showing conclusively rebut an inference of a discriminatory pattern or practice? Are such statistics consistent with a plausible account of a discriminatorily motivated employer?

C. DISPARATE IMPACT

HAZEN PAPER COMPANY v. BIGGINS
Supreme Court of the United States, 1993.
507 U.S. 604, 113 S.Ct. 1701, 123 L.Ed.2d 338.

JUSTICE O'CONNOR delivered the opinion of the Court.

In this case we clarify the standards for liability and liquidated damages under the Age Discrimination in Employment Act of 1967 (ADEA), 81 Stat. 602, as amended, 29 U.S.C. § 621 et seq.

Petitioner Hazen Paper Company manufactures coated, laminated, and printed paper and paperboard. The company is owned and operated by two cousins, petitioners Robert Hazen and Thomas N. Hazen. The Hazens hired respondent Walter F. Biggins as their technical director in 1977. They fired him in 1986, when he was 62 years old.

Respondent brought suit against petitioners in the United States District Court for the District of Massachusetts, alleging a violation of the ADEA. He claimed that age had been a determinative factor in petitioners' decision to fire him. Petitioners contested this claim, asserting instead that respondent had been fired for doing business with competitors of Hazen Paper. The case was tried before a jury, which rendered a verdict for respondent on his ADEA claim and also found violations of the Employee Retirement Income Security Act of 1974 (ERISA), 88 Stat. 895, § 510, 29 U.S.C. § 1140, and state law. On the ADEA count, the jury specifically found that petitioners "willfully" violated the statute. Under § 7(b) of the ADEA, 29 U.S.C. § 626(b), a "willful" violation gives rise to liquidated damages.

Petitioners moved for judgment notwithstanding the verdict. The District Court granted the motion with respect to a state-law claim and the finding of "willfulness" but otherwise denied it. An appeal ensued. The United States Court of Appeals for the First Circuit affirmed judgment for respondent on both the ADEA and ERISA counts, and reversed judgment notwithstanding the verdict for petitioners as to "willfulness."

In affirming the judgments of liability, the Court of Appeals relied heavily on the evidence that petitioners had fired respondent in order to prevent his pension benefits from vesting. That evidence, as construed most favorably to respondent by the court, showed that the Hazen Paper pension plan had a 10–year vesting period and that respondent would have reached the 10–year mark had he worked "a few more weeks" after being fired. There was also testimony that petitioners had offered to retain respondent as a consultant to Hazen Paper, in which capacity he would not have been entitled to receive pension benefits. The Court of Appeals found this evidence of pension interference to be sufficient for ERISA liability, and also gave it considerable emphasis in upholding ADEA liability.

* * *

We long have distinguished between "disparate treatment" and "disparate impact" theories of employment discrimination. * * * The disparate treatment theory is of course available under the ADEA, as the language of that statute makes clear. "It shall be unlawful for an employer * * * to fail or refuse to hire or to discharge any individual or otherwise discriminate against any individual with respect to his compensation, terms, conditions, or privileges of employment, *because of such individual's age.*" 29 U.S.C. § 623 (a)(1) (emphasis added). See [*Trans World Airlines, Inc. v.*] *Thurston*[, 469 U.S. 111,] at 120–125 [(1985)] (affirming ADEA liability under disparate treatment theory). By contrast, we have never decided whether a disparate impact theory of liability is available under the ADEA, see *Markham v. Geller*, 451 U.S. 945, 68 L. Ed. 2d 332, 101 S. Ct. 2028 (1981) (REHNQUIST, J., dissenting from denial of certiorari), and we need not do so here. Respondent claims only that he received disparate treatment.

In a disparate treatment case, liability depends on whether the protected trait (under the ADEA, age) actually motivated the employer's decision. The employer may have relied upon a formal, facially discriminatory policy requiring adverse treatment of employees with that trait. Or the employer may have been motivated by the protected trait on an ad hoc, informal basis. Whatever the employer's decisionmaking process, a disparate treatment claim cannot succeed unless the employee's protected trait actually played a role in that process and had a determinative influence on the outcome.

Disparate treatment, thus defined, captures the essence of what Congress sought to prohibit in the ADEA. It is the very essence of age discrimination for an older employee to be fired because the employer believes that productivity and competence decline with old age. As we explained in *EEOC v. Wyoming*, 460 U.S. 226, 75 L. Ed. 2d 18, 103 S. Ct. 1054 (1983), Congress' promulgation of the ADEA was prompted by its concern that older workers were being deprived of employment on the basis of inaccurate and stigmatizing stereotypes. * * * Thus the ADEA commands that "employers are to evaluate [older] employees * * * on their merits and not their age." *Western Air Lines, Inc. v. Criswell*, 472 U.S. 400, 422, 86 L. Ed. 2d 321, 105 S. Ct. 2743 (1985). The employer cannot rely on age as a proxy for an employee's remaining characteristics, such as productivity, but must instead focus on those factors directly.

When the employer's decision is wholly motivated by factors other than age, the problem of inaccurate and stigmatizing stereotypes disappears. This is true even if the motivating factor is correlated with age, as pension status typically is. Pension plans typically provide that an employee's accrued benefits will become nonforfeitable, or "vested," once the employee completes a certain number of years of service with the employer. See 1 J. Mamorsky, Employee Benefits Law § 5.03 (1992). On average, an older employee has had more years in the work force than a younger employee, and thus may well have accumulated more years of service with a particular employer. Yet an employee's age is analytically distinct from his years of service. An employee who is younger than 40, and therefore outside the class of older workers as defined by the ADEA, see 29 U.S.C. § 631(a), may have worked for a particular employer his entire career, while an older worker may have been newly hired. Because age and years of service are analytically distinct, an employer can take account of one while ignoring the other, and thus it is incorrect to say that a decision based on years of service is necessarily "age-based."

The instant case is illustrative. Under the Hazen Paper pension plan, as construed by the Court of Appeals, an employee's pension benefits vest after the employee completes 10 years of service with the company. Perhaps it is true that older employees of Hazen Paper are more likely to be "close to vesting" than younger employees. Yet a decision by the company to fire an older employee solely because he has nine-plus years of service and therefore is "close to vesting" would not constitute discriminatory treatment on the basis of age. The prohibited stereotype ("Older employees are likely to be ___") would not have figured in this decision, and the attendant stigma would not ensue. The decision would not be the result of an inaccurate and denigrating generalization about age, but would rather represent an accurate judgment about the employee—that he indeed is "close to vesting."

We do not mean to suggest that an employer lawfully could fire an employee in order to prevent his pension benefits from vesting. Such conduct is actionable under § 510 of ERISA, as the Court of Appeals rightly found in affirming judgment for respondent under that statute. See *Ingersoll-Rand Co. v. McClendon*, 498 U.S. 133, 142–143, 112 L. Ed. 2d 474, 111 S. Ct. 478 (1990). But it would not, without more, violate the ADEA. That law requires the employer to ignore an employee's age (absent a statutory exemption or defense); it does not specify further characteristics that an employer must also ignore. Although some language in our prior decisions might be read to mean that an employer violates the ADEA whenever its reason for firing an employee is improper in any respect, see *McDonnell Douglas Corp. v. Green*, 411 U.S. 792, 802, 36 L. Ed. 2d 668, 93 S. Ct. 1817 (1973) * * * (employer must have "legitimate, nondiscriminatory reason" for action against employee), this reading is obviously incorrect. For example, it cannot be true that an employer who fires an older black worker because the worker is black thereby violates the ADEA. The employee's race is an improper reason, but it is improper under Title VII, not the ADEA.

We do not preclude the possibility that an employer who targets employees with a particular pension status on the assumption that these employees are likely to be older thereby engages in age discrimination. Pension status may be a proxy for age, not in the sense that the ADEA makes the two factors equivalent, cf. *Metz* [*v. Transit Mix, Inc.*, 828 F.2d 1202, 1208 (7th Cir., 1987)] (using "proxy" to mean statutory equivalence), but in the sense that the employer may suppose a correlation between the two factors and act accordingly. Nor do we rule out the possibility of dual liability under ERISA and the ADEA where the decision to fire the employee was motivated both by the employee's age and by his pension status. Finally, we do not consider the special case where an employee is about to vest in pension benefits as a result of his age, rather than years of service, see 1 Mamorsky, *supra*, at § 5.02[2], and the employer fires the employee in order to prevent vesting. That case is not presented here. Our holding is simply that an employer does not violate the ADEA just by interfering with an older employee's pension benefits that would have vested by virtue of the employee's years of service.

Besides the evidence of pension interference, the Court of Appeals cited some additional evidentiary support for ADEA liability. Although there was no direct evidence of petitioners' motivation, except for two isolated comments by the Hazens, the Court of Appeals did note the following indirect evidence: Respondent was asked to sign a confidentiality agreement, even though no other employee had been required to do so, and his replacement was a younger man who was given a less onerous agreement. In the ordinary ADEA case, indirect evidence of this kind may well suffice to support liability if the plaintiff also shows that the employer's explanation for its decision—here, that respondent had been disloyal to Hazen Paper by doing business with its competitors—is " 'unworthy of credence.' " But inferring age-motivation from the implausibility of the employer's explanation may be problematic in cases where other unsavory motives, such as pension interference, were present. This issue is now before us in the Title VII context, see *Hicks v. St. Mary's Honor Center*, 970 F.2d 487 (C.A.8 1992), cert. granted, 506 U.S. 1042 (1993), and we will not address it prematurely. We therefore remand the case for the Court of Appeals to reconsider whether the jury had sufficient evidence to find an ADEA violation.

[*Eds.*: The Court's discussion of the standard for "willful" violations under § 7(b) of ADEA is omitted.]

[*Eds.* The opinion of JUSTICE KENNEDY, with whom THE CHIEF JUSTICE and JUSTICE THOMAS join, concurring, is omitted.]

Notes and Questions

1. *Irrelevance of Higher Cost of Hiring or Retaining Older Workers?* Before *Hazen Paper* some lower courts had begun to interpret the ADEA more broadly to condemn discrimination on the basis of age-correlated criteria such as seniority, vested tenure, higher wages, or pension eligibility, and thus provide an extra measure of job security for long-term employees who might face difficulties in securing re-employment. This interpretation was given support by some of the economic analysis cited in the introduction to this chapter. This analysis assumed the prevalence of long-term "relational" contracts and suggested the need to protect employees from employers' incentives to breach these contracts in certain circumstances. Consider this excerpt from the dissenting opinion of Judge Frank Easterbrook in *Metz v. Transit Mix, Inc.*, one of the cases adopting a broader interpretation of the ADEA, which was both cited and apparently rejected in *Hazen Paper*:

A growing literature on education, training, employment, and other aspects of human capital suggests that there may be times when employers will pay wages that do not represent the employees' marginal products. For example, while receiving firm-specific training the employee may receive a wage exceeding his product; this is how the firm finances the training (for which the employee will not pay, because it has no use outside the firm). Later the firm will recoup its investment by paying less than the marginal product. See Becker, *Human Capital* 26–37, 216–23. Other firms that give their employees access to trade secrets or put them in positions of trust may try to cement the employees' loyalty (or honesty) with "golden handcuffs"—wages in excess of the employees' marginal product, a form of special compensation the employee forfeits if he leaves the firm. E.g., Gary S. Becker & George J. Stigler, *Law Enforcement, Malfeasance, and Compensation of Enforcers,* 3 J. Legal Studies 1 (1974). Still other firms may pay employees slightly less than their marginal product early in their careers, knowing that as each employee's productivity declines at the end of his career, the firm will be paying more than marginal product (thus paying the employee his due over the life cycle). This gives employees strong reasons to stick with their firms and be more productive throughout their careers, which in turn yields society the benefit of everyone's abilities.

* * *

Whenever the age-wage profile of a class of employees includes a period of compensation at more than marginal product, the firm may be inclined to behave opportunistically—to fire the employee as soon as his current productivity no longer covers his current wage. A firm's desire to attract new employees will curtail this opportunism, to the extent new hires learn of the firm's reputation (or depend on a union to police the firm's behavior). When the firm encounters economic trouble or for some other reason plans to shrink, it need not worry about scaring away bright new employees; it is out of that market. The distressed or shrinking firm may try to dispose of higher paid, older employees, cheating them out of the high compensation at the end of their careers.

828 F.2d 1202, at 1220, 1221.

The majority in *Metz* held that the employer could not advance cost saving as a justification for replacing an older worker with a younger worker who was paid a lower salary. *Metz* seems no longer to be good law even in the Seventh Circuit. See, e.g., Anderson v. Baxter Healthcare Corp., 13 F.3d 1120, 1126 (7th Cir.1994) ("Anderson could not prove age discrimination even if he was fired simply because Baxter desired to reduce its salary costs by discharging him."). See also, e.g., Dilla v. West, 179 F.3d 1348 (11th Cir.1999) ("the mere fact that there exists a perfect correlation, or even a direct link" with age does not mean reliance on age); Schiltz v. Burlington Northern Railroad, 115 F.3d 1407 (8th Cir.1997).

2. *Encouraging the Employment of Older Workers?* Regardless of *Hazen Paper*, do you think that the statute's goals of encouraging the employment of older workers would be advanced by prohibiting any employer from

using its own rising wage scale as a justification for refusing to hire or for terminating an older worker? What if employers subject to this prohibition were allowed to adjust any wage premium they pay for experience to any extent they wish as long as older workers are not treated more poorly than comparable younger workers? See Harper, ADEA Doctrinal Impediments, supra, at 779–790; Christine Jolls, Hands–Tying and the Age Discrimination in Employment Act, 74 Tex. L. Rev. 1813 (1996).

3. *Disparate Impact Claims After* Hazen Paper. Might the ADEA still be used after *Hazen Paper* to protect the job security of older workers through disparate impact-based challenges to the termination of employees on the basis of age-correlated criteria such as seniority or high compensation levels? The *Hazen* Court expressly reserved judgment on whether disparate impact claims are available under the ADEA. Twelve years later the Court decided the issue.

SMITH v. CITY OF JACKSON, MISSISSIPPI

Supreme Court of the United States, 2005.

544 U.S. 228, 125 S.Ct. 1536, 161 L.Ed.2d 410.

Justice Stevens announced the judgment of the Court and delivered the opinion of the Court with respect to Parts I, II, and IV, and an opinion with respect to Part III, in which Justice Souter, Justice Ginsburg, and Justice Breyer join.

* * *

I

On October 1, 1998, the City adopted a pay plan granting raises to all City employees. The stated purpose of the plan was to "attract and retain qualified people, provide incentive for performance, maintain competitiveness with other public sector agencies and ensure equitable compensation to all employees regardless of age, sex, race and/or disability." On May 1, 1999, a revision of the plan, which was motivated, at least in part, by the City's desire to bring the starting salaries of police officers up to the regional average, granted raises to all police officers and police dispatchers. Those who had less than five years of tenure received proportionately greater raises when compared to their former pay than those with more seniority. Although some officers over the age of 40 had less than five years of service, most of the older officers had more.

Petitioners are a group of older officers who filed suit under the ADEA claiming both that the City deliberately discriminated against them because of their age (the "disparate-treatment" claim) and that they were "adversely affected" by the plan because of their age (the "disparate-impact" claim). The District Court granted summary judgment to the City on both claims. The Court of Appeals held that the ruling on the former claim was premature because petitioners were entitled to further discovery on the issue of intent, but it affirmed the dismissal of the disparate-impact claim. 351 F.3d 183 (CA5 2003). Over one judge's dissent, the majority concluded that disparate-impact claims are categorically unavailable under the ADEA. Both the majority and the dissent assumed that the facts alleged by petitioners would entitle them to relief under the reasoning of *Griggs v. Duke Power Co.*, 401 U.S. 424, 28 L.Ed. 2d 158, 91 S.Ct. 849 (1971).

* * *

III

In determining whether the ADEA authorizes disparate-impact claims, we begin with the premise that when Congress uses the same language in two statutes having similar purposes, particularly when one is enacted shortly after the other, it is appropriate to presume that Congress intended that text to have the same meaning in both statutes. *Northcross v. Board of Ed. of Memphis City Schools*, 412 U.S. 427, 428, 37 L. Ed. 2d 48, 93 S. Ct. 2201 (1973) (per curiam). We have consistently applied that presumption to language in the ADEA that was "derived in haec verba from Title VII." *Lorillard v. Pons*, 434 U.S. 575, 584, 55 L. Ed. 2d 40, 98 S. Ct. 866 (1978). Our unanimous interpretation of § 703(a)(2) of the Title VII in Griggs is therefore a precedent of compelling importance.

In *Griggs*, * * * [w]e explained that Congress had "directed the thrust of the Act to the consequences of employment practices, not simply the motivation." Ibid. We relied on the fact that history is "filled with examples of men and women who rendered highly effective performance without the conventional badges of accomplishment in terms of certificates, diplomas, or degrees. Diplomas and tests are useful servants, but Congress has mandated the commonsense proposition that they are not to become masters of reality." Id., at 433, 28 L. Ed. 2d 158, 91 S. Ct. 849. And we noted that the Equal Employment Opportunity Commission (EEOC), which had enforcement responsibility, had issued guidelines that accorded with our view. Id., at 433–434, 28 L. Ed. 2d 158, 91 S. Ct. 849. We thus squarely held that § 703(a)(2) of Title VII did not require a showing of discriminatory intent.

While our opinion in *Griggs* relied primarily on the purposes of the Act, buttressed by the fact that the EEOC had endorsed the same view, we have subsequently noted that our holding represented the better reading of the statutory text as well. See *Watson v. Fort Worth Bank & Trust*, 487 U.S. 977, 991, 101 L. Ed. 2d 827, 108 S. Ct. 2777 (1988), Neither § 703(a)(2) nor the comparable language in the ADEA simply prohibits actions that "limit, segregate, or classify" persons; rather the language prohibits such actions that "deprive any individual of employment opportunities or otherwise adversely affect his status as an employee, because of such individual's" race or age. Ibid. (explaining that in disparate-impact cases, "the employer's practices may be said to 'adversely affect [an individual's status] as an employee'" (alteration in original) (quoting 42 U.S.C. § 2000e-2(a)(2))). Thus the text focuses on the effects of the action on the employee rather than the motivation for the action of the employer.[2]

Griggs, which interpreted the identical text at issue here, thus strongly suggests that a disparate-impact theory should be cognizable under the ADEA. Indeed, for over two decades after our decision in *Griggs*, the Courts of Appeal uniformly interpreted the ADEA as authorizing recovery on a "disparate-impact" theory in appropriate cases. It was only after our decision in *Hazen Paper Co. v. Biggins*, 507 U.S. 604, 123 L. Ed. 2d 338, 113 S. Ct. 1701 (1993), that some of those courts concluded that the ADEA did not authorize a disparate-impact theory of liability. Our opinion in *Hazen Paper*, however, did not address or comment on the issue we decide today. * * *

The Court of Appeals' categorical rejection of disparate-impact liability, like Justice O'Connor's, rested primarily on the RFOA provision and the majority's analysis of legislative history. [W]e think the history of the enactment of the ADEA, with particular reference to the Wirtz Report, supports the pre-Hazen Paper consensus concerning disparate-impact liability. And Hazen Paper itself contains the response to the concern over the RFOA provision.

The RFOA provision provides that it shall not be unlawful for an employer "to take any action otherwise prohibited under subsectio[n] (a) ... where the differentiation is based on reasonable factors other than age discrimination ...." 81 Stat. 603. In most disparate-treatment cases, if an employer in fact acted on a factor other than age, the action would not be prohibited under subsection (a) in the first place. See *Hazen Paper*, 507 U.S., at 609, 123 L. Ed. 2d 338, 113 S. Ct. 1701 ("[T]here is no disparate treatment under the ADEA when the factor motivating the employer is some feature other than the employee's age."). In those disparate-treatment cases, such as in *Hazen Paper* itself, the RFOA provision is simply unnecessary to avoid liability under the ADEA, since there was no prohibited action in the first place. The RFOA provision is not, as Justice O'Connor suggests, a "safe harbor from liability," since there would be no liability under § 4(a). See *Texas Dep't of Community Affairs v. Burdine*, 450 U.S. 248, 254, 67 L. Ed. 2d 207, 101 S. Ct. 1089 (1981) (noting, in a Title VII case, that an employer can

---

2. In reaching a contrary conclusion, Justice O'Connor ignores key textual differences between § 4(a)(1), which does not encompass-disparate-impact liability, and § 4(a)(2). Section 4(a)(1) makes it unlawful for an employer "to fail or refuse to hire ... any individual ... because of such individual's age." (Emphasis added.) The focus of the section is on the employer's actions with respect to the targeted individual. Paragraph (a)(2), however, makes it unlawful for an employer "to limit ... his employees in any way that would deprive or tend to deprive any individual of employment opportunities or otherwise adversely affect his status as an employee, because of such individual's age." (Emphasis added.) Unlike in paragraph (a)(1), there is thus an incongruity between the employer's actions—which are focused on his employees generally—and the individual employee who adversely suffers because of those actions. Thus, an employer who classifies his employees without respect to age may still be liable under the terms of this paragraph if such classification adversely affects the employee because of that employee's age—the very definition of disparate impact. Justice O'Connor is therefore quite wrong to suggest that the textual differences between the two paragraphs are unimportant.

defeat liability by showing that the employee was rejected for "a legitimate, nondiscriminatory reason" without reference to an RFOA provision).

In disparate-impact cases, however, the allegedly "otherwise prohibited" activity is not based on age. Ibid. (" '[C]laims that stress "disparate impact" [by contrast] involve employment practices that are facially neutral in their treatment of different groups but that in fact fall more harshly on one group than another . . .' " (quoting *Teamsters v. United States*, 431 U.S. 324, 335–336, n. 15, 52 L. Ed. 2d 396, 97 S. Ct. 1843 (1977))). It is, accordingly, in cases involving disparate-impact claims that the RFOA provision plays its principal role by precluding liability if the adverse impact was attributable to a nonage factor that was "reasonable." Rather than support an argument that disparate impact is unavailable under the ADEA, the RFOA provision actually supports the contrary conclusion.[11]

Finally, we note that both the Department of Labor, which initially drafted the legislation, and the EEOC, which is the agency charged by Congress with responsibility for implementing the statute, 29 U.S.C. § 628 [29 USCS § 628], have consistently interpreted the ADEA to authorize relief on a disparate-impact theory. The initial regulations, while not mentioning disparate impact by name, nevertheless permitted such claims if the employer relied on a factor that was not related to age. 29 CFR § 860.103(f)(1)(i) (1970) (barring physical fitness requirements that were not "reasonably necessary for the specific work to be performed"). See also § 1625.7 (2004) (setting forth the standards for a disparate-impact claim).

The text of the statute, as interpreted in *Griggs*, the RFOA provision, and the EEOC regulations all support petitioners' view. We therefore conclude that it was error for the Court of Appeals to hold that the disparate-impact theory of liability is categorically unavailable under the ADEA.

IV

Two textual differences between the ADEA and Title VII make it clear that even though both statutes authorize recovery on a disparate-impact theory, the scope of disparate-impact liability under ADEA is narrower than under Title VII. The first is the RFOA provision, which we have already identified. The second is the amendment to Title VII contained in the Civil Rights Act of 1991, 105 Stat. 1071. One of the purposes of that amendment was to modify the Court's holding in *Wards Cove Packing Co. v. Atonio*, 490 U.S. 642, 104 L. Ed. 2d 733, 109 S. Ct. 2115 (1989), a case in which we narrowly construed the employer's exposure to liability on a disparate-impact theory. See Civil Rights Act of

11. We note that if Congress intended to prohibit all disparate-impact claims, it certainly could have done so. For instance, in the Equal Pay Act of 1963, 29 U.S.C. § 206(d)(1), Congress barred recovery if a pay differential was based "on any other factor"—reasonable or unreasonable—"other than sex." The fact that Congress provided that employees could use only reasonable factors in defending a suit under the ADEA is therefore instructive.

1991, § 2, 105 Stat. 1071. While the relevant 1991 amendments expanded the coverage of Title VII, they did not amend the ADEA or speak to the subject of age discrimination. Hence, *Wards Cove's* pre-1991 interpretation of Title VII's identical language remains applicable to the ADEA.

Congress' decision to limit the coverage of the ADEA by including the RFOA provision is consistent with the fact that age, unlike race or other classifications protected by Title VII, not uncommonly has relevance to an individual's capacity to engage in certain types of employment. To be sure, Congress recognized that this is not always the case, and that society may perceive those differences to be larger or more consequential than they are in fact. However, as Secretary Wirtz noted in his report, "certain circumstances ... unquestionably affect older workers more strongly,as a group, than they do younger workers." Wirtz Report 28. Thus, it is not surprising that certain employment criteria that are routinely used may be reasonable despite their adverse impact on older workers as a group. Moreover, intentional discrimination on the basis of age has not occurred at the same levels as discrimination against those protected by Title VII. While the ADEA reflects Congress' intent to give older workers employment opportunities whenever possible, the RFOA provision reflects this historical difference.

Turning to the case before us, we initially note that petitioners have done little more than point out that the pay plan at issue is relatively less generous to older workers than to younger workers. They have not identified any specific test, requirement, or practice within the pay plan that has an adverse impact on older workers. As we held in *Wards Cove*, it is not enough to simply allege that there is a disparate impact on workers, or point to a generalized policy that leads to such an impact. Rather, the employee is ' "responsible for isolating and identifying the specific employment practices that are allegedly responsible for any observed statistical disparities." ' 490 U.S., at 656, 104 L. Ed. 2d 733, 109 S. Ct. 2115 (emphasis added) (quoting *Watson*, 487 U.S., at 994, 101 L. Ed. 2d 827, 108 S. Ct. 2777). Petitioners have failed to do so. Their failure to identify the specific practice being challenged is the sort of omission that could "result in employers being potentially liable for 'the myriad of innocent causes that may lead to statistical imbalances ....' " 490 U.S., at 657, 104 L. Ed. 2d 733, 109 S. Ct. 2115. In this case not only did petitioners thus err by failing to identify the relevant practice, but it is also clear from the record that the City's plan was based on reasonable factors other than age.

The plan divided each of five basic positions—police officer, master police officer, police sergeant, police lieutenant, and deputy police chief—into a series of steps and half-steps. The wage for each range was based on a survey of comparable communities in the Southeast. Employees were then assigned a step (or half-step) within their position that corresponded to the lowest step that would still give the individual a 2% raise. Most of the officers were in the three lowest ranks; in each of those ranks there were officers under age 40 and officers over 40. In none did their age affect their compensation. The few officers in the two highest ranks are all over 40. Their raises, though higher in dollar amount than the raises given to junior officers, represented a smaller percentage of their salaries, which of course are higher than the salaries paid to their juniors. They are members of the class complaining of the "disparate impact" of the award.

Petitioners' evidence established two principal facts: First, almost two-thirds (66.2%) of the officers under 40 received raises of more than 10% while less than half (45.3%) of those over 40 did. Second, the average percentage increase for the entire class of officers with less than five years of tenure was somewhat higher than the percentage for those with more seniority. Because older officers tended to occupy more senior positions, on average they received smaller increases when measured as a percentage of their salary. The basic explanation for the differential was the City's perceived need to raise the salaries of junior officers to make them competitive with comparable positions in the market.

Thus, the disparate impact is attributable to the City's decision to give raises based on seniority and position. Reliance on seniority and rank is unquestionably reasonable given the City's goal of raising employees' salaries to match those in surrounding communities. In sum, we hold that the City's decision to grant a larger raise to lower echelon employees for the purpose of bringing salaries in line with that of surrounding police forces was a decision based on a "reasonable factor other than age" that responded to the City's legitimate goal of retaining police officers. Cf. *MacPherson v. University of Montevallo*, 922 F.2d 766, 772 (CA11 1991).

While there may have been other reasonable ways for the City to achieve its goals, the one selected was not unreasonable. Unlike the business necessity test, which asks whether there are other ways for the employer to achieve its goals that do not result in a disparate impact on a protected class, the reasonableness inquiry includes no such requirement.

The Chief Justice took no part in the decision of this case.

JUSTICE SCALIA, concurring in part and concurring in the judgment.

* * *

This is an absolutely classic case for deference to agency interpretation. The Age Discrimination in Employment Act of 1967 (ADEA), 29 U.S.C. § 621 et seq., confers upon the EEOC authority to issue "such rules and regulations as it may consider necessary or appropriate for carrying out the" ADEA. § 628. Pursuant to this authority, the EEOC promulgated, after notice-and-comment rulemaking, see 46 Fed. Reg. 47724, 47727 (1981), a regulation that reads as follows:

"When an employment practice, including a test, is claimed as a basis for different treatment of employees or applicants for employment on the grounds that it is a 'factor other than' age, and such a practice has an adverse impact on individuals within the protected age group, it can only be justified as a business necessity." 29 CFR § 1625.7(d) (2004).

The statement of the EEOC which accompanied publication of the agency's final interpretation of the ADEA said the following regarding this regulation: "Paragraph (d) of § 1625.7 has been rewritten to make it clear that employment criteria that are age-neutral on their face but which nevertheless have a disparate impact on members of the protected age group must be justified as a business necessity. See *Laugesen v. Anaconda Co.*, 510 F.2d 307 (6th Cir. 1975); *Griggs v. Duke Power Co.*, 401 U.S. 424 [28 L. Ed. 2d 158, 91 S. Ct. 849] (1971)." 46 Fed. Reg., at 47725. The regulation affirmed, moreover, what had been the longstanding position of the Department of Labor, the agency that previously administered the ADEA. * * *

JUSTICE O'CONNOR, with whom JUSTICE KENNEDY and JUSTICE THOMAS join, concurring in the judgment.

* * *

Congress' decision not to authorize disparate impact claims is understandable in light of the questionable utility of such claims in the age-discrimination context. No one would argue that older workers have suffered disadvantages as a result of entrenched historical patterns of discrimination, like racial minorities have. See *Massachusetts Bd. of Retirement v. Murgia*, 427 U.S. 307, 313–314, 49 L. Ed. 2d 520, 96 S. Ct. 2562 (1976) (per curiam); see also Wirtz Report 5–6. Accordingly, disparate impact liability under the ADEA cannot be justified, and is not necessary, as a means of redressing the cumulative results of past discrimination. Cf. *Griggs*, 401 U.S., at 430, 28 L. Ed. 2d 158, 91 S. Ct. 849 (reasoning that disparate impact liability is necessary under Title VII to prevent perpetuation of the results of past racial discrimination).

Moreover, the Wirtz Report correctly concluded that—unlike the classifications protected by Title VII—there often is a correlation between an individual's age and her ability to perform a job. Wirtz Report 2, 11–15. That is to be expected, for "physical ability generally declines with age," *Murgia*, supra, at 315, 49 L. Ed. 2d 520, 96 S. Ct. 2562, and in some cases, so does mental capacity, see *Gregory v. Ashcroft*, 501 U.S. 452, 472, 115 L. Ed. 2d 410, 111 S. Ct. 2395 (1991). Perhaps more importantly, advances in technology and increasing access to formal education often leave older workers at a competitive disadvantage vis-a-vis younger workers. Wirtz Report 11–15. Beyond these performance-affecting factors, there is also the fact that many employment benefits, such as salary, vacation time, and so forth, increase as an employee gains experience and seniority. See, e.g., *Finnegan v. Trans World Airlines, Inc.*, 967 F.2d 1161, 1164 (CA7 1992) ("[V]irtually all elements of a standard compensation package are positively correlated with age"). Accordingly, many employer decisions that are intended to cut costs or respond to market forces will likely have a disproportionate effect on older workers. Given the myriad ways in which legitimate business practices can have a disparate impact on older workers, it is hardly surprising that Congress declined to subject employers to civil liability based solely on such effects.

Notes and Questions

1. *ADEA Disparate Impact vs. Title VII Disparate Impact.* In light of the Court's opinion in *Smith* in what ways does disparate impact analysis under ADEA differ from disparate impact analysis under Title VII? Which of these differences, if any, might have mattered in the *Smith* case? For instance, would it have mattered in *Smith* if the City of Jackson had to establish that its reliance on seniority and rank in setting raises was necessary to achieve its "legitimate [business] goal of retaining police officers" rather than just a "reasonable" means of achieving that goal? Would it have mattered if the plaintiffs would have had an opportunity to present other "reasonable" ways for the City to achieve its goal without the same disparate impact on older workers?

2. *Likely Effect on Common Business Practices of the Availability of ADEA Disparate Impact.* Is the availability of the disparate impact theory of discrimination in ADEA litigation likely to have a significant effect on common legitimate employer business practices? Consider, for instance, the concerns expressed by Justice O'Connor in her dissenting opinion. If "advances in technology and increasing access to formal education ... leave older workers at a competitive disadvantage", will employers not be able to defend use of technological and educational standards as "reasonable" business practices? If employer decisions "that are intended to cut costs or respond to market forces ... have a disproportionate effect on older workers" because labor costs generally increase with the age of workers, will employers not be able to cite cost reduction as a "reasonable" business goal?

Some lower court decisions before *Smith* had held that personnel policies that have an adverse effect on older workers by limiting the hiring of more senior or tenured employees who had to be paid higher salaries could not be justified by a desire to cut labor costs. See, e.g., Leftwich v. Harris-Stowe State College, 702 F.2d 686 (8th Cir. 1983) (policy for reducing full-time higher-paid faculty by limiting number of tenured positions); Geller v. Markham, 635 F.2d 1027 (2d Cir. 1980) (policy against recruitment of teachers with more than five years of experience paid at high salary grade). Are these decisions consistent with the *Smith* Court's allowance of a "reasonable factor other than age" defense? Furthermore, is there not a cost defense even under Title VII litigation? For instance, does Title VII not permit employers to use validated tests despite adverse impact because of the costs of individualized selection processes?

3. *Does the ADEA Require Individualized Assessments?* Does the theory of disparate impact under Title VII require employers to provide at least as much individualized assessment as is efficient? See, e.g., *Dothard v. Rawlinson*, supra, where the Court rejected the prison system's reliance on size as a proxy for strength. If so, is such a requirement relevant to the ADEA, which, as stated in *Smith*, does not "ask[] whether there are other ways for the employer to achieve its goals that do not result in a disparate impact ..."? For example, could an employer use a weight-height ratio requirement as a proxy for physical agility, despite the requirement's disparate impact on older workers? Cf. Ellis v. United Airlines, Inc., 73 F.3d 999 (10th Cir. 1996) (airline's weight standards challenged because of their

disparate impact on older workers). Can an employer use the temporal proximity of technology training as a proxy for technological proficiency?

4. *Use of Disparate Impact in ADEA Cases Challenging Subjective Decisionmaking.* Can older workers use disparate impact proof to challenge an employer for allowing managers to make termination or promotion decisions on the basis of unguided subjective assessments? If so, are such challenges likely to be successful under a disparate impact framework of proof, as established in *Smith*, that does not allow consideration of less restrictive alternatives? See, e.g., Meacham v. Knolls Atomic Power Lab, 461 F.3d 134 (2d Cir. 2006) (finding "reasonable" delegating managers discretion to choose employees to terminate based on subjective assessments of "flexibility" and "criticality").

5. *Burden of Proof on Reasonable Justification?* Which party bears the burden of proving whether there is a "reasonable" justification for an employment practice that disparately impacts older workers? Does the "reasonable factors other than age" provision offer an affirmative defense to employers, or does the *Smith* Court's affirmation of *Wards Cove* for ADEA litigation place the burden of persuasion on plaintiffs? The Supreme Court has agreed to review a lower court decision holding that while employers bear a burden of producing a reasonable justification, ADEA plaintiffs, unlike Title VII plaintiffs, must carry the ultimate burden of persuasion on the adequacy of the justification. See, e.g., *Meacham*, supra, cert. granted, 128 S. Ct. 1118, 169 L.Ed.2d 846 (2007).

6. *Disparate Impact and Benefits.* Can the disparate impact framework be used under the ADEA to challenge the level of benefits provided by employers? Will the capping of benefits for all workers often have more of an impact on older than on younger workers? Is it always a reasonable policy to reduce labor costs? Recall Justice Rehnquist's aggregation of benefits approach to disparate impact as expressed in *Gilbert* and *Satty*, supra pp. 311–316. See also Finnegan v. Trans World Airlines, Inc., 967 F.2d 1161 (7th Cir.1992) (holding an employer's restriction of benefits to all workers not subject to disparate impact ADEA challenge), and the following note.

D. BENEFITS

1. *Note on Employee Benefit Plans and Age Discrimination*

In 1974 Congress enacted the Employee Retirement Income Security Act (ERISA), Pub.L. No. 93–406, 88 Stat. 829, codified at various places in the Internal Revenue Code (Code) and at 29 U.S.C. § 1000 et seq. Congress entered the retirement benefits area in the belief that state laws governing contracts and pension trusts had proven incapable of protecting the pension benefits of workers who lost their jobs prior to retirement age or who learned upon retirement that their employer lacked sufficient assets to satisfy its pension obligations. See generally Richard Ippolito, Pensions, Economics, and Public Policy (1986). There are two basic types of ERISA pension plans: "defined contribution" plans that provide for an individual account for each participant and for benefits based solely upon the amount contributed to that account plus any income or other gain; and "defined benefit" plans which are defined as any other pension plan but generally involve plans where the employer promises to pay a specific or definitely determinable benefit. Once vesting has occurred (normally after five years of employment), employees have a nonforfeitable right to their accrued retirement benefits. In addition to "employee pension benefit" plans, ERISA also covers "employee welfare benefit" plans, defined in 29 U.S.C. § 1002(1). Welfare benefit plans are not subject to an ERISA vesting requirement, however. ERISA issues are treated at length in chapter 16.

In 1979, the Department of Labor, acting pursuant to § 4(f)(2) of ADEA, 29 U.S.C. § 623(f)(2), issued an "Interpretative Bulletin," 29 C.F.R. § 660.120, 44 Fed.Reg. 30648 (May 25, 1979), which permitted employers to cease contributions and accruals for employees working beyond normal retirement age. Responding to pressure from the courts, see American Ass'n of Retired Persons v. EEOC, 823 F.2d 600 (D.C.Cir.1987), the EEOC initiated a rulemaking proceeding to reverse this policy. Then in 1986, by adding a new section § 4(i) to ADEA (as well as amending the Code and ERISA), Congress required all pension plans to continue contributions and accruals regardless of an employee's age, for plan years commencing on or after January 1, 1988. See Omnibus Budget Reconciliation Act of 1986 (OBRA), Pub.L. 99–509, 100 Stat. 1973–80. Congress expressly provided, however, that employers may limit the "amount of benefits that [a] plan provides" or limit "the number of years which are taken into account for purposes of determining benefit accrual under the plan." 29 U.S.C. § 623(i)(2).

2. *Note on Title I of the Older Workers Benefit Protection Act of 1990*

In Public Employees Retirement System of Ohio v. Betts, 492 U.S. 158, 109 S.Ct. 2854, 106 L.Ed.2d 134 (1989), the Supreme Court issued a broad ruling immunizing from challenge under ADEA virtually all uses of age classifications in bona fide employee benefit plans. Justice Kennedy's opinion for the majority was premised on an interpretation of § 4(f)(2) of ADEA. The Court held that employer conduct in accordance with plans adopted prior to ADEA's effective date could never be "a subterfuge to evade the purposes of" the statute within the meaning of § 4(f)(2). Since the disability retirement plan at issue in the case before it had been amended in 1976, however, the Court went on to consider the scope of the § 4(f)(2) exemption for post-Act plans. Reading § 4(f)(2) not as a defense but as a description of prohibited employer conduct, the Court held that Congress intended broadly to shield the use of age classifications in benefit plans, even if the plans provided less valuable benefits for older workers than their younger counterparts and the difference in benefits could not be justified in terms of the higher costs of providing the same level of benefits for the older workers. Justice Kennedy's opinion for the majority read the reference to "subterfuge" in § 4(f)(2) to require proof of an intent to discriminate in other, nonfringe-benefits aspects of the employment relationship. For example, an employer's decision to reduce salaries of all employees while substantially increasing benefits for younger workers might be challenged as a subterfuge to accomplish pay discrimination in violation of § 4(a)(1) of ADEA.

Betts was a problematic ruling on a number of grounds. First, the decision rejected the longstanding interpretation of the Department of Labor, which was reaffirmed by the EEOC when it assumed enforcement responsibility for ADEA, that age-based reductions in benefits were permissible only if justified by "significant cost considerations," and hence "benefit levels for older workers may be reduced to the extent necessary to achieve approximate equivalency in cost for older and younger workers," 29 C.F.R. § 1625.10(a)(1). Second, the Court's interpretation of § 4(f)(2) appeared to go well beyond the purpose of the provision's sponsors—i.e., to remove the disincentive to hire older workers because of the higher costs of providing insurance and other benefits for such workers. Finally, the Court appeared to be sanctioning a form of age discrimination in compensation levels without even requiring some reasonable business justification for the differential benefit levels.

The *Betts* Court's ruling placed in question a string of lower-court holdings that retirement-eligible employees could not, on account of such eligibility, be denied severance pay afforded other workers. See, e.g., EEOC v. Westinghouse Elec. Corp., 869 F.2d 696 (3d Cir.1989), vacated and remanded, 493 U.S. 801, 110 S.Ct. 37, 107 L.Ed.2d 7 (1989)); cf. EEOC v. Borden's, Inc., 724 F.2d 1390 (9th Cir.1984). It also gave employers broad latitude to structure early retirement incentives in a manner that significantly favored younger workers.

On October 16, 1990, Congress passed the Older Workers Benefit Protection Act (OWBPA), Public L. No. 101–433, 104 Stat. 978. Title I overturns *Betts* in its entirety. OWBPA amends § 4(f)(2) of ADEA: (i) to clarify that benefit plans may be illegally discriminatory, regardless of their date of adoption; (ii) to remove the "subterfuge" requirement as a condition of illegality; (iii) to place the burden of proof of justification of a discriminatory plan on the employer; and (iv) to require that "for each benefit or benefit package, the actual amount of payment made or cost incurred on behalf of an older worker is no less than that made or incurred on behalf of the younger worker, as permissible under section 1625.10, title 29, Code of Federal Regulations (as in effect on June 22, 1989) * * *." See, e.g., Quinones v. Evanston, 58 F.3d 275 (7th Cir.1995) (defined benefit plan may provide lower benefits to those hired at older age, but only to the extent necessary to equalize costs). (As provided in the EEOC regulations, cost justification for age-based benefit reductions may be made on either a "benefit-by-benefit" or a "benefit package" basis and by placing employees into five-year age brackets.)

OWBPA allows certain exceptions from the equal benefit/equal cost rule: (i) minimum-age conditions for eligibility for normal or early retirement; (ii) subsidized early retirement benefits under defined-benefit pension plans; (iii) defined-benefit pension plan "bridge payments" that do not exceed Social Security benefits and that terminate with Social Security eligibility; (iv) reduction of long-term disability benefits by the amount of employer-funded pension funds; and (v) limited benefit coordination by which employers can offset against severance pay obligations triggered by a "contingent event unrelated to age" (e.g., a plant closing or staff reduction) the value of retiree health benefits, and if the employees are eligible for not less than an immediate and unreduced pension, any additional pension benefits triggered by the contingent event.

The OWBPA Statement of Managers indicates that reductions in a retiree's post-retirement medical coverage once the retiree becomes eligible for Medicare are permitted, even when the employer's retiree health benefits exceed the value of the retiree's Medicare benefits. See S. 1511, Final Substitute of the Managers (Managers' Report), 53 (BNA) FEP Decisions Special Supplement, October 15, 1990, at S–13. Although no explanation is given in the Managers' Report, the implication seems to be that the equal benefit/equal cost rule applies only to active employees.

In Erie County Retirees Ass'n v. County of Erie, 220 F.3d 193 (3d Cir.2000), however, the court of appeals found the Managers' Report not controlling, and held that the equal benefit/equal cost rule applies to retirees and thus restricts how employers structure post-retirement medical coverage. The EEOC filed an amicus brief in support of the older retirees in *Erie* and at first embraced the result in its compliance manual. In 2001, however, the EEOC rescinded the portions of its manual discussing *Erie*, and on July 14, 2003, proposed an exemption that allows employers to reduce or end retiree health benefits when retirees become eligible for Medicare or a state-sponsored retiree health benefits program. 68 Fed. Reg. 41542. The proposal stated that the "Commission is concerned that many employers will respond to [*Erie*] * * * not by incurring additional costs for retiree benefits that supplement Medicare, but rather by reducing or eliminating health coverage for retirees who are not yet eligible for Medicare" Id. at 41546. The rule became final on December 26, 2007. 29 C.F.R. 1625.32. See also AARP v. EEOC, 489 F.3d 558 (3d Cir. 2007) (affirming EEOC's authority under § 9 of the ADEA to issue the "narrow exemption").

Title I of OWBPA also permits some departure from the equal benefit/equal cost cost rule in the structuring of voluntary early retirement plans; this is discussed at pp. 475–477 infra. In addition, Title II of the statute requires certain minimum safeguards for ADEA waiver agreements; these are discussed at pp. 485–490 infra.

The OWBPA amended the ADEA to clarify that an employee pension benefit plan, as defined by ERISA (treated in chapter 16 infra), may specify "a minimum age as a condition of eligibility for normal or early retirement." 29 U.S.C. § 623(l)(1)(A). As noted, ADEA and ERISA had already been amended in 1986 to require all pension plans to continue contributions and accruals regardless of an employee's age. 29 U.S.C. § 623(i)(1). This earlier amendment, however, also provided that employers may limit the "amount of benefits that [a] plan provides" or limit "the number of years which are taken into account for purposes of determining benefit accrual under the plan." 29 U.S.C. § 623(i)(2). See, e.g., Atkins v. Northwest Airlines, Inc., 967 F.2d 1197 (8th Cir.1992) (employer may cap benefit accrual for employees who have completed a specified number of years of service even where it lowers retirement benefits for workers who retire before a "normal" retirement age).

E. RETIREMENT

Note on Mandatory Retirement

ADEA and analogous state laws take a very restrictive position on mandatory retirement. Congress in 1978 rejected the Court's holding in

United Air Lines, Inc. v. McMann, 434 U.S. 192, 98 S.Ct. 444, 54 L.Ed.2d 402 (1977), that mandatory retirement provisions in bona fide employee retirement plans were lawful under § 4(f)(2). In light of the 1978 amendments, involuntary terminations pursuant to a retirement plan are to be treated by the Act like any other involuntary terminations. With the removal of the age 70 cap on protected workers in 1986, and similar movement in the states, age-based mandatory retirement policies are now generally prohibited. See generally Martin Levine, Age Discrimination and the Mandatory Retirement Controversy (1988). Individuals within the protected class may be severed from their employment only for performance or other legitimate business reasons not because of the arrival of a particular birthday. Generally, ADEA imposes no obligation to renew definite-term employment contracts, although presumably age cannot be a factor in the non-renewal decision. For an interesting case involving a contract that provided for termination upon the employee's reaching the age of 70—at a time prior to the 1986 ADEA amendments—see Harrington v. Aetna–Bearing Co., 921 F.2d 717 (7th Cir.1991).

After the 1986 amendments, the ADEA contained four limited exceptions to the no-mandatory retirement rule. The most general, the BFOQ, is considered at pp. 438–445. A second, for firefighters and law enforcement officers, was later modified by Congress and is discussed in note 6 on page 444 supra. A third, for employees who attained the age of 70 "serving under a contract of unlimited tenure * * * at an institution of higher education," expired in 1994. The 1986 amendments required the EEOC to commission the National Academy of Sciences (NAS) to study the potential consequences of the elimination of mandatory retirement for institutions of higher education. Predicting that few faculty members will work beyond the age of 70, the NAS-appointed panel concluded that mandatory retirement for tenured university faculty should be ended. See National Research Council, Ending Mandatory Retirement For Tenured Faculty: The Consequences for Higher Education (P.B. Hammond & H.P. Morgan eds. 1991). The issue is explored in Richard A. Epstein & MacLane, Keep Mandatory Retirement for Tenured Faculty, 14 Regulation (Spring 1991), pp. 85–96; Oscar Reubhausen, Commentary: The Age Discrimination in Employment Act Amendments of 1986: Implications for Tenure and Retirement, 14 J.Coll. & Univ.L. 561 (1988); Matthew Finkin, Commentary: Tenure After an Uncapped ADEA: A Different View, 15 J.Coll. & Univ.L. 43 (1988); John Burton, Tenured Faculty and the "Uncapped" Age Discrimination in Employment Act, 7 Yale L. & Pol'y Rev. 450 (1987). The problem of applying performance standards to employees who work past the age of 70 is usefully surveyed in Charles Craver, The Application of the Age Discrimination in Employment Act to Persons Over Seventy, 58 Geo.Wash.L.Rev. 52 (1989).

A fourth exception, § 12(c)(1), continues to permit the mandatory retirement of employees who have attained the age of 65, who are entitled to a specified level of nonforfeitable annual retirement benefit from their employers' plans—raised from $27,000 to $44,000 in 1985—and who for two years prior to retirement were "employed in a bona fide executive or high policy making position * * *." 29 U.S.C. § 631(c)(1). This exemption is narrowly construed in the EEOC regulations, 29 C.F.R. § 1625.12. "Bona fide executive" status applies "only to a very few top level employees who exercise substantial executive authority over a significant number of employees and a large volume of business," such as heads of major divisions in a corporate headquarters operation. Id. § 1625(d)(2). Similarly, "high policy making" status is limited to "certain top level employees * * * 'whose position and responsibility are such that they play a significant role in the development of corporate policy and effectively recommend the implementation thereof,' " such as a company's chief economist or research scientist who effectively recommends policy direction to the top corporate officers. Id. § 1625.12(e), quoting H.R.Rep. 950, 95th Cong., 2d Sess. 10 (1978). The EEOC's view has received judicial approval. Compare, e.g., Passer v. American Chem. Society, 935 F.2d 322 (D.C.Cir.1991) (exemption applies to head of division with 25 employees and $4 million budget); Colby v. The Graniteville Company, 635 F.Supp. 381 (S.D.N.Y.1986) (exemption applies to company's senior vice president of finance and administration), with Whittlesey v. Union Carbide Corp., 567 F.Supp. 1320 (S.D.N.Y.1983), affirmed, 742 F.2d 724 (2d Cir.1984) (exemption inapplicable to company's chief labor counsel because of minimal contribution to policy making).

Of course, mandatory retirement also is permitted for employees who are completely excluded from the Act's coverage. State and local elected officials and appointed policymakers, for instance, are expressly excluded from the Act's coverage by the definition of employee in § 11(f) (excluding "any person elected to public office in any State or political subdivision of any State by the qualified voters thereof * * * or an appointee on the policymaking level"). In Gregory v. Ashcroft, 501 U.S. 452, 111 S.Ct. 2395, 115 L.Ed.2d 410 (1991), the Supreme Court held that this exclusion was sufficiently broad to insulate Missouri's constitutional provision requiring mandatory retirement of appointed judges at age 70. Although the appointed judges in that state were subject to periodic unopposed retention elections, the Court's rationale appears to reach all appointed state judges.

Note on Early Retirement Plans

Early retirement normally means retirement at reduced benefit levels because defined-benefit pension plans typically require some combination of age and years of service for eligibility for a full pension benefit and provide, as a general matter, larger pension benefits with increased length of service. Some early retirement plans seek to remove some of these disincentives by providing a "window" period during which eligibility requirements for full benefits are relaxed or early retirees are given benefits which would have required additional years of service. Under such plans, early retirees can obtain the equivalent (or a pro rata adjustment) of the full pension benefits they would have obtained had they worked to normal retirement age. Other plans, however, offer employees of a certain age, who take early retirement during a "window" period, specially enhanced retirement benefits which they would not be able to obtain after the "window" period of eligibility regardless of how much longer they worked.

Age Bias in the Structure of the Incentives?

ADEA has been the basis for two types of challenges to early retirement incentive plans. The first has been to age-based plans that offer a less valuable retirement incentive to older workers than is offered to their younger counterparts, or that exclude some older workers from the incentive program entirely. Before *Betts* the lower courts uniformly recognized that such plans, by depriving older workers of a possible benefit offered to their younger counterparts, constitute a prima facie violation of § 4(a) of ADEA. The courts differed, however, on the possible protection of such plans by § 4(f)(2). Compare Karlen v. City Colleges of Chicago, 837 F.2d 314 (7th Cir.1988) (applying the EEOC "cost justification" interpretation of § 4(f)(2) in striking down a plan), with Cipriano v. Board of Educ. of City School Dist., 785 F.2d 51 (2d Cir.1986) (applying a broader legitimate business reason interpretation of § 4(f)(2)); Patterson v. Independent School Dist. No. 709, 742 F.2d 465 (8th Cir.1984).

The OWBPA expressly excludes "voluntary early retirement plan[s]" from the equal cost/equal benefit principle, provided such plans are "consistent with the relevant purpose or purposes of the Act." Apparently, Congress meant by the latter clause to prohibit "arbitrary" age distinctions in early retirement incentive plans, but without defining what would constitute an arbitrary distinction. Consider the following language from the Managers' Report, supra, at S–12:

> 1. * * * Early retirement incentive plans that withhold benefits to older workers above a specific age while continuing to make them available to younger workers may conflict with the purpose of prohibiting arbitrary age discrimination in employment. The purpose of prohibiting arbitrary age discrimination is also undermined by denying or reducing benefits to older workers based on age-related stereotypes. For example, it would be unlawful under this substitute to exclude older workers from an early retirement incentive plan based on stereotypical assumptions that "older workers would be retiring anyway."

> 2. It is also clear that a wide variety of voluntary early retirement incentive plans would be lawful under the ADEA. For example, early retirement incentives that provide a flat dollar amount (e.g., $20,000), service-based benefits (e.g., $1000 multiplied by the number of years of service) or a percentage of all salary to all employees above a certain age * * * would remain lawful. * * * Finally, early retirement incentives that impute years of service and/or age would satisfy the ADEA. For example, a plan that gives employees who have attained the age of 55 and who retire during a specified window period credit for 5 additional years of service and/or age would be lawful.

Does the text of the OWBPA prevent an employer from seeking to mitigate the younger workers' disincentive to retire by crediting those workers with additional years of service necessary for a normal retirement benefit—a credit that is less valuable to employees closer to normal retirement age? Would such a plan necessarily be based on an invidious age-based stereotype?

Since passage of the OWBPA, some courts have struck down retirement plans that offered greater benefits to younger workers than those offered to older workers. See, e.g., Jankovitz v. Des Moines Independent Community School Dist., 421 F.3d 649 (8th Cir. 2005); Solon v. Gary Community School Corp., 180 F.3d 844 (7th Cir.1999); EEOC v. Hickman Mills Consolidated

School Dist. No. 1, 99 F.Supp.2d 1070 (W.D.Mo. 2000). But see Auerbach v. Board of Educ. of Harborfields Central School Dist. of Greenlawn, 136 F.3d 104 (2d Cir.1998) (employer can provide extra benefits to those retiring when they are first eligible for retirement, even though eligibility is in part based on age); Lyon v. Ohio Educ. Assn'n, 53 F.3d 135 (6th Cir.1995) (employer can give more encouragement to younger workers to retire by granting them greater benefits through imputation of more years of foregone service). In EEOC v. Jefferson County Sheriff's Dept., 467 F.3d 571 (6th Cir. 2006) (en banc), the court of appeals overruled "in part" its decision in *Lyon*. The court held illegally discriminatory a plan that used the concept of foregone service to increase benefits to disabled workers the further they were from their normal retirement age when initially disabled. The Supreme Court granted certiorari to review *Jefferson County* in Kentucky Retirement Systems v. EEOC, ___ U.S. ___, 128 S.Ct. 36, 168 L.Ed.2d 805 (2007). Might the court of appeals have been wrong in both *Lyon* and *Jefferson County*?

Voluntariness?

The other type of ADEA attack on retirement resignation incentives has been made against plans offering benefits only to older employees on the ground that they place undue pressure on such employees to exit the workforce. This litigation has been brought by those who have been offered and accepted incentives, but who later decide to sue to challenge the circumstances of their retirement. The following case is an example.

HENN v. NATIONAL GEOGRAPHIC SOCIETY

United States Court of Appeals, Seventh Circuit, 1987.
819 F.2d 824.

EASTERBROOK, CIRCUIT JUDGE.

Experiencing a decline in advertising, the National Geographic Society decided to reduce the number of employees selling ads. The Society offered every ad salesman over age 55 the option of early retirement. The Society made the offer in June 1983; the recipients had more than two months to think it over. The Society offered: a severance payment of one year's salary, retirement benefits calculated as if the retiree had quit at 65, medical coverage for life as if the employee were still on the payroll, and some supplemental life insurance coverage. The letter extending the offer stated that this was a one-time opportunity. Twelve of the fifteen recipients took the offer; the three who declined are still employed by the Society. All twelve have received the promised benefits. Four of the twelve filed this suit, contending that their separation violated the Age Discrimination in Employment Act, 29 U.S.C. §§ 621–34.

The district court granted summary judgment to the Society. It concluded that early retirement violates the ADEA only if the alternative is "constructive discharge"—that is, working conditions so onerous or demeaning that the employee has effectively been fired in place and compelled to leave. See *Bartman v. Allis–Chalmers Corp.,* 799 F.2d 311, 314 (7th Cir.1986); *Brown v. Brienen,* 722 F.2d 360, 365 (7th Cir.1983).

The court thought it undisputed that plaintiffs' working conditions were unchanged from what they had always been; there was pressure to perform and dark hints that failure to sell more ads would have unpleasant consequences, but the judge concluded that these went with the territory. Each person's decision to retire was his own, and any pressure he felt was the product of the downturn in sales and the risks of a salesman's job.

The plaintiffs' brief on appeal is principally devoted to insisting that there was enough evidence of constructive discharge to require a trial. The case has been complicated, however, by *Paolillo v. Dresser Industries, Inc.*, 813 F.2d 583 (2d Cir.1987), which holds that *every* retirement under an early retirement plan creates a prima facie case of age discrimination, and that the employer must show both that the details of the plan have solid business justification and that each decision to retire is "voluntary"—by which the Second Circuit apparently meant "without undue strain". If *Paolillo* correctly interprets the ADEA, this case must be tried. We conclude, however, that the parties and the district court, rather than *Paolillo,* took the right approach. Only a constructive discharge, where an actual discharge would violate the ADEA, supports a claim of the sort plaintiffs pursue.

* * *

In characterizing retirement under an early retirement program as presumptively discriminatory, *Paolillo* overlooked the regulation governing early retirement plans, 29 C.F.R. § 1625.9(f). This provides: "Neither section 4(f)(2) nor any other provision of the Act makes it unlawful for a plan to permit individuals to elect early retirement at a specified age at their own option." This plausible construction of the ADEA is entitled to considerable weight where, as here, Congress never considered the matter. *Chevron U.S.A., Inc. v. Natural Resources Defense Council, Inc.,* 467 U.S. 837, 843, 104 S.Ct. 2778, 2781, 81 L.Ed.2d 694 (1984). The legislative history of the ADEA is unilluminating about early retirement plans. Given that, § 1625.9(f), and the fact that the offer of early retirement is beneficial to the recipient, there is no reason to treat every early retirement as presumptively an act of age discrimination.

* * * Retirement is an innocuous event, coming once to many employees and more than once to some. Retirement is not itself a prima facie case of age discrimination, not unless all separations from employment are. And * * * an offer of incentives to retire early is a benefit to the recipient, not a sign of discrimination. Taken together, these two events—one neutral, one beneficial to the older employee—do not support an inference of age discrimination.

What distinguishes early retirement from discharge is the power of the employee to choose to keep working. This must mean a "voluntary" choice. But what does "voluntary" mean? We could ask, as the court did in *Paolillo,* whether the employee had enough time to mull over the offer and whether the choice was free from "pressure". (In *Paolillo* the employees had less than a week, which the court thought suspiciously short.) Yet the need to make a decision in a short time, under pressure, is an unusual definition of "involuntary". A criminal defendant may be offered a plea bargain on a take-it-or-leave-it basis, knowing that if he does not act quickly the prosecutor may strike a deal with another defendant instead; the need to act in haste does not make the plea "involuntary" if the defendant knows and accepts the terms of the offer.

* * *

The "voluntariness" question in these and many more examples of important choices turns on such things as: did the person receive information about what would happen in response to the choice? was the choice free from fraud or other misconduct? did the person have an opportunity to say no? A very short period to make a complex choice may show that the person could not digest the information necessary to the decision. This would show that the offer of information was illusory and there was no informed choice. But when the employee has time to consult spouse and financial adviser, the fact that he still found the decision hard cannot be decisive. * * *

The plaintiffs in this case do not say that they lacked information about the terms of the offer. All had time to discuss the offer with families and financial advisers. They complain that they felt pressure and perceived the choice to be excruciating, but that is not important. They could prevail only by showing that the Society manipulated the options so that they were driven to early retirement not by its attractions but by the terror of the alternative. If the terms on which they would have remained at the Society were themselves violations of the ADEA, then taking the offer of early retirement was making the best of things, a form of minimization of damages.

* * *

The plaintiffs complain of two things that made their positions untenable: the "silent treatment" and threats (real and implied) of unpleasant consequences if they did not start selling more ads. The "silent treatment" was principally that no one in the Society would tell them whether they ought to take the offer of early retirement; the Society says this was caused by its policy of sticking to the facts (doubtless to avoid charges of placing undue pressure on the employees), while the plaintiffs say that their inability to get straight answers about whether they should take the offer led them to fear the worst. The threats came about because all four plaintiffs had experienced bad years, and their supervisors told them they needed to sell more ads; this led them to fear for their jobs.

The record contains extensive admissions by the plaintiffs tending to support the district judge's conclusion that any threats made to these plaintiffs while they were considering the offer were no greater than justified by their lack of sales. Selling is a risky profession, and it does not make a salesman's job unbearable to remind him that he must produce and that there are penalties for failure. The plaintiffs say, however, that the Society's warnings were not justified on a more complete review of their performance. They also believe that the Society hassled them more than their sluggish sales performance warranted. To support this belief Henn states that Bill Hughes, his supervisor, said to him early in 1983: "[s]ome of you older guys will not be around at the end of the year". All four plaintiffs rely on a passage in a memorandum that was part of the bureaucratic process that ended in the offer of early retirement: "Of the total twenty sales members one out of two are over 55 years, six are over age 62 and four are presently over age 65. (sic: actually 5 under 55; 5 between 55–61; 6 from 62–65; 4 over 65) Only one sales person over 65 plans to retire this year and an undetermined number desire to continue toward age 70. If an age balance is not struck soon our average age will obviously increase. Serious repercussions will result if younger sales personnel are not available to cultivate clients in new growth industries and insure future sales. To attract youthful qualified sales personnel we must be cognizant of industry practices and offer required incentives." The author of the memo recommended that salesmen be fired; the Society did not take that advice. It maintains that neither comment supports an inference that it acted or would have acted improperly to any person on the payroll.

The district court concluded that neither these nor other comments and incidents added up to constructive discharge or supported a reasonable belief by the plaintiffs that, had they remained at the Society, they would have been fired unlawfully. They were at risk of discipline or discharge for their performance (or lack of performance), and all four were producing less than their quota. The Society turned down the recommendation that it fire people, so the author of the memorandum did not speak for the Society. And although the record may well support an inference that the Society wanted to reduce the average age of its sales staff, this does not show that it used illegal means. Any early retirement program reduces average age, because only older employees are eligible to retire. That the Society favored the results of its program does not condemn the program. We passed that point when we accepted the conclusion of the EEOC, stated in 29 C.F.R. § 1625.9(f), that early retirement programs do not violate the ADEA. See also *Kier v. Commercial Union Insurance Cos.*, 808 F.2d 1254, 1258 (7th Cir.1987) (the fact that a reduction in force reduces the average age of the remaining employees does not support an inference that a particular employee was fired because of age).

The argument based on constructive discharge depends not on the Society's beliefs about the effects of retirements but on what it communicated to the employees. The district court properly concluded that salesmen must endure adverse reactions and other signs of displeasure when their productivity falls off. An employer's communication of the risks of the job does not spoil the employee's decision to avoid those risks by quitting. Were it otherwise, any employee about whom there was dissatisfaction would have a jury case under the ADEA, even if the dissatisfaction were supported by objective indicators (such as low productivity). In passing on a motion for summary judgment, a court must indulge inferences in favor of the non-moving party, but it need not indulge all possible inferences. The reasonable inferences from this record would not allow a jury to infer that the plaintiffs would have been fired (in violation of the ADEA) had they turned down the offer of early retirement, and without such a constructive discharge they cannot undo their choice to retire.

Notes and Questions

1. *Presumptive Validity Under "Constructive Discharge" Standard.?* Is the Seventh Circuit's affirmation of the district court's grant of summary judgment to the Society based on a conclusion that the plaintiffs did not advance adequate proof of age bias? If all the plaintiffs and other offerees had turned down the early retirement offers and then been discharged, would they have had adequate evidence of age bias to withstand a summary judgment motion? Is the Seventh Circuit's decision instead based on the plaintiffs' failure to show that they or other members of their age-defined class of offerees were coerced to retire? Do you agree with Judge Easterbrook that a "prima facie" case of coercion was not made out by allegations, taken as true for summary judgment purposes, that (i) the plaintiffs had insufficient time to consider their options, (ii) had been led to fear the worst by the firm's "silent treatment", and (iii) had shortly before been criticized for poor sales performance, coupled with (iv) the employer's written statement identifying a need to reduce the average age of its sales staff? Does the court's constructive-discharge standard express a strong rule of presumptive validity that takes into account only the effects of any overt threats, rather than the effects of threats and retirement incentives together?

2. *"Take Early Retirement or Be Discharged."* If an employee is given an explicit choice between forced termination and early retirement at enhanced benefits, should the *Henn* presumption of a knowing, voluntary decision apply? In Ackerman v. Diamond Shamrock Corp., 670 F.2d 66 (6th Cir.1982), an ADEA claim was dismissed on a motion for summary judgment in such a situation. *Ackerman* was narrowly distinguished by the Sixth Circuit in Ruane v. G.F. Business Equipment, Inc., 828 F.2d 20 (6th Cir.1987), as a case where the employee was represented by counsel, given 30 days to make up his mind, received $100,000 in additional consideration, and "was not otherwise distinctly informed that he had no right to remain in his present employment * * *." See also Hebert v. Mohawk Rubber Co., 872 F.2d 1104, 1112–13 (1st Cir.1989):

> In our view, to accept the reasoning of the Sixth Circuit [in *Ackerman*] that a person's acceptance of an early retirement package is voluntary when faced with the "choice" between the Scylla of forced retirement and the Charybdis of discharge * * * is to turn a blind eye upon the "take-it-or-leave-it" nature of such an "offer". * * * Absent the right to decline an employer's offer of early retirement and keep working under lawful conditions, the "decision" to take the early retirement "option" is no decision at all. A "choice" between not working with benefits and not working without benefits amounts to, in effect, compulsory retirement.

See also Adams v. Ameritech Services, Inc., 231 F.3d 414 (7th Cir.2000) (holding that coercing employees into accepting positions with lower pay by threatening them with discriminatory reduction in force would constitute illegal "constructive demotion").

3. *"Take Early Retirement or a Position at Lower Pay or Reduced Responsibilities."* Might less extreme coercion also meet the *Henn* constructive discharge standard? What if an employer states that it will significantly reduce the pay and responsibilities of an older employee if he does not accept an offer of early retirement incentives? See Vega v. Kodak Caribbean, Ltd., 3 F.3d 476, 480 (1st Cir.1993) ("the law regards as the functional equivalent of a discharge those offers of early retirement which, if refused, will result in work so arduous or unappealing, or working conditions so intolerable, that a reasonable person would feel compelled to forsake his job rather than to submit to looming indignities"). Should it be sufficiently coercive to indicate that an offeree who declines the offer will be placed in a position that is to any extent worse than his status quo? See Mitchell v. Mobil Oil Corp., 896 F.2d 463, 467 (10th Cir.1990) (adopting this standard). Was there at least this much coercion in *Henn*?

4. *Effect of the OWBPA.?* Does the Seventh Circuit's approach in *Henn* survive the OWBPA? The new law also requires that the early retirement be "voluntary," but again without defining the term. According to the Senate labor committee report, "window" periods are permitted, provided—

> [e]mployees eligible for these programs [are] given sufficient time to consider their options, particularly in circumstances when no previous retirement counseling has been provided. * * * The critical question involving allegations of involuntary retirement is whether, under the circumstances, a reasonable person would have concluded that there was no choice but to accept the offer. See Paolillo v. Dresser Industries, Inc., 821 F.2d 81, 84 (2d Cir.1987). Thus, threats of imminent layoffs, intimidation or subtle coercion may, either individually or collectively, "require or permit" involuntary retirement in any particular case.

S.Rep. No. 101–263, 101st Cong., 2d Sess. 27 (1990). Does this language direct courts to consider not only any employer threats, but also the conditions, including time constraints, under which the retirement decisions had to be made? Can courts also consider the likelihood of the incentives not being again available after the "window" for the offer is closed? For an analysis of the OWBPA and its legislative history that concludes that Congress intended to endorse both the *Henn* constructive-discharge standard and a fair process approach suggested in the *Paolillo* decision, see Michael C. Harper, Age–Based Exit Incentives, Coercion, and the Prospective Waiver of ADEA Rights: The Failure of the Older Workers Benefit Protection Act, 79 Va. L. Rev. 1271, 1309–1328 (1993).

The Managers' Report, supra, at S–12, expressly disavows a statement in the Senate committee report that assigns the burden of proof to the employer to show that the retirement was voluntary. Does the text of the OWBPA, however, assign the burden of persuasion on the issue of voluntariness to the employer? See 29 U.S.C. § 623(f)(2).

5. *Do Conditional Retirement Incentives and Threats Together Enable Employers to Circumvent the ADEA?* Should the law, contrary to the analysis

in *Henn*, take into account the time conditioned nature of early retirement incentives, as well as employer threats, when assessing whether a retirement is truly voluntary? Consider the following:

A post-fifty-five-year-old offeree in this typical exit window scenario might well rationally accept early retirement even though she prefers continuing employment. The reason is that the offeree must include in her calculations the chance that she will be terminated without the extra benefits offered for voluntary retirement. Thus, an offeree who prefers employment to retirement with increased benefits might prefer the latter to the perceived chance of continued employment plus the perceived chance of termination without enhanced benefits. Clearly it is the conditional nature of the retirement incentive that makes the two preferences consistent, that, in other words, makes it rational for an offeree to accept the incentive even though she prefers continued employment.

This is highly significant for an employer wanting to rid itself of more older workers than could be justified by individualized comparisons of the productivity of all its workers. For instance, assume an employer wanted to cut a section of its workforce in half and that one half of the employees in this section were over fifty. Assume further that the employer could eliminate half of these post-fifty-year-old employees on the basis of individualized analyses of relative productivity. Also, assume that by offering a conditional incentive, the employer could convince three-fourths of the post-fifty-year-olds to accept retirement, even though many of these employees would prefer continuing to work. Even if none of the other one-fourth that declined retirement were vulnerable to discharge, the employer increased by 50% (from 50% to 75%) the proportion of its older workforce that it could displace. * * *

An employer is thus able to use an age-based retirement plan to eliminate significantly more older workers than it could terminate by individualized consideration of their productivity, despite the fact that many of these older workers prefer continued employment. * * *

Harper, Age–Based Exit Incentives, supra, at 1277–79.

6. *Should Retirement Incentive Plans Be Able to Incorporate Age–Based Considerations Not Allowed in Mandatory Retirement Plans?* Does the following analysis in the Seventh Circuit's post-*Henn* ruling in Karlen v. City Colleges of Chicago, 837 F.2d 314 (7th Cir.1988), provide a good response to Professor Harper?

The purpose of such programs often is to ease out older employees, whether because they cost the employer more in salary or fringe benefits, or have gone stale, or are blocking advancement for the ambitious young. Often, therefore, the discussions leading up to the adoption of such programs will generate evidence of age discrimination. Yet the discrimination seems to be in favor of rather than against older employees, by giving them an additional option and one prized by many older employees. Nor can it be seriously argued that the concept of early retirement for workers over a specified age stigmatizes such workers, as would a program designed to change not the age but the racial composition of the work force by allowing blacks but not whites to retire early.

Entitlement to early retirement is a valued perquisite of age—an additional option available only to the older worker and only slightly tarnished by the knowledge that sometimes employers offer it because they want to ease out older workers.

Id. at 317. Are you convinced that age-based generalizations that would taint a mandatory termination policy should be permissible for a voluntary termination plan? Is judicial (and congressional) tolerance of such generalizations a practical concession to employer needs after the abolition of mandatory retirement? See Issacharoff and Harriss, supra, at 814–15.

7. *Would Full Disclosure Promote Voluntariness?* The Senate committee that reported out the bill that was ultimately enacted as the OWBPA stated that, as a condition of voluntariness, "[e]ligible employees must be provided complete and accurate information regarding the benefits available under the plan. If subsequent layoffs or terminations are contemplated or discussed, employees should be advised of the criteria by which those decisions will be made." S.Rep. No. 101–263, at 27. Is this disclosure requirement reflected in the text of the statute? Would such disclosures themselves create a coercive environment in which retirement decisions could not be assumed to be truly voluntary? Or do such disclosures just clarify what will always be a question in an employee's mind when offered early retirement incentives for some limited "window" period, especially during a reduction in force? If so, would such disclosures help employees who would prefer voluntary retirement with a bonus to the risk of involuntary layoff? Note that the Managers' Report, supra, at S–12, "expressly disavows" the sentence from the Senate report that is quoted at the beginning of this note.

8. *Can the Window for Early Retirement Benefits in Part Be Defined by Age?* Assuming that early retirement incentive offers cannot be limited by maximum age cutoffs, can employers nonetheless use a particular age to help define when employees reach their "window" of eligibility? In Auerbach v. Board of Educ. of the Harborfields Central Sch. Dist., 136 F.3d 104 (2d Cir.1998), the court held that the employer could offer special retirement benefits only during the school year that an employee first reached both 20 years of service and 55 years of age. The court reasoned that every teacher regardless of age theoretically could meet these requirements at some point. Do you agree? Would the case be different if the employer had defined the window of eligibility only by age?

9. *Coercion, Discrimination, and No Waiver.* Note again that an employee who accepts early retirement and associated enhanced benefits cannot establish a violation of the ADEA simply by proving that his retirement was coerced; he also must demonstrate that the employer's efforts to compel him to retire were at least in part driven by consideration of his age. In many cases the employee also will probably have a third hurdle to clear; he will have to invalidate as involuntary any waiver of his rights to bring a claim under the ADEA that he signed as a condition of receiving the enhanced benefits.

F. WAIVER

The extent to which waiver agreements between employers and employees are enforceable is an issue that arises under Title VII as well as the ADEA. In Alexander v. Gardner–Denver Co., 415 U.S. 36, 52 n. 15, 94 S.Ct. 1011, 1022 n. 15, 39 L.Ed.2d 147 (1974), p. 1132 infra, the Court endorsed the "voluntary and knowing" test applied by the lower courts to agreements of individual employees to waive Title VII claims against their employers for any discrimination that may have already occurred. Title VII courts continue to apply this test, considering either "ordinary contract principles", see, e.g., O'Shea v. Commercial Credit Corp., 930 F.2d 358 (4th Cir.1991), or the "totality of circumstances" under which the agreement was signed, see, e.g., Riley v. American Family Mut. Ins. Co., 881 F.2d 368 (7th Cir.1989). These circumstances include: the plaintiff's business experience and education, the amount of time the employee had to consider the agreement before signing, whether the employee was given additional consideration beyond that to which she was already entitled, the clarity of the agreement, whether the employee was encouraged or discouraged to consult with an attorney, and whether the employee had a fair opportunity to do so. See, e.g., Puentes v. United Parcel Service, Inc., 86 F.3d 196 (11th Cir.1996) (a day was inadequate period for consideration). Even those courts that have applied "ordinary contract principles" have considered some of these factors. See, e.g., Pilon v. University of Minn., 710 F.2d 466 (8th Cir.1983) (representation by attorney and clarity of language).

For a number of reasons, however, the waiver issue in ADEA litigation engaged the particular attention of Congress. First, because the ADEA borrows enforcement procedures from the Fair Labor Standards Act (FLSA), the courts had to distinguish Supreme Court decisions interpreting the FLSA as not allowing waivers unsupervised by the government. See D.A. Schulte, Inc. v. Gangi, 328 U.S. 108, 66 S.Ct. 925, 90 L.Ed. 1114 (1946); Brooklyn Savings Bank v. O'Neil, 324 U.S. 697, 65 S.Ct. 895, 89 L.Ed. 1296 (1945). This was true both for ADEA courts professing to apply "ordinary contract principles", see, e.g., Runyan v. National Cash Register Corp., 787 F.2d 1039 (6th Cir.1986), and for those considering the "totality of circumstances", see, e.g., Coventry v. United States Steel Corp., 856 F.2d 514 (3d Cir.1988). More importantly, the waiver issue has arisen frequently in ADEA litigation, perhaps because employers are more likely to offer extra benefits to retiring older workers who have rendered considerable past service, but only if those employees are willing to waive any possible legal claims. In any event, an EEOC interpretative regulation permitting unsupervised ADEA waiver agreements resulted in riders to EEOC appropriations in 1988 and 1989 blocking implementation of the regulation. Then in 1990 in Title II of the OWBPA Congress specified minimum conditions for the waiver of rights under the ADEA.

Note on Waiver Agreements Under the OWBPA

Title II of the OWBPA provides that an individual "may not waive any right or claim under" ADEA unless the waiver is "knowing and voluntary", and stipulates that a waiver may not be considered knowing and voluntary unless it satisfies certain minimum conditions. The party asserting the validity of a waiver has the burden of proof on the "knowing and voluntary" issue.

Individual ADEA Waiver Agreements

For individual waiver agreements, seven minimum conditions must be satisfied: (i) the waiver must be part of an intelligible written agreement; (ii) it must specifically refer to waiver of ADEA rights or claims; (iii) it may not waive rights or claims arising after the date of the agreement; (iv) it must be "in exchange for consideration in addition to anything of value to which the individual already is entitled"; (v) the individual must be advised in writing to consult with an attorney prior to executing the agreement; (vi) the individual must be given at least 21 days to consider the agreement; and (vii) the individual must be given at least seven days following execution to revoke the agreement.

These conditions were given further elaboration in EEOC regulations that became final in July, 1998. See 14 C.F.R. Part 1625. For instance, "the entire waiver agreement must be in writing" in "plain language geared to the level of understanding of the individual party to the agreement or individuals eligible to participate." § 1625.22(b)(2) and (3). The bar to waiver of rights or claims arising after the date of the agreement does not preclude "agreements to perform future employment-related actions such as * * * to retire or otherwise terminate employment at a future date." § 1625.22(c)(2).

The regulations also clarify that an employer is not required to provide workers in the ADEA protected class consideration beyond that provided to workers outside this class, but only "consideration in addition" to that which the protected worker is already entitled. § 1625.22(d)(4). Accord, DiBiase v. SmithKline Beecham Corp., 48 F.3d 719 (3d Cir.1995). The extra consideration does not have to be of any particular kind or level, but it cannot be the return of some benefit that "was eliminated in contravention of law or contract, express or implied." § 1625.22(d)(3).

The 21–day mandatory consideration period begins to run from the date of the employer's final offer and is not restarted by changes that are not "material." § 1625.22(e)(4). Furthermore, the parties may agree that even material changes to the offer do not restart the period, and an employee may sign the agreement before the end of the period as long as his doing so is knowing and voluntary and is not induced by fraud, misrepresentation, a threat to alter the offer before the end of the period, or by the provision of different terms to employees who sign early. § 1625.22(e)(4) and (6). The seven-day revocation period, however "cannot be shortened by the parties, by agreement or otherwise." § 1625.22(e)(5).

Waivers in Connection With Group Terminations

Title II treats somewhat differently waivers "requested in connection with an exit incentive or other employment termination program offered to a group or class of employees * * *." To be effective, such waivers require a longer consideration period (45 days instead of 21 days). In addition, employers must disclose any eligibility factors for individuals covered by the program and "the job titles and ages of all individuals eligible or selected for the program, and the ages of all individuals in the same job classification or organizational unit who are not eligible or selected for the program." The regulations state that a covered "program" exists "when an employer offers additional consideration for the signing of a waiver pursuant to an exit incentive or other employment termination (e.g., a reduction in force) to two or more employees." § 1625.22(f)(1)(iii)(B).

The regulations also attempt to clarify the meaning of "job classification or organizational unit", whose members' ages must be disclosed, by stating that such a "decisional unit" is "that portion of the employer's organization structure from which the employer chose the persons who would be offered consideration for the signing of a waiver and those who would not be offered consideration for the signing of a waiver." § 1625.22(f)(3)(i)(B). For instance, if the employer intends to reduce its force of accountants by ten percent, then the ages of all its accountants must be provided. § 1625.22(f)(iii)(E) and (iv)(E). This applies even if the "terminees" are to be "selected from a subset of a decisional unit", such as where the employer intends that the ten percent reduction in accountants "will come from the accountants whose performance is in the bottom one-third" of all accountants. § 1625.22(f)(3)(v). For analysis of these disclosure requirements, *see, e.g.* Burlison v. McDonald's Corp., 455 F.3d 1242 (11th Cir. 2006); Kruchowski v. Weyerhauser Co., 446 F.3d 1090 (10th Cir. 2006).

Settlements of Charges Filed with the EEOC or in Court

Title II also requires that effective settlements of charges already filed with a governmental authority are to be knowing and voluntary, and provides that the first five minimum conditions must be met to satisfy this standard. For such claims, however, the minimum 21 or 45 consideration period and the seven-day revocation period do not apply; the Act instead only requires that the charging party be "given a reasonable period of time within which to consider the settlement agreement." The regulations provide that what is a "reasonable period" should be affected by whether the charging "individual is represented by counsel". § 1625.22(g)(4).

Notes and Questions

1. *Legal Effect of a Defective Waiver?* What is the legal significance of a waiver deemed ineffective under the OWBPA standards? Does the employer who requires such a waiver violate ADEA, without more, or must employees who signed the ineffective waiver still prove that the exit incentive plan, or their individual discharges, were otherwise unlawful?

Consider how your answers to these questions apply to the following case. An employer offered its employees a "Voluntary Big Ticket Severance Allowance Plan", under which employees were given only five days to decide whether to participate in the Plan or to remain employed at reduced wages. Employees who decided to resign under the Plan could earn greater severance benefits if they agreed to waive all their claims under the ADEA, including those unrelated to their termination. Did the employer violate the ADEA if it gave the employees only five days to sign the waiver to receive enhanced benefits? What if it provided 45 days to decide whether to sign the waiver, but only five days to decide whether to resign to receive any benefits under the Plan? See EEOC v. Sears, Roebuck & Co., 857 F.Supp. 1233 (N.D.Ill.1994).

2. *Does Title II Provide Adequate Protection?* Do you agree with the approach of Title II of the OWBPA? Should EEOC supervision be required where the ADEA plaintiff is a nonlegal professional, an unsophisticated low-level manager, or an unskilled maintenance worker? Given the EEOC's limited resources, is it likely that the agency could provide effective oversight in any event? For a further discussion of the "knowing and voluntary" standard, see Note, Waiver of Rights Under the Age Discrimination in Employment Act of 1967, 86 Colum.L.Rev. 1067 (1986).

3. *Does Title II Adequately Protect the EEOC's Statutory Role?* Under Title II, employees cannot waive their right to file a charge with the EEOC or to otherwise cooperate with an EEOC investigation. Cf. EEOC v. Cosmair, Inc., L'Oreal Hair Care Div., 821 F.2d 1085 (5th Cir.1987) (finding such a waiver to be against public policy); EEOC v. Astra, 94 F.3d 738 (1st Cir.1996) (upholding injunction of enforcement of promises in settlement agreements to not assist EEOC in investigation of Title VII charges). Does the right to file charges with the EEOC provide sufficient opportunity for government scrutiny of the voluntary and knowing character of the waiver agreement? Does it provide sufficient opportunity for the agency to learn of systemic discriminatory practices and, possibly, file suit for injunctive relief and on behalf of individuals who have not executed waiver agreements? Does this depend on whether the EEOC may recover damages for those who have signed waivers? Review these questions again after studying the materials in chapters 17 and 18.

4. *When Might a Release that Meets the OWBPA Minimum Conditions Be Void?* How might an employer cause a waiver that meets the OWBPA conditions to be defective? What if the employer tells the offerees that their positions will soon be eliminated, but then immediately after their benefit-induced resignation, it hires younger workers to take their place? Can intentional misrepresentations preclude a knowing and voluntary waiver? See Bennett v. Coors Brewing Co., 189 F.3d 1221 (10th Cir.1999) (fraud, duress, or mutual mistake, as defined by state law, may render an ADEA waiver void).

5. *Must an Employee Return the Consideration for an Ineffective Waiver Before Suit?* In Oubre v. Entergy Operations, Inc., 522 U.S. 422, 118 S.Ct. 838, 139 L.Ed.2d 849 (1998), the Supreme Court held that an employee's ADEA suit against her employer was not barred by her retention of monies that she took from her employer in exchange for a release that did not satisfy the OWBPA. The Court stressed that the retention, like the release itself, did not constitute an effective waiver of her ADEA claims because it did not comply with the OWBPA mandates. The Court also noted that many employees already will have spent any monies received and that barring suit because of retention thus would tempt employers to evade the requirements of the OWBPA. The Court did allow, however, that "courts may need to inquire whether the employer has claims for restitution, recoupment, or setoff against the employee, and these questions may be more complex where

a release is effective as to some claims but not as to ADEA claims." 522 U.S. at 428.

The EEOC has issued a final legislative rule amending its regulations on ADEA waivers in light of *Oubre*. See 29 C.F.R. 1625.22. The amendment takes the following positions. First, the *Oubre* Court's rejection of application of the common law ratification and tender back doctrines applies to waivers that are not knowing and voluntary because of common law principles like fraud, duress, coercion, or mistake of material fact, not just to waivers that do not meet the minimum OWBPA conditions. Accord, *Bennett v. Coors Brewing Co.*, note 4 supra. Second, "tender back" clauses in waiver agreements are ineffective so that the holding of *Oubre* cannot be circumvented by contract. Third, also to prevent a contractual circumvention of *Oubre*, a "covenant not to sue, or other equivalent arrangement", as well as a waiver agreement, is included under the no "tender back" rule. This means that an employer cannot enforce a "covenant not to sue" that does not meet the knowing and voluntary standards. Fourth, the new rule prohibits and renders ineffective any ADEA waiver agreement, covenant not to sue, or other equivalent arrangement that imposes any condition precedent or penalty or any other limitation, beyond attorney's fees and costs specifically authorized under law, that would discourage challenging the waiver agreement or covenant not to sue under the OWBPA.

Fifth, where an employee successfully challenges a waiver or covenant not to sue, and prevails on the merits of the ADEA claim, courts have the discretion to determine whether the employer is entitled to restitution, recoupment or setoff against the employee's monetary award. But a reduction cannot exceed the lesser of the amount the employee recovered, on the one hand, and the consideration the employee received for signing the waiver or covenant, on the other. Finally, an employer may not abrogate its duties to any signatory under a waiver agreement or covenant, even if one or more of the signatories or the EEOC successfully challenges the validity of the agreement. The last position is supported by Justice Breyer's concurring opinion in *Oubre*, arguing that the Court's decision makes waiver agreements voidable, but not void, as well as the holding of a district court, Butcher v. Gerber Prods. Co., 8 F.Supp.2d 307 (S.D.N.Y. 1998). For an application of *Oubre* to an ineffective prospective waiver of Title VII claims, see Richardson v. Sugg, 448 F.3d 1046 (8th Cir. 2006).

6. *Should Time Periods Be Relaxed for Settlements?* Do you understand why the OWBPA does not demand the same set minimum periods for consideration and revocation of waivers of charges that have already been filed with the EEOC or a court? Do employees need less time when charges have been filed? Is time pressure more justified for settlements of filed charges?

7. *Why Does the OWBPA Not Allow Prospective Waiver?* The OWBPA's prohibition of the waiver of rights or claims arising after the date of the agreement is consistent with the analysis of the Supreme Court in Alexander v. Gardner–Denver, supra. In that case the Court held that a collective bargaining representative could not prospectively trade an individual employee's Title VII cause of action for a right to private arbitration of a discrimination claim. This holding was in part an elaboration of the more

general "clear" proposition "that there can be no prospective waiver of an employee's rights under Title VII." 415 U.S. at 51, 94 S.Ct. at 1021. This means that an employee cannot agree to trade being protected against discrimination in the future for a higher salary or other enhanced benefits.

Do you understand why employees should be able to waive Title VII or ADEA claims against discrimination that has already occurred, but not against future discrimination? Is there more reason to be paternalistic toward employees before possible discriminatory acts have occurred? Are prospective waivers of rights to be protected against discrimination more likely to encourage, rather than discourage, future discrimination?

8. *Do Conditional Exit Incentive Plans Effectively Induce Prospective Waivers?* Consider the following argument:

> [E]mployees within the ADEA's post-forty-year-old protected class may accept a conditional exit offer because of the fear of future age-based terminations without extra benefits. They may do so in part because they are unaware of or uncertain about the protection the ADEA would afford against some possible future termination. * * * The retirement incentive enables * * * an employer to accomplish its age-based goals without worrying about an ADEA challenge. The employee's resignation obviates a future age-based discharge. * * * These is no clear reason why an employer should be able to insulate its disparate treatment of an older employee more easily by explicitly or implicitly telling that employee that she might be fired and can obtain a bonus by resigning instead, than by firing the employee and then telling her that she will receive higher severance pay if she signs a release of any right to sure for her discharge.

Harper, Age–Based Exit Incentives, supra, at 1294–95. Does the OWBPA at least implicitly reject this argument?.

9. *Does Title II Apply to Exit Incentive Programs That Do Not Seek Waivers?* An employer may offer enhanced retirement benefits to a group of its employees to induce their resignation or retirement without requiring those who accept to waive ADEA or other claims. If such a group is defined by age, should the employer's failure to meet the Title II minimum conditions for voluntary and knowing waiver render any resignations involuntary and coerced for purposes of finding underlying liability under Title I of the OWBPA? Would that be consistent with the apparent approval of the *Henn* decision in the legislative history of the OWBPA? With the structure of Title I and Title II? Reconsider note 1 above.

Even if Title II standards under current law only apply to determine the validity of waivers, should the ADEA be amended to require any employer who offers an early retirement incentive plan, but does not request formal waivers, to be subject to disclosure requirements like those in Title II of the OWBPA? Reconsider the argument in note 8.

Chapter Seven

DISABILITY DISCRIMINATION

A. INTRODUCTION

In the aggregate individuals with disabilities have occupied an inferior economic position in American society. As highlighted in the House Report on the legislation that became the Americans with Disabilities Act of 1990 (ADA), Pub. L. No. 101–336, 104 Stat. 327, codified at 42 U.S.C. §§ 12101 et seq., before passage of the ADA, two out of every three disabled Americans of working-age were not employed and two of three who were not working wanted to be, the income of disabled workers was about thirty six percent less than that of their nondisabled counterparts, and in 1984 fifty percent of adults with disabilities had household incomes of $15,000 or less, compared to only twenty-five percent of nondisabled adults. See H.R. Rep. No. 485, 101st Cong., 2d sess., pt. 2, at 32 (1990). See also Jane West, The Social and Policy Context of the Act, in The Americans with Disabilities Act: From Policy to Practice 5 (Jane West, ed. 1991).

1. *Prejudice.* Furthermore, there was reason for the Congress that passed the ADA to believe that the relative economic deprivation of the disabled at least in part derived from some of the same forms of employment discrimination that historically have plagued racial and other minorities in our society. See generally United States Commission on Civil Rights, Accommodating the Spectrum of Individual Abilities (1983); Jacobus tenBroek & Floyd W. Matson, The Disabled and the Law of Welfare, 54 Cal.L.Rev. 809, 814 & nn. 21–22 (1966). Impairments which are physically disfiguring or socially stigmatizing, such as epilepsy and mental retardation, often provoke prejudice in the form of unreasoned dislike and a preference for nonassociation. See Harold E. Yuker, The Measurement of Attitudes Toward Disabled Persons (1966); Frank Bowe, Handicapping America (1978); Harlan Hahn, Paternalism and Public Policy, 20 Society 36 (March/April 1983). Moreover, even employers who are free of such prejudice may, because of their unfamiliarity with impaired workers, engage in false stereotyping—overestimating the limiting effects of impairment, the difficulties of shifting impaired workers among tasks, and the costs of supervision and training. See Jean

Ruth Schroedel, Employer Attitudes Towards Hiring Persons with Disabilities (1978).

2. *Statistical Discrimination.* In addition, as may be true for race, sex, and age discrimination, employers may have economic incentives to discriminate against the disabled. Discrimination against the disabled may be efficient if it caters to the prejudice of other workers or customers. It also may be efficient when there is some truth to the stereotype underlying the prejudice—when indulgence of the prejudice more efficiently screens workers than would relatively expensive individualized assessment to determine which disabled workers disprove the general stereotype. The likelihood of efficient "statistical discrimination" against the handicapped seems particularly great because employers must confront a confusing variety of both types and severities of disabilities. Furthermore, just as retirement pensions and the increasing costs of insurance with age may discourage the employment of older workers, disability insurance programs, however desirable for other reasons, may make the employment of certain types of disabled workers more expensive.

3. *Need for Workplace Accommodations.* The relatively poor experience of the disabled in the employment market, however, cannot be explained fully by the types of employment discrimination treated in earlier chapters of this book. Many disabilities are sufficiently serious to prevent the effective performance of a broad range of jobs. Moreover, employers may find it efficient to refuse to hire anyone with particular disabilities, regardless of their ability to perform the basic jobs they seek, because employers have structured their work processes and physical facilities for the average nondisabled worker. For instance, the removal of physical access barriers to buildings or work stations may be necessary to enable workers with particular disabilities to function as productively as their nonimpaired counterparts, and in many cases the costs of removal may be far greater than any potential savings in labor costs.

The lowering of this last kind of barrier to the equal participation of disabled individuals in the workforce requires regulation beyond the mere condemnation of unequal treatment on the basis of disability as a suspect, protected classification. It requires asking difficult questions about the extent to which employers must provide equal opportunities for the disabled, not simply formally equal treatment. Should the law compel employers to modify their work processes and physical facilities to accommodate the disabled, even where this involves increased costs for the employer and the economy? Will the costs of accommodation be repaid to society in the long run by enabling more citizens to reach their full productive potential? Even if these costs are not fully repaid, are they well spent in giving these citizens an opportunity to achieve the dignity of productive work? If the social judgment is made that the benefits of enhancing the employability of impaired workers outweigh the costs of accommodation, should the costs be spread through taxation and subsidization by the government or through price increases caused by extra regulations on all private employers?

4. *The Rehabilitation Act of 1973.* In its first significant treatment of these questions Congress stopped short of imposing obligations on private employers that could not pass on the costs of regulation to the federal government. The Rehabilitation Act of 1973, 29 U.S.C. §§ 701–795(i), reflects the judgment that some costs appropriately may be assessed from federal sector employers and contractors and from employers receiving federal financial assistance. The 1973 Act, in addition to increasing funding for vocational rehabilitation, sought to eradicate discriminatory and other barriers to the hiring of disabled workers. Section 501 imposes affirmative action obligations on federal agencies. Section 502 seeks to remove physical access barriers in federal buildings. Section 503 levies affirmative action duties on all federal contractors with contracts in excess of $10,000. These duties extend to all of the contractors' operations. Finally, § 504 prohibits federal programs and any program or activity receiving federal financial assistance from discriminating against "otherwise qualified individual[s] with a disability * * * solely by reason of [their] disability * * *." 42 U.S.C. § 794(a).

5. *The Americans with Disabilities Act of 1990.* By enacting Title I of the ADA in 1990, however, Congress took the additional step of imposing on all employers subject to Title VII the duty to not discriminate against any "qualified individual with a disability" (§ 102(a)). Moreover, by defining "qualified individual with a disability" to mean "an individual with a disability who, with or without reasonable accommodation, can perform the essential functions of the employment position that such individual holds or desires" (§ 101(8)), and by expressly including "not making reasonable accommodations to the known physical or mental limitations of an otherwise qualified individual with a disability" as a category of prohibited discrimination (§ 102(b)(5)(A)), the Act clearly seems to require employers to offer disabled workers something more than formally neutral treatment.

In part because of its broader goals, the ADA—to a greater extent than Title VII or even the ADEA—remains a controversial statute. The fact that the ADA thus far seems not to have improved employment levels for the disabled—see the studies and data cited in Samuel R. Bagenstos, The Americans with Disabilities Act as Welfare Reform, 44 Wm. & Mary L. Rev. 921,1017–18 (2003) and Susan Schwochau & Peter David Blanck, The Economics of the Americans with Disabililties Act, Part III: Does the ADA Disable the Disabled, 21 Berk. J. Emp. & Lab.L. 271 (2000)—has provided fuel both for those who would repeal and those who would strengthen the statute. In addition, the ADA's broad and sometimes confusing provisions seem to have helped generate an unexpected proliferation of litigation and legal issues.

In this chapter we focus on the two special sets of legal issues that have generated most of the litigation under the ADA: (i) the meaning of the Act's "reasonable accommodation" requirement, and (ii) the specification of the Act's protected class through the definition of "disability". There has been no cognate for the second of these issues highlighted in prior chapters because defining inclusion in a protected class has not been difficult under Title VII or the ADEA. We address this issue first in this chapter because determining whether an aggrieved worker suffers from a "disability" and thus is protected may be the first step in the analysis of a claim brought under the ADA. However, the two issues highlighted in this chapter are related; the scope of the special reasonable accommodation requirement of the ADA may be relevant to placing limitations on the workers who may be covered by the ADA.

B. DEFINITION OF "DISABILITY"

The definition of "disability" in the ADA (at § 3(2)) is included in preliminary provisions applicable to all Titles of the Act, including Title I, governing employment, and Title III, governing public accommodations, as applied in the following decision.

BRAGDON v. ABBOTT

Supreme Court of the United States, 1998.
524 U.S. 624, 118 S.Ct. 2196, 141 L.Ed.2d 540.

JUSTICE KENNEDY delivered the opinion of the Court.

We address in this case the application of the Americans with Disabilities Act of 1990 (ADA), 104 Stat. 327, 42 U.S.C. § 12101 et seq., to persons infected with the human immunodeficiency virus (HIV). We granted certiorari to review, first, whether HIV infection is a disability under the ADA when the infection has not yet progressed to the so-called symptomatic phase; and, second, whether the Court of Appeals, in affirming a grant of summary judgment, cited sufficient material in the record to determine, as a matter of law, that respondent's infection with HIV posed no direct threat to the health and safety of her treating dentist.

I

Respondent Sidney Abbott has been infected with HIV since 1986. When the incidents we recite occurred, her infection had not manifested its most serious symptoms. On September 16, 1994, she went to the office of petitioner Randon Bragdon in Bangor, Maine, for a dental appointment. She disclosed her HIV infection on the patient registration form. Petitioner completed a dental examination, discovered a cavity, and informed respondent of his policy against filling cavities of HIV-infected patients. He offered to perform the work at a hospital with no added fee for his services, though respondent would be responsible for the cost of using the hospital's facilities. Respondent declined.

Respondent sued petitioner under state law and § 302 of the ADA, 104 Stat. 355, 42 U.S.C. § 12182, alleging discrimination on the basis of her disability. The state law claims are not before us. Section 302 of the ADA provides: "No individual shall be discriminated against on the basis of disability in the full and equal enjoyment of the goods, services, facilities, privileges, advantages, or accommodations of any place of public accommodation by any person who * * * operates a place of public accommodation." § 12182(a). The term "public accommodation" is defined to include the "professional office of a health care provider." § 12181(7)(F).

A later subsection qualifies the mandate not to discriminate. It provides: "Nothing in this subchapter shall require an entity to permit an individual to participate in or benefit from the goods, services, facilities, privileges, advantages and accommodations of such entity where such individual poses a direct threat to the health or safety of others." § 12182(b)(3).

* * * After discovery, the parties filed cross-motions for summary judgment. The District Court ruled in favor of the plaintiffs, holding that respondent's HIV infection satisfied the ADA's definition of disability. The court held further that petitioner raised no genuine issue of material fact as to whether respondent's HIV infection would have posed a direct threat to the health or safety of others during the course of a dental treatment. The court relied on affidavits submitted by Dr. Donald Wayne Marianos, Director of the Division of Oral Health of the Centers for Disease Control and Prevention (CDC). The Marianos affidavits asserted it is safe for dentists to treat patients infected with HIV in dental offices if the dentist follows the so-called universal precautions described in the Recommended Infection–Control Practices for Dentistry issued by CDC in 1993 (1993 CDC Dentistry Guidelines).

The Court of Appeals affirmed. It held respondent's HIV infection was a disability under the ADA, even though her infection had not yet progressed to the symptomatic stage. The Court of Appeals also agreed that treating the respondent in petitioner's office would not have posed a direct threat to the health and safety of others. Unlike the District Court, however, the Court of Appeals declined to rely on the Marianos affidavits. Instead the court relied on the 1993 CDC Dentistry Guidelines, as well as the Policy on AIDS, HIV Infection and the Practice of Dentistry, promulgated by the American Dental Association in 1991 (1991 American Dental Association Policy on HIV).

II

We first review the ruling that respondent's HIV infection constituted a disability under the ADA. The statute defines disability as:

"(A) a physical or mental impairment that substantially limits one or more of the major life activities of such individual;

"(B) a record of such an impairment; or

"(C) being regarded as having such impairment." § 12102(2).

We hold respondent's HIV infection was a disability under subsection (A) of the definitional section of the statute. In light of this conclusion, we need not consider the applicability of subsections (B) or (C).

* * *

A

The ADA's definition of disability is drawn almost verbatim from the definition of "handicapped individual" included in the Rehabilitation Act of 1973, 29 U.S.C. § 706(8)(B) (1988 ed.), and the definition of "handicap" contained in the Fair Housing Amendments Act of 1988, 42 U.S.C. § 3602(h)(1) (1988 ed.). Congress' repetition of a well-established term carries the implication that Congress intended the term to be construed in accordance with pre-existing regulatory interpretations. * * * In this case, Congress did more than suggest this construction; it adopted a specific statutory provision in the ADA directing as follows:

"Except as otherwise provided in this chapter, nothing in this chapter shall be construed to apply a lesser standard than the standards applied under title V of the Rehabilitation Act of 1973 (29 U.S.C. § 790 et seq.) or the regulations issued by Federal agencies pursuant to such title." 42 U.S.C. § 12201(a).

The directive requires us to construe the ADA to grant at least as much protection as provided by the regulations implementing the Rehabilitation Act.

1

The first step in the inquiry under subsection (A) requires us to determine whether respondent's condition constituted a physical impairment. The Department of Health, Education and Welfare (HEW) issued the first regulations interpreting the Rehabilitation Act in 1977. The regulations are of particular significance because, at the time, HEW was the agency responsible for coordinating the implementation and enforcement of § 504. *Consolidated Rail Corporation v. Darrone*, 465 U.S. 624, 634, 104 S.Ct. 1248, 1254–1255, 79 L.Ed.2d 568, (1984) (citing Exec. Order No. 11914, 3 CFR § 117 (1976–1980 Comp.) The HEW regulations, which appear without change in the current regulations issued by the Department of Health and Human Services, define "physical or mental impairment" to mean:

"(A) any physiological disorder or condition, cosmetic disfigurement, or anatomical loss affecting one or more of the following body systems: neurological; musculoskeletal; special sense organs; respiratory, including speech organs; cardiovascular; reproductive, digestive, genito-urinary; hemic and lymphatic; skin; and endocrine; or

"(B) any mental or psychological disorder, such as mental retardation, organic brain syndrome, emotional or mental illness, and specific learning disabilities." 45 CFR § 84.3(j)(2)(i) (1997).

In issuing these regulations, HEW decided against including a list of disorders constituting physical or mental impairments, out of concern that any specific enumeration might not be comprehensive. 42 Fed.Reg. 22685 (1977), reprinted in 45 CFR pt. 84, App. A, p. 334 (1997). The commentary accompanying the regulations, however, contains a representative list of disorders and conditions constituting physical impairments, including "such diseases and conditions as orthopedic, visual, speech, and hearing impairments, cerebral palsy, epilepsy, muscular dystrophy, multiple sclerosis, cancer, heart disease, diabetes, mental retardation, emotional illness, and * * * drug addiction and alcoholism.'' *Ibid*.

In 1980, the President transferred responsibility for the implementation and enforcement of § 504 to the Attorney General. See, e.g., Exec. Order No. 12250, 3 CFR § 298 (1981). The regulations issued by the Justice Department, which remain in force to this day, adopted verbatim the HEW definition of physical impairment quoted above. 28 CFR § 41.31(b)(1) (1997). In addition, the representative list of diseases and conditions originally relegated to the commentary accompanying the HEW regulations were incorporated into the text of the regulations. *Ibid*.

HIV infection is not included in the list of specific disorders constituting physical impairments, in part because HIV was not identified as the cause of AIDS until 1983. [*Eds*. All scientific citations are omitted throughout.] HIV infection does fall well within the general definition set forth by the regulations, however.

The disease follows a predictable and, as of today, an unalterable course. Once a person is infected with HIV, the virus invades different cells in the blood and in body tissues. Certain white blood cells, known as helper T-lymphocytes or CD4+ cells, are particularly vulnerable to HIV. The virus attaches to the CD4 receptor site of the target cell and fuses its membrane to the cell's membrane. HIV is a retrovirus, which means it uses an enzyme to convert its own genetic material into a form indistinguishable from the genetic material of the target cell. The virus' genetic material migrates to the cell's nucleus and becomes integrated with the cell's chromosomes. Once integrated, the virus can use the cell's own genetic machinery to replicate itself. Additional copies of the virus are released into the body and infect other cells in turn. Although the body does produce antibodies to combat HIV infection, the antibodies are not effective in eliminating the virus.

The virus eventually kills the infected host cell. CD4+ cells play a critical role in coordinating the body's immune response system, and the decline in their number causes corresponding deterioration of the body's ability to fight infections from many sources. Tracking the infected individual's CD4+ cell count is one of the most accurate measures of the course of the disease.

The initial stage of HIV infection is known as acute or primary HIV infection. In a typical case, this stage lasts three months. The virus concentrates in the blood. The assault on the immune system is immediate. The victim suffers from a sudden and serious decline in the number of white blood cells. There is no latency period. Mononucleosis-like symptoms often emerge between six days and six weeks after infection, at times accompanied by fever, headache, enlargement of the lymph nodes (lymphadenopathy), muscle pain (myalgia), rash, lethargy, gastrointestinal disorders, and neurological disorders. Usually these symptoms abate within 14 to 21 days. HIV antibodies appear in the bloodstream within 3 weeks; circulating HIV can be detected within 10 weeks.

After the symptoms associated with the initial stage subside, the disease enters what is referred to sometimes as its asymptomatic phase. The term is a misnomer, in some respects, for clinical features persist throughout, including lymphadenopathy, dermatological disorders, oral lesions, and bacterial infections. Although it varies with each individual, in most instances this stage lasts from 7 to 11 years. * * *

In light of the immediacy with which the virus begins to damage the infected person's white blood cells and the severity of the disease, we hold it is an impairment from the moment of infection. As noted earlier, infection with HIV causes immediate abnormalities in a person's blood, and the infected person's white cell count continues to drop throughout the course of the disease, even when the attack is concentrated in the lymph nodes. In light of these facts, HIV infection must be regarded as a physiological disorder with a constant and detrimental effect on the infected person's hemic and lymphatic systems from the moment of infection. HIV infection satisfies the statutory and regulatory definition of a physical impairment during every stage of the disease.

2

The statute is not operative, and the definition not satisfied, unless the impairment affects a major life activity. Respondent's claim throughout this case has been that the HIV infection placed a substantial limitation on her ability to reproduce and to bear children. Given the pervasive, and invariably fatal, course of the disease, its effect on major life activities of many sorts might have been relevant to our inquiry. * * * We have little doubt that had different parties brought the suit they would have maintained that an HIV infection imposes substantial limitations on other major life activities.

From the outset, however, the case has been treated as one in which reproduction was the major life activity limited by the impairment. It is our practice to decide cases on the grounds raised and considered in the Court of Appeals and included in the question on which we granted certiorari. * * * We ask, then, whether reproduction is a major life activity.

We have little difficulty concluding that it is. As the Court of Appeals held, "[t]he plain meaning of the word 'major' denotes comparative importance" and "suggest[s] that the touchstone for determining an activity's inclusion under the statutory rubric is its significance." Reproduction falls well within the phrase "major life activity." Reproduction and the sexual dynamics surrounding it are central to the life process itself.

While petitioner concedes the importance of reproduction, he claims that Congress intended the ADA only to cover those aspects of a person's life which have a public, economic, or daily character. The argument founders on the statutory language. Nothing in the definition suggests that activities without a public, economic, or daily dimension may somehow be regarded as so unimportant or insignificant as to fall outside the meaning of the word "major." The breadth of the term confounds the attempt to limit its construction in this manner.

As we have noted, the ADA must be construed to be consistent with regulations issued to implement the Rehabilitation Act. See 42 U.S.C. § 12201(a). Rather than enunciating a general principle for determining what is and is not a major life activity, the Rehabilitation Act regulations instead provide a representative list, defining term to include "functions such as caring for one's self, performing manual tasks, walking, seeing, hearing, speaking, breathing, learning, and working." 45 CFR § 84.3(j)(2)(ii) (1997); 28 CFR § 41.31(b)(2) (1997). As the use of the term "such as" confirms, the list is illustrative, not exhaustive.

These regulations are contrary to petitioner's attempt to limit the meaning of the term "major" to public activities. The inclusion of activities such as caring for one's self and performing manual tasks belies the suggestion that a task must have a public or economic character in order to be a major life activity for purposes of the ADA. On the contrary, the Rehabilitation Act regulations support the inclusion of reproduction as a major life activity, since reproduction could not be regarded as any less important than working and learning. * * *

3

The final element of the disability definition in subsection (A) is whether respondent's physical impairment was a substantial limit on the major life activity she asserts. The Rehabilitation Act regulations provide no additional guidance. 45 CFR pt. 84, App. A, p. 334 (1997).

Our evaluation of the medical evidence leads us to conclude that respondent's infection substantially limited her ability to reproduce in two independent ways. First, a woman infected with HIV who tries to conceive a child imposes on the man a significant risk of becoming infected. The cumulative results of 13 studies collected in a 1994 text-book on AIDS indicates that 20% of male partners of women with HIV became HIV-positive themselves, with a majority of the studies finding a statistically significant risk of infection.

Second, an infected woman risks infecting her child during gestation and childbirth, i.e., perinatal transmission. Petitioner concedes that women infected with HIV face about a 25% risk of transmitting the virus to their children. Published reports available in 1994 confirm the accuracy of this statistic.

Petitioner points to evidence in the record suggesting that antiretro-viral therapy can lower the risk of perinatal transmission to about 8%. The Solicitor General questions the relevance of the 8% figure, pointing to regulatory language requiring the substantiality of a limitation to be assessed without regard to available mitigating measures. We need not resolve this dispute in order to decide this case, however. It cannot be said as a matter of law that an 8% risk of transmitting a dread and fatal disease to one's child does not represent a substantial limitation on reproduction.

The Act addresses substantial limitations on major life activities, not utter inabilities. Conception and childbirth are not impossible for an HIV victim but, without doubt, are dangerous to the public health. This meets the definition of a substantial limitation. The decision to reproduce carries economic and legal consequences as well. There are added costs for antiretroviral therapy, supplemental insurance, and long-term health care for the child who must be examined and, tragic to think, treated for the infection. The laws of some States, moreover, forbid persons infected with HIV from having sex with others, regardless of consent.

In the end, the disability definition does not turn on personal choice. When significant limitations result from the impairment, the definition is met even if the difficulties are not insurmountable. For the statistical and other reasons we have cited, of course, the limitations on reproduction may be insurmountable here. Testimony from the respondent that her HIV infection controlled her decision not to have a child is unchallenged. In the context of reviewing summary judgment, we must take it to be true. We agree with the District Court and the Court of Appeals that no triable issue of fact impedes a ruling on the question of statutory coverage. Respondent's HIV infection is a physical impairment which substantially limits a major life activity, as the ADA defines it. In view of our holding, we need not address the second question presented, i.e., whether HIV infection is a per se disability under the ADA.

[*Eds.* The concurring opinion of JUSTICE STEVENS, joined by JUSTICE BREYER, is omitted.]

JUSTICE GINSBURG concurring.

HIV infection, as the description set out in the Court's opinion documents, has been regarded as a disease limiting life itself. The disease inevitably pervades life's choices: education, employment, family and financial undertakings. It affects the need for and, as this case shows, the ability to obtain health care because of the reaction of others to the impairment. No rational legislator, it seems to me apparent, would require nondiscrimination once symptoms become visible but permit discrimination when the disease, though present, is not yet visible. I am therefore satisfied that the statutory and regulatory definitions are well met. HIV infection is "a physical * * * impairment that substantially limits * * * major life activities," or is so perceived, 42 U.S.C. §§ 12102(2)(A),(C), including the afflicted individual's family relations, employment potential, and ability to care for herself, see 45 CFR § 84.3(j)(2)(ii) (1997); 28 CFR § 41.31(b)(2) (1997).

CHIEF JUSTICE REHNQUIST with whom JUSTICE SCALIA and JUSTICE THOMAS join, and with whom JUSTICE O'CONNOR joins as to Part II, concurring in the judgment in part and dissenting in part.

I

Petitioner does not dispute that asymptomatic HIV-positive status is a physical impairment. I therefore assume this to be the case, and proceed to the second and third statutory requirements for "disability."

According to the Court, the next question is "whether reproduction is a major life activity." That, however, is only half of the relevant question. As mentioned above, the ADA's definition of a "disability" requires that the major life activity at issue be one "of such individual." § 12102(2)(A). The Court truncates the question, perhaps because there is not a shred of record evidence indicating that, prior to becoming infected with HIV, respondent's major life activities included reproduction (assuming for the moment that reproduction is a major life activity at all). At most, the record indicates that after learning of her HIV status, respondent, whatever her previous inclination, conclusively decided that she would not have children. There is absolutely no evidence that, absent the HIV, respondent would have had or was even considering having children. Indeed, when asked during her deposition whether her HIV infection had in any way impaired her ability to carry out any of her life functions, respondent answered "No."

* * *

But even aside from the facts of this particular case, the Court is simply wrong in concluding as a general matter that reproduction is a "major life activity." Unfortunately, the ADA does not define the phrase "major life activities." But the Act does incorporate by reference a list of such activities contained in regulations issued under the Rehabilitation Act. 42 U.S.C. § 12201(a); 45 CFR § 84.3(j)(2)(ii) (1997). The Court correctly recognizes that this list of major life activities "is illustrative, not exhaustive," but then makes no attempt to demonstrate that reproduction is a major life activity in the same sense that "caring for one's self, performing manual tasks, walking, seeing, hearing, speaking, breathing, learning, and working" are.

* * *

No one can deny that reproductive decisions are important in a person's life. But so are decisions as to whom to marry, where to live, and how to earn one's living. Fundamental importance of this sort is not the common thread linking the statute's listed activities. The common thread is rather that the activities are repetitively performed and essential in the day-to-day existence of a normally functioning individual. They are thus quite different from the series of activities leading to the birth of a child.

* * *

But even if I were to assume that reproduction is a major life activity of respondent, I do not agree that an asymptomatic HIV infection "substantially limits" that activity. The record before us leaves no doubt that those so infected are still entirely able to engage in sexual intercourse, give birth to a child if they become pregnant, and perform the manual tasks necessary to rear a child to maturity. While individuals infected with HIV may choose not to engage in these activities, there is no support in language, logic, or our case law for the proposition that such voluntary choices constitute a "limit" on one's own life activities.

[*Eds*. The opinion of JUSTICE O'CONNOR concurring in the judgment in part and dissenting in part is omitted. For the Court's consideration of Abbott's defense that his treatment of Bragdon was justified by health and safety risks, see below at page 570.]

Note on the Rehabilitation Act of 1973 and the ADA

The *Bragdon* Court's reliance on administrative and judicial interpretation of the Rehabilitation Act in its interpretation of the ADA suggests one reason why the former statute continues to be relevant. There are other reasons, however, why the Rehabilitation Act continues to be of direct interest after passage of the ADA, even though the amendments to the Rehabilitation Act expressly adopt the employment discrimination standards contained in Title I of the ADA, see 29 U.S.C. §§ 791(g), 794(d), and the range of employers covered by the ADA is much broader than that of the Rehabilitation Act. First, § 501 of the Rehabilitation Act covers one very important employer not reached by the ADA, the federal government. Second, the Rehabilitation Act's enforcement procedures and remedies differ somewhat from those provided by the ADA.

Perhaps most importantly, the Rehabilitation Act's prohibition in § 504(a) of disability discrimination "under any program or activity receiving Federal financial assistance" can be enforced directly in court through a private right of action without exhausting the administrative procedure mandated for the ADA by the incorporation of Title VII "remedies and procedures" (ADA, § 107(a)). The Supreme Court has recognized that this direct private right of action is afforded by § 505(a)(2) of the Rehabilitation Act, which provides § 504 plaintiffs the "remedies, procedures, and rights set forth in Title VI of the Civil Rights Act of 1964." See Consolidated Rail Corp. v. Darrone, 465 U.S. 624, 626, 104 S.Ct. 1248, 79 L.Ed.2d 568 (1984). *Darrone* itself was a pre-ADA case involving an equitable action alleging intentional discrimination and seeking back pay; however, the courts of appeals have allowed private damages actions under § 504, even after passage of the ADA. See, e.g., Freed v. Consolidated Rail Corp., 201 F.3d 188 (3d Cir.2000). Furthermore, with the passage of the Civil Rights Restoration Act of 1987, Pub.L. 100–259, 102 Stat. 28, § 504 covers more than simply the specific program or activity to which federal funds are allotted. For private firms that are not "principally engaged in the business of providing education, health care, housing, social services, or parks and recreation" (§ 504(b)(3)(A)(ii)), it reaches "the entire plant or other comparable, geographically separate facility" to which assistance is extended (§ 504(b)(3)(B)). For other recipients, it reaches their entire institution. But see United States Dept. of Transp. v. Paralyzed Veterans of America, 477 U.S. 597, 605–06, 106 S.Ct. 2705, 91 L.Ed.2d 494 (1986) (§ 504 covers only employers who are the direct recipients of federal assistance, and not simply the ultimate beneficiaries of such assistance). See also Schrader v. Fred A.

Ray, M.D., P.C., 296 F.3d 968 (10th Cir.2002) (coverage of federal fund recipients under § 504, in contrast to ADA, not dependent on having 15 employees).

Federal employees alleging disability discrimination under the Rehabilitation Act, however, have not been extended a direct private right of action independent of EEOC administrative procedures. See, e.g., Spence v. Straw, 54 F.3d 196 (3d Cir.1995). Section 505(a) does provide that the "remedies, procedures, and rights" accorded federal employees by § 717 of Title VII shall be made available to enforce § 501's proscription of disability discrimination in federal sector employment. This allows federal employees to achieve de novo consideration of disability discrimination complaints in federal court when they are dissatisfied with any administrative resolution. See also Civil Service Reform Act of 1978, 5 U.S.C. § 2302(b)(1)(D) (prohibiting disability discrimination against employees in the civil service).

The Rehabilitation Act does not provide a private right of action, even after the exhaustion of administrative review, for employees of federal contractors who allege that their employer has failed to comply with the affirmative action obligations imposed on such contractors pursuant to the mandate of § 503 of the Rehabilitation Act. However, § 503(b) directs the Department of Labor to investigate promptly and take action on any complaints filed by disabled workers of a federal contractor's failure to comply with its contractual obligations. Under regulations issued by the Labor Department's Office of Federal Contract Compliance, see 41 C.F.R. pt. 60–741, such action may include equitable relief for the discriminatee, as well as contract termination and disbarment.

The Rehabilitation Act also seems to have particular relevance for Title II of the ADA. Section 202 in Title II provides that:

> no qualified individual with a disability shall, by reason of such disability, be excluded from participation in or be denied the benefits of the services, programs, or activities of a public entity, or be subjected to discrimination by any such entity.

The Department of Justice, with the concurrence of some lower courts, has interpreted this provision to cover public employment, and has issued regulations incorporating both the EEOC regulations on Title I of the ADA and its own regulations under § 504 of the Rehabilitation Act. 28 C.F.R. § 35.140(b). See, e.g., Bledsoe v. Palm Beach County Soil and Water Conservation District, 133 F.3d 816 (11th Cir.1998) (public employers can be sued under Title II without meeting Title I jurisdictional requirements). But see, e.g., Zimmerman v. Oregon, 170 F.3d 1169 (9th Cir.1999) (Title II was intended to cover only discrimination against those who may benefit from public services, not discrimination against those who may provide labor or other inputs for the production of those services). Section 203 of the ADA provides that § 202 is to be enforced pursuant to the remedies and procedures of § 505 of the Rehabilitation Act, 505(a)(2), affording the same direct private right of action allowed for § 504 plaintiffs. See S.Rep. No. 116, 101st Cong., 1st Sess. 57–58 (1989).

Notes and Questions

1. *A Holding for Title I?* Is there any reason to believe that the *Bragdon* Court's analysis and holdings concerning the meaning of "disability" do not apply for employment discrimination cases under Title I of the ADA? The EEOC regulations interpreting the ADA define "physical or mental impairment", see 29 C.F.R. § 1630.2(h), and "major life activities", see 29 C.F.R. § 1630.2(i) and (j), in the same manner as the HEW Rehabilitation Act regulations relied on in *Bragdon*.

2. *Implications of Treating Reproduction as a Major Life·Activity.* Does the *Bragdon* Court's holding that "reproduction is a major life activity for the purposes of the ADA" mean that infertility is a disability so that employers must at least consider accommodating employees who wish to take some time off work for fertility treatments or for alternative conception procedures? Compare Krauel v. Iowa Methodist Medical Center, 915 F.Supp. 102, 108 (S.D.Iowa 1995), affirmed, 95 F.3d 674 (8th Cir.1996); Zatarain v. WDSU–Television, 881 F.Supp. 240, 243 (E.D.La.1995), affirmed, 79 F.3d 1143 (5th Cir.1996), with Pacourek v. Inland Steel Co., 858 F.Supp. 1393, 1404 (N.D.Ill.1994); Erickson v. Board of Governors, 911 F.Supp. 316 (N.D.Ill.1995). Does the inclusion of reproduction as a major life activity also mean that all sexually transmitted diseases may be disabilities?

Given the *Bragdon* Court's treatment of reproduction as a major life activity, is HIV infection always a disability? Assume that Abbott at the time of Bragdon's refusal to treat in his office had already undergone a hysterectomy, and therefore was unable to conceive, or that Abbott was a male homosexual with no interest in participating in sexual reproduction. Does the majority's silent response to the Chief Justice's argument that the definition of disability demands consideration of the impact of the impairment on the life activity of the particular plaintiff constitute an implicit holding that the plaintiff's particular life status need not be considered? Or is this silence better explained as adopting a rebuttable presumption that the plaintiff's ability to reproduce safely was affected by the HIV infection?

3. *Alternative Routes to the Coverage of HIV Carriers.* If Bragdon's HIV infection had not yet progressed to the "so-called symptomatic phase", could she argue that some major life activity other than reproduction was substantially limited? Does the Court's statement that "[r]eproduction and the sexual dynamics surrounding it are central to the life process" suggest that sexual activity unconnected to reproduction could be a major life activity? Does sexual activity, in any event, fit even Chief Justice Rehnquist's criteria of "activities that are repetitively performed and essential to the day-to-day existence of a normally functioning individual?" Compare McAlindin v. County of San Diego, 192 F.3d 1226 (9th Cir.1999) (impairment resulting in substantial limitation on sexual intercourse is a disability), with Contreras v. Suncast Corp., 237 F.3d 756 (7th Cir.2001) (affidavit asserting decline in frequency of sexual relations is not sufficient to avert summary judgment). Is sexual activity substantially limited by HIV infection?

Alternatively, as suggested by Justice Ginsburg's concurring decision, should life planning be treated as a major life activity that would be substantially limited by the contraction of any terminal disease? See Note, Evaluating Purely Reproductive Disorders Under the Americans with Disabilities Act, 96 Mich.L.Rev. 724, 736–38 (1997).

4. *Other Major Life Activities.* Does the *Bragdon* Court's method of determining that reproduction is a major life activity—considering its comparative importance in life—help answer whether other life activities not listed in the Rehabilitation Act or ADA regulations are also major life activities? Should reading be treated as a major life activity? See Head v. Glacier Northwest, Inc., 413 F.3d 1053 (9th Cir. 2005); Hileman v. City of Dallas, 115 F.3d 352 (5th Cir.1997). Climbing? See Rogers v. International Marine Terminals, Inc., 87 F.3d 755 (5th Cir.1996). Sleeping? See *Head*, supra; McAlinden v. County of San Diego, supra. Interacting with other people? See id; Soileau v. Guilford of Maine, Inc., 105 F.3d 12 (1st Cir.1997). Moving in crowds? See Reeves v. Johnson Controls World Services, 140 F.3d 144 (2d Cir.1998): Thinking? See *Head*, supra.

5. *Independent Definition of "Impairment".* How does the Court, in accord with the administrative regulations under both the Rehabilitation Act and the ADA, define "impairment"? Does this definition exclude from coverage certain conditions, such as being overweight, that might at least be regarded as substantially limiting major life activities? See note 9 at p. 522 infra. Could the Court have interpreted the statute more broadly to include its own definition of impairment as any physical or mental condition that substantially limits a major life activity?

6. *Does Impairment Require At Least Some Effect on an Internal Body System?* Does the *Bragdon* Court's treatment of HIV infection as an impairment, even before its "so-called symptomatic phase", suggest that any disease, such as multiple sclerosis, that will inevitably later develop serious symptoms should be treated as an impairment as soon as it is diagnosed? Or must there at least be some significant current effect on an internal body system, even if that effect has no external symptoms?

7. *Can Contagiousness Alone Constitute an Impairment?* In School Bd. of Nassau Cty. v. Arline, 480 U.S. 273, 107 S.Ct. 1123, 94 L.Ed.2d 307 (1987), the Court held that discrimination against an individual because of the contagiousness, or perceived contagiousness, of an otherwise substantially limiting disease (tuberculosis) is discrimination on the basis of handicap, now disability, under the Rehabilitation Act. The *Arline* Court also stated that an impairment that "might not diminish a person's physical or mental capabilities * * * could nevertheless substantially limit that person's ability to work as a result of the negative reactions of others to the impairment"; and that by covering those who are "regarded as impaired", "Congress acknowledged that society's accumulated myths and fears [including fear of contagion] are as handicapping as are the physical limitations that flow from actual impairment". The *Arline* Court, however, disclaimed reaching the issue of whether a person without any physical or mental symptoms could be considered handicapped "solely on the basis of contagiousness." Does the Court's analysis in *Bragdon* suggest how it would decide whether contagiousness alone could constitute an impairment so that a totally asymptomatic carrier of a serious disease might be protected under the ADA?

8. *Coverage of Carriers of Disease–Associated Genes?* The questions posed in the last two notes also raise the issue of ADA and Rehabilitation Act coverage of individuals who carry genes that either determine the later onset of a disease or make that onset more likely. Employers may have an economic interest in, and may soon have the technical capability for, conducting genetic testing on current and potential employees. See Larry Gostin, Genetic Discrimination: The Use of Genetically Based Diagnostic and Prognostic Tests by Employers and Insurers, 17 Am. J.L. & Med. 109, 116 (1991). Does the ADA prevent employers from not hiring or firing workers because the workers' genes predict some future impairment? Is the gene itself an "impairment"? On the one hand, the EEOC has advised that "the term impairment * * * does not include characteristic predisposition to illness or disease." 29 C.F.R. pt. 1630, app. § 1630.2(h). On the other hand, in a Policy Guidance issued in 1995 the EEOC asserted that the ADA proscribes discrimination on the basis of "genetic information relating to illness, disease, or other disorders," because such discrimination would be against those "regarded as" having an impairment. EEOC Order No. 915.002 § 902. Is the EEOC's position consistent? Does a disease-associated gene, before becoming symptomatic, substantially limit some major life activity? See Pauline T. Kim, Genetic Discrimination, Genetic Privacy: Rethinking Employee Protections for a Brave New Workplace, 96 Nw. U.L.Rev. 1497, 1528–30 (2002) (arguing that ADA prohibitions do not comfortably fit genetic discrimination). See also Mark A. Rothstein, Genetic Discrimination in Employment and the Americans with Disabilities Act, 29 Hous. L. Rev. 23 (1992).

If the ADA does not cover discrimination against genetic characteristics, should new legislation be enacted that does so? A majority of states have passed such laws, see Sonia M. Suter, The Allure and Peril of Genetics Exceptionalism: Do We Need Special Genetics Legislation?, 79 Wash. U. L.Q. 669, 691–96 (2001), and President Clinton issued an Executive Order protecting federal employees from genetic discrimination. Exec. Order No. 13145, 3 C.F.R. § 235 (2000). See also EEOC Policy Guidance on Executive Order 13145, issued July 26, 2000. Furthermore, a bill that would bar all employers from discriminating on the basis of genetic information passed the House of Representatives with only three dissenting votes in 2007. H.R. 493, 110th Cong., 1st Sess. Similar legislation unanimously passed the Senate in 2003. See S.B. 1053, 108th Cong., 1st Sess. This legislation also would ban employers from collecting genetic information, except to monitor the effects of work place health hazards. Is regulation of the collection of genetic information a better way to address the new developments in genetics? See also the discussion of medical testing under the ADA at pp. 576–578 infra.

9. *Treatment of Drug and Alcohol Addiction.* Section 104(a) of the ADA provides that protected individuals "shall not include any employee or applicant who is currently engaging in the illegal use of drugs, when the covered entity acts on the basis of such use." This express exclusion does not extend, however, to those who have successfully completed a supervised drug rehabilitation program, or are currently in such a program and not engaged in drug use, or are "erroneously regarded as engaged in such use." (§ 104(b)) Section 510 of the ADA also amends § 504 of the Rehabilitation Act to effect a similar exclusion of illegal drug users, and hence negate for

drug users any possibly contrary implications from a footnote in *Arline*, 480 U.S. at 285 n.14. The EEOC's Interpretive Guidance states that the "term 'currently engaging' is not intended to be limited to the use of drugs on the day of, or within a matter of days or weeks before, the employment action in question. Rather, the provision is intended to apply to the illegal use of drugs that has occurred recently enough to indicate that the individual is actively engaged in such conduct." 29 C.F.R. pt. 1630, app. § 1630.3(a) through (c). See also Shafer v. Preston Memorial Hosp. Corp., 107 F.3d 274, 278 (4th Cir.1997) (current use of drugs can be within prior week or month even where individual is in a rehabilitation program at time of allegedly discriminatory act).

The ADA does not exclude even current alcoholics from coverage, although § 104(c)(4) expressly authorizes employers to hold alcoholics as well as drug users to the same job standards as it holds other employees. See Mararri v. WCI Steel, Inc., 130 F.3d 1180 (6th Cir.1997) (current alcoholics may be protected). Does § 104 indicate that all alcoholics are treated as having a disability within the meaning of the ADA? Anyone with a "drinking problem?" Is there a difference? Would all illegal drug users be covered by the ADA but for the express exclusion in § 104? If not, would an individual who has been erroneously perceived as a drug user by an employer necessarily be protected? The courts have not treated alcohol or drug addiction as per se disabilities. See, e.g., Burch v. Coca–Cola Co., 119 F.3d 305 (5th Cir.1997) (alcoholism is not always a disability; must show substantial limitation).

Does the ADA protect those who are not current drug users from discrimination based on their past use? Would ADA coverage prevent an employer from applying a company rule against hiring previously terminated workers to a worker whom it once discharged for drug use? In Raytheon Co. v. Hernandez, 540 U.S. 44, 124 S.Ct. 513, 157 L.Ed.2d 357 (2003), the Court assumed that an employer would have engaged in ADA-proscribed disparate treatment only if it did not rehire a worker because of his past addiction, rather than because of the company's neutral rule against hiring previously terminated workers.

SUTTON v. UNITED AIR LINES, INC.

Supreme Court of the United States, 1999.
527 U.S. 471, 119 S.Ct. 2139, 144 L.Ed.2d 450.

Justice O'Connor delivered the opinion of the Court.

I

* * *

Petitioners are twin sisters, both of whom have severe myopia. Each petitioner's uncorrected visual acuity is 20/200 or worse in her right eye and 20/400 or worse in her left eye, but "[w]ith the use of corrective lenses, each * * * has vision that is 20/20 or better." Consequently, without corrective lenses, each "effectively cannot see to conduct numerous activities such as driving a vehicle, watching television or shopping in public stores," but with corrective measures, such as glasses or contact lenses, both "function identically to individuals without a similar impairment."

In 1992, petitioners applied to respondent for employment as commercial airline pilots. They met respondent's basic age, education, experience, and FAA certification qualifications. After submitting their applications for employment, both petitioners were invited by respondent to an interview and to flight simulator tests. Both were told during their interviews, however, that a mistake had been made in inviting them to interview because petitioners did not meet respondent's minimum vision requirement, which was uncorrected visual acuity of 20/100 or better. Due to their failure to meet this requirement, petitioners' interviews were terminated, and neither was offered a pilot position.

In light of respondent's proffered reason for rejecting them, petitioners filed a charge of disability discrimination under the ADA with the Equal Employment Opportunity Commission (EEOC). After receiving a right to sue letter, petitioners filed suit in the United States District Court for the District of Colorado, alleging that respondent had discriminated against them "on the basis of their disability, or because [respondent] regarded [petitioners] as having a disability" in violation of the ADA. Specifically, petitioners alleged that due to their severe myopia they actually have a substantially limiting impairment or are regarded as having such an impairment, and are thus disabled under the Act.

* * *

II

* * *

The parties agree that the authority to issue regulations to implement the Act is split primarily among three Government agencies. * * *

No agency, however, has been given authority to issue regulations implementing the generally applicable provisions of the ADA, see §§ 12101–12102, which fall outside Titles I–V. Most notably, no agency has been delegated authority to interpret the term "disability." § 12102(2). Justice Breyer's contrary, imaginative interpretation of the Act's delegation provisions is belied by the terms and structure of the ADA. The EEOC has, nonetheless, issued regulations to provide additional guidance regarding the proper interpretation of this term. After restating the definition of disability given in the statute, see 29 CFR § 1630.2(g) (1998), the EEOC regulations define the three elements of disability: (1) "physical or mental impairment," (2) "substantially limits," and (3) "major life activities." See id., at §§ 1630.2(h)-(j). Under the regulations, a "physical impairment" includes "[a]ny physiological disorder, or condition, cosmetic disfigurement, or anatomical loss affecting one or more of the following body systems: neurological, musculoskeletal, special sense organs, respiratory (including speech organs), cardiovascular, reproductive, digestive, genito-urinary, hemic and lymphatic, skin, and endocrine." § 1630.2(h)(1). The term "substantially limits" means, among other things, "[u]nable to perform a major life activity that the average person in the general population can perform"; or "[s]ignificantly restricted as to the condition, manner or duration under which an individual can perform a particular major life activity as compared to the condition, manner, or duration under which the average person in the general population can perform that same major life activity." § 1630.2(j). Finally, "[m]ajor [l]ife [a]ctivities means functions such as caring for oneself, performing manual tasks, walking, seeing, hearing, speaking, breathing, learning, and working." § 1630.2(i). Because both parties accept these regulations as valid, and determining their validity is not necessary to decide this case, we have no occasion to consider what deference they are due, if any.

The agencies have also issued interpretive guidelines to aid in the implementation of their regulations. For instance, at the time that it promulgated the above regulations, the EEOC issued an "Interpretive Guidance," which provides that "[t]he determination of whether an individual is substantially limited in a major life activity must be made on a case by case basis, without regard to mitigating measures such as medicines, or assistive or prosthetic devices." 29 CFR pt. 1630, App. § 1630.2(j) (1998) (describing § 1630.2(j)). The Department of Justice has issued a similar guideline. See 28 CFR pt. 35, App. A, § 35.104 ("The question of whether a person has a disability should be assessed without regard to the availability of mitigating measures, such as reasonable modification or auxiliary aids and services"); pt. 36, App. B, § 36.104 (same). Although the parties dispute the persuasive force of these interpretive guidelines, we have no need in this case to decide what deference is due.

III

* * *

We conclude that respondent is correct that the approach adopted by the agency guidelines—that persons are to be evaluated in their hypothetical uncorrected state—is an impermissible interpretation of the ADA. Looking at the Act as a whole, it is apparent that if a person is taking measures to correct for, or mitigate, a physical or mental impairment, the effects of those measures—both positive and negative—must be taken into account when judging whether that person is "substantially limited" in a major life activity and thus "disabled" under the Act. The dissent relies on the legislative history of the ADA for the contrary proposition that individuals should be examined in their uncorrected state. Because we decide that, by its terms, the ADA cannot be read in this manner, we have no reason to consider the ADA's legislative history.

Three separate provisions of the ADA, read in concert, lead us to this conclusion. The Act defines a "disability" as "a physical or mental impairment that substantially limits one or more of the major life activities" of an individual. § 12102(2)(A) (emphasis added). Because the phrase "substantially limits" appears in the Act in the present indicative verb form, we think the language is properly read as requiring that a person be presently—not potentially or hypothetically—substantially limited in order to demonstrate a disability. A "disability" exists only where an impairment "substantially limits" a major life activity, not where it "might," "could," or "would" be substantially limiting if mitigating measures were not taken. A person whose physical or mental impairment is corrected by medication or other measures does not have an impairment that presently "substantially limits" a major life activity. To be sure, a person whose physical or mental impairment is corrected by mitigating measures still has an impairment, but if the impairment is corrected it does not "substantially limi[t]" a major life activity.

The definition of disability also requires that disabilities be evaluated "with respect to an individual" and be determined based on whether an impairment substantially limits the "major life activities of such individual." § 12102(2). Thus, whether a person has a disability under the ADA is an individualized inquiry. See *Bragdon v. Abbott*, 524 U.S. 624, 118 S.Ct. 2196, 141 L.Ed.2d 540 (1998) (declining to consider whether HIV infection is a per se disability under the ADA); 29 CFR pt. 1630, App. § 1630.2(j) ("The determination of whether an individual has a disability is not necessarily based on the name or diagnosis of the impairment the person has, but rather on the effect of that impairment on the life of the individual").

The agency guidelines' directive that persons be judged in their uncorrected or unmitigated state runs directly counter to the individualized inquiry mandated by the ADA. The agency approach would often require courts and employers to speculate about a person's condition and would, in many cases, force them to make a disability determination based on general information about how an uncorrected impairment usually affects individuals, rather than on the individual's actual condition. For instance, under this view, courts would almost certainly find all diabetics to be disabled, because if they failed to monitor their blood sugar levels and administer insulin, they would almost certainly be substantially limited in one or more major life activities. A diabetic whose illness does not impair his or her daily activities would therefore be considered disabled simply because he or she has diabetes. Thus, the guidelines approach would create a system in which persons often must be treated as members of a group of people with similar impairments, rather than as individuals. This is contrary to both the letter and the spirit of the ADA.

The guidelines approach could also lead to the anomalous result that in determining whether an individual is disabled, courts and employers could not consider any negative side effects suffered by an individual resulting from the use of mitigating measures, even when those side effects are very severe. * * *

Finally, and critically, findings enacted as part of the ADA require the conclusion that Congress did not intend to bring under the statute's protection all those whose uncorrected conditions amount to disabilities. Congress found that "some 43,000,000 Americans have one or more physical or mental disabilities, and this number is increasing as the population as a whole is growing older." § 12101(a)(1). This figure is inconsistent with the definition of disability pressed by petitioners.

* * *

The dissents suggest that viewing individuals in their corrected state will exclude from the definition of "disab[led]" those who use prosthetic limbs, or take medicine for epilepsy or high blood pressure. This suggestion is incorrect. The use of a corrective device does not, by itself, relieve one's disability. Rather, one has a disability under subsection A if, notwithstanding the use of a corrective device, that individual is substantially limited in a major life activity. For example, individuals who use prosthetic limbs or wheelchairs may be mobile and capable of functioning in society but still be disabled because of a substantial limitation on their ability to walk or run. The same may be true of individuals who take medicine to lessen the symptoms of an impairment so that they can function but nevertheless remain substantially limited. Alternatively, one whose high blood pressure is "cured" by medication may be regarded as disabled by a covered entity, and thus disabled under subsection C of the definition. The use or nonuse of a corrective device does not determine whether an individual is disabled; that determination depends on whether the limitations an individual with an impairment actually faces are in fact substantially limiting.

Applying this reading of the Act to the case at hand, we conclude that the Court of Appeals correctly resolved the issue of disability in respondent's favor. As noted above, petitioners allege that with corrective measures, their visual acuity is 20/20, and that they "function identically to individuals without a similar impairment." In addition, petitioners concede that they "do not argue that the use of corrective lenses in itself demonstrates a substantially limiting impairment." Accordingly, because we decide that disability under the Act is to be determined with reference to corrective measures, we agree with the courts below that petitioners have not stated a claim that they are substantially limited in any major life activity.

IV

Our conclusion that petitioners have failed to state a claim that they are actually disabled under subsection (A) of the disability definition does not end our inquiry. Under subsection (C), individuals who are "regarded as" having a disability are disabled within the meaning of the ADA. See § 12102(2)(C). Subsection (C) provides that having a disability includes "being regarded as having," § 12102(2)(C), "a physical or mental impairment that substantially limits one or more of the major life activities of such individual," § 12102(2)(A). There are two apparent ways in which individuals may fall within this statutory definition: (1) a covered entity mistakenly believes that a person has a physical impairment that substantially limits one or more major life activities, or (2) a covered entity mistakenly believes that an actual, nonlimiting impairment substantially limits one or more major life activities. In both cases, it is necessary that a covered entity entertain misperceptions about the individual—it must believe either that one has a substantially limiting impairment that one does not have or that one has a substantially limiting impairment when, in fact, the impairment is not so limiting. These misperceptions often "resul[t] from stereotypic assumptions not truly indicative of * * * individual ability." See 42 U.S.C. § 12101(7). * * *

There is no dispute that petitioners are physically impaired. Petitioners do not make the obvious argument that they are regarded due to their impairments as substantially limited in the major life activity of seeing. They contend only that respondent mistakenly believes their physical impairments substantially limit them in the major life activity of working. To support this claim, petitioners allege that respondent has a vision requirement, which is allegedly based on myth and stereotype. Further, this requirement substantially limits their ability to engage in the major life activity of working by precluding them from obtaining the job of global airline pilot, which they argue is a "class of employment." In reply, respondent argues that the position of global airline pilot is not a class of jobs and therefore petitioners have not stated a claim that they are regarded as substantially limited in the major life activity of working.

Standing alone, the allegation that respondent has a vision requirement in place does not establish a claim that respondent regards petitioners as substantially limited in the major life activity of working. By its terms, the ADA allows employers to prefer some physical attributes over others and to establish physical criteria. An employer runs afoul of the ADA when it makes an employment decision based on a physical or mental impairment, real or imagined, that is regarded as substantially limiting a major life activity. Accordingly, an employer is free to decide that physical characteristics or medical conditions that do not rise to the level of an impairment—such as one's height, build, or singing voice— are preferable to others, just as it is free to decide that some limiting, but not substantially limiting, impairments make individuals less than ideally suited for a job.

* * *

When the major life activity under consideration is that of working, the statutory phrase "substantially limits" requires, at a minimum, that plaintiffs allege they are unable to work in a broad class of jobs. Reflecting this requirement, the EEOC uses a specialized definition of the term "substantially limits" when referring to the major life activity of working:

> "significantly restricted in the ability to perform either a class of jobs or a broad range of jobs in various classes as compared to the average person having comparable training, skills and abilities. The inability to perform a single, particular job does not constitute a substantial limitation in the major life activity of working." § 1630.2(j)(3)(i).

The EEOC further identifies several factors that courts should consider when determining whether an individual is substantially limited in the major life activity of working, including the geographical area to which the individual has reasonable access, and "the number and types of jobs utilizing similar training, knowledge, skills or abilities, within the geographical area, from which the individual is also disqualified." §§ 1630.2(j)(3)(ii)(A), (B). To be substantially limited in the major life activity of working, then, one must be precluded from more than one type of job, a specialized job, or a particular job of choice. If jobs utilizing an individual's skills (but perhaps not his or her unique talents) are available, one is not precluded from a substantial class of jobs. Similarly, if a host of different types of jobs are available, one is not precluded from a broad range of jobs.

Because the parties accept that the term "major life activities" includes working, we do not determine the validity of the cited regulations. We note, however, that there may be some conceptual difficulty in defining "major life activities" to include work, for it seems "to argue in a circle to say that if one is excluded, for instance, by reason of [an impairment, from working with others] * * * then that exclusion constitutes an impairment, when the question you're asking is, whether the exclusion itself is by reason of handicap." Tr. of Oral Arg. in *School Bd. of Nassau Co. v. Arline*, O.T.1986, No. 85–1277, p. 15 (argument of Solicitor General). Indeed, even the EEOC has expressed reluctance to define "major life activities" to include working and has suggested that working be viewed as a residual life activity, considered, as a last resort, only "[i]f an individual is not substantially limited with respect to any other major life activity." 29 CFR pt. 1630, App. § 1630.2(j) (1998) (emphasis added) ("If an individual is substantially limited in any other major life activity, no determination should be made as to whether the individual is substantially limited in working" (emphasis added)).

Assuming without deciding that working is a major life activity and that the EEOC regulations interpreting the term "substantially limits" are reasonable, petitioners have failed to allege adequately that their poor eyesight is regarded as an impairment that substantially limits them in the major life activity of working. They allege only that respondent regards their poor vision as precluding them from holding positions as a "global airline pilot." Because the position of global airline pilot is a single job, this allegation does not support the claim that respondent regards petitioners as having a substantially limiting impairment. See 29 CFR § 1630.2(j)(3)(i) ("The inability to perform a single, particular job does not constitute a substantial limitation in the major life activity of working"). Indeed, there are a number of other positions utilizing petitioners' skills, such as regional pilot and pilot instructor to name a few, that are available to them. Even under the EEOC's Interpretative Guidance, to which petitioners ask us to defer, "an individual who cannot be a commercial airline pilot because of a minor vision impairment, but who can be a commercial airline co-pilot or a pilot for a courier service, would not be substantially limited in the major life activity of working." 29 CFR pt. 1630, App. § 1630.2.

Petitioners also argue that if one were to assume that a substantial number of airline carriers have similar vision requirements, they would be substantially limited in the major life activity of working. Even assuming for the sake of argument that the adoption of similar vision requirements by other carriers would represent a substantial limitation on the major life activity of working, the argument is nevertheless flawed. It is not enough to say that if the physical criteria of a single employer were imputed to all similar employers one would be regarded as substantially limited in the major life activity of working only as a result of this imputation. An otherwise valid job requirement, such as a height requirement, does not become invalid simply because it would limit a person's employment opportunities in a substantial way if it were adopted by a substantial number of employers. Because petitioners have not alleged, and cannot demonstrate, that respondent's vision requirement reflects a belief that petitioners' vision substantially limits them, we agree with the decision of the Court of Appeals affirming the dismissal of petitioners' claim that they are regarded as disabled.

JUSTICE GINSBURG concurring.

I agree that 42 U.S.C. § 12102(2)(A) does not reach the legions of people with correctable disabilities. The strongest clues to Congress' perception of the domain of the Americans with Disabilities Act (ADA), as I see it, are legislative findings that "some 43,000,000 Americans have one or more physical or mental disabilities," § 12101(a)(1), and that "individuals with disabilities are a discrete and insular minority," persons "subjected to a history of purposeful unequal treatment, and relegated to a position of political powerlessness in our society," § 12101(a)(7). * * *

JUSTICE STEVENS, with whom JUSTICE BREYER joins, dissenting.

I

* * *

In my view, when an employer refuses to hire the individual "because of" his prosthesis, and the prosthesis in no way affects his ability to do the job, that employer has unquestionably discriminated against the individual in violation of the Act. Subsection (B) of the definition, in fact, sheds a revelatory light on the question whether Congress was concerned only about the corrected or mitigated status of a person's impairment. If the Court is correct that "[a] 'disability' exists only where" a person's "present" or "actual" condition is substantially impaired, there would be no reason to include in the protected class those who were once disabled but who are now fully recovered. Subsection (B) of the Act's definition, however, plainly covers a person who previously had a serious hearing impairment that has since been completely cured. See *School Bd. of Nassau Cty. v. Arline*, 480 U.S. 273, 281, 107 S.Ct. 1123, 94 L.Ed.2d 307 (1987). Still, if I correctly understand the

Court's opinion, it holds that one who continues to wear a hearing aid that she has worn all her life might not be covered—fully cured impairments are covered, but merely treatable ones are not. The text of the Act surely does not require such a bizarre result.

The three prongs of the statute, rather, are most plausibly read together not to inquire into whether a person is currently "functionally" limited in a major life activity, but only into the existence of an impairment—present or past—that substantially limits, or did so limit, the individual before amelioration. This reading avoids the counterintuitive conclusion that the ADA's safeguards vanish when individuals make themselves more employable by ascertaining ways to overcome their physical or mental limitations.

To the extent that there may be doubt concerning the meaning of the statutory text, ambiguity is easily removed by looking at the legislative history. * * *

The ADA originated in the Senate. The Senate Report states that "whether a person has a disability should be assessed without regard to the availability of mitigating measures, such as reasonable accommodations or auxiliary aids." S.Rep. No. 101–116, p. 23 (1989). The Report further explained, in discussing the "regarded as" prong:

> "[An] important goal of the third prong of the [disability] definition is to ensure that persons with medical conditions that are under control, and that therefore do not currently limit major life activities, are not discriminated against on the basis of their medical conditions. For example, individuals with controlled diabetes or epilepsy are often denied jobs for which they are qualified. Such denials are the result of negative attitudes and misinformation." *Id.*, at 24.

When the legislation was considered in the House of Representatives, its Committees reiterated the Senate's basic understanding of the Act's coverage, with one minor modification: They clarified that "correctable" or "controllable" disabilities were covered in the first definitional prong as well. The Report of the House Committee on the Judiciary states, in discussing the first prong, that, when determining whether an individual's impairment substantially limits a major life activity, "[t]he impairment should be assessed without considering whether mitigating measures, such as auxiliary aids or reasonable accommodations, would result in a less-than-substantial limitation." H.R.Rep. No. 101–485, pt. III, p. 28 (1990). The Report continues that "a person with epilepsy, an impairment which substantially limits a major life activity, is covered under this test," *ibid.*, as is a person with poor hearing, "even if the hearing loss is corrected by the use of a hearing aid." *Id.*, at 29.

The Report of the House Committee on Education and Labor likewise states that "[w]hether a person has a disability should be assessed without regard to the availability of mitigating measures, such as reasonable accommodations or auxiliary aids." Id., pt. II, at 52. To make matters perfectly plain, the Report adds:

> "For example, a person who is hard of hearing is substantially limited in the major life activity of hearing, even though the loss may be corrected through the use of a hearing aid. Likewise, persons with impairments, such as epilepsy or diabetes, which substantially limit a major life activity are covered under the first prong of the definition of disability, even if the effects of the impairment are controlled by medication." Ibid. (emphasis added).

All of the Reports, indeed, are replete with references to the understanding that the Act's protected class includes individuals with various medical conditions that ordinarily are perfectly "correctable" with medication or treatment. * * *

In addition, each of the three Executive agencies charged with implementing the Act has consistently interpreted the Act as mandating that the presence of disability turns on an individual's uncorrected state. * * *

The EEOC's Interpretive Guidance provides that "[t]he determination of whether an individual is substantially limited in a major life activity must be made on a case by case basis, without regard to mitigating measures such as medicines, or assistive or prosthetic devices." 29 CFR pt. 1630, App. § 1630.2(j) (1998). The EEOC further explains:

> "[A]n individual who uses artificial legs would * * * be substantially limited in the major life activity of walking because the individual is unable to walk without the aid of prosthetic devices. Similarly, a diabetic who without insulin would lapse into a coma would be substantially limited because the individual cannot perform major life activities without the aid of medication." Ibid.

The Department of Justice has reached the same conclusion. [See majority opinion.] 28 CFR pt. 35, App. A, § 35.104 (1998). The Department of Transportation has issued a regulation adopting this same definition of "disability." See 49 CFR pt. 37.3 (1998).

In my judgment, the Committee Reports and the uniform agency regulations merely confirm the message conveyed by the text of the Act—at least insofar as it applies to impairments such as the loss of a limb, the inability to hear, or any condition such as diabetes that is substantially limiting without medication. * * *

II

* * *

This case * * * is not about whether petitioners are genuinely qualified or whether they can perform the job of an airline pilot without posing an undue safety risk. The case just raises the threshold question whether petitioners are members of the ADA's protected class. It simply asks whether the ADA lets petitioners in the door in the same way as the

Age Discrimination in Employment Act of 1967 does for every person who is at least 40 years old, see 29 U.S.C. § 631(a), and as Title VII of the Civil Rights Act of 1964 does for every single individual in the work force. Inside that door lies nothing more than basic protection from irrational and unjustified discrimination because of a characteristic that is beyond a person's control. Hence, this particular case, at its core, is about whether, assuming that petitioners can prove that they are "qualified," the airline has any duty to come forward with some legitimate explanation for refusing to hire them because of their uncorrected eyesight, or whether the ADA leaves the airline free to decline to hire petitioners on this basis even if it is acting purely on the basis of irrational fear and stereotype.

* * *

III

* * *

* * * Since the purpose of the ADA is to dismantle employment barriers based on society's accumulated myths and fears, see 42 U.S.C. § 12101(a)(8); *Arline*, 480 U.S., at 283–284, 107 S.Ct. 1123, it is especially ironic to deny protection for persons with substantially limiting impairments that, when corrected, render them fully able and employable. Insofar as the Court assumes that the majority of individuals with impairments such as prosthetic limbs or epilepsy will still be covered under its approach because they are substantially limited "notwithstanding the use of a corrective device," I respectfully disagree as an empirical matter. Although it is of course true that some of these individuals are substantially limited in any condition, Congress enacted the ADA in part because such individuals are not ordinarily substantially limited in their mitigated condition, but rather are often the victims of "stereotypic assumptions not truly indicative of the individual ability of such individuals to participate in, and contribute to, society." 42 U.S.C. § 12101(a)(7).

It has also been suggested that if we treat as "disabilities" impairments that may be mitigated by measures as ordinary and expedient as wearing eyeglasses, a flood of litigation will ensue. The suggestion is misguided. Although vision is of critical importance for airline pilots, in most segments of the economy whether an employee wears glasses—or uses any of several other mitigating measures—is a matter of complete indifference to employers. It is difficult to envision many situations in which a qualified employee who needs glasses to perform her job might be fired—as the statute requires—"because of," 42 U.S.C. § 12112, the fact that she cannot see well without them. Such a proposition would be ridiculous in the garden-variety case. On the other hand, if an accounting firm, for example, adopted a guideline refusing to hire any incoming accountant who has uncorrected vision of less than 20/100—or, by the same token, any person who is unable without medication to avoid having seizures—such a rule would seem to be the essence of invidious discrimination.

JUSTICE BREYER, dissenting.

We must draw a statutory line that either (1) will include within the category of persons authorized to bring suit under the Americans with Disabilities Act of 1990 some whom Congress may not have wanted to protect (those who wear ordinary eyeglasses), or (2) will exclude from the threshold category those whom Congress certainly did want to protect (those who successfully use corrective devices or medicines, such as hearing aids or prostheses or medicine for epilepsy). Faced with this dilemma, the statute's language, structure, basic purposes, and history require us to choose the former statutory line, as JUSTICE STEVENS (whose opinion I join) well explains. I would add that, if the more generous choice of threshold led to too many lawsuits that ultimately proved without merit or otherwise drew too much time and attention away from those whom Congress clearly sought to protect, there is a remedy. The Equal Employment Opportunity Commission (EEOC), through regulation, might draw finer definitional lines, excluding some of those who wear eyeglasses (say, those with certain vision impairments who readily can find corrective lenses), thereby cabining the overly broad extension of the statute that the majority fears.

The majority questions whether the EEOC could do so, for the majority is uncertain whether the EEOC possesses typical agency regulation-writing authority with respect to the statute's definitions. The majority poses this question because the section of the statute, 42 U.S.C. § 12116, that says the EEOC "shall issue regulations" also says these regulations are "to carry out this subchapter" (namely, § 12111 to § 12117, the employment subchapter); and the section of the statute that contains the three-pronged definition of "disability" precedes "this subchapter," the employment subchapter, to which § 12116 specifically refers. (Emphasis added).

Nonetheless, the employment subchapter, i.e., "this subchapter," includes other provisions that use the defined terms, for example a provision that forbids "discriminat[ing] against a qualified individual with a disability because of the disability." § 12112(a). The EEOC might elaborate through regulations the meaning of "disability" in this last-mentioned provision, if elaboration is needed in order to "carry out" the substantive provisions of "this subchapter." An EEOC regulation that elaborated the meaning of this use of the word "disability" would fall within the scope both of the basic definitional provision and also the substantive provisions of "this" later subchapter, for the word "disability" appears in both places.

There is no reason to believe that Congress would have wanted to deny the EEOC the power to issue such a regulation, at least if the regulation is consistent with the earlier statutory definition and with the relevant interpretations by other enforcement agencies. The physical location of the definitional section seems to reflect only drafting or stylistic, not substantive, objectives. And to pick and choose among which of "this subchapter['s]" words the EEOC has the power to explain would inhibit the development of law that coherently interprets this important statute.

Notes and Questions

1. *Companion Cases.* On the same day that it announced its decision in *Sutton*, the Court also announced decisions in two other cases to which the analysis of *Sutton* was relevant. In Murphy v. United Parcel Service, Inc., 527 U.S. 516, 119 S.Ct. 2133, 144 L.Ed.2d 484 (1999), the Court held that for purposes of assessing "disability" under the first prong of the ADA definition, Murphy's high blood pressure, like the severe myopia of the Sutton sisters, must be considered in its mitigated, medicated state. The Court in *Murphy* also held that Murphy failed to advance sufficient evidence to prove that he was regarded as being unable to work in "a class of jobs utilizing his skills" as a mechanic; he "put forward no evidence that he is regarded as unable to perform any mechanic job that does not call for driving a commercial motor vehicle * * *." Id. at 524.

In Albertsons, Inc. v. Kirkingburg, 527 U.S. 555, 119 S.Ct. 2162, 144 L.Ed.2d 518 (1999), the Court held that mitigating measures "undertaken, whether consciously or not, with the body's own systems" also must be taken into account when assessing whether an impairment is substantially limiting. In considering whether Kirkingburg's impaired, effectively monocular vision constituted a disability, therefore, it was necessary to consider the extent to which his brain and visual system were able to compensate for the weakness of one of his eyes.

2. *Congressional Intent.* Did the majority in *Sutton* or Justice Stevens have the better of the argument over probable congressional intent on the coverage of impaired individuals who avoid substantial limitations on major life activities through mitigating measures? For criticisms of the Court, see, e.g., Aviam Soifer, The Disability Term: Dignity, Default, and Negative Capability, 47 UCLA L.Rev. 1279 (2000); Bonnie Poitras Tucker, The Supreme Court's Definition of Disability Under the ADA: A Return to the Dark Ages, 52 Ala. L. Rev. 321 (2000); Matthew Diller, Judicial Backlash, the ADA, and the Civil Rights Model, 21 Berk. J. Emp. & Lab.L. 19 (2000); Linda Hamilton Krieger, Socio–Legal Backlash, 21 Berk. J. Emp. & Lab. L. 476 (2000). But cf. Samuel R. Bagenstos, The Americans with Disabilities Act as Welfare Reform, 44 Will. & Mary L.Rev. 921 (2003) (critics misinterpret legislative history of ADA). Some state courts have interpreted similar language in their definition of disability to cover those who are substantially limited in the absence of mitigation. See, e.g., Dahill v. Police Dept. of Boston, 434 Mass. 233, 748 N.E.2d 956 (2001).

If Justice Breyer correctly surmised that Congress did not anticipate protecting "those who wear ordinary eyeglasses", but did contemplate protecting "those who successfully use corrective devices or medicines, such as hearing aids or prostheses or medicine for epilepsy", how should the Court have ruled? Could the Court have decided the case by holding that those whose vision can be corrected with ordinary eyeglasses do not suffer from an impairment, because they are not socially stigmatized as abnormal? Cf. Samuel R. Bagenstos, Subordination, Stigma, and "Disability", 86 Va. L. Rev. 397 (2000) (ADA protects only those individuals subjected to stigma).

3. *Relevance of EEOC Regulations and Interpretive Guidance?* Why did the Court in *Sutton* not give deference to the views of the EEOC on the mitigating measures issue, given uncertain congressional intent and the Court's *Chevron* doctrine? See Chevron U.S.A., Inc. v. Natural Resources Defense Council, Inc., 467 U.S. 837, 104 S.Ct. 2778, 81 L.Ed.2d 694 (1984) ("if the statute is silent or ambiguous with respect to the specific issue, the question for the court is whether the agency's answer is based on a permissible construction of the statute"). Is it because the definition of disability is contained in "the generally applicable provisions of the ADA" for which "[n]o agency * * * has been given authority to issue regulations?" If so, why did the Court nonetheless state that it did not have to consider "what deference is due" the EEOC's regulations or its interpretive guidelines on the meaning of disability? Does the Court indicate that the EEOC's view on the mitigation issue cannot withstand review even under the *Chevron* "permissible construction" standard? See generally Ruth Colker, The Americans with Disabilities Act: A Windfall for Defendants, 34 Harv. C.R.-C.L. L.Rev. 99 (1999) (criticizing the courts for failing, inter alia, to give deference to the EEOC regulations and guidelines).

4. *Does* Sutton *Preclude Per Se Disabilities?* Does the analysis in *Sutton* answer the question left open in *Bragdon* concerning "whether HIV infection is a per se disability under the ADA?" Does *Sutton*'s stress on the "with respect to an individual" language in the ADA's definition of disability indicate that neither the EEOC or the courts can define a particular condition as a "per se disability"? In *Albertsons* the Court cited *Bragdon* for the proposition that "some impairments may invariably cause a substantial limitation of a major life activity", though it doubted this is true for monocular vision and stressed the importance of "case-by-case" determination of disability. See also Toyota Motor Mfg. v. Williams, 534 U.S. 184, 122 S.Ct. 681, 151 L.Ed.2d 615 (2002), infra p. 524.

The EEOC's Interpretive Guidance states that the "determination of whether an individual is substantially limited in a major life activity must be made on a case by case basis * * *." 29 C.F.R. pt. 1630, app. § 1630.2(j) (1996). On the other hand, the Guidance also states that some "impairments * * * such as HIV infection, are inherently substantially limiting." Id. Is that guideline consistent with *Sutton*? Even if not, might the EEOC based on scientific analysis of certain diseases and conditions at least articulate a list of physical and mental conditions that are "impairments" and thus satisfy the first element of the ADA's definition of disability? The EEOC's Enforcement Guidance seems to take this step for mental illnesses, discussed in note 14 infra. See also Sharona Hoffman, Corrective Justice and Title I of the ADA, 52 Am. Univ.L.Rev. 1213 (2003) (Congress should authorize EEOC to develop an exclusive list of covered impairments).

5. *When Are Mitigated Impairments Still Substantially Limiting?* When might those with mitigated impairments be substantially limited? This question presumably turns in part on what are defined as major life activities. Are individuals with prosthetic legs normally substantially limited

in their ability to run? Are those with prosthetic arms or hands necessarily substantially limited in lifting or writing? Cf. Gillen v. Fallon Ambulance Service, Inc., 283 F.3d 11 (1st Cir.2002) (genetic amputee with only one completely functioning arm may be substantially limited in major life activity of lifting). In which major life activities might an effectively medicated diabetic or epileptic be limited? See, e.g., Lawson v. CSX Transp., Inc., 245 F.3d 916, 923 (7th Cir.2001) (diabetes can substantially limit the major life activity of eating); EEOC v. Sara Lee Corp., 237 F.3d 349 (4th Cir. 2001) (medicated epileptic who could drive, work and care for son is not disabled); Otting v. J.C. Penney Co., 223 F.3d 704 (8th Cir.2000) (since sporadic severe seizures continued after medication and prevented driving and solitary bathing, epilepsy remained a disability). Can controlled hypertension be substantially limiting? A hearing dysfunction mitigated by an auditory device?

6. *Is It Sufficient That the Effects of Treatment Are Substantially Limiting?* Consider the *Sutton* Court's argument that it would be "anomalous" to ignore the negative side effects of mitigating measures when assessing whether an individual is disabled. Must the treatment having these side effects be shown to be medically necessary or prudent? See, e.g., Hill v. Kansas City Area Transportation Authority, 181 F.3d 891 (8th Cir.1999) (medication must be medically required); Christian v. St. Anthony Medical Ctr., 117 F.3d 1051 (7th Cir.1997) (necessary and prescribed treatment may cause protected disability). Can an employer discriminate against an employee because of a minor side effect, such as an unattractive facial twitch, of an effective treatment that is necessary to avoid death or the aggravation of a serious disability such as cancer?

7. *Coverage of Individuals Whose Conditions Could Be, but Have not Been, Mitigated?* How should courts treat conditions that could be mitigated, but have not been? Should it make a difference at what risk, at what effort, and at what expense the condition can be alleviated or eliminated? In Hein v. All America Plywood Co., Inc., 232 F.3d 482, 487 (6th Cir.2000), the court held that a truck driver with hypertension was not protected as a person with a disability because he was able to function normally in a medicated state, and his "voluntary failure to obtain medication, rather than the physical condition of hypertension itself * * * was the direct cause of his temporary inability to work." See also Tangires v. Johns Hopkins, 79 F.Supp.2d 587 (D.Md.), aff'd, 230 F.3d 1354 (4th Cir.2000) (plaintiff who refused to take asthma medication because of "unsubstantiated" fear of its effect was not substantially limited). See generally Lisa E. Key, Voluntary Disabilities and the ADA: A Reasonable Interpretation of "Reasonable Accommodations", 48 Hastings L. J. 75, 96 (1996) (mutability of a condition should be relevant to what employer accommodation is reasonable, rather than to definition of disability).

8. *"Record" of a Substantially Limiting Impairment.* Might the Sutton sisters have been more successful had they alleged discrimination because of their having a "record" of an impairment? Presumably each sister suffered from severe myopia and was substantially limited in her ability to see before receiving prescriptions for corrective lenses. Does § 12102(2)(B) of the ADA provide protection only against discrimination for having once been disabled, rather than against discrimination due to the potential for a future reoccur-

rence of past disability? But why would anyone ever discriminate against someone for having once been disabled except out of fear of a reoccurrence? Would it matter whether the Sutton sisters could have proven that they were not hired because of an irrational fear that their vision would deteriorate into an uncorrectable state, rather than because of a concern, whether or not rational, that they would temporarily lose their mitigating lenses because of extreme in-flight turbulence or inadvertence?

9. *"Regarded As" Impaired.* The *Sutton* Court states that there are "two apparent ways" that individuals may come within ADA coverage under the third prong of the definition of disability in § 12102(2)(C) of the ADA. The Court contemplates coverage (i) where an employer mistakenly believes that an individual has a condition that would satisfy the definition of disability if it existed, and (ii) where an employer mistakenly believes that a real impairment substantially limits a major life function. The *Sutton* Court, however, does not suggest coverage where an employer has a third kind of mistaken belief: that an actual condition is physiologically abnormal when it is in fact normal and thus not an impairment.

The *Sutton* Court's delineation of coverage is consistent with the EEOC's regulations. While the EEOC's definition of "regarded as having such an impairment" allows the "substantially limits" element to be totally dependent on "the attitudes of others toward such impairment", 29 C.F.R. § 1630.2(*l*)(2), the "impairment" element cannot be totally dependent on the subjective perceptions of employers or others. This explains why individuals cannot be protected under the "regarded as" prong when an employer refuses to hire them because they have, or are regarded as having, some characteristic, "such as eye color, hair color, left-handedness, or height, weight or muscle tone that are within 'normal' range and are not the result of a physiological disorder." 29 C.F.R. pt. 1630, app. § 1630.2(h). See, e.g., EEOC v. Watkins Motor Lines, Inc., 463 F.3d 436 (6th Cir. 2006) (non-physiologically caused "morbid obesity" not an impairment); Francis v. City of Meriden, 129 F.3d 281 (2d Cir.1997) (since being overweight is not an impairment, being regarded as overweight is also not); Tsetseranos v. Tech Prototype, Inc., 893 F.Supp. 109, 119 (D.N.H.1995) (pregnancy not an impairment); de la Torres v. Bolger, 781 F.2d 1134, 1138 (5th Cir.1986) (left-handedness not an impairment).

10. *Working as a Major Life Activity.* Why does the *Sutton* Court in dicta question the EEOC's assumption that working is a major life activity, an assumption that the Court in *Arline* had seemed to endorse? Do you understand the "conceptual" circle that apparently troubles at least some members of the majority? Is that circle in part broken by the limitation on the meaning of "being regarded as" highlighted in the last note, so that employment decisions based on "normal" conditions do not qualify disadvantaged workers for coverage? Is it also in part broken by the EEOC's requirement, endorsed at least as a "minimum" standard by the *Sutton* majority, that ADA plaintiffs must allege that they are unable, or are regarded as being unable, to work in a broad class or range of jobs?

11. *Rationale for not Treating the Exclusion from a Single or Narrow Class of Jobs as Substantially Limiting?* If working is treated as a major life activity, are the EEOC's restrictions justifiable? Does it make sense to read

the ADA as not reaching an employer's failure to reasonably accommodate a worker whose development of an abnormal physiological condition, such as carpal-tunnel syndrome, affects the employer's assumptions about her ability to perform the particular job that she presumably chose as her best employment opportunity before her impairment? Hasn't such a worker been substantially affected by her impairment? Or does the potential economic burden of the reasonable accommodation requirement provide a rationale for not protecting those who cannot establish that their impairment affects their ability to perform a range of alternative jobs as well?

12. *Do Plaintiffs Have to Prove Absence of Any Work Utilizing Their Skills?* Does the *Sutton* Court's application of the EEOC's standard mean that plaintiffs claiming substantial limits on their ability to work must at least establish that there is no available alternative work utilizing their "training, skills, and abilities"? In *Murphy* the Court noted evidence that the plaintiff "could perform jobs such as diesel mechanic, automotive mechanic, gas-engine repairer, and gas-welding mechanic, all of which utilize petitioner's mechanical skills." 527 U.S. at 524–25. Might it be sufficient for plaintiffs to show that they have in fact been excluded from a large number and broad range of jobs, regardless of the remaining alternatives? What do the EEOC regulations indicate? See 29 C.F.R. § 1630.2(j)(3)(i) and (ii)(B), (C). What if a plaintiff has found alternative employment? In *Murphy* the Court noted that the plaintiff had "secured another job as a mechanic shortly after leaving" the defendant's employ. 527 U.S. at 524.

Should plaintiffs be able to prove a substantial limitation on their ability to work by relying only on testimony on the effects of their impairment? See, e.g., McKay v. Toyota Motor Mfg., U.S.A., Inc., 110 F.3d 369 (6th Cir.1997) (considering expert witness testimony on the effects of plaintiff's carpal tunnel syndrome on her ability to lift and to engage in repetitive activities, and thus to perform a range of manufacturing jobs). Some courts have demanded that plaintiffs present detailed vocational data. See, e.g., Duncan v. Washington Metropolitan Area Transit Authority, 240 F.3d 1110 (D.C.Cir. 2001) (en banc) (plaintiff must introduce quantitative evidence of the number and type of jobs available in the geographical area, for persons with similar skills, from which plaintiff would be disqualified because of his disability).

13. *"Substantially Limiting" in "Regarded as" Impaired Cases.* The Sutton sisters did not aver that they were actually substantially limited in their ability to work, but only that United's management regarded them as being unable to do work for which they had special training and skills. Does the Court's treatment of this claim, especially in the final full paragraph of the majority opinion, rest on the position of "global airline pilot" being only a single job? Or would the Court also require plaintiffs to prove that they are regarded as being unable to work by other alternative employers as well as by the defendant? The lower courts have not required Title VII plaintiffs to prove that employers other than the defendant share the defendant's bias. See, e.g., EEOC v. Heartway Corp., 466 F.3d 1156 (10th Cir. 2006). Cf. Cook v. Rhode Island Dep't of Mental Health, 10 F.3d 17, 25–26 (1st Cir.1993) (holding that the Rehabilitation Act does not require plaintiffs to seek other jobs unsuccessfully to prove that an employer's discrimination had a substantially limiting effect: "If the rationale proffered by an employer in the

context of a single refusal to hire adequately evinces that the employer treats a particular condition as a disqualifier for a wide range of employment opportunities, proof of a far-flung pattern of rejections may not be necessary."); E.E. Black, Ltd. v. Marshall, 497 F.Supp. 1088, 1100 (D.Haw.1980) ("In evaluating whether there is a substantial handicap to employment, it must be assumed that all employers offering the same job or similar jobs would use the same requirement or screening process.").

14. *Application to Emotional or Mental Illness.* Will plaintiffs who can establish that they suffer, or are regarded as suffering, from an emotional or mental illness covered as an impairment also be able readily to establish that it affects their ability to be employed in a broad range of jobs? After *Sutton* this presumably is not true for those suffering from mental illnesses that can be controlled through medication. Does *Sutton* mean that such individuals can be discharged because of an employer's general, or even irrational, fears that their medication will lose its efficacy or will not be taken? Or might proof of such fears establish that the employees are being regarded as substantially limited in their ability to do any work or perhaps to engage in some other major life activity?

15. *Alternatives to Working as Major Life Activities.* After *Sutton* would plaintiffs be well advised to attempt to establish coverage by claiming substantial limitations on some major life activity other than working? Will there be many cases where plaintiffs could meet the EEOC standards for showing a substantial limitation on their ability to work, as applied in *Sutton*, without also being able to show a substantial limitation on some other major life activity? In *Kirkingburg*, see 527 U.S. at 565, the Court reiterated *Bragdon*'s conclusion that substantial limitations need not be "utter inabilities" and also cited with apparent approval the EEOC's definition of "substantially limits" as being "significantly restricted * * * compared to the condition, manner, or duration under which the average person in the general population can perform." See 29 C.F.R. § 1639.2(j)(1)(ii). See also Steven S. Locke, The Incredible Shrinking Protected Class: Redefining the Scope of Disability Under the Americans with Disabilities Act, 68 U. Colo. L. Rev. 107 (1997) (arguing that eliminating working as a major life activity could benefit ADA plaintiffs by refocusing courts' attention on the ability to perform particular physical and mental tasks, rather than on employment effects).

Consider, however, how the following decision affects using other life activities to substitute for work.

TOYOTA MOTOR MFG. v. WILLIAMS
Supreme Court of the United States, 2002.
534 U.S. 184, 122 S.Ct. 681, 151 L.Ed.2d 615.

JUSTICE O'CONNOR delivered the opinion of the Court.

I

Respondent began working at petitioner's automobile manufacturing plant in Georgetown, Kentucky, in August 1990. She was soon placed on an engine fabrication assembly line, where her duties included work with pneumatic tools. Use of these tools eventually caused pain in respondent's hands, wrists, and arms. She sought treatment at petitioner's in-house medical service, where she was diagnosed with bilateral carpal tunnel syndrome and bilateral tendinitis. Respondent consulted a personal physician who placed her on permanent work restrictions that precluded her from lifting more than 20 pounds or from "frequently lifting or carrying of objects weighing up to 10 pounds," engaging in "constant repetitive ... flexion or extension of [her] wrists or elbows," performing "overhead work," or using "vibratory or pneumatic tools."

In light of these restrictions, for the next two years petitioner assigned respondent to various modified duty jobs. Nonetheless, respondent missed some work for medical leave, and eventually filed a claim under the Kentucky Workers' Compensation Act. The parties settled this claim, and respondent returned to work. She was unsatisfied by petitioner's efforts to accommodate her work restrictions, however, and responded by bringing an action in the United States District Court for the Eastern District of Kentucky alleging that petitioner had violated the ADA by refusing to accommodate her disability. That suit was also settled, and as part of the settlement, respondent returned to work in December 1993.

Upon her return, petitioner placed respondent on a team in Quality Control Inspection Operations (QCIO). QCIO is responsible for four tasks: (1) "assembly paint"; (2) "paint second inspection"; (3) "shell body audit"; and (4) "ED surface repair." Respondent was initially placed on a team that performed only the first two of these tasks, and for a couple of years, she rotated on a weekly basis between them. In assembly paint, respondent visually inspected painted cars moving slowly down a conveyor. She scanned for scratches, dents, chips, or any other flaws that may have occurred during the assembly or painting process, at a rate of one car every 54 seconds. When respondent began working in assembly paint, inspection team members were required to open and shut the doors, trunk, and/or hood of each passing car. Sometime during respondent's tenure, however, the position was modified to include only visual inspection with few or no manual tasks. Paint second inspection required team members to use their hands to wipe each painted car with a glove as it moved along a conveyor. The parties agree that respondent was physically capable of performing both of these jobs and that her performance was satisfactory.

During the fall of 1996, petitioner announced that it wanted QCIO employees to be able to rotate through all four of the QCIO processes. Respondent therefore received training for the shell body audit job, in which team members apply a highlight oil to the hood, fender, doors, rear quarter panel, and trunk of passing cars at a rate of approximately one car per minute. The highlight oil has the viscosity of salad oil, and employees spread it on cars with a sponge attached to a block of wood. After they wipe each car with the oil, the employees visually inspect it for flaws. Wiping the cars required respondent to hold her hands and arms up around shoulder height for several hours at a time.

A short while after the shell body audit job was added to respondent's rotations, she began to experience pain in her neck and shoulders. Respondent again sought care at petitioner's in-house medical service, where she was diagnosed with myotendinitis bilateral periscapular, an inflammation of the muscles and tendons around both of her shoulder blades; myotendinitis and myositis bilateral forearms with nerve compression causing median nerve irritation; and thoracic outlet compression, a condition that causes pain in the nerves that lead to the upper extremities. Respondent requested that petitioner accommodate her medical conditions by allowing her to return to doing only her original two jobs in QCIO, which respondent claimed she could still perform without difficulty.

The parties disagree about what happened next. According to respondent, petitioner refused her request and forced her to continue working in the shell body audit job, which caused her even greater physical injury. According to petitioner, respondent simply began missing work on a regular basis. Regardless, it is clear that on December 6, 1996, the last day respondent worked at petitioner's plant, she was placed under a no-work-of-any-kind restriction by her treating physicians. On January 27, 1997, respondent received a letter from petitioner that terminated her employment, citing her poor attendance record.

Respondent filed a charge of disability discrimination with the Equal Employment Opportunity Commission (EEOC). After receiving a right to sue letter, respondent filed suit against petitioner in the United States District Court for the Eastern District of Kentucky. Her complaint alleged that petitioner had violated the ADA and the Kentucky Civil Rights Act, Ky. Rev. Stat. Ann. §§ 344.010 et seq. (1997 and Supp. 2000), by failing to reasonably accommodate her disability and by terminating her employment. * * *

Respondent based her claim that she was "disabled" under the ADA on the ground that her physical impairments substantially limited her in (1) manual tasks; (2) housework; (3) gardening; (4) playing with her children; (5) lifting; and (6) working, all of which, she argued, constituted major life activities under the Act. Respondent also argued, in the alternative, that she was disabled under the ADA because she had a record of a substantially limiting impairment and because she was regarded as having such an impairment. See 42 U.S.C. §§ 12102(2)(B–C) (1994 ed.).

After petitioner filed a motion for summary judgment and respondent filed a motion for partial summary judgment on her disability claims, the District Court granted summary judgment to petitioner. The court found that respondent had not been disabled, as defined by the ADA, at the time of petitioner's alleged refusal to accommodate her, and that she had therefore not been covered by the Act's protections or by the Kentucky Civil Rights Act, which is construed consistently with the ADA. * * *

* * * The Court of Appeals for the Sixth Circuit reversed the District Court's ruling on whether respondent was disabled at the time she sought an accommodation * * *. The Court of Appeals held that in order for respondent to demonstrate that she was disabled due to a substantial limitation in the ability to perform manual tasks at the time of her accommodation request, she had to "show that her manual disability involved a 'class' of manual activities affecting the ability to perform tasks at work." Respondent satisfied this test, according to the Court of Appeals, because her ailments "prevented her from doing the tasks associated with certain types of manual assembly line jobs, manual product handling jobs and manual building trade jobs (painting, plumbing, roofing, etc.) that require the gripping of tools and repetitive work with hands and arms extended at or above shoulder levels for extended periods of time." * * * Because the Court of Appeals concluded that respondent had been substantially limited in performing manual tasks and, for that reason, was entitled to partial summary judgment on the issue of whether she was disabled under the Act, it found that it did not need to determine whether respondent had been substantially limited in the major life activities of lifting or working, or whether she had had a "record of" a disability or had been "regarded as" disabled.

* * *

III

The question presented by this case is whether the Sixth Circuit properly determined that respondent was disabled under subsection (A) of the ADA's disability definition at the time that she sought an accommodation from petitioner. 42 U.S.C. § 12102(2)(A). The parties do not dispute that respondent's medical conditions, which include carpal tunnel syndrome, myotendinitis, and thoracic outlet compression, amount to physical impairments. The relevant question, therefore, is whether the Sixth Circuit correctly analyzed whether these impairments substantially limited respondent in the major life activity of performing manual tasks. Answering this requires us to address an issue about which the EEOC regulations are silent: what a plaintiff must demonstrate to establish a substantial limitation in the specific major life activity of performing manual tasks.

Our consideration of this issue is guided first and foremost by the words of the disability definition itself. "Substantially" in the phrase "substantially limits" suggests "considerable" or "to a large degree." See Webster's Third New International Dictionary 2280 (1976) (defining "substantially" as "in a substantial manner" and "substantial" as "considerable in amount, value, or worth" and "being that specified to a large degree or in the main"); see also 17 Oxford English Dictionary 66–67 (2d ed. 1989) ("substantial": "relating to or proceeding from the essence of a thing; essential"; "of ample or considerable amount, quantity, or dimensions"). The word "substantial" thus clearly precludes impairments that interfere in only a minor way with the performance of manual tasks from qualifying as disabilities. Cf. *Albertson's, Inc. v.*

Kirkingburg, 527 U.S. at 565 (explaining that a "mere difference" does not amount to a "significant restriction" and therefore does not satisfy the EEOC's interpretation of "substantially limits").

"Major" in the phrase "major life activities" means important. See Webster's, *supra*, at 1363 (defining "major" as "greater in dignity, rank, importance, or interest"). "Major life activities" thus refers to those activities that are of central importance to daily life. In order for performing manual tasks to fit into this category—a category that includes such basic abilities as walking, seeing, and hearing—the manual tasks in question must be central to daily life. If each of the tasks included in the major life activity of performing manual tasks does not independently qualify as a major life activity, then together they must do so.

That these terms need to be interpreted strictly to create a demanding standard for qualifying as disabled is confirmed by the first section of the ADA, which lays out the legislative findings and purposes that motivate the Act. See 42 U.S.C.§ 12101. When it enacted the ADA in 1990, Congress found that "some 43,000,000 Americans have one or more physical or mental disabilities." § 12101(a)(1). If Congress intended everyone with a physical impairment that precluded the performance of some isolated, unimportant, or particularly difficult manual task to qualify as disabled, the number of disabled Americans would surely have been much higher. * * *

We therefore hold that to be substantially limited in performing manual tasks, an individual must have an impairment that prevents or severely restricts the individual from doing activities that are of central importance to most people's daily lives. The impairment's impact must also be permanent or long-term. See 29 CFR §§ 1630.2(j)(2)(ii)-(iii) (2001).

* * *

An individualized assessment of the effect of an impairment is particularly necessary when the impairment is one whose symptoms vary widely from person to person. Carpal tunnel syndrome, one of respondent's impairments, is just such a condition. While cases of severe carpal tunnel syndrome are characterized by muscle atrophy and extreme sensory deficits, mild cases generally do not have either of these effects and create only intermittent symptoms of numbness and tingling. Carniero, Carpal Tunnel Syndrome: The Cause Dictates the Treatment 66 Cleveland Clinic J. Medicine 159, 161–162 (1999). Studies have further shown that, even without surgical treatment, one quarter of carpal tunnel cases resolve in one month, but that in 22 percent of cases, symptoms last for eight years or longer. See DeStefano, Nordstrom, & Uierkant, Long-term Symptom Outcomes of Carpal Tunnel Syndrome and its Treatment, 22A J. Hand Surgery 200, 204–205 (1997). When pregnancy is the cause of carpal tunnel syndrome, in contrast, the symptoms normally resolve within two weeks of delivery. See Ouellette, Nerve Compression Syndromes of the Upper Extremity in Women, 17

Journal of Musculoskeletal Medicine 536 (2000). Given these large potential differences in the severity and duration of the effects of carpal tunnel syndrome, an individual's carpal tunnel syndrome diagnosis, on its own, does not indicate whether the individual has a disability within the meaning of the ADA.

IV

* * *

The Court of Appeals relied on our opinion in *Sutton v. United Air Lines, Inc.*, for the idea that a "class" of manual activities must be implicated for an impairment to substantially limit the major life activity of performing manual tasks. But *Sutton* said only that "when the major life activity under consideration is that of working, the statutory phrase 'substantially limits' requires ... that plaintiffs allege that they are unable to work in a broad class of jobs." 527 U.S. 471 at 491. Because of the conceptual difficulties inherent in the argument that working could be a major life activity, we have been hesitant to hold as much, and we need not decide this difficult question today. In *Sutton*, we noted that even assuming that working is a major life activity, a claimant would be required to show an inability to work in a "broad range of jobs," rather than a specific job. *Id.*, at 492. But *Sutton* did not suggest that a class-based analysis should be applied to any major life activity other than working. * * * Nothing in the text of the Act, our previous opinions, or the regulations suggests that a class-based framework should apply outside the context of the major life activity of working.

While the Court of Appeals in this case addressed the different major life activity of performing manual tasks, its analysis circumvented *Sutton* by focusing on respondent's inability to perform manual tasks associated only with her job. This was error. When addressing the major life activity of performing manual tasks, the central inquiry must be whether the claimant is unable to perform the variety of tasks central to most people's daily lives, not whether the claimant is unable to perform the tasks associated with her specific job. Otherwise, *Sutton*'s restriction on claims of disability based on a substantial limitation in working will be rendered meaningless because an inability to perform a specific job always can be recast as an inability to perform a "class" of tasks associated with that specific job.

There is also no support in the Act, our previous opinions, or the regulations for the Court of Appeals' idea that the question of whether an impairment constitutes a disability is to be answered only by analyzing the effect of the impairment in the workplace. Indeed, the fact that the Act's definition of "disability" applies not only to Title I of the Act, 42 U.S.C. §§ 12111–12117 (1994 ed.), which deals with employment, but also to the other portions of the Act, which deal with subjects such as public transportation, §§ 12141–12150, 42 U.S.C. §§ 12161–12165 (1994 ed. and Supp. V), and privately provided public accommodations, §§ 12181–12189, demonstrates that the definition is intended to cover individuals with disabling impairments regardless of whether the individuals have any connection to a workplace.

Even more critically, the manual tasks unique to any particular job are not necessarily important parts of most people's lives. As a result, occupation-specific tasks may have only limited relevance to the manual task inquiry. In this case, "repetitive work with hands and arms extended at or above shoulder levels for extended periods of time," the manual task on which the Court of Appeals relied, is not an important part of most people's daily lives. The court, therefore, should not have considered respondent's inability to do such manual work in her specialized assembly line job as sufficient proof that she was substantially limited in performing manual tasks.

At the same time, the Court of Appeals appears to have disregarded the very type of evidence that it should have focused upon. It treated as irrelevant "the fact that [respondent] can ... tend to her personal hygiene [and] carry out personal or household chores." Yet household chores, bathing, and brushing one's teeth are among the types of manual tasks of central importance to people's daily lives, and should have been part of the assessment of whether respondent was substantially limited in performing manual tasks.

The District Court noted that at the time respondent sought an accommodation from petitioner, she admitted that she was able to do the manual tasks required by her original two jobs in QCIO. In addition, according to respondent's deposition testimony, even after her condition worsened, she could still brush her teeth, wash her face, bathe, tend her flower garden, fix breakfast, do laundry, and pick up around the house. The record also indicates that her medical conditions caused her to avoid sweeping, to quit dancing, to occasionally seek help dressing, and to reduce how often she plays with her children, gardens, and drives long distances. But these changes in her life did not amount to such severe restrictions in the activities that are of central importance to most people's daily lives that they establish a manual-task disability as a matter of law. On this record, it was therefore inappropriate for the Court of Appeals to grant partial summary judgment to respondent on the issue whether she was substantially limited in performing manual tasks, and its decision to do so must be reversed. * * *

Notes and Questions

1. *Substituting Other Life Activities for Working.* Does the *Toyota* decision prevent ADA plaintiffs from using restrictions on their ability to do particular work as the basis for claiming a disability, at least unless they can demonstrate that those restrictions prevent them from performing a broad range of jobs otherwise suitable for their knowledge, skills, and abilities? After *Toyota* what must a plaintiff who is no longer able to do particular work, but who cannot meet the standard for showing a substantial limitation on her general ability to work, demonstrate about her condition to establish a disability?

2. *General Teaching of* Toyota *for Meaning of Major Life Activity.* Does the Court's analysis in part IV of its *Toyota* opinion suggest a distinction between, on the one hand, physical, or perhaps mental, functions that are of importance only because they may enable an individual to engage in a major life activity, and, on the other hand, functions that are normally themselves of "central importance to most people's daily lives"? The Court asserts that "repetitive work with hands and arms extended at or above shoulder levels for extended periods of time" "is not an important part of most people's daily lives." The inability to do such work thus makes an impairment a disability only if it prevents an individual from engaging in some other derivative function of "central importance." Similar analysis might suggest that internal bodily functions, such as those associated with critical organs like the lungs or kidney or liver, only contribute to, rather than themselves constitute major life activities. Compare Fiscus v. Wal-Mart Stores, Inc., 385 F.3d 378, 384 (3d Cir. 2004) (kidneys' elimination of waste from blood is major life activity because essential to life), with Furnish v. SVI Systems, Inc., 270 F.3d 445, 450 (7th Cir. 2001) (liver function is not a major life activity). The Court, however, presumably would not draw the same conclusion about "seeing" or "hearing" or "reasoning". See, e.g., Sutton v. United Airlines, Inc., supra (seeing); Mattice v. Memorial Hospital of South Bend, Inc., 249 F.3d 682 (7th Cir. 2001) ("cognitive thinking" is major life activity). These physical or mental functions would seem to have intrinsic value to most people. How are courts to determine which other functions are themselves of central importance, however? The *Toyota* Court also lists "walking" as a major life activity. Is that because physical mobility is of intrinsic worth, or because it is always of central import to most people because of derivative tasks it enables people to perform? Is lifting a major life activity? See, e.g., Gillen v. Fallon Ambulance Service, Inc., 283 F.3d 11 (1st Cir. 2002) (lifting may be a major life activity, substantially limited for individual missing a hand).

3. *Use of "Regarded as" Prong for Other Major Life Activities.* By its teaching on the meaning of major life activity, does the *Toyota* decision also make it more difficult for individuals to secure disability status by claiming that their employer regarded them as being substantially limited in some major life activity other than working? It seems doubtful that Williams would have strengthened her case by contending that Toyota's management regarded her as substantially limited in some major activity away from work. Could the Sutton sisters have convincingly claimed that they were regarded by United as being substantially limited in their ability to see? Are there likely to be many cases where employers reject employees because of misconceptions about the employees' ability to function outside of work? But cf. Mattice v. Memorial Hospital, supra (hospital's alleged opinion that doctor was substantially limited in cognition could be basis for disability status); Doane v. City of Omaha, 115 F.3d 624, 627 (8th Cir.1997) (employer regarded worker who lost sight in one eye as being substantially limited in major life activity of seeing).

4. *Coverage of Nonpermanent Diseases or Injuries?* Does the coverage of individuals with "a record of * * * an impairment" mean that the temporary nature of an impairment should not exclude it from coverage under the ADA? Should abnormal conditions that affect a body system and

substantially limit a major life activity for only a limited period be treated as a disability? The EEOC's regulations state that the "duration or expected duration" of an impairment "should be considered in determining whether an individual is substantially limited in a major life activity." 29 C.F.R. § 1630.2(j)(2)(ii). The courts generally have held that temporary conditions should not be covered. See, e.g., Pollard v. High's of Baltimore, Inc., 281 F.3d 462 (4th Cir. 2002) (temporary back injury not a disability); Branch v. City of New Orleans, 78 F.3d 582 (5th Cir.1996) (ulcerative colitis causing intermittent episodes of limited duration not a disability); McDonald v. Pennsylvania Dep't of Public Welfare, 62 F.3d 92, 96–97 (3d Cir.1995) (worker fired because of inability to work for two months following abdominal surgery not protected by ADA or Rehabilitation Act). But see Aldrich v. Boeing Co., 146 F.3d 1265 (10th Cir.1998) (whether temporary disability substantially limits major life function must be decided on case-by-case basis); Mark v. Burke Rehabilitation Hosp., 6 A.D. Cases 1156 (S.D.N.Y. 1997) (record of disabling cancer of limited duration sufficient).

Is there a convincing policy rationale for not covering temporary conditions? Would Congress have been more concerned about requiring employers to bear the costs of accommodating temporary disabilities than of permanent disabilities? Cf. also Mark Kelman, Market Discrimination and Groups, 53 Stan. L. Rev. 833, 889 (contending that accommodation law should only protect those who suffer continuing social segregation). Recall that the Family and Medical Leave Act of 1993, see page 419 supra, now requires employers to grant employees up to 12 weeks of unpaid leave to address serious health condition, which is defined to include "an illness, injury, impairment or physical or mental condition that involves" "inpatient care" or "continuing treatment by a health care provider." 29 U.S.C. § 2611(11).

5. *Fixed Criteria for Disability Status?* There are certain human characteristics, such as eyesight, hearing, and intelligence, that can be described along a continuum. Accepting the EEOC's use of " 'normal' range" as a criterion for an "impairment", see 29 C.F.R. pt. 1630, app. § 1630.2(h), and the performance of the "average person" as a criterion for "substantially limits", see 29 C.F.R. § 1630.2(j), can fixed lines be drawn for all cases? For instance, could the EEOC establish, based on scientific evidence, 20/200 vision as a cut-off point for a visual impairment that substantially limits the major life activity of seeing? Cf. Chandler v. City of Dallas, 2 F.3d 1385, 1390 (5th Cir.1993) (vision that can be corrected to 20/200 is not a handicap under Rehabilitation Act). Based on psychological studies, could the EEOC stipulate an intelligent quotient of 65 for mental retardation that substantially limits the major life activity of learning?

Should this approach be taken when a plaintiff claims that his impairment, such as a significant learning disability, substantially limits his own potential for reading and learning, even though his high intelligence nonetheless allows him to read and learn at an average level? Cf. Calef v. Gillette Co., 322 F.3d 75 (1st Cir. 2003) (employee with Attention Deficit Hyperactivity Disorder not substantially limited in learning where academic skills are within normal range); Bartlett v. New York State Bd. of Law Examiners, 970 F.Supp. 1094 (S.D.N.Y.1997), affirmed, 156 F.3d 321 (2d Cir.1998), vacated and remanded, 527 U.S. 1031, 119 S.Ct. 2388, 144 L.Ed.2d 790 (1999) (must compare dyslexic's performance with other "high achievers", not with general population). Does the decision in *Kirkingburg*, discussed in note 1 page 519 supra, answer this question by holding that an individual's ability to compensate for an impairment is relevant to whether it is substantially limiting? Does the *Toyota* decision also suggest an answer, by focusing on effects on an ultimately valuable major life activity, rather than on contributory processes? Or might both of these Supreme Court decisions be distinguished?

6. *Should All Physical and Mental Impairments Be Protected?* Should the holdings of *Sutton, Toyota, and Kirkingburg* be overturned by Congress? Legislation to do so has been introduced under the title of the ADA Restoration Act of 2007. H.R. 3195, 110th Cong. 1st Sess. This legislation would define "disability" to be "a physical or mental impairment" or having a record of or being regarded as having such an impairment. This would eliminate the "substantially limits" a "major life activity" condition. The legislation also expressly provides that "mitigating measures" are not to be considered. Should this legislation be enacted? Are there good reasons that a disability discrimination statute should not be even more comprehensively (and simply) structured to proscribe discrimination against any physical or mental condition, including being left-handed or being overweight or being prone to irritability? If we want to prevent "myths, fears and stereotypes" about physical and mental conditions from affecting employment opportunities, why should we insist that there be some actual or perceived abnormal disorder? For an argument that the ADA's coverage should be extended in this way, at least for the overweight, see Jane Byeff Korn, Fat, 77 B.U.L.Rev. 25 (1997).

Reconsider these questions as you study in the following pages the reasonable accommodation requirements imposed on employers by the ADA. Might these obligations explain the hesitancy of some, including many who would condemn discrimination on the basis of any irrelevant condition, to broaden the ADA protected class? Compare, e.g., Kelman, supra (suggesting a normative distinction between those who should benefit from on the one hand anti-discrimination and on the other hand accommodation obligations), with Samuel R. Bagenstos,"Rational Discrimination," Accommodation, and the Politics of (Disability) Civil Rights, 89 Vir. L. Rev. 825 (2003) (denying the normative distinction between accommodation and antidiscrimination requirements).

C. THE DUTY OF REASONABLE ACCOMMODATION

The ADA's imposition of a duty of reasonable accommodation toward individuals with disabilities presents the disability statute's sharpest contrast with the antidiscrimination provisions thus far treated in this book. This duty is asserted through several key provisions of Title I of the Act. First, the core prohibition of employment discrimination expressed in § 102 (a) provides that "[n]o covered entity shall discriminate against a qualified individual with a disability because of the disability of such individual", and § 101(8) defines "qualified individual with a disability" to mean "an individual with a disability who, *with or without reasonable accommodation*, can perform the essential functions of the employment position that such individual holds or desires." (Emphasis supplied). This definition requires employers to evaluate disabled individuals' job performance potential taking into account reasonable accommodations of their disabilities.

Second, § 102(b) lists several ways in which the proscribed discrimination against a "qualified individual with a disability" can occur, including (in subsection (b)(5)):

> (A) not making reasonable accommodation to the known physical or mental limitations of an otherwise qualified individual with a disability who is an applicant or employee, unless [the alleged discriminator] can demonstrate that the accommodation would impose an undue hardship on the operation of the business * * *; or (B) denying employment opportunities to a job applicant or employee who is an otherwise qualified individual with a disability, if such denial is based on the need * * * to make reasonable accommodation to the physical or mental impairments of the employee or applicant;

42 U.S.C. § 12112(b)(5). These provisions together pose a number of difficult procedural and substantive issues.

US AIRWAYS, INC. v. BARNETT
Supreme Court of the United States, 2002.
535 U.S. 391, 122 S.Ct. 1516, 152 L.Ed.2d 589.

JUSTICE BREYER delivered the opinion of the Court.

I

In 1990, Robert Barnett, the plaintiff and respondent here, injured his back while working in a cargo-handling position at petitioner US Airways, Inc. He invoked seniority rights and transferred to a less physically demanding mailroom position. Under US Airways' seniority system, that position, like others, periodically became open to seniority-based employee bidding. In 1992, Barnett learned that at least two employees senior to him intended to bid for the mailroom job. He asked US Airways to accommodate his disability-imposed limitations by making an exception that would allow him to remain in the mailroom. After permitting Barnett to continue his mailroom work for five months while it considered the matter, US Airways eventually decided not to make an exception. And Barnett lost his job.

Barnett then brought this ADA suit claiming, among other things, that he was an "individual with a disability" capable of performing the essential functions of the mailroom job, that the mailroom job amounted to a "reasonable accommodation" of his disability, and that US Airways, in refusing to assign him the job, unlawfully discriminated against him. US Airways moved for summary judgment. It supported its motion with appropriate affidavits, Fed. Rule Civ. Proc. 56, contending that its "well-established" seniority system granted other employees the right to obtain the mailroom position.

The District Court found that the undisputed facts about seniority warranted summary judgment in US Airways' favor. * * *

An en banc panel of the United States Court of Appeals for the Ninth Circuit reversed. It said that the presence of a seniority system is merely "a factor in the undue hardship analysis." And it held that "[a] case-by-case fact intensive analysis is required to determine whether any particular reassignment would constitute an undue hardship to the employer." * * *

II

[W]e must consider the following statutory provisions. First, the ADA says that an employer may not "discriminate against a qualified individual with a disability." 42 U.S.C. § 12112(a). Second, the ADA says that a "qualified" individual includes "an individual with a disability who, with or without reasonable accommodation, can perform the essential functions of" the relevant "employment position." § 12111(8). Third, the ADA says that "discrimination" includes an employer's "not making reasonable accommodations to the known physical or mental limitations of an otherwise qualified ... employee, unless [the employer] can demonstrate that the accommodation would impose an undue hardship on the operation of [its] business." § 12112(b)(5)(A) (emphasis added). Fourth, the ADA says that the term " 'reasonable accommodation' may include ... reassignment to a vacant position." § 12111(9)(B).

* * *

A

US Airways' claim that a seniority system virtually always trumps a conflicting accommodation demand rests primarily upon its view of how the Act treats workplace "preferences." Insofar as a requested accommodation violates a disability-neutral workplace rule, such as a seniority rule, it grants the employee with a disability treatment that other workers could not receive. Yet the Act, US Airways says, seeks only "equal" treatment for those with disabilities See, e.g., 42 U.S.C. § 12101(a)(9). It does not, it contends, require an employer to grant preferential treatment. Cf. H. R. Rep. No. 101–485, pt. 2, p. 66 (1990); S. Rep. No. 101–116, pp. 26–27 (1989) (employer has no "obligation to prefer applicants with disabilities over other applicants"). Hence it does not require the employer to grant a request that, in violating a disability-neutral rule, would provide a preference.

While linguistically logical, this argument fails to recognize what the Act specifies, namely, that preferences will sometimes prove necessary to achieve the Act's basic equal opportunity goal. The Act requires preferences in the form of "reasonable accommodations" that are needed for those with disabilities to obtain the same workplace opportunities that those without disabilities automatically enjoy. By definition any special "accommodation" requires the employer to treat an employee with a disability differently, i.e., preferentially. And the fact that the difference in treatment violates an employer's disability-neutral rule cannot by itself place the accommodation beyond the Act's potential reach.

Were that not so, the "reasonable accommodation" provision could not accomplish its intended objective. Neutral office assignment rules would automatically prevent the accommodation of an employee whose disability-imposed limitations require him to work on the ground floor. Neutral "break-from-work" rules would automatically prevent the accommodation of an individual who needs additional breaks from work, perhaps to permit medical visits. Neutral furniture budget rules would automatically prevent the accommodation of an individual who needs a different kind of chair or desk. Many employers will have neutral rules governing the kinds of actions most needed to reasonably accommodate a worker with a disability. See 42 U.S.C. § 12111(9)(b) (setting forth examples such as "job restructuring," "part-time or modified work schedules," "acquisition or modification of equipment or devices," "and other similar accommodations"). Yet Congress, while providing such examples, said nothing suggesting that the presence of such neutral rules would create an automatic exemption. * * *

In sum, the nature of the "reasonable accommodation" requirement, the statutory examples, and the Act's silence about the exempting effect of neutral rules together convince us that the Act does not create any such automatic exemption. The simple fact that an accommodation would provide a "preference"—in the sense that it would permit the worker with a disability to violate a rule that others must obey—cannot, in and of itself, automatically show that the accommodation is not "reasonable." * * *

US Airways also points to the ADA provisions stating that a " 'reasonable accommodation' may include . . . reassignment to a vacant position." § 12111(9)(B). And it claims that the fact that an established seniority system would assign that position to another worker automatically and always means that the position is not a "vacant" one. Nothing in the Act, however, suggests that Congress intended the word "vacant" to have a specialized meaning. And in ordinary English, a seniority system can give employees seniority rights allowing them to bid for a "vacant" position. The position in this case was held, at the time of suit, by Barnett, not by some other worker; and that position, under the US Airways seniority system, became an "open" one. * * * Moreover, US Airways has said that it "reserves the right to change any and all" portions of the seniority system at will. Consequently, we cannot agree with US Airways about the position's vacancy; nor do we agree that the Act would automatically deny Barnett's accommodation request for that reason.

B

Barnett argues that the statutory words "reasonable accommodation" mean only "effective accommodation," authorizing a court to consider the requested accommodation's ability to meet an individual's disability-related needs, and nothing more. On this view, a seniority rule violation, having nothing to do with the accommodation's effectiveness, has nothing to do with its "reasonableness." It might, at most, help to prove an "undue hardship on the operation of the business." But, he adds, that is a matter that the statute requires the employer to demonstrate, case by case.

In support of this interpretation Barnett points to Equal Employment Opportunity Commission (EEOC) regulations stating that "reasonable accommodation means.... modifications or adjustments ... that enable a qualified individual with a disability to perform the essential functions of [a] position." 29 CFR § 1630(o)(ii) (2001). See also H.R. Rep. No. 101–485, pt. 2, at 66; S. Rep. No. 101–116, at 35 (discussing reasonable accommodations in terms of "effectiveness," while discussing costs in terms of "undue hardship"). Barnett adds that any other view would make the words "reasonable accommodation" and "undue hardship" virtual mirror images—creating redundancy in the statute. And he says that any such other view would create a practical burden of proof dilemma.

The practical burden of proof dilemma arises, Barnett argues, because the statute imposes the burden of demonstrating an "undue hardship" upon the employer, while the burden of proving "reasonable accommodation" remains with the plaintiff, here the employee. This allocation seems sensible in that an employer can more frequently and easily prove the presence of business hardship than an employee can prove its absence. But suppose that an employee must counter a claim of "seniority rule violation" in order to prove that an "accommodation" request is "reasonable." Would that not force the employee to prove what is in effect an absence, i.e., an absence of hardship, despite the statute's insistence that the employer "demonstrate" hardship's presence?

These arguments do not persuade us that Barnett's legal interpretation of "reasonable" is correct. For one thing, in ordinary English the word "reasonable" does not mean "effective." It is the word "accommodation," not the word "reasonable," that conveys the need for effectiveness. An ineffective "modification" or "adjustment" will not accommodate a disabled individual's limitations. Nor does an ordinary English meaning of the term "reasonable accommodation" make of it a simple, redundant mirror image of the term "undue hardship." The statute refers to an "undue hardship on the operation of the business." 42 U.S.C. § 12112 (b)(5)(A). Yet a demand for an effective accommodation could prove unreasonable because of its impact, not on business operations, but on fellow employees—say because it will lead to dismissals, relocations, or modification of employee benefits to which an employer, looking at the matter from the perspective of the business itself, may be relatively indifferent.

Neither does the statute's primary purpose require Barnett's special reading. The statute seeks to diminish or to eliminate the stereotypical thought processes, the thoughtless actions, and the hostile reactions that far too often bar those with disabilities from participating fully in the Nation's life, including the workplace. See generally § 12101(a) and (b). These objectives demand unprejudiced thought and reasonable responsive reaction on the part of employers and fellow workers alike. They will sometimes require affirmative conduct to promote entry of disabled people into the workforce. They do not, however, demand action beyond the realm of the reasonable.

Neither has Congress indicated in the statute, or elsewhere, that the word "reasonable" means no more than "effective." The EEOC regulations do say that reasonable accommodations "enable" a person with a disability to perform the essential functions of a task. But that phrasing simply emphasizes the statutory provision's basic objective. The regulations do not say that "enable" and "reasonable" mean the same thing.
* * *

Finally, an ordinary language interpretation of the word "reasonable" does not create the "burden of proof" dilemma to which Barnett points. Many of the lower courts, while rejecting both US Airways' and Barnett's more absolute views, have reconciled the phrases "reasonable accommodation" and "undue hardship" in a practical way.

They have held that a plaintiff/employee (to defeat a defendant/employer's motion for summary judgment) need only show that an "accommodation" seems reasonable on its face, i.e., ordinarily or in the run of cases. See, e.g., *Reed v. LePage Bakeries, Inc.*, 244 F.3d 254, 259 (CA1 2001) (plaintiff meets burden on reasonableness by showing that, "at least on the face of things," the accommodation will be feasible for the employer) * * *.

Once the plaintiff has made this showing, the defendant/employer then must show special (typically case-specific) circumstances that demonstrate undue hardship in the particular circumstances. See *Reed*, 244 F.3d at 258–259 ("undue hardship inquiry focuses on the hardships imposed ... in the context of the particular [employer's] operations' ")
* * *.

* * * In our opinion, that practical view of the statute, applied consistently with ordinary summary judgment principles, see Fed. Rule Civ. Proc. 56, avoids Barnett's burden of proof dilemma, while reconciling the two statutory phrases ("reasonable accommodation" and "undue hardship").

III

The question in the present case focuses on the relationship between seniority systems and the plaintiff's need to show that an "accommodation" seems reasonable on its face, i.e., ordinarily or in the run of cases. We must assume that the plaintiff, an employee, is an "individual with a disability." He has requested assignment to a mailroom position as a "reasonable accommodation." We also assume that normally such a request would be reasonable within the meaning of the statute, were it not for one circumstance, namely, that the assignment would violate the rules of a seniority system. See § 12111(9) ("reasonable accommodation" may include "reassignment to a vacant position"). Does that circumstance mean that the proposed accommodation is not a "reasonable" one?

In our view, the answer to this question ordinarily is "yes." The statute does not require proof on a case-by-case basis that a seniority system should prevail. That is because it would not be reasonable in the run of cases that the assignment in question trump the rules of a seniority system. To the contrary, it will ordinarily be unreasonable for the assignment to prevail.

A

Several factors support our conclusion that a proposed accommodation will not be reasonable in the run of cases. Analogous case law supports this conclusion, for it has recognized the importance of seniority to employee-management relations. This Court has held that, in the context of a Title VII religious discrimination case, an employer need not adapt to an employee's special worship schedule as a "reasonable accommodation" where doing so would conflict with the seniority rights of other employees. *Trans World Airlines, Inc. v. Hardison,* 432 U.S. 63, 79–80, 53 L. Ed. 2d 113, 97 S.Ct. 2264 (1977). The lower courts have unanimously found that collectively bargained seniority trumps the need for reasonable accommodation in the context of the linguistically similar Rehabilitation Act. * * * And several Circuits, though differing in their reasoning, have reached a similar conclusion in the context of seniority and the ADA. * * * All these cases discuss collectively bargained seniority systems, not systems (like the present system) which are unilaterally imposed by management. But the relevant seniority system advantages, and related difficulties that result from violations of seniority rules, are not limited to collectively bargained systems.

For one thing, the typical seniority system provides important employee benefits by creating, and fulfilling, employee expectations of fair, uniform treatment. These benefits include "job security and an opportunity for steady and predictable advancement based on objective standards." [citations omitted] They include "an element of due process," limiting "unfairness in personnel decisions." Gersuny, Origins of Seniority Provisions in Collective Bargaining, 33 Lab.L.J. 518, 519 (1982). And they consequently encourage employees to invest in the employing company, accepting "less than their value to the firm early in their careers" in return for greater benefits in later years. J. Baron & D. Kreps, Strategic Human Resources: Frameworks for General Managers 288 (1999).

Most important for present purposes, to require the typical employer to show more than the existence of a seniority system might well undermine the employees' expectations of consistent, uniform treatment—expectations upon which the seniority system's benefits depend. That is because such a rule would substitute a complex case-specific "accommodation" decision made by management for the more uniform, impersonal operation of seniority rules. Such management decision making, with its inevitable discretionary elements, would involve a matter of the greatest importance to employees, namely, layoffs; it would take place outside, as well as inside, the confines of a court case; and it might well take place fairly often. Cf. ADA, 42 U.S.C. § 12101(a)(1), (estimating that some 43 million Americans suffer from physical or mental disabilities). We can find nothing in the statute that suggests Congress intended to undermine seniority systems in this way. And we consequently conclude that the employer's showing of violation of the rules of a seniority system is by itself ordinarily sufficient.

B

The plaintiff (here the employee) nonetheless remains free to show that special circumstances warrant a finding that, despite the presence of a seniority system (which the ADA may not trump in the run of cases), the requested "accommodation" is "reasonable" on the particular facts. That is because special circumstances might alter the important expectations described above. * * * The plaintiff might show, for example, that the employer, having retained the right to change the seniority system unilaterally, exercises that right fairly frequently, reducing employee expectations that the system will be followed—to the point where one more departure, needed to accommodate an individual with a disability, will not likely make a difference. The plaintiff might show that the system already contains exceptions such that, in the circumstances, one further exception is unlikely to matter. We do not mean these examples to exhaust the kinds of showings that a plaintiff might make. But we do mean to say that the plaintiff must bear the burden of showing special circumstances that make an exception from the seniority system reasonable in the particular case. And to do so, the plaintiff must explain why, in the particular case, an exception to the employer's seniority policy can constitute a "reasonable accommodation" even though in the ordinary case it cannot.

IV

In its question presented, US Airways asked us whether the ADA requires an employer to assign a disabled employee to a particular position even though another employee is entitled to that position under the employer's "established seniority system." We answer that ordinarily the ADA does not require that assignment. Hence, a showing that the assignment would violate the rules of a seniority system warrants summary judgment for the employer—unless there is more. The plaintiff must present evidence of that "more," namely, special circumstances surrounding the particular case that demonstrate the assignment is nonetheless reasonable.

Because the lower courts took a different view of the matter, and because neither party has had an opportunity to seek summary judgment in accordance with the principles we set forth here, we vacate the Court of Appeals' judgment and remand the case for further proceedings consistent with this opinion.

JUSTICE STEVENS, concurring.

Although the Court of Appeals did not apply the standard that the Court endorses today, it correctly rejected the per se rule that petitioner has pressed upon us and properly reversed the District Court's entry of summary judgment for petitioner. The Court of Appeals also correctly held that there was a triable issue of fact precluding the entry of summary judgment with respect to whether petitioner violated the statute by failing to engage in an interactive process concerning respondent's three proposed accommodations. This latter holding is untouched by the Court's opinion today.

Among the questions that I have not been able to answer on the basis of the limited record that has been presented to us are: (1) whether the mailroom position held by respondent became open for bidding merely in response to a routine airline schedule change, or as the direct consequence of the layoff of several thousand employees; (2) whether respondent's requested accommodation should be viewed as an assignment to a vacant position, or as the maintenance of the status quo; and (3) exactly what impact the grant of respondent's request would have had on other employees. As I understand the Court's opinion, on remand, respondent will have the burden of answering these and other questions in order to overcome the presumption that petitioner's seniority system justified respondent's discharge.

JUSTICE O'CONNOR, concurring.

I agree with portions of the opinion of the Court, but I find problematic the Court's test for determining whether the fact that a job reassignment violates a seniority system makes the reassignment an unreasonable accommodation under the Americans with Disabilities Act of 1990 (ADA or Act), 42 U.S.C. §§ 12101 et seq. (1994 ed. and Supp. V). Although a seniority system plays an important role in the workplace, for the reasons I explain below, I would prefer to say that the effect of a seniority system on the reasonableness of a reassignment as an accommodation for purposes of the ADA depends on whether the seniority system is legally enforceable. * * * [I]n order that the Court may adopt a rule, and because I believe the Court's rule will often lead to the same outcome as the one I would have adopted, I join the Court's opinion despite my concerns. * * *

* * * In the context of a workplace, a vacant position is a position in which no employee currently works and to which no individual has a legal entitlement. For example, in a workplace without a seniority system, when an employee ceases working for the employer, the employee's former position is vacant until a replacement is hired. Even if the replacement does not start work immediately, once the replacement

enters into a contractual agreement with the employer, the position is no
longer vacant because it has a "possessor." In contrast, when an
employee ceases working in a workplace with a legally enforceable
seniority system, the employee's former position does not become vacant
if the seniority system entitles another employee to it. Instead, the
employee entitled to the position under the seniority system immediately
becomes the new "possessor" of that position. In a workplace with an
unenforceable seniority policy, however, an employee expecting assignment to a position under the seniority policy would not have any type of
contractual right to the position and so could not be said to be its
"possessor." The position therefore would become vacant.

* * *

Although I am troubled by the Court's reasoning, I believe the
Court's approach for evaluating seniority systems will often lead to the
same outcome as the test I would have adopted. Unenforceable seniority
systems are likely to involve policies in which employers "retain the
right to change the system," and will often "permit exceptions". They
will also often contain disclaimers that "reduce employee expectations
that the system will be followed." Thus, under the Court's test, disabled
employees seeking accommodations that would require exceptions to
unenforceable seniority systems may be able to show circumstances that
make the accommodation "reasonable in their particular case." Because
I think the Court's test will often lead to the correct outcome, and
because I think it important that a majority of the Court agree on a rule
when interpreting statutes, I join the Court's opinion.

JUSTICE SCALIA, with whom JUSTICE THOMAS joins, dissenting.

* * * The right to be given a vacant position so long as there are no
obstacles to that appointment (including another candidate who is better
qualified, if "best qualified" is the workplace rule) is of considerable
value. If an employee is hired to fill a position but fails miserably, he will
typically be fired. Few employers will search their organization charts for
vacancies to which the low-performing employee might be suited. The
ADA, however, prohibits an employer from firing a person whose disability is the cause of his poor performance without first seeking to place
him in a vacant job where the disability will not affect performance.
Such reassignment is an accommodation to the disability because it
removes an obstacle (the inability to perform the functions of the
assigned job) arising solely from the disability. * * *

The phrase "reassignment to a vacant position" appears in a subsection describing a variety of potential "reasonable accommodations":

"(A) making existing facilities used by employees readily accessible to and usable by individuals with disabilities; and

"(B) job restructuring, part-time or modified work schedules,
reassignment to a vacant position, acquisition or modification of
equipment or devices, appropriate adjustment or modifications of
examinations, training materials or policies, the provision of quali-

fied readers or interpreters, and other similar accommodations for individuals with disabilities." § 12111(9).

Subsection (A) clearly addresses features of the workplace that burden the disabled because of their disabilities. Subsection (B) is broader in scope but equally targeted at disability-related obstacles. Thus it encompasses "modified work schedules" (which may accommodate inability to work for protracted periods), "modification of equipment and devices," and "provision of qualified readers or interpreters." There is no reason why the phrase "reassignment to a vacant position" should be thought to have a uniquely different focus. It envisions elimination of the obstacle of the current position (which requires activity that the disabled employee cannot tolerate) when there is an alternate position freely available. If he is qualified for that position, and no one else is seeking it, or no one else who seeks it is better qualified, he must be given the position. But "reassignment to a vacant position" does not envision the elimination of obstacles to the employee's service in the new position that have nothing to do with his disability—for example, another employee's claim to that position under a seniority system, or another employee's superior qualifications. Cf. 29 CFR pt. 1630, App. 1630.2(*o*), p. 357 (2001) (explaining "reasonable accommodation" as "any change in the work environment or in the way things are customarily done that enables an individual with a disability to enjoy equal employment opportunities") * * *.

JUSTICE SOUTER, with whom JUSTICE GINSBURG joins, dissenting.

With US Airways itself insisting that its seniority system was noncontractual and modifiable at will, there is no reason to think that Barnett's accommodation would have resulted in anything more than minimal disruption to US Airways's operations, if that. Barnett has shown his requested accommodation to be "reasonable," and the burden ought to shift to US Airways if it wishes to claim that, in spite of surface appearances, violation of the seniority scheme would have worked an undue hardship. I would therefore affirm the Ninth Circuit.

Notes and Questions

1. *Presumption Against Modification of Seniority Systems.* Does *US Airways* correctly conclude that a requested accommodation that "conflicts with the rules of a seniority system" is "ordinarily" not reasonable? If Congress would have wanted a special presumption protecting seniority systems from accommodation requests, why would it not have included in the ADA a provision governing seniority systems, as it did in Title VII and the ADEA? Is the *US Airways* Court's presumption a justifiable use of an implied judicial authority to provide interpretive rules to clarify elastic terms like "reasonable" that ultimately must entail some kind of balancing analysis?

2. *"Special Circumstances" for Overriding Seniority–Based Expectations?* What "special circumstances" does the Court indicate might be

sufficient to make an accommodating departure from a seniority system "reasonable"? Can you think of other sufficient circumstances? Consider also Justice O'Connor's alternative test. In which cases, if any, might it yield a different result? Would it provide clearer guidance? Consider that the various states treat differently the enforceability of commitments made unilaterally by employers in employment manuals. See pp. 745–750, infra.

3. *Must Collective Bargaining Agreements Accommodate the Disabled in "Special Circumstances"?* Should any departure from collectively bargained seniority rules be treated as not "reasonable", or might an employer, in "special circumstances", have an obligation to request that a union with which it has a collective agreement accept a variance that allows a less senior disabled worker to have priority for a necessary reassignment? Might the ADA be read to require a union, in "special circumstances", to consent during the term of a bargaining agreement to such a reassignment?

4. *Rejection of Efficacious–Only Reading of "Reasonable Accommodation".* Note the argument made by Barnett, based on the Act's inclusion of an "undue hardship" defense, to convince the Court that a "reasonable" accommodation, for purposes of the ADA, must mean an "effective" accommodation. How does the Court reconcile the requirement of "reasonable accommodation" with the "undue hardship" defense in answering this argument? If an employee can demonstrate "special circumstances" that warrant a departure from a seniority system in his particular case, could the employer still prove that such an accommodation would be an "undue hardship"?

5. *Burden of Proof on Reasonable Accommodation.* Does the Court's opinion in *US Airways* confirm that a plaintiff ultimately must carry the burden of persuasion on the reasonableness of some particular accommodation? Is this conclusion dictated by the wording of § 102(b)(5)? Should employers nonetheless bear some burden of production, at least after the employee identifies some plausible accommodations? Do employers typically possess the best information on the costs and other effects of plausible accommodations suggested by employees, just as employees have the best information on their physical and mental condition? Does plaintiffs' ability to conduct discovery obviate imposing any burden of production on employers? See Benson v. Northwest Airlines, Inc., 62 F.3d 1108, 1112 (8th Cir.1995) ("once the plaintiff makes 'a facial showing that reasonable accommodation is possible,' the burden of production shifts to the employer to show that it is unable to accommodate the employee.").

6. *Must Disabled Individuals Qualified for a Vacant Position Be Given Preferences Over Those Deemed More Qualified?* The Court in *US Airways* rejects the airline's argument that the ADA never requires employers to grant "preferences" to disabled employees by departing from neutral rules. What neutral rules, other than seniority, might be used by employers in making job assignments? See, e.g., Shapiro v. Township of Lakewood, 292 F.3d 356 (3d Cir. 2002) (employer's neutral rule that employee must check posting board and apply to particular vacant positions is governed by *Barnett* analysis).

Are employers, at least in some circumstances, obligated to reassign disabled employees to vacant positions for which they are qualified, even though the employers would prefer assigning other employees whom they deem more qualified? The Supreme Court first granted, and then after settlement dismissed, a writ of certiorari on this issue in Huber v. Wal-Mart Stores, Inc., 486 F.3d 480 (8th Cir.), cert. granted, ___ U.S. ___, 128 S.Ct. 742, 169 L.Ed.2d 579 (2007) (ADA does not require employers to give disabled employees preferences in reassignments over more qualified non-disabled applicants). For a different view, see Smith v. Midland Brake, Inc., 180 F.3d 1154 (10th Cir.1999) (en banc) (unless it would impose an undue hardship, qualified individual with a disability must be reassigned a vacant position even if a "better qualified" employee is available). Why would Congress want the disabled to be given preferences in competing for reassignment to a new job with their current employer, if they are not to be given preferences when applying for jobs with new employers? On the other hand, if no preferences are given to the disabled when considering their reassignment, does the reasonable accommodation duty add anything to a nondiscrimination command for such decisions? Would it be consistent with the statute to require an employer to reassign the qualified disabled to a vacant position unless the employer can prove others are clearly more qualified? Cf. Aka v. Washington Hosp. Ctr., 156 F.3d 1284, 1304 (D.C.Cir. 1998) (en banc) (reassignment obligation requires "some active effort on the part of the employer").

7. *For Which Positions Must Reassignment Be Considered?* The ADA obligates employers to consider disabled employees' reassignment to existing vacant jobs that would not constitute a promotion. The EEOC's Interpretive Guidance would impose a duty to consider reassignment to "wholly distinct and different" positions in "different offices and facilities." See Gile v. United Airlines, Inc., 95 F.3d 492 (7th Cir.1996). Should employers even be required to consider positions outside commuting distance from the employee's home if the employee expresses a willingness to move and to pay moving expenses? The EEOC Enforcement Guidance on Reasonable Accommodation states that an employer's obligation is not necessarily limited by "department, facility, personnel system, or geographical area"; the obligation is limited only by "undue hardship." But cf. 29 C.F.R. § 1614.203(g) (Rehabilitation Act regulation requiring reassignment only in the "same commuting area").

Must employers always offer an individual with a disability who can no longer perform in his current position reassignment to an inferior position with a lower wage? Or can an employer assert nondiscriminatory policies against demotions? See Dalton v. Subaru–Isuzu Automotive, Inc., 141 F.3d 667 (7th Cir.1998) (suggesting that employers may have legitimate nondiscriminatory reasons for such policies).

8. *For How Long Must an Employer Consider Reassignment?* For how long must an employer's personnel officers look for another position for a newly disabled employee? Until he informs them that he is no longer interested or at least ceases cooperating with them? Or does the statutory definition of a "qualified individual with a disability" suggest a more limited duration for the obligation to consider reassignment? The Interpretive Guidance only directs employers to consider "equivalent" positions that will become vacant "within a reasonable amount of time * * * in light of the totality of circumstances", giving the example of a position that would

become open in a week. 29 C.F.R. pt. 1630, app. § 1630.2(*o*). In its Enforcement Guidance on Reasonable Accommodation, the EEOC uses examples with periods between 4 weeks and six months.

Note on "Interactive Process" and ADA

Employer's Failure to Engage in "Interactive Process" as Itself a Violation of the ADA? Justice Stevens notes that the majority does not disturb the holding of the court of appeals that the airline violated the ADA "by failing to engage in an interactive process" concerning Barnett's proposed accommodations. If an employee can prove that her employer had failed to fulfill its obligations to cooperate in the search for a viable reassignment or other reasonable accommodation, should she necessarily win her case, or should she also have to prove that a reasonable accommodation actually existed? Most courts have held that the plaintiff must demonstrate that a reasonable accommodation existed. See, e.g., Smith v. Midland Brake; Mengine v. Runyon, 114 F.3d 415 (3d Cir.1997). But cf. Hendricks–Robinson v. Excel Corp., 154 F.3d 685 (7th Cir.1998) (employer may have violated ADA by implementing medical layoff policy that did not provide adequate opportunity to identify reasonable accommodations). See also 29 C.F.R. § 1630.2(*o*)(3), and the accompanying Interpretive Guidance, see 29 C.F.R. pt. 1630, app. 1630.9 (Process of Determining the Appropriate Reasonable Accommodation).

Is there a rationale for penalizing employers who fail to engage in a good faith, interactive effort to discover a reasonable accommodation in cases in which no such accommodation ultimately can be identified? Could such a rationale be similar to one that justifies finding employers to violate antidiscrimination provisions in cases where they unjustifiably consider a protected status classification, even where they would have made the same decision but for this consideration? Cf. § 107 of the Civil Rights Act of 1991 (prohibiting discrimination where "race, color, religion, sex, or national origin was a motivating factor for any employment practice, even though other factors also motivated the practice").

On the other hand, have courts been correct to demand the identification of a reasonable accommodation given the fact that § 102(a) only condemns discrimination against "a qualified individual with a disability" and the definition of "a qualified individual with a disability" requires that the individual be able to perform essential employment functions "with or without reasonable accommodation"? Can there be any discrimination under § 102 if there is no reasonable accommodations available to make a disabled individual "qualified"? Does this logic apply to all cases, or might there be distinguishable instances in which an individual is qualified to perform her job, but seeks some accommodation, such as a ramp to provide more direct wheelchair access to an office suite, to make her work conditions equal to those of the nondisabled? If the employer refused to even consider the costs and benefits of a ramp, or the possible alternatives, might such a case be covered by § 102(b)(5)(a) regardless of whether the ramp, or any alternative, could be shown to constitute a "reasonable" accommodation?

Employee's Failure to Engage in the Interactive Process of Identifying Accommodations. If a plaintiff can demonstrate reasonable accommodation during a trial, is her claim nonetheless defective if she failed previously to suggest such an accommodation to the employer? Should this depend on whether her failure to do so derived from the employer's nonresponsiveness or from her failure to work with the employer in exploring alternatives? In Beck v. University of Wisconsin Bd. of Regents, 75 F.3d 1130, 1135–36 (7th Cir.1996), the Seventh Circuit affirmed summary judgment for the defendant employer because the court concluded that the plaintiff employee had failed to participate in good faith with the employer in an effort to identify a reasonable accommodation. See also Derbis v. United States Shoe Corp., 67 F.3d 294 (4th Cir.1995) (plaintiff failed to provide employer with information about the injury to her injured hand necessary to identify reasonable accommodations). Can such decisions be supported by the wording of § 101(8)? By § 102(b)(5)?

Relevance of Defendant's Knowledge of Plaintiff's Disability. Section 102(b)(5)(A) proscribes "not making reasonable accommodation to the *known* physical or mental limitation of an otherwise qualified individual with a disability" (emphasis supplied). This presumably means that an employer that has not been apprised of the existence of a disability has no accommodation responsibilities and can take adverse action against the employee for conduct caused by his disability. See 29 C.F.R. pt. 1630, app. § 1630.9 ("an employer would not be expected to accommodate disabilities of which it is unaware"). See also, e.g., Hedberg v. Indiana Bell Tel. Co., Inc., 47 F.3d 928, 931 (7th Cir.1995) (employer can discharge employee because of behavior caused by disability, where employer did not know of disability's existence); Miller v. National Casualty Co., 61 F.3d 627, 629–30 (8th Cir. 1995) (accord). Does this also mean that workers with known disabilities always must advise employers of their need for at least some type of accommodation? Or might the ADA require employers in some cases to ask employees or applicants if they need accommodation? See Bultemeyer v. Fort Wayne Community Sch., 100 F.3d 1281, 1285 (7th Cir.1996) ("properly participating in the interactive process means that an employer cannot expect an employee to read its mind and know that he or she must specifically say I want a reasonable accommodation, particularly when the employee has a mental illness.").

If an employer learns of a disability and the need for accommodation only after the disability has caused inadequate performance or other delinquencies that would normally result in a discharge, does the employer have an obligation to attempt reasonable accommodation first? Should it matter whether the employee's disability was an emotional or mental illness that obscured his perception of the need for accommodation? See Stola v. Joint Indus. Bd., 889 F.Supp. 133, 136 (S.D.N.Y.1995) (employer did not violate ADA when it terminated plaintiff before learning of his mental impairment, but this does not mean employer can then reject plaintiff's reapplication without considering reasonable accommodation).

VANDE ZANDE v. STATE OF WISCONSIN DEPARTMENT OF ADMINISTRATION

United States Court of Appeals, Seventh Circuit, 1995.
44 F.3d 538.

POSNER, CHIEF JUDGE.

It is plain enough what "accommodation" means. The employer must be willing to consider making changes in its ordinary work rules, facilities, terms, and conditions in order to enable a disabled individual to work. The difficult term is "reasonable." The plaintiff in our case, a paraplegic, argues in effect that the term just means apt or efficacious. An accommodation is reasonable, she believes, when it is tailored to the particular individual's disability. A ramp or lift is thus a reasonable accommodation for a person who like this plaintiff is confined to a wheelchair. Considerations of cost do not enter into the term as the plaintiff would have us construe it. Cost is, she argues, the domain of "undue hardship"—a safe harbor for an employer that can show that it would go broke or suffer other excruciating financial distress were it compelled to make a reasonable accommodation in the sense of one effective in enabling the disabled person to overcome the vocational effects of the disability.

These are questionable interpretations both of "reasonable" and of "undue hardship." To "accommodate" a disability is to make some change that will enable the disabled person to work. * * * So "reasonable" may be intended to qualify (in the sense of weaken) "accommodation," in just the same way that if one requires a "reasonable effort" of someone this means less than the maximum possible effort, or in law that the duty of "reasonable care," the cornerstone of the law of negligence, requires something less than the maximum possible care. It is understood in that law that in deciding what care is reasonable the court considers the cost of increased care. (This is explicit in Judge Learned Hand's famous formula for negligence. *United States v. Carroll Towing Co.*, 159 F.2d 169, 173 (2d Cir.1947).) Similar reasoning could be used to flesh out the meaning of the word "reasonable" in the term "reasonable accommodations." It would not follow that the costs and benefits of altering a workplace to enable a disabled person to work would always have to be quantified, or even that an accommodation would have to be deemed unreasonable if the cost exceeded the benefit however slightly. But, at the very least, the cost could not be disproportionate to the benefit. Even if an employer is so large or wealthy—or, like the principal defendant in this case, is a state, which can raise taxes in order to finance any accommodations that it must make to disabled employees—that it may not be able to plead "undue hardship," it would not be required to expend enormous sums in order to bring about a trivial improvement in the life of a disabled employee. If the nation's employers have potentially unlimited financial obligations to 43 million disabled persons, the Americans with Disabilities Act will have imposed an indirect tax potentially greater than the national debt. We do not find an intention to bring about such a radical result in either the language of the Act or its history. The preamble actually "markets" the Act as a cost saver, pointing to "billions of dollars in unnecessary expenses resulting from dependency and nonproductivity." § 12101(a)(9). The savings will be illusory if employers are required to expend many more billions in accommodation than will be saved by enabling disabled people to work.

The concept of reasonable accommodation is at the heart of this case. The plaintiff sought a number of accommodations to her paraplegia that were turned down. The principal defendant as we have said is a state, which does not argue that the plaintiff's proposals were rejected because accepting them would have imposed undue hardship on the state or because they would not have done her any good. The district judge nevertheless granted summary judgment for the defendants on the ground that the evidence obtained in discovery, construed as favorably to the plaintiff as the record permitted, showed that they had gone as far to accommodate the plaintiff's demands as reasonableness, in a sense distinct from either aptness or hardship—a sense based, rather, on considerations of cost and proportionality—required. On this analysis, the function of the "undue hardship" safe harbor, like the "failing company" defense to antitrust liability, * * * is to excuse compliance by a firm that is financially distressed, even though the cost of the accommodation to the firm might be less than the benefit to disabled employees.

This interpretation of "undue hardship" is not inevitable—in fact probably is incorrect. It is a defined term in the Americans with Disabilities Act, and the definition is "an action requiring significant difficulty or expense." 42 U.S.C. § 12111(10)(A). The financial condition of the employer is only one consideration in determining whether an accommodation otherwise reasonable would impose an undue hardship. See 42 U.S.C. §§ 12111(10)(B)(ii), (iii). The legislative history equates "undue hardship" to "unduly costly." These are terms of relation. We must ask, "undue" in relation to what? Presumably (given the statutory definition and the legislative history) in relation to the benefits of the accommodation to the disabled worker as well as to the employer's resources.

So it seems that costs enter at two points in the analysis of claims to an accommodation to a disability. The employee must show that the accommodation is reasonable in the sense both of efficacious and of proportional to costs. Even if this prima facie showing is made, the employer has an opportunity to prove that upon more careful consideration the costs are excessive in relation either to the benefits of the accommodation or to the employer's financial survival or health. In a classic negligence case, the idiosyncrasies of the particular employer are irrelevant. Having above-average costs, or being in a precarious financial situation, is not a defense to negligence. *Vaughan v. Menlove*, 3 Bing. (N.C.) 468, 132 Eng.Rep. 490 (Comm.Pl.1837). One interpretation of "undue hardship" is that it permits an employer to escape liability if he can carry the burden of proving that a disability accommodation reasonable for a normal employer would break him. *Barth v. Gelb*, 2 F.3d 1180, 1187 (D.C.Cir.1993).

Lori Vande Zande, aged 35, is paralyzed from the waist down as a result of a tumor of the spinal cord. Her paralysis makes her prone to develop pressure ulcers, treatment of which often requires that she stay at home for several weeks. * * * We hold that Vande Zande's pressure ulcers are a part of her disability, and therefore a part of what the State of Wisconsin had a duty to accommodate—reasonably.

Vande Zande worked for the housing division of the state's department of administration for three years, beginning in January 1990. The housing division supervises the state's public housing programs. Her job was that of a program assistant, and involved preparing public information materials, planning meetings, interpreting regulations, typing, mailing, filing, and copying. In short, her tasks were of a clerical, secretarial, and administrative-assistant character. In order to enable her to do this work, the defendants, as she acknowledges, "made numerous accommodations relating to the plaintiff's disability." As examples, in her words, "they paid the landlord to have bathrooms modified and to have a step ramped; they bought special adjustable furniture for the plaintiff; they ordered and paid for one-half of the cost of a cot that the plaintiff needed for daily personal care at work; they sometimes adjusted the plaintiff's schedule to perform backup telephone duties to accommodate the plaintiff's medical appointments; they made changes to the plans for a locker room in the new state office building; and they agreed to provide some of the specific accommodations the plaintiff requested in her October 5, 1992 Reasonable Accommodation Request."

But she complains that the defendants did not go far enough in two principal respects. One concerns a period of eight weeks when a bout of pressure ulcers forced her to stay home. She wanted to work full time at home and believed that she would be able to do so if the division would provide her with a desktop computer at home (though she already had a laptop). Her supervisor refused, and told her that he probably would have only 15 to 20 hours of work for her to do at home per week and that she would have to make up the difference between that and a full work week out of her sick leave or vacation leave. In the event, she was able to work all but 16.5 hours in the eight-week period. She took 16.5 hours of sick leave to make up the difference. As a result, she incurred no loss of income, but did lose sick leave that she could have carried forward indefinitely. She now works for another agency of the State of Wisconsin, but any unused sick leave in her employment by the housing division would have accompanied her to her new job. Restoration of the 16.5 hours of lost sick leave is one form of relief that she seeks in this suit.

She argues that a jury might have found that a reasonable accommodation required the housing division either to give her the desktop computer or to excuse her from having to dig into her sick leave to get paid for the hours in which, in the absence of the computer, she was unable to do her work at home. No jury, however, could in our view be permitted to stretch the concept of "reasonable accommodation" so far. Most jobs in organizations public or private involve team work under supervision rather than solitary unsupervised work, and team work under supervision generally cannot be performed at home without a substantial reduction in the quality of the employee's performance. This will no doubt change as communications technology advances, but is the situation today. Generally, therefore, an employer is not required to accommodate a disability by allowing the disabled worker to work, by himself, without supervision, at home. * * * An employer is not required to allow disabled workers to work at home, where their productivity inevitably would be greatly reduced. No doubt to this as to any generalization about so complex and varied an activity as employment there are exceptions, but it would take a very extraordinary case for the employee to be able to create a triable issue of the employer's failure to allow the employee to work at home.

And if the employer, because it is a government agency and therefore is not under intense competitive pressure to minimize its labor costs or maximize the value of its output, or for some other reason, bends over backwards to accommodate a disabled worker—goes further than the law requires—by allowing the worker to work at home, it must not be punished for its generosity by being deemed to have conceded the reasonableness of so far-reaching an accommodation. That would hurt rather than help disabled workers. Wisconsin's housing division was not required by the Americans with Disabilities Act to allow Vande Zande to work at home; even more clearly it was not required to install a computer in her home so that she could avoid using up 16.5 hours of sick leave. It is conjectural that she will ever need those 16.5 hours; the expected cost of the loss must, therefore, surely be slight. An accommodation that allows a disabled worker to work at home, at full pay, subject only to a slight loss of sick leave that may never be needed, hence never missed, is, we hold, reasonable as a matter of law.

Her second complaint has to do with the kitchenettes in the housing division's building, which are for the use of employees during lunch and coffee breaks. Both the sink and the counter in each of the kitchenettes were 36 inches high, which is too high for a person in a wheelchair. The building was under construction, and the kitchenettes not yet built, when the plaintiff complained about this feature of the design. But the defendants refused to alter the design to lower the sink and counter to 34 inches, the height convenient for a person in a wheelchair. Construction of the building had begun before the effective date of the Americans with Disabilities Act, and Vande Zande does not argue that the failure to include 34–inch sinks and counters in the design of the building violated the Act. She could not argue that; the Act is not retroactive. * * * But she argues that once she brought the problem to the attention of her supervisors, they were obliged to lower the sink and counter, at least on the floor on which her office was located but possibly on the other floors in the building as well, since she might be moved to another floor. All that the defendants were willing to do was to install a shelf 34 inches high in the kitchenette area on Vande Zande's floor. That took care of the counter problem. As for the sink, the defendants took the position that since the plumbing was already in place it would be too costly to lower the sink and that the plaintiff could use the bathroom sink, which is 34 inches high.

Apparently it would have cost only about $150 to lower the sink on Vande Zande's floor; to lower it on all the floors might have cost as much as $2,000, though possibly less. Given the proximity of the bathroom sink, Vande Zande can hardly complain that the inaccessibility of the kitchenette sink interfered with her ability to work or with her physical comfort. Her argument rather is that forcing her to use the bathroom sink for activities (such as washing out her coffee cup) for which the other employees could use the kitchenette sink stigmatized her as different and inferior; she seeks an award of compensatory damages for the resulting emotional distress. We may assume without having to decide that emotional as well as physical barriers to the integration of disabled persons into the workforce are relevant in determining the reasonableness of an accommodation. But we do not think an employer has a duty to expend even modest amounts of money to bring about an absolute identity in working conditions between disabled and nondisabled workers. The creation of such a duty would be the inevitable consequence of deeming a failure to achieve identical conditions "stigmatizing." That is merely an epithet. We conclude that access to a particular sink, when access to an equivalent sink, conveniently located, is provided, is not a legal duty of an employer. The duty of reasonable accommodation is satisfied when the employer does what is necessary to enable the disabled worker to work in reasonable comfort.

Notes and Questions

1. *"Reasonable" as Cost–Benefit Analysis?* Note that Vande Zande, also without success, made the same argument about the meaning of "reasonable" that Barnett made in *US Airways*. What definition of "reasonable" does the *Vande Zande* court instead embrace? Is its definition consistent with the Supreme Court's later opinion in *US Airways*? Does the *Vande Zande* court's definition turn on whether the accommodation will be cost efficient for the employer in the long run? Or does Judge Posner's test ask whether the costs of accommodation are disproportionate to the total benefits to society, including those that will accrue to the plaintiff employee? Cf. Borkowski v. Valley Cent. Sch. Dist., 63 F.3d 131, 138 n. 3 (2d Cir.1995) (costs of reasonable accommodation must not be clearly disproportionate to its benefits, but § 504 of Rehabilitation Act "does not require that the employer receive a benefit commensurate with the cost of the accommodation"). Are there reasons why employers may not make socially efficient accommodations without a legal mandate? Cf. Christine Jolls, Antidiscrimination and Accommodation, 115 Harv. L. Rev. 643 (2001) (demonstrating

how accommodation requirement overlaps with social cost and benefit balancing under disparate impact analysis). See also J.H. Verkerke, Is the ADA Efficient?, 50 U.C.L.A. L.Rev. 903 (2003); Stewart J. Schwab & Steven L. Willborn, Reasonable Accommodation of Workplace Disabilities, 44 Will. & Mary L. Rev. 1199 (2003); J.H. Verkerke, Disaggregating Antidiscrimination and Accommodation, 44. Will & Mary L. Rev. 1385 (2003); Amy L. Wax, Disability, Reciprocity, and "Real Efficiency": Unified Approach, 44 Wm. & Mary L. Rev. 1421 (2003); Pamela S. Karlan & George Rutherglen, Disabilities, Discrimination, and Reasonable Accommodation, 46 Duke L. J. 1 (1996).

If the reasonableness of an accommodation depends in part on the benefits that it might bring to an employee, must employers incur higher accommodation costs for disabled employees who would be more affected by the loss of their position, perhaps because of their greater job tenure or because of their higher salary or even because of their greater vulnerability to social degradation? Cf. McElrath v. Kemp, 714 F.Supp. 23, 28 (D.D.C. 1989) (§ 501 of the Rehabilitation Act requires employer to provide further opportunity for rehabilitation to relapsed alcoholic in part because of the likely devastating impact of loss of job).

The EEOC rejects use of cost-benefit analysis to define either reasonable accommodation or undue hardship. See Enforcement Guidance: Reasonable Accommodation and Undue Hardship Under the Americans With Disabilities Act, Question 44, March 1, 1999. In Olmstead v. L.C., 527 U.S. 581, 119 S.Ct. 2176, 144 L.Ed.2d 540 (1999), however, at least five members of the Court (see opinion of Justice Ginsburg for four Justices on this issue and concurring opinion of Justice Kennedy) suggested that application of an analogous "reasonable modifications" standard in the definition of "qualified individual with a disability" in Title II (the public services portion) of the ADA requires consideration of all the costs of modifications, at least when those modifications threaten a "fundamental alteration" in state programs. Was a "fundamental alteration" of defendant's operations threatened by Vande Zande's proposed accommodations?

2. *"Undue Hardship"*. What did Vande Zande argue concerning the meaning of "undue hardship"? How did the court of appeals treat it? Was Vande Zande's interpretation of "undue hardship" consistent with the definition provided in § 101(10) of the ADA? What alternative interpretation of "undue hardship" is offered by the court of appeals? Is it consistent with the statutory definition? With the Supreme Court's opinion in *US Airways*?

Consider further the statutory definition. Why might Congress have directed consideration of the "overall financial resources of the covered entity"? (§ 101(10)(B)(iii)). Does this suggest that a larger or more profitable firm should have to bear extra costs of accommodation? Is that fair? Isn't it likely that a larger firm with more employees also will be asked to make more accommodations? Is that why it is relevant to consider "the overall size of the business of a covered entity with respect to the number of its employees"? Might a larger employer also be able to reap some economies of scale in its expenditures for some accommodations which, like the modification of facilities or equipment, will be useful for multiple employees? Is that one reason why the facility-specific factors listed in § 101(10)(B)(ii) are also relevant? Are these factors, on the other hand, relevant to individualized accommodations of the type sought in *Vande Zande*?

Note that the undue hardship language is used only in § 102(b)(5)(A). Is the undue hardship defense available for § 102(b)(5)(B) claims? For any other of the kinds of discrimination listed in § 102(b)?

3. *Application of "Reasonable Accommodation" Standard in* Vande Zande. Does the court of appeals in *Vande Zande* actually apply its own cost-benefit reasonable accommodation standard? Consider first the lowering of the sink on Vande Zande's floor. Apparently that would have cost only $150. If Vande Zande worked four more years on this floor, the cost for each work day would have been less than twenty cents. Wouldn't the benefit to Vande Zande of not having to go to the bathroom sink be at least this much, especially if emotional as well as physical costs are taken into account? Or does the court, at the end of the excerpted opinion, effectively qualify its cost-benefit paradigm? If so, is this qualification sensible?

Does the court also qualify its cost-benefit paradigm in its analysis of Vande Zande's claim that Wisconsin should have provided her with a desktop computer, or alternatively given her paid leave? Does the court compare the costs of a desktop computer to the benefits of allowing her the flexibility of homework? Or does it instead announce a general rule about whether the ADA requires employers to allow disabled workers to work at least temporarily at home when necessary? If so, is the rule sensible? Might it be justified, within the cost-benefit paradigm, as a bright line rule to guide employers, similar to a speed limit violation, per se negligence rule? Or should the court have reviewed the particular costs to Wisconsin of Vande Zande doing home work? Should it have reviewed the general policies of Wisconsin toward home work? Cf. Langon v. Department of Health & Human Services, 959 F.2d 1053, 1055 (D.C.Cir.1992) (denying summary judgment to defendant, noting that it often allowed home work). Given the rapid development of communications technology, should courts assume the durability of any general rules on home work?

Is the court influenced by the numerous accommodations that Wisconsin did afford Vande Zande? Should it have been? Does the ADA direct an assessment of the overall efforts of an employer toward a particular employee, or should the level of accommodation to each need of a disabled employee be evaluated separately?

4. *Discrimination Between Disabled Individuals?* The court of appeals suggests that Wisconsin did more than the ADA requires by allowing Vande Zande to work many hours at home. What if Wisconsin had not permitted any home work for another disabled worker whose duties were similar to those of Vande Zande? Assuming the court's approach to home work is correct, would the second worker have a strong claim of discrimination under the ADA? What if the disability of the second worker was caused by some disease, such as cancer or AIDS, and thus differed from Vande Zande's disability? Would allowing a discrimination claim discourage extra accommodation to some disabled workers? Cf. Myers v. Hose, 50 F.3d 278, 284 (4th Cir.1995) ("the fact that certain accommodations may have been offered * * * to some employees as a matter of good faith does not mean that they must be extended to Myers as a matter of law."). Does such an argument

justify especially generous treatment of white or male workers? If not, why should discrimination between disabilities be treated differently?

In *Olmstead*, supra, a majority of the Court held that a state could discriminate against some mentally ill individuals by failing to provide them with the community care services granted to other mentally ill persons. In a portion of her opinion joined by five Justices, Justice Ginsburg, responding to a dissent by Justice Thomas that no case of discrimination was presented, cited O'Connor v. Consolidated Coin Caterers Corp., 517 U.S. 308, 116 S.Ct. 1307, 134 L.Ed.2d 433 (1996), supra p. 429, for the proposition that discrimination can occur within a protected class. Assuming that the plaintiffs in *Olmstead* were denied community care for reasons other than the severity or nature of their disability, however, was *O'Connor* a relevant precedent? Justice Kennedy, in a concurring opinion, argued that the plaintiffs should have to "show that persons needing psychiatric or other medical services to treat a mental disability are subject to a more onerous condition than are persons eligible for other existing state medical services."

5. *Reduced Wages as an Accommodation?* What if Vande Zande had requested as an accommodation a reduced wage proportionate to the quantity of work that she could complete during a bout of pressure ulcers? Many jobs that require coordination with the efforts of other employees can only be completed effectively at a regulated pace, but some jobs involve independent work that can proceed at any pace. For instance, a visually impaired lawyer might be able independently to do legal work of high quality, but at a slower rate. Would accommodating the lawyer's reduced production rate through a reduced wage impose any significant costs on an employer? Should the reactions of coworkers be taken into account? Cf. 29 C.F.R. pt. 1630, app. 1630.15(d) (employer should not "be able to demonstrate undue hardship by showing that the provision of the accommodation has a negative impact on the morale of its other employees but not on the ability of these employees to perform their jobs.").

Is it relevant to the questions raised in the last paragraph that the ADA lists "part-time or modified work schedules" as possible reasonable accommodations? § 101(9)(b). Does this listing suggest that employers in some cases may have to accommodate employees whose stamina has been reduced by a disability by offering these employees reduced hours, depending on the nature of the employees' work and whether it can be sufficiently separated into discrete components to permit part-time employment? If such an accommodation is required, or granted voluntarily by an employer, the employee presumably would have to be paid only on a part-time basis. See Rhodes v. Bob Florence Contractor, 890 F.Supp. 960, 967 (D.Kan.1995).

6. *Providing Leave as a Reasonable Accommodation.* If Vande Zande's symptoms could have been brought under control by some period of treatment or rehabilitation so that she would have been qualified to work after this period, would Wisconsin have been obligated to provide unpaid leave as a reasonable accommodation? What are the costs to employers of providing unpaid leave to weigh against the potential benefits to disabled employees? Note that the ADA covers employees who may not be able to claim the benefits of the Family Medical Leave Act (FMLA), 29 U.S.C. § 2601 et seq. This may be true for a number of reasons, including the employees having

worked insufficient hours or being employed at a worksite with fewer than 50 employees or already having claimed twelve workweeks of unpaid leave in the past twelve months.

The EEOC's Interpretive Guidance states that other reasonable accommodations that are not specifically mentioned in the ADA's nonexhaustive list "could include permitting the use of accrued paid leave or providing additional unpaid leave for necessary treatment." 29 C.F.R. pt. 1630, app. 1630.2(o). Should any duty to provide leave depend on the probable duration of the treatment period? Most courts have held that requests for indefinite leaves for an indefinite period or for over a year are not reasonable. See, e.g., Wood v. Green, 323 F.3d 1309 (11th Cir. 2003); Hudson v. MCI Telecommunications Corp., 87 F.3d 1167, 1169 (10th Cir.1996) (employer not required by ADA to provide indefinite leave, but a "reasonable allowance of time for medical care and treatment" may be mandated in some cases); Myers v. Hose, 50 F.3d 278, 283 (4th Cir.1995) (providing indefinite leave is not required by the ADA because to be "qualified individual with a disability" employee must be qualified in the present "or in the immediate future"). Should reasonableness also turn on the probability that the treatment will be successful? See, e.g., Humphrey v. Memorial Hosps. Ass'n, 239 F.3d 1128, 1136 (9th Cir. 2001) (specified leave period must "plausibly enable" employee to be qualified on return). For a discussion of the collected cases, see Stephen F. Befort, The Most Difficult ADA Reasonable Accommodation Issues: Reassignment and Leave of Absence, 37 Wake For. L. Rev. 439 (2002).

7. *Accommodations Beyond Those Necessary for Job Performance.* By considering Vande Zande's request for a lower kitchenette sink, did the court assume that the reasonable accommodation obligation in the ADA is not limited to accommodations necessary to enable disabled employees to perform their jobs? The EEOC's Regulations define "reasonable accommodation" to include "[m]odifications or adjustments to a job application process that enable a qualified applicant with a disability to be considered for the position such qualified applicant desires", and "[m]odifications or adjustments that enable a covered entity's employee with a disability to enjoy equal benefits and privileges of employment as are enjoyed by its other similarly situated employees without disabilities." 29 C.F.R. § 1630.2(o)(1). Is this regulatory definition in accord with the statute?

"Modifications or adjustments" to provide "equal benefits and privileges of employment" might include modifications of amenities generally provided to employees, such as kitchenettes and restrooms. Must employers in some cases also provide disabled employees with benefits, such as convenient parking spaces for those whose walking is impaired, even where nondisabled employees are not provided comparable benefits? Should any obligation depend on a demonstration that the disabled employee requires the accommodation in order to perform his job, or should it be sufficient to demonstrate that the accommodation is not costly and is necessary to provide the disabled employee with a work experience of equal quality as that enjoyed by the nondisabled? Compare Lyons v. Legal Aid Society, 68 F.3d 1512, 1517 (2d Cir.1995) (convenient parking might be required because plaintiff could not work without parking close to office), with Harmer v. Virginia Elec. & Power Co., 831 F.Supp. 1300, 1307 (E.D.Va.1993) (asthmatic employee cannot demand smoking ban because he could perform essential functions even in smoke-filled room). The EEOC's Enforcement Guidance on Reasonable Accommodation states that only job-related needs must be specially addressed. The Guidance also states that "if an adjustment or modification assists the individual throughout his or her daily activities, on and off the job, it will be considered a personal item that the employer is not required to provide. Accordingly, an employer would generally not be required to provide an employee with a disability with a prosthetic limb, wheelchair, or eyeglasses." 29 C.F.R. pt. 1630, app. § 1630.9.

"Modifications or adjustments to a job application process" might include accommodations during some kind of screening examination. See, e.g., Fink v. New York City Dep't of Personnel, 53 F.3d 565, 567 (2d Cir.1995) (considering the adequacy of accommodations, including tape recordings, afforded visually impaired applicants during civil service examination). To the extent that the screening examination seeks to determine applicants' qualifications for employment, disabled applicants presumably would not have to first independently demonstrate their qualifications before becoming eligible for accommodation during the normal examination. On the other hand, any suggested accommodations that would prevent the examination from establishing qualifications for essential job functions presumably would not be reasonable.

8. *Must an Employee's Relationship or Association with an Individual with a Disability Be Reasonably Accommodated?* Section 102(b)(4) of the ADA proscribes discrimination against a qualified individual because of his or her "relationship or association" with another individual with a "known disability." Does this mean that the association or relationship must be reasonably accommodated? For instance, what if Vande Zande had requested to work at home sometimes to care for a disabled child? See, e.g., Den Hartog v. Wasatch Academy, 129 F.3d 1076, 1083–84 (10th Cir.1997) (no accommodation required); 29 C.F.R. pt. 1630, app. § 1630.8 (same).

9. *Relation Between Substantially Limiting Condition and Condition Requiring Accommodation.* Note that the court in *Vande Zande* holds that Wisconsin had a duty to accommodate Vande Zande's pressure ulcers as a part of her disability of paralysis without determining that the ulcers themselves substantially limited a major life activity. This holding is in accord with the statutory language, which requires accommodation to "known physical or mental limitations", not only the "disabilities", of the disabled. However, courts have not required employers to accommodate nondisabling injuries simply because they arose from the same trauma or accident that resulted in a separate disability. See, e.g., Wood v. Crown Redi-Mix, Inc., 339 F.3d 682, 686 (8th Cir. 2003); Felix v. New York City Transit Authority, 324 F.3d 102 (2d Cir. 2003).

10. *Discrimination Against the Nondisabled or Affirmative Action for the Disabled?* If a disabled worker has an ADA claim against her employer for denying her more than reasonable accommodations simply because the accommodations were afforded to another disabled worker, does a nondisabled worker also have such a claim? Does the ADA protect against discrimination symmetrically, like Title VII generally, or is it asymmetrical, like the ADEA and the PDA? (Might a pregnant woman, who presumably is not

within the ADA protected class, see 29 C.F.R. pt. 1630, app. § 1630.2(h), in any event, have a Title VII claim for being denied an accommodation granted to a disabled employee?)

Even if the ADA is asymmetrical, might a nondisabled public employee have a claim under the equal protection clause? Would any such claim necessarily be futile because disability status is not a suspect classification? See City of Cleburne v. Cleburne Living Center, 473 U.S. 432, 105 S.Ct. 3249, 87 L.Ed.2d 313 (1985). See also pages 189–197 supra. Or might the ADA itself even be challenged to the extent that it requires employers to make special expenditures to help the disabled that are not made to benefit the nondisabled? Should the general goal of equal employment opportunity justify affirmative action for the disabled, if it does not justify affirmative action for racial minorities or women? Is it relevant that the ADA requires each impaired person to be treated as an individual in determining disabled status and the need for accommodation? That the affirmative action required by the ADA involves additional expenditures to enable the disabled to meet neutral standards set by employers, rather than any adjustment of those standards? See Jeffrey O. Cooper, Overcoming Barriers to Employment: The Meaning of Reasonable Accommodation and Undue Hardship in the Americans with Disabilities Act, 139 U. Pa. L. Rev. 1423 (1991).

Note that in Board of Trustees of the Univ. of Alabama v. Garrett, 531 U.S. 356, 121 S.Ct. 955, 148 L.Ed.2d 866 (2001), the Court held that the equal protection clause does not obligate state governments "to make special accommodations for the disabled", id. at 367, and that the Congress that enacted the ADA did not have before it a record of irrational discrimination by state governments against the disabled adequate to support use of congressional authority under § 5 of the fourteenth amendment to abrogate state immunity from private suit. Contrast *Garrett* with Tennessee v. Lane, 541 U.S. 509, 124 S.Ct. 1978, 158 L.Ed.2d 820 (2004), where the Court held that Congress did have sufficient authority under § 5 of the fourteenth amendment to abrogate state immunity for private suits under Title II of the ADA that claim unequal access to court houses. The Court found that before passing the ADA Congress considered a substantial record of state and local government discrimination in the provision of public services and programs covered by Title II, including access to courthouses and the courts. Are *Garrett* and *Lane* relevant to the questions posed in the last paragraph?

11. *Does the Reasonable Accommodation Requirement Help or Hurt the Disabled?* Two economic studies since the passage of the ADA have concluded that the sometimes costly accommodation obligations imposed on employers by the statute have led to a decline in the employment of disabled workers. See Daron Acemoglu & Joshua D. Angrist, Consequences of Employment Protection? The Case of the Americans with Disabilities Act, 109 J. Po. Econ. 915 (2001); Thomas DeLeire, The Wage and Employment Effects of the Americans with Disabilities Act, 35 J. Hum. Res. 691 (2000). But see Susan Schowochau & Peter David Blanck, The Economics of the Americans with Disabilities Act, Part III: Does the ADA Disable the Disabled, 21 Berk. J. Emp. & Lab. L. 271 (2000); Michael Ashley Stein, Empirical Implications of Title I, 85 Iowa L. Rev. 1671 (2000) (criticizing the methodologies of the studies). Assuming that the studies do accurately report a resultant decline in the employment of the disabled, what should be the legislative response?

Should Congress increase the penalties that can be imposed on employers for discriminating against disabled employment applicants? Should it provide subsidies for the costs of accommodation to supplement or supplant enforcement? Should Congress permit employers to pay the disabled less to compensate for the extra costs of accommodation? Or should at least some decline in the quantity of jobs for the disabled be accepted as an at least temporary cost for an enhancement of the quality of accommodated employment? For a thorough treatment, see Christine Jolls, Accommodation Mandates, 53 Stan. L. Rev. 223, 273–82 (discussing the studies and their possible implications for policy).

DEANE v. POCONO MEDICAL CENTER

United States Court of Appeals, Third Circuit, 1998 (en banc).

142 F.3d 138.

BECKER, CHIEF JUDGE.

I.

In April 1990, PMC hired Deane as a registered nurse to work primarily on the medical/surgical floor. On June 22, 1991, while lifting a resistant patient, she sustained a cartilage tear in her right wrist causing her to miss approximately one year of work. In June 1992, Deane and Barbara Manges, a nurse assigned to Deane's workers' compensation case, telephoned PMC and advised Charlene McCool, PMC's Benefits Coordinator, that Deane intended to return to work with certain restrictions. According to Deane, she informed McCool that she was unable to lift more than 15–20 pounds or perform repetitive manual tasks such as typing, but that her physician, Dr. Osterman, had released her to return to "light duty" work. Deane further explained to McCool that, if she could not be accommodated in a light duty position on the medical/surgical floor, she was willing to move to another area of the hospital, as long as she could remain in nursing. Unfortunately, this telephone call was PMC's only meaningful interaction with Deane during which it could have assessed the severity of or possible accommodation for her injuries. PMC never requested additional information from Deane or her physicians, and, according to Deane, when she subsequently attempted to contact PMC on several occasions, she was treated rudely by McCool and told not to call again.

After speaking with Deane and Manges, McCool advised Barbara Hann, PMC's Vice President of Human Resources, of Deane's request to return to work, of her attendant work restrictions, and of her stated need for accommodation. Shortly after considering the information conveyed by McCool and after comparing it to the job description of a medical/surgical nurse at PMC, Hann determined that Deane was unable to return to her previous position. Hann then asked Carol Clarke, PMC's Vice President of Nursing, and Susan Stine, PMC's Director of Nursing Resources/Patient Care Services, to review Deane's request to return to PMC and to explore possible accommodations for her. Both Clarke and Stine concluded that Deane could not be accommodated in her previous job as a nurse on the medical/surgical floor or in any other available position at the hospital. Finally, Hann asked Marie Werkheiser, PMC's Nurse Recruiter, whether there were any current or prospective job openings for registered nurses at PMC. According to Werkheiser, there were no such openings at that time.

As a result of the collective determination that Deane could not be accommodated in her previous job or in any other available position in the hospital, PMC sent Deane an "exit interview" form on August 7, 1992. On August 10, 1992, Hann notified Deane by telephone that she could not return to work because of her "handicap", and this litigation ensued. In March 1993, Deane accepted a registered nurse position at a non-acute care facility, where she remained until May 1993. Deane has been employed by a different non-acute care facility since July 1993. Neither of these positions require heavy lifting, bathing patients, or the like. * * *

* * * [Deane contends] that she was disabled under the terms of the ADA by virtue of the fact that PMC regarded her limitations as being far worse than they actually were, that PMC failed to accommodate her lifting restriction, and that she was eventually terminated on account of PMC's perception that she was disabled. In support of her perception claim, Deane relies on a "laundry list" of PMC's allegedly erroneous perceptions. According to Deane, PMC believed that she was unable to lift more than ten pounds, push or pull anything, assist patients in emergency situations, move or assist patients in the activities of daily living, perform any patient care job at PMC or any other hospital, perform CPR, use the rest of her body to assist patients, work with psychiatric patients, or use medical equipment. Deane refutes each of these perceptions—or, in her view, misperceptions—and contends that her injury was, in fact, relatively minor in nature. Deane further contends that PMC should be held responsible for these misperceptions because they were the result of PMC's "snap judgment" arrived at without making a good faith analysis, investigation, or assessment of the nature of her injury.

Finally, Deane maintains that she requires and is entitled to accommodation for her lifting restriction. In this regard, Deane contends that she could be accommodated either in her previous position as a nurse on the medical/surgical floor or through reassignment to another position that would not require heavy lifting. As to the former, Deane has suggested the following accommodations: (1) use of an assistant to help her move or lift patients; (2) implementation of a functional nursing approach, in which nurses would perform only certain types of nursing tasks; and (3) use of a Hoyer lift to move patients. Deane also maintains that she could have been transferred to another unit within the medical center such as the pediatrics, oncology, or nursery units, which would not have required heavy lifting. In the alternative, Deane submits that she can perform the essential functions of her previous job in the medical/surgical floor without accommodation because lifting is not an essential function of nursing. * * *

II.

A.

[*Eds.* The court first concluded that Deane adduced sufficient evidence to create an issue of material fact over whether PMC regarded her as being disabled: "there are factual disputes over how impaired PMC regarded Deane as being compared with her actual level of impairment, and whether PMC's perception of Deane constituted a 'significant[ ] restriction in [Deane's] ability to perform either a class of jobs or a broad range of jobs in various classes as compared to the average person having comparable training, skills and abilities.' " 29 C.F.R. § 1630.2(j)(3)(i).]

B.

The second element of Deane's prima facie case under the ADA requires her to demonstrate that she is a "qualified individual". The ADA defines this term as an individual "who, with or without reasonable accommodation, can perform the essential functions of the employment position that such individual holds or desires." 42 U.S.C. § 12111(8). * * *

Determining whether an individual can, with or without reasonable accommodation, perform the essential functions of the position held or sought * * * is relatively straightforward. First, a court must consider whether the individual can perform the essential functions of the job without accommodation. If so, the individual is qualified (and, a fortiori, is not entitled to accommodation). If not, then a court must look to whether the individual can perform the essential functions of the job with a reasonable accommodation. If so, the individual is qualified. If not, the individual has failed to set out a necessary element of the prima facie case. * * *

* * *

2.

* * * [W]e must now determine whether Deane has, in fact, adduced sufficient evidence to survive summary judgment on the question whether she can perform the essential functions of the job without accommodation as to those functions. Deane claims that the heavy lifting she is restricted from doing is not an essential job function of a nurse. Deane describes nursing as a profession that focusses primarily on skill, intellect, and knowledge. While conceding that lifting constitutes part of a nurse's duties, she submits that it is only a small part.

* * *

PMC urges that lifting is an essential function of a nurse. In support, PMC cites its job description, which details under the heading "MAJOR TASKS, DUTIES AND RESPONSIBILITIES" that one of the "WORKING CONDITIONS" for a staff registered nurse is the "frequent lifting of patients." PMC also notes that Deane conceded that the PMC job description was "an accurate reflection of the tasks, duties and responsibilities as well as the qualifications, physical requirements and working conditions of a registered nurse at [PMC]," and that among her "critical job demands" at PMC were: (1) the placement of patients in water closets, tub chairs or gurneys, (2) the changing of position of patients, and (3) the lifting of laundry bags. These pieces of evidence, contends PMC, constitute multiple admissions by Deane that lifting is an essential function of a staff registered nurse at PMC. Finally, PMC asserts that the consequences of a nurse's inability to lift patients could create a dangerous situation in the hospital for Deane and her patients.

We decline to apply conclusive effect to either the job description or PMC's judgment as to whether heavy lifting is essential to Deane's job. The EEOC's Interpretive Guidance indicates that "the employer's judgment as to which functions are essential" and "written job descriptions prepared before advertising or interviewing applicants" are two possible types of evidence for determining the essential functions of a position, but that such evidence is not to be given greater weight simply because it is included in the non-exclusive list set out in 29 C.F.R. § 1630.2(n)(3). See 29 C.F.R. pt. 1630, app. § 1630.2(n). Thus, the job description is not, as PMC contends, incontestable evidence that unassisted patient lifting is an essential function of Deane's job. Moreover, the EEOC Regulations also provide that while "inquiry into the essential functions is not intended to second guess an employer's business judgment with regard to production standards," whether a particular function is essential "is a factual determination that must be made on a case by case basis [based upon] all relevant evidence." Id. (emphasis added). Finally, the import of the rest of PMC's evidence (e.g., her alleged admissions, etc.) is disputed by Deane. For all these reasons, we find that there is a genuine issue of material fact on the issue of whether Deane was a qualified individual under the ADA.[12] * * *

---

12. In view of this conclusion, we need not reach the more difficult question addressed by the panel whether "regarded as" disabled plaintiffs must be accommodated by their employers if they cannot perform the essential functions of their jobs. Deane contends that, as a matter of statutory interpretation, "regarded as" plaintiffs are entitled to the same reasonable accommodations from their employers as are actually disabled plaintiffs. She reasons that, just as we found that a plain reading of the ADA only requires plaintiffs to show that they can perform the essential functions of the job, a plain reading of the definition of "qualified individual" demonstrates that a "regarded as" plaintiff is qualified so long as she can perform the essential functions with reasonable accommodation. See 42 U.S.C. § 12111(8) (defining a "qualified individual" as one "who, with or without reasonable accommodation, can perform the essential functions of the employment position that such individual

holds or desires"); see also 29 C.F.R. § 1630.2(m). Moreover, Deane submits that this plain reading of the statute is buttressed by the Supreme Court's decision in [School Bd. of Nassau Cty. v.] Arline, 480 U.S. [273,] 288–89 (holding that, under the Rehabilitation Act, employers have an affirmative obligation to make reasonable accommodations for employees who are perceived to be handicapped). More importantly, according to Deane, failure to mandate reasonable accommodations for "regarded as" plaintiffs would undermine the role the ADA plays in ferreting out disability discrimination in employment. This is because, following Deane's logic, the "regarded as" prong of the disability definition is premised upon the reality that the perception of disability, socially constructed and reinforced, is difficult to destroy, and in most cases, merely informing the employer of its misperception will not be enough.

GREENBERG, CIRCUIT JUDGE, dissenting.

* * * The issue * * * is whether a person who is not actually disabled can demand a reasonable accommodation from an employer. After all it was Deane who claimed to need the lifting restriction and who claimed that she had to avoid repetitive manual tasks. To me the answer has to be no. * * * Congress did not pass the ADA to permit persons without a disability to demand accommodations. * * *

The majority believes that there is a genuine issue of material fact as to "whether PMC misperceived Deane as being disabled." But that dispute does not matter, for the critical issue is not how PMC viewed Deane because there is simply no escape from the fact that an essential element of Deane's case is that "PMC failed to accommodate her lifting restriction." After all, as the majority explains, "Deane maintains that she requires and is entitled to accommodation for her lifting restriction." * * * Thus, even if PMC regarded her as more substantially impaired than she actually was, this misperception does not matter for she was not entitled to any accommodation. * * *

The majority indicates that there is a genuine dispute of material fact regarding whether heavy lifting is an essential function of her former job. I agree that there is a genuine dispute of fact as to whether heavy lifting is an essential function of the job. But, just as the dispute of fact regarding PMC's perception of Deane does not matter, neither does the heavy lifting dispute because it is not material. Inasmuch as Deane is not actually disabled, she has no right to an accommodation whether or not the accommodation would impact on her ability to perform the essential functions of the job.

Notes and Questions

1. *Must "Regarded As" Disabled Individuals Be Accommodated?* Note the arguments presented in footnote 12 in the *Deane* court's opinion. Are you persuaded more by the argument, based on the language of the statute, that the "qualified" status *vel non* of individuals who meet the "regarded as" part of the ADA's definition of "disability" must be assessed with reasonable accommodations, just as is the status of those who meet the

In countering Deane's position, PMC notes preliminarily that a "regarded as" plaintiff's only disability is the employer's irrational response to her illusory condition. Under these circumstances, reasons PMC, it simply makes no sense to talk of accommodations for any physical impairments because, by definition, the impairments are not the statutory cause of the plaintiff's disability. Adopting Deane's interpretation of the ADA would, in PMC's view: (1) permit healthy employees to, through litigation (or the threat of litigation) demand changes in their work environments under the guise of "reasonable accommodations" for disabilities based upon misperceptions; and (2) create a windfall for legitimate "regarded as" disabled employees who, after disabusing their employers of their misperceptions, would nonetheless be entitled to accommodations that their similarly situated co-workers are not, for admittedly non-disabling conditions.

While we acknowledge the considerable force of PMC's argument, especially the latter point, we express no position on the accommodation issue, and note that the Equal Employment Opportunity Commission has not taken an official position yet either. * * *

definition of disability because of their actual condition? Or are you more persuaded by the policy argument that those who are not actually disabled do not warrant accommodation? Compare D'Angelo v. ConAgra Foods, Inc., 422 F.3d 1220 (11th Cir. 2005); Williams v. Philadelphia Hous. Auth. Police Dep't, 380 F.3d 751(3d Cir. 2004) (both holding that "regarded as disabled" employees are entitled to reasonable accommodation), with Kaplan v. North Las Vegas, 323 F.3d 1226 (9th Cir. 2003); Weber v. Strippit, Inc., 186 F.3d 907 (8th Cir.1999) (both finding no accommodation obligation toward "regarded as" disabled).

Do you understand Judge Greenberg's position on this issue? He states that it does not matter whether heavy lifting is an essential function of Deane's former job because the medical center had no duty to accommodate someone who did not have an actual disability. But if heavy lifting is not an essential function, Deane could be a qualified individual with a disability even if she could not do such lifting. Does Judge Greenberg mean that the reasonable accommodation obligations imposed on employers by § 102 (b)(5) of the ADA do not apply for "qualified" individuals whose disability status is based on how they are regarded? Is that why he indicates that the medical center could reject Deane because of her inability to lift heavy patients, regardless of whether that lifting was an essential function of her nursing job? Is this a sensible reading of the statute, consistent with both its language and its policy concerns?

2. *Relevance of Distinction of "Essential Functions"*. Do you understand, based on the language of the statute, why the en banc court in *Deane* concluded that in order to be a "qualified individual" under the ADA a plaintiff must be able to perform, with or without reasonable accommodation, only the"essential functions" of the relevant job, rather than all of its functions? Does the distinction of "essential functions" have further relevance to the operation of the statute? Should an employer's obligation to reasonably accommodate qualified individuals with a disability include the obligation not to adversely treat a qualified disabled individual because of his or her inability to perform a function that is not "essential"? See, e.g., Lovejoy–Wilson v. NOCO Motor Fuel, Inc., 263 F.3d 208 (2d Cir. 2001) (employer could not refuse to promote epileptic, based on her inability to drive, to position for which driving was not an essential job function).

3. *Determining What Functions Are Essential*. Should the *Deane* court have given "conclusive effect" to the medical center's judgment and job description in deciding whether heavy lifting was essential to Deane's job? Note the last sentence in § 101(8) of the ADA. What should "consideration" entail? Consider also the nonexhaustive lists of reasons for finding a job function essential, or "fundamental" rather than "marginal", and of evidence for whether a function is essential, as presented in the EEOC's regulations, 29 C.F.R. § 1630.2(n)(2) and (3), and explained further in its Interpretive Guidance, 29 C.F.R. pt. 1630, app. § 1630.2(n).

4. *Job Attendance as an Essential Function*. The import of "essential function" analysis and of the EEOC's regulations on this issue may turn somewhat on the essential function claimed by the employer and the accommodation desired by the employee. For instance, employers sued under the ADA have often claimed that the disability-caused absences of plaintiffs

from work render the plaintiffs unqualified because adherence to attendance rules is an essential function of their employment. The plaintiffs in these cases claim that flexibility on attendance would be a reasonable accommodation to their disabilities. Some courts have held that employees whose disabilities have required them to commit major breaches of established attendance policies are not qualified individuals with a disability. See, e.g., Spangler v. Federal Home Loan Bank, 278 F.3d 847 (8th Cir. 2002); EEOC v. Yellow Freight Sys., 253 F.3d 943 (7th Cir. 2001); Hypes v. First Commerce Corp., 134 F.3d 721 (5th Cir.1998); Price v. S–B Power Tool, 75 F.3d 362, 365–66 (8th Cir.1996); Tyndall v. National Educ. Ctrs., Inc., 31 F.3d 209, 213–14 (4th Cir.1994); Jackson v. Veterans Admin., 22 F.3d 277, 278–79 (11th Cir.1994). Other courts, however, have held that temporary medical leave might constitute reasonable accommodation in some cases. See, e.g., Cehrs v. Northeast Ohio Alzheimer's Research Center, 155 F.3d 775 (6th Cir.1998) (severe psoriasis flareup); Criado v. IBM Corp., 145 F.3d 437 (1st Cir.1998) (mental depression).

Can the essential-functions standard in the ADA, or the EEOC's elaboration of this standard, help decide these cases, or must they turn on individualized balancing of costs and benefits? Cf. Fritz v. Mascotech Automotive Systems Group, Inc., 914 F.Supp. 1481, 1490 (E.D.Mich.1996) (employee's attendance raised issue of reasonable accommodation that must be resolved by jury). See generally James A. Passamano, Employee Leave Under the Americans with Disabilities Act and the Family Medical Leave Act, 38 S. Tex. L. Rev. 861 (1997).

5. *Essential Function Analysis in Job Restructuring Cases.* Might essential function analysis and the EEOC guidelines be helpful in cases where plaintiffs claim that employers should accommodate their disabilities by restructuring job duties between employees, see § 101(9)(b) (expressly listing "job restructuring" as a possible reasonable accommodation), so that the plaintiffs will have jobs for which they are fully qualified? Might Deane have requested job restructuring as an accommodation? See also, e.g., Haysman v. Food Lion, Inc., 893 F.Supp. 1092, 1101 (S.D.Ga.1995) (lifting seventy pounds is an essential function of assistant store manager position because it was on job description, assistant managers regularly performed such lifting, and the consequences of not doing so would be reduced efficiency); Kuntz v. City of New Haven, 2 A.D. Cases (BNA) 905 (D.Conn. 1993), affirmed without opinion, 29 F.3d 622 (2d Cir.1994) ("physically strenuous aspects" of New Haven police lieutenant's job are proportionately insignificant relative to supervisory and administrative duties).

6. *Does Infrequency Mean Nonessential?* Are infrequently performed functions necessarily not essential? The EEOC's Interpretive Guidance notes that "although a firefighter may not regularly have to carry an unconscious adult out of a burning building, the consequence of failing to require the firefighter to be able to perform this function would be serious." 29 C.F.R. pt. 1630, app. § 1630.2(n).) Should frequency nonetheless be a relevant factor in some cases?

7. *Hiring Assistants as an Accommodation?* Section 101(9)(B) of the ADA lists "the provision of qualified readers or interpreters" as a reasonable accommodation. The EEOC's Interpretive Guidance further states that

reasonable accommodation may include providing personal assistants, "such as a page turner for an employee with no hands or a travel attendant to act as a sighted guide to assist a blind employee on occasional business trips." 29 C.F.R. pt. 1630, app. § 1630.2(*o*). However, the Guidance also states that employers need not "reallocate essential functions" to assistants:

> For example, suppose a security guard position requires the individual who holds the job to inspect identification cards. An employer would not have to provide an individual who is legally blind with an assistant to look at the identification cards for the legally blind employee. In this situation the assistant would be performing the job for the individual with a disability rather than assisting the individual to perform the job.

Id. Do you understand the distinction drawn by the EEOC? If an employee must turn pages in his job, why is page turning assisting rather than performing an essential function of a job, just as is inspecting identification cards in the EEOC's last example? Might the EEOC be suggesting that employers may have to provide assistants to help disabled employees perform relatively mundane parts of their jobs that do not require use of the disabled employees' special skills, but they do not have to provide assistants to do part of disabled employees' skill-demanding work? If so, does this distinction import a class bias into the accommodation standard, requiring greater expenditures for more highly skilled disabled employees? Does the distinction nonetheless accord with a statutory goal of providing more equal opportunities for the disabled? With a standard of reasonableness that weighs all costs and benefits of a suggested accommodation? See also Reigel v. Kaiser Foundation Health Plan of N.C., 859 F.Supp. 963, 973 (E.D.N.C. 1994) (employer not required to provide assistant to physician practicing internal medicine who was unable to perform tasks demanding hand or arm strength).

8. *Attractiveness to Customers as an Essential Function?* In light of the development of BFOQ law under Title VII, might essential function analysis and the EEOC guidelines be helpful in cases where plaintiffs claim that employers include job qualifications only to appeal to customer stereotypes and prejudices? Can such cases be decided by a direct cost-benefit analysis? Consider, for instance, the claim of a dwarf that he should be able to be employed as a guard at an exclusive, high fashion store despite the employer's desire to project a glamorous image. Or the claim of a cosmetically disfigured woman that she should be able to be employed as a receptionist at a restaurant despite the employer's demand for an especially attractive greeter. Would the woman's claim be stronger than if she applied for work as a model or an exotic dancer? Compare the Wilson v. Southwest Airlines Co. case at p. 334 and the accompanying notes. Compare Kuehl v. Wal–Mart Stores, Inc., 909 F.Supp. 794, 801 (D.Colo.1995) (Wal–Mart door greeter must be able to greet standing, rather than sitting, because essence of Wal–Mart's greeting policy was aggressive hospitality), with EEOC v. Wal–Mart Stores, Inc., 477 F.3d 561 (8th Cir. 2007) (EEOC presented prima facie case that applicant with cerebral palsy could be greeter with use of motorized scooter).

9. *Can an Individual Receiving Disability Benefits Be a "Qualified Individual with a Disability"?* If an individual successfully applies for

disability benefits from the social security system, from a state's workers' compensation system, or from a private disability insurer, should that individual be estopped from claiming that she "can perform the essential functions of the employment position" that she seeks? Indeed, should an individual's mere assertion of "total and permanent disability" in an application for benefits be sufficient to preclude her from claiming that she is capable of fulfilling the functions of any job?

In Cleveland v. Policy Management Systems Corp., 526 U.S. 795, 119 S.Ct. 1597, 143 L.Ed.2d 966 (1999), the Supreme Court held that the pursuit and receipt of social security benefits for total disability does not "estop" or even "erect a strong presumption against the recipient's success under the ADA." The Court stressed that determinations of eligibility for social security disability benefits are made on the basis of necessarily simplifying presumptions about the general ability to work of people with particular impairments, and without individualized assessment of a claimant's capacities or consideration of either essential job functions or of reasonable accommodations. The Court also noted that social security disability benefits may be granted to individuals after they begin working again so that their reentry into the labor market can be facilitated as their condition changes over time. Finally, the Court cited the "ordinary rules" of the legal system that allow parties to make two or more legally inconsistent claims in the alternative as relevant to an ADA plaintiff who "has merely applied for, but has not been awarded" benefits. The Court did hold, however, that an ADA plaintiff must "proffer a sufficient explanation" of "the apparent contradiction that arises out of the earlier social security disability claim." "To defeat summary judgment, that explanation must be sufficient to warrant a reasonable juror's concluding that, assuming the truth of, or the plaintiff's good faith belief in, the earlier [claim of total disability], the plaintiff could nonetheless 'perform the essential functions' of her job, with or without 'reasonable accommodation.'" Since Cleveland, some plaintiffs who have filed for social security disability benefits have been able to defeat motions for summary judgment by offering evidence that they would have been qualified to work had they been reasonably accommodated. See, e.g., Vera v. Williams Hospitality Group, 73 F.Supp.2d 161 (D.P.R. 1999); Donahue v. Consolidated Rail Corp., 52 F.Supp.2d 476 (E.D.Pa. 1999).

Note on Establishing Discriminatory Intent Under the ADA

In few cases litigated under Title I of the ADA have plaintiffs had to establish the basic element of a disparate treatment case—that the defendant took into account plaintiff's protected status in making a personnel decision adverse to the plaintiff. Instead, in most ADA employment discrimination cases, like US Airways, Vande Zande, and Deane, plaintiffs have claimed that defendant employers have failed to provide reasonable accommodations. Defendants have responded, not by claiming neutrality toward plaintiffs' physical or mental conditions and the behavior caused by such conditions, but rather by denying (i) that these conditions constitute disabilities under the ADA's definition, (ii) that the plaintiffs requested accommodations that would be reasonable, or (iii) that plaintiffs requested accommodations that could be granted without undue hardship. Where more traditional disparate treatment claims have been asserted in Rehabilitation Act cases, however, the lower courts generally have applied the *McDonnell Douglas–Burdine* burden-shifting rules. See, e.g., Crawford v. Runyon, 37 F.3d 1338, 1341 (8th Cir.1994); Teahan v. Metro–North Commuter R.R. Co., 951 F.2d 511, 514 (2d Cir.1991); Smith v. Barton, 914 F.2d 1330, 1339–40 (9th Cir.1990); Norcross v. Sneed, 755 F.2d 113, 116–17 (8th Cir.1985). The courts in ADA cases have followed this precedent. See, e.g., Ennis v. NABER, Inc., 53 F.3d 55, 57 (4th Cir.1995).

As illustrated by *Ennis*, however, there are some disparate treatment issues that are special to the ADA. Relying on the ADA's proscription of discrimination against individuals for having a relationship or association with an individual with a disability, § 102(b)(4), the plaintiff in *Ennis* claimed that she was discharged because of her adoption of a disabled child who would impose special costs on the employer's health care plan. The Fourth Circuit held that in order to establish a prima facie case, the plaintiff would have to show membership in the protected class, being discharged, performance before discharge at a level meeting her employer's legitimate expectations, and "circumstances that raise a reasonable inference of unlawful discrimination." Id. at 58. The court posited the last condition as an alternative to showing being replaced by someone without a disability or with a disability easier to accommodate, which it suggested would be too difficult because of a plaintiff's lack of knowledge about the conditions of other employees. However, the court also found that the plaintiff had failed to demonstrate any circumstances raising an inference of discrimination beyond her discharge. Do you agree with the approach of the *Ennis* court? Why shouldn't satisfaction of the first three conditions be an adequate prima facie case of discriminatory discharge? Do you also agree that replacement with someone with a more easily accommodated disability raises an inference of a violation of the ADA? See Hutchinson v. United Parcel Service, 883 F.Supp. 379, 395 (N.D.Iowa 1995).

Most lower courts now hold that an ADA plaintiff does not have to prove that his disability was the sole cause of the adverse personnel action he challenges. See, e.g., Head v. Glacier Northwest, Inc., 413 F.3d 1053, 1065 (9th Cir. 2005) (motivating cause); McNely v. Ocala Star–Banner Corp., 99 F.3d 1068, 1076–77 (11th Cir.1996) (but-for causation). But see Hedrick v. Western Reserve Care Sys., 355 F.3d 444, 454 (6th Cir. 2004) (sole cause). The *McNely* court stressed legislative history suggesting that Congress intended to reject a sole causation standard when it did not repeat in the ADA the "solely by reason of her or his disability" phrase of § 504 of the Rehabilitation Act. 99 F.3d at 1076. The *McNely* court also noted that when Congress enacted the ADA it was aware of the Supreme Court's interpretation in *Price Waterhouse* of Title VII to not require proof of sole causation. Does this mean that the *Price Waterhouse* Court's burden shifting on the but-for causation issue should also apply to ADA cases? If so, should ADA courts further apply Congress's modification of the *Price Waterhouse* holding in § 107 of the Civil Rights Act of 1991, as interpreted by the Supreme Court in Desert Palace, Inc. v. Costa, 539 U.S. 90, 123 S.Ct. 2148, 156 L.Ed.2d 84 (2003), supra p. 75? Or is that provision not applicable to the ADA because it expressly amends only Title VII? The lower courts have not reached a consensus. See, e.g., *Head*, supra, at 1065–66 (interpreting and applying *Desert Palace*, but not 1991 Civil Rights Act); Pedigo v. P.A.M. Transport, Inc., 60 F.3d 1300, 1301 (8th Cir.1995) (following the 1991 Act). See also § 107(a) of the ADA (incorporating Title VII "powers, remedies, and procedures").

Employers might acknowledge that they have treated an employee adversely because of inappropriate or unproductive behavior associated with his disability, but may deny that discrimination against that behavior should be treated as discrimination "because of" the disability. In Raytheon Co. v. Hernandez, supra p. 507, at fn. 6, the Supreme Court seemed to approve such a defense by noting that in Hazen Paper Co. v. Biggins, supra p. 457, it had rejected an argument that discrimination against something "related to" a protected status is discrimination against that status. Thus, the Court suggested, termination for "testing positive" for drugs would be termination because of violation of a rule against illegal drug use, and not because of a related drug addiction. See also, e.g., Despears v. Milwaukee County, 63 F.3d 635, 636 (7th Cir.1995) (discharging an alcoholic for having his license revoked for multiple convictions of drunk driving was not a decision based on his alcoholism because the alcoholism did not compel him to drive while drunk); EEOC v. Amego, Inc., 110 F.3d 135, 149 (1st Cir.1997) (firing employee for abuse of drug prescribed for her disabling depression not caused by disability); Palmer v. Circuit Court of Cook County, 117 F.3d 351 (7th Cir.1997) ("if an employer fires an employee because of the employee's unacceptable behavior, the fact that that behavior was precipitated by a mental illness does not present an issue" under the ADA). Should a court's treatment of these kinds of cases turn on whether the employer would have penalized the behavior in the same manner had it not been caused by the disability?

Section 103 of the ADA provides an express general defense for even overt intentional discrimination against individuals with disabilities. Section 103(a) allows qualification standards, tests, or selection criteria that deny a job or benefit to an individual with a disability if they are "shown to be job-related and consistent with business necessity" and job "performance cannot be accomplished by reasonable accommodation. * * * " Does this defense do more than reiterate the requirement that an individual with a disability must be qualified, with or without reasonable accommodation, to "perform the essential functions" of the desired job in order to be a victim of the discrimination condemned by Title I of the ADA? Might an individual be "qualified" under the § 101(8) definition and still, based on the § 103(a) defense, be legitimately excluded from a job because of his disability? For instance, should an employer be able to justify the blanket exclusion from a class of jobs of all individuals with a particular disability based on the costs of individualized, predictive assessments of which individuals with this disability could perform the jobs? Cf. EEOC v. Exxon Corp., 203 F.3d 871 (5th Cir. 2000) ("business necessity" defense applicable to generally applied safety rules, rather than safety rules imposed on particular individuals); International Union, UAW v. Johnson Controls, Inc., 499 U.S. 187, 111 S.Ct. 1196, 113 L.Ed.2d 158 (1991), supra page 457.

Section 103(b) offers a specific defense for overt intentional discrimination against an individual with a disability by providing that an employer "may include a requirement that an individual shall not pose a direct threat to the health or safety of other individuals in the workplace" as one of the "qualification standards" allowed by § 103(a). Section 101(3) defines "direct threat" as a "significant risk to the health or safety of others that cannot be eliminated by reasonable accommodation." The EEOC regulations state that the "determination that an individual poses a 'direct threat' shall be based on an individualized assessment of the individual's present ability to safely perform the essential functions of the job." 29 C.F.R. § 1630.2(r). The EEOC directs consideration of four factors: "(1) The duration of the risk; (2) The nature and severity of the potential harm; (3) The likelihood that the potential harm will occur; and (4) The imminence of the potential harm." Id.

Consider how the *Bragdon* Court viewed a parallel defense applicable to public accommodation discrimination claims under Title III of the ADA:

BRAGDON v. ABBOTT

Supreme Court of the United States, 1998.
524 U.S. 624, 118 S.Ct. 2196, 141 L.Ed.2d 540.

JUSTICE KENNEDY delivered the opinion of the Court.

III

* * * Notwithstanding the protection given respondent by the ADA's definition of disability, petitioner could have refused to treat her if her infectious condition "pose[d] a direct threat to the health or safety of others." 42 U.S.C. § 12182(b)(3). The ADA defines a direct threat to be "a significant risk to the health or safety of others that cannot be eliminated by a modification of policies, practices, or procedures or by the provision of auxiliary aids or services." Ibid. Parallel provisions appear in the employment provisions of Title I. §§ 12111(3), 12113(b).

The ADA's direct threat provision stems from the recognition in *School Bd. of Nassau Cty. v. Arline*, 480 U.S. 273, 287, 107 S.Ct. 1123, 1130–1131, 94 L.Ed.2d 307 (1987), of the importance of prohibiting discrimination against individuals with disabilities while protecting others from significant health and safety risks, resulting, for instance, from a contagious disease. In *Arline*, the Court reconciled these objectives by construing the Rehabilitation Act not to require the hiring of a person who posed "a significant risk of communicating an infectious disease to others." *Id.*, at 287, n. 16, 107 S.Ct., at 1131, n. 16. Congress amended the Rehabilitation Act and the Fair Housing Act to incorporate the language. See 29 U.S.C. § 706(8)(D) (excluding individuals who "would constitute a direct threat to the health or safety of other individuals"); 42 U.S.C. § 3604(f)(9) (same). It later relied on the same language in enacting the ADA. See 28 CFR pt. 36, App. B, p. 626 (1997) (ADA's direct threat provision codifies *Arline*). Because few, if any, activities in life are risk free, *Arline* and the ADA do not ask whether a risk exists, but whether it is significant. *Arline*, supra, at 287, and n. 16, 107 S.Ct., at 1131, and n. 16; 42 U.S.C. § 12182(b)(3).

The existence, or nonexistence, of a significant risk must be determined from the standpoint of the person who refuses the treatment or accommodation, and the risk assessment must be based on medical or other objective evidence. *Arline*, supra, at 288, 107 S.Ct., at 1131; 28 CFR § 36.208(c) (1997); id., pt. 36, App. B, p. 626. As a health care professional, petitioner had the duty to assess the risk of infection based on the objective, scientific information available to him and others in his profession. His belief that a significant risk existed, even if maintained in good faith, would not relieve him from liability. To use the words of the question presented, petitioner receives no special deference simply because he is a health care professional. * * *

Our conclusion that courts should assess the objective reasonableness of the views of health care professionals without deferring to their individual judgments does not answer the implicit assumption in the question presented, whether petitioner's actions were reasonable in light of the available medical evidence. In assessing the reasonableness of petitioner's actions, the views of public health authorities, such as the U.S. Public Health Service, CDC, and the National Institutes of Health, are of special weight and authority. *Arline*, supra, at 288, 107 S.Ct., at 1130–1131; 28 CFR pt. 36, App. B, p. 626 (1997). The views of these organizations are not conclusive, however. A health care professional who disagrees with the prevailing medical consensus may refute it by citing a credible scientific basis for deviating from the accepted norm. See W. Keeton, D. Dobbs, R. Keeton, & D. Owen, Prosser and Keeton on Law of Torts § 32, p. 187 (5th ed.1984).

We have reviewed so much of the record as necessary to illustrate the application of the rule to the facts of this case. For the most part, the Court of Appeals followed the proper standard in evaluating the petitioner's position and conducted a thorough review of the evidence. Its rejection of the District Court's reliance on the Marianos affidavits was a correct application of the principle that petitioner's actions must be evaluated in light of the available, objective evidence. The record did not show that CDC had published the conclusion set out in the affidavits at the time petitioner refused to treat respondent.

* * * Petitioner testified that he believed hospitals had safety measures, such as air filtration, ultraviolet lights, and respirators, which would reduce the risk of HIV transmission. Petitioner made no showing, however, that any area hospital had these safeguards or even that he had hospital privileges. His expert also admitted the lack of any scientific basis for the conclusion that these measures would lower the risk of transmission. Petitioner failed to present any objective, medical evidence showing that treating respondent in a hospital would be safer or more efficient in preventing HIV transmission than treatment in a well-equipped dental office.

We are concerned, however, that the Court of Appeals might have placed mistaken reliance upon two other sources. In ruling no triable issue of fact existed on this point, the Court of Appeals relied on the 1993 CDC Dentistry Guidelines and the 1991 American Dental Association Policy on HIV. This evidence is not definitive. As noted earlier, the

CDC Guidelines recommended certain universal precautions which, in CDC's view, "should reduce the risk of disease transmission in the dental environment." * * * In our view, the Guidelines do not necessarily contain implicit assumptions conclusive of the point to be decided. The Guidelines set out CDC's recommendation that the universal precautions are the best way to combat the risk of HIV transmission. They do not assess the level of risk.

Nor can we be certain, on this record, whether the 1991 American Dental Association Policy on HIV carries the weight the Court of Appeals attributed to it. The Policy does provide some evidence of the medical community's objective assessment of the risks posed by treating people infected with HIV in dental offices. * * *

We note, however, that the Association is a professional organization, which, although a respected source of information on the dental profession, is not a public health authority. It is not clear the extent to which the Policy was based on the Association's assessment of dentists' ethical and professional duties in addition to its scientific assessment of the risk to which the ADA refers. * * *

* * *

There are reasons to doubt whether petitioner advanced evidence sufficient to raise a triable issue of fact on the significance of the risk. Petitioner relied on two principal points: First, he asserted that the use of high-speed drills and surface cooling with water created a risk of airborne HIV transmission. The study on which petitioner relied was inconclusive, however, determining only that "[f]urther work is required to determine whether such a risk exists." Johnson & Robinson, Human Immunodeficiency Virus–1 (HIV–1) in the Vapors of Surgical Power Instruments, 33 J. of Medical Virology 47, 47 (1991). Petitioner's expert witness conceded, moreover, that no evidence suggested the spray could transmit HIV. His opinion on airborne risk was based on the absence of contrary evidence, not on positive data. Scientific evidence and expert testimony must have a traceable, analytical basis in objective fact before it may be considered on summary judgment. See General Electric Co. v. Joiner, 522 U.S. 136, 118 S.Ct. 512, 518, 519, 139 L.Ed.2d 508 (1997).

Second, petitioner argues that, as of September 1994, CDC had identified seven dental workers with possible occupational transmission of HIV. These dental workers were exposed to HIV in the course of their employment, but CDC could not determine whether HIV infection had resulted. It is now known that CDC could not ascertain whether the seven dental workers contracted the disease because they did not present themselves for HIV testing at an appropriate time after their initial exposure. It is not clear on this record, however, whether this information was available to petitioner in September 1994. If not, the seven cases might have provided some, albeit not necessarily sufficient, support for petitioner's position. Standing alone, we doubt it would meet the objective, scientific basis for finding a significant risk to the petitioner.

Our evaluation of the evidence is constrained by the fact that on these and other points we have not had briefs and arguments directed to the entire record. * * *

We conclude the proper course is to give the Court of Appeals the opportunity to determine whether our analysis of some of the studies cited by the parties would change its conclusion that petitioner presented neither objective evidence nor a triable issue of fact on the question of risk. In remanding the case, we do not foreclose the possibility that the Court of Appeals may reach the same conclusion it did earlier. A remand will permit a full exploration of the issue through the adversary process.

CHIEF JUSTICE REHNQUIST, with whom JUSTICE SCALIA and JUSTICE THOMAS join, and with whom JUSTICE O'CONNOR joins as to Part II, concurring in the judgment in part and dissenting in part.

I agree with the Court that "the existence, or nonexistence, of a significant risk must be determined from the standpoint of the person who refuses the treatment or accommodation," as of the time that the decision refusing treatment is made. I disagree with the Court, however, that "[i]n assessing the reasonableness of petitioner's actions, the views of public health authorities * * * are of special weight and authority." Those views are, of course, entitled to a presumption of validity when the actions of those authorities themselves are challenged in court, and even in disputes between private parties where Congress has committed that dispute to adjudication by a public health authority. But in litigation between private parties originating in the federal courts, I am aware of no provision of law or judicial practice that would require or permit courts to give some scientific views more credence than others simply because they have been endorsed by a politically appointed public health authority (such as the Surgeon General). In litigation of this latter sort, which is what we face here, the credentials of the scientists employed by the public health authority, and the soundness of their studies, must stand on their own. * * *

Notes and Questions

1. *An Objectively "Significant Risk" from the Standpoint of the Decisionmaker.* Why does the *Bragdon* Court require the significance of the risk to be evaluated on the basis only of evidence that was available at the time of the exclusionary decision? What does the Court assume about how Congress weighed health and safety risks against the disadvantaging of the disabled? Why does the Court then reject a subjective, good faith standard for the "health and safety" defense? Should the compulsory force of the law operate against someone like Bragdon who without animus toward the disabled, sincerely wants to protect his own health or that of others? Whether or not you agree with the Court's standard as a matter of policy, is there any reason not to apply it in Title I as well as Title III cases under the ADA?

2. *Should Courts Rely on Administrative or Privately Developed Risk Standards?* Note the *Bragdon* Court's statement that the "views of public

health authorities * * * are of special weight and authority", though "not conclusive", in assessing the reasonableness of exclusionary decisions like that of Abbott's. Note also the Court's treatment of the 1993 Center for Disease Control (CDC) Dentistry Guidelines and the 1991 American Dental Association (ADA) Policy on HIV. Had the CDC Guidelines directly assessed risk, should the lower court have given them "special weight"? Should the lower court also have given "special weight" to the ADA Policy had it expressly assessed risk levels and separated that assessment from considerations of professional duty? Would your answers differ if the Department of Health and Human Services (HHS), or the EEOC, had adopted either the CDC Guidelines or the ADA Policy by rulemaking, even without express statutory rulemaking authority? Should the HHS or the EEOC attempt to engage in such rulemaking for serious prevalent and contagious diseases such as HIV?

3. *Special Regulatory Authority for Food Handling.* The ADA does provide express administrative authority for one category of health risk. Section 103(d) of the ADA directs the Secretary of HHS to promulgate a list of infectious and communicable diseases that may be transmitted through the handling of food. Employers may refuse to assign a job involving food handling to any individual with a listed disease for which the risk of transmission cannot be eliminated by reasonable accommodation.

4. *Treatment of HIV Infection Risk in the Lower Courts.* A number of courts have recognized that there is no evidence of HIV being transmitted through the air, rather than through bodily fluids. See, e.g., Chalk v. United States District Ct., 840 F.2d 701, 706 (9th Cir.1988) (AIDS-infected teacher may be returned to classroom, in view of "an overwhelming evidentiary consensus of medical and scientific opinion regarding the nature and transmission of AIDS"); Harris v. Thigpen, 941 F.2d 1495, 1525 (11th Cir.1991) (must do case-by-case determination of risk of transmission of AIDS virus); Saladin v. Turner, 936 F.Supp. 1571, 1580–81 (N.D.Okl.1996) (ADA prohibits discharge of waiter for associating with an HIV-infected partner).

On the other hand, some courts have held that employers may determine that HIV-infected individuals do not meet reasonable qualification standards for jobs involving invasive surgical procedures. See, e.g., Mauro v. Borgess Medical Center, 137 F.3d 398 (6th Cir.1998); Bradley v. University of Texas M.D. Anderson Cancer Ctr., 3 F.3d 922, 924 (5th Cir.1993); Doe v. Washington Univ., 780 F.Supp. 628, 632–34 (E.D.Mo.1991). See also Doe v. Aliquippa Hospital Ass'n, 3 (BNA) A.D. Cases 1244 (W.D. Pa. 1994) (operating room technician erroneously perceived to have HIV virus was not "otherwise qualified" because of perceived risk of infecting others); Local 1812, Am. Fed'n of Gov't Employees v. United States Dep't of State, 662 F.Supp. 50, 54 (D.D.C.1987) (AIDS carrier not "otherwise qualified" for worldwide Foreign Service). Are the last two decisions good law after *Bragdon*? On remand in *Bragdon* the First Circuit held that Bragdon's evidence of a direct threat in performing the dental work with proper precautions in his office rather than in a hospital was too speculative to present a genuine issue of material fact. See Abbott v. Bragdon, 163 F.3d 87 (1st Cir.1998).

5. *"Direct Threat" to the Individual with a Disability.* Note again the ADA's definition of "direct threat" as a "significant risk to the health or safety of others." In light of this definition can an employer refuse to hire an individual because the individual's disability poses a direct threat to his or her own safety, regardless of whether the disability also threatens others? In Chevron U.S.A. Inc. v. Echazabal, 536 U.S. 73, 122 S.Ct. 2045, 153 L.Ed.2d 82 (2002) a unanimous Court upheld as a reasonable application of the statute an EEOC regulation stating that an employer can guard against a "direct threat" to the health or safety of the "individual" as well as to others. 29 C.F.R. § 1630.2(r). What justification might there be for this administrative gloss? Does the statute's framing of the "direct threat" defense as being included in permissible "qualification standards" give the EEOC more discretion to suggest further related standards?

6. *Purpose of the "Direct Threat" Defense?* What exactly does the "direct threat" defense add to the requirement in § 101(8) of the ADA that in order to be protected from employment discrimination an individual with a disability must be qualified to perform essential job functions? Might a contagious worker, like the teacher with tuberculosis in the *Arline* case, be considered qualified to work and still to pose a health or safety threat? How about a worker with a mental disorder that caused violent, threatening outbursts, but who could function productively between outbursts? Would an employer need to assert the "direct threat" defense to justify not hiring for a job requiring exposure to a particular chemical an individual with a genetic predisposition to a type of cancer that could be triggered by the chemical, or would that individual not be within the ADA protected class in any event? (If Title VII included a defense like the "direct threat" defense, would the *Johnson Controls* case, p. 321 supra, have had to be decided differently?)

7. *Reversing the Burden of Proof?* Does the *Bragdon* Court assume that Bragdon had the burden of proving the direct threat as an affirmative defense? Should employers always have this burden under the provisions of Title I? Can an employer effectively reverse the burden of proof by asserting, as suggested in the last note, that a plaintiff is not a qualified individual with a disability because insuring safety is an essential function of the job she seeks? See Bates v. United Parcel Service, Inc., 511 F.3d 974 (9th Cir.2007) (hearing impaired plaintiffs must show that they are capable of safely filling driving positions they seek, but employer would have to prove its hearing standard was a business necessity). See also Albertson's, Inc. v. Kirkingburg, 527 U.S. 555, 578, 119 S.Ct. 2162, 2174, 144 L.Ed.2d 518 (1999) (Thomas, J. concurring) (suggesting that plaintiffs should have burden of proving safety where it is essential to job); Ann Hubbard, Understanding and Implementing the ADA's Direct Threat Defense, 95 Nw. L. Rev. 1279 (2001) (statute places burden on employer).

8. *Does the "Direct Threat" Defense Justify Rational Statistical Discrimination?* Does the "direct threat" defense do more than clarify for the ADA that essential job functions always may include protecting the safety of others? Does it also justify an employer's exclusion of an individual with a disability on the basis of a general employment standard that efficiently, but imperfectly, screens out those who provide significant health and safety threats? Or is this precluded by the EEOC's assertion that an employer's determination of the existence of a "direct threat" must be based on an

"individualized assessment of the individual's present ability to safely perform"? If so, is this a correct interpretation of § 103(b) of the Act? What if individualized predictive assessments are too expensive to be practical? Or does the EEOC just intend that employers consider each condition individually to the extent practical? Cf. Western Air Lines v. Criswell, 472 U.S. 400, 414, 105 S.Ct. 2743, 86 L.Ed.2d 321 (1985), p. 438 supra (interpreting bona fide occupational qualification defense under the ADEA to allow age-based qualifications when it is "impossible or highly impractical" to assess older employees as safety risks on an individualized basis). See also EEOC v. Exxon Corp., supra, (employers may use "business necessity" defense to justify general, safety-based qualification standards).

In *Albertsons* the Government argued that any safety standard that tends to screen out individuals with disabilities can only be applied in accord with the EEOC's reading of the "direct threat" provision in § 103(b) of the ADA—i.e., each disabled employee must be given an "individualized assessment." The Court did not rule on the Government's argument because it found the safety standard applied in that case to be required by the Department of Transportation.

Note on the ADA and Medical Examinations and Inquiries

Section 102(d) of the ADA may discourage some intentional discrimination against disabled workers by restricting the use of medical examinations and inquiries (other than testing for the illegal use of drugs, which § 104(d)(1) provides "shall not be considered a medical examination.") Section 102(d)(2) is designed to discourage intentional hiring discrimination by prohibiting medical exams or inquiries of "a job applicant as to whether such applicant is an individual with a disability or as to the nature or severity of such disability." Section 102(d)(3) allows an offer of employment to be conditioned on the results of a post-offer, confidential medical examination required of all entering employees; it is presumably difficult to revoke an offer after a medical examination without highlighting the results of the exam as the probable cause of the revocation.

Section 102(d)(2)(B), however, raises a challenging interpretive issue by permitting pre-employment offer "inquiries into the ability of an applicant to perform job-related functions." What kind of inquiries only probe the ability to perform job functions without also probing the existence or the nature of a disability?

The EEOC's "Enforcement Guidance" on "Preemployment Disability–Related Questions and Medical Examinations"(October, 1995) defines a prohibited medical inquiry broadly as one "likely to elicit information" about a disability. An "employer cannot ask questions that are closely related to disability." However, "if there are many possible answers to a question and only some of those answers would contain disability-related information", the question may be asked. For instance, an employer may ask whether an applicant "can perform any or all job functions." An employer also may inquire about attendance records in prior employment, but may not ask about the applicant's worker-compensation claims history because this would be likely to elicit information about the individual's disability. Tests that measure a candidate's ability to perform a discrete task, such as a physical fitness test or a simulated task test, are not improper pre-offer tests under the ADA. Similarly, psychological tests used to measure an applicant's ability or propensity to perform a job successfully, such as personality or honesty tests, are not automatically barred, unless application of the test shows that it is designed to detect mental disability. *See, e.g.,* Karraker v. Rent–A–Center, Inc., 411 F.3d 831 (7th Cir. 2005) (barring use of test originally designed to detect mental disorders). Vision tests are not automatically barred, but may constitute a medical exam if they are likely to reveal an applicant's disability. For further elaboration, see also the EEOC's "Enforcement Guidance: Disability–Related Inquiries and Medical Examinations of Employees Under the Americans with Disabilities Act (ADA)" (July, 2000).

Is § 102(d)(2)'s restriction on pre-offer inquiries only to insure that unrevealed disabilities stay hidden before employment offers so that employers cannot as easily construct pretexts for discrimination? Can an employer insist on testing a job applicant who claims to have a disability to confirm the need for reasonable accommodation? See Grenier v. Cyanamid Plastics, 70 F.3d 667, 675 (1st Cir.1995) (permissible to request medical documentation to establish claim of disability and ability to perform job). What if the applicant is a former employee who previously requested accommodation? See Harris v. Harris & Hart, 206 F.3d 838, 844 (9th Cir. 2000) "[d]efendant had no reason to believe plaintiff's condition had cured itself"). The EEOC's Enforcement Guidance on Reasonable Accommodation states that employers may ask for documentation of any particular disability for which an individual requests reasonable accommodation unless the disability is obvious or already known.

Are the purposes of the ADA served by allowing applicants who have been asked inappropriate questions about their medical histories to sue without proving that they are disabled? Compare, e.g., Cossette v. Minnesota Power & Light, 188 F.3d 964 (8th Cir.1999); Griffin v. Steeltek, Inc., 160 F.3d 591 (10th Cir.1998) (proof of disability not required), with Armstrong v. Turner Industries, 141 F.3d 554 (5th Cir.1998) (must be some cognizable injury from improper examination).

Section 102(d)(4)(A) also prohibits any medical examination or inquiry of current employees concerning disability status, "unless such examination or inquiry is shown to be job-related and consistent with business necessity." The EEOC's Interpretive Guidance states that:

> The purpose of this provision is to prevent the administration to employees of medical tests or inquiries that do not serve a legitimate business purpose. For example, if an employee suddenly starts to use increased amounts of sick leave or starts to appear sickly, an employer could not require that employee to be tested for AIDS, HIV infection, or cancer unless the employer can demonstrate that such testing is job-related and consistent with business necessity. 29 C.F.R. pt. 1630, app. § 1630.13(b).

Would the EEOC's interpretation prevent an employer from protecting against employee abuse of sick leave by requiring employees to provide some general medical documentation before returning from substantial leave? Would it prevent an employer from requiring employees returning from substantial leave to provide medical certification that they do not pose a threat to the safety or health of other workers? See Conroy v. New York State Dept. of Correctional Services, 333 F.3d 88 (2d Cir. 2003) (to show business necessity, employer must justify policy requiring medical certification by demonstrating reason to believe covered jobs might pose threat to health or safety or that covered employees might be abusers of sick leave). Is this an adequate accommodation of legitimate employer concerns? Are not the risks of contagion and abuse of sick leave always present?

What remedies might be available to plaintiffs who can establish that an employer has conducted a medical examination or inquiry that is illegal under § 102(d)? To obtain more than attorney's fees and a prospective order would plaintiffs have to show loss of some employment opportunity? Would plaintiffs at least have to establish that they were qualified individuals with a disability?

Can an applicant who answers illegal questions on a preemployment medical examination untruthfully to hide his or her disability claim the protection of the statute from a subsequent employment rejection or discharge? Compare Armstrong, supra, with Downs v. Massachusetts Bay Transportation Authority, 13 F.Supp.2d 130 (D.Mass.1998).

Some states also have passed laws barring the use of medical tests for determining the presence of particular conditions. See, e. g., Vt. Stat. Ann. Tit. 21, 495 (1995); Wis. State. Ann. § 103.15 (West 1996) (both restricting HIV testing). Other states have prohibited pre-employment genetic screening. See, e.g., Or.Rev.Stat. § 659A.300 (2001); Iowa Code § 729.6(2) (1995).

Note on the ADA and the Disparate Impact Theory of Discrimination

The list of alternative definitions of disability discrimination contained in § 102(b) of the ADA expressly authorizes disparate impact challenges. Section 102(b)(3) prohibits "utilizing standards, criteria, or methods of administration—(A) that have the effect of discrimination on the basis of disability. * * * " Section 102(b)(6) prohibits "using qualification standards, employment tests or other selection criteria that screen out or tend to screen out an individual with a disability or a class of individuals with disabilities unless the standard, test or other selection criteria * * * is shown to be job-related * * * and is consistent with business necessity. * * * " And § 102(b)(1), which prohibits "limiting, segregating, or classifying a job applicant or employee in a way that adversely affects the opportunities or status of such applicant or employee because of the disability of such applicant or employee", seems more clearly to rest on disparate effects than § 703(a)(2) of Title VII, on which disparate impact theory was first based. But see 29 C.F.R. pt. 1630, app. § 1630.5 (suggesting that the EEOC views (b)(1) to cover only intentional discrimination).

Only the § (b)(6) prohibition includes an express job relatedness and business necessity qualification; however, the EEOC's ADA regulations also include the qualification when repeating the § (b)(3) prohibition. See 29 C.F.R. § 1630.7. Is this inclusion appropriate? Can the disparate impact theory be applied without allowing some kind of cost-based defense? Should the qualification also be applied to the prohibition in § 102(b)(1)? These questions are further complicated by the statute's additional express inclusion in § 103(a) of the ADA of a job-relatedness and business necessity "defense" to charges framed under language that tracks only § 102(b)(6), and by the fact that this defense is framed to be advanced in tandem with a demonstration that no "reasonable accommodation" can be accomplished.

The EEOC's Interpretive Guidance states that the selection criteria that may be challenged under § (b)(6) include "all types of selection criteria, including safety requirements, vision or hearing requirements, walking requirements, lifting requirements, and employment tests." 29 C.F.R. pt. 1630, app. § 1630.10. The Guidance also asserts that although "it is not the intent of this part to second guess an employer's judgment with regard to production standards", selection criteria that "do not concern an essential function of the job would not be consistent with business necessity", and even "selection criteria that are related to an essential function of the job may not be used to exclude an individual with a disability if that individual could satisfy the criteria with the provision of a reasonable accommodation." Id. Is it clear that selection criteria should have to relate to some essential job function to be justified as a business necessity?

Does disparate impact analysis play any useful independent role in ADA cases? Presumably in most cases it would be harder to advance statistical proof that an employment practice has a disparate impact on a group of individuals with disabilities than it would be to demonstrate a failure to provide reasonable accommodation in a particular case. Might there be any cases where an ADA plaintiff could establish an unjustified disparate impact, but the same plaintiff could not establish a failure to provide reasonable accommodations? Wouldn't the application of an unjustified standard, test, or criteria to affect the employment opportunities of a disabled individual also constitute a failure to provide reasonable accommodation? Of what ultimate, additional benefit to ADA plaintiffs, then, is the availability of disparate impact analysis? Might disparate impact proof more easily support a broader remedial order enjoining the use of some employment standards?

Individuals with disabilities clearly would benefit from the availability of disparate impact proof under the ADA if that proof could be used to challenge limitations or exclusions in employer-provided health or disability insurance plans. Most such limitations or exclusions disproportionately affect some group of disabled workers, but do not seem to be reachable by the reasonable accommodation requirements in § 102(b)(5). Might they be reachable by § 102(b)(3) or even § 102(b)(1)? However, relying on a decision of the Supreme Court interpreting the Rehabilitation Act, the EEOC has taken the position that benefit limitations that are framed neutrally toward all disabilities, are not adopted for the purpose of affecting the disabled, and have only a disparate impact on individuals with disabilities, are permissible. "Thus, for example, an employer that reduces the number of paid sick leave days that it will provide to all employees, or reduces the amount of medical insurance coverage that it will provide to all employees, is not in violation of [§ 102(b)(3)], even if the benefits reduction has an impact on employees with disabilities in need of greater sick leave and medical coverage. * * * See Alexander v. Choate, 469 U.S. 287, 105 S.Ct. 712, 83 L.Ed.2d 661 (1985)." 29 U.S.C. pt. 1630, app. § 1630.5. In *Choate* the Supreme Court assumed that § 504 of the Rehabilitation Act could be applied against some practices that have an unjustified impact on the disabled, but held that § 504 of the Rehabilitation Act did not reach a decision by the State of Tennessee to limit the number of annual days of inpatient hospital care covered by its state Medicaid program, without proof of a discriminatory motive. As explained in the following Note, however, the application of *Choate* in accord with the EEOC's stance does not preclude ADA challenges to employer-provided health or disability insurance plans based on allegations of discriminatory intent.

Note on the ADA and Insurance

Section 102(a) of the ADA prohibits discrimination against a qualified individual with a disability in regard to "terms, conditions, and privileges of employment." Furthermore, § 102(b)(2) provides that this discrimination includes "participating in a contractual or other arrangement or relationship", including a "relationship with * * * an organization providing fringe benefits", that subjects a qualified applicant or employee to disability discrimination. In an "Interim Enforcement Guidance", the EEOC not surprisingly interprets § 102 to cover employers' discrimination on the basis of disability in the provision of health insurance to their employees. See EEOC Interim Enforcement Guidance on the Application of the ADA to Disability–Based Distinctions in Employer Provided Health Insurance (Aug. 7, 2000).

The EEOC's 2000 Enforcement Guidance further states that "disability-based insurance plan distinctions are permitted only if they are within the protective ambit of section 501(c) of the ADA." Section 501(c) states that the Act's employment provisions shall not be construed to prohibit insurers or self-insured employers or health care organizations that administer bona fide benefit plans from "underwriting risks, classifying risks, or administering such risks that are based on or not inconsistent with State law", unless such decisions are "used as a subterfuge to evade the purposes" of the employment provisions. As explained in the Senate Committee Report:

> [W]hile a plan which limits certain kinds of coverage based on classification of risk would be allowed under this section, the plan may not refuse to insure, or refuse to continue to insure, or limit the amount, extent, or kind of coverage available to an individual, or charge a different rate for the same coverage solely because of a physical or mental impairment, except where the refusal, limitation, or rate differential is based on sound actuarial principles or is related to actual or reasonably anticipated experience.

S.Rep. No. 101–116, 101st Cong., 1st Sess. at 85 (1989), reprinted in 1 Legislative History of the Americans with Disabilities Act, at 183 (1991).

The EEOC's 2000 Guidance states that limitations or exclusions in employer-provided health benefit plans are only proscribed by the ADA if both (1) intentionally based on disability and (2) not "within the protective ambit of section 501(c) * * *." EEOC Interim Enforcement Guidance on the Application of the ADA to Disability–Based Distinctions in Employer Provided Health Insurance, supra. The first condition is based on the assumption, as explained in the prior Note, that the disparate "impact theory of discrimination is unavailable in this context". Id. at n.7. It also conveys the agency's view that universal, nondisease-specific restrictions on coverage, such as limits on "mental/nervous" conditions or "eye care," blanket preexisting condition clauses or caps on annual benefits for the treatment of any physical condition, do not constitute intentional discrimination on the basis of disability. The Interim Guidance states: "Such broad distinctions, which apply to the treatment of a multitude of dissimilar conditions and which constrain individuals both with and without disabilities, are not distinctions based on disability." However, "[a] term or provision is 'disability-based' if it singles out a particular disability (e.g. deafness, AIDS, schizophrenia), a discrete group of disabilities (e.g., cancers, muscular dystrophies, kidney diseases), or disability in general * * *."

Do you understand the EEOC's distinction between broad exclusions, such as for "mental/nervous" conditions, and exclusions of a class of diseases, such as cancers? Is it based on the fact that an exclusion of "mental/nervous" conditions also excludes many individuals not having a disability within the ADA's definition? Is everyone afflicted with cancer within the ADA's protected class? In any event, notwithstanding *Choate,* why should the ADA not condemn limitations or exclusions that have the effect of disproportionately disadvantaging the disabled, even if they also may disadvantage some who are not disabled? Is it because cost-saving limitations or exclusions in health insurance plans are likely to disproportionately affect disabled individuals by the denial of extra benefits, rather than by the imposition of additional burdens? Compare the treatment of pregnancy-related benefits in General Electric v. Gilbert, page 311 supra, and Nashville Gas Co. v. Satty, page 313 supra.

The lower courts generally have been unsympathetic to charges that more restrictive treatment of certain conditions in health or disability insurance plans constitutes discrimination against the disabled under the ADA. Some decisions seem to adopt the EEOC's approach, finding the different insurance coverage of certain treatments or broadly defined conditions not to be facial discrimination on the basis of disability. See, e.g., EEOC v. CNA Insurance Cos., 96 F.3d 1039, 1044 (7th Cir.1996) (shorter temporal limitation on disability benefits for mental disorders not disability discrimination); Krauel v. Iowa Methodist Medical Center, 95 F.3d 674 (8th Cir.1996) (exclusion of benefits for infertility treatments does not single out particular disabilities). Cf. Rogers v. Department of Health and Environmental Control, 174 F.3d 431 (4th Cir.1999) (Title II of ADA does not require benefits for mental conditions to be equal to those for physical conditions). Other decisions assert a broader claim that the ADA does not prohibit insurance plans from limiting benefits for particular disabilities, as long as the plans are open to all regardless of disability. See, e.g., EEOC v. Staten Island Savings Bank, 207 F.3d 144 (2d Cir. 2000); Weyer v. Twentieth Century Fox Film Corp., 198 F.3d 1104 (9th Cir.2000); Kimber v. Thiokol Corp., 196 F.3d 1092 (10th Cir., 1999); Ford v. Schering–Plough Corp., 145 F.3d 601 (3d Cir.1998); Parker v. Metropolitan Life Ins. Co., 121 F.3d 1006, 1015–16 (6th Cir.1997) (en banc). Cf. Doe v. Mutual of Omaha Ins. Co., 179 F.3d 557 (7th Cir.1999) (Title III of ADA does not regulate content of insurance plans). But see Lewis v. Aetna Life Insurance Co., 982 F.Supp. 1158 (E.D.Va.1997) (it may violate ADA to terminate mental health benefits, but not physical health benefits, after 24 months); Sharona Hoffmann, Aids

Caps, Contraceptive Coverage, and the Law, 23 Card L. Rev. 1315 (2002) (criticizing judicial trends). Cf. Mental Health Parity Act, 42 U.S.C. § 300gg–5 (1996) (prohibiting in certain health insurance plans, annual or lifetime limits for mental health benefits not imposed for general medical and surgical benefits, unless parity would cause a rise in costs of more than 1%).

With respect to the meaning of § 501(c), of the ADA, the EEOC's Enforcement Guidance rejects the view of several circuit courts, see, e.g., EEOC v. Aramark Corp., 208 F.3d 266 (D.C.Cir.2000); Ford, supra; Modderno v. King, 82 F.3d 1059, 1065 (D.C.Cir.1996), that the section's "subterfuge" language should be read in the same manner as the Supreme Court in Public Employees Retirement System of Ohio v. Betts, 492 U.S. 158, 109 S.Ct. 2854, 106 L.Ed.2d 134 (1989), interpreted the "subterfuge" language in § 4(f)(2) of the ADEA; see discussion at p. 471 supra. The Enforcement Guidance explains that "both the language of the ADA, expressly covering 'fringe benefits,' and the Act's legislative history, rejecting the concept of a 'safe harbor' for pre-ADA plans, make plain congressional intent that the Betts approach not be applied in the context of the ADA." Enforcement Guidance at n. 10. Thus, the EEOC's position is that the ADA reaches pre-ADA plans, does not require a showing of specific intent to discriminate in a non-benefit aspect of the employment relationship, and does not impose the burden of proving "subterfuge" on the plaintiff.

In the EEOC's view, once a term or provision is found to be disability-related, the employer has "the burden of proving that the challenged disability-based insurance distinction" is within § 501(c)'s protection. For insured plans, the employer must prove that "1) the health insurance plan is bona fide in that it exists and pays benefits, and its terms have been accurately communicated to eligible employees; and 2) the health insurance plan's terms are not inconsistent with applicable state law as interpreted by the appropriate state authorities." For self-insured plans, only the first criterion applies.

After this showing is made, the employer must still prove that the disability-based distinction is not a "subterfuge" to evade the purposes of ADA. The EEOC offers a "non-exclusive list of potential business/insurance justifications", including:

> b. The respondent may prove that the disparate treatment is justified by legitimate actuarial data, or by actual or reasonably anticipated experience, and that conditions with comparable actuarial data and/or experience are treated in the same fashion. In other words, the respondent may prove that the disability-based disparate treatment is attributable to the application of legitimate risk classification and underwriting procedures to the increased risks (and thus increased cost to the health insurance plan) of the disability, and not to the disability per se.

> c. The respondent may prove that the disparate treatment is necessary (i.e., that there is no nondisability-based health insurance plan change that could be made) to ensure that the challenged health insurance plan satisfies the commonly accepted or legally required standards for the fiscal soundness of such an insurance plan. * * *

> d. The respondent may prove that the challenged insurance practice or activity is necessary (i.e., that there is no nondisability-based

change that could be made) to prevent the occurrence of an unacceptable change either in the coverage of the health insurance plan, or in the premiums charged for the health insurance plan. An "unacceptable" change is a drastic increase in premium payments (or in co-payments or deductibles), or a drastic alteration to the scope of coverage or level of benefits provided, that would: 1) make the health insurance plan effectively unavailable to a significant number of other employees, 2) make the health insurance plan so unattractive as to result in significant adverse selection, or 3) make the health insurance plan so unattractive that the employer cannot compete in recruiting and maintaining qualified workers due to the superiority of health insurance plans offered by other employers in the community.

e.   Where the charging party is challenging the respondent's denial of coverage for a disability-specific treatment, the respondent may prove that this treatment does not provide any benefit (*i.e.*, has no medical value). * * *

Can these "justifications" be readily construed and applied by courts? Is there some interpretation of the meaning of "subterfuge" that connects the justifications? What statutory purpose do they insure is not evaded? A requirement that the disabled, or those with particular disabilities, not be given at least equal consideration and attention? Is an employer protected under § 501(c) if it denies a benefit for a particular disability based upon a good faith, but erroneous actuarial calculation? Is it understandable that the courts have resisted the EEOC's approach?

Workers have challenged employer-provided health and disability insurance plans under Title III of the ADA, which governs disability discrimination in public accommodations, as well as under the employment discrimination provisions of Title I. Title I may seem insufficient both because it requires any plaintiff to be "qualified" to work and by the time a challenged insurance limitation is applicable the plaintiff may be totally disabled from work, see, e.g., Morgan v. Joint Administration Board, 268 F.3d 456 (7th Cir.2001); *Weyer*, supra; Gonzales v. Garner Food Servs., 89 F.3d 1523, 1528 (11th Cir.1996); but see, e.g., *Ford,*, supra; Castellano v. City of New York, 142 F.3d 58 (2d Cir.1998) (coverage extends to discrimination related to or arising out of an employment relationship as under Title VII); and because allegedly discriminating insurance companies may not be covered entities under Title I, but see Carparts Distribution Ctr. v. Automotive Wholesaler's Ass'n of New England, Inc., 37 F.3d 12, 16–17 (1st Cir.1994) (association offering self-funded health insurance plan and trust that administers plan are covered entities to the extent they are agents of employers or exert control over employment opportunities). Title III's applicability is also uncertain, however: The lower courts are split over whether this Title's proscription of disability discrimination "in the full and equal enjoyment of the goods, services, facilities, privileges, advantages, or accommodations of any place of public accommodation" (§ 302), is limited to physical structures. Compare Pallozzi v. Allstate Life Ins. Co., 198 F.3d 28 (2d Cir.1999), as amended, 204 F.3d 392 (2d Cir.2000); *Doe*, supra and *Carparts Distribution Ctr.*, supra, (not limited), with *Weyer*, supra; Parker v. Metropolitan Life Insurance Co., 121 F.3d 1006 (6th Cir.1997) (en banc) and *Ford*, supra (limited). Section 501(c) is expressly applicable to Title III as well as Title I challenges, and might be read to imply potential coverage outside its safe harbor under one Title or the other.

Workers also may attempt to invoke state law to challenge exclusions or limitations in employer-provided insurance plans. ERISA, however, may preempt any state regulation of self-funded plans, see FMC Corp. v. Holliday, 498 U.S. 52, 111 S.Ct. 403, 112 L.Ed.2d 356 (1990), page 1177, infra as well as any state human rights laws that attempt to regulate employer benefit plan practices that are not also violative of federal law, see Shaw v. Delta Air Lines, Inc., 463 U.S. 85, 103 S.Ct. 2890, 77 L.Ed.2d 490 (1983) discussed at p. 1184 infra.

Part Three

PROTECTING SOCIALLY
VALUED ACTIVITY

This Part of the book shifts attention from employment regulations framed to prevent unfair treatment of individuals because of an immutable status, to laws intended to protect certain kinds of individual choice. Although the line between the two kinds of employment regulation may not always be sharply drawn, their nature and possible justifications vary.

The distinctive character of employment laws designed to protect the choice to engage in some valued activity is highlighted by the topic of chapter 8, religious discrimination. As evidenced by its inclusion in Title VII, discrimination against members of particular religious groups may in part be a form of status discrimination. Indeed, religious bigotry is often a breed of racism. Those who hate, stigmatize, assign subordinate roles, or otherwise show unequal respect to those of particular religious faiths may have the same attitudes toward the descendants of members of these faiths, regardless of the descendants' religious or cultural identifications. Moreover, religious affiliations often are more ascribed than chosen. For powerful psychological reasons, most humans throughout history have accepted the faith of their parents.

Nevertheless, religious discrimination cannot be viewed entirely or primarily as a form of status discrimination. Religion is not an immutable status. Individuals can and often do choose to change or totally reject their faiths. Further, in modern societies such choices increasingly can be made against ancestral wishes and the culture into which one is born. Most importantly, little of the workplace religious discrimination in our society reflects prejudice against some assumed genetic pool; the discrimination would cease altogether if the individuals agreed to forsake their religious beliefs and practices. Yet, as will be stressed, our laws prohibit discrimination against religious beliefs and practices, not simply membership in a particular religious group. This raises the question why religious choices are insulated from the coercion of employment decisions, while comparable protection is not given to other salient human choices. That reason presumably has something to do with the value the society assigns to religious freedom.

The other forms of employment regulation examined in this part of the book are more sharply distinct from status discrimination regulation. Thus, chapter 9 considers the protection afforded by the first amendment to public employees' choice of particular forms of expressive activity. Chapter 10 reviews legislatively and judicially created rules designed to protect employees' efforts to claim some substantive, government-conferred right, including the right to be free of status discrimination. Finally, chapter 11 considers the emerging common law and statutory protection of the decisions of employees to discharge some duty that they owe, or that they believe they owe, society.

Society may choose to protect particular forms of employee activity for at least two different kinds of reasons. The first kind of reason derives from collective social judgments about the intrinsic value of particular activities for the employees who engage in them. The second derives from judgments about the instrumental worth of the activity, either for employees or for third parties.

As suggested, our laws prohibit religious discrimination in large part because we deem religious expression to be an activity of high intrinsic worth. Similarly, we protect political activity in part because of a collective judgment that political participation is important to the full development of all human beings. There are, of course, also instrumental reasons for these regulations: protection of religious minorities promotes a social climate of tolerance that redounds to the benefit of all; protection of political expression by public employees contributes in important ways to the public debate.

Instrumental justifications are more central to the regulations considered in the remaining chapters of this section. The materials in those chapters suggest that such justifications can be grouped in three categories. First, society may recognize that the effective enforcement of particular substantive rights may require some protection of employee efforts to assert those rights. If employers can use their power over personnel decisionmaking to penalize such efforts with impunity, the underlying substantive rights may be robbed of all practical significance. Although some employee self-help may be very disruptive and impose substantial costs, the protection of other efforts may require little more justification than the original justifications for the underlying rights.

Second, society may determine that protecting certain employee self-help efforts is an effective way not only to protect rights granted by the state, but also to promote a process for determining terms and conditions of employment that is thought to be preferable to direct government regulation. Such a determination in part underlies the National Labor Relations Act's protection of employee efforts to organize unions and to bargain collectively with their employer. Unions might insure the protection of rights more effectively than can governmental action because they have continuing and internal relationships with employers.

Third, society might wish to protect employee activity because of its contribution to goals that are not related to employee, or employer, interests. The readiest justification for such regulatory protection is simply that employees cannot be expected to bargain for third parties, or for the general society. Employer-employee bargains will not account for the external effects of certain types of employment decisionmaking. If society wants employees to engage in activity that will in some way be costly to employers, but will not directly benefit employees, it must offer employees a guarantee of protection against employer retaliation.

This last instrumental reason for choosing particular activity to protect from employment discrimination, however, may be the most open-ended. It may warrant protection of a broad range of activity that would impose substantial costs on employers. In this section of the book, as in the previous section, our analysis must include consideration of the costs as well as the benefits of particular forms of regulation.

Our analysis in this Part may also have to consider some issues that were not salient in the previous section. Two should be noted here. First, the first amendment chapter highlights the important issue of whether there are strong justifications for offering different protection to public sector employees than to those in the private sector. Is regulation of the private sector likely to entail higher costs of enforcement and over-enforcement? Second, the common law development of some of the regulations included in this section raises the legal process issue of whether protection of socially valued employee activity is best undertaken by legislatures or by courts.

Chapter Eight

RELIGIOUS DISCRIMINATION

A. INTRODUCTION

The statutory and constitutional prohibition of religious discrimination might be viewed as a form of status discrimination regulation. Certainly, some of history's more vicious religious bigots have considered those who practice particular religions to constitute a different and inferior race. Not surprisingly, the Supreme Court has ruled that the proscription of "racial" discrimination in the 1866 Civil Rights Act, 42 U.S.C. §§ 1981, 1982, 1985(3), encompasses discrimination against Jews. See Shaare Tefila Congregation v. Cobb, 481 U.S. 615, 107 S.Ct. 2019, 95 L.Ed.2d 594 (1987). Furthermore, discrimination against religious minorities sometimes also may be closely related to bias on account of national origin.

But existing law cannot be explained completely in these terms. For example, Title VII defines discrimination on account of "religion" to include "all aspects of religious observance and practice, as well as belief," § 701, 42 U.S.C. § 2000e(j), and explicitly requires "reasonable accommodat[ion]" of an employee's or applicant's religious observance or practice. As suggested in the last chapter, a duty of reasonable accommodation reflects a qualified claim to special treatment. Similarly, the Constitution requires government in some cases to suppress legitimate interests in deference to a claim of free exercise of religion under the first amendment. The decision to protect religious observance and practices, even at some cost to the efficiency of government programs or private employer policies, may reflect a judgment that religious choices are critical to human dignity and autonomy, and therefore should be given special protection. It may also reflect a societal commitment to religious pluralism. Without protection of religious practices, as well as beliefs, religious minorities might be driven either to assimilate or to accept confinement in isolated communities where they could find employment with coreligionists. Either choice could impoverish the larger society.

B. THE TITLE VII DUTY OF ACCOMMODATION

TRANS WORLD AIRLINES, INC. v. HARDISON

Supreme Court of the United States, 1977.
432 U.S. 63, 97 S.Ct. 2264, 53 L.Ed.2d 113.

MR. JUSTICE WHITE delivered the opinion of the Court.

Petitioner Trans World Airlines (TWA) operates a large maintenance and overhaul base in Kansas City, Mo. On June 5, 1967, respondent Larry G. Hardison was hired by TWA to work as a clerk in the Stores Department at its Kansas City base. Because of its essential role in the Kansas City operation, the Stores Department must operate 24 hours per day, 365 days per year, and whenever an employee's job in that department is not filled, an employee must be shifted from another department, or a supervisor must cover the job, even if the work in other areas may suffer.

Hardison, like other employees at the Kansas City base, was subject to a seniority system contained in a collective-bargaining agreement that TWA maintains with petitioner International Association of Machinists and Aerospace Workers (IAM). The seniority system is implemented by the union steward through a system of bidding by employees for particular shift assignments as they become available. The most senior employees have first choice for job and shift assignments, and the most junior employees are required to work when the union steward is unable to find enough people willing to work at a particular time or in a particular job to fill TWA's needs.

In the spring of 1968 Hardison began to study the religion known as the Worldwide Church of God. One of the tenets of that religion is that one must observe the Sabbath by refraining from performing any work from sunset on Friday until sunset on Saturday. The religion also proscribes work on certain specified religious holidays.

When Hardison informed Everett Kussman, the manager of the Stores Department, of his religious conviction regarding observance of the Sabbath, Kussman agreed that the union steward should seek a job swap for Hardison or a change of days off; that Hardison would have his religious holidays off whenever possible if Hardison agreed to work the traditional holidays when asked; and that Kussman would try to find Hardison another job that would be more compatible with his religious beliefs. The problem was temporarily solved when Hardison transferred to the 11 p.m.–7 a.m. shift. Working this shift permitted Hardison to observe his Sabbath.

The problem soon reappeared when Hardison bid for and received a transfer from Building 1, where he had been employed, to Building 2, where he would work the day shift. The two buildings had entirely separate seniority lists; and while in Building 1 Hardison had sufficient seniority to observe the Sabbath regularly, he was second from the bottom on the Building 2 seniority list.

In Building 2 Hardison was asked to work Saturdays when a fellow employee went on vacation. TWA agreed to permit the union to seek a change of work assignments for Hardison, but the union was not willing to violate the seniority provisions set out in the collective-bargaining contract, and Hardison had insufficient seniority to bid for a shift having Saturdays off.

A proposal that Hardison work only four days a week was rejected by the company. Hardison's job was essential and on weekends he was the only available person on his shift to perform it. To leave the position empty would have impaired supply shop functions, which were critical to airline operations; to fill Hardison's position with a supervisor or an employee from another area would simply have undermanned another operation; and to employ someone not regularly assigned to work Saturdays would have required TWA to pay premium wages.

When an accommodation was not reached, Hardison refused to report for work on Saturdays. A transfer to the twilight shift proved unavailing since that schedule still required Hardison to work past sundown on Fridays. After a hearing, Hardison was discharged on grounds of insubordination for refusing to work during his designated shift.

* * *

III

The Court of Appeals held that TWA had not made reasonable efforts to accommodate Hardison's religious needs under the 1967 EEOC guidelines in effect at the time the relevant events occurred. In its view, TWA had rejected three reasonable alternatives, any one of which would have satisfied its obligation without undue hardship. First, within the framework of the seniority system, TWA could have permitted Hardison to work a four-day week, utilizing in his place a supervisor or another worker on duty elsewhere. * * * Second—according to the Court of Appeals, also within the bounds of the collective-bargaining contract— the company could have filled Hardison's Saturday shift from other available personnel competent to do the job, of which the court said there were at least 200. * * * Third, TWA could have arranged a "swap between Hardison and another employee either for another shift or for the Sabbath days." * * *

We disagree with the Court of Appeals in all relevant respects. It is our view that TWA made reasonable efforts to accommodate and that each of the Court of Appeals' suggested alternatives would have been an undue hardship within the meaning of the statute as construed by the EEOC guidelines.

A

It might be inferred from the Court of Appeals' opinion and from the brief of the EEOC in this Court that TWA's efforts to accommodate were no more than negligible. The findings of the District Court, supported by the record, are to the contrary. In summarizing its more detailed findings, the District Court observed:

> "TWA established as a matter of fact that it did take appropriate action to accommodate as required by Title VII. It held several meetings with plaintiff at which it attempted to find a solution to plaintiff's problems. It did accommodate plaintiff's observance of his special religious holidays. It authorized the union steward to search for someone who would swap shifts, which apparently was normal procedure."

It is also true that TWA itself attempted without success to find Hardison another job. The District Court's view was that TWA had done all that could reasonably be expected within the bounds of the seniority system.

The Court of Appeals observed, however, that the possibility of a variance from the seniority system was never really posed to the union. This is contrary to the District Court's findings and to the record. The District Court found that when TWA first learned of Hardison's religious observances in April 1968, it agreed to permit the union's steward to seek a swap of shifts or days off but that "the steward reported that he was unable to work out scheduling changes and that he understood that no one was willing to swap days with plaintiff". Later, in March 1969, at a meeting held just two days before Hardison first failed to report for his Saturday shift, TWA again "offered to accommodate plaintiff's religious observance by agreeing to any trade of shifts or change of sections that plaintiff and the union could work out * * *. Any shift or change was impossible within the seniority framework and the union was not willing to violate the seniority provisions set out in the contract to make a shift or change." As the record shows, Hardison himself testified that Kussman was willing, but the union was not, to work out a shift or job trade with another employee.

* * *

B

We are also convinced, contrary to the Court of Appeals, that TWA itself cannot be faulted for having failed to work out a shift or job swap for Hardison. Both the union and TWA had agreed to the seniority system; the union was unwilling to entertain a variance over the objections of men senior to Hardison; and for TWA to have arranged unilaterally for a swap would have amounted to a breach of the collective-bargaining agreement.

(1)

Hardison and the EEOC insist that the statutory obligation to accommodate religious needs takes precedence over both the collective-bargaining contract and the seniority rights of TWA's other employees. We agree that neither a collective-bargaining contract nor a seniority system may be employed to violate the statute, but we do not believe that the duty to accommodate requires TWA to take steps inconsistent with the otherwise valid agreement.

* * *

It was essential to TWA's business to require Saturday and Sunday work from at least a few employees even though most employees preferred those days off. Allocating the burdens of weekend work was a matter for collective bargaining. In considering criteria to govern this allocation, TWA and the union had two alternatives: adopt a neutral system, such as seniority, a lottery, or rotating shifts; or allocate days off in accordance with the religious needs of its employees. TWA would have had to adopt the latter in order to assure Hardison and others like him of getting the days off necessary for strict observance of their religion, but it could have done so only at the expense of others who had strong, but perhaps nonreligious, reasons for not working on weekends. There were no volunteers to relieve Hardison on Saturdays, and to give Hardison Saturdays off, TWA would have had to deprive another employee of his shift preference at least in part because he did not adhere to a religion that observed the Saturday Sabbath.

Title VII does not contemplate such unequal treatment. The repeated, unequivocal emphasis of both the language and the legislative history of Title VII is on eliminating discrimination in employment, and such discrimination is proscribed when it is directed against majorities as well as minorities. Indeed, the foundation of Hardison's claim is that TWA and IAM engaged in religious *discrimination* in violation of § 703(a)(1) when they failed to arrange for him to have Saturdays off. It would be anomalous to conclude that by "reasonable accommodation" Congress meant that an employer must deny the shift and job preference of some employees, as well as deprive them of their contractual rights, in order to accommodate or prefer the religious needs of others, and we conclude that Title VII does not require an employer to go that far.

(2)

Our conclusion is supported by the fact that seniority systems are afforded special treatment under Title VII itself. * * * "[T]he unmistakable purpose of § 703(h) was to make clear that the routine application of a bona fide seniority system would not be unlawful under Title VII." *International Brotherhood of Teamsters v. United States,* 431 U.S. 324, 352, 97 S.Ct. 1843, 1863, 52 L.Ed.2d 396 (1977). See also *United Air Lines, Inc. v. Evans,* 431 U.S. 553, 97 S.Ct. 1885, 52 L.Ed.2d 571 (1977). Section 703(h) is "a definitional provision; as with the other provisions of § 703, subsection (h) delineates which employment practices are illegal and thereby prohibited and which are not." *Franks v. Bowman Transportation Co.,* 424 U.S. 747, 758, 96 S.Ct. 1251, 1261, 47 L.Ed.2d 444 (1976). Thus, absent a discriminatory purpose, the operation of a seniority system cannot be an unlawful employment practice even if the system has some discriminatory consequences.

There has been no suggestion of discriminatory intent in this case. * * * The Court of Appeals' conclusion that TWA was not limited by the terms of its seniority system was in substance nothing more than a ruling that operation of the seniority system was itself an unlawful employment practice even though no discriminatory purpose had been shown. That ruling is plainly inconsistent with the dictates of § 703(h), both on its face and as interpreted in the recent decisions of this Court.

As we have said, TWA was not required by Title VII to carve out a special exception to its seniority system in order to help Hardison to meet his religious obligations.

C

The Court of Appeals also suggested that TWA could have permitted Hardison to work a four-day week if necessary in order to avoid working on his Sabbath. Recognizing that this might have left TWA shorthanded on the one shift each week that Hardison did not work, the court still concluded that TWA would suffer no undue hardship if it were required to replace Hardison either with supervisory personnel or with qualified personnel from other departments. Alternatively, the Court of Appeals suggested that TWA could have replaced Hardison on his Saturday shift with other available employees through the payment of premium wages. Both of these alternatives would involve costs to TWA, either in the form of lost efficiency in other jobs or higher wages.

To require TWA to bear more than a *de minimis* cost in order to give Hardison Saturdays off is an undue hardship.[1] Like abandonment of the seniority system, to require TWA to bear additional costs when no such costs are incurred to give other employees the days off that they want would involve unequal treatment of employees on the basis of their religion. By suggesting that TWA should incur certain costs in order to give Hardison Saturdays off the Court of Appeals would in effect require TWA to finance an additional Saturday off and then to choose the employee who will enjoy it on the basis of his religious beliefs. While incurring extra costs to secure a replacement for Hardison might remove the necessity of compelling another employee to work involuntarily in Hardison's place, it would not change the fact that the privilege of having Saturdays off would be allocated according to religious beliefs.

As we have seen, the paramount concern of Congress in enacting Title VII was the elimination of discrimination in employment. In the absence of clear statutory language or legislative history to the contrary, we will not readily construe the statute to require an employer to

---

1. The dissent argues that "the costs to TWA of either paying overtime or not replacing respondent would [not] have been more than *de minimis*." This ignores, however, the express finding of the District Court that "[b]oth of these solutions would have created an undue burden on the conduct of TWA's business," and it fails to take account of the likelihood that a company as large as TWA may have many employees whose religious observances, like Hardison's, prohibit them from working on Saturdays or Sundays.

discriminate against some employees in order to enable others to observe their Sabbath.

MR. JUSTICE MARSHALL, with whom MR. JUSTICE BRENNAN joins, dissenting.

The accommodation issue by definition arises only when a neutral rule of general applicability conflicts with the religious practices of a particular employee. In some of the reported cases, the rule in question has governed work attire; in other cases it has required attendance at some religious function; in still other instances, it has compelled membership in a union; and in the largest class of cases, it has concerned work schedules. What all these cases have in common is an employee who could comply with the rule only by violating what the employee views as a religious commandment. In each instance, the question is whether the employee is to be exempt from the rule's demands. To do so will always result in a privilege being "allocated according to religious beliefs," unless the employer gratuitously decides to repeal the rule *in toto*. What the statute says, in plain words, is that such allocations are required unless "undue hardship" would result.

* * *

Once it is determined that the duty to accommodate sometimes requires that an employee be exempted from an otherwise valid work requirement, the only remaining question is whether this is such a case: Did TWA prove that it exhausted all reasonable accommodations, and that the only remaining alternatives would have caused undue hardship on TWA's business?

* * *

To begin with, the record simply does not support the Court's assertion, made without accompanying citations, that "[t]here were no volunteers to relieve Hardison on Saturdays." Everett Kussman, the manager of the department in which respondent worked, testified that he had made no effort to find volunteers, and the union stipulated that its steward had not done so either. * * * Of course, it is * * * possible that no trade—or none consistent with the seniority system—could have been arranged. But the burden under the EEOC regulation is on TWA to establish that a reasonable accommodation was not possible. 29 CFR § 1605.1(c) (1976). Because it failed either to explore the possibility of a voluntary trade or to assure that its delegate, the union steward, did so, TWA was unable to meet its burden.

Nor was a voluntary trade the only option open to TWA that the Court ignores; to the contrary, at least two other options are apparent from the record. First, TWA could have paid overtime to a voluntary replacement for respondent—assuming that someone would have been willing to work Saturdays for premium pay—and passed on the cost to respondent. In fact, one accommodation Hardison suggested would have done just that by requiring Hardison to work overtime when needed at regular pay. Under this plan, the total overtime cost to the employer—

and the total number of overtime hours available for other employees—would not have reflected Hardison's Sabbath absences. Alternatively, TWA could have transferred respondent back to his previous department where he had accumulated substantial seniority, as respondent also suggested. Admittedly, both options would have violated the collective-bargaining agreement; the former because the agreement required that employees working over 40 hours per week receive premium pay, and the latter because the agreement prohibited employees from transferring departments more than once every six months. But neither accommodation would have deprived any other employee of rights under the contract or violated the seniority system in any way.

ANSONIA BOARD OF EDUC. v. PHILBROOK
Supreme Court of the United States, 1986.
479 U.S. 60, 107 S.Ct. 367, 93 L.Ed.2d 305.

CHIEF JUSTICE REHNQUIST delivered the opinion of the Court.

Petitioner Ansonia Board of Education has employed respondent Ronald Philbrook since 1962 to teach high school business and typing classes in Ansonia, Connecticut. In 1968, Philbrook was baptized into the Worldwide Church of God. The tenets of the church require members to refrain from secular employment during designated holy days, a practice that has caused respondent to miss approximately six school days each year.

* * *

Since the 1967–1968 school year, the school board's collective-bargaining agreements with the Ansonia Federation of Teachers have granted to each teacher 18 days of leave per year for illness, cumulative to 150 and later to 180 days. Accumulated leave may be used for purposes other than illness as specified in the agreement. A teacher may accordingly use five days' leave for a death in the immediate family, one day for attendance at a wedding, three days per year for attendance as an official delegate to a national veterans organization, and the like. With the exception of the agreement covering the 1967–1968 school year, each contract has specifically provided three days' annual leave for observance of mandatory religious holidays, as defined in the contract. Unlike other categories for which leave is permitted, absences for religious holidays are not charged against the teacher's annual or accumulated leave.

The school board has also agreed that teachers may use up to three days of accumulated leave each school year for "necessary personal business." Recent contracts limited permissible personal leave to those uses not otherwise specified in the contract. This limitation dictated, for example, that an employee who wanted more than three leave days to attend the convention of a national veterans organization could not use personal leave to gain extra days for that purpose. Likewise, an employee already absent three days for mandatory religious observances could not later use personal leave for "[a]ny religious activity," or "[a]ny religious observance."

* * * Until the 1976–1977 year, Philbrook observed mandatory holy days by using the three days granted in the contract and then taking unauthorized leave. His pay was reduced accordingly. In 1976, however, respondent stopped taking unauthorized leave for religious reasons, and began scheduling required hospital visits on church holy days. He also worked on several holy days. Dissatisfied with this arrangement, Philbrook repeatedly asked the school board to adopt one of two alternatives. His preferred alternative would allow use of personal business leave for religious observance, effectively giving him three additional days of paid leave for that purpose. Short of this arrangement, respondent suggested that he pay the cost of a substitute and receive full pay for additional days off for religious observances.[3] Petitioner has consistently rejected both proposals.

* * *

We find no basis in either the statute or its legislative history for requiring an employer to choose any particular reasonable accommodation. By its very terms the statute directs that any reasonable accommodation by the employer is sufficient to meet its accommodation obligation. The employer violates the statute unless it "demonstrates that [it] is unable to reasonably accommodate * * * an employee's * * * religious observance or practice without undue hardship on the conduct of the employer's business." Thus, where the employer has already reasonably accommodated the employee's religious needs, the statutory inquiry is at an end. The employer need not further show that each of the employee's alternative accommodations would result in undue hardship. As *Hardison* illustrates, the extent of undue hardship on the employer's business is at issue only where the employer claims that it is unable to offer any reasonable accommodation without such hardship. Once the Court of Appeals assumed that the school board had offered to Philbrook a reasonable alternative, it erred by requiring the board to nonetheless demonstrate the hardship of Philbrook's alternatives.

* * *

The remaining issue in the case is whether the school board's leave policy constitutes a reasonable accommodation of Philbrook's religious beliefs. Because both the District Court and the Court of Appeals applied what we hold to be an erroneous view of the law, neither explicitly considered this question. We think that there are insufficient factual findings as to the manner in which the collective bargaining agreement has been interpreted in order for us to make that judgment initially. We think that the school board policy in this case, requiring respondent to take unpaid leave for holy day observance that exceeded the amount

---

3. The suggested accommodation would reduce the financial costs to Philbrook of unauthorized absences. In 1984, for example, a substitute cost $30 per day, and respondent's loss in pay from an unauthorized absence was over $130.

allowed by the collective-bargaining agreement, would generally be a reasonable one. In enacting § 701(j), Congress was understandably motivated by a desire to assure the individual additional opportunity to observe religious practices, but it did not impose a duty on the employer to accommodate at all costs. *TWA v. Hardison,* 432 U.S. 63, 97 S.Ct. 2264, 53 L.Ed.2d 113 (1977). The provision of unpaid leave eliminates the conflict between employment requirements and religious practices by allowing the individual to observe fully religious holy days and requires him only to give up compensation for a day that he did not in fact work. Generally speaking, "[t]he direct effect of [unpaid leave] is merely a loss of income for the period the employee is not at work; such an exclusion has no direct effect upon either employment opportunities or job status." *Nashville Gas Co. v. Satty,* 434 U.S. 136, 145, 98 S.Ct. 347, 353, 54 L.Ed.2d 356 (1977).

But unpaid leave is not a reasonable accommodation when paid leave is provided for all purposes *except* religious ones. A provision for paid leave "that is part and parcel of the employment relationship may not be doled out in a discriminatory fashion, even if the employer would be free * * * not to provide the benefit at all." *Hishon v. King & Spalding,* 467 U.S. 69, 75, 104 S.Ct. 2229, 2234, 81 L.Ed.2d 59 (1984). Such an arrangement would display a discrimination against religious practices that is the antithesis of reasonableness. Whether the policy here violates this teaching turns on factual inquiry into past and present administration of the personal business leave provisions of the collective-bargaining agreement. The school board contends that the necessary personal business category in the agreement, like other leave provisions, defines a limited purpose leave. Philbrook, on the other hand, asserts that the necessary personal leave category is not so limited, operating as an open-ended leave provision that may be used for a wide range of secular purposes in addition to those specifically provided for in the contract, but not for similar religious purposes. We do not think that the record is sufficiently clear on this point for us to make the necessary factual findings, and we therefore affirm the judgment of the Court of Appeals remanding the case to the District Court.

JUSTICE MARSHALL, concurring in part and dissenting in part.

* * * I do not find the specificity of the personal business leave, or the possibility that it may be used for activities similar to the religious activities Philbrook seeks leave to pursue, necessarily dispositive of whether the board has satisfied its affirmative duty under § 701(j), 42 U.S.C. § 2000e(j), to reasonably accommodate Philbrook's religious needs. Even if the District Court should find that the personal leave is restricted to specific secular uses having no similarity with Philbrook's religious activities, Philbrook would still encounter a conflict between his religious needs and work requirements. In my view, the question would remain whether, without imposing an undue hardship on the conduct of its educational program, the school board could further reasonably accommodate Philbrook's need for additional religious leave.

If, for example, the personal business leave were so limited that it allowed teachers paid leave for the sole purpose of meeting with their accountants to prepare their income tax returns (a purely secular activity), a proposal from Philbrook that he be allowed to prepare his tax return on his own time and use this paid leave for religious observance might be found imminently reasonable and lacking in undue hardship. The board's prior determination that the conduct of its educational program can withstand the paid absence of its teachers for up to six days each year for religious and personal reasons tends to indicate that granting Philbrook's similar request in this case for a total of six days paid religious leave and no personal leave is reasonable, would cause the board no undue hardship, and hence falls within the scope of the board's affirmative obligation under Title VII.

JUSTICE STEVENS, concurring in part and dissenting in part.

Respondent does not contend that the leave policy is discriminatory because he is eligible for, or has actually received, fewer days of paid leave than members of other religious faiths or than teachers who have no religious obligations on school days. The basis of his principal discrimination argument is that the total of six days for mandated religious observances and necessary personal business is not adequate to enable him to take care of "the personal business that is most important and pressing to him: religious activity and observance," whereas this combination of six days of paid leave is adequate for some teachers who have different religious and ethical commitments. Quite clearly, however, this argument rests on the premise that the respondent's special, that is, religious, needs entitle him to extraordinary treatment. Respondent's "discrimination" argument states a grievance against equal treatment rather than a claim that he has been the recipient of unequal treatment.[2]

This point comes into sharp focus when the contractual prohibition against using the three days of personal leave for "any religious observance" is seen for what it is, merely a part of the broader prohibition against using personal business leave for any of the purposes specifically authorized in the contract. The existing leave policy denies paid days to any teacher who proposes to take more paid days of personal business leave per year to fulfill his or her commitments than the contract allows. Respondent's wish to use his secular leave for religious purposes is thwarted by the same policy that denies an avid official delegate to a National Veterans' Organization use of secular leave days for that activity in excess of the days specifically allotted for it under the contract. In fact, since three days are expressly authorized for mandated religious observances—events that recur each year—whereas most other categories of paid leave cover relatively infrequent contingencies such as a death in the family or attendance at a family wedding, it is highly

2. Denying the use of personal business days for religious purposes is no more discriminatory against religion than if the personal business leave category were entirely absent from the contract. Neither a decision to refuse personal business leave days altogether nor a decision to provide these days for specific purposes not otherwise provided for in the contract represents a discrimination against religion.

probable that the leave policy as a whole tends to favor, rather than to disfavor, persons who must observe religious days during the school year. For example, an atheist who attends a wedding, a funeral, and a graduation on school days receives a total of three days of paid personal leave, but a religious person who attends the same three events on paid days also receives pay for three religious days.

Notes and Questions

1. *Did* Hardison *Turn on the Existence of a Collectively Bargained Seniority System?* Would the Court's view of Hardison's claim have been different if TWA did not have to deal with a union and could have accommodated Hardison by departing from a unilaterally imposed, seniority-based job allocation system, rather than from a system collectively bargained with a union? Cf. Balint v. Carson City, 180 F.3d 1047 (9th Cir.1999) (en banc) (*Hardison* teaches that accommodation is reasonable only if no disruption to any seniority system and no more than *de minimus* cost). Note that the seniority system in *US Airways, Inc. v. Barnett*, p. 534 supra, had been unilaterally promulgated by a nonunion employer.

Would the case have been decided differently if Hardison had sued the union, as well as TWA, for failing to accommodate him by agreeing to accept a variance from the collectively bargained system? Note that the reasonable accommodation requirement in the definition of religion in § 701(j) does not expressly apply to labor organizations. Numerous lower courts have required unions to accommodate employees who assert religious reasons for not wanting to pay union dues. See, e.g., EEOC v. University of Detroit, 904 F.2d 331 (6th Cir.1990); Tooley v. Martin–Marietta Corp., 648 F.2d 1239 (9th Cir.1981). See also note 2, p. 606 infra.

2. *Does* Hardison *Hold That Title VII Does Not Require the Subordination of Employees' Secular Interests to Religious Interests?* If the case did not turn on the union's resistance to accommodating Hardison, why would requiring TWA to assign other employees to Saturday work have been unreasonable or have imposed an undue hardship? Is it because even a unilaterally adopted seniority system for job assignments creates expectations, the frustration of which might affect general employee morale? Or does *Hardison* hold that Title VII does not require employers to discount the secular interests of some employees when accommodating the religious interests of other employees? Is this an appropriate weighing of the interests reflected in § 701(j)?

3. *Residual Content of Duty of Reasonable Accommodation?* If, as the Court states, requiring "TWA to bear more than a *de minimis* cost in order to give Hardison Saturdays off is an undue hardship", and if Title VII does not require subordination of the secular interests of some employees to the religious interests of others, what content is left of the "reasonable accommodation" requirement? Does it require employers to incur some minimal administrative costs to accommodate religious practices? The lower courts have so held. See, e.g., EEOC v. Ilona of Hungary, Inc., 108 F.3d 1569, 1576 (7th Cir.1997) (employer must provide two employees unpaid day off for Yom Kippur); Opuku–Boateng v. California, 95 F.3d 1461, 1470 (9th Cir.1996)

(employer may have to accommodate Seventh Day Adventist who could not work on Saturdays); Protos v. Volkswagen of America, Inc., 797 F.2d 129 (3d Cir.1986) (employer who had crew of relief operators to substitute for absent employees could reasonably accommodate plaintiff's religious need to have Saturdays free).

4. Hardison *and the ADA.* Is the *Hardison* Court's interpretation of "reasonable accommodation" and "undue hardship" relevant to the meaning of these terms in the American with Disabilities Act (ADA)? Based in part on the ADA's legislative history, the EEOC has taken the position that "[t]o demonstrate undue hardship pursuant to the ADA * * *, an employer must show substantially more difficulty or expense than would be needed to satisfy the "de minimis" title VII standard of undue hardship." 29 C.F.R. § 1630.15(d). Why would Congress use the same phrases in two employment discrimination statutes and intend two different meanings? Did the Court in *Hardison* veer from congressional intent for Title VII because of constitutional considerations? Is the Court likely to interpret the ADA in a similarly restricted fashion?

5. *Holding of* Philbrook? Does the Court in *Philbrook* hold that Ansonia had a duty to reasonably accommodate Philbrook with paid leave, or simply that it had a duty not to discriminate against religious purposes in the allocation of such leave? What does the Court expect the district court to determine on remand? Whether the employer intended to treat leave for religious purposes less favorably than leave for secular purposes? Whether its policies effectively treated religious leave less favorably without any significant business justification? What if the district court determines that Ansonia treats any secular purpose, other than those allotted specific days, as "necessary personal business" for purposes of allowing the three general purpose leave days? Would that show a preference for secular purposes?

6. *Do the Religiously Observant Have a Right to Unpaid Leave?* Does the *Philbrook* majority agree with Justice Stevens's apparent position that Title VII requires equal treatment of religiously observant employees, but does not require any affirmative subsidization? The majority seems to agree that an employer may refuse to provide any paid leave whatsoever for any purpose. But does this mean that an employer also may refuse to provide even unpaid leave exceptions to its general mandatory attendance rules? Note that religious majorities face no conflict comparable to Philbrook's because their religious holidays usually coincide with general vacation days. Must the reasonable accommodation requirement in Title VII demand some minimal special, affirmative efforts on behalf of religious workers if those workers, like disabled workers through the ADA and pregnant workers through the PDA, are to be granted equal employment opportunities? Does this analysis help explain why the majority cites *Nashville Gas Co.* v. *Satty,* p. 313 supra, in distinguishing the effects of denying paid leave and unpaid leave?

7. *Accommodation of Religious Garb and Grooming?* Does Title VII require employers to allow special clothing or grooming that their employees claim is dictated by their religion? Should an employer's obligation turn on whether it would accept the garb or grooming if adopted by an employee for secular reasons? Or must an employer at least provide some reason, other

than the prejudice of customers or coworkers, why allowing a departure from a dress and grooming code for religious reasons would impose more than de minimis costs? Would any variation from an established uniform or conventional grooming be likely to impose such costs? See, e.g., Cloutier v. Costco Wholesale Corp., 390 F.3d 126 (1st Cir. 2004) (employer may require member of "Church of Body Modification" to cover facial piercing to avoid "undue hardship" of losing "control over its public image"); EEOC v. United Parcel Serv., 94 F.3d 314, 320 (7th Cir.1996) (whether UPS policy of placing employees who are not clean shaven in positions without public contact reasonably accommodates religious reasons for not shaving is a question of material fact). Cf. Goldman v. Weinberger, 475 U.S. 503, 106 S.Ct. 1310, 89 L.Ed.2d 478 (1986) (first amendment does not restrict Air Force's application of general dress code to prohibit observant Jew's wearing of a yarmulke).

Might an employer, such as a public school, justify refusing to allow employees in public positions to assert their religious beliefs through their clothing, while allowing other employees to dress unusually for secular purposes? In United States v. Board of Educ. for Sch. Dist. of Philadelphia, 911 F.2d 882 (3d Cir.1990), the court held that the state's interest in preserving religious neutrality in the public classroom justified a "religious garb" prohibition that barred a teacher from wearing Muslim religious dress. Do you agree?

8. *Does Title VII Protect the Non–Religious?* Title VII's condemnations of discrimination are generally symmetrical, applying to discrimination in favor of, as well as against, traditionally disadvantaged groups. Does this symmetry also apply to the prohibition against religious discrimination? Does Title VII proscribe discrimination against an employee for rejecting a favored religious faith? For rejecting religion altogether? See, e.g., Shapolia v. Los Alamos Nat'l Lab., 992 F.2d 1033, 1038 (10th Cir.1993) (plaintiff stated cause of action by claiming he was terminated for not being a Mormon like his supervisors). Does protection of the atheist from discrimination under Title VII require the accommodation of his rejection of religious practices? See, e.g., Young v. Southwestern Savings & Loan Association, 509 F.2d 140 (5th Cir.1975) (atheist cannot be required by secular employer to participate in prayer activities). How far does the equal protection principle apply in this context? If the state is required by the free exercise clause to accommodate religious needs of employees, is it similarly required to accommodate the secular needs of nonreligious employees? Cf. Frazee v. Illinois Dept. of Emp. Security, 489 U.S. 829, 109 S.Ct. 1514, 103 L.Ed.2d 914 (1989) (free exercise clause violated by denial of unemployment compensation benefits to non-denominational Christian who refused to work on Sunday based on his religious beliefs).

9. *Must Religious Proselytizing Be Accommodated?* By requiring reasonable accommodation to "all aspects of religious observance and practice", does Title VII demand that employers indulge the efforts of employees to press their religious views on fellow workers and customers? The courts have assumed that the nondisruptive assertion of religious beliefs around the workplace may have to be accommodated, but also have held that employers do not have to abide religious expression that injures working relationships or otherwise affects productivity. See, e.g., Peterson v. Hewlett–Packard Co.,

358 F.3d 599 (9th Cir. 2004) (employer could terminate employee for refusing to remove prominent posting in his work cubicle of Biblical passages condemning homosexuality in violation of employer's anti-harassment policy); Knight v. State of Connecticut Dept. Of Public Health, 275 F.3d 156 (2d Cir.2001) (state may prohibit public health professionals from evangelizing while delivering services to clients); Anderson v. U.S.F. Logistics (IMC), Inc., 274 F.3d 470 (7th Cir.2001) (employer can prohibit employee using "Have a Blessed Day" in communications with customers); Chalmers v. Tulon Co. of Richmond, 101 F.3d 1012, 1021 (4th Cir.1996) (letters written to supervisor and subordinate charging them with immoral and ungodly behavior justify discharge); Wilson v. U.S. West Communications, 58 F.3d 1337, 1341–42 (8th Cir.1995) (wearing of graphic anti-abortion pin around workplace caused disruptions not based on religious prejudice and could not be accommodated without undue hardship). See also Banks v. Service America Corp., 952 F.Supp. 703, 709–10 (D.Kan.1996) (greeting customers with "God Bless You" and "Praise the Lord" may be a religious practice subject to reasonable accommodation). Cf. Tucker v. California Dep't of Educ., 97 F.3d 1204, 1216 (9th Cir.1996) (striking down under first amendment a policy prohibiting the display of religious objects outside closed offices and prohibiting religious advocacy in the workplace during work hours).

10. *Religious Harassment.* The basic prohibition of religious discrimination in Title VII condemns discharging an employee because of that employee's religion, regardless of whether the employer first provides the employee with the opportunity to convert to the employer's favored religion. Conditioning an employee's job on the employee's willingness to convert indeed might be viewed as analogous to "quid pro quo" sexual harassment, proscribed as discriminatory under Title VII under similar analysis. See Venters v. City of Delphi, 123 F.3d 956, 975–76 (7th Cir.1997) (accepting this theory). See also Kent Greenawalt, Title VII and Religious Liberty, 33 Loy. Univ. Ch. L.J. 1 (2001). Furthermore, an employer's acceptance of anti-Semitic, anti-Catholic, anti-Muslim or similarly bigoted remarks, as well as other general harassment of employees because of their religion, presumably also is prohibited by Title VII as the discriminatory imposition of different working conditions or a hostile work environment.

Would an employer's acceptance of aggressive religious proselytizing at the workplace constitute a form of hostile work environment harassment? See *Venters*, supra (Police Chief allegedly engaged in discriminatory religious harassment by subjecting subordinate to intimidating and intrusive religious proselytizing). How are employers to determine to what extent they must accommodate some employees' asserted religious need to proselytize, on the one hand, and other employees' right to have a nonhostile workplace, on the other hand? Should any objecting employees first be required to assert that they find particular religious overtures offensive? Should employees be required to listen to nonthreatening religious views? To have religious symbols or graphics placed before them? Consider, for instance, the Biblical scriptures in *Peterson*, supra, or the graphic anti-abortion pin in *Wilson*, supra. Should it make any difference whether the proselytizing employee is a supervisor?

The EEOC in 1993 suggested guidelines on discriminatory workplace harassment that would have applied the same standards for actionable hostile work environment sex-based harassment, see pp. 349–360 supra, to religion and other Title VII protected categories, as well as to age and disability. 58 Fed Reg. 51,266 (proposed Oct. 1, 1993). The guidelines had to be withdrawn within a year because of strongly expressed concern from members of Congress that the inclusion of religion would lead to the stifling of religious expression. See generally Betty L. Dunkum, Where to Draw the Line: Handling the Religious Harassment Issues in the Wake of the Failed EEOC Guidelines, 71 Notre D. L. Rev. 953 (1996).

11. *Accommodating Religious Association.* In order to improve morale and productivity, a large automobile manufacturer uses company resources to support "affinity groups" among its employees. These groups are to be based on the status characteristics of employees, and the company has supported disability and gay and lesbian as well as various ethnically defined groups such as African-Americans, Hispanics, and Chinese-Americans. Company guidelines prohibit affinity groups being based on interests, such as theatre or golf, however, and the guidelines also prohibit any group being based on religious affiliation or interest. Does the company violate Title VII by refusing the request of employees to establish a non-denominational "Christian affinity group"? See Moranski v. General Motors Corp., 433 F.3d 537 (7th Cir. 2005) (treating all religious positions alike did not constitute actionable discrimination).

C. THE CONSTITUTIONAL SETTING

THORNTON v. CALDOR

Supreme Court of the United States, 1985.
472 U.S. 703, 105 S.Ct. 2914, 86 L.Ed.2d 557.

CHIEF JUSTICE BURGER delivered the opinion of the Court.

I

* * *

In 1977, following the state legislature's revision of the Sunday-closing laws,[2] respondent opened its Connecticut stores for Sunday business. In order to handle the expanded store hours, respondent required its managerial employees to work every third or fourth Sunday. Thornton, a Presbyterian who observed Sunday as his Sabbath, initially complied with respondent's demand and worked a total of 31 Sundays in 1977 and 1978. In October 1978, Thornton was transferred to a management position in respondent's Torrington store; he continued to work on Sundays during the first part of 1979. In November 1979, however, Thornton informed respondent that he would no longer work on Sun-

---

2. The state legislature revised the Sunday-closing laws in 1976 after a state court held that the existing laws were unconstitutionally vague. *State v. Anonymous,* 33 Conn.Supp. 55, 364 A.2d 244 (Com.Pl. 1976). The legislature modified the laws to permit certain classes of businesses to re- main open. Conn.Gen.Stat. § 53–302a (1985). At the same time, a new provision was added, § 53–303e, which prohibited employment of more than six days in any calendar week and guaranteed employees the right not to work on the Sabbath of their religious faith.

days because he observed that day as his Sabbath; he invoked the protection of Conn.Gen.Stat. § 53–303e(b) (1985), which provides:

"No person who states that a particular day of the week is observed as his Sabbath may be required by his employer to work on such day. An employee's refusal to work on his Sabbath shall not constitute grounds for his dismissal."

Thornton rejected respondent's offer either to transfer him to a management job in a Massachusetts store that was closed on Sundays, or to transfer him to a nonsupervisory position in the Torrington store at a lower salary.[4] In March 1980, respondent transferred Thornton to a clerical position in the Torrington store; Thornton resigned two days later and filed a grievance with the State Board of Mediation and Arbitration alleging that he was discharged from his manager's position in violation of Conn.Gen.Stat. § 53–303e(b) (1985).

[*Eds.* On review of the Board's decision sustaining Thornton's grievance, the Supreme Court of Connecticut reversed, holding that the statute did not have "a clear secular purpose."]

II

Under the Religion Clauses, government must guard against activity that impinges on religious freedom, and must take pains not to compel people to act in the name of any religion. In setting the appropriate boundaries in Establishment Clause cases, the Court has frequently relied on our holding in *Lemon* [v. *Kurtzman,* 403 U.S. 602, 91 S.Ct. 2105, 29 L.Ed.2d 745 (1971),] for guidance, and we do so here. To pass constitutional muster under *Lemon* a statute must not only have a secular purpose and not foster excessive entanglement of government with religion, its primary effect must not advance or inhibit religion.

The Connecticut statute challenged here guarantees every employee, who "states that a particular day of the week is observed as his Sabbath," the right not to work on his chosen day. Conn.Gen.Stat. § 53–303e(b) (1985). The State has thus decreed that those who observe a Sabbath any day of the week as a matter of religious conviction must be relieved of the duty to work on that day, no matter what burden or inconvenience this imposes on the employer or fellow workers. The statute arms Sabbath observers with an absolute and unqualified right not to work on whatever day they designate as their Sabbath.[8]

In essence, the Connecticut statute imposes on employers and employees an absolute duty to conform their business practices to the particular religious practices of the employee by enforcing observance of the Sabbath the employee unilaterally designates. The State thus com-

---

4. The collective-bargaining agreement in effect for nonsupervisory employees provided that they were not required to work on Sundays if it was "contrary [to the employee's] personal religious convictions."

8. The State Board of Mediation and Arbitration construed the statute as providing Thornton with the absolute right not to work on his Sabbath. *Caldor, Inc. v. Thornton,* Conn.Bd.Med. & Arb.No. 7980–A–727 (Oct. 20, 1980) * * *.

mands that Sabbath religious concerns automatically control over all secular interests at the workplace; the statute takes no account of the convenience or interests of the employer or those of other employees who do not observe a Sabbath. The employer and others must adjust their affairs to the command of the State whenever the statute is invoked by an employee.

There is no exception under the statute for special circumstances, such as the Friday Sabbath observer employed in an occupation with a Monday through Friday schedule—a school teacher, for example; the statute provides for no special consideration if a high percentage of an employer's work force asserts rights to the same Sabbath. Moreover, there is no exception when honoring the dictates of Sabbath observers would cause the employer substantial economic burdens or when the employer's compliance would require the imposition of significant burdens on other employees required to work in place of the Sabbath observers.[9] Finally, the statute allows for no consideration as to whether the employer has made reasonable accommodation proposals.

* * * As such, the statute goes beyond having an incidental or remote effect of advancing religion. See, *e.g., Roemer v. Maryland Bd. of Public Works,* 426 U.S. 736, 747, 96 S.Ct. 2337, 2345, 49 L.Ed.2d 179 (1976); *Board of Education v. Allen,* 392 U.S. 236, 88 S.Ct. 1923, 20 L.Ed.2d 1060 (1968). The statute has a primary effect that impermissibly advances a particular religious practice.

JUSTICE O'CONNOR, with whom JUSTICE MARSHALL joins, concurring.

I do not read the Court's opinion as suggesting that the religious accommodation provisions of Title VII of the Civil Rights Act of 1964 are similarly invalid. These provisions preclude employment discrimination based on a person's religion and require private employers to reasonably accommodate the religious practices of employees unless to do so would cause undue hardship to the employer's business. 42 U.S.C. §§ 2000e(j) and 2000e–2(a)(1). Like the Connecticut Sabbath law, Title VII attempts to lift a burden on religious practice that is imposed by *private* employers, and hence it is not the sort of accommodation statute specifically contemplated by the Free Exercise Clause. See *Wallace v. Jaffree,* 472 U.S. 38, 83–84, 105 S.Ct. 2479, 2504–2505, 86 L.Ed.2d 29 (1985) (opinion concurring in judgment). The provisions of Title VII must therefore manifest a valid secular purpose and effect to be valid under the Establishment Clause. In my view, a statute outlawing employment discrimination based on race, color, religion, sex, or national origin has

---

9. Section 53–303e(b) gives Sabbath observers the valuable right to designate a particular weekly day off—typically a weekend day, widely prized as a day off. Other employees who have strong and legitimate, but non-religious, reasons for wanting a weekend day off have no rights under the statute. For example, those employees who have earned the privilege through seniority to have weekend days off may be forced to surrender this privilege to the Sabbath observer; years of service and payment of "dues" at the workplace simply cannot compete with the Sabbath observer's absolute right under the statute. Similarly, those employees who would like a weekend day off, because that is the only day their spouses are also not working, must take a back seat to the Sabbath observer.

the valid secular purpose of assuring employment opportunity to all groups in our pluralistic society. See *Trans World Airlines, Inc. v. Hardison,* 432 U.S. 63, 90, n. 4, 97 S.Ct. 2264, 2280, n. 4, 53 L.Ed.2d 113 (1977) (MARSHALL, J., dissenting). Since Title VII calls for reasonable rather than absolute accommodation and extends that requirement to all religious beliefs and practices rather than protecting only the Sabbath observance, I believe an objective observer would perceive it as an anti-discrimination law rather than an endorsement of religion or a particular religious practice.

Notes and Questions

1. *Does* Caldor *Call into Question Title VII?* Are you persuaded by Justice O'Connor's concurrence in *Caldor* that the Court's holding does not call into question the constitutionality of the religious accommodation clause of Title VII? Consider footnote 9 in the majority opinion. Does this suggest that Title VII's reasonable accommodation clause would not pass constitutional muster if it required employers to subordinate the secular interests of some employees in competitive seniority rights to the religious interests of other employees? Even under *Hardison*'s reading of Title VII requirements, is not the Sabbatarian's claim superior to that of the secular employee, for only the former need be honored in the absence of "undue hardship"? The majority in *Caldor* also stresses that the challenged Connecticut law could cause some employers "substantial economic burdens". Why should the incidence of unusual hardship on particular employers be relevant to the question of whether a statute "establishes" religion? Does the Court's analysis, in any event, suggest that the establishment clause requires Title VII to allow employers a broad undue hardship defense and prevents Congress from expanding the accommodation requirement beyond that imposed under *Hardison*? See also Protos v. Volkswagen of America, Inc., 797 F.2d 129 (3d Cir.1986) (distinguishing *Caldor* by noting that "Title VII does not require absolute deference to the religious practices of the employee, allows for consideration of the hardship to other employees and to the company, and permits an evaluation of whether the employer has attempted to accommodate the employee").

2. *Is* Caldor *Relevant to the NLRA?* Section 19 of the National Labor Relations Act allows employees who are members or adhere to "established and traditional tenets * * * of a bona fide religion, body, or sect which has historically held conscientious objection to joining or financially supporting labor organizations" to withhold the union dues otherwise required under a collective bargaining agreement and contribute such sums to a charitable organization listed in the agreement or, in the absence of such list, to a charity of the employee's choosing. Does this provision violate the establishment clause? See Wilson v. NLRB, 920 F.2d 1282 (6th Cir.1990). On the other hand, is it required by the free exercise clause?

3. *Free Exercise Claims for Reasonable Accommodation?* The free exercise clause in the first amendment balances, and some would argue, limits the establishment clause applied in *Caldor*. Indeed, in three cases, the Supreme Court invalidated state unemployment compensation rules that conditioned the availability of benefits upon an applicant's willingness to

work under conditions forbidden by his religion. See Sherbert v. Verner, 374 U.S. 398, 83 S.Ct. 1790, 10 L.Ed.2d 965 (1963); Thomas v. Review Bd. of Indiana Employment Sec. Div., 450 U.S. 707, 101 S.Ct. 1425, 67 L.Ed.2d 624 (1981); Hobbie v. Unemployment Appeals Comm'n of Florida, 480 U.S. 136, 107 S.Ct. 1046, 94 L.Ed.2d 190 (1987). In *Sherbert* and its progeny the Court required the state to justify a substantial burden on a religious practice with some "compelling governmental interest." It might be argued that these cases limit the reach of *Caldor* by not only permitting, but also requiring at least public employers to give some degree of special treatment to religiously motivated requests for exemption from general work rules, and perhaps also requiring state regulation to account for the special needs of the religious.

However, in Employment Div., Oregon Dept. of Human Resources v. Smith, 494 U.S. 872, 110 S.Ct. 1595, 108 L.Ed.2d 876 (1990), the Court narrowed the *Sherbert* line of cases by holding them not applicable where state law denies unemployment benefits to applicants who are discharged for conduct violative of laws of general application not specifically targeted at religious practice or belief. The *Smith* Court explained that the *Sherbert* line of cases stand only "for the proposition that where the State has in place a system of individual exemptions, it may not refuse to extend that system to cases of 'religious hardship' without compelling reason." 494 U.S. at 884. In other situations, "generally applicable, religion-neutral laws that have the effect of burdening a particular religious practice need not be justified by a compelling governmental interest." Id. at 886 n.3.

Reacting negatively to the *Smith* decision, Congress passed the Religious Freedom Restoration Act of 1993 (RFRA). 42 U.S.C. § 2000bb to bb–4 (1994). RFRA announced that "Government shall not substantially burden a person's exercise of religion even if the burden results from a rule of general applicability, except * * * in furtherance of a compelling governmental interest * * * [and where it uses] the least restrictive means of furthering that compelling governmental interest." 42 U.S.C. § 2000bb–1(a)-(b) (1994). In City of Boerne v. Flores, 521 U.S. 507, 117 S.Ct. 2157, 138 L.Ed.2d 624 (1997), however, the Court declared that Congress did not have the constitutional authority to apply RFRA to state governments. Congress had relied on its fourteenth amendment enforcement power, but the *Boerne* Court stressed that this power allowed Congress only to remedy past unconstitutional action and to prevent future unconstitutional action, such as that which would deny the free expression of religion. Given the broad sweep of RFRA and its application to neutral laws that are not likely to have been motivated by any religious bigotry, the Court concluded, RFRA could not be "considered remedial, preventive legislation, if those terms are to have any meaning." Id. at 2170.

In the wake of *Smith* and *Boerne*, could Congress justify an enlargement of the reasonable accommodation of religion requirement interpreted in *Hardison* by citing the first amendment's free exercise clause? Or might even the *Hardison de minimis* standard be unenforceable in private suits against state employers because it cannot be based on the fourteenth amendment? See Endres v. Indiana State Police, 334 F.3d 618 (7th Cir. 2002)(holding private suit based on § 703(j) accommodation requirement barred in at least federal court by sovereign immunity).

D. DISCRIMINATION BY RELIGIOUS INSTITU-TIONS

Section 702(a) of Title VII provides that the statute "shall not apply * * * to a religious corporation, association, educational institution, or society with respect to the employment of individuals of a particular religion to perform work connected with the carrying on by such corporation, association, educational institution, or society of its activities." Prior to 1972, § 702 exempted only the religious activities of such employers, but the provision was then amended to reach all activities of religious organizations, to "take the political hands of Caesar off of the institutions of God, where they have no place to be." 118 Cong.Rec. 4503 (1972) (remarks of Sen. Ervin). In a 1987 ruling, the Supreme Court held that application of the amended exemption to the nonprofit activities of such organizations—in that case, a public gymnasium operated by the Church of Jesus Christ of the Latter Day Saints—does not contravene the establishment clause. Corporation of Presiding Bishop of Church of Jesus Christ of Latter–Day Saints v. Amos, 483 U.S. 327, 107 S.Ct. 2862, 97 L.Ed.2d 273 (1987).

Justice White's majority opinion in *Amos* finds acceptable under the establishment clause Congress's purpose in expanding the exemption: minimizing governmental "interfer[ence] with the decision-making process in religions." Justice White acknowledged that an employee's freedom of choice in religious matters could be affected by decisions of employers insulated from challenge by the expanded § 702 exemption, but stressed that this effect would derive from choices forced on employees by religious employers, rather than directly by the government. The Court distinguished *Caldor* as a case where "Connecticut had given the force of law to the employee's designation of a Sabbath day and required accommodation by the employer regardless of the burden which that constituted for the employer or other employees." 483 U.S. at 337 n.15.

As stressed in the separate concurring opinions of Justices Brennan, O'Connor and Blackmun, *Amos* leaves open whether § 702's categorical exemption can be constitutionally applied to commercial, for-profit activities of religious organizations. As stated by Justice Brennan, the majority opinion seems based on a recognition that "[w]hile not every nonprofit activity may be operated for religious purposes, the likelihood that many are makes a categorical rule a suitable means to avoid chilling the exercise of religion." 483 U.S. at 345. This reasoning, however, does not support a categorical exemption for all for-profit activities. The lower courts generally have avoided ruling on the constitutionality of applying a categorical exemption to for-profit activities by rejecting a commercial enterprise's claim to be "religious" for purposes of § 702(a). For example, in EEOC v. Townley Engineering & Mfg. Co., 859 F.2d 610 (9th Cir.1988), the court held that a mining equipment company that was founded as a Christian, "faith-oriented" business, included bible tracts in every piece of outgoing mail, and conducted devotional services in the workplace, had to permit an atheist employee to excuse himself from mandatory prayer services. The court rejected Townley's contention that it was a "religious employer" on the ground that its business was "primarily secular." Judge Noonan dissented on free exercise grounds.

Even if construed not to exempt for-profit commercial activities, does § 702(a), as applied in *Amos*, provide too great an insulation of religious-based discrimination? Does it mean, for instance, that any research university owned and operated under religious auspices could refuse to hire members of other religious faiths to teach secular subjects or to perform other nonsectarian duties? Might many such universities, like most commercial enterprises, be outside the protection of § 702(a) because they are not primarily "religious"? Cf. EEOC v. Kamehameha Schools/Bishop Estate, 990 F.2d 458, 460 (9th Cir.1993) (applying *Townley* to find particular private primary and secondary schools to be primarily secular rather than religious). Might the provision of significant government grants to research universities classified as "religious" for purposes of the § 702(a) exemption be challenged under the establishment clause?

Educational institutions can also assert another exemption from Title VII's prohibition of religious discrimination. Section 703(e)(2) provides: "[I]t shall not be an unlawful employment practice for a school, college, university, or other educational institution or institution of learning to hire and employ employees of a particular religion" if the discriminating employer "is, in whole or in substantial part, owned, supported, controlled, or managed by a particular religion" or religious institution, or if the curriculum "is directed toward the propagation of a particular religion." This exemption was included in Title VII as originally enacted and was not amended when the § 702(a) exemption was enlarged. Might some educational institutions, whose instruction and activities are not primarily religious, be insulated by § 703(e)(2), perhaps because they receive substantial support from some religious denomination? Cf. Killinger v. Samford University, 113 F.3d 196 (11th Cir.1997) (university exempt under § 702(a) also exempt under § 703(e)(2) because it received substantial support from Baptist church). In light of *Amos* and *Caldor*, is § 703(e)(2) constitutional?

Even if an institution with a religious affiliation is not within the protective ambit of § 702(a) or § 703(e)(2), it may still attempt to invoke Title VII's bona fide occupational qualification (BFOQ) defense to religion-based discrimination. For instance, in Pime v. Loyola University of Chicago, 803 F.2d 351 (7th Cir. 1986), the court upheld the right of a university with a Jesuit tradition that did not qualify it as a religious employer for § 702(a) purposes to reserve seven out of 31 positions in its philosophy department for those with Jesuit training. The court stated that "[i]t appears to be significant to the educational tradition and character of the institution that students be assured a degree of contact with teachers who have received the training and accepted the obligations which are essential to membership in the Society of Jesus." Id. at 353. Is this approach consistent with the interpretation of the BFOQ defense given by the Supreme Court in cases like *Johnson Controls*, supra page 34, and *Criswell*, supra page 438? Was Jesuit training "reasonably necessary" to advance the "central mission" or "essence" of the university's philosophy department?

The § 702(a) exemption does not authorize race, color, national origin or sex discrimination by religious institutions. Similarly, courts have held that the ADEA does not contain an implied exemption for religious institutions. See, e.g., DeMarco v. Holy Cross High School, 4 F.3d 166 (2d Cir.1993). However, the lower courts also have ruled that the free exercise clause does not permit Title VII or the ADEA to proscribe discriminatory hiring for ministerial positions. See, e.g., Petruska v. Gannon University, 462 F.3d 294 (3d Cir.2006); Young v. Northern Illinois Conference of United Methodist Church, 21 F.3d 184, 187 (7th Cir.1994); McClure v. Salvation Army, 460 F.2d 553 (5th Cir.1972). See also Elvig v. Calvin Presbyterian Church, 375 F.3d 951 (9th Cir.2004) (allowing sexual harassment claim for damages, but not to overturn termination). Some courts have applied this "ministerial exception" to lay employees whose "primary duties consist of teaching, spreading the faith, church governance, supervision of a religious order, or supervision or participation in religious ritual and worship...." Rayburn v. General Conference of Seventh–Day Adventists, 772 F.2d 1164, 1169 (4th Cir.1985); see also, e.g., Tomic v. Catholic Diocese of Peoria, 442 F.3d 1036 (7th Cir.2006) (music director and organist cannot assert ADEA claim). Should application of the ministerial exception be dependent on the defendant showing that discriminatory hiring is mandated by religious doctrine? See generally Caroline Corbin, 75 Ford L. Rev. 1965 (2007); Ira Lupu, Free Exercise Exemption and Religious Institutions: The Case of Employment Discrimination, 67 B.U.L.Rev. 391 (1987); Douglas Laycock, Towards a General Theory of the Religion Clauses: The Case of Church Labor Relations and the Right to Church Autonomy, 81 Colum.L.Rev. 1373 (1981).

In EEOC v. Catholic University of America, 83 F.3d 455, 461–62 (D.C.Cir.1996), the court held that the Supreme Court's decision in *Smith* did not render inappropriate a broad ministerial exception based on the first amendment because *Smith* dealt with the state's accommodation of individuals seeking to observe a religious command, while the ministerial exception was framed to protect the freedom of the church to manage its own religious mission and to avoid state entanglement in that mission. Other courts of appeals have agreed. See, e.g., Gellington v. Christian Methodist Episcopal Church, Inc., 203 F.3d 1299 (11th Cir. 2000); Combs v. Central Texas Annual Conference of the United Methodist Church, 173 F.3d 343 (5th Cir.1999). Does RFRA, in any event, implicitly amend the federal anti-discrimination laws to protect religious institutions from actions by the EEOC, if not private parties? Cf. Hankins v. Lyght, 441 F.3d 96 (2d Cir.2006) (RFRA amends the ADEA and can be asserted against private plaintiff).

Chapter Nine

PROTECTION OF EMPLOYEE EXPRESSION AND ASSOCIATION BY THE FIRST AMENDMENT

A. INTRODUCTION

As the religion clauses of the first amendment seek affirmatively to protect religious activity from unreasonable and unnecessarily burdensome government action, the other clauses place a similarly high value on an important range of secular activity, most significantly freedom of expression. It is established that the first amendment erects a virtually absolute shield for expressive activity against suppression by the government in its regulatory, law enforcement role. The questions considered by this chapter are whether and to what extent this constitutional guarantee should operate as a limit on public employer personnel decisions.

A brief account of the theoretical justifications for the "free speech principle" will assist consideration of these questions. See generally R. Kent Greenawalt, Free Speech Justifications, 89 Colum.L.Rev. 119 (1989). Two dominant theories have emerged from the decisions and the secondary literature. The first posits that the primary purpose of the first amendment is the protection of the preconditions for public debate. As originally formulated, this justification was thought limited to those matters of government and public affairs directly relevant to an informed citizenry intelligently exercising its franchise. See, e.g., Alexander Meikeljohn, Free Speech and Its Relation to Self–Government (1948). In time, the range of topics has been expanded to include "expression about philosophical, social, artistic, economic, literary, or ethical matters," Abood v. Detroit Bd. of Educ., 431 U.S. 209, 231, 97 S.Ct. 1782, 1797, 52 L.Ed.2d 261 (1977), and indeed any matter of general interest.

Under this view, the first amendment values unrestrained debate for an instrumental reason: it is more likely to yield an enlightened public. In Justice Holmes's famous formulation, the first amendment assures a "marketplace of ideas" in which competing conceptions of the good are ventilated for citizens to digest, appraise and possibly act upon. Government's role in this marketplace should be one of neutrality between competing viewpoints. This instrumental purpose of the first amendment would seem to argue for rules protecting from adverse personnel decisions employees who make contributions to the public debate. The fact that an individual works for the government would seem to provide no justification for depriving the public of his or her contribution. The growth in the size of the government sector indeed suggests that much public employee expression is likely to be of increasing general interest. Moreover, if suppression of such expressive activity were permitted, government control of access to a major sector of employment opportunities would enable it to compel an orthodoxy of belief indirectly, through its leverage over public employees, that the first amendment bars it from compelling directly. See generally Mark Yudoff, When Government Speaks (1983).

A rival conception of the first amendment holds that human expressive activity is valued not merely because it may contribute to enlightenment on political, or even more personal, questions, but also because such activity, like religious activity for many, may have intrinsic value. It may contribute to a sense of personal autonomy or to the full development of the human potential. This formulation of the purpose of the constitutional guarantee argues for even broader restrictions on personnel decisions, because it does not require that the communication make any contribution to public debate or enlightenment. See, e.g., David Richards, Free Speech and Obscenity Law: Toward a Moral Theory of the First Amendment, 123 U.Pa.L.Rev. 45 (1974).

Unlike many of the regulations treated in this book, the restrictions addressed in this chapter are based on constitutional rights. This constitutional basis raises certain issues not presented by statutory schemes. First, the Constitution in general, and the first amendment in particular, reaches only governmental action. This "state action" requirement presents the question of why society would wish to control public employers' personnel decisions more than those of private employers. Second, the Constitution, by and large, is enforced by the courts. Because of institutional limitations, courts lack the capacity of a legislative body to develop special administrative mechanisms for the efficient adjudication and conciliation of disputes; to fashion rough compromises between competing values; or to compose comprehensive regulations for an area without regard to the submissions of particular parties. Finally, constitutional restrictions are not subject to revision by ordinary political processes; constitutional decisions can be changed only when political movements succeed in amending the Constitution or in changing the political perspective on the Supreme Court. It therefore does not suffice to say that a particular restriction would be desirable policy; rather, it is necessary to show why the interests at stake require such an extraordinary degree of insulation from majoritarian preferences.

Why might a society want to regulate, through a fundamental document insulated from ordinary majoritarian processes, the personnel decisions of only public employers? Are such decisions significantly more likely to threaten free expression because such employers have greater power over their employees or are less subject to the discipline of market forces than private employers? Might a society be more skeptical that ordinary political controls would adequately police the discretionary decisions of public employers? Or does the society place a higher value on the public-employee speech that is likely to be inhibited by adverse personnel decisions? Finally, can giving special constitutional protection to public employees be explained in part by our society's valuation of private ordering and the additional costs of enforcement in the large private sector?

Historical Note

Until midpoint in this century, the courts did not employ the first amendment to impose restrictions on public employers' personnel decisions. During the 1800s and the first half of the 1900s, the view prevailed that a citizen "may have a constitutional right to talk politics, but he has no constitutional right to be a policeman." McAuliffe v. Mayor of New Bedford, 155 Mass. 216, 220, 29 N.E. 517 (1892) (Holmes, J.). This position made the first amendment largely irrelevant as a legal limitation on the decisions of public employers, and it corresponded to the prevailing doctrine of employment "at will" that governed the decisions of their private counterparts (see chapter 12). The Supreme Court adhered to this view as late as 1952. See Adler v. Board of Educ., 342 U.S. 485, 72 S.Ct. 380, 96 L.Ed. 517 (1952) (upholding a New York law barring from public school employment anyone who advocated the violent overthrow of the government or belonged to an organization found to advocate or teach such an overthrow).

However, in the same year that *Adler* was decided, the Court began eroding the absolute position suggested by Holmes' formulation. In Wieman v. Updegraff, 344 U.S. 183, 73 S.Ct. 215, 97 L.Ed. 216 (1952), it struck down on due process grounds an oath requiring public employees to affirm the absence of past affiliation with the Communist Party irrespective of whether the employee had knowledge of any unlawful or subversive activity by that organization. The erosion of the Holmes dictum continued apace in the 1960s. For instance, in Shelton v. Tucker, 364 U.S. 479, 81 S.Ct. 247, 5 L.Ed.2d 231 (1960), the Court invalidated as an impairment of first amendment-protected associational rights an Arkansas statute that required public school teachers to make annual disclosure of their organizational affiliations.

Perhaps most importantly, in a series of cases invalidating state government loyalty oaths, the Court in the sixties elaborated on the implications of *Wieman* to expand the protection of public employees. See Cramp v. Board of Pub. Instruc., 368 U.S. 278, 82 S.Ct. 275, 7 L.Ed.2d 285 (1961); Baggett v. Bullitt, 377 U.S. 360, 84 S.Ct. 1316, 12 L.Ed.2d 377 (1964); Elfbrandt v. Russell, 384 U.S. 11, 86 S.Ct. 1238, 16 L.Ed.2d 321 (1966); Keyishian v. Board of Regents, 385 U.S. 589, 87 S.Ct. 675, 17 L.Ed.2d 629 (1967). These cases found oaths to threaten first amendment protected activity because they were excessively vague. *Keyishian* was the culminating decision. Not only did it reject the New York law originally upheld in *Adler,* but it also expressly repudiated the "major premise" of that opinion—"that public employment, including academic employment, may be conditioned upon the surrender of constitutional rights which could not be abridged by direct government action." Id. at 605, 87 S.Ct. at 681.

The repudiation of Holmes's premise that public employment is a privilege that can be denied for any reason, forced the Court to confront more directly the extent to which the first amendment should restrict public employers. What kinds of employee speech, or other expressive activity, should receive protection from adverse personnel decisions? What kinds of governmental justifications should be adequate to warrant the inhibition of public-employee speech?

B. FREE SPEECH AND PUBLIC EMPLOYMENT

PICKERING v. BOARD OF EDUCATION

Supreme Court of the United States, 1968.
391 U.S. 563, 88 S.Ct. 1731, 20 L.Ed.2d 811.

JUSTICE MARSHALL delivered the opinion of the Court.

Appellant Marvin L. Pickering, a teacher in Township High School District 205, Will County, Illinois, was dismissed from his position by the appellee Board of Education for sending a letter to a local newspaper in connection with a recently proposed tax increase that was critical of the way in which the Board and the district superintendent of schools had handled past proposals to raise new revenue for the schools.

* * *

In February of 1961 the appellee Board of Education asked the voters of the school district to approve a bond issue to raise $4,875,000 to erect two new schools. The proposal was defeated. Then, in December of 1961, the Board submitted another bond proposal to the voters which called for the raising of $5,500,000 to build two new schools. This second proposal passed and the schools were built with the money raised by the bond sales. In May of 1964 a proposed increase in the tax rate to be used for educational purposes was submitted to the voters by the Board and was defeated. Finally, on September 19, 1964, a second proposal to increase the tax rate was submitted by the Board and was likewise defeated. It was in connection with this last proposal of the School Board that appellant wrote the letter to the editor that resulted in his dismissal.

* * *

The letter constituted, basically, an attack on the School Board's handling of the 1961 bond issue proposals and its subsequent allocation of financial resources between the schools' educational and athletic programs. It also charged the superintendent of schools with attempting to prevent teachers in the district from opposing or criticizing the proposed bond issue.

The Board dismissed Pickering for writing and publishing the letter. Pursuant to Illinois law, the Board was then required to hold a hearing on the dismissal. At the hearing the Board charged that numerous statements in the letter were false and that the publication of the statements unjustifiably impugned the "motives, honesty, integrity, truthfulness, responsibility and competence" of both the Board and the school administration. The Board also charged that the false statements damaged the professional reputations of its members and of the school administrators, would be disruptive of faculty discipline, and would tend to foment "controversy, conflict and dissension" among teachers, administrators, the Board of Education, and the residents of the district. * * * The Board found the statements to be false as charged. No evidence was introduced at any point in the proceedings as to the effect of the publication of the letter on the community as a whole or on the administration of the school system in particular, and no specific findings along these lines were made.

* * *

The Board contends that "the teacher by virtue of his public employment has a duty of loyalty to support his superiors in attaining the generally accepted goals of education and that, if he must speak out publicly, he should do so factually and accurately, commensurate with his education and experience." Appellant, on the other hand, argues that the test applicable to defamatory statements directed against public officials by persons having no occupational relationship with them, namely, that statements to be legally actionable must be made "with knowledge that [they were] * * * false or with reckless disregard of whether [they were] * * * false or not," *New York Times Co. v. Sullivan,* 376 U.S. 254, 280, 84 S.Ct. 710, 726, 11 L.Ed.2d 686 (1964), should also be applied to public statements made by teachers. * * *

An examination of the statements in appellant's letter objected to by the Board reveals that they, like the letter as a whole, consist essentially of criticism of the Board's allocation of school funds between educational and athletic programs, and of both the Board's and the superintendent's methods of informing, or preventing the informing of, the district's taxpayers of the real reasons why additional tax revenues were being sought for the schools. The statements are in no way directed towards any person with whom appellant would normally be in contact in the course of his daily work as a teacher. Thus no question of maintaining either discipline by immediate superiors or harmony among coworkers is presented here. Appellant's employment relationships with the Board and, to a somewhat lesser extent, with the superintendent are not the kind of close working relationships for which it can persuasively be claimed that personal loyalty and confidence are necessary to their proper functioning. Accordingly, to the extent that the Board's position here can be taken to suggest that even comments on matters of public concern that are substantially correct * * * may furnish grounds for dismissal if they are sufficiently critical in tone, we unequivocally reject it.[3]

3. It is possible to conceive of some positions in public employment in which the need for confidentiality is so great that even completely correct public statements might furnish a permissible ground for dismissal. Likewise, positions in public employment in which the relationship between superior and subordinate is of such a personal and

We next consider the statements in appellant's letter which we agree to be false. The Board's original charges included allegations that the publication of the letter damaged the professional reputations of the Board and the superintendent and would foment controversy and conflict among the Board, teachers, administrators, and the residents of the district. However, no evidence to support these allegations was introduced at the hearing. So far as the record reveals, Pickering's letter was greeted by everyone but its main target, the Board, with massive apathy and total disbelief. The Board must, therefore, have decided, perhaps by analogy with the law of libel, that the statements were *per se* harmful to the operation of the schools.

However, the only way in which the Board could conclude, absent any evidence of the actual effect of the letter, that the statements contained therein were *per se* detrimental to the interest of the schools was to equate the Board members' own interests with that of the schools. Certainly an accusation that too much money is being spent on athletics by the administrators of the school system (which is precisely the import of that portion of appellant's letter containing the statements that we have found to be false) cannot reasonably be regarded as *per se* detrimental to the district's schools. Such an accusation reflects rather a difference of opinion between Pickering and the Board as to the preferable manner of operating the school system, a difference of opinion that clearly concerns an issue of general public interest.

In addition, the fact that particular illustrations of the Board's claimed undesirable emphasis on athletic programs are false would not normally have any necessary impact on the actual operation of the schools, beyond its tendency to anger the Board. For example, Pickering's letter was written after the defeat at the polls of the second proposed tax increase. It could, therefore, have had no effect on the ability of the school district to raise necessary revenue, since there was no showing that there was any proposal to increase taxes pending when the letter was written.

More importantly, the question whether a school system requires additional funds is a matter of legitimate public concern on which the judgment of the school administration, including the School Board, cannot, in a society that leaves such questions to popular vote, be taken as conclusive. On such a question free and open debate is vital to informed decision-making by the electorate. Teachers are, as a class, the members of a community most likely to have informed and definite opinions as to how funds allotted to the operation of the schools should be spent. Accordingly, it is essential that they be able to speak out freely on such questions without fear of retaliatory dismissal.

intimate nature that certain forms of public criticism of the superior by the subordinate would seriously undermine the effectiveness of the working relationship between them can also be imagined. We intimate no views as to how we would resolve any specific instances of such situations, but merely note that significantly different considerations would be involved in such cases.

In addition, the amounts expended on athletics which Pickering reported erroneously were matters of public record on which his position as a teacher in the district did not qualify him to speak with any greater authority than any other taxpayer. The Board could easily have rebutted appellant's errors by publishing the accurate figures itself, either via a letter to the same newspaper or otherwise. We are thus not presented with a situation in which a teacher has carelessly made false statements about matters so closely related to the day-to-day operations of the schools that any harmful impact on the public would be difficult to counter because of the teacher's presumed greater access to the real facts. Accordingly, we have no occasion to consider at this time whether under such circumstances a school board could reasonably require that a teacher make substantial efforts to verify the accuracy of his charges before publishing them.[4]

What we do have before us is a case in which a teacher has made erroneous public statements upon issues then currently the subject of public attention, which are critical of his ultimate employer but which are neither shown nor can be presumed to have in any way either impeded the teacher's proper performance of his daily duties in the classroom[5] or to have interfered with the regular operation of the schools generally. In these circumstances we conclude that the interest of the school administration in limiting teachers' opportunities to contribute to public debate is not significantly greater than its interest in limiting a similar contribution by any member of the general public.

* * *

While criminal sanctions and damage awards have a somewhat different impact on the exercise of the right to freedom of speech from dismissal from employment, it is apparent that the threat of dismissal from public employment is nonetheless a potent means of inhibiting speech. * * * [I]n a case such as the present one, in which the fact of employment is only tangentially and insubstantially involved in the subject matter of the public communication made by a teacher, we conclude that it is necessary to regard the teacher as the member of the general public he seeks to be.[6]

---

4. There is likewise no occasion furnished by this case for consideration of the extent to which teachers can be required by narrowly drawn grievance procedures to submit complaints about the operation of the schools to their superiors for action thereon prior to bringing the complaints before the public.

5. We also note that this case does not present a situation in which a teacher's public statements are so without foundation as to call into question his fitness to perform his duties in the classroom. In such a case, of course, the statements would mere-

ly be evidence of the teacher's general competence, or lack thereof, and not an independent basis for dismissal.

6. Because we conclude that appellant's statements were not knowingly or recklessly false, we have no occasion to pass upon the additional question whether a statement that was knowingly or recklessly false would, if it were neither shown nor could reasonably be presumed to have had any harmful effects, still be protected by the First Amendment. See also n. 5, supra.

GIVHAN v. WESTERN LINE CONSOLIDATED
SCHOOL DISTRICT

Supreme Court of the United States, 1979.

439 U.S. 410, 99 S.Ct. 693, 58 L.Ed.2d 619.

MR. JUSTICE REHNQUIST delivered the opinion of the Court.

Petitioner Bessie Givhan was dismissed from her employment as a junior high English teacher at the end of the 1970–1971 school year. * * * In an effort to show that its decision was justified, respondent School District introduced evidence of, among other things, a series of private encounters between petitioner and the school principal in which petitioner allegedly made "petty and unreasonable demands" in a manner variously described by the principal as "insulting," "hostile," "loud," and "arrogant." After a two-day bench trial, the District Court held that petitioner's termination had violated the First Amendment. Finding that petitioner had made "demands" on but two occasions and that those demands "were neither 'petty' nor 'unreasonable,' insomuch as all the complaints in question involved employment policies and practices at [the] school which [petitioner] conceived to be racially discriminatory in purpose or effect," the District Court concluded that "the primary reason for the school district's failure to renew [petitioner's] contract was her criticism of the policies and practices of the school district, especially the school to which she was assigned to teach."

* * * Although it found the District Court's findings not clearly erroneous, the Court of Appeals concluded that because petitioner had privately expressed her complaints and opinions to the principal, her expression was not protected under the First Amendment. * * * We are unable to agree that private expression of one's views is beyond constitutional protection, and therefore reverse the Court of Appeals' judgment and remand the case so that it may consider the contentions of the parties freed from this erroneous view of the First Amendment.[4]

Notes and Questions

1. *Reasons for Special Protection of Public Employee Speech.* Do these cases help explain why the speech of public employees should be given special protection not afforded to the speech of private employees? Did Pickering's and Givhan's employers have greater economic power over their staff than do private employers? Is a local polity more likely to be interested in its school board's budget allocation than in the budgetary decisions of a

---

4. Although the First Amendment's protection of government employees extends to private as well as public expression, striking the *Pickering* balance in each context may involve different considerations. When a teacher speaks publicly, it is generally the *content* of his statements that must be assessed to determine whether they "in any way either impeded the teacher's proper performance of his daily duties in the classroom or * * * interfered with the regular operation of the schools generally." Private expression, however, may in some situations bring additional factors to the *Pickering* calculus. When a government employee personally confronts his immediate superior, the employing agency's institutional efficiency may be threatened not only by the content of the employee's message but also by the manner, time, and place in which it is delivered.

major local manufacturer, or more concerned about race discrimination in
the school system than at the manufacturing plant?

2. *Why Protect Internal Speech?* Has the Court in *Givhan* adopted the
personal autonomy, noninstrumental view of the first amendment? Or is the
decision better understood as holding that although speech must contribute
to public debate, the relevant "public" may be the employer and coworkers
in the restricted internal "polity" of the workplace? Is protection of internal
speech necessary to the effective or orderly development of speech for public
debate?

3. *Should "Public Figure" Libel Law Be Applied?* Given New York
Times v. Sullivan, 376 U.S. 254, 84 S.Ct. 710, 11 L.Ed.2d 686 (1964), which
permits libel suits to proceed against speakers uttering knowing or intentionally false statements about public officials or public figures, is there any
reason why such statements when uttered by public employees about their
employer should ever receive the special protection of the Constitution?
Justice White argued not, in a separate opinion in *Pickering* (not included
above). Cf. also Johnson v. Multnomah County, Oregon, 48 F.3d 420, 423–24
(9th Cir.1995) (holding that even "recklessly false statements are not per se
unprotected", but noting split in circuits on issue.)

The *Pickering* majority suggests that some false statements regarding
matters of public interest, even if not intentional or recklessly false, may be
sufficiently harmful to a public employer to warrant discipline. Why should
public employees receive less protection than nonemployees who defame
public officials or public figures? From the speaker's standpoint, does liability in damages have more of a silencing effect than loss of employment or
other discipline? Are false statements by public employees likely to cause
greater harm?

4. *Protecting Truthful Speech.* Should the government's interest in the
public good be weighed in the *Pickering* balancing analysis at all, given the
purposes of the first amendment? Should the government have to show an
adverse impact that derives from the manner of the speech, rather than its
content? An adverse impact on the "clients" of the government services
being challenged, rather than on general public opinion? See generally
Andersen v. McCotter, 100 F.3d 723, 728 (10th Cir.1996) (government must
show actual undermining of public confidence); Jefferson v. Ambroz, 90 F.3d
1291, 1297 (7th Cir.1996) (government could discharge probation officer for
calling talk show and criticizing criminal justice system, in part because of
effect on officer's probationers' confidence in system).

5. *To Which Personnel Decisions Does* Pickering *Extend?* The *Pickering* balancing analysis presumably can be applied to any personnel decision
that punishes a public employee's protected speech. Does *Pickering* apply to
government actions that might discourage such speech by eliminating external financial incentives? In United States v. National Treasury Employees
Union, 513 U.S. 454, 115 S.Ct. 1003, 130 L.Ed.2d 964 (1995), the Court
applied the *Pickering* analysis to a challenge to a law that prohibited federal
employees from accepting any compensation, including honoraria and traveling expenses, for making speeches or writing articles. The Court held that
the government's burden under *Pickering* was especially "heavy" because
the challenged ban applied prospectively to a broad range of speech, rather

than just to that of particular individual employees, and that the "speculative benefits" of the ban were not sufficient "to justify this crudely crafted burden" on the speech of federal workers. Id. at 477. Do you agree that the government's burden should be heavier when it attempts to influence all employees through a general ban, rather than to sanction prior speech of a particular employee? See Crue v. Aiken, 370 F.3d 668 (7th Cir.2004) (finding illegal a university's general prohibition of communications with potential athletic recruits concerning "racial stereotyping" through mascot); Swartzwelder v. McNeilly, 297 F.3d 228 (3d Cir. 2002) (upholding injunction against enforcement of restriction on police officers testifying as experts in court without prior clearance).

6. *Threats to Working Relationships?* The Court stresses that Pickering's statements were not "directed towards any person with whom [he] would normally be in contact in the course of his daily work as a teacher." Cases where an employee breaches a duty of confidentiality or publicly criticizes a superior for whom he or she serves as a close personal assistant seem easily distinguishable. But should all employee criticism of immediate superiors or coworkers be unprotected? Should a public employer at least be required to wait until the impairment of a working relationship harms its operations before disciplining an employee for making such statements? Compare Tyler v. City of Mountain Home, Arkansas, 72 F.3d 568 (8th Cir.1995), with Voigt v. Savell, 70 F.3d 1552, 1560 (9th Cir.1995).

7. *Protection of Policymaking Employees?* Does *Pickering* apply to public officials in a policymaking position? Should elected public officials be able to demand unqualified loyalty from those with significant delegated policymaking authority? See, e.g., Silberstein v. City of Dayton, 440 F.3d 306 (6th Cir. 2006) (when employee is in policymaking position, there is a "presumption" that balance favors the government); Bonds v. Milwaukee County, 207 F.3d 969, 981 (7th Cir.2000) (policymaking exception does not apply to nonpolitical speech, but "policymaking status remains critical factor" in balance); McEvoy v. Spencer, 124 F.3d 92, 103 (2d Cir.1997) ("an employee's policymaking role does not provide an employer with complete insulation for adverse employment action, but does weigh, normally heavily, on the employer's side in the *Pickering* balance"). Cf. Wilbur v. Mahan, 3 F.3d 214, 217–19 (7th Cir.1993) (political speech and affiliation of policymakers not protected).

8. *Constitutional Protection of "Whistleblowers"?* To what extent is "whistleblowing"—involving an employee's public disclosure of potential wrongdoing by his or her public employer—protected by the first amendment, as construed in *Pickering?* Should a whistleblower's protection wane if investigations do not support his allegations? Should protection depend on following "proper channels" before going public? Compare Jurgensen v. Fairfax County, 745 F.2d 868 (4th Cir.1984), criticized in Tony Massaro, Significant Silences: Freedom of Speech in the Public Sector Workplace, 61 So.Cal.L.Rev. 1, 66 (1987), with Solomon v. Royal Oak Township, 842 F.2d 862, 866 (6th Cir.1988) ("public interest in the disclosure of corruption outweighs the state's interest in confidentiality"). By statute, Congress has provided significant protections for federal sector employees engaged in whistleblowing activity. These provisions are discussed at pp. 716–718 infra.

9. *"Manner, Time, and Place"*. Consider also footnote 4 in the *Givhan* opinion. Why should manner, time, and place be more relevant to determining the protection of nonpublic, internal expressions of views? Are comments critical of a superior at general employee meetings more or less likely to be protected than comments in private, individual conferences with the superior?

10. *Costs of a Balancing Test?* Does the balancing test used in *Pickering* and *Givhan* generate excessive uncertainty? On the one hand, might the costs of litigation, including pretrial discovery and the prospect of large jury awards, lead to more tentative employer personnel policies than otherwise would seem desirable? On the other hand, might the uncertainties of a balancing test augment the threat of possible adverse personnel actions on protected employee speech? Is a balancing test nonetheless necessary, notwithstanding these concerns?

11. *Remedies for First Amendment Violations.* Congress can significantly affect the remedies available for first amendment violations. In Bush v. Lucas, 462 U.S. 367, 103 S.Ct. 2404, 76 L.Ed.2d 648 (1983), the Court held that it would not create a damages remedy for nonprobationary federal employees in the civil service who are subjected to an adverse personnel action on account of protected first amendment activity. The Court explained that the comprehensive civil service system established by Congress provides meaningful remedies against the United States government for the violation of first amendment rights. The *Bush* opinion, and Congress's enforcement authority under § 5 of the fourteenth amendment, suggests that Congress could choose to fashion reasonable enforcement systems, that include use of administrative processes, to protect the first amendment rights of state and local government employees as well as those of federal employees. The Court's decision in City of Boerne v. Flores, 521 U.S. 507, 117 S.Ct. 2157, 138 L.Ed.2d 624 (1997), however, indicates that Congress could not invoke § 5 to design an enforcement system that *expanded* public employees' rights to free speech, and decisions such as Kimel v. Florida Board of Regents, 528 U.S. 62, 120 S.Ct. 631, 145 L.Ed.2d 522 (2000), indicate that Congress does not have authority outside § 5 to abrogate states' sovereign immunity to actions brought by their employees.

CONNICK v. MYERS

Supreme Court of the United States, 1983.
461 U.S. 138, 103 S.Ct. 1684, 75 L.Ed.2d 708.

JUSTICE WHITE delivered the opinion of the Court.

I

The respondent, Sheila Myers, was employed as an Assistant District Attorney in New Orleans for five and a half years. She served at the pleasure of petitioner Harry Connick, the District Attorney for Orleans Parish. During this period Myers competently performed her responsibilities of trying criminal cases.

In the early part of October 1980, Myers was informed that she would be transferred to prosecute cases in a different section of the criminal court. Myers was strongly opposed to the proposed transfer[1] and expressed her view to several of her supervisors, including Connick. Despite her objections, on October 6 Myers was notified that she was being transferred. Myers again spoke with Dennis Waldron, one of the First Assistant District Attorneys, expressing her reluctance to accept the transfer. A number of other office matters were discussed and Myers later testified that, in response to Waldron's suggestion that her concerns were not shared by others in the office, she informed him that she would do some research on the matter.

That night Myers prepared a questionnaire soliciting the views of her fellow staff members concerning office transfer policy, office morale, the need for a grievance committee, the level of confidence in supervisors, and whether employees felt pressured to work in political campaigns. Early the following morning, Myers typed and copied the questionnaire. She also met with Connick who urged her to accept the transfer. She said she would "consider" it. Connick then left the office. Myers then distributed the questionnaire to 15 Assistant District Attorneys. Shortly after noon, Dennis Waldron learned that Myers was distributing the survey. He immediately phoned Connick and informed him that Myers was creating a "mini-insurrection" within the office. Connick returned to the office and told Myers that she was being terminated because of her refusal to accept the transfer. She was also told that her distribution of the questionnaire was considered an act of insubordination.

* * *

Myers filed suit under 42 U.S.C. § 1983 (1976 ed., Supp. V), contending that her employment was wrongfully terminated because she had exercised her constitutionally protected right of free speech.

* * *

II

* * * Our task, as we defined it in *Pickering,* is to seek "a balance between the interests of the [employee], as a citizen, in commenting upon matters of public concern and the interest of the State, as an employer, in promoting the efficiency of the public services it performs through its employees." 391 U.S., at 568, 88 S.Ct., at 1734. The District Court, and thus the Court of Appeals as well, misapplied our decision in *Pickering* and consequently, in our view, erred in striking the balance for respondent.

* * *

The District Court got off on the wrong foot in this case by initially finding that, "[t]aken as a whole, the issues presented in the question-

---

1. Myers' opposition was at least partially attributable to her concern that a conflict of interest would have been created by the transfer because of her participation in a counseling program for convicted defendants released on probation in the section of the criminal court to which she was to be assigned.

naire relate to the effective functioning of the District Attorney's Office and are matters of public importance and concern." Connick contends at the outset that no balancing of interests is required in this case because Myers' questionnaire concerned only internal office matters and that such speech is not upon a matter of "public concern," as the term was used in *Pickering*. Although we do not agree that Myers' communication in this case was wholly without First Amendment protection, there is much force to Connick's submission. The repeated emphasis in *Pickering* on the right of a public employee "as a citizen, in commenting upon matters of public concern," was not accidental. This language, reiterated in all of *Pickering*'s progeny, reflects both the historical evolvement [sic] of the rights of public employees, and the common-sense realization that government offices could not function if every employment decision became a constitutional matter.

* * *

In all of these cases, the precedents in which *Pickering* is rooted, the invalidated statutes and actions sought to suppress the rights of public employees to participate in public affairs. The issue was whether government employees could be prevented or "chilled" by the fear of discharge from joining political parties and other associations that certain public officials might find "subversive." The explanation for the Constitution's special concern with threats to the right of citizens to participate in political affairs is no mystery. The First Amendment "was fashioned to assure unfettered interchange of ideas for the bringing about of political and social changes desired by the people." *Roth v. United States*, 354 U.S. 476, 484, 77 S.Ct. 1304, 1308, 1 L.Ed.2d 1498 (1957); *New York Times Co. v. Sullivan*, 376 U.S. 254, 269, 84 S.Ct. 710, 720, 11 L.Ed.2d 686 (1964). "[S]peech concerning public affairs is more than self-expression; it is the essence of self-government." *Garrison v. Louisiana*, 379 U.S. 64, 74–75, 85 S.Ct. 209, 215–216, 13 L.Ed.2d 125 (1964). Accordingly, the Court has frequently reaffirmed that speech on public issues occupies the " 'highest rung of the hierarchy of First Amendment values,' "and is entitled to special protection.

* * *

Pickering, its antecedents, and its progeny lead us to conclude that if Myers' questionnaire cannot be fairly characterized as constituting speech on a matter of public concern, it is unnecessary for us to scrutinize the reasons for her discharge. When employee expression cannot be fairly considered as relating to any matter of political, social, or other concern to the community, government officials should enjoy wide latitude in managing their offices, without intrusive oversight by the judiciary in the name of the First Amendment.

* * *

We do not suggest, however, that Myers' speech, even if not touching upon a matter of public concern, is totally beyond the protection of the First Amendment. "[T]he First Amendment does not protect speech and assembly only to the extent it can be characterized as political. 'Great secular causes, with smaller ones, are guarded.' " *Mine Workers v. Illinois Bar Assn.,* 389 U.S. 217, 223, 88 S.Ct. 353, 356, 19 L.Ed.2d 426 (1967), quoting *Thomas v. Collins,* 323 U.S. 516, 531, 65 S.Ct. 315, 323, 89 L.Ed. 430 (1945). We in no sense suggest that speech on private matters falls into one of the narrow and well-defined classes of expression which carries so little social value, such as obscenity, that the State can prohibit and punish such expression by all persons in its jurisdiction. See *Chaplinsky v. New Hampshire,* 315 U.S. 568, 62 S.Ct. 766, 86 L.Ed. 1031 (1942); *Roth v. United States, supra; New York v. Ferber,* 458 U.S. 747, 102 S.Ct. 3348, 73 L.Ed.2d 1113 (1982). For example, an employee's false criticism of his employer on grounds not of public concern may be cause for his discharge but would be entitled to the same protection in a libel action accorded an identical statement made by a man on the street. We hold only that when a public employee speaks not as a citizen upon matters of public concern, but instead as an employee upon matters only of personal interest, absent the most unusual circumstances, a federal court is not the appropriate forum in which to review the wisdom of a personnel decision taken by a public agency allegedly in reaction to the employee's behavior. Our responsibility is to ensure that citizens are not deprived of fundamental rights by virtue of working for the government; this does not require a grant of immunity for employee grievances not afforded by the First Amendment to those who do not work for the State.

Whether an employee's speech addresses a matter of public concern must be determined by the content, form, and context of a given statement, as revealed by the whole record. In this case, with but one exception, the questions posed by Myers to her co-workers do not fall under the rubric of matters of "public concern." We view the questions pertaining to the confidence and trust that Myers' co-workers possess in various supervisors, the level of office morale, and the need for a grievance committee as mere extensions of Myers' dispute over her transfer to another section of the criminal court. Unlike the dissent, we do not believe these questions are of public import in evaluating the performance of the District Attorney as an elected official. Myers did not seek to inform the public that the District Attorney's Office was not discharging its governmental responsibilities in the investigation and prosecution of criminal cases. Nor did Myers seek to bring to light actual or potential wrongdoing or breach of public trust on the part of Connick and others. Indeed, the questionnaire, if released to the public, would convey no information at all other than the fact that a single employee is upset with the status quo. While discipline and morale in the workplace are related to an agency's efficient performance of its duties, the focus of Myers' questions is not to evaluate the performance of the office but rather to gather ammunition for another round of controversy with her superiors. These questions reflect one employee's dissatisfaction with a transfer and an attempt to turn that displeasure into a cause celebre.[8]

8. This is not a case like *Givhan,* where an employee speaks out as a citizen on a matter of general concern, not tied to a personal employment dispute, but arranges

To presume that all matters which transpire within a government office are of public concern would mean that virtually every remark—and certainly every criticism directed at a public official—would plant the seed of a constitutional case. While as a matter of good judgment, public officials should be receptive to constructive criticism offered by their employees, the First Amendment does not require a public office to be run as a roundtable for employee complaints over internal office affairs.

One question in Myers' questionnaire, however, does touch upon a matter of public concern. Question 11 inquires if assistant district attorneys "ever feel pressured to work in political campaigns on behalf of office supported candidates." We have recently noted that official pressure upon employees to work for political candidates not of the worker's own choice constitutes a coercion of belief in violation of fundamental constitutional rights. *Branti v. Finkel,* 445 U.S. [507,] 515–516, 100 S.Ct. [1287 (1980)]; *Elrod v. Burns,* 427 U.S. 347, 96 S.Ct. 2673, 49 L.Ed.2d 547 (1976). In addition, there is a demonstrated interest in this country that government service should depend upon meritorious performance rather than political service. *CSC v. Letter Carriers,* 413 U.S. 548, 93 S.Ct. 2880, 37 L.Ed.2d 796 (1973); *Public Workers v. Mitchell,* 330 U.S. 75, 67 S.Ct. 556, 91 L.Ed. 754 (1947). Given this history, we believe it apparent that the issue of whether assistant district attorneys are pressured to work in political campaigns is a matter of interest to the community upon which it is essential that public employees be able to speak out freely without fear of retaliatory dismissal.

Because one of the questions in Myers' survey touched upon a matter of public concern and contributed to her discharge, we must determine whether Connick was justified in discharging Myers.

* * *

The *Pickering* balance requires full consideration of the government's interest in the effective and efficient fulfillment of its responsibilities to the public.

* * *

We agree with the District Court that there is no demonstration here that the questionnaire impeded Myers' ability to perform her responsibilities. The District Court was also correct to recognize that "it is important to the efficient and successful operation of the District Attorney's office for Assistants to maintain close working relationships with their superiors." Connick's judgment, and apparently also that of his first assistant Dennis Waldron, who characterized Myers' actions as causing a "mini-insurrection," was that Myers' questionnaire was an act of insubordination which interfered with working relationships.[11] When

to do so privately. Mrs. Givhan's right to protest racial discrimination—a matter inherently of public concern—is not forfeited by her choice of a private forum. * * *

11. Waldron testified that from what he had learned of the events on October 7, Myers "was trying to stir up other people

close working relationships are essential to fulfilling public responsibilities, a wide degree of deference to the employer's judgment is appropriate. Furthermore, we do not see the necessity for an employer to allow events to unfold to the extent that the disruption of the office and the destruction of working relationships is manifest before taking action. We caution that a stronger showing may be necessary if the employee's speech more substantially involved matters of public concern.

* * * Questions, no less than forcefully stated opinions and facts, carry messages and it requires no unusual insight to conclude that the purpose, if not the likely result, of the questionnaire is to seek to precipitate a vote of no confidence in Connick and his supervisors. Thus, Question 10, which asked whether or not the Assistants had confidence in and relied on the word of five named supervisors, is a statement that carries the clear potential for undermining office relations.

Also relevant is the manner, time, and place in which the questionnaire was distributed. * * * Here the questionnaire was prepared and distributed at the office; the manner of distribution required not only Myers to leave her work but others to do the same in order that the questionnaire be completed.[13] Although some latitude * * * is to be allowed when professional employees are involved, and Myers did not violate announced office policy, the fact that Myers, unlike Pickering, exercised her rights to speech at the office supports Connick's fears that the functioning of his office was endangered.

Finally, the context in which the dispute arose is also significant. This is not a case where an employee, out of purely academic interest, circulated a questionnaire so as to obtain useful research. Myers acknowledges that it is no coincidence that the questionnaire followed upon the heels of the transfer notice. When employee speech concerning office policy arises from an employment dispute concerning the very application of that policy to the speaker, additional weight must be given to the supervisor's view that the employee has threatened the authority of the employer to run the office. Although we accept the District Court's factual finding that Myers' reluctance to accede to the transfer order was not a sufficient cause in itself for her dismissal, and thus does not constitute a sufficient defense under *Mt. Healthy City Board of Ed. v. Doyle,* 429 U.S. 274, 97 S.Ct. 568, 50 L.Ed.2d 471 (1977), this does not render irrelevant the fact that the questionnaire emerged after a persis-

not to accept the changes [transfers] that had been made on the memorandum and that were to be implemented." In his view, the questionnaire was a "final act of defiance" and that, as a result of Myers' action, "there were going to be some severe problems about the changes." Connick testified that he reached a similar conclusion after conducting his own investigation. "After I satisfied myself that not only wasn't she accepting the transfer, but that she was affirmatively opposing it and disrupting the

routine of the office by this questionnaire. I called her in * * * [and dismissed her]."

13. The record indicates that some, though not all, of the copies of the questionnaire were distributed during lunch. Employee speech which transpires entirely on the employee's own time, and in nonwork areas of the office, bring different factors into the *Pickering* calculus, and might lead to a different conclusion. Cf. *NLRB v. Magnavox Co.,* 415 U.S. 322, 94 S.Ct. 1099, 39 L.Ed.2d 358 (1974).

tent dispute between Myers and Connick and his deputies over office transfer policy.

III

Myers' questionnaire touched upon matters of public concern in only a most limited sense; her survey, in our view, is most accurately characterized as an employee grievance concerning internal office policy. The limited First Amendment interest involved here does not require that Connick tolerate action which he reasonably believed would disrupt the office, undermine his authority, and destroy close working relationships. Myers' discharge therefore did not offend the First Amendment.

JUSTICE BRENNAN, with whom JUSTICE MARSHALL, JUSTICE BLACKMUN, and JUSTICE STEVENS join, dissenting.

The Court seeks to distinguish *Givhan* on the ground that speech protesting racial discrimination is "inherently of public concern." In so doing, it suggests that there are two classes of speech of public concern: statements "of public import" because of their content, form, and context, and statements that, by virtue of their subject matter, are "inherently of public concern." In my view, however, whether a particular statement by a public employee is addressed to a subject of public concern does not depend on where it was said or why. The First Amendment affords special protection to speech that may inform public debate about how our society is to be governed—regardless of whether it actually becomes the subject of a public controversy.

* * * I would hold that Myers' questionnaire addressed matters of public concern because it discussed subjects that could reasonably be expected to be of interest to persons seeking to develop informed opinions about the manner in which the Orleans Parish District Attorney, an elected official charged with managing a vital governmental agency, discharges his responsibilities.

* * *

The Court's adoption of a far narrower conception of what subjects are of public concern seems prompted by its fears that a broader view "would mean that virtually every remark—and certainly every criticism directed at a public official—would plant the seed of a constitutional case." Obviously, not every remark directed at a public official by a public employee is protected by the First Amendment.[3] But deciding whether a particular matter is of public concern is an inquiry that, by its very nature, is a sensitive one for judges charged with interpreting a constitutional provision intended to put "the decision as to what views shall be voiced largely into the hands of each of us." *Cohen v. California*, 403 U.S. 15, 24, 91 S.Ct. 1780, 1788, 29 L.Ed.2d 284 (1971).

3. Perhaps the simplest example of a statement by a public employee that would not be protected by the First Amendment would be answering "No" to a request that the employee perform a lawful task within the scope of his duties. Although such a refusal is "speech," which implicates First Amendment interests, it is also insubordination, and as such it may serve as the basis for a lawful dismissal.

Note on Rankin v. McPherson

Rankin v. McPherson, 483 U.S. 378, 381, 107 S.Ct. 2891, 2895, 97 L.Ed.2d 315 (1987), involved a 19 year old clerical employee of a county law enforcement agency who reacted to news of an attempted assassination of President Reagan by remarking to her co-worker and apparent boyfriend "he's cutting back medicaid and food stamps * * * shoot, if they go for him again, I hope they get him." The remark was overheard by another of McPherson's co-workers and resulted in her discharge. The Court, in an opinion by Justice Marshall, held that the statement was on a matter of public concern protected by *Pickering*:

> Considering the statement in context, as *Connick* requires, discloses that it plainly dealt with a matter of public concern. The statement was made in the course of a conversation addressing the policies of the President's administration. It came on the heels of a news bulletin regarding what is certainly a matter of heightened public attention * * *. The inappropriate or controversial character of a statement is irrelevant to the question whether it deals with a matter of public concern.

Id. at 386–87, 107 S.Ct. at 2897–98. Having found the *Pickering* threshold satisfied, the Court proceeded to inquire whether the statement impaired the effective functioning of the constable's office. The defendant acknowledged that McPherson's conduct had not interfered with the internal operations of its office. Nor was there any danger that the plaintiff had discredited the office by making her statement in public. Given her level of responsibility within the agency, the statement did not compromise the mission of the employer: "Where, as here, an employee serves no confidential, policymaking, or public contact role, the danger to the agency's successful function from that employee's speech is minimal." Id. at 391–92, 107 S.Ct. at 2900. Justice Scalia, joined by Chief Justice Rehnquist and Justices White and O'Connor, dissented.

Was *Rankin* consistent with *Connick*? Would the Court have protected McPherson's speech had she said that "I hope they get" some private citizen who had been unkind to her family?

Notes and Questions

1. *Reduced Protection for Speech About Labor Disputes?* For over a half century, the Court has taken the position that "the dissemination of information concerning the facts of a labor dispute must be regarded as within that area of free discussion that is guaranteed by the Constitution * * *. Free discussion concerning the conditions in industry and the causes of labor disputes [is] indispensable * * *." Thomas v. Collins, 323 U.S. 516, 532, 65 S.Ct. 315, 323, 89 L.Ed. 430 (1945) (quoting Thornhill v. Alabama, 310 U.S. 88, 102–03, 60 S.Ct. 736, 744–45, 84 L.Ed. 1093 (1940)); see also NLRB v. Virginia Elec. & Power Co., 314 U.S. 469, 477, 62 S.Ct. 344, 348, 86 L.Ed. 348 (1941); Senn v. Tile Layers Protective Union, 301 U.S. 468, 478, 57 S.Ct. 857, 862, 81 L.Ed. 1229 (1937). Is *Connick* reconcilable with this position? See generally Michael C. Harper, The Consumer's Emerging Right to Boy-

cott: *NAACP v. Claiborne Hardware* and Its Implications for American Labor Law, 93 Yale L.J. 409 (1984).

2. *No Protection At All of Speech on Non-"Public Concern" Matters?* Does *Connick* mean that public employee speech on matters not of "public concern" has no protection under the first amendment from injunctions, criminal prosecution, or other forms of state censorship? Or does Justice White hold that such speech receives no greater protection than that afforded the speech of private employees from the state as law-enforcement authority?

3. *Should Courts Decide What Is of Concern to the Public?* How are courts to determine what is a matter of "public concern"? Can a court assume that the general public would not be concerned about the efficiency or the fairness of personnel operations that its tax dollars support, or about the conduct of an important public agency such as the district attorney's office? Might the denial of full protection to particular issues, such as the labor relations issues in *Connick*, itself discourage public interest in those issues? Would it be better to reject all content-based thresholds and simply ask whether the public employer's actions were reasonably based on the operational requirements of the workplace rather than on a desire to suppress the expression of viewpoints? For criticism of *Connick*, see Tony Massaro, Significant Silences: Freedom of Speech in the Public Sector Workplace, 61 S.Cal.L.Rev. 1 (1987) (especially pp. 20–25 for lower court applications); Risa Lieberwitz, Freedom of Speech in Public Sector Employment: The Deconstitutionalization of the Public Sector Workplace, 19 U.Cal. Dav.L.Rev. 597 (1986).

4. *Importance of Myers's Immediate Audience?* Was the critical fact in *Connick* that there was no indication that Myers intended to release the questionnaire or its results to the public? Would Myers have fared better if she had framed her opposition in the form of a petition served on her supervisors rather than a questionnaire directed at coworkers? Could not the organization of coworkers, like preliminary discussions with supervisors, eventually lead to communication to the general public about the operations of government? How could the identity of the addressees of Myers' questionnaire have been determinative when the Court was willing to find that question 11 and McPherson's comments about the President were worthy of greater protection? Does *Rankin*, in any event, minimize the importance of a public employee's addressees?

5. *Importance of Myers's Motivation?* Was Myers's apparent motivation for distributing the questionnaire the critical fact in *Connick?* Should the level of first amendment protection turn on the altruism or civic-mindedness of the speaker? Is a motive test sensible given the ease with which private disputes can be framed as appeals to a matter of public concern? Most courts have focused on the content, as well as form and context, of the speech, rather than on its motivation. See, e.g., Banks v. Wolfe County Bd. Of Educ., 330 F.3d 888 (6th Cir. 2003); Azzaro v. County of Allegheny, 110 F.3d 968, 978 (3d Cir. 1997) (en banc); Zamboni v. Stamler, 847 F.2d 73 (3d Cir.1988); Rode v. Dellarciprete, 845 F.2d 1195, 1201 (3d Cir.1988) (all cases holding that an employee's personal stake in a matter of public concern does not require *Connick* treatment). But see Callaway v. Hafeman, 832 F.2d 414 (7th

Cir.1987) (internal speech on matter of public interest not protected because employee's "concern was personal, not public").

6. *Protecting Challenges to Supervisors' Authority?* Does the *Connick* Court's treatment of question 11 suggest that any speech that calls into question the personnel policies of the speaker's immediate supervisor can be the basis for an adverse personnel decision, even without a showing of actual work disruption? Is there not always a risk that such speech may undermine the authority of supervisors? Was it the questionnaire itself or the manner in which it was distributed that justified Myers's supervisors' concern? Should it matter whether the criticism is part of a political campaign in opposition to the election of the speaker's superiors? See Kinsey v. Salado Indep. Sch. Dist., 950 F.2d 988, 992–93 (5th Cir.1992) (en banc).

7. *Should Courts Now Weigh the Importance of the Public Concern?* The *Connick* Court cautions "that a stronger showing [of government interest] may be necessary if the employee's speech more substantially involved matters of public concern." Does this mean that the courts should determine the level of first amendment protection not only by judging whether a topic is a matter of public concern, but also by weighing the importance of the concern? Why would question 11, an inquiry concerning possible violations of an established constitutional right, not meet any threshold of importance? Does question 11 carry little weight for the Court only because it was part of a questionnaire that did not otherwise address a "public concern" and that generally seemed to be motivated by a personal grievance? Does this suggest that some kinds of employee criticism of supervisors should be protected even if managerial authority is, in fact, undermined?

8. *Was* Connick *a "Mixed Motive" Case?* Should the mode of proof for "mixed motive" § 1983 cases set out in Mt. Healthy City School Dist. Bd. of Educ. v. Doyle, 429 U.S. 274, 97 S.Ct. 568, 50 L.Ed.2d 471 (1977), have been used in *Connick*? Under *Mt. Healthy*, if a plaintiff proves that protected speech was a motivating factor in an adverse personnel decision, the defendant employer must prove that it would have made the same decision but for this illegitimate motive. Did the Court hold that the plaintiff had not established her affirmative case of showing that her protected speech (question 11) was a motivating factor in her dismissal, that the plaintiff had not shown that this motivation was unacceptable given the government's legitimate interests, or that the defendant had sustained its affirmative defense that Myers would have been dismissed for the other parts of the questionnaire?

9. *Protecting Public Employees From Their Employer's Misconstruction of Protected Speech?* Should the *Connick* test be applied to what the public employer thought was said, or to what the trier of fact ultimately determines was actually said? In Waters v. Churchill, 511 U.S. 661, 667, 114 S.Ct. 1878, 128 L.Ed.2d 686 (1994), the Supreme Court concluded that governmental managers could discharge an employee for making statements that they "reasonably found", based on interviews with two witnesses, included comments that criticized her supervisor and discouraged transfers into her department and thus were not protected under *Connick*'s restatement of the *Pickering* balance (whether or not the comments also involved a matter of

"public concern"). Justice O'Connor, writing for herself, Chief Justice Rehnquist, and Justices Souter and Ginsburg, held that an employer only must conduct an investigation that is reasonable in light of what the employee has been alleged to have said: "This need not be the care with which trials, with their rules or evidence and procedure, are conducted. It should, however, be the care that a reasonable manager would use before making an employment decision * * * of the sort involved in the particular case." Id. at 677–78. Justice Scalia, joined by Justices Kennedy and Thomas, objected to requiring any investigation, contending that the first amendment only demands that the employer not assert a legitimate reason as a pretext in bad faith. Justice Stevens, joined by Justice Blackmun, penned a strong dissent, arguing that the first amendment is violated "when a public employee is fired for uttering speech on a matter of public concern that is not unduly disruptive of the operation of the relevant agency," regardless of whether "the firing was based upon a reasonable mistake about what the employee said." Id. at 698.

10. *Can the First Amendment Protect Employees Who Have Not Actually Engaged in Protected Activity?* Is a public employee protected from a discharge prompted by an employer's erroneous belief that the employee engaged in activity that would be protected by the first amendment had it actually occurred? Does *Waters* dictate an answer? Would protection help avoid the chilling of appropriate speech? Would it in any way impede public administration? Cf. Fogarty v. Boles, 121 F.3d 886, 890 (3d Cir.1997) (absence of actual protected speech is fatal to cause of action).

11. *Protection of Artistic or Personal Expression?* Under *Connick* can the writing of fictional works be protected from adverse personnel actions by the first amendment? The presentation of photographs, paintings, music, or dance? Must the employee-artist first establish that his work somehow conveys a "message" of "public concern"? In City of San Diego v. Roe, 543 U.S. 77, 125 S.Ct. 521, 160 L.Ed.2d 410 (2004), the Court held that a police officer's videotapes featuring him performing sexual acts in a police uniform did not involve a matter of public concern and thus did not require *Pickering* balancing. But cf. Eberhardt v. O'Malley, 17 F.3d 1023, 1026 (7th Cir.1994) (holding that the writing of a novel, or of love songs, short stories or scripts, is presumptively protected, regardless of the subject matter or the relationship to the author's job).

12. *Protecting Government Contractors?* In Board of County Comm's v. Umbehr, 518 U.S. 668, 116 S.Ct. 2342, 2348–49, 135 L.Ed.2d 843 (1996), the Court held that *Pickering* balancing provides the appropriate flexible analysis for claims of government retaliation against government contractors for engaging in protected speech activities. Should public officials have greater discretion to control the speech of independent contractors than the speech of public employees because of the greater delegation of authority to contractors? Or do public employers have a reduced legitimate interest in restraining the speech of independent contractors because of the lack of close working relationships?

13. *Petitioning the Government on Matters of Private Concern?* Petitioning the government, including through lawsuits, is protected under the first amendment. Does *Connick* limit this protection? For instance, what if a public employee is discharged in retaliation for suing his supervisor for

breach of a real estate contract? What if the employee is discharged for filing for an abatement of his real estate taxes? Compare Grigley v. Atlanta, 136 F.3d 752 (11th Cir.1998) ("rationale of *Connick* applies to expression that takes the form of a petition as well as expression that takes the form of speech"), with San Filippo v. Bongiovanni, 30 F.3d 424 (3d Cir. 1994) ("public concern" limitation does not apply under the petition clause of the first amendment to claims of retaliation for invoking formal grievance mechanism).

GARCETTI, ET AL. v. CEBALLOS

Supreme Court of the United States, 2006.
547 U.S. 410, 126 S.Ct. 1951, 164 L.Ed.2d 689.

JUSTICE KENNEDY delivered the opinion of the Court.

I

Respondent Richard Ceballos has been employed since 1989 as a deputy district attorney for the Los Angeles County District Attorney's Office. During the period relevant to this case, Ceballos was a calendar deputy in the office's Pomona branch, and in this capacity he exercised certain supervisory responsibilities over other lawyers. In February 2000, a defense attorney contacted Ceballos about a pending criminal case. The defense attorney said there were inaccuracies in an affidavit used to obtain a critical search warrant. The attorney informed Ceballos that he had filed a motion to traverse, or challenge, the warrant, but he also wanted Ceballos to review the case. According to Ceballos, it was not unusual for defense attorneys to ask calendar deputies to investigate aspects of pending cases.

After examining the affidavit and visiting the location it described, Ceballos determined the affidavit contained serious misrepresentations. The affidavit called a long driveway what Ceballos thought should have been referred to as a separate roadway. Ceballos also questioned the affidavit's statement that tire tracks led from a stripped-down truck to the premises covered by the warrant. His doubts arose from his conclusion that the roadway's composition in some places made it difficult or impossible to leave visible tire tracks.

Ceballos spoke on the telephone to the warrant affiant, a deputy sheriff from the Los Angeles County Sheriff's Department, but he did not receive a satisfactory explanation for the perceived inaccuracies. He relayed his findings to his supervisors, petitioners Carol Najera and Frank Sundstedt, and followed up by preparing a disposition memorandum. The memo explained Ceballos' concerns and recommended dismissal of the case. On March 2, 2000, Ceballos submitted the memo to Sundstedt for his review. A few days later, Ceballos presented Sundstedt with another memo, this one describing a second telephone conversation between Ceballos and the warrant affiant.

Based on Ceballos' statements, a meeting was held to discuss the affidavit. Attendees included Ceballos, Sundstedt, and Najera, as well as the warrant affiant and other employees from the sheriff's department. The meeting allegedly became heated, with one lieutenant sharply criticizing Ceballos for his handling of the case.

Despite Ceballos' concerns, Sundstedt decided to proceed with the prosecution, pending disposition of the defense motion to traverse. The trial court held a hearing on the motion. Ceballos was called by the defense and recounted his observations about the affidavit, but the trial court rejected the challenge to the warrant.

Ceballos claims that in the aftermath of these events he was subjected to a series of retaliatory employment actions. The actions included reassignment from his calendar deputy position to a trial deputy position, transfer to another courthouse, and denial of a promotion. Ceballos initiated an employment grievance, but the grievance was denied based on a finding that he had not suffered any retaliation. Unsatisfied, Ceballos sued in the United States District Court for the Central District of California, asserting, as relevant here, a claim under Rev. Stat. § 1979, 42 U.S.C. § 1983. He alleged petitioners violated the First and Fourteenth Amendments by retaliating against him based on his memo of March 2.

* * *

II

* * *

* * * Government employers, like private employers, need a significant degree of control over their employees' words and actions; without it, there would be little chance for the efficient provision of public services. Cf. *Connick [v. Myers,* 461 U.S. 138,] 143, 103 S. Ct. 1684, 75 L. Ed. 2d 708 ("[G]overnment offices could not function if every employment decision became a constitutional matter"). Public employees, moreover, often occupy trusted positions in society. When they speak out, they can express views that contravene governmental policies or impair the proper performance of governmental functions.

At the same time, the Court has recognized that a citizen who works for the government is nonetheless a citizen. The *First Amendment* limits the ability of a public employer to leverage the employment relationship to restrict, incidentally or intentionally, the liberties employees enjoy in their capacities as private citizens. See *Perry v. Sindermann,* 408 U.S. 593, 597, 92 S. Ct. 2694, 33 L. Ed. 2d 570 (1972). So long as employees are speaking as citizens about matters of public concern, they must face only those speech restrictions that are necessary for their employers to operate efficiently and effectively. See, *e.g., Connick, supra,* at 147, 103 S. Ct. 1684, 75 L. Ed. 2d 708 ("Our responsibility is to ensure that citizens are not deprived of fundamental rights by virtue of working for the government'').

* * *

The Court's decisions, then, have sought both to promote the individual and societal interests that are served when employees speak as citizens on matters of public concern and to respect the needs of government employers attempting to perform their important public functions. * * * Underlying our cases has been the premise that while the *First Amendment* invests public employees with certain rights, it does not empower them to ''constitutionalize the employee grievance.'' *Connick*, 461 U.S., at 154, 103 S. Ct. 1864, 75 L. Ed. 2d 708.

III

With these principles in mind we turn to the instant case. Respondent Ceballos believed the affidavit used to obtain a search warrant contained serious misrepresentations. He conveyed his opinion and recommendation in a memo to his supervisor. That Ceballos expressed his views inside his office, rather than publicly, is not dispositive. Employees in some cases may receive First Amendment protection for expressions made at work. See, *e.g., Givhan v. Western Line Consol. School Dist.*, 439 U.S. 410, 414, 99 S. Ct. 693, 58 L. Ed. 2d 619 (1979). Many citizens do much of their talking inside their respective workplaces, and it would not serve the goal of treating public employees like ''any member of the general public,'' *Pickering [v. Board of Educ.]*, 391 U.S. [563], 573, 88 S. Ct. 1731, 20 L. Ed. 2d 811, to hold that all speech within the office is automatically exposed to restriction.

The memo concerned the subject matter of Ceballos' employment, but this, too, is nondispositive. The *First Amendment* protects some expressions related to the speaker's job. See, *e.g., ibid.; Givhan, supra*, at 414, 99 S. Ct. 693, 58 L. Ed. 2d 619. As the Court noted in *Pickering*: ''Teachers are, as a class, the members of a community most likely to have informed and definite opinions as to how funds allotted to the operation of the schools should be spent. Accordingly, it is essential that they be able to speak out freely on such questions without fear of retaliatory dismissal.'' 391 U.S., at 572, 88 S. Ct. 1731, 20 L. Ed. 2d 811. The same is true of many other categories of public employees.

The controlling factor in Ceballos' case is that his expressions were made pursuant to his duties as a calendar deputy. That consideration— the fact that Ceballos spoke as a prosecutor fulfilling a responsibility to advise his supervisor about how best to proceed with a pending case— distinguishes Ceballos' case from those in which the *First Amendment* provides protection against discipline. We hold that when public employees make statements pursuant to their official duties, the employees are not speaking as citizens for First Amendment purposes, and the Constitution does not insulate their communications from employer discipline.

Ceballos wrote his disposition memo because that is part of what he, as a calendar deputy, was employed to do. It is immaterial whether he experienced some personal gratification from writing the memo; his First Amendment rights do not depend on his job satisfaction. The significant point is that the memo was written pursuant to Ceballos' official duties. Restricting speech that owes its existence to a public employee's professional responsibilities does not infringe any liberties the employee might have enjoyed as a private citizen. It simply reflects the exercise of employer control over what the employer itself has commissioned or created. Cf. *Rosenberger v. Rector and Visitors of Univ. of Va.*, 515 U.S. 819, 833, 115 S. Ct. 2510, 132 L. Ed. 2d 700 (1995) ("[W]hen the government appropriates public funds to promote a particular policy of its own it is entitled to say what it wishes"). Contrast, for example, the expressions made by the speaker in *Pickering*, whose letter to the newspaper had no official significance and bore similarities to letters submitted by numerous citizens every day.

Ceballos did not act as a citizen when he went about conducting his daily professional activities, such as supervising attorneys, investigating charges, and preparing filings. In the same way he did not speak as a citizen by writing a memo that addressed the proper disposition of a pending criminal case. When he went to work and performed the tasks he was paid to perform, Ceballos acted as a government employee. The fact that his duties sometimes required him to speak or write does not mean his supervisors were prohibited from evaluating his performance.

This result is consistent with our precedents' attention to the potential societal value of employee speech. Refusing to recognize First Amendment claims based on government employees' work product does not prevent them from participating in public debate. The employees retain the prospect of constitutional protection for their contributions to the civic discourse. This prospect of protection, however, does not invest them with a right to perform their jobs however they see fit.

Our holding likewise is supported by the emphasis of our precedents on affording government employers sufficient discretion to manage their operations. Employers have heightened interests in controlling speech made by an employee in his or her professional capacity. Official communications have official consequences, creating a need for substantive consistency and clarity. Supervisors must ensure that their employees' official communications are accurate, demonstrate sound judgment, and promote the employer's mission. Ceballos' memo is illustrative. It demanded the attention of his supervisors and led to a heated meeting with employees from the sheriff's department. If Ceballos' superiors thought his memo was inflammatory or misguided, they had the authority to take proper corrective action.

Ceballos' proposed contrary rule, adopted by the Court of Appeals, would commit state and federal courts to a new, permanent, and intrusive role, mandating judicial oversight of communications between and among government employees and their superiors in the course of official business. This displacement of managerial discretion by judicial supervision finds no support in our precedents. When an employee speaks as a citizen addressing a matter of public concern, the First Amendment requires a delicate balancing of the competing interests surrounding the speech and its consequences. When, however, the employee is simply performing his or her job duties, there is no warrant for a similar degree of scrutiny. To hold otherwise would be to demand permanent judicial intervention in the conduct of governmental operations to a degree inconsistent with sound principles of federalism and the separation of powers.

* * *

Proper application of our precedents * * * leads to the conclusion that the First Amendment does not prohibit managerial discipline based on an employee's expressions made pursuant to official responsibilities. Because Ceballos' memo falls into this category, his allegation of unconstitutional retaliation must fail.

Two final points warrant mentioning. First, as indicated above, the parties in this case do not dispute that Ceballos wrote his disposition memo pursuant to his employment duties. We thus have no occasion to articulate a comprehensive framework for defining the scope of an employee's duties in cases where there is room for serious debate. We reject, however, the suggestion that employers can restrict employees' rights by creating excessively broad job descriptions. The proper inquiry is a practical one. Formal job descriptions often bear little resemblance to the duties an employee actually is expected to perform, and the listing of a given task in an employee's written job description is neither necessary nor sufficient to demonstrate that conducting the task is within the scope of the employee's professional duties for First Amendment purposes.

Second, JUSTICE SOUTER suggests today's decision may have important ramifications for academic freedom, at least as a constitutional value. There is some argument that expression related to academic scholarship or classroom instruction implicates additional constitutional interests that are not fully accounted for by this Court's customary employee-speech jurisprudence. We need not, and for that reason do not, decide whether the analysis we conduct today would apply in the same manner to a case involving speech related to scholarship or teaching.

IV

Exposing governmental inefficiency and misconduct is a matter of considerable significance. As the Court noted in *Connick*, public employers should, "as a matter of good judgment," be "receptive to constructive criticism offered by their employees." *461 U.S., at 149, 103 S. Ct. 1684, 75 L. Ed. 2d 708.* The dictates of sound judgment are reinforced by the powerful network of legislative enactments—such as whistle-blower protection laws and labor codes—available to those who seek to expose wrongdoing. See, *e.g.,* 5 U.S.C. § 2302(b)(8); Cal. Govt. Code Ann. § 8547.8 (West 2005); Cal. Lab. Code Ann. § 1102.5 (West Supp. 2006). Cases involving government attorneys implicate additional safeguards in the form of, for example, rules of conduct and constitutional obligations apart from the First Amendment. See, *e.g.*, Cal. Rule Prof. Conduct 5–110 (2005) ("A member in government service shall not institute or cause to be instituted criminal charges when the member knows or should know that the charges are not supported by probable cause"); *Brady v. Maryland, 373 U.S. 83, 83 S. Ct. 1194, 10 L. Ed. 2d 215 (1963).* These imperatives, as well as obligations arising from any other applicable constitutional provisions and mandates of the criminal and civil laws, protect employees and provide checks on supervisors who would order unlawful or otherwise inappropriate actions.

We reject, however, the notion that the First Amendment shields from discipline the expressions employees make pursuant to their professional duties. Our precedents do not support the existence of a constitutional cause of action behind every statement a public employee makes in the course of doing his or her job.

JUSTICE STEVENS, dissenting.

* * * The notion that there is a categorical difference between speaking as a citizen and speaking in the course of one's employment is quite wrong. Over a quarter of a century has passed since then-Justice Rehnquist, writing for a unanimous Court, rejected "the conclusion that a public employee forfeits his protection against governmental abridgment of freedom of speech if he decides to express his views privately rather than publicly." *Givhan v. Western Line Consol. School Dist.*, 439 U.S. 410, 414, 99 S. Ct. 693, 58 L. Ed. 2d 619 (1979). We had no difficulty recognizing that the First Amendment applied when Bessie Givhan, an English teacher, raised concerns about the school's racist employment practices to the principal. See *id., at 413–416, 99 S. Ct. 693, 58 L. Ed. 2d 619.* Our silence as to whether or not her speech was made pursuant to her job duties demonstrates that the point was immaterial. That is equally true today, for it is senseless to let constitutional protection for exactly the same words hinge on whether they fall within a job description. Moreover, it seems perverse to fashion a new rule that provides employees with an incentive to voice their concerns publicly before talking frankly to their superiors.

JUSTICE SOUTER, with whom JUSTICE STEVENS and JUSTICE GINSBURG join, dissenting.

The difference between a case like *Givhan* and this one is that the subject of Ceballos's speech fell within the scope of his job responsibilities, whereas choosing personnel was not what the teacher was hired to do. The effect of the majority's constitutional line between these two cases, then, is that a *Givhan* schoolteacher is protected when complaining to the principal about hiring policy, but a school personnel officer would not be if he protested that the principal disapproved of hiring minority job applicants. This is an odd place to draw a distinction,[1] and while necessary judicial line-drawing sometimes looks arbitrary, any distinction obliges a court to justify its choice. Here, there is no adequate justification for the majority's line categorically denying *Pickering* protection to any speech uttered "pursuant to ... official duties,".[1]

As all agree, the qualified speech protection embodied in *Pickering* balancing resolves the tension between individual and public interests in the speech, on the one hand, and the government's interest in operating efficiently without distraction or embarrassment by talkative or head-line-grabbing employees. The need for a balance hardly disappears when an employee speaks on matters his job requires him to address; rather, it seems obvious that the individual and public value of such speech is no less, and may well be greater, when the employee speaks pursuant to his duties in addressing a subject he knows intimately for the very reason that it falls within his duties.

* * *

[W]hy do the majority's concerns, which we all share, require categorical exclusion of First Amendment protection against any official retaliation for things said on the job? Is it not possible to respect the unchallenged individual and public interests in the speech through a *Pickering* balance without drawing the strange line I mentioned before? * * *

Two reasons in particular make me think an adjustment using the basic *Pickering* balancing scheme is perfectly feasible here. First, the extent of the government's legitimate authority over subjects of speech required by a public job can be recognized in advance by setting in effect a minimum heft for comments with any claim to outweigh it. Thus, the risks to the government are great enough for us to hold from the outset that an employee commenting on subjects in the course of duties should not prevail on balance unless he speaks on a matter of unusual importance and satisfies high standards of responsibility in the way he does it. The examples I have already given indicate the eligible subject matter, and it is fair to say that only comment on official dishonesty, deliberately unconstitutional action, other serious wrongdoing, or threats to health and safety can weigh out in an employee's favor. If promulgation of this standard should fail to discourage meritless actions premised on 42 U.S.C. § 1983 (or *Bivens v. Six Unknown Fed. Narcotics Agents*, 403 U.S. 388, 91 S. Ct. 1999, 29 L. Ed. 2d 619 (1971)) before they get filed, the standard itself would sift them out at the summary-judgment stage.[5]

1. It seems stranger still in light of the majority's concession of some First Amendment protection when a public employee repeats statements made pursuant to his duties but in a separate, public forum or in a letter to a newspaper.

5. As I also said, a public employer is entitled (and obliged) to impose high standards of honesty, accuracy, and judgment on employees who speak in doing their work. These criteria are not, however, likely to discourage meritless litigation or provide a handle for summary judgment. The employee who has spoken out, for example, is unlikely to blame himself for prior bad judgment before he sues for retaliation.

My second reason for adapting *Pickering* to the circumstances at hand is the experience in Circuits that have recognized claims like Ceballos's here. First Amendment protection less circumscribed than what I would recognize has been available in the Ninth Circuit for over 17 years, and neither there nor in other Circuits that accept claims like this one has there been a debilitating flood of litigation. For that matter, the majority's position comes with no guarantee against factbound litigation over whether a public employee's statements were made "pursuant to ... official duties,". In fact, the majority invites such litigation by describing the enquiry as a "practical one," apparently based on the totality of employment circumstances. Are prosecutors' discretionary statements about cases addressed to the press on the courthouse steps made "pursuant to their official duties"? Are government nuclear scientists' complaints to their supervisors about a colleague's improper handling of radioactive materials made "pursuant" to duties?

* * * [S]peech addressing official wrongdoing may well fall outside protected whistle-blowing, defined in the classic sense of exposing an official's fault to a third party or to the public; the teacher in *Givhan*, for example, who raised the issue of unconstitutional hiring bias, would not have qualified as that sort of whistle-blower, for she was fired after a private conversation with the school principal. In any event, the combined variants of statutory whistle-blower definitions and protections add up to a patchwork, not a showing that worries may be remitted to legislatures for relief.

JUSTICE BREYER, dissenting [omitted].

Notes and Questions

1. *An Appropriate Threshold?* The Court in *Garcetti* adds a second threshold, in addition to that set in *Connick*, that public employees claiming first amendment protection must cross before they can subject their employers' personnel actions to the judicial balancing of *Pickering*. How does the Court articulate this threshold? Given *Connick*, why did the Court find it appropriate to posit the additional threshold? Could adjusting the *Pickering* balance as suggested by Justice Souter have adequately protected government interests without any new threshold?

2. *Applications.* What precisely is the scope of the employee expressions "pursuant to official responsibilities" or "employment duties" exempted from *Pickering* balancing by *Garcetti*? Consider the following.

a. *Job–Required or Job–Related?* Ceballos charged that he was retaliated against for speech other than the disposition memorandum treated by the Court in *Garcetti*. The Court remanded to the Court of Appeals in part to consider these other charges. How might the *Garcetti* Court's standard apply to retaliation against Ceballos for a speech delivered to the Mexican-American Bar Association about misconduct in the Sheriff's Department in the criminal case on which he wrote the disposition memorandum? For testifying in the hearing to suppress evidence in the case that the affidavit he investigated contained intentional fabrications? If Ceballos had filed a complaint with the office of Garcetti, the District Attorney, alleging that his superiors were colluding with the Sheriff's Department to obtain evidence illegally, would retaliation against the complaint be subject to *Pickering* balancing? Is the test to be applied in these cases whether the speech is required by the job or whether it is related to the job?

b. *Functional not Formal Definition of Job.* Justice Kennedy, for the Court in *Garcetti*, rejects "the suggestion that employers can restrict employees' rights by creating excessively broad job descriptions." He states that "[f]ormal job descriptions" are not controlling, and that the "proper inquiry" is instead a "practical one" to determine whether "conducting the task is within the scope of the employee's professional duties". Would your answers to any of the questions in the last paragraph be influenced by the description of Ceballos's job in formal documents? By what was taken into account in his job evaluations? By legal standards for vicarious liability?

c. *Internal Grievance Process.* Does *Garcetti* mean that if a public employer provides formal internal complaint procedures that its employees are required to use before going public with their grievance, employees will have no first amendment protection for speech made while using such procedures? Would this be consistent with the Court's statement that "[g]iving employees an internal forum for their speech will discourage them from concluding that the safest avenue of expression is to state their views in public?"

3. *Relevance of Alternative Legal Remedies?* Is it relevant to the reach of the first amendment that public employees who suffer retaliation for work-related expression may have alternative legal remedies like those noted at the end of the *Garcetti* Court's opinion? (See the discussion of whistleblower protections at pp. 636–37 supra.) Should the availability of such remedies for some public employees affect the first amendment protections of other public employees for whom they are not available? Note that the Court has found the existence of a comprehensive civil service system relevant to the remedies available to federal employees for adverse personnel actions taken against them in retaliation for first amendment activity. See *Bush v. Lucas*, discussed in note 11, page 621 supra. Rather than restricting the reach of the first amendment protections for all public employees, could the Court in *Garcetti* instead have encouraged state whistleblower laws by restricting the judicial remedies available to those with adequate alternative remedies, or was that option foreclosed by Congress' express provision in § 1983 of a remedy for the deprivation of constitutional rights under color of state law?

Even if expression like that of Ceballos's memorandum is not protected under some whistleblower law, might it be protected by an implied contractual covenant from an employer toward its employees that it will not terminate their employment for their good faith and effective performance of their jobs? The Reporters for the Restatement (Third) of Employment Law have proposed acceptance of such a covenant. See generally pp. 774–82 infra; see also Cynthia Estlund, Harmonizing Work and Citizenship: A Due Process Solution to a First Amendment Problem, The Supreme Court Review 2006, 115 (2007) (suggesting that such an interest could be protected under the due process clause and thus require that an employer provide "some kind of hearing" to insure against its deprivation).

4. *Academic Freedom.* Note the *Garcetti* Court's reservation of whether its analysis "would apply in the same manner to a case involving speech related to scholarship or teaching." Application of *Connick*'s "public concern" limit on the protection of public employee speech also could result in the exemption of much academic expression from *Pickering* balancing. Should "academic freedom" be equally protected on all subjects, no matter how esoteric or of limited public interest? Cf. Keyishian v. Board of Regents, 385 U.S. 589, 693, 87 S.Ct. 675, 17 L.Ed.2D 629 (1967) (academic freedom is a "special concern of the First Amendment"). See generally Richard H. Hiers, New Restrictions on Academic Free Speech, 2 J.C. & U.L. 217 (1995).

C. FREE ASSOCIATION AND PUBLIC EMPLOYMENT

McLAUGHLIN v. TILENDIS

United States Court of Appeals, Seventh Circuit, 1968.
398 F.2d 287.

CUMMINGS, J.

This action was brought under Section 1 of the Civil Rights Act of 1871 (42 U.S.C. § 1983) by John Steele and James McLaughlin who had been employed as probationary teachers by Cook County, Illinois, School District No. 149. Each sought damages of $100,000 from the Superintendent of School District No. 149 and the elected members of the Board of Education of that District.

Steele was not offered a second-year teaching contract and McLaughlin was dismissed before the end of his second year of teaching. Steele alleged that he was not rehired and McLaughlin alleged that he was dismissed because of their association with Local 1663 of the American Federation of Teachers, AFL–CIO. Neither teacher had yet achieved tenure.

* * *

It is settled that teachers have the right of free association, and unjustified interference with teachers' associational freedom violates the Due Process clause of the Fourteenth Amendment. *Shelton v. Tucker,* 364 U.S. 479, 485–487, 81 S.Ct. 247, 5 L.Ed.2d 231.

* * *

The trial judge was motivated by his conclusion that more than free speech was involved here, stating:

"The union may decide to engage in strikes, to set up machinery to bargain with the governmental employer, to provide machinery for arbitration, or may seek to establish working conditions. Overriding community interests are involved. The very ability of the governmental entity to function may be affected. The judiciary, and particularly this Court, cannot interfere with the power or discretion of the state in handling these matters."

It is possible of course that at some future time plaintiffs may engage in union-related conduct justifying their dismissal. But the Supreme Court has stated that

"Those who join an organization but do not share its unlawful purposes and who do not participate in its unlawful activities surely pose no threat, either as citizens or as public employees." *Elfbrandt v. Russell*, 384 U.S. 11, 17, 86 S.Ct. 1238, 1241, 16 L.Ed.2d 321.

Even if this record disclosed that the union was connected with unlawful activity, the bare fact [of] membership does not justify charging members with their organization's misdeeds. A contrary rule would bite more deeply into associational freedom than is necessary to achieve legitimate state interests, thereby violating the First Amendment.

Illinois has not prohibited membership in a teachers' union, and defendants do not claim that the individual plaintiffs engaged in any illegal strikes or picketing.[3] Moreover, collective bargaining contracts between teachers' unions and school districts are not against the public policy of Illinois. *Chicago, etc., Education Association v. Board of Education of City of Chicago*, 76 Ill.App.2d 456, 222 N.E.2d 243 (1966). Illinois even permits the automatic deduction of union dues from the salaries of employees of local governmental agencies. Ill.Rev.Stats.1967, Ch. 85, Sec. 472. These very defendants have not adopted any rule, regulation or resolution forbidding union membership. Accordingly, no paramount public interest of Illinois warranted the limiting of Steele's and McLaughlin's right of association.

Notes and Questions

1. *Protecting Freedom of Association.* Although the first amendment does not expressly mention freedom of association, the Supreme Court in Shelton v. Tucker, relied upon in *McLaughlin* and in the loyalty oath cases, see, e.g., Elfbrandt v. Russell, 384 U.S. 11, 86 S.Ct. 1238, 16 L.Ed.2d 321 (1966), held that the amendment's express protection of free speech, assembly and the right to petition government implicitly includes the guaranty of free association.

The right of association also includes a right to avoid political associations. Thus, the Court has held that public employees who do not occupy policymaking or confidential positions have a constitutional right not to be

---

3. In Illinois, strikes and certain picketing by public employees are enjoinable. Board of Education of Community Unit School Dist. No. 2 v. Redding, 32 Ill.2d 567, 207 N.E.2d 427 (1965).

discharged solely because of their failure to affiliate with a particular political party. Branti v. Finkel, 445 U.S. 507, 100 S.Ct. 1287, 63 L.Ed.2d 574 (1980); Elrod v. Burns, 427 U.S. 347, 96 S.Ct. 2673, 49 L.Ed.2d 547 (1976). The Court in these decisions rejected the view that patronage hiring is necessary to the effective functioning of the democratic political process. As stated in *Elrod:* "Patronage can result in the entrenchment of one or a few parties to the exclusion of others. And most indisputably * * *, patronage is a very effective impediment to the associational and speech freedoms which are essential to a meaningful system of democratic government." Id. at 369–70, 96 S.Ct. at 2687–88. In Rutan v. Republican Party, 497 U.S. 62, 110 S.Ct. 2729, 111 L.Ed.2d 52 (1990), the Court held that *Branti* and *Elrod* apply to hiring, promotion, transfer and layoff-recall decisions as well as discharges. And in O'Hare Truck Serv., Inc. v. City of Northlake, 518 U.S. 712, 116 S.Ct. 2353, 2355, 135 L.Ed.2d 874 (1996), it held that these cases also apply where government officials retaliate against independent contractors because of their "political association or the expression of political allegiance."

Should a public employer be able to harass even a policymaking or confidential subordinate because of the subordinate's political associations, or should only discharge of the subordinate be permitted? See Wallace v. Benware, 67 F.3d 655, 662 (7th Cir.1995) (finding *Elrod*'s policymaking exception not to extend to retaliatory harassment).

2. *Freedom of Association After Connick?* Does *Connick* suggest that to be protected from adverse personnel actions, a public employee's association must relate to an issue of "public concern", and thus that *McLaughlin* may no longer be good law? Or does *Connick* limit only the protection of expression, without limiting the protection of association? Compare Cobb v. Pozzi, 363 F.3d 89 (2d Cir. 2003) (*Connick* applies to free association claims), with Hatcher v. Board of Public Educ., 809 F.2d 1546, 1558 (11th Cir.1987) (*Connick* does not apply).

In *O'Hare Truck Service*, supra, the Court distinguished cases like *Pickering*, and *Umbehr*, discussed in note 12 at p. 631, where specific speech activity is punished and a balancing of governmental interests is required, from cases "where the raw test of political affiliation [is] suffic[ient] to show a constitutional violation, without the necessity of an inquiry more detailed than asking whether the requirement was appropriate for the employment in question." 518 U.S. at 719. Does this distinction also suggest that *Connick* is not applicable to freedom of association cases? Is the distinction intelligible and workable? For a view that it is not, see Justice Scalia's dissent, id. at 668.

3. *Mandatory Union Dues.* In light of the right of public employees to refuse to associate, does *McLaughlin*'s holding that a public employer cannot discharge employees for their union affiliation mean that a public employer also cannot require its employees to contribute to a union that has been selected to represent them in collective negotiations? In Abood v. Detroit Bd. of Educ., 431 U.S. 209, 97 S.Ct. 1782, 52 L.Ed.2d 261 (1977), the Supreme Court upheld a state law that authorized the negotiation of "agency shop" clauses requiring public employees who decline union membership to pay a service fee equal to regular union dues. The Court found that any interfer-

ence with employees' associational rights was justified by the state's interest in peaceful labor relations and its judgment that such relations could be obtained best through a system of exclusive representation by a union selected by a majority of employees. State law could require that such a system be maintained by compulsory payment of fees by all employees represented in the bargaining unit so as to ensure that all who benefit share fairly in the costs of collective representation. The *Abood* Court, however, also held that the first amendment prevents public employers and unions from requiring objecting employees to pay fees to be used for contributions to political candidates or for the expression of political or ideological views unrelated to the grievance adjustment and collective bargaining functions of unions. Unions also must take steps to ensure that objecting agency shop employees do not suffer even a temporary use of dues for purposes impermissible under *Abood*. See Chicago Teachers Union v. Hudson, 475 U.S. 292, 106 S.Ct. 1066, 89 L.Ed.2d 232 (1986). See generally Mancur Olson, The Logic of Collective Action: Public Goods and the Theory of Groups, ch. 3 (1971).

The Supreme Court has avoided deciding whether the first amendment prevents private employers and unions regulated by either the National Labor Relations Act or the Railway Labor Act from compelling employees to pay fees to support union political activities. Employee plaintiffs have argued that federal regulation of labor relations in general and the authorization of exclusive representation in particular make any such compulsion state action. The Court has sidestepped this argument by holding that both federal labor relations statutes authorize the exaction of only those fees necessary to union performance of core grievance adjustment and collective bargaining duties. See Communications Workers v. Beck, 487 U.S. 735, 108 S.Ct. 2641, 101 L.Ed.2d 634 (1988) (NLRA); Ellis v. Brotherhood of Railway Clerks, 466 U.S. 435, 104 S.Ct. 1883, 80 L.Ed.2d 428 (1984), and International Ass'n of Machinists v. Street, 367 U.S. 740, 81 S.Ct. 1784, 6 L.Ed.2d 1141 (1961) (RLA).

4. *Protecting Union–Related Activity?* The first amendment neither requires public employers to deal with unions as employee representatives, see Smith v. Arkansas State Highway Employees, Local 1315, 441 U.S. 463, 99 S.Ct. 1826, 60 L.Ed.2d 360 (1979), nor requires the government to force private employers to do so, see Babbitt v. United Farm Workers, 442 U.S. 289, 313, 99 S.Ct. 2301, 2316, 60 L.Ed.2d 895 (1979). Moreover, while there are strong first amendment arguments to support the right of employees to form unions, it is doubtful that constitutional protection extends to strikes or other forms of concerted economic pressure. Cf. Lyng v. International Union, United Auto. Workers, 485 U.S. 360, 108 S.Ct. 1184, 99 L.Ed.2d 380 (1988) (associational and expressive rights of union members not infringed by statute that denies food stamps to households including any individual on strike); U.A.W.–A.F.L. Local 232 v. Wisconsin Employment Relations Bd., 336 U.S. 245, 69 S.Ct. 516, 93 L.Ed. 651 (1949) (neither thirteenth amendment prohibition of slavery nor first amendment prevents state from enjoining concerted intermittent work stoppages). Indeed, notwithstanding some expansive language in earlier cases, see Thornhill v. Alabama, 310 U.S. 88, 60 S.Ct. 736, 84 L.Ed. 1093 (1940), the Court also has now made clear that union picketing is not fully insulated from reasonable state regulation. See,

e.g., NLRB v. Retail Store Employees Union, Local 1001, 447 U.S. 607, 100 S.Ct. 2372, 65 L.Ed.2d 377 (1980); Teamsters v. Vogt, Inc., 354 U.S. 284, 77 S.Ct. 1166, 1 L.Ed.2d 1347 (1957); Hughes v. Superior Court, 339 U.S. 460, 70 S.Ct. 718, 94 L.Ed. 985 (1950); but cf. NAACP v. Claiborne Hardware, 458 U.S. 886, 102 S.Ct. 3409, 73 L.Ed.2d 1215 (1982) (consumer boycott motivated by opposition to racial segregation protected by first amendment); Harper, The Consumer's Emerging Right to Boycott, supra, 93 Yale L.J. 409. The Court has indicated, however, that union handbilling should be afforded more first amendment protection than picketing, see Edward J. DeBartolo Corp. v. Florida Gulf Coast Building & Construction Trades Council, 485 U.S. 568, 108 S.Ct. 1392, 99 L.Ed.2d 645 (1988).

5. *Protecting Partisan Political Activity in the Workplace?* Does the right of association include public employee participation in partisan political campaigns? The Court has broadly sustained civil service law restrictions on such participation. See United Public Workers of America v. Mitchell, 330 U.S. 75, 67 S.Ct. 556, 91 L.Ed. 754 (1947) (provision of federal Hatch Act, 5 U.S.C § 7324(a)), reaffirmed in a pair of post-*Pickering* decisions, see Broadrick v. Oklahoma, 413 U.S. 601, 93 S.Ct. 2908, 37 L.Ed.2d 830 (1973); United States Civil Serv. Comm'n v. National Ass'n of Letter Carriers, 413 U.S. 548, 93 S.Ct. 2880, 37 L.Ed.2d 796 (1973). Justice White's opinion for the *Letter Carriers* Court explains that Congress could act to ensure that "the rapidly expanding Government work force should not be employed to build a powerful, invincible, and perhaps corrupt political machine," and that government employees not be pressured to "vote in a certain way or perform political chores in order to curry favor with their superiors rather than to act out their own beliefs." Id. at 565–66, 93 S.Ct. at 2890–91. Do these rulings effectively deprive public employees of the full rights of citizenship in the service of a sanitized conception of the political process? Do they permit bans on mere affiliation with political parties? Do they bar public employees from wearing partisan political buttons or displaying party propaganda in their lockers or on their bumper stickers? See Biller v. U.S. Merit Sys. Protection Bd., 863 F.2d 1079 (2d Cir.1988) (union president's statement of support of a Presidential candidate does not violate Hatch Act absent showing of concerted action with campaign); Blaylock v. U.S. Merit Sys. Protection Bd., 851 F.2d 1348 (11th Cir.1988) (same); but cf. Burrus v. Vegliante. 336 F.3d 82 (2d Cir. 2003) (upholding United States Postal Service (USPS) removal from union bulletin boards in nonpublic areas of post offices, of posters comparing positions of candidates in the 2000 presidential election).

6. *Protecting Personal Association?* Does the first amendment prevent a public employer from discriminating against an employee because of her personal association with an individual in disfavor with the employer? Should it make a difference whether the personal relationship was formed for the purpose of engaging in first amendment protected activity? See Rode v. Dellarciprete, 845 F.2d 1195, 1204 (3d Cir.1988). For a discussion of the constitutional protection afforded the intimate associations of public employees, see p. 869 infra.

Chapter Ten

PROTECTION FOR THE ASSERTION OF EMPLOYEE STATUTORY RIGHTS

A. INTRODUCTION

This chapter explores antiretaliation provisions of federal and state laws regulating the employment relationship. These provisions protect a particular kind of socially valued employee activity—activity intended to facilitate the enforcement of laws securing employee rights. The justification for the provisions is thus derivative. The activity protected is socially valued because the employee rights it helps secure have been deemed valuable by the particular statutory scheme.

All modern antidiscrimination laws depend on employee assertion of claims as a principal means of identifying infractions and promoting compliance. For the principal federal antidiscrimination laws—Title VII, ADEA, and the ADA—the filing of a charge with the Equal Employment Opportunity Commission (EEOC)—is a prerequisite to any private lawsuit. For other statutes, such as the federal wage and hour law, the Fair Labor Standards Act of 1938 (FLSA), 29 U.S.C. §§ 201 et seq. (the subject of chapter 15), such a filing (here, with the U.S. Department of Labor) is not a formal requirement; but as a practical matter, most claimants will not be able to vindicate their rights without government intervention, and the government will not typically intervene unless apprised of the situation by a private complaint.

Virtually every federal and most state employment laws contain some form of express antiretaliation provision. See, e.g., FLSA, § 15(a)(3), 29 U.S.C. § 215(a)(3); Occupational Safety and Health Act, § 11(c), 29 U.S.C. § 660(c); the Employee Retirement Security Act of 1974 (ERISA), §§ 502(a), 510, 29 U.S.C. §§ 1132(a), 1140. These provisions, however, come in different stripes. The narrower variant provides protection only for invoking or participating in the formal processes of the statute. Thus, § 704(a) of Title VII prohibits discrimination against an employee or applicant "because he has made a charge, testified, assisted, or participated in any manner in an investigation, proceeding, or hearing under this title." This type of clause is often referred to as a "participation" clause. In addition, a broader form of antiretaliation provision privileges some forms of self-help opposition to unlawful practices. Section 704(a) also contains an "opposition" clause prohibiting discrimination against an employee or applicant "because he has opposed any practice made an unlawful employment practice by this title."

An example of a third type of antiretaliation provision, § 510 of ERISA, 29 U.S.C. § 1140, is discussed at pp. 1039–50 infra. Section 510, in addition to protecting the assertion of statutory claims, protects against a form of status discrimination, that which occurs for the purpose of interfering with employees obtaining contractual benefits regulated by ERISA. See, e.g., Dister v. The Continental Group, Inc., 859 F.2d 1108 (2d Cir.1988) (employee fired on the eve of entitlement to enhanced pension benefits for the retaliatory purpose of preventing the obtainment of such benefits).

This chapter focuses on the first two types of antiretaliation provisions, treating examples under Title VII and the Occupational Safety and Health Act (OSHA). The chapter then concludes with a consideration of implied antiretaliation remedies.

Retaliation claims have become a very significant feature of the employment litigation landscape. In 2006, for instance, 29.8% of all charges filed with the EEOC alleged illegal retaliation. See www.eeoc. gov/stats/charges.html. For general treatments, see Deborah L. Brake, Retaliation, 90 Minn. L. Rev. 18 (2005); Douglas E. Ray, Title VII Retaliation Cases: Creating a New Protected Class, 58 U.Pitt. L. Rev. 405 (1997).

B. EXPRESS ANTIRETALIATION PROVISIONS: PARTICIPATION CLAUSE

BURLINGTON NORTHERN v. WHITE

Supreme Court of the United States, 2006.

548 U.S. 53, 126 S. Ct. 2405, 165 L. Ed. 2d 345.

JUSTICE BREYER delivered the opinion of the Court.

I

A

This case arises out of actions that supervisors at petitioner Burlington Northern & Santa Fe Railway Company took against respondent Sheila White, the only woman working in the Maintenance of Way department at Burlington's Tennessee Yard. In June 1997, Burlington's roadmaster, Marvin Brown, interviewed White and expressed interest in her previous experience operating forklifts. Burlington hired White as a "track laborer," a job that involves removing and replacing track components, transporting track material, cutting brush, and clearing litter and cargo spillage from the right-of-way. Soon after White arrived on the job, a co-worker who had previously operated the forklift chose to assume other responsibilities. Brown immediately assigned White to operate the forklift. While she also performed some of the other track laborer tasks, operating the forklift was White's primary responsibility.

In September 1997, White complained to Burlington officials that her immediate supervisor, Bill Joiner, had repeatedly told her that women should not be working in the Maintenance of Way department. Joiner, White said, had also made insulting and inappropriate remarks to her in front of her male colleagues. After an internal investigation, Burlington suspended Joiner for 10 days and ordered him to attend a sexual-harassment training session.

On September 26, Brown told White about Joiner's discipline. At the same time, he told White that he was removing her from forklift duty and assigning her to perform only standard track laborer tasks. Brown explained that the reassignment reflected co-worker's complaints that, in fairness, a "more senior man" should have the "less arduous and cleaner job" of forklift operator. 364 F.3d 789, 792 (CA 6 2004).

On October 10, White filed a complaint with the Equal Employment Opportunity Commission (EEOC or Commission). She claimed that the reassignment of her duties amounted to unlawful gender-based discrimination and retaliation for her having earlier complained about Joiner. In early December, White filed a second retaliation charge with the Commission, claiming that Brown had placed her under surveillance and was monitoring her daily activities. That charge was mailed to Brown on December 8.

A few days later, White and her immediate supervisor, Percy Sharkey, disagreed about which truck should transport White from one location to another. The specific facts of the disagreement are in dispute, but the upshot is that Sharkey told Brown later that afternoon that White had been insubordinate. Brown immediately suspended White without pay. White invoked internal grievance procedures. Those procedures led Burlington to conclude that White had *not* been insubordinate. Burlington reinstated White to her position and awarded her backpay for the 37 days she was suspended. White filed an additional retaliation charge with the EEOC based on the suspension.

B

After exhausting administrative remedies, White filed this Title VII action against Burlington in federal court. As relevant here, she claimed that Burlington's actions—(1) changing her job responsibilities, and (2) suspending her for 37 days without pay—amounted to unlawful retaliation in violation of Title VII. § 2000e–3(a). A jury found in White's favor on both of these claims. It awarded her $ 43,500 in compensatory damages, including $ 3,250 in medical expenses. The District Court denied Burlington's post-trial motion for judgment as a matter of law. See Fed. Rule Civ. Proc. 50(b).

Initially, a divided Sixth Circuit panel reversed the judgment and found in Burlington's favor on the retaliation claims. The full Court of Appeals vacated the panel's decision, however, and heard the matter en banc. The court then affirmed the District Court's judgment in White's favor on both retaliation claims. While all members of the en banc court voted to uphold the District Court's judgment, they differed as to the proper standard to apply. Compare 364 F.3d at 795–800, with *id.*, at 809 (Clay, J., concurring).

II

Title VII's anti-retaliation provision forbids employer actions that "discriminate against" an employee (or job applicant) because he has "opposed" a practice that Title VII forbids or has "made a charge, testified, assisted, or participated in" a Title VII "investigation, proceeding, or hearing." § 2000e–3(a). No one doubts that the term "discriminate against" refers to distinctions or differences in treatment that injure protected individuals. * * * But different Circuits have come to different conclusions about whether the challenged action has to be employment or workplace related and about how harmful that action must be to constitute retaliation. * * *

A

Petitioner and the Solicitor General both argue that the Sixth Circuit is correct to require a link between the challenged retaliatory action and the terms, conditions, or status of employment. They note that Title VII's substantive anti-discrimination provision protects an individual only from employment-related discrimination. They add that the anti-retaliation provision should be read *in pari materia* with the anti-discrimination provision. And they conclude that the employer actions prohibited by the anti-retaliation provision should similarly be limited to conduct that "affects the employee's compensation, terms, conditions, or privileges of employment."

We cannot agree. The language of the substantive provision differs from that of the anti-retaliation provision in important ways. Section 703(a) sets forth Title VII's core anti-discrimination provision in the following terms:

"It shall be an unlawful employment practice for an employer—

"(1) *to fail or refuse to hire or to discharge* any individual, or otherwise to discriminate against any individual *with respect to his compensation, terms, conditions, or privileges of employment*, because of such individual's race, color, religion, sex, or national origin; or

"(2) to limit, segregate, or classify his employees or applicants for employment in any way *which would deprive or tend to deprive any individual of employment opportunities or otherwise adversely affect his status as an employee*, because of such individual's race, color, religion, sex, or national origin." § 2000e–2(a) (emphasis added).

Section 704(a) sets forth Title VII's anti-retaliation provision in the following terms: "It shall be an unlawful employment practice for an employer *to discriminate against* any of his employees or applicants for employment ... because he has opposed any practice made an unlawful employment practice by this subchapter, or because he has made a charge, testified, assisted, or participated in any manner in an investigation, proceeding, or hearing under this subchapter." § 2000e–3(a) (emphasis added).

The underscored words in the substantive provision—"hire," "discharge," "compensation, terms, conditions, or privileges of employment," "employment opportunities," and "status as an employee"— explicitly limit the scope of that provision to actions that affect employment or alter the conditions of the workplace. No such limiting words appear in the anti-retaliation provision. Given these linguistic differences, the question here is not whether identical or similar words should be read *in pari materia* to mean the same thing. * * * Rather, the question is whether Congress intended its different words to make a legal difference. We normally presume that, where words differ as they differ here, "Congress acts intentionally and purposely in the disparate inclusion or exclusion." *Russello v. United States,* 464 U.S. 16, 23, 104 S. Ct. 296, 78 L. Ed. 2d 17 (1983).

There is strong reason to believe that Congress intended the differences that its language suggests, for the two provisions differ not only in language but in purpose as well. The anti-discrimination provision seeks a workplace where individuals are not discriminated against because of their racial, ethnic, religious, or gender-based status. See *McDonnell Douglas Corp. v. Green,* 411 U.S. 792, 800–801, 93 S. Ct. 1817, 36 L. Ed. 2d 668 (1973). The anti-retaliation provision seeks to secure that primary objective by preventing an employer from interfering (through retaliation) with an employee's efforts to secure or advance enforcement of the Act's basic guarantees. The substantive provision seeks to prevent injury to individuals based on who they are, *i.e.,* their status. The anti-retaliation provision seeks to prevent harm to individuals based on what they do, *i.e.,* their conduct.

To secure the first objective, Congress did not need to prohibit anything other than employment-related discrimination. The substantive provision's basic objective of "equality of employment opportunities" and the elimination of practices that tend to bring about "stratified job environments," *id.,* at 800, 93 S. Ct. 1817, 36 L. Ed. 2d 668, would be achieved were all employment-related discrimination miraculously eliminated.

But one cannot secure the second objective by focusing only upon employer actions and harm that concern employment and the workplace. Were all such actions and harms eliminated, the anti-retaliation provision's objective would *not* be achieved. An employer can effectively retaliate against an employee by taking actions not directly related to his employment or by causing him harm *outside* the workplace. See, *e.g.,*

Rochon v. Gonzales, 438 F.3d at 1213 (FBI retaliation against employee "took the form of the FBI's refusal, contrary to policy, to investigate death threats a federal prisoner made against [the agent] and his wife"); *Berry v. Stevinson Chevrolet*, 74 F.3d 980, 984, 986 (CA10 1996) (finding actionable retaliation where employer filed false criminal charges against former employee who complained about discrimination). A provision limited to employment-related actions would not deter the many forms that effective retaliation can take. Hence, such a limited construction would fail to fully achieve the anti-retaliation provision's "primary purpose," namely, "maintaining unfettered access to statutory remedial mechanisms." *Robinson v. Shell Oil Co.*, 519 U.S. 337, 346, 117 S. Ct. 843, 136 L. Ed. 2d 808 (1997).

* * *

[W]e conclude that Title VII's substantive provision and its anti-retaliation provision are not coterminous. The scope of the anti-retaliation provision extends beyond workplace-related or employment-related retaliatory acts and harm. We therefore reject the standards applied in the Courts of Appeals that have treated the anti-retaliation provision as forbidding the same conduct prohibited by the anti-discrimination provision and that have limited actionable retaliation to so-called "ultimate employment decisions." * * *

B

The anti-retaliation provision protects an individual not from all retaliation, but from retaliation that produces an injury or harm. As we have explained, the Courts of Appeals have used differing language to describe the level of seriousness to which this harm must rise before it becomes actionable retaliation. * * * In our view, a plaintiff must show that a reasonable employee would have found the challenged action materially adverse, "which in this context means it well might have dissuaded a reasonable worker from making or supporting a charge of discrimination." *Rochon*, 438 F.3d at 1219 (quoting *Washington*, 420 F.3d at 662).

We speak of *material* adversity because we believe it is important to separate significant from trivial harms. Title VII, we have said, does not set forth "a general civility code for the American workplace." *Oncale v. Sundowner Offshore Services, Inc.*, 523 U.S. 75, 80, 118 S. Ct. 998, 140 L. Ed. 2d 201 (1998); see *Faragher*, 524 U.S., at 788, 118 S. Ct. 2275, 141 L. Ed. 2d 662 (judicial standards for sexual harassment must "filter out complaints attacking the ordinary tribulations of the workplace, such as the sporadic use of abusive language, gender-related jokes, and occasional teasing"). An employee's decision to report discriminatory behavior cannot immunize that employee from those petty slights or minor annoyances that often take place at work and that all employees experience. See 1 B. Lindemann & P. Grossman, Employment Discrimination Law 669 (3d ed. 1996) (noting that "courts have held that personality conflicts at work that generate antipathy" and "snubbing by supervisors and co-workers" are not actionable under § 704(a)). The anti-retaliation provision seeks to prevent employer interference with "unfettered access" to Title VII's remedial mechanisms. *Robinson*, 519 U.S., at 346, 117 S. Ct. 843, 136 L. Ed. 2d 808. It does so by prohibiting employer actions that are likely "to deter victims of discrimination from complaining to the EEOC," the courts, and their employers. *Ibid.* And normally petty slights, minor annoyances, and simple lack of good manners will not create such deterrence. See 2 EEOC 1998 Manual § 8, p. 8–13.

We refer to reactions of a *reasonable* employee because we believe that the provision's standard for judging harm must be objective. An objective standard is judicially administrable. It avoids the uncertainties and unfair discrepancies that can plague a judicial effort to determine a plaintiff's unusual subjective feelings. We have emphasized the need for objective standards in other Title VII contexts, and those same concerns animate our decision here. See, *e.g.*, [*Pa. State Police v.*] *Suders*, 542 U.S. [129,] 141, 124 S. Ct. 2342, 159 L. Ed. 2d 204 [(2004)] (constructive discharge doctrine); *Harris v. Forklift Systems, Inc.*, 510 U.S. 17, 21, 114 S. Ct. 367, 126 L. Ed. 2d 295 (1993) (hostile work environment doctrine).

We phrase the standard in general terms because the significance of any given act of retaliation will often depend upon the particular circumstances. Context matters. "The real social impact of workplace behavior often depends on a constellation of surrounding circumstances, expectations, and relationships which are not fully captured by a simple recitation of the words used or the physical acts performed." *Oncale, supra*, at 81–82, 118 S. Ct. 998, 140 L. Ed. 2d 201. A schedule change in an employee's work schedule may make little difference to many workers, but may matter enormously to a young mother with school age children. Cf., *e.g.*, *Washington, supra*, at 662 (finding flex-time schedule critical to employee with disabled child). A supervisor's refusal to invite an employee to lunch is normally trivial, a nonactionable petty slight. But to retaliate by excluding an employee from a weekly training lunch that contributes significantly to the employee's professional advancement might well deter a reasonable employee from complaining about discrimination. See 2 EEOC 1998 Manual § 8, p. 8–14. Hence, a legal standard that speaks in general terms rather than specific prohibited acts is preferable for an "act that would be immaterial in some situations is material in others." *Washington, supra*, at 661.

* * *

III

Applying this standard to the facts of this case, we believe that there was a sufficient evidentiary basis to support the jury's verdict on White's retaliation claim. See *Reeves v. Sanderson Plumbing Products, Inc.*, 530 U.S. 133, 150–151, 120 S. Ct. 2097, 147 L. Ed. 2d 105 (2000). The jury found that two of Burlington's actions amounted to retaliation: the reassignment of White from forklift duty to standard track laborer tasks and the 37-day suspension without pay.

Burlington does not question the jury's determination that the motivation for these acts was retaliatory. But it does question the statutory significance of the harm these acts caused. The District Court instructed the jury to determine whether respondent "suffered a materially adverse change in the terms or conditions of her employment," and the Sixth Circuit upheld the jury's finding based on that same stringent interpretation of the anti-retaliation provision (the interpretation that limits § 704 to the same employment-related conduct forbidden by § 703). Our holding today makes clear that the jury was not required to find that the challenged actions were related to the terms or conditions of employment. And insofar as the jury also found that the actions were "materially adverse," its findings are adequately supported.

First, Burlington argues that a reassignment of duties cannot constitute retaliatory discrimination where, as here, both the former and present duties fall within the same job description. We do not see why that is so. Almost every job category involves some responsibilities and duties that are less desirable than others. Common sense suggests that one good way to discourage an employee such as White from bringing discrimination charges would be to insist that she spend more time performing the more arduous duties and less time performing those that are easier or more agreeable. That is presumably why the EEOC has consistently found "retaliatory work assignments" to be a classic and "widely recognized" example of "forbidden retaliation." 2 EEOC 1991 Manual § 614.7, pp. 614–31 to 614–32; see also 1972 Reference Manual § 495.2 (noting Commission decision involving an employer's ordering an employee "to do an unpleasant work assignment in retaliation" for filing racial discrimination complaint); EEOC Dec. No. 74–77, 1974 EEOC LEXIS 2, 1974 WL 3847, *4 (Jan. 18, 1974) ("Employers have been enjoined" under Title VII "from imposing unpleasant work assignments upon an employee for filing charges").

To be sure, reassignment of job duties is not automatically actionable. Whether a particular reassignment is materially adverse depends upon the circumstances of the particular case, and "should be judged from the perspective of a reasonable person in the plaintiff's position, considering all the circumstances." *Oncale*, 523 U.S., at 81, 118 S. Ct. 998, 140 L. Ed. 2d 201. But here, the jury had before it considerable evidence that the track labor duties were "by all accounts more arduous and dirtier"; that the "forklift operator position required more qualifications, which is an indication of prestige"; and that "the forklift operator position was objectively considered a better job and the male employees resented White for occupying it." 364 F.3d at 803 (internal quotation marks omitted). Based on this record, a jury could reasonably conclude that the reassignment of responsibilities would have been materially adverse to a reasonable employee.

Second, Burlington argues that the 37–day suspension without pay lacked statutory significance because Burlington ultimately reinstated White with backpay. Burlington says that "it defies reason to believe that Congress would have considered a rescinded investigatory suspension with full back pay" to be unlawful, particularly because Title VII, throughout much of its history, provided no relief in an equitable action for victims in White's position.

We do not find Burlington's last mentioned reference to the nature of Title VII's remedies convincing. After all, throughout its history, Title VII has provided for injunctions to "bar like discrimination in the future," *Albemarle Paper Co.* v. *Moody,* 422 U.S. 405, 418, 95 S. Ct. 2362, 45 L. Ed. 2d 280 (1975) (internal quotation marks omitted), an important form of relief. Pub. L. 88–352, § 706(g), 78 Stat. 261, as amended, 42 U.S.C. § 2000e–5(g). And we have no reason to believe that a court could not have issued an injunction where an employer suspended an employee for retaliatory purposes, even if that employer later provided backpay. In any event, Congress amended Title VII in 1991 to permit victims of intentional discrimination to recover compensatory (as White received here) and punitive damages, concluding that the additional remedies were necessary to "help make victims whole." *West* v. *Gibson,* 527 U.S. 212, 219, 119 S. Ct. 1906, 144 L. Ed. 2d 196 (1999) (quoting H. R. Rep. No. 102–40, pt. 1, pp. 64–65 (1991)); see 42 U.S.C. §§ 1981a(a)(1), (b). We would undermine the significance of that congressional judgment were we to conclude that employers could avoid liability in these circumstances.

Neither do we find convincing any claim of insufficient evidence. White did receive backpay. But White and her family had to live for 37 days without income. They did not know during that time whether or when White could return to work. Many reasonable employees would find a month without a paycheck to be a serious hardship. And White described to the jury the physical and emotional hardship that 37 days of having "no income, no money" in fact caused. ("That was the worst Christmas I had out of my life. No income, no money, and that made all of us feel bad. ... I got very depressed"). Indeed, she obtained medical treatment for her emotional distress. A reasonable employee facing the choice between retaining her job (and paycheck) and filing a discrimination complaint might well choose the former. That is to say, an indefinite suspension without pay could well act as a deterrent, even if the suspended employee eventually received backpay. Cf. *Mitchell,* 361 U.S., at 292, 80 S. Ct. 332, 4 L. Ed. 2d 323 ("It needs no argument to show that fear of economic retaliation might often operate to induce aggrieved employees quietly to accept substandard conditions"). Thus, the jury's conclusion that the 37-day suspension without pay was materially adverse was a reasonable one.

JUSTICE ALITO, concurring in the judgment [omitted].

Notes and Questions

1. *Holding?* Did the *Burlington* Court have to decide whether § 704 reaches employer conduct that does not implicates wages and working conditions? Didn't the conduct complained of by White—the change in job duties and the temporary suspension—involve aspects of her working conditions?

2. *Retaliatory Harassment.* Given the Court's reasoning, employer conduct in actionable retaliation for protected activity need not involve a "tangible employment action" under *Faragher* and *Ellerth*. *Burlington* thus rejects the view previously held by the Fourth Circuit that § 704(a) reaches only "ultimate" employment decisions—a position that effectively precluded § 704(a) protection for retaliatory workplace harassment not implicating formal employment decisions such as hiring, firing, promotion and pay. See Mattern v. Eastman Kodak Co., 104 F.3d 702 (5th Cir.1997).

3. *"Material Adversity."* Does the Court's "material adversity" standard provide a manageable limiting principle? Do any of these cases come out differently after *Burlington*? See Wanamaker v. Columbian Rope Co., 108 F.3d 462, 463 (2d Cir.1997) ("barring a terminated employee from using an office and phone to conduct a job hunt presents only a minor, ministerial stumbling block toward securing future employment"); Munday v. Waste Mgt. of North America, Inc., 126 F.3d 239, 243 (4th Cir.1997) (coworkers' shunning of plaintiff not material adverse emplyment action). For a pre-*Burlington* review of the decisions, see Joel E. Kravetz, Deterrence v. Material Harm: Finding the Appropriate Standard to Define an "Adverse Action" in Retaliation Claims, 4 U.Pa.J. of Lab. & Emp. L. 315 (2002).

4. *"Causation".* A critical issue under both clauses of § 704(a) is whether the adverse employment action suffered by the plaintiff was "caused" by the employee's protected activity. See, e.g., McDonnell v. Cisneros, 84 F.3d 256 (7th Cir.1996) (harassing conduct complained of was merely continuation of alleged conduct giving rise to the initial sexual harassment complaint). Should a short time span between the protected activity and the adverse action be sufficient to raise an inference of § 704(a) discrimination? See Clark County School Dist. v. Breeden, 532 U.S. 268, 273, 274, 121 S.Ct. 1508, 149 L.Ed.2d 509 (2001) (cases relying on temporal proximity alone suggest that such proximity must be "very close"; "[a]ction taken (as here) 20 months later suggests, by itself no causality at all"). See also, e.g., Quinn v. Green Tree Credit Corp., 159 F.3d 759, 769 (2d Cir.1998); Oliver v. Digital Equipment Corp., 846 F.2d 103, 110 (1st Cir.1988). See generally Note, Weighing Temporal Proximity in Title VII Retaliation Claims, 43 Bost. Coll. L. Rev. 741 (2002).

5. *"Participation"*: *Activity Prior to the Filing of a Charge?* Even though the Title VII clause refers to participation in proceedings "under this title," its protective reach presumably extends to filings with state civil rights deferral agencies, which constitute formal "participation" required by Title VII as a prelude to filing a charge with the EEOC. See Title VII, § 706 (b)–(d), 29 U.S.C. § 2000e–5(b)–(d). But to what extent does the participation clause protect activity prior to any administrative filing?

a. *Collection of Information.* What about an employee's attempt to collect information prior to the filing of a charge? What if the information is sought from clients of the employer who might prefer not to be disturbed by the internal disagreements of the employer? See EEOC v. Kallir, Philips, Ross, Inc., 401 F.Supp. 66 (S.D.N.Y.1975), affirmed, 559 F.2d 1203 (1977).

b. *Internal Complaints.* Does Title VII's participation clause protect discrimination complaints lodged internally with the employer? This issue has arisen in connection with the antiretaliation provision of the Fair Labor Standards Act, 29 U.S.C. § 215(a)(3), which provides that it is unlawful for any person

> (3) to discharge or in any other manner discriminate against any employee because such employee has filed any complaint or instituted or caused to be instituted any proceedings under or related to this chapter, or has testified or is about to testify in any such proceeding * * *.

In Lambert v. Genesee Hospital, 10 F.3d 46, 55 (2d Cir. 1993), drawing a distinction between the FLSA provision and Title VII's broader opposition clause, the Second Circuit held that the "plain language of this provision limits the cause of action to retaliation for filing formal complaints, instituting a proceeding, or testifying, but does not encompass complaints made to a supervisor." Other courts hold that this provision protects employees who file complaints internally with the employer even if no formal charge or complaint is ever filed. See, e.g., Valerio v. Putnam Assocs. Inc., 173 F.3d 35, 41 (1st Cir.1999); Lambert v. Ackerley, 180 F.3d 997, 1004 (9th Cir.1999) (en banc decision vacating contrary panel ruling).

c. *Employer's Internal Investigation.* Does the participation clause also extend to statements made by employees during an employer's internal investigation of a discrimination or harassment complaint after or prior to the filing of an EEOC charge? See Vasconcelos v. Meese, 907 F.2d 111, 112 (9th Cir.1990). Consider the dilemma created for employers by Merritt v. Dillard Paper, 120 F.3d 1181 (11th Cir.1997). In that case, a female receptionist filed a sexual harassment suit. Rather than conduct a complete investigation, the company agreed to take depositions of five current employees identified by the receptionist as participants in the harassing environment, including Merritt, a manager. In his deposition, Merritt admitted to some of the alleged behavior and acknowledged that some of the other offensive comments "sounded like" his own. After settling with the receptionist, the company fired Merritt who then sued under § 704(a)'s participation clause. The Eleventh Circuit reversed a grant of summary judgment for the employer, holding that under § 704(a)'s literal language, Merritt could not be fired for his deposition testimony. Was *Merritt* rightly decided?

In Clover v. Total System Services, Inc., 176 F.3d 1346 (11th Cir.1999), the court of appeals panel held that § 704(a) does extend to an employer's internal investigation if conducted in response to notice of an EEOC charge:

> [W]e recognize that at least where an employer conducts its investigation in response to [an EEOC] notice of charge of discrimination, and is thus aware that the evidence gathered in that inquiry will be considered by the EEOC as part of its investigation, the employee's participation is participation "in any manner" in the EEOC investigation.

Id. at 1353. In EEOC v. Total System Services, Inc., 221 F.3d 1171 (11th Cir. 2000), however, the appeals court held that participation clause protection does not extend to internal investigations conducted *before* an employer receives notice of an EEOC charge. Since only the opposition clause applied, the employer could discharge an employee based on a reasonable belief that the employee had lied in the investigation.

d. *Requests for Reasonable Accommodation of One's Disability.* In the ADA context, is an employee's request for a reasonable accommodation protected "participation" activity under § 503(a) of the statute? Some courts have relied on the anti-"interference" provisions in § 503(b). See Brown v. City of Tuscon, 336 F.3d 1181, 1193 (9th Cir.2003). What if the employee is not in fact disabled for ADA purposes? What if he acted reasonably and in good faith in believing he was? Compare, e.g., Sarno v. Douglas Elliman–Gibbons & Ives, Inc., 183 F.3d 155, 159–60 (2d Cir. 1999), with Standard v. A.B.E.L. Servs., Inc., 161 F.3d 1318, 1322 (11th Cir. 1998); see also note 4 below. Reasonable accommodation duties under the ADA are discussed at pp. 533–67 supra.

6. *Implied Participation Clauses?* In Jackson v. Birmingham Bd. of Educ., 544 U.S. 167, 174 (2005), the Court held that protection against retaliation for filing a complaint with the government could be implied from the prohibition of gender discrimination in Title IX of the Education Amendments of 1972, 20 U.S.C. § 1681 et seq.: "when a funding recipient retaliates against a person because he complains of sex discrimination, this constitutes intentional discrimination 'on the basis of sex,' in violation of Title IX." The Court will be deciding in 2008 whether federal sector employees have an implied retaliation claim under Section 15 of ADEA, 29 U.S.C. § 633a, see Gomez–Perez v. United States Postal Service, 476 F.3d 54 (1st Cir. 2007), cert. granted, No. 06–1321; and whether plaintiffs have such a claim under 42 U.S.C. § 1981, see Humphries v. CBOCS West, Inc., 474 F.3d 387 (7th Cir. 2007), cert. granted, No. 06–1431.

7. *False or Baseless Accusations.* Is the employee protected even when the charge filed or the testimony given is false? Or without a reasonable basis? See Wyatt v. Boston, 35 F.3d 13, 15 (1st Cir.1994); Novotny v. Great American Federal Savings & Loan Assn., 539 F.Supp. 437 (W.D.Pa.1982), on remand from 442 U.S. 366, 99 S.Ct. 2345, 60 L.Ed.2d 957 (1979); Pettway v. American Cast Iron Pipe Co., 411 F.2d 998 (5th Cir.1969) (false charge that employer bought off EEOC investigator). But cf. Wideman v. Wal–Mart Stores, Inc., 141 F.3d 1453, 1454 (11th Cir.1998) (courts have not resolved whether the participation clause contains a "good faith, reasonable basis requirement").

The EEOC urges a rule of absolute protection:

[C]ourts have consistently held that a respondent is liable for retaliating against an individual for filing an EEOC charge regardless of the validity or reasonableness of the charge. To permit an employer to retaliate against a charging party based on its unilateral determination that the charge was unreasonable or otherwise unjustified would chill the rights of all individuals protected by the anti-discrimination statutes.

EEOC Guidance on Investigating, Analyzing Retaliation Claims, reprinted in (BNA) Daily Labor Report, No. 100, May 26, 1998, pp. E–3, E–6 (hereafter "EEOC Retaliation Guidance").

Is the Commission accurate in stating that without absolute protection for participation-clause activity, employers could make a "unilateral determination" of its reasonableness? Would this be true of a rule that gave the employer a defense if it could prove to the court's satisfaction that the charge was indeed unreasonable or intentionally false? What about the litigious employee who repeatedly files baseless charges? Would it strike a better accommodation of the competing policies to read § 704(a) as protecting only non-intentional falsehoods? Cf. Linn v. United Plant Guard Workers, 383 U.S. 53, 86 S.Ct. 657, 15 L.Ed.2d 582 (1966) (federal labor policy precludes state libel action for misstatements during union organizing campaigns, absent a showing of intentional or reckless disregard of truth).

Does an employer violate § 704(a) by instituting a libel action against an employee who files an unmeritorious charge? Cf. Bill Johnson's Restaurants, Inc. v. NLRB, 461 U.S. 731, 103 S.Ct. 2161, 76 L.Ed.2d 277 (1983) (NLRB may not halt prosecution of state libel action unless there is a retaliatory motive and the suit lacks a reasonable basis in fact or law).

8. *Former Employees.* Section 704(a) proscribes any form of retaliation against "employees or applicants for employment." Does *Burlington* confirm that it also proscribes retaliation, such as through a negative letter of reference, against former employees? In Robinson v. Shell Oil Co., 519 U.S. 337, 117 S.Ct. 843, 136 L.Ed.2d 808 (1997), discussed in *Burlington*, the Supreme Court unanimously held that former employees are protected by § 704(a). Justice Thomas explained:

> Finding that the term "employees" in § 704(a) is ambiguous, we are left to resolve that ambiguity. The broader context provided by other sections of the statute provides considerable assistance in this regard. [S]everal sections of the statute plainly contemplate that former employees will make use of the remedial mechanisms of Title VII. * * * Insofar as § 704(a) expressly protects employees from retaliation for filing a "charge" under Title VII, and a charge under § 703(a) alleging unlawful discharge would necessarily be brought by a former employee, it is far more consistent to include former employees within the scope of "employees" protected by § 704(a).

Is there a danger, under *Robinson*, that plaintiffs will be able to revive time-barred claims simply by applying for positions with, or seeking references from, former employers?

9. *Prohibited "Discrimination" under § 704(a)?* a. *Defensive Measures in Litigation.* Is it "discrimination" violative of § 704(a) for an employer to refuse to refer complaints to its internal EEO office, instead referring them to its legal department, where litigation or an outside agency is involved? See United States v. N.Y.C. Transit Auth., 97 F.3d 672, 677 (2d Cir.1996) ("Reasonable defensive measures" taken during or in preparation for litigation do not violate § 704(a), "even though such steps are adverse to the charging employee and result in differential treatment"; moreover, these defensive measures "[did] not affect the complainant's work, working conditions, or compensation").

b. *Exhaustion of Remedies Provisions.* Is it "discrimination" to provide in a collective bargaining agreement that contractual grievances could not proceed to arbitration if the employee brought an ADEA or other statutory claim in court? See EEOC v. Board of Governors of State Colleges and Universities, 957 F.2d 424 (7th Cir.1992), where the clause in question provided:

> If prior to filing a grievance hereunder, or while a grievance proceeding is in progress, an employee seeks resolution of the matter in any other forum, whether administrative or judicial, the Board or any University shall have no obligation to entertain or proceed further with the matter pursuant to this grievance procedure.

Id. at 426. The court held that the provision involved retaliation in violation of § 4(d) of ADEA, 29 U.S.C. § 623(d). The Seventh Circuit panel reasoned that § 4(d) does not require a showing of retaliatory intent:

> * * * Section 4(d) is concerned with the effect of discrimination against employees who pursue their federal rights, not the motivation of the employer who discriminates. * * * [T]he employer may not proffer a good faith reason for taking retaliatory action. For example, the Board's asserted justification * * *, avoiding duplicative litigation, does not rebut the claim that the Board discriminated against employees who engaged in protected activity. * * * Congress chose not to enact any affirmative defenses to a charge of retaliation * * *, and did not provide an exception to Section 4(d) when such discrimination would be rational or financially prudent.

Id. at 428. Accord, Johnson v. Palma, 931 F.2d 203 (2d Cir.1991); EEOC v. General Motors Corp., 826 F.Supp. 1122 (N.D.Ill.1993). Does it ultimately make sense as a policy matter to treat election-of-remedies provisions as a form of retaliation? See pp. 1139–40 infra.

In *N.Y.C. Transit Auth.,* supra, the Second Circuit distinguished *Board of Governors* and *Johnson* as cases where "assertion of Title VII rights costs employees the right, contractually guaranteed in a collective bargaining agreement, to proceed against their employers in a binding arbitration that would control the outcome of an ultimate employment decision * * *." 97 F.3d at 679. Is there really a contractual guaranty of binding arbitration where the collective agreement expressly reserves paying the costs of such arbitrations only for those employees who elect it as their remedy of choice?

   c. *Closer Scrutiny of Complaining Employees.* Generally, discriminatory application of performance standards, including closer scrutiny of complaining employees, on account of protected activity is actionable. See, e.g., Harrison v. Metropolitan Government of Nashville, 80 F.3d 1107 (6th Cir.1996). However, the employer may have legitimate business reasons for more closely monitoring a particular employee, say, because of an unusual absenteeism problem. See, e.g., Morgan v. Hilti, Inc., 108 F.3d 1319, 1324 (10th Cir.1997).

   d. *Refusal to Hire or Discharge for Refusing to Sign an Arbitration Agreement.* A company has decided to implement an otherwise lawful arbitration program covering all future employment claims by its employees. Is it actionable retaliation to refuse to hire an applicant, or discharge an employee, who refuses to agree to such a predispute arbitration clause? See, e.g., Weeks v. Harden Mfg. Corp., 291 F.3d 1307 (11th Cir.2002) (refusal to agree to such a clause is not protected activity); EEOC v. Luce, Forward, Hamilton & Scripps, 345 F.3d 742, 754 (9th Cir.2003) (en banc) (leaving question open for remand). What if the arbitration program is implemented firmwide after the employer learns that a few employees have filed charges with the EEOC?

10. *Retaliation Suits by In–House Counsel.* The prevailing view appears to be that in-house counsel are protected by the anti-retaliation provisions of federal discrimination laws despite employer claims that such suits will inevitably lead to disclosure of confidential attorney-client communications; confidentiality presumably can be protected short of disallowing the action. See, e.g., Kachmar v. SunGard Data Systems, Inc., 109 F.3d 173 (3d Cir.1997); cf. General Dynamics Corp. v. Superior Court, 7 Cal.4th 1164, 32 Cal.Rptr.2d 1, 876 P.2d 487, 490 (1994) (suggesting that there may be situations "where the attorney-employee's retaliatory discharge claim is incapable [of] complete resolution without breaching the attorney-client privilege"). See also note 6, p. 704 infra.

11. *Retaliation Because of Complaint by Relative or Working Associate?* Does § 704(a)'s participation clause protect employees from retaliation by their employer because a relative or other close associate has filed a charge against that employer?

12. *Retaliation Because of Complaint Against Other Employer.* Does § 704(a) protect employees who complain about discriminatory treatment by some other employer with whom their employer has a business relationship? Consider, for instance, an employee assigned by her employer to work on the premises of another employer where the employee encounters harassing conduct. See Flowers v. Columbia College Chicago, 397 F.3d 532 (7th Cir. 2005) (Easterbrook, J.) (finding coverage).

C. EXPRESS ANTIRETALIATION PROVISIONS: THE SPECIAL CASE OF SELF–HELP REMEDIES

HOCHSTADT v. WORCESTER FOUNDATION

United States Court of Appeals, First Circuit, 1976.
545 F.2d 222.

CAMPBELL, J.

The Worcester Foundation for Experimental Biology is a nonprofit institution primarily committed to basic biomedical research, employing some 250 persons. The Foundation devotes $1.8 million of its annual budget to cancer research in what is known as the Cell Biology Program. The principal investigator is Dr. Mahlan Hoagland, who is also the Director of the Foundation. Dr. Hoagland has recruited other scientists to join the program since its inception, and in 1971 recruited Dr. Harvey Ozer, a virologist, to fill a specific need in the program.

Dr. Ozer informed Dr. Hoagland of the availability and interest of his wife, Dr. Joy Hochstadt, in joining the Foundation. Dr. Hochstadt is a microbiologist, whose research into cell membrane functions, described by one scientist at the hearing as "pioneering", fit into the Foundation's research program. In September, 1971, Dr. Hoagland offered both Dr. Ozer and Dr. Hochstadt positions as senior scientists. Dr. Ozer's salary was set at $24,000, while Dr. Hochstadt's salary was set at $18,000. These salaries reflected the needs of the institution. Dr. Ozer and Dr. Hochstadt accepted the employment offers on October 1, but thereafter Dr. Hochstadt sought to renegotiate her salary, claiming it was discriminatory and illegal. The Foundation reluctantly acceded to readjust the salaries of Dr. Hochstadt and Dr. Ozer so that each would receive $21,000.

After starting her employment in January, 1972, Dr. Hochstadt joined the small group of cell biologists and participated in the periodic meetings of the group held to discuss policies, recruitment, and direction of research. At these meetings, Dr. Hochstadt early began to interpose personal grievances and salary complaints, to discuss the inadequacy of the Foundation's affirmative action program, and to criticize the Foundation's administration and its director, Dr. Hoagland, and assistant director, Dr. Welsch. These complaints interfered with the meetings, disrupted the discussions, and eventually caused discontinuation of the meetings.

In January, 1973, after they had been at the Foundation for over a year, Dr. Hochstadt and Dr. Ozer each sought from the Foundation $3,000 in lump sum back pay and a $3,000 salary increase to compensate for unanticipated moving expenses and the cost of living increase. In March, 1973, plaintiff was given a $1,500 (4.5%) increase as a result of the Foundation's annual salary review. Dr. Hoagland indicated that she would receive a larger raise the following year "when you've effectively joined the team."

In July, 1973, Dr. Hochstadt filed formal charges with the Massachusetts Commission Against Discrimination (MCAD), the EEOC, and the Department of Labor, alleging that the Foundation had discriminated against her by setting her starting salary much lower than that for male scientists starting work at the same time. One month later, she filed a class action complaint with the Department of Health, Education, and Welfare on behalf of all female employees at the Foundation. The complaint filed with HEW caused the Department to request the Foundation to implement an affirmative action plan. In June, 1974, the MCAD found reasonable cause to credit Dr. Hochstadt's complaint, but deferred further consideration of the charge pending action by the EEOC. In September, 1974, Dr. Hochstadt filed suit against the Foundation pursuant to § 2000e–5(f)(1), removing the case from the jurisdiction of the EEOC. In December, 1974, the Foundation settled with Dr. Hochstadt for $20,000.

Subsequent to her minimal increase and the filing of these charges, plaintiff sought to elicit salary information from other scientists and personnel at the Foundation, and on several occasions this conduct interfered with ongoing research and upset the other scientists and research assistants who were approached.

Plaintiff also circulated rumors that the Foundation would lose much of its federal funding because it was not complying with regulations concerning affirmative action programs. To allay the apprehension created by these rumors, on at least three occasions the Foundation had to invite an official from HEW to assure scientists at the Foundation that they were in no danger of losing federal funding.

In April, 1974, Dr. Hochstadt invited Dr. Helene Guttman, an officer of the Association of Women in Science, to conduct a covert affirmative action survey at the Foundation, ostensively [sic] while attending a scientific seminar. Dr. Guttman later wrote to Congressman Edwards indicating her findings that the Foundation was not in compliance with federal regulations and [was] critical of HEW's handling of Dr. Hochstadt's complaint of discrimination against the Foundation, and she sent copies of the letter to eight other members of Congress.

Also in 1974, Dr. Hochstadt invited a reporter from the Worcester Telegram to examine her files containing confidential salary information for employees at the Foundation. The reporter wrote several articles in the Telegram.

In mid–1974, the associate director, Dr. Welsch, complained to Dr. Hochstadt about her use of the Foundation's telephone for personal calls to her lawyer and to Dr. Guttman amounting to over $950 and her misuse of secretarial assistance and xeroxing services.

In late 1974, two research assistants in Dr. Hochstadt's laboratory left the Foundation because of their difficulties with Dr. Hochstadt. Complaints from subordinates in other laboratories never reached the level of the complaints of Dr. Hochstadt's research assistants.

* * *

[The question in this case is] whether plaintiff's overall conduct was so generally inimical to her employer's interests, and so "excessive", as to be beyond the protection of section 704(a) even though her actions were generally associated with her complaints of illegal employer conduct. We conclude that although plaintiff's original salary complaint may have been justified, and although her later complaint over her poor rating—whether or not justified—was one which she was entitled to make in an appropriate way, still neither of these could insulate her deportment from adverse scrutiny insofar as it went beyond the pale of reasonable opposition activity.

* * *

* * * Congress certainly did not mean to grant sanctuary to employees to engage in political activity for women's liberation on company time, and an employee does not enjoy immunity from discharge for misconduct merely by claiming that at all times she was defending the rights of her sex by "opposing" discriminatory practices. An employer remains entitled to loyalty and cooperativeness from employees:

> "[M]anagement prerogatives * * * are to be left undisturbed to the greatest extent possible. Internal affairs of employers * * * must not be interfered with except to the limited extent that correction is required in discrimination practices."

Additional views on H.R. 7152, U.S.Code Cong. & Admin.News, p. 2516 (88th Cong., 2d Sess., 1964). On the other hand, section 704(a) clearly does protect an employee against discharge for filing complaints in good faith before federal and state agencies and for registering grievances through channels appropriate in the particular employment setting.

It is less clear to what extent militant self-help activity falling between these two poles, such as particular types of on-the-job opposition to alleged discrimination, vociferousness, expressions of hostility to an employer or superior and the like, are protected. In the instant case, the issue is clouded by a sophisticated employment setting which lacks a rigid structure and within which it is not always easy to assess when an employee—in this case a highly educated senior scientist—clearly oversteps the bounds.

In such instances, we think courts have in each case to balance the purpose of the Act to protect persons engaging reasonably in activities opposing sexual discrimination, against Congress' equally manifest desire not to tie the hands of employers in the objective selection and control of personnel. Allowing an employee to invoke the protection of section 704(a) for conduct aimed at achieving purely ulterior objectives, or for conduct aimed at achieving even proper objectives through the use of improper means, could have an effect directly contrary to Congress' goal, by discouraging employers from hiring persons whom the Act is designed to protect. The standard can be little more definitive than the rule of reason applied by a judge or other tribunal to given facts. The requirements of the job and the tolerable limits of conduct in a particular setting must be explored. The present case, therefore, raises the question, put simply, of whether plaintiff went "too far" in her particular employment setting.

This approach is consistent with that taken by other courts when interpreting section 704(a). In *EEOC v. Kallir, Philips, Ross, Inc.*, 401 F.Supp. 66 (S.D.N.Y.1975), a case cited by both parties, the plaintiff was discharged for discreetly obtaining from a customer of her employer a written description of her job which had been requested by the New York City Commission on Human Rights during its investigation of the employee's charge of sex discrimination. Stressing the broad language of section 704(a) protecting an employee for assisting "in any manner" with a proceeding under Title VII, the court held that plaintiff's solicitation of the letter was protected. Noting that plaintiff's action had no negative effect on the client relationship, the court observed:

> "Under some circumstances, an employee's conduct in gathering or attempting to gather evidence to support his charge may be so

excessive and so deliberately calculated to inflict needless economic hardship on the employer that the employee loses the protection of section 704(a), just as other legitimate civil rights activities lose the protection of section 704(a) when they progress to deliberate and unlawful conduct against the employer."

Id. at 71–72. The Supreme Court too has made passing reference to the limits of protected conduct under section 704(a), stating that an employer may properly deny employment to a former employee who participated in an unlawful "stall-in" to protest the employer's civil rights record. "Nothing in Title VII compels an employer to absolve and rehire one who has engaged in such deliberate, unlawful activity against it." *McDonnell Douglas Corp. v. Green,* 411 U.S. 792, 803, 93 S.Ct. 1817, 1825, 36 L.Ed.2d 668 (1973).

* * *

Cases discussing limitations upon the right of union employees to engage in "concerted activity" against their employer provide a helpful point of comparison. Even if the ends sought to be achieved by the employees are protected by the National Labor Relations Act, the means chosen by the employees may be excessive. For example, in *NLRB v. Local 1229, IBEW, (Jefferson Standard Broadcasting Co.),* 346 U.S. 464, 74 S.Ct. 172, 98 L.Ed.2d 195 (1953), the Court reinstated the Board's order upholding an employer's discharge of nine employees for distributing during lawful picketing handbills accusing the employer television station of not serving the public interest.

* * *

Under the principles of the labor cases, the district court was entitled to conclude that Dr. Hochstadt's actions went beyond the scope of protected opposition because they damaged the basic goals and interests of the Foundation. * * * The district court was entitled to find that Dr. Hochstadt's constant complaints to colleagues damaged relationships among members of the cell biology group and sometimes even interfered with laboratory research. Even if justified, they occurred upon some occasions when the employer was entitled to expect her full commitment and loyalty. Section 704(a) does not afford an employee unlimited license to complain at any and all times and places.

* * *

Keeping in mind the legitimate interests both of Dr. Hochstadt and the Foundation, we face the ultimate question, whether the district court could properly on this record determine that Dr. Hochstadt "went too far" in her activities and deportment. We think it could. A permissible interpretation of the evidence was that the Foundation had wiped the slate clean in December, 1974, after its settlement with Dr. Hochstadt, and that the administration was willing to accept her as a member of the team. But Dr. Hochstadt's extreme hostility toward Dr. Welsch, Dr.

Gibbons,[7] and Dr. Hoagland in response to the April, 1975, evaluation indicated that there would be no change in her attitude or her behavior from that encountered since she was hired in 1972. The continuation of the general conflict forced the Foundation to make a critical choice: either it would retain Dr. Hochstadt and tolerate not only her complaints against the Foundation but also the complaints against Dr. Hochstadt's behavior raised by other scientists and research personnel, or it would terminate her employment. We cannot disagree with the district court's conclusion that the Foundation was justified in choosing the latter course.

Notes and Questions

1. *Rationale for Opposition Clause.* Why did Congress, in addition to the participation clause in § 704(a), also provide for an opposition clause, which protects some measure of oppositional activity outside of the formal processes of Title VII? Does this provision reflect a judgment that these formal processes might prove inadequate to the task of eliminating employment discrimination? Or was Congress seeking to promote informal dispute resolution without requiring the intercession of government? Does the scope of protection, and hence the extent to which employers must tolerate the costs incident to on-the-job oppositional activity, differ depending on which conception of the congressional purpose is accurate?

2. *Implied Opposition Clauses?* Some statutes, like the FLSA , including its Equal Pay Act (EPA) amendment, 29 U.S.C. § 206(d), do not contain an express opposition clause. See, e.g., FLSA, 29 U.S.C. § 215(a)(3). In EEOC v. Romeo Community Schools, 976 F.2d 985 (6th Cir. 1992), a female temporary custodian was denied a promotion to a permanent position because she had lodged informal complaints of gender-based wage discrimination allegedly violative of the EPA. The court held that "it is the assertion of statutory rights which is the triggering factor, not the filing of a formal complaint." Id. at 989. Is this a defensible reading? Is this "implied" opposition clause coextensive with § 704(a) of Title VII?

3. *Erroneous, Good Faith Opposition.* Given that protected opposition must be to a practice "made unlawful by this title," did Congress mean to limit protection to situations where the practices are in fact unlawful? See Clark County School District v. Breeden, 532 U.S. 268, 270, 121 S.Ct. 1508, 149 L.Ed.2d 509 (2001) (expressly leaving question open). Most courts have held that reasonable, good-faith opposition is protected even if the underlying practice is found to be lawful. See, e.g., EEOC v. Crown Zellerbach Corp., 720 F.2d 1008 (9th Cir.1983); De Anda v. St. Joseph Hosp., 671 F.2d 850

---

7. Because Dr. Gibbons was the EEOC officer at the Foundation, there is some merit in the plaintiff's argument that she was entitled to show a high degree of hostility towards the Foundation in her conversation with Dr. Gibbons charging that her low evaluation was discriminatory. Even assuming, however, that a higher degree of protection attaches to an employee's contacts with her employer's EEOC officer, Dr. Hochstadt's hostile confrontation with Dr. Welsch, the assistant director of the Foundation, must be judged against the normal standard for protected opposition, and that confrontation, the precipitating factor of her discharge, went beyond the scope of protected activity.

(5th Cir.1982); Rucker v. Higher Educ. Aids Bd., 669 F.2d 1179 (7th Cir.1982); Berg v. La Crosse Cooler Co., 612 F.2d 1041 (7th Cir.1980). Is there any justification for insisting on a greater degree of accuracy in accusation here than in the participation-clause context? Are the costs to the employer greater?

In *Clark County*, the Supreme Court stated that Title VII's opposition clause does not protect opposition to activity that the employee could not reasonably believe violated the statute. In that case, the Court held that a female employee could not reasonably believe that the chuckling in her presence of two male co-workers in response to a job applicant's sexually explicit comment was actionable sexual harassment. Other courts, adopting a similar objectively reasonable belief standard, have held that opposition to a single racially derogatory remark by a coworker is not protected by the opposition clause. See Little v. United Technologies, Carrier Transicold Div., 103 F.3d 956 (11th Cir.1997); Silver v. KCA, Inc., 586 F.2d 138 (9th Cir.1978).

What if the opposition is not to activity unlawful under Title VII but, rather, to an employer's laggard compliance with other antidiscrimination laws, such as Executive Order 11246 (workforce utilization analysis and possible affirmative action requirements for federal contractors)? See Holden v. Owens–Illinois, Inc., 793 F.2d 745 (6th Cir.1986). Opposition clearly must relate to employment concerns, not other unlawful or improper employer activity. See, e.g., Trent v. Valley Electric Assn. Inc., 41 F.3d 524 (9th Cir.1994) (complaint about practices of outside consultant).

4. *Unreasonable Opposition*. *Hochstadt* involves the question of how far an employee may pursue self-help opposition while remaining within the protection of § 704(a). In what precise ways did the plaintiff go beyond the pale? Would an equally contentious male have been treated the same way? Employee opposition is always unsettling to supervisors and coworkers. At what point can it be said that an employee was discharged because of the intraoffice disruption she caused, or because of the "poor judgment" she has shown, rather than because of her opposition as such? Would you support a test that keys propriety to an employee's position on the management ladder, so that higher-level supervisors or managers must be more circumspect than other employees?

Some courts have been more tolerant of the type of activity present in *Hochstadt*. See Grant v. Hazelett Strip–Casting Corp., 880 F.2d 1564, 1569 (2d Cir.1989) (plaintiff had destroyed documents but, unlike Hochstadt, had not engaged in "prolonged obstreperous acts" and misconduct); Wrighten v. Metropolitan Hospitals, Inc., 726 F.2d 1346, 1355 (9th Cir.1984) (nurse made numerous complaints of allegedly racist treatment of patients and eventually held a press conference).

Some decisions hold that employees engage in protected opposition by picketing their employer and even complaining to customers about their employer's discriminatory practices? See, e.g., Sumner v. United States Postal Serv., 899 F.2d 203, 209 (2d Cir. 1990); EEOC v. Crown Zellerbach Corp., 720 F.2d 1008, 1010 (9th Cir. 1983). Are employees also protected when they refuse to perform discriminatory work assignments? When they walk off the job to protest the employer's practices? For a suggestion that

Title VII's opposition clause should be read this broadly, see Benjamin I. Sachs, Employment Law as Labor Law: Toward a New Model, 29 Cardozo L. Rev. forthcoming, 2008 (n.208).

5. *Public Opposition.* Under what circumstances can an employee go public with her opposition? Note that Dr. Hochstadt invited assistance not only from an officer of the Association of Women in Science, but also from a newspaper reporter. Is it realistic to expect lone employees, not represented by unions, to engage in opposition without attempting to secure assistance from the outside community? See Wrighten v. Metropolitan Hosps., supra (black nurse held press conference to charge employer with poor health care for black patients); EEOC v. Crown Zellerbach Corp., 720 F.2d 1008 (9th Cir.1983) (employees sent letter to local school board, which was a major customer of their employer, protesting manager's receipt of affirmative action award).

6. *Relevance of Collective Labor Law.* The *Hochstadt* court relies on NLRA precedents. Should Title VII, a statute that focuses principally on the rights of individuals and does not provide a mechanism for group assertion and resolution of claims with management, be read to incorporate the NLRA's ground-rules for group protest activity?

7. *"Opposition"?* How pointed does the employee's statement have to be to trigger opposition clause protection? See, e.g., Majewski v. Automatic Data Processing, Inc., 274 F.3d 1106, 1117–18 (6th Cir.2001) (isolated statement in letter reviewing performance issues overall that "I was doing not anything different than my co-workers and I felt like they were trying to fire me because I was forty" held insufficient).

8. *Opposition in Violation of Other Laws.* Can a Title VII court take into account the fact that oppositional activity itself may contravene other laws? Or does the congressional policy embodied in § 704(a) require a measure of protection even in such circumstances? Note that in McDonnell Douglas Corp. v. Green, p. 54 supra, Green's opposition activity took the form of a "stall-in" tactic whereby he parked his car on an access road to the plant causing serious traffic problems. Green's § 704(a) claim was rejected by the district court, and he did not take a further appeal. The Supreme Court observed: "Nothing in Title VII compels an employer to absolve and rehire one who has engaged in * * * deliberate, unlawful activity against it." 411 U.S. at 803.

In Emporium Capwell Co. v. Western Addition Community Organization, 420 U.S. 50, 95 S.Ct. 977, 43 L.Ed.2d 12 (1975), the Supreme Court (per Justice Marshall) held that the NLRA did not protect consumer picketing by black employees intended to pressure the employer to deal directly with them to resolve race discrimination complaints and thus circumvent its NLRA obligation to deal exclusively with the union authorized by the NLRA to represent the plaintiffs. A § 704(a) claim was not presented in that case; the court noted that "[e]ven assuming that § 704(a) protects employees' picketing and instituting a consumer boycott, the same conduct is not necessarily entitled to affirmative protection from the NLRA." Id. at 71–72. Should the opposition activity in *Emporium Capwell* be protected by Title VII if the plaintiffs sought to compel the employer to violate the NLRA?

9. *Special Rule for Firm's EEO Officers?* Are personnel directors simply doing their jobs when they point out possible employment law violations to their employers, or are they engaged in § 704(a)-protected opposition activity? See, e.g., McKenzie v. Renberg's Inc., 94 F.3d 1478, 1486–87 (10th Cir. 1996). Are employees who perform EEO, human resources or other personnel functions for their employer under a special duty of loyalty? At what point does a firm EEO officer's opposition to his employer's employment practices render him unable to fulfill the functions of his position? See Smith v. Singer Co., 650 F.2d 214 (9th Cir.1981); Pendleton v. Rumsfeld, 628 F.2d 102 (D.C.Cir.1980). If the purpose of the opposition clause is to supplement the reach of Title VII's formal processes, does it make sense to exclude from the protective ambit of § 704(a) those employees who are likely to have the best access to information about the employer's systemic practices? Are there countervailing considerations which should be taken into account? Is there a significant danger that such employees will be able to transform a disagreement over the manner in which their personnel functions have been performed into a retaliation claim? See, e.g., Dranchak v. Akzo Nobel Inc., 88 F.3d 457 (7th Cir.1996).

10. *Retaliation Against Spouse.* Does § 704 protect from retaliation the spouse of an employee who has engaged in protected activity opposing arguably actionable discrimination? Compare EEOC v. Ohio Edison Co., 7 F.3d 541, 544 (6th Cir.1993), with Holt v. JTM Industries, 89 F.3d 1224 (5th Cir.1996) (no ADEA protection).

11. *Opposition on Behalf of Third Parties.* In Childress v. City of Richmond, 134 F.3d 1205 (4th Cir.1998), the court held that white male employees opposing hostile work environment discrimination directed at black coworkers were protected from retaliation under § 704(a). The plaintiff must still have engaged in protected activity to sue under § 704(a), even if she is not complaining of discrimination directed at her. See Smith v. Riceland Foods, 151 F.3d 813 (8th Cir.1998). Does § 704(a) extend to an employee who participates in an internal investigation of a charge on behalf of management and in the course of that investigation opposes certain conduct of the employer? Cf. Twisdale v. Snow 325 F.3d 950 (7th Cir. 2003) (interpreting § 704 not to protect opposition to charge of discrimination).

12. *Opposition to Practices of Prior Employer or Other Third–Party Employer.* Does the entity charged with retaliation under § 704(a) have to be the same entity who was the object of the plaintiff's opposition? See, e.g., McMenemy v. City of Rochester, 241 F.3d 279, 283–84 (2d Cir. 2001) (answering in the negative).

13. *Availability of Preliminary Injunctive Relief?* Dr. Hochstadt had sought preliminary injunctive relief pending resolution of her charge before the EEOC, even though § 706(f)(2) of Title VII expressly authorizes only the EEOC to seek this remedy. Because the *Hochstadt* court affirmed the denial of injunctive relief, it reserved decision as to its authority to award such relief. Is there a compelling case to allow such applications in § 704 cases given the plaintiff's dependence on the uncoerced testimony of other employees? What was Congress's justification in limiting preliminary injunctive relief to EEOC applications? Some courts have found implied authority to issue a preliminary injunction in private Title VII retaliation litigation. See

Wagner v. Taylor, 836 F.2d 566, 570–575 (D.C. Cir. 1988); Sheehan v. Purolator Courier Corp., 676 F.2d 877 (2d Cir. 1982).

14. *Causation in Retaliation Cases.* As explained in Desert Palace, Inc. v. Costa, pp. 75–80 supra, in Price Waterhouse v. Hopkins, pp. 434–36 supra, the Supreme Court (following precedent under the NLRA and 42 U.S.C. § 1983) held that where a Title VII plaintiff proves that a discriminatory motive was a motivating factor in a challenged decision, an employer can avoid liability altogether by proving that at the time of the decision it would have made the same decision on wholly legitimate grounds. In response, Congress amended Title VII in § 107 of the Civil Rights Act of 1991, now § 703(m) of Title VII, to provide that proof of a discriminatory motive establishes a violation despite an employer's successfully shouldering its "same decision" defense. In such circumstances, the plaintiff will have shown a § 703 (m) violation but will not be able to obtain certain relief, including damages, backpay and reinstatement. See § 706(g)(2).

Some courts have taken the view that because § 107 of the 1991 Civil Rights Act does not by its terms cover retaliation claims, *Price Waterhouse* (and its provision of a complete defense) continues to apply. Compare Medlock v. Ortho Biotech, 164 F.3d 545, 552 (10th Cir.1999); McNutt v. Board of Trustees, 141 F.3d 706 (7th Cir. 1998); Woodson v. Scott Paper, 109 F.3d 913 (3d Cir.1997); Merritt v. Dillard Paper Co., 120 F.3d 1181, 1191 (11th Cir.1997), with Fields v. New York State Office of Mental Retardation and Developmental Disabilities, 115 F.3d 116 (2d Cir.1997). The EEOC disagrees: such a reading "undermines the purpose of the anti-retaliation provisions of maintaining unfettered access to the statutory remedial mechanism." EEOC Retaliation Guidance, supra, at E–8 n. 45.

Note on the Occupational Safety and Health Act and Other Minimum–Terms Laws

The Occupational Safety and Health Act of 1970 (OSHA), 29 U.S.C. § 651 et seq., represents a somewhat different type of regulation of labor markets than does Title VII and other discrimination laws or the state contract law doctrines surveyed in subsequent chapter 12. The rules and decisions in chapter 12 are principally concerned with determining the joint intentions of the parties to the employment contract. The antidiscrimination laws seek to purge certain influences from the contracting process, but otherwise allow the parties to set their own terms of compensation, benefits, hours, etc. By contrast, OSHA, by requiring employers to adhere to minimum safety and health standards, regulates the *substantive* terms of the employment relationship. Its principal federal antecedent was the 1938 enactment of the FLSA, which sets the minimum wages and maximum hours of all employees within its reach (see chapter 15). Employees cannot waive or trade their OSHA or FLSA protection in contracts with their employer. See generally Samuel Estreicher & Gillian Lester, Employment Law, ch. 12 (2008).

Substantive regulations—which are more common on the state level and in other countries—may have a number of justifications, some of which concern weaknesses in the operations of labor markets. The FLSA is in part a corrective for the limited bargaining power and employment options of the lowest paid, poorly skilled segment of the nation's workers. OSHA, which reaches all workers employed by firms engaged in interstate commerce, also might be justified by other kinds of market failures. Some OSHA regulation, see, e.g., OSHA's hazard communication standard, 29 C.F.R. § 1910.1200, 52 Fed.Reg. 31852 et seq., treated in Dole v. United Steelworkers, 494 U.S. 26, 110 S.Ct. 929, 108 L.Ed.2d 23 (1990) (reviewing authority of President's Office of Management and Budget under Paperwork Reduction Act), attempts to perfect the operation of labor markets by eliminating disparate access to information between employers and workers: Employers are better situated to know of hidden or long-term hazards and have little incentive to explain these hazards to their employees.

OSHA's imposition of minimum safety and health standards cannot be waived by employees or their union representatives irrespective of information availability. This suggests that the Act also rests on other perceived labor market weaknesses in addition to informational imbalance, for presumably collective bargaining agents should do an acceptable job in ferreting out potential safety problems in the workplace. See David Weil, Individual Rights and Collective Agents: The Role of Old and New Workplace Institutions in the Regulation of Labor Markets? (NBER Working Paper 9565, 2003). These possible market defects include the possibility that even fully informed workers may not be able fully to appreciate long-term, probabilistic risk. See generally W. Kip Viscusi, Risk By Choice 59–87 (1983); and his Risk Perceptions in Regulation, Tort Liability, and the Market, 14 Regulation (Fall 1991), pp. 50–57; Mary Loring Lyndon, Information Economics and Chemical Toxicity: Designing Laws to Produce and Use Data, 87 Mich.L.Rev. 1795 (1989); Cass R. Sunstein, Legal Interference with Private Preferences, 53 U.Chi.L.Rev. 1129 (1986). In addition, unregulated bargaining may not fully account for the external or public costs of declining worker health and safety. See Susan Rose–Ackerman, Progressive Law and Economics—And the New Administrative Law, 98 Yale L.J. 341, 356 (1988).

Like the FLSA and child labor laws, OSHA may have another explanation unrelated to market failure. These statutes may express a collective social judgment about standards of fairness and decency. Our society may have decided that it simply does not want people subjected to work unless certain minimum wage and health standards are met. The law, in effect, stipulates the minimum terms upon which a worker may be engaged. For a consideration of the "standard economic objection" to "minimum standards" legislation, see Steven L. Willborn, Individual Employment Rights and the Standard Economic Objection: Theory and Empiricism, 67 U.Neb. L.Rev. 101 (1988); see also (former U.S. Secretary of the Treasury and Harvard president) Lawrence Summers, Some Simple Economics of Mandated Benefits, 79 AEA Papers & Proc. (May 1989), pp. 177–83.

To the extent the law covers all of the nation's employers, OSHA creates no competitive disadvantage within American product markets. To the extent other countries with whom we compete have similar laws, it creates no competitive disadvantage in those foreign markets. However, such laws do increase the cost of hiring workers at the margin, and hence may reduce employment levels in some situations. See Finis Welch, Minimum Wages: Issues and Evidence (1978) (the cost of minimum wage protection may include a decline in the demand for those workers whom the law seeks to protect).

Responsibility for the administration of OSHA is lodged with two different federal agencies. The Occupational Safety and Health Administration, located in the Department of Labor, is responsible for promulgating standards and enforcement. The adjudication of violations of the statute is committed to the Occupational Safety and Health Review Commission, (OSHRC), an independent agency. See Martin v. OSHRC, 499 U.S. 144, 111 S.Ct. 1171, 113 L.Ed.2d 117 (1991) (Secretary of Labor's interpretation controls over conflicting OSHRC interpretation).

WHIRLPOOL CORP. v. MARSHALL, SECRETARY OF LABOR

Supreme Court of the United States, 1980.
445 U.S. 1, 100 S.Ct. 883, 63 L.Ed.2d 154.

Mr. Justice Stewart delivered the opinion of the Court.

The Occupational Safety and Health Act of 1970 (Act) prohibits an employer from discharging or discriminating against any employee who exercises "any right afforded by" the Act.[2] The Secretary of Labor (Secretary) has promulgated a regulation providing that, among the rights that the Act so protects, is the right of an employee to choose not to perform his assigned task because of a reasonable apprehension of death or serious injury coupled with a reasonable belief that no less drastic alternative is available.[3] The question presented in the case before us is whether this regulation is consistent with the Act.

2. Section 11(c)(1) of the Act, 84 Stat. 1603, 29 U.S.C. § 660(c)(1), provides in full:

"No person shall discharge or in any manner discriminate against any employee because such employee has filed any complaint or instituted or caused to be instituted any proceeding under or related to this Act or has testified or is about to testify in any such proceeding or because of the exercise by such employee on behalf of himself or others of any right afforded by this Act."

3. The regulation, 29 CFR § 1977.12 (1979), provides in full:

"(a) In addition to protecting employees who file complaints, institute proceedings, or testify in proceedings under or related to the Act, section 11(c) also protects employees from discrimination occurring because of the exercise 'of any right afforded by this Act.' Certain rights are explicitly provided in the Act; for example, there is a right to participate as a party in enforcement proceedings (sec. 10). Certain other rights exist by necessary implication. For example, employees may request information from the Occu-

pational Safety and Health Administration; such requests would constitute the exercise of a right afforded by the Act. Likewise, employees interviewed by agents of the Secretary in the course of inspections or investigations could not subsequently be discriminated against because of their cooperation.

"(b)(1) On the other hand, review of the Act and examination of the legislative history discloses that, as a general matter, there is no right afforded by the Act which would entitle employees to walk off the job because of potential unsafe conditions at the workplace. Hazardous conditions which may be violative of the Act will ordinarily be corrected by the employer, once brought to his attention. If corrections are not accomplished, or if there is dispute about the existence of a hazard, the employee will normally have opportunity to request inspection of the workplace pursuant to section 8(f) of the Act, or to seek the assistance of other public agencies which have responsibility in the field of safety and health. Under such circumstances, therefore, an employer would not ordinarily be in violation of

I

The petitioner company maintains a manufacturing plant in Marion, Ohio, for the production of household appliances. Overhead conveyors transport appliance components throughout the plant. To protect employees from objects that occasionally fall from these conveyors, the petitioner has installed a horizontal wire-mesh guard screen approximately 20 feet above the plant floor. This mesh screen is welded to angle-iron frames suspended from the building's structural steel skeleton.

Maintenance employees of the petitioner spend several hours each week removing objects from the screen, replacing paper spread on the screen to catch grease drippings from the material on the conveyors, and performing occasional maintenance work on the conveyors themselves. To perform these duties, maintenance employees usually are able to stand on the iron frames, but sometimes find it necessary to step onto the steel mesh screen itself.

In 1973, the company began to install heavier wire in the screen because its safety had been drawn into question. Several employees had fallen partly through the old screen, and on one occasion an employee had fallen completely through to the plant floor below but had survived. A number of maintenance employees had reacted to these incidents by bringing the unsafe screen conditions to the attention of their foremen. The petitioner company's contemporaneous safety instructions admonished employees to step only on the angle-iron frames.

On June 28, 1974, a maintenance employee fell to his death through the guard screen in an area where the newer, stronger mesh had not yet been installed.[4] Following this incident, the petitioner effectuated some repairs and issued an order strictly forbidding maintenance employees from stepping on either the screens or the angle-iron supporting struc-

section 11(c) by taking action to discipline an employee for refusing to perform normal job activities because of alleged safety or health hazards.

"(2) However, occasions might arise when an employee is confronted with a choice between not performing assigned tasks or subjecting himself to serious injury or death arising from a hazardous condition at the workplace. If the employee, with no reasonable alternative, refuses in good faith to expose himself to the dangerous condition, he would be protected against subsequent discrimination. The condition causing the employee's apprehension of death or injury must be of such a nature that a reasonable person, under the circumstances then confronting the employee, would conclude that there is a real danger of death or serious injury and that there is insufficient time due to the urgency of the situation, to eliminate the danger through resort to regular stat-

utory enforcement channels. In addition, in such circumstances, the employee, where possible, must also have sought from his employer, and been unable to obtain, a correction of the dangerous condition."

4. As a result of this fatality, the Secretary conducted an investigation that led to the issuance of a citation charging the company with maintaining an unsafe walking and working surface in violation of 29 U.S.C. § 654(a)(1). The citation required immediate abatement of the hazard and proposed a $600 penalty. Nearly five years following the accident, the Occupational Safety and Health Review Commission affirmed the citation, but decided to permit the petitioner six months in which to correct the unsafe condition. *Whirlpool Corp.,* 1979 CCH OSHD ¶ 23,552. A petition to review that decision is pending in the United States Court of Appeals for the District of Columbia Circuit.

ture. An alternative but somewhat more cumbersome and less satisfactory method was developed for removing objects from the screen. This procedure required employees to stand on power-raised mobile platforms and use hooks to recover the material.

On July 7, 1974, two of the petitioner's maintenance employees, Virgil Deemer and Thomas Cornwell, met with the plant maintenance superintendent to voice their concern about the safety of the screen. The superintendent disagreed with their view, but permitted the two men to inspect the screen with their foreman and to point out dangerous areas needing repair. Unsatisfied with the petitioner's response to the results of this inspection, Deemer and Cornwell met on July 9 with the plant safety director. At that meeting, they requested the name, address, and telephone number of a representative of the local office of the Occupational Safety and Health Administration (OSHA). Although the safety director told the men that they "had better stop and think about what [they] were doing," he furnished the men with the information they requested. Later that same day, Deemer contacted an official of the regional OSHA office and discussed the guard screen.

The next day, Deemer and Cornwell reported for the night shift at 10:45 p.m. Their foreman, after himself walking on some of the angle-iron frames, directed the two men to perform their usual maintenance duties on a section of the old screen.[6] Claiming that the screen was unsafe, they refused to carry out this directive. The foreman then sent them to the personnel office, where they were ordered to punch out without working or being paid for the remaining six hours of the shift.[7] The two men subsequently received written reprimands, which were placed in their employment files.

A little over a month later, the Secretary filed suit in the United States District Court for the Northern District of Ohio, alleging that the petitioner's actions against Deemer and Cornwell constituted discrimination in violation of § 11(c)(1) of the Act. * * *

Following a bench trial, the District Court found that the regulation in question justified Deemer's and Cornwell's refusals to obey their foreman's order on July 10, 1974. * * * The District Court nevertheless denied relief, holding that the Secretary's regulation was inconsistent with the Act and therefore invalid.

The Court of Appeals for the Sixth Circuit reversed the District Court's judgment. * * *

II

The Act itself creates an express mechanism for protecting workers from employment conditions believed to pose an emergent threat of

---

6. This order appears to have been in direct violation of the outstanding company directive that maintenance work was to be accomplished without stepping on the screen apparatus.

7. Both employees apparently returned to work the following day without further incident.

death or serious injury. Upon receipt of an employee inspection request stating reasonable grounds to believe that an imminent danger is present in a workplace, OSHA must conduct an inspection. 29 U.S.C. § 657(f)(1). In the event this inspection reveals workplace conditions or practices that "could reasonably be expected to cause death or serious physical harm immediately or before the imminence of such danger can be eliminated through the enforcement procedures otherwise provided by" the Act,[11] 29 U.S.C. § 662(a), the OSHA inspector must inform the affected employees and the employer of the danger and notify them that he is recommending to the Secretary that injunctive relief be sought. § 662(c). At this juncture, the Secretary can petition a federal court to restrain the conditions or practices giving rise to the imminent danger. By means of a temporary restraining order or preliminary injunction, the court may then require the employer to avoid, correct, or remove the danger or to prohibit employees from working in the area. § 662(a).[12]

To ensure that this process functions effectively, the Act expressly accords to every employee several rights, the exercise of which may not subject him to discharge or discrimination. An employee is given the right to inform OSHA of an imminently dangerous workplace condition or practice and request that OSHA inspect that condition or practice. 29 U.S.C. § 657(f)(1). He is given a limited right to assist the OSHA inspector in inspecting the workplace, §§ 657(a)(2), (e), and (f)(2), and the right to aid a court in determining whether or not a risk of imminent danger in fact exists. See § 660(c)(1). Finally, an affected employee is given the right to bring an action to compel the Secretary to seek injunctive relief if he believes the Secretary has wrongfully declined to do so. § 662(d).

In the light of this detailed statutory scheme, the Secretary is obviously correct when he acknowledges in his regulation that, "as a general matter, there is no right afforded by the Act which would entitle employees to walk off the job because of potential unsafe conditions at the workplace."

* * *

As this case illustrates, however, circumstances may sometimes exist in which the employee justifiably believes that the express statutory arrangement does not sufficiently protect him from death or serious injury. Such circumstances will probably not often occur, but such a

---

11. These usual enforcement procedures involve the issuance of citations and imposition of penalties. When an OSHA inspection reveals a violation of 29 U.S.C. § 654 or of any standard promulgated under the Act, the Secretary may issue a citation for the alleged violation, fix a reasonable time for the dangerous condition's abatement, and propose a penalty. §§ 658(a), 659(a), 666. The employer may contest the citation and proposed penalty. § 659(a), (c). Should he do so, the effective date of the abatement order is postponed until the completion of all administrative proceedings initiated in good faith. §§ 659(b), 666(d). Such proceedings may include a hearing before an administrative law judge and review by the Occupational Safety and Health Review Commission. §§ 659(c), 661(i).

12. Such an order may continue pending the consummation of the Act's normal enforcement proceedings. § 662(b).

situation may arise when (1) the employee is ordered by his employer to work under conditions that the employee reasonably believes pose an imminent risk of death or serious bodily injury, and (2) the employee has reason to believe that there is not sufficient time or opportunity either to seek effective redress from his employer or to apprise OSHA of the danger.

Nothing in the Act suggests that those few employees who have to face this dilemma must rely exclusively on the remedies expressly set forth in the Act at the risk of their own safety. But nothing in the Act explicitly provides otherwise. Against this background of legislative silence, the Secretary has exercised his rulemaking power under 29 U.S.C. § 657(g)(2) and has determined that, when an employee in good faith finds himself in such a predicament, he may refuse to expose himself to the dangerous condition, without being subjected to "subsequent discrimination" by the employer.

The question before us is whether this interpretative regulation constitutes a permissible gloss on the Act by the Secretary, in light of the Act's language, structure, and legislative history. Our inquiry is informed by an awareness that the regulation is entitled to deference unless it can be said not to be a reasoned and supportable interpretation of the Act. *Skidmore v. Swift & Co.,* 323 U.S. 134, 139–140, 65 S.Ct. 161, 164, 89 L.Ed. 124. See *Ford Motor Credit Co. v. Milhollin,* 444 U.S. 555, 100 S.Ct. 790, 63 L.Ed.2d 22; *Mourning v. Family Publications Service, Inc.,* 411 U.S. 356, 93 S.Ct. 1652, 36 L.Ed.2d 318.

The regulation clearly conforms to the fundamental objective of the Act—to prevent occupational deaths and serious injuries.

* * *

To accomplish this basic purpose, the legislation's remedial orientation is prophylactic in nature. See *Atlas Roofing Co. v. Occupational Safety and Health Review Comm'n,* 430 U.S. 442, 444–445, 97 S.Ct. 1261, 1263–1264, 51 L.Ed.2d 464. The Act does not wait for an employee to die or become injured. It authorizes the promulgation of health and safety standards and the issuance of citations in the hope that these will act to prevent deaths or injuries from ever occurring. It would seem anomalous to construe an Act so directed and constructed as prohibiting an employee, with no other reasonable alternative, the freedom to withdraw from a workplace environment that he reasonably believes is highly dangerous.

Moreover, the Secretary's regulation can be viewed as an appropriate aid to the full effectuation of the Act's "general duty" clause. That clause provides that "[e]ach employer * * * shall furnish to each of his employees employment and a place of employment which are free from recognized hazards that are causing or are likely to cause death or serious physical harm to his employees." 29 U.S.C. § 654(a)(1). As the legislative history of this provision reflects, it was intended itself to deter the occurrence of occupational deaths and serious injuries by placing on employers a mandatory obligation independent of the specific health and safety standards to be promulgated by the Secretary. Since OSHA inspectors cannot be present around the clock in every workplace, the Secretary's regulation ensures that employees will in all circumstances enjoy the rights afforded them by the "general duty" clause.

The regulation thus on its face appears to further the overriding purpose of the Act, and rationally to complement its remedial scheme.

[*Eds.* The Court's discussion of the legislative history is omitted.]

Notes and Questions

1. *Limits of Self–Help Remedy.* The OSHA regulation, sustained in *Whirlpool,* does not create a general right to walk off the job whenever workers suspect a safety hazard. Rather, the workers must show that (i) they have a good faith, reasonably grounded fear of "a real danger of death or serious injury"; (ii) "there is insufficient time due to the urgency of the situation, to eliminate the danger through resort to regular statutory channels"; and (iii) "where possible," they "have sought from the employer, and been unable to obtain, a correction of the dangerous condition." 29 C.F.R. § 1977.12(b)(2), quoted in footnote 3 of the *Whirlpool* opinion.

2. *Role of Administrative Agency?* Is the provision of self-help remedies in the OSHA scheme best understood as a controlled experiment authorized by the administrative agency to whom Congress has delegated policymaking authority and subject to the ongoing superintendence of that agency? Should courts develop similar self-help remedies in other statutory schemes in which either the element of imminent hazard or administrative supervision is lacking?

Effective March 21, 2003 a new OSHA rule protects airline employees against retaliation by their employers, their contractors or subsidiaries for providing information to authorities on air carrier safety violations. See 29 C.F.R. Part 1979.

3. *Self-Help Under the National Labor Relations Act.* Federal labor law provides additional self-help protection. Workers have a § 7 right to strike over safety issues, see NLRB v. Washington Aluminum Co., 370 U.S. 9, 82 S.Ct. 1099, 8 L.Ed.2d 298 (1962), and under § 502 of the LMRA, 29 U.S.C. § 143, may even strike in the face of a contractual no-strike promise if they have an objective, good-faith fear of "abnormally dangerous conditions," see Gateway Coal v. United Mine Workers, 414 U.S. 368, 385–86, 94 S.Ct. 629, 640–41, 38 L.Ed.2d 583 (1974); e.g., TNS, Inc. v. NLRB, 296 F.3d 384 (6th Cir. 2002). The collective bargaining agreement may itself privilege refusals to perform work under unsafe conditions, thus creating an exception to a general "work now/grieve later" principle, see NLRB v. City Disposal Systems, 465 U.S. 822, 104 S.Ct. 1505, 79 L.Ed.2d 839 (1984).

4. *Refusal to Perform Work Assignments Under Title VII's Opposition Clause & "Constructive Discharge" Doctrine.* Are there circumstances where § 704(a) of Title VII provides protection for oppositional activity taking the form of a refusal to work? Can an employee subjected to insufferably discriminatory working conditions refuse to work as long as those conditions

continue? Courts have developed a "constructive discharge" doctrine to privilege employees to quit their employment in such circumstances without the quit being treated as a voluntary separation. See, e.g., Pennsylvania State Police v. Suders, 542 U.S. 129, 124 S.Ct. 2342, 159 L.Ed.2d 204 (2004). See also pp. 477–81 supra.

D. IMPLIED ANTIRETALIATION PROVISIONS

As noted above, most federal and state employment statutes now include some form of antiretaliation provision. As the next decision suggests, however, this is not universally the case. Furthermore, some federal and state statutes that do contain antiretaliation provisions expressly authorize only administrative or criminal enforcement; they do not expressly provide a private right of action to workers claiming to be victims of retaliation. When should state or federal courts imply antiretaliation guarantees and afford employees a right of action to enforce them? Does a statutory scheme that does not provide for such actions reflect a considered legislative judgment that they are inappropriate? May a court infer from the existence of substantive restrictions on employer action and the provision of some remedies a declaration of legislative policy permitting judicial implication of a private right of action?

KELSAY v. MOTOROLA, INC.
Supreme Court of Illinois, 1978.
74 Ill.2d 172, 23 Ill.Dec. 559, 384 N.E.2d 353.

RYAN, J.

Plaintiff, Marilyn Jo Kelsay, filed a complaint in the circuit court of Livingston County, seeking compensatory and punitive damages against her ex-employer, Motorola, Inc. The plaintiff alleged that her employment with defendant had been terminated as retaliation for her filing a workmen's compensation claim. The trial court directed a verdict in plaintiff's favor and the jury assessed damages in the amount of $1,000 compensatory damages and $25,000 punitive damages. The court remitted the compensatory damages to $749, which represents the wages plaintiff lost between the time she was discharged and the time she found a new job. On appeal, the Fourth District Appellate Court reversed the judgment of the trial court, holding that an employee has no cause of action against an employer for retaliatory discharge.

* * *

The Workmen's Compensation Act (Ill.Rev.Stat.1973, ch. 48, par. 138.1 *et seq.*) substitutes an entirely new system of rights, remedies, and procedure for all previously existing common law rights and liabilities between employers and employees subject to the Act for accidental injuries or death of employees arising out of and in the course of the employment. (37 Ill.L. & Prac. *Workmen's Compensation* sec. 2 (1958).) Pursuant to the statutory scheme implemented by the Act, the employee gave up his common law rights to sue his employer in tort, but recovery for injuries arising out of and in the course of his employment became automatic without regard to any fault on his part. The employer, who gave up the right to plead the numerous common law defenses, was compelled to pay, but his liability became fixed under a strict and comprehensive statutory scheme, and was not subjected to the sympathies of jurors whose compassion for fellow employees often led to high recovery. (See 81 Am.Jur.2d *Workmen's Compensation* sec. 1 *et seq.* (1976).) This trade-off between employer and employee promoted the fundamental purpose of the Act, which was to afford protection to employees by providing them with prompt and equitable compensation for their injuries.

* * *

While noting that in 1975, subsequent to plaintiff's discharge, the Workmen's Compensation Act was amended making it unlawful for an employer to interfere with or to coerce the employee in the exercise of his rights under the Act (Ill.Rev.Stat.1975, ch. 48, par. 138.4(h)), the employer argues that as of the time of plaintiff's discharge, the legislature had neither prohibited nor provided for any remedy for a discharge resulting from the filing of a workmen's compensation claim. As such, its authority to terminate the employee, whose contract was at will, was absolute.

* * *

We are not convinced that an employer's otherwise absolute power to terminate an employee at will should prevail when that power is exercised to prevent the employee from asserting his statutory rights under the Workmen's Compensation Act. As we have noted, the legislature enacted the workmen's compensation law as a comprehensive scheme to provide for efficient and expeditious remedies for injured employees. This scheme would be seriously undermined if employers were permitted to abuse their power to terminate by threatening to discharge employees for seeking compensation under the Act. We cannot ignore the fact that when faced with such a dilemma many employees, whose common law rights have been supplanted by the Act, would choose to retain their jobs, and thus, in effect, would be left without a remedy either common law or statutory. This result, which effectively relieves the employer of the responsibility expressly placed upon him by the legislature, is untenable and is contrary to the public policy as expressed in the Workmen's Compensation Act. We cannot believe that the legislature, even in the absence of an explicit proscription against retaliatory discharge, intended such a result.

* * *

The employer argues that the exclusivity provision of section 11 of the Act, which provides that the provisions of the Act "shall be the measure of the responsibility of any employer" (Ill.Rev.Stat.1973, ch. 48, par. 138.11), precludes an action for retaliatory discharge. Motorola argues that this conclusion is compelled because the section clearly shows that the legislature intended that the Act should be exclusive in providing for employees' rights and remedies. We do not agree. First, that section was meant to limit recovery by employees to the extent provided by the Act in regard to work-related injuries, and was not intended to insulate the employer from independent tort actions. Second, we cannot accept a construction of section 11 which would allow employers to put employees in a position of choosing between their jobs and seeking their remedies under the Act.

* * *

The employer argues that the absence of any provisions for civil remedies for retaliatory discharge in the 1975 amendments, which make it a criminal offense for an employer to threaten or effect such a discharge (Ill.Rev.Stat.1975, ch. 48, par. 138.4(h)), is a conscious decision by the legislature that no such civil remedy shall exist. We do not agree. As we have noted, retaliatory discharge is offensive to the public policy of this State as stated in the Workmen's Compensation Act. This policy can only be effectively implemented and enforced by allowing a civil remedy for damages, distinct from any criminal sanctions which may be imposed on employers for violating the Act after 1975. The imposition of a small fine, enuring to the benefit of the State, does nothing to alleviate the plight of those employees who are threatened with retaliation and forgo their rights, or those who lose their jobs when they proceed to file claims under the Act. It is conceivable, moreover, that some employers would risk the threat of criminal sanction in order to escape their responsibility under the Act. Further, the fact that an act is penal in nature does not bar a civil remedy, and where a statute is enacted for the benefit of a particular class of individuals a violation of its terms may result in civil as well as criminal liability, even though the former remedy is not specifically mentioned. *Heimgaertner v. Benjamin Electric Manufacturing Co.* (1955), 6 Ill.2d 152, 128 N.E.2d 691.

* * *

We now consider the award of $25,000 punitive damages. In this connection, two points merit consideration, first, whether punitive damages may generally be awarded in cases for retaliatory discharge, and second, whether the jury's award for such damages was proper in the instant case.

* * *

In the absence of the deterrent effect of punitive damages there would be little to dissuade an employer from engaging in the practice of discharging an employee for filing a workmen's compensation claim. For example in this case, the plaintiff was entitled to only $749 compensatory damages. We noted above the very real possibility that some employers would risk the threat of criminal sanction in order to escape their responsibilities under the Act. The statute makes such conduct, as is involved in this case, a petty offense (Ill.Rev.Stat.1975, ch. 48, par. 138.26), which is punishable by a fine not to exceed $500 (Ill.Rev.Stat.

1975, ch. 38, par. 1005–9–1(4)). The imposition on the employer of the small additional obligation to pay a wrongfully discharged employee compensation would do little to discourage the practice of retaliatory discharge, which mocks the public policy of this State as announced in the Workmen's Compensation Act. In the absence of other effective means of deterrence, punitive damages must be permitted to prevent the discharging of employees for filing workmen's compensation claims.

* * *

However, under the facts of the present case, we are compelled to conclude that the award of $25,000 as punitive damages was improper. [T]he function of punitive damages is similar to that of a criminal penalty, *i.e.,* as a punishment to the wrongdoer and as a means to deter such a wrongdoer and others from committing like offenses in the future. (See *Mattyasovszky v. West Towns Bus Co.* (1975), 61 Ill.2d 31, 330 N.E.2d 509.) Because of their penal nature, punitive damages are not favored in the law, and the courts must take caution to see that punitive damages are not improperly or unwisely awarded. (See *Eshelman v. Rawalt* (1921), 298 Ill. 192, 197, 131 N.E. 675.) Adherence to this rule compels us to conclude that punitive damages should not be awarded where, as here, the cause of action forming the basis for their award is a novel one.

* * *

At the time of plaintiff's discharge there was no provision in the Act making it unlawful to discharge an employee for seeking relief under its provisions. Also, at that time there was no decision of this court holding that a retaliatory discharge in such cases was actionable.

Note on Workers' Compensation Laws

Workers' compensation legislation was developed by the states in the early part of the twentieth century. This legislation replaced the employee's common law negligence action against his or her employer with a no-fault insurance scheme funded by mandatory employer contributions and providing for a statutory schedule of compensation. This legislation expresses a compromise by which employees avoid the common law doctrines of assumption of risk, contributory negligence and nonliability for fellow-servant negligence, and employers avoid the risk of high or unpredictable jury awards. See generally Lawrence M. Friedman, A History of American Law, ch. 14 (1973); Richard A. Epstein, The Historical Origins and Economic Structure of Workers' Compensation Law, 16 Ga.L.Rev. 775 (1982).

The disparity between the limited compensation available under the workers' compensation schedules with the much more substantial verdicts obtainable in jury-tried civil actions has created pressure on the courts to recognize exceptions to the exclusivity of the workers' compensation scheme. See, e.g., Johns–Manville Products v. Contra Costa Superior Court, 27 Cal.3d 465, 165 Cal.Rptr. 858, 612 P.2d 948 (1980) (employee suffering from a disease caused by exposure to workplace asbestos could recover in tort for

the aggravation of the disease attributable to the alleged fraudulent concealment by company doctors' misdiagnosis, as distinct from the hazards of the
employment that caused the disease to have been contracted); Bell v.
Industrial Vangas, Inc., 30 Cal.3d 268, 179 Cal.Rptr. 30, 637 P.2d 266 (1981)
("dual capacity" exception permitted suit by a salesman injured by product
of his employer that he was delivering in the course of his employment).

Notes and Questions

1. *Implications of Absence of Express Private Remedy.* Why might the
Illinois legislature prior to 1975 have established a workers' compensation
scheme without making it unlawful for an employer to retaliate against an
employee for filing a claim under that scheme? Could this have been part of
a legislative compromise? Could it have been mere oversight? Might the
legislature have wanted the courts to develop protections? How should
courts treat such incomplete legislation? May courts properly exercise a kind
of equity jurisprudence to ensure the efficacy of the stated "public" goals of
the measure? See Jonathan R. Macey, Promoting Public–Regarding Legislation Through Statutory Interpretation: An Interest Group Model, 86 Co-
lum.L.Rev. 223 (1986); see also (now U.S. Court of Appeals Judge) Guido
Calabresi, A Common Law for the Age of Statutes (1982); Samuel Estreicher,
Review Essay: Judicial Nullification: Guido Calabresi's Uncommon Common
Law for a Statutory Age, 57 N.Y.U.L.Rev. 1126 (1982).

Is the case for an implied right of action stronger or weaker after 1975,
when the Illinois legislature provided for criminal remedies? For an example
of judicial reluctance to recognize a supplementary civil action, see Bottijliso
v. Hutchison Fruit Co., 96 N.M. 789, 635 P.2d 992 (1981).

2. *Implied Federal Causes of Action.* For federal statutes, the Supreme
Court articulated in Cort v. Ash, 422 U.S. 66, 95 S.Ct. 2080, 45 L.Ed.2d 26
(1975), a set of criteria for deciding whether to recognize an implied right of
action:

> First, is the plaintiff "one of the class for whose especial benefit the
> statute was enacted"—that is, does the statute create a federal right in
> favor of the plaintiff? Second, is there any indication of legislative
> intent, explicit or implicit, either to create such a remedy or to deny
> one? Third, is it consistent with the underlying purpose of the legislative
> scheme to imply such a remedy? And finally, is the cause of action one
> traditionally relegated to state law, so that it would be inappropriate to
> infer a cause of action based solely on federal law?

Id. at 78 (citations and emphasis omitted). Applying this test, the Court
recognized an implied right of action under § 901(a) of Title IX of the
Education Amendments of 1972, 42 U.S.C. § 681, in Cannon v. University of
Chicago, 441 U.S. 677, 99 S.Ct. 1946, 60 L.Ed.2d 560 (1979). Moreover the
Court seems to have set aside the *Cort* test. Generally, in post-*Cannon*
decisions, the Court has stressed the second factor, insisting that Congress
signal its intent to authorize private actions. See, e.g., Alexander v. Sandoval, 532 U.S. 275, 287, 121 S.Ct. 1511, 149 L.Ed.2d 517 (2001) ("[l]ike
substantive federal law itself, private rights of action to enforce federal law
must be created by Congress"); Karahalios v. National Fed. of Federal

Employees. Local 1263, 489 U.S. 527, 109 S.Ct. 1282, 103 L.Ed.2d 539 (1989).

3. *Punitive Damages?* Are you persuaded by the *Kelsay* court's refusal to sustain the award of punitive damages? Did the employer have any legitimate reliance interest arguing against retrospective application?

4. *Absenteeism Due to Workplace Injury.* Does the cause of action recognized in *Kelsay* extend to a situation where the reason for a termination is not the assertion of a workers' compensation claim but, rather, the employee's extended absence from work due to the workplace injury? Most courts have declined to find such a termination actionable. See, e.g., Clifford v. Cactus Drilling Corp., 419 Mich. 356, 353 N.W.2d 469 (1984). For a proposed legislative remedy, see Mark A. Rothstein, Statute: A Proposed Model Act for the Reinstatement of Employees Upon Recovery from Work–Related Injury or Illness, 26 Harv.J. on Legis. 263 (1989). Does the Americans with Disabilities Act provide a remedy? See note 4, p. 531 supra.

Chapter Eleven

PROTECTION OF THE PUBLIC INTEREST

A. INTRODUCTION

The previous chapter considered rules protecting employee activity because of its contribution to a statutory scheme that is intended to secure benefits for employees. In this chapter, we consider more generally the extent to which common law decisions and statutes protect employee activity that is valued primarily because of benefits generated for third parties, typically the general public. Despite the nominal adherence of most jurisdictions to the "employment at will" doctrine, state courts increasingly have carved out exceptions to restrict discharges that offend what these courts deem to be their state's "public policy." We are also witnessing a substantial growth in legislation prohibiting retaliation against "whistleblowers"—individuals who disclose unlawful or other improper conduct by their employers.

The primary rationale for the "public policy" cause of action seems to be that employers should not use their contractual right to terminate the employment relationship in a manner that might frustrate the third-party interests of the public. Such frustration is likely where a termination retaliates against and thereby discourages employee activity that serves some public interest. By analogy to the doctrine holding certain contracts void as a matter of public policy, the public policy exceptions to the employment-at-will rule "are aimed at controlling the external effects" of private employment decisionmaking. See Jeffrey L. Harrison, "New" Terminable–at–Will Employment Contract: An Interest and Cost Incidence Analysis, 69 Iowa L.Rev. 327, 349 (1984). The public policy cause of action also owes an intellectual debt to Lawrence Blades, Employment at Will vs. Individual Freedom: On Limiting the Abusive Exercise of Employer Power, 67 Colum.L.Rev. 1404 (1967), which argued that much like the French doctrine of *abus de droit* and the American tort doctrines of malicious prosecution and abuse of process, American employment law should restrict abusive exercise of employer power for a socially unjustified purpose.

B. PERFORMANCE OF PUBLIC OBLIGATIONS

NEES v. HOCKS
Supreme Court of Oregon, 1975.
272 Or. 210, 536 P.2d 512.

DENECKE, J.

The jury found for plaintiff; therefore, we must consider the facts as established by the evidence most favorable to plaintiff. The plaintiff performed clerical duties for defendants. She started work in 1971. In 1972 she was called for jury duty; however, as she informed defendants, she requested and was granted a 12–month postponement because of her honeymoon. On February 2, 1973, plaintiff was again subpoenaed to serve on the jury. She told defendants and they stated that a month was too long for her "to be gone." Defendants gave her a letter which stated defendants could spare plaintiff "for awhile" but not for a month and asked that she be excused. Plaintiff presented this letter to the court clerk and told the clerk that she had been called before and had to be excused, but she would like to serve on jury duty. The clerk told plaintiff she would not be excused. The plaintiff immediately came back to the office and told defendants that she would have to serve a minimum of two weeks' jury duty. She did not tell defendants she had told the court clerk she really wanted to serve.

Plaintiff started her jury duty on February 26, 1973. On March 1, 1973, she received a termination letter from defendants. The letter stated, in part: "Although we asked you to request an excusal from Jury Duty and wrote a letter confirming the [defendants'] position, it has been brought to our attention you, in fact, requested to be placed on Jury Duty." The letter went on to state the defendants also were not otherwise satisfied with plaintiff's work. Based upon other evidence, however, the jury could have found plaintiff was not terminated because of dissatisfaction with the quality of plaintiff's work.

* * *

We recognize, as defendants assert, that, generally, in the absence of a contract or legislation to the contrary, an employer can discharge an employee at any time and for any cause. Conversely, an employee can quit at any time for any cause. Such termination by the employer or employee is not a breach of contract and ordinarily does not create a tortious cause of action. The question to us is, however, are there instances in which the employer's reason or motive for discharging harms or interferes with an important interest of the community and, therefore, justifies compensation to the employee?

Other courts have held that there are such instances. In *Petermann v. International Brotherhood of Teamsters*, 174 Cal.App.2d 184, 344 P.2d 25 (1959), the plaintiff was discharged by his employer for refusing to give perjured testimony before a committee of the legislature. A judgment on the pleadings for the defendant employer was reversed.

* * *

We conclude that there can be circumstances in which an employer discharges an employee for such a socially undesirable motive that the employer must respond in damages for any injury done. The next question is, does the evidence in this case permit a finding that such circumstances are present?

There is evidence from which the jury could have found that the defendants discharged the plaintiff because, after being subpoenaed, and contrary to the defendants' wishes, plaintiff told the clerk she would like to serve and she did serve on jury duty.[2] Therefore, the immediate question can be stated specifically—is the community's interest in having its citizens serve on jury duty so important that an employer, who interferes with that interest by discharging an employee who served on a jury, should be required to compensate his employee for any damages she suffered?

Art. VII, § 3, of the Oregon Constitution provides that jury trial shall be preserved in civil cases. Art. I, § 11, provides a defendant in a criminal case has a right of trial by jury. Art. VII, § 5, provides: "The Legislative Assembly shall so provide that the most competent of the permanent citizens of the county shall be chosen for jurors."

ORS 10.040 provides for certain exemptions from jury duty. ORS 10.050 provides for certain excuses from jury duty including health, age and "(c) When serving as a juror would result in extreme hardship to the person including but not limited to unusual and extraordinary financial hardship." ORS 10.055 provides for deferment of jury duty "for good cause shown" for not more than one year. ORS 10.990 provides that if a juror "without reasonable cause" neglects to attend for jury service the sheriff may impose a fine, not exceeding $20 for each day the juror does not attend.

People v. Vitucci, 49 Ill.App.2d 171, 199 N.E.2d 78 (1964), stated that an employer who discharged an employee who was absent because of jury duty was guilty of contempt of court. Massachusetts has a statute making such conduct contemptuous. 44 Mass.G.L.A., ch. 268, § 14A.

These actions by the people, the legislature and the courts clearly indicate that the jury system and jury duty are regarded as high on the scale of American institutions and citizen obligations. If an employer were permitted with impunity to discharge an employee for fulfilling her obligation of jury duty, the jury system would be adversely affected. The will of the community would be thwarted. For these reasons we hold that

---

2. If the only evidence was that the defendants would have suffered a substantial hardship if plaintiff served this particular month [and] defendants requested only a postponement of jury service but the plaintiff nevertheless asked to serve this particular month, we probably would regard the discharge as justifiable.

the defendants are liable for discharging plaintiff because she served on the jury.

Notes and Questions

1. *Citizen's Duty of Cooperation.* The public obligation to respond in good faith to calls for jury service seems clear. Note, for example, the "extreme hardship" showing required by Oregon state law for deferments. The jury system plainly would break down if evasion—whether due to individual predilection or employer pressures—were to become the rule. If the system is to continue to rely on self-assessment of availability, must some public remedies be provided against employer coercion, whether administrative sanctions or civil actions? Does it seem fair for the law to force citizens to perform some public duty at the cost of their jobs?

2. *Volunteering for Jury Duty.* Does the reasoning of *Nees* bar an employer from retaliating against an employee for volunteering for jury duty?

3. *Employer Interests.* Are the employer's legitimate interests adequately protected by footnote 2 of the court's opinion in *Nees*? After *Nees,* could employers and employees in Oregon agree in an employment contract that the employees would not accept a call for jury duty without the employer's approval? That employees will make clear their unavailability for a particular period if asked to do so by their employer?

4. *Statutory Developments.* The holding of *Nees* has now been codified. See Ore.Rev.Stat. 10.090. Many states have comparable provisions. See, e.g., West's Ann.Cal.Labor Code § 230(a); N.Y.Jud.Law § 532; Tex.Civ.Code Art. § 122.001–003. Some statutes also expressly protect employees who leave work to testify as witnesses in court, see, e.g., West's Ann.Cal.Labor Code § 230; N.Y.—McKinney's Penal Law § 215.11; Or.Rev.Stat. 659.270, or before a legislature, see, e.g., Nev.Rev.Stat. 50.070. Also, the Federal Jury System Improvement Act, 28 U.S.C. § 1875, prohibits penalizing employees who serve on a federal court jury. See Shea v. County of Rockland, 810 F.2d 27 (2d Cir.1987) (only lost wages, not compensatory damages, may be recovered).

5. *"Citizen Crime Fighters"?* How broadly does the *Nees* rationale extend? Law enforcement authorities in some sense also rely on public cooperation in detecting and apprehending wrongdoers. Yet, under current law, while citizens may be obligated to respond honestly to grand jury inquiries, in most states they are under no affirmative duty to report suspected wrongdoing. Should employees who report illegal behavior by their fellow employees or employer be protected from employer retaliation? See Palmateer v. International Harvester Co., 85 Ill.2d 124, 52 Ill.Dec. 13, 421 N.E.2d 876 (1981), and materials on "whistleblowers," at pp. 705–23 infra.

C. REFUSAL TO PERFORM ASSIGNMENT IN CONTRAVENTION OF PUBLIC POLICY

TAMENY v. ATLANTIC RICHFIELD CO.

Supreme Court of California, 1980.

27 Cal.3d 167, 164 Cal.Rptr. 839, 610 P.2d 1330.

TOBRINER, J.

Plaintiff Gordon Tameny instituted the present action against his former employer, Atlantic Richfield Company (Arco), alleging that Arco had discharged him after 15 years of service because he refused to participate in an illegal scheme to fix retail gasoline prices. Plaintiff sought recovery from Arco on a number of theories, contending, inter alia, that Arco's conduct in discharging him for refusing to commit a criminal act was tortious and subjected the employer to liability for compensatory and punitive damages under normal tort principles.

* * *

Because this appeal arises from a judgment entered after the sustaining of a general demurrer, we must, under established principles, assume the truth of all properly pleaded material allegations of the complaint in evaluating the validity of the trial court's action.

* * *

According to the complaint, plaintiff was hired by Arco as a relief clerk in 1960, received regular advancements, merit increases and commendatory evaluations in his initial years with the company, and, in 1966, was promoted to the position of retail sales representative, the position he held when discharged by Arco in 1975. His duties as a retail sales representative included among other matters the management of relations between Arco and the various independent service station dealers (franchisees) in his assigned territory of Bakersfield.

The complaint alleges that beginning in the early 1970s, Arco, Arco's district manager McDermott, and others engaged in a combination "for the purpose of reducing, controlling, stabilizing, fixing, and pegging the retail gasoline prices of Arco service station franchisees." According to the complaint, defendants' conduct in this regard violated express provisions of the Sherman Antitrust Act (15 U.S.C. § 1 et seq.), the Cartwright Act (Bus. & Prof.Code, § 16720 et seq.), and a specific consent decree which had been entered in a federal antitrust prosecution against Arco.

The complaint further asserts that during the early 1970s, defendants increasingly pressured plaintiff to "threaten [and] cajole * * * the so-called 'independent' service station dealers in [his] territory to cut their gasoline prices to a point at or below a designated level specified by Arco." When plaintiff refused to yield to his employer's pressure to engage in such tactics, his supervisor told him that his discharge was imminent, and soon thereafter plaintiff was fired, effective March 25, 1975. Although at the time of the discharge Arco indicated in its personnel records that plaintiff was being fired for "incompetence" and for "unsatisfactory performance," the complaint alleges that "the sole reason" for plaintiff's discharge was his refusal to commit the "grossly illegal and unlawful acts which defendants tried to force him to perform."

* * *

Under the traditional common law rule, codified in Labor Code section 2922,[6] an employment contract of indefinite duration is in general terminable at "the will" of either party. Over the past several decades, however, judicial authorities in California and throughout the United States have established the rule that under both common law and the statute an employer does not enjoy an absolute or totally unfettered right to discharge even an at-will employee. In a series of cases arising out of a variety of factual settings in which a discharge clearly violated an express statutory objective or undermined a firmly established principle of public policy, courts have recognized that an employer's traditional broad authority to discharge an at-will employee "may be limited by statute * * * or by considerations of public policy." (*Petermann v. International Brotherhood of Teamsters* (1959) 174 Cal. App.2d 184, 188, 344 P.2d 25, 27 (discharge for refusal to commit perjury); see, e.g., * * * *Nees v. Hocks* (1975) 272 Or. 210, 536 P.2d 512 (discharge for serving on jury); *Frampton v. Central Indiana Gas Co.* (1973) 260 Ind. 249, 297 N.E.2d 425 (discharge for filing worker's compensation claim); *Harless v. First Nat. Bank in Fairmont* (W.Va. 1978) 246 S.E.2d 270 (discharge for reporting violations of consumer protection laws).)

Petermann v. International Brotherhood of Teamsters, supra, one of the seminal California decisions in this area, imposes a significant condition upon the employer's broad power of dismissal by nullifying the right to discharge because an employee refuses to perform an unlawful act. In *Petermann,* the plaintiff, who had been employed as a business agent by defendant union, brought a "wrongful discharge" action against the union alleging that he had been dismissed from his position because he had refused to follow his employer's instructions to testify falsely under oath before a legislative committee, and instead had given truthful testimony. Emphasizing that the employer's instructions amounted to a directive to commit perjury, a criminal offense, plaintiff maintained that the employer acted illegally in discharging him for refusing to follow such an order.

The *Petermann* court recognized that in the absence of contractual limitations an employer enjoys broad discretion to discharge an employee, but concluded that as a matter of "public policy and sound morality" the employer's conduct, as alleged in the complaint, could not be con-

---

6. Section 2922 provides in relevant part: "An employment, having no specified term, may be terminated at the will of either party on notice to the other. * * * * "

doned. The court explained: "The commission of perjury is unlawful. (Pen.Code, § 118). * * * It would be obnoxious to the interests of the state and contrary to public policy and sound morality to allow an employer to discharge any employee, whether the employment be for a designated or unspecified duration, on the ground that the employee declined to commit perjury, an act specifically enjoined by statute. * * * The public policy of this state as reflected in the penal code sections referred to above would be seriously impaired if it were to be held that one could be discharged by reason of his refusal to commit perjury. To hold that one's continued employment could be made contingent upon his commission of a felonious act at the instance of his employer would be to encourage criminal conduct upon the part of both the employee and employer and serve to contaminate the honest administration of public affairs. * * * " (174 Cal.App.2d at pp. 188–189, 344 P.2d at p. 27.)

Thus, *Petermann* held that even in the absence of an explicit statutory provision prohibiting the discharge of a worker on such grounds, fundamental principles of public policy and adherence to the objectives underlying the state's penal statutes require the recognition of a rule barring an employer from discharging an employee who has simply complied with his legal duty and has refused to commit an illegal act.[8]

As the statement of facts set out above demonstrates, the present case closely parallels *Petermann* in a number of essential respects. Here, as in *Petermann,* the complaint alleges that the defendant employer instructed its employee to engage in conduct constituting a criminal offense. Plaintiff, like the employee in *Petermann,* refused to violate the law and suffered discharge as a consequence of that refusal.

Arco concedes, as it must in light of *Petermann,* that the allegations of the complaint, if true, establish that defendants acted unlawfully in discharging plaintiff for refusing to participate in criminal activity. Arco maintains, however, that plaintiff's remedy for such misconduct sounds only in contract and not in tort. Accordingly, Arco asserts that the trial court properly sustained its demurrer to plaintiff's tort causes of action, and correctly precluded plaintiff from recovering either compensatory tort damages or punitive damages.

In support of its contention that an action for wrongful discharge sounds only in contract and not in tort, Arco argues that because of the contractual nature of the employer-employee relationship, an injury which an employer inflicts upon its employee by the improper termination of such a relationship gives rise only to a breach of contract

---

8. Although the *Petermann* court did not rely upon Labor Code section 2856, that statute provides additional support for the *Petermann* ruling. Section 2856 declares that "[a]n employee shall substantially comply with all the directions of his employer concerning the service on which he is engaged, *except where such obedience is* im-possible or *unlawful* * * *." (Italics added.) While this statute does not specifically refer to an employer's authority to discharge an employee, the statute does reflect direct legislative approval of the basic proposition that an employer enjoys no authority to direct an employee to engage in unlawful conduct.

action. California decisions, however, have long recognized that a wrongful act committed in the course of a contractual relationship may afford both tort and the contractual relief, and in such circumstances the existence of the contractual relationship will not bar the injured party from pursuing redress in tort.

* * *

[W]e conclude that an employee's action for wrongful discharge is ex delicto and subjects an employer to tort liability. As the *Petermann* case indicates, an employer's obligation to refrain from discharging an employee who refuses to commit a criminal act does not depend upon any express or implied " 'promises set forth in the [employment] contract' " * * *, but rather reflects a duty imposed by law upon all employers in order to implement the fundamental public policies embodied in the state's penal statutes. As such, a wrongful discharge suit exhibits the classic elements of a tort cause of action. As Professor Prosser has explained: "[Whereas] [c]ontract actions are created to protect the interest in having promises performed," "[t]ort actions are created to protect the interest in freedom from various kinds of harm. The duties of conduct which give rise to them are imposed by law, and are based primarily upon social policy, and not necessarily upon the will or intention of the parties. * * * " (Prosser, Law of Torts (4th ed. 1971) p. 613.)

* * *

We hold that an employer's authority over its employee does not include the right to demand that the employee commit a criminal act to further its interests, and an employer may not coerce compliance with such unlawful directions by discharging an employee who refuses to follow such an order. An employer engaging in such conduct violates a basic duty imposed by law upon all employers, and thus an employee who has suffered damages as a result of such discharge may maintain a tort action for wrongful discharge against the employer.

MANUEL, J., concurring.

I concur in the judgment.

In my view the cause of action here in question flows from a clear statutory source—i.e., the provisions of section 2856 of the Labor Code. (Cf. *Montalvo v. Zamora* (1970) 7 Cal.App.3d 69, 73–75, 86 Cal.Rptr. 401.) Accordingly, I see no reason to search further for it among the vague and ill-defined dictates of "fundamental public policy."

CLARK, J., dissenting.

In the instant case the alleged actionable conduct is only contractual, that is, the alleged wrongful termination of an employment contract. In terminating that contract defendant did not *also* breach a duty giving rise to a cause of action in tort. (See *Petermann v. International Brotherhood of Teamsters, supra,* 174 Cal.App.2d 184, 344 P.2d 25.) As in *Petermann* there is no delictual breach in the termination itself, although it is alleged that defendants' *reason* for the termination—plaintiff's refusal to cooperate with defendants in committing acts contrary to public policy—was improper. There does not exist in the instant case * * * the least connection between defendants' actionable conduct (breach of contract) and *any* tort.

Notes and Questions

1. *Stages in the Development of the "Public Policy" Cause of Action.* *Kelsay* (the concluding case in chapter 10), *Nees* and *Tameny* represent three stages in the judicial recognition of the public policy cause of action. *Kelsay* involves judicial implication of a private civil remedy for employees who have been retaliated against for the assertion of a statutory claim; the public policy is defined by the statute, and the court is engaged in a rather traditional enterprise of deciding whether a private right of action is both necessary to effectuate the scheme and also consistent with the legislative design. *Nees* involves a somewhat more difficult problem because the public policy is not centrally located in a particular statute, but must be gleaned from a variety of state statutory and constitutional provisions. Nevertheless, once a public policy in favor of promoting public cooperation with the jury service requirement is identified, the question for the court becomes whether a civil remedy is needed against employer pressures to report falsely unavailability for jury service. *Tameny* requires the court to determine whether in some circumstances employee refusals to perform assigned work contravenes public policy. Although the source of the public policy is readily identified, the interference with the employer's operations is greater than in *Kelsay* or *Nees*. See Samuel Estreicher & Beverly Wolff, At–Will Employment and the Problem of Unjust Dismissal, 36 Record of the Assn. of the Bar of the City of N.Y. 170 (April 1981).

2. *"Hobson's Choice"?* Both *Tameny* and *Petermann* on which it relies seek to relieve an employee from a pernicious Hobson's choice: either comply with the employer's directive and violate the law, or refuse to comply and suffer discharge. In both, to allow the employer to use the power of discharge to enlist employee intermediaries in unlawful conduct would be to permit the employer to do indirectly what it could not do directly. Yet, how does the *Tameny* court square its ruling with § 2922 of the Cal.Lab.Code (quoted in footnote 6)? Interestingly, there may have been a statutory basis for recognizing the cause of action in *Tameny* (see footnote 8). Would the case have come out differently if the latter statute were not on the books?

3. *Contract vs. Tort.* What is the significance of the fact that the majority in *Tameny* permits the plaintiff to sue in either contract or tort? How should courts determine whether a cause of action sounds in tort or contract? Is the dissent right that there is no independent wrongful act in this case other than the termination of employment itself, and hence no basis for tort recovery? Is it relevant that the primary interests to be served by the cause of action seem to be those of the public, rather than those of employees or employers? Is it relevant whether an employee could agree to an enforceable contract provision that waived any right to refuse to do an illegal act for the employer?

In Foley v. Interactive Data Corp., 47 Cal.3d 654, 254 Cal.Rptr. 211, 765 P.2d 373 (1988), reprinted in part at pp. 763–66 supra, the California high court offered the following explanation for why a *Tameny* claim affords a tort recovery:

> As *Tameny* explained, the theoretical reason for labeling the discharge wrongful in such a case is not based on the terms and conditions of the contract but rather arises out of duty implied in law on the part of the employer to conduct its affairs in compliance with public policy. * * * [T]here is no logical basis to distinguish in cases of wrongful termination for reasons violative of fundamental principles of public policy between situations in which the employee is an at-will employee and [those] in which the employee has a contract for a specified term. The tort is independent of the term of employment.

Id. at 667, 254 Cal.Rptr. at 215, 765 P.2d at 377, citing Koehrer v. Superior Court, 181 Cal.App.3d 1155, 1166, 226 Cal.Rptr. 820, 826 (1986).

Although the New Hampshire Supreme Court initially analogized the public policy claim to an action in assumpsit to recover damages for the employer's breach of an implied contractual obligation not to exercise contractual authority in contravention of state public policy, see Monge v. Beebe Rubber Co., 114 N.H. 130, 316 A.2d 549, 550 (1974), it now permits suit in either contract or tort, see Cloutier v. Great Atlantic & Pacific Tea Co., 121 N.H. 915, 920, 436 A.2d 1140, 1143 (1981). Most courts follow *Tameny, Foley* and *Cloutier* in permitting tort recovery. But see Johnson v. Kreiser's Inc., 433 N.W.2d 225 (S.D.1988) (contract recovery only).

4. *Preclusion of Common Law Remedy by Available Administrative Remedy*? The courts may have been receptive to the public policy cause of action in *Kelsay* and *Tameny* in part because of the absence of any retaliatory discharge remedy in the statute that gave rise to the public policy claim. Should courts recognize an additional tort remedy even where the statute provides an administrative remedy? A private cause of action? Compare, e.g., Makovi v. Sherwin–Williams Co., 316 Md. 603, 561 A.2d 179 (1989) (statutory remedies are available for discharge on account of pregnancy); Wolk v. Saks Fifth Ave., Inc., 728 F.2d 221 (3d Cir.1984) (exclusive remedy for sexual harassment is state civil rights statute), with Rojo v. Kliger, 52 Cal.3d 65, 276 Cal.Rptr. 130, 801 P.2d 373 (1990) (statutory remedy does not bar public policy tort action for workplace sexual harassment); Collins v. Elkay Mining Co., 179 W.Va. 549, 371 S.E.2d 46, 48 (W.Va. 1988) (failure to file charge under Federal Coal Mine Safety Act or West Virginia Mine Safety Act does not bar retaliatory discharge claim by coal mine foreman for refusing to falsify company safety reports); Holien v. Sears, Roebuck and Co., 298 Or. 76, 689 P.2d 1292 (1984) (same); Phillips v. Gemini Moving Specialists, 63 Cal.App.4th 563, 74 Cal.Rptr.2d 29 (2d Dist. 1998) (employee fired after complaining about improper wage setoff may proceed under *Tameny* theory, despite statutory remedy).

5. *Statutes Principally Concerned with Private, Proprietary Interests*. Are some statutes inappropriate bases for public policy claims because they are primarily concerned with private and proprietary, rather than public, interests? See Campbell v. Ford Industries, Inc., 274 Or. 243, 546 P.2d 141 (1976).

In Foley v. Interactive Data Corp., supra, plaintiff who worked as defendant's product manager had learned that his new supervisor was under FBI investigation for embezzlement from his former employer, the Bank of America. Believing that corporate management would want to know of a high executive's alleged prior criminal conduct, he disclosed this information to his former supervisor, and was allegedly fired for that reason. The California high court held that these facts did not state a claim under California law:

> In the present case, plaintiff alleges that defendant discharged him in "sharp derogation" of a substantial public policy that imposes a legal duty on employees to report relevant business information to management. * * *
>
> Whether or not there is a statutory duty requiring an employee to report information relevant to his employer's interest, we do not find a substantial public policy prohibiting an employer from discharging an employee for performing that duty. * * * When the duty of an employee to disclose information to his employer serves only the private interest of the employer, the rationale underlying the *Tameny* cause of action is not implicated.

47 Cal.3d at 669–71, 254 Cal.Rptr. at 217–18, 765 P.2d at 379–80.

By contrast, in Paolella v. Browning–Ferris Inc., 158 F.3d 183 (3d Cir.1998), the Third Circuit (applying Delaware law) held that an employee fired after accusing his company of fraudulently inflating client bills stated a "public policy" claim under state law. Acknowledging that "mere questioning of the propriety of a supervisor's business practices" is not actionable under E.I. DuPont de Nemours & Co. v. Pressman, 679 A.2d 436 (Del. 1996), the appeals court emphasized that plaintiff's claim raised legal rather than merely ethical concerns, Paolella having presented evidence that defendant's billing practice "was illegally designed to defraud [its] customers by leading them to believe the increase in their monthly fees was due solely to a state imposed increase in [its] dumping costs and was therefore authorized under the terms of the service agreements." 158 F.3d at 191. Was there a third-party interest present in *Paolella* that was not present in *Foley*?

6. *Adverse Actions Short of Discharge.* Would Tameny have had a cause of action if instead of being discharged, he was reassigned to a less desirable position or was presented with a cut in salary? Is there any reason why the "public policy" cause of action should be limited to discharges rather than other retaliatory personnel decisions? Cf. Scott v. Pacific Gas and Electric Co., 11 Cal.4th 454, 46 Cal.Rptr.2d 427, 904 P.2d 834 (1995) (recognized implied-in-fact contract cause of action for "wrongful demotion").

7. *Refusal to Perform Assignment Erroneously Believed to be Unlawful.* Should employees be protected from discharge, or from other discipline, for refusing to perform work that they sincerely and reasonably thought was illegal, even if it turns out that there is no illegality?

8. *State Law Incorporation of Federal Norms.* To what extent may or should the public policy of a state incorporate federal concerns? Compare, e.g., Guy v. Travenol Labs., Inc., 812 F.2d 911 (4th Cir.1987) (claim of retaliatory discharge for refusing to falsify records required by federal law; federal diversity decision holding that North Carolina has no obligation to use its tort system to supplement federal scheme); Rachford v. Evergreen Int'l Airlines, 596 F.Supp. 384 (N.D.Ill.1984) (state has general policy in favor of aviation safety, but it has no interest in enforcing FAA regulations), with Coman v. Thomas Mfg. Co., 325 N.C. 172, 381 S.E.2d 445 (1989) (discharge allegedly for refusing to violate federal safety and recordkeeping requirements); Phipps v. Clark Oil & Refining Corp., 408 N.W.2d 569 (Minn.1987) (service station employee discharged for refusing to violate federal law by pumping leaded gasoline into vehicle designed for only unleaded gasoline states claim); Thompson v. St. Regis Paper Co., 102 Wash.2d 219, 685 P.2d 1081 (1984) (accountant fired for instituting accurate accounting system in compliance with Foreign Corrupt Practices Act of 1977).

Is there a danger that state courts will misconstrue complex federal regulations? Consider Green v. Ralee Engineering Co., 19 Cal.4th 66, 78 Cal.Rptr.2d 16, 960 P.2d 1046 (1998), where the California high court held that the *Tameny* "public policy" cause of action could be based on federal safety regulations of the federal Aviation Authority (FAA)implementing the Federal Aviation Act of 1958 (FAA), 49 U.S.C. formerly § 1301 et seq., now § 40101 et seq. Justice Chin's opinion for the majority states:

> Plaintiff performed the FAA-required inspections on the parts intended for use in Boeing aircraft to further a fundamental public policy: "to ensure that each article produced conforms to the type design and is in a condition for safe operation." (14 C.F.R. § 21.143(a).) Therefore, this regulation-based fundamental public policy may serve as the foundation for plaintiff's *Tameny* claim. * * *

* * *

> * * * By informing defendant that he believed it was shipping defective parts for use in passenger aircraft, plaintiff gave defendant adequate notice that his concern involved potentially significant public policy matters because the FAA requires manufacturers to establish quality control procedures for the component parts they produce (14 C.F.R. § 21.143.) Thus, unlike some cases where an employer's violations of its own procedures does not implicate public policy, the internal quality control procedures at issue in this case are part of a statutory and regulatory scheme established by Congress and the FAA, designed to ensure the manufacture of safe aircraft.

* * *

> To the extent defendant * * * claims that the FAA regulations do not even apply to its operations because it apparently never applied for certification under the FAA provisions, its argument * * * fails at the summary judgment stage of proceedings. If plaintiff's allegations are true, then defendant arguably misinterpreted the safety of the parts shipped to prime manufacturers such as Boeing, on which information

these manufacturers would foreseeably rely for their own certification program. * * *

78 Cal.Rptr.2d at 24–26, 28–29, 960 P.2d at 1054–56, 1058–59.

Justice Baxter's dissent charges the majority with judicial activism, noting in part:

> [T]he majority never explains why a parts manufacturer such as defendant should have thought to focus upon a regulation pertaining to FAA certification and oversight of prime manufacturers. Indeed, the majority apparently are unable to identify any FAA regulation applicable to parts suppliers.

Id. at 34, 960 P.2d at 1064.

9. *Federal Preemption.* In English v. General Electric Co., 496 U.S. 72, 110 S.Ct. 2270, 110 L.Ed.2d 65 (1990), the Supreme Court unanimously held that a state-law intentional infliction of emotional distress claim by a laboratory technician who was allegedly terminated for reporting violations of nuclear-safety standards was not preempted by the antiretaliation provision of § 210 of the Energy Reorganization Act of 1974 (see Stat.Supp.). Relying on the Court's easing of federal preemption principles for state-law claims in nuclear safety disputes in Silkwood v. Kerr–McGee Corp., 464 U.S. 238, 104 S.Ct. 615, 78 L.Ed.2d 443 (1984) (allowing punitive damages for plutonium radiation injuries), Justice Blackmun's opinion notes: "Ordinarily, the mere existence of a federal regulatory or enforcement scheme, even one as detailed as § 210, does not by itself imply pre-emption of state remedies." 496 U.S. at 80. A pre—*English* ruling finds state-law protection of whistleblowing consistent with and not preempted by federal nuclear industry regulatory standards. See Norris v. Lumbermen's Mutual Cas. Co., 881 F.2d 1144 (1st Cir.1989). See also Parten v. Consolidated Freightways Corp., 923 F.2d 580 (8th Cir.1991) (rejecting federal preemption of retaliatory discharge claim of foreman who complained of truck safety based on § 405 of the Surface Transportation Act of 1983); Schweiss v. Chrysler Motors Corp., 922 F.2d 473 (8th Cir.1990) (rejecting OSHA preemption argument in light of *English*); Sargent v. Central National Bank & Trust Co. of Enid, 809 P.2d 1298 (Okl.1991) (bank officer's claim of discharge in retaliation for refusing to destroy or alter bank records not preempted by § 24 (Fifth) of National Bank Act's authorization of bank directors to dismiss officers "at pleasure"). For further discussion of federal preemption, see pp. 1167–98 infra.

10. *Implied Federal Causes of Action.* Whether a court will recognize a federal civil action for discharge in violation of federal statutory norms will turn on whether Congress has signaled an intent to create a right of action. See, e.g., Alexander v. Sandoval, 532 U.S. 275, 287, 121 S.Ct. 1511, 149 L.Ed.2d 517(2001),The Court's earlier approach in Cort v. Ash, 422 U.S. 66, 95 S.Ct. 2080, 45 L.Ed.2d 26 (1975), envisioned a broader policy inquiry into whether private suits would promote the purpose of the legislation. For an illustration of the shift, see, e.g., Le Vick v. Skaggs Companies, Inc., 701 F.2d 777 (9th Cir.1983) (overruling earlier decision that private right of action exists under 15 U.S.C. § 1674(a) for discharge of an employee because his wages had been subjected to garnishment). See also note 2, p. 681 supra.

D. REFUSAL TO VIOLATE ETHICAL OBLIGATIONS

PIERCE v. ORTHO PHARMACEUTICAL CORP.

Supreme Court of New Jersey, 1980.
84 N.J. 58, 417 A.2d 505.

Pollock, J.

Ortho specializes in the development and manufacture of therapeutic and reproductive drugs. Dr. Pierce is a medical doctor who was first employed by Ortho in 1971 as an Associate Director of Medical Research. She signed no contract except a secrecy agreement, and her employment was not for a fixed term. She was an employee at will. In 1973, she became the Director of Medical Research/Therapeutics, one of three major sections of the Medical Research Department. Her primary responsibilities were to oversee development of therapeutic drugs and to establish procedures for testing those drugs for safety, effectiveness, and marketability. Her immediate supervisor was Dr. Samuel Pasquale, Executive Medical Director.

In the spring of 1975, Dr. Pierce was the only medical doctor on a project team developing loperamide, a liquid drug for treatment of diarrhea in infants, children, and elderly persons. The proposed formulation contained saccharin. Although the concentration was consistent with the formula for loperamide marketed in Europe, the project team agreed that the formula was unsuitable for use in the United States. An alternative formulation containing less saccharin might have been developed within approximately three months.

By March 28, however, the project team, except for Dr. Pierce, decided to continue with the development of loperamide. That decision was made apparently in response to a directive from the Marketing Division of Ortho. This decision meant that Ortho would file an investigational new drug application (IND) with the Federal Food and Drug Administration (FDA), continuing laboratory studies on loperamide, and begin work on a formulation. FDA approval is required before any new drug is tested clinically on humans. 21 U.S.C. § 355; 21 C.F.R. §§ 310.3 *et seq.* Therefore, loperamide would be tested on patients only if the FDA approved the saccharin formulation.

Dr. Pierce knew that the IND would have to be filed with and approved by the FDA before clinical testing could begin. Nonetheless, she continued to oppose the work being done on loperamide at Ortho. On April 21, 1975, she sent a memorandum to the project team expressing her disagreement with its decision to proceed with the development of the drug. In her opinion, there was no justification for seeking FDA permission to use the drug in light of medical controversy over the safety of saccharin.

Dr. Pierce met with Dr. Pasquale on May 9 and informed him that she disagreed with the decision to file an IND with the FDA. She felt that by continuing to work on loperamide she would violate her interpretation of the Hippocratic oath. She concluded that the risk that saccharin might be harmful should preclude testing the formula on children or elderly persons, especially when an alternative formulation might soon be available.

Dr. Pierce recognized that she was joined in a difference of "viewpoints" or "opinion" with Dr. Pasquale and others at Ortho concerning the use of a formula containing saccharin. In her opinion, the safety of saccharin in loperamide pediatric drops was medically debatable. She acknowledged that Dr. Pasquale was entitled to his opinion to proceed with the IND. On depositions, she testified concerning the reason for her difference of opinion about the safety of using saccharin in loperamide pediatric drops:

> Q. That was because in your medical opinion that was an unsafe thing to do. Is that so?
>
> A. No. I didn't know. The question of saccharin was one of potential harm. It was controversial. Even though the rulings presently look even less favorable for saccharin it is still a controversial issue.

After their meeting on May 9, Dr. Pasquale informed Dr. Pierce that she would no longer be assigned to the loperamide project. On May 14, Dr. Pasquale asked Dr. Pierce to choose other projects. After Dr. Pierce returned from vacation in Finland, she met on June 16 with Dr. Pasquale to discuss other projects, but she did not choose a project at that meeting. She felt she was being demoted, even though her salary would not be decreased. Dr. Pierce summarized her impression of that meeting in her letter of resignation submitted to Dr. Pasquale the following day. In that letter, she stated:

> Upon learning in our meeting June 16, 1975, that you believe I have not 'acted as a Director', have displayed inadequacies as to my competence, responsibility, productivity, inability to relate to the Marketing Personnel, that you, and reportedly Dr. George Braun and Mr. Verne Willaman consider me to be non-promotable and that I am now or soon will be demoted, I find it impossible to continue my employment at Ortho.

The letter made no specific mention of her difference of opinion with Dr. Pasquale over continuing the work on loperamide. Nonetheless, viewing the matter most favorably to Dr. Pierce, we assume the sole reason for the termination of her employment was the dispute over the loperamide project. Dr. Pasquale accepted her resignation.

In her complaint, which was based on principles of tort and contract law, Dr. Pierce claimed damages for the termination of her employment. Her complaint alleged:

> The Defendant, its agents, servants and employees requested and demanded Plaintiff follow a course of action and behavior which was impossible for Plaintiff to follow because of the Hippocratic oath she

had taken, because of the ethical standards by which she was governed as a physician, and because of the regulatory schemes, both federal and state, statutory and case law, for the protection of the public in the field of health and human well-being, which schemes Plaintiff believed she should honor.

However, she did not specify that testing would violate any state or federal statutory regulation. Similarly, she did not state that continuing the research would violate the principles of ethics of the American Medical Association. She never contended her participation in the research would expose her to a claim for malpractice.

* * *

As discussed below, our careful examination of Dr. Pierce's allegations and the record reveals no genuine issue of material fact requiring disposition at trial. Although this case raises important policy considerations, all the relevant facts are before us, and there is no reason to defer a decision. Accordingly, we reverse the Appellate Division and reinstate the summary judgment in favor of defendant.

* * *

In recognizing a cause of action to provide a remedy for employees who are wrongfully discharged, we must balance the interests of the employee, the employer, and the public. Employees have an interest in knowing they will not be discharged for exercising their legal rights. Employers have an interest in knowing they can run their businesses as they see fit as long as their conduct is consistent with public policy. The public has an interest in employment stability and in discouraging frivolous lawsuits by dissatisfied employees.

Although the contours of an exception are important to all employees at will, this case focuses on the special considerations arising out of the right to fire an employee at will who is a member of a recognized profession. One writer has described the predicament that may confront a professional employed by a large corporation:

> Consider, for example, the plight of an engineer who is told that he will lose his job unless he falsifies his data or conclusions, or unless he approves a product which does not conform to specifications or meet minimum standards. Consider also the dilemma of a corporate attorney who is told, say in the context of an impending tax audit or antitrust investigation, to draft backdated corporate records concerning events which never took place or to falsify other documents so that adverse legal consequences may be avoided by the corporation; and the predicament of an accountant who is told to falsify his employer's profit and loss statement in order to enable the employer to obtain credit. [Blades, Employment at Will vs. Individual Freedom: On Limiting the Abusive Exercise of Employer Power, 67 Colum.L.Rev. 1404, 1408–09 (1967).]

Employees who are professionals owe a special duty to abide not only by federal and state law, but also by the recognized codes of ethics of their professions. That duty may oblige them to decline to perform acts required by their employers. However, an employee should not have the right to prevent his or her employer from pursuing its business because the employee perceives that a particular business decision violates the employee's personal morals, as distinguished from the recognized code of ethics of the employee's profession. *See* Comment, 28 *Vand.L.Rev.* 805, 832 (1975).

We hold that an employee has a cause of action for wrongful discharge when the discharge is contrary to a clear mandate of public policy. The sources of public policy include legislation; administrative rules, regulations or decisions; and judicial decisions. In certain instances, a professional code of ethics may contain an expression of public policy. However, not all such sources express a clear mandate of public policy. For example, a code of ethics designed to serve only the interests of a profession or an administrative regulation concerned with technical matters probably would not be sufficient. Absent legislation, the judiciary must define the cause of action in case-by-case determinations. An employer's right to discharge an employee at will carries a correlative duty not to discharge an employee who declines to perform an act that would require a violation of a clear mandate of public policy. However, unless an employee at will identifies a specific expression of public policy, he may be discharged with or without cause.

* * *

We now turn to the question whether Dr. Pierce was discharged for reasons contrary to a clear mandate of public policy. As previously stated, granting Ortho's motion for summary judgment is appropriate at this juncture only if there is no genuine issue as to any material fact.

The material facts are uncontroverted. In opposing the motion for summary judgment, Dr. Pierce did not contend that saccharin was harmful, but that it was controversial. Because of the controversy she said she could not continue her work on loperamide. Her supervisor, Dr. Pasquale, disagreed and thought that research should continue.

As stated above, before loperamide could be tested on humans, an IND had to be submitted to the FDA to obtain approval for such testing. 21 U.S.C. § 355. The IND must contain complete manufacturing specifications, details of pre-clinical studies (testing on animals) which demonstrate the safe use of the drug, and a description of proposed clinical studies. The FDA then has 30 days to withhold approval of testing. 21 C.F.R. § 312.1. Since no IND had been filed here, and even giving Dr. Pierce the benefit of all doubt regarding her allegations, it is clear that clinical testing of loperamide on humans was not imminent.

Dr. Pierce argues that by continuing to perform research on loperamide she would have been forced to violate professional medical ethics expressed in the Hippocratic oath. She cites the part of the oath that reads: "I will prescribe regimen for the good of my patients according to my ability and my judgment and never do harm to anyone." Clearly, the general language of the oath does not prohibit specifically research that does not involve tests on humans and that cannot lead to such tests without governmental approval.

We note that Dr. Pierce did not rely on or allege violation of any other standards, including the "codes of professional ethics" advanced by the dissent. Similarly, she did not allege that continuing her research would constitute an act of medical malpractice or violate any statute, including N.J.S.A. 45:9–16(h).

In this case, Dr. Pierce has never contended that saccharin would necessarily cause harm to anyone. She alleged that the current controversy made continued investigation an unnecessary risk. However when she stopped work on loperamide, there was no risk. Our point here is not that participation in unethical conduct must be imminent before an employee may refuse to work. The more relevant consideration is that Dr. Pierce does not allege that preparation and filing of the IND was unethical. Further Dr. Pierce does not suggest that Ortho would have proceeded with human testing without FDA approval. The case would be far different if Ortho had filed the IND, the FDA had disapproved it, and Ortho insisted on testing the drug on humans. The actual facts are that Dr. Pierce could not have harmed anyone by continuing to work on loperamide.

Viewing the matter most favorably to Dr. Pierce, the controversy at Ortho involved a difference in medical opinions. Dr. Pierce acknowledged that Dr. Pasquale was entitled to his opinion that the oath did not forbid work on loperamide. Nonetheless, implicit in Dr. Pierce's position is the contention that Dr. Pasquale and Ortho were obliged to accept her opinion. Dr. Pierce contends, in effect, that Ortho should have stopped research on loperamide because of her opinion about the controversial nature of the drug.

Dr. Pierce espouses a doctrine that would lead to disorder in drug research. Under her theory, a professional employee could redetermine the propriety of a research project even if the research did not involve a violation of a clear mandate of public policy. Chaos would result if a single doctor engaged in research were allowed to determine, according to his or her individual conscience, whether a project should continue. *Cf. Report of the Ad Hoc Committee on the Principles of Medical Ethics,* American Medical Association 3 (1979). An employee does not have a right to continued employment when he or she refuses to conduct research simply because it would contravene his or her personal morals. An employee at will who refuses to work for an employer in answer to a call of conscience should recognize that other employees and their employer might heed a different call. However, nothing in this opinion should be construed to restrict the right of an employee at will to refuse to work on a project that he or she believes is unethical. In sum, an employer may discharge an employee who refuses to work unless the refusal is based on a clear mandate of public policy.

PASHMAN, J., dissenting.

The majority's analysis recognizes that the ethical goals of professional conduct are of inestimable social value. By maintaining informed standards of conduct, licensed professions bring to the problems of their public responsibilities the same expertise that marks their calling. The integrity of codes of professional conduct that result from this regulation deserves judicial protection from undue economic pressure. Employers are a potential source of this pressure, for they can provide or withhold—until today, at their whim—job security and the means of enhancing a professional's reputation. Thus, I completely agree with the majority's ruling that "an employee has a cause of action for wrongful discharge when the discharge is contrary to a clear mandate of public policy" as expressed in a "professional code of ethics."

* * *

Three * * * points made by the majority require discussion, for they reflect the majority's failure to follow the well-established rule that the claims of a party opposing summary judgment are to be "indulgently treated" * * *. The first is the majority's characterization of the effect of plaintiff's ethical position. It appears to believe that Dr. Pierce had the power to determine whether defendant's proposed development program would continue at all. This is not the case, nor is plaintiff claiming the right to halt defendant's development efforts. Interpreted "indulgently," yet realistically, plaintiff claims only the right to her professional autonomy. She contends that she may not be discharged for expressing her view that the clinical program is unethical or for refusing to continue her participation in the project. She has done nothing else to impede continued development of defendant's proposal; moreover, it is undisputed that defendant was able to continue its program by reassigning personnel. Thus, the majority's view that granting doctors a right to be free from abusive discharges would confer on any one of them complete veto power over desirable drug development is ill-conceived.

The second point concerns the role of governmental approval of the proposed experimental program. In apparent ignorance of the past failures of official regulation to safeguard against pharmaceutical horrors, the majority implies that the necessity for administrative approval for human testing eliminates the need for active, ethical professionals within the drug industry. * * * But we do not know whether the United States Food and Drug Administration (FDA) would be aware of the safer alternative to the proposed drug when it would pass upon defendant's application for the more hazardous formula. The majority professes no such knowledge. We must therefore assume the FDA would have been left in ignorance. This highlights the need for ethically autonomous professionals within the pharmaceutical industry—a need which the majority's approach does nothing to satisfy.

The final point to which I must respond is the majority's observation that plaintiff expressed her opposition prematurely, before the FDA had approved clinical experimentation. * * * Essentially, the majority holds that a professional employee may not express a refusal to engage in illegal or clearly unethical conduct until his actual participation and the resulting harm is imminent. This principle grants little protection to the ethical autonomy of professionals that the majority proclaims. Would the majority have Dr. Pierce wait until the first infant was placed before her, ready to receive the first dose of a drug containing 44 times the concentration of saccharin permitted in 12 ounces of soda? The majority minimizes the scope of plaintiff's ethical obligation. The "clear mandate of public policy" was no less clear when she made known her opposition and refusal to participate. A professional's opposition to unethical conduct should not be considered untimely when its unethical nature is apparent. By contrast, the majority's requirement that proposed conduct be imminent would require, for example, an associate in a law firm to withhold his opposition to the preparation of perjured testimony or false evidence, see *DR* 7–102(A)(4), (5) & (6), until he is actually ordered to begin the preparation. This narrow view of an employee's duty to obey codes of ethics does little to promote such clear mandates of public policy. It will allow unscrupulous employers to forestall discussion on proposed unethical conduct, and to evade the spirit of the majority's new principle by carefully timing such conduct to prevent meaningful dissent.

Notes and Questions

1. Given the New Jersey Supreme Court's reasoning in *Pierce,* under what circumstances would Dr. Pierce have been justified in (i) expressing her concerns to her superiors; (ii) refusing to work further on a particular project; or (iii) reporting her objections to the FDA?

2. *Professional Norms as a Source of "Public Policy"? Pierce* raises the question whether "public policy" may be found in sources other than state constitutional, statutory, or administrative provisions. What justification is there for incorporating private professional codes of ethics into the public policy of a state? Employers may not like particular labor laws, but they participate in the democratic process of selecting the members of the legislature that enact such laws. Are professional associations acting in some sense on behalf of the state, as proxy regulators for the state? Are there reasons why society might wish to protect the autonomy even of professionals who are employed in corporations? For a particularly insightful discussion, see General Dynamics Corp. v. Superior Ct., 7 Cal.4th 1164, 32 Cal.Rptr.2d 1, 876 P.2d 487 (1994). See also Elliot Freidson, Professional Powers (1986); Note, A Remedy for the Discharge of Professional Employees Who Refuse to Perform Unethical or Illegal Acts: A Proposal in Aid of Professional Ethics, 28 Vand.L.Rev. 805 (1975). Would Dr. Pierce have stated a "public policy" cause of action if Ortho had forced her to conduct research that would have exposed her to a claim of professional malpractice under AMA standards?

3. *Promoting Drug Safety or Hamstringing Drug Research?* Should Dr. Pierce have been protected from discharge if, while continuing work on the loperamide project, she informed the FDA that the company could have produced a safer alternative formula? Would protection of professional autonomy in such a case promote the release of information concerning the potential risks of a product like a new drug? On the one hand, government regulators are limited in their ability independently to assess the safety of a new drug or product and hence are critically dependent on the information they receive from regulated firms. Creation of a privilege of professional dissent might well aid the government's regulatory objectives. On the other hand, protection of the confidentiality of internal company deliberations and research may help encourage the development of drugs that produce substantial benefits. A drug may promote the well-being of the vast majority of its intended users while causing great harm to a small subset of users whose characteristics may not be readily identifiable at the early stages of a drug's development and use. Where safety is a matter of such probabilistic risk-assessment, is it clearly violative of public policy to permit an employer to insist that the professionals it employs, while free to vent disagreements internally, not discuss those disagreements outside the firm? Who should be making the decision on the proper role of professional "watchdogs"? The professional association? The state courts? The state legislature? The FDA? See generally Whistleblowing in Biomedical Research (J. Swazey and S. Scher eds. 1981).

4. *Professional Norms as Source of Public Policy or Internal Regulation?* The *Pierce* court drew a distinction between professional norms that "contain an expression of public policy" and "a code of ethics designed to serve only the interests of a profession or an administrative regulation concerned with technical matters * * *." In Warthen v. Toms River Hospital, 199 N.J.Super. 18, 488 A.2d 229, appeal denied, 101 N.J. 255, 501 A.2d 926 (1985), a nurse claimed that ethical considerations in the Code for Nurses supported her refusal to dialyze a terminally-ill patient. The Code provided in relevant part:

> The nurse's concern for human dignity and the provision of quality nursing care is not limited by personal attitudes or beliefs. If personally opposed to the delivery of care in a particular case because of the nature of the health problem or the procedures to be used, the nurse is justified in refusing to participate. Such refusal should be made known in advance and in time for other appropriate arrangements to be made for the client's nursing care.

The state intermediate appellate court held that this passage "defines a standard of conduct beneficial only to the individual nurse and not to the public at large. The overall purpose of the language cited by plaintiff is to preserve human dignity; however, it should not be at the expense of the patient's life or contrary to the family's wishes." 199 N.J.Super. at 27, 488 A.2d at 233.

5. *Relevance of Extensive Government Regulation of Employer.* Should the claim of professional autonomy be rejected when government extensively regulates the conduct of the employer? See Suchodolski v. Michigan Consol. Gas Co., 412 Mich. 692, 316 N.W.2d 710 (1982) (rejecting public policy cause

of action based on Code of Ethics of Institute of Internal Auditors, in view of extensive state regulation of the accounting systems of public utilities and fact that plaintiff did not allege he was discharged for falsifying reports to regulatory commission). Would Dr. Pierce have had a cause of action had there been no expectation of FDA review before the drug would be tested on humans?

6. *In-House Counsel's Duty of Loyalty to the Firm?* On the legal professional's duty of loyalty, see, e.g., Balla v. Gambro, 145 Ill.2d 492, 164 Ill.Dec. 892, 584 N.E.2d 104 (Ill. 1991) (attorney-client privilege bars retaliatory discharge suit even though in-house counsel had operational as well as legal responsibilities and his disclosures led to FDA removal of defective dialyzers from market); Herbster v. North American Co. for Life & Health Insur., 150 Ill.App.3d 21, 103 Ill.Dec. 322, 501 N.E.2d 343, appeal denied, 114 Ill.2d 545, 108 Ill.Dec. 417, 508 N.E.2d 728 (1987) (in-house counsel allegedly fired for refusing to destroy records sought in discovery failed to state claim). In July 1990, Governor Thompson of Illinois vetoed a bill that would have overturned *Herbster,* explaining that the proposed law would have fundamentally altered the lawyer-client relationship for only one class of lawyers—in-house counsel.

A number of courts have permitted in-house counsel to pursue "public policy" damages actions against their former employer-clients. See GTE Products Corp. v. Stewart, 421 Mass. 22, 653 N.E.2d 161, 166 (Mass. 1995) (retaliatory discharge claim lies "if it depends on 1) explicit and unequivocal statutory or ethical norms, 2) [that] embody policies of importance to the public at large in the circumstances of the particular case, and 3) the claim can be proved without any violation of the attorney's obligation to respect client confidences and secrets."); General Dynamics Corp. v. Superior Ct. of San Bernardino Co., 7 Cal.4th 1164, 32 Cal.Rptr.2d 1, 876 P.2d 487 (1994) (provided cause of action can be maintained without breaching attorney-client privilege or "unduly endangering the values lying at the heart of the professional relationship"); Nordling v. Northern States Power Co., 478 N.W.2d 498 (Minn.1991) (alleged retaliation for opposing firm proposal to conduct "personal lifestyle" surveillance of employees); Shearin v. E.F. Hutton Group, Inc., 652 A.2d 578 (Del.Ch.1994) (in-house counsel fired for attempting to expose impropriety by corporate parent); Mourad v. Automobile Club Insurance Ass'n, 186 Mich.App. 715, 465 N.W.2d 395 (1991) (alleged retaliatory demotion for refusal to violate ethical duty to policyholders; contract claims also alleged); Parker v. M & T Chemicals, Inc., 236 N.J.Super. 451, 566 A.2d 215 (App.Div.1989) (alleged retaliation for refusing to join scheme to cheat competitor; claim under state whistleblower statute).

The American Bar Association's Model Rule 1.13(b) authorizes in-house counsel to disclose to highest levels of the corporation any act, or refusal to act, "that is a violation of law which might reasonably be imputed to the organization, and is likely to result in substantial injury to the organization." Rule 1.13(b) does not require or authorize disclosure to shareholders or to third parties outside of the firm, even where the highest authority in the organization declines to disclose or remedy such serious wrongdoing. See also "Note on the Sarbanes–Oxley Act of 2002," pp. 721–23 infra.

7. *Professional Obligations and the Implied Covenant of Good Faith and Fair Dealing.* As elaborated in note 5, p. 780 infra, the New York courts have rejected the "public policy" cause of action in Murphy v. American Home Products Corp., 58 N.Y.2d 293, 304–05, 461 N.Y.S.2d 232, 237, 448 N.E.2d 86, 91 (1983), and have narrowly construed the implied covenant of good faith and fair dealing in *Murphy* and Sabetay v. Sterling Drug, Inc., 69 N.Y.2d 329, 514 N.Y.S.2d 209, 506 N.E.2d 919 (1987). However, in Wieder v. Skala, 80 N.Y.2d 628, 593 N.Y.S.2d 752, 609 N.E.2d 105 (1992), a law firm associate fired because he had reported alleged ethical misconduct by a fellow associate stated a violation of an "implied-in-law obligation" inherent in his relationship with his employer.

Wieder's potential reach was narrowed in Horn v. New York Times, 100 N.Y.2d 85, 760 N.Y.S.2d 378, 790 N.E.2d 753 (2003). In that case, the newspaper's associate medical director, whose duties included medical advice to its employees and review of workers' compensation claims filed by employees to determine whether claimed injuries were work-related, alleged she was discharged because she refused to provide her employer with confidential medical records of employees without their consent; plaintiff further alleged that she sought advice from the state's department of health and was informed that such disclosure would violate her legal and ethical duties to patients. The New York high court essentially restricted *Wieder* to cases involving lawyer's ethical duties, where the judiciary plays a special supervisory role.

8. *Malpractice Liability for Nondisclosure of Improper Practices?* Some professionals may be subject to liability if they fail to disclose improper practices. See generally George C. Harris, Taking the Entity Theory Seriously: Lawyer Liability for Failure to Prevent Harm to Organizational Clients Through Disclosure of Constituent Wrongdoing, 11 Geo. J. Leg. Eth. 598 (1998); Joseph I. Goldstein & Catherine Dixon, New Teeth for the Public's Watchdog: The Expanded Role of the Independent Accountant in Detecting, Preventing, and Reporting Financial Fraud, 44 Bus.Lawy. 439 (Feb. 1989).

E. WHISTLEBLOWERS

GEARY v. UNITED STATES STEEL CORP.

Supreme Court of Pennsylvania, 1974.
456 Pa. 171, 319 A.2d 174.

POMEROY, J.

The complaint avers that appellant, George B. Geary, was continuously employed by appellee, United States Steel Corporation (hereinafter "company"), from 1953 until July 13, 1967, when he was dismissed from his position. Geary's duties involved the sale of tubular products to the oil and gas industry. His employment was at will. The dismissal is said to have stemmed from a disagreement concerning one of the company's new products, a tubular casing designed for use under high pressure. Geary alleges that he believed the product had not been adequately tested and constituted a serious danger to anyone who used it; that he voiced his misgivings to his superiors and was ordered to "follow directions", which he agreed to do; that he nevertheless continued to express his reservations, taking his case to a vice-president in charge of sale of the product; that as a result of his efforts the product was reevaluated and withdrawn from the market; that he at all times performed his duties to the best of his ability and always acted with the best interests of the company and the general public in mind; and that because of these events he was summarily discharged without notice. Geary asserts that the company's conduct in so acting was "wrongful, malicious and abusive", resulting in injury to his reputation in the industry, mental anguish, and direct financial harm, for which he seeks both punitive and compensatory damages.[2]

The case having been dismissed on a demurrer, all properly pleaded facts are taken as admitted for the purpose of testing the sufficiency of the complaint.[3]

* * *

* * * The facts alleged show only that there was a dispute over the merits of the new product; that Geary vigorously expressed his own point of view in the matter, by-passing his immediate superiors and taking his case to a company vice-president, and that he was ultimately discharged. There is nothing here from which we could infer that the company fired Geary for the specific purpose of causing him harm, or coercing him to break any law[9] or otherwise to compromise himself. According to his own averments, Geary had already won his own battle within the company. The most natural inference from the chain of events recited in the complaint is that Geary had made a nuisance of himself, and the company discharged him to preserve administrative order in its own house. * * *

Appellant's final argument is an appeal to considerations of public policy. Geary asserts in his complaint that he was acting in the best interests of the general public as well as of his employer in opposing the marketing of a product which he believed to be defective. Certainly, the potential for abuse of an employer's power of dismissal is particularly serious where an employee must exercise independent, expert judgment in matters of product safety, but Geary does not hold himself out as this sort of employee. So far as the complaint shows, he was involved only in the sale of company products. There is no suggestion that he possessed any expert qualifications, or that his duties extended to making judgments in matters of product safety. In essence, Geary argues that his

2. Following his discharge Geary filed a claim for unemployment benefits with the Bureau of Employment Security. The Unemployment Compensation Board of Review found that Geary was not guilty of willful misconduct in the company's employ, and allowed the claim. * * *

3. The company in its brief denies that the new product was withdrawn from the market as a result of Geary's efforts, and has offered to prove that it has been marketed successfully without incident for several years. This factual contention is irrelevant at the preliminary objection stage.

9. Appellant suggests in his brief that continued sale of the defective product might have entailed both criminal and civil liability. This is mere speculation, particularly since the product was allegedly withdrawn from the market.

conduct should be protected because his intentions were good. No doubt most employees who are dismissed from their posts can make the same claim. We doubt that establishing a right to litigate every such case as it arises would operate either in the best interest of the parties or of the public.

Given the rapidity of change in corporate personnel in the areas of employment not covered by labor agreements, suits like the one at bar could well be expected to place a heavy burden on our judicial system in terms of both an increased case load and the thorny problems of proof which would inevitably be presented. We agree with appellant, however, that these considerations do not in themselves justify denying a legal forum to a plaintiff with a justiciable claim. See *Niederman v. Brodsky*, 436 Pa. 401, 261 A.2d 84 (1970). Of greater concern is the possible impact of such suits on the legitimate interest of employers in hiring and retaining the best personnel available. The ever present threat of suit might well inhibit the making of critical judgments by employers concerning employee qualifications.

The problem extends beyond the question of individual competence, for even an unusually gifted person may be of no use to his employer if he cannot work effectively with fellow employees. Here, for example, Geary's complaint shows that he by-passed his immediate superiors and pressed his views on higher officers, utilizing his close contacts with a company vice president.[14] The praiseworthiness of Geary's motives does not detract from the company's legitimate interest in preserving its normal operational procedures from disruption.[15] In sum, while we agree that employees should be encouraged to express their educated views on the quality of their employer's products, we are not persuaded that creating a new non-statutory cause of action of the sort proposed by appellant is the best way to achieve this result. On balance, whatever public policy imperatives can be discerning here seem to militate against such a course.

ROBERTS, J., dissenting.

In the particular circumstances of this case, appellant's discharge demonstrates the arbitrary dismissal power exercisable by an employer.

14. " * * * [T]he claimant was critical of the program and objected to his superiors * * *. [He] was ordered to follow directions and agreed that he would do so even though he was still opposed to the program * * *. [He] took the problem to a vice president of the company with whom he was in close contact and as a result of re-evaluation the program was withdrawn * * *." Findings of Fact of Unemployment Compensation Board, attached to and made a part of the amended complaint as Exhibit "A". In pursuing this course, Geary exceeded any duty imposed on him under the rule of the Restatement (Second) of Agency § 381: Duty to Give Information, cited in the dissenting opinion. We do not conceive that § 381 bears any relation to the case before us.

15. We see no basis for inferring that Geary's discharge was a spiteful retaliatory gesture designed to punish him for noticing and calling attention to the asserted defect in the company's product. This is particularly true in view of the fact that the product was withdrawn from the market. It does not follow that, because Geary's motives were good, the company's motives in discharging him were bad. In scrutinizing the complaint we are not required to put aside our common sense or attribute to parties a perversity which the facts alleged do not warrant.

The managers of this publicly-held corporation determined that George B. Geary should be dismissed because he called to the attention of his superiors that the steel pipe manufactured by his employer and which Geary was required to sell was a defective and dangerous product. His suggestion that the unsafe steel pipe be withdrawn from the market to protect both the public from danger and his employer from liability was in complete harmony with his employer's best interest. Nevertheless, Geary was discharged.

As a salesman, Geary was required to know intimately the products he was selling. He represented United States Steel and it was expected that he would be alert to protect his employer's reputation. Likewise, it was natural that he would seek to shield himself and his employer from the consequences of a dangerous product. When he correctly recognized that the defective steel pipe had strong potential for causing injury and damage, he immediately notified his superiors. His reward for loyalty was dismissal. Of course, had Geary not informed his superiors of the defective product, he may well have been discharged for his failure to do so.

Geary's assessment of the danger of the steel pipe was correct, since after his notification, the corporation removed the steel pipe from the market. On these pleadings, it is manifestly clear that the employer realized Geary was right and that its interest lay in withdrawing from the market the dangerous product. Despite Geary's candor in seeking within the corporation family to advance the corporation's best interest, his employer fired him.

There is no doubt that strong public policies of this Commonwealth have been offended by Geary's discharge. First, the product asserted by appellant to be defective was, after appellant notified his superiors, withdrawn from the market. The manufacture and distribution of defective and potentially dangerous products does not serve either the public's or the employer's interest. Our courts have granted relief to those injured by defective merchandise. E.g., *Kassab v. Central Soya*, 432 Pa. 217, 246 A.2d 848 (1968); *Webb v. Zern*, 422 Pa. 424, 220 A.2d 853 (1966). See Restatement (Second) of Torts § 402A (1965). The majority, however, fails to perceive that the prevention of injury is a fundamental and highly desirable objective of our society.

Second, appellant as an employee was "subject to a duty to use reasonable efforts to give his [employer] information which is relevant to affairs entrusted to him, and which, as the [employee] has notice, the [employer] would desire to have and which can be communicated without violating a superior duty to a third person." Restatement (Second) of Agency § 381 (1958). Had Geary refrained from notifying his superiors of the defective product, he could have been discharged for violating this duty to come forward with information. No responsible policy is served which permits an employee to be discharged solely for obeying his legal duty to communicate information to his superiors. Indeed, the policy underlying this duty to communicate is frustrated by denying Geary the opportunity to present his case to the court.

PALMATEER v. INTERNATIONAL HARVESTER CO.

Supreme Court of Illinois, 1981.

85 Ill.2d 124, 52 Ill.Dec. 13, 421 N.E.2d 876.

SIMON, J.

The plaintiff, Ray Palmateer, complains of his discharge by International Harvester Company (IH). He had worked for IH for 16 years, rising from a unionized job at an hourly rate to a managerial position on a fixed salary. Following his discharge, Palmateer filed a four-count complaint against IH, alleging in count II that he had suffered a retaliatory discharge. According to the complaint, Palmateer was fired both for supplying information to local law-enforcement authorities that an IH employee might be involved in a violation of the Criminal Code of 1961 (Ill.Rev.Stat.1979, ch. 38, par. 1–1 *et seq.*) and for agreeing to assist in the investigation and trial of the employee if requested. The circuit court of Rock Island County ruled the complaint failed to state a cause of action and dismissed it; the appellate court affirmed in a divided opinion. We granted Palmateer leave to appeal to determine the contours of the tort of retaliatory discharge approved in *Kelsay v. Motorola, Inc.* (1978), 74 Ill.2d 172, 23 Ill.Dec. 559, 384 N.E.2d 353.

* * *

By recognizing the tort of retaliatory discharge, *Kelsay* acknowledged the common law principle that parties to a contract may not incorporate in it rights and obligations which are clearly injurious to the public. * * * But the Achilles heel of the principle lies in the definition of public policy. When a discharge contravenes public policy in any way the employer has committed a legal wrong. However, the employer retains the right to fire workers at will in cases "where no clear mandate of public policy is involved" (*Leach v. Lauhoff Grain Co.,* (1977), 51 Ill.App.3d 1022, 1026, 9 Ill.Dec. 634, 366 N.E.2d 1145). But what constitutes clearly mandated public policy?

There is no precise definition of the term. In general, it can be said that public policy concerns what is right and just and what affects the citizens of the State collectively. It is to be found in the State's constitution and statutes and, when they are silent, in its judicial decisions. (*Smith v. Board of Education* (1950), 405 Ill. 143, 147, 89 N.E.2d 893.) Although there is no precise line of demarcation dividing matters that are the subject of public policies from matters purely personal, a survey of cases in other States involving retaliatory discharges shows that a matter must strike at the heart of a citizen's social rights, duties, and responsibilities before the tort will be allowed.

* * *

It is clear that Palmateer has here alleged that he was fired in violation of an established public policy. The claim is that he was discharged for supplying information to a local law-enforcement agency that an IH employee might be violating the Criminal Code, for agreeing to gather further evidence implicating the employee, and for intending to testify at the employee's trial, if it came to that. Because of the procedural posture of the case, these allegations must be accepted as true. (*Fitzgerald v. Chicago Title & Trust Co.* (1978), 72 Ill.2d 179, 187, 20 Ill.Dec. 581, 380 N.E.2d 790.) There is no public policy more basic, nothing more implicit in the concept of ordered liberty (see *Palko v. Connecticut* (1937), 302 U.S. 319, 325, 58 S.Ct. 149, 152, 82 L.Ed. 288, 292), than the enforcement of a State's criminal code. (See *Hewitt v. Hewitt* (1979), 77 Ill.2d 49, 61–62, 31 Ill.Dec. 827, 394 N.E.2d 1204; *Jarrett v. Jarrett* (1979), 78 Ill.2d 337, 345, 36 Ill.Dec. 1, 400 N.E.2d 421.) There is no public policy more important or more fundamental than the one favoring the effective protection of the lives and property of citizens. See Ill. Const.1970, Preamble; *Marbury v. Madison* (1803), 5 U.S. (1 Cranch) 137, 163, 2 L.Ed. 60, 69.

No specific constitutional or statutory provision requires a citizen to take an active part in the ferreting out and prosecution of crime, but public policy nevertheless favors citizen crime-fighters. "Public policy favors the exposure of crime, and the cooperation of citizens possessing knowledge thereof is essential to effective implementation of that policy. Persons acting in good faith who have probable cause to believe crimes have been committed should not be deterred from reporting them by the fear of unfounded suits by those accused." (*Joiner v. Benton Community Bank* (1980), 82 Ill.2d 40, 44, 44 Ill.Dec. 260, 411 N.E.2d 229.) Although *Joiner* involved actions for malicious prosecution, the same can be said for the citizen employee who fears discharge. Public policy favors Palmateer's conduct in volunteering information to the law-enforcement agency. Once the possibility of crime was reported, Palmateer was under a statutory duty to further assist officials when requested to do so. (Ill.Rev.Stat.1979, ch. 38, par. 31–8). Public policy thus also favors Palmateer's agreement to assist in the investigation and prosecution of the suspected crime.

The foundation of the tort of retaliatory discharge lies in the protection of public policy, and there is a clear public policy favoring investigation and prosecution of criminal offenses. Palmateer has stated a cause of action for retaliatory discharge.

RYAN, J. * * * dissenting.

Kelsay relied on the fact that the legislature had clearly established the public policy that injured workers had a right to file claims for compensation with the Industrial Commission. We there held that discharging the employee for filing such a claim violated that public policy. Here the public policy supporting the cause of action cannot be found in any expression of the legislature, but only in the vague belief that public policy requires that we all become "citizen crime-fighters" (85 Ill.2d at 132, 52 Ill.Dec. at 17, 421 N.E.2d at 880).

* * *

It is indeed praiseworthy that the plaintiff in our case is interested in ferreting out crime. His complaint, however, does not allege conduct on his part that will bring it within the area of any public policy that has been articulated by the legislature. The plaintiff was not discharged for failing to violate or for complying with the requirements of our obstruction-of-justice statute (Ill.Rev.Stat.1979, ch. 38, par. 31–4), or of the section of our statute concerning refusing to aid an officer (Ill.Rev.Stat. 1979, ch. 38, par. 31–8). * * * If the plaintiff would have been discharged for such a reason, *strong, clear, fundamental* articulated public policy would have been contravened and an action in tort would then be appropriate. The complaint, however, does not even allege that a crime had been committed or that the plaintiff reported to the law-enforcement agency that a crime had been committed. It only alleges that plaintiff was discharged because he reported to a law-enforcement agency that an employee of the defendant *might* be involved in a violation of the criminal code and that he had agreed to assist the law-enforcement agency in gathering further information. It should be remembered that the plaintiff was not a unionized employee, but held a position in management. By assuming the role of a "citizen crime-fighter" undertaking to ferret out crime for the police the plaintiff, through his spying, could seriously affect labor relations of his employer. Also, his conduct, without consulting with the proper management personnel, could impair the company's internal security program. In other words, the plaintiff here had taken it upon himself to become involved in crime fighting when it was neither required by law, nor by his employment, and obviously was against the wishes of his employer.

Notes and Questions

1. *"Active" vs. "Passive" Whistleblowers.* The Pennsylvania high court's ruling in *Geary* reflects the reluctance of some courts, in the absence of an express statute, to extend the "public policy" cause of action to what might be termed "active whistleblowers"—employees who are not being asked to commit unlawful acts, as in *Petermann* and *Tameny,* but who observe unlawful acts being committed by supervisors or their coworkers and wish to report those observations to the firm's higher management or law enforcement authorities. See, e.g., Adler v. American Standard Corp., 830 F.2d 1303 (4th Cir.1987) (assistant general manager of defendant's printing division claimed he was discharged for refusing to include in annual sales projections certain accounts obtained by means of kickbacks; federal diversity court held that "an employment termination motivated by a desire to conceal wrongdoing by preventing its disclosure to higher corporate officers does not violate Maryland's public policy"); Murphy v. American Home Products Corp., 58 N.Y.2d 293, 461 N.Y.S.2d 232, 448 N.E.2d 86 (1983) (assistant treasurer claimed that he was fired in retaliation for having

revealed to corporate officers and directors at least $50 million in illegal account manipulations of secret pension reserves which improperly inflated growth projections); see generally Estreicher & Wolff, supra, 36 Record of Ass'n of Bar of City of New York at 185–87, 192–93.

Do rulings like *Geary, Murphy,* and *Adler* reflect simply a judicial failure of nerve or adherence to outmoded conceptions of employee loyalty? The employees in these cases may have been under no legal duty to report wrongdoing. But is there any reason why the state would not want to further its regulatory objectives by, as it were, deputizing employees as law enforcement agents and hence internalizing regulatory norms? See Christopher Stone, Where the Law Ends: The Social Control of Corporate Behavior 200–14 (1975); Whistle Blowing: The Report of the Conference on Professional Responsibility (R. Nader, P. Petkas & K. Blackwell eds. 1972); Blowing the Whistle: Dissent in the Public Interest (C. Peters & T. Branch eds. 1972).

2. Palmateer's *Holding? Palmateer* seems a somewhat ambiguous ruling in view of the hazy facts presented in the pleadings sustained on demurrer. It is unclear, for example, what crime was committed. Should it matter whether the crime affected third parties or was, rather, an offense against the employer's property?

It is also unclear whether the police initially focused on International Harvester without any prompting from Palmateer and were simply soliciting his assistance. Does *Palmateer* stand only for the proposition that an employee may respond to requests for assistance from law enforcement authorities, without necessarily sanctioning an employee's unsolicited reports to such authorities? But see Barr v. Kelso–Burnett Co., 106 Ill.2d 520, 88 Ill.Dec. 628, 478 N.E.2d 1354, 1356 (1985) (citation omitted) ("In *Palmateer* the public policy of allowing citizens to freely go to the police with information concerning possible criminal conduct was clearly mandated by the enactment of the Criminal Code of 1961 and the need to enforce the Code in order to carry out the purpose behind its enactment."). If the state wants to protect its citizens' cooperation in criminal investigations, why would it not also want to protect their initiation of such investigations? Are there costs to protecting employee-initiated whistleblowing that are not incurred when employees are simply responding candidly to the inquiries of law enforcement agencies? In the absence of legislation, are courts on firmer ground in reading state common law to protect the latter situation and not the former?

3. *Other Rulings Protecting "Active" Whistleblowers.* For other rulings protective of the active whistleblower, see Wholey v. Sears Roebuck, 370 Md. 38, 803 A.2d 482 (2002) (recognizing claim in principle based on criminal statute outlawing retaliation against those reporting crimes, but protecting only reports to appropriate law enforcement authorities); Belline v. K–Mart Corp., 940 F.2d 184 (7th Cir.1991) (protection under Illinois law of employee who reported to management that his supervisor gave away merchandise); Brown v. Physicians Mutual Ins. Co., 679 S.W.2d 836 (Ky.App.1984) (protection of report of regulatory violations to state insurance department); Harless v. First National Bank in Fairmont, 162 W.Va. 116, 246 S.E.2d 270 (1978) (protection of office manager of bank consumer credit department

discharged in retaliation for efforts to bring to attention of employer compliance obligations under state consumer credit statute); cf. Sheets v. Teddy's Frosted Foods, Inc., 179 Conn. 471, 427 A.2d 385 (1980) (protection of employee with quality control responsibility for reporting false and illegal food labeling to supervisor); Sanchez v. Unemployment Ins. Appeals Board, 36 Cal.3d 575, 205 Cal.Rptr. 501, 685 P.2d 61 (1984) (employee subjected to discrimination because of reports to public authorities concerning employer's misuse of public funds had "good cause" to resign and was therefore qualified for unemployment compensation).

4. *"Internal" Whistleblowing.* As the Maryland high court's ruling in *Wholey* illustrates, there is a general judicial reluctance to protect wholly intracorporate disclosures, even though as an initial matter, a requirement of exhaustion of internal remedies might both facilitate compliance and minimize avoidable reputational harm to the employer. Consider also the post-*Palmateer* rulings of the Illinois intermediate courts. Compare Johnson v. World Color Press, Inc., 147 Ill.App.3d 746, 101 Ill.Dec. 251, 498 N.E.2d 575 (5th Dist.1986), appeal denied, 113 Ill.2d 575, 106 Ill.Dec. 47, 505 N.E.2d 353 (1987) (employee should be free to report accounting improprieties to superiors even if no report is made to law enforcement officials), with Zaniecki v. P.A. Bergner & Co., 143 Ill.App.3d 668, 97 Ill.Dec. 756, 493 N.E.2d 419 (3d Dist.1986) (*Palmateer* does not extend to wholly internal disclosure of suspected wrongdoing); but cf. Lanning v. Morris Mobile Meals, Inc., 308 Ill.App.3d 490, 242 Ill.Dec. 173, 720 N.E.2d 1128 (3d Dist. 1999) (without expressly disturbing *Zaniecki*, the court held that plaintiff's complaint of improper food storage necessarily implicated public interests and plaintiff's retaliatory discharge was "not precluded based on her failure to report an alleged health code violation to a public official."). See Belline v. K–Mart Corp., 940 F.2d 184 (7th Cir.1991) (applying Illinois law; siding with majority position among Illinois intermediate courts). Ironically, in Geary's case internal disclosure prompted the company to withdraw the defective product from the market but also permitted the court to characterize the situation as an internal squabble.

Although the California whistleblower statute, Calif.Labor Code § 1102.5, expressly protects active whistleblowers only when they make disclosures to government agencies, some California appellate decisions have recognized a "public policy" tort action for active whistleblowers who confine their disclosures internally within the firm. Compare Collier v. The Superior Court of Los Angeles County, 228 Cal.App.3d 1117, 279 Cal.Rptr. 453 (2d Dist.1991); Verduzco v. General Dynamics, Convair Div., 742 F.Supp. 559 (S.D.Cal.1990), with American Computer Corp. v. Superior Court, 213 Cal.App.3d 664, 668, 261 Cal.Rptr. 796, 798 (4th Dist.1989).

5. *Mode of Internal Disclosure.* Should the method of internal disclosure make a difference? Note that Geary complained to officers superior to his immediate supervisor. If the employer has in place an internal complaint mechanism, must it be utilized by the whistleblowing employee? Cf. Burlington Industries, Inc. v. Ellerth, 524 U.S. 742, 118 S.Ct. 2257, 141 L.Ed.2d 633 (1998); Faragher v. City of Boca Raton, 524 U.S. 775, 118 S.Ct. 2275, 141 L.Ed.2d 662 (1998) (both recognizing an affirmative defense in Title VII cases where supervisors engage in sexual harassment not resulting in a termination or other "tangible employment action," in part to encourage

plaintiffs to minimize harm by utilizing effective internal complaint procedure).

6. *Relevance of Expertise of Whistleblower*. Should courts also make some assessment of the expertise of the employee whistleblower? Note that in *Geary, Adler* and *Murphy* the plaintiffs were making disclosures about matters that were part of the responsibilities of their jobs. Was Geary, a salesman, nevertheless not sufficiently "expert"? See Smith v. Calgon Carbon Corp., 917 F.2d 1338 (3d Cir.1990) (*Geary* extended to internal disclosure of plant operations causing environmental hazard by employee "not charged with the specific responsibility of protecting the public's interest in health and safety").

7. *Nature of Suspected Illegality*. a. *Rules Protecting Shareholders vs. General Public*. Should it matter whether the employee is disclosing a possible violation of a law that is intended to protect the general public, or just the employer or its stockholders? In *Murphy* the stockholders were the victims of the illegal manipulations that the plaintiff exposed. But see "Note on Sarbanes–Oxley Act of 2002," p. 721 infra.

b. *Negligence vs. Intentional Wrongdoing*. What if the plaintiff is "blowing the whistle" not on intentional wrongdoing but on arguably negligent activity, such as the manufacture of a product which the employee believes violates a tort duty of care? Is this a fair characterization of the facts in *Geary?*

8. *Erroneous, Good–Faith Whistleblowing*. Should employees be protected for erroneously, but in good faith, reporting something that would have been illegal had it in fact occurred? If their mistake was one of law, rather than fact? Should the answers differ depending on whether we are dealing with intracorporate disclosure rather than disclosure to public authorities? With nonexpert whistleblowers? With regulatory offenses rather than criminal misconduct? With negligent activity rather than intentional wrongdoing?

9. *First Amendment Protections for Public Employees*. The public employee whistleblower enjoys substantial protection under the first amendment. See, e.g., Monsanto v. Quinn, 674 F.2d 990 (3d Cir.1982) (revenue officer's letters to Tax Division of IRS complaining of poor management and low employee morale); Rookard v. Health and Hospitals Corp., 710 F.2d 41 (2d Cir.1983) (municipal hospital nursing director's complaints of waste and corruption). See also United States v. Garde, 673 F.Supp. 604 (D.D.C.1987), appeal dismissed, 848 F.2d 1307 (D.C.Cir.1988) (associational right of organization that acts as whistleblower informants' advocate infringed by broad subpoena seeking identity of informants). In addition, as explained below, federal sector employees enjoy statutory protection for whistleblowing activities.

Note on Statutory Protection of Whistleblowers

1. *State Legislation*

As reflected in the Statutory Supplement, a growing number of states have passed legislation to protect both passive and active whistleblowing by private-sector employees. See, e.g., West's Ann.Cal.Labor Code § 1102.5; Fla. Stat. § 448.102; Mich.Comp.Laws Ann. §§ 15.361–15.369; Minn. Stat. § 181.932; N.J.Stat.Ann. §§ 34:19–1 et seq.; N.Y.Labor Law, art. 20–C, § 740; 43 Pa.Stat. §§ 1421 et seq. Laws protecting whistleblowing in the public sector are even more common.

The state whistleblower laws exhibit the following features:

(1) *Scope of Coverage.* Whistleblowing may extend to violation of federal as well as state laws, and agency regulations as well as statutes. Coworker misconduct is likely to be covered because most of these laws, like New Jersey's, extend to "any activity, policy or practice" possibly constituting a violation. See Higgins v. Pascack Valley Hospital, 158 N.J. 404, 730 A.2d 327 (1999) (en banc). The New Jersey high court has even ruled that violations of Japanese Petroleum Association guidelines prohibiting the sale of gasoline containing more than 5 percent benzene, a carcinogen, come within the state whistleblower law. See Mehlman v. Mobil Oil Corp., 153 N.J. 163, 707 A.2d 1000 (1998) (sustaining $7 million verdict for former Mobil toxicologist who was discharged for objection to Japanese subsidiary's sale of gasoline containing excessive levels of benzene).

New York's statute is especially narrow, applying only to disclosures of wrongdoing presenting "a substantial and specific danger to public health or safety". See Remba v. Federation Empl. & Guidance Serv., 76 N.Y.2d 801, 559 N.Y.S.2d 961, 559 N.E.2d 655 (1990); Vail–Ballou Press, Inc. v. Tomasky, 266 A.D.2d 662, 698 N.Y.S.2d 98 (3d Dept.1999). The New York law also contains an election-of-remedies provision foreclosing other state-law claims. See Pipas v. Syracuse Home Assn., 226 A.D.2d 1097, 641 N.Y.S.2d 768 (4th Dept.1996).

Similarly, Ohio Rev. Code Ann. § 4113.52 requires reasonable belief "that the violation either is a criminal offense that is likely to cause an imminent risk of physical harm to persons or a hazard to public health or safety or is a felony * * *." See Brooks v. Martin Marietta Utility Serv., 166 F.3d 1213 (6th Cir. 1998) (unpublished) (employee belief of a likely criminal violation, not simply regulatory violation, required).

(2) *Protected Class.* There is typically no limitation on the class of employees who are protected. Hence, even highly placed corporate officers would be able to challenge terminations for whistleblowing. In May 1997, New Jersey's law was amended to cover licensed or certified health care professionals who protest or report what they believe to be improper patient care practices.

(3) *Scienter Requirement.* Most of the laws protect erroneous whistleblowing as long as the plaintiff reasonably believed illegality had occurred. Compare, e.g., 43 Pa.Stat. § 1423(a), with N.Y.Labor Law § 740(6). New York's law has been interpreted, however, to require proof of actual violations. See Bordell v. General Electric Co., 88 N.Y.2d 869, 644 N.Y.S.2d 912, 667 N.E.2d 922 (1996).

(4) *Exhaustion of Internal Remedies.* As a general matter, the statutes carry an obligation to exhaust internal channels of redress before public disclosure. New Jersey provides, however, that "[d]isclosure shall not be

required where the employee is reasonably certain that the activity, policy or practice is known to one or more supervisors of the employer or where the employee reasonably fears physical harm as a result of the disclosure provided, however, that the situation is emergency in nature." Similar exceptions to an exhaustion requirement may be implicit in other statutes. The California statute reaches only disclosure to public authorities, but the courts have extended the common law to reach internal whistleblowing.

(5) *Remedies.* Remedies generally include damages, attorney's fees, and, in some cases, reinstatement.

2. *Whistleblower Provisions in Federal Health and Safety Legislation*

Virtually every federal health and safety law contains an antiretaliation provision which either expressly protects whistleblowing or is capable of being read in this manner. See generally Eugene R. Fidell, Federal Protection of Private Sector Health and Safety Whistleblowers, 2 Admin.L.J. 1 (1988). The federal courts, however, have shown some reluctance to interpret such provisions to cover whistleblowing that is not explicitly protected. For example, the circuits are split over whether nuclear facility inspectors who file intracorporate quality control reports without contacting federal authorities are covered by a provision protecting participation "in any other action to carry out the purposes of" the Energy Reorganization Act, 42 U.S.C. § 5851(a)(3). Compare Brown & Root v. Donovan, 747 F.2d 1029 (5th Cir.1984) (not protected), with Kansas Gas & Electric Co. v. Brock, 780 F.2d 1505 (10th Cir.1985); Mackowiak v. University Nuclear Systems, 735 F.2d 1159 (9th Cir.1984); Consolidated Edison v. Donovan, 673 F.2d 61 (2d Cir.1982).

See also Mayo v. Questech, Inc., 727 F.Supp. 1007 (E.D.Va.1989) (whistleblower protections afforded to employees of Department of Defense contractors, 10 U.S.C. § 2409, are not enforceable by private right of action); Adams v. Dole, 927 F.2d 771 (4th Cir.1991) (whistleblower protections of the Energy Reorganization Act apply only to employees of Nuclear Regulatory Commission (NRC) licensees or applicants for NRC licenses, and their contractors, and hence did not extend to employees of Department of Energy (DOE)-owned nuclear facilities operated by private contractors who must look to internal DOE whistleblowing process).

Rulings holding that flight officers complaining of a discharge for refusal to fly allegedly unsafe aircraft lack protection under the Federal Aviation Act or the regulations of the Federal Aviation Administration. See Buethe v. Britt Airlines, Inc., 749 F.2d 1235 (7th Cir.1984); Pavolini v. Bard–Air Corp., 645 F.2d 144 (2d Cir.1981), would seem superseded by the 1999 "Whistleblower Protection Program" (WPP) amendment to the Airline Deregulation Act, 49 U.S.C. § 42121. The WPP requires the filing of a complaint with the Secretary of Labor, id. § 42121(b)(1), and does not appear to authorize a private right of action. For discussion of the general problem, see Peter R. Marksteiner, The Flying Whistleblower: It's Time for Federal Statutory Protection for Aviation Industry Workers, 25 J. Legis. 39 (1999) (discussing White House Commission on Aviation Safety and Security, Final Report to President Clinton).

Federal preemption of state whistleblower protection may be an issue in some cases. See, e.g., Branche v. Airtran Airways, Inc., 342 F.3d 1248 (11th Cir. 2003) (state retaliatory discharge action was not preempted by Airline Deregulation Act, 49 U.S.C. § 41713, whose preemptive force is limited to matters relating to airline prices, routes or services; 1999 WPP amendment to the Act, 49 U.S.C. § 42121, did not expand preemptive scope of the Deregulation Act); Botz v. Omni Air Int'l, 286 F.3d 488, 496 (8th Cir. 2002) (invocation of state whistleblower law by flight attendant refusing a flight assignment for safety reasons held preempted by Deregulation Act because state law claim would interfere with "carrier's ability to provide its scheduled services"). The general issue of coordination between federal and state remedies in this area is surveyed in Trystan Phifer O'Leary, Silencing the Whistleblower: The Gap Between Federal and State Retaliatory Discharge Laws, 85 Iowa L. Rev. 663 (2000).

3. *Federal Civil Service Sector*

As a result of the Civil Service Reform Act of 1978 (CSRA), 5 U.S.C. § 2301 et seq., federal employees are protected from reprisals for whistleblowing. Title I of the CSRA provides:

> Employees should be protected against reprisal for the lawful disclosure of information which the employees reasonably believe evidences—
>
> (A) a violation of any law, rule, or regulation, or
>
> (B) mismanagement, a gross waste of funds, an abuse of authority, or a substantial danger to public health or safety.

Id. § 2301(b)(9). "[P]rohibited personnel practices" include actions taken in retaliation for whistleblowing, id. § 2302(b)(8), and those taken as a reprisal "for the exercise of any appeal right granted by any law, rule, or regulation," id. § 2302(b)(9). Challenges to adverse personnel decisions may be brought by individual employees to the Merit Systems Protections Board (MSPB) for final administrative determination. Alternatively, in the case of nontenured employees, the Special Counsel may petition the MSPB for "corrective action" against agencies or employees engaged in prohibited personnel practices. The courts have generally held that there is no private right of action; redress must be sought either through an appeal of agency action to the MSPB or through a petition for corrective action with the Special Counsel. See Borrell v. United States International Communications Agency, 682 F.2d 981 (D.C.Cir.1982). This legislation is usefully described in Robert G. Vaughn, Statutory Protection of Whistleblowers in the Federal Executive Branch, 1982 U.Ill.L.Rev. 615.

In April 1989, President Bush signed the Whistleblower Protection Act of 1989, Pub.L. 101–12, 103 Stat. 16, which seeks to strengthen the CSRA whistleblower provisions in a number of respects, the most important of which are as follows: First, the Office of Special Counsel is reconstituted as an independent agency charged with the responsibility for protecting whistleblowing employees (rather than protecting the merit system) and empowered to investigate and initiate corrective action. Second, while employees generally must first seek the assistance of the Special Counsel, they now have an independent right of action to seek corrective action from the MSPB should the Special Counsel decline to act on their behalf. Third, in the proceeding before the MSPB, the burden of proof has been eased to enable the employee to establish a prima facie case by demonstrating that his or her disclosure was "a contributing factor in the personnel decision," while placing on the agency the burden of proving its affirmative defense "by clear and convincing evidence that it would have taken the same personnel action in the absence of such disclosure." Finally, employees who are prevailing parties in the MSPB proceeding are entitled to attorney's fees. For a discussion of the relationship between CSRA remedies and the Federal Tort Claims Act, see Rivera v. United States, 924 F.2d 948 (9th Cir.1991). For criticism of the 1989 legislation, see Bruce D. Fisher, The Whistleblower Protection Act of 1989: A False Hope for Whistleblowers, 43 Rutg.L.Rev. 355 (1991).

4. *RICO*

The omnipresent Racketeer Influenced and Corrupt Organizations Act of 1970 (RICO), 18 U.S.C. §§ 1961–1968, may also be of aid to whistleblowers. A federal jury verdict in Kentucky, relying in part on RICO, awarded two former Ashland Oil Inc. executives $70 million after finding they had been wrongfully discharged for protesting illegal payments to Mideast oil middlemen to obtain crude oil after the 1979 Arab oil embargo. See Jury Awards 2 Ashland Oil Ex–Officials $70 Million in Suit Over Their Dismissal, Wall St. J., June 14, 1988, p. 5, col. 1.; Williams v. Hall, 683 F.Supp. 639 (E.D.Ky.1988) (executives have standing to sue). The Supreme Court has held that whistleblowers lack standing under § 1964(c), 18 U.S.C. § 1964(c), in the absence of proof that the relevant injury was caused by the alleged racketeering activities themselves, rather than by retaliation for nonparticipation in or disclosure of such activities. See Beck v. Prupis, 529 U.S. 494, 120 S.Ct. 1608, 146 L.Ed.2d 561 (2000).

Employees have been held to lack standing under the Clayton Act to sue for retaliatory discharge for refusal to engage in anticompetitive practices. See Vinci v. Waste Management, Inc., 80 F.3d 1372, 1376 (9th Cir.1996) ("The loss of a job is not the type of injury that the antitrust laws were designed to prevent.").

5. *"Qui Tam" and Whistleblower Provisions of the False Claims Act*

The civil False Claims Act (FCA), 31 U.S.C. §§ 3729–31, may also provide a means for whistleblowers (or others) to sue employers (or their agents) who present false or fraudulent claims to the government. The suit is in the nature of a *qui tam* action on behalf of the government (which has the right to assume primary responsibility for the suit or, with court approval, seek its dismissal). In 1986, the civil penalty was increased to "not less than $5,000 and not more than $10,000 plus 3 times the amount of damages which the government sustains because of the act of that person," id. § 3729, of which the private plaintiff can recover 15–25%.

As part of the 1986 amendments to the FCA, Congress provided affirmative protection for a limited category of employee whistleblowers:

(h) Any employee who is discharged, demoted, suspended, threatened, harassed, or in any other manner discriminated against in the terms and conditions of employment by his or her employer because of lawful acts done by the employee on behalf of the employee or others in furtherance of an action under this section, including investigation for, initiation of, testimony for, or assistance in an action filed or to be filed under this section, shall be entitled to all relief necessary to make the employee whole. Such relief shall include reinstatement with the same seniority status such employee would have had but for the discrimination, 2 times the amount of back pay, interest on the back pay, and compensation for any special damages sustained as a result of the discrimination, including litigation costs and reasonable attorneys' fees. An employee may bring an action in the appropriate district court of the United States for the relief provided in this subsection. 31 U.S.C. § 3730(h).

Most often, the employee-whistleblower invokes § 3730(h) in tandem with the *qui tam* provisions. Whistleblower protection may be limited, however, to actions taken "in furtherance of an action" under the FCA. This includes lawful investigations conducted by the employee but may not include refusals to perform work assignments. Cf. Hardin v. DuPont Scandinavia, 731 F.Supp. 1202 (S.D.N.Y.1990) ("Plaintiff alleges only that 'she refused to go along with the scheme, and * * * she was cut out of the ongoing coal contracts.' Thus, plaintiff's alleged loss was the result of her refusal to participate in the alleged scheme, not the result of steps taken in furtherance of an action.") (dicta).

The "action filed or to be filed under this section" language of § 3730(h) has generated litigation over whether a cause of action lies where the plaintiff never filed or intended to file a FCA action. In Childree v. UAP/GA AG CHEM, Inc., 92 F.3d 1140 (11th Cir.1996), the plaintiff, responsible for billing customers, raised concerns to her supervisors about a request by Varner Bass, a principal customer, to re-bill certain invoices—which plaintiff believed was part of a scheme to defraud the Government. In response to a subpoena to appear before a Department of Agriculture (DOA) hearing, plaintiff reluctantly testified about the re-billing request and turned over copies of the Varner Bass re-billing form. She was subsequently terminated for removing confidential customer files from the company's premises without its authorization. The district court held that plaintiff failed to show "some nexus between her conduct and the furtherance of a potential False Claims Act action," noting that the DOA administrative hearing was not an "action" contemplated by § 3730(h). On appeal, the Eleventh Circuit held that a cause of action under § 3730(h) could be maintained, adopting a "prospective" interpretation of the "filed or to be filed" language "as linking protection to events as they were understood at the time of the investigation or report." Id. at 1144, quoting Neal v. Honeywell, Inc., 33 F.3d 860, 864 (7th Cir.1994). As long as there was a "distinct possibility" of a FCA action when the plaintiff reported what she learned, she could claim protection under § 3730(h):

> Childree concedes that she never even considered filing a § 3730(b) qui tam action, so it is obvious that such an action was never a distinct possibility. The question, then, is whether the government's filing of a § 3730(a) action was a distinct possibility at the time Childree rendered her assistance. We think that summary judgment should not have been granted against Childree on this issue.

92 F.3d at 1146.

Whether the underlying *qui tam* action can be brought will depend on (i) whether the information on which the action was brought was "publicly disclos[ed] * * * in a criminal, civil, or administrative hearing, in a congressional, administrative, or Government Accounting Office report, hearing, audit, or investigation, or from news media"; and (ii) if such "public disclosure" has occurred, whether the plaintiff nevertheless was "an original source of the information." 31 U.S.C. § 3730(e)(4)(A)–(B).

Some decisions have expanded the standing of federal and other government employees to bring *qui tam* actions under the FCA against federal contractors and others who defraud the Government, even though the information was obtained by the federal employees in the course of their employment. Compare United States ex rel. LeBlanc v. Raytheon Co., 913 F.2d 17 (1st Cir.1990) (information acquired by quality assurance specialist for U.S. Defense Contract Administrative Service belonged to the Government because plaintiff's job for the Government was to uncover fraud), with United States ex rel. Findley v. FPC–Boron Employees' Club, 105 F.3d 675 (D.C.Cir.1997) (disappointed vendors complaining of preferential arrangements for employees' club to service vending machines could not sue because the government had previously questioned these arrangements, even though relators added specific information about particular clubs that was not in the public domain); United States ex rel. Hagood v. Sonoma County Water Agency, 929 F.2d 1416 (9th Cir.1991) (information obtained by an assistant district counsel of the Army Corps of Engineers in the course of preparing contract with county water agency was not "publicly disclosed" and hence relator need not show he was an "original source"). See also United States ex rel. Laird v. Lockheed Martin Engineering and Science Servs., 336 F.3d 346 (5th Cir. 2003) (plaintiff learning of employer's failure to report excessive costs to federal agency claimed he was discharged because of his internal inquiry, and filed unsuccessful state wrongful termination action; federal court had jurisdiction under "original source" exception, 31 U.S.C. § 3730(e)(4), even though his federal FCA action was based on information previously disclosed in his state action; the exception is satisfied as long as plaintiff had " 'direct and independent knowledge' " of the " 'information' " on which the allegations in the public disclosure are based"; split in the circuits on this issue).

In State of Vermont Agency of Natural Resources v. United States ex rel. Stevens, 529 U.S. 765, 120 S.Ct. 1858, 146 L.Ed.2d 836 (2000), the Supreme Court held that qui tam relators have article III standing to bring FCA suits because the FCA in effect makes a partial assignment of the Government's claim to the private relator.

Some states have passed statutes modeled after the FCA. See Calif.Government Code § 10548, a part of the Reporting of Improper Government Activities Act of 1986, Stats.1986, ch. 353, §§ 4–5. See Steve Seidenberg, Joining the Feds: States Passing Whistleblower Statutes, National L. J., Jan. 13, 2003, p. A24.

Note on the Sarbanes–Oxley Act of 2002

In July 2002, President George W. Bush signed the Sarbanes–Oxley Act of 2002 mandating sweeping accounting and corporate governance reforms. The Act was passed in reaction to accounting scandals that resulted in the failure of Enron, a major public company, and significant regulatory problems for other corporations. The Act contains two whistleblower provisions, §§ 806 and 1107. Section 806 protects individuals who report or cooperate in the investigation of conduct alleged to violate certain federal securities and antifraud laws, and provides a private civil action, 18 U.S.C.§ 1514A. Section 1107 makes it a felony to intentionally retaliate against individuals who provide a law enforcement officer with "truthful information" concerning the actual or potential commission of "any Federal offense," id. § 1513. Section 806 complaints have to be lodged initially with the U.S. Department of Labor (DOL). See Sarbanes–Oxley Claims Represent Largest Category of Non–Health, Safety Cases for DOL, (BNA) Daily Lab. Rep., No. 237, Dec, 10, 2003, p. A–1.

1. *Section 806—Civil Whistleblower Provision*

a. Scope. Individuals employed by any public company, or its agents, are protected against retaliation "because of any act done" to provide information or assist in an investigation "regarding any conduct which the employee reasonably believes" to violate 18 U.S.C. §§ 1341 (mail fraud), 1343 (fraud by wire, radio or television), 1344 (bank fraud), 1348 (securities fraud), or "any rule or regulation of the Securities and Exchange Commission, or any provision of Federal law relating to fraud against shareholders. . . . " 18 U.S.C. § 1514(a)(1). The information or assistance has to be provided to an investigation conducted by a federal agency, a member of Congress or any committee of Congress, or "a person with supervisory authority over the employee (or such other person working for the employer who has the authority to investigate, discover, or terminate misconduct). . . ." This whistleblower provision does not preempt other federal or state law retaliation claims or collectively bargained rights, 18 U.S.C. § 1514(A)(d).

The Act also contains a "participation" clause, § 1514(a)(2), protecting individuals who "file, cause to be filed, testify, participate in, or otherwise assist in a proceeding filed or about to be filed (with any knowledge of the employer) relating to an alleged violation" of the enumerated federal statutes, rules and regulations. Section 806's structure suggests that the reasonable-belief requirement applies only to § 1514(a)(1) disclosure or assistance, not participation activity under § 1514(a)(2).

b. Procedure. An employee seeking relief under § 806 must file a complaint with the DOL within 90 days of the alleged violation. The Act incorporates procedures and evidentiary standards from the Airline Deregulation Act of 2000, 49 U.S.C. § 42121. Within 60 days of receiving a complaint, DOL is authorized to commence an investigation if there is a reasonable cause to believe a violation has occurred. If so, the Secretary must notify the charged party of the finding and issue a preliminary order curing the alleged violation, reinstating the charging party, and providing other affirmative relief. There is then an opportunity to lodge objections and request a hearing. The Secretary's final order after such hearing is appealable to a court of appeals.

If the Secretary has not issued a final order within 180 days after the filing of a complaint, and the charging party is not responsible for any delay, the charging party may bring a compliance action directly in federal district court.

c. Remedies. An employee prevailing in a § 806 action is entitled to "make whole" relief, including reinstatement, back pay, and "compensation for any special damages sustained as a result of the discrimination, including litigation costs, expert witness fees, and reasonable attorney fees." 18 U.S.C. § 1514A(c). There is no express provision for compensatory or punitive damages.

The Act also authorizes a provisional reinstatement remedy. See generally Samuel Estreicher & Wendy C. Butler, Preliminary Reinstatement Under Sarbanes-Oxley, N.Y.L.J., May 9, 2006, p. 3. In Bechtel v. Competitive Techs., Inc., 369 F.Supp.2d 233 (D.Conn. 2005), vacated, 448 F.3d 469 (2d Cir. 2006), the district court enforced an ALJ order under Sarbanes-Oxley requiring preliminary reinstatement of former vice presidents of a technology company fired after complaining about corporate fraud. The Second Circuit, however, reversed, holding that the district court lacked jurisdiction because the statute did not authorize judicial enforcement of the Secretary's preliminary reinstatement orders.

In Welch v. Cardinal Bankshares Corp., 2005 WL 990535 (Feb. 15, 2005), a case decided before the Second Circuit's decision in *Bechtel*, the Labor Department's ALJ ruled that a bank must reinstate its former chief financial officer who blew the whistle on alleged violations of the Sarbanes-Oxley Act, and also awarded $172,839 in damages and attorney's fees: "Although Welch will be required to report to a CEO and board of directors who have been openly critical of Welch since this litigation was initiated, that circumstance is not sufficiently unusual in the context of a Sarbanes-Oxley whistleblower case to warrant denying him reinstatement."

d. Open Questions. Section 806 presents a number of issues: (1) Can individual agents of the company be sued under § 806? (2) If the complaining party had previously agreed to arbitrate all employment-related disputes, will this arbitration provision be read to encompass § 806 claims? (3) To what extent does the participation clause protect activity prior to the filing of a formal proceeding? (4) Is a whistleblower who provides information that is already publicly known protected under § 806? (5) Which company officials have the requisite "authority to investigate, discover, or terminate misconduct"? To what extent will whistleblowers be protected in making disclosures to coworkers or first-line supervisors?

2. *Section 1107—Criminal Sanctions*

Section 1107 of the Act makes it a felony to "knowingly, with the intention to retaliate, take[] any action harmful to any person, including interference with lawful employment or livelihood of any person, for providing to a law enforcement officer any truthful information relating to the commission or possible commission of any Federal offense." 18 U.S.C.

§ 1513(e). Note that the criminal provision covers disclosures of any violations of federal law, not just employee reports of securities violations or shareholder fraud.

F. ASSERTION OF POLITICAL FREEDOM

NOVOSEL v. NATIONWIDE INSURANCE CO.
United States Court of Appeals, Third Circuit, 1983.
721 F.2d 894.

Adams, J.

Novosel was an employee of Nationwide from December 1966 until November 18, 1981. He had steadily advanced through the company's ranks in a career unmarred by reprimands or disciplinary action. At the time his employment was terminated, he was a district claims manager and one of three candidates for the position of division claims manager.

In late October 1981, a memorandum was circulated through Nationwide's offices soliciting the participation of all employees in an effort to lobby the Pennsylvania House of Representatives. Specifically, employees were instructed to clip, copy, and obtain signatures on coupons bearing the insignia of the Pennsylvania Committee for No–Fault Reform. This Committee was actively supporting the passage of House Bill 1285, the "No–Fault Reform Act," then before the state legislature.

The allegations of the complaint charge that the sole reason for Novosel's discharge was his refusal to participate in the lobbying effort and his privately stated opposition to the company's political stand. Novosel contends that the discharge for refusing to lobby the state legislature on the employer's behalf constituted the tort of wrongful discharge on the grounds it was willful, arbitrary, malicious and in bad faith, and that it was contrary to public policy. Alternatively, the complaint avers a breach of an implied contract promising continued long-term employment so long as Novosel's job performance remained satisfactory. Novosel sought damages, reinstatement and declaratory relief. Nationwide did not file an answer to the complaint; instead it presented a motion to dismiss. Following the submission of briefs on the motion to dismiss, and without benefit of either affidavits or oral argument, the district court granted the motion on January 14, 1983.

* * *

Novosel's tort allegations raise two separate issues: first, whether a wrongful discharge claim is cognizable under Pennsylvania law; second, if such a claim can go forward under state law, by what standard is a court to determine whether the facts set forth in the complaint present a sufficient basis for a successful tort action.

* * *

Applying the logic of *Geary* [*v. United States Steel Corp.*, 456 Pa. 171, 319 A.2d 174 (1974),] we find that Pennsylvania law permits a cause of action for wrongful discharge where the employment termination abridges a significant and recognized public policy. The district court did not consider the question whether an averment of discharge for refusing to support the employer's lobbying efforts is sufficiently violative of such public policy as to state a cause of action. Nationwide, however, now proposes that "the only prohibition on the termination of an employee is that the termination cannot violate a *statutorily* recognized public policy."

This Court has recognized that the "only Pennsylvania cases applying public policy exceptions have done so where no statutory remedies were available." *Bruffett* [*v. Warner Communications, Inc.*, 692 F.2d 910, 919 (3d Cir.1982)]. Moreover, [the state courts have] allowed causes of action to be implied directly from the Pennsylvania Constitution. Given that there are no statutory remedies available in the present case and taking into consideration the importance of the political and associational freedoms of the federal and state Constitutions, the absence of a statutory declaration of public policy would appear to be no bar to the existence of a cause of action. Accordingly, a cognizable expression of public policy may be derived in this case from either the First Amendment of the United States Constitution or Article I, Section 7 of the Pennsylvania Constitution.[6]

* * *

An extensive case law has developed concerning the protection of constitutional rights, particularly First Amendment rights, of government employees.

* * *

In striking down the use of patronage appointments for federal government employees, the [Supreme Court has] noted that one of its goals was to insure that "employees themselves are to be sufficiently free from improper influences." *CSC v. Letter Carriers,* 413 U.S. 548, 564, 93 S.Ct. 2880, 2890, 37 L.Ed.2d 796 (1973). It was not, however, simply the abuse of state authority over public employees that fueled the Court's concern over patronage political appointments; no less central is the fear that the political process would be irremediably distorted. If employers such as federal, state or municipal governments are allowed coercive control of the scope and direction of employee political activities, it is argued, their influence will be geometrically enhanced at the expense of both the individual rights of the employees and the ability of the lone political actor to be effectively heard.

We further note that the Pennsylvania Supreme Court has similarly voiced its concern over the threat posed by discharges to the constitu-

---

6. The relevant portion of Article I, Section 7 of the Pennsylvania Constitution states:

The free communication of thoughts and opinions is one of the invaluable rights of man, and every citizen may freely speak, write and print on any subject, being responsible for the abuse of that liberty.

tionally protected rights of employees. In *Sacks v. Commonwealth of Pennsylvania, Department of Public Welfare,* 502 Pa. 201, 465 A.2d 981 (Pa.Sup.Ct.1983), the court ordered a state employee reinstated following a discharge for public comments critical of his agency employer.

* * *

Although Novosel is not a government employee, the public employee cases do not confine themselves to the narrow question of state action. Rather, these cases suggest that an important public policy is in fact implicated wherever the power to hire and fire is utilized to dictate the terms of employee political activities. In dealing with public employees, the cause of action arises directly from the Constitution rather than from common law developments. The protection of important political freedoms, however, goes well beyond the question whether the threat comes from state or private bodies. The inquiry before us is whether the concern for the rights of political expression and association which animated the public employee cases is sufficient to state a public policy under Pennsylvania law. While there are no Pennsylvania cases squarely on this point, we believe that the clear direction of the opinions promulgated by the state's courts suggests that this question be answered in the affirmative. * * * The Pennsylvania Supreme Court's rulings in *Geary* and *Sacks* are thus interpreted to extend to a non-constitutional claim where a corporation conditions employment upon political subordination. This is not the first judicial recognition of the relationship between economic power and the political process:

> the special status of corporations has placed them in a position to control vast amounts of economic power which may, if not regulated, dominate not only the economy but also the very heart of our democracy, the electoral process * * *. [The desired end] is not one of equalizing the resources of opposing candidates or opposing positions, but rather of preventing institutions which have been permitted to amass wealth as a result of special advantages extended by the State for certain economic purposes from using that wealth to acquire an unfair advantage in the political process * * *.

First National Bank of Boston v. Bellotti, 435 U.S. 765, 809, 98 S.Ct. 1407, 1433, 55 L.Ed.2d 707 (1978) (White, J., dissenting).

* * * [O]n remand the district court should employ the four part inquiry the *Sacks* court derived from [*Connick v. Myers,* 461 U.S. 138, 103 S.Ct. 1684, 75 L.Ed.2d 708 (1983), and *Pickering v. Board of Education,* 391 U.S. 563, 88 S.Ct. 1731, 20 L.Ed.2d 811 (1968)]:

> 1.   Whether, because of the speech, the employer is prevented from efficiently carrying out its responsibilities;

> 2.   Whether the speech impairs the employee's ability to carry out his own responsibilities;

> 3.   Whether the speech interferes with essential and close working relationships;

4. Whether the manner, time and place in which the speech occurs interferes with business operations.

Sacks, supra, 502 Pa. at 216, 465 A.2d at 988.

In weighing these issues, a court should employ the balancing test factors set forth for wrongful discharge cases by the Pennsylvania Superior Court in *Yaindl* [*v. Ingersoll–Rand Co.,* 281 Pa.Super. 560, 422 A.2d 611 (1980)]:

(a) the nature of the actor's conduct,

(b) the actor's motive,

(c) the interests of the other with which the actor's conduct interferes,

(d) the interests sought to be advanced by the actor,

(e) the social interests in protecting the freedom of action of the actor and the contractual interests of the other,

(f) the proximity or remoteness of the actor's conduct to the interference, and

(g) the relations between the parties.

[*id.*] at 574, 422 A.2d at 618, *quoting* Restatement (Second) of Torts § 767 (1979).

Notes and Questions

1. *Statutes Protecting Political Activity.* Several states have passed statutes expressly barring employers from using the threat of discharge or loss of job rights as a means of coercing or influencing employees "to adopt or follow or refrain from adopting or following any particular course or line of political action or political activity." Cal. Labor Code § 1102. See Conn. Pub. Act 83–578 (barring discharge on grounds violative of the first amendment); La. Rev.Stat. §§ 23:961–962; Nev.Rev.Stat. §§ 614.040.

2. *"State Action" Requirement in* Novosel? The Third Circuit, sitting in diversity, may have exceeded the position of the Pennsylvania courts in holding that the state's public policy incorporated federal constitutional norms. The *Sacks* case, for example, involved public employees with respect to whom federal and state constitutional guarantees plainly apply. On the other hand, in the eighteenth and early nineteenth centuries, when the state constitutions were drafted, the principal threat to liberty was thought to stem from government not private activity. With the rise of the multistate corporation and other centers of accumulated wealth and power, is there a need for a new constitutional order applicable to private as well as state action? If the political conscience and autonomy of public employees require protection from their employers, should not the law give similar protection to the conscience and autonomy of private employees? For an example of judicial reluctance to grant this protection, see Barr v. Kelso–Burnett Co., 106 Ill.2d 520, 88 Ill.Dec. 628, 478 N.E.2d 1354 (1985). See generally Note, Free Speech, The Private Employee and State Constitutions, 91 Yale L.J. 522 (1982).

3. *State Constitutional Provisions Applicable to Private Conduct.* The *Novosel* decision has not been followed in Pennsylvania state courts or other jurisdictions principally because of the state action requirement of federal and state constitutions. However, a number of state courts have held that the state constitutional guarantee of free speech operates as a limitation on the rights of private property owners, including private employers. See Jones v. Memorial Hospital System, 677 S.W.2d 221 (Tex.App.1984); cf. PruneYard Shopping Center v. Robins, 447 U.S. 74, 100 S.Ct. 2035, 64 L.Ed.2d 741 (1980) (sustaining California decision requiring private shopping malls to permit leafletting); see generally Note, Private Abridgement of Speech and the State Constitution, 90 Yale L.J. 165 (1980).

4. *Statutory Extension of Constitutional Protections.* A Connecticut statute applies federal and state free-speech guarantees to the private sector, "provided such activity does not substantially or materially interfere with the employee's bona fide job performance or the working relationship between the employee and the employer * * *." Conn. Gen. Stat. § 31–51q. See Cotto v. United Technologies Corp., 251 Conn. 1, 738 A.2d 623 (1999) (statute provides remedy for private-sector employees, but court rejects employee's challenge to requirement that American flags be placed at employee workstations because of absence of allegations that employee was directed to manifest his patriotism in a particular way or to affix the flag to his personal property).

5. *Legitimate Employer Interests?* Might private employers more easily than public employers be able to justify a requirement that their employees support the political goals of the firm? First amendment jurisprudence is based on an assumption of government neutrality. Can that premise be applied to nongovernmental actors? Would the raison d'etre of certain private organizations, such as the ACLU and the National Right to Work League, be undermined if they cannot prefer like-minded job applicants and cannot call upon the off-hours support of their employees for the goals of the organization? Even where a corporation is principally concerned with the sale of goods or services, rather than advocacy of a cause, it has a first amendment right to be a partisan on matters of concern to it (or at least to assert the public's first amendment right to receive such partisan views). See First National Bank of Boston v. Bellotti, 435 U.S. 765, 98 S.Ct. 1407, 55 L.Ed.2d 707 (1978). Note that the insurance company in *Novosel* sought to enlist its employees' aid in defeating no-fault legislation that might have jeopardized the company's goals and reduced its staffing needs. After *Novosel,* is the company confined to the use of professional lobbyists in pursuing its rights under *Bellotti?* See Korb v. Raytheon Corp., 410 Mass. 581, 574 N.E.2d 370 (1991) (firm can dismiss executive functioning as liaison with Defense Department for speaking out against defense budget as private citizen, even though state statute extends free speech protections to private sector employees).

6. *Distinguishing* Pierce? Should Novosel's refusal to follow his employer's commands be protected from retaliation, while Dr. Pierce's refusal to follow her employer's commands was not?

7. *"Voluntary" Participation?* Can a company after *Novosel* encourage employees voluntarily to participate in a campaign against no-fault legisla-

tion? Even if an employer does not overtly threaten discharge or other detriment to job rights, can a decision whether to participate ever be truly voluntary when an employee's response to the solicitation will not go unnoticed by her superiors?

8. *Use of "Public Policy" Cause of Action in Absence of "Political Activity" Law.* Can an attorney in a law firm be discharged for representing an unpopular client with which the attorney finds common political cause? Is the state-law "public policy" cause of action available in jurisdictions lacking express statutory protection for employee political activity? See Greenwood v. Taft, Stettinius & Hollister, 105 Ohio App.3d 295, 663 N.E.2d 1030 (Ohio App. 1995), lv. denied, 75 Ohio St.3d 1204, 662 N.E.2d 22 (1996) (denying attorney's claim that he was fired for representing gay-rights organization because alleged public policy against discrimination in employment for participation in the political process not of requisite "uniform statewide application").

Part Four

PROTECTING EMPLOYEES
FROM
ARBITRARY OR INTRUSIVE
DECISIONMAKING

In this part of the book, we consider to what extent courts and legislatures have established rules to limit the ability of employers to engage in arbitrary or intrusive decisionmaking. To some extent, employees protected from group status discrimination by laws like Title VII, ADEA and the ADA are also protected from arbitrary or intrusive decisions because, once a prima facie case has been established, the employer's lack of compelling reasons for the adverse decision may lead a trier of fact to find pretextual discrimination. However, not all workers are fully protected by these laws and inquiry into whether an employer has made an arbitrary or intrusive decision is an indirect one, for in theory employers can be arbitrary under the status discrimination laws so long as they are not motivated by prohibited discrimination. In Part Three, we also looked at statutes and court decisions that provided some indirect basis for challenging arbitrary or intrusive employer decisions, but only where such decisions implicated socially valued employee activity.

In chapter 12, we begin with a discussion of the American common law doctrine of "employment at will," and look at the growing statutory and decisional exceptions to the rule that have emerged over the last two decades; we also consider whether the United States should follow the lead of the developed European countries in enacting comprehensive wrongful dismissal legislation. Chapter 13 takes up the issue of workplace privacy—an area of law that is highly developed for government employees, but is still in its nascent stages for private sector workers. The final chapter in this part presents the law governing post-termination restraints, where employers by express contract or implied rules seek to prevent departing employees from competitive activity or misappropriation of confidential, proprietary information obtained during the prior employment.

Chapter Twelve

THE EMPLOYMENT CONTRACT

A. THE DOCTRINE OF "EMPLOYMENT AT WILL"

American common law generally construes employment for an indefinite or unstated term as a relationship which may be terminated "at will" by either party. In the absence of a contractual or statutory limitation (of the sort set forth in chapters two through nine of this book), or a recognized common law exception (such as the "public policy" cause of action discussed in chapter 11), "at will" employees have no protection against arbitrary employer action, regardless of prior years of service, any firm-specific human capital investments, the absence of alternative employment opportunities, or the insubstantiality of the grounds for termination.

The American doctrine of employment-at-will has been criticized on two distinct grounds. First, it has been argued that the doctrine erects a virtually irrebuttable presumption of at-will status that may be at variance with the actual intentions of the parties to establish a different rule. This is the view taken in the reading by Professor Feinman which follows this introduction. Second, the doctrine has been challenged on the ground that it provides an inadequate level of job security. The two criticisms lead to distinct modes of legal intervention. The response to the former criticism is to abandon any presumption of at-will status and instead allow open consideration of the available evidence as to the intentions of the parties. Such a program is in keeping with the traditional function of contract law—to facilitate private determination. The response to the latter criticism is to mandate some form of job security irrespective of the agreement of the parties. This is not a traditional role for contract law but rather a call for regulation that must be justified as such.

This chapter initially sets forth the current status of the employment-at-will doctrine through an examination of the ways courts have responded to these two different sources of disquiet over the doctrine. It then turns to a consideration of the policy arguments for and against legislative enactment of just–cause protections comparable to those afforded public sector and union-represented employees. Such legislation, while common in Western Europe and Canada, has, to date, been enacted only in Montana, although proposals have been presented to many state legislatures and have been considered by the National Conference of Commissioners on Uniform State Laws and other organizations.

We begin with a discussion of the origins of this central doctrine of U.S. employment law.

JAY M. FEINMAN, THE DEVELOPMENT OF THE EMPLOYMENT AT WILL RULE*

I. THE ENGLISH LAW

* * *

The duration of service relationships was a concern in earliest ages of English law, but the law was best formulated and made prominent only with the statement of a rule and policy by Blackstone:

> If the hiring be general, without any particular time limited, the law construes it to be a hiring for a year; upon a principle of natural equity, that the servant shall serve, and the master maintain him, throughout all the revolutions of the respective seasons, as well when there is work to be done as when there is not.

The rule thus stated expressed a sound principle: injustice would result if, for example, masters could have the benefit of servants' labor during planting and harvest seasons but discharge them to avoid supporting them during the unproductive winter, or if servants who were supported during the hard season could leave their masters' service when their labor was most needed. But the source of the yearly hiring rule was not solely, as might be supposed from Blackstone's statement, in the judges' concern for fairness between master and servant. The rule was also shaped by the requirements of the Statutes of Labourers, which prescribed a duty to work and prohibited leaving an employment or discharging a servant before the end of a term, and by the Poor Laws, which used a test of residence and employment to determine which community was responsible for the support of a person. Thus, despite a concern with the "revolution of the seasons," the rule articulated by Blackstone was not restricted to agricultural and domestic workers. The presumption that an indefinite hiring was a hiring for a year extended to all classes of servants. * * *

As the law was faced with an increasing variety of employment situations, mostly far removed from the domestic relations which had shaped the earlier law, the importance of the duration of contract question diminished and the second issue, the notice required to terminate the contract, moved to the fore. Even when they recognized hirings as yearly ones, the courts refused to consider the contracts as entire and

* 20 Amer.J. of Legal Hist. 118 (1976).

instead developed the rule that, unless specified otherwise, service contracts could be terminated on reasonable notice.

* * *

English law thus attempted to adapt to changing conditions and new situations, but more was involved than a simple desire to do justice between the parties. The Master and Servant Act of 1824 made breach of a service contract by an employee a criminal offense, while breach by an employer was still only a civil wrong. Thereafter, workers often sought shorter periods of notice.

* * *

II. The American Development

A. *The Early Law*

In colonial times some hirings, such as of day laborers, were conventionally terminable at will. Agricultural and domestic service relations often followed the English rule of yearly hirings. In the nineteenth century, however, whatever consensus existed about the state of the law dissolved.

* * *

C. *Wood and His Rule: Termination at Will*

By the 1870's the dissolution of the earlier law was apparent. Although the presumption of yearly hiring was recognized as anachronistic, the concept of reasonable notice had not caught on. Attempts were made to provide new, more fitting rules.

* * *

Thus the time was ripe for a sure resolution of the problem; it was achieved by an Albany lawyer and prolific treatise writer named Horace Gray Wood. Wood sliced through the confusion and stated the employment at will doctrine in absolutely certain terms:

> With us the rule is inflexible, that a general or indefinite hiring is *prima facie* a hiring at will, and if the servant seeks to make it out a yearly hiring, the burden is upon him to establish it by proof. * * * [I]t is an indefinite hiring and is determinable at the will of either party, and in this respect there is no distinction between domestic and other servants.

The puzzling question is what impelled Wood to state the rule that has since become identified with his name. Wood's master and servant treatise, like his other works, won him acclaim for his painstaking scholarship, but that comprehensiveness and concern for detail were absent in his treatment of the duration of service contracts. First, the four American cases he cited in direct support of the rule were in fact far off the mark. Second, his scholarly disingenuity was extraordinary; he stated incorrectly that no American courts in recent years had approved the English rule, that the employment at will rule was inflexibly applied in the United States, and that the English rule was only for a yearly hiring, making no mention of notice. Third, in the absence of valid legal support, Wood offered no policy grounds for the rule he proclaimed.

Whatever its origin and the inadequacies of its explanation, Wood's rule spread across the nation until it was generally adopted. New York, for example, of special interest here, adopted the rule in 1895, the Court of Appeals noting that the rule was "correct" and by then widely in use.

* * *

D.   *The New York Development*

* * *

The Court of Appeals settled the issue in 1895 by adopting Wood's rule in *Martin v. New York Life Insurance Co.* [, 148 N.Y. 117, 42 N.E. 416 (1895)]. The facts in *Martin* were an extreme example of the type of fact situation that had become common. Martin was the head of New York Life's real estate department at an annual salary of $10,000. On being discharged he sued, alleging that his indefinite hiring was an annual one, relying on the leading New York case of *Adams v. Fitzpatrick* [125 N.Y. 124, 26 N.E. 143 (1891)]. The trial court granted judgment to Martin but the general term reversed and the Court of Appeals upheld the reversal. The Court of Appeals disingenuously misread *Adams* and announced a two-fold rule: that an indefinite hiring was presumed to be a hiring at will, and that stating a rate of payment (*e.g.*, $10,000 per year) did not raise a presumption that the contract was intended to be of that duration.

* * *

III.   Evaluating the Employment at Will Doctrine
* * *

The participants in the litigation that resulted in the change to Wood's rule were what could loosely be called middle-level employees and their employers. During a period when annual wages in the United States averaged considerably less than $1,000, many of the discharged employees bringing the duration of contract suits received salaries of several thousand dollars, up to the $10,000 salary of the plaintiff in *Martin* and the $15,000 salary, plus commission, plus expenses, of the plaintiff in *Cuppy v. Stollwerck Bros.* [, 216 N.Y. 591, 111 N.E. 249,] in 1916. Typical positions held by these employees included corporate secretary, sales agent, attorney, plant superintendent, general manager and cashier, and chief building engineer.

Of course, there had always been managers, sales agents, and factory superintendents better paid than average workers. But through the first half of the nineteenth century owners and managers of smaller businesses comprised the bulk of the commercial middle class. Enterprises were not usually impersonal; the managers were frequently the owners of the businesses. The primary identifying feature of the old middle group of workers was that most members had an "independent means of livelihood." As the century progressed and the scale of production increased, however, enterprises became larger and more impersonal and many workers became farther removed from ownership. There were still many independent business people, of course, but salaried employees with little control of their employment situation became a larger proportion of the work force and an important segment of the economy. Engineers, foremen, and the new specialists in the management of larger enterprises were an important component of the new economic system, but for the most part they had less control over their positions than many of their predecessors. Thus the many suits brought to establish interests in their jobs were an attempt by a newly-important group in the economy to apply a traditional doctrine to their new situation, but the courts rejected the attempt and instead announced the new principle of employment at will. The reasons for this lie in the class division fundamental to the capitalist system: the distinction between owners and non-owners of capital. The effects of this division are felt in the control of labor and the discharge of employees.

* * *

Employment at will is the ultimate guarantor of the capitalist's authority over the worker. The rule transformed long-term and semi-permanent relationships into non-binding agreements terminable at will. If employees could be dismissed on a moment's notice, obviously they could not claim a voice in the determination of the conditions of work or the use of the product of their labor.

Notes and Questions

1. *Other Historical Accounts.* For other historical accounts reaching similar conclusions, see Mary Ann Glendon & Edward R. Lev, Changes in the Bonding of the Employment Relationship: An Essay on the New Property, 20 B.C.L.Rev. 457 (1979); Sanford Jacoby, The Duration of Indefinite Employment Contracts in the United States and England: A Historical Analysis, 5 Comp.Lab.L. 85 (1982); Charles McCurdy, The Roots of "Liberty of Contract" Reconsidered: Major Premises in the Law of Employment, 1867–1937, 1984 Y.B.Sup.Ct.Hist. Soc'y 20; Gary Minda, The Common Law of Employment At Will in New York, 36 Syracuse L.Rev. 939, 966–90 (1985). For a discussion of the 19th century common law's treatment of claims under long-term employment contracts, see Wythe Holt, Recovery by the Worker Who Quits: A Comparison of the Mainstream, Legal Realist, and Critical Legal Studies Approaches to a Problem of Nineteenth Century Contract Law, 1986 Wis.L.Rev. 677.

2. *Effect of Adherence to English Precedent?* a. *Yearly Hiring vs. Customary Notice of Dismissal?* If the American courts had been more faithful to the English precedents, should they have presumed a yearly hiring? Or, rather, should they have permitted termination only after furnishing customary notice of termination? The latter remains the premise

of the common law in Canada. See, e.g., Wallace v. United Grain Growers, [1997] 3 S.C.R. 701.

b. *Restrictions on Employee Quits?* Could American courts have adopted either of these approaches without importing some of the underlying domestic relations and feudalist assumptions of the English decisions? Does Feinman's discussion of the Master and Servant Act of 1824 suggest that workers in some circumstances would have chafed under such restrictions on their freedom to quit at will? Indeed, some American decisions penalized employees who quit their jobs without notice or cause. See Jacoby, supra, at 105–07; Holt, supra, at 686–87. Could an American court in this period, working either from English or American precedents, have implied a *one-sided* "cause" limitation on discharge applicable only to employers?

3. *Contract–Law Grounds for Wood's Rule?* a. *Absence of Independent Consideration?* Feinman suggests that Wood's rule, as applied by the American courts, erected a virtually irrebuttable presumption that a hiring for an indefinite or unstated term was a hiring terminable at will. To what extent is this presumption justified by the requirements of contract law? Does the doctrine of consideration require that, in order to secure a binding promise of job security, an employee must furnish consideration *in addition* to his promise to work for stated wages? Professor Farnsworth writes that "by the end of the nineteenth century, at least in the United States, the traditional requirement that the consideration be either a benefit to the promisor or a detriment to the promisee had begun to give way to a requirement that the consideration be 'bargained for.' " E. Allan Farnsworth, Contracts, § 2.2, at 43 (1990). Could not an employee's promise to work at stated wages provide consideration for a number of "bargained for" promises on the employer's side, including a promise of job security absent "cause" for termination?

b. *Mutuality of Obligation?* Does the problem lie, rather, in the fact that the employee's promise to work at stated wages is "illusory" given the right, possibly safeguarded by the thirteenth amendment to the Constitution, to quit work at any time and for any reason? Perhaps this is what the nineteenth century court meant when it spoke in terms of a lack of mutuality of obligation. Can the requisite mutuality now be found in the various practical forces, such as seniority rules and pension vesting requirements, that bind many employees to their jobs? See Glendon & Lev, supra; Samuel Estreicher & Beverly Wolff, At–Will Employment and the Problem of Unjust Dismissal, 36 Record of Assn. of the Bar of the City of N.Y. 170, 187–88 (April 1981). Moreover, modern decisions suggest that a promise is not illusory if the power to terminate is conditioned by an obligation to give notice, however brief, or on the occurrence of events beyond the promisor's control. See Farnsworth, supra, § 2.14, at 77–79; 1A A. Corbin, Contracts, § 163 (1963) ("The giving of the notice relieves [the other party] from obligation as well as the notice-giver himself."). Consider also the following analysis from a 1921 Illinois ruling:

> While consideration is essential to the validity of a contract, mutuality of obligation is not. Where there is no other consideration for a contract,

the mutual promises of the parties constitute the consideration, and these promises must be binding on both parties or the contract fails for want of consideration, but, where, there is any other consideration for the contract, mutuality of obligation is not essential. If mutuality, in a broad sense, were held to be an essential element in every valid contract to the extent that both contracting parties could sue on it, there could be no such thing as a valid unilateral or option contract.

Armstrong Paint & Varnish Works v. Continental Can Co., 301 Ill. 102, 108, 133 N.E. 711, 714 (1921). See also Mark Pettit, Jr., Modern Unilateral Contracts, 63 B.U.L.Rev. 551 (1983).

c. *Why Didn't Middle–Class Employees "Contract Out" of Wood's Rule?* If the contract law of the period did not inflexibly require construing indefinite hirings as at-will relationships, why were the American courts unreceptive to the claims of largely white, middle class employees that they had bargained for some measure of job security? Once the pattern of judicial decisions became clear, why did these middle class employees not insist on definite-term contracts with express provisions for termination without "cause"? Or did they? What answers does Feinman offer?

4. *Property Law vs. Contract Law?* a. *A Property Right in One's Job?* Some writers have suggested that contract law is the wrong starting point for analyzing the termination of the employment relationship. Rather, the employee should be viewed as having a property right in his job defeasible only upon "cause" for termination. See William B. Gould, IV, The Idea of the Job as Property in Contemporary America: The Legal and Collective Bargaining Framework, 1986 B.Y.U.L.Rev. 885; Jack Beermann & Joseph Singer, Baseline Questions in Legal Reasoning: The Example of Property in Jobs, 23 Ga.L.Rev. 911 (1989). On what basis should the courts recognize such property rights?

b. *Procedural Due Process?* Government sector workers may claim some protection under the Fourteenth Amendment's due process clause which states that "property" may not be taken by the state without "due process of law". The Supreme Court has held that the clause does not create property rights, but rather reaches only interests already recognized by state or other positive law, including in some cases interests in continued public employment absent "cause" for termination. See Board of Regents of State Colleges v. Roth, 408 U.S. 564, 92 S.Ct. 2701, 33 L.Ed.2d 548 (1972); Perry v. Sindermann, 408 U.S. 593, 92 S.Ct. 2694, 33 L.Ed.2d 570 (1972). For interests so recognized, there is a constitutional requirement of due process before they may be impaired; sometimes an appropriate combination of a limited hearing prior to termination of employment and a prompt post-termination hearing. See Cleveland Board of Educ. v. Loudermill, 470 U.S. 532, 105 S.Ct. 1487, 84 L.Ed.2d 494 (1985); Gilbert v. Homar, 520 U.S. 924, 117 S.Ct. 1807, 138 L.Ed.2d 120 (1997).

B. WRONGFUL TERMINATION: CONTRACT THEORIES OF RECOVERY

The courts have proceeded on two fronts to mitigate the rigid presumption erected by early formulations of the employment-at-will doctrine. One approach has been to show greater receptivity to finding express contractual promises of job security. The second has been to recognize in appropriate circumstances implied promises restricting the employer's at-will authority. However, because contract-law approaches are principally directed at effectuating the underlying intentions of the parties, they are not likely sources of job-security arrangements where at-will status is established by the parties' underlying agreement.

1. *Personnel Manuals/Employee Handbooks*

WOOLLEY v. HOFFMANN–LA ROCHE, INC.

Supreme Court of New Jersey, 1985.
99 N.J. 284, 491 A.2d 1257.

WILENTZ, C.J.

Plaintiff, Richard Woolley, was hired by defendant, Hoffmann–La Roche, Inc., in October 1969, as an Engineering Section Head in defendant's Central Engineering Department at Nutley. There was no written employment contract between plaintiff and defendant. Plaintiff began work in mid-November 1969. Some time in December, plaintiff received and read the personnel manual on which his claims are based.

In 1976, plaintiff was promoted, and in January 1977 he was promoted again, this latter time to Group Leader for the Civil Engineering, the Piping Design, the Plant Layout, and the Standards and Systems Sections. In March 1978, plaintiff was directed to write a report to his supervisors about piping problems in one of defendant's buildings in Nutley. This report was written and submitted to plaintiff's immediate supervisor on April 5, 1978. On May 3, 1978, stating that the General Manager of defendant's Corporate Engineering Department had lost confidence in him, plaintiff's supervisors requested his resignation. Following this, by letter dated May 22, 1978, plaintiff was formally asked for his resignation, to be effective July 15, 1978.

Plaintiff refused to resign. Two weeks later defendant again requested plaintiff's resignation, and told him he would be fired if he did not resign. Plaintiff again declined, and he was fired in July.

* * *

The trial court, relying on *Savarese v. Pyrene Mfg. Co.,* 9 *N.J.* 595, 89 A.2d 237 (1952), *Hindle v. Morrison Steel Co.,* 92 N.J.Super. 75, 223 A.2d 193 (App.Div.1966), and *Piechowski v. Matarese,* 54 N.J.Super. 333, 148 A.2d 872 (App.Div.1959), held that in the absence of a "most convincing[ ]" demonstration that "it was the intent of the parties to enter into such long-range commitments * * * clearly, specifically and definitely expressed" (using, almost verbatim, the language of *Savarese, supra,* 9 N.J. at 601, 89 A.2d 237), supported by consideration over and above the employee's rendition of services, the employment is at will. Finding that the personnel policy manual did not contain any such clear and definite expression and, further, that there was no such additional consideration, the court granted summary judgment in favor of defendant, sustaining its right to fire plaintiff with or without cause.

The Appellate Division, viewing plaintiff's claim as one for a "permanent or lifetime employment," found that the company's policy manual did not specifically set forth the term, work, hours or duties of the employment and "appear[ed] to be a unilateral expression of company policies and procedures * * * not bargained for by the parties," this last reference being similar to the notion, relied on by the trial court, that additional consideration was required. Based on that view, it held that the "promulgation and circulation of the personnel policy manual by defendant did not give plaintiff any enforceable contractual rights." * * *

We are thus faced with the question of whether this is the kind of employment contract—a "long-range commitment"—that must be construed as one of indefinite duration and therefore at will unless the stringent requirements of *Savarese* are met, or whether ordinary contractual doctrine applies. In either case, the question is whether Hoffmann–La Roche retained the right to fire with or without cause or whether, as Woolley claims, his employment could be terminated only for cause. * * *

This Court has clearly announced its unwillingness to continue to adhere to rules regularly leading to the conclusion that an employer can fire an employee-at-will, with or without cause, for any reason whatsoever. Our holding in *Pierce v. Ortho Pharmaceutical Corp.*, 84 N.J. 58, 72, 417 A.2d 505 (1980), while necessarily limited to the specific issue of that case (whether employer can fire employee-at-will when discharge is contrary to a clear mandate of public policy), implied a significant questioning of that rule in general.

* * *

The rule of *Savarese, supra,* 9 N.J. 595, 89 A.2d 237, which the trial court and the Appellate Division transported to this case, was derived in a very different context from that here. The case involved an unusual transaction not likely to recur (promise by company officer, made to induce employee to play baseball with company team, for lifetime employment even if employee became disabled as a result of playing baseball). * * *

What is before us in this case is not a special contract with a particular employee, but a general agreement covering all employees. There is no reason to treat such a document with hostility.

* * *

Given the facts before us and the common law of contracts interpreted in the light of sound policy applicable to this modern setting, we conclude that the termination clauses of this company's Personnel Policy Manual, including the procedure required before termination occurs, could be found to be contractually enforceable. Furthermore, we conclude that when an employer of a substantial number of employees circulates a manual that, when fairly read, provides that certain benefits are an incident of the employment (including, especially, job security provisions), the judiciary, instead of "grudgingly" conceding the enforceability of those provisions, *Saverese, supra,* 9 N.J. at 601, 89 A.2d 237, should construe them in accordance with the reasonable expectations of the employees.

* * *

In determining the manual's meaning and effect, we must consider the probable context in which it was disseminated and the environment surrounding its continued existence. The manual, though apparently not distributed to all employees ("in general, distribution will be provided to supervisory personnel * * * "), covers all of them. Its terms are of such importance to all employees that in the absence of contradicting evidence, it would seem clear that it was intended by Hoffmann–La Roche that all employees be advised of the benefits it confers.

We take judicial notice of the fact that Hoffmann–La Roche is a substantial company with many employees in New Jersey. The record permits the conclusion that the policy manual represents the most reliable statement of the terms of their employment. At oral argument counsel conceded that it is rare for any employee, except one on the medical staff, to have a special contract. Without minimizing the importance of its specific provisions, the context of the manual's preparation and distribution is, to us, the most persuasive proof that it would be almost inevitable for an employee to regard it as a binding commitment, legally enforceable, concerning the terms and conditions of his employment. Having been employed, like hundreds of his co-employees, without any individual employment contract, by an employer whose good reputation made it so attractive, the employee is given this one document that purports to set forth the terms and conditions of his employment, a document obviously carefully prepared by the company with all of the appearances of corporate legitimacy that one could imagine.

* * *

The mere fact of the manual's distribution suggests its importance. Its changeability—the uncontroverted ability of management to change its terms—is argued as supporting its non-binding quality, but one might as easily conclude that, given its importance, the employer wanted to keep it up to date, especially to make certain, given this employer's good reputation in labor relations, that the benefits conferred were sufficiently competitive with those available from other employers, including benefits found in collective bargaining agreements. The record suggests that the changes actually made almost always favored the employees.

Given that background, then, unless the language contained in the manual were such that no one could reasonably have thought it was intended to create legally binding obligations, the termination provisions of the policy manual would have to be regarded as an obligation undertaken by the employer. It will not do now for the company to say it did not mean the things it said in its manual to be binding. Our courts will not allow an employer to offer attractive inducements and benefits to the workforce and then withdraw them when it chooses, no matter how sincere its belief that they are not enforceable.

* * *

Many of these workers undoubtedly know little about contracts, and many probably would be unable to analyze the language and terms of the manual. Whatever Hoffmann–La Roche may have intended, that which was read by its employees was a promise not to fire them except for cause

Having concluded that a jury could find the Personnel Policy Manual to constitute an offer, we deal with what most cases deem the major obstacle to construction of the terms as constituting a binding agreement, namely, the requirement under contract law that consideration must be given in exchange for the employer's offer in order to convert that offer into a binding agreement.

We conclude that these job security provisions contained in a personnel policy manual widely distributed among a large workforce are supported by consideration and may therefore be enforced as a binding commitment of the employer.

* * * In most of the cases involving an employer's personnel policy manual, the document is prepared without any negotiations and is voluntarily distributed to the workforce by the employer. It seeks no return promise from the employees. It is reasonable to interpret it as seeking continued work from the employees, who, in most cases, are free to quit since they are almost always employees at will, not simply in the sense that the employer can fire them without cause, but in the sense that they can quit without breaching any obligation. Thus analyzed, the manual is an offer that seeks the formation of a unilateral contract—the employees' bargained-for action needed to make the offer binding being their continued work when they have no obligation to continue.

The unilateral contract analysis is perfectly adequate for that employee who was aware of the manual and who continued to work intending that continuation to be the action in exchange for the employer's promise; it is even more helpful in support of that conclusion if, but for the employer's policy manual, the employee would have quit. *See generally* M. Pettit, "Modern Unilateral Contracts," 63 B.U.L.Rev. 551 (1983) (judicial use of unilateral contract analysis in employment cases is widespread).

* * * In *Toussaint* [*v. Blue Cross and Blue Shield of Michigan,*] 408 Mich. 579, 292 N.W.2d 880 [1980,] one main issue was the contractual force of an oral assurance given to the employee when he was hired that he would not be discharged so long as he was "doing his job." In addition to that assurance, Toussaint was at the same time handed a manual, which provided that an employee would not be discharged without cause and without following certain procedures. The court noted in *dictum* that the oral assurance was not necessary to its holding. The court's discussion of the effect of distributing a manual is worth noting:

> * * * It is enough that the employer chooses, presumably in its own interest, to create an environment in which the employee believes that, whatever, the personnel policies and practices, they are established and official at any given time, purport to be fair, and are applied consistently and uniformly to each employee. The employer has then created a situation "instinct with an obligation." [292 *N.W.*2d at 892 (footnotes omitted).]

A footnote concluded that "[i]t was therefore unnecessary for Toussaint to prove reliance on the policies set forth in the manual."

Similarly, in *Anthony v. Jersey Cent. Power & Light Co.,* 51 N.J.Super. 139, 143 *A.*2d 762 [(1958)], practically every contractual objection that could be made here was disposed of by the Appellate Division in the context of a claim for pension rights by supervisory personnel based on a company manual (entitled "General Rules"). There, the defendant-employer argued that its severance-pay rule was a mere gratuitous promise, not supported by consideration. The court responded, analyzing the promise as an offer of a unilateral contract and the employees' continued services as sufficient acceptance and consideration therefor. *Id.* at 143, 143 A.2d 762. To the defendant's argument that there was no evidence of reliance upon its promise, the *Anthony* court responded that reliance was to be presumed under the circumstances. *Id.* at 145–46, 143 A.2d 762. We agree.[10]

The lack of definiteness concerning the other terms of employment—its duration,[11] wages, precise service to be rendered, hours of work, etc., does not prevent enforcement of a job security provision.

---

10. If reliance is not presumed, a strict contractual analysis might protect the rights of some employees and not others. For example, where an employee is not even aware of the existence of the manual, his or her continued work would not ordinarily be thought of as the bargained-for detriment. See S. Williston, *Contracts* §§ 101, 102A (1957). But see A. Corbin, *Contracts* 59 (1963) (suggesting that knowledge of an offer is not a prerequisite to acceptance). Similarly, if it is quite clear that those employees who knew of the offer knew that it sought their continued work, but nevertheless continued without the slightest intention of putting forth that action as consideration for the employer's promise, it might not be sufficient to form a contract. See S. Williston, Contracts § 67 (1957). But see *Pine River* [*State Bank* v. *Mettille,*] 333 N.W.2d at 622, 627, 630 [(Minn.1983).] In this case there is no proof that plaintiff, Woolley, relied on the policy manual in continuing his work. Furthermore, as the Appellate Division correctly noted, Woolley did "not bargain for" the employer's promise. The implication of the presumption of reliance is that the manual's job security provisions became binding the moment the manual was distributed. Anyone employed before or after became one of the beneficiaries of those provisions of the manual. And if *Toussaint* is followed, employees neither had to read it, know of its existence, or rely on it to benefit from its provisions any more than employees in a plant that is unionized have to read or rely on a collective-bargaining agreement in order to obtain its benefits.

11. The parties agree that Woolley's employment was for an indefinite period. We therefore need not determine the impact of a job security clause where the employment is alleged to be for a fixed term, *e.g.,* because of the stated salary period. *See Willis v. Wyllys Corp.,* 98 N.J.L. 180, 119 A. 24 (E. & A. 1922) (when employment contract states annual salary, the term of employment is not indefinite, but by the year).

Realistically, the objection has force only when the agreement is regarded as a special one between the employer and an individual employee. There it might be difficult to determine whether there was good cause for termination if one could not determine what it was that the employee was expected to do. That difficulty is one factor that suggests the employer did not intend a lifetime contract with one employee. Here the question of good cause is made considerably easier to deal with in view of the fact that the agreement applies to the entire workforce, and the workforce itself is rather large. Even-handedness and equality of treatment will make the issue in most cases far from complex; the fact that in some cases the "for cause" provision may be difficult to interpret and enforce should not deprive employees in other cases from taking advantage of it. If there is a problem arising from indefiniteness, in any event, it is one caused by the employer.

* * *

We therefore reverse the Appellate Division's affirmance of the trial court's grant of summary judgment and remand this matter to the trial court for further proceedings consistent with this opinion. Those proceedings should have the benefit of the entire manual that was in force at the time Woolley was discharged. The provisions of the manual concerning job security shall be considered binding unless the manual elsewhere prominently and unmistakably indicates that those provisions shall not be binding or unless there is some other similar proof of the employer's intent not to be bound. The ordinary division of issues between the court and the jury shall apply. If the court concludes that the job security provisions are binding (or submits that issue to the jury), it shall either determine their meaning or, if reasonable men could differ as to that meaning, submit that issue as well to the jury. If either the court or the jury under those circumstances concludes that the Personnel Policy Manual constituted a promise that an employee in Woolley's position could not be fired except for good cause, the only issue remaining shall be Woolley's damages. Woolley need not prove consideration—that shall be presumed. Furthermore, it shall not be open to defendant to prove that good cause in fact existed on the basis of which Woolley could have been terminated. If the court or jury concludes that the manual's job security provisions are binding, then, according to those provisions, even if good cause existed, an employee could not be fired unless the employer went through the various procedures set forth in the manual, steps designed to rehabilitate that employee in order to *avoid* termination. On the record before us the employer's failure to do so is undeniable. If that is the case, we believe it would be unfair to allow this employer to try now to recreate the facts as they might have existed had the employer given to Woolley that which the manual promised, namely, a set of detailed procedures, all for Woolley's benefit, designed to see if there was some way he could be retained by Hoffmann–La Roche. This is especially so in view of Woolley's death. Hoffmann–La Roche chose to act without complying with those procedures. It would not be fair now to allow the employer to claim that these procedures, of which it wrongfully deprived him, would have done him no good, when the only party who could effectively counter that claim—Woolley—is dead.

* * *

We are aware that problems that do not ordinarily exist when collective bargaining agreements are involved may arise from the enforcement of employment manuals. Policy manuals may not generally be as comprehensive or definite as typical collective bargaining agreements. Further problems may result from the employer's explicitly reserved right unilaterally to change the manual. We have no doubt that, generally, changes in such a manual, including changes in terms and conditions of employment, are permitted. We express no opinion, however, on whether or to what extent they are permitted when they adversely affect a binding job security provision.

* * *

All that this opinion requires of an employer is that it be fair. It would be unfair to allow an employer to distribute a policy manual that makes the workforce believe that certain promises have been made and then to allow the employer to renege on those promises. What is sought here is basic honesty: if the employer, for whatever reason, does not want the manual to be capable of being construed by the court as a binding contract, there are simple ways to attain that goal. All that need be done is the inclusion in a very prominent position of an appropriate statement that there is no promise of any kind by the employer contained in the manual; that regardless of what the manual says or provides, the employer promises nothing and remains free to change wages and all other working conditions without having to consult anyone and without anyone's agreement; and that the employer continues to have the absolute power to fire anyone with or without good cause.

APPENDIX [TO *WOOLLEY V. HOFFMAN-LAROCHE, INC.*]

The following are the termination provisions included in the portion of the Personnel Policy Manual submitted to the courts below.

Termination

I. Purpose

This policy states the company's philosophy with respect to terminations of employees and provides uniform guidelines for the administration of this policy.

II. Policy

It is the policy of Hoffmann–La Roche to retain to the extent consistent with company requirements, the services of all employees who perform their duties efficiently and effectively. However, it may become necessary under certain conditions to terminate employment for the good of the employee and/or the company. The types of terminations that exist are lay-off, discharge due to performance, disciplinary discharge, retirement, and resignation.

III.   General

The definitions of the types of termination are as follows:

— *Layoff* means termination of employment on the initiative of the company under circumstances, normally lack of work, such that the employee is subject to recall. He/she may be reinstated without loss of seniority if recalled within one year of the date of layoff.

— *Discharge due to Performance* means termination of employment on the initiative of the company under circumstances generally related to the quality of the employee's performance, whereby the employee is considered unable to meet the requirements of the job. In this case, the employee is not subject to recall or reinstatement.

— *Discharge, Disciplinary* means termination of employment on the initiative of the company for reasons of misconduct or willful negligence in the performance of job duties such that the employee will not be considered for re-employment.

— *Retirement* means termination of active work by the employee at the age or under conditions set forth in the company's retirement plan, under which the employee receives retirement pay and enjoys other benefits.

— *Resignation* means termination of employment on the initiative of the employee. Employees are expected to give no less than two weeks notice of resignation. An employee who resigns will retain no reinstatement or re-employment rights.

Resignation requested is a category of information on the Personnel Action Form and means termination of employment, for cause, on the initiative of the company. "Mutual Agreement" terminations must be further identified as either discharge due to performance or disciplinary for purposes of severance pay eligibility * * *.

IV.   Guidelines for Discharge Due to Performance

In keeping with the company's concern for all employees, termination of employment on the initiative of the company under circumstances generally related to the quality of the employee's job performance deserves special consideration. We would like to insure that every reasonable step has been taken to help the employee continue in a productive capacity. It is the responsibility of each manager and supervisor to develop the people working for him/her. In cases of unsatisfactory job performance, which may develop into termination of employment, each manager and supervisor should consider the following:

    A.   Has the employee been made aware of the problem in specific terms?

    B.   Are the suggestions as to how these problems can be eliminated in writing?

    C.   Has assistance been offered to the employee to help the employee remedy the situation?

D. Has the employee been given a sufficient amount of time and help to remedy the situation?

If a situation related to poor job performance has just come to a manager's or supervisor's attention, joint evaluation between the employee and the manager is recommended. The manager should try to determine the cause of the problem. Is it lack of experience in the job, education, motivation, employee personal problems, or personality conflict? Once the cause is identified, the employee should be given time, if possible, to remedy the situation. The manager should also be considering ways to remedy the situation and to improve the individual's performance. This may mean the use of outside sources to develop the employee and/or the job to put the employee on an appropriate career path. Other alternatives are:

A. Changing the employee's responsibilities in his/her present job.

B. Reassignment to a different job in the department.

C. Encouraging the employee to bid into an area where his/her chances of success are felt to be better.

D. A change to a position of lesser responsibility.

If, after sufficient time and consideration of the above, the employee does not remedy the situation, the supervisor should then proceed with the termination of the employee * * *.

Notes and Questions

1. *Other "Handbook" Rulings.* Virtually all jurisdictions that have considered the question have concluded that unilaterally promulgated personnel manuals and employee handbooks can give rise to enforceable promises of job security. In addition to *Woolley,* see, e.g., Dillon v. Champion Jogbra, Inc., 819 A.2d 703 (Vt. 2002); Demasse v. ITT Corp., 194 Ariz. 500, 984 P.2d 1138 (1999) (en banc); Leikvold v. Valley View Community Hospital, 141 Ariz. 544, 688 P.2d 170 (1984); O'Brien v. New England Telephone & Telegraph Co., 422 Mass. 686, 664 N.E.2d 843 (1996); Feges v. Perkins Restaurants, Inc., 483 N.W.2d 701 (Minn. 1992); cf. Pine River State Bank v. Mettille, 333 N.W.2d 622 (Minn.1983); Duldulao v. St. Mary of Nazareth Hospital Center, 115 Ill.2d 482, 106 Ill.Dec. 8, 505 N.E.2d 314 (1987); Thompson v. St. Regis Paper Co., 102 Wash.2d 219, 685 P.2d 1081 (1984); Gates v. Life of Montana Ins. Co., 205 Mont. 304, 668 P.2d 213 (1983); Weiner v. McGraw–Hill, Inc., 57 N.Y.2d 458, 457 N.Y.S.2d 193, 443 N.E.2d 441 (1982); Simpson v. Western Graphics Corp., 293 Or. 96, 643 P.2d 1276 (1982); Toussaint v. Blue Cross and Blue Shield of Michigan, 408 Mich. 579, 292 N.W.2d 880 (1980). See generally Stephen F. Befort, Employee Handbooks and the Legal Effect of Disclaimers, 13 Indus. Rels. L.J. 326 (1991/1992).

Iowa's formulation of the "handbook exception" requires that "the traditional requirements of contract formation have been met." Fogel v. Trustees of Iowa College, 446 N.W.2d 451, 456 (Iowa 1989) (manual containing no for–cause restriction for dismissal held "too indefinite to create an enforceable unilateral contract").

2. *Handbook Statements as Binding "Promises"?* Not all statements in a personnel manual or employee handbook will be deemed "promises" of sufficient "specificity and commitment" to raise "an employer's policy to the level of a promise." Lytle v. Malady, 458 Mich. 153, 579 N.W.2d 906, 911 (1998) (en banc). The Michigan high court, which first recognized the "handbook" exception to employment at-will in *Toussaint*, found the following language insufficient to create a binding promise:

> The contents of this booklet are not intended to establish, and should not be construed to constitute any contract between the [employer] and any employee, or group of employees.

> * * *

> No employee will be terminated without proper cause or reason and not until management has made a careful review of the facts.

458 Mich. at 162–63. The court explained:

> This contractual disclaimer clearly communicated to employees that the employer did not intend to be bound by the policies stated in the handbook. At the very least, we find that the disclaimer renders the "proper cause" statement too vague and indefinite to constitute a promise. * * * that could form the basis of a legitimate-expectation claim.

Id. at 166. Was the problem here of insufficient specificity to the employer's promise? The mutually contradictory language used? What result if there had not been an express disclaimer in this case? On disclaimers, see notes 6–8 below.

3. Woolley *and "Unilateral Contract" Theory.* The *Woolley* court reasons that employer promises contained in a personnel manual or employee handbook are simply a form of "unilateral contract" that invites acceptance of this new term by the continued performance of employees. Presumably, the employer does not ask for a promise from the employees because "what is of value is their continued performance." Farnsworth, supra, Contracts, Sec. 3.12, at 146. See generally Mark Petit, Jr., Modern Unilateral Contracts, 63 B.U. L. Rev. 551 (1983).

Can the *Woolley* rationale be fully explained in these terms? Consider the following: (1) Did the employer make a promise at all in stating its "philosophy" in "guidelines" for management? (2) Is it clear that the employer intended the manual "promises" to induce further work performance? (3) If reliance on the employees' part is required, can such reliance be irrebuttably presumed even though the handbook was not generally distributed to the workforce? (4) If widespread knowledge of the handbook's contents is assumed, is it clear that employees relied to their detriment when their behavior/performance continued in precisely the same manner as before? Was there any evidence that the employees in *Woolley* were reluctant promisees who had been encouraged not to quit, or who had forsworn union representation, because of the promises contained in the handbook? (5) Does the fact that the employer had reserved the power to modify the provisions of the handbook, and had unilaterally modified those provisions in the past, raise the question of whether any reliance on the handbook would have been justifiable? (6) Does the "unilateral contract" theory permit or restrict unilateral employer changes in the job security term through new unilateral contracts "accepted" by continued performance of the employees? See "Note on Unilateral Modification," below. For an argument that cases like *Woolley* nonetheless reflect an application of traditional contract-law principles to modern employment systems, see Matthew W. Finkin, The Bureaucratization of Work: Employer Policies and Contract Law, 1986 Wis.L.Rev. 733.

4. Woolley *and Promissory Estoppel Theory*. Would the doctrine of promissory estoppel have provided a firmer basis for a handbook exception to the at-will rule? Some courts like the New York Court of Appeals in *Weiner* (cited in note 1 supra) effectively have limited the exception to circumstances that would support a promissory estoppel claim. Professor Hillman criticizes the limited use of promissory estoppel in employment cases. See Robert A. Hillman, The Unfulfilled Promise of Promissory Estoppel in the Employment Setting, 31 Rutgers L.J. 1 (1999). One reason for its limited use may be that the element of detrimental reliance often cannot be shown, as arguably was the case in *Woolley* itself? Moreover, some states like Texas recognize only defensive uses of the doctrine (when, say, an oral contract fails because of the statute of frauds) rather than as a basis for an affirmative cause of action. See Cortlan H. Maddux, Employers Beware! The Emerging Use of Promissory Estoppel as an Exception to the Employment At Will, 49 Bayl. L. Rev. 197 (1997).

5. *Is Dissemination of the Manual Required?* In a post-*Woolley* ruling, the New Jersey Supreme Court seemed to reaffirm that dissemination of the personnel manual in its entirety is not required. See Nicosia v. Wakefern Food Corp., 136 N.J. 401, 408–12, 643 A.2d 554, 558–59 (1994) (entire manual was distributed to only 300 of 1500 nonunion employees; plaintiff received only eleven-page section of the manual dealing with discipline procedures but had to rest his claim on the manual as a whole). By contrast, the Pennsylvania Supreme Court appears to require actual dissemination to employees before a handbook will create binding commitments. See Morosetti v. Louisiana Land and Exploration Co., 522 Pa. 492, 495, 564 A.2d 151, 152 (1989): "A handbook distributed to employees as inducement for employment may be an offer and its acceptance a contract. The employees here, however, could * * * show [only] an internal consideration of policy for what might be given, if and when they announced a policy for all employees. It is not sufficient to show only that they had a policy. It must be shown that they intended to offer it as a binding contract."

6. *A Doctrine Akin to "Administrative Estoppel"?* Are *Woolley* and similar cases best understood not as a species of traditional contract law but as an instance of estoppel akin to the administrative law doctrine that agencies are bound to self-imposed restrictions on their discretionary authority until they have formally rescinded those restrictions? See Accardi v. Shaughnessy, 347 U.S. 260, 74 S.Ct. 499, 98 L.Ed. 681 (1954). For a similar rationale, see Bankey v. Storer Broadcasting, discussed in "Note on Unilateral Modfication," below. This "administrative law model," also discussed in Henry H. Perritt, Jr., Employee Dismissal Law & Practice Sec. 4.44 (4th ed.

1997), is expressly rejected in Demasse v. ITT Corp., discussed in the "Note on Unilateral Modification," below.

7. *"Permanent" Employment.* Note the *Woolley* court's discussion of contracts for "permanent" or "lifetime" employment which, under the prior decision in *Savarese*, require explicit specification of such a term as well as additional consideration from the offeree. Some decisions appear to hold that such contracts are never enforceable: "The promise of 'permanent' employment alone is too broad to be enforced." Scott v. Extracorporeal, Inc., 376 Pa.Super. 90, 545 A.2d 334 (1988). Can such an approach be squared with the modern willingness to consider what the parties have in fact bargained for, rather than erect a per se barrier to promises of indefinite employment? The New Jersey high court in *Woolley* nevertheless suggests that a special level of scrutiny is required of bilateral promises of permanent or indefinite employment. What reasons are given? Is the court's treatment of in its prior decision in *Savarese* ultimately consistent with its approach in *Woolley* to handbook promises?

8. *Effect of Disclaimers of Job Security Promises?* In keeping with the suggestion in the last paragraph of the *Woolley* opinion and similar invitations in such cases as *Toussaint,* 408 Mich. at 610, 292 N.W.2d at 890–91 (as further confirmed in *Lytle,* supra), and *Thompson,* 102 Wash.2d at 230, 685 P.2d at 1088, employers have revised their manuals and handbooks by inserting prominent disclaimers of any promise of job security. The courts generally have held that such language is sufficient prospectively to defeat a *Woolley*-type contract claim. See, e.g., Rowe v. Montgomery Ward & Co., 437 Mich. 627, 473 N.W.2d 268 (1991); Suter v. Harsco Corp., 184 W.Va. 734, 403 S.E.2d 751 (1991); Pratt v. Brown Machine Co., 855 F.2d 1225 (6th Cir.1988); Uebelacker v. Cincom Systems Inc., 48 Ohio App.3d 268, 549 N.E.2d 1210 (Ohio App.1988) (disclaimer in employee benefit book held effective); Eldridge v. Evangelical Lutheran Good Samaritan Soc'y, 417 N.W.2d 797 (N.D.1987); Reid v. Sears, Roebuck & Co., 790 F.2d 453 (6th Cir.1986); Larose v. Agway, Inc., 147 Vt. 1, 508 A.2d 1364 (1986); Bailey v. Perkins Restaurants, Inc., 398 N.W.2d 120, 122–23 (N.D.1986).

9. *Ineffective Disclaimers.* The employer's disclaimer may be ineffective if the wording is ambiguous or if it has not been adequately communicated to the employee. See Schipani v. Ford Motor Co., 102 Mich.App. 606, 302 N.W.2d 307 (1981); Ferraro v. Koelsch, 124 Wis.2d 154, 368 N.W.2d 666 (1985). In Nicosia v. Wakefern Food Corp., 136 N.J. 401, 643 A.2d 554 (1994), the employer's manual contained the following disclaimer:

> This manual contains statements of Wakefern Food Corp. and its subsidiaries' Human Resource policies and procedures. * * * The terms and procedures contained therein are not contractual and are subject to change and interpretation at the sole discretion of the Company, and without prior notice or consideration to any employee.

The New Jersey Supreme Court held the disclaimer to be ineffective both because it was not "set off in a way to attract attention" and its message did not make clear the employer's reservation of at-will authority:

> Nicosia should not be expected to understand that Wakefern's characterization of its manual as "not contractual" or "subject to change and interpretation at the sole discretion of the Company" meant that the

employer, despite the discipline and termination provisions of its manual, reserved the "absolute power to fire anyone with or without cause" without actually changing those provisions.

Id. at 560–61.

Some courts have asked juries to evaluate disclaimers in light of the employer's actual practice. See McGinnis v. Honeywell, Inc., 110 N.M. 1, 791 P.2d 452, 457 (1990); Zaccardi v. Zale Corp., 856 F.2d 1473, 1476–77 (10th Cir.1988). The Wyoming Supreme Court will permit juries to disregard disclaimers in employee handbooks upon proof of detrimental reliance on the representations contained therein. See McDonald v. Mobil Coal Producing, Inc., 789 P.2d 866 (Wyo.1990).

10. *"Wrongful Demotion"?* Does the cause of action recognized in *Woolley* extend to adverse personnel decisions short of dismissal. In Scott v. Pacific Gas and Electric Co., 11 Cal.4th 454, 46 Cal.Rptr.2d 427, 904 P.2d 834 (1995), Scott and Johnson were engineers employed by the defendant utility in a managerial capacity who were demoted for failure to properly supervise overtime and establishing a side business that gave rise to a number of conflicts of interest with their employer. The demotion resulted in a 25 percent reduction in salary and benefits, as well as loss of all supervisory authority. Plaintiffs claimed their demotion violated the employer's implied "cause" promise gleaned in part from its discipline guidelines that stressed "positive," i.e., progressive discipline. The California high court held:

> Conceptually, there is no rational reason why an employer's policy that its employees will not be demoted except for good cause, like a policy restricting termination or providing for severance pay, cannot become an implied term of an employment contract. In each of these instances, an employer promises to confer a significant benefit on the employee, and it is a question of fact whether that promise was reasonably understood by the employee to create a contractual obligation.

Id. at 464, 904 P.2d at 839. See generally Gregory Mark Munson, A Straightjacket for Employment At–Will: Recognizing Breach of Implied Contract Actions for Wrongful Demotion, 50 Vand. L. Rev. 1577 (1997). Recall that antidiscrimination laws are generally held to reach all adverse employment decisions, whether or not they result in a termination of employment.

11. *Can the Dispute–Resolution Mechanism Contained in a Handbook Displace a Court Action for Breach?* Can an employee handbook or personnel manual preclude enforcement of its substantive terms in the civil courts by setting forth a particular dispute resolution mechanism as exclusive? In O'Brien v. New England Telephone & Telegraph, 422 Mass. 686, 664 N.E.2d 843 (1996), the court held that the plaintiff was barred from pursuing his *Woolley*-type claim for failure to follow the procedures required by the personnel manual:

> O'Brien knew of the grievance procedure * * * and had used it successfully. She cannot assert a right against unfair treatment under one part of her employment contract and fail to follow procedures set forth in another part of that contract that could provide relief from that unfair treatment.

> When a collective bargaining agreement provides a grievance procedure, the general rule is that the remedies specified in the agreement must be exhausted before an employee may resort to the courts. * * * We see no justification for treating differently an employee asserting rights under a personnel manual where none of the limited exceptions to the exhaustion requirement * * * applies.

Id. at 695, 664 N.E.2d at 849–50 (citations omitted). If O'Brien had pursued her internal remedies but was not satisfied with the company's disposition, could she then go to court? Would she be able to secure a de novo reconsideration of the merits of her claim? For the employer's internal complaint procedure to have a preclusive effect, would the manual or handbook at least have to expressly state that the procedure is the "exclusive" remedy for such claims? See *Demasse*, 194 Ariz. at 515, 984 P.2d at 1153 (leaving question open). On these issues, see generally Samuel Estreicher, Arbitration of Employment Disputes Without Unions, 66 Chi.–Kent L.Rev. 753, 769–72 (1990). For the extent to which the employers may as a condition of employment require arbitration not only of contractual claims but also statutory and public policy claims, see pp. 1132–58 infra.

12. *Efficiency and Distributional Implications of the "Handbook" Exception?* An economist might argue that the *Woolley–Toussaint* rule should have no efficiency consequences as long as the parties are permitted to contract out of prior job security arrangements, and there are no significant transaction costs to making such contracts. If employers value flexibility over discharges more than employees value job security, employers could simply repurchase the discretion to discharge without cause. The *Woolley–Toussaint* rule, however, may ultimately affect the tenure afforded some employees if transaction costs are significant; and could have at least short-term distributional consequences, if any transfer of the right requires a transfer of wealth to its previous holder, here the employees. See generally Stewart J. Schwab, Collective Bargaining and the Coase Theorem, 72 Corn. L.Rev. 245 (1987); Jeffrey Harrison, "New" Terminable-at-Will Employment Contract: An Interest and Cost Incidence Analysis, 69 Iowa L.Rev. 327 (1984). Dean Morriss argues that in the overwhelming majority of cases, employers have contracted out of the "handbook" exception by inserting disclaimers into their employee handbooks. See Andrew P. Morriss, Bad Data, Bad Economics, and Bad Policy: Time to Fire Wrongful Discharge Law, 74 Tex. L. Rev. 1901 (1996).

Note on Unilateral Modification/Rescission of Handbook Promises

Consider the *Woolley* court's reservation of the question whether the employer could unilaterally change the handbook in a manner that would "adversely affect a job security provision." From the standpoint of traditional contract law, an employer cannot effect a midterm modification of a prior contractual commitment to employ an individual for a stated term (or under stated conditions) simply by announcing that it is changing the contract for the future. The employee's continued performance of services in the face of such an announcement would not constitute an agreement to the change; and the employer's continued provision of employment (albeit under different terms) would not provide consideration for the midterm modification because of the employer's pre-existing duty. See generally Farnsworth, Contracts, supra, §§ 4.21–.22 (questioning pre-existing duty rule). By contrast, where employment is truly at will, each day provides the setting for a new contract. Under the New Jersey high court's reasoning, could an employer argue that just as its unilateral contract offer to impose a job security term could be accepted by the employees' continued performance, so could its new unilateral contract offer to remove the job security term be accepted by the employees' continued performance? Consider three groups of employees: (1) one group hired during the earlier at-will era; (2) one group hired after the job security term was imposed; and (3) a third group hired after the job security term was rescinded. Do the rights of these employees differ? If employees in group (2) are terminated after the job security term was rescinded, are their rights based on the job security term or the revived at-will rule?

a. *Michigan–California Position.* In Bankey v. Storer Broadcasting Co., 432 Mich. 438, 443 N.W.2d 112 (1989) (en banc), the Michigan Supreme Court, responding to a certified question from the Sixth Circuit, rejected the implications of the "unilateral contract" theory utilized in *Woolley.* The court held that contractual rights based on the "handbook exception" to the "at will" rule recognized in *Toussaint* could be unilaterally modified by an employer even without explicit reservation at the outset of the right to do so:

> Without rejecting the applicability of unilateral contract theory in other situations, we find it inadequate [here]. We look, instead, to the analysis employed in *Toussaint* which focused upon the benefit that accrues to an employer when it establishes desirable personnel policies. Under *Toussaint,* written personnel policies are not enforceable because they have been "offered and accepted" as a unilateral contract; rather, their enforceability arises from the benefit the employer derives by establishing such policies. * * *

> Under the *Toussaint* analysis, an employer who chooses to establish desirable personnel policies, such as a discharge-for-cause employment policy, is not seeking to induce each individual employee to show up for work day after day, but rather is seeking to promote an environment conducive to collective productivity. The benefit to the employer of promoting such an environment, rather than the traditional contract-forming mechanisms of mutual assent or individual detrimental reliance, gives rise to a situation "instinct with an obligation." When * * * the employer changes its discharge-for-cause policy to one of employment-at-will, the employer's benefit is correspondingly extinguished, as is the rationale for the court's enforcement of the discharge-for-cause policy. * * *

> It is one thing to expect that a discharge-for-cause policy will be uniformly applied while it is in effect; it is quite a different proposition to expect that such a personnel policy, having no fixed duration, will be immutable unless the right to revoke the policy was expressly reserved. * * *

> Were we to [hold] that once an employer adopted a policy of discharge-for-cause, such a policy could never be changed short of

successful renegotiation with each employee who worked while the policy was in effect, the uniformity stressed in *Toussaint* * * * would be sacrificed. If an employer had amended its policy from time to time * * *, the employer could find itself obligated in a variety of different ways to any number of different employees, depending on the modifications that had been adopted and the extent of the work force turnover.

443 N.W.2d at 119–20. The *Bankey* court stressed, however, that changes cannot be made in "bad faith," giving the example of a temporary suspension of a for-cause policy for the purpose of facilitating the termination of a particular employee; and that "reasonable notice of the change must be uniformly given to affected employees." Id. at 120.

For the California Supreme Court's view, see Asmus v. Pacific Bell, 24 Cal.4th 1, 23 Cal.4th 1, 96 Cal.Rptr.2d 179, 999 P.2d 71, 73–78–79 (2000) (en banc) (on certified question from Ninth Circuit) (citations omitted):

> * * * An employer may unilaterally terminate a policy that contains a specified condition, if the condition is one of indefinite duration, and the employer effects the change after a reasonable time, on reasonable notice, and without interfering with the employees' vested benefits.
>
> * * *
>
> * * * The general rule governing the proper termination of unilateral contracts is that once the promisor determines after a reasonable time that it will terminate or modify the contract, and provides employees with reasonable notice of the change, additional consideration is not required. The mutuality of obligation principle requiring new consideration for contract termination applies to bilateral contracts only. In the unilateral contract context, there is no mutuality of obligation. For an effective modification, there is consideration in the form of continued employee services. * * * [A] rule requiring separate consideration in addition to continued employment as a limitation on the ability to terminate or modify an employee security agreement would contradict the general principle that the law will not concern itself with the adequacy of consideration.
>
> * * * Just as employers must accept the employees' continued employment as consideration for the original contract terms, employees must be bound by amendments to those terms, with the availability of continuing employment serving as adequate consideration from the employer. When Pacific Bell terminated its original ["Management Employee Security Policy"] MESP and then offered continuing employment to employees who received notice and signed an acknowledgment to that effect, the employees accepted the new terms, and the subsequent modified contract, by continuing to work. Continuing to work after the policy termination and subsequent modification constituted acceptance of the new employment terms.

In rejecting the plaintiffs' argument that the employer's job security promise should not be treated as an illusory promise, the California high court added: "[T]he MESP was not illusory because plaintiffs obtained the benefits of the policy while it was operable. In other words, Pacific Bell was obligated to follow it as long as the MESP remained in effect. * * * As long as the MESP remained in force, Pacific Bell could not treat the contract as illusory by refusing to adhere to its terms; the promise was not optional with the employer and was fully enforceable until terminated or modified." 999 P.2d at 79. The court also rejected the view that the MESP created a vested benefit: "[V]ested benefits cannot be stretched to include obligations created by an employer's written policy statements applicable to the general workforce." Id. (citing *Bankey*).

b. *Illinois–Connecticut–Wyoming Position.* The Illinois high court took a very different view in Doyle v. Holy Cross Hospital, 186 Ill.2d 104, 237 Ill.Dec. 100, 708 N.E.2d 1140 (1999):

> * * * Given the contractual rationale of *Duldulao* [v. *St. Mary of Nazareth Hospital Center*, 115 Ill.2d 482, 106 Ill.Dec. 8, 505 N.E.2d 314 (1987)], we find it difficult to reconcile defendant's position with the requirements for contract formation and modification. Applying "traditional principles" of contract law, as *Duldulao* did, we conclude * * * that the defendant's unilateral modification to the employee handbook lacked consideration and therefore is not binding on the plaintiffs. A modification of an existing contract, like a newly formed contract, requires consideration to be valid and enforceable. * * * Consideration consists of some detriment to the offeror, some benefit to the offeree, or some bargained-for exchange between them. * * * In the present case, we are unable to conclude that consideration exists that would justify our enforcement of the modification against existing employees. Because the defendant was seeking to reduce the rights enjoyed by the plaintiffs, it was the defendant, and not the plaintiffs, who would properly be required to provide consideration for the modification. But in adding the disclaimer, the defendant provided nothing of value to the plaintiffs and did not itself incur any disadvantage. * * *

> * * *

> * * * [T]o accept the defendant's reasoning, that the plaintiffs must supply consideration for a change in the contract to their detriment, and to locate consideration in the plaintiffs' continued work, * * * would paradoxically require the plaintiffs to quit their jobs in order to preserve the rights they previously claimed under the employee handbook. * * *

Id. at 111–15, 708 N.E.2d at 1144–46. The Connecticut and Wyoming supreme courts follow the same approach. See Torosyan v. Boehringer Ingelheim Pharm., 234 Conn. 1, 662 A.2d 89 (1995) (Peters, C.J.; arguably prior "cause" term was based on bilateral agreement); Brodie v. General Chem. Corp., 934 P.2d 1263 (Wyo.1997). See also Demasse v. ITT Corp., 194 Ariz. 500, 984 P.2d 1138 (1999) (on certified questions from the Ninth Circuit); McIlravy v. Kerr–McGee Corp., 119 F.3d 876 (10th Cir.1997) (applying Arizona law).

Is the problem identified in *Doyle* one of lack of consideration for the sought-for modification or one of lack of adequate notice? The Arizona Supreme Court in *Demasse*, for example, left open the question whether continued employment could provide consideration for a rescission of an "implied in fact" job security term where the employee was given "adequate notice of the modification": "An employee must be informed of any new term, aware of its impact on the pre-existing contract, and affirmatively consent to it to accept the offered modification." 194 Ariz. at 508, 984 P.2d at 1146.

What would be adequate consideration for changing a handbook-based job security term? The Wyoming high court in *Brodie* stated: "Consideration to modify an employment contract to restore at-will status would consist of either some benefit to the employee, detriment to the employer, or a bargained for exchange. The question of what type of consideration is sufficient cannot be answered with specificity because we have long held that absent fraud or unconscionability, we will not look into the adequacy of consideration." 934 P.2d at 1268 (citations omitted). Does the employer provide sufficient consideration by conditioning some improvement in benefits or a promotion on the employee's continuing to work in accordance with the terms of the modified employee handbook? Are employees likely to change their position by quitting? If, say, a promotion is withheld on this basis, does the disappointed employee have a retaliation claim (see note 6, p. ____ supra)? What about the firm's interest in uniform treatment of employees otherwise similarly situated: Does it make sense to have some of the workers covered by a "good cause" and others subject to "at will" status, when the terms and conditions of the workers are supposedly governed by the same underlying, ostensibly uniform personnel manual/employee handbook?

c. *Proposed Restatement of Employment Law.* The proposed Restatement (Third) of Employment Law (§ 2.04) takes the position that "[p]olicy statements by an employer—made in such documents as employee manuals, personnel handbooks and employment policy directives provided, or made accessible, to employees—that, reasonably read in context, establish limits on the employer's power to terminate the employment relationship are binding on the employer until modified or revoked." Such obligations can be revoked prospectively under § 2.05:

> § 2.05. Modification or Revocation of Binding Employer Policy Statements

>> (a) An employer may modify or revoke its binding policy statement by providing reasonable notice of the modified statement or revocation to the affected employees.

>> (b) Modifications and revocations apply to all employees hired, and all employees who continue working, after the effective date of the notice of modification or revocation.

>> (c) Modifications and revocations cannot adversely affect vested or accrued employee rights that may have been created by the statement, by an employment agreement based on the statement (covered by § 2.03), or by reasonable detrimental reliance on a promise in the statement (covered by § 2.02(c)).

d. *Effect of Unilateral Modification/Rescission of Other Promises?* If an employer, under *Bankey* and *Asmus*, can unilaterally modify the job-security term contained in an employment manual, are other promises made to the employees similarly modifiable? In Bullock v. Automobile Club of Michigan,

432 Mich. 472, 444 N.W.2d 114 (1989), handed down the same day as *Bankey,* the employer terminated a sales representative for failing to meet production quotas as set forth in its unilaterally promulgated sales rules manual. Plaintiff alleged that when hired, before publication of the manual, he was assured "he would have a lifetime job as long as he did not steal" and that the employer never terminated employees for unsatisfactory production. The court held that these allegations stated a claim under *Toussaint:* "The employment manuals * * *, to the extent they do not constitute unilateral modification of the policy basis of plaintiff's claim, must be seen on this record as an *offer* to modify the discharge-for-cause provision of Bullock's alleged express contract and do not entitle the defendant to summary disposition." 444 N.W.2d at 119 (emphasis in original).

In Dumas v. Auto Club Insurance Assn., 437 Mich. 521, 473 N.W.2d 652 (1991), upon commencing employment plaintiff insurance salesmen were told they would be paid under an "Accrued Commission Plan." Under the plan, they would receive seven percent commissions on insurance policies sold and policy renewals. The commission amounts were tied to policy premiums. Subsequently, the employer changed the compensation plan from commissions based on a percentage of premiums to a flat rate for each policy sold or renewed. Plaintiffs challenged the new system as it applied to renewals of old policies purchased before the change in compensation plan. The court held that while vested rights that already accrued may give rise to a claim in contract, the "legitimate expectations" approach of *Toussaint* would not be extended outside of the wrongful-discharge setting:

> While the deferred compensation cases are subject to contract law, the "legitimate expectations" doctrine of *Toussaint* does not follow traditional contract analysis. Therefore, it does not logically follow that *Toussaint* should be extended to the area of compensation. Also, since employees' accrued benefits are protected by the presence of traditional contract remedies, there is no need to extend the expectations rationale to compensation.

Id. at 531, 473 N.W.2d at 656. The promise to a subset of plaintiffs that they would receive seven percent commissions "forever," was enforceable under the Michigan statute of frauds. (For further discussion of the statute of frauds, see pp. 757–63 infra.)

2. *Express Oral Contracts*

OHANIAN v. AVIS RENT A CAR SYSTEM, INC.
United States Court of Appeals, Second Circuit, 1985.
779 F.2d 101.

Cardamone, J.

Defendant Avis Rent A Car System (Avis) appeals from a judgment entered on a jury verdict in the Eastern District of New York (Weinstein, Ch.J.) awarding $304,693 in damages to plaintiff Robert S. Ohanian for lost wages and pension benefits arising from defendant's breach of a lifetime employment contract made orally to plaintiff.

* * *

Plaintiff Ohanian began working for Avis in Boston in 1967. Later he was appointed District Sales Manager in New York, and subsequently moved to San Francisco. By 1980 he had become Vice President of Sales for Avis's Western Region. Robert Mahmarian, a former Avis general manager, testified that Ohanian's performance in that region was excellent. During what Mahmarian characterized as "a very bad, depressed economic period," Ohanian's Western Region stood out as the one region that was growing and profitable. According to the witness, Ohanian was directly responsible for this success.

In the fall of 1980, Avis's Northeast Region—the region with the most profit potential—was "dying." Mahmarian and then Avis President Calvano decided that the Northeast Region needed new leadership and Ohanian was the logical candidate. They thought plaintiff should return to New York as Vice President of Sales for the Northeast Region. According to Mahmarian, "nobody anticipated how tough it would be to get the guy." Ohanian was happy in the Western Region, and for several reasons did not want to move. First, he had developed a good "team" in the Western Region; second, he and his family liked the San Francisco area; and third, he was secure in his position where he was doing well and did not want to get involved in the politics of the Avis "World Headquarters," which was located in the Northeast Region. Mahmarian and Calvano were determined to bring Ohanian east and so they set out to overcome his reluctance. After several phone calls to him, first from then Vice President of Sales McNamara, then from Calvano, and finally Mahmarian, Ohanian was convinced to accept the job in the Northeast Region. In Mahmarian's words, he changed Ohanian's mind

> On the basis of promise, that a good man is a good man, and he has proven his ability, and if it didn't work out and he had to go back out in the field, or back to California, or whatever else, fine. As far as I was concerned, his future was secure in the company, unless— and I always had to qualify—unless he screwed up badly. Then he is on his own, and even then I indicated that at worst he would get his [severance] because there was some degree of responsibility on the part of management, Calvano and myself, in making this man make this change.

Ohanian's concerns about security were met by Mahmarian's assurance that "[u]nless [he] screwed up badly, there is no way [he was] going to get fired * * * [he would] never get hurt here in this company." Ohanian accepted the offer and began work in the Northeast Region in early February 1981.

In April 1981 Ohanian told Fred Sharp, Vice President of Personnel, that he needed relocation money that had been promised, but not yet received. Sharp subsequently sent two form letters to Ohanian: one from Sharp to Ohanian and the other, prepared by Avis, from Ohanian to Sharp. The second letter was a form with boxes for Ohanian to check to signify his choice of relocation expense plans. Ohanian checked one of the boxes, signed the form, and returned it to Sharp.

The following language appeared on the form that Ohanian signed and returned:

> I also hereby confirm my understanding that nothing contained herein or in connection with the change in my position with Avis shall be deemed to constitute an obligation on the part of Avis to employ me for any period of time, and both the company and I can terminate my employment at will.

> There are no other agreements or understandings in respect of my change in position with Avis or the moving of my residence except as is set forth or referred to herein, and in your confirmation letter to me dated April 21, 1981, and the agreements and undertakings set forth therein cannot be modified or altered except by an instrument in writing signed by me and by an executive officer of Avis.

At trial, Ohanian said that he did not believe he read the letter other than to check the relocation plan he desired. He testified that he did not intend this letter to be a contract or to change the terms of his prior agreement with Avis.

Seven months after Ohanian moved to the Northeast Region, he was promoted to National Vice President of Sales and began work at Avis World Headquarters in Garden City, New York. He soon became dissatisfied with this position and in June 1982, pursuant to his request, returned to his former position as Vice President of Sales for the Northeast Region. A month later, on July 27, 1982, at 47 years of age, plaintiff was fired without severance pay. He then instituted this action. Within three months of termination, plaintiff obtained a job as Vice President of Sales for American International Rent A Car. His first year's salary at American International was $50,000 plus a $20,000 bonus. When Ohanian was fired by Avis, his yearly salary was $68,400, and the jury found that he was owed a $17,100 bonus that he had earned before being fired.

* * *

Avis does not challenge the jury's finding that it had not proved that plaintiff was terminated for just cause. Neither has it appealed the awards for the bonus and relocation expenses. Both parties agree that New York law applies.

Defendant's principal argument is that the oral contract that the jury found existed is barred under the statute of frauds, § 5–701 (subd. a, para. 1) of the General Obligations Law. Section 5–701 provides in relevant part:

> Every agreement, promise or undertaking is void, unless it or some note or memorandum thereof be in writing, and subscribed by the party to be charged therewith, or by his lawful agent, if such agreement, promise or undertaking * * * [b]y its terms is not to be performed within one year from the making thereof or the performance of which is not to be completed before the end of a lifetime.

It has long been held that the purpose of the statute is to raise a barrier to fraud when parties attempt to prove certain legal transactions that are deemed to be particularly susceptible to deception, mistake, and perjury. *See D & N Boening, Inc. v. Kirsch Beverages*, 63 N.Y.2d 449, 453–54, 483 N.Y.S.2d 164, 472 N.E.2d 992 (1984). The provision making void any oral contract "not to be performed within one year" is to prevent injustice that might result either from a faulty memory or the absence of witnesses that have died or moved. *See id.; 2 Corbin on Contracts* § 444 at 534 (1950).

* * *

In fact, New York courts perhaps * * * believing that strict application of the statute causes more fraud than it prevents, have tended to construe it warily. The one-year provision has been held not to preclude an oral contract unless there is "not * * * the slightest possibility that it can be fully performed within one year." 2 *Corbin on Contracts* § 444 at 535; *Warner v. Texas and Pacific Railway*, 164 U.S. 418, 434, 17 S.Ct. 147, 153, 41 L.Ed. 495 (1896) ("The question is not what the probable, or expected, or actual performance of the contract was; but whether the contract, according to the reasonable interpretation of its terms, required that it should not be performed within the year."); *Boening*, 63 N.Y.2d at 455, 483 N.Y.S.2d 164, 472 N.E.2d 992. ("this court has continued to analyze oral agreements to determine if, according to the parties' terms, there might be any possible means of performance within one year"). * * *

When does an oral contract not to be performed within a year fall within the strictures of the statute? A contract is not "to be performed within a year" if it is terminable within that time only upon the breach of one of the parties. *Boening*, 63 N.Y.2d at 456, 483 N.Y.S.2d 164, 472 N.E.2d 992. That rule derives from logic because "[p]erformance, if it means anything at all, is 'carrying out the contract by doing what it requires or permits' * * * and a breach is the unexcused failure to do so." *Id.* (*citing Blake v. Voigt*, 134 N.Y. at 72, 31 N.E. 256) [(1892)]. The distinction is between an oral contract that provides for its own termination at any time on the one hand, and an oral contract that is terminable within a year only upon its breach on the other. The former may be proved by a plaintiff and the latter is barred by the statute.

Avis contends that its oral agreement with Ohanian is barred by the statute of frauds because it was not performable within a year. Avis claims that it could only fire plaintiff if he breached the contract, and breach of a contract is not performance. * * *

What defendant fails to recognize is that under New York law "just cause" for termination may exist for reasons other than an employee's breach. * * *

In the instant case, just cause for dismissing Ohanian would plainly include any breach of the contract, such as drinking on the job or refusing to work, since the agreement contemplates plaintiff giving his best efforts. But, as noted, just cause can be broader than breach and here there may be just cause to dismiss without a breach. To illustrate, under the terms of the contract it would be possible that despite plaintiff's best efforts the results achieved might prove poor because of adverse market conditions. From defendant's standpoint that too would force Avis to make a change in its business strategy, perhaps reducing or closing an operation. That is, there would be just cause for plaintiff's dismissal. But if this is what occurred, it would not constitute a breach of the agreement. Best efforts were contemplated by the parties, results were not. Defendant was anxious to have plaintiff relocate because of his past success, but plaintiff made no guarantee to produce certain results. Thus, this oral contract could have been terminated for just cause within one year, without any breach by plaintiff, and is therefore not barred by the statute of frauds.

* * *

Defendant next urges that any claims based on the oral agreement between Ohanian and Avis are barred by the parol evidence rule. Avis says that the clear and unambiguous letter of April 21, 1981 was signed by plaintiff, and it contradicts plaintiff's assertion that he was promised lifetime employment and severance on termination. It is, of course, a fundamental principle of contract law "that, where parties have reduced their bargain, or any element of it, to writing, the parol evidence rule applies to prevent its variance by parol evidence." *Laskey v. Rubel Corp.,* 303 N.Y. 69, 71, 100 N.E.2d 140 (1951).

Avis's argument fails for a very basic reason: the jury found that the April 21st letter did not constitute a contract between it and Ohanian. The trial judge had correctly instructed the jury that if it found the letter to be a contract it could not find for plaintiff, and the jury found for plaintiff. Parol evidence is excluded only when used as an attempt to vary or modify the terms of an existing written contract. *See Kirtley v. Abrams,* 299 F.2d 341, 345 (2d Cir.1962) (the rule does not preclude a party "from attempting to show that there never was any agreement such as the writing purported to be"); *Whipple v. Brown Brothers Co.,* 225 N.Y. 237, 244, 121 N.E. 748 (1919) ("One cannot be made to stand on a contract he never intended to make."); 3 *Corbin on Contracts* § 577 at 385 (1960).

* * *

Avis says that inasmuch as the evidence of an oral promise of lifetime employment was insufficient as a matter of law, that issue should not have gone to the jury. It relies on *Brown v. Safeway Stores, Inc.,* 190 F.Supp. 295 (E.D.N.Y.1960), as support for this argument. Defendant can draw little solace from *Brown.* In that case the claimed assurances were made in several ways including meetings of a group of employees—the purpose of which was not to discuss length of employment—or during casual conversation. *Id.* at 299–300. The conversations were not conducted in an atmosphere, as here, of critical one-on-one negotiation regarding the terms of future employment. Further, in *Brown* the district court found as a matter of fact that the alleged promise of lifetime employment was never made. In contrast, in the instant case the evidence was ample to permit the jury to decide whether statements made to Ohanian by defendant were more than casual comments or mere pep talks delivered by management to a group of employees. All of the surrounding circumstances—fully related earlier— were sufficient for the jury in fact to find that there was a promise of lifetime employment to a "star" employee who, it was hoped, would revive a "dying" division of defendant corporation.

Notes and Questions

1. *Promises of "Lifetime" or "Permanent" Employment.* Modern courts generally have rejected the position of the early common law that express promises of "permanent" or "lifetime" employment are per se unenforceable either for want of consideration or mutuality of obligation. See, e.g., Weiner v. McGraw–Hill, Inc., 57 N.Y.2d 458, 457 N.Y.S.2d 193, 443 N.E.2d 441 (1982). The courts remain, however, wary of purported *oral* agreements of lifetime employment. See e.g., the *Woolley* court's discussion of Savarese v. Pyrene Mfg. Co., at p. 738 supra; note 7, p. 748 supra; see also Murray v. Commercial Union Insurance Co., 782 F.2d 432 (3d Cir.1986) (applying Pennsylvania law); Veno v. Meredith, 357 Pa.Super. 85, 515 A.2d 571 (1986).

2. *Sophisticated Employees and Oral Contracts.* The Second Circuit in *Ohanian* submitted to the jury the question of whether Avis had promised Ohanian a lifetime job absent "just cause," notwithstanding his signing forms reciting that "both the company and I can terminate my employment at will." Should sophisticated employees be able to rely on oral assurances of a term as significant as lifetime employment absent "just cause"? Does *Ohanian*'s analysis render the statute of frauds a dead letter for most oral employment contracts? Is there any argument for not requiring a written commitment in a case like *Ohanian,* yet requiring it of a two-year term contract? Is there any reason why employees who count on assurances of job security cannot be expected to obtain written commitments?

In McInerney v. Charter Golf, Inc., 176 Ill.2d 482, 223 Ill.Dec. 911, 680 N.E.2d 1347 (1997), the court rejected the approach taken in *Ohanian*, holding an oral promise of lifetime employment unenforceable under the statute of frauds:

> A "lifetime" employment contract is, in essence, a permanent employ-
> ment contract. Inherently, it anticipates a relationship of long dura-
> tion—certainly longer than one year. In the context of an employment-
> for-life contract, we believe that the better view is to treat the contract
> as one "not to be performed within the space of one year from the
> making thereof." To hold otherwise would eviscerate the policy underly-
> ing the statute of frauds and would invite confusion, uncertainty and
> outright fraud. Accordingly, we hold that a writing is required for the
> fair enforcement of lifetime employment contracts.

Id. at 490–91, 680 N.E.2d at 1351–52.

3. *Must Express Oral Contracts be of Definite Duration?* At the beginning of Mike Tyson's boxing career, he was placed under the supervision of Cus D'Amato, a renowned boxing figure and manager, who became Tyson's legal guardian. In 1982 D'Amato and Kevin Rooney, a trainer, agreed they would train Tyson without compensation until he became a professional fighter. The two further agreed that when Tyson advanced to professional ranks, Rooney would be Tyson's trainer "for as long as [Tyson] fought professionally." Rooney trained Tyson for 28 months without compensation. After Tyson entered professional ranks in 1985, D'Amato died and James Jacobs became Tyson's manager in 1986. To quell rumors, Tyson authorized Jacobs to state publicly that Rooney would be Tyson's trainer "as long as Mike Tyson is a professional fighter." In 1988, Tyson terminated his relationship with Rooney. The latter then sued Tyson in federal court claiming breach of the 1982 oral agreement. On certified questions from the Second Circuit, the New York Court of Appeals agreed that Rooney's suit could proceed under New York law:

> A sensible path to declare New York law starts with these two steps: (1) if the duration is definite, the at-will doctrine is inapplicable, on the other hand, (2) if the employment term is indefinite or undefined, the rebuttable at-will presumption is operative and other facts come into the equation. * * *

> * * *

> When an agreement is silent as to duration * * * it is presumptively at-will, absent an express or implied limitation on an employer's otherwise unfettered ability to discharge an employee. * * * Only when we discern no term of definiteness or no express limitation does the analysis switch over to the rebuttable presumption line of cases. They embody the principle that an employment relationship is terminable upon even the whim of either the employer or the employee. The agreement in this case is not silent and manifestly provides a sufficiently limiting framework.

> * * *

> * * * [A]lthough the exact end-date of Tyson's professional boxing career was not precisely calculable, the boundaries of beginning and end of the employment period are sufficiently ascertainable. That is enough to defeat a matter-of-law decision by a judge, in substitution for resolution * * * by jury verdict. * * *

> The range of the employment relationship * * * is established by the definable commencement and conclusion of Tyson's boxing career. Though the times are not precisely predictable and calculable to dates certain, they are legally and experientially limited and ascertainable by objective benchmarks. * * *

Rooney v. Tyson, 91 N.Y.2d 685, 689–90, 692–93, 674 N.Y.S.2d 616, 697 N.E.2d 571 (1998). The court did not consider the applicability of the statute of frauds, which presumably would not have barred the action because Tyson's professional career might have ended within a year.

Judge Smith, dissenting, would have required Rooney to "show consideration independent of a mere promise to work for an employer to overcome the presumption of at-will employment" because "a promise of employment which might last anywhere from a day to a decade is insufficient, standing alone, to indicate an actual intention to be potentially and absolutely bound to obligations far in excess of an ordinary employment at-will relationship." 91 N.Y.2d at 702, 704. The dissent also faulted the majority for circumventing the statute of frauds by recognizing a binding oral contract for what was in essence an indefinite term. See id. at 704–705.

4. *Promissory Estoppel Theory?* Can a promissory estoppel claim be pursued when the alleged promise is for an employment-at-will rather than employment for a definite term? In Bower v. AT & T Technologies, Inc., 852 F.2d 361 (8th Cir.1988), the court of appeals held that a claim under Missouri law was stated by employees alleging detrimental reliance on their employer's promise that they would be rehired as clerical workers once their repair jobs were phased out as a result of the divestiture of AT & T subsidiaries. Subsequently, the Missouri Court of Appeals held that promissory estoppel theory was not available to enforce a promise for at-will employment. See Rosatone v. GTE Sprint Communications, 761 S.W.2d 670 (Mo.App.1988). But cf. Peck v. Imedia, Inc., 293 N.J.Super. 151, 679 A.2d 745 (App.Div.1996) (worker's moving from Boston to New Jersey and giving up her desktop business for promise of employment, stated claim); Comeaux v. Brown & Williamson Tobacco Co., 915 F.2d 1264, 1272–73 (9th Cir.1990) (damages under California law for detrimental reliance on withdrawn job offer). Judicial reluctance to embrace the promissory estoppel theory is evaluated in Robert A. Hillman, Questioning the "New Consensus" on Promissory Estoppel: An Empirical and Theoretical Study, 98 Colum. L.Rev. 580 (1998); Hillman, The Unfulfilled Promise of Promissory Estoppel in the Employment Setting, 31 Rutgers L.J. 1 (1999); Cortlan H. Maddux, Employers Beware! The Emerging Use of Promissory Estoppel as an Exception to Employment At Will, 49 Baylor L. Rev. 197 (1997).

Does the promissory-estoppel approach always avoid difficulties under the statute of frauds? The Illinois Supreme Court in *McInerney* thought not:

> In the context of an employment relationship, reasonable reliance is insufficient to bar application of the statute of frauds. Some authorities—reflected in the view of the Second Restatement—have used promissory estoppel to bar application of the statute of frauds in a narrow class of cases in which a performing party would otherwise be without an adequate remedy and there is some element of unjust enrichment. Restatement (Second) of Contracts Sec. 139, Comment c, at 355–56 (1981). We do not believe that this case is one which requires us to adopt such a rule. [Here,] McInerney has been compensated for his services, and the sole injustice of which he complains is his employer's failure to honor its promise of lifetime employment. Our plaintiff, however, is a salesman—a sophisticated man of commerce—and arguably should have realized that his employer's oral promise was unenforceable under the statute of frauds and that his reliance on that promise was misplaced.

176 Ill.2d at 492–93, 680 N.E.2d at 1352–53.

5. *Effect of Stating Salary as Payable for a Stipulated Period?* Should hiring an employee at a stated salary "per year" create a presumption that the hiring is for such a period? A Georgia statute appears to contain such a rule: "If a contract of employment provides that wages are payable at a stipulated period, the presumption shall arise that the hiring is for such period," but it also states that "[a]n indefinite hiring may be terminated at will by either party." O.C.G.A. § 34–7–1 (1988). The Georgia decisions hold that mere reference to an annual salary does not require application of the presumption. See Tipton v. Canadian Imperial Bank of Commerce, 872 F.2d 1491, 1496–97 (11th Cir.1989) (collecting authorities).

3. *"Implied in Fact" Contracts*

FOLEY v. INTERACTIVE DATA CORPORATION

Supreme Court of California, En Banc, 1988.
47 Cal.3d 654, 254 Cal.Rptr. 211, 765 P.2d 373.

Lucas, C.J.

According to the complaint, plaintiff is a former employee of defendant, a wholly owned subsidiary of Chase Manhattan Bank that markets computer-based decision-support services. Defendant hired plaintiff in June 1976 as an assistant product manager at a starting salary of $18,500. As a condition of employment defendant required plaintiff to sign a "Confidential and Proprietary Information Agreement" whereby he promised not to engage in certain competition with defendant for one year after the termination of his employment for any reason. The agreement also contained a "Disclosure and Assignment of Information" provision that obliged plaintiff to disclose to defendant all computer-related information known to him, including any innovations, inventions or developments pertaining to the computer field for a period of one year following his termination. Finally, the agreement imposed on plaintiff a continuing obligation to assign to defendant all rights to his computer-related inventions or innovations for one year following termination. It did not state any limitation on the grounds for which plaintiff's employment could be terminated.

Over the next six years and nine months, plaintiff received a steady series of salary increases, promotions, bonuses, awards and superior performance evaluations. In 1979 defendant named him consultant manager of the year and in 1981 promoted him to branch manager of its Los Angeles office. His annual salary rose to $56,164 and he received an additional $6,762 merit bonus two days before his discharge in March 1983. He alleges defendant's officers made repeated oral assurances of job security so long as his performance remained adequate.

Plaintiff also alleged that during his employment, defendant maintained written "Termination Guidelines" that set forth express grounds for discharge and a mandatory seven-step pretermination procedure. Plaintiff understood that these guidelines applied not only to employees under plaintiff's supervision, but to him as well. On the basis of these representations, plaintiff alleged that he reasonably believed defendant would not discharge him except for good cause, and therefore he refrained from accepting or pursuing other job opportunities.

The event that led to plaintiff's discharge was a private conversation in January 1983 with his former supervisor, vice president Richard Earnest. During the previous year defendant had hired Robert Kuhne and subsequently named Kuhne to replace Earnest as plaintiff's immediate supervisor. Plaintiff learned that Kuhne was currently under investigation by the Federal Bureau of Investigation for embezzlement from his former employer, Bank of America. Plaintiff reported what he knew about Kuhne to Earnest, because he was "worried about working for Kuhne and having him in a supervisory position * * *, in view of Kuhne's suspected criminal conduct." Plaintiff asserted he "made this disclosure in the interest and for the benefit of his employer," allegedly because he believed that because defendant and its parent do business with the financial community on a confidential basis, the company would have a legitimate interest in knowing about a high executive's alleged prior criminal conduct.

In response, Earnest allegedly told plaintiff not to discuss "rumors" and to "forget what he heard" about Kuhne's past. In early March, Kuhne informed plaintiff that defendant had decided to replace him for "performance reasons" and that he could transfer to a position in another division in Waltham, Massachusetts. Plaintiff was told that if he did not accept a transfer, he might be demoted but not fired. One week later, in Waltham, Earnest informed plaintiff he was not doing a good job, and six days later, he notified plaintiff he could continue as branch manager if he "agreed to go on a 'performance plan.' Plaintiff asserts he agreed to consider such an arrangement." The next day, when Kuhne met with plaintiff, purportedly to present him with a written "performance plan" proposal, Kuhne instead informed plaintiff he had the choice of resigning or being fired. Kuhne offered neither a performance plan nor an option to transfer to another position.

* * *

Although plaintiff describes his cause of action as one for breach of an oral contract, he does not allege explicit words by which the parties agreed that he would not be terminated without good cause. Instead he alleges that a course of conduct, including various oral representations, created a reasonable expectation to that effect. Thus, his cause of action is more properly described as one for breach of an implied-in-fact contract.* * *

The absence of an express written or oral contract term concerning termination of employment does not necessarily indicate that the employment is actually intended by the parties to be "at will," because the presumption of at-will employment may be overcome by evidence of contrary intent. Generally, courts seek to enforce the actual understanding of the parties to a contract, and in so doing may inquire into the parties' conduct to determine if it demonstrates an implied contract. "[I]t must be determined, as a question of fact, whether the parties acted in such a manner as to provide the necessary foundation for [an implied contract], and evidence may be introduced to rebut the inferences and show that there is another explanation for the conduct." (*Silva v. Providence Hosp. of Oakland* (1939) 14 Cal.2d 762, 774, 97 P.2d 798; * * *). Such implied-in-fact contract terms ordinarily stand on equal footing with express terms. (Rest.2d Contracts * * , §§ 4, 19.) At issue here is whether the foregoing principles apply to contract terms establishing employment security, so that the presumption of Labor Code section 2922 [of at-will employment] may be overcome by evidence of contrary implied terms, or whether such agreements are subject to special substantive or evidentiary limitations.

* * *

The limitations on employment security terms on which defendant relies were developed during a period when courts were generally reluctant to look beyond explicit promises of the parties to a contract. "The court-imposed presumption that the employment contract is terminable at will relies upon the formalistic approach to contract interpretation predominant in late nineteenth century legal thought: manifestations of assent must be evidenced by definite, express terms if promises are to be enforceable." (Note, *Protecting At Will Employees,* 93 Harv.L.Rev. [1816, 1825 (1980)]. In the intervening decades, however, courts increasingly demonstrated their willingness to examine the entire relationship of the parties to commercial contracts to ascertain their actual intent, and this trend has been reflected in the body of law guiding contract interpretation. (See, Goetz & Scott, *The Limits of Expanded Choice: An Analysis of the Interactions Between Express and Implied Contract Terms* (1985) 73 Cal.L.Rev. 261, 273–276 ["The (Uniform Commercial) Code, now joined by the Second Restatement of Contracts, effectively reverses the common law presumption that the parties' writing and the official law of contract are the definitive elements of the agreement. Evidence derived from experience and practice can now trigger the incorporation of additional, implied terms"].)

* * *

In the employment context, factors apart from consideration and express terms may be used to ascertain the existence and content of an employment agreement, including "the personnel policies or practices of the employer, the employee's longevity of service, actions or communications by the employer reflecting assurances of continued employment, and the practices of the industry in which the employee is engaged." * * * Pursuant to Labor Code section 2922, if the parties reach no express or implied agreement to the contrary, the relationship is terminable at any time without cause. But when the parties have enforceable expectations concerning either the term of employment or the grounds or manner of termination, Labor Code section 2922 does not diminish the force of such contractual or legal obligations. The presumption that an employment relationship of indefinite duration is intended to be terminable at will is therefore "subject, like any presumption, to contrary evidence. This may take the form of an agreement, express or implied, that * * * the employment relationship will continue indefinitely, pending the occurrence of some event such as the employer's dissatisfaction with the employee's services or the existence of some 'cause' for termination." * * *

Finally, we do not agree with the Court of Appeal that employment security agreements are so inherently harmful or unfair to employers, who do not receive equivalent guarantees of continued service, as to merit treatment different from that accorded other contracts. On the contrary, employers may benefit from the increased loyalty and productivity that such agreements may inspire. * * * Permitting proof of and reliance on implied-in-fact contract terms does not nullify the at-will rule, it merely treats such contracts in a manner in keeping with general contract law. * * *

Defendant's remaining argument is that even if a promise to discharge "for good cause only" could be implied in fact, the evidentiary factors * * * relied on by plaintiff are inadequate as a matter of law. This contention fails on several grounds.

First, defendant overemphasizes the fact that plaintiff was employed for "only" six years and nine months. Length of employment is a relevant consideration but six years and nine months is sufficient time for conduct to occur on which a trier of fact could find the existence of an implied contract. * * *

Second, an allegation of breach of written "Termination Guidelines" implying self-imposed limitations on the employer's power to discharge at will may be sufficient to state a cause of action for breach of an employment contract. * * *

Finally, * * * plaintiff alleges that he supplied the company valuable and separate consideration by signing an agreement whereby he promised not to compete or conceal any computer-related information from defendant for one year after termination. The noncompetition agreement and its attendant "Disclosure and Assignment of Proprietary Information, Inventions, etc." may be probative evidence that "it is more probable that the parties intended a continuing relationship, with limitations upon the employer's dismissal authority [because the] employee has provided some benefit to the employer, or suffers some detriment, beyond the usual rendition of service."

In sum, plaintiff has pleaded facts which, if proved, may be sufficient for a jury to find an implied-in-fact contract limiting defendant's right to discharge him arbitrarily—facts sufficient to overcome the presumption of Labor Code section 2922. On demurrer, we must assume these facts to be true. In other words, plaintiff has pleaded an implied-in-fact contract and its breach, and is entitled to his opportunity to prove those allegations.

Notes and Questions

1. *"Implied in Fact" Contract and the Presumption of At–Will Employment.* How does the court in *Foley* reconcile its recognition of an "implied in fact" contract with the otherwise applicable (indeed, in California, statutorily grounded) presumption of at-will employment? Under the reasoning in *Foley*, will it be difficult for most plaintiffs, at least with significant years of service with the employer, to make out an "implied in fact" contract?

2. *Implied Terms or Implied Contract?* Is the *Foley* court right that modern contract law has dispensed with the need for express promises or other manifestations of intention? Do implied terms play more than a supplementary role? Should they? Is the use of implied terms in contracts between merchants, the principal focus of the Uniform Commercial Code, fully transferable to the employment context? What exactly does the court mean by the "implied-in-fact contract"?

Does the approach of the *Foley* court invite juries to find implied contracts having no real basis in the parties' bargained-for exchange, out of solicitude for long-term employees who may find re-employment difficult? Is it a sufficient response that the parties can readily disclaim any intention of creating binding job security arrangements?

3. *"Implied in Fact" Doctrine in Other Jurisdictions.* In other jurisdictions, courts may invoke the language of "implied in fact" contracts to permit enforcement of indefinite oral obligations contained in unilateral employer promulgations or allow incorporation of implied in employment agreements negotiated between employers and employees. For example, in Torosyan v. Boehringer Ingelheim Pharms., 234 Conn. 1, 662 A.2d 89 (1995); see also Boothby v. Texon, Inc., 414 Mass. 468, 608 N.E.2d 1028 (1993), the court used the terminology of "implied contract" apparently in the belief that "express" contracts, at least in that jurisdiction, require a particular form of words. The case would appear to have involved sufficient evidence of an agreement for indefinite employment containing a limit on termination of employment by the employer. As the state high court noted and held to be not clearly erroneous: "The trial court found that, in the circumstances of this case, the oral and written statements constituted promises to the plaintiff" and "that, by working for the defendant, the plaintiff accepted those promises." 234 Conn. at 22. The state supreme court further reasoned:

> Pursuant to traditional contract principles... the default rule of employment at will can be modified by the agreement of the parties. "Accordingly, to prevail on the ... count of his complaint (that) alleged the existence of an implied agreement, the plaintiff had the burden of proving by the fair preponderance of the evidence that (the employer) had agreed either by words or conduct, to undertake (some) form of actual contract commitment to him under which he could not be terminated without cause."

Id. at 15.

GUZ v. BECHTEL NATIONAL, INC.

Supreme Court of California, En Banc, 2000.
24 Cal.4th 317, 100 Cal.Rptr.2d 352, 8 P.3d 1089.

BAXTER, J.

* * *

Guz alleges he had an agreement with Bechtel that he would be employed so long as he was performing satisfactorily and would be discharged only for good cause. Guz claims no express understanding to this effect. However, he asserts that such an agreement can be inferred by combining evidence of several *Foley* factors, including (1) his long service; (2) assurances of continued employment in the form of raises, promotions, and good performance reviews; (3) Bechtel's written personnel policies, which suggested that termination for poor performance would be preceded by progressive discipline, that layoffs during a work force reduction would be based on objective criteria, including formal ranking, and that persons laid off would receive placement and reassignment assistance; and (4) testimony by a Bechtel executive that company practice was to terminate employees for a good reason and to reassign, if possible, a laid-off employee who was performing satisfactorily.

* * *

As we shall explain, we find triable evidence that Bechtel's written personnel documents set forth implied contractual limits on the circumstances under which Guz, and other Bechtel workers, would be terminated. On the other hand, we see no triable evidence of an implied agreement between Guz and Bechtel on additional, different, or broader terms of employment security. As Bechtel suggests, the personnel documents themselves did not restrict Bechtel's freedom to reorganize, reduce, and consolidate its work force for whatever reasons it wished. Thus, contrary to the Court of Appeal's holding, Bechtel had the absolute right to eliminate Guz's work unit and to transfer the unit's responsibilities to another company entity, even if the decision was influenced by dissatisfaction with the eliminated unit's performance, and even if the personnel documents entitled an individual employee to progressive discipline procedures before being fired for poor performance.

* * *

At the outset, Bechtel insists that the existence of implied contractual limitations on its termination rights is negated because Bechtel expressly disclaimed all such agreements. Bechtel suggests the at-will presumption of Labor Code § 2922 was conclusively reinforced by language Bechtel inserted in Policy 1101, which specified that the company's employees "have no ... agreements guaranteeing continuous service and may be terminated at [Bechtel's] option." As Bechtel points out, Guz concedes he understood Policy 1101 applied to him.

This express disclaimer, reinforced by the statutory presumption of at-will employment, satisfied Bechtel's initial burden, if any, to show that Guz's claim of a contract limiting Bechtel's termination rights had no merit. But neither the disclaimer nor the statutory presumption necessarily foreclosed Guz from proving the existence and breach of such an agreement.

* * *

Cases in California and elsewhere have held that at-will provisions in personnel handbooks, manuals, or memoranda do not bar, or necessarily overcome, other evidence of the employer's contrary intent * * *[10]
* * *

We agree that disclaimer language in an employee handbook or policy manual does not necessarily mean an employee is employed at will. But even if a handbook disclaimer is not controlling * * * in every case, neither can such a provision be ignored in determining whether the parties' conduct was intended, and reasonably understood, to create binding limits on an employer's statutory right to terminate the relationship at will. Like any direct expression of employer intent, communicated to employees and intended to apply to them, such language must be taken into account, along with all other pertinent evidence, in ascertaining the terms on which a worker was employed. We examine accordingly the evidence cited by Guz in support of his implied contract claim.

[I]t is undisputed that Guz received no individual promises or representations that Bechtel would retain him except for good cause, or upon other specified circumstances. * * * Nor does Guz seriously claim that the practice in Bechtel's industry was to provide secure employment. Indeed, the undisputed evidence suggested that because Bechtel, like other members of its industry, operated by competitive bidding from project to project, its work force fluctuated widely and, in terms of raw numbers, was in general decline.

However, Guz insists his own undisputed long and successful service at Bechtel constitutes strong evidence of an implied contract for permanent employment except upon good cause. Guz argues that by retaining him for over 20 years, and by providing him with steady raises, promotions, commendations, and good performance reviews during his tenure, Bechtel engaged in "actions ... reflecting assurances of continued employment." (*Foley, supra*, 47 Cal. 3d 654, 680.) Bechtel responds that an individual employee's mere long and praiseworthy service has little or no tendency to show an implied agreement between the parties that the employee is no longer terminable at will.

* * *

We agree that an employee's mere passage of time in the employer's service, even where marked with tangible indicia that the employer

---

10. On the other hand, most cases applying California law, both pre- and post-Foley, have held that an at-will provision in an express written agreement, signed by the employee, cannot be overcome by proof of an implied contrary understanding. * * *

approves the employee's work, cannot alone form an implied-in-fact contract that the employee is no longer at will. Absent other evidence of the employer's intent, longevity, raises and promotions are their own rewards for the employee's continuing valued service; they do not, in and of themselves, additionally constitute a contractual guarantee of future employment security. A rule granting such contract rights on the basis of successful longevity alone would discourage the retention and promotion of employees.

On the other hand, long and successful service is not necessarily irrelevant to the existence of such a contract. Over the period of an employee's tenure, the employer can certainly communicate, by its written and unwritten policies and practices, or by informal assurances, that seniority and longevity do create rights against termination at will. The issue is whether the employer's words or conduct, on which an employee reasonably relied, gave rise to that specific understanding.

Read in context, *Foley, supra*, 47 Cal. 3d 654, did not hold otherwise. In the first place, *Foley*'s reference to lengthy, successful service as evidence of an implied contract not to terminate at will was simply quoted, with little independent analysis, from *Pugh [v. See's Candies, Inc.,]* 116 Cal. App. 3d 311, at page 328 [(1981)]. *Pugh*, in turn, had adopted wholesale the reasoning of *Cleary v. American Airlines, Inc.* (1980) 111 Cal. App. 3d 443, 168 Cal. Rptr. 722 that " 'termination of employment without legal cause [after long service] offends the implied-in-law covenant of good faith and fair dealing contained in all contracts, including employment contracts.' " (*Pugh, supra*, 116 Cal. App. 3d at p. 328, quoting *Cleary*, supra, 111 Cal. App. 3d at p. 455 * * *.) In other words, these cases suggested, because the arbitrary termination of a veteran employee is neither fair nor in good faith, such conduct violates the implied covenant contained in every employment contract, regardless of its terms.

But *Foley* itself discredited this line of reasoning. There we "reiterated that the employment relationship is fundamentally contractual" (*Foley, supra*, 47 Cal. 3d 654, 696), and we made clear that the implied covenant of good faith and fair dealing cannot supply limitations on termination rights to which the parties have not actually agreed.* * *

We therefore decline to interpret *Foley* as holding that long, successful service, standing alone, can demonstrate an implied-in-fact contract right not to be terminated at will. In the case before us, there is no indication that employee longevity is a significant factor in determining the existence or content of an implied contract limiting the employer's termination rights. Guz claims no particular "actions or communications by [Bechtel]" (*Foley, supra*, 47 Cal. 3d 654, 680), and no industry customs, practices, or policies, which suggest that by virtue of his successful longevity in Bechtel's employ, he had earned a contractual right against future termination at will.

If anything, Bechtel had communicated otherwise. The company's Policy 1101 stated that Bechtel employees had no contracts guaranteeing their continuous employment and could be terminated at Bechtel's option. Nothing in this language suggested any exception for senior workers, or for those who had received regular raises and promotions. While occasional references to seniority appear in other sections of Bechtel's personnel documents, the narrow context of these references undermines an inference that Bechtel additionally intended, or employees had reason to expect, special immunities from termination based on their extended or successful service.

* * *

Finally, Guz asserts there is evidence that, industry custom and written company personnel policies aside, Bechtel had an unwritten "policy or practice[]" (*Foley, supra*, 47 Cal. 3d 654, 680) to release its employees only for cause. As the sole evidence of this policy, Guz points to the deposition testimony of Johnstone, BNI's president, who stated his understanding that Bechtel terminated workers only with "good reason" or for "lack of [available] work." But there is no evidence that Bechtel employees were aware of such an unwritten policy, and it flies in the face of Bechtel's general disclaimer. This brief and vague statement, by a single Bechtel official, that Bechtel sought to avoid arbitrary firings is insufficient as a matter of law to permit a finding that the company, by an unwritten practice or policy on which employees reasonably relied, had contracted away its right to discharge Guz at will.

In sum, if there is any significant evidence that Guz had an implied contract against termination at will, that evidence flows exclusively from Bechtel's written personnel documents. It follows that there is no triable issue of an implied contract on terms broader than the specific provisions of those documents. In reviewing the Court of Appeal's determination that Bechtel may have breached contractual obligations to Guz by eliminating his work unit, we must therefore focus on the pertinent written provisions.

As noted above, Bechtel's written personnel provisions covering termination from employment fell into two categories. The parties do not dispute that certain of these provisions, expressly denominated "Policies" (including Policies 1101 and 302), were disseminated to employees and were intended by Bechtel to inform workers of rules applicable to their employment. There seems little doubt, and we conclude, a triable issue exists that the specific provisions of these Policies did become an implicit part of the employment contracts of the Bechtel employees they covered, including Guz.

Guz also points to another Bechtel document, the RIF Guidelines, that addressed procedures for implementing reductions in the workforce. Evidence suggesting the contractual status of this document is somewhat closer. On the one hand, the "Guidelines" label and evidence indicating this document was distributed primarily to supervisors for their use, weighs against an inference that Bechtel intended a widely disseminated policy on which employees might directly rely. * * * Moreover, there was some evidence that even some Bechtel managers were unaware of the force ranking system set forth in Policy 302 and the RIF Guidelines.

On the other hand, the formality, tone, length, and detail of the RIF Guidelines suggests they were not intended as merely precatory. The RIF Guidelines comprised a minimum of six single-spaced pages, and were distributed under a cover letter suggesting that they represented "corporate policy." In some instances, the RIF Guidelines defined or supplemented terms and provisions directly set forth in Policies 302 and 1101, such as the holding status described in Policy 1101 and the formal personnel ranking system described in Policy 302. There was also some evidence that Bechtel employees, including Guz, were aware of RIF Guideline procedures such as force ranking, had observed that the company followed these procedures in the past, and believed them to be Bechtel's policy. Goldstein, Guz's supervisor at BNI–MI, declared that as a supervisor, he received and was "instructed to follow" the RIF Guidelines. On balance, we are persuaded a triable issue exists that the RIF Guidelines, like the formally denominated Policies, formed part of an implied contract between Bechtel and its employees.

As Bechtel stresses, Policy 1101 itself purported to disclaim any employment security rights. However, Bechtel had inserted other language, not only in Policy 1101 itself, but in other written personnel documents, which described detailed rules and procedures for the termination of employees under particular circumstances. Moreover, the specific language of Bechtel's disclaimer, stating that employees had no contracts "guaranteeing ... continuous service" * * * and were terminable at Bechtel's "option," did not foreclose an understanding between Bechtel and all its workers that Bechtel would make its termination decisions within the limits of its written personnel rules. Given these ambiguities, a fact finder could rationally determine that despite its general disclaimer, Bechtel had bound itself to the specific provisions of these documents.

In holding that Bechtel may have breached the terms of an implied contract with Guz by eliminating his work unit, the Court of Appeal relied on two premises. Focusing on one reason Guz was given for this decision—a "downturn in ... workload"—the Court of Appeal concluded that even if this reason were taken at face value, the evidence permitted a determination that it was arbitrary and unreasonable, and thus without good cause, because it lacked support in the facts. Second, the Court of Appeal found triable evidence that this stated reason was pretextual, in that it masked Bechtel's true purpose to dismiss BNI–MI's workers on the basis of the unit's poor performance, but without affording each member the benefit of the progressive discipline rules set forth in the company's personnel documents.

On the facts before us, we conclude that both these premises were in error. Bechtel's written personnel documents—which, as we have seen, are the sole source of any contractual limits on Bechtel's rights to terminate Guz—imposed no restrictions upon the company's prerogatives to eliminate jobs or work units, for any or no reason, even if this would lead to the release of existing employees such as Guz.

Policy 1101 itself did address a category of termination labeled "Layoff." However, this section simply defined that term as a "Bechtel-initiated termination[] of employees caused by a reduction in workload, reorganizations, changes in job requirements, or other circumstances such as failure to meet [a] client's site access requirements." [Italics omitted.] Policy 1101 further provided that persons scheduled for layoff were entitled to advance notice to facilitate reassignment efforts and job search assistance, and that "[a] surplus employee[] [might] be placed on 'holding status' if there [was] a possible Bechtel reassignment within the following 3–month period." By proceeding in this fashion, Policy 1101 confirmed that Bechtel was free to "reorganize" itself, or to "change[] ... job requirements," and to "initiate[]" employee "terminations ... caused by" this process, so long as Bechtel provided the requisite advance notice.

The RIF Guidelines set forth more detailed procedures for selecting individual layoff candidates, and for helping such persons obtain jobs elsewhere within the company. But the RIF Guidelines, like the Policies, neither stated nor implied any limits on Bechtel's freedom to implement the reorganization itself.

Guz, like the Court of Appeal, focuses on a separate section of Policy 1101, titled "Unsatisfactory Performance." This section, the so-called progressive discipline provision, stated that "employees who fail to perform their jobs in a satisfactory manner may be terminated, provided the employees have been advised of the specific shortcomings and given an opportunity to improve their performance." * * * Like the Court of Appeal, Guz cites BNI president Johnstone's disclosure that he was unhappy with BNI–MI's work product as evidence that the elimination of BNI–MI was a pretext for firing its individual members without resort to the progressive discipline policy.

However, as Bechtel suggests, Policy 1101 cannot reasonably be construed to conflate the separate Unsatisfactory Performance and Layoff provisions in this manner. Whatever rights Policy 1101 gave an employee threatened with replacement on account of his or her individual poor performance, we see nothing in Bechtel's personnel documents which, despite Bechtel's general disclaimer, limited Bechtel's prerogative to eliminate an entire work unit, and thus its individual jobs, even if the decision was influenced by a belief that the unit's work would be better performed elsewhere within the company.

Accordingly, we conclude the Court of Appeal erred in finding, on the grounds it stated, that Guz's implied contract claim was triable. Insofar as the Court of Appeal used these incorrect grounds to overturn the trial court's contrary determination, and thus to reinstate Guz's contractual cause of action, the Court of Appeal's decision must be reversed.

[*Eds.* The concurring opinions of Justices Mosk and Chin (the latter joined by Justice Brown) and the concurring and dissenting opinion of Justice Kennard, are omitted.]

Notes and Questions

1. *Future of "Implied in Fact" Contracts in California?* In what respects has the *Guz* court narrowed the scope of the "implied in fact" contract doctrine in California, and in what respects does the doctrine continue to be viable in that jurisdiction? Do you understand why the court agreed there was a triable issue of fact with respect to Bechtel's RIF guidelines but not the other aspects of Guz's implied contract claims?

2. *Role of Handbook Disclaimer?* Is the *Guz* court, in its general approach, giving undue effect to the disclaimer of a job security term contained in Bechtel's policy handbook? In footnote 9 in its opinion (not included in the excerpt above), the court notes that "we do not understand Guz to claim that he had an employment security agreement that predated and arose independently of Policy 1101 and therefore could not be rescinded or cancelled by virtue of Policy 1101's [subsequent] disclaimer. On the contrary, Guz admits Policy 1101 (necessarily including its disclaimer) applied to him, and he premises his contractual claim on an amalgam of factors, significantly including certain language in Policy 1101 itself."

4. Implied Covenant of Good Faith and Fair Dealing

FORTUNE v. NATIONAL CASH REGISTER CO.

Supreme Judicial Court of Massachusetts, 1977.
373 Mass. 96, 364 N.E.2d 1251.

ABRAMS, J.

Orville E. Fortune (Fortune), a former salesman of The National Cash Register Company (NCR), brought a suit to recover certain commissions allegedly due as a result of a sale of cash registers to First National Stores Inc. (First National) in 1968. Counts 1 and 2 of Fortune's amended declaration claimed bonus payments under the parties' written contract of employment. The third count sought recovery in quantum meruit for the reasonable value of Fortune's services relating to the same sales transaction. Judgment on a jury verdict for Fortune was reversed by the Appeals Court, and this court granted leave to obtain further appellate review. We affirm the judgment of the Superior Court. We hold, for the reasons stated herein, there was no error in submitting the issue of "bad faith" termination of an employment at will contract to the jury.

The issues before the court are raised by NCR's motion for directed verdicts. Accordingly, we summarize the evidence most favorable to the plaintiff. * * *

Fortune was employed by NCR under a written "salesman's contract" which was terminable at will, without cause, by either party on written notice. The contract provided that Fortune would receive a weekly salary in a fixed amount plus a bonus for sales made within the "territory" (i.e., customer accounts or stores) assigned to him for "coverage or supervision," whether the sale was made by him or someone else.[2] The amount of the bonus was determined on the basis of "bonus credits," which were computed as a percentage of the price of products sold. Fortune would be paid a percentage of the applicable bonus credit as follows: (1) 75% if the territory was assigned to him at the date of the order, (2) 25% if the territory was assigned to him at the date of delivery and installation, or (3) 100% if the territory was assigned to him at both times. The contract further provided that the "bonus interest" would terminate if shipment of the order was not made within eighteen months from the date of the order unless (1) the territory was assigned to him for coverage at the date of delivery and installation, or (2) special engineering was required to fulfil the contract. In addition, NCR reserved the right to sell products in the salesman's territory without paying a bonus. However, this right could be exercised only on written notice.

In 1968, Fortune's territory included First National. This account had been part of his territory for the preceding six years; he had been successful in obtaining several orders from First National, including a million dollar order in 1963. Sometime in late 1967, or early 1968, NCR introduced a new model cash register, Class 5. Fortune corresponded with First National in an effort to sell the machine. He also helped to arrange for a demonstration of the Class 5 to executives of First National on October 4, 1968. NCR had a team of men also working on this sale.

On November 27, 1968, NCR's manager of chain and department stores, and the Boston branch manager, both part of NCR's team, wrote to First National regarding the Class 5. The letter covered a number of subjects, including price protection, trade-ins, and trade-in protection against obsolescence. While NCR normally offered price protection for only an eighteen-month term, apparently the size of the proposed order from First National caused NCR to extend its price protection terms for either a two-year or four-year period. On November 29, 1968, First National signed an order for 2,008 Class 5 machines to be delivered over a four-year period at a purchase price of approximately $5,000,000. Although Fortune did not participate in the negotiation of the terms of the order,[3] his name appeared on the order form in the space entitled "salesman credited." The amount of the bonus credit as shown on the order was $92,079.99.

---

2. Apparently, NCR's use of a "guaranteed territory" was designed to motivate "the salesman to develop good will for the company and also avoided a damaging rivalry among salesmen." D. Boorstin, The Americans: The Democratic Experience at 202 (1973).

3. Fortune was not authorized to offer the price protection terms which appeared in the November 27 letter, as special covenant A, par. 3 of his contract prohibited him from varying the prices of items.

On January 6, 1969, the first working day of the new year, Fortune found an envelope on his desk at work. It contained a termination notice addressed to his home dated December 2, 1968. Shortly after receiving the notice, Fortune spoke to the Boston branch manager with whom he was friendly. The manager told him, "You are through," but, after considering some of the details necessary for the smooth operation of the First National order, told him to "stay on," and to "[k]eep on doing what you are doing right now." Fortune remained with the company in a position entitled "sales support." In this capacity, he coordinated and expedited delivery of the machines to First National under the November 29 order as well as servicing other accounts.

Commencing in May or June, Fortune began to receive some bonus commissions on the First National order. Having received only 75% of the applicable bonus due on the machines which had been delivered and installed, Fortune spoke with his manager about receiving the full amount of the commission. Fortune was told "to forget about it." Sixty-one years old at that time, and with a son in college, Fortune concluded that it "was a good idea to forget it for the time being."

NCR did pay a systems and installations person the remaining 25% of the bonus commissions due from the First National order although contrary to its usual policy of paying *only* salesmen a bonus. NCR, by its letter of November 27, 1968, had promised the services of a systems and installations person; the letter had claimed that the services of this person, Bernie Martin (Martin), would have a forecasted cost to NCR of over $45,000. As promised, NCR did transfer Martin to the First National account shortly after the order was placed.

Approximately eighteen months after receiving the termination notice, Fortune, who had worked for NCR for almost twenty-five years, was asked to retire. When he refused, he was fired in June of 1970. Fortune did not receive any bonus payments on machines which were delivered to First National after this date.

At the close of the plaintiff's case, the defendant moved for a directed verdict, arguing that there was no evidence of any breach of contract, and adding that the existence of a contract barred recovery under the quantum meruit count. Ruling that Fortune could recover if the termination and firing were in bad faith, the trial judge, without specifying on which count, submitted this issue to the jury. NCR then rested and, by agreement of counsel, the case was sent to the jury for special verdicts on two questions:

    "1. Did the Defendant act in bad faith * * * when it decided to terminate the Plaintiff's contract as a salesman by letter dated December 2, 1968, delivered on January 6, 1969?

    "2. Did the Defendant act in bad faith * * * when the Defendant let the Plaintiff go on June 5, 1970?"

The jury answered both questions affirmatively, and judgment entered in the sum of $45,649.62.[6]

* * *

The contract at issue is a classic terminable at will employment contract. It is clear that the contract itself reserved to the parties an explicit power to terminate the contract without cause on written notice. It is also clear that under the express terms of the contract Fortune has received all the bonus commissions to which he is entitled. Thus, NCR claims that it did not breach the contract, and that it has no further liability to Fortune.[7] According to a literal reading of the contract, NCR is correct.

However, Fortune argues that, in spite of the literal wording of the contract, he is entitled to a jury determination on NCR's motives in terminating his services under the contract and in finally discharging him. We agree. We hold that NCR's written contract contains an implied covenant of good faith and fair dealing, and a termination not made in good faith constitutes a breach of the contract.

We do not question the general principles that an employer is entitled to be motivated by and to serve its own legitimate business interests; that an employer must have wide latitude in deciding whom it will employ in the face of the uncertainties of the business world; and that an employer needs flexibility in the face of changing circumstances. We recognize the employer's need for a large amount of control over its work force. However, we believe that where, as here, commissions are to be paid for work performed by the employee, the employer's decision to terminate its at will employee should be made in good faith. NCR's right to make decisions in its own interest is not, in our view, unduly hampered by a requirement of adherence to this standard.

On occasion some courts have avoided the rigidity of the "at will" rule by fashioning a remedy in tort. We believe, however, that in this case there is remedy on the express contract. In so holding we are merely recognizing the general requirement in this Commonwealth that parties to contracts and commercial transactions must act in good faith toward one another. Good faith and fair dealing between parties are pervasive requirements in our law; it can be said fairly, that parties to contracts or commercial transactions are bound by this standard. See G.L. c. 106,

---

6. The amount apparently represented 25% of the commission due during the eighteen months the machines were delivered to First National, and which was paid to Martin, and 100% of the commissions on the machines delivered after Fortune was fired.

7. Damages were, by stipulation of the parties, set equal to the unpaid bonus amounts. Thus we need not consider whether other measures of damages might be justified in cases of bad faith termination. Nor do we now decide whether a tort action, with possible punitive damages,

might lie in such circumstances. See, e.g., Blades, Employment at Will vs. Individual Freedom: On Limiting the Abusive Exercise of Employer Power, 67 Colum.L.Rev. 1404, 1421–1427 (1967).

Although the order called for purchase of 2,008 Class 5 machines for a total sale of $5,040,080, at trial the parties stipulated that "1,503 machines were actually delivered and installed" under the First National order. The stipulated damages in the instant case were based on the number of registers actually delivered and installed.

§ 1–203 (good faith in contracts under Uniform Commercial Code); G.L. c. 93B, § 4(3)(c) (good faith in motor vehicle franchise termination).

* * *

In the instant case, we need not * * * speculate as to whether the good faith requirement is implicit in every contract for employment at will. It is clear, however, that, on the facts before us, a finding is warranted that a breach of the contract occurred. Where the principal seeks to deprive the agent of all compensation by terminating the contractual relationship when the agent is on the brink of successfully completing the sale, the principal has acted in bad faith and the ensuing transaction between the principal and the buyer is to be regarded as having been accomplished by the agent. Restatement (Second) of Agency § 454, and Comment a (1958). The same result obtains where the principal attempts to deprive the agent of any portion of a commission due the agent. Courts have often applied this rule to prevent over-reaching by employers and the forfeiture by employees of benefits almost earned by the rendering of substantial services. See, e.g., *RLM Assocs. v. Carter Mfg. Corp.*, 356 Mass. 718, 248 N.E.2d 646 (1969); *Lemmon v. Cedar Point, Inc.*, 406 F.2d 94, 97 (6th Cir.1969); *Coleman v. Graybar Elec. Co.*, 195 F.2d 374 (5th Cir.1952); *Zimmer v. Wells Management Corp.*, 348 F.Supp. 540 (S.D.N.Y.1972); *Sinnett v. Hie Food Prods., Inc.*, 185 Neb. 221, 174 N.W.2d 720 (1970). In our view, the Appeals Court erroneously focused only on literal compliance with payment provisions of the contract and failed to consider the issue of bad faith termination. Restatement (Second) of Agency § 454, and Comment a (1958).

NCR argues that there was no evidence of bad faith in this case; therefore, the trial judge was required to direct a verdict in any event. We think that the evidence and the reasonable inferences to be drawn therefrom support a jury verdict that the termination of Fortune's twenty-five years of employment as a salesman with NCR the next business day after NCR obtained a $5,000,000 order from First National was motivated by a desire to pay Fortune as little of the bonus credit as it could. The fact that Fortune was willing to work under these circumstances does not constitute a waiver or estoppel; it only shows that NCR had him "at their mercy." *Commonwealth v. DeCotis*, 366 Mass. 234, 243, 316 N.E.2d 748 (1974).

NCR also contends that Fortune cannot complain of his firing in June, 1970, as his employment contract clearly indicated that bonus credits would be paid only for an eighteen-month period following the date of the order. As we have said, the jury could have found that Fortune was stripped of his "salesman" designation in order to disqualify him for the remaining 25% of the commissions due on cash registers delivered prior to the date of his first termination. Similarly, the jury could have found that Fortune was fired (or not assigned to the First National account) so that NCR could avoid paying him *any* commissions on cash registers delivered after June, 1970.

Conversely, the jury could have found that Fortune was assigned by NCR to the First National account; that all he did in this case was arrange for a demonstration of the product; that he neither participated in obtaining the order nor did he assist NCR in closing the order; and that nevertheless NCR credited him with the sale. This, however, did not obligate the trial judge to direct a verdict.

Notes and Questions

1. *Implied Good–Faith Covenant vs. "Implied in Fact" Contract?* How is the approach to implied terms taken in *Fortune* different, if at all, from that taken in the *Foley* decision?

2. *Origin of Good–Faith Covenant.* The implied covenant of good faith and fair dealing can be viewed as an example of contract law supplying the implied background rules which inform the expectations of the parties when they enter into a particular contract. Absent such implied terms, the parties would have to negotiate prolix documents setting forth all of the obligations underlying their proposed relationship. For example, in Wood v. Lucy, Lady Duff–Gordon, 222 N.Y. 88, 118 N.E. 214 (1917), a well-known creator of fashions gave the exclusive right to market her designs for a period of at least a year to Wood in return for half of the proceeds he obtained from such marketing, but the agreement said nothing about Wood's duty to market the designs. Lady Duff Gordon's attempt to justify a breach of the agreement because of lack of consideration was rejected by the New York Court of Appeals. Judge Cardozo explained that in view of the "exclusive privilege" granted to Wood, the court would not "suppose that one party was to be placed at the mercy of the other," and held that consideration was supplied by Wood's implied promise to use "reasonable efforts to * * * market her designs * * *." Id. at 90–91, 118 N.E. at 214.

3. *Did* Fortune *Really Involve a Strategic Firing? Fortune* may seem a straightforward application of the implied good-faith covenant. A commission salesman who arranges a major sale reasonably assumes that he will not be terminated for the purpose of preventing him from earning commissions due on completion of the sale. For Professor Epstein, however, the decision is "wrong in principle":

> The contractual provisions concerning commissions represent a rough effort to match payment with performance where the labor of more than one individual was necessary to close the sale. The case is not simply one where a strategically timed firing allowed the company to deprive a dismissed employee of the benefits due him upon completion of performance. Indeed, the firm kept none of the commission at all, so that when the case went to the jury, the only issue was whether the company should be called upon to pay the same commission twice. * * * In its enthusiastic meddling in private contracts, the court nowhere suggested an alternative commission structure that would have better served the joint interests of the parties at the time of contract formation.

Epstein, In Defense of the Contract at Will, 51 U.Chi.L.Rev. 947, 981–82 (1984), excerpted at pp. 825–29 infra. Is Epstein really disagreeing with the principle of *Fortune,* or with the finding of employer bad-faith on these facts?

If the latter, is Epstein or the court correct? On the issue of strategic dismissals by employers to avoid employee benefit obligations, see pp. 1039–50 infra.

4. *A Basis for Overturning the Dismissal vs. Obtaining Compensation Due?* As interpreted by the Massachusetts courts, *Fortune* seems confined to situations involving forfeiture of compensation for past services on the eve of entitlement. See Gram v. Liberty Mutual Ins. Co., 384 Mass. 659, 666–67, 429 N.E.2d 21, 25–26 (1981). Moreover, the *Fortune* ruling has been construed to provide a basis only for securing the compensation withheld rather than for overturning the termination itself. See Wakefield v. Northern Telecom, Inc., 769 F.2d 109 (2d Cir.1985) (applying either New York or New Jersey law). As Judge Winter observed in *Wakefield*:

> Wakefield may not * * * recover for his termination *per se*. However, the contract for payment of commissions creates rights distinct from the employment relation, and * * * obligations derived from the covenant of good faith implicit in the commission contract may survive the termination of the employment relationship.

> * * *

> A covenant of good faith should not be implied as a modification of an employer's right to terminate an at-will employee because even a whimsical termination does not deprive the employee of benefits expected in return for the employee's performance. This is so because performance and the distribution of benefits occur simultaneously, and neither party is left high and dry by the termination. Where, however, a covenant of good faith is necessary to enable one party to receive the benefits promised for performance, it is implied by the law as necessary to effectuate the intent of the parties.

Id. at 112.

For rulings similar to *Fortune* and *Wakefield,* see Metcalf v. Intermountain Gas Co., 116 Idaho 622, 627, 778 P.2d 744, 749 (1989); Wagenseller v. Scottsdale Memorial Hospital, 147 Ariz. 370, 710 P.2d 1025, 1040 (1985) (en banc); Nolan v. Control Data Corp., 243 N.J.Super. 420, 579 A.2d 1252 (App.Div.1990).

The good-faith covenant plays a significant role in deferred compensation cases. See generally Samuel J. Samaro, The Case for Fiduciary Duty as a Restraint on Employer Opportunism Under Sales Commission Agreements, 8 U. Pa. L. Rev. J. of Lab. & Emp. L. 441 (2006).

5. *The Good–Faith Covenant in New York.* The New York courts have insisted that an implied good-faith covenant cannot be read so as to override an at-will employment contract: "[I]t would be incongruous to say that an inference may be drawn that the employer impliedly agreed to a provision which would be destructive of his right of termination." Murphy v. American Home Products Corp., 58 N.Y.2d 293, 304–05, 461 N.Y.S.2d 232, 237, 448 N.E.2d 86, 91 (1983). Does this language from *Murphy* overstate the incongruity between the good-faith covenant and at-will contracts? Consider Sabetay v. Sterling Drug, Inc., 69 N.Y.2d 329, 514 N.Y.S.2d 209, 506 N.E.2d 919 (1987). In that case, a director of financial projects responsible for

administering the dissolution of his employer's Greek facility claimed that he
was discharged because he disclosed to upper management an illegal tax
avoidance scheme, and that such a discharge for faithfully performing the
obligations of his job contravened the implied good-faith covenant. As
counsel for Sabetay argued:

> Such an implied covenant to cooperate with or not to hinder a promi-
> sor's performance should logically include a prohibition on retaliatory
> acts against a promisor who performs as promised. * * * In this case,
> Sabetay promised to comply with the rules of the Company requiring
> him to refrain from certain improper and illegal activities and requiring
> him to report knowledge of such activities to higher management. In
> accordance with that promise, Sabetay signed written statements certi-
> fying his compliance with those rules. [T]he law imposes upon Sterling a
> covenant not to hinder or obstruct Sabetay in carrying out his promise,
> and not to retaliate against him for fulfilling the terms of his promise;
> such retaliation obviously serves to hinder performance. * * * Sterling
> breached its implied covenant of good faith and fair dealing with
> Sabetay when it terminated him because he complied with Company
> rules as he had promised * * *.

Br. for Pl.-Appellant, pp. 41–4. The New York high court disagreed. *Sabetay*
is criticized in Gary Minda & Katie R. Raab, Time for an Unjust Dismissal
Statute in New York, 54 Brooklyn L.Rev. 1137, 1154 (1989).

However, in Wieder v. Skala, 80 N.Y.2d 628, 593 N.Y.S.2d 752, 609
N.E.2d 105 (1992), New York opened the door a crack, in a case involving a
law firm's discharge of an associate allegedly for reporting the professional
misconduct of another associate to disciplinary authorities as required by the
legal's profession's Code of Professional Responsibility. The high court held
that the plaintiff stated a claim for breach of contract based on an "implied-
in-law obligation" inherent in his relationship with his employer. *Wieder's*
potential reach was narrowed in Horn v. New York Times, note 7, p. 705
supra.

6. *The Good–Faith Covenant as a Basis for a Broader Protection
Against Retaliatory Discharge in Violation of Public Policy?* Some courts
have been willing to invoke the good-faith covenant well beyond the contractual gap-filler role envisioned by the Massachusetts and New York courts (in
Lady Duff–Gordon and *Wakefield*). Perhaps the broadest statement to this
effect is Monge v. Beebe Rubber Co., 114 N.H. 130, 133, 316 A.2d 549, 551–
52 (1974):

> In all employment contracts, whether at will or for a definite term, the
> employer's interest in running his business as he sees fit must be
> balanced against the interest of the employee in maintaining his employ-
> ment, and the public's interest in maintaining a proper balance between
> the two. * * * We hold that a termination by the employer of a contract
> of employment at will which is motivated by bad faith or malice or based
> on retaliation is not [in] the best interest of the economic system or the
> public good and constitutes a breach of the employment contract.

Monge involved a claim of retaliatory discharge for refusing sexual advances
from a supervisor. The New Hampshire high court has subsequently narrowed *Monge* to situations "where an employee is discharged because he has

performed an act that public policy would encourage, or refused to do that which public policy would condemn." Howard v. Dorr Woolen Co., 120 N.H. 295, 297, 414 A.2d 1273, 1274 (1980). The widely-recognized state law cause of action for retaliatory discharge in violation of public policy is the subject of chapter 11 of this book.

5. What Constitutes "Good Cause"?

If we assume that the jurisdiction has adopted some form of a "cause" or "good cause" limitation on the employer's at-will authority, does this mean that employers are liable if they cannot demonstrate "cause" in fact, even if they acted on a reasonable, good-faith belief that they had cause for the decision? The following decision from California takes up this issue.

COTRAN v. ROLLINS HUDIG HALL INT'L
Supreme Court of California, 1998.
17 Cal.4th 93, 69 Cal.Rptr.2d 900, 948 P.2d 412.

Brown, J.

When an employee hired under an implied agreement not to be dismissed except for "good cause" is fired for misconduct and challenges the termination in court, what is the role of the jury in deciding whether misconduct occurred? Does it decide whether the acts that led to the decision to terminate happened? Or is its role to decide whether the employer had reasonable grounds for believing they happened and otherwise acted fairly? * * *

* * * The better reasoned view, we conclude, prescribes the jury's role as deciding whether the employer acted with " 'a fair and honest cause or reason, regulated by good faith.' " That language is from *Pugh v. See's Candies, Inc.* (1981) 116 Cal. App. 3d 311, 330 [171 Cal. Rptr. 917] (*Pugh I*), the font of implied-contract-based wrongful termination law in California. Recently, in *Scott* v. *Pacific Gas & Electric Co.* (1995) 11 Cal. 4th 454, 467 [46 Cal. Rptr. 2d 427, 904 P.2d 834](*Scott*), we elaborated on the content of good or just cause by enumerating what it is not: reasons that are " 'trivial, capricious, unrelated to business needs or goals, or pretextual.' " * * *[8]

I. Facts and Procedural Background * * *

8. In this case, the contractual limitation on the employer's at-will power of termination is implied, arising, as the trial judge apparently determined, from preliminary negotiations and the text of a letter defendants sent plaintiff in response to a request for additional assurances of "permanent employment" before accepting their employment offer. The letter stated that if plaintiff's efforts to develop an international brokerage department failed to succeed, "other opportunities" within the organization would be "made available" to him. The Court of Appeal held it was error for the trial court to take from the jury the issue whether there was an implied contract not to terminate plaintiff except for good cause, a holding we do not review. Wrongful termination claims founded on an explicit promise that termination will not occur except for just or good cause may call for a different standard, depending on the precise terms of the contract provision.

In 1987, Rollins Hudig Hall International, Inc. (Rollins), an insurance brokerage firm, approached plaintiff, then a vice-president of a competitor, with a proposal to head its new West Coast international office. Following a series of telephone conferences, meetings and exchanges of letters, plaintiff joined Rollins in January 1988 as senior vice-president and western regional international manager. He held that position until 1993 when he was fired.

The events leading to plaintiff's termination began in March 1993, when an employee in Rollins's international department reported to Deborah Redmond, the firm's director of human resources, that plaintiff was sexually harassing two other employees, Carrie Dolce and Shari Pickett. On March 24, Redmond called both women to her office. In separate interviews, she asked each if they had been harassed. Both said yes; each accused plaintiff as the harasser. Two days later, both women furnished statements to Redmond stating that plaintiff had exposed himself and masturbated in their presence more than once; both also accused plaintiff of making repeated obscene telephone calls to them at home. Redmond sent copies of these statements to Rollins's equal employment opportunity (EEO) office in Chicago. Rollins's president, Fred Feldman, also was given copies. He arranged for a meeting with plaintiff at Rollins's Chicago office, attended by Robert Hurvitz, the firm's head of EEO, and Susan Held, Rollins's manager for EEO compliance. At the meeting, Feldman reviewed the accusations made by Dolce and Pickett against plaintiff. He explained that an investigation would ensue and that its outcome would turn on credibility. After reading the Dolce and Pickett statements to plaintiff, Held explained how the investigation would proceed. Plaintiff said nothing during the meeting about having had consensual relations with either of his two accusers, and offered no explanation for the complaints.

Pending completion of the EEO investigation, Rollins suspended plaintiff. Over the next two weeks, Held interviewed 21 people who had worked with plaintiff, including 5 he had asked her to interview. Held concluded that both Dolce and Pickett, who reiterated the incidents described in their statements, appeared credible. Her investigation failed to turn up anyone else who accused plaintiff of harassing them while at Rollins. One Rollins account executive, Gail Morris, told Held that plaintiff had made obscene telephone calls to her when they both worked for another company, soon after a sexual relationship between the two had ended. Susan Randall, one of those plaintiff had asked to be interviewed and who had described plaintiff as a "perfect gentleman," later called Held to relate "a strange early morning phone call" from plaintiff which "was not for any business purpose." Randall "couldn't figure out what [plaintiff] wanted, * * * yelled at him, told him to leave her alone, and never to call her in the middle of the night again." Held's investigation also confirmed that plaintiff had telephoned Dolce and Pickett at home. In April, both women signed sworn affidavits reciting in detail the charges made against plaintiff in their original statements.

On the basis of her investigation, her assessment of Dolce's and Pickett's credibility, and the fact that no one she interviewed had said it was "impossible" to believe plaintiff had committed the alleged sexual harassment, Held concluded it was more likely than not the harassment had occurred. She met with Feldman and Hurvitz to present her conclusions and gave Feldman copies of the affidavits of Dolce, Pickett, and Gail Morris. After reviewing Held's investigative report and the affidavits, Feldman fired plaintiff on April 23, 1993. This suit followed.

II. The Trial

* * *

Rollins defended its decision to fire plaintiff on the ground that it had been reached honestly and in good faith, not that Rollins was required to prove the acts of sexual harassment occurred. Plaintiff objected to Rollins's defense theory, and the trial court rejected it as not available in a breach of contract action, the only one of plaintiff's claims to go to the jury. Boiled down, the trial judge remarked, the case was nothing more than "a contract dispute" and it was Rollins's burden to prove plaintiff committed the acts that led to his dismissal; "whether [Rollins] in good faith believed [plaintiff] did it is not at issue." THE TRIAL COURT TOLD THE JURY: "What is at issue is whether the claimed acts took place. * * * The issue for the jury to determine is whether the acts are in fact true. * * * Those are issues that the jury has to determine." The trial court also read * * * the standard instruction defining "good cause" in employment discharge litigation.[9] It refused an instruction requested by Rollins directing the jury not to substitute its opinion for the employer's.

The jury returned a special verdict. Asked whether plaintiff "engaged in any of the behavior on which [Rollins] based its decision to terminate plaintiff's employment," it answered "no." It set the present cash value of plaintiff's lost compensation at $1.78 million. Rollins appealed from the judgment entered on the verdict. The Court of Appeal reversed. We granted review to clarify the standard juries apply in wrongful termination litigation to evaluate an employer's "good cause" defense based on employee misconduct. We decide, in other words, the question the jury answers when the discharged employee denies committing the acts that provoked the decision to terminate employment. The question of the jury's role in resolving the related but separate issue of whether the reasons assigned by an employer for termination are legally sufficient to constitute good cause is one we leave for another case.

III. Discussion

* * *

9. [This standard instruction] states: "Where there is an employment agreement not to terminate an employee except for good cause, an employer may not terminate the employment of an employee unless such termination is based on a fair and honest cause or reason. In determining whether there was good cause, you must balance the employer's interest in operating the business efficiently and profitably with the interest of the employee in maintaining employment."

* * * As several courts have pointed out, a standard permitting juries to reexamine the factual basis for the decision to terminate for misconduct—typically gathered under the exigencies of the workaday world and without benefit of the slow-moving machinery of a contested trial—dampens an employer's willingness to act, intruding on the "wide latitude" the court in [*Pugh v. See's Candies, Inc.*, 203 Cal.App.3d 743, 250 Cal.Rptr. 195 (1st Dist.1988) (*Pugh II*),] recognized as a reasonable condition for the efficient conduct of business. We believe the [actual-cause] standard is too intrusive, that it tips unreasonably the balance between the conflicting interests of employer and employee that California courts have sought to sustain as a hallmark of the state's modern wrongful termination employment law. * * *

Equally significant is the jury's relative remoteness from the everyday reality of the workplace. The decision to terminate an employee for misconduct is one that not uncommonly implicates organizational judgment and may turn on intractable factual uncertainties, even where the grounds for dismissal are fact specific. If an employer is required to have in hand a signed confession or an eyewitness account of the alleged misconduct before it can act, the workplace will be transformed into an adjudicatory arena and effective decisionmaking will be thwarted. Although these features do not justify a rule permitting employees to be dismissed arbitrarily, they do mean that asking a civil jury to reexamine in all its factual detail the triggering cause of the decision to dismiss— including the retrospective accuracy of the employer's comprehension of that event—months or even years later, in a context distant from the imperatives of the workplace, is at odds with an axiom underlying the jurisprudence of wrongful termination. That axiom, clearly enunciated in *Pugh II*, supra, 203 Cal. App. 3d at page 769, is the need for a sensible latitude for managerial decisionmaking and its corollary, an optimum balance point between the employer's interest in organizational efficiency and the employee's interest in continuing employment.

* * *

The proper inquiry for the jury, in other words, is not, "Did the employee in fact commit the act leading to dismissal?" It is, "Was the factual basis on which the employer concluded a dischargeable act had been committed reached honestly, after an appropriate investigation and for reasons that are not arbitrary or pretextual?" The jury conducts a factual inquiry in both cases, but the questions are not the same. In the first, the jury decides the ultimate truth of the employee's alleged misconduct. In the second, it focuses on the employer's response to allegations of misconduct. * * *

* * * We give operative meaning to the term "good cause" in the context of implied employment contracts by defining it, under the combined *Scott–Pugh* standard * * * as fair and honest reasons, regulated by good faith on the part of the employer, that are not trivial, arbitrary or capricious, unrelated to business needs or goals, or pretextual. A reasoned conclusion, in short, supported by substantial evidence

gathered through an adequate investigation that includes notice of the claimed misconduct and a chance for the employee to respond.

The law of wrongful discharge is largely a creature of the common law. Hence, it would be imprudent to specify in detail the essentials of an adequate investigation. * * *

* * * Justice Tobriner wrote on behalf of a unanimous court in *Pinsker* v. *Pacific Coast Society of Orthodontists* (1974) 12 Cal. 3d 541 [116 Cal. Rptr. 245, 526 P.2d 253], that "[t]he common law requirement of a fair procedure does not compel formal proceedings with all the embellishments of a court trial * * *, nor adherence to a single mode of process. It may be satisfied by any one of a variety of procedures which afford a fair opportunity for an applicant to present his position. * * * "

All of the elements of the governing standard are triable to the jury.

IV. The Disposition

Because it was error to instruct that Rollins could prevail only if the jury was satisfied sexual harassment actually occurred, the case must be retried. On retrial, the jury should be instructed, in accordance with the views we have expressed, that the question critical to defendants' liability is not whether plaintiff in fact sexually harassed other employees, but whether at the time the decision to terminate his employment was made, defendants, acting in good faith and following an investigation that was appropriate under the circumstances, had reasonable grounds for believing plaintiff had done so. * * *

Mosk, J. [concurring in part].

* * * I write separately to make three points. First, "substantial evidence" that the employee committed misconduct is not synonymous with "any" evidence. The ultimate determination is whether a reasonable employer could have found that an employee committed the charged misconduct based on all the evidence before it. * * * Similarly, the requirement that an employee receive notice and an opportunity to be heard is not fulfilled by a charade of due process by an employer that has already made up its mind, but rather signifies "adequate notice of the 'charges' * * * and a reasonable opportunity to respond." * * * Although we do not dictate the precise form that the employer must adopt, fair procedure requires that the employee have a truly meaningful opportunity to tell his or her side of the story and to influence the employer's decision.

Second, there is nothing, of course, in the majority's standard that precludes an employer and an employee from negotiating or impliedly forming a contract with a "good cause" clause that defines that term more explicitly, in which case the jury's good cause determination would be shaped by this contractual definition. For example, the employment contract may spell out in greater detail the due process protections enjoyed by the employee. * * * A court may also reasonably interpret an implied or express employment agreement that contains particularly strong promises of employment security to embody a more protective good cause standard. In short, the majority's definition of "good cause" is a "default" definition that applies only in the absence of more specific contractual provisions.

Third, I note that nothing in the majority opinion is intended to alter the different manner in which the term "good cause" is construed by arbitrators pursuant to a collective bargaining agreement between unions and employers. In such agreements the contract is express, the remedies more limited, the role of the arbitrator in policing collective bargaining agreements well established both contractually and customarily, and the contractual language supplemented by a well developed body of arbitration law concerning the meaning of "good cause" that the parties can be presumed to be aware of at the time they entered the agreement. * * * The majority's good cause standard does not extend beyond the context in which it is articulated, i.e., implied contracts between employers and individual employees.

KENNARD, J. [dissenting in part].

* * * To determine the parties' intent, a court or jury must examine all evidence relating to the formation of the implied agreement. Only if the court or jury concludes that the parties' intent cannot be determined from this evidence should it undertake to bridge this gap by supplying the meaning that comports with community standards of fairness and public policy.

Moreover, if the court must flesh out the meaning of an implied "good cause" limitation, it should choose the meaning that achieves the fairest and most workable result consistent with the normal practices and expectations of employers and employees in modern society. In my view, the meaning that best satisfies these requirements is one that permits the employer to discharge the employee only for specific acts of misconduct that the employee actually committed. Recognizing that a limitation of this kind puts the employer in a difficult position, and that it may impose liability even on employers who have used their best efforts to determine the truth of misconduct allegations fairly and accurately, I would hold that if an employer agrees to reinstate a falsely accused and wrongfully discharged employee, it should be liable in damages only for backpay.

Notes and Questions

1. *Justification for a Partially Subjective Standard?* Are you convinced by the court's explanation of why the jury should not apply an objective standard of whether "good cause" actually existed? Is this explanation based on concerns about preserving employer discretion or on the court's assumptions about the likely intent of the parties, or both? Do you agree with Justice Mosk that the court's standard is only a "default" rule that the parties could modify by express contract terms? If so, what sort of language would suffice to give Cotran the protection of an objective standard? Is it likely that the parties will in fact negotiate over the terms of an "implied in

fact" contract? For an example of a contrary ruling, see Sanders v. Parker Drilling Co., 911 F.2d 191 (9th Cir.1990) (applying Alaska law).

2. *"Second–Class" Contracts?* Is the *Cotran* court suggesting that the "implied in fact" contract is not entitled to the full level of protection that would be accorded an express contract for a definite term requiring "cause" for mid-term dismissal? How else should one understand the suggestion in footnote 8 that an "explicit promise that termination will not occur except for just or good cause may call for a different standard"? Or that "just cause" provisions in collective labor agreements might be interpreted differently?

3. *After-Acquired Evidence of Misconduct?* How would the *Cotran* court treat a situation where an employer acquires post-discharge evidence of the employee's resume fraud? Can the good-faith standard be met by an employer who did not know of the fraud at the time of its initial decision? Is there any reason to treat "implied in fact" contract cases differently from Title VII claims, where after-acquired evidence of misconduct may affect entitlement to reinstatement and other prospective relief but does not negate the underlying violation? See pp. 85–90 supra. But see Crawford Rehabilitation Services, Inc. v. Weissman, 938 P.2d 540 (Colo.1997) (holding that "after-acquired" evidence of "resume fraud" provided a complete defense to claims of breach of implied contract and promissory estoppel).

4. *"Cause" in Definite–Term Contracts.* According to the Restatement (Second) of Agency § 409(1):

> A principal is privileged to discharge before the time fixed by contract of employment an agent who has committed such a violation of duty that his conduct constitutes a material breach of contract, or who, without committing a violation of duty, fails to perform or reasonably appears unable to perform a material part of the promised service because of physical or mental disability.

Notice that the focus is on the employee-agent's material breach or inability to perform; ordinarily, changes in the employer's business circumstances will not supply "cause". See, e.g., Drake v. Geochemistry and Environmental Chemistry Research, Inc., 336 N.W.2d 666 (S.D. 1983); Ryan v. Brown Motors, Inc., 132 N.J.L. 154, 39 A.2d 70 (N.J. 1944). The traditional rule is also that the employer's subjective motivation is irrelevant, as long as adequate cause in fact existed. In some jurisdictions, however, the emphasis placed on the employer's good faith and honesty in the implied-contract cases has prompted courts in definite-term contract cases to require that the employer's stated justification must be the actual reason for the termination. See, e.g., Wilde v. Houlton Regional Hospital, 537 A.2d 1137 (Me.1988).

Consider the approach to the definition of "cause" in the proposed Restatement (Third) of Employment Law § 3.06, comments h–i:

> h. *Cause for Termination: Substantive Dimension:* (i) *Definite–Term Agreements.* When parties negotiate an express agreement for a fixed term of employment, they ordinarily provide in the agreement for a special payout in the event of early termination without cause; in the absence of such a provision, the default rule generally applied by the courts is that termination without cause requires payment of the con-

tractual salary and other benefits for the duration of the term, subject to any mitigation of damages under applicable law. "Cause," if not defined in the parties' agreement, will in these circumstances usually refer to misconduct, other malfeasance by the employee, or other material breach of the agreement, such as persistent neglect of duties, gross negligence, or a failure to perform the duties of the position due to a permanent disability. The parties are, of course, free to define in the agreement their own special understanding of what would constitute cause sufficient to terminate the agreement without breach. However, absent explicit language in the agreement, cause does not include changes in the economic condition of the employer, such as a downturn in demand for the employer's product, a fall in the employer's share price, or the sale of the business.

(ii) *Indefinite-Term Agreements.* Where an employer and employee have negotiated an indefinite-term agreement with limits on the employer's power of termination, the definition of cause for termination expressly agreed to by the parties controls. However, if the agreement is silent on the question, then, given the potential length of indefinite-term agreements, the reasonable presumption is that the parties intended not only that the employee's misconduct, malfeasance, inability to perform the work due to permanent disability, or other material breach may constitute cause for termination, but also that significant changes in the economic circumstances of the employer can supply such cause.

(iii) *Factual Cause.* Where the parties have provided for a definite term of employment or for an indefinite term with a cause limitation on the employer's power of termination, the reasonable presumption is that the parties intended any cause requirement to be confined to situations of undisputed or otherwise proven employee misconduct, malfeasance, failure to perform the work due to permanent disability, or other material breach; and did not intend also to permit termination based on the employer's reasonable, good faith but erroneous belief that the employee engaged in such conduct. This is in keeping with conventional views of cause as an objective concept, and with the concomitant understanding that an erroneous belief of justification for early termination of a definite-term contract, even if grounded in good faith and based upon facts obtained after an appropriate investigation, does not constitute legally sufficient cause to terminate under the agreement.

i. *Cause for Termination: Procedural Dimension.* The cause required to terminate an agreement under § 2.03 also may have a procedural dimension, with respect to both the employer and the employee. Where the agreement specifies the procedures for termination, its terms control. If those terms, for example, require the terminated employee to exhaust certain internal remedies, such as an appeal to the board of directors, those remedies ordinarily—absent proof of futility—must be reasonably exhausted before the employee may bring a lawsuit claiming that the termination was not based on a proper cause. However, even where the agreement is silent on procedures for termination, the fact the parties have provided for a cause limitation on the employer's power to terminate normally requires the employer to give reasons for the termination and be held to the regular and even-handed application of the grounds for terminating an employee for cause.

C. WRONGFUL DISCHARGE: TORT THEORIES OF RECOVERY

1. *"Bad–Faith Breach"*

FOLEY v. INTERACTIVE DATA CORP.
Supreme Court of California, En Banc 1988.
47 Cal.3d 654, 254 Cal.Rptr. 211, 765 P.2d 373.

[*Eds.* For previous excerpt from this decision, see pp. 763–67 supra.]

We turn now to plaintiff's cause of action for tortious breach of the implied covenant of good faith and fair dealing. Relying on *Cleary* [*v. American Airlines, Inc.,*] (1980), 111 Cal.App.3d 443, 168 Cal.Rptr. 722, and subsequent Court of Appeal cases, plaintiff asserts we should recognize tort remedies for such a breach in the context of employment termination.

The distinction between tort and contract is well grounded in common law, and divergent objectives underlie the remedies created in the two areas. Whereas contract actions are created to enforce the intentions of the parties to the agreement, tort law is primarily designed to vindicate "social policy." (Prosser, Law of Torts (4th ed. 1971) p. 613.) The covenant of good faith and fair dealing was developed in the contract arena and is aimed at making effective the agreement's promises. Plaintiff asks that we find that the breach of the implied covenant in employment contracts also gives rise to an action seeking an award of tort damages.

* * *

"Every contract imposes upon each party a duty of good faith and fair dealing in its performance and its enforcement." (Rest.2d Contracts, § 205.) This duty has been recognized in the majority of American jurisdictions, the Restatement, and the Uniform Commercial Code. (Burton, *Breach of Contract and the Common Law Duty to Perform in Good Faith* (1980) 94 Harv.L.Rev. 369.) Because the covenant is a contract term, however, compensation for its breach has almost always been limited to contract rather than tort remedies. As to the scope of the covenant, " '[t]he precise nature and extent of the duty imposed by such an implied promise will depend on the contractual purposes.' " (*Egan v. Mutual of Omaha Ins. Co.* (1979) 24 Cal.3d 809, 818, 169 Cal.Rptr. 691, 620 P.2d 141.) Initially, the concept of a duty of good faith developed in contract law as "a kind of 'safety valve' to which judges may turn to fill gaps and qualify or limit rights and duties otherwise arising under rules of law and specific contract language." (Summers, *The General Duty of Good Faith—Its Recognition and Conceptualization* (1982) 67 Cornell L.Rev. 810, 812, fn. omitted; see also Burton, supra, 94 Harv.L.Rev. 369,

371 ["the courts employ the good faith doctrine to effectuate the intentions of parties, or to protect their reasonable expectations" (fn. omitted)].) As a contract concept, breach of the duty led to imposition of contract damages determined by the nature of the breach and standard contract principles.

An exception to this general rule has developed in the context of insurance contracts where, for a variety of policy reasons, courts have held that breach of the implied covenant will provide the basis for an action in tort. California has a well-developed judicial history addressing this exception. In *Comunale v. Traders & General Ins. Co.* (1958) 50 Cal.2d 654, 658, 328 P.2d 198, we stated, "There is an implied covenant of good faith and fair dealing in every contract that neither party will do anything which will injure the right of the other to receive the benefits of the agreement." (See also *Egan v. Mutual of Omaha Ins. Co.,* supra, 24 Cal.3d 809, 818, 169 Cal.Rptr. 691, 620 P.2d 141.) Thereafter, in *Crisci v. Security Ins. Co.* (1967) 66 Cal.2d 425, 58 Cal.Rptr. 13, 426 P.2d 173, for the first time we permitted an insured to recover in tort for emotional damages caused by the insurer's breach of the implied covenant. We explained in *Gruenberg v. Aetna Ins. Co.* (1973) 9 Cal.3d 566, 108 Cal.Rptr. 480, 510 P.2d 1032, that "[t]he duty [to comport with the implied covenant of good faith and fair dealing] is immanent [sic] in the contract whether the company is attending [on the insured's behalf] to the claims of third persons against the insured or the claims of the insured itself. Accordingly, when the insurer unreasonably and in bad faith withholds payment of the claim of its insured, it is subject to liability in tort." (Id., at p. 575, 108 Cal.Rptr. 480, 510 P.2d 1032.)

* * *

In our view, the underlying problem in the line of cases relied on by plaintiff lies in the decisions' uncritical incorporation of the insurance model into the employment context, without careful consideration of the fundamental policies underlying the development of tort and contract law in general or of significant differences between the insurer/insured and employer/employee relationships. When a court enforces the implied covenant it is in essence acting to protect "the interest in having promises performed" (Prosser, Law of Torts (4th ed. 1971) p. 613)—the traditional realm of a contract action—rather than to protect some general duty to society which the law places on an employer without regard to the substance of its contractual obligations to its employee. * * * An allegation of breach of the implied covenant of good faith and fair dealing is an allegation of breach of an "ex contractu" obligation, namely one arising out of the contract itself. The covenant of good faith is read into contracts in order to protect the express covenants or promises of the contract, not to protect some general public policy interest not directly tied to the contract's purposes. The insurance cases thus were a major departure from traditional principles of contract law. We must, therefore, consider with great care claims that extension of the exceptional approach taken in those cases is automatically appropriate if certain hallmarks and similarities can be adduced in another contract setting. With this emphasis on the historical purposes of the covenant of good faith and fair dealing in mind, we turn to consider the bases upon which extension of the insurance model to the employment sphere has been urged.

The "special relationship" test gleaned from the insurance context has been suggested as a model for determining the appropriateness of permitting tort remedies for breach of the implied covenant of the employment context. One commentary has observed, "[j]ust as the law of contracts fails to provide adequate principles for construing the terms of an insurance policy, the substantial body of law uniquely applicable to insurance contracts is practically irrelevant to commercially oriented contracts * * *. These [unique] features characteristic of the insurance contract make it particularly susceptible to public policy considerations." (Louderback & Jurika, *Standards for Limiting the Tort of Bad Faith Breach of Contract* (1982) 16 U.S.F.L.Rev. 187, 200–201, fns. omitted.) These commentators assert that tort remedies for breach of the covenant should not be extended across the board in the commercial context, but that, nonetheless, public policy considerations suggest extending the tort remedy if certain salient factors are present. (Id., at pp. 216–218.) "The tort of bad faith should be applied to commercial contracts only if four of the features characteristic of insurance bad faith actions are present. The features are: (1) one of the parties to the contract enjoys a superior bargaining position to the extent that it is able to dictate the terms of the contract; (2) the purpose of the weaker party in entering into the contract is not primarily to profit but rather to secure an essential service or product, financial security or peace of mind; (3) the relationship of the parties is such that the weaker party places its trust and confidence in the larger entity; and (4) there is conduct on the part of the defendant indicating an intent to frustrate the weaker party's enjoyment of the contract rights." (Id., at p. 227.) The discussion of these elements includes an assumption that a tort remedy should be recognized in employment relationships within the stated limitations.

* * *

[W]e are not convinced that a "special relationship" analogous to that between insurer and insured should be deemed to exist in the usual employment relationship which would warrant recognition of a tort action for breach of the implied covenant. Even if we were to assume that the special relationship model is an appropriate one to follow in determining whether to expand tort recovery, a breach in the employment context does not place the employee in the same economic dilemma that an insured faces when an insurer in bad faith refuses to pay a claim or to accept a settlement offer within policy limits. When an insurer takes such actions, the insured cannot turn to the marketplace to find another insurance company willing to pay for the loss already incurred. The wrongfully terminated employee, on the other hand, can (and must, in order to mitigate damages [see *Parker v. Twentieth Century–Fox Film Corp.* (1970) 3 Cal.3d 176, 181–182, 89 Cal.Rptr. 737, 474 P.2d 689] make reasonable efforts to seek alternative employment. * * * Moreover, the role of the employer differs from that of the "quasi-public" insurance company with whom individuals contract specifically in order to obtain protection from potential specified economic harm. The employer does not similarly "sell" protection to its employees; it is not providing a public service. Nor do we find convincing the idea that the employee is necessarily seeking a different kind of financial security than those entering a typical commercial contract. If a small dealer contracts for goods from a large supplier, and those goods are vital to the small dealer's business, a breach by the supplier may have financial significance for individuals employed by the dealer or to the dealer himself. Permitting only contract damages in such a situation has ramifications no different from a similar limitation in the direct employer-employee relationship.

Finally, there is a fundamental difference between insurance and employment relationships. In the insurance relationship, the insurer's and insured's interest are financially at odds. If the insurer pays a claim, it diminishes its fiscal resources. The insured of course has paid for protection and expects to have its losses recompensed. When a claim is paid, money shifts from insurer to insured, or, if appropriate, to a third party claimant.

Putting aside already specifically barred improper motives for termination which may be based on both economic and noneconomic considerations, as a general rule it is to the employer's economic benefit to retain good employees. The interests of employer and employee are most frequently in alignment. If there is a job to be done, the employer must still pay someone to do it. This is not to say that there may never be a "bad motive" for discharge not otherwise covered by law. Nevertheless, in terms of abstract employment relationships as contrasted with abstract insurance relationships, there is less inherent relevant tension between the interests of employers and employees than exists between that of insurers and insureds. Thus the need to place disincentives on an employer's conduct in addition to those already imposed by law simply does not rise to the same level as that created by the conflicting interests at stake in the insurance context. Nor is this to say that the Legislature would have no basis for affording employees additional protections. It is, however, to say that the need to extend the special relationship model in the form of judicially created relief of the kind sought here is less compelling.

* * * [I]n traditional contract law, the *motive* of the breaching party generally has no bearing on the scope of damages that the injured party may recover for the breach of the implied covenant; the remedies are limited to contract damages. Thus, recitation of the parameters of the

implied covenant alone is unsatisfactory. If the covenant is implied in every contract, but its breach does not in every contract give rise to tort damages, attempts to define when tort damages are appropriate simply by interjecting a requirement of "bad faith" do nothing to limit the potential reach of tort remedies or to differentiate between those cases properly and traditionally compensable by contract damages and those in which tort damages should flow. Virtually any firing (indeed any breach of a contract term in any context) could provide the basis for a pleading alleging the discharge was in bad faith under the cited standards.

Notes and Questions

1. *Covenant of Good Faith Law in California.* Before *Foley,* some of the California appellate courts had construed the implied good-faith covenant as a substantive limitation on discharge, apparently irrespective of the actual agreement of the parties. The most prominent example was Cleary v. American Airlines, Inc., 111 Cal.App.3d 443, 455, 168 Cal.Rptr. 722, 729 (1980), a case involving the discharge of an employee with 18 years of service: "Termination of employment without legal cause after such a period of time offends the implied-in-law covenant of good faith and fair dealing contained in all contracts including employment contracts." *Cleary* left ambiguous whether the "implied-in-law covenant" was a nonwaivable term, or, rather, a waivable background rule read into the contract whether or not it plausibly effectuated the expectations of the parties. Nevertheless, *Cleary* and Pugh v. See's Candies, Inc., 116 Cal.App.3d 311, 171 Cal.Rptr. 917 (1981), worked a sea-change in California employment law, producing hefty jury awards. See David J. Jung & Richard Harkness, The Facts of Wrongful Discharge, 4 Lab.Lawy. 257, 261 (1988) (criticizing reported statistics but acknowledging that the "expected average award" is approximately $220,000).

Foley reflects the California Supreme Court's determination to limit such awards, in part by rejecting tort-based recovery, and by confining the good-faith covenant to a supplementary, gap-filler role: "[B]ecause the implied covenant protects only the parties' right to receive the benefit of their agreement, and in at-will relationships there is no agreement to terminate only for cause, the implied covenant standing alone cannot be read to impose such a duty." 47 Cal.3d at 698 n.39. This holding was reaffirmed by the state high court in *Guz.*

The contributions of Professor Joseph Grodin, who as an appeals court judge authored *Cleary* and *Pugh,* are assessed in Christopher David Ruiz Cameron, No Ordinary Joe: Joseph R. Grodin and His Influence on California's Law of the Workplace, 52 Hastings L. J. 253 (2001).

2. *The Analogy to"Bad–Faith Breach" in Insurance Law.* Does the *Foley* court persuasively distinguish the insurance law principle of "bad-faith breach," which states a tort in California and other states? Consider Justice Broussard's partial dissent in *Foley:*

> The principal reason we permit tort damages for breach of the covenant of good faith and fair dealing in an insurance contract is that persons do not generally purchase insurance to obtain a commercial advantage, but

to secure the peace of mind and security it will provide in protecting against accidental loss. * * * That reason applies equally to the employer-employee relationship. A man or a woman usually does not enter into employment solely for the money; a job is status, reputation, a way of defining one's self worth and worth in the community. It is also essential to financial security, offering assurance of future income needed to repay present debts and future obligations. * * *

Because workers value their jobs as more than merely a source of money, contract damages, if limited to loss of income, are inadequate. * * * [I]nsured and employees both depend on the contracts "for their security, well-being, and peace of mind. If insurance companies or employers act in bad faith, the consequences can be very severe, indeed much greater than those that result from breach of contract.

In contrast, commercial contracts, generally speaking, are negotiated between parties of more nearly equal bargaining strength, and are entered into for purpose of profit. Breach entails only lost profits, and often a market exists in which the damaged party can cover its loss. * * *

A tort action for bad faith breach requires that the discharge be wrongful—that is, in breach of contract. But once that prerequisite is satisfied, it focuses not upon the employee's right to enforce a particular contractual provision, but upon society's right to deter and demand redress for arbitrary or malicious conduct which inflicts harm on one of its members. That is the proper and traditional function of tort law * * *.

47 Cal.3d at 709–12, 254 Cal.Rptr. at 246–48, 47 Cal.3d 654, 254 Cal.Rptr. 211, 765 P.2d 373, 408–10. Does the *Foley* majority explain why tort damages should not generally be available to deter intentional breach of a contractual obligation? Are most employers likely to damage themselves in the marketplace for new hires if they are known to discharge long-service employees without cause? Could it similarly be argued that tort recovery should not be available in insurance coverage disputes because insurers are adequately deterred from bad-faith behavior by reputational costs? On the general issue of tort damages for contract breach, see William S. Dodge, The Case for Punitive Damages in Contracts, 48 Duke L.J. 629 (1999); John A. Sebert, Punitive and Nonpecuniary Damages in Actions Based Upon Contract: Toward Achieving the Objective of Full Compensation, 33 U.C.L.A. L.Rev. 1565, 1633–42 (1986).

If the views of the dissent had prevailed in *Foley,* would an employee be able to plead a tort cause of action in every discharge case? What principled limitations could be placed on this theory? Would the parties be able to contract out of the tort regime, say, where employees are not willing to "purchase" this additional protection?

3. *Tort Damages in "Forfeiture"–Type Cases?* In K Mart Corp. v. Ponsock, 103 Nev. 39, 732 P.2d 1364 (1987), the Nevada high court held that an employee discharged after nearly 10 years of service for the purpose of preventing the vesting of retirement benefits could recover in tort. Apparently, Nevada limits the bad-faith discharge theory recognized in *K Mart* to contexts where employers breach without justification a "contractual obli-

gation of continued employment". Sands Regent v. Valgardson, 105 Nev. 436, 777 P.2d 898, 899 (1989). Should tort damages be available in a case like *Fortune,* p. 774 supra?

2. *Fraud or Deceit*

HUNTER v. UP–RIGHT, INC.

Supreme Court of California, 1993.

6 Cal.4th 1174, 26 Cal.Rptr.2d 8, 864 P.2d 88.

PANELLI, J.

We granted review in this case to determine whether *Foley* v. *Interactive Data Corp.* (1988) 47 Cal.3d 654 [, 254 Cal.Rptr. 211, 765 P.2d 373](*Foley*) precludes recovery of tort damages for fraud and deceit predicated on a misrepresentation made to effect termination of employment. *Foley* made clear that the employment relationship is "fundamentally contractual," and that—terminations in violation of public policy aside—contract damages are the appropriate remedy for wrongful termination. * * * Analyzing the circumstances of this case in light of *Foley* and of the traditional elements of fraud, we conclude that wrongful termination of employment ordinarily does not give rise to a cause of action for fraud or deceit, even if some misrepresentation is made in the course of the employee's dismissal. Tort recovery is available only if the plaintiff can establish all of the elements of fraud with respect to a misrepresentation that is separate from the termination of the employment contract, i.e., when the plaintiff's fraud damages cannot be said to result from termination itself. The record in this case does not support such recovery. Accordingly, we reverse the judgment of the Court of Appeal.

FACTUAL BACKGROUND

Charles Hunter began working as a welder for Up–Right, Inc. (Up–Right) in January 1973. In 1980 he was promoted to welding supervisor and worked in that capacity until his employment was terminated on September 10, 1987.

In August 1988 Hunter sued Up–Right and his former supervisor, Pat Nelson, alleging causes of action for breach of contract, breach of the implied covenant of good faith and fair dealing, and various torts. After this court filed its decision in *Foley,* supra, 47 Cal.3d 654, Hunter sought and obtained permission to amend his complaint to allege a cause of action for fraud, based on the same facts as alleged in the original complaint.

The evidence presented at trial was in conflict regarding the circumstances of Hunter's termination. Hunter testified that he enjoyed his job at Up–Right, got along well with coworkers, and received excellent performance evaluations. He testified that at the end of the workday on September 10, 1987, he was called in to meet with Nelson. According to Hunter, Nelson told him that there had been a corporate decision to eliminate his position and that if he did not resign he would be terminated. Hunter testified he asked Nelson for the opportunity to work in a lesser position within the company, but was refused. Hunter then signed a document setting forth his resignation. The next day he picked up his final paycheck, which included $5,200 in severance pay.

Nelson testified to a different series of events. On several occasions during a period prior to September 9, 1987, Nelson testified he had admonished Hunter regarding excessive absences to attend to personal matters. On September 9, 1987, Nelson testified, Hunter told him he was thinking of resigning due to personal problems. Nelson told him to think about it overnight and come back the next day. Nelson directed his secretary, Catherine Olson, to prepare a resignation form for Hunter's signature. On September 10, Hunter returned and told Nelson he had decided to resign. Hunter then signed the resignation form. Nelson had Olson prepare a final paycheck. Nelson testified that no corporate decision had been made to eliminate Hunter's job.

John Maricich, who had been plant superintendent for Up–Right for eight years until his resignation in January 1988, testified that Up–Right had a policy of terminating employees only for good cause. He testified that Hunter was an excellent employee.

* * *

The jury found in favor of Hunter on three theories: breach of implied contract not to terminate employment without good cause, breach of implied covenant of good faith and fair dealing, and fraud. By special verdict, it awarded Hunter $38,013 on the contractual theories and $120,000 for misrepresentation. The parties agreed that the $120,000 figure represented the jury's finding as to Hunter's total damages, and thus included the $38,013 awarded as contractual damages. The trial court entered judgment in favor of Hunter in the amount of $120,000, and the Court of Appeal affirmed.

Discussion
* * *

The Court of Appeal erred in inferring that an employer that misrepresents a fact in the course of wrongfully terminating an employee has committed a fraud. The court contrasted Hunter's testimony (that Nelson told him his job had been eliminated by corporate decision) with Nelson's testimony (that no such corporate decision had been made and that Hunter would not have been dismissed had he not signed a resignation). From this, the court concluded that Hunter had proved a knowing misrepresentation (the supposed corporate decision) that was intended to defraud Hunter into resigning his job, Hunter's detrimental reliance (in resigning), and his resulting damage. Thus, according to the Court of Appeal, Hunter established each of the elements of fraud: (a) misrepresentation; (b) defendant's knowledge of the statement's falsity; (c) intent to defraud (i.e., to induce action in reliance on the misrepresentation); (d) justifiable reliance; and (e) resulting damage. (5 Witkin,

Summary of Cal. Law (9th ed. 1988) Torts, § 676, p. 778; Civ. Code, § 1709; *Hobart* v. *Hobart Estate Co.* (1945) 26 Cal.2d 412, 422 [159 P.2d 958].)

The problem with the Court of Appeal's analysis is that the result of Up–Right's misrepresentation is indistinguishable from an ordinary constructive wrongful termination. The misrepresentation transformed what would otherwise have been a resignation into a constructive termination. As the jury found that Up–Right lacked good cause to dismiss Hunter, the constructive termination was wrongful. Thus, Up–Right simply employed a falsehood to do what it otherwise could have accomplished directly. It cannot be said that Hunter relied to his detriment on the misrepresentation in suffering constructive dismissal. Thus, the fraud claim here is without substance.

Moreover, it is difficult to conceive of a wrongful termination case in which a misrepresentation made by the employer to effect termination could ever rise to the level of a separately actionable fraud. In essence, such misrepresentations are merely the means to the end desired by the employer, i.e., termination of employment. They cannot serve as a predicate for tort damages otherwise unavailable under *Foley*. If the termination itself is wrongful, either because it breaches the employment contract or because it violates some well-established public policy articulated in a statute or constitutional provision, then the employee is entitled to recover damages sounding in contract or tort, respectively. But no independent fraud claim arises from a misrepresentation aimed at termination of employment.

Recognition of a fraud cause of action in the context of wrongful termination of employment not only would contravene the logic of *Foley*, but also potentially would cause adverse consequences for industry in general. Fraud is easily pleaded, and in all likelihood it would be a rare wrongful termination complaint that omitted to do so. Much harder, however, is the defense of such claims and their resolution at the summary judgment or demurrer stage of litigation. The resultant costs and inhibition of employment decisionmaking are precisely the sort of consequences we cited in *Foley* in disapproving tort damages for breaches of the implied covenant of good faith and fair dealing.

We note, however, that a misrepresentation not aimed at effecting termination of employment, but instead designed to induce the employee to alter detrimentally his or her position in some other respect, might form a basis for a valid fraud claim even in the context of a wrongful termination. The Court of Appeals for the Ninth Circuit addressed such a situation in *Miller* v. *Fairchild Industries, Inc.* (9th Cir.1989) 885 F.2d 498, 509–510. In that case, the employees had filed complaints against Fairchild with the Equal Employment Opportunity Commission, which resulted in negotiation of settlement agreements by which the employees gave up their right to sue under title VII of the 1964 Civil Rights Act (42 U.S.C. § 2000e–3(a)) in return for Fairchild's promise to provide training opportunities. Soon after the settlement, however, the employees were laid off. They sued Fairchild, alleging, as one of their causes of action, that Fairchild fraudulently induced them to enter into the settlement agreements by concealing the fact that they were probable candidates for future layoff, and by making promises that Fairchild had no intention of keeping. The court concluded that Fairchild's failure to provide the promised training opportunities supported an inference that it had not intended to perform when it signed the settlement agreements. (885 F.2d at p. 509.) Thus, the trial court's entry of directed verdict on the fraud causes of action was improper. (Id. at p. 510.)

In *Miller* v. *Fairchild Industries, Inc.,* supra, the allegedly fraudulent settlement agreement was collateral to the employment contract itself. The *Miller* plaintiffs demonstrated that they had changed their position in reliance on Fairchild's misrepresentations by foregoing their rights to sue under title VII. *Miller* is thus readily distinguishable from the present case, where plaintiff has shown only that Up–Right engineered his resignation without good cause by telling him his position had been eliminated.

* * * It is suggested that the fraud cause of action serves to vindicate such a public policy. While fraud and deceit are defined by statute (see Civ. Code, § 1572, 1573, 1709, 1710, 3294), and while fraudulent conduct is generally condemned by society, we cannot agree that the prohibitions embodied in the statutes concern society at large in the *Foley* sense. At root, fraud and deceit affect only the individual interests of the employer and employee. A claim of fraud or deceit is essentially a private dispute seeking a monetary remedy, not an action to vindicate a broader public interest.

Although tort damages are unavailable in this case, Hunter has established his claim to contractual damages for constructive wrongful termination, and on remand the judgment must be modified accordingly.

Mosk, J. [dissenting].

I dissent. The record in this case reveals that plaintiff was deceived into resigning so that the employer could terminate his employment without the risk of a wrongful discharge lawsuit. Six months after his discharge, plaintiff accidentally discovered that the inducement to resign, based on representations his position was about to be eliminated, had been a ruse. The majority hold[s] that the use of fraud in the termination of an employment contract under these circumstances is not actionable, and that only a breach of contract action lies.

* * *

[W]hile the duty to treat a party with whom one enters into contract in good faith can be seen as only a contractual duty, the obligation to refrain from committing fraud is a duty imposed by society to govern commercial and other human relationships, regardless of whether those relationships are contractual. And, unlike the tortious breach of the covenant of good faith and fair dealing, the tort of fraud has never depended on the existence of a "special relationship" between the tortfeasor and the tort victim. * * *

[I]n the promissory fraud cases, tort recovery is allowed, despite the fact that fraud and contract damages arise from the same set of facts, because the judicial system seeks to vindicate a social policy of preventing injurious, deliberate falsehoods. Although it is a fact of life that parties breach contracts because of changes in circumstance, the tort system is used to send a signal that the breach of a contract a party calculatingly never intended to fulfill is a different, and greater, wrong than an ordinary breach, and should receive greater sanction.

The circumstances in the present case are analogous to promissory fraud. Although plaintiff's damages are presumably the same for being tricked into resigning as they would be if he had been simply wrongfully discharged outright, the former behavior involves a fraud for which the law of tort provides special disincentives. The purpose of the fraud in this case, as the jury fairly inferred, was to dupe plaintiff into forfeiting his contractual and employment rights by deceiving him into resigning. The corporation sought through this artful deception to extricate itself from its contractual obligations, rather than to straightforwardly discharge him and risk potential liability for breach of contract. The law of fraud is designed to deter the use of such strategms.

Notes and Questions

1. *No Stopping Point?* Is the majority in *Hunter* right that the tort of fraud could be used to cover all cases potentially encompassed by a bad-faith breach of contract tort, or might its reach, as Justice Mosk suggests, be more limited? Does the dissent require a showing of detrimental reliance on the employer's misrepresentation? Could such a showing have been made? See further note 3, below.

2. *Purpose of Allowing Tort Recovery for Fraudulent Inducement of Resignation?* What public purpose would be served by allowing tort damages for a fraudulently induced resignation in cases where a direct discharge could support only contract damages? Justice Mosk asserts that an employee whose resignation is fraudulently induced is "in a different, and worse, position than an employee who is straightforwardly discharged." Why? Assuming that the fraud is accepted as a basis for tolling any applicable statute of limitations (which, in any event, is usually quite long for breach of contract claims), isn't the misled employee in as good a position to sue for contract damages as the directly discharged employee? Or is Justice Mosk's concern that some misled employees will never learn that they were deceived, and therefore deceit, when discovered, requires greater penalties to ensure adequate deterrence?

3. *Tort of Fraudulent Inducement.* Andrew Lazar, who worked for 20 years for a family business in New York, was lured to California by a new employer promising a long-term job in a thriving business. The California firm, however, was having serious financial problems when the representations were made, and, moreover, was planning a merger that eventually

would result in the elimination of Lazar's position. Two years after his move to California, Lazar's position was eliminated. He sued for damages for lost income, loss of contact with New York market, payments on his California home he could no longer afford, and emotional distress. The California Supreme Court held that his action could proceed, distinguishing *Hunter* on the ground that, in this case, the plaintiff detrimentally relied on the employer's misrepresentations by taking actions (moving to California and resigning his prior employment) that placed him in a worse position. Lazar v. Superior Court of Los Angeles Co., 12 Cal.4th 631, 49 Cal.Rptr.2d 377, 909 P.2d 981 (1996); accord, Stewart v. Jackson & Nash, 976 F.2d 86, 88 (2d Cir. 1992) (plaintiff's injuries, which involved damage to her career growth, "commenced well before her termination and were, in several respects, unrelated to it"; extended in Hyman v. IBM Corp., 2000 WL 1538161 (S.D.N.Y.2000); both applying New York law); Kidder v. AmSouth Bank, N.A., 639 So.2d 1361 (1994).

Should cases like *Lazar* be treated differently than cases like *Hunter*? If contract damages are sufficient to compensate for a wrongfully induced resignation, why are they not sufficient for wrongfully induced career decisions? Is additional deterrence more important in cases like *Lazar*? For a contrary ruling asserting the unreasonableness of reliance on promises of permanent employment by an at-will employee, see Shelby v. Zayre Corp., 474 So.2d 1069 (Ala.1985). *Lazar* is criticized in William L. Kandel & Lloyd C. Loomis, Fraud Claims in the Employment Relationship: The Unsettling Resurgence of a Tort, 22 Employee Rels. L.J. 103 (no. 2, Autumn 1996).

Note also that California Labor Code § 970 prohibits employers from inducing "employees to move to, from, or within California by misrepresentation of the nature, length or physical conditions of employment." Tyco Indus. v. Superior Court (Richards), 164 Cal.App.3d 148, 155, 211 Cal.Rptr. 540, 544 (1985); see Funk v. Sperry Corp., 842 F.2d 1129, 1133–34 (9th Cir.1988) (§ 970 claim requires proof of knowingly false representations). Should this statute have been read to provide the exclusive remedy for fraudulent inducement in employment cases? On the question whether statutory remedies preempt common law approaches for the same wrong, see notes 4 & 9, pp. 692, 695 supra.

Does the tort of fraudulent inducement also extend to misrepresentations that induce an at-will employee to continue her employment? See Mackenzie v. Miller Brewing Co., 241 Wis.2d 700, 623 N.W.2d 739 (2001) (rejecting as impermissible blurring of the line between contract and tort).

4. *Decisions in Other Jurisdictions on the Tort of Fraud or Deceit.* For decisions finding fraud actionable in the employment context, see, e.g., Sea–Land Service, Inc. v. O'Neal, 224 Va. 343, 297 S.E.2d 647 (1982) (action against employer for intentionally breaching promise of employment in a particular new position if she resigned from her present job with the company); O'Neal v. Stifel, Nicolaus & Co., 996 S.W.2d 700 (Mo. App. 1999) (same); cf. Bower v. AT & T Technologies, Inc., 852 F.2d 361 (8th Cir.1988) (damages for "detrimental reliance" on promise that employees would be rehired as clerical employees after their telephone repair jobs were phased out as a result of divestiture of subsidiaries).

5. *Tort of Negligent Breach?* A few courts have used negligence concepts to permit tort recovery for breach of the employment contract. See, e.g., Flanigan v. Prudential Federal, 221 Mont. 419, 720 P.2d 257 (1986) (negligent failure to follow employer's stated termination policies; tort recovery not barred by exclusivity of workers' compensation scheme); Chamberlain v. Bissell, Inc., 547 F.Supp. 1067 (W.D.Mich.1982). Contra, Heltborg v. Modern Machinery, 244 Mont. 24, 795 P.2d 954, 962 (1990); Demars v. General Dynamics Corp., 779 F.2d 95, 99–100 (1st Cir.1985) (Massachusetts law); Boresen v. Rohm & Haas, Inc., 526 F.Supp. 1230, 1235–36 (E.D.Pa. 1981) (Pennsylvania law).

In *Chamberlain,* the court held that a long-term employee had been discharged for cause, but that the employer could be held liable in tort for negligent performance of its contractual obligation to give annual performance reviews, including the giving of prior notice that discharge could result if performance did not improve. The court found the following principle in Michigan law:

> [W]hile a complete failure to perform a contractual obligation may be actionable only as a breach of contract, the negligent *performance* of the obligation is actionable as a tort. The fact that no actionable breach of contract may have occurred does not preclude a finding that the performance of a contractual obligation has been negligent and resulted in harm. * * *
>
> Since Bissell had a contractual obligation to conduct performance reviews and since it actually undertook to conduct those reviews, it follows that Bissell had a duty to use ordinary or reasonable care in performing the plaintiff's reviews. * * *
>
> * * * [A] reasonable person, under the circumstances of this case, would have told Chamberlain that discharge was being considered, or was possible, without a rapid and drastic change in his job performance.

547 F.Supp. at 1081 (emphasis in original). *Chamberlain* apparently misreads Michigan law, which requires "a duty imposed by the law upon all," rather than "a duty arising out of the intention of the parties themselves and owed only to those specific individuals to whom the promise runs." Ferrett v. General Motors Corp., 438 Mich. 235, 475 N.W.2d 243, 247 (1991) (rejecting tort of negligent evaluation), quoting Hart v. Ludwig, 347 Mich. 559, 565–66, 79 N.W.2d 895 (1956). We know from medical malpractice actions that negligent performance of contractual duties may give rise to tort liability. Why should this principle not hold equally true in the employment context?

Is the problem here not the absence of a duty by the employer to perform contractual obligations without negligence, but rather the difficulty of allowing tort damages for a partial breach when a complete breach (termination of employment) receives only recovery in contract?

Should an employer be held liable for negligent administration of company rules, such as a drug control policy? In Huegerich v. IBP Inc., 547 N.W.2d 216 (Iowa 1996), plaintiff argued that his discharge for violating IBP's policy prohibiting on-premises possession of illegal drugs or "lookalike" drugs (having the same appearance or effect of an illegal drug) should be set aside because IBP was negligent in failing to specifically advise him that possession of "look-alike" drugs violated company policy. The Iowa high court set aside a damages verdict for "negligent discharge": "To recognize a theory of negligent discharge would require the imposition of a duty of care upon an employer when discharging an employee. Such a duty would radically alter the long recognized doctrine allowing discharge for any reason or no reason at all." Id. at 220.

6. *Corporate Punitive Damages?* The commission of an otherwise actionable tort by an agent of the employer does not necessarily translate into employer liability for punitive damages. Calif. Civil Code Sec. 3294, subd. (a), for example, allows a plaintiff to seek punitive damages "for the breach of an obligation not arising from contract" when the plaintiff can show by "clear and convincing evidence" that a defendant "has been guilty of oppression, fraud or malice." However, subd. (b), added in 1980, states that an employer cannot be held liable for punitive damages unless

> the employer has advance knowledge of the unfitness of the employee and employed him with a conscious disregard of the rights or safety of others or authorized or ratified the wrongful conduct for which the damages are awarded or was personally guilty of oppression, fraud or malice.

The statute also includes an additional qualification for corporate employers who will not be liable for punitive damages unless "the advance knowledge and conscious disregard, authorization, ratification or act of oppression, fraud, or malice [is] on the part of an officer, director, or managing agent of the corporation."

In White v. Ultramar, 21 Cal.4th 563, 88 Cal.Rptr.2d 19, 981 P.2d 944 (1999), the California Supreme Court held that under the 1980 amendment,

> the Legislature intended the term "managing agent" to include only those corporate employees who exercise substantial independent authority and judgment in their corporate decisionmaking so that their decisions ultimately determine corporate policy. The scope of a corporate employee's discretion and authority under our test is therefore a question of fact for decision on a case-by-case basis.

* * *

> * * * Although the Court of Appeal did not review her job functions in detail, it concluded that Salla, the zone manager who fired plaintiff, was his supervisor and therefore a managing agent under section 3294, subdivision (b). Under our construction of the term, however, * * * Salla's supervision of plaintiff and her ability to fire him alone were insufficient to make her a managing agent. Nonetheless, viewing all the facts in favor of the trial court's judgment, we conclude that Salla was a managing agent as we construe the term.

> As the zone manager * * *, Salla was responsible for managing eight stores, including two stores in the San Diego area, and at least sixty-five employees. The individual store managers reported to her, and Salla reported to department heads in the corporation's retail management department.

The supervision of eight stores and sixty-five employees is a significant aspect of [the employer's] business. The testimony of Salla's superiors establishes that they delegated most, if not all, of the responsibility for running these stores to her. The fact that Salla spoke with other employees and consulted the human resources department before firing plaintiff does not detract from her admitted ability to act independently of those sources. * * *

21 Cal.App.4th at 566, 577, 981 P.2d at 947, 954. For the approach to these issues in the Title VII context, see Kolstad v. American Dental Assn., 527 U.S. 526, 119 S.Ct. 2118, 144 L.Ed.2d 494 (1999), p. 378 supra.

7. *Preemption by Workers' Compensation Laws?* When dealing with possible tort or other claims for the recovery of personal injury in the employment context, consideration needs to be given to the exclusivity provision of workers' compensation laws. The California courts have generally taken a narrow view of the exclusivity provision and have allowed conduct which is not "a legitimate risk of employment" and "which falls outside of the compensation bargain" to be challenged in civil actions. See, e.g., Shoemaker v. Myers, 52 Cal.3d 1, 276 Cal.Rptr. 303, 801 P.2d 1054 (1990) (claim under whistleblower statute for public employees, West's Ann.Cal. Government Code § 19683, held not barred by exclusivity provision; "public policy" tort action remanded). Should the fraud claim in *Hunter* or *Lazar* have been barred by the exclusivity provision?

Arguments have been made that discrimination and retaliation claims seeking recovery for personal injury fall under the exclusivity provision of workers' compensation laws. In City of Moorpark v. Superior Court of Ventura County, 18 Cal.4th 1143, 77 Cal.Rptr.2d 445, 959 P.2d 752 (1998), the court held that the prohibition against discrimination against employees "who are injured in the course and scope of their employment," in Calif. Labor Code § 132a, did not provide the exclusive remedy for disability-based discrimination and hence did not bar statutory antidiscrimination and common law wrongful discharge remedies. For discussion of the effect of the exclusivity provision on emotional-distress and harassment, see "Note on Emotional Distress in the Workplace Claims," p. 810 infra.

3. *Intentional Interference with Contractual Relations*

CAPPIELLO v. RAGEN PRECISION INDUSTRIES, INC.
Superior Court of New Jersey, Appellate Division, 1984.
192 N.J.Super. 523, 471 A.2d 432.

DREIER, J.

Alexander A. Cappiello (plaintiff) was an employee at will of defendant, Ragen Precision Industries, Inc. (Ragen). At the time of his firing his immediate superior was defendant George Van de Wegh, and the corporate president was defendant Eugene Lopata. Plaintiff was a commission salesman and alleges he was terminated as a result of an agreement between the individual defendants to appropriate his right to accrued commissions, as well as a substantial commission about to be paid as a result of his efforts to sell Ragen's data retrieval system to the Superior Court of New Jersey. Other commissions are in dispute, but it is clear from the jury's verdict that it accepted *in toto* plaintiff's allegations concerning the commissions owed to him. The evidence as to some of them will be discussed later, but the total jury award was $117,188.01. In addition, the jury awarded plaintiff punitive damages in the amount of $25,000, and additionally awarded plaintiff's wife, Pauline Cappiello, $10,000 *per quod* damages for loss of consortium and $10,000 in punitive damages. The award is against all defendants, and the individuals were found to have maliciously conspired to discharge the plaintiff. An additional individual defendant, the chairman of the board, was exonerated.

Any discussion of the legal consequences of firing an employee at will in this State must start with an analysis of *Pierce v. Ortho Pharmaceutical Corp.*, 84 N.J. 58, 417 A.2d 505 (1980)[, excerpted at p. 696 supra.] * * *

The Court specifically noted that the action may be maintained in contract or tort or both, but in either case the employee must show that he was fired for refusing to perform an act that is "a violation of a clear mandate of public policy," and, insofar as the action is maintained in tort, punitive damages can be awarded "to deter improper conduct in an appropriate case, * * * [which] remedy is not available under the law of contracts." *Id.* at 72–73, 417 A.2d 505. The Court was specific, however, in noting that "[o]ur holding should not be construed to preclude employees from alleging a breach of the express terms of an employment agreement." *Id.* at 73, 417 A.2d 505.

* * *

It is not disputed that, although plaintiff's employment was at will, he had an agreement with Ragen for the payment of commissions. Therefore, a breach of this agreement may be separately recognized as a basis for compensatory damages, even under *Pierce,* notwithstanding that plaintiff's discharge must be upheld if he does not meet the *Pierce* abusive discharge test. The problem lies with the award of punitive damages. They are unavailable unless the *Pierce* rationale can be invoked or another basis found, such as the malicious interference with contractual advantage alleged by plaintiff.

The jury interrogatories firmly establish that plaintiff was terminated maliciously and wrongfully to deprive him of his commissions, and that this deprivation was the responsibility of the individual defendants. Although the trial court in the jury interrogatory unfortunately used the language "guilty of maliciously *conspiring* to discharge the plaintiff," from its context in the interrogatories and the whole of the court's charge it is clear that the court was referring merely to the general conduct and inquiring into which, if any, of the individuals had engaged in the action of depriving plaintiff of his commissions—rather than raising the tort of conspiracy as a separate basis of recovery.

* * *

We must next examine plaintiff's allegation of a malicious interference with contractual rights. In New Jersey we have described the tort succinctly as "one who unjustifiably interferes with the contract of another is guilty of a wrong." *Harris v. Perl,* 41 N.J. 455, 461, 197 A.2d 359 (1964). Defendants claim that this tort is inapplicable here, since plaintiff must show the action of a third party. * * *

> * * * The defendant's breach of his own contract with the plaintiff is of course not a basis for the tort. [*Prosser, The Law of Torts* (4 ed. 1971), § 129 at 934, *and see* cases at n. 9]

The interference with one's own contract is merely a breach of that contract. The tort requires the meddling into the affairs of another, in which case punitive damages may follow. As this court noted in *Sandler v. Lawn–A–Mat Chem. & Equip. Corp.,* 141 N.J.Super. 437, 358 A.2d 805 (App.Div.), certif. den. 71 N.J. 503, 366 A.2d 658 (1976):

> Penn–Jersey urges that the cause of action herein is equated with the tort of malicious interference with a contractual relationship where punitive damages may be appropriate. [Citations omitted]. We reject this thesis as inapplicable to the cause of action herein, where the claim is by one party against the other party to the contract and not against a third party interloper who has interfered with the contractual relationship. The latter claim is clearly a tortious wrong whereas the former is only contractual in nature. [141 N.J.Super. at 450, 358 A.2d 805]

Under this analysis it is clear that the punitive damage award against plaintiff's employer, Ragen, will not satisfy these standards, since one cannot interfere with one's own contract. The same is not true, however, of the individual defendants whom the jury found to have acted out of their own greed to procure plaintiff's commissions for their own economic benefit.

* * *

In our case, it was shown that plaintiff's superior and the president of the corporation acting for the corporation in order to secure sizeable commissions owing to plaintiff, terminated him. As tortfeasors they are personally liable, notwithstanding their corporate status. *McGlynn v. Schultz,* 95 N.J.Super. 412, 416, 231 A.2d 386 (App.Div.), certif. den. 50 N.J. 409, 235 A.2d 901 (1967); *Trustees of Structural Steel v. Huber,* 136 N.J.Super. 501, 505, 347 A.2d 10 (App.Div.1975), certif. den. 70 N.J. 143, 358 A.2d 190 (1976). Yet the case law apparently provides no direct remedy against the corporation apart from compensatory damages. Since this is so, there is no incentive for a corporation to refrain from conduct such as that in this case. But there is little difference between what Ragen has done here and any other failure of a party to pay what it knows is justly due. Punitive damages may be called for morally, but in light of the *Pierce* statement, they are not legally assessable here directly against Ragen. *Cf. Garden State Community Hospital v. Watson,* 191 N.J.Super. 225, 227, 465 A.2d 1225 (App.Div.1982), and *Milcarek v.*

Nationwide Ins. Co., 190 N.J.Super. 358, 368, 463 A.2d 950 (App.Div. 1983).

Even if there is no *direct* liability for punitive damages, Ragen can still be responsible for the same on a *vicarious* liability basis under the particular facts of this case. As was noted in *Winkler v. Hartford Acc. and Indem. Co.,* 66 N.J.Super. 22, 168 A.2d 418 (App.Div.), certif. den. 34 N.J. 581, 170 A.2d 544 (1961):

> * * * A corporate employer may be held for exemplary damages if its employee who committed the wrongful act or authorized or ratified it was so high in authority as to be fairly considered executive in character. *Wendelken v. New York, S. & W.R. Co.,* 88 N.J.L. 270 [86 A. 377] (E. & A.1913). See also *Gindin v. Baron,* 16 N.J.Super. 1 [83 A.2d 790] (App.Div.1951), and 11 N.J.Super. 215 [78 A.2d 297] (App.Div.1951). * * *.

Here there is little question that the actions of Eugene Lopata, Ragen's president, were those of an employee "so high in authority as to be fairly considered executive in character." Also, since Ragen here has participated in a single defense with its executives in an effort to retain plaintiff's commissions, we can well find a specific ratification of Lopata's and Van de Wegh's actions. *Security Corp. v. Lehman Associates, Inc.,* 108 N.J.Super. 137, 146–147, 260 A.2d 248 (App.Div.1970). Therefore, although not *directly* responsible for the assessed punitive damages, Ragen is vicariously liable for the same.

Notes and Questions

1. *Origin of Interference Tort.* The interference tort has a long lineage, beginning, interestingly, with the employment contract case of Lumley v. Gye, 2 El. & Bl. 216, 118 Eng.Rep. 749 (1853), in which a singer under contract to sing at plaintiff's theater was induced by the defendant, who owned a rival theater, to break her contract with plaintiff in order to perform for defendant. Even though no violence, fraud or defamation was alleged, such enticement of another's servants was held tortious. See also Walker v. Cronin, 107 Mass. 555 (1871) (union held liable for inducing its members to leave their jobs in the course of a strike). See generally Harvey S. Perlman, Interference with Contract and Other Economic Expectancies: A Clash of Tort and Contract Doctrine, 49 U.Chi.L.Rev. 61 (1982); Note, An Analysis of the Formation of Property Rights Underlying Tortious Interference with Contracts and Other Economic Relations, 50 U.Chi.L.Rev. 1116 (1983); Note, Tortious Interference with Contract: A Reassertion of Society's Interest in Commercial Stability and Contractual Integrity, 81 Colum.L.Rev. 1491 (1981).

2. *The Restatement (Second) of Torts Position.* As set forth in the Restatement (Second) of Torts § 766, the tort is quite open-ended:

> One who intentionally and improperly interferes with the performance of a contract (except a contract to marry) between another and a third person by inducing or otherwise causing the third person not to perform the contract, is subject to liability to the other for the pecuniary loss

resulting to the other from the failure of the third person to perform the contract.

The tort plainly extends to interference with prospective contractual relations, see id. § 766B, and to contracts terminable at will, see id. § 766, comment g ("Until he has so terminated it, the contract is valid and subsisting, and the defendant may not improperly interfere with it."). See Truax v. Raich, 239 U.S. 33, 38, 36 S.Ct. 7, 9, 60 L.Ed. 131 (1915) ("The fact that the employment is at the will of the parties, respectively, does not make it at the will of others.").

3. *Factors Governing Whether Wrongful Interference Has Occurred.* Under Restatement (Second) of Torts § 767, whether there has been wrongful interference depends on an assessment of seven factors:

    (a) the nature of the actor's conduct,

    (b) the actor's motive,

    (c) the interests of the other with which the actor's conduct interferes,

    (d) the interests sought to be advanced by the actor,

    (e) the social interests in protecting the freedom of action of the actor and the contractual interests of the other,

    (f) the proximity or remoteness of the actor's conduct to the interference and

    (g) the relations between the parties.

Unlike other intentional torts such as intentional injury to person or property, or defamation, this branch of tort law has not developed a crystallized set of definite rules as to the existence or nonexistence of a privilege to act. * * *

Id. § 767, comment (b).

4. *Supervisor's Good–Faith Defense.* As a general matter, supervisors acting in good faith within the scope of their authority in effecting a discharge will not be held liable under this tort. See, e.g., Wells v. Thomas, 569 F.Supp. 426 (E.D.Pa.1983); Menefee v. Columbia Broadcasting System, Inc., 458 Pa. 46, 329 A.2d 216 (1974). "The rule assigning liability to corporate officials only when their actions are motivated by actual, and not merely implied, malice has particular force because 'their freedom of action directed toward corporate purposes should not be curtailed by fear of personal liability.'" Gram v. Liberty Mutual Insur. Co., 384 Mass. 659, 663–64, 429 N.E.2d 21, 24 (1981).

Consider, however, the facts in Yaindl v. Ingersoll–Rand Co., 281 Pa.Super. 560, 422 A.2d 611 (1980). Yaindl, a technical services manager at Ingersoll–Rand's Standard Pump–Aldrich Division (SP–AD), had been sent to Italy to inspect pumps sold by SP–AD. His report critical of the manufacture of pump rods antagonized Burns, the manager of SP–AD's manufacturing department, which resulted in a heated argument eventuating in Yaindl's discharge for insubordination. Several weeks later, Yaindl interviewed for a position at Ingeroll–Rand's Turbo Products Division, but did not get the job because Bennett, the group manager for the SP–AD division, had balked at the prospect of Yaindl's being rehired at a different corporate division. While rejecting a wrongful discharge action against the company, the court held that these allegations stated a claim against Bennett. Bennett could not be held liable for furnishing his honest opinion about Yaindl's performance. But, here, "[h]e used his position as a group manager to eliminate [Yaindl's] job possibilities at Turbo by threatening * * * a subordinate within the Ingersoll–Rand's corporate hierarchy, that if [Yaindl] was hired, he would discuss the matter with a vice-president." Id. at 583, 422 A.2d at 623. The court further explained that "a manager's pursuit of a former employee and interference with the employee's employment opportunities at another company constitutes a far greater infringement upon the employee's right to make a living than does the manager's discharge of the employee from the manager's own company." Id. at 584–85, 422 A.2d at 624. *Yaindl* is narrowed in Daniel Adams Assoc., Inc. Rimbach Publishing, Inc., 360 Pa.Super. 72, 82, 519 A.2d 997, 1002 (1987). For other cases sustaining claims against supervisors, see, e.g., Haupt v. International Harvester Co., 582 F.Supp. 545 (N.D.Ill.1984); Harless v. First National Bank, 162 W.Va. 116, 246 S.E.2d 270 (1978); cf. Wagenseller v. Scottsdale Mem. Hosp., 147 Ariz. 370, 710 P.2d 1025, 1043 (1985).

   5. *Third–Party Interference?* The interference tort may be difficult to assert in the employment context both in view of the malice requirement and because the wrongful interference must be the work of a third party. Some courts have held flatly that a supervisor's exercise of authority cannot constitute third-party interference, lest the employer be held liable for interfering with its own contract. See, e.g., Becket v. Welton Becket & Assoc., 39 Cal.App.3d 815, 114 Cal.Rptr. 531 (1974); Ryan v. Brooklyn Eye and Ear Hospital, 46 A.D.2d 87, 360 N.Y.S.2d 912 (1974). On the other hand, *Cappiello* imposes respondeat superior liability on the employer for the intentional wrongdoing of its executives. Does it make sense to impose vicarious liability where the agent of the employer, by definition, must have been acting outside the scope of his authority? Does *Cappiello* support an interference claim by any discharged employee against his former supervisor, and vicariously against his former employer, for wrongfully interfering with his employment contract by inducing his discharge without cause? What aspects of the case arguably provide limiting principles? See also Bell Atlantic Network Services, Inc. v. P.M. Video Corp., 322 N.J.Super. 74, 730 A.2d 406 (N.J. Super. 1999).

   In *Yaindl,* the court found the requisite third party in the fact that SP–AD and Turbo were separate corporate divisions that "had only a distant relationship with each other," but suggested that "the employer could be held vicariously liable when one of its employees intentionally and improperly interferes with another's prospective contractual relation with the employer." 281 Pa.Super. at 585 n. 13, 422 A.2d at 624 n. 13; see *Daniel Adams Assoc.,* 519 A.2d at 1002 (absent special facts of *Yaindl,* "where plaintiff has entered into a contract with a corporation, and that contract is terminated by a corporate agent who has acted within the scope of his or her authority, the corporation and its agent are considered one so that there is no third party against whom a claim for contractual interference will lie.").

   For commentary, see Frank J. Cavico, Tortious Interference with Contract in the At–Will Employment Context, 79 U. Det. Mercy L. Rev. 503

(2002); Alex B. Long, Tortious Interference with Business Relations: "The Other White Meat" of Employment Law, 84 Minn. L. Rev. 863 (2000).

6. *Workplace Violence/Harassment and "Negligent Hiring/Retention" Liability.* Employers may be held liable for negligence in hiring and retaining personnel that commit acts of violence on customers and coworkers. See, e.g., Southeast Apartments Mgmt., Inc. v. Jackman, 257 Va. 256, 513 S.E.2d 395, 397 (1999) (cause of action "for harm resulting from the employer's negligence in retaining a dangerous employee who the employer knew or should have known was dangerous and likely to harm" others); Geise v. Phoenix Co. of Chicago, 246 Ill.App.3d 441, 186 Ill.Dec. 122, 615 N.E.2d 1179 (1993). See generally Jeffrey Bennett Cohen, Injured Customers Make Customers Pay Under the Negligent Hiring Doctrine: Evolution, Explanation, and Avoidance of Negligent Hiring Litigation, 6 J. Indiv. Employee Rights 305 (no.4, 1998); Alfred G. Feliu, Workplace Violence and the Duty of Care: The Scope of an Employer's Obligation to Protect Against the Violent Employee, 20 Employee Rels. L.J. 381 (no. 3, Winter 1994/95). For the effect of the exclusivity feature of workers' compensation laws, see "Note on Emotional Stress in the Workplace Claims," below.

4. *Intentional Infliction of Emotional Distress*

Note on Emotional Distress in the Workplace Claims

a. *Intentional Infliction of Emotional Distress*

Damage claims for the intentional infliction of emotional distress have met with some success in cases where the investigation leading to the discharge or the discharge itself is conducted in an abusive manner. See, e.g., Agis v. Howard Johnson Co., 371 Mass. 140, 355 N.E.2d 315 (1976) (discharge of waitresses in alphabetical order as a means of uncovering employee theft; tort lies even in the absence of accompanying physical injury); Holmes v. Oxford Chemicals, Inc., 672 F.2d 854 (11th Cir.1982) (Alabama recognizes "tort of outrage" for damages arising from arbitrary reduction of employee's monthly disability benefit).

Some jurisdictions, however, decline to permit recovery under this tort unless the emotional distress is accompanied by and results from physical injury. See, e.g., Forde v. Royal's, Inc., 537 F.Supp. 1173 (S.D.Fla.1982) (applying Florida law). The tort may also lie as a supplementary remedy for employment discrimination claims such as sexual harassment, see, e.g., College–Town v. Massachusetts Comm'n Against Discrimination, 400 Mass. 156, 508 N.E.2d 587 (1987), or retaliation for filing discrimination charges, see, e.g., Moffett v. Gene B. Glick Co., 621 F.Supp. 244 (N.D.Ind.1985). But see Fox v. Terre Haute Ind. Broadcasters, 701 F.Supp. 172 (S.D.Ind.1988) (Indiana law's exception to "physical impact" rule does not extend to age discrimination claim). Some decisions have extended the tort to negligent, as well as intentional, conduct causing extreme emotional distress even without accompanying physical injury. See Miller v. Fairchild Industries, 797 F.2d 727 (9th Cir.1986) (California law). See generally Regina Austin, Employer Abuse, Worker Resistance, and the Tort of Intentional Infliction of Emotional Distress, 41 Stan.L.Rev. 1 (1988); Daniel J. Givelber, The Right to Minimum Social Decency and the Limits of Evenhandedness: Intentional

Infliction of Emotional Distress by Outrageous Conduct, 82 Colum.L.Rev. 42 (1982).

b. *Recovery for Workplace Stress*

In addition to the emotional-distress tort, employees have also begun to assert claims for mental disorders caused by workplace stress. See Bureau of National Affairs, Stress in the Workplace: Costs, Liability and Prevention (1987); National Council on Compensation Insurance, Emotional Stress in the Workplace—New Legal Rights in the Eighties (1985).

c. *Exclusivity Barrier of Workers' Compensation Laws*

Both emotional-distress and workplace-stress claims may be precluded by the exclusivity of the workers' compensation scheme, at least to the extent they are based on conduct normally occurring in the workplace. Compare, e.g., Konstantopoulos v. Westvaco Corp., 690 A.2d 936 (Del.1996) (no sexual-harassment or sexual-assault exception to exclusivity provision); Hibben v. Nardone, 137 F.3d 480 (7th Cir.1998) (exclusivity provision under Wisconsin law applies to emotional-distress claims even when such claims are based on sexual harassment by coworker); Cole v. Fair Oaks Fire Protection Dist., 43 Cal.3d 148, 160, 233 Cal.Rptr. 308, 729 P.2d 743 (1987) (exclusivity provision applies to emotional-distress claim if the employer's actions giving rise to the claim are "a normal part of the employment relationship"), with GTE Southwest, Inc. v. Bruce, 42 Tex. Sup. J. 907, 998 S.W.2d 605 (1999) (supervisor abuse over extended period); Hart v. National Mortgage & Land Co., 189 Cal.App.3d 1420, 235 Cal.Rptr. 68 (1987) (supervisor allegedly grabbed employee's genitals and made sexually suggestive gestures). See generally Thomas S. Cook, Workers' Compensation and Stress Claims: Remedial Intent and Restrictive Application, 62 Notre Dame L.Rev. 879 (1987).

5. *Defamation*

LEWIS v. EQUITABLE LIFE ASSUR. SOCIETY

Supreme Court of Minnesota, 1986.

389 N.W.2d 876.

AMDAHL, C.J.

Plaintiffs, Carole Lewis, Mary Smith, Michelle Rafferty, and Suzanne Loizeaux, former employees of defendant, the Equitable Life Assurance Society of the United States (company), all hired for indefinite, at-will terms, were discharged for the stated reason of "gross insubordination." They claim that they were discharged in breach of their employment contracts, as determined by an employee handbook, and that they were defamed because the company knew that they would have to repeat the reason for their discharges to prospective employers. A Ramsey county jury awarded plaintiffs compensatory and punitive damages. The Minnesota Court of Appeals affirmed the award but remanded on the issue of contract damages for future harm. We affirm in full the award of compensatory damages but reverse the award of punitive damages.

* * *

In seeking new employment, plaintiffs were requested by prospective employers to disclose their reasons for leaving the company, and each indicated that she had been "terminated." When plaintiffs received interviews, they were asked to explain their terminations. Each stated that she had been terminated for "gross insubordination" and attempted to explain the situation. The company neither published nor stated to any prospective employer that plaintiffs had been terminated for gross insubordination. Its policy was to give only the dates of employment and the final job title of a former employee unless specifically authorized in writing to release additional information.

Only one plaintiff found employment while being completely forthright with a prospective employer about her termination by the company. A second plaintiff obtained employment after she misrepresented on the application form her reason for leaving the company. She did, however, explain the true reason in her interview. A third plaintiff obtained employment only when she left blank the question on the application form requesting her reason for leaving her last employment; the issue never arose in her interview. The fourth plaintiff has been unable to find full-time employment. All plaintiffs testified to suffering emotional and financial hardship as a result of being discharged by the company.

* * *

Defamation Claim

With regard to plaintiffs' defamation claims, the company argues that the trial court's conclusion of liability on the part of the company was erroneous because: (1) the only publications of the allegedly defamatory statement were made by plaintiffs; (2) the statement in question was true; and (3) the company was qualifiedly privileged to make the statement.

1. Publication

In order for a statement to be considered defamatory, it must be communicated to someone other than the plaintiff, it must be false, and it must tend to harm the plaintiff's reputation and to lower him or her in the estimation of the community. * * * Generally, there is no publication where a defendant communicates a statement directly to a plaintiff, who then communicates it to a third person. Restatement (Second) of Torts § 577, comment m (1977). Company management told plaintiffs that they had engaged in gross insubordination, for which they were being discharged. This allegedly defamatory statement was communicated to prospective employers of each plaintiff. The company, however, never communicated the statement. Plaintiffs themselves informed prospective employers that they had been terminated for gross insubordination. They did so because prospective employers inquired why they had left their previous employment. The question raised is whether a defendant can ever be held liable for defamation when the statement in question was published to a third person only by the plaintiff.

We have not previously been presented with the question of defamation by means of "self-publication." Courts that have considered the question, however, have recognized a narrow exception to the general rule that communication of a defamatory statement to a third person by the person defamed is not actionable. *See, e.g., McKinney v. County of Santa Clara,* 110 Cal.App.3d 787, 168 Cal.Rptr. 89 (1980); *Colonial Stores, Inc. v. Barrett,* 73 Ga.App. 839, 38 S.E.2d 306 (1946); *Belcher v. Little,* 315 N.W.2d 734 (Iowa 1982); *Grist v. Upjohn Co.,* 16 Mich.App. 452, 168 N.W.2d 389 (1969); *Bretz v. Mayer,* 1 Ohio Misc. 59, 203 N.E.2d 665 (1963); *First State Bank of Corpus Christi v. Ake,* 606 S.W.2d 696 (Tex.Civ.App.1980). These courts have recognized that if a defamed person was in some way compelled to communicate the defamatory statement to a third person, and if it was foreseeable to the defendant that the defamed person would be so compelled, then the defendant could be held liable for the defamation.

* * *

The company presents two arguments against recognition of the doctrine of compelled self-publication. It argues that such recognition amounts to creating tort liability for wrongful discharge which, it asserts, has been rejected by this court. In *Wild v. Rarig,* 302 Minn. [419,] 442, 234 N.W.2d [775, 790 (1975)], we held that bad-faith termination of contract is not an independent tort of the kind that will permit a tort recovery. The company, however, misreads our holding regarding tort liability for wrongful discharge. We did not hold that the harm resulting from a bad-faith termination of a contract could never give rise to a tort recovery. Indeed, we recognized such a possibility by stating that a plaintiff is limited to contract damages "except in exceptional cases where the defendant's breach of contract constitutes or is accompanied by an independent tort." *Id.* at 440, 234 N.W.2d at 789. If plaintiffs here can establish a cause of action for defamation, the fact that the defamation occurred in the context of employment discharge should not defeat recovery.

The company also argues that recognition of the doctrine of self-publication would discourage plaintiffs from mitigating damages. This concern does not appear to be a problem, however, if liability for self-publication of defamatory statements is imposed *only* where the plaintiff was in some significant way compelled to repeat the defamatory statement and such compulsion was, or should have been, foreseeable to the defendant. Also, the duty to mitigate can be further protected by requiring plaintiffs when they encounter a situation in which they are compelled to repeat a defamatory statement to take all reasonable steps to attempt to explain the true nature of the situation and to contradict the defamatory statement. In such circumstances, there would be no voluntary act on the part of a plaintiff that would constitute a failure to mitigate. This point is clearly illustrated by the present action. The company points to no reasonable course of conduct that plaintiffs could have taken to mitigate their damages.

The trend of modern authority persuades us that Minnesota law should recognize the doctrine of compelled self-publication. We acknowledge that recognition of this doctrine provides a significant new basis for maintaining a cause of action for defamation and, as such, it should be cautiously applied. However, when properly applied, it need not substantially broaden the scope of liability for defamation. The concept of compelled self-publication does no more than hold the originator of the defamatory statement liable for damages caused by the statement where the originator knows, or should know, of circumstances whereby the defamed person has no reasonable means of avoiding publication of the statement or avoiding the resulting damages; in other words, in cases where the defamed person was compelled to publish the statement. In such circumstances, the damages are fairly viewed as the direct result of the originator's actions.

* * *

In the present action, the record indicates that plaintiffs were compelled to repeat the allegedly defamatory statement to prospective employers and that the company knew plaintiffs would be so compelled. The St. Paul office manager admitted that it was foreseeable that plaintiffs would be asked by prospective employers to identify the reason that they were discharged. Their only choice would be to tell them "gross insubordination" or to lie. Fabrication, however, is an unacceptable alternative.

2. Issue of Truth

Finding that there was a publication, we next turn to the issue of truth. True statements, however disparaging, are not actionable. * * * Since it is true that plaintiffs were fired for gross insubordination, the company argues, they cannot maintain an action for defamation. The company contends the relevant statement to consider when analyzing the defense of truth is the one that plaintiffs made to their prospective employers, that is, that they had been fired for gross insubordination. Plaintiffs counter that it is the truth or falsity of the underlying statement—that plaintiffs engaged in gross insubordination—that is relevant.

The company relies for its authority solely upon language of this court in *Johnson v. Dirkswager*, 315 N.W.2d 215, 218–19 (Minn.1982), where we raised the question whether truth as a defense goes to the verbal accuracy of the statement or to the underlying implication of the statement. In *Dirkswager*, however, it was unnecessary to resolve the question. Moreover, that case is distinguishable from the present case because there the underlying statements were presented merely as "allegations of misconduct." *Id.* at 219 n. 4. Here, the company's charges against plaintiffs went beyond accusations and were conclusory statements that plaintiffs had engaged in gross insubordination.

Requiring that truth as a defense go to the underlying implication of the statement, at least where the statement involves more than a simple allegation, appears to be the better view. *See* Restatement (Second) of Torts § 581A, comment e (1977). Moreover, the truth or falsity of a statement is inherently within the province of the jury. This court will not overturn a jury finding on the issue of falsity unless the finding is manifestly and palpably contrary to the evidence. Thus, we find no error on this point because the record amply supports the jury verdict that the charge of gross insubordination was false.

3. *Qualified Privilege*

* * *

The doctrine of privileged communication rests upon public policy considerations. As other jurisdictions recognize, the existence of a privilege results from the court's determination that statements made in particular contexts or on certain occasions should be encouraged despite the risk that the statements might be defamatory. *See Calero v. Del Chemical Corp.*, 68 Wis.2d 487, 498, 228 N.W.2d 737, 744 (1975). Whether an occasion is a proper one upon which to recognize a privilege is a question of law for the court to determine. *Jacron Sales Co. v. Sindorf*, 276 Md. 580, 350 A.2d 688 (1976); *Fisher v. Myers*, 339 Mo. 1196, 100 S.W.2d 551 (1936); *Cash v. Empire Gas Corp.*, 547 S.W.2d 830, 833 (Mo.Ct.App.1976). In the context of employment recommendations, the law generally recognizes a qualified privilege between former and prospective employers as long as the statements are made in good faith and for a legitimate purpose.

* * *

* * * A qualified privilege may be lost if it is abused. The burden is on the plaintiff to show that the privilege has been abused. While the initial determination of whether a communication is privileged is a question of law for the court to decide, the question of whether the privilege was abused is a jury question. Restatement (Second) of Torts, § 619 (1977). * * *

The company * * * argues that the court's instructions incorrectly stated the standard of malice which plaintiffs must prove if the existence of a qualified privilege is demonstrated. The law recognizes essentially two definitions of malice in defamation cases: the "actual malice" definition as set forth in *New York Times Co. v. Sullivan*, 376 U.S. 254, 279–80, 84 S.Ct. 710, 726, 11 L.Ed.2d 686 (1964), and the common-law definition. *See Stuempges* [*v. Parke, Davis & Co.*, 297 N.W.2d 252, 257 (Minn.1980)]. The common-law definition is more appropriate in the employer-employee situation because it focuses on the employer's attitude toward the plaintiff. *See id.* at 258. Under the common-law definition, malice exists where the defendant " 'made the statement from ill will and improper motives, or causelessly and wantonly for the purpose of injuring the plaintiff.' " *Id.* at 257 (quoting *McKenzie v. William J. Burns International Detective Agency, Inc.*, 149 Minn. 311, 312, 183 N.W. 516, 517 (1921)). In its instructions, the court informed the jurors that if they found that the company was entitled to a qualified privilege, plaintiff had to prove that the statement was made "with actual malice." In defining malice for the jury, the court correctly set forth the common-law definition. We therefore find no error in the jury instructions.

DAMAGES

1. Compensatory Damages

* * * Neither expungement of the company's records nor vindication at trial eliminate all future harm to the plaintiffs' earning capacity. The fact that plaintiffs brought suit against the company may itself have future detrimental effects. A person who brings suit against a former employer is likely to be a less attractive employment candidate to prospective employers. No amount of vindication with respect to the gross insubordination charge can eliminate this impact on plaintiffs' future work lives. We conclude that there was no error in including damages for future harm in plaintiffs' awards. The trial court awards of compensatory damages are supported by the evidence, and we therefore reverse the court of appeals directive remanding the issue of compensatory damages.

2. Punitive Damages

* * * [W]e deny the imposition of punitive damages in defamation actions involving compelled self-publication. We are concerned that the availability of punitive damages may tend to encourage publication of defamatory statements in actions where the plaintiff, rather than the defendant, does the actual publication. More importantly, in the context of an employee discharge, the availability of punitive damages in such an action may significantly deter employer communication of the reason for discharge.

Notes and Questions

1. *Defamation as an "Independent" Tort?* Are you persuaded by the Minnesota high court's explanation that while "bad-faith termination of contract is not an independent tort of the kind that will permit a tort recovery," defamation is an independent tort that may provide redress for "the harm resulting from a bad-faith termination"? Particularly in light of *Lewis's* endorsement of the "self-publication" concept, in what sense was the tort independent of the wrongful termination?

2. *Publication Requirement.* Publication is an essential element of common law defamation. See Restatement (Second) of Torts § 577(1) (1977).

a. *Self-Publication?* The "self-publication" concept originated in the wartime case of Colonial Stores, Inc. v. Barrett, 73 Ga.App. 839, 38 S.E.2d 306 (1946). Under the regulations of the War Manpower Commission, employers were required to furnish discharged employees with written statements of availability, and prospective employees were required to display this certificate to prospective employers. In this case, Barrett's former employer wrote on the certificate that he had been fired for "improper conduct toward fellow employees," in violation of the Manpower Commission's prohibition of information "prejudicial to the employee in seeking new employment." *Id.* at 841, 38 S.E.2d at 308. As *Lewis* illustrates, some courts have extended this concept to situations involving a less direct compulsion to reveal the reasons for the prior termination. See also Frank B. Hall v. Buck, 678 S.W.2d 612 (Tex.App.1984) (statements made to private investigator hired by plaintiff). Contra, e.g., White v. Blue Cross & Blue Shield of Mass., 442 Mass. 64, 809 N.E.2d 1034 (2004); Gore v. Health–Tex, Inc., 567 So.2d 1307 (Ala.1990); Yetter v. Ward Trucking Corp., 401 Pa.Super. 467, 585 A.2d 1022 (1991). See generally Note, Self–Publication of Defamation and Employee Discharge, 6 Rev. of Litig. 313 (1987).

b. *"Publication" Despite Wholly Intrafirm Communication?* Even in jurisdictions that do not follow *Lewis,* publication may be found in internal communications between employees or officers of the same corporation. See, e.g., Torosyan v. Boehringer Ingelheim Pharm., 234 Conn. 1, 27–28, 662 A.2d 89 (1995); Pirre v. Printing Developments, Inc., 468 F.Supp. 1028, 1041–42 (S.D.N.Y.1979); Hanrahan v. Kelly, 269 Md. 21, 305 A.2d 151 (1973); Restatement (Second) of Torts § 577(1), comment (i); Rodney Smolla, Law of Defamation Sec. 15.02 (1994). But see Otteni v. Hitachi America Ltd., 678 F.2d 146 (11th Cir.1982) (no publication if communication is limited to employer's officers or members of their immediate staff).

3. *Privileges*. The key issues in defamation suits in the employment context are likely to be those of privilege and malice.

a. *Absolute Privilege*. An absolute privilege is likely to be limited to communications made in the context of judicial and quasi-judicial proceedings. See, e.g., Rogozinski v. Airstream by Angell, 152 N.J.Super. 133, 377 A.2d 807, 816 (1977) (even statements mandated by an unemployment compensation commission are entitled only to qualified privilege because no judicial or quasi-judicial proceeding was pending at the time). Some courts have been willing to extend absolute-privilege treatment to statements required by collective bargaining agreements or arising out of grievance proceedings. See Hasten v. Phillips Petroleum Co., 640 F.2d 274 (10th Cir.1981); General Motors Corp. v. Mendicki, 367 F.2d 66 (10th Cir.1966). But see Overall v. University of Pennsylvania, 412 F.3d 492 (3d Cir.2005).

In the securities industry, employers are required by the stock exchanges to complete a Form U–5 setting forth the reasons for every termination of employment of a registered representative. Information contained in the Form U–5 is available to prospective employers and investors. Responding to a certified question from the Second Circuit, the New York Court of Appeals held in Rosenberg v. MetLife, Inc., 8 N.Y.3d 359, 834 N.Y.S.2d 494, 866 N.E.2d 439 (2007), that an employer's statements on a National Association of Securities Dealers' (NASD)'s employee termination notice (Form U-5) are protected by an absolute privilege in defamation lawsuits. The court emphasized the public function of the Form U-5 reporting system: "The Form U-5 plays a significant role in the NASD's self-regulatory process. * * * Upon receipt of the Form U-5, the NASD routinely investigates terminations for cause to determine whether the representative violated any securities rules." Id. at 367.

b. *Qualified Privilege.* For statements made in the course of internal company investigations or in response to inquiries about the performance of former employees, only a qualified privilege is likely to be available. Such a privilege is defeated, as was the case in *Lewis,* on a showing of "malice." "Good faith or lack of malice does not mean lack of hostility or ill feeling; it means that '(t)he person making the statement must have reasonable grounds for believing that it is true and he must honestly believe it is a correct statement.' " Rouly v. Enserch Corp., 835 F.2d 1127, 1130 (5th Cir.1988) (applying Mississippi law). As a practical matter, however, much will depend on how juries assess the reasonableness of the manner by which the employer has conducted its investigation and communicated its grounds for termination to the employee (or prospective employer). Compare, e.g., Loughry v. Lincoln First Bank, 67 N.Y.2d 369, 502 N.Y.S.2d 965, 494 N.E.2d 70 (1986), with Kasachkoff v. The City of New York, 107 A.D.2d 130, 485 N.Y.S.2d 992 (1st Dept.1985), affirmed, 68 N.Y.2d 654, 505 N.Y.S.2d 67, 496 N.E.2d 226 (1986).

4. *Coworker Liability for Libel?* Can coworkers be sued, in libel or under the intentional-interference tort, for misrepresenting the performance of an employee resulting in his wrongful termination? See, e.g., Sheppard v. Freeman, 67 Cal.App.4th 339, 79 Cal.Rptr.2d 13 (4th Dist.1998) ("except where a statutory exception applies, an employee or former employee cannot sue other employees based on their conduct relating to personnel decisions").

5. *Laws Seeking to Mitigate Reemployment Difficulties.* Cases like *Lewis* may be viewed as a common law response to the plight of improperly discharged employees who find employment opportunities barred because of their prior work record. Some states have passed legislation to further mitigate such reemployment difficulties. (These provisions can be found in the Stat.Supp.)

a. *Missouri's "Service Letter" Statute.* Missouri requires employers on request to furnish a written statement "setting forth the nature and character of service rendered by such employee * * * and truly stating for what cause, if any, such employee was discharged or voluntarily quit such service." Inaccuracies in such a "service letter" may result in liability for compensatory but not punitive damages. Vernon's Ann.Mo.Stat. § 290.140; see Neb.Rev.Stat. § 48–211; Vernon's Texas Ann.Civ.St. art. 5196, subd. 3. For a decision under the Missouri statute, see Gibson v. Hummel, 688 S.W.2d 4 (Mo.App.1985).

b. *Access to Personnel Files.* Following the Federal Privacy Act, 5 U.S.C. § 552a, some states have also mandated employee access to personnel files and a right to correct inaccurate information in such files. See, e.g., Cal. Labor Code § 1198.5; Conn. Gen. Stat. Ann.§ 21–128e (West 1997); Nev. Rev.Stat. 613.075; Wis.Stat.Ann. 103.13. See pp. 873–74 infra for discussion of the Fair Credit Reporting Act.

c. *Anti–"Blacklisting" Laws.* A few states also prohibit employers from "blacklisting" or from conspiring or acting to prevent a discharged employee from securing new employment. See, e.g., Cal. Labor Code § 1050; Nev.Rev. Stat. 613.210; Vernon's Ann.Texas Civ.St. art. 5196. Typically, such provisions privilege "truthfully stating in writing, on request of such former employee or other persons to whom such former employee has applied for employment, the reason why such employee was discharged, and why his relationship to such company ceased." Vernon's Ann. Texas Civ.St. art. 5196, subd. 1.

d. *Retaliatory References*. Former employees may have a claim under the discrimination laws if negative references are used as a means of retaliating against them for their prior claims or opposition activity, even if the claimed retaliation occurs after employment was terminated. See Robinson v. Shell Oil Co., 519 U.S. 337, 117 S.Ct. 843, 136 L.Ed.2d 808 (1997).

6. *Impact of "Negligent Hiring/Retention" Tort?* Should the rules that govern the process of obtaining information about prior work records from an applicant's previous employers be affected by decisions holding an employer liable for negligence in hiring or retention of violent or abusive employees? See, e.g., Doe v. Garcia, 131 Idaho 578, 961 P.2d 1181 (1998); Welsh Manufacturing v. Pinkerton's Inc., 474 A.2d 436 (R.I.1984), appeal after remand, 494 A.2d 897 (R.I.1985).

7. *Employer Liability for Favorable References?* In Randi W. v. Muroc Joint Unified School Dist., 14 Cal.4th 1066, 60 Cal.Rptr.2d 263, 929 P.2d 582 (1997), several school districts provided glowing references for Robert Gadams, a former school administrator, failing to disclose frequent allegations against Gadams of sexual improprieties with students and his forced resignation from at least one job due to complaints of improper sexual behavior. Relying on these recommendations, a school district hired Gadams, and he shortly thereafter allegedly molested a 13–year old student, Randy W. The California Supreme Court sustained Randy W.'s right to seek tort damages from the former employers because of their unqualified letters of reference, suggesting that liability could have been avoided either by providing "full disclosure" letters or "no comment" letters containing only "basic employment dates and details." The court reasoned that "the writer of a letter of recommendation owes to prospective employers and third persons a duty not to misrepresent the facts in describing the qualifications and character of a former employee, if making these misrepresentations would present a substantial, foreseeable risk of physical injury to the prospective employer or third persons." There would be no duty, however, in the absence of "resulting physical injury, or some special relationship between the parties * * *." Id. at 1081, 929 P.2d at 591 (citing Restatement (Second) of Torts §§ 310–11).

Nor presumably would the former employer have faced any liability in refusing any reference or merely verifying employment dates. See *Randi W.*, 929 P.2d at 589. What about an incomplete "neutral" reference that states the employee was released for restructuring reasons without revealing his violent misconduct triggering the release? See, e.g., Jerner v. Allstate Ins., Fla. Cir. Ct. No. 93–09472 (1993) (setting the case for trial); the parties ultimately settled out of court. See Vickie Chachere, Suit Settled in Rocky Point Shootings: The Gunman Reaches a Pact with the Victims and the Families, Tampa Trib., Oct. 3, 1995, p. 1, available at 1995 WL 14264532.

8. *Laws Seeking to Reduce Employer Liability for References.* In an effort to encourage employers to avoid "no comment" letters which may hamstring reemployment of the former employee and certainly deprive new employers of material information about the prospective employee they are not likely to acquire from interviews and background checks, a number of states have enacted statutes conferring a "good faith" immunity on those who provide employment references. See, e.g., Alaska Stat. § 9.65.10 (Michie 1996); Colo. Rev. Stat. § 8–2–114 (1997); Ill. Comp. Stat. Ann. 46/10 (West Supp. 1997); Mich. Comp. Laws Ann. 423.452 (West Supp. 1998) These laws typically take the form of a presumption of an employer's good faith in providing a reference, to be rebutted on a showing of reckless, knowing or maliciously motivated disclosure of false or misleading information. Do these laws do more than simply codify the conventional qualified privilege available under common law? See generally Markita D. Cooper, Job Reference Immunity Statutes: Prevalent But Irrelevant, 11 Cornell J.L. & Pub. Pol'y 1 (2001).

9. *Social Optimum?* What would be the optimal regulatory regime for employment references. Consider some of the alternatives, as developed in J. Hoult Verkerke, Legal Regulation of Employment Reference Practices, 65 U. Chi.L. Rev. 115 (1998):

a. *Strict Employer Liability for Erroneous References.* This extreme would lead to widespread "no comment" letters complicating reemployment and depriving future employers of material adverse information about prospective hires (what Verkerke terms "churning").

b. *Absolute Privilege.* This extreme offers inadequate incentives for employers to be careful about the references they provide (what Verkereke calls "scarring").

c. *Qualified Privilege.* Although in theory the employer is not held responsible for references made in good faith, in practice many employers seek to avoid the costs of litigation by providing falsely positive references or "no comment" letters. Professor Verkerke notes: "Both anecdotal accounts and survey evidence demonstrate that employers presently provide a substantial amount of information about former employees. And yet complaints about an inadequate supply of certain types of reference information persist." 65 U.Chi.L.Rev. at 161.

d. *Mandatory Disclosure.* If a qualified privilege will result in "no comment" letters, especially where previous employers have negative information about the violent proclivities of former employees, should employers at least be required to disclose prior violent workplace conduct by employees about whom a reference is requested? See Markita D. Cooper, Beyond Name, Rank and Serial Number: "No Comment" Job Reference Policies, Violent Employees and the Need for Disclosure–Shield Legislation, 5 Va. J. Soc. Pol'y & L. 287 (1998) (noncompliance with disclosure obligation could result in liability to new employers or customers/employees harmed by former employee's violence).

For a proposal that would mandate disclosure upon an employee's written request and waiver of right to sue, coupled with an opportunity for the employee to identify errors and demand correction before any waiver would take effect, see Deborah A. Ballam, Employment References—Speak No Evil, Hear No Evil: A Proposal for Meaningful Reform, 39 Am. Bus. L. J. 445 (2002). If an employer declined to make the demanded corrections, the employee could seek a resolution through arbitration but would retain the right to sue for defamation.

e. *Paying for References.* Prospective employers do not pay for references perhaps because of difficulties in pricing the information:

> A flat rate for each reference would have to be low enough to make the purchase worthwhile even though, in the majority of cases, the former employer will have nothing valuable to disclose. If the price per reference is therefore quite low, employers who know particularly damaging information will be disinclined to expose themselves to potential defamation liability in return for such a trivial sum.

Verkerke, supra, at 171.

D. EVALUATING THE CASE FOR WRONGFUL DISCHARGE LEGISLATION

The preceding sections of this chapter have surveyed the various approaches the courts have taken to modify the employment-at-will doctrine in response to the job-security claims of employees who are not covered by collective bargaining agreements or civil service laws. However, judicial action, whether based on contract, tort or property principles, is not a likely (or arguably even legitimate) source for enduring "just cause" protection for all employees. Because of the limits of the common law both in working a radical change in background employment norms and in fashioning the necessary procedures and exceptions from coverage, general "just cause" protection requires legislation. The case for and against such legislation, and the form such measures might take, is treated in this section. Consider first Professor Epstein's defense of existing arrangements.

1. Is Legislation Warranted?

RICHARD EPSTEIN, IN DEFENSE OF THE CONTRACT AT WILL*

* * * [I]t is possible to identify a number of reasons why the at-will contract usually works for the benefit of both sides in employment as well as partnership contexts.

1. *Monitoring Behavior.* The shift in the internal structure of the firm from a partnership to an employment relation eliminates neither bilateral opportunism nor the conflicts of interest between employer and employee. Begin for the moment with the fears of the firm, for it is the firm's right to maintain at-will power that is now being called into question. In all too many cases, the firm must contend with the recur-

* 51 U.Chi. L. Rev. 947 (1984).

rent problem of employee theft and with the related problems of unauthorized use of firm equipment and employee kickback arrangements. * * * [T]he proper concerns of the firm are not limited to obvious forms of criminal misconduct. The employee on a fixed wage can, at the margin, capture only a portion of the gain from his labor, and therefore has a tendency to reduce output. The employee who receives a commission equal to half the firm's profit attributable to his labor may work hard, but probably not quite as hard as he would if he received the entire profit from the completed sale, an arrangement that would solve the agency-cost problem only by undoing the firm. * * * The conflicts between employer and employee may sometimes call for the severance of the relationship, just as they do in the partnership context. But the rational response is to counteract the tendency for employee abuse only to the point where private gain equals private cost. Agency costs are like other costs that must be minimized in order for production to proceed, and the persistence of firms shows that this can be done.

The problem of management then is to identify the forms of social control that are best able to minimize these agency costs. * * *

* * * Internal auditors may help control some forms of abuse, and simple observation by coworkers may well monitor employee activities. (There are some very subtle tradeoffs to be considered when the firm decides whether to use partitions or separate offices for its employees.) Promotions, bonuses, and wages are also critical in shaping the level of employee performance. But the carrot cannot be used to the exclusion of the stick. In order to maintain internal discipline, the firm may have to resort to sanctions against individual employees. It is far easier to use those powers that can be unilaterally exercised: to fire, to demote, to withhold wages, or to reprimand. These devices can visit very powerful losses upon individual employees without the need to resort to legal action, and they permit the firm to monitor employee performance continually in order to identify both strong and weak workers and to compensate them accordingly. The principles here are constant, whether we speak of senior officials or lowly subordinates, and it is for just this reason that the contract at will is found at all levels in private markets.

* * *

Thus far, the analysis generally has focused on the position of the employer. Yet for the contract at will to be adopted ex ante, it must work for the benefit of workers as well. And indeed it does, for the contract at will also contains powerful limitations on employers' abuses of power. * * *

[W]here the employer makes increased demands under a contract at will[,] the worker can quit whenever the net value of the employment contract turns negative. As with the employer's power to fire or demote, the threat to quit (or at a lower level to come late or leave early) is one that can be exercised without resort to litigation. Furthermore, that threat turns out to be most effective when the employer's opportunistic behavior is the greatest because the situation is one in which the worker has least to lose. * * *

The case for the contract at will is further strengthened by another feature common to contracts of this sort. The employer is often required either to give notice or to pay damages in lieu of notice; damages are traditionally equal to the wages that the employee would have earned during the notice period. These provisions for "severance pay" provide the worker with some protection against casual or hasty discharges, but they do not interfere with the powerful efficiency characteristics of the contract at will. First, lump-sum transfers do not require the introduction of any "for cause" requirement, which could be the source of expensive litigation. Second, because the sums are definite, they can be easily computed, so that administrative costs are minimized. Third, because the payments are unconditional, they do not create perverse incentives for the employee or heavy monitoring costs for the employer: the terminated employee will not be tempted to avoid gainful employment in order to run up his damages for wrongful discharge; the employer, for his part, will not have to monitor the post-termination behavior of the employee in order to guard against that very risk. Thus, provisions for severance pay can be used to give employees added protection against arbitrary discharge without sacrificing the advantages of a clean break between the parties.

2. *Reputational Losses.* * * * The employer who decides to act for bad reason or no reason at all may not face any legal liability under the classical common law rule. But he faces very powerful adverse economic consequences. If coworkers perceive the dismissal as arbitrary, they will take fresh stock of their own prospects, for they can no longer be certain that their faithful performance will ensure their security and advancement. The uncertain prospects created by arbitrary employer behavior is functionally indistinguishable from a reduction in wages unilaterally imposed by the employer. At the margin some workers will look elsewhere, and typically the best workers will have the greatest opportunities. By the same token the large employer has more to gain if he dismisses undesirable employees, for this ordinarily acts as an implicit increase in wages to the other employees, who are no longer burdened with uncooperative or obtuse coworkers.

The existence of both positive and negative reputational effects is thus brought back to bear on the employer. The law may tolerate arbitrary behavior, but private pressures effectively limit its scope. Inferior employers will be at a perpetual competitive disadvantage with enlightened ones and will continue to lose in market share and hence in relative social importance. The lack of legal protection to the employees is therefore in part explained by the increased informal protections that they obtain by working in large concerns.

3. *Risk Diversification and Imperfect Information.*

* * *

The contract at will is also a sensible private adaptation to the problem of imperfect information over time. In sharp contrast to the purchase of standard goods, an inspection of the job before acceptance is far less likely to guarantee its quality thereafter. The future is not clearly known. More important, employees, like employers, *know what they do not know*. They are not faced with a bolt from the blue, with an "unknown unknown." Rather they face a known unknown for which they can plan. The at-will contract is an essential part of that planning because it allows both sides to take a wait-and-see attitude to their relationship so that new and more accurate choices can be made on the strength of improved information. * * *

4. *Administrative Costs.* There is one last way in which the contract at will has an enormous advantage over its rivals. It is very cheap to administer. Any effort to use a for-cause rule will in principle allow all, or at least a substantial fraction of, dismissals to generate litigation. Because motive will be a critical element in these cases, the chances of either side obtaining summary judgment will be negligible. Similarly, the broad modern rules of discovery will allow exploration into every aspect of the employment relation. * * *

Nonetheless, it may be said that this inquiry is worth conducting because employers err in making decisions to fire and injustices will be done unless legal sanctions are imposed. But this analysis entirely ignores the fact that error costs always run in both directions. It has already been shown that there are powerful correctives against capricious discharge even under an at-will rule. The chances of finding an innocent employee wronged by a firm vendetta are quite remote. By the same token, jury sympathy with aggrieved plaintiffs may result in a very large number of erroneous verdicts for employees. In principle it might be proper to tolerate the high error rate if the consequences of erroneous dismissal to the innocent employee were more severe than the consequences of erroneous reinstatement to the innocent employer. But quite the opposite is apt to be the case. Able employees are the very persons who have the greatest opportunity of obtaining alternate employment in the marketplace and who can therefore best mitigate their losses. Although their search for new work may be complicated because of the previous dismissal, the dismissed employee usually can get other persons, e.g., representatives of other companies with whom he has dealt, to help overcome the negative inference from the dismissal. Indeed there is less trouble in explaining away the dismissal if it is generally understood that contracts are terminable at will, since termination no longer implies employee misconduct.

Notes and Questions

1. *Costs of a "Cause" Regime?* Professor Epstein's essay argues that the employment-at-will doctrine offers advantages for both parties to the employment relationship. Is it likely that movement to a "cause" regime will make employers significantly less likely to hire at the margin, and to

forestall hiring until completion of extensive pre-employment screening and satisfactory performance of a probationary period? Some Japanese firms that are accustomed to long-term employment relationships insist on extensive testing of American applicants even for entry-level manufacturing positions. See Labor Letter, Wall St.J., December 29, 1987, p. 1, col. 5. If the employment relationship is deemed to embody a set of implicit mutual obligations, might a "cause" regime also lead to obligations on the employee's part to furnish reasonable notice of termination and greater judicial receptivity to post-employment restraints on working for competitors? For further discussion, see "Note on Measuring the Costs of Wrongful Dismissal Protections" below.

2. *Is Wrongful Discharge Ever in the Firm's Interest?* Is Epstein right that, at least in the absence of racial, gender or ethnic discrimination or retaliation for whistleblowing, it is never in the interest of the employer to discharge long-term productive employees?

a. *Agency Costs of Delegating Decisionmaking to Supervisors?* Even if the firm as a whole may be likened to the rational economic actor underlying microeconomic analysis, can the same be said for line supervisors who may be acting out of pique or preservation of a power relationship and whose decisions are routinely deferred to by the firm? Cf. Douglas L. Leslie, Labor Bargaining Units, 70 Va.L.Rev. 353, 373–74 (1984) (discussing principal-agency problems).

b. *Adverse Selection?* Is the market likely to under-produce "cause" agreements because isolated employers offering such terms are likely to attract poor performers and thus be magnets for "lemons"? See Walter Kamiat, Labor and Lemons: Efficient Norms in the Internal Labor Market and Possible Failures of Individual Contracting, 144 U.Pa. L. Rev. 1953 (1996); David I. Levine, Just–Cause Employment Policies in the Presence of Worker Adverse Selection, 9 J. Lab. Econ. 294 (1991). But see J. Hoult Verkerke, An Empirical Perspective on Indefinite Term Employment Contracts: Resolving the Just Cause Debate, 1995 Wis. L. Rev. 837, 903–904:

> A significant theoretical criticism of these arguments is that the signaling problems are symmetrical. Just as prospective employees send an adverse signal by demanding just cause, so an employer might signal, by demanding an at-will relationship or refusing to agree to a just cause term that it is unusually likely to discharge such workers. * * *

> An empirical implication of the adverse selection argument is that employers should be more willing to offer just cause protection when they have other reliable sources of information about worker quality. Since adverse selection depends on the inability of employers to distinguish good from bad workers, reliable information would tend to overcome this difficulty and diminish the importance of contractual choice as an indicator of worker quality. * * * Thus, we should observe contractual just cause terms in industries and occupations in which employers engage in extensive search before hiring or in which worker quality is a function of easily observable variables. After a trial period of employment, firms also should be willing to extend just cause protection. * * *

> [T]he survey data do not reveal a pattern of contracting that seems consistent with these implications. * * * [A]nd there is no evidence that

many employers grant contractual protection against discharge after employees complete a probationary period. Employers' failure to extend [such] protection to postprobationary employees can only be explained by something other than adverse selection or signaling.

c. *Employer Opportunism in Internal Labor Markets?* A decision to fire a productive employee may be economically rational if the employee's compensation exceeds his or her marginal productivity to the firm. Professors Wachter and Cohen suggest that a "backloaded" compensation structure may be characteristic of firms seeking to promote long-term commitment and investment by employees in "firm-specific skills" (which add value to the employer but do not enhance the employee's portable skills). Such a compensation structure is often referred in the economics literature as an "internal labor market" or "relational" contract. Although descriptions vary, the central feature of the arrangement is that after an initial training period, both the firm and the employee derive gains that they would not achieve in its absence: The employee's productivity exceeds not only his wage but what he could earn in the external labor market; and the firm reaps the benefit of a specially trained, committed workforce. During this phase, because both sides benefit, the arrangement is fully self-enforcing. However, because compensation is backloaded over the course of the employee's career—in part to motivate long-term commitment and in part because employees derive satisfaction from a compensation structure that improves over time—there comes a point where the interests of the firm and the employee begin to diverge: The employee continues to enjoy a wage exceeding what he could obtain elsewhere, but his wage also exceeds his productivity contribution to the firm. See Michael L. Wachter & George Cohen, The Law and Economics of Collective Bargaining: An Introduction and Application to the Problems of Subcontracting, Partial Closure, and Relocation, 136 U.Pa.L.Rev. 1349, 1362–64 (1988). In bad times, employers may have an incentive to "cheat" on this relational contract; hence, candidates for staff reductions are likely to come from the ranks of long-term, usually older, workers who are being paid above their marginal value. Age discrimination laws may be animated by similar concerns. Dean Schwab applies such reasoning to explain California decisions like *Pugh*, *See's Candies*, and *Foley* finding an "implied in fact" job security term in the case of long-service employee facing late-career discharges. See Stewart J. Schwab, Life–Cycle Justice: Accommodating Just Cause and Employment at Will, 92 Mich. L. Rev. 8 (1993). A similar analysis may apply as an explanation for age discrimination laws., see p. 427 supra.

Professor Ehrenberg has argued, on the other hand, that long-term employees do not need the law's assistance because reputational costs would discourage firms from unjustly dismissing workers who were in the stage of their life-cycles in which marginal productivity falls below wages. In his view, the problem of unjust dismissal is largely confined to low-skilled workers in casual labor markets. For such workers, the appropriate legal response is not to increase marginal labor costs (through mandatory job security), but to prod state unemployment insurance systems to more rigorously examine dismissals for "misconduct" and to encourage the award of unemployment benefits without extra waiting periods. See Ronald Ehrenberg, Workers' Rights: Rethinking Protective Labor Legislation, in Rethinking Employment Policy 137, 142–50 (D.L. Bawden & F. Skidmore eds. 1989).

Professor Issacharoff, while sympathetic to the "internal labor market" or "life-cycle justice" model, questions whether these analytic concepts can be readily translated into legal rules:

> But what is it that the law can or should protect? The difficulty comes in transforming the life-cycle employment model from an analytic device for understanding the operation of labor markets into a legal definition of rights for determining liability. The * * * model places a great deal of stress on the transformative moment when an employee is subject to special legal solicitude for having entered into the category of employees at risk for opportunistic discharges. This in turn raises a constant concern in imprecise contractual arrangements: how to verify the impropriety of the actions of the allegedly breaching party. Moreover, * * * these problems are compounded in the employment setting in which any measure of low employee productivity could indicate that the employee has reached [the point in the implicit deferred compensation scheme whereby wages are expected to exceed productivity as the employee is recouping on prior investments,] but could also "characterize a late-career employee who has breached his or her side of the implicit contract by 'shirking' under the cover of the life-cycle just cause standard for discharge."

Samuel Issacharoff, Contracting for Employment: The Limited Return of the Common Law, 74 Tex. L. Rev. 1783, 1804–05 (1996), quoting Verkerke, An Empirical Perspective, supra, at 883. Would avoiding these difficulties and protecting employees who are over a certain age and thus are likely not to be able to obtain comparable employment provide a sensible compromise? What would be the problems with such an approach?

3. *Effectiveness of Reputational Costs?* Are Ehrenberg and Epstein right that if "unjust dismissals" do occur, employers will be sufficiently penalized by reputational losses in the marketplace not to engage in such conduct again? Might individual terminations be so fact-specific, and mass staff reductions so shrouded in economic necessity that little in the way of reputational loss will be incurred? Moreover, is the exit of some incumbent employees likely to be only of marginal significance as a deterrent of employer arbitrariness—given: (i) the bilateral monopoly that Epstein elsewhere in the article recognizes will occur in the course of an ongoing relationship in which "each side gains from the contract more than it could obtain by returning to the open market"; (ii) the prevalence of seniority-based compensation and benefits that tie incumbent employees to their jobs; (iii) age discrimination barriers to older workers finding new employment; and (iv) the difficulty in securing new employment without a favorable reference from previous employers?

4. *Incidence of Wrongful Dismissal.* Does the fact that arbitrators under collective bargaining agreements overturn approximately one-third of all discharges that go to arbitration suggest that unjust dismissal does in fact occur with some regularity? See Jack Stieber & Michael Murray, Protection Against Unjust Discharge: The Need for a Federal Statute, 16 U. Mich. J.L. Ref. 319 (1983); Jack Stieber, The Case for Protection of Unorganized

Employees Against Unjust Discharge, IRRA 32nd Annual Proc. 155, 160–61 (1979).

Estimates of the incidence of wrongful dismissal vary. Extrapolating from the labor arbitration experience, and on the assumption that the reversal rate in the arbitration setting would also hold true for nonunion firms under a statutory "cause" regime, Professor Peck estimated that approximately 300,000 discharge or discipline cases would be overturned annually. See Cornelius J. Peck, Unjust Discharges from Employment: A Necessary Change in the Law, 40 Ohio St.L.J. 1, 8–10 (1979). Professor Frug puts the figure at 150,000 cases a year. See Gerald E. Frug, Why Courts Are Always Making Law, Fortune, Sept. 25, 1989, at 247, 248. Professors Freed and Polsby estimate that a nonunion worker faces a probability of wrongful dismissal of no more than .5769% (under Peck's estimate) or .2083% (under Frug's): "All of these probabilities are low enough that a person who disregarded them would not be acting unreasonably." Mayer Freed & Daniel Polsby, Just Cause for Termination Rules and Economic Efficiency, 38 Emory L.J. 1097, 1106–07 (1989). The methodology of the Stieber–Peck estimates is criticized in Andrew P. Morriss, Bad Data, Bad Economics, and Bad Policy: Time to Fire Wrongful Discharge Law, 74 Tex. L. Rev. 1901 (1996).

5. *Weighing Error Costs.* Does Epstein give away the store when he acknowledges that "[i]n principle it might be proper to tolerate the high error rate [of a cause regime] if the consequences of erroneous dismissal to the innocent employee were more serious than the consequences of erroneous reinstatement to the innocent employer"? If the costs of erroneous dismissal to the innocent employee have been underestimated, and the costs of erroneous termination to the employer can be reduced by, say, placing review of dismissal decisions in the hands of expert arbitrators rather than overly sympathetic juries, might not the overall benefit to employees of such recourse and to employers of such a check on supervisory misjudgments outweigh the attendant costs?

Note on the Critique of the Employment–At–Will Doctrine

An economist might defend Epstein's position and the employment-at-will doctrine by arguing that employers and employees who would benefit from checks on arbitrary terminations could freely contract for such checks without governmental regulation. To the extent that any such check is more valuable to a group of employees than its absence is valuable to their employer, they will "purchase" the check by trading other parts of the compensation package that their labor market position enables them to command. Such purchases do in fact occur, the economist might note, when employees support unions that negotiate "just cause" provisions in collective agreements and when some high-level management employees negotiate contracts for a definite term containing sanctions for termination without cause. Mandatory job security protection, however, may force employees to accept a benefit that is more expensive to their employers than it is valuable to them. Employers may respond by eliminating (or reducing) other compensation that the employees would have preferred or by hiring fewer employees because of increased marginal labor costs. Either way, under this view, private autonomy will be frustrated and net social welfare will be reduced. See Jeffrey L. Harrison, The "New" Terminable-at-Will Employment Contract: An Interest and Cost Incidence Analysis, 69 Iowa L.Rev. 327 (1984).

There are two kinds of counterarguments that can be made to this kind of criticism of governmental regulation. First, a society may wish to reject the valuation that many individual workers are willing to give a particular good, such as job security. It may wish to do so because the rejected individual priorities offend certain fundamental values by which the society wishes to be defined, such as the importance of assuring some minimum level of dignity to all who work, or the principle reflected in § 6 of the Clayton Act of 1914 that the labor of a human being is not a commodity to be dispensed with at will. A society may also reject certain individual values because it is convinced that requiring people to live under new values will transform their priorities, creating a different welfare calculus in accord with the new values. Such paternalistic justifications, however, may be more difficult to accept for a general mandatory job security law than for minimum employment terms such as those established by the Occupational Safety and Health Act and minimum wage legislation.

The second kind of counterargument questions some of the assumptions of the free market economist's attack on regulation. Some would argue, for instance, that the grant of minimum benefits to workers, whether it be minimum job safety or job security, can help effect some redistribution of social wealth from the holders of capital to the contributors of labor. Employers operating in imperfect labor markets cannot necessarily recoup what they must grant workers by lowering other parts of the compensation package. Most economists would view unrestricted redistributions of social wealth in the form of tax and spending power subsidies as more efficient and therefore preferable vehicles. Those interested in pursuing wealth redistribution policies, however, may find that redistribution is socially acceptable only when it occurs as an incident to rules that accord with dominant social values.

Furthermore, some would question the assumption that the rarity of individual employee bargaining for job security protections proves that workers are not willing to incur the costs of such protections. The inclusion in almost all collective bargaining agreements of prohibitions of termination without "just cause" certainly suggests that many employees are willing to bargain and pay for job security. It may be that free bargaining over job security does not occur in most nonunionized labor markets—because of barriers to information about the availability of such protections, inaccurate assessments of the likelihood of unjust dismissal, difficulties in raising questions concerning termination at the outset of a relationship, obstacles to mobility, or employer monopsony. Consider the following excerpt.

PAUL C. WEILER, THE CASE OF WRONGFUL DISMISSAL*

Contractual guarantees against dismissal without just cause are an almost universal fact of life under collective agreements between union-

* From Paul C. Weiler, Governing the Workplace: The Future of Labor and Employment Law, ch. 2, pp. 72–78 (Cambridge, Mass.: Harvard Univ. Press, 1990).

ized firms and their workers. A fundamental difference between a union and a nonunion firm is that in the former, management's decision is ultimately challengeable by the employee in a neutral arbitral forum which will appraise the facts, the process, the proportionality of the penalty and even the substance of the alleged offense itself (such as the refusal to submit to a random drug test unilaterally adopted as company policy). This collective bargaining experience provides strong evidence both that workers would really like to have this broad protection if they had a union representative which was able to secure it, and also that employers can and do readily concede this right without thereby increasing their labor costs and depressing employee compensation. There is little reason to suppose that workers who happen to be employed in a union shop have qualitatively different preferences than those employed in a nonunion shop. One would infer, instead, that a number of features of the nonunion labor market obstruct the satisfaction of this worker preference for contractual guarantees against unjust dismissal, and that these features are remedied by collective bargaining.

* * *

Information. There is reason to doubt that workers are actually making an informed sacrifice of any such guarantee even if they do obtain somewhat higher wages and benefits in return for giving their employer a free hand in making dismissal decisions. The incidence of unjust discharge is low and varies considerably across firms, but the worker who is shopping for a job will find it very difficult to learn (and certainly will not want to ask) about the actual dismissal risks in the firms being interviewed. Worse, even if accurate comparative statistics were made broadly available, people have a psychological tendency to discount unduly the present risk value of low incidence/high severity events in choosing whether to trade these off for immediate tangible benefits or costs.[53] For the same reasons the community has concluded that workers may underinvest in insurance against severely disabling physical injuries and thus mandates workers' compensation benefits, it could also support a law which requires protection against the rather unlikely occurrence of an unfair firing of a long-service employee, which does severe harm to the individual victim when it does occur.

Public Good. Even the unusual well-informed individual who believes it worthwhile to trade a modicum of present compensation for protection against the future possibility of unfair dismissal from a valuable job may find it hard to persuade his employer to make that kind

---

53. To some extent this is because the experience of being fired is such a rare event that we are simply unable to estimate realistically that it will happen to us. An obvious rejoinder * * * is that the absence of accurate information makes us as prone to overestimate as to underestimate the true odds. However, what is special about dismissal (as compared, say, to a natural mishap) is that one's own behavior and job performance is likely to play a role in the employer's decision. If people feel—as I assume most do—that they can and do perform acceptably in their jobs, the phenomenon of cognitive dissonance is likely to make workers discount rather than inflate the chances that they (rather than others) will be singled out for dismissal. * * *

of exchange. One difficulty is that protection against unfair firings is not secured by a simple undertaking in a contract of employment; it requires the development of an elaborate program of progressive discipline, personnel documentation and record-keeping, and some procedure for appeal and even adjudication. Development and maintenance of such a program involves a considerable investment by the employer, and once it is in place the program would almost certainly be made available to all employees. This produces the classic problem of the public good in an individualistic market. Even though all the employees might prefer to make this exchange, and even though the employer might be prepared to incur these costs if all the employees were to agree to whatever sacrifice in compensation was needed to pay for it, each individual employee lacks the full incentive to make that investment in securing the desired guarantee, because he can hope that some of his fellow employees will do this for him.[55]

Employee Power. The problem of coordinating employee action is likely to be a major factor only in smaller firms. In larger enterprises with sophisticated personnel departments management could take the initiative on behalf of all its employees if it believed that the bulk of them would like such a program and were willing to pay the price for it. The package would then be instituted as part of standard working conditions for all workers, whether or not any might have been tempted to be free riders. The information gap alluded to above is likely to be much less a problem for incumbent employees than for new hires. The longer-service worker will have some sense of the incidence of arbitrary firings, will not be as likely to downplay the consequences when he sees them inflicted on his colleagues, and will develop greater interest in the issue as his personal investment in his job increases with time. The problem is that the labor market tends to undervalue these concerns of the *average* long-service employee, and instead to focus the firm's attention on the interests of the *marginal* employee, the one who is being newly recruited (or who is likely to leave and have to be replaced). Because the latter has much less knowledge and concern about the risk of discharge, his comparison shopping will not serve as an adequate surrogate for the wishes and priorities of the majority of the incumbent employees. * * *

Management Power. Up to this point I have treated the job issue as though it involved an inherent conflict between the worker's interest in fair treatment and the employer's interest in efficient and lower-cost labor. The true conflict is more complicated than that. * * * Although the capital markets deploy a variety of techniques for the alignment of management interests with those of the shareholders, inevitably these leave managers with significant slack for making self-regarding decisions on behalf of the firm. Recognition of this fact is crucial in this context, because although any mutual advantage from a contractual undertaking

---

55. The classic treatment of this issue in the labor market and other contexts is Mancur Olson, *The Logic of Collective Ac-* *tion and the Theory of Groups* (Cambridge, Mass.: Harvard University Press, 1965).

about unjust dismissal would be shared between workers and shareholders, the tangible and immediate costs would be borne by managers. They would have to take much greater care in investigating and documenting the case for dismissal, they would have to defend their decisions and policies against challenges in an outside forum, and they would lose the felt benefit that comes from wielding unreviewable power over their subordinates. As I observed earlier, senior managers in an increasing number of firms have become more receptive to the idea of their entertaining appeals by employees from the decisions of lower management: so far as I know, though, no senior management in a nonunion firm now allows external appeals about its own dismissal *policies.* * * *

* * * The fact that this kind of protection is provided as a matter of course under collective agreements is a much better index of the mutual advantage that exists on this issue. Whatever the other deficiencies of union representation * * *, it is designed to repairing each of the flaws noted earlier in the way the nonunion relationship responds to dismissal. Union representation provides the institutional memory to secure a true understanding of the dimensions of the discharge problem in different firms and industries; collective bargaining gives much more emphatic voice to the needs and priorities of the longer-service employee who has invested much of his working life with his firm; the collective agreement erects a broad structure of rules and procedures into which the just cause guarantee can be fitted; and the organization of the employees into a cohesive bargaining unit gives them the kind of leverage necessary to extract such an undertaking from recalcitrant management, insistent on the maintenance of its unilateral prerogatives. If "just cause" is nearly always the product of such a process, then it does stake out a fair claim for enactment and enforcement by protective employment legislation.

Notes and Questions

1. *Implications of Prevalence of "Cause" Regime in Union Settings?* Professor Weiler suggests credible explanations for the concurrent prevalence of the guarantee of external review of termination decisions in union-negotiated collective agreements and the rarity of such guarantees in nonunion employment relationships. See also Steven L. Willborn, Individual Employment Rights and the Standard Economic Objection: Theory and Empiricism, 67 Neb.L.Rev. 101, 125–134 (1988). For an alternative account, see Freed & Polsby, Just Cause for Termination Rules, supra, 38 Emory L.J. at 1119–26.

a. *Less Costly External Review?* Are there reasons to believe that external review of dismissals in a union setting is less costly for employers than external review in a nonunion setting? Consider two important realities of labor-management relations in this country: First, unions have general authority, consistent with their duty of fair representation, to control and screen which grievances are pressed to arbitration. Second, as a "quid pro quo" for agreeing to external arbitration, most employers negotiate commitments from unions not to strike over arbitrable grievances.

b. *Better Informed Employees?* Do non-union employees systematically overstate the degree to which they are protected from unjust dismissal under existing law? See Pauline T. Kim, Bargaining with Imperfect Information: A Study of Worker Perceptions of Legal Protection in an At–Will World, 83 Corn. L. Rev. 105 (1997). If so, might unions serve as a repeat-player in the labor market collecting and disseminating information about the true incidence of unjust dismissals?

c. *Different Employee Preferences?*

Is Weiler necessarily correct to assume that "there is little reason to suppose that workers who happen to be employed in a union shop have qualitatively different preferences than those employed in a nonunion shop"? Might the choice of a union itself reflect a preference for the kinds of benefits that unions normally advertise and obtain, including external review of discipline?

Does the introduction of majoritarian decisionmaking through a labor union allow a majority to "purchase" just-cause protection at the expense of a minority of the workforce? See Freed & Polsby, supra, at 1124: "The fact that employees choose unjust dismissal rules under unionization may well be an artifact of the employees' collectivized status, given that collectivization lowers the price that employees must pay in order to extract such rules from the employer." These authors also argue that such rules may reflect unduly the preferences of the union leadership for a "stable constituency" and a process that can "generate demand for their services. * * *" Id. at 1125.

2. *Union Representation as "Exit" Option for At–Will Employees?* If unions can adequately protect job security, why is it necessary for the state to mandate job security protection to workers who are free to choose unions? Might some of the same information-related imperfections in the labor market that distort employee valuation of job security also distort employee valuation of union representation? It is also worth questioning whether employee choice of unions is adequately protected by American law from employer coercion. Some commentators, including Weiler, think not. See Paul C. Weiler, Promises to Keep: Securing Workers' Rights to Self–Organization Under the NLRA, 96 Harv.L.Rev. 1769 (1983); Striking a New Balance: Freedom of Contract and the Prospects for Union Representation, 98 Harv.L.Rev. 351 (1984). Indeed, the overall conclusion of the book excerpted from above is a call for greater protection of the collective representation option. In addition, union representation is not a legally protected option in this country for supervisors and managers. See NLRB v. Kentucky River Community Care, Inc., 532 U.S. 706, 121 S.Ct. 1861, 149 L.Ed.2d 939 (2001); NLRB v. Bell Aerospace Co., 416 U.S. 267, 94 S.Ct. 1757, 40 L.Ed.2d 134 (1974).

3. *Changing the "Background" Rule?* Would it be desirable to reverse the background rule from a presumption of at-will status to a presumption of job tenure absent "cause," while permitting the parties to contract for different arrangements? Professor Verkerke argues, based on some empirical results, that this new background rule would be "inefficient" in that most parties will waste resources bargaining back to an at-will regime. See Verkerke, Indefinite Term Employment Contracts, supra. Are significant

resources likely to be wasted if employers demand that job applicants, as a condition of employment, agree to at-will status?

4. *Limiting Wrongful Dismissal Protection to Long–Term Employees?* Should wrongful discharge legislation be narrowly framed if its major purpose is the protection of long-term employees who have made firm-specific investments in their firms that cannot be recouped by working elsewhere? Would it be preferable that such legislation take the form of mandatory severance compensation keyed to, say, years of service? Or that it be an explicit aspect of age discrimination legislation? See Michael C. Harper, ADEA Doctrinal Impediments to the Fulfillment of the Wirtz Report Agenda, 31 U. Rich. L.Rev. 757, 787–93 (1997); Stewart J. Schwab, Life–Cycle Justice, supra; Issacharoff, Contracting for Employment, supra, at 1806 ff.

2. *What Form Should the Legislation Take?*

As an example of how wrongful discharge legislation might be framed, consider the Montana Wrongful Discharge from Employment Act, the first of its kind in this country.

MONTANA WRONGFUL DISCHARGE FROM EMPLOYMENT ACT

Mont.Code Ann. §§ 39–2–901 to –914.

For text, consult Statutory Supplement.

Notes and Questions

1. *"Good Cause" Standard.* The substantive standard for wrongful termination—"good cause"—is defined only in general terms and arguably resembles the open-ended "just cause" formulation of collective bargaining agreements. Some commentators have urged that the principles developed in labor arbitration awards should be used as persuasive authority in wrongful discharge litigation. See, e.g., Clyde W. Summers, Individual Protection Against Unjust Dismissal: Time for a Statute, 62 Va.L.Rev. 481, 499 (1976). Then–Judge Joseph R. Grodin, a former labor lawyer, California Supreme Court justice and later a law professor, writing in Pugh v. See's Candies, 116 Cal.App.3d 311, 330, 171 Cal.Rptr. 917, 927 (1981), has cautioned against uncritical reliance on arbitral precedent:

> Care must be taken, however, not to interfere with legitimate exercise of managerial discretion.[26] * * * And where, as here, the employee occupies a sensitive managerial or confidential position, the employee must of necessity be allowed substantial scope for the exercise of subjective judgment.

> > 26. Labor arbitrators have generated a large body of decisions interpreting and applying such terms as "just cause" (see Elkouri & Elkouri, How Arbitration Works (1973) ch. 15), and some of their work may be useful. It must be remembered, however, that arbitrators are selected by the parties and on the basis, partly, of the

> confidence which the parties have in their knowledge and judgment concerning labor relations matters. * * * For courts to apply the same standards may prove overly intrusive in some cases.

See Samuel Estreicher, Arbitration of Employment Disputes Without Unions, 66 U.Chi.–Kent L. Rev. 753, 794–95 (1990).

Montana decisions make clear that a considerably more deferential standard than the "just cause" required in labor agreements applies. In Buck v. Billings Montana Chevrolet, Inc., 248 Mont. 276, 811 P.2d 537 (1991), the court held that a new purchaser of an automobile dealership had "a legitimate business reason," within the meaning of the "good cause" concept as defined in the statute, to terminate the former manager and replace him with a manager from the purchaser's other operations, even though the decision was admittedly not based on the prior work performance of the former manager. The *Buck* court defined a "legitimate business reason" as one that is

> neither false, whimsical or capricious, and it must have some logical relationship to the needs of the business. In applying this definition, one must take into account the right of an employer to exercise discretion over who it will employ and keep in employment. Of equal importance to this right, however, is the legitimate interest of the employee to secure employment.

Id. at 281–82, 811 P.2d at 540. The court explained, however, that its holding was limited "to those who occupy sensitive managerial confidential positions," and that the balance might tip the other way in the case of non-managerial employees. Id. at 283, 811 P.2d at 541. The Montana high court also apparently draws a distinction between decisions eliminating managerial positions and decisions replacing one employee with another. See Kestell v. Heritage Health Care Corp., 259 Mont. 518, 858 P.2d 3 (1993) (setting aside summary judgment against former director of hospital's chemical dependency unit). See generally Donald C. Robinson, The First Decade of Judicial Interpretation of the Montana Wrongful Discharge from Employment Act, 57 Mont. L. Rev. 375 (1996).

2. *Post–Dispute Arbitration Option*. The Montana statute contemplates resort to a civil action and presumably a jury trial. However, final and binding arbitration is offered as an alternative and is creatively encouraged by fee-shifting provisions. Are there advantages to this approach over either committing disputes exclusively to the courts or to arbitration? Does the Montana statute require that there must be an agreement to arbitrate before the attorney's fees provisions are triggered? In 1993, the Montana legislature amended the statute to make clear that a unilateral offer to arbitrate that is refused triggers the attorney's fees provisions. See Mont. Code Ann. § 39–2–915. In May v. First National Pawn Brokers, 269 Mont. 19, 887 P.2d 185 (1994), the court adopted the "manifest disregard of the law" standard for vacating arbitration awards, in view of the limited judicial review available under Montana law. For a model post-dispute arbitration agreement, see Center for Public Resources, Model Procedure for Employment Termination Dispute Adjudication (Nov.1986).

3. *Implications of Damages Cap.* Why did the Montana legislature place a four-year "cap" on lost wages and fringe benefits, exclude recovery for emotional distress and compensatory damages, and limit punitive damages to cases of fraud or malice? In view of the statutory cap on recovery and the preemption of preexisting common law contract remedies, are plaintiffs as a class made less well off than they were under an at-will regime? Is the legislative compromise reflected in the Montana statute similar to the compromise that led to passage of workers' compensation systems (see p. ____ supra)? Does the Montana measure, in effect, confer upon employees as a group some measure of job security in exchange for a ceiling on employer liability? Or is the measure more favorable to employer interests by limiting liability yet retaining a fault-based system invocable only by court action? Would it have been preferable from a policy standpoint, and fairer to employee interests, to have provided either for (i) a strict liability-based administrative process resembling workers' compensation systems, or (ii) if a fault-based civil action were desired, authority to award attorney's fees to prevailing claimants, as is true under Title VII and ADEA?

The Montana Supreme Court rejected a challenge to the Montana statute brought under the state constitution's guaranty of equal protection and "full legal redress for injury incurred in employment" in Meech v. Hillhaven West, Inc., 238 Mont. 21, 776 P.2d 488 (1989). The history of the Montana statute is developed in Andrew P. Morriss, The Story of the Montana Wrongful Discharge from Employment Act: A Drama in 5 Acts, in Employment Law Stories, ch. 9 (Samuel Estreicher & Gillian Lester eds. 2007).

4. *Exclusions from Coverage.* Note that the act contains several exclusions from coverage. The "good cause" standard only applies to employees who have completed a probationary period, presumably to give employers time to determine the suitability of a new hire. In addition, the act exempts any discharge (i) that is remediable by any other state or federal statute; (ii) that affects employees covered by a collective bargaining agreement; or (iii) that affects employees "covered by a written contract for a specific term." The first exemption avoids duplicative adjudication. The second exemption may do so as well, but it raises the question of whether the state should require unionized employees to expend bargaining leverage to extract protection that is granted as a statutory right to nonunion workers. Could not duplicative adjudication be avoided by requiring a discharged employee to choose between a statutory and contractual remedy, as commonly occurs in civil service systems?

What is the explanation for the third exclusion? Is the legislature effectively providing an opportunity for the parties to "contract out" of the statute? Will employees be better off if they are compelled to enter into written contracts for two- or one-year, or even shorter terms, rather than open-ended indefinite employment arrangements? Montana decisions make clear that nonrenewal of specific-term contracts are not covered by the "good cause" requirement. See Farris v. Hutchinson, 254 Mont. 334, 838 P.2d 374 (1992).

5. *Adverse Actions Short of Discharge.* Note also that the statute covers constructive discharges, but this term does not include refusals to promote or improve wages or other working conditions. Some courts have applied the new common law "wrongful discharge" doctrine to constructive discharges. See, e.g., Scott v. Pacific Gas and Electric Co., 11 Cal.4th 454, 46 Cal.Rptr.2d 427, 904 P.2d 834 (1995), discussed at note 10, p. 749 supra; Mitchell v. Connecticut General Life Ins. Co., 697 F.Supp. 948 (E.D.Mich.1988) (applying Michigan's *Toussaint* doctrine). Is the Montana statute's coverage adequate? Under their negotiated agreements, union-represented employees generally enjoy protection from any arbitrary discipline, not just terminations. Why should nonunionized employees be forced to resign, and to prove that resignation was effectively compelled, before being granted protection?

6. *Preemption of Common Law Claims.* Note also that implied-contract claims are barred by the preemption provision of the statute, Mont. Code Ann.§ 39–2–913; however, contract claims bearing on matters other than discharge, such as compensation, are not barred. See Beasley v. Semitool, Inc., 258 Mont. 258, 853 P.2d 84 (1993). Should the preemptive sweep of a wrongful dismissal law be broader?

Note on the Uniform Law Commissioners' Model Employment Termination Act

In August 1991, the National Conference of Commissioners of Uniform State Laws approved a "Model Employment Termination Act" and recommended its enactment in every state; for text, see Stat.Supp. The proposed model act embodies essentially the tradeoff reflected in the Montana law: certainty of a right of action to challenge wrongful termination in exchange for limitations on remedies, particularly the exclusion of punitive damages, compensatory damages, or other recovery for emotional distress and pain and suffering. Covered employees are granted a substantive right to "good cause" protections against discharge, which cannot be waived except by an individually executed agreement guaranteeing a minimum schedule of severance payments keyed to length of service. The proposed law contemplates that state-appointed arbitrators will adjudicate claims with authority to award reinstatement, with or without backpay, and severance pay if reinstatement is infeasible. Unlike the Montana law, attorney's fees may be awarded to a prevailing claimant. For a somewhat similar proposal, see Calif. State Bar Ad Hoc Comm. on Termination At Will and Wrongful Discharge, To Strike a New Balance: A Report of the Ad Hoc Comm. on Termination At Will and Wrongful Discharge (Feb.1984). For the general views of the reporter for the National Conference of Commissioners' drafting committee, see Theodore J. St. Antoine, The Making of the Model Employment Termination Act, 69 Wash. L. Rev. 361 (1994); and A Seed Germinates: Unjust Discharge Reform Heads Toward Full Flower, 67 Neb.L.Rev. 56 (1988). See also Kenneth A. Sprang, Beware the Toothless Tiger: A Critique of the Model Employment Termination Act, 43 Am. U. L. Rev. 849 (1994).

SAMUEL ESTREICHER, UNJUST DISMISSAL LAWS: SOME CAUTIONARY NOTES*

III. SOME GENERAL CHARACTERISTICS OF UNJUST DISMISSAL LAWS ABROAD

A. Reinstatement

The most striking point about the foregoing schemes is that, irrespective of formal legal position, reinstatement is simply not an important feature in practice (at least outside of Canada, Italy and perhaps Germany). The measures surveyed here do not in fact vindicate a right to a job. At best, they provide a much needed transfer payment to cushion displacement and perhaps an opportunity to clear one's name.

The evidence from England and from studies of NLRB reinstatees, as compared with labor arbitration reinstatees, suggests that the reinstatement remedy is difficult to police effectively outside of the context of union representation. Germany's works councils seem to play a supportive role, similar to that of a union, and Italy's statute is aided by its labor movement's willingness to assist nonmember dischargees (in the hopes of recruiting them). One may venture here the generalization that perhaps such protective support mechanisms are necessary to the success of the reinstatement remedy.

B. Size of Awards

Outside of Canada and possibly Italy, the monetary awards, while not insignificant, are at modest, predictable levels—certainly in comparison to American jury recoveries. The English awards are striking in this regard, which goes a long way toward explaining the English employers' reluctance to reinstate and the high settlement rate prior to hearing.** Punitive damages are also not a significant feature, although punitive concepts explain the additional award in Great Britain's statute and other similar provisions.

C. Exclusions from Coverage and Fixed–Term Contracts

None of the countries in question provides universal protection; throughout we find qualifying periods of continuous service (in Great Britain, now 52 continuous weeks and two years for small firms); and exclusions or special provision for small sized companies (again, in Great Britain, by nearly doubling the qualifying period).

Managerial employees apparently are not per se excluded from coverage. (Italy does provide a separate set of procedures.) Great Britain's exclusion of employees under fixed-term contract of at least one year's duration may operate to disqualify most managers. Even if formal-

* 33 Am.J.Comp.L. 310 (1985) updated in Global Issues in Employment Law 74–85 (Samuel Estreicher & Miriam A. Cherry eds. 2008).

** [Eds. Under pressure from the European Community's International Court of Justice, the United Kingdom has amended its laws to provide for uncapped monetary recoveries in discrimination cases, and has raised its monetary cap for unfair dismissal cases to £50,000 (approximately $75,000).]

ly excluded, however, managerial employees may have common law rights to dismissal only upon notice.

As to fixed-term contracts, Great Britain permits exclusion in the case of employees under a fixed-term contract of at least one year's duration who sign a written waiver of statutory rights. On the other hand, Germany, France and Italy, sensing here a potentially significant evasive tactic, seek to discourage repeated renewal of fixed-term contracts.

D. Delegation of "Just Cause" Criteria to the Tribunal

None of the statutes here attempt to spell out the standards, the criteria of "just cause." Rather, they are broad delegations to the tribunals to develop procedural and substantive criteria, usually without guidance from a well-developed body of labor arbitration law.

The British model, as it has evolved, seems to be one of deferential review of managerial prerogative, rather than *de novo* review—similar in theory to our judicial review of administrative agency action. This model of thoroughgoing deference seems not to have taken hold elsewhere on the Continent.

E. Use of Specialized Tribunals

With the exception of Japan and Italy, the statutes in question all utilize specialized labor tribunals that, at least in theory, are thought to dispense a cheaper, quicker, more accessible and expert justice. These tribunals, while often tripartite, do not offer the same opportunity for party selection of decisionmaker as would U.S. labor arbitration.

F. Absence of Labor Union Opposition

Although at first unions were skeptical, even opposed, to these new statutes, the evidence strongly suggests that the European unions have not only made their peace but also have assisted nonmember utilization of the statutory procedures (as an organizing tactic).

G. Relation to Redundancy Dismissal Legislation

Virtually all of the countries under review have also enacted some protections against economic dismissals, individual or group. In Great Britain, redundancy laws preceded the unjust dismissal statute. Although I am not sure of the precise relationship between these schemes, I suspect that unjust dismissal laws appeared to many as at least logically inevitable once the inviolability of the at-will concept was breached by redundancy laws. Moreover, in many situations, both disciplinary and economic reasons may be potentially available to an employer bent on terminating an employee. Effective policing of either scheme may well require enactment of the other.

Notes and Questions

1. *Relationship Between Discrimination and Unfair Dismissal Claims.* Because of the availability of unfair dismissal remedies in most of the European countries, there is less of an incentive to frame one's case as a discrimination case where the gravamen of the claim is a challenge to the fairness of a termination decision. Thus, for example, 31% of cases resolved in 2005–06 in the U.K. employment tribunal system involved discrimination claims. See Employment Tribunal Service, Annual Report & Accounts 2005–06, App., table 2, at 29 (available at www.governmenttribunals.gov.uk). In the U.S., by contrast, given the absence of unfair dismissal legislation (outside of Montana), plaintiffs look to the anti-discrimination laws as their principal recourse. Over time, litigants in Europe may be more attracted to pursuing discrimination claims which, under EU law, cannot be subject to a maximum level of recovery.

2. *Relatively Low U.K. Tribunal Awards.* By U.S. standards, U.K. employment tribunal awards would seem low, even in discrimination cases where caps are no longer imposed on awards. What factors might explain this? The extent of discrimination in the U.K.? The absence of a civil jury? The legal culture in the U.K.? Is the fairly widespread acceptance by European employers of "just cause" regimes attributable to their ability readily to insure themselves without excessive costs? Might this be the source of a desirable trade-off for the U.S.—relatively prompt recovery provided in employee-friendly employment tribunals but lower awards?

3. *Reinstatement Remedy.* Under what conditions is an effective reinstatement remedy possible in a nonunionized environment or one without a support mechanism similar to the German works councils? Who would police post-reinstatement compliance? Should the law require the reinstatement of of wrongly dismissed high-level executives or other employees whose jobs depend on maintenance of a high degree of employer trust and confidence? Does a "no waiver" rule make sense in the context of employees who have a fair measure of individual bargaining power?

4. *Special Tribunals?* Why have the Europeans tended to provide for special administrative tribunals or labor courts to handle employment cases, including discrimination claims? Would the U.S. need a similar set of institutions to administer a general unfair dismissal regime? Is the Canadian federal government's use of "adjudicators" from the ranks of private labor arbitrators an attractive possibility for the U.S.? Who would pay for the adjudicators? Should such adjudicators be permitted freely to rely on labor arbitration principles that were developed in a consensual setting as part of an ongoing process of collective bargaining? Should those principles apply to disputes involving employees whose jobs involve considerable unsupervised time and the daily exercise of discretion and judgment?

5. *Resistance to Change?* Although many European observers believe that a greater measure of flexibility is needed in dismissal laws to encourage employment growth, change to these laws faces considerable obstacles. See, e.g., John C. Reitz, Political Economy and Contract Law, in New Features in Contract Law (Reiner Schulze, ed., 2007) (available at http://ssrn.com/abstract = 964476):

In April–May, 2006, French students and labor unions, joined by teachers, the jobless, and even retirees, took to the streets in an escalating series of actions to protest government proposals to amend the labor laws to give employers a limited right to terminate young, first-time permanent employees on an at will basis. The proposed law would have created a new two-year labor contract (the so-called *contrat première embauche* or *C.P.E.*) for businesses with over twenty workers and for workers younger than twenty–six [when] employed for their first job. The new contract would have permitted employers to terminate without notice, severance pay, or the obligation to show that the employee has violated the contract. Over a two–month period of disruptions, the protestors managed to * * * shut down universities, threatened to hurt tourism and economy, and brought violent clashes between young people and police. Eventually, the French political leaders bowed to public opposition and rescinded the law that promulgated the *C.P.E.* contract.

Chapter Thirteen

PROTECTION FROM INTRUSIVE EMPLOYMENT PRACTICES

A. INTRODUCTION

This chapter presents a distinct form of labor market regulation—one intended to protect employee interests in privacy or autonomy. Rather than simply seeking protection from the abuse of accepted employer authority to pursue economic goals, such regulation directly challenges the legitimacy of employer authority over aspects of the lives of employees. We encountered a similar claim in *Novosel*, p. 723 supra, where the Third Circuit (applying Pennsylvania law) recognized a public policy against employer-coerced political activity by employees.

The protection of employee privacy, like the protection of religious freedom and political expression, preserves a zone of personal choice. However, unlike the activity at issue in Part II, the varied personal choices that may be protected by the establishment of workplace privacy rights are not necessarily especially valued by society, either intrinsically or instrumentally. Instead, they may be protected simply because the society determines that a sphere of life should be immune from employer control even at the workplace.

For general treatments of the subject of privacy in the workplace, see Matthew W. Finkin, Privacy in Employment Law (1995); Ira Michael Shepard et al., Workplace Privacy (2d ed. 1989); Pauline T. Kim, Privacy Rights, Public Policy and the Employment Relationship, 57 Ohio St. L.J. 671 (1996).

B. CONSTITUTIONAL PROTECTIONS IN THE PUBLIC SECTOR

1. Physical Privacy

O'CONNOR v. ORTEGA

Supreme Court of the United States, 1987.
480 U.S. 709, 107 S.Ct. 1492, 94 L.Ed.2d 714.

Justice O'Connor, J., announced the judgment of the Court and delivered an opinion in which Chief Justice Rehnquist, and Justices White and Powell, JJ., joined.

I

Dr. Magno Ortega, a physician and psychiatrist, held the position of Chief of Professional Education at Napa State Hospital (Hospital) for 17 years, until his dismissal from that position in 1981. As Chief of Professional Education, Dr. Ortega had primary responsibility for training young physicians in psychiatric residency programs.

In July 1981, Hospital officials, including Dr. Dennis O'Connor, the Executive Director of the Hospital, became concerned about possible improprieties in Dr. Ortega's management of the residency program. In particular, the Hospital officials were concerned with Dr. Ortega's acquisition of an Apple II computer for use in the residency program. The officials thought that Dr. Ortega may have misled Dr. O'Connor into believing that the computer had been donated, when in fact the computer had been financed by the possibly coerced contributions of residents. Additionally, the Hospital officials were concerned with charges that Dr. Ortega had sexually harassed two female Hospital employees, and had taken inappropriate disciplinary action against a resident.

On July 30, 1981, Dr. O'Connor requested that Dr. Ortega take paid administrative leave during an investigation of these charges. * * *

Dr. O'Connor selected several Hospital personnel to conduct the investigation, including an accountant, a physician, and a Hospital security officer. Richard Friday, the Hospital Administrator, led this "investigative team." At some point during the investigation, Mr. Friday made the decision to enter Dr. Ortega's office. The specific reason for the entry into Dr. Ortega's office is unclear from the record. The petitioners claim that the search was conducted to secure state property. Initially, petitioners contended that such a search was pursuant to a Hospital policy of conducting a routine inventory of state property in the office of a terminated employee. At the time of the search, however, the Hospital had not yet terminated Dr. Ortega's employment; Dr. Ortega was still on administrative leave. Apparently, there was no policy of inventorying the offices of those on administrative leave. Before the search had been initiated, however, the petitioners had become aware that Dr. Ortega had taken the computer to his home. Dr. Ortega contends that the purpose of the search was to secure evidence for use against him in administrative disciplinary proceedings.

The resulting search of Dr. Ortega's office was quite thorough. The investigators entered the office a number of times and seized several items from Dr. Ortega's desk and file cabinets, including a Valentine's card, a photograph, and a book of poetry all sent to Dr. Ortega by a former resident physician. These items were later used in a proceeding before a hearing officer of the California State Personnel Board to impeach the credibility of the former resident, who testified on Dr. Ortega's behalf. The investigators also seized billing documentation of one of Dr. Ortega's private patients under the California Medicaid program. The investigators did not otherwise separate Dr. Ortega's property from state property because, as one investigator testified, "[t]rying to sort State from non-State, it was too much to do, so I gave it up and boxed it up." Thus, no formal inventory of the property in the office was ever made. Instead, all the papers in Dr. Ortega's office were merely placed in boxes, and put in storage for Dr. Ortega to retrieve.

* * *

II

* * *

Within the workplace context, this Court has recognized that employees may have a reasonable expectation of privacy against intrusions by police. See *Mancusi v. DeForte,* 392 U.S. 364, 88 S.Ct. 2120, 20 L.Ed.2d 1154 (1968). As with the expectation of privacy in one's home, such an expectation in one's place of work is "based upon societal expectations that have deep roots in the history of the Amendment." * * * Thus, in *Mancusi v. DeForte, supra,* the Court held that a union employee who shared an office with other union employees had a privacy interest in the office sufficient to challenge successfully the warrantless search of that office:

"It has long been settled that one has standing to object to a search of his office, as well as of his home * * *. [I]t seems clear that if DeForte had occupied a 'private' office in the union headquarters, and union records had been seized from a desk or a filing cabinet in that office, he would have had standing * * *. In such a 'private' office, DeForte would have been entitled to expect that he would not be disturbed except by personal or business invitees, and that records would not be taken except with his permission or that of his union superiors." 392 U.S., at 369, 88 S.Ct., at 2124.

Given the societal expectations of privacy in one's place of work * * *, we reject the contention made by the Solicitor General and petitioners that public employees can never have a reasonable expectation of privacy in their place of work. Individuals do not lose Fourth Amendment rights merely because they work for the government instead of a private employer. The operational realities of the workplace, however, may make *some* employees' expectations of privacy unreasonable when an intrusion is by a supervisor rather than a law enforcement official. Public employees' expectations of privacy in their offices, desks, and file cabinets, like similar expectations of employees in the private sector, may be reduced by virtue of actual office practices and procedures, or by legitimate regulation. Indeed, in *Mancusi* itself, the Court suggested that the union employee did not have a reasonable expectation of privacy against his union supervisors. 392 U.S., at 369, 88 S.Ct., at 2124. The employee's expectation of privacy must be assessed in the context of the employment relation. An office is seldom a private enclave free from entry by supervisors, other employees and business and personal invitees. Instead, in many cases offices are continually entered by fellow employees and other visitors during the workday for conferences, consultations, and other work-related visits. Simply put, it is the nature of government offices that others—such as fellow employees, supervisors, consensual visitors, and the general public—may have frequent access to an individual's office. * * * Given the great variety of work environments in the public sector, the question of whether an employee has a reasonable expectation of privacy must be addressed on a case-by-case basis.

The Court of Appeals concluded that Dr. Ortega had a reasonable expectation of privacy in his office, and five Members of this Court agree with that determination. * * * Because the record does not reveal the extent to which Hospital officials may have had work-related reasons to enter Dr. Ortega's office, we think the Court of Appeals should have remanded the matter to the District Court for its further determination. But regardless of any legitimate right of access the Hospital staff may have had to the office as such, we recognize that the undisputed evidence suggests that Dr. Ortega had a reasonable expectation of privacy in his desk and file cabinets. The undisputed evidence discloses that Dr. Ortega did not share his desk or file cabinets with any other employees. Dr. Ortega had occupied the office for 17 years and he kept materials in his office, which included personal correspondence, medical files, and correspondence from private patients unconnected to the Hospital, personal financial records, teaching aids and notes, and personal gifts and mementos. The files on physicians in residency training were kept outside Dr. Ortega's office. Indeed, the only items found by the investigators were apparently personal items because, with the exception of the items seized for use in the administrative hearings, all the papers and effects found in the office were simply placed in boxes and made available to Dr. Ortega. Finally, we note that there was no evidence that the Hospital had established any reasonable regulation or policy discouraging employees such as Dr. Ortega from storing personal papers and effects in their desks or file cabinets, although the absence of such a policy does not create an expectation of privacy where it would not otherwise exist.

* * *

III

Having determined that Dr. Ortega had a reasonable expectation of privacy in his office, the Court of Appeals simply concluded without discussion that the "search * * * was not a reasonable search under the fourth amendment." * * *

* * *

There is surprisingly little case law on the appropriate Fourth Amendment standard of reasonableness for a public employer's work-related search of its employee's offices, desks, or file cabinets. * * *

The legitimate privacy interests of public employees in the private objects they bring to the workplace may be substantial. Against these privacy interests, however, must be balanced the realities of the workplace, which strongly suggest that a warrant requirement would be unworkable. While police, and even administrative enforcement personnel, conduct searches for the primary purpose of obtaining evidence for use in criminal or other enforcement proceedings, employers most frequently need to enter the offices and desks of their employees for legitimate work-related reasons wholly unrelated to illegal conduct. Employers and supervisors are focused primarily on the need to complete the government agency's work in a prompt and efficient manner. An employer may have need for correspondence, or a file or report available only in an employee's office while the employee is away from the office. Or, as is alleged to have been the case here, employers may need to safeguard or identify state property or records in an office in connection with a pending investigation into suspected employee misfeasance.

In our view, requiring an employer to obtain a warrant whenever the employer wished to enter an employee's office, desk, or file cabinets for a work-related purpose would seriously disrupt the routine conduct of business and would be unduly burdensome. Imposing unwieldy warrant procedures in such cases upon supervisors, who would otherwise have no reason to be familiar with such procedures, is simply unreasonable. In contrast to other circumstances in which we have required warrants, supervisors in offices such as at the Hospital are hardly in the business of investigating the violation of criminal laws. Rather, work-related searches are merely incident to the primary business of the agency. * * *

Whether probable cause is an inappropriate standard for public employer searches of their employees' offices presents a more difficult issue. For the most part, we have required that a search be based upon probable cause, but as we noted in *New Jersey v. T.L.O.,* [469 U.S. 325, 105 S.Ct. 733, 83 L.Ed.2d 720 (1985)], "[t]he fundamental command of the Fourth Amendment is that searches and seizures be reasonable, and although 'both the concept of probable cause and the requirement of a warrant bear on the reasonableness of a search, * * * in certain limited circumstances neither is required.'" [*Id.*] at 340, 105 S.Ct., at 743 (quoting *Almeida–Sanchez v. United States,* 413 U.S. 266, 277, 93 S.Ct. 2535, 2541, 37 L.Ed.2d 596 (1973) (Powell, J., concurring)). * * * We have concluded, for example, that the appropriate standard for administrative searches is not probable cause in its traditional meaning. Instead, an administrative warrant can be obtained if there is a showing that reasonable legislative or administrative standards for conducting an inspection are satisfied. See *Marshall v. Barlow's, Inc.,* 436 U.S. [307, 320, 98 S.Ct. 1816, 1824 (1978)]; *Camara v. Municipal Court,* 387 U.S. [523, 538, 87 S.Ct. 1727, 1735 (1967)].

As an initial matter, it is important to recognize the plethora of contexts in which employers will have an occasion to intrude to some extent on an employee's expectation of privacy. Because the parties in this case have alleged that the search was either a noninvestigatory work-related intrusion or an investigatory search for evidence of suspected work-related employee misfeasance, we undertake to determine the appropriate Fourth Amendment standard of reasonableness *only* for these two types of employer intrusions and leave for another day inquiry into other circumstances.

The governmental interest justifying work-related intrusions by public employers is the efficient and proper operation of the workplace. Government agencies provide myriad services to the public, and the work of these agencies would suffer if employers were required to have probable cause before they entered an employee's desk for the purpose of finding a file or piece of office correspondence. Indeed, it is difficult to give the concept of probable cause, rooted as it is in the criminal investigatory context, much meaning when the purpose of a search is to retrieve a file for work-related reasons. Similarly, the concept of probable cause has little meaning for a routine inventory conducted by public employers for the purpose of securing state property. * * * To ensure the efficient and proper operation of the agency, therefore, public employers must be given wide latitude to enter employee offices for work-related, noninvestigatory reasons.

We come to a similar conclusion for searches conducted pursuant to an investigation of work-related employee misconduct. Even when employers conduct an investigation, they have an interest substantially different from "the normal need for law enforcement." *New Jersey v. T.L.O., supra,* 469 U.S., at 351, 105 S.Ct., at 749 (Blackmun, J., concurring in judgment). Public employers have an interest in ensuring that their agencies operate in an effective and efficient manner, and the work of these agencies inevitably suffers from the inefficiency, incompetence, mismanagement or other work-related misfeasance of its employees. Indeed, in many cases, public employees are entrusted with tremendous responsibility, and the consequences of their misconduct or incompetence to both the agency and the public interest can be severe. In contrast to law enforcement officials, therefore, public employers are not enforcers of the criminal law; instead, public employers have a direct and overriding interest in ensuring that the work of the agency is conducted in a proper and efficient manner. In our view, therefore, a probable cause requirement for searches of the type at issue here would impose intolerable burdens on public employers. The delay in correcting the employee misconduct caused by the need for probable cause rather than reasonable suspicion will be translated into tangible and often irreparable damage to the agency's work, and ultimately to the public interest. * * * Additionally, while law enforcement officials are expected to "schoo[l] themselves in the niceties of probable cause," *id.,* at 343, 105 S.Ct., at 744, no such expectation is generally applicable to public employers, at least when the search is not used to gather evidence of a criminal offense. It is simply unrealistic to expect supervisors in most government agencies to learn the subtleties of the probable cause standard.

* * *

In sum, we conclude that the "special needs, beyond the normal need for law enforcement make the * * * probable-cause requirement impracticable," [*New Jersey* v. *T.L.O*,] 469 U.S., at 351, 105 S.Ct., at 749 (Blackmun, J., concurring in judgment), for legitimate work-related, noninvestigatory intrusions as well as investigations of work-related misconduct. A standard of reasonableness will neither unduly burden the efforts of government employers to ensure the efficient and proper operation of the workplace, nor authorize arbitrary intrusions upon the privacy of public employees. We hold, therefore, that public employer intrusions on the constitutionally protected privacy interests of government employees for noninvestigatory, work-related purposes, as well as for investigations of work-related misconduct, should be judged by the standard of reasonableness under all the circumstances. Under this reasonableness standard, both the inception and the scope of the intrusion must be reasonable.

* * *

Ordinarily, a search of an employee's office by a supervisor will be "justified at its inception" when there are reasonable grounds for suspecting that the search will turn up evidence that the employee is guilty of work-related misconduct, or that the search is necessary for a noninvestigatory work-related purpose such as to retrieve a needed file. Because the petitioners had an "individualized suspicion" of misconduct by Dr. Ortega, we need not decide whether individualized suspicion is an essential element of the standard of reasonableness that we adopt today.

* * *

IV

In the procedural posture of this case, we do not attempt to determine whether the search of Dr. Ortega's office and the seizure of his personal belonging, satisfy the standard of reasonableness we have articulated in this case. No evidentiary hearing was held in this case because the District Court acted on cross-motions for summary judgment, and granted petitioners summary judgment. * * * The Court of Appeals, on the other hand, concluded that the record in this case justified granting partial summary judgment on liability to Dr. Ortega.

* * * [T]he District Court was in error in granting the petitioners summary judgment. There was a dispute of fact about the character of the search, and the District Court acted under the erroneous assumption that the search was conducted pursuant to a Hospital policy. Moreover, no findings were made as to the scope of the search that was undertaken.

The Court of Appeals concluded that Dr. Ortega was entitled to partial summary judgment on liability. It noted that the Hospital had no policy of inventorying the property of employees on administrative leave, but it did not consider whether the search was otherwise reasonable. Under the standard of reasonableness articulated in this case, however, the absence of a Hospital policy did not necessarily make the search unlawful. A search to secure state property is valid as long as the petitioners had a reasonable belief that there was government property in Dr. Ortega's office which needed to be secured, and the scope of the intrusion was itself reasonable in light of this justification. Indeed, the petitioners have put forward evidence that they had such a reasonable belief; at the time of the search, petitioners knew that Dr. Ortega had removed the computer from the Hospital. The removal of the computer—together with the allegations of mismanagement of the residency program and sexual harassment—may have made the search reasonable at its inception under the standard we have put forth in this case. As with the District Court order, therefore, the Court of Appeals' conclusion that summary judgment was appropriate cannot stand.

On remand, therefore, the District Court must determine the justification for the search and seizure, and evaluate the reasonableness of both the inception of the search and its scope.*

JUSTICE SCALIA, concurring in the judgment.

* * * There is no reason why [the] determination that a legitimate expectation of privacy exists should be affected by the fact that the government, rather than a private entity, is the employer. Constitutional protection against *unreasonable* searches by the government does not disappear merely because the government has the right to make reasonable intrusions in its capacity as employer.

I cannot agree, moreover, with the plurality's view that the reasonableness of the expectation of privacy (and thus the existence of Fourth Amendment protection) changes "when an intrusion is by a supervisor rather than a law enforcement official." The identity of the searcher (police vs. employer) is relevant not to whether Fourth Amendment protections apply, but only to whether the search of a protected area is reasonable.

* * *

The case turns, therefore, on whether the Fourth Amendment was violated—*i.e.,* whether the governmental intrusion was reasonable. It is here that the government's status as employer, and the employment-related character of the search, become relevant. * * * I would hold that government searches to retrieve work-related materials or to investigate violations of workplace rules—searches of the sort that are regarded as reasonable and normal in the private-employer context—do not violate the Fourth Amendment. Because the conflicting and incomplete evidence in the present case could not conceivably support summary judgment

---

* We have no occasion in this case to reach the issue of the appropriate standard for the evaluation of the Fourth Amendment reasonableness of the seizure of Dr. Ortega's personal items. Neither the District Court nor the Court of Appeals addressed this issue * * *. [We also] do not address the appropriate standard when an employee is being investigated for criminal misconduct or breaches of other nonwork-related statutory or regulatory standards.

that the search did not have such a validating purpose, I agree with the plurality that the decision must be reversed and remanded.

Notes and Questions

1. On remand, Ortega recovered $436,000 in damages. In affirming the judgment, the Ninth Circuit observed:

> The search was at best, a general and unbounded pursuit of anything that might tend to indicate any sort of malfeasance–a search that is almost by definition, unreasonable. * * *

> There is no reason to suspect that office Lotharios in general keep incriminating evidence of their activities in their desk drawers or files.

Ortega v. O'Connor, 146 F.3d 1149, 1163 (9th Cir.1998).

2. *Government as Regulator vs. Government as Manager?* The Court in *O'Connor inter alia* determined the extent to which constitutional norms fashioned to restrain government as regulator apply to government in its role as manager of a workplace. Are you satisfied with the *O'Connor* plurality's compromise, eschewing the polar extremes presented by the law-enforcement and private employer analogies? Does the plurality dispense with the probable cause and warrant requirements because of (i) the employee's low expectation of privacy in his desk, file cabinets and office space, (ii) the absence of a law enforcement objective on the employer's part, or (iii) the special needs of government as an employer? Does Justice O'Connor's opinion suggest that privacy interests thought sufficiently weighty to restrict law enforcement investigations do not similarly restrict investigations of work-related misconduct? Is this a tenable distinction, particularly in view of the fact that evidence of work-related misconduct may also constitute evidence of a criminal offense and may well be furnished to law enforcement authorities?

3. *Utility of the Private–Employer Analogy?* How does Justice Scalia's position differ from that of the plurality? Does the reference to "the private-employer context" suggest that what private employers "normal[ly]" do defines the scope of permissible governmental action? Does this make sense in view of the paucity of restrictions under current law on searches in the nonunion, "at-will" private sector?

4. *Providing Advance Notice of "Unreasonable" Searches?* If a government employer notified all of its employees that as a condition of their employment their desks or lockers could be searched at any time for any or no reason, it presumably could render unreasonable any expectations of privacy. Would this enable the employer to conduct searches totally unrestrained by the fourth amendment? See American Postal Workers v. Postal Service, 871 F.2d 556, 560 (6th Cir.1989) (permitting search of lockers provided for in collective bargaining agreement because employees had acknowledged in writing that lockers could be searched at any time as long as the union steward was afforded opportunity to be present). Are there other interests in addition to reasonable expectations of privacy that should be protected by the fourth amendment?

How much and what kind of advance notice is required to defeat a reasonable expectation of privacy? See United States v. Taketa, 923 F.2d 665, 673 (9th Cir.1991) (government relied on a Drug Enforcement Agency regulation requiring employees to maintain clean desks as a basis for subjecting defendant's office to inspection at any time; court held that such a regulation, unenforced by a practice of inspections, did not defeat privacy expectation); Brambrinck v. City of Philadelphia, 1994 WL 649342 (E.D.Pa. 1994) (police directive putting officers on notice of random locker inspections did not make clear that personal items (e.g., pockets of clothing) would be subject to search).

Can an employee by consent effectively waive his or her fourth amendment rights to be free of search without individualized suspicion or probable cause? Cf. Kraslawsky v. Upper Deck Co., 56 Cal.App.4th 179, 193 65 Cal.Rptr.2d 297, 306 (4th Dist.1997) (consent was not given but, in any event, would only be one factor in balancing test).

5. *Searches of Employee's Private Property.* Should a different rule (perhaps a probable cause requirement) apply to the search of Ortega's personal effects? See Gossmeyer v. McDonald, 128 F.3d 481 (7th Cir.1997) (upholding search of privately purchased file cabinet by employer and law enforcement officials acting on anonymous tip of employee's possession of child pornography).

6. *Physical Detention.* Physical detention of an employee during an investigatory interview may also raise fourth amendment issues. In INS v. Delgado, 466 U.S. 210, 104 S.Ct. 1758, 80 L.Ed.2d 247 (1984), the Court held that the government's "factory survey" of a work force in search of illegal aliens did not constitute a search of the entire work force, and the questioning which occurred could only be challenged by individuals who were actually detained or seized. Justice Rehnquist's opinion for the Court explained:

> We reject the claim that the entire work forces of the two factories were seized for the duration of the surveys when the INS placed agents near the exits of the factory sites. Ordinarily, when people are at work their freedom to move about has been meaningfully restricted, not by the actions of law enforcement officials, but by the workers' voluntary obligations to their employers.

Id. at 217.

7. *Video and Other Surveillance as a "Search"?* Does O'Connor indicate that there would be no constitutional restraints on a public employer's monitoring of its employees' on-premises activity, perhaps through the use of video cameras? How about monitoring of phone calls? Should it matter whether the surveillance is surreptitious or openly disclosed? Compare Vega–Rodriguez v. Puerto Rico Telephone Co., 110 F.3d 174 (1st Cir.1997) (relying on O'Connor to hold that employees lacked a reasonable expectation of privacy against disclosed video surveillance in open work area), with United States v. Taketa, supra, 923 F.2d at 673 (finding a reasonable expectation of privacy against drug enforcement agents' surreptitious video surveillance of an office reserved for the defendant's exclusive use). Do employees have reasonable privacy expectations not to be videotaped by third parties, such

as television reporters? See Sanders v. American Broadcasting Companies Inc., 20 Cal.4th 907, 85 Cal.Rptr.2d 909, 978 P.2d 67 (1999).

8. *Investigatory Searches.* The plurality opinion in *O'Connor* purports to leave open the question whether individualized suspicion is required for an investigatory rather than inventory search. The plurality refers to footnote 8 of New Jersey v. T.L.O., 469 U.S. 325, 342 n. 8, 105 S.Ct. 733, 744 n. 8, 83 L.Ed.2d 720 (1985) (school authority's search of student's purse based on individualized suspicion), quoting United States v. Martinez–Fuerte, 428 U.S. 543, 560–61, 96 S.Ct. 3074, 3084–85, 49 L.Ed.2d 1116 (1976), and citing Camara v. Municipal Court, 387 U.S. 523, 87 S.Ct. 1727, 18 L.Ed.2d 930 (1967).

The reference to *Martinez–Fuerte* and *Camara* suggest two different arguments for dispensing with an individualized-suspicion requirement. In *Martinez–Fuerte,* the Court upheld the constitutionality of the Border Patrol's policy of slowing all oncoming traffic to a halt and then referring some vehicles to an area for a few minutes of questioning. The Court reasoned that the government's strong interest in maintaining the integrity of its borders justified the limited intrusion effected by the checkpoint halt and questioning system.

Camara involved systematic administrative investigations of regulated firms. In general, the Court has required as a predicate for such investigations an "administrative search warrant," in order to ensure supervision by a neutral magistrate of the reasonableness of the scope of the investigation and the selection criteria employed. See *Camara*; Marshall v. Barlow's Inc., 436 U.S. 307, 98 S.Ct. 1816, 56 L.Ed.2d 305 (1978). In highly regulated industries where the Court has found only attenuated expectations of privacy, however, it has permitted dispensing with even an administrative warrant. See New York v. Burger, 482 U.S. 691, 107 S.Ct. 2636, 96 L.Ed.2d 601 (1987) (junkyards); Donovan v. Dewey, 452 U.S. 594, 101 S.Ct. 2534, 69 L.Ed.2d 262 (1981) (mining); United States v. Biswell, 406 U.S. 311, 92 S.Ct. 1593, 32 L.Ed.2d 87 (1972) (firearms); Colonnade Catering Corp. v. United States, 397 U.S. 72, 90 S.Ct. 774, 25 L.Ed.2d 60 (1970) (alcoholic beverages).

For a decision refusing to extend this *Biswell–Colonnade* exception to permit warrantless searches of the track-side lodging of employees of horse-racing tracks, see Serpas v. Schmidt, 827 F.2d 23 (7th Cir.1987). But see Dimeo v. Griffin, 943 F.2d 679 (7th Cir.1991) (en banc) (racing officials did not need person-specific cause, or warrants, before conducting drug testing of jockeys, drivers and other participants in horse races—*Serpas* distinguished as a residential search); Shoemaker v. Handel, 795 F.2d 1136 (3d Cir. 1986) (sustaining scheme subjecting jockeys to breathalyzer and urine tests where discretion of officials conducting search was circumscribed by regulation).

9. *Uncorroborated Tips and "Individualized Suspicion".* If individualized suspicion is required for an investigatory search, is an uncorroborated tip of an informant of unknown reliability sufficient for a desk search? See Gossmeyer v. McDonald, supra, 128 F.3d at 491 (finding anonymous tip contained indicia of reliability—informant identified himself as coworker, made specific allegations of serious misconduct, and stated where pictures of

child pornography could be found—and search occurred one day after receipt of tip).

To require a urinalysis of a police officer, is the uncorroborated allegation of the officer's former girlfriend (also a police officer) that she had seen the officer use drugs in her presence sufficient? See Copeland v. Philadelphia Police Dept., 840 F.2d 1139, 1144 (3d Cir.1988) (held reasonable under *O'Connor*).

10. *"State Action"*. Federal constitutional challenges can only be lodged against "governmental" "state action". Are there circumstances where the employment decisions of privately owned enterprises should be considered "state action"? See Sullivan v. Barnett, 139 F.3d 158, 170 (3d Cir.1998) (workers' compensation law "inextricably entangles [private] insurance companies in a partnership with the Commonwealth such that they become an integral part of the state in administering the statutory scheme"); Holodnak v. Avco Corp., 514 F.2d 285 (2d Cir.1975) (state action found in operations of defense contractor). The Supreme Court has insisted on direct government involvement in the conduct in question and has declined to find state action present even in the case of intensely regulated private firms. See Jackson v. Metropolitan Edison Co., 419 U.S. 345, 95 S.Ct. 449, 42 L.Ed.2d 477 (1974); Moose Lodge No. 107 v. Irvis, 407 U.S. 163, 92 S.Ct. 1965, 32 L.Ed.2d 627 (1972). On state constitutions, see note 6, p. 89 infra.

SKINNER v. RAILWAY LABOR EXECUTIVES' ASSOCIATION

Supreme Court of the United States, 1989.
489 U.S. 602, 109 S.Ct. 1402, 103 L.Ed.2d 639.

JUSTICE KENNEDY delivered the opinion of the Court.

The Federal Railroad Safety Act of 1970 authorizes the Secretary of Transportation to "prescribe, as necessary, appropriate rules, regulations, orders, and standards for all areas of railroad safety." 84 Stat. 971, 45 U.S.C. § 431(a). Finding that alcohol and drug abuse by railroad employees poses a serious threat to safety, the Federal Railroad Administration (FRA) has promulgated regulations that mandate blood and urine tests of employees who are involved in certain train accidents. The FRA also has adopted regulations that do not require, but do authorize, railroads to administer breath and urine tests to employees who violate certain safety rules. The question presented by this case is whether these regulations violate the Fourth Amendment.

I

* * *

After reviewing further comments from representatives of the railroad industry, labor groups, and the general public, the FRA, in 1985, promulgated regulations addressing the problem of alcohol and drugs on the railroads. The final regulations apply to employees assigned to perform service subject to the Hours of Service Act of 1907, ch. 2939, 34

Stat. 1415, 45 U.S.C. § 61 *et seq.* The regulations prohibit covered employees from using or possessing alcohol or any controlled substance. 49 CFR § 219.101(a)(1) (1987). * * *

To the extent pertinent here, two subparts of the regulations relate to testing. Subpart C, which is entitled "Post–Accident Toxicological Testing," is mandatory. It provides that railroads "shall take all practicable steps to assure that all covered employees of the railroad directly involved * * * provide blood and urine samples for toxicological testing by FRA," § 219.203(a), upon the occurrence of certain specified events. Toxicological testing is required following a "major train accident," which is defined as any train accident that involves (i) a fatality, (ii) the release of hazardous material accompanied by an evacuation or a reportable injury, or (iii) damage to railroad property of $500,000. § 219.201(a)(1). The railroad has the further duty of collecting blood and urine samples for testing after an "impact accident," which is defined as a collision that results in a reportable injury, or in damage to railroad property of $50,000 or more. § 219.201(a)(2). Finally, the railroad is also obligated to test after "[a]ny train incident that involves a fatality to any on-duty railroad employee." § 219.201(a)(3).

After occurrence of an event which activates its duty to test, the railroad must transport all crew members and other covered employees directly involved in the accident or incident to an independent medical facility where both blood and urine samples must be obtained from each employee.[2] After the samples have been collected, the railroad is required to ship them by prepaid air freight to the FRA laboratory for analysis. § 219.205(d). There, the samples are analyzed using "state-of-the-art equipment and techniques" to detect and measure alcohol and drugs. The FRA proposes to place primary reliance on analysis of blood samples, as blood is "the only available body fluid * * * that can provide a clear indication not only of the presence of alcohol and drugs but also their current impairment effects." 49 Fed.Reg. 24291 (1984). Urine samples are also necessary, however, because drug traces remain in the urine longer than in blood, and in some cases it will not be possible to transport employees to a medical facility before the time it takes for certain drugs to be eliminated from the bloodstream. In those instances, a "positive urine test, taken with specific information on the pattern of elimination for the particular drug and other information on the behavior of the employee and the circumstances of the accident, may be crucial to the determination of" the cause of an accident. *Ibid.*

The regulations require that the FRA notify employees of the results of the tests and afford them an opportunity to respond in writing before

---

2. The regulations provide a limited exception from testing "if the railroad representative can immediately determine, on the basis of specific information, that the employee had no role in the cause(s) of the accident/incident." 49 CFR 219.203(a)(3)(i) (1987). No exception may be made, however, in the case of a "major train accident."

Ibid. In promulgating the regulations, the FRA noted that, while it is sometimes possible to exonerate crew members in other situations calling for testing, it is especially difficult to assess fault and degrees of fault in the aftermath of the more substantial accidents. See 50 Fed.Reg. 31544 (1985).

preparation of any final investigative report. See § 219.211(a)(2). Employees who refuse to provide required blood or urine samples may not perform covered service for nine months, but they are entitled to a hearing concerning their refusal to take the test. § 219.213.

Subpart D of the regulations, which is entitled "Authorization to Test for Cause," is permissive. It authorizes railroads to require covered employees to submit to breath or urine tests in certain circumstances not addressed by Subpart C. Breath or urine tests, or both, may be ordered (1) after a reportable accident or incident, where a supervisor has a "reasonable suspicion" that an employee's acts or omissions contributed to the occurrence or severity of the accident or incident, § 219.301(b)(2); or (2) in the event of certain specific rule violations, including noncompliance with a signal and excessive speeding, § 219.301(b)(3). A railroad also may require breath tests where a supervisor has a "reasonable suspicion" that an employee is under the influence of alcohol, based upon specific, personal observations concerning the appearance, behavior, speech, or body odors of the employee. § 219.301(b)(1). Where impairment is suspected, a railroad, in addition, may require urine tests, but only if two supervisors make the appropriate determination, § 219.301(c)(2)(i), and, where the supervisors suspect impairment due to a substance other than alcohol, at least one of those supervisors must have received specialized training in detecting the signs of drug intoxication. § 219.301(c)(2)(ii).

Subpart D further provides that whenever the results of either breath or urine tests are intended for use in a disciplinary proceeding, the employee must be given the opportunity to provide a blood sample for analysis at an independent medical facility. § 219.303(c). If an employee declines to give a blood sample, the railroad may presume impairment, absent persuasive evidence to the contrary, from a positive showing of controlled substance residues in the urine. The railroad must, however, provide detailed notice of this presumption to its employees, and advise them of their right to provide a contemporaneous blood sample. As in the case of samples procured under Subpart C, the regulations set forth procedures for the collection of samples, and require that samples "be analyzed by a method that is reliable within known tolerances." § 219.307(b).

* * *

II

* * *

We have long recognized that a "compelled intrusio[n] into the body for blood to be analyzed for alcohol content" must be deemed a Fourth Amendment search. See *Schmerber v. California,* 384 U.S. 757, 767–768, 86 S.Ct. 1826, 1833–1834, 16 L.Ed.2d 908 (1966). * * *

Unlike the blood-testing procedure at issue in *Schmerber,* the procedures prescribed by the FRA regulations for collecting and testing urine samples do not entail a surgical intrusion into the body. It is not disputed, however, that chemical analysis of urine, like that of blood, can reveal a host of private medical facts about an employee, including whether she is epileptic, pregnant, or diabetic. Nor can it be disputed that the process of collecting the sample to be tested, which may in some cases involve visual or aural monitoring of the act of urination, itself implicates privacy interests. [*Eds.* The Court at this point concludes that the collection and subsequent analysis of the requisite biological samples must be deemed fourth amendment searches.]

III

A

To hold that the Fourth Amendment is applicable to the drug and alcohol testing prescribed by the FRA regulations is only to begin the inquiry into the standards governing such intrusions. *O'Connor v. Ortega,* 480 U.S. 709, 719, 107 S.Ct. 1492, 1499, 94 L.Ed.2d 714 (1987) (plurality opinion); *New Jersey v. T.L.O.,* 469 U.S. 325, 337, 105 S.Ct. 733, 741, 83 L.Ed.2d 720 (1985). For the Fourth Amendment does not proscribe all searches and seizures, but only those that are unreasonable.

* * *

The Government's interest in regulating the conduct of railroad employees to ensure safety, like its supervision of probationers or regulated industries, or its operation of a government office, school, or prison, "likewise presents 'special needs' beyond normal law enforcement that may justify departures from the usual warrant and probable-cause requirements." *Griffin v. Wisconsin,* [483 U.S. 868, 873, 107 S.Ct. 3164, 3168, 97 L.Ed.2d 709 (1987).] The Hours of Service employees covered by the FRA regulations include persons engaged in handling orders concerning train movements, operating crews, and those engaged in the maintenance and repair of signal systems. 50 Fed.Reg. 31511 (1985). It is undisputed that these and other covered employees are engaged in safety-sensitive tasks. * * *

The FRA has prescribed toxicological tests, not to assist in the prosecution of employees but rather "to prevent accidents and casualties in railroad operations that result from impairment of employees by alcohol or drugs." 49 CFR § 219.1(a) (1987).[5] This governmental interest

---

5. The regulations provide that "[e]ach sample provided under [Subpart C] is retained for not less than six months following the date of the accident or incident and may be made available to * * * a party in litigation upon service of appropriate compulsory process on the custodian * * *." 49 CFR § 219.211(d) (1987). The Agency explained, when it promulgated this provision, that it intends to retain such samples primarily "for its own purposes (*e.g.,* to permit reanalysis of a sample if another laboratory reported detection of a substance not tested for in the original procedure)." 50 Fed.Reg. 31545 (1985). While this provi-

sion might be read broadly to authorize the release of biological samples to law enforcement authorities, the record does not disclose that it was intended to be, or actually has been, so used. * * * Absent a persuasive showing that the FRA's testing program is pretextual, we assess the FRA's scheme in light of its obvious administrative purpose. We leave for another day the question whether routine use in criminal prosecutions of evidence obtained pursuant to the administrative scheme would give rise to an inference of pretext, or otherwise

in ensuring the safety of the traveling public and of the employees themselves plainly justifies prohibiting covered employees from using alcohol or drugs on duty, or while subject to being called for duty. This interest also "require[s] and justif[ies] the exercise of supervision to assure that the restrictions are in fact observed." *Griffin v. Wisconsin,* 483 U.S., at 875, 107 S.Ct., at 3168. The question that remains, then, is whether the Government's need to monitor compliance with these restrictions justifies the privacy intrusions at issue absent a warrant or individualized suspicion.

B

An essential purpose of a warrant requirement is to protect privacy interests by assuring citizens subject to a search or seizure that such intrusions are not the random or arbitrary acts of government agents. A warrant assures the citizen that the intrusion is authorized by law, and that it is narrowly limited in its objectives and scope. * * * A warrant also provides the detached scrutiny of a neutral magistrate, and thus ensures an objective determination whether an intrusion is justified in any given case. * * * In the present context, however, a warrant would do little to further these aims. Both the circumstances justifying toxicological testing and the permissible limits of such intrusions are defined narrowly and specifically in the regulations that authorize them, and doubtless are well known to covered employees. Cf. *United States v. Biswell,* 406 U.S. 311, 316, 92 S.Ct. 1593, 1596, 32 L.Ed.2d 87 (1972). Indeed, in light of the standardized nature of the tests and the minimal discretion vested in those charged with administering the program, there are virtually no facts for a neutral magistrate to evaluate. Cf. *Colorado v. Bertine,* 479 U.S. 367, 376, 107 S.Ct. 738, 744, 93 L.Ed.2d 739 (1987) (Blackmun, J., concurring).[6]

We have recognized, moreover, that the Government's interest in dispensing with the warrant requirement is at its strongest when, as here, "the burden of obtaining a warrant is likely to frustrate the

---

impugn the administrative nature of the Agency's program.

6. Subpart C of the regulations, for example, does not permit the exercise of any discretion in choosing the employees who must submit to testing, except in limited circumstances and then only if warranted by objective criteria. Subpart D, while conferring some discretion to choose those who may be required to submit to testing, also imposes specific constraints on the exercise of that discretion. Covered employees may be required to submit to breath or urine tests only if they have been directly involved in specified rule violations or errors, or if their acts or omissions contributed to the occurrence or severity of specified accidents or incidents. To be sure, some discretion necessarily must be used in determining whether an employee's acts or omissions contributed to the occurrence or severity of an event, but this limited assessment of the objective circumstances surrounding the event does not devolve unbridled discretion upon the supervisor in the field. Cf. *Marshall v. Barlow's, Inc.,* 436 U.S. 307, 323, 98 S.Ct. 1816, 1825–1826, 56 L.Ed.2d 305 (1978).

In addition, the regulations contain various safeguards against any possibility that discretion will be abused. A railroad that requires post-accident testing in bad faith, 49 CFR § 219.201(c) (1987), or that willfully imposes a program of authorized testing that does not comply with Subpart D, § 219.9(a)(3), or that otherwise fails to follow the regulations, § 219.9(a)(5), is subject to civil penalties, in addition to whatever damages may be awarded through the [labor] arbitration process.

governmental purpose behind the search." *Camara v. Municipal Court,* 387 U.S., at 533, 87 S.Ct., at 1733. * * * As the Agency recognized, alcohol and other drugs are eliminated from the bloodstream at a constant rate, see 49 Fed.Reg. 24291 (1984), and blood and breath samples taken to measure whether these substances were in the bloodstream when a triggering event occurred must be obtained as soon as possible. See *Schmerber v. California,* 384 U.S., at 770–771, 86 S.Ct., at 1835–1836. Although the metabolites of some drugs remain in the urine for longer periods of time and may enable the Agency to estimate whether the employee was impaired by those drugs at the time of a covered accident, incident, or rule violation, 49 Fed.Reg. 24291 (1984), the delay necessary to procure a warrant nevertheless may result in the destruction of valuable evidence.

* * *

C

Our cases indicate that even a search that may be performed without a warrant must be based, as a general matter, on probable cause to believe that the person to be searched has violated the law. See *New Jersey v. T.L.O.,* 469 U.S., at 340, 105 S.Ct., at 742. When the balance of interests precludes insistence on a showing of probable cause, we have usually required "some quantum of individualized suspicion" before concluding that a search is reasonable. See, *e.g., United States v. Martinez–Fuerte,* 428 U.S. [543, 560, 96 S.Ct. 3074, 3084, 49 L.Ed.2d 1116 (1976)]. We made it clear, however, that a showing of individualized suspicion is not a constitutional floor, below which a search must be presumed unreasonable. *Id.,* at 561, 96 S.Ct., at 3084. In limited circumstances, where the privacy interests implicated by the search are minimal, and where an important governmental interest furthered by the intrusion would be placed in jeopardy by a requirement of individualized suspicion, a search may be reasonable despite the absence of such suspicion. We believe this is true of the intrusions in question here.

By and large, intrusions on privacy under the FRA regulations are limited. To the extent transportation and like restrictions are necessary to procure the requisite blood, breath, and urine samples for testing, this interference alone is minimal given the employment context in which it takes place. Ordinarily, an employee consents to significant restrictions in his freedom of movement where necessary for his employment, and few are free to come and go as they please during working hours. See, *e.g., INS v. Delgado,* 466 U.S., at 218, 104 S.Ct., at 1763. Any additional interference with a railroad employee's freedom of movement that occurs in the time it takes to procure a blood, breath, or urine sample for testing cannot, by itself, be said to infringe significant privacy interests.

Our decision in *Schmerber v. California,* 384 U.S. 757, 86 S.Ct. 1826, 16 L.Ed.2d 908 (1966), indicates that the same is true of the blood tests required by the FRA regulations. In that case, we held that a State could direct that a blood sample be withdrawn from a motorist suspected of driving while intoxicated, despite his refusal to consent to the intrusion. We noted that the test was performed in a reasonable manner, as the motorist's "blood was taken by a physician in a hospital environment according to accepted medical practices." *Id.*, at 771, 86 S.Ct., at 1836. We said also that the intrusion occasioned by a blood test is not significant, since such "tests are a commonplace in these days of periodic physical examinations and experience with them teaches that the quantity of blood extracted is minimal, and that for most people the procedure involves virtually no risk, trauma, or pain." *Ibid.* * * *

The breath tests authorized by Subpart D of the regulations are even less intrusive than the blood tests prescribed by Subpart C. Unlike blood tests, breath tests do not require piercing the skin and may be conducted safely outside a hospital environment and with a minimum of inconvenience or embarrassment. Further, breath tests reveal the level of alcohol in the employee's bloodstream and nothing more. * * *

A more difficult question is presented by urine tests. Like breath tests, urine tests are not invasive of the body and, under the regulations, may not be used as an occasion for inquiring into private facts unrelated to alcohol or drug use.[7] We recognize, however, that the procedures for collecting the necessary samples, which require employees to perform an excretory function traditionally shielded by great privacy, raise concerns not implicated by blood or breath tests. While we would not characterize these additional privacy concerns as minimal in most contexts, we note that the regulations endeavor to reduce the intrusiveness of the collection process. The regulations do not require that samples be furnished under the direct observation of a monitor, despite the desirability of such a procedure to ensure the integrity of the sample. See 50 Fed.Reg. 31555 (1985). See also Field Manual B–15; *id.*, at D–1. The sample is also collected in a medical environment, by personnel unrelated to the railroad employer, and is thus not unlike similar procedures encountered often in the context of a regular physical examination.

More importantly, the expectations of privacy of covered employees are diminished by reason of their participation in an industry that is regulated pervasively to ensure safety, a goal dependent, in substantial part, on the health and fitness of covered employees.

* * *

By contrast, the government interest in testing without a showing of individualized suspicion is compelling. Employees subject to the tests

---

7. When employees produce the blood and urine samples required by Subpart C they are asked by medical personnel to complete a form stating whether they have taken any medications during the preceding 30 days. The completed forms are shipped with the samples to the FRA's laboratory. See Field Manual B–15. This information is used to ascertain whether a positive test result can be explained by the employee's lawful use of medications. While this procedure permits the Government to learn certain private medical facts that an employee might prefer not to disclose, there is no indication that the Government does not treat this information as confidential, or that it uses the information for any other purpose. Under the circumstances, we do not view this procedure as a significant invasion of privacy. Cf. *Whalen v. Roe*, 429 U.S. 589, 602, 97 S.Ct. 869, 878, 51 L.Ed.2d 64 (1977).

discharge duties fraught with such risks of injury to others that even a momentary lapse of attention can have disastrous consequences. * * * An impaired employee, the Agency found, will seldom display any outward "signs detectable by the lay person or, in many cases, even the physician." 50 Fed.Reg. 31526 (1985). * * *

While no procedure can identify all impaired employees with ease and perfect accuracy, the FRA regulations supply an effective means of deterring employees engaged in safety-sensitive tasks from using controlled substances or alcohol in the first place. 50 Fed.Reg. 31541 (1985). * * * By ensuring that employees in safety-sensitive positions know they will be tested upon the occurrence of a triggering event, the timing of which no employee can predict with certainty, the regulations significantly increase the deterrent effect of the administrative penalties associated with the prohibited conduct, * * * concomitantly increasing the likelihood that employees will forgo using drugs or alcohol while subject to being called for duty.

* * *

Without quarreling with the importance of these governmental interests, the Court of Appeals concluded that the post-accident testing regulations were unreasonable because "[b]lood and urine tests intended to establish drug use other than alcohol * * * cannot measure current drug intoxication or degree of impairment." * * *

* * * Even if urine test results disclosed nothing more specific than the recent use of controlled substances by a covered employee, this information would provide the basis for further investigative work designed to determine whether the employee used drugs at the relevant times. See Field Manual B–4. The record makes clear, for example, that a positive test result, coupled with known information concerning the pattern of elimination for the particular drug and information that may be gathered from other sources about the employee's activities, may allow the Agency to reach an informed judgment as to how a particular accident occurred.

More importantly, the Court of Appeals overlooked the Agency's policy of placing principal reliance on the results of blood tests, which unquestionably can identify very recent drug use, see, *e.g.*, 49 Fed.Reg. 24291 (1984), while relying on urine tests as a secondary source of information designed to guard against the possibility that certain drugs will be eliminated from the bloodstream before a blood sample can be obtained. The court also failed to recognize that the FRA regulations are designed not only to discern impairment but also to deter it. Because the record indicates that blood and urine tests, taken together, are highly effective means of ascertaining on-the-job impairment and of deterring the use of drugs by railroad employees, we believe the Court of Appeals erred in concluding that the post-accident testing regulations are not reasonably related to the Government objectives that support them.

MARSHALL, J., with whom BRENNAN, J. joins, dissenting.

It is the probable-cause requirement * * * that the FRA's testing regime most egregiously violates, a fact which explains the majority's ready acceptance and expansion of the countertextual "special needs" exception. By any measure, the FRA's highly intrusive collection and testing procedures qualify as full-scale personal searches. Under our precedents, a showing of probable cause is therefore clearly required. But even if these searches were viewed as entailing only minimal intrusions on the order, say, of a police stop-and-frisk, the FRA's program would still fail to pass constitutional muster, for we have, without exception, demanded that even minimally intrusive searches of the person be founded on individualized suspicion.

Note on National Treasury Employees Union v. Von Raab

On the same day as its *Skinner* decision, in National Treasury Employees Union v. Von Raab, 489 U.S. 656, 109 S.Ct. 1384, 103 L.Ed.2d 685 (1989), the Court upheld (5–4) the United States Customs Service's drug testing program. In May 1986, the Commissioner of Customs announced that drug tests through urine specimens would be required as a condition of employment for (1) employees directly involved in drug interdiction or the enforcement of related laws, (2) employees authorized to carry firearms, and (3) employees authorized to handle "classified" materials. Here, as in *Skinner,* the principal issue was not whether a warrant or probable cause was required, but whether individualized suspicion was necessary. Justice Kennedy's opinion for the Court held that the program was constitutionally reasonable even in the absence of individualized suspicion for testing. The opinion stressed the strength of the government's interests in ensuring that "front-line interdiction personnel" and those carrying firearms not themselves be involved with illegal substances. The majority also asserted that employees involved in policing the integrity of the nation's borders, like employees of the United States Mint or the military or intelligence services, "have a diminished expectation of privacy in respect to the intrusions occasioned by a urine test."

The Court conceded that there was little evidence of drug abuse on the part of Customs Service personnel, but maintained that the program was justified as a deterrent to such abuse:

> There is little reason to believe that American workplaces are immune from this pervasive social problem * * *. Detecting drug impairment on the part of employees can be a difficult task, especially where, as here, it is not feasible to subject employees and their work-product to the kind of day-to-day scrutiny that is the norm in more traditional office environments. Indeed, the almost unique mission of the Service gives the Government a compelling interest in ensuring that many of these employees do not use drugs even off-duty, for such use creates risks of bribery and blackmail against which the Government is entitled to guard * * *.

109 S.Ct. at 1395.

The principal dissent, penned by Justice Scalia, stressed the absence of a demonstrated drug problem in the Service:

The Court's response to this lack of evidence is that "[t]here is little reason to believe that American workplaces are immune from [the] pervasive social problem" of drug abuse. * * * Perhaps such a generalization would suffice if the workplace at issue could produce such catastrophic social harm that no risk whatever is tolerable—the secured areas of a nuclear power plant, for example, see *Rushton* v. *Nebraska Public Power District*, 844 F.2d 562 (C.A.8 1988). But if such a generalization suffices to justify demeaning bodily searches, without particularized suspicion, to guard against the bribing or blackmailing of a law enforcement agent, or the careless use of a firearm, then the Fourth Amendment has become frail protection indeed. In *Skinner, Bell* [v. *Wolfish*, 441 U.S. 520, 99 S.Ct. 1861, 60 L.Ed.2d 447 (1979)], *T.L.O.,* and *Martinez–Fuerte,* we took pains to establish the existence of a special need for the search and seizure—a need not based upon the existence of a "pervasive social problem" combined with speculation as to the effect of that problem in the field at issue, but rather upon well known or well demonstrated evils in *that field,* with well known or well demonstrated consequences.

109 S.Ct. at 1400–01 (emphasis in original).

Notes and Questions

1. *Executive Order 12,564.* On September 15, 1986, President Reagan issued Executive Order 12,564, 51 Fed.Reg. 32,889, requiring each executive agency to establish a program to identify drug abuse on the part of employees in "sensitive positions," broadly defined to include over a million federal employees. The Executive Order requires testing of all job applicants for such positions, and of employees as to whom there is reasonable suspicion of illegal drug use, following involvement in an accident, or as part of employee counseling or rehabilitation under an employee assistance program (EAP). Id. at 32,891. Employees testing positive (presumably after confirmatory tests) are to be removed from duty pending successful rehabilitation through an EAP. Refusal to participate in an EAP results in dismissal. Following the Executive Order, a number of federal agencies promulgated regulations requiring drug testing, particularly of employees in safety- or security-sensitive positions. The regulations affect not only agency staff but often also employees of firms regulated by the agencies, see, e.g., 49 C.F.R. Part 40, 53 Fed.Reg. 47002 (Nov. 15, 1988) (Department of Transportation), or employees of firms contracting with the agencies, see, e.g., 49 C.F.R. Parts 223 & 252, 53 Fed.Reg. 37,763 (1988) (Department of Defense contractors must test all employees in "sensitive positions"). Pursuant to 1987 legislation appropriating funds to implement the Executive Order, the Department of Health and Human Services promulgated scientific and technical guidelines for federal testing programs. See 53 Fed.Reg. 11,970 (1988).

2. *Drug–Free Workplace Act.* Congress also enacted drug-free workplace requirements for federal contractors as part of 1988 omnibus drug legislation, Pub.L. 100–690, Title V subtitle D, 102 Stat. 4304 (Drug–Free Workplace Act of 1988), which does not mandate testing but requires, inter alia, that contractors ensure that any employee convicted of a drug violation committed in the workplace be subject to discipline (up to dismissal) absent

successful participation in an EAP. Implementing regulations are found at 10 C.F.R. § 707.1 (Dept. of Energy); 13 C.F.R. § 145.600 (Small Business Admin.); 29 C.F.R.§ 98.600 (Dept. of Labor).

3. *Narrow "Special Needs" Exception for "Safety Sensitive" and "Drug Enforcement" Positions?* Do *Skinner* and *Von Raab* yield a blanket endorsement of the federal government's drug testing policies or are these decisions properly confined to their special railroad safety and drug-interdiction contexts? Note that in *Von Raab,* the Court remanded to the lower courts for a determination whether the employees covered by the Service's classified-material category in fact had access to sensitive material which could fall into the hands of smugglers. Absent individualized suspicion of on-the-job drug use, what justification does the government have for testing employees who are not involved in safety-related or drug-enforcement functions?

In Vernonia School District v. Acton, 515 U.S. 646, 653, 115 S.Ct. 2386, 132 L.Ed.2d 564 (1995), the Court recognized yet another "special" circumstance justifying suspicion-less testing: the custodial authority of school officials in requiring drug testing of students participating in interscholastic sports. The *Vernonia* rationale was further extended in Board of Ed. of Indep. School Dist. No. 92 of Pottawatomie Co. v. Earls, 536 U.S. 822, 122 S.Ct. 2559, 153 L.Ed.2d 735 (2002) (permitting drug testing of all students engaged in extracurricular activities). However, in Chandler v. Miller, 520 U.S. 305, 117 S.Ct. 1295, 137 L.Ed.2d 513 (1997), the Court reaffirmed the "main rule," striking down a Georgia statute requiring candidates for high state office to submit and pass drug test:

Our precedents establish that the proffered special need for drug testing must be substantial—important enough to override the individual's acknowledged privacy interest, sufficiently vital to suppress the Fourth Amendment's normal requirement of individualized suspicion. * * *

Respondents' defense of the statute rests primarily on the incompatibility of unlawful drug use with holding high state office. * * * Notably lacking in respondents' presentation is any indication of a concrete danger demanding departure from the Fourth Amendment's main rule.

* * * In *Von Raab*, the Customs Service had defended its officer drug-test program in part as a way to demonstrate the agency's commitment to enforcement of the law. * * * The * * * Court, however, did not rely on that justification. Indeed, if a need of the "set a good example" genre were sufficient to overwhelm a Fourth Amendment objection, then the care this Court took to explain why the needs in *Skinner*, *Von Raab*, and *Vernonia* ranked as "special" wasted many words in entirely unnecessary, perhaps even misleading, elaborations.

117 S.Ct. at 1303, 1305.

4. *Access to Confidential Information.* Do the Court's drug-testing rulings suggest that the government's interest in protecting confidential information supports suspicion less testing of all employees with potential access to such information? See, e.g., National Treasury Employees Union v.

U.S. Customs Service, 27 F.3d 623 (D.C.Cir.1994) (upholding testing of customs employees with access to database containing information about targeting of certain imports and identifying times and places of particular scrutiny); Harmon v. Thornburgh, 878 F.2d 484 (D.C.Cir.1989) (testing permitted of Justice Department lawyers with "top secret national security clearance" even when they do not handle "truly sensitive" information on a regular basis). On what basis can employees be tested if they lack access to such information? See, e.g., National Treasury Employees Union v. Yeutter, 918 F.2d 968 (D.C.Cir.1990).

5. *"Safety Sensitive" Positions.* How far does the "safety sensitive" concept of *Skinner* extend? Are public school teachers and custodians employed in safety-sensitive positions simply because of their access to children, thus justifying drug testing without individualized suspicion? See Aubrey v. School Board of Lafayette, 148 F.3d 559 (5th Cir.1998) (upholding application of drug testing policy to school custodian because he interacted regularly with children, used hazardous substances in work, and operated potentially dangerous equipment); Knox County Educ. Assn. v. Knox County Bd. Of Educ., 158 F.3d 361 (6th Cir.1998) ("'in loco parentis" responsibility of, and inability to closely monitor, public-school teachers justifies suspicion-less testing). But cf. United Teachers of New Orleans v. Orleans Parish School Board, 142 F.3d 853, 857 (5th Cir.1998) (unconstitutional to require any teacher, aide, or clerical worker injured on the job to submit to drug test "absent adequate individualized suspicion of wrongful drug use"). What about access to patients in a health-care facility? See Pierce v. Smith, 117 F.3d 866 (5th Cir.1997) ("special needs" situation found to force physician enrolled in state medical residency program to undergo urinalysis). Access to the President? See Stigile v. Clinton, 110 F.3d 801 (D.C.Cir.1997) (testing of U.S. Office of Management and Budget employees holding permanent passes to Old Executive Office building that the Chief Executive frequently visits).

6. *"Random" Testing as Discretionary Testing?* Does *Skinner* suggest that random drug testing of government employees in safety- or security-sensitive positions will always be found constitutional? Does the Court's reference to "random" testing mean that such testing can be entirely discretionary, or does the testing have to be pursuant to established criteria that cabin discretion? The Court has not permitted random searches of motorists, compare Delaware v. Prouse, 440 U.S. 648, 99 S.Ct. 1391, 59 L.Ed.2d 660 (1979), with Michigan Department of State Police v. Sitz, 496 U.S. 444, 110 S.Ct. 2481, 110 L.Ed.2d 412 (1990), and it has generally insisted on an "administrative warrant" to limit official discretion as to targets of a search of commercial enterprises. See *Camara*; Marshall v. Barlow's, Inc., 436 U.S. 307, 98 S.Ct. 1816, 56 L.Ed.2d 305 (1978). Would requiring an administrative warrant in *Skinner* and *Von Raab* have made sense? Were there equivalent safeguards in place? Consider footnote 6 of *Skinner*.

7. *Testing of Applicants vs. Incumbent Employees.* May testing of job applicants be conducted under less demanding standards than for existing employees? Is it reasonable to assume that job applicants have diminished privacy expectations? See, e.g., Willner v. Thornburgh, 928 F.2d 1185 (D.C.Cir.1991); American Postal Workers Union, Boston Metro Area v. Frank, 734 F.Supp. 40 (D.Mass.1990); Fowler v. New York City Dept. of

Sanitation, 704 F.Supp. 1264 (S.D.N.Y.1989). See also Yin v. State of California, 95 F.3d 864 (9th Cir.1996) (state's request that plaintiff submit to an independent medical examination for ADA claim held reasonable). But see O'Keefe v. Passaic Valley Water Comm'n, 253 N.J.Super. 569, 602 A.2d 760 (1992) (neither water meter readers nor reader applicants could be subject to drug testing absent individualized suspicion); cf. Doe v. Roe, Inc., 143 Misc.2d 156, 539 N.Y.S.2d 876 (Sup.Ct.N.Y.Co.1989) (finding violation of state human rights law both in private employer's urinalysis drug screen for job applicants without demonstrating that such test was job related and also in refusal to hire because of test results).

Can the public employer treat newly promoted employees as akin to new hires for purposes of administering a drug test without individualized suspicion? See Loder v. City of Glendale, 14 Cal.4th 846, 59 Cal.Rptr.2d 696, 927 P.2d 1200 (1997) (individualized suspicion required under fourth amendment for testing of incumbent employees offered a promotion to another position; but not required under fourth amendment or Cal. Const. art. I, § 1 for testing of new hires). For further discussion of state constitutional limits, see pp. 891–92 infra.

8. *Effect of Release of Investigatory Samples to Law–Enforcement Authorities?* Does footnote 5 of *Skinner* suggest that government testing will be measured under the fourth amendment rules applicable to criminal law-enforcement activity if steps are not taken to prevent release of samples to law-enforcement authorities?

9. *Private Information Contained in Test Results?* Does drug testing potentially threaten employee privacy because of the other information, such as pregnancy or AIDS infection, that it may reveal? If so, can these privacy implications be adequately addressed without barring the tests? See Mares v. ConAgra Poultry Co., 971 F.2d 492 (10th Cir.1992) (in order to assure accuracy of test results, employer can ask—as long as confidentiality is maintained—about nature of illness for which prescription drugs are taken, the length of time medication is to be taken, and name of physician); but cf. Roe v. Cheyenne Mountain Conference Resort, Inc., 124 F.3d 1221, 1236 (10th Cir.1997) (views of the Colorado supreme court required because in *Mares*, "plaintiff stressed that she was not complaining about the drug testing and was willing to submit to the tests. The *Mares* case, therefore, did not deal with the random drug issue raised in this case."). Cf. Pierce v. Smith, 117 F.3d 866 (5th Cir.1997) (test did not probe or reveal whether plaintiff was pregnant, epileptic or diabetic).

10. *Additional Privacy Safeguards in Test Administration.* What other steps must government take to minimize infringement of privacy interests? Note, for example, that the Customs Service's program in *Von Raab* permits employees to produce urine samples in the privacy of a bathroom stall, and that HHS regulations require that only after employees have tested positive for illicit drugs are they required to supply medication records to ensure that the positive indication was not caused by legal drugs. See HHS Regulations § 2.7, 53 Fed.Reg. 11985–86 (1988). The D.C. Circuit in National Treasury Employees Union v. Yeutter, supra, held that where the test is based on reasonable suspicion alone, it violates the fourth amendment to require visual observation of urination, absent an individualized determination that

the worker might tamper with the specimen. See HHS Mandatory Guidelines for Federal Workplace Drug Testing Programs, 53 Fed.Reg. 11,970, at 11,981 (1988) (visual monitoring is ordinarily unnecessary). Compare also Wilcher v. City of Wilmington, 139 F.3d 366 (3d Cir.1998) (direct observation by monitors of giving of urine samples was reasonable, where monitors refrained from looking at firefighters' genitalia and direct observation served government's interest in preventing cheating), with Hansen v. California Dept. of Correction, 868 F.Supp. 271 (N.D.Cal.1994) (violation of California right to privacy in requiring direct observation, absent showing of specific reason to fear employee would tamper with sample).

11. *Drug Testing Methodology*. The most commonly used specimen for drug testing is urine, although blood, saliva and hair have also been used. The test often employed for the initial screen is the enzyme multiplied immunoassay technique (EMIT). The advantage of EMIT is that it applies to a broad spectrum of drugs and is fast and cheap to administer. Because the EMIT screen will identify a high number of false positives, *see* Mark A. Rothstein, Drug Testing in the Workplace: The Challenge to Employment Relations and Employment Law, 63 Chi.–Kent L.Rev. 683, 697 (1987) ("Two out of three positives identified by the test will be false positives."), a confirmatory test is necessary before one may conclude that a positive result indicates drug use. The most widely used confirmatory test is gas chromatography/mass spectrometry (GC/MS), which is both time-consuming (only one sample and one drug per sample may be used at a time) and quite expensive. Although a blood test may reveal presence of drugs in their active state, a positive result on a urine test does not necessarily reveal recency of use or offer direct proof of actual impairment. Commission on Labor and Employment Law, Drug Testing in the Workplace, 43 Record of Assn. of the Bar of City of New York 447, 454–56 (1988).See generally Tyler D. Hartwell, Paul D. Steele & Nathaniel F. Rodman, Workplace Alcohol–Testing Programs: Prevalence and Trends, Monthly Lab. Rev. (June 1998), pp. 27ff.; and their Prevalence of Drug Testing in the Workplace, Monthly Lab. Rev. (Nov. 1996), pp. 35 ff.; Barnum & Gleason, The Credibility of Drug Tests: A Multi–Stage Bayesian Analysis, 47 Indus. & Lab. Rels. Rev. 610 (1994).

On use of hair testing, see Tom Mieczkowski, Harvey J. Landress, Richard Newel & Shirley D. Coletti, Testing Hair for Illicit Drug Use (U.S. Dept. of Justice, Nat'l Instit. of Health, Research in Brief, Jan. 1993).

On liability of testing laboratories for faulty tests, see Stinson v. Physicians Immediate Care, Ltd., 269 Ill.App.3d 659, 207 Ill.Dec. 96, 646 N.E.2d 930 (1995); Elliott v. Laboratory Specialists, Inc., 588 So.2d 175 (1991); see generally Karen Manfield, Imposing Liability on Drug Testing Laboratories for "False Positives": Getting Around Privity, 64 U.Chi. L. Rev. 287 (1997) (drawing analogy to accountants' liability). See also Carroll v. Federal Express Corp., 113 F.3d 163 (9th Cir. 1997) (employer could delegate drug-testing duty under DOT regulations to laboratory).

12. *Implications of "False Positive" Results?* Congress in the Americans with Disabilities Act of 1990 (ADA) attempted to leave undisturbed drug testing programs by exempting such tests from the prohibition of preoffer medical examinations, § 104(d), 42 U.S.C. § 12112(d), and excluding current users of illegal drugs from the definition of "qualified individual

with a disability," § 104(a), id. § 12114(a). Some open questions include whether former drug abusers or workers who are subjected to adverse personnel action on the basis of "false positive" results come within the ADA's protection.

False-positive results in some circumstances may also give rise to state-law claims for defamation, *see* Elaine Shoben, Test Defamation in the Workplace: False Positive Results in Attempting to Detect Lies, AIDS, or Drug Use, 1988 U.Chi.L.F. 181; or, possibly, claims under the Federal Privacy Act, 5 U.S.C. § 552a (and its state analogues), see Comment, Drug Testing of Federal Government Employees: Is Harm Resulting from Negligent Record Maintenance Actionable?, 1988 U.Chi.L.F. 239.

What procedural safeguards are necessary to ensure that public employees at least do not suffer disadvantage because of false positive tests? Does the due process clause require that particular procedures be followed before public employees may be tested? Before adverse personnel action may be taken on the basis of test results?

13. *Implications of Inability to Test for Current Impairment?* In view of the limitations of urinalysis as a means of detecting current impairment, can a public employer's drug testing program be challenged as an impermissible inquiry into the off-the-premises behavior of its employees? Does *Von Raab* suggest, however, that the government employer can test even for off-premises use because of its interest in ensuring that its employees are not susceptible to bribery or blackmail? Would the more general societal interest in eliminating the demand for drugs be an adequate justification? For a pre-*Von Raab* view, see Allan Adler, Probative Value and the Unreasonable Search: A Constitutional Perspective on Workplace Drug Testing, 1988 U.Chi.L.F. 113 (drug testing is probative only of possibly unlawful behavior and should trigger the more demanding standards applicable to government in its role as law enforcer rather than employer).

14. *Testing for AIDS and Hepatitis.* Blood testing by public employers for presence of the AIDS antibody or hepatitis B virus also raises fourth amendment questions. Conceivably, testing may be sought by insurance carriers who wish to exclude high medical risks from general policy coverage. Employers may also wish to engage in such testing either to reduce insurance costs or out of fear of transmission of the disease. See Glover v. Eastern Nebraska Community Office of Retardation, 867 F.2d 461 (8th Cir.1989) (Nebraska facility for the mentally retarded lacked a factual basis for believing that its clients were exposed to a meaningful risk of transmission of the AIDS virus from its employees). See generally Mark A. Rothstein, Screening Workers for AIDS, in AIDS and the Law 126 (H. Dalton & S. Barris eds. 1987). Do *Skinner* and *Von Raab* provide any support for the constitutionality of AIDS testing of any class of government employees? Such testing also may raise issues under the ADA and state disability discrimination laws.

15. *Self–Incrimination Issues.* There would seem to be no viable argument that the provision of a blood or urine sample could constitute self-incrimination under the fifth amendment. See Schmerber v. California, 384 U.S. 757, 86 S.Ct. 1826, 16 L.Ed.2d 908 (1966) (state can compel nontestimonial evidence, such as blood-alcohol test, without violating fifth amendment).

However, the self-incrimination clause may restrict more traditional government employer investigations. See, e.g., Gardner v. Broderick, 392 U.S. 273, 88 S.Ct. 1913, 20 L.Ed.2d 1082 (1968) (voiding dismissal of policeman because of refusal to sign waiver of immunity after being called before grand jury investigating police misconduct); Lefkowitz v. Turley, 414 U.S. 70, 94 S.Ct. 316, 38 L.Ed.2d 274 (1973) (cancellation of public contracts for failure to waive immunity found unconstitutional). If immunity from subsequent prosecution is granted, refusal to answer questions closely related to a legitimate interest of the public employer may permissibly be treated as insubordination warranting dismissal. See *Gardner,* 392 U.S. at 278, 88 S.Ct. at 1916; Uniformed Sanitation Men Ass'n v. Commissioner of Sanitation, 392 U.S. 280, 88 S.Ct. 1917, 20 L.Ed.2d 1089 (1968). Does this line of authority adequately address the public employer's interest in monitoring the behavior of high-level policy making officials? See Lefkowitz v. Cunningham, 431 U.S. 801, 810, 97 S.Ct. 2132, 2138, 53 L.Ed.2d 1 (1977) (Stevens, J., dissenting).

In National Treasury Employees Union v. U.S. Dept. of Treasury, 838 F.Supp. 631, 639 (D.D.C.1993), a union was permitted to challenge on self-incrimination clause grounds the Customs Service's policy requiring employees to complete a questionnaire inquiring into matters such as prior arrests, drug use and financial status. The court observed, in granting a preliminary injunction:

> The government attempts to deflect attention from the compulsion issue by asserting that the employee can always plead self-incrimination, and that such an answer could not be used as evidence in a criminal proceeding. However, * * * the forms do not inform respondent of this "choice." Additionally, as the Supreme Court has said, the privilege applies not only to disclosures that may be used in a criminal prosecution but also when the disclosures "could lead to other evidence that might be so used." Devine v. Goldstein, 680 F.2d 243, 247 (1982). Here, there has been no indication that the act of pleading the Fifth Amendment is not a disclosure in and of itself which could lead to investigation by the Justice Department. A reasonable person could certainly so conclude.

> By requiring employees to answer incriminating questions, coupled with a warning that the answers could be used against the employee, the government is effectively coercing a waiver of immunity. An employee who is discharged for refusing to answer under these circumstances is, in fact, being discharged for a refusal to waive his constitutional privilege.

Under Baxter v. Palmigiano, 425 U.S. 308, 96 S.Ct. 1551, 47 L.Ed.2d 810 (1976), the trier of fact in a civil case may properly draw an adverse inference against a party that declines to answer relevant questions on fifth amendment grounds. This raises difficult problems for employees accused of misconduct that may trigger criminal as well as civil liability. See generally Vincent C. Alexander, 'Pleading the Fifth' in Civil Actions, N.Y.L.J., Mar. 17, 2003, p. 3.

16. *First Amendment Limits.* Questions unjustifiably probing into beliefs or associations are vulnerable to first amendment challenges. See, e.g.,

Shelton v. Tucker, 364 U.S. 479, 81 S.Ct. 247, 5 L.Ed.2d 231 (1960); NAACP v. Alabama ex rel. Patterson, 357 U.S. 449, 78 S.Ct. 1163, 2 L.Ed.2d 1488 (1958). For a case refusing to sustain a first amendment-based objection to undergoing urinalysis for drug and alcohol abuse, see Rushton v. Nebraska Public Power District, 844 F.2d 562 (8th Cir.1988) (religious objection to "alcoholism is a disease" premise of testing program). First amendment rights of public employees are the subject of chapter 9.

2. Associational Privacy

Note on Associational Privacy

Unlike claims of physical privacy, claims of associational privacy typically directly question some governmental objective. Are there ever justifiable reasons for government employers to be concerned with an employee's associational choices, even when those choices affect only conduct that occurs outside of the workplace?

Associational privacy suits have been brought against inquiries into the cohabitation decisions of police officers and teachers. Such inquiries have been challenged on due process grounds. Compare, e.g., Fraternal Order of Police, Lodge No. 5 v. City of Philadelphia, 859 F.2d 276 (3d Cir.1988) (sustaining police department's background investigation into family financial status and organizational memberships of applicants for elite anticorruption unit); City of Sherman v. Henry, 39 Tex. Sup. J. 920, 928 S.W.2d 464 (1996) (rejecting substantive due process-privacy challenge to city's denial of promotion to a police officer for having committed adultery with a coworker's spouse, holding that neither U.S. nor state constitutions give officer right to engage in adultery), with Briggs v. North Muskegon Police Dept., 563 F.Supp. 585 (W.D.Mich.1983), affirmed, 746 F.2d 1475 (6th Cir.1984) (voiding dismissal of policeman for cohabiting with married woman not his wife). They also have been subject to first-amendment scrutiny. See, e.g., Cybyske v. Independent School Dist. No. 196, 347 N.W.2d 256 (Minn.1984) (refusal to hire teacher because of political views of her spouse violates associational rights). See generally Michael A. Woronoff, Note, Public Employees or Private Citizens: The Off–Duty Sexual Activities of Police Officers and the Constitutional Right of Privacy, 18 U.Mich.J.L.Ref. 195 (1984). See also Walls v. City of Petersburg, 895 F.2d 188 (4th Cir.1990) (rejecting Title VII disparate-impact and privacy challenge to police department questionnaire asking whether applicant had immediate relatives with criminal records, ever had sexual relations with a person of the same sex, or was previously married and if so why previous marriages failed, and inquiring into debts incurred by applicant's children and their spouses).

Do public employees have a right to engage in nontraditional lifestyle choices without fear of suffering disadvantage on the job? Should the Constitution be read broadly to protect a right of "intimate association"? See Kenneth Karst, The Freedom of Intimate Association?, 89 Yale L.J. 624 (1980).

C. EMERGING PROTECTION OF PRIVATE-SEC-TOR EMPLOYEES

However "state action" and the public sector are defined, legal recognition of privacy claims, like recognition of job security rights, has been more certain within this sector of the economy. Privacy developments governing the private sector, by contrast, are in a nascent state— a patchwork of rights and theories from a variety of sources.

1. Federal Statutory Law

a. 1988 Employee Polygraph Protection Act

As a means of avoiding the difficulties inherent in subjective assessment of credibility, employers confronting instances of theft or pilferage have often resorted to mechanical devices such as polygraphs to determine the truthfulness of employee accounts. The use of such devices has generated two distinct concerns. One questions the reliability of the devices as a means of ascertaining the truth. See, e.g., William G. Iacono & David T. Lykken, The Scientific Status of Research on Polygraph Techniques: The Case Against Polygraph Tests, in 1 Modern Scientific Evidence § 14–3.0 (D. Faigman, D. Kaye, M. Saks & J. Sanders eds., 1997); David T. Lykken, A Tremor in the Blood (1981). The second concern is that such devices may violate privacy interests because they involve elements of physical intrusion and self-incrimination. See, e.g., Report of the Privacy Protection Study Commission, Personal Privacy in an Information Society 239–40 (1977).

Until the 1980s, the regulation of polygraph testing was a matter of state law. See, e.g., Johnson v. Delchamps, Inc., 846 F.2d 1003 (5th Cir.1988) (negligent administration of lie detector test). In 1988, however, Congress passed the Employee Polygraph Protection Act (EPPA), 29 U.S.C. §§ 2001–09. This Act prohibits the use of lie detector tests outside certain limited situations. Moreover, even where permitted, any tests must be conducted in conformity with strict procedural requirements. The statute broadly defines the term "lie detector" to include "a polygraph, deceptograph, voice stress analyzer, psychological stress evaluator, or any other similar device (whether mechanical or electrical) that is used * * * for the purpose of rendering a diagnostic opinion regarding the honesty or dishonesty of an individual" (§ 2).

The exemptions from the statutory prohibition include (i) testing by the federal government for national defense, security and counterintelligence functions (§ 7(b)–(c)); (ii) testing of incumbent employees in connection with an ongoing investigation (§ 7(d)); (iii) testing of prospective employees by private employers involved in provision of guard and security services (§ 7(e)); and (iv) testing by any employer authorized to manufacture, distribute, or dispense controlled substances (§ 7(f)).

The provision likely to have the greatest importance for private employers is the limited exemption for testing in connection with an ongoing investigation in § 7(d), 29 U.S.C. § 2006(d). The statute imposes several preconditions for such testing. First, it must be administered in connection with "an ongoing investigation involving economic loss or injury to the employer's business * * *." Second, the employee must have had "access to the property" in question. Third, the employer must have "a reasonable suspicion" that the employee was involved in the incident. Finally, the employer must provide to the employee a statement that sets forth the particulars of the specific incident, including the identification of the economic loss, the basis for believing the employee had the requisite access, and the basis for reasonable suspicion of the employee's involvement. Section 8(a) further provides that "without additional supporting evidence" an employee may not be disciplined because of the results of even a permissible polygraph test under § 7(d), or because of the refusal to take such a test. However, the same evidence that creates the reasonable suspicion that warrants the testing may also serve as this additional supporting evidence.

In Mennen v. Easter Stores, 951 F.Supp. 838 (N.D.Iowa 1997), the court held that a store's cooperating with a police request that a suspected manager take a polygraph test in connection with the investigation of in-store theft did not violate 29 U.S.C. § 2002(1), which prohibits employers from asking employees to submit to such tests:

> * * * The police department needed [the store's] permission to request that Mennen take the polygraph; however, at that point in time [the store] had not taken an active role in the investigation, used the results from the polygraph examination, or taken any adverse employment action against Mennen. Although [the store] had the power to veto the administration of the polygraph examination, it did not require, request, suggest or cause Mennen to take or submit to a polygraph examination.

Id. at 853. However, the employer violated 29 U.S.C. § 2002(3) in later using the results of the test in demoting the manager. Damages for emotional distress were held available under the EPPA. Note also that the EPPA contains a no-waiver provision, and the employee's consent to a polygraph test in violation of the law "does not, in and of itself, confer on [the employer] the reasonable suspicion necessary to request that [the employee] take a polygraph." Long v. Mango's Tropical Café, Inc., 958 F.Supp. 612, 616 (S.D.Fla.1997).

In situations where an exemption applies, and hence testing is permissible, the statute sets forth additional limitations, including a detailed list of the rights of the examinee. These rights include being represented by counsel, having an opportunity to review questions that will be proposed, and not being asked questions concerning sexual behavior, beliefs and associations (§ 8(b)). Examiners are also placed under certain restrictions, including obligations to produce a written opinion that does not contain information irrelevant to the purpose of the test, and to maintain for three years all opinions and questions used (§ 8(c)). Under § 9, the results of a polygraph may not be disclosed except to the examinee (or his designee), the employer, or to any court or agency pursuant to court order. An employer may make disclosures to government agencies only of information that constitutes an admission of criminal conduct. Section 10 provides that more restrictive state laws or collective bargaining agreement provisions are not preempted.

Do polygraph test examiners become the "employer" for EPPA purposes because of their influence over the employer's compliance with EPPA requirements? See 29 C.F.R. § 801.2(c) ("The term employer means any person acting directly or indirectly in the interest of the employer"). Compare James v. Professionals' Detective Agency, 876 F.Supp. 1013 (N.D.Ill.1995), with Fallin v. Mindis Metals, Inc., 865 F.Supp. 834 (N.D.Ga.1994) (no examiner liability when examiner does not select which employees to test).

A "lie detector" for EPPA purposes includes "a polygraph, deceptograph, voice stress analyzer, psychological stress evaluator, or any other similar device (whether mechanical or electrical) that is used, or the results of which are used, for the purpose of rendering a diagnostic opinion regarding the honesty or dishonesty of an individual." 29 U.S.C. § 2001(3). In Veazey v. Communications & Cable of Chicago, Inc., 194 F.3d 850 (7th Cir.1999), the court held that an employer could violate the EPPA by requiring an employee to read into a tape recorder a verbatim transcript of a threatening message that had been found on the voicemail of another employee: "[A] tape recorder might very well be considered as an adjunct to a 'lie detector' determination under the EPPA because the results of a tape recording (a voice exemplar) can be used to render a diagnostic opinion regarding the honesty or dishonesty of an individual when evaluated by a voice stress analyzer or similar device." Id. at 859.

The scientific validity of written "honesty" tests—not covered by the express terms of the EPPA—has been questioned. See Office of Technology Assessment, The Use of Integrity Tests for Pre-employment Screening (OTA/SET/4421990) (doubting predictive validity for identifying potentially dishonest employees and raising questions about possibly discriminatory effects).

b. 1974 Privacy Act

Another important federal measure is the Privacy Act of 1974, 5 U.S.C. § 552(a), which grants certain rights and remedies to individuals who are the subject of records maintained by federal agencies, see, e.g., Dickson v. Office of Personnel Management, 828 F.2d 32 (D.C.Cir.1987) (agency's maintenance of record in violation of statutory fairness standard exposes agency to liability for damages); Brune v. Internal Revenue Service, 861 F.2d 1284 (D.C.Cir.1988) (agency not required by Privacy Act to interview employees under investigation for possible misconduct before questioning third parties about the incident).

c. HIPAA Privacy Regulations of 2000

In December 2000, the U.S. Dept. of Health and Human Services (HHS) published final regulations on the Standards for Privacy of

Individually Identifiable Health Information ("Privacy Regulations"), pursuant to the Health Insurance Portability and Accountability Act of 1996 (HIPAA). 63 Fed. Reg. 50312 (Aug. 17, 2000). In general, these regulations require that (1) all "protected health information" (identifiable health information provided by health care providers and insurers relating to the physical or mental health of individuals or payments for provision of health care) be held confidential, unless a specific exemption applies to the information; (2) all entities subject to the regulations treat such information as confidential; and (3) patients are given certain protections against the misuse or disclosure of their health record. See generally Kathryn L. Bakich, Countdown to HIPAA Compliance: Understanding EDI, Privacy, and Security, 15 Benefits L.J. 45 (Summer 2002).

d. 1970 Fair Crediting Report Act

The Fair Credit Reporting Act of 1970 (FCRA), 15 U.S.C. §§ 1681*l*–1681t, requires employers who decline to hire a job applicant because of the results of a credit investigation to inform the rejected applicant of the name and address of the reporting agency. Id. § 1681m. The individual then has certain disclosure rights against the reporting agency.

In 1996, the FCRA was amended to create new obligations for employers who obtain "consumer report[s]," i.e., credit checks, on applicants or employees; or who use credit reporting agencies to access "investigative consumer report[s]," which are broadly defined as information "concerning a consumer's character, general reputation, personal characteristics and mode of living," 15 U.S.C. § 1681a(e). Investigative reports generally involve interviews with people acquainted with the consumer-employee.

Under the 1996 amendments, the employer must provide a "clear and conspicuous" written disclosure stating that a consumer report may be obtained for employment purposes, and employee authorization is required before a report may be requested. Certification that these disclosures have been made must be provided to the credit reporting agency. Before taking adverse action based in whole or in part on a consumer report, the employer must provide the employee with a copy of the report and written explanation of the employee's rights under the FCRA. 15 U.S.C. § 1681b(b)(1)–(3).

With respect to "investigative consumer reports," the employer must disclose in writing to the applicant or employee that an investigative consumer report may be obtained and may include information about character, general reputation, personal characteristics and mode of living. The disclosure must also inform the individual that he may request additional information concerning the nature and scope of the investigation. Certification must be made to the credit reporting agency that these disclosures have been provided. 15 U.S.C. § 1681d. The FCRA also requires consumer reporting agencies to maintain procedures for reinvestigating and correcting inaccuracies (§ 1681i).

In 1999, the Federal Trade Commission (FTC) took the position that applicants or employees must be told of a company's plans to have an outside party (including a law firm) probe any alleged workplace sexual harassment or other wrongdoing:

> [O]nce an employer turns to an outside organization for assistance in investigation of harassment claims * * *, the assisting entity [if it "regularly engage[s] in assisting employers with investigations for a fee"] is a [consumer reporting agency (CRA)] because it furnishes "consumer reports" to a "third party" (the employer). For purposes of determining whether the entity is a CRA, the FCRA does not distinguish whether the information on consumers is obtained from "internal" records or from outside the employer's workforce. The source and scope of information *does* enter into a determination whether the information is a "consumer report" or an "investigative consumer report."

Letter from Christopher Keller, FTC Div. Of Financial Practices, to Judi A. Vail, Esq. dated April 5, 1999. In a subsequent letter, the FTC staff noted that "the FRCA does not apply to investigations [employers] conduct themselves through their own personnel," and "would not apply where the employer uses a third party that does not 'regularly engage' in preparing such reports and thus does not fall under the definition of 'consumer reporting agency' * * *."

Employers' concerns that the FTC view would interfere with their ability to use third parties to investigate employee misconduct, including instances of sexual harassment, led Congress to enact the Fair and Accurate Credit Transactions Act of 2003. Section 611 of the Act amends the FCRA definition of "consumer report" to exclude communications made by a third party to an employer in connection with the investigation of suspected misconduct relating to employment or compliance with applicable laws, regulations and company policies. After taking an adverse action against an employee based on such a third-party report, the employer is required to disclose to the employee a summary of the report, but need not disclose sources of information for the report.

On the liability of credit reporting agencies for inaccuracies in credit reports, see Philbin v. Trans Union Corp., 101 F.3d 957 (3d Cir.1996). For state-law restrictions on background checks, see note 3, p. 889 infra.

e.   1968 Omnibus Crime Control and Safe Streets Act

The Federal wiretapping statute, Title III of the Omnibus Crime Control and Safe Streets Act of 1968, as amended by the Electronic Communications Privacy Act of 1986, 18 U.S.C. §§ 2510–20, generally prohibits both public and private parties from intercepting the contents of telephone calls and certain other communications without judicial authority. The statute contains two important exemptions.

i.   *Consent.* First, § 2511(2)(d) authorizes interception where one of the parties to the conversation has given prior consent. The courts, however, are not predisposed to find implied consent. See, e.g., Watkins

v. L.M. Berry & Co., 704 F.2d 577 (11th Cir.1983) (employer's announced policy of intercepting sales calls did not establish consent to monitoring of personal calls beyond determining the nature of the call); see also Williams v. Poulos, 11 F.3d 271, 281–82 (1st Cir.1993) (employees were told monitoring might occur, but were not told of the manner of monitoring or which employees would be monitored); Deal v. Spears, 980 F.2d 1153, 1157 (8th Cir.1992). But see Griffin v. City of Milwaukee, 74 F.3d 824 (7th Cir.1996) (openness of monitoring can establish consent, where city dispatchers were told calls might be monitored and that incoming emergency calls would be recorded, and the recording equipment was in a glass case in the middle of plaintiff's work area). One-party consent suffices under the federal law, see 18 U.S.C. § 2511(2)(d), but not under all state laws.

ii. *Business–Extension Exception.* In addition, § 2510(5)(a)(i)—the "business extension" provision—exempts from the statutory prohibition any equipment used by the telephone subscriber or user "in the ordinary course of its business. * * * " Do employers have unlimited discretion under this exception to listen on employee calls on a telephone company-provided extension? In *Watkins,* supra, for example, the court held that an employer's interception of a telephone discussion concerning an employee's job interview with another company was not "in the ordinary course of its business" because the employee was free to resign at will; moreover, "a personal call may be intercepted in the ordinary course of business to determine its nature but never its contents." 704 F.2d at 583. See Briggs v. American Air Filter Co., 630 F.2d 414 (5th Cir.1980) (where employer has reasonable suspicion about disclosure of confidential information, has previously warned employee not to make such disclosure, has reason to believe that the employee will continue to disclose the information, and knows a particular call is with a competitor, it is within the ordinary course of business for an employer to listen in to the extent the conversation is revealing the feared disclosure); *Deal,* supra, 980 F.2d at 1158 (listening to all 22 hours of employee's tape-recorded calls "without regard to their relation to * * * business interests"); Arias v. Mutual Central Alarm Svcs., Inc., 182 F.R.D. 407 (S.D.N.Y. 1998) (employer had reasonable suspicion of wrongdoing to justify eavesdropping as "in the ordinary course of business").

The courts have also held that this exception applies only to recording instruments provided by the telephone company. See Williams v. Poulos, supra, 11 F.3d at 280 (custom-made device); *Deal,* supra, 980 F.3d at 1157–58; Sanders v. Robert Bosch Corp., 38 F.3d 736 (4th Cir.1994).

f. 1986 Electronic Communications Privacy Act

In the Electronic Communications Privacy Act of 1986 (ECPA), 100 Stat. 1848, 18 U.S.C. §§ 2510, 2701, Congress amended Title III of the federal wiretapping law to regulate emerging forms of electronic communications.The ECPA protects most electronic communications, including e-mail, from interception, attempted interception, disclosure, use and unauthorized access of stored messages. The ECPA does not cover silent video surveillance. See Thompson v. Johnson County Community College, 930 F.Supp. 501 (D.Kan.1996) (Title I regulates only "any wire, oral or electronic communication," 18 U.S.C. § 2511(1)(a)). In addition to the consent and telephone-extension exceptions discussed above, the ECPA further limits its use as a basis for employee privacy claims in the e-mail context.

The statute distinguishes between (1) intercepting communications during their transmission (Title I), and (2) accessing previously-stored communications (Title II, also called the "Stored Communications Act"), with restrictions on the former more stringent than the latter. Unlike a telephone communication, e-mail is stored in a service-provider computer until the addressee accesses the computer to retrieve and read the message.

The ECPA is a complicated piece of legislation, enacted before the advent of the Internet. Consider the following decision in which the Ninth Circuit panel on rehearing vacated an earlier ruling, replacing it with what follows.

KONOP v. HAWAIIAN AIRLINES, INC.
United States Court of Appeals for the Ninth Circuit, 2002.
302 F.3d 868.

BOOCHEVER, J.

[Robert] Konop, a pilot for Hawaiian [Airlines, Inc.], created and maintained a website where he posted bulletins critical of his employer, its officers, and the incumbent union, Air Line Pilots Association ("ALPA"). * * *

Konop controlled access to his website by requiring visitors to log in with a user name and password. He created a list of people, mostly pilots and other employees of Hawaiian, who were eligible to access the website. Pilots Gene Wong and James Gardner were included on this list. Konop programmed the website to allow access when a person entered the name of the eligible person, created a password, and clicked the "SUBMIT" button on the screen, indicating acceptance of the terms and conditions of use. These terms and conditions prohibited any member of Hawaiian's management from viewing the website and prohibited users from disclosing the website's contents to anyone else.

In December 1995, Hawaiian vice president James Davis asked Wong for permission to use Wong's name to access Konop's website. Wong agreed. Davis claimed he was concerned about untruthful allegations that he believed Konop was making on the website. * * * Davis also logged in with the name of another pilot, Gardner, who had similarly consented to Davis' use of his name. * * *

Konop filed suit alleging claims under the federal Wiretap Act and the Stored Communications Act [(SCA)—essentially Titles I and II of the ECPA], the Railway Labor Act, and state law, arising from Davis' viewing and use of Konop's secure website. Konop also alleged that Hawaiian placed him on medical suspension for his opposition [to company wage policy], in violation of the Railway Labor Act. The district court granted summary judgment to Hawaiian on all but the retaliatory suspension claim, and entered judgment against Konop on that claim after a short bench trial.

* * *

B. Wiretap Act

Konop argues that Davis' conduct constitutes an interception of an electronic communication in violation of the Wiretap Act. The Wiretap Act makes it an offense to "intentionally intercept[] ... any wire, oral, or electronic communication." 18 U.S.C. § 2511(1)(a). * * *

* * * Konop's website fits the definition of "electronic communication" [in § 2510(12).]

The Wiretap Act, however, prohibits only "interception" of electronic communications. "Intercept" is defined as "the aural or other acquisition of the contents of any wire, electronic, or oral communication through the use of any electronic, mechanical, or other device." Id. § 2510(4). Standing alone, this definition would seem to suggest that an individual "intercepts" an electronic communication by "acquiring" its contents, regardless of when or under what circumstances the acquisition occurs. * * *

[, in] Steve Jackson Games, Inc. v. United States Secret Service, 36 F.3d 457 (5th Cir. 1994), the Fifth Circuit held that the government's acquisition of email messages stored on an electronic bulletin board system, but not yet retrieved by the intended recipients, was not an "interception" under the Wiretap Act. The court observed that, prior to the enactment of the ECPA, the word "intercept" had been interpreted to mean the acquisition of communication contemporaneous with transmission. * * * The court further observed that Congress, in passing the ECPA, intended to retain [this] definition of "intercept" with respect to wire and oral communications, while amending the Wiretap Act to cover interceptions of electronic communications. * * * The court reasoned, however, that the word "intercept" could not describe the exact same conduct with respect to wire and electronic communications because [these terms] were defined differently in the statute. Specifically, the term "wire communication" was defined to include storage of the communications, while "electronic communication" was not. [This reflected] Congress' understanding that, although one could "intercept" a wire communication in storage, one could not "intercept" an electronic communication in storage. * * *

The Ninth Circuit endorsed the reasoning of *Steve Jackson Games* in *United States v. Smith*, 155 F.3d 1051 [9th Cir. 1998)]. * * *

We agree with the *Steve Jackson* and *Smith* courts that the narrow definition of "intercept" applies to electronic communications. Notably,

Congress has since amended the Wiretap Act to eliminate storage from the definition of wire communication, see USA PATRIOT Act § 209, 115 Stat. at 283, such that the textual definition relied upon by the *Steve Jackson* and *Smith* courts no longer exists. This change, however, supports the analysis of those case. By eliminating storage from the definition of wire communication, Congress essentially reinstated the pre-ECPA definition of "intercept"—acquisition contemporaneous with transmission—with respect to wire communication. * * * The purpose of the recent amendment was to reduce protection of voice mail messages to the lower level of protection provided other stored communications. See H.R. Rep. 107–236(I), at 158–59 (2001). * * *

We therefore hold that for a website such as Konop's to be "intercepted" in violation of the Wiretap Act, it must be acquired during transmission, not while it is in electronic storage. * * * [The SCA, i.e., Title II of the ECPA was enacted] for the express purpose of addressing "access to stored electronic communication and transactional records." * * * The level of protection provided stored communications under the SCA is considerably less than that provided communications covered by the Wiretap Act. * * * [I]f Konop's position were correct and acquisition of a stored communication were an interception under the Wiretap Act, the government would have to comply with the more burdensome, more restrictive procedures of the Wiretap Act to do exactly what Congress apparently authorized it to do under the less burdensome procedures of the SCA. Congress could not have intended this result. * * *

Because we conclude that Davis' conduct did not constitute an "interception" of an electronic communication in violation of the Wiretap Act, we affirm the district court's grant of summary judgment against Konop on his Wiretap Act claim.

C. Stored Communications Act

Konop also argues that, by viewing his secure, website, Davis accessed a stored electronic communication without authorization in violation of the SCA. The SCA makes it an offense to "intentionally access[] without authorization a facility through which an electronic communication service is provided . . . and thereby obtain[] . . . access to a wire or electronic communication while it is in electronic storage in such system." 18 U.S.C. § 2701(a)(1). The SCA excepts from liability, however, "conduct authorized by a user of that service with respect to a communication of or intended for that user." 18 U.S.C. § 2701(c)(2). The district court found that [this exception] applied because Wong and Gardner consented to Davis' use of Konop's website. * * *

The parties agree that the relevant "electronic communications service" is Konop's website, and the website was in "electronic storage." In addition, for purposes of this opinion, we accept the parties' assumption that Davis' conduct constituted "access without authorization" to "a facility through which an electronic communication service is provided."

We therefore address only the narrow question of whether the district court properly found Hawaiian exempt from liability under § 2701(c)(2). * * *

[T]he plain language of § 2701(c)(2) indicates that only a "user" of the service can authorize a third party's access to the communication statute defines "user" as one who 1) uses the service and 2) is duly authorized to do so. Because the statutory language is unambiguous, it must control our construction of the statute, notwithstanding the legislative history [suggesting that] "addressees" or "intended recipients" of electronic communications would have the authority under the SCA to allow third party access to those communications. See H.R. Rep. No. 99–647, at 66–67 * * * .

Based on the common definition of the word "use," we cannot find any evidence in the record that Wong ever used Konop's website. There is some evidence, however, that Gardner may have used the website, but it is unclear when that use occurred. At any rate, the district court did not make any findings on whether Wong and Gardner actually used Konop's website—it simply assumed that Wong and Gardner, by virtue of being eligible to view the website, could authorize Davis' use. The problem with this approach is that it essentially reads the "user" requirement out of § 2701(c)(2). Taking the facts in the light most favorable to Konop, we must assume that neither Wong nor Gardner was a "user" of the website at the time he authorized Davis to view it. We therefore reverse the district court's grant of summary judgment to Hawaiian on Konop's SCA claim.

[*Eds.*—The court's discussion of Konop's Railway Labor Act and retaliation claims is omitted.]

Notes and Questions

1. *Contemporaneity Requirement for Interception of Electronic Communications in Storage?* Judge Reinhardt, in his partial dissent in *Konop*, argued that the majority's contemporaneity requirement for interception of stored electronic communications

> would result in eliminating stored electronic communications from the purview of the intercept prohibition altogether because a stored communication cannot be acquired contemporaneously with its transmission—it has already been transmitted. * * * The nature of electronic communication is that it spends infinitesimal amounts of time "en route," unlike a phone call. Therefore, in order to "intercept" an electronic communication, one ordinarily obtains one of the copies made en route or at the destination. These copies constitute "stored electronic communications," as acknowledged by the majority. 18 U.S.C. § 2510(17)(A) * * * . If intercept is defined as solely contemporaneous acquisition, then in contravention of Congressional intent, at most all acquisitions of the contents of electronic communications would escape the intercept prohibition entirely.

Does the majority or the dissent have the better interpretation of the statutory text? The Congressional purpose? See generally Jay P. Kesan, Cyber–Working or Cyber–Shirking?": A First Principles Examination of Electronic Privacy in the Workplace, 54 Fla. L. Rev. 289 (2002); Note, Proposal for a Fair Statutory Interpretation: E–Mail Stored in a Service Provider Computer is Subject to an Interception Under the Federal Wiretap Act, 7 J.L. & Pol'y 519 (1999).

2. *"Access" to Stored Communications: "User" Exception.* The *Konop* court's remand suggests that intended recipients of a stored communication can without restriction authorize third-party access, as long as they actually have used the electronic communications service in question. Is this a necessary reading of § 2701(c)(2)? A plausible one? Judge Reinhardt did not dissent on the SCA portion of the panel ruling.

3. *"Access" to Stored Communications: "Service Provider" Exception.* Under § 2701(c), the prohibition on access to stored communications does not apply "with respect to conduct authorized—(1) by the person or entity providing a wire or electronic communications system; [or] (2) by a user of that service with respect to a communication of or intended for that user * * *." Under 18 U.S.C. § 2702(b), the prohibition on disclosure of stored messages does not apply, inter alia, "(4) to a person employed or authorized or whose facilities are used to forward such communication to its destination; [or] (5) as may be necessarily incident to the rendition of the service or to the protection of the rights or property of the provider of that service * * *."

May an employer that provides its own service or owns its own communications system lawfully access and disclose stored employee e-mail insofar as the ECPA is concerned? In Bohach v. City of Reno, 932 F.Supp. 1232 (D.Nev.1996), the court answered affirmatively, noting that the police officers in that case were warned that messages on their electronic pagers were subject to monitoring and, in any event, the ECPA "allows service providers to do as they wish when it comes to accessing communications in electronic storage." Id. at 1236. Cf. Smyth v. Pillsbury Co., 914 F.Supp. 97 (E.D.Pa. 1996) (no invasion of privacy despite previous assurances by employer that e-mail would be confidential). Is there a policy justification for limiting eavesdropping over the employer's telephone system but not over its e-mail system?

4. *"Access" to Messages Already Received by Intended Recipients?* In Fraser v. Nationwide Mutual Ins. Co., 352 F.3d 107 (3d Cir. 2003), the lower court held that retrieval of an e-mail message after it has been received falls entirely outside of the ECPA, reasoning that Congress intended to address only electronic messages in the course of transmission. The Third Circuit affirmed but on the basis of the service-provider exception, as discussed in note 3 above.

2. *State Law Developments*

a. Personal Intrusion

BORSE v. PIECE GOODS SHOP, INC.

United States Court of Appeals for the Third Circuit, 1992.
963 F.2d 611.

BECKER, CIRCUIT JUDGE.

Plaintiff Sarah Borse brought suit against her former employer, Piece Goods Shop, Inc. ("the Shop"), in the district court for the Eastern District of Pennsylvania. She claimed that, by dismissing her when she refused to submit to urinalysis screening and personal property searches (conducted by her employer at the workplace pursuant to its drug and alcohol policy), the Shop violated a public policy that precludes employers from engaging in activities that violate their employees' rights to privacy and to freedom from unreasonable searches. [T]he district court dismissed her complaint for failure to state a claim on which relief could be granted. This appeal requires us to decide whether an at-will employee who is discharged for refusing to consent to urinalysis screening for drug use and to searches of her personal property states a claim for wrongful discharge under Pennsylvania law.

* * *

I. THE ALLEGATIONS OF THE COMPLAINT

Because of the procedural posture of this case, we begin with a summary of the allegations of the complaint. Borse was employed as a sales clerk by the Piece Goods Shop for almost fifteen years. In January 1990, the Shop adopted a drug and alcohol policy which required its employees to sign a form giving their consent to urinalysis screening for drug use and to searches of their personal property located on the Shop's premises.

Borse refused to sign the consent form. On more than one occasion, she asserted that the drug and alcohol policy violated her right to privacy and her right to be free from unreasonable searches and seizures as guaranteed by the United States Constitution. The Shop continued to insist that she sign the form and threatened to discharge her unless she did. On February 9, 1990, the Shop terminated Borse's employment.

The complaint alleges that Borse was discharged in retaliation for her refusal to sign the consent form and for protesting the Shop's drug and alcohol policy. It asserts that her discharge violated a public policy, embodied in the First and Fourth Amendments to the United States Constitution, which precludes employers from engaging in activities that violate their employees' rights to privacy and to freedom from unreasonable searches of their persons and property. Plaintiff seeks compensatory damages for emotional distress, injury to reputation, loss of earnings, and diminished earning capacity. She also alleges that the discharge was willful and malicious and, accordingly, seeks punitive damages.

II.   OVERVIEW OF THE PUBLIC POLICY EXCEPTION TO THE EMPLOYMENT-AT-WILL DOCTRINE IN PENNSYLVANIA

* * *

Pennsylvania Supreme Court has not addressed the question whether discharging an at-will employee who refuses to consent to urinalysis and to searches of his or her personal property located on the employer's premises violates public policy[. We] must predict how that court would resolve the issue should it be called upon to do so. * * *

B.   *Recognition of the Exception by the Pennsylvania Supreme Court*

* * *

In Geary v. United States Steel Corp., 456 Pa. 171, 319 A.2d 174 (1974) * * * the Pennsylvania Supreme Court recognized the possibility that an action for wrongful discharge might lie when the firing of an at-will employee violates public policy. Geary, a salesperson, complained to his immediate superiors about the safety of his employer's product. After being told to "follow directions," Geary took his complaints to the vice-president in charge of the product. As a result, the company withdrew the product from the market, but discharged Geary.

Geary argued that an exception to the at-will doctrine was warranted in his case because his dismissal was contrary to public policy. The Pennsylvania Supreme Court disagreed, relying upon two factors to decide that Geary's case did not merit an exception. First, the court observed that Geary was not responsible for monitoring product safety and that he did not possess expertise in that area. 319 A.2d at 178–79. Second, the court noted that Geary had violated the internal chain of command by pressing his concerns before the vice-president. Id. at 179–80.

* * *

The Pennsylvania Supreme Court did not revisit the validity of the public policy exception to the employment-at-will doctrine until fifteen years after *Geary*. In Clay v. Advanced Computer Applications, Inc., 522 Pa. 86, 559 A.2d 917 (1989), a married couple employed by the same company alleged that they were fired because the wife rejected the sexual advances of a company manager. The court held that their claims were barred because they had failed to seek recourse under the Pennsylvania Human Relations Act, which provides a statutory remedy for wrongful discharges based upon sexual harassment. The court did not deny that it had recognized a public policy exception to the employment-at-will doctrine in *Geary*, but it did stress the narrowness of that exception. The court stated:

> As a general rule, there is no common law cause of action against an employer for termination of an at-will employment rela-

tionship.... Exceptions to this rule have been recognized only in the most limited of circumstances, where discharges of at-will employees would threaten clear mandates of public policy.... Nevertheless, inasmuch as appellees failed to pursue their exclusive statutory remedy for sexual harassment and discrimination in the workplace, they are precluded from relief.

Id. at 918–19 (citations omitted).

One year later, the Pennsylvania Supreme Court returned to the issue again. In Paul v. Lankenau Hospital, 524 Pa. 90, 569 A.2d 346 (1990), a doctor alleged that a hospital had forced him to resign because he removed five refrigerators, which he claimed that he was authorized to take. He argued that because he had permission to remove the refrigerators, the hospital was estopped from discharging him for taking them. The court held that the doctrine of equitable estoppel is not an exception to the employment-at-will doctrine. Id. at 348. The court also appeared to question the validity of the public policy exception, but it did not expressly inter it.

* * *

As we have noted above, the Pennsylvania Supreme Court has not addressed the public policy exception since its decision in Paul. We are aware of no "persuasive evidence of a change in Pennsylvania law." As we have also explained, the Pennsylvania Superior Court continues to interpret Pennsylvania law as recognizing the public policy exception. Accordingly, we continue to interpret *Geary* as recognizing a cause of action for wrongful discharge when dismissal of an at-will employee violates a clear mandate of public policy.

III.   Sources of Public Policy

In order to evaluate Borse's claim, we must attempt to "discern whether any public policy is threatened" by her discharge. As evidence of a public policy that precludes employers from discharging employees who refuse to consent to the practices at issue, Borse primarily relies upon the First and Fourth Amendments to the United States Constitution and the right to privacy included in the Pennsylvania Constitution. As will be seen, we reject her reliance on these constitutional provisions, concluding instead that, to the extent that her discharge implicates public policy, the source of that policy lies in Pennsylvania common law.

A.   Constitutional Provisions

[*Eds.* The court rejects the argument that federal or state constitutional principles support a public policy claim, largely because these constitutional provisions do not reach the conduct of private employers.]

B.   Pennsylvania Common Law

Although we have rejected Borse's reliance upon constitutional provisions as evidence of a public policy allegedly violated by the Piece Goods Shop's drug and alcohol program, our review of Pennsylvania law reveals other evidence of a public policy that may, under certain circumstances, give rise to a wrongful discharge action related to urinalysis or to personal property searches. Specifically, we refer to the Pennsylvania common law regarding tortious invasion of privacy. Pennsylvania recognizes a cause of action for tortious "intrusion upon seclusion." Marks v. Bell Telephone Co., 460 Pa. 73, 331 A.2d 424, 430 (1975). The Restatement defines the tort as follows:

> One who intentionally intrudes, physically or otherwise, upon the solitude or seclusion of another or his private affairs or concerns, is subject to liability to the other for invasion of his privacy, if the intrusion would be highly offensive to a reasonable person.

Restatement (Second) of Torts § 652B.

Unlike the other forms of tortious invasion of privacy, an action based on intrusion upon seclusion does not require publication as an element of the tort. Harris by Harris v. Easton Publishing Co., 335 Pa. Super. 141, 483 A.2d 1377, 1383 (1984). The tort may occur by (1) physical intrusion into a place where the plaintiff has secluded himself or herself; (2) use of the defendant's senses to oversee or overhear the plaintiff's private affairs; or (3) some other form of investigation or examination into plaintiff's private concerns. 483 A.2d at 1383. Liability attaches only when the intrusion is substantial and would be highly offensive to "the ordinary reasonable person." Id. at 1383–84.

We can envision at least two ways in which an employer's urinalysis program might intrude upon an employee's seclusion. First, the particular manner in which the program is conducted might constitute an intrusion upon seclusion as defined by Pennsylvania law. The process of collecting the urine sample to be tested clearly implicates "expectations of privacy that society has long recognized as reasonable," Skinner v. Railway Labor Executives Association, 489 U.S. 602, 109 S. Ct. 1402, 1413, 103 L. Ed. 2d 639 (1989). In addition, many urinalysis programs monitor the collection of the urine specimen to ensure that the employee does not adulterate it or substitute a sample from another person. See, for example, 109 S. Ct. at 1413 (noting that in some cases, visual or aural observation of urination is required). See also National Treasury Employees Union v. Von Raab, 489 U.S. 656, 109 S. Ct. 1384, 1388, 103 L. Ed. 2d 685 (1989). Monitoring collection of the urine sample appears to fall within the definition of an intrusion upon seclusion because it involves the use of one's senses to oversee the private activities of another. Restatement (Second) of Torts § 652B, comment b. See also *Harris*, 483 A.2d at 1383.

* * *

Second, urinalysis "can reveal a host of private medical facts about an employee, including whether she is epileptic, pregnant, or diabetic." *Skinner*, 109 S. Ct. at 1413. A reasonable person might well conclude that submitting urine samples to tests designed to ascertain these types of information constitutes a substantial and highly offensive intrusion upon seclusion.

The same principles apply to an employer's search of an employee's personal property. If the search is not conducted in a a discreet manner or if it is done in such a way as to reveal personal matters unrelated to the workplace, the search might well constitute a tortious invasion of the employee's privacy. See, for example, K-Mart Corp. Store No. 7441 v. Trotti, 677 S.W.2d 632 (Tex. App. 1984) (search of employee's locker). See also Bodewig v. K-Mart, Inc., 54 Or. App. 480, 635 P.2d 657 (1981) (subjecting cashier accused of stealing to strip search).

The Pennsylvania courts have not had occasion to consider whether a discharge related to an employer's tortious invasion of an employee's privacy violates public policy. The district court for the Western District of Pennsylvania has addressed this question in applying Pennsylvania law, however. In Rogers v. International Business Machines Corp., 500 F. Supp. 867 (W.D. Pa. 1980), plaintiff argued that IBM's decision to discharge him violated public policy because it was based upon an investigation of a personal matter (an alleged affair with a co-worker) that invaded his right of privacy. The court examined the record to determine whether the investigation intruded upon plaintiff's seclusion. After determining that IBM had confined its investigation to interviewing other employees and examining company records, the court concluded that IBM's procedures were reasonable and did not violate public policy.

We predict that the Pennsylvania Supreme Court would follow the approach taken in *Rogers*. In other words, we believe that when an employee alleges that his or her discharge was related to an employer's invasion of his or her privacy, the Pennsylvania Supreme Court would examine the facts and circumstances surrounding the alleged invasion of privacy. * * * If the court determined that the discharge was related to a substantial and highly offensive invasion of the employee's privacy, we believe that it would conclude that the discharge violated public policy.

* * *

Only a handful of other jurisdictions have considered urinalysis programs implemented by private employers. The majority of these decisions balance the employee's privacy interest against the employer's interests in order to determine whether to uphold the programs. See, for example, Luedtke v. Nabors Alaska Drilling, Inc., 768 P.2d 1123 (Alaska 1989). In *Luedtke*, two employees challenged their employer's urinalysis program, alleging violation of their state constitutional right of privacy, common-law invasion of privacy, wrongful discharge, and breach of the covenant of good faith and fair dealing. (Under Alaska law, the public policy exception to the employment-at-will doctrine is "largely encompassed within the implied covenant of good faith and fair dealing." 768 P.2d at 1130, quoting Knight v. American Guard & Alert, Inc., 714 P.2d

788, 792 (Alaska 1986)). After determining that the relevant provision of the Alaska constitution did not apply to private action, the Alaska Supreme Court concluded that a public policy protecting an employee's right to withhold private information from his employer exists in Alaska and that violation of that policy "may rise to the level of a breach of the implied covenant of good faith and fair dealing," 768 P.2d at 1130.

* * *

The court then turned to the question "whether employer monitoring of employee drug use outside the work place is such a prohibited intrusion," id. at 1133. The court reasoned that the boundaries of the employee's right of privacy "are determined by balancing [that right] against other public policies, such as the health, safety, rights and privileges of others." Id. at 1135–36 (quoting Ravin v. State, 537 P.2d 494, 504 (Alaska 1975)). Because the *Luedtke* plaintiffs performed safety-sensitive jobs, the court concluded that the public policy supporting the protection of the health and safety of other workers justified their employer's urinalysis program. 768 P.2d at 1136.

The West Virginia Supreme Court also applied a balancing test in Twigg v. Hercules Corp., 406 S.E.2d 52 (W. Va. 1990). The case arose when the district court for the Northern District of West Virginia certified the following question to the court:

> Can the discharge of an employee for refusing to submit to urinalysis as part of a random drug test violate a substantial public policy of West Virginia and subject the employer to damages under [West Virginia law] when the employer has no individualized suspicion of drug usage and the drug test is not prohibited by state statute?

In response, the court observed that it had previously held that requiring employees to submit to polygraph tests violated the state's public policy of protecting individual privacy rights. The court then reasoned: It is unquestionable that since we do recognize a "legally protected interest in privacy" and have previously found that requiring employees to submit to polygraph examinations violates public policy based upon this privacy right, we likewise recognize that it is contrary to public policy in West Virginia for an employer to require an employee to submit to drug testing, since such testing portends an invasion of an individual's right to privacy. Id. at 55.

Even some courts that have held that urinalysis programs conducted by private employers do not violate the public policy exception to the employment-at-will doctrine have balanced the employee's interests against the employer's. Hennessey v. Coastal Eagle Point Oil Company, 247 N.J. Super. 297, 589 A.2d 170, certif. granted, 598 A.2d 897 (1991), provides an example of this approach. After refusing to apply federal and state constitutional prohibitions against unreasonable searches to private employers, the *Hennessey* court conceded, for the sake of argument, that the right of privacy may serve as a source of public policy. The court opined, however, that the the intrusion upon privacy implicated by urinalysis had been "overstated." 589 A.2d at 177. The court also observed that the urinalysis program served public policy by deterring drug use and that the employer had a legitimate interest in eliminating drug use in the workplace. Because the court considered the invasion of privacy minimal and the employer's interests substantial, it concluded, on the basis of this balancing, that the employer had not violated a clear mandate of public policy and hence that discharging an employee who tested positive for drugs did not fall within the public policy exception to the employment-at-will doctrine.

The court in *Hennessey* was much more reluctant than the *Luedtke* and *Twigg* courts to recognize the privacy interest raised by the employer's urinalysis program. We find it significant, however, that in *Hennessey* it was clear that the particular program at issue did not constitute a substantial and highly offensive invasion of privacy. First, the urine specimens were tested solely for drugs. 589 A.2d at 173. Second, although monitors were present during the collection of the specimens, the monitors stood behind the employees and were specifically instructed "not to look at any of the employees' genitalia or private parts." Id. We suspect that given these circumstances, a reasonable person would not find the program highly offensive.

Although most other jurisdictions have applied a balancing test to urinalysis programs conducted by private employers, not all have done so. In Jennings v. Minco Technology Labs, Inc., 765 S.W.2d 497 (Tex. App. 1989), for example, the Texas Court of Appeals upheld an employer's random urinalysis program without balancing the employee's interests against the employer's. The court upheld the program for two reasons. First, the court reasoned that although the Texas Supreme Court had on one occasion recognized an exception to the employment-at-will doctrine based on public policy, see Sabine Pilot, Inc. v. Hauck, 687 S.W.2d 733 (Tex. 1985), the "lower courts are not free to create additional exceptions," 765 S.W.2d at 501, particularly in the absence of a statute explicitly recognizing the public policy allegedly violated by the discharge, id. at 501 & 501 n3. Second, the court reasoned that the employer's urinalysis program would not violate plaintiff's privacy because her urine would be tested only if she consented. Id. at 502. Jennings argued that her consent would be ineffective because if she did not consent, she would lose her job, which she could not afford to do. The court rejected her argument, however, because "there cannot be one law of contracts for the rich and another for the poor." Id.

The balancing test is more consistent with Pennsylvania law than the approach taken by the Texas court in *Jennings*. Unlike the Texas courts, Pennsylvania's intermediate appellate courts have recognized a public policy exception to the employment-at-will doctrine on three occasions and have emphasized the need to examine all the circumstances in a wrongful discharge action. Moreover, although two of those cases in part relied upon public policies expressed in statutes, the

Pennsylvania courts have also recognized other sources as competent evidence of public policy. More importantly, under Pennsylvania law an employee's consent to a violation of public policy is no defense to a wrongful discharge action when that consent is obtained by the threat of dismissal.

In view of the foregoing analysis, we predict that the Pennsylvania Supreme Court would apply a balancing test to determine whether the Shop's drug and alcohol program (consisting of urinalysis and personal property searches) invaded Borse's privacy. Indeed, determining whether an alleged invasion of privacy is substantial and highly offensive to the reasonable person necessitates the use of a balancing test. The test we believe that Pennsylvania would adopt balances the employee's privacy interest against the employer's interest in maintaining a drug-free workplace in order to determine whether a reasonable person would find the employer's program highly offensive. We recognize that other jurisdictions have considered individualized suspicion and concern for safety as factors to be considered in striking the balance, see, for example, *Twigg*, 406 S.E.2d at 55 (allowing urinalysis based on individualized suspicion or when employee's job implicates safety concerns). We do not doubt that, in an appropriate case, Pennsylvania would include these factors in the balance, but we do not believe that the Pennsylvania Supreme Court would require private employers to limit urinalysis programs or personal property searches to employees suspected of drug use or to those performing safety-sensitive jobs.

Notes and Questions

1. *Intrusion Upon Seclusion?* In what way is an employer's drug testing of an employee an intrusion upon "seclusion"? Is the *Borse* court stretching or is this an appropriate application of the tort?

Consider an employer's search of an employee's locked desk or locker or personal effects? Might such a search constitute an intrusion that would require some adequate business justification? Does employer covert surveillance of private areas such as restrooms or changing rooms also constitute a potentially actionable intrusion on seclusion tort?

2. *Developments Under Massachusetts Privacy Law.* Massachusetts is one of the few states to have enacted a general privacy statute applicable to public and private employers. See G.L. c. 214, § 1B. The Massachusetts courts have dealt with drug testing policies under that statute. In Webster v. Motorola, Inc., 637 N.E.2d 203, 418 Mass. 425 (1994), the employer manufactured and sold electronic equipment, and was permitted to engage in suspicion-less testing of an account executive whose responsibilities required him to drive a company-owned vehicle 20–25,000 miles a year. The plaintiff's privacy interest was deemed outweighed by the employer's interest in ensuring that its vehicle was not operated by a person under the influence of illegal drugs. See also Folmsbee v. Tech Tool Grinding & Supply, Inc., 417 Mass. 388, 630 N.E.2d 586 (1994) (rejecting public-policy challenge to dismissal of employee for refusing to submit to mandatory drug testing):

* * * The nature of Tech Tool's business requires extreme alertness and precision. Even a slight error could result in serious harm to both employees and customers. Morin had a strong basis for suspecting that Tech Tool employees were using drugs. Thus, he was concerned for the safety of both Tech Tool's employees and its customers.

Tech Tool provided thirty days' notice prior to initiating any testing. All full-time employees, including the two owners, were required to take the test. Morin promised that anyone who tested positive would not be fired, but would be retested in thirty days and given an opportunity to undergo drug counselling at company expense.

Id. at 393, 630 N.E.2d at 589.

3. *Range of State Privacy Legislation.* Massachusetts is unusual in providing by statute for a general right to privacy. However, virtually all states have enacted laws that protect some aspects of privacy in the workplace.

a. *Access to Personnel Files.* State laws analogous to the Federal Privacy Act provide for both employee access to personnel files and also rights to obtain corrections of inaccurate information in such files. See, e.g., Mich.Comp.Laws Ann. §§ 423.501–.512.

b. *Fair Credit Reporting Laws.* There are also state analogues to the Fair Credit and Reporting Act. See, e.g., N.Y. General Business Law § 380–b(b).

c. *Regulation of Investigative Techniques or Particular Inquiries.* One category of state laws focus on particular investigative techniques. See, e.g., D.C., tit. 36, ch. 8, § 36–802 (prohibiting all use of lie detector tests); Md. Ann. Code, Cts. & Jud. Proc., § 10–401 to 410 (regulating willful interception of any wire, oral or electronic communication absent consent of all of the parties), interpreted in Schmerling v. Injured Workers' Insurance Fund, 368 Md. 434, 795 A.2d 715 (2002); N.Y. Penal Law §§ 250.00, 250.05 (class E felony to engage in unlawful wiretapping, mechanical overhearing of a conversation, or interception of an electronic communication); Cal. Penal Code § 632 (monitoring of cellular communication requires consent of all parties). New York prohibits fingerprinting of employees. See N.Y.Labor Law § 201–a (banning fingerprinting of applicants and employees).

Another category of laws focus on particular pre-employment inquiries thought invasive of personal privacy, see, e.g., Md.Ann.Code, art. 100, § 95A (questions pertaining to any physical, psychological or psychiatric illness or treatment not bearing "a direct, material, and timely relationship" to applicant's fitness); or improperly attaching adverse consequences to arrest or conviction records, see, e.g., Md.Ann.Code, art. 27, § 740 (inquiry into criminal charges not resulting in conviction); Mass.G.L.A., c. 151B, § 4(9) (same); Va. Code 19.2–392.4 (no inquiry into arrest not resulting in conviction or which was expunged; inquiry into convictions must be job-related). In some states, inquiry into convictions records is permitted, but adverse action cannot be taken unless conviction meets job-related test. See, e.g., N.Y. Executive Law § 296 (15) & N.Y. Correction Law Art. 23–A & §§ 752–53. California allows public safety officers an opportunity to review adverse comments in their personnel files and file written responses within 30 days.

See Calif. Gov. Code §§ 630 et seq., interpreted in Riverside County v. Superior Court, 27 Cal.4th 793, 118 Cal.Rptr.2d 167, 42 P.3d 1034 (2002).

Curbs on certain types of surveillance of employees can be found in, e.g., West's Ann.Cal.Pub.Utility Code § 8251; Kan.Stat.Ann. § 44–808(6); Nev. Rev.Stat., vol. 32, Detectives & Spotters Law § 613.160; N.Y.Labor Law § 704(1).

d. *Medical Records Privacy & Identity Privacy.* In Pettus v. Cole, 49 Cal.App.4th 402, 57 Cal.Rptr.2d 46 (1st Dist.1996), employer-selected psychiatrists who examined Pettus in connection with a disability-leave request violated the Calif. Medical Information Act (CMIA) by providing his employer with a detailed report of their examinations without the employee's authorization; and the employer was held to have violated both Pettus's CMIA and state constitutional privacy rights by using this medical information to force him, under pain of discharge, to enroll in an inpatient alcohol treatment program. See also HIPAA privacy regulations, pp. 872–73 supra.

Restrictions on use of employee social security numbers are contained in Cal. Civ. Code § 1798.85. See generally Michael J. Gray, The New Identity Crisis, Corporate Counsel, Dec. 2003, p. 57.

4. *State Drug Testing Laws.* A number of state laws significantly regulate private employer drug testing programs. See, e.g., Conn.Gen.Stat. Ann., P.A. 87–551 L.1987 (1987 App.) (permitting random testing only of applicants and where authorized by federal law or where the employee serves in a "high-risk" or "safety-sensitive" occupation; otherwise, "reasonable suspicion required for testing); Vt.Stat.Ann., tit. 21 §§ 511–20 (random testing permitted only of applicants and where required by federal law; otherwise, only probable-cause testing is permitted and only where employer has an employee assistance program (EAP) and will not terminate employee unless employee tests positive after completion of EAP).

State civil rights laws may impose additional restrictions on employer testing programs. See Doe v. Roe, Inc., 160 A.D.2d 255, 553 N.Y.S.2d 364 (App.Div. 1st Dept.1990), affirming 143 Misc.2d 156, 539 N.Y.S.2d 876 (Sup.Ct.N.Y.Co.1989) (test which cannot accurately distinguish between opiate users and consumers of lawful foodstuffs or medications may discriminate against individuals who are inaccurately perceived as disabled).

5. *Role of "Public Policy" Cause of Action.* A number of states relying on statutory and state constitutional provisions have recognized a "public policy" cause of action to protect employee privacy interests. See, e.g., Baughman v. Wal–Mart Stores, Inc., 215 W.Va. 45, 592 S.E.2d 824, 20 (BNA) IER Cas. 1199 (2003) (state public policy permits pre-employment testing of applicants, but not testing of incumbent employees absent "good faith objective suspicion" of drug use or safety considerations); Hennessey v. Coastal Eagle Point Oil Co., 129 N.J. 81, 609 A.2d 11 (1992) (incorporating state constitutional privacy protections into "public policy" cause of action regulating drug-testing policy, but holding that oil refinery's firing of at-will employee in safety-sensitive position for failing urine test was not actionable); Borse v. Piece Goods Shop, Inc., 963 F.2d 611, 622 (3d Cir.1992) (public policy embodied in Pennsylvania common law for tortious intrusion on seclusion renders discharge unlawful where it is "related to a substantial and highly offensive invasion of employee's privacy"—applied to aspects of

drug-testing policy); Luedtke v. Nabors Alaska Drilling Inc., 768 P.2d 1123, 1133 (Alaska 1989) ("there is sufficient evidence to support the conclusion that there exists a public policy protecting spheres of employee conduct into which employers may not intrude"; however, monitoring of oil drilling rig employees for off-duty drug use held permissible); cf. Novosel v. Nationwide Insurance Co., p. 723 supra.

6. *Role of State Constitutions.* State constitutions can also provide a direct source of protection for the privacy of private sector employees. For instance, the right of privacy under the California Constitution, art. I, sec. 1, reaches private action; see White v. Davis, 13 Cal.3d 757, 120 Cal.Rptr. 94, 533 P.2d 222 (1975); Hill v. National Collegiate Athletic Assn., 7 Cal.4th 1, 26 Cal.Rptr.2d 834 865 P.2d 633 (1994) (en banc). But see Cisco v. United Parcel Services, 328 Pa.Super. 300, 476 A.2d 1340 (1984) (employer need not rehire former employee acquitted of suspected theft; constitutional guarantees applicable to criminal defendants do not extend to private-sector employees).

In light of the reach of the California constitutional privacy guaranty, Loder v. City of Glendale, 14 Cal.4th 846, 59 Cal.Rptr.2d 696, 927 P.2d 1200 (1997), although a public sector case, is relevant to the private sector. In *Loder*, the California high court held that the city's suspicion less drug testing of all current employees was not reasonable under the fourth amendment, but neither the federal nor state constitutional privacy guarantee was violated by requiring all job applicants offered positions to submit to drug testing as part of pre-employment medical examinations:

> [U]rinalysis drug testing of job applicants that is administered as part of an otherwise lawful preemployment medical examination represents much less of an intrusion on reasonable expectations of privacy than does drug testing in other contexts. As a general matter, a job applicant reasonably must anticipate that a prospective employer may require that he or she undergo [such an] examination before the hiring process is completed. When drug testing is conducted as part of a required preemployment medical examination that typically includes a urinalysis for medical conditions or diseases, the testing does not impose the usual intrusion on privacy that results when an individual is required to provide a separate urine sample on demand. * * *

> [B]ecause of the significant problems—absenteeism, increased safety concerns, tardiness, reduced productivity, and increased risk of turnover— typically posed by an employee who abuses drugs or alcohol, an employer has a legitimate and substantial interest in determining whether or not an applicant currently is engaging in such conduct before the employer finalizes any hiring decision. And because an employer normally has had no opportunity to observe a job applicant over a period of time under circumstances that might alert the employer to a potential drug or alcohol problem, the employer has a greater need to conduct suspicionless drug testing of job applicants than it does to conduct such testing of current employees. * * *

Id. at 897, 59 Cal.Rptr.2d at 728–29, 927 P.2d at 1232–33. The court remanded the question whether the city could enact a properly limited urinalysis testing program for those seeking promotions. See id. at 899, 59 Cal.Rptr.2d at 730, 927 P.2d at 1234.

7. *Federal Preemption?* State statutes and decisions protective of employee privacy may be found to be preempted by federal law in certain circumstances. See, e.g., French v. Pan Am Express, Inc., 869 F.2d 1 (1st Cir.1989) (Rhode Island law barring drug testing as a condition of employment impinges on Federal Aviation Act's regulation of pilot qualification requirements); Jackson v. Liquid Carbonic Corp., 863 F.2d 111 (1st Cir.1988) (§ 301 of Labor Management Relations Act (LMRA), 29 U.S.C. § 185, preempts reliance on Massachusetts privacy statute to bar drug testing of union-represented employees); but see Cramer v. Consolidated Freightways, Inc., 255 F.3d 683 (9th Cir. 2001) (en banc) (no preemption where privacy right is not negotiable or there is no clear waiver in the collective agreement). The Oregon drug testing law (Okla. Stat. tit. 40, §§ 551–565) was sustained against § 301, LMRA preemption challenge in Karnes v. Boeing Co., 335 F.3d 1189(10th Cir. 2003). Federal preemption issues are further considered at pp. 1167–97 infra.

b. *Personal Autonomy*

RULON–MILLER v. IBM CORP.

California Court of Appeals, First District, 1984.
162 Cal.App.3d 241, 208 Cal.Rptr. 524.

RUSHING, J.

International Business Machines (IBM) appeals from the judgment entered against it after a jury awarded $100,000 compensatory and $200,000 punitive damages to respondent (Virginia Rulon–Miller) on claims of wrongful discharge and intentional infliction of emotional distress. Rulon–Miller was a low-level marketing manager at IBM in its office products division in San Francisco. Her termination as a marketing manager at IBM came about as a result of an accusation made by her immediate supervisor, defendant Callahan, of a romantic relationship with the manager of a rival office products firm, QYX.

IBM is an international manufacturer of computers, office equipment and telecommunications systems. As well, it offers broad general services in the data processing field. It is reputed to be the single most successful high technology firm in the world. It is also a major force in the low technology field of typewriters and office equipment.

IBM is an employer traditionally thought to provide great security to its employees as well as an environment of openness and dignity. The company is organized into divisions, and each division is, to an extent, independent of others. The company prides itself on providing career opportunities to its employees, and respondent represents a good example of this. She started in 1967 as a receptionist in the Philadelphia Data Center. She was told that "career opportunities are available to [employees] as long as they are performing satisfactorily and are willing to accept new challenges." While she worked at the data center in Philadelphia, she attended night school and earned a baccalaureate degree. She was promoted to equipment scheduler and not long after received her first merit award. The company moved her to Atlanta, Georgia where she spent 15 months as a data processor. She was transferred to the office products division and was assigned the position of "marketing support representative" in San Francisco where she trained users (i.e., customers) of newly-purchased IBM equipment. Respondent was promoted to "product planner" in 1973 where her duties included overseeing the performance of new office products in the marketplace. As a product planner, she moved to Austin, Texas and later to Lexington, Kentucky. Thereafter, at the urging of her managers that she go into sales in the office products division, she enrolled at the IBM sales school in Dallas. After graduation, she was assigned to San Francisco.

Her territory was the financial district. She was given a performance plan by her management which set forth the company's expectations of her. She was from time to time thereafter graded against that plan on a scale of one through five with a grade of one being the highest. After her first year on the job, she was given a rating of one and was felt by her manager to be a person who rated at the top of IBM's scale.

A little over a year after she began in San Francisco, IBM reorganized its office products division into two separate functions, one called office systems and another called office products. Respondent was assigned to office systems; again she was given ratings of one and while there received a series of congratulatory letters from her superiors and was promoted to marketing representative. She was one of the most successful sales persons in the office and received a number of prizes and awards for her sales efforts. IBM's system of rewarding salespersons has a formalistic aspect about it that allows for subtle distinctions to be made while putting great emphasis on performance; respondent exercised that reward system to its fullest. She was a very successful seller of typewriters and other office equipment.

She was then put into a program called "Accelerated Career Development Program" which was a way of rewarding certain persons who were seen by their superiors as having management potential. IBM's prediction of her future came true and in 1978 she was named a marketing manager in the office products branch.

IBM knew about respondent's relationship with Matt Blum well before her appointment as a manager. Respondent met Blum in 1976 when he was an account manager for IBM. That they were dating was widely known within the organization. In 1977 Blum left IBM to join QYX, an IBM competitor, and was transferred to Philadelphia. When Blum returned to San Francisco in the summer of 1978, IBM personnel were aware that he and respondent began dating again. This seemed to present no problems to respondent's superiors, as Callahan confirmed when she was promoted to manager. Respondent testified: "Somewhat in passing, Phil said: I heard the other day you were dating Matt Blum, and I said: Oh. And he said, I don't have any problem with that. You're my number one pick. I just want to assure you that you are my selection." The relationship with Blum was also known to Regional Manager Gary Nelson who agreed with Callahan. Neither Callahan nor Nelson raised any issue of conflict of interest because of the Blum relationship.

Respondent flourished in her management position, and the company, apparently grateful for her efforts, gave her a $4,000 merit raise in 1979 and told her that she was doing a good job. A week later, her manager, Phillip Callahan, left a message that he wanted to see her.

When she walked into Callahan's office he confronted her with the question of whether she was dating Matt Blum. She wondered at the relevance of the inquiry and he said the dating constituted a "conflict of interest," and told her to stop dating Blum or lose her job and said she had a "couple of days to a week" to think about it.

The next day Callahan called her in again, told her "he had made up her mind for her," and when she protested, dismissed her. IBM and Callahan claim that he merely "transferred" respondent to another division.

The initial discussion between Callahan and respondent of her relationship with Blum is important. We must accept the version of the facts most favorable to the respondent herein. (*Nestle v. City of Santa Monica* (1972) 6 Cal.3d 920, 925, 101 Cal.Rptr. 568, 496 P.2d 480.) When Callahan questioned her relationship with Blum, respondent invoked her right to privacy in her personal life relying on existing IBM policies. A threshold inquiry is thus presented whether respondent could reasonably rely on those policies for job protection. Any conflicting action by the company would be wrongful in that it would constitute a violation of her contract rights. (*Lord v. Goldberg* (1889) 81 Cal. 596, 22 P. 1126; *Pugh v. See's Candies, Inc.* (1981) 116 Cal.App.3d 311, 171 Cal.Rptr. 917.)

* * * The covenant of good faith and fair dealing embraces a number of rights, obligations, and considerations implicit in contractual relations and certain other relationships. At least two of those considerations are relevant herein. The duty of fair dealing by an employer is, simply stated, a requirement that like cases be treated alike. Implied in this, of course, is that the company, if it has rules and regulations, apply those rules and regulations to its employees as well as affording its employees their protection.

* * *

In this case, there is a close question of whether those rules or regulations permit IBM to inquire into the purely personal life of the employee. If so, an attendant question is whether such a policy was applied consistently, particularly as between men and women. The distinction is important because the right of privacy, a constitutional right in California (*City and County of San Francisco v. Superior Court* (1981) 125 Cal.App.3d 879, 883, 178 Cal.Rptr. 435), could be implicated by the IBM inquiry. Much of the testimony below concerned what those policies were. The evidence was conflicting on the meaning of certain

IBM policies. We observe ambiguity in the application but not in the intent. The "Watson Memo" (so called because it was signed by a former chairman of IBM) provided as follows:

"TO ALL IBM MANAGERS:

"The line that separates an individual's on-the-job business life from his other life as a private citizen is at times well-defined and at other times indistinct. But the line does exist, and you and I, as managers in IBM, must be able to recognize that line.

"I have seen instances where managers took disciplinary measures against employees for actions or conduct that are not rightfully the company's concern. These managers usually justified their decisions by citing their personal code of ethics and morals or by quoting some fragment of company policy that seemed to support their position. Both arguments proved unjust on close examination. What we need, in every case, is balanced judgment which weighs the needs of the business and the rights of the individual.

"Our primary objective as IBM managers is to further the business of this company by leading our people properly and measuring quantity and quality of work and effectiveness on the job against clearly set standards of responsibility and compensation. This is performance—and performance is, in the final analysis, the one thing that the company can insist on from everyone.

"We have concern with an employee's off-the-job behavior only when it reduces his ability to perform regular job assignments, interferes with the job performance of other employees, or if his outside behavior affects the reputation of the company in a major way. When on-the-job performance is acceptable, I can think of few situations in which outside activities could result in disciplinary action or dismissal.

"When such situations do come to your attention, you should seek the advice and counsel of the next appropriate level of management and the personnel department in determining what action—if any—is called for. Action should be taken only when a legitimate interest of the company is injured or jeopardized. Furthermore the damage must be clear beyond reasonable doubt and not based on hasty decisions about what one person might think is good for the company.

"IBM's first basic belief is respect for the individual, and the essence of this belief is a strict regard for his right to personal privacy. This idea should never be compromised easily or quickly.

"/s/ Tom Watson, Jr."

It is clear that this company policy insures to the employee both the right of privacy and the right to hold a job even though "off-the-job behavior" might not be approved of by the employee's manager.

IBM had adopted policies governing employee conduct. Some of those policies were collected in a document known as the "Performance and Recognition" (PAR) Manual. IBM relies on the following portion of the PAR Manual:

"A conflict of interest can arise when an employee is involved in activity for personal gain, which for any reason is in conflict with IBM's business interests. Generally speaking, 'moonlighting' is defined as working at some activity for personal gain outside of your IBM job. If you do perform outside work, you have a special responsibility to avoid any conflict with IBM's business interests.

"Obviously, you cannot solicit or perform in competition with IBM product or service offerings. Outside work cannot be performed on IBM time, including 'personal' time off. You cannot use IBM equipment, materials, resources, or 'inside' information for outside work. Nor should you solicit business or clients or perform outside work on IBM premises.

"Employees must be free of any significant investment or association of their own or of their immediate family's [sic], in competitors or suppliers, which might interfere or be thought to interfere with the independent exercise of their judgment in the best interests of IBM."

This policy of IBM is entitled "Gifts" and appears to be directed at "moonlighting" and soliciting outside business or clients on IBM premises. It prohibits "significant investment" in competitors or suppliers of IBM. It also prohibits "association" with such persons "which might interfere or be thought to interfere with the independent exercise of their judgment in the best interests of IBM."

Callahan based his action against respondent on a "conflict of interest." But the record shows that IBM did not interpret this policy to prohibit a romantic relationship. Callahan admitted that there was no company rule or policy requiring an employee to terminate friendships with fellow employees who leave and join competitors. Gary Nelson, Callahan's superior, also confirmed that IBM had no policy against employees socializing with competitors.

This issue was hotly contested with respondent claiming that the "conflict of interest" claim was a pretext for her unjust termination. Whether it was presented a fact question for the jury.

Do the policies reflected in this record give IBM a right to terminate an employee for a conflict of interest? The answer must be yes, but whether respondent's conduct constituted such was for the jury. We observe that while respondent was successful, her primary job did not give her access to sensitive information which could have been useful to competitors. She was, after all, a seller of typewriters and office equipment. Respondent's brief makes much of the concession by IBM that there was no evidence whatever that respondent had given any information or help to IBM's competitor QYX. It really is no concession at all;

she did not have the information or help to give. Even so, the question is one of substantial evidence. The evidence is abundant that there was no conflict of interest by respondent.

* * *

The contract rights in an employment agreement or the covenant of good faith and fair dealing gives both employer and employee the right to breach and to respond in damages. Here, however, the question is whether if IBM elected to exercise that right it should also be liable for punitive damages, because of its intentional infliction of emotional distress. The issue is whether the conduct of the marketing manager of IBM was "extreme and outrageous," a question involving the objective facts of what happened in the confrontation between the employee and employer as well as the special susceptibility of suffering of the employee. * * *

To determine if Callahan's conduct could reach the level of extreme, outrageous, and atrocious conduct, requires detailed examination. First, there was a decided element of deception in Callahan acting as if the relationship with Blum was something new. The evidence was clear he knew of the involvement of respondent and Blum well before her promotion. Second, he acted in flagrant disregard of IBM policies prohibiting him from inquiring into respondent's "off job behavior." By giving respondent "a few days" to think about the choice between job and lover, he implied that if she gave up Blum she could have her job. He then acted without giving her "a few days to think about it" or giving her the right to choose.

So far the conduct is certainly unfair but not atrocious. What brings Callahan's conduct to an actionable level is the way he brought these several elements together in the second meeting with respondent. He said, after calling her in, "I'm making the decision for you." The implications of his statement were richly ambiguous, meaning she could not act or think for herself, or that he was acting in her best interest, or that she persisted in a romantic involvement inconsistent with her job. When she protested, he fired her.

The combination of statements and conduct would under any reasoned view tend to humiliate and degrade respondent. To be denied a right granted to all other employees for conduct unrelated to her work was to degrade her as a person. His unilateral action in purporting to remove any free choice on her part contrary to his earlier assurances also would support a conclusion that his conduct was intended to emphasize that she was powerless to do anything to assert her rights as an IBM employee. And such powerlessness is one of the most debilitating kinds of human oppression. The sum of such evidence clearly supports the jury finding of extreme and outrageous conduct.

Notes and Questions

1. *"Implied in Fact" Contract?* After the California high court's decision in *Guz*, p. 768 supra, would *Rulon–Miller* come out the same way on the contract cause of action?

2. *Anti–Fraternization Policies.* Might the public policy tort actions surveyed in chapter 11 also have provided a model for a cause of action for Rulon–Miller that was not dependent on any promises from IBM? Do anti-fraternization policies offend any clear public policy? Do employers have any legitimate interest in such policies? For cases in the public sector, compare Briggs v. North Muskegon Police Dept., 563 F.Supp. 585 (W.D.Mich.1983) (striking down dismissal of part-time police officer for living with someone not his spouse), with Shawgo v. Spradlin, 701 F.2d 470 (5th Cir.1983) (sustaining constitutional privacy challenge to rule prohibiting cohabitation among police officers); also Montgomery v. Carr, 101 F.3d 1117 (6th Cir. 1996) (rational-basis scrutiny applies to rule against married teachers in the same school). Consider also the following statutory theories for challenging no-dating and no-spouse policies.

a. *"Legal Activities" Laws.* In New York State v. Wal–Mart Stores, Inc., 207 A.D.2d 150, 621 N.Y.S.2d 158 (3d Dept.1995), Wal–Mart terminated two employees for violating its "fraternization" policy, which prohibited a "dating relationship" between a married employee and another employee not the former's spouse. Plaintiffs, a man and a woman (separated but not divorced from her husband), sued under New York Labor Law § 201–d, which prohibits discriminatory treatment for engaging in "legal recreational activities" off-premises and during nonworking hours. The appellate court held that dating activity was not a "recreational activity" within the meaning of the statute. Contra, Pasch v. Katz Media Group, No. 94 Civ. 8554, 1995 WL 469710, 10 (BNA) IER Cas. 1574 (S.D.N.Y. Aug.8, 1995).

b. *"Marital Status" Laws.* Do anti-fraternization polices violate state laws barring discrimination on account of "marital status," on the theory that married couples are more favorably treated under these policies? Do these laws protect only those who are married? For a decision sustaining a challenge to an anti-fraternization policy alleging discrimination against the non-married, see Ross v. Stouffer Hotel Co., 72 Haw. 350, 816 P.2d 302 (1991).

c. *Antidiscrimination Laws.* For Title VII challenges, see Sarsha v. Sears, Roebuck & Co., 3 F.3d 1035 (7th Cir.1993) (rejecting Title VII challenge to no-dating policy applied to supervisory employees); Yuhas v. Libbey–Owens–Ford Co., 562 F.2d 496 (7th Cir.1977) (finding employer's "no spouse" policy had disparate impact on women under Title VII, but was job related as rule to minimize perception of favoritism among coworkers).

See generally Timothy D. Chandler, Rafael Gely, Jack Howard & Robin Cheramie, Spouses Need Not Apply: The Legality of Antinepotism and Non–Spouse Rules, 39 San Diego L. Rev. 31 (2002); Anna M. Depaolo, Note, Antifraternizing Policies and At–Will Employment: Counseling for a Better Relationship, 1996 Ann. Survey of Amer. L. 59.

4. *Should Employers Promulgate Privacy Policies?* In view of *Rulon–Miller,* why might an employer still want to issue a policy memorandum that suggests limits on its authority over employees' off-premises conduct? For the view that employers should promulgate policies broadly protective of employee privacy interests, see David Ewing, Freedom Inside the Organization: Bringing Civil Liberties in the Workplace (1977).

5. *When Is Off–Premises Conduct Job–Related?* What off-premises employee conduct should be the basis for discipline or discharge? How should an employer treat an employee arrested for tax fraud who, in return for a guilty plea, receives a suspended sentence and is available for work? How about an employee who negotiates a similar suspension on a child battery charge? An employee who gets intimately involved with the son or daughter of an important client? Job applicants who smoke? See City of North Miami v. Kurtz, 653 So.2d 1025 (Fla. 1995) (smoker refused to sign pre-employment statement that he had not smoked in previous two years; rejecting state constitutional challenge); Grusendorf v. City of Oklahoma, 816 F.2d 539 (10th Cir. 1987) (off-duty smoking by firefighter-trainee in contravention of department policy; rejecting federal due process challenge).

6. *Confidentiality and Employee Assistance Programs.* The breach of a promise of confidentiality made as part of company drug rehabilitation assistance program may be actionable. See, e.g., Bratt v. IBM Corp., 785 F.2d 352 (1st Cir.1986); see generally John M. Capron & Myra K. Creighton, No Good Deed Goes Unpunished: Employee Assistance Programs as Sources of Liability, 24 Employee Rels. L.J. 79 (no.3, Winter 1998).

3. *Collective Bargaining Agreements*

Unionized private sector employees generally enjoy more protection of their privacy, as well as of their job security, than do their nonunionized counterparts. Unions can help protect employee privacy both by the negotiation of express contractual provisions and by encouraging arbitrators to find implied protections when construing labor agreements. The NLRB has ruled that employers subject to the NLRA have a duty to bargain with exclusive bargaining representatives before implementing a drug testing program for existing employees, see Johnson–Bateman Co., 295 N.L.R.B. No. 26 (1989), but need not bargain over the testing of applicants who are not yet part of the bargaining unit, see Minneapolis Star Tribune, 295 N.L.R.B. No. 63 (1989). The Supreme Court, however, has held that an employer subject to the Railway Labor Act could implement a drug testing program without bargaining when it had an "arguable" claim that it was authorized to initiate the program by the union's acceptance of its past practices during periodic examinations. This claim was to be resolved by the Act's grievance and arbitration process as a "minor dispute." See Consolidated Rail Corp. v. Railway Labor Executives' Ass'n, 491 U.S. 299, 109 S.Ct. 2477, 105 L.Ed.2d 250 (1989); see also Teamsters v. Southwest Airlines, Inc., 875 F.2d 1129 (5th Cir.1989) (arguable justification for drug program in management rights clause).

Even where unions have not negotiated explicit privacy-protective provisions, they have often been successful in persuading arbitrators to find in the labor agreement implied privacy guarantees. Such arbitrators have used as bases for such awards the same sources that have been invoked for construing the meaning of "just cause": past firm or industry practice, negotiating history, or perhaps general social standards of fairness that the parties can be assumed to have accepted. There is a division among arbitrators over the extent to which the "just cause" standard incorporates constitutional norms limiting unreasonable searches and discipline for off-premises conduct. The majority of arbitrators reject per se application of constitutional doctrine, but some nonetheless refer to the doctrine as a guide for gauging past practice or accepted principles defining the "common law of the shop." See generally Proceedings of the 23rd Annual Meeting of the National Academy of Arbitrators, Surveillance and the Labor Arbitration Process: Arbitration and the Expanding Role of Neutrals (G. Somers & B. Dennis, eds. 1970).

Arbitration cases treating employee drug testing are illustrative. Although these cases evidence a division of authority, they also indicate that even in the absence of any specific restrictions on employer authority many arbitrators have questioned both the institution of drug tests and discipline resulting from such tests. Arbitrators have sometimes demanded individualized suspicion of impairment or on-the-premises drug use; they have sometimes imposed a higher standard of proof for discipline based on positive test results; and they have sometimes required, under progressive discipline principles, an opportunity for rehabilitation before discharge. See generally Denenberg & Denenberg, Drug Testing from the Arbitrator's Perspective, 11 Nova L.Rev. 377 (1987); Levin & Denenberg, How Arbitrators View Drug Abuse, 31 Arb.J. 97 (1976); Wynns, Arbitration Standards in Drug Discharge Cases, 34 Arb.J. 19 (1976). For arbitrator scrutiny of employer surveillance practices, see Edward Hertenstein, Electronic Monitoring in the Workplace: How Arbitrators Have Ruled, Dispute Resol. J. (Fall 1997), pp. 36 ff.

Chapter Fourteen

POST–TERMINATION RESTRAINTS

A. INTRODUCTION

In this chapter, we explore the extent to which employers lawfully may restrict the freedom of departing employees to compete in the same business and to use information these employees acquired in their prior positions. The issues treated here have taken on greater saliency in recent years as "knowledge" workers have become a growing segment of the U.S. workforce and as many "internal labor market" arrangements are undergoing change. As we move to a more mobile labor force, post-termination restraints will become an ever more prominent feature of U.S. employment law.

B. NO–COMPETE COVENANTS

BDO SEIDMAN v. HIRSHBERG
Court of Appeals of New York, 1999.
93 N.Y.2d 382, 690 N.Y.S.2d 854, 712 N.E.2d 1220.

LEVINE, J.

BDO Seidman (BDO), a general partnership of certified public accountants, appeals from the affirmance of an order of the Supreme Court granting summary judgment dismissing its complaint against defendant, who was formerly employed as an accountant with the firm. The central issue before us is whether the "reimbursement clause" in an agreement between the parties, requiring defendant to compensate BDO for serving any client of the firm's Buffalo office within 18 months after the termination of his employment, is an invalid and unenforceable restrictive covenant. The courts below so held.

FACTS AND PROCEDURAL HISTORY

BDO is a national accounting firm having 40 offices throughout the United States, including four in New York State. Defendant began employment in BDO's Buffalo office in 1984, when the accounting firm he had been working for was merged into BDO, its partners becoming

901

BDO partners. In 1989, defendant was promoted to the position of manager, apparently a step immediately below attaining partner status. As a condition of receiving the promotion, defendant was required to sign a "Manager's Agreement," the provisions of which are at issue. In Paragraph "SIXTH" defendant expressly acknowledged that a fiduciary relationship existed between him and the firm by reason of his having received various disclosures which would give him an advantage in attracting BDO clients. Based upon that stated premise, defendant agreed that if, within 18 months following the termination of his employment, he served any former client of BDO's Buffalo office, he would compensate BDO "for the loss and damages suffered" in an amount equal to one and one half times the fees BDO had charged that client over the last fiscal year of the client's patronage. Defendant was to pay such amount in five annual installments.

Defendant resigned from BDO in October 1993. This action was commenced in January 1995. During pretrial discovery, BDO submitted a list of 100 former clients of its Buffalo office, allegedly lost to defendant, who were billed a total of $138,000 in the year defendant left the firm's practice.

Defendant denied serving some of the clients, averred that a substantial number of them were personal clients he had brought to the firm through his own outside contacts, and also claimed that with respect to some clients, he had not been the primary BDO representative servicing the account. * * *

Discussion

Concededly, the Manager's Agreement defendant signed does not prevent him from competing for new clients, nor does it expressly bar him from serving BDO clients. Instead, it requires him to pay "for the loss and damages" sustained by BDO in losing any of its clients to defendant within 18 months after his departure, an amount equivalent to one and one half times the last annual billing for any such client who became the client of defendant.

Nonetheless, it is not seriously disputed that the agreement, in its purpose and effect, is a form of ancillary employee anti-competitive agreement that is not per se unlawful but will be carefully scrutinized by the courts. * * *

The modern, prevailing common law standard of reasonableness for employee agreements not to compete applies a three-pronged test. A restraint is reasonable only if it: (1) is no greater than is required for the protection of the legitimate interest of the employer, (2) does not impose undue hardship on the employee, and (3) is not injurious to the public (see, e.g., *Technical Aid Corp. v. Allen*, 134 N.H. 1, 8, 591 A.2d 262, 265–266 * * *; Restatement [Second] of Contracts § 188). A violation of any prong renders the covenant invalid.

New York has adopted this prevailing standard of reasonableness in determining the validity of employee agreements not to compete. "In this context a restrictive covenant will only be subject to specific enforcement to the extent that it is reasonable in time and area, necessary to protect the employer's legitimate interests, not harmful to the general public and not unreasonably burdensome to the employee" (*Reed, Roberts Assocs. v. Strauman*, 40 N.Y.2d 303, 307, 386 N.Y.S.2d 677, 353 N.E.2d 590).

In general, we have strictly applied the rule to limit enforcement of broad restraints on competition. Thus, in *Reed, Roberts Assocs.* (supra), we limited the cognizable employer interests under the first prong of the common law rule to the protection against misappropriation of the employer's trade secrets or of confidential customer lists, or protection from competition by a former employee whose services are unique or extraordinary (40 N.Y.2d at 308).

With agreements not to compete between professionals, however, we have given greater weight to the interests of the employer in restricting competition within a confined geographical area. In *Gelder Med. Group v. Webber* (41 N.Y.2d 680, 394 N.Y.S.2d 867, 363 N.E.2d 573) and *Karpinski v. Ingrasci* (28 N.Y.2d 45, 320 N.Y.S.2d 1, 268 N.E.2d 751), we enforced total restraints on competition, in limited rural locales, permanently in *Karpinski* and for five years in *Gelder*. The rationale for the differential application of the common law rule of reasonableness expressed in our decisions was that professionals are deemed to provide "unique or extraordinary" services (see, *Reed, Roberts Assocs. v. Strauman*, supra, 40 N.Y.2d at 308).

BDO urges that accountancy is entitled to the status of a learned profession and, as such, the *Karpinski* and *Gelder Medical Group* precedents militate in favor of the validity of the restrictive covenant here. We agree that accountancy has all the earmarks of a learned profession * * *. [However, t]his Court's rationale for giving wider latitude to covenants between members of a learned profession[1] because their services are unique or extraordinary (*Reed, Roberts Assocs.*, supra) does not realistically apply to the actual context of the anti-competitive agreement here. In the instant case, BDO is a national accounting firm seeking to enforce the agreement within a market consisting of the entirety of a major metropolitan area. Moreover, defendant's unchallenged averments indicate that his status in the firm was not based upon the uniqueness or extraordinary nature of the accounting services he generally performed on behalf of the firm, but in major part on his ability to attract a corporate clientele. Nor was there any proof that defendant possessed any unique or extraordinary ability as an accountant that would give him a competitive advantage over BDO. Moreover,

---

1. Law firm partnership agreements represent an exception to the liberality with which we have previously treated restraints on competition in the learned professions. Our decisions invalidating anti-competitive clauses in such agreements were not based on application of the common law rule, but upon enforcement of the public policy reflected in DR 2–108(A) of the Code of Professional Responsibility (see, 22 NYCRR 1200.13). There is no counterpart to DR 2–108(A) in the rules regulating the ethical conduct of accountants. * * *

the contexts of the agreements not to compete in *Karpinski* and *Gelder Medical Group* were entirely different. In each case, the former associate would have been in direct competition with the promisee-practitioner for referrals from a narrow group of primary health providers in a rural, geographical market for their medical or dental practice specialty.

Thus, our learned profession precedents do not obviate the need for independent scrutiny of the anti-competitive provisions of the Manager's Agreement under the tripartite common law standard. Close analysis of Paragraph SIXTH of the agreement under the first prong of the common law rule, to identify the legitimate interest of BDO and determine whether the covenant is no more restrictive than is necessary to protect that interest, leads us to conclude that the covenant as written is overbroad in some respects. BDO claims that the legitimate interest it is entitled to protect is its entire client base, which it asserts a modern, large accounting firm expends considerable time and money building and maintaining. However, the only justification for imposing an employee agreement not to compete is to forestall unfair competition (see, *Columbia Ribbon & Carbon Mfg. Co. v. A–1–A Corp.*, 42 N.Y.2d at 499). It seems self-evident that a former employee may be capable of fairly competing for an employer's clients by refraining from use of unfair means to compete. If the employee abstains from unfair means in competing for those clients, the employer's interest in preserving its client base against the competition of the former employee is no more legitimate and worthy of contractual protection than when it vies with unrelated competitors for those clients.

* * * Protection of customer relationships the employee acquired in the course of employment may indeed be a legitimate interest. [Where employees work closely with clients or customers over a long period of time,] the employee has been enabled to share in the goodwill of a client or customer which the employer's overall efforts and expenditures created. The employer has a legitimate interest in preventing former employees from exploiting or appropriating the goodwill of a client or customer, which had been created and maintained at the employer's expense, to the employer's competitive detriment.

It follows from the foregoing that BDO's legitimate interest here is protection against defendant's competitive use of client relationships which BDO enabled him to acquire through his performance of accounting services for the firm's clientele during the course of his employment. Extending the anti-competitive covenant to BDO's clients with whom a relationship with defendant did not develop through assignments to perform direct, substantive accounting services would, therefore, violate the first prong of the common law rule: it would constitute a restraint "greater than is needed to protect" these legitimate interests (Restatement [Second] of Contracts § 188[1][a]). * * *

To the extent, then, that paragraph SIXTH of the Manager's Agreement requires defendant to compensate BDO for lost patronage of clients with whom he never acquired a relationship through the direct provision of substantive accounting services during his employment, the covenant is invalid and unenforceable. By a parity of reasoning, it would be unreasonable to extend the covenant to personal clients of defendant who came to the firm solely to avail themselves of his services and only as a result of his own independent recruitment efforts, which BDO neither subsidized nor otherwise financially supported as part of a program of client development. Because the goodwill of those clients was not acquired through the expenditure of BDO's resources, the firm has no legitimate interest in preventing defendant from competing for their patronage. Indeed, enforcement of the restrictive covenant as to defendant's personal clients would permit BDO to appropriate goodwill created and maintained through defendant's efforts, essentially turning on its head the principal justification to uphold any employee agreement not to compete based on protection of customer or client relationships.

Except for the overbreadth in the foregoing two respects, the restrictions in paragraph SIXTH do not violate the tripartite common law test for reasonableness. The restraint on serving BDO clients is limited to 18 months, and to clients of BDO's Buffalo office. The time constraint appears to represent a reasonably brief interlude to enable the firm to replace the client relationship and goodwill defendant was permitted to acquire with some of its clients. Defendant is free to compete immediately for new business in any market and, if the overbroad provisions of the covenant are struck, to retain his personal clients and those clients of BDO's that he had not served to any significant extent while employed at the firm. He has averred that BDO's list of lost accounts contains a number of clients in both categories. Thus, there is scant evidence suggesting that the covenant, if cured of overbreadth, would work an undue hardship on defendant.

Moreover, given the likely broad array of accounting services available in the greater Buffalo area, and the limited remaining class of BDO clientele affected by the covenant, it cannot be said that the restraint, as narrowed, would seriously impinge on the availability of accounting services in the Buffalo area from which the public may draw, or cause any significant dislocation in the market or create a monopoly in accounting services in that locale. These factors militate against a conclusion that a reformed paragraph SIXTH would violate the third prong of the common law test, injury to the public interest. * * *

Severance or Partial Enforcement

We conclude that the Appellate Division erred in holding that the entire covenant must be invalidated, and in declining partially to enforce the covenant to the extent necessary to protect BDO's legitimate interest. * * * The issue of whether a court should cure the unreasonable aspect of an overbroad employee restrictive covenant through the means of partial enforcement or severance has been the subject of some debate among courts and commentators. * * * A legitimate consideration against the exercise of this power is the fear that employers will use their superior bargaining position to impose unreasonable anti-competitive restrictions, uninhibited by the risk that a court will void the entire agreement, leaving the employee free of any restraint. The prevailing, modern view rejects a per se rule that invalidates entirely any overbroad employee agreement not to compete. Instead, when, as here, the unenforceable portion is not an essential part of the agreed exchange, a court should conduct a case specific analysis, focusing on the conduct of the employer in imposing the terms of the agreement (see, Restatement [Second] of Contracts § 184). Under this approach, if the employer demonstrates an absence of overreaching, coercive use of dominant bargaining power, or other anti-competitive misconduct, but has in good faith sought to protect a legitimate business interest, consistent with reasonable standards of fair dealing, partial enforcement may be justified. * * *

Here, the undisputed facts and circumstances militate in favor of partial enforcement. The covenant was not imposed as a condition of defendant's initial employment, or even his continued employment, but in connection with promotion to a position of responsibility and trust just one step below admittance to the partnership. There is no evidence of coercion or that the Manager's Agreement was part of some general plan to forestall competition. Moreover, no proof was submitted that BDO imposed the covenant in bad faith, knowing full well that it was overbroad. Indeed, as already discussed, the existence of our "learned profession" precedents, and decisions in other States upholding the full terms of this type of agreement, support the contrary conclusion. Therefore, partial enforcement of Paragraph SIXTH is warranted.

The Appellate Division's fear that partial enforcement will require rewriting the parties' agreement is unfounded. No additional substantive terms are required. The time and geographical limitations on the covenant remain intact. The only change is to narrow the class of BDO clients to which the covenant applies. * * *

DAMAGES

Since defendant does not dispute that at least some BDO clients to which the restrictive covenant validly applies were served by him during the contractual duration of the restraint, plaintiff is entitled to partial summary judgment on the issue of liability. Remittal is required in order to establish plaintiff's damages, including resolution of any contested issue as to which of BDO's former clients served by defendant the restrictive covenant validly covers.

As to those clients, the measure of plaintiff's damages will depend in the first instance on the validity of the clause in paragraph SIXTH of the Manager's Agreement requiring defendant to compensate BDO "for the loss and damages suffered" in an amount equal to one and one half times the fees charged each lost client over the last full year the client was served by the firm. This provision essentially represents a liquidated damages clause, as BDO conceded at nisi prius.

Liquidated damages provisions, under our precedents, are valid if the "damages flowing from a breach are difficult to ascertain [and under] a provision fixing damages in advance * * * the amount is a reasonable measure of the anticipated probable harm" (*City of Rye v. Public Serv. Mut. Ins. Co.*, 34 N.Y.2d 470, 473, 358 N.Y.S.2d 391, 315 N.E.2d 458). On the other hand, if "the amount fixed is plainly or grossly disproportionate to the probable loss, the provision calls for a penalty and will not be enforced" (*Truck Rent–A–Center, Inc. v. Puritan Farms 2nd, Inc.*, 41 N.Y.2d 420, 425, 393 N.Y.S.2d 365, 361 N.E.2d 1015).

The damages here are sufficiently difficult to ascertain to satisfy the first requirement of a valid liquidated damages provision. Because of the inability to project with any degree of certainty how long a given client would have remained with BDO if defendant had not made himself available as an alternative source of accounting services, BDO's actual lost profits from defendant's breach would be impossible to determine with any precision.

In our view, however, the averment regarding the basis of the liquidated damages formula by no means conclusively demonstrates the absence of gross disproportionality. * * * We note that other courts have remitted on the issue of the validity of these types of liquidated damages provisions in accountant employee anti-competitive agreements when they found the record insufficiently developed to establish that the amount fixed in the agreement was not so excessive to actual damages as to constitute a penalty * * * The sparse proof on this issue here persuades us that we, similarly, should remit for further development of the record on the liquidated damages formula.

Notes and Questions

1. *Competition by Current Employees Against Their Employer.* Even without an express agreement, employees are under a common law duty not to compete against their employer. In the interest of facilitating the ability to pursue new employment, employees may engage in preparatory steps towards seeking new employment such as inquiring with prospective employers, and once they decide to leave, they may give notice of such departure to coworkers and clients of the employer. See, e.g., Maryland Metals, Inc. v. Metzner, 282 Md. 31, 382 A.2d 564, 568–69 (1978) ("A departing employee may not solicit his employer's customers but he may advise the customers of his intention to leave and set up a competing business."). This common law duty does not apply to former employees. If an employer desires to bar competition by employees after they leave its employ, an express agreement is normally required. But cf. *PepsiCo, Inc. v. Redmond*, p. 915.

Consider the Colorado high court's balancing of these principles in Jet Courier Service, Inc. v. Mulei, 771 P.2d 486, 493 (1989):

> The court of appeals affirmed the trial court's holding that Mulei's pre-termination meetings with customers did not violate a duty of loyalty since ACT did not become operational and commence competing

with Jet until after Mulei left Jet's employ. * * * This reasoning fails to accord adequate scope to the duty of loyalty outlined in the Restatement. * * * While still employed by Jet, Mulei was subject to a duty of loyalty to act solely for the benefit of Jet in all matters connected with his employment. * * * [T]he key inquiry is whether Mulei's meetings amounted to solicitation, which would be a breach of his duty of loyalty. Generally under his privilege to make preparations to compete after the termination of his employment, an employee may advise current customers that he will be leaving his current employment. * * * However, any pre-termination solicitation of those customers for a new competing business violates an employee's duty of loyalty.

With respect to the solicitation of co-employees, the *Jet Courier* court urged a "flexible" approach:

It is normally permissible for employees of a firm, or for some of its partners, to agree among themselves, while still employed, that they will engage in a competition with the firm. * * * However, a court may find that it is a breach of duty for a number of the key officers or employees to agree to leave their employment simultaneously and without giving the employer an opportunity to hire and train replacements.

771 P.2d at 497 (discussing Restatement (Second) Agency § 393, comment e).

A breach of the duty of loyalty will permit recovery of damages resulting from such breach, including, as in *Jet Courier*, denial of monthly salary compensation to an employee "for any month during which he engaged in acts breaching his duty of loyalty" and denial of contractual quarterly bonus payments "for any quarter" during which he engaged in such acts. Id. at 500.

2. *Freedom of Contract?* Consider a number of possible justifications for regulation of post-termination no-compete covenants:

a. "Employers should not be able to insulate themselves from competition by precluding highly-skilled employees from working for their competitors."

b. "Employees should not be able to bind themselves in a way that hampers their ability to exit the firm and thereby tempt their employers to impose unreasonable terms during the employment relationship."

c. "Employees should not be able to bind themselves in a way that hampers their ability to exit the firm because employees will not be able properly to value the opportunity costs of such restraints, particularly at the stage when they are hired."

Which of these justifications do you find persuasive? Do these justifications provide support for a per se rule barring no-compete covenants, or something more akin to New York's reasonable-restraint rule? Do these justifications retain any force where the previous employer continues the employee's salary during the no-compete period (what in the United Kingdom is called a "gardening leave")? Cf. Maltby v. Harlow Meyer Savage, Inc., 166 Misc.2d 481, 633 N.Y.S.2d 926 (N.Y.Sup.1995).

An early article that has proved influential in the case law is Harlan Blake, Employee Agreements Not to Compete, 73 Harv. L. Rev. 625 (1960).

3. *Indistinguishable from a No–Compete Clause?* Is the *Seidman* court correct that the forfeiture clause was indistinguishable in effect from a no-compete clause? Do forfeiture clauses, because they do not directly restrain working for competitors, warrant a more tolerant judicial attitude? See "Note on Forfeiture-for-Competition Clauses and 'Employee Choice' Doctrine," below.

4. *Expanding the Categories of Protectible Interests?*

a. *"Unique" Employees.* What sort of employees have "unique" skills? Actors? Professional Athletes? Heart surgeons? Why does the difficulty their employer would have replacing them provide a justification for a no-compete covenant that presumably would not be enforceable if they had more easily replaceable skills? Is there an assumption that the employer made certain human capital investments enabling these employees to acquire such skills? Is this always true?

b. *Client Relationships.* Does *Seidman* hold that New York will enforce reasonable no-compete clauses justified only by the former employer's concern that ex-employees should not be able to disturb existing client relationships? Are such clauses enforceable in New York even where (i) there is no risk to the first employer's trade secrets; (ii) the former employee has not acted in a manner inconsistent with his duties to the former employer before leaving employment; and (iii) the former employee does not possess "unique" skills?

For another decision enlarging the "unique" skills category to encompass client relationships, see Ticor Title Insurance Co. v. Cohen, 173 F.3d 63, 71 (2d Cir.1999), where an account executive for a title insurance company was barred for six months from working for a competitor. The court reasoned that the employee had a "unique relationship with Ticor and its clients":

> [A]ll of Cohen's clients came to him during his time at Ticor, and were developed, in part, at Ticor's expense. For example, about half of Cohen's clients he had attracted himself, but the other half were inherited from other departing Ticor salesmen. Cohen maintained these relationships, at least in part, by the use of the substantial entertainment expense account provided by Ticor.

5. *Inquiry into Reasonable Scope of Constraint.* Even where a protectible interest is found, courts will still inquire whether the geographical and durational limits on the no-compete clause are reasonable. For a recent case holding that in the dynamic internet-based information technology (IT) industry, a one-year limitation is unreasonable, see EarthWeb, Inc. v. Schlack, 71 F.Supp.2d 299 (S.D.N.Y. 1999): "When measured against the IT industry in the internet environment, a one-year hiatus from the workforce is several generations, if not an eternity." 71 F. Supp.2d at 316. Unlike the *Seidman* court, the *EarthWeb* court declined to "blue pencil" the covenant to make it shorter and thus enforceable, stating that "retroactive alterations distort the terms of the employment relationship." Id. at 311. The court may have reached this conclusion because it questioned whether Schlack's admit-

ted access to his previous employer's "strategic content planning" deserved trade-secrets protection given that such planning is "necessarily revealed when those Web sites are launched on the Internet." Id. at 315.

6. *Per Se Prohibitions of No–Compete Clauses.* Section 16600 of California's Labor Code provides that "every contract by which anyone is restrained from engaging in a lawful profession, trade or business of any kind is to that extent void." The statute allows no-compete clauses that are given in connection with the sale of substantially all of the assets of a corporation (§ 16600(1)–(2)), or are given in connection with the sale of a partnership interest (§ 166002(2)). In addition, the California statute does not itself bar the enforcement of clauses barring solicitation of the former employer's customers or employees or of clauses protecting the former employer's trade secrets.

Colorado has similar legislation, which also contains exceptions for clauses "providing for recovery of the expense of educating and training an employee who has served an employer for a period of less than two years" and for executive and management personnel. Colo. C.R.S. 8–2–113 (1998); Atmel Corp. v. Vitesse Semiconductor Corp., 30 P.3d 789 (Colo.App.2001) ("This management personnel exception applies to those employees who are 'in charge' of the business and who act in an unsupervised manner."). Some states have statutes that appear in terms similar to California's, but still have been construed to allow "reasonable" no-compete clauses. See, e.g., Dobbins, DeGuire & Tucker, P.C. v. Rutherford, 218 Mont. 392, 708 P.2d 577 (1985); Bayly, Martin & Fay v. Pickard, 780 P.2d 1168 (Okl.1989). For criticism of judicial tolerance of no-compete covenants, see Phillip J. Closius & Henry M. Schaffer, Involuntary Nonservitude: The Current Judicial Enforcement of Employee Covenants Not to Compete—A Proposal for Reform, 57 S. Cal. L. Rev. 531 (1984).

Law firms may be restricted by ethical rules in seeking no-compete or no-solicit covenants from departing associates. See, e.g., R.I. Supreme Ct. Ethics Advisory Panel, Op. 2003–07 (Nov., 18, 2003) (law firm may not condition severance benefits on agreement not to solicit clients because, except for agreements concerning benefits upon retirement, ethics rules prohibit restrictions on "the rights of a lawyer to practice after termination of the [employment or partnership] relationship"; interpreting R.I. Rule of Professional Conduct 5.6).

In Don Frumer and Checkpoint Ltd. v. Radguard Ltd., reprinted in ILLR 20, pp. 45–60, the National Labour Court of Israel changed prior law to hold no-compete covenants unenforceable absent a basis for believing former employee will reveal trade secrets or special consideration having been given for the covenant.

7. *Competing Interests.* What legitimate interests, if any, of employers and employees are undermined by the California statute?

a. *Disincentive to Train?* Will employers be willing to provide training to improve the general (i.e., transportable) skills of employees without some protection from competition by departing employees? Consider Colo. C.R.S. 8–2–113(2)(c). See generally Daron Acemoglu &

Jorn–Steffen Pischke, Beyond Becker: Training in Imperfect Labour Markets, 109 Economics J. F112 (Feb. 1999).

b. *Disincentive to Innovate?* Will employers be able adequately to protect investments in confidential proprietary information? To the extent no-compete clauses are needed to prevent employees from trading on confidential information developed with their previous employer, standard economic theory would suggest a suboptimal level of investment in such information. By contrast, Professor Hyde argues that the economic success of the computer industry in Santa Clara County, California, better known as "Silicon Valley," is due in large measure to a culture permitting a high degree of employee interfirm mobility and weak trade secret protections. See Alan Hyde, Working in Silicon Valley: Economic and Legal Analysis of a High–Velocity Labor Market (2003).

8. *Consideration for No–Compete Clauses?* Presumably, consideration is not a problem when employees are required to sign no-compete agreements as a condition of employment. Is separate consideration required to support no-compete agreements signed by incumbent employees? Some courts hold that continued at-will employment beyond the date of signing of the agreement provides sufficient consideration. See, e.g., Copeco, Inc. v. Caley, 91 Ohio App.3d 474, 632 N.E.2d 1299 (Ohio App. 1992). Other courts require that employment continue for a "substantial" or "reasonable" time before a no-compete promise will be enforced—a kind of ex post theory of consideration. See, e.g., Zellner v. Conrad, 183 A.D.2d 250, 589 N.Y.S.2d 903 (App. Div. 1992).

Texas apparently requires separate consideration. See Travel Masters, Inc. v. Star Tours, Inc., 827 S.W.2d 830, 833 (Tex.1991):

> Because employment at-will is not binding upon either the employee or the employer and is not an otherwise enforceable agreement, we conclude that a covenant not to compete executed either at the inception of or during an employment at-will relationship cannot be ancillary to an otherwise enforceable agreement and is unenforceable as a matter of law. Since [the] covenant not to compete is not ancillary to an otherwise enforceable agreement, we hold that the covenant * * * is an unreasonable restraint of trade and unenforceable on grounds of public policy.

In In re Halliburton Co. and Brown & Root Energy Services, Relators, 45 Tex. Sup. 57, 80 S.W.3d 566 (Tex. 2002), the Texas high court held that an employer-promulgated arbitration program was enforceable against at-will employees as long as the employees were notified of the program and continued their employment following the date on which the program took effect. The court distinguished prior rulings such as Light v. Centel Cellular Co., 37 Tex. Sup., J. 838, 883 S.W.2d 642 (1994), which held that no-compete covenants were unenforceable against at-will employees if the purported consideration running to such employees consisted only of "continued employment". The employer's promise of continued employment in *Light* was illusory because the employer was under no binding obligation whereas the employee would continue to be bound by the covenant. In the instant case, the court explained, the mutual promise to arbitrate disputes was binding on both parties and would survive termination of the relationship.

Is Texas's insistence on independent consideration consistent with the way courts have treated other limitations on at-will employment, as explored in chapter 12, or is there something special about the restraint imposed by no-compete covenants that should require bargained-for exchange? See generally Tracy L. Staidl, The Enforceability of Noncompetition Agreements When Employment Is At–Will: Reformulating the Analysis, 2 Employee Rights & Employment Pol'y J. 95 (1998).

Can employers satisfy an independent-consideration requirement by terminating the at-will employee and conditioning his rehire on execution of an otherwise reasonable no-compete covenant? See, e.g., International Paper Co. v. Suwyn and Louisiana–Pacific Corp., 951 F.Supp. 445 (S.D.N.Y. 1997). If so, do employees gain anything by the law requiring such a process?

9. *Wrongful Discharge for Refusing to Sign a No–Compete Agreement?* Can an incumbent employee lawfully be fired for refusing to sign a no-compete agreement in a jurisdiction that enforces "reasonable" agreements? Most courts would not find the discharge actionable. See, e.g., Tatge v. Chambers & Owen, Inc., 219 Wis.2d 99, 579 N.W.2d 217, 224 (Wis. 1998) (employees are protected from compliance with an unreasonable covenant "by rendering that covenant void and unenforceable. * * * The public policy is not to create a cause of action, but to void the covenant"). But see D'sa v. Playhut, Inc., 85 Cal.App.4th 927, 102 Cal.Rptr.2d 495 (2000) (in view of state's prohibition of no-compete covenants, discharge for failure to sign a confidentiality agreement containing such a covenant states "public policy" cause of action, despite severability provisions).

10. *Choice of Law Issues.* AGI, a California corporation, and Hunter, a Maryland firm, are competitors providing computer consulting services for businesses that use human resources software. Pike, a Maryland resident, worked for Hunter for 16 months in Baltimore; her employment agreement contained a one-year no-compete clause and a Maryland choice of law clause, both of which are lawful under Maryland law. AGI recruits Pike to work in California during the one-year period. Does California's statute prohibiting no-compete agreements apply? See The Application Group, Inc. v. The Hunter Group, 61 Cal.App.4th 881, 892, 72 Cal.Rptr.2d 73, 86 (1st Dist. 1998) (holding it does):

> We are * * * convinced that California has a materially greater interest than does Maryland in the application of its law to the parties' dispute, and that California's interests would be more seriously impaired if its policy were subordinated to the policy of Maryland. Accordingly, the trial court did not err when it declined to enforce the contractual conflict of law provision in Hunter's employment agreements. To have done so would have been to allow an out-of-state employer/competitor to limit employment and business opportunities in California.

11. *"No–Solicitation" Agreements.* Should the law treat differently agreements that allow the employee to enter into a competitive business but do not allow raiding of employees or customers of the previous employer? The California courts, for example, have held that restrictions on client solicitations are enforceable despite the statutory ban on no-compete covenants. See Loral Corp. v. Moyes, 174 Cal.App.3d 268, 219 Cal.Rptr. 836

(1985). In Chernoff Diamond & Co. v. Fitzmaurice, 234 A.D.2d 200, 651 N.Y.S.2d 504 (App.Div. 1996), a two-year bar on solicitation of an insurance agency's clients was upheld but on an analysis that presumably also would have been used in evaluating a no-compete agreement:

> * * * [N]either the duration of the restriction, i.e., two years, nor its scope is unduly burdensome. The covenant does not prohibit defendant from pursuing his profession * * * or limit him geographically. Indeed, the only restriction imposed upon him is that he is not permitted to deal with [his previous employer's] clients. There is no reason to suppose that this limitation will prevent defendant * * * from operating a successful insurance agency.

> Although, within the context of this case, the restriction imposed is relatively limited in scope, we are mindful that even such a restriction on defendant's right to pursue his livelihood should not be enforced if it is not necessary to protect the employer's "legitimate interests". * * * In this regard, the issue is not only whether plaintiff's client list was confidential (which it apparently was, but only in part) but also whether defendant obtained, while in plaintiff's employ, invaluable and otherwise unobtainable information concerning the business practices and resulting insurance needs of these clients due to his position as their trusted professional advisor.

In view of the rationale of the *Chernoff* court, can a no-solicitation clause legally prohibit an employee from soliciting a former employer's customers even if the employee did not service those customers? See, e.g., Amex Distributing Co. v. Mascari, 150 Ariz. 510, 724 P.2d 596 (App. 1986).

12. *"Raiding" by Customers.* Do the considerations differ when the employer's concern is not raiding of customers by former employees but, rather, the raiding of employees by its customers? Is the following clause, insisted on as a condition of employment by a consulting agency of all newly hired employees, enforceable in New York or California?

> You shall not for a period of 12 months following the termination of your employment either alone or jointly with others whether as principal, agent, director, shareholder, employee, consultant or in any other capacity whether or directly or indirectly through any other person, firm or company and whether for your own benefit or that of others:

> > (a) Solicit, canvass or seek to obtain or accept business * * * of any person, firm or company who has at any time during the twelve months preceding the date of termination of your employment been a client or customer of the Employer. Should you violate this section you will pay the employer, within thirty days after receipt, twenty-five percent of the gross fees you receive from Employer's client and customers for a period of five years.

Does it make a difference if the company also requires new hires to sign standard one-year no-compete and "trade secrets" clauses?

13. *No–Hire Agreements Between Employers.* Can firms agree not to raid each other's employees? In Heyde Cos. d/b/a Greenbriar Rehabilitation v. Dove Healthcare LLC, 258 Wis.2d 28, 654 N.W.2d 830 (2002), under agreements between supplier Greenbriar and 34 nursing homes, including

Dove, Greenbriar provided physical therapists who worked in the nursing homes but remained Greenbriar employees; the agreements provided that the nursing homes could not hire Greenbriar therapists without its consent. The Wisconsin high court held that the no-hire covenant contravened public policy. But cf. Webb v. West Side Dist. Hosp., 144 Cal.App.3d 946, 193 Cal.Rptr. 80 (Cal. App. 1983) (sustaining provision restricting a hospital from hiring any doctor who had been assigned by a supplier without paying the latter a fee).

14. *"Faithless Servant" Doctrine.* Employees who violate their duty of loyalty to their employers may forfeit their compensation as "faithless servants". Traditionally, New York allowed forfeiture of the defaulting employee's entire compensation, but recent decisions limit the forfeiture to the compensation owed during the period of disloyalty; where compensation is paid on a transaction-by-transaction basis and the disloyalty is held not to taint the entire relationship, the forfeiture may be limited accordingly. See, e.g., Phansalkar v. Andersen Weinroth & Co., L.P., 344 F.3d 184 (2d Cir. 2003).

Note on Forfeiture-for-Competition Clauses and "Employee Choice" Doctrine

Provisions in incentive compensation or other employee benefit plans that provide for forfeiture of stock rights or other special benefits if the employee leaves to work for a competitor are likely to receive more lenient judicial treatment, even in jurisdictions generally unreceptive to no-compete covenants. For example, in IBM v. Bajorek, 191 F.3d 1033 (9th Cir.1999), the court held that a forfeiture provision in a stock option plan that was triggered when an optionee went to work for a competitor did not violate Calif. Labor Code § 16600 (or state law prohibiting employees from collecting wages already paid), as Bajorek had failed to show that the forfeiture provision "completely restrained" him from pursuing his profession.

New York employs an "employee choice" doctrine that draws a distinction between voluntary and involuntary termination of employment. Where an employee voluntarily terminates his or her employment, a forfeiture-for-competition agreement is generally enforceable, without regard to its reasonableness. See Post v. Merrill Lynch, Pierce, Fenner & Smith, 48 N.Y.2d 84, 421 N.Y.S.2d 847, 397 N.E.2d 358 (1979); Kristt v. Whelan, 4 A.D.2d 195, 199, 164 N.Y.S.2d 239 (1st Dep. 1957), affirmed without opinion, 5 N.Y.2d 807, 181 N.Y.S.2d 205, 155 N.E.2d 116 (1958). The theory is that "[a] contract that affords an ex-employee the choice between working for a competitor (and thereby forgoing divested benefits) or retaining those benefits by not working for a competitor is not an unreasonable restraint of trade." Murphy v. Gutfreund, 583 F.Supp. 957, 965 (S.D.N.Y. 1984), dismissed on other grounds, 624 F.Supp. 444 (S.D.N.Y. 1985).

Where employment has been involuntarily terminated, however, the same forfeiture-for-competition agreement is evaluated for the presence of a protectible interest and reasonableness of scope and duration, as would be a conventional no-compete clause. As in other situations, plaintiffs will try to argue that what may look like a voluntary separation or retirement is in fact a compelled termination. See, e.g., Lucente v. IBM Corp., 310 F.3d 243 (2d

Cir. 2002) (whether termination was voluntary is a question for the jury). Even in the event of an involuntary termination, should the reasonableness inquiry be less stringent than that which would apply to a no-compete covenant directly restraining work for a competitor? Does this depend on whether the forfeiture provision affects a central element of compensation, such as salary or pension benefits, or a more conjectural element like stock option rights? See, e.g., York v. Actmedia, Inc., 1990 WL 41760 (S.D.N.Y. 1990).

Should a clause requiring repayment of training costs be treated differently? In Heartland Securities Corp. v. Gerstenblatt, 2000 WL 303274 (S.D.N.Y. 2000), the employer sought to enforce an agreement making employees liable to repay a portion of the $200,000 it costs to train them, if they go to work for a competitor within four years of their date of hire. Likening the repayment obligation to "indentured servitude," the court found that the employer had no protectible interest and declined enforcement.

More generally, should no-compete covenants be enforced in cases where the employee has been involuntarily terminated? See Kenneth J. Vanko, "You're Fired! And Don't Forget Your Non–Compete . . .": The Enforceability of Restrictive Covenants in Involuntary Discharge Cases, 1 DePaul Bus. & Comm. L.J. 1 (2002).

C. "INEVITABLE DISCLOSURE" AND OTHER IMPLIED RESTRAINTS

PEPSICO, INC. v. REDMOND

U.S. Court of Appeals for the Seventh Circuit, 1995.
54 F.3d 1262.

FLAUM, J.

Plaintiff PepsiCo, Inc., sought a preliminary injunction against defendants William Redmond and the Quaker Oats Company to prevent Redmond, a former PepsiCo employee, from divulging PepsiCo trade secrets and confidential information in his new job with Quaker and from assuming any duties with Quaker relating to beverage pricing, marketing, and distribution. The district court agreed with PepsiCo and granted the injunction. We now affirm that decision.

I

The facts of this case lay against a backdrop of fierce beverage-industry competition between Quaker and PepsiCo, especially in "sports drinks" and "new age drinks." Quaker's sports drink, "Gatorade," is the dominant brand in its market niche. PepsiCo introduced its Gatorade rival, "All Sport," in March and April of 1994, but sales of All Sport lag far behind those of Gatorade. Quaker also has the lead in the new-age-drink category. Although PepsiCo has entered the market through joint ventures with the Thomas J. Lipton Company and Ocean Spray Cranberries, Inc., Quaker purchased Snapple Beverage Corp., a large new-age-drink maker, in late 1994. PepsiCo's products have about half of Snapple's market share. Both companies see 1995 as an important year for their products: PepsiCo has developed extensive plans to increase its market presence, while Quaker is trying to solidify its lead by integrating Gatorade and Snapple distribution. Meanwhile, PepsiCo and Quaker each face strong competition from Coca Cola Co., which has its own sports drink, "PowerAde," and which introduced its own Snapple-rival, "Fruitopia," in 1994, as well as from independent beverage producers.

William Redmond, Jr. worked for PepsiCo in its PepsiCola North America division ("PCNA") from 1984 to 1994. Redmond became the General Manager of the Northern California Business Unit in June, 1993, and was promoted one year later to General Manager of the business unit covering all of California, a unit having annual revenues of more than 500 million dollars and representing twenty percent of PCNA's profit for all of the United States.

Redmond's relatively high-level position at PCNA gave him access to inside information and trade secrets. Redmond, like other PepsiCo management employees, had signed a confidentiality agreement with PepsiCo. That agreement stated in relevant part that he

> would not disclose at any time, to anyone other than officers or employees of [PepsiCo], or make use of, confidential information relating to the business of [PepsiCo] * * * obtained while in the employ of [PepsiCo], which shall not be generally known or available to the public or recognized as standard practices.

Donald Uzzi, who had left PepsiCo in the beginning of 1994 to become the head of Quaker's Gatorade division, began courting Redmond for Quaker in May, 1994. Redmond met in Chicago with Quaker officers in August, 1994, and on October 20, 1994, Quaker, through Uzzi, offered Redmond the position of Vice President—On Premise Sales for Gatorade. Redmond did not then accept the offer but continued to negotiate for more money. Throughout this time, Redmond kept his dealings with Quaker secret from his employers at PCNA.

On November 8, 1994, Uzzi extended Redmond a written offer for the position of Vice President—Field Operations for Gatorade and Redmond accepted. Later that same day, Redmond called William Bensyl, the Senior Vice President of Human Resources for PCNA, and told him that he had an offer from Quaker to become the Chief Operating Officer of the combined Gatorade and Snapple company but had not yet accepted it. Redmond also asked whether he should, in light of the offer, carry out his plans to make calls upon certain PCNA customers. Bensyl told Redmond to make the visits.

Redmond also misstated his situation to a number of his PCNA colleagues, including Craig Weatherup, PCNA's President and Chief Executive Officer, and Brenda Barnes, PCNA's Chief Operating Officer and Redmond's immediate superior. As with Bensyl, Redmond told them that he had been offered the position of Chief Operating Officer at

Gatorade and that he was leaning "60/40" in favor of accepting the new position.

On November 10, 1994, Redmond met with Barnes and told her that he had decided to accept the Quaker offer and was resigning from PCNA. Barnes immediately took Redmond to Bensyl, who told Redmond that PepsiCo was considering legal action against him.

True to its word, PepsiCo filed this diversity suit on November 16, 1994, seeking a temporary restraining order to enjoin Redmond from assuming his duties at Quaker and to prevent him from disclosing trade secrets or confidential information to his new employer. * * *

From November 23, 1994, to December 1, 1994, the district court conducted a preliminary injunction hearing on the same matter. At the hearing, PepsiCo offered evidence of a number of trade secrets and confidential information it desired protected and to which Redmond was privy. First, it identified PCNA's "Strategic Plan," an annually revised document that contains PCNA's plans to compete, its financial goals, and its strategies for manufacturing, production, marketing, packaging, and distribution for the coming three years. Strategic Plans are developed by Weatherup and his staff with input from PCNA's general managers, including Redmond, and are considered highly confidential. The Strategic Plan derives much of its value from the fact that it is secret and competitors cannot anticipate PCNA's next moves. PCNA managers received the most recent Strategic Plan at a meeting in July, 1994, a meeting Redmond attended. PCNA also presented information at the meeting regarding its plans for Lipton ready-to-drink teas and for All Sport for 1995 and beyond, including new flavors and package sizes.

Second, PepsiCo pointed to PCNA's Annual Operating Plan ("AOP") as a trade secret. The AOP is a national plan for a given year and guides PCNA's financial goals, marketing plans, promotional event calendars, growth expectations, and operational changes in that year. The AOP, which is implemented by PCNA unit General Managers, including Redmond, contains specific information regarding all PCNA initiatives for the forthcoming year. The AOP bears a label that reads "Private and Confidential—Do Not Reproduce" and is considered highly confidential by PCNA managers.

In particular, the AOP contains important and sensitive information about "pricing architecture"—how PCNA prices its products in the marketplace. Pricing architecture covers both a national pricing approach and specific price points for given areas. Pricing architecture also encompasses PCNA's objectives for All Sport and its new age drinks with reference to trade channels, package sizes and other characteristics of both the products and the customers at which the products are aimed. Additionally, PCNA's pricing architecture outlines PCNA's customer development agreements. These agreements between PCNA and retailers provide for the retailer's participation in certain merchandising activities for PCNA products. As with other information contained in the AOP, pricing architecture is highly confidential and would be extremely valuable to a competitor. Knowing PCNA's pricing architecture would allow a competitor to anticipate PCNA's pricing moves and underbid PCNA strategically whenever and wherever the competitor so desired. PepsiCo introduced evidence that Redmond had detailed knowledge of PCNA's pricing architecture and that he was aware of and had been involved in preparing PCNA's customer development agreements with PCNA's California and California-based national customers. Indeed, PepsiCo showed that Redmond, as the General Manager for California, would have been responsible for implementing the pricing architecture guidelines for his business unit.

PepsiCo also showed that Redmond had intimate knowledge of PCNA "attack plans" for specific markets. Pursuant to these plans, PCNA dedicates extra funds to supporting its brands against other brands in selected markets. To use a hypothetical example, PCNA might budget an additional $500,000 to spend in Chicago at a particular time to help All Sport close its market gap with Gatorade. Testimony and documents demonstrated Redmond's awareness of these plans and his participation in drafting some of them.

Finally, PepsiCo offered evidence of PCNA trade secrets regarding innovations in its selling and delivery systems. Under this plan, PCNA is testing a new delivery system that could give PCNA an advantage over its competitors in negotiations with retailers over shelf space and merchandising. Redmond has knowledge of this secret because PCNA, which has invested over a million dollars in developing the system during the past two years, is testing the pilot program in California.

Having shown Redmond's intimate knowledge of PCNA's plans for 1995, PepsiCo argued that Redmond would inevitably disclose that information to Quaker in his new position, at which he would have substantial input as to Gatorade and Snapple pricing, costs, margins, distribution systems, products, packaging and marketing, and could give Quaker an unfair advantage in its upcoming skirmishes with PepsiCo. Redmond and Quaker countered that Redmond's primary initial duties at Quaker as Vice President–Field Operations would be to integrate Gatorade and Snapple distribution and then to manage that distribution as well as the promotion, marketing and sales of these products. Redmond asserted that the integration would be conducted according to a pre-existing plan and that his special knowledge of PCNA strategies would be irrelevant. This irrelevance would derive not only from the fact that Redmond would be implementing pre-existing plans but also from the fact that PCNA and Quaker distribute their products in entirely different ways: PCNA's distribution system is vertically integrated (i.e., PCNA owns the system) and delivers its product directly to retailers, while Quaker ships its product to wholesalers and customer warehouses and relies on independent distributors. The defendants also pointed out that Redmond had signed a confidentiality agreement with Quaker preventing him from disclosing "any confidential information belonging to others," as well as the Quaker Code of Ethics, which prohibits employees from engaging in "illegal or improper acts to acquire a competitor's trade secrets." Redmond additionally promised at the hearing that should he be faced with a situation at Quaker that might involve the use or disclosure of PCNA information, he would seek advice from Quaker's in-house counsel and would refrain from making the decision. * * *

On December 15, 1994, the district court issued an order enjoining Redmond from assuming his position at Quaker through May, 1995, and permanently from using or disclosing any PCNA trade secrets or confidential information. The court entered its findings of fact and conclusions of law on January 26, 1995, nunc pro tunc December 15, 1994. The court, which completely adopted PepsiCo's position, found that Redmond's new job posed a clear threat of misappropriation of trade secrets and confidential information that could be enjoined under Illinois statutory and common law. The court also emphasized Redmond's lack of forthrightness both in his activities before accepting his job with Quaker and in his testimony as factors leading the court to believe the threat of misappropriation was real. This appeal followed.

II

Both parties agree that the primary issue on appeal is whether the district court correctly concluded that PepsiCo had a reasonable likelihood of success on its various claims for trade secret misappropriation and breach of a confidentiality agreement. * * *

A

The Illinois Trade Secrets Act ("ITSA"), which governs the trade secret issues in this case, provides that a court may enjoin the "actual or threatened misappropriation" of a trade secret. 765 ILCS 1065/3(a) * * *. A party seeking an injunction must therefore prove both the existence of a trade secret and the misappropriation. The defendants' appeal focuses solely on misappropriation; although the defendants only reluctantly refer to PepsiCo's marketing and distribution plans as trade secrets, they do not seriously contest that this information falls under the ITSA.[5]

The question of threatened or inevitable misappropriation in this case lies at the heart of a basic tension in trade secret law. Trade secret law serves to protect "standards of commercial morality" and "encourage[] invention and innovation" while maintaining "the public interest in having free and open competition in the manufacture and sale of unpatented goods." 2 [Melvin F.] Jager, [Trade Secrets Law] § IL.03, at

---

5. Under the ITSA, trade secret "means information, including but not limited to, technical or non-technical data, a formula, pattern, compilation, program, device, method, technique, drawing, process, financial data, or list of actual or potential customers that:

(1) is sufficiently secret to derive economic value, actual or potential, from not generally being known to other persons who can obtain economic value from its disclosure or use; and

(2) is the subject of efforts that are reasonable under the circumstances to maintain its secrecy or confidentiality."

765 ILCS 1065/2(d). * * *

IL–12 [Clark Boardman rev. ed. 1994)]. Yet that same law should not prevent workers from pursuing their livelihoods when they leave their current positions. * * *

This tension is particularly exacerbated when a plaintiff sues to prevent not the actual misappropriation of trade secrets but the mere threat that it will occur. While the ITSA plainly permits a court to enjoin the threat of misappropriation of trade secrets, there is little law in Illinois or in this circuit establishing what constitutes threatened or inevitable misappropriation.[6] * * *

In *AMP* [*Inc.* v. *Fleischhacker*, 823 F.2d 1199 (7th Cir.1987), see p. ___ infra] we affirmed the denial of a preliminary injunction on the grounds that the plaintiff AMP had failed to show either the existence of any trade secrets or the likelihood that defendant Fleischhacker, a former AMP employee, would compromise those secrets or any other confidential business information. AMP, which produced electrical and electronic connection devices, argued that Fleishhacker's new position at AMP's competitor would inevitably lead him to compromise AMP's trade secrets regarding the manufacture of connectors. *AMP*, 823 F.2d at 1207. In rejecting that argument, we emphasized that the mere fact that a person assumed a similar position at a competitor does not, without more, make it "inevitable that he will use or disclose * * * trade secret information" so as to "demonstrate irreparable injury." *Id.*

It should be noted that *AMP*, which we decided in 1987, predates the ITSA, which took effect in 1988. The ITSA abolishes any common law remedies or authority contrary to its own terms. 765 ILCS 1065/8. The ITSA does not, however, represent a major deviation from the Illinois common law of unfair trade practices. * * * The ITSA mostly codifies rather than modifies the common law doctrine that preceded it. Thus, we believe that *AMP* continues to reflect the proper standard under Illinois's current statutory scheme.[7]

The ITSA * * * and *AMP* lead to the same conclusion: a plaintiff may prove a claim of trade secret misappropriation by demonstrating that defendant's new employment will inevitably lead him to rely on the plaintiff's trade secrets. * * * Questions remain, however, as to what constitutes inevitable misappropriation and whether PepsiCo's submissions * * * meet that standard. We hold that they do.

---

6. The ITSA definition of misappropriation relevant to this discussion is "the disclosure or use of a trade secret of a person without express or implied consent by another person who * * * at the time of disclosure or use, knew or had reason to know that the knowledge of the trade secret was * * * acquired under circumstances giving rise to a duty to maintain its secrecy * * *." 765 ILCS 1065/2(b).

7. The ITSA has overruled *AMP's* implications regarding the durability of an agreement to protect trade secrets. *AMP* followed a line of Illinois cases questioning the validity of agreements to keep trade secrets confidential where those agreements did not have durational or geographical limits. *AMP*, 823 F.2d at 1202. The ITSA, in reversing those cases, provides that "a contractual or other duty to maintain secrecy or limit use of a trade secret shall not be deemed to be void or unenforceable solely for lack of durational or geographical limitation on the duty." 765 ILCS 1065/8(b)(1). * * *

PepsiCo presented substantial evidence at the preliminary injunction hearing that Redmond possessed extensive and intimate knowledge about PCNA's strategic goals for 1995 in sports drinks and new age drinks. The district court concluded on the basis of that presentation that unless Redmond possessed an uncanny ability to compartmentalize information, he would necessarily be making decisions about Gatorade and Snapple by relying on his knowledge of PCNA trade secrets. It is not the "general skills and knowledge acquired during his tenure with" PepsiCo that PepsiCo seeks to keep from falling into Quaker's hands, but rather "the particularized plans or processes developed by [PCNA] and disclosed to him while the employer-employee relationship existed, which are unknown to others in the industry and which give the employer an advantage over his competitors." *AMP*, 823 F.2d at 1202. The [plaintiff in] *AMP* * * * could do nothing more than assert that skilled employees were taking their skills elsewhere; PepsiCo has done much more.

Admittedly, PepsiCo has not brought a traditional trade secret case, in which a former employee has knowledge of a special manufacturing process or customer list and can give a competitor an unfair advantage by transferring the technology or customers to that competitor. * * * PepsiCo has not contended that Quaker has stolen the All Sport formula or its list of distributors. Rather PepsiCo has asserted that Redmond cannot help but rely on PCNA trade secrets as he help plots Gatorade and Snapple's new course, and that these secrets will enable Quaker to achieve a substantial advantage by knowing exactly how PCNA will price, distribute, and market its sports drinks and new age drinks and being able to respond strategically. * * *

Quaker and Redmond assert that they have not and do not intend to use whatever confidential information Redmond has by virtue of his former employment. They point out that Redmond has already signed an agreement with Quaker not to disclose any trade secrets or confidential information gleaned from his earlier employment. They also note with regard to distribution systems that even if Quaker wanted to steal information about PCNA's distribution plans, they would be completely useless in attempting to integrate the Gatorade and Snapple beverage lines.

The defendants' arguments fall somewhat short of the mark. Again, the danger of misappropriation in the present case is not that Quaker threatens to use PCNA's secrets to create distribution systems or coopt PCNA's advertising and marketing ideas. Rather, PepsiCo believes that Quaker, unfairly armed with knowledge of PCNA's plans, will be able to anticipate its distribution, packaging, pricing, and marketing moves. Redmond and Quaker even concede that Redmond might be faced with a decision that could be influenced by certain confidential information that he obtained while at PepsiCo. In other words, PepsiCo finds itself in the position of a coach, one of whose players has left, playbook in hand, to join the opposing team before the big game. Quaker and Redmond's protestations that their distribution systems and plans are entirely different from PCNA's are thus not really responsive.

The district court also concluded from the evidence that Uzzi's actions in hiring Redmond and Redmond's actions in pursuing and accepting his new job demonstrated a lack of candor on their part and proof of their willingness to misuse PCNA trade secrets, findings Quaker and Redmond vigorously challenge. * * *

The facts of the case do not ineluctably dictate the district court's conclusion. Redmond's ambiguous behavior toward his PepsiCo superiors might have been nothing more than an attempt to gain leverage in employment negotiations. The discrepancy between Redmond's and Uzzi's comprehension of what Redmond's job would entail may well have been a simple misunderstanding. * * * The court also pointed out that Quaker, through Uzzi, seemed to express an unnatural interest in hiring PCNA employees: all three of the people interviewed for the position Redmond ultimately accepted worked at PCNA. Uzzi may well have focused on recruiting PCNA employees because he knew they were good and not because of their confidential knowledge. Nonetheless, the district court, after listening to the witnesses, determined otherwise. That conclusion was not an abuse of discretion. * * *

Thus, when we couple the demonstrated inevitability that Redmond would rely on PCNA trade secrets in his new job at Quaker with the district court's reluctance to believe that Redmond would refrain from disclosing these secrets in his new position (or that Quaker would ensure Redmond did not disclose them), we conclude that the district court correctly decided that PepsiCo demonstrated a likelihood of success on its statutory claim of trade secret misappropriation.

* * *

C

For the same reasons we concluded that the district court did not abuse its discretion in granting the preliminary injunction on the issue of trade secret misappropriation, we also agree with its decision on the likelihood of Redmond's breach of his confidentiality agreement should he begin working at Quaker. Because Redmond's position at Quaker would initially cause him to disclose trade secrets, it would necessarily force him to breach his agreement not to disclose confidential information acquired while employed in PCNA. Cf. *George S. May Int'l*, 628 N.E.2d at 653 ("An employer's trade secrets are considered a protectable interest for a restrictive covenant under Illinois law.").

Quaker and Remond do not assert that the confidentiality agreement is invalid; such agreements are enforceable when supported by adequate consideration. * * *

III

Finally, Redmond and Quaker have contended in the alternative that the injunction issued against them is overbroad. They disagree in particular with the injunction's prohibition against Redmond's participation in the integration of the Snapple and Gatorade distribution systems. The defendants claim that whatever trade secret and confidential information Redmond has, that information is completely irrelevant to Quaker's integration task. They further argue that, because Redmond would only be implementing a plan already in place, the injunction is especially inappropriate. A district court ordinarily has wide latitude in fashioning injunctive relief, and we will restrict the breadth of an injunction only where the district court has abused its discretion. * * *

While the defendants' arguments are not without some merit, the district court determined that the proposed integration would require Redmond to do more than execute a plan someone else had drafted. It also found that Redmond's knowledge of PCNA's trade secrets and confidential information would inevitably shape that integration and that Redmond could not be trusted to avoid that conflict of interest. If the injunction permanently enjoined Redmond from assuming these duties at Quaker, the defendants' argument would be stronger. However, the injunction against Redmond's immediate employment at Quaker extends no further than necessary and was well within the district court's discretion. * * *

Notes and Questions

1. *Implied No–Compete Agreement?* Is it a justifiable reading of the employment agreement between Pepsi and Redmond that Redmond impliedly agreed not to work at all for competitor firms after he left Pepsi? Note that the district court on remand narrowed the injunction, permitting Redmond to take the job at Quaker, but merely enjoining any disclosure of confidential information. See PepsiCo, Inc. v. Redmond, 1996 WL 3965 (N.D.Ill.1996). Is this narrowing consistent with the Seventh Circuit's opinion?

The New York courts, by contrast, have stated a strong presumption against implied, post-employment no-compete covenants:

> Although in a proper case an implied-in-fact covenant not to compete for the term of the employment may be found to exist, anticompetitive covenants covering the postemployment period will not be implied.

American Broadcasting Companies v. Wolf, 52 N.Y.2d 394, 406, 438 N.Y.S.2d 482, 420 N.E.2d 363 (1981); see American Federal Group Ltd. v. Rothenberg, 136 F.3d 897, 909 (2d Cir.1998) (applying New York law). See also note 3 below.

2. *"Inevitable Disclosure"*. The theory of inevitable disclosure appeared in a New York decision as early as 1919 in Eastman Kodak Co. v. Powers Film Products, Inc., 189 A.D. 556, 179 N.Y.S. 325 (4th Dept.), a case involving an express no-compete covenant. The court stated that the departing employee's "rendition of services along the lines of his training would almost necessarily impart such knowledge to some degree. [The employee] cannot be loyal both to his promise to his former employer and to his new obligations to the defendant company." Id. at 330. In *Eastman Kodak*,

however, the theory did not provide a basis for judicial implication of a covenant, but rather only helped identify a protectible interest justifying enforcement of an express no-compete clause.

Decisions invoking the theory as an independent basis for injunctive relief, in situations where a no-compete clause is absent or unenforceable, are relatively rare. The doctrine is explored in Susan Street Whaley, Comment, The Inevitable Disaster of Inevitable Disclosure, 67 U. Cinn. L. Rev. 809 (1999); Jay L. Koh, From Hoops to Hard Drives: An Accession Law Approach to the Inevitable Misappropriation of Trade Secrets, 48 Am U. L. Rev. 271 (1998); Suellen Lowry, Inevitable Disclosure Trade Secret Disputes: Dissolutions of Concurrent Property Interests, 40 Stan. L. Rev. 519 (1998).

Is the doctrine a useful default rule embodying what the parties likely intended, a default rule that the parties could readily modify in bargaining?

3. *Misappropriation of Trade Secrets.* Courts may also be willing to enjoin, for a time, working for competitors where the employee has misappropriated trade secrets or otherwise breached a fiduciary duty to the former employer, even in the absence of an enforceable no-compete covenant. For example, in DoubleClick, Inc. v. Henderson, 1997 WL 731413 (Sup. Ct. N.Y. Co. 1997), a case often cited as resting on the inevitable-discovery theory, the defendants were caught misappropriating trade secrets from their former Internet advertising company to aid their effort to start up a competitor company. The court enjoined defendants from working on Internet-advertising projects for six months because defendants' past conduct gave rise to a presumption of prospective use of plaintiff's trade secrets:

> In the instant case it appears to the court that the defendants will inevitably use DoubleClick's trade secrets * * *. [T]he centrality of Henderson and Dickey in DoubleClick's operations make it unlikely that they could "eradicate [DoubleClick's] secrets from their mind." * * * Moreover the actual use of DoubleClick's trade secrets * * * demonstrate defendants' cavalier attitude toward their duties to their former employer. This gives rise to a reasonable inference that they would use DoubleClick's confidential information against it.

1997 WL 731413, citing Lumex, Inc. v. Highsmith, 919 F.Supp. 624, 631 (E.D.N.Y.1996).

For a decision questioning the application of the "inevitable disclosure" doctrine in the absence of actual misappropriation of trade secrets, see EarthWeb, Inc. v. Schlack, 71 F.Supp.2d 299 (S.D.N.Y.1999), vacated and remanded (to clarify basis for denying plaintiff's motion for preliminary injunctive relief), 205 F.3d 1322 (2d Cir.2000) (unpubl.). In October 1998, Schlack had joined EarthWeb as vice-president for Worldwide Content, and was responsible for overseeing the editorial content of the company's web site. EarthWeb's sites contained information technology (IT) information obtained through licensing agreements with third parties. Schlack at the time agreed to a broad confidentiality clause and a 12–month no-compete covenant barring his post-termination employment with a directly competing entity, defined as:

> (i) an on-line service for Information Professionals whose primary business is to provide information technology professionals with a direc-

tory of third-party technology, software, and/or developer resources; and/or an on-line reference library, and/or

(ii) an on-line store, the primary purpose of which is to sell or distribute third-party software or products used for Internet sites or software development.

After less than a year with EarthWeb, Schlack left to join ITworld.com, a web site that would consolidate four on-line IT publications into a single on-line source for IT professionals. Unlike EarthWeb, his new employer generated its own content rather than rely on the services of third parties. Expressing skepticism over a doctrine that had the potential of creating "an implied in-fact restrictive covenant," the *EarthWeb* court held that the no-compete clause was in fact a limited one applying only to entities in "specific IT areas," and that EarthWeb's claims would have to rise or fall on "the restrictive covenant it drafted, and not on a confidentiality provision conflated with the theory of inevitable disclosure," 1999 WL 980165, at *11.

Given *Redmond*, *DoubleClick* and *EarthWeb*, how would you formulate the test for when a court will grant an injunction on the inevitable-disclosure theory?

4. *Was There an Actual or Threatened Misappropriation of Trade Secrets in* Redmond? What was the trade secret information threatened in *Redmond*? The general rule is that "general information" of a former employer's business operations is not a protectible trade secret. See Reed, Roberts Associates, Inc. v. Strauman, 40 N.Y.2d 303, 308, 386 N.Y.S.2d 677, 353 N.E.2d 590, 594 (1976):

> Apparently, the employer is more concerned with Strauman's knowledge of the intricacies of their business operation. However, absent any wrongdoing, we cannot agree that Strauman should be prohibited from utilizing his knowledge and talents in this area (see Restatement, Agency 2d, § 396, comment b). A contrary holding would make those in charge of operations or specialists in certain aspects of an enterprise virtual hostages of their employers. Where the knowledge does not qualify for protection as a trade secret and there has been no conspiracy or breach of trust resulting in commercial piracy we see no reason to inhibit the employee's ability to realize his potential both professionally and financially by availing himself of opportunity.

Consider Professor Hyde's critique of the *Redmond* ruling:

> What *did* Redmond know? He was far from the key figure in All Sport; he was one of many regional managers. He had access to Pepsi–Cola's "Strategic Plan" and "Annual Operating Plan" of "financial goals, marketing plans, promotional event calendars, growth expectations and operational changes." He knew which markets Pepsi–Cola would focus on and something about a new delivery system. In other words, he knew what any manager knows.

Alan Hyde, Working in Silicon Valley: Economic Analysis of a High-Velocity Labor Market 35 (2003). Is this a fair characterization of the facts in *Redmond*?

D.   TRADE SECRETS

AMP INC. v. FLEISCHHACKER

U.S. Court of Appeals for the Seventh Circuit, 1987.
823 F.2d 1199.

Cummings, J.

Plaintiff appeals the district court's entry of final judgment in favor of the defendants after a bench trial. We affirm.

The plaintiff, AMP Incorporated, brought this action against a former employee, James Fleischhacker, and one of its competitors, Molex, alleging unfair competition and misappropriation of trade secrets. AMP is the world's leading producer of electrical and electronic connection devices. It is by far the largest company in the connector industry, with over 21,000 employees and 1983 reported sales of over one-and-one-half billion dollars and net income of about $163 million. AMP's Components & Assemblies Division, headquartered in Winston–Salem, North Carolina, is one of its major divisions, generating in excess of $100 million in gross sales per year.

Molex is a principal competitor of AMP's Components & Assemblies Division and has its principal place of business in Lisle, Illinois. Molex's annual sales are in excess of $250 million, with foreign sales accounting for over half of that total. A significant portion of Molex's total sales is attributable to products that compete directly with products manufactured by AMP's Components & Assemblies Division.

The present controversy involves the 1984 hiring by Molex of defendant James Fleischhacker, formerly the Division Manager of AMP's Components & Assemblies Division, to fill the position of Director of Marketing for Molex's Commercial Products Division. Mr. Fleischhacker, who holds a Bachelor of Science degree from the University of Minnesota and a Master's degree from the Massachusetts Institute of Technology, joined AMP in 1973. He rapidly advanced through the corporation and in 1982 was named Manager of the Components & Assemblies Division, the position he held until he resigned in 1984. As Division Manager, Mr. Fleischhacker supervised approximately 1200 people who were responsible for the manufacture and sale of 10,000 different component parts. His duties as Division Manager included reviewing and approving business programs, interfacing with group management, implementing strategic policies and plans, and developing personnel. His primary energies, however, were devoted to motivating and coordinating the efforts of others. His ability and performance at AMP were rated as exceptional and he was told that he had the potential of rising higher within AMP's corporate structure and even of becoming president of the corporation. His honesty, integrity, loyalty, discretion, and judgment while employed by AMP were consistently rated as good to excellent in formal evaluations and by the testimony of his co-workers.

In 1982 Molex decided to create a new position, Director of Marketing, in its Commercial Products Division. An executive search firm directed Molex to Mr. Fleischhacker, whom Molex found to be a desirable and highly qualified candidate for the position as a result of his background, education, skill, and ability, including demonstrated product management capabilities, and especially because of his knowledge of the connector industry. Molex made a written offer of employment to Mr. Fleischhacker at the end of 1983, which he accepted in February 1984.

AMP has alleged that Molex's hiring of Mr. Fleischhacker is part of a larger pattern of conduct by Molex involving the misappropriation and threatened misappropriation of AMP's trade secrets and other confidential information, and the solicitation and hiring of AMP personnel. Given the nature of the competition between Molex and AMP, the nature of the respective positions held by Mr. Fleischhacker at AMP and Molex, and an alleged propensity on the part of Molex to misappropriate AMP's internal information without regard to its proprietary nature, AMP maintains that it is inevitable that Mr. Fleischhacker and other AMP personnel hired by Molex will use and disclose AMP trade secrets and confidential information for the benefit and unjust enrichment of Molex. * * *

After a trial on the merits, the district court entered judgment in favor of the defendants, denying injunctive relief and damages against Molex for unfair competition, and denying injunctive relief against Molex and Mr. Fleischhacker to prevent trade secret misappropriation. In its judgment order and subsequent order clarifying the original order, the district court explained that because of their relatively simple design and the ease with which they could be copied, the products manufactured by AMP's Components & Assemblies Division did not constitute protectible trade secrets. The district court also held that although AMP had established the existence of protectible business information, it had failed to show any likelihood that Mr. Fleischhacker would compromise any confidential information known to him. AMP appeals the district court's judgment.

Resolution of the issues presented by this appeal requires an analysis of the Illinois law of trade secrets. We must first take note of the distinction drawn by Illinois law between the protection afforded an employer who has bound his employee by an enforceable post-employment restrictive covenant not to compete and one who relies exclusively upon common law restrictions against disclosure of confidential information. To our considerable dismay, this distinction is one which the parties have chosen largely to ignore. While an enforceable restrictive covenant may protect material, such as confidential information revealed to an employee during the course of his employment, which does not constitute a trade secret, an employer's protection absent a restrictive covenant is narrower and extends only to trade secrets or near-permanent customer relationships. * * *

Thus the initial question to be resolved is whether Mr. Fleischhacker was bound by a valid and enforceable restrictive covenant or was merely restricted by common law principles. The record indicates that he was not bound by a restrictive covenant not to compete. He did, however, sign a confidentiality agreement when he first became employed at AMP whereby he agreed inter alia:

> (3) To keep confidential during and subsequent to the period of said employment, except for those whom his authorized activities for the Company require should be informed, all information relating to the Company's business, its research or engineering activities, its manufacturing processes or trade secrets, its sources of supply or lists of customers and its plans or contemplated actions.

* * * The language of this confidentiality agreement purports to prohibit Mr. Fleischhacker from disclosing to any non-AMP personnel any information relating to AMP and its operations forever. The Illinois courts have held unenforceable nearly identical provisions in confidentiality agreements because (1) they contain no limitation on the duration of the nondisclosure provision, instead restricting disclosure "during and subsequent to the period of said employment," and (2) they contain no geographical limitation or other kind of limit on the parties to whom the employee is prohibited from disclosing information. See *Cincinnati Tool Steel Co. v. Breed*, 136 Ill. App. 3d [267,] 275–276, 482 N.E.2d [170,] 175 [(2d Dist. 1985)]; *Disher v. Fulgoni*, 124 Ill. App. 3d 257, 262, 464 N.E.2d 639, 643, 79 Ill. Dec. 735 (1st Dist. 1984). Confidentiality agreements without such limitations constitute, in the view of the Illinois courts, unreasonable restraints on trade which unduly restrict the free flow of information necessary for business competition. * * *

Because Mr. Fleischhacker is not subject to any enforceable contractual restrictions, AMP was first required to establish the existence of genuine trade secrets in order for injunctive relief to be warranted. The Illinois Supreme Court has defined a trade secret as "a plan or process, tool, mechanism, compound, or informational data utilized by a person in his business operations and known only to him and such limited other persons to whom it may be necessary to confide it." *ILG Industries, Inc. v. Scott*, 49 Ill. 2d 88, 92, 273 N.E.2d 393, 395 (1971). It is generally recognized in Illinois that at the termination of employment, an employee may not take with him confidential, particularized plans or processes developed by his employer and disclosed to him while the employer-employee relationship existed, which are unknown to others in the industry and which give the employer an advantage over his competitors. On the other hand, an employee is free to take with him general skills and knowledge acquired during his tenure with his former employer. * * * Furthermore, while recognizing that a business must be afforded protection against the wrongful appropriation of confidential information by a prior employee who held a position of confidence and trust, the Illinois Supreme Court has emphasized that:

the right of an individual to follow and pursue the particular occupation for which he is best trained is a most fundamental right. Our society is extremely mobile and our free economy is based upon competition. One who has worked in a particular field cannot be compelled to erase from his mind all of the general skills, knowledge and expertise acquired through his experience. These skills are valuable to such employee in the market place for his services. Restraints cannot be lightly placed upon his right to compete in the area of his greatest worth.

ILG Industries v. Scott, 49 Ill. 2d at 93–94, 273 N.E.2d at 396.

The district court initially found that AMP had failed to establish any protectable trade secrets with respect to the products manufactured by its Components & Assemblies Division. The court found that the electronic components produced were low technology commodity products which could be easily reproduced, and that much of the AMP product information possessed by Mr. Fleischhacker was already known to virtually all of AMP's competitors and easily available from widely circulated public sources. AMP does not contest this finding on appeal, asserting that it never contended that its connectors themselves constituted trade secrets. * * * Rather AMP contends that it has protectible trade secrets in a host of confidential information to which Mr. Fleischhacker had access during the course of his employment at AMP. This information, it alleges, includes: business and strategic planning information for the Components & Assemblies Division; new product development information; manufacturing information, including equipment, processes, cost and capacity information; financial information, including product-line profit-margin, sales, and budget information; and marketing and customer information.

AMP has consistently failed throughout this litigation to identify any particularized trade secrets actually at risk. Prior to trial, AMP submitted six single-spaced, typewritten pages listing by general item and category hundreds of pieces of AMP internal information. Other courts have warned plaintiffs of the risks they run by failing to identify specific trade secrets and instead producing long lists of general areas of information which contain unidentified trade secrets. See, e.g., *Litton Systems, Inc. v. Sundstrand Corp.*, 750 F.2d 952, 954, 956–957, 224 U.S.P.Q. (BNA) 252 (1984). In its principal brief to this Court, AMP has again refused to specify precisely what trade secrets it believes to be at risk by identifying particular documents or other sources of information. * * *

In its original judgment order, the district court held that AMP had failed to establish the existence of any trade secrets. * * * In a subsequent order clarifying its original order, however, the court held that AMP had demonstrated the existence of "protectible business secrets" * * *, although significantly it too failed to list any particular pieces or type of information that warranted protection. Despite this finding, the court nevertheless concluded that no relief was warranted because AMP had not shown any likelihood that Mr. Fleischhacker would compromise any of the information known to him. AMP now argues that this clarifying order precludes the defendants from contesting the existence of trade secrets and that under Illinois law irreparable harm is presumed to follow if a protectable interest is not protected.

Our examination of Illinois law reveals that the district court erred as a matter of law when it held that the general confidential information identified by AMP constituted protectible business secrets. As explained above, where the parties have entered into a restrictive covenant not to compete, the scope of protection afforded a former employer is quite broad and may extend to the type of generalized confidential business information to which AMP points. * * * Absent such a covenant, however, the plaintiff must demonstrate the existence of a genuine trade secret to obtain injunctive relief. As Judge Shadur noted in *Fleming Sales Co. v. Bailey*, 611 F. Supp. 507, 511 (N.D.Ill.1985), the "right to impose contractual restraints does not render the same knowledge 'trade secrets' in the absence of such restraints."

In marked contrast to those cases involving the enforceability of a restrictive covenant, the Illinois courts have not extended protection under the common law of trade secrets to the kind of generalized confidential business information on which AMP relies. In *Cincinnati Tool Steel Co. v. Breed*, 136 Ill. App. 3d 267, 482 N.E.2d 170, 90 Ill. Dec. 463, the plaintiff alleged that a former office manager/sales manager had misappropriated confidential pricing information, including cost, special discounts and supply information. The court refused to find that the plaintiff had a protectible interest in this information warranting injunctive relief. The defendant former manager had not taken any documents or other material with her when she left the plaintiff's employ, and the court concluded that the fact that the defendant might be able to recollect pricing information that could potentially be used to the plaintiff's detriment while later working for one of plaintiff's competitors was simply too conjectural to establish a prima facie showing of a protectible interest. Similarly, in *Smith Oil Corp. v. Viking Chemical Co.*, 127 Ill. App. 3d 423, 468 N.E.2d 797, 82 Ill. Dec. 250, the plaintiff alleged that former employees had misappropriated customer lists, customer orders, pricing information, cost information, sample formulas, product formulas, customer correspondence and other special customer information when they left to work for a competitor. Other than the exact formulas for the plaintiff's products, the court held that the information which the plaintiff wanted protected fell into the category of "general skills and knowledge" which an employee is free to take with him when his employment is terminated. * * *

These cases are controlling here. The district court credited the testimony of Mr. Fleischhacker that after he tendered his resignation he hurriedly packed his personal papers and belongings under the surveillance of an AMP employee and did not deliberately take with him anything of a confidential nature. AMP has offered no proof to the contrary. See *Smith Oil Corp.*, 127 Ill. App. 3d at 431, 468 N.E.2d at

802–803 (injunctive relief requires that plaintiff produce evidence that former employee actually took or possessed trade secret information) * * * The record is similarly devoid of any evidence that Mr. Fleischhacker ever systematically recorded, copied, compiled, or even purposefully memorized any of AMP's confidential business information while he was still employed at AMP for use in his new position at Molex. * * *

This is not a case where the plaintiff can point to any tangible work product, such as blueprints, designs, plans, processes, or other technical specifications, at risk of misappropriation. * * * Nor is this a case, like many cited by AMP, involving a former employee who held a technical or engineering position and was responsible for distinct areas of technology and research. Mr. Fleischhacker was a high-level managerial executive who had broad supervisory responsibility for 1200 employees and over 10,000 different products at AMP. AMP now requests that we restrain him from in any way making use of or relying on his independent recollections of generalized business and technical information to which he had access while employed at AMP. Illinois law simply does not authorize such relief.

* * *

* * * [T]he practical effect of any grant of injunctive relief in favor of AMP would be to prohibit Mr. Fleischhacker from working in the connector industry. In its brief AMP disingenuously claims that the injunctive relief requested would not deny Mr. Fleischhacker his choice of employer, i.e., Molex, but would only remove him from the conflicting position he now holds. Molex, however, obviously hired Mr. Fleischhacker as a result of his expertise, skill, and experience as a Director of Marketing in the connector industry. It is unlikely that Mr. Fleischhacker would be of much use to Molex in a position wholly unrelated to the duties he performed at AMP. The same would undoubtedly be true of any other company in the connector industry.

Our holding by no means leaves an employer helpless against a former employee using the skills and knowledge he acquired during the course of employment to obtain an undue competitive advantage. An employer is always free to protect its interests through a reasonable, restrictive covenant not to compete. * * * But when an employer has failed to take such a simple step on its own, a court will not raise to trade secret status "the fruits of ordinary experience in * * * business, thus compelling former employees to reinvent the wheel as the price for entering the competitive market." *Fleming Sales Co.*, 611 F. Supp. at 515.

* * *

The district court found that AMP had failed to show any likelihood that Mr. Fleischhacker would compromise any of AMP's confidential business information known to him. AMP presented no evidence that he had disclosed or used AMP confidences since he began working at Molex. According to the district court, AMP further failed to prove that "any confidences, if obtained, would be useful to Molex or would give it any advantages over AMP in the marketplace." * * * AMP's lame protestations that Mr. Fleischhacker's assumption of the Director of Marketing position for Molex's Consumer Products Division has created an inherent conflict of interest making it inevitable that he will use or disclose AMP trade secret information are entirely insufficient to demonstrate irreparable injury. The district court was thus correct in ruling that even if AMP had established the existence of particular, protectible trade secrets, no injunctive relief was warranted because it had failed to show that any such information had been misappropriated or was at risk of misappropriation.

Finally AMP challenges the district court's judgment in favor of defendant Molex on its unfair competition claim. AMP had alleged that Molex's recruitment of Mr. Fleischhacker was part of a larger scheme to obtain AMP confidential business and technical information. While the district court found that in the past Molex had indeed hired employees from AMP as well as from its other competitors, it concluded that there was simply no evidence that Molex had systematically pursued those employees to gain the confidences of AMP. Similarly, the district court found that Molex had come into possession of an AMP internal document, the "MTA Plan," in 1980, but concluded that there was no evidence that the document was obtained through improper means or that Molex had benefited from its possession of the document to the detriment of AMP. [*Eds.*—The court concluded that the district court's findings as to the unfair competition claim were not clearly erroneous.]

Notes and Questions

1. *Requirement of "Particularized Trade Secrets".* Can the *AMP* court's emphasis on plaintiff's need "to identify any particularized trade secrets at risk," as opposed to "generalized confidential business information," be reconciled with the later decision in *Redmond*, which purports also to be based on Illinois law? Under the Restatement (Third) of Unfair Competition, § 39, comment d:

> A person claiming rights in a trade secret bears the burden of defining the information for which protection is sought with sufficient definiteness to permit a court * * * to determine the fact of an appropriation. * * * [A] court may require greater specificity when the plaintiff's claim involves information that is closely integrated with the general skill and knowledge that is properly retained by former employees.

2. *Influence of Restatement (Third) of Unfair Competition/Uniform Trade Secrets Act. Redmond* states that *AMP* was decided before enactment of Illinois's adoption of the Uniform Trade Secrets Act (UTSA), which took effect in 1988, and arguably *Redmond* reflects the influence of the new trade secret legislation. According to one commentator, the trade secret provisions of the Restatement (Third) of Unfair Competition, also modeled after the UTSA and accompanying case law, significantly expanded "the remedies available to protect confidential information in private hands," by eliminat-

ing the distinction between trade secrets and other confidential information and treating "[a]ll secret information of economic value" as falling within the definition of a protectible trade secret. Edmund W. Kitch, The Expansion of Trade Secrecy Protection and the Mobility of Management Employees, 47 S.C. L. Rev. 659, 663 (1996).

Forty-two states have enacted the UTSA in one form or another since its promulgation in 1979; eight states have not (Massachusetts, Michigan, New York, New Jersey, Pennsylvania, Tennessee, Texas and Wyoming). Massachusetts has its own trade secrets law that is not based on the UTSA. See Mass. Ann. Laws ch. 93, §§ 42–42A. The other seven states have developed decisional law based in part on § 757 of the Restatement (First) of Torts. See 2 Melvin F. Jager, Trade Secrets Law (1985).

The UTSA differs from the earlier Restatement of Torts in several respects: (i) its definition of the term "trade secret" is broader than the Restatement's; (ii) it does not require use by the trade secret owner as a prerequisite to legal protection; (iii) individuals who obtain the trade secret by improper means are subject to liability even if they never use this information; (iv) third parties who acquire the trade secret with actual or constructive knowledge of its having been obtained by improper means are liable, irrespective of actual use; (v) perpetual injunctions are not favored, with injunctions lasting only until good faith competitors learn the trade secret by proper means (e.g., "reverse engineering"); and (vi) the UTSA provides for a three-year statute of limitations from date misappropriation is discovered or should have been discovered. See discussion in Kitch, supra; Marina Lao, Federalizing Trade Secrets Law in an Information Economy, 59 Ohio St. L.J. 1633 (1998); Ramon A. Klitzke, The Uniform Trade Secrets Act, 64 Marq. L. Rev. 277 (1980).

3. *Effect on Mobility of Managerial Employees.* Professor Kitch believes that the Restatement (Third) of Unfair Competition has significantly expanded the class of employees brought within its prohibitions:

> These are employees who are privy to information about the plans and strategies of the firm, information that is not used continuously in the business because it is constantly changing, but information that is of economic value to competitors because they can use it to adapt and modify their own strategies. Under previous law, there was no possibility that the generalist managerial employee, unfamiliar with the concrete details of production processes, ongoing research efforts, or particular customers, would be faced with trade secrecy restraint. For such employees, their knowledge of the industry, indeed their detailed knowledge of their ex-employer, may be the only marketable attribute they have. Stripped of the ability to use that knowledge, these employees may have little to offer beyond the knowledge of a freshly-minted (and far cheaper) M.B.A. graduate.

Does this view overstate the extent to which departing employees will be kept from their trades, given the transferability of managerial skills and the care most courts take to enforce only provisions of reasonable duration?

4. *Implications of Absence of Express No–Compete Clause.* Note the *AMP* court's view that an express no-compete clause might have provided protection for "the type of generalized confidential business information"

AMP sought to protect. Is this advice consistent with the court's refusal to enforce the confidentiality provision that Fleischbacker had agreed to? Is there any policy reason to favor broad no-compete covenants over broad confidentiality provisions? Are employees better able to appreciate the likely consequences of signing the former as opposed to the latter. For a case illustrating greater judicial willingness to protect information through the vehicle of a no-compete clause, see Sigma Chemical Co. v. Harris, 794 F.2d 371 (8th Cir.1986).

5. *Do We Need a Trade Secret Law?* Professor Bone questions the efficiency case for presuming an agreement to protect trade secrets, as championed by, among others, David D. Friedman, William Landes & Richard Posner, Some Economics of Trade Secret Law, 5 J. Econ. Persp. 61 (1991):

> Suppose there were no trade secret law. X [i.e., the prospective inventor] would estimate the economic value of [the prospective invention] by considering the protection afforded by existing laws * * * and the benefits of extra-legal measures, such as lead-time and learning-curve advantages. * * *
>
> The critical question is how X's ex ante calculation changes with the addition of trade secret law. There is reason to question the substantiality of any such change. For one thing, trade secret law gives little, if any, protection to the nonpatentable invention that is relatively easy to reinvent or reverse-engineer. Moreover, inventions that are exceptionally difficult to reinvent are likely to be "nonobvious" and hence patentable. * * *

Robert G. Bone, A New Look at Trade Secret Law: Doctrine in Search of Justification, 86 Calif. L. Rev. 241, 266–68 (1998).

Bone argues for a general narrowing of trade secret protections not contained in express contractual limitations:

> * * * A no-confidentiality default [rule] would force the employer, who has superior private information about trade secrets, to contract around the default and thus signal the employee that valuable secrets are involved.
>
> In addition, express confidentiality agreements should be enforced mainly according to their terms. For example, trade secret owners should not have to prove actual secrecy or reasonable secrecy precautions to recover for breach unless the contract so provides. Such an approach can benefit both sides. The trade secret owner is not likely to sue over publicly available information because the benefit of doing so is small relative to the cost. This means that a broad confidentiality agreement is likely to create little additional risk to the recipient of the secret.

Id. at 302. Do you agree? See also Pamela Samuelson & Suzanne Scotchmer, The Law and Economics of Reverse Engineering, 111 Yale L.J. 1575 (2002).

6. *The Silicon Valley Experience?* On terms somewhat similar to Bone's, Professor Hyde argues that the innovative culture of California's Silicon Valley is attributable in large part to attenuated trade secret protections:

To sum up the experience of Silicon Valley confirms the economic theory that high employee mobility creates no tendency to underproduce technical information. On the contrary, such information will continue to be produced despite the fact, and perhaps sometimes because of the fact, that employees will be back in the job market soon and may share that information with rivals. Information is produced because the firm can make more money from the production even of nonrivalrous information than from other investments; because mobile information lowers the firm's cost; and because such a labor market provides maximum incentives for employees to produce information.

Hyde, Working in Silicon Valley, supra. Hyde, too, argues for a general narrowing of trade secrets protection: The plaintiff employer should bear the burden of identifying a particular trade secret the employee would be likely to disclose on his new job. * * * As part of the definition of trade secret', the plaintiff employer should have to demonstrate that the information in question would not have been created unless it could have been kept secret." Id. at ___. Does Professor Hyde offer a workable standard for courts to administer? Also, if information of the sort PepsiCo tried to protect in *Redmond* (the principal focus of Hyde's critique) were normally disclosable, would this cause firms to engage in inefficient management practices to ensure that no employee when he or she departs could cause competitive harm? Should information on a firm's business strategy (as in *Redmond*) be offered more protection than the kind of technical information that Silicon Valley firms have used creatively?

7. *Economic Espionage Act of 1996.* Largely in response to the problem of misappropriation of U.S. proprietary information by foreign states and companies, Congress enacted the Economic Espionage Act of 1996 (EEA), 18 U.S.C. §§ 1831–39. The EEA criminalizes trade secret thefts by or for the benefit of foreign states or entities; it also penalizes thefts by domestic actors (with somewhat lesser penalties). Congress plainly intended sparing use of this law; Attorney General Reno felt obliged to give assurances that each case must receive the prior approval and close supervision of either the Attorney General, Deputy Attorney General, or the Assistant Attorney General for the Criminal Division. See 1 Jager, Trade Secrets Law, app. P, at 46–47. The EEA is criticized in Alan Farnham, How Safe Are Your Secrets?, Fortune, Sept. 8, 1997, pp. 114 ff.

Note on Employee Rights to Intellectual Property

Under U.S. copyright law, the employer is considered the author of a "work made for hire" when it is prepared by an employee in the scope of his employment. The "scope of employment" criterion is developed in Restatement (Second) of Agency § 228. The default rule under U.S. patent law, however, is different: absent agreement, the invention belongs to the inventing party, whether he be an employee or an independent contractor. "In many cases, this is true even where the employer paid for the invention or otherwise had some expectation of ownership in the invention." Bruce H. Little & Craig W. Trepanier, Untangling the Intellectual Property Rights of Employers, Employees, Inventors, and Independent Contractors, 22 Employee Rels. 49, 56 (No. 4, Spring 1997).

Employers often require their employees to assign their inventions to the firm. Some states restrict such assignments. For example, Cal. Labor Code § 2870 (1999) provides in relevant part:

§ 2870 Application of provision that employee shall assign or offer to assign rights to invention to employer

(a) Any provision in an employment agreement which provides that an employee shall assign, or offer to assign, any of his or her rights to an invention to his or her employer shall not apply to an invention that the employee developed entirely on his or her own time without using the employer's equipment, supplies, facilities, or trade secret information except for those inventions that either:

(1) Relate at the time of conception or reduction to practice of the invention to the employer's business, or actual or demonstrably anticipated research or development of the employer; or

(2) Result from any work performed by the employee for the employer.

Some employers also require employees to sign so-called "holdover" agreements, which purport to reach inventions conceived after termination of employment "if conceived as a result of and [are] attributable to work done during such employment and [which] relate[] to a method, substance, machine, article of manufacture or improvements therein within the scope of business" of the employer. Ingersoll–Rand Co. v. Ciavatta, 110 N.J. 609, 615, 542 A.2d 879 (1988). Recognizing the value of a company-sponsored culture of "creative brainstorming" and the legitimacy in some circumstances of providing protection to employers even in the absence of trade secrets or other confidential information, the *Ingersoll–Rand* court declined to adopt a rule of per se invalidity but barred enforcement of the putative assignment in that case as a matter of state common law:

The record shows that Armand Ciavatta [a program manager for Ingersoll–Rand Research, Inc.] was not hired to invent or work on design improvements or other variations of the split set friction stabilizer [i.e., a device used in the mining industry to prevent the fall of rock from the roofs and walls of underground mines]. * * * Ingersoll–Rand did not assign Ciavatta to a "think tank" division in which he would likely have encountered on a daily basis the ideas of fellow Ingersoll–Rand personnel regarding how the split set stabilizer could be improved or how a more desirable alternative stabilizer might be designed.

More importantly, the information needed to invent the split set stabilizer is not that unique type of information that we would deem protectable even under our expanded definition of a protectable interest. All of the specifications and capabilities of the Ingersoll–Rand split set stabilizer were widely publicized throughout industry and trade publications.

Id. at 641.

Part Five

"MINIMUM TERMS" LAWS: FILLING OUT THE EMPLOYMENT CONTRACT

Until this point the book has treated two the principal approaches of the American legal regime toward the regulation employer decisions; first, the prohibition of decisions having particular "bad" reasons or unjustified "bad" effects; and second, the enforcement of contractual commitments, both express and implied. In general, U.S. employment law allows the parties to the relationship to write their own contracts, unlike the tradition in at least continental Europe of a significant government role in the process.

In this part, we look at two areas where the federal government has established minimum substantive standards that set a floor for private bargaining. Chapter 15 explores the federal requirement that employers pay specified minimum wages and overtime premiums for work in excess of 40 hours in a workweek. Chapter 16 covers the federal statute regulating employee benefit plans that cover pension and welfare benefits.

Chapter Fifteen

REGULATION OF COMPENSATION AND HOURS

A. INTRODUCTION

The principal federal law regulating compensation and work hours is the Fair Labor Standards Act (FLSA), which was enacted in 1938, in President Franklin D. Roosevelt's words, to give "all our able-bodied working men and women a fair day's pay for a fair day's work. * * * A self-supporting and self-respecting democracy can plead no justification for the existence of child labor, no economic reason for chiseling workers' wages or stretching workers' hours." Jonathan Grossman, Fair Labor Standards Act of 1938: Maximum Struggle for a Minimum Wage, 101 Monthly Lab. Rev. 22 (1978) (quoting FDR's May 24, 1937 message to Congress accompanying the Administration's bill). The law was in keeping with the Progressive Era views of the President and his advisors that minimum labor standards should provide a floor below which competition among workers should not descend. See note 4, p. __ infra.

As indicated by President Roosevelt's message, the FLSA contains three core substantive obligations: (1) payment of a prescribed minimum wage (§ 206 (a)); (2) payment of an overtime premium (1 1/2 times the employee's basic rate of pay) for work in excess of 40 hours in any workweek (§ 207(a)); and (3) prohibition of employment of children under the age of 12, with special exceptions for certain types of agricultural work and child actors (§ 212). Other provisions impose on employers (4) recordkeeping (§ 211) and (5) non-retaliation (§ 215(a)(3)) duties.

The Act is enforced by the Wage Hour Division of the Department of Labor (DOL). DOL has authority to subpoena records and bring lawsuits for injunctive relief and for backpay relief on behalf of present or former employees. Employees also may sue on their own, without any requirement to file a complaint with DOL, and can do so both individually and on behalf of others "similarly situated" (who consent to be represented in this manner). See note 6, p. __ infra.

The FLSA does not preempt state laws that offer greater protections to employees; and indeed several states maintain higher minimum wages than the federal level. Moreover, while the federal government does not set a maximum limit on the numbers of hours a day or week an individual can work (other than to require payment of the overtime premium for work in excess of 40 hours a week), some states like California have set an 8–hour workday and require payment of an overtime premium for work beyond 8 hours a day. States also have enacted laws to require regular payment of wages and to prohibit employers from making unauthorized deductions from an employee's pay.

We first consider the FLSA's minimum wage obligation and then turn to the Act's overtime regulations. In the final section, we treat state wage payment laws.

B. MINIMUM WAGE LAWS

1. The Policy Debate

Whenever proposals are made to raise the minimum wage, invariably they have been challenged on the ground that such hikes will do more harm than good for low-wage employees because employers will respond to the externally imposed rise in their labor costs by either reducing work hours of incumbent workers or declining to hire new workers at the same rate as before. In 1995, prominent labor economists David Card and Alan Krueger published *Myth and Measurement: The New Economics of the Minimum Wage*, a book reporting their empirical studies of the effects of past hikes in the minimum wage. Card and Krueger found no disemployment effect, and indeed their data suggested a slight rise in employment levels. Rare for academics, their book markedly influenced the policy debates over the 1996–97 increase. Professor Shaviro evaluates the Card–Krueger work in the excerpt that follows.

DANIEL SHAVIRO, THE MINIMUM WAGE AND OPTIMAL SUBSIDY POLICY*

* * * The widely shared view, based on empirical research concerning teenagers that was assumed to apply more generally, was that a 10 percent increase in the minimum wage would likely reduce the hours worked by low wage workers by 1 to 3 percent, while a 25 percent hike would reduce such hours by 3.5 to 5.5 percent. * * *

Some noted that these estimates might support the claim that minimum wage hikes increase low-wage income overall. Suppose, for example, that a 20 percent increase in the minimum wage (the approximate magnitude of the 1996 change) increased affected workers' wages by an average of 10 percent (since some were already being paid more

* From The Minimum Wage, the Earned Income Tax Credit, and Optimal Subsidy   Policy, 64 U. Chi. L. Rev. 405 (1997).

than the old minimum wage), while reducing their hours by 5 percent. The net result would be a nearly 5 percent increase in their overall earnings. One could argue that they gained still more from increased leisure. * * *

Thus, the minimum wage arguably made low-wage workers as a group better off, unless they were sufficiently risk-averse to dislike the "lottery" to which it subjected them by increasing hourly wages but reducing work opportunities. Under this view, the minimum wage might even have strengthened marginal workers' workplace affiliation, by increasing the ex ante expected return. Such a claim was countered, however, by two strong arguments. *First*, the resulting disemployment might be borne disproportionately by those who were both least skilled and least affiliated in the workplace. Their ex ante expected return might drop even if it increased for the group as a whole, and they might be the ones who really needed the encouragement. * * * *Second*, suppose that low-wage jobs are an important stepping stone to better work opportunities in the future. If the reduction in hours worked means fewer jobs, not just fewer hours per job, then a minimum wage increase might reduce the present value of expected lifetime income for low-wage workers, even if upon enactment it increased their current-year income.

... David Card and Alan Krueger's *Myth and Measurement: The New Economics of the Minimum Wage*, published in 1995, boldly asserts that the economic consensus of the last fifty years, holding that the minimum wage results in disemployment, has simply been wrong. Based mainly on four empirical studies that Card, Krueger, and Lawrence Katz conducted in various combinations in the early 1990s, * * * they assert the following: (1) modest minimum wage hikes do not reduce, and may even increase, low-wage employment; (2) improved econometric research techniques * * * permit them to assert this with confidence; and (3) the standard prediction of disemployment is based on a faulty theoretical understanding of the labor market. * * *

* * *

[*Eds.* Professor Shaviro proceeds to evaluate the four case studies relied on by Card and Krueger: (1) California's 1988 increase in the state minimum wage, from the federally mandated $3.35, to $4.25 an hour; (2) the 1990 increase in the federal minimum which, when compared to the states' prior wage levels, made it a larger relative increase in some states than others; (3) the effects within Texas of the 1990 federal minimum wage increase; and (4) New Jersey's increase in the state minimum wage from $4.25 to $5.05 per hour. In each of the examples, Card and Krueger found the particular minimum wage increase had no negative effect on employment levels among low-wage workers. * * *]

[I]n Paul Samuelson's words, "it takes a theory to kill a theory; facts can only dent a theorist's hide." The theory behind the standard view is obvious enough: raise low-wage labor's price and demand for it will drop; or, bar certain agreements between employers and prospective workers and they will agree less frequently or for fewer hours. How could one explain the opposite result: that, when the price increases, demand does too, or that the imposition of a cartel by legal fiat increases output?

Card and Krueger make three suggestions, each of which relies on rejecting the premise of competitive markets that underlies the law of demand.

Monopsony Theory: [One argument holds that] the mandate might increase low-wage employment under two conditions: (1) low-wage employers exercise monopsony power, permitting them to set wages noncompetitively and below labor's productive value; and (2) employers cannot wage-discriminate by paying different salaries to workers who perform the same job. If both of these assumptions hold, it may make perfect sense to decline to hire an additional employee, even though the value of her labor exceeds the wage that she is asking [because the marginal cost of hiring the additional employee is not only the additional employee's wage but also an increase in the wages paid underpaid incumbent employees].

* * *

While logically coherent, the monopsony theory is widely regarded as utterly implausible as to low-wage workers. It requires lack of competition between employers, either because there is only one or because they all collude. * * * In the fast-food industry alone, numerous powerful companies compete nationwide. Their franchises can be found side-by-side nearly everywhere, competing for workers no less than for customers. A range of other employers * * * compete for low-wage workers as well. * * *

Card and Krueger concede this point, but claim that monopsony arises after all because employees, once they have a job, are reluctant to leave. Habituation, search costs, and the like give the employer a kind of monopsony power over current employees who cannot with sufficient ease find and accept competing offers. This explanation does not fit well, however, with conditions in the fast-food industry where, as Card and Krueger note, fewer than one-half of the nonsupervisory personnel in a typical restaurant have been on the job as long as six months, and more than 80 percent of the restaurants have vacancies at any given time. * * *

Even if there were monopsony in low-wage labor markets and a minimum wage could therefore, in principle, increase employment, it might be unlikely to do so in practice. [T]o set the monopsony-offsetting minimum wage at the right level one would need accurate information about the value of various workers' actual and prospective labor. In practice, * * * such value is both virtually impossible to observe and subject to substantial variation, both over time and as between different occupations, firms, plants, and even individual workers. "A uniform national minimum wage, infrequently changed, is wholly unsuited to these diversities of conditions."

* * *

Efficiency or Incentive Wages: Card and Krueger next rely on recent insights from labor economics that reflect human workers' being more complicated, less controllable, harder to monitor, and thus more variable in their output, than inanimate productive inputs such as commodities and machines. Hiring and firing workers is expensive, given search and training costs, but workers are free to quit and often cannot bond effectively against doing so. Moreover, they can shirk, or provide less than their best efforts, but whether they are doing so is hard to observe (and thus comparatively hard for them to bond against). * * *

These considerations often lead employers to pay what economists call efficiency or incentive wages. These are wages set high enough to make job loss more of a sanction than it would be at the reservation wage where the employee was close to indifferent about continuing at the same job. * * *

The implications are twofold. *First*, employers may receive some compensation in the form of greater output when they are required to pay employees higher wages. * * * *Second*, employers often choose between low-wage-high-turnover and high-wage-low-turnover strategies. When the minimum wage bars the former strategy and employers switch to the latter, the result, at least in the short run, may be a stable higher-employment equilibrium.

Unfortunately, Card and Krueger, while rightly * * * noting the second implication, ignore the first. Where an employer would have chosen the low-wage-high-turnover strategy but for the minimum wage, there is a strong inference that it was superior overall from the employer's standpoint. Thus, the minimum wage remains a net tax on low-wage employment despite the creation of some offsetting benefit. Over the long run, one would expect this tax to reduce low-wage employment by shifting resources out of low-wage industries, or by encouraging other substitution, as of capital for low-wage labor. * * * Thus, the positive employment effect, if any, may be purely short-term.

* * *

Employers also sometimes offer efficiency wages in order to increase the average quality of their job applicants, thus increasing the average quality of those they hire if quality is imperfectly observable. * * * Once again, if employers must pay more simply to get the same benefit, the extra cost is a tax in full, not offset by increased output.

Notes and Questions

1. *Justifications for Minimum Wage Laws.* In addition to the "market failure" arguments advanced by Card and Krueger, consider the following justifications that have been offered for minimum wage laws:

a. *Antipoverty Measure.* Professor Shaviro argues that such laws offer a poor mechanism for reducing poverty because (i) benefits are not tailored to family income but, rather, are given to low-wage jobholders, many of whom are young members of middle-class households; and (ii) the costs of such laws (principally disemployment) may be borne disproportionately by individuals from poorer households. See generally John T. Addison & McKinley L. Blackburn, Minimum Wages and Poverty, 52 Indus. & Lab. Rels. Rev. 393 (April 1999) (finding evidence of poverty-reducing effect among teenagers and older junior high school dropouts for the period 1983–96); see also note 3 below.

b. *Progressive Wealth Redistribution.* Professor Gottesman argues that minimum wage laws offer a politically feasible, if less than optimal, means of effecting progressive wealth redistribution, because political majorities will support "making work pay" where they will not vote for outright wealth transfers. Michael H. Gottesman, Whither Goest Labor Law: Law and Economics in the Workplace, 100 Yale L.J. 2767, 2790–93 (1991). The redistributive (and any displacement) effects of a minimum wage increase are multiplied because pay structures in collective bargaining agreements (and even among nonunion employers that pay wages comparable to the union sector) are often keyed to a multiple of the statutory minimum wage.

c. *Strengthening Workplace Affiliation.* A related argument for "making work pay" is that higher wages will improve incentives for marginal workers to leave welfare rolls and enter (and remain) in the workforce. Nobel laureate economist Edmund Phelps is prominently associated with this view. See Edmund S. Phelps, Rewarding Work: How to Restore Participation and Self–Support to Free Enterprise (1997). Phelps's policy recommendation, however, is not to legislate increases in the minimum wage but, rather, to offer firms a subsidy for each low income worker they hire. Professor Shaviro similarly urges, 64 U. Chi. L. Rev. at 459, a well-designed "earned income tax credit" financed out of general revenues ("Why not, instead of imposing a tax on the very thing one wants to encourage, pay for a low-wage subsidy (if one is desired) through general revenues? To the extent its preferred recipients are poor, why not try to target it somewhat better?").

2. *Implications of Small Disemployment Effects?* Even if Card and Krueger's finding of an employment-*increasing* effect can be challenged, the principal thrust of their work is that the disemployment effects of *modest* increases in the minimum wages are likely to be rather limited. Note that Professor Shaviro concedes that given the current state of the empirical literature, the magnitude of any disemployment effect cannot be readily ascertained, even if indicated as a theoretical matter. If so, consider the following assessment of the Card–Krueger studies:

> The new research on the minimum wage reinforces and strengthens rather considerably prior evidence concluding that employment effects associated with changes in the minimum wage [(MW)], at least at levels historically adopted in the U.S., are rather small. Our understanding of *why* MW employment effects are so small is on less firm grounds. But

the absence of large effects of MW on employment clearly undercuts the case for opposing moderate increases in the minimum.

John T. Addison & Barry T. Hirsch, The Economic Effects of Employment Regulation: What Are the Limits?, ch. 4 in Government Regulation of the Employment Relationship 145 (Bruce E. Kaufman ed., 1997). Professors Addison and Hirsch further observe:

> It should be noted that weak employment effects from the MW are not a result of low compliance. Evidence from Card and Krueger and others indicates clearly that MW laws do increase wages. Nor does the evidence support the proposition that small employment effects can be explained by a changed mix in the compensation package, with higher wages offset by lower wages and fringes. Fringes and training costs are low on most MW jobs. A higher MW does, in fact, increase costs to businesses, some of which are passed forward to consumers. Card and Krueger provide evidence from an events study surrounding the 1989 legislation showing that expectations of a higher MW are associated with lower market values among companies that are low-skill labor intensive.

Id. at 168 n.16.

For studies finding limited disemployment effects from minimum-wage increases in the U.K. and France, see Richard Dickens, Stephen Machin & Alan Manning, The Effects of Minimum Wages on Employment: Theory and Evidence from Britain, 17 J. Labor Econ. 1 (no. 1, 1999); John M. Abowd, Francis Kramarz & David N. Margolis,, Minimum Wages and Employment in France and the United States (National Bur. Econ. Res., Working Paper 6996, March 1999); John M. Abowd, Francis Kramarz, Thomas Lemieux & David N. Margolis, Minimum Wages and Youth Employment in France and the United States (National Bur. Econ. Res., Working Paper 6111, July 1997).

3. *Differential Disemployment Effects?* Even if the aggregate disemployment effects of minimum-wage increases are small, are these effects visited disproportionately among certain subgroups? Or, put differently, are the benefits of such increases disproportionately extended to particular subgroups? Compare David Neumark, Mark Schweitzer & William Wascher, The Effects of Minimum Wages Throughout the Wage Distribution (National Bur. Econ. Res., Working Paper 7519, Feb. 2000) (relatively low-wage union members gain at the expense of the lowest-wage nonunion workers when minimum wage increases); Jeffrey A. Mills, Kakoli Rou & Nicolas Williams, Recent Wage Increases and the Minimum Wage Labor Force, 20 J. Labor Res. 479, 488–89 (Fall 1999) (1996 federal minimum-wage increase indicates a shift in food-service employment away from teenagers and toward adults and full-time workers; 1997 increase had a negative effect on female employment in this industry), with Kevin Lang & Shulamit Kahn, The Effect of Minimum Wage Laws on the Distribution of Employment: Theory and Evidence, 69 J. Public Econ. 67 (July 1998) (1990–91 minimum-wage increase shifted food-service employment toward young workers, students and part-timers). See also Addison & Blackburn, Minimum Wages and Poverty, supra (minimum-wage increases in the 1990s reduced poverty among junior high dropouts and teenagers but increases in the 1980s did not reduce

poverty for these groups, principally because of absence of any disemployment effect from higher-wage minima in the 1990s).

For a view from the "critical race" perspective that minimum-wage laws should be reevaluated because of their harmful effects on minority, low-skilled workers, see Harry Hutchinson, Toward a Critical Race Reformist Conception of Minimum Wage Regimes: Exploding the Power of Myth, Fantasy, and Hierarchy, 34 Harv. J. on Legis. 93 (1997).

4. *Should Public Policy be Concerned with Employment Losses?* Consider Marc Linder, The Minimum Wage as Industrial Policy: A Forgotten Role, 16 J. Legis. 151, 155–56 (1990):

> [B]y downplaying the number of jobs destroyed by a statutory minimum wage, proponents unwittingly undermine the most cogent grounds for supporting it—namely, that the jobs it destroys are low-wage and unproductive. * * * Thus, the appropriate response to the argument that the minimum wage hurts the very people it is supposed to protect is: the minimum wage helps those marginal workers by forcing their inefficient employers either to rationalize or be driven out of business by more efficient competitors paying higher wages.

Similar views were held by certain policymakers during the 1920s and 1930s. See Jason Taylor & George Selgin, By Our Bootstraps: Origins and Effects of the High–Wage Doctrine and the Minimum Wage, 20 J. Labor Res. 447 (Fall 1999); cf. Robert E. Prasch, American Economics in the Progressive Era on the Minimum Wage, 13 J. Econ. Persp. 221 (Spring 1999). On the implications of monopsony theory, see Alan Manning, Monopsony in Motion: Imperfect Competition in Labor Markets (2003); and his Monopsony and the Efficiency of Labour Market Interventions, 11 Labour Econ. 145 (April 2004).

5. *Looking Abroad.* Professor Shaviro suggests that one problem with a nationally uniform minimum wage is that it fails to reflect the diversity of local conditions; the FLSA permits "upward" variability—as states can enact higher minimum wages—but not "downward" variability below the FLSA "floor". Would it be preferable, instead of the FLSA model, to adopt (i) what until recently had been the British approach of allowing regional and local wage councils (comprised of workers' and employers' representatives with an odd number of independent members) to set wage minima (see David Metcalf, The Low Pay Commission and the National Minimum Wage, 109 Econ. J. F46 (No. 453, Feb. 1999)); or (ii) the German approach of dispensing with statutory wage minima in favor of collectively bargained standards?

2. The Substantive Obligation

a. Coverage

SECRETARY OF LABOR v. LAURITZEN

U.S. Court of Appeals for the Seventh Circuit, 1987.

835 F.2d 1529.

[*Eds.* This decision is excerpted at pp. 12–18 supra.]

Notes and Questions

1. *"Suffer or Permit"*. Does the FLSA's definition of "[e]mploy" to include "suffer or permit to work" (29 U.S.C. § 203(g)) and the courts' use of the "economic realities" test argue for an expansive scope of coverage for the statute? See Bruce Goldstein, Marc Linder, Laurence E. Nortion, II, and Catherine K. Ruckelshaus, Enforcing Fair Labor Standards in the Modern American Sweatshop: Rediscovering the Statutory Definition of Employment, 46 U.C.L.A. L. Rev. 993 (1999). Review the materials in chapter 1 of this book. Should an FLSA-covered employment relationship be found in the following situations?:

a. *Putative Independent Contractors*. Defendant employs piece-rate workers to pick and peel the seafood it processes and packs. The workers provide their own hairnets, aprons, gloves and knives. Defendant enforces hygiene rules but otherwise does not regulate their work. The workers come and go as they please and are free to work for competitors (though few in fact do so). Employees or independent contractors? See McLaughlin v. Seafood, Inc., 867 F.2d 875, modifying 861 F.2d 450 (5th Cir.1988).

b. *Home Work*. Defendant hires both in-house and home researchers to find subscriber telephone numbers for the purpose of increasing magazine sales. Home researchers are not required to comply with any labor standards. Nor is there any obligation to complete a certain number of "cards". The home workers are paid on a piece-rate basis, while in-house researchers are paid the FLSA minimum wage for all hours worked. Are the home workers employees covered by the FLSA? See McLaughlin v. DialAmerica Mktg., Inc., 716 F.Supp. 812 (D.N.J. 1989); see also Silent Woman, Ltd. v. Donovan, 585 F.Supp. 447 (E.D.Wis.1984).

c. *"Workfare"*. Pursuant to state law, Social Security Income (SSI) recipients are required to work in order to receive benefits. Are they employees covered by the FLSA? Compare Johns v. Stewart, 57 F.3d 1544 (10th Cir.1995), with Archie v. Grand Central Partnership, Inc., 997 F.Supp. 504 (S.D.N.Y.1998). See generally David Finegold, Is the Fair Labor Standards Act Fair to Welfare Recipients?, 19 J. Labor Res. 245 (Spring 1998); Kevin J. Miller, Comment, Welfare and the Minimum Wage: Are Workfare Participants "Employees" Under the Fair Labor Standards Act?, 66 U.Chi.L. Rev. 183 (1999).

d. *Rehabilitation Programs*. Plaintiff enters a Salvation Army rehabilitative program which requires him to assign his food stamps and welfare benefits to the program and perform assigned work while in the program. Is he an employee for FLSA purposes? See Williams v. Strickland, 87 F.3d 1064 (9th Cir.1996).

e. *Volunteers*. The city's firefighters are required to be certified to render Basic Life Support (BLS) services to individuals they encounter in the performance of their duties. It is not uncommon for firefighters to be dispatched on emergency medical calls if they are able to arrive before a rescue squad. Rescue squads are separately organized nonprofit entities that provide "Advanced Life Support" (ALS). The city itself does not possess an ALS license and does not require its firefighters to become certified to provide ALS care. Benshoff, a city firefighter, freely volunteered to join a rescue squad and now seeks compensation from the city for time he spends on rescue squad service rendered on occasions when he is dispatched on emergency calls. See Benshoff v. City of Virginia Beach, 180 F.3d 136 (4th Cir.1999).

2. *Statutory Exceptions to the Minimum–Wage Requirement.* The FLSA exempts certain categories of workers from the minimum-wage requirement. These include (i) a miscellany of groups such as, inter alia, amusement and recreational employees (29 U.S.C. § 213(a)(3)), agricultural employees (§ 213(a)(6)), employees of limited circulation newspapers (§ 213(a)(10)), persons who deliver newspapers to the consumers (§ 213(d)), and casual babysitters (§ 213(a)(15)); (ii) workers hired under the "opportunity wage" provision (§ 206(g); see note 4 below); (iii) learners, apprentices and disabled workers hired pursuant to a special certificate issued by the Secretary of Labor under § 14 of the FLSA (§§ 213 (a)(7) & 214)); and (iv) "tipped employees" who must receive at least $2.25 an hour with the remainder of the minimum wage to be made up in tips actually received (§ 203(n), (t)); and (iv) outside salesmen (§ 213(a)(1)), see, e.g., Myers v. Copper Cellar Corp., 192 F.3d 546 (6th Cir. 1999); see also Walter John Wessels, Minimum Wages and Tipped Servers, 35 Econ. Inquiry 334 (1997); Samuel Estreicher & Jonathan Remy Nash, The Law and Economics of Tipping: The Laborer's Perspective (unpubl., available ssrn.com).

3. *Domestic Service Workers.* In Long Island Care at Home v. Coke, 127 S.Ct. 2339, 168 L.Ed.2d 54 (2007), a unanimous Court (per Justice Breyer) held that the U.S. Department of Labor acted within its statutory authority in issuing a regulation that included as "companionship" workers exempt under the FLSA workers "employed by an ... agency other than the family or household using their services." 29 C.F.R. § 552.109(a). The statutory exemption spoke in terms of persons "employed in domestic service employment to provide companionship services for individuals ... unable to care for themselves," 29 U.S.C. § 213(a)(15). Justice Breyer explained for the Court:

> In this case the FLSA explicitly leaves gaps, for example as to the scope and definition of statutory terms such as "domestic service employment" and "companionship services." 29 U.S.C. § 213(a)(15). It provides the Department of Labor with the power to fill these gaps through rules and regulations. Ibid.; 1974 Amendments, § 29(b), 88 Stat. 76 (authorizing the Secretary of Labor "to prescribe necessary rules, regulations, and orders with regard to the amendments made by this Act"). The subject matter of the regulation in question concerns a matter in respect to which the agency is expert, and it concerns an interstitial matter, i.e., a portion of a broader definition, the details of which, as we said, Congress entrusted the agency to work out.

> The Department focused fully upon the matter in question. It gave notice, it proposed regulations, it received public comment, and it issued final regulations in light of that comment. 39 Fed. Reg. 35383 (1974); 40 Fed. Reg. 7404. * * * The resulting regulation says that employees who

provide "companionship services" fall within the terms of the statutory exemption irrespective of who pays them. * * *

Although the FLSA in 1974 already covered *some* of the third-party-paid workers, it did not at that point cover others. It did not cover, for example, companionship workers employed directly by the aged person's family; nor did it cover workers employed by many smaller private agencies. The result is that whether, or how, the definition should apply to workers paid by third parties raises a set of complex questions. Should the FLSA cover *all* companionship workers paid by third parties? Or should the FLSA cover *some* such companionship workers, perhaps those working for some (say, large but not small) private agencies, or those hired by a son or daughter to help an aged or infirm mother living in a distant city? Should it cover *none*? How should one weigh the need for a simple, uniform application of the exemption against the fact that some (but not all) third-party employee were previously covered? Satisfactory answers to such questions may well turn upon the kind of thorough knowledge of the subject matter and ability to consult at length with affected parties that an agency, such as the Department of Labor, possesses. And it is consequently reasonable to infer (and we do infer) that Congress intended its broad grant of definitional authority to the Department to include the authority to answer these kinds of questions.

4. *Outside Salesmen.* Why are outside salesmen, as opposed to their counterparts working inside employer facilities, exempt from the FLSA altogether? Note that on-premises salesmen are exempt from the overtime but not minimum-wage provisions of the FLSA, if more than half of their compensation "represents commissions on goods or services" (§ 207(i)). Does the outside-salesmen exemption reflect (i) the difficulty employers have controlling the hours of outside-sales work, (ii) the difficulty of computing wages when compensation is principally in the form of commissions on sales, (iii) a recognition that outside-sales personnel in some sense function as entrepreneurs in that their pay is so directly tied to sales, or (iv) all of the above? The outside-salesman exemption requires a difficult determination of which duties are "incidental and in conjunction with" sales activities, and which duties should be treated as nonexempt. See, e.g., Ackerman v. Coca–Cola Enterprises, Inc., 179 F.3d 1260 (10th Cir.1999).

5. *"Opportunity" Wage.* To minimize perceived negative effects on young marginal workers, Congress in the 1989 FLSA amendments allowed employers to pay a "training wage" of 85 percent of the increased federal minimum for up to 180 days for individuals with less than 60 days of cumulative work experience. Pub. L. No. 101–157, § 6 (1989). The training-wage provision expired on March 31, 1993, and was not renewed by Congress. However, the 1996 amendments provide that an "opportunity wage" of $4.25 per hour may be paid to employees who are under age 20 for the first 90 consecutive calendar days of employment. 29 U.S.C. § 206(g).

b. *Other Issues*

Because the minimum-wage obligation is fairly straightforward, it occasions little litigation other than with respect to coverage issues.

Generally the minimum wage if applicable must be paid in cash or negotiable instruments. However, under § 3(m) the "wage" paid can include "the reasonable cost, as determined by the Secretary of Labor, to the employer of furnishing such employee with board, lodging or other facilities, if such board, lodging or other facilities are customarily furnished by such employer to his employees * * *." 29 U.S.C. § 203(m). An employer may not, however, set off against the required minimum wages the value of goods, including gas and supplies from the company store, furnished to employees. See, e.g., Brennan v. Heard, 491 F.2d 1 (5th Cir.1974).

Note on Prevailing Wage Laws

The federal government and many states require employers who have contracted to provide materials, services or construction work for government entities to pay locally prevailing wages (and sometimes also fringe benefits). The Walsh–Healy Government Contracts Act, 41 U.S.C. §§ 35 et seq., imposes such an obligation on all companies engaged in providing manufacturing services or supplies to the federal government pursuant to contracts in excess of $10,000. The Davis–Bacon Act, 40 U.S.C. §§ 276a et seq., requires payment of prevailing wages and benefits as determined by the Secretary of Labor to all laborers and mechanics engaged in the construction, alteration or repair of a public work project pursuant to a contract with the federal government (in excess of $2000). The Service Contract Labor Standards Act, 41 U.S.C. §§ 351 et seq., is a similar measure applicable to all contracts for services to the federal government in excess of $2500. Overtime obligations for federal construction contractors are set out in the Contract Work Hours and Safety Standards Act, 40 U.S.C. §§ 327 et seq.

Many states impose similar or even more demanding obligations on their contractors. For example, California requires not only payment of prevailing wages and benefits on state-funded public works projects, but also the payment of overtime after 8 hours of work in a day. Cal. Labor Code § 1815.

The Secretary of Labor now allows a weighted average of the rates paid in a locality to be used to determine the prevailing wage if no single rate is paid to more than half of the employees in a locality. Previous regulations allowed the prevailing wage to be any single rate paid to more than 30% of the employees in a locality (such as the single rate fixed by a multiemployer collective bargaining agreement). See Building & Construction Trades' Dept. v. Donovan, 712 F.2d 611 (D.C.Cir.1983).

See generally Armand J. Thieblot, Jr., Prevailing Wage Legislation: The Davis–Bacon Act, State "Little Davis–Bacon" Acts, the Walsh–Healey Act, and the Service Contract Act (U.Pa. Wharton School, Indus. Rels. Unit, No. 27, 1986); Daniel P. Kessler & Lawrence Katz, Prevailing Wage Laws and Construction Labor Markets (National Bur. Econ. Res. Working Paper 7454, Dec. 1999).

A number of cities have passed ordinances requiring municipal contractors to pay "living" wages to their employees. Cambridge, MA, for example, requires employees of city contractors with contracts over $10,000 to be paid

$10.68 per hour with annual cost-of-living adjustments. See Econ. Policy Institute Issue Guide—Living Wage, available at www.epi.org/content.cfm/issueguides_livingwage_lwo-table; Symposium, Full–Time Workers Should Not be Poor: The Living Wage Movement, 70 Miss. L.J. 889 (2001).

Note on Portal–to–Portal Act of 1947

Congress enacted the Portal-to-Portal Act amendments of 1947 to the FLSA ("Portal Act") in reaction to a series of Supreme Court decisions which held that the FLSA required compensation for time spent by employees traveling from "portal to portal"—walking from iron ore portals to underground working areas and walking from time clocks located near the plant entrance to the areas where they began productive labor—and that the "workweek" for FLSA purposes included all time the employee is required to be on the employer's premises. See Tennessee Coal, Iron & R. Co. v. Muscoda Local No. 123, 321 U.S. 590, 64 S.Ct. 698, 88 L.Ed. 949 (1944); Armour & Co. v. Wantock, 323 U.S. 126, 65 S.Ct. 165, 89 L.Ed. 118 (1944); Anderson v. Mt. Clemens Pottery Co., 328 U.S. 680, 66 S.Ct. 1187, 90 L.Ed. 1515 (1946). In the Portal Act amendments, 29 U.S.C. § 254 seq., Congress repealed any past liability for these "portal to portal" rulings. With respect to future claims, Congress rendered non-compensable any time spent walking to and from "actual place of performance of the principal activity or activities which such employee is employed to perform," as well as time spent on "activities which are preliminary or postliminary to said principal activities" that occur prior to and subsequent to the workday. (§ 4(a), 29 U.S.C. § 254(a)).

In Steiner v. Mitchell, 350 U.S. 247, 76 S.Ct. 330, 100 L.Ed. 267 (1956), the Supreme Court held that certain activities that are an "integral and indispensable" part of a principal activity are also compensable even when they do not themselves involve productive labor. In IBP, Inc. v. Alvarez, 546 U.S. 21, 126 S.Ct. 514, 163 L.Ed.2d 288 (2005), the Court extended the reasoning of *Steiner* to hold (1) compensable pre-production time spent walking from the changing area to the place of production and the post-production time spent waiting to take off required equipment; but (2) non-compensable pre-production time spent walking to the changing area and waiting to don such equipment because such time was excluded as "preliminary" to principal work activities. Importantly, the *Alvarez* Court adopted the concept of a continuous workday that is started by the performance of a principal activity under *Steiner*:

> Indeed, IBP has not offered any support for the unlikely proposition that Congress intended to create an intermediate category of activities that would be sufficiently "principal" to be compensable, but not sufficiently principal to commence the workday. Accepting the necessary import of our holding in *Steiner*, we conclude that the locker rooms where the special safety gear is donned and doffed are the relevant "place of performance" of the principal activity that the employee was employed to perform within the meaning of § 4(a)(1). Walking to that place before starting work is excluded from FLSA coverage, but the statutory text does not exclude walking from that place to another area within the plant immediately after the workday has commenced.

* * *

[W]e hold that any activity that is "integral and indispensable" to a "principal activity" is itself a "principal activity" under § 4(a) of the Portal-to-Portal Act. Moreover, during a continuous workday, any walking time that occurs after the beginning of the employee's first principal activity and before the end of the employee's last principal activity is excluded from the scope of that provision, and as a result is covered by the FLSA.

546 U.S. at 34, 37.

C. OVERTIME REGULATION

1. *Determining Overtime Pay*

BRIGHT v. HOUSTON NORTHWEST MEDICAL CENTER SURVIVOR, INC.

U.S. Court of Appeals for the Fifth Circuit (en banc), 1991.
934 F.2d 671.

GARWOOD, J.

This is a former employee's suit for overtime compensation under section 7(a)(1) of the Fair Labor Standards Act (FLSA), 29 U.S.C. § 207(a)(1). The question presented is whether "on-call" time the employee spent at home, or at other locations of his choosing substantially removed from his employer's place of business, is to be included for purposes of section 7 as working time in instances where the employee was not actually "called." The district court granted the motion for summary judgment of the employer, defendant-appellee Houston Northwest Medical Center Survivor, Inc. (Northwest), ruling that this on-call time was not working time and dismissing the suit of the employee, plaintiff-appellant Frederick George Bright (Bright). A divided panel of this Court reversed and remanded. Disagreeing with the panel majority's contrary conclusion, this Court en banc now holds that the undisputed facts afford no basis for a finding that the employee's on-call time was working time for purposes of section 7. We accordingly affirm the district court's summary judgment for the employer.

FACTS AND PROCEEDINGS BELOW

Bright went to work for Northwest at its hospital in Houston in April 1981 as a biomedical equipment repair technician, and remained in that employment until late January 1983 when, for reasons wholly unrelated to any matters at issue here, he was in effect fired. Throughout his employment at Northwest, Bright worked a standard forty-hour week at the hospital, from 8:00 a.m. to 4:30 p.m., with half an hour off for lunch, Monday through Friday, and he was paid an hourly wage. Overtime in this standard work week was compensated at time and a half rates, and it was understood that overtime work required advance approval by the department head, Jim Chatterton. When Bright started at the hospital, his immediate supervisor was Howard Culp, the senior biomedical equipment repair technician. Culp had the same work schedule as Bright. However, throughout his off-duty hours, Culp was required to wear an electronic paging device or "beeper" and to be "on call" to come to the hospital to make emergency repairs on biomedical equipment. Culp, as Bright knew, was not compensated for this "on-call" time (although Culp apparently was compensated when he was called). In February 1982 Culp resigned, and Bright succeeded him as the senior biomedical equipment repair technician and likewise succeeded Culp in wearing the beeper and being on call throughout all his off-duty time. Bright remained in that role throughout the balance of his employment at Northwest. The only period of time at issue in this lawsuit is that when Bright had the beeper, namely from February 1982 to the end of his employment in January 1983.

Bright was not compensated for his on-call time, and knew this was the arrangement with him as it had been with Culp. During the "on-call" time, if Bright were called, and came to the hospital, he was compensated by four hours [of] compensatory time at his then regular hourly rate (which apparently was some $9 or $10 per hour) for each such call. This compensation was effected by Bright simply working that many less hours the following workday or days: for example, if Bright were called on a Monday evening, he might work in his regular workshift only from 8:00 a.m. until noon on the following Tuesday, but would be paid for the entire eight hours on that day. There is no evidence that these calls on average (or, indeed, in any given instance) took as much as two hours and forty minutes (two-thirds of four hours) of Bright's time. This case does not involve any claim respecting entitlement to compensation (overtime or otherwise) for time that Bright actually spent pursuant to a call from Northwest received while he was on call.

It is undisputed that during the on-call time at issue Bright was not required to, and did not, remain at or about the hospital or any premises of or designated by his employer. He was free to go wherever and do whatever he wanted, subject only to the following three restrictions: (1) he must not be intoxicated or impaired to the degree that he could not work on medical equipment if called to the hospital, although total abstinence was not required (as it was during the daily workshift); (2) he must always be reachable by the beeper; and (3) he must be able to arrive at the hospital within, in Bright's words, "approximately twenty minutes" from the time he was reached on the beeper. Bright's answer to interrogatories reflect that in February 1982, when he commenced wearing the beeper and being on call, he was living about three miles, on average a fifteen-minute drive, from the hospital, but that in about July 1982 he moved his residence to a location some seventeen miles, on average a thirty-minute drive, from the hospital, and continued living there throughout all the remaining some five or six months of his Northwest employment. * * * Bright admitted while on call he not only stayed at home and watched television and the like, but also engaged in other activities away from home, including his "normal shopping" (including supermarket and mall shopping) and "occasionally" going out to restaurants to eat. * * * Bright also testified on deposition that he was "called" on "average" two times during the working week (Monday through Friday) and "ordinarily two to three times" on the weekend. * * *

DISCUSSION

At issue here is whether the time Bright spent on call, but uncalled on, is working time under section 7, which provides in relevant part as follows:

> "Except as otherwise provided in this section, no employer shall employ any of his employees * * * for a workweek longer than forty hours unless such employee receives compensation for his employment in excess of the hours above specified at a rate not less than one and one-half times the regular rate at which he is employed." 29 U.S.C. § 207(a)(1).

* * *

Here, the undisputed facts show that the on-call time is not working time. In such a setting, we have not hesitated to so hold as a matter of law. * * *

Armour [*& Co.* v. *Wantock*, 323 U.S. 126, 65 S. Ct. 165, 89 L.Ed. 118 (1944)], and *Skidmore* [*v. Swift & Co.*, 323 U.S. 134, 65 S.Ct. 161, 89 L.Ed. 124 (1944)] clearly stand for the proposition that, in a proper setting, on-call time may be working time for purposes of section 7. But those decisions also plainly imply that that is not true of employer-required on-call time in all settings. In *Skidmore* the Court noted, with at least some degree of implied approval, the administrative interpretations that

> "in some occupations * * * periods of inactivity are not properly counted as working time even though the employee is subject to call. Examples are an operator of a small telephone exchange where the switchboard is in her home and she ordinarily gets several hours of uninterrupted sleep each night; or a pumper of a stripper well or watchman of a lumber camp during the off season, who may be on duty twenty-four hours a day but ordinarily 'has a normal night's sleep, has ample time in which to eat his meals, and has a certain amount of time for relaxation and entirely private pursuits.' Exclusion of all such hours the Administrator thinks may be justified." *Id.* 65 S. Ct. at 163–64.

* * *

Bright's case is wholly different from *Armour* and *Skidmore* and similar cases in that Bright did not have to remain on or about his employer's place of business, or some location designated by his employer, but was free to be at his home or at any place or places he chose, without advising his employer, subject only to the restrictions that he be reachable by beeper, not be intoxicated, and be able to arrive at the hospital in "approximately" twenty minutes.[7] During the period in issue he actually moved his home—as Northwest knew and approved—to a location seventeen miles and twenty-five or thirty minutes away from the hospital, as compared to the three miles (and some fifteen minutes) away that it had been when he started carrying his beeper. Bright was not only able to carry on his normal personal activities at his own home, but could also do normal shopping, eating at restaurants, and the like, as he chose. * * *

[W]e have described "the critical issue" in cases of this kind as being "whether the employee can use the [on-call] time effectively for his or her own purposes." *Halferty* [*v. Pulse Drug Co., Inc.*], 864 F.2d [1185,] 1189 [5th Cir. 1989)]. This does not imply that the employee must have substantially the same flexibility or freedom as he would if not on call, else all or almost all on-call time would be working time, a proposition that the settled case law and the administrative guidelines clearly reject. Only in the very rarest of situations, if ever, would there be any point in an employee being on call if he could not be reached by his employer so as to shortly thereafter—generally at least a significant time before the next regular workshift could take care of the matter—be able to perform a needed service, usually at some particular location.

Within such accepted confines, Bright was clearly able to use his on-call time effectively for his own personal purposes. * * *

The panel majority * * * placed crucial reliance on the fact that Bright throughout the nearly one year in issue never had any relief from his on-call status during his nonworking hours. * * * [T]he panel majority inferentially conceded that for any given day or week of on-call time, Bright was as free to use the time for his own purposes. * * * But the panel majority claims that a different result should apply here because Bright's arrangement lasted nearly a year.

We are aware of no authority that supports this theory, and we decline to adopt it. * * *

Further, the FLSA is structured on a workweek basis. Section 7, at issue here, requires time and a half pay "for a workweek longer than forty hours." What Bright was or was not free to do in the last week in September is wholly irrelevant to whether he worked any overtime in the first week of that month. As we said in *Halferty*, the issue "is whether the employee can use the time effectively for his or her own

---

7. The administrative interpretations reflect the difference in kind between situations where the on-call employee has to remain at or about the employer's place of business and those where the on-call employee can be at home or other accessible places of his choosing. See 29 CFR § 785.17:

"An employee who is required to remain on call on the employer's premises or so close thereto that he cannot use the time effectively for his own purposes is work-

ing while 'on call.' An employee who is not required to remain on the employer's premises but is merely required to leave word at his home or with company officials where he may be reached is not working while on call."

We recognize that these interpretations do not have the force of law and that we are not required to defer to them, although they may properly be considered as to some degree persuasive. *Skidmore*, 65 S.Ct. at 163.

purposes," and that must be decided, under the statutory framework, on the basis of each workweek at the most.

JERRE S. WILLIAMS, J., with whom JOHNSON, J., joins, dissenting.

[T]he opinion for the Court falls back, as it must, upon the proposition that Bright was in the same situation as someone holding a job in a remote part of Alaska where, after an eight hour day, the use of his or her own time obviously is limited. This reliance is wholly foreign to the thrust of the Fair Labor Standards Act. Admittedly, there are jobs which because of location are in isolated areas. That is in the nature of the jobs. But the isolation is not the result of an employer's direction requiring employee on-call availability during off-duty hours. The employer has nothing to do with the restricted recreational and living accommodations in an isolated job. That is not an on-call situation at all. In contrast, here it is the employer who is enforcing a unique restriction upon a particular employee as part of the particular on-call work assignment. This is of the essence of the thrust of potential work time under the Fair Labor Standards Act. * * *

Finally, the opinion for the Court asserts that all overtime issues under the statute must be based upon a week by week analysis. We have said this in a case where it is relevant, but there are instances where the courts have recognized that the week by week test is not adequate. While the FLSA calls for the calculation of the payment of overtime on a weekly basis, it does not require that each individual week be a wholly separate entity in determining whether an employee is working or not. * * *

Notes and Questions

1. *Justifications for Overtime Regulations.* Consider the following justifications for regulating overtime work:

a. *Work–Sharing.* A principal justification offered for requiring payment of an overtime premium is that employment levels should increase when it becomes more expensive for employers to use incumbent workers for work beyond the normal workweek. In a similar effort to reduce double-digit unemployment through work-sharing, France has enacted an economy-wide 35 hour week. Professors Addision and Hirsch observe:

> An overtime premium mandated *economywide* cannot increase employment significantly * * * unless there exists excess unemployment. * * * If there exists high unemployment, then the argument that an overtime premium increases employment is possible *if the straight-time wage (W) remains fixed.* Firms determine the optimal mix between employment and hours per worker; an increase in marginal wage costs from W to 1.5W may shift firms' mix toward employment and away from overtime hours, although this need not follow given the increase in costs favored by employers.
>
> The argument that an overtime premium will increase employment is weakened further by the possibility that as a result of the

premium the straight-time wage will *decrease* so that the wages-hours combination is of equivalent value to workers. That is, the availability of jobs offering overtime hours may result in an equilibrium straight-time wage that is slightly lower than it would be in the absence of the premium

We know even less about the costs of the FLSA overtime provisions resulting from reduced scheduling flexibility. Absent overtime pay regulation, firms requiring workers to regularly or occasionally work long or variable hours would be required to pay a compensating differential only if workers regarded long hours with pay as a disamenity. Labor market sorting would result in what is likely to be a rather modest wage premium for long hours. With the overtime premium in place, firms will often choose to employ existing workers at 1.5W rather than hire additional workers at W, owing to variable product demand and fixed employment and training costs. But the overtime premium does raise the cost to firms of using variable work hours and is likely to increase reliance on temporary workers in positions where firm-specific skills are minimal. * * *

Addison & Hirsch, The Economic Effects of Employment Regulation, supra, at 141–42 (citations omitted; emphasis in original).

b. *Leisure.* A related justification for the overtime premium is that by creating a financial disincentive for work beyond the regular workweek, the FLSA expands the leisure-time (with associated health benefits) available to workers. However, there is often a tradeoff between earnings and hours of work, see generally Daniel Hecker, How Hours of Work Affect Occupational Earnings, Monthly Labor Review (Oct. 1998), pp. 8 ff., and some workers might prefer working longer hours even at straight-time wages to compelled leisure. What justification is there for not permitting the affected workers to choose for themselves between work and leisure? Is the premise that at least in the absence of a collective bargaining agent, most workers will be presented with ultimatums from their employers to work overtime? Note that the FLSA, unlike some of the European laws, does not prohibit employers from compelling employees to work overtime as long as the overtime premium is paid. See generally Todd D. Rakoff, A Time for Every Purpose: Law and the Balance of Life 65–66 (2002); Shirley Lung, Overwork and Overtime, 34 Ind.L.Rev. 51 (2005).

c. *"Making Work Pay".* Like the minimum wage requirement, the overtime premium requirement benefits incumbents workers who would not receive such a premium in the absence of a legal mandate, assuming that the employer does not impose a work hour reduction that dissipates the wage gain.

2. *Compensable "Work Time".* As *Bright* illustrates, overtime regulations require a definition of what constitutes compensable work time.

a. *"On Call" Time.* For rulings finding on-call time to be compensable, see, e.g., Renfro v. City of Emporia, Kansas, 948 F.2d 1529 (10th Cir.1991) (firefighters had to report to firehouse with 20 minutes of being paged, on-call periods were 24 hours in length, and plaintiffs received on average 3–5 calls per on-call period). See generally 29 U.S.C. §§ 553.221, 785.17; Eric

Phillips, On–Call Time Under the Fair Labor Standards Act, 95 Mich. L. Rev. 2633 (1997); Christopher S. Miller, Steven J. Whitehead & Elizabeth Clark–Morrison, The Impact of Electronic Paging and On–Call Policies on Overtime Pay Under the FLSA, 11 Labor Lawy. 231 (1995).

     b. *"Off the Clock" Time.* In view of the FLSA definition that to "[e]mploy includes to suffer or permit to work," 29 U.S.C. § 203(g), employers may be held liable for "off the clock" work that they require or permit employees to perform in order to complete job assignments, even in the face of a policy prohibiting off-the-clock work. See, e.g., Lyle v. Food Lion, Inc., 954 F.2d 984 (4th Cir.1992). Moreover, the " 'Working' commences at the time [teh employee] reports * * * to work in accordance with the employer's requirement, even though through a cause beyond the employee's control, he is not able to commence performance of his productive activities until a later time." 29 C.F.R. § 790.6(b).

     c. *Pre–Shift and Post–Shift Time.* The general rule is that activities preliminary to beginning work or subsequent to completing work are not compensable. Time spent changing clothes or showering need not be compensated unless done at the site at the employer's request or required by the nature of the principal duties. See Steiner v. Mitchell, 350 U.S. 247, 76 S.Ct. 330, 100 L.Ed. 267 (1956); Reich v. Monfort, Inc., 144 F.3d 1329 (10th Cir.1998) (time spent by meat processing employees after their shift cleaning protective equipment and cutting knives held compensable).

     "Normal" travel time to and from work is generally not compensable. See 29 C.F.R. § 785.35; Kavanagh v. Grand Union, 192 F.3d 269, 272 (2d Cir.1999):

> We interpret "normal travel" as used in the regulation to refer to the time normally spent by a specific employee traveling to work. The term does not represent an objective standard of how far most workers commute or how far they may reasonably be expected to commute. Instead, it represents a subjective standard, defined by what is usual within the confines of a particular employment relationship.

     d. *"Sleep Time".* In Skidmore v. Swift & Co., 323 U.S. 134, 137, 65 S.Ct. 161, 89 L.Ed. 124 (1944), the Supreme Court held that whether waiting time or sleep time must be compensated is a question of fact which

> involves scrutiny and construction of the agreements between the particular parties, appraisal of their practical construction of the working agreement by conduct, consideration of the nature of the service, and its relation to the waiting time, and all of the surrounding circumstance. * * * The law does not impose an arrangement upon the parties. It imposes upon the courts the task of finding what the arrangement was.

The Labor Department's regulations permit agreements between an employer and an employee on 24–hour duty to exclude not more than 8 hours for "a bona fide regularly scheduled sleeping period," provided (i) adequate facilities are provided, (ii) the employee can usually enjoy an uninterrupted night's sleep, (iii) sleep time interruptions are compensated, and (iv) the entire sleep period is compensated if the employee cannot receive at least 5 hours' sleep during the scheduled period. 29 C.F.R. § 785.22. For employees residing at their employer's premises on a permanent basis or "for extended periods of time," the regulations (§ 785.23) state:

> It is, of course, difficult to determine the exact hours worked under these circumstances and any reasonable agreement of the parties which takes into consideration all of the pertinent facts will be accepted.

See, e.g., Bouchard v. Regional Governing Board of Region V Mental Retardation Services, 939 F.2d 1323 (8th Cir. 1991) (upholding arrangement in which weekday "Life Skill Trainers" (LSTs) resided at the facility during weekdays and were paid for 40 duty hours; unpaid time included "Off Duty Hours" from 8:00 a.m. to 3:30 p.m. each day, when the clients were away from the group homes, and "Evening Hours" from 10:00 p.m. to 6:00 a.m., when LSTs were expected to sleep in private quarters at the group home; compensation was provided for actual time on duty when client needed attention for at least 5–8 minutes during sleep time, and for entire 8–hour sleep period whenever interruptions totaled three hours or more).

3. *"Regular Rate"*. The FLSA requires computation of a "regular rate" of pay, which will provide the basis for calculation of the overtime premium. Under 29 U.S.C. § 207(e), the "regular rate" includes "all remuneration for employment paid to, or on behalf of, the employee."

a. *Statutory Exclusions*. There are seven statutory exclusions from the definition of "regular rate".

(1) sums paid as gifts; payments in the nature of gifts * * * as a reward for service, the amount of which are not measured by or dependent on hours worked, production, or efficiency;

(2) payments made for occasional periods when no work is performed due to vacation, holiday, illness, failure of the employer to provide sufficient work, or other similar cause * * *;

(3) [s]ums paid in recognition of services performed during a given period if either (a) both the fact that payment is to be made and the amount of the payment are determined at the sole discretion of the employer at or at the end of the period and not pursuant to any prior contract, agreement, or promise causing the employee to expect such payments regularly; or (b) the payments are made pursuant to a bona fide profit-sharing plan * * *;

(4) contributions irrevocably made * * * to a bona fide plan providing old-age, retirement, life, accident, or health insurance or similar benefits for employees;

(5) extra compensation provided by a premium rate paid for certain hours worked * * * because such hours are ... in excess of eight in day or * * * in excess of the employee's normal working hours * * *;

(6) extra compensation provided by a premium rate for work [on weekends, holidays, or regular day of rest] * * *; or

(7) extra compensation provided by a premium rate * * * for work outside of the hours established in good faith by the [employment contract or collective agreement] as the basic, normal, or regular workday (not exceeding eight hours) or workweek applicable to such employee. * * *

29 U.S.C. § 207(e).

b. *Bonuses?* An investment bank provides its traders an annual "discretionary performance bonus" keyed to the profitability of the firm generally and the profits generated by the trading department. In existence for five years, the bank has awarded such a bonus, amounting to 25% of average compensation, in four of the years. Is the bonus part of "regular pay"? See 29 C.F.R. § 778.211(b); Walling v. Harnischfeger Corp., 325 U.S. 427, 432, 65 S.Ct. 1246, 89 L.Ed. 1711 (1945); Walling v. Richmond Screw Anchor Co., 154 F.2d 780, 784 (2d Cir.1946). If the bonus is included but covers a period of more than a week, the employer must apportion the amount of the bonus over the number of workweeks covered to determine the regular rate. 29 C.F.R. § 778.209.

c. *Stock Options?* The Labor Department had taken the position that employers offering certain types of stock option plans to hourly employees may be required to include the amount of profit realized when options are exercised, in calculating the employees' "regular rate" of pay. See U.S. Dept. of Labor, Wage and Hour Div., Opinion Letter, Fair Labor Standards Act, 1999 WL 1002365 (DOL Wage–Hour, Feb. 12, 1999). The proposed plan addressed in the opinion letter offered all eligible employees (i.e., full-time employees on the payroll more than three months) options for 100 shares with a grant price for the options fixed for five years. The employees' right to purchase the shares would occur after the two-year anniversary date or immediately upon the stock being traded at or above the designated price for a certain number of days, whichever occurred earliest. Once exercisable, employees could purchase shares at any time before the options' expiration date. Moreover, upon notice of exercise by the employee, the company would lend the money necessary to purchase the shares at the grant price. Employee profit would be the difference between the grant price and the price of the stock at the time the options were exercised. According to the DOL opinion letter, the profit was to be allocated over the period in which the option is exercised, but if an employee exercised options more than 104 weeks into the program, all profit earned would be allocated to his regular rate of pay for the preceding 104 weeks.

Is the Labor Department's position a sensible one? Congress, believing the ruling would discourage stock option programs, enacted the Worker Economic Opportunity Act of 2000, Pub.L. 106–202, to exempt from the § 7(e) definition of "regular rate" of pay, "any value or income derived from employer-provided grants or rights pursuant to a stock option, stock appreciation right, or bona fide employee stock purchase plan." The exception applies only if employee participation is voluntary; there is at least a six-month delay between the grant of an option and its exercise by the employee; and options offered at a discount do not exceed 15 percent of fair market value at time of the grant.

d. *Excludable vs. Creditable Items.* Some items are excluded from compensation for purpose of determining the "regular rate", but are nevertheless creditable to any overtime due (e.g., amounts paid as premium compensation for hours in excess of 8 in a day or 40 in a week or for work on weekends). Some items are excluded and are also not creditable to any overtime due (e.g., paid vacation and holidays, see Dunlop v. Gray–Goto, Inc., 528 F.2d 792 (10th Cir.1976)).

e. *Calculated for Each Workweek.* As the *Bright* court stressed, the "regular rate" must be calculated for each week worked. 29 C.F.R. § 778.109:

> The regular rate of pay of an employee is determined by dividing his total remuneration for employment (except for statutory exclusions) in any workweek by the total of hours actually worked by him in that workweek for which such compensation was paid.

Was the court right that the workweek basis for overtime supported its view that the on-call time in that case was not compensable?

4. *Departures from General Rule of Overtime Pay for Work Over 40 Hours a Week.* In general, the overtime calculation—both the "regular rate" and hours worked—is based on each workweek. Thus, for example, an employee whose regular rate is $10 an hour and who works 50 hours in the first week and 30 hours in the second week is entitled to an overtime premium for the first week ($10 × 40 hrs. plus $15 × 10 hrs. or $550), even though he averaged only 40 hours a week. A private employer also cannot pay employee owed overtime in compensatory time even if calculated at the premium rate, because under the workweek rule, what the employee does in another workweek has no bearing on his overtime entitled for a week in which he works more than 40 hours. There are a few narrow exceptions from this rule:

a. *Fixed Salary for Fluctuating Workweeks.* The regulations (29 C.F.R. § 778.114) provide:

> An employee employed on a salary basis may have hours of work which fluctuate from week to week and the salary may be paid him pursuant to an understanding * * * that he will receive such fixed amount * * * for whatever hours he is called upon to work in a workweek. * * * Since the salary in such a situation is intended to compensate the employee at straight time rates * * *, the regular rate of the employee will vary from week to week. * * * Payment for overtime hours at one-half such rate in addition to the salary satisfies the overtime pay requirement because such hours have already been compensated at the straight time regular rate, under the salary arrangement.

Thus, in the example given in the regulations, take an employee whose hours vary from week to week, whose overtime is never in excess of 50 hours in a workweek, and whose salary of $250 a week is paid with the understanding that it constitutes his compensation, except for overtime premiums, for all hours worked in a workweek. If over four weeks he works 40, 44, 50 and 48 hours, his regular rate of pay in each of these weeks is approximately $6.25, $5.68, $5, $5.21, respectively. Only additional half-time is due: for the second week, $261.36 ($250 plus $2.84 × 4 hrs., or 40 hrs. @ $5.68 and 4 hrs. @ $8.52); for the third week, $275 ($250 plus 10 hrs. @ $2.50, or 40 hrs. @ $5 plus 10 hrs. @ $7.50); and for the fourth week, approximately $270.88 ($250 plus 8 hrs. at $2.61, or 40 hrs. at $5.21 plus 8 hrs. at $7.82).

For this method to be applicable, (i) the employee must not "customarily" work a "regular schedule of hours," (ii) the salary is paid whether or not the employee works "a full schedule of hours" and (iii) is large enough that the employee is never paid below the minimum wage in a given week, and (iv) "the employee clearly understands that the salary covers whatever hours the job may demand in a particular week". 29 U.S.C. § 778.114(c).

Some Issues: Is this method available where salaried employees are improperly docked for partial-day absences? See Cash v. Conn Appliances, Inc., 2 F.Supp. 2d 884 (E.D.Tex.1997) (answering yes). For individuals improperly classified as salaried exempt employees? See Blackmon v. Brookshire Grocery Co., 835 F.2d 1135, 1138–39 (5th Cir. 1988); Donihoo v. Dallas Automotive, Inc., 1998 WL 47632 (N.D. Tex. Feb. 2, 1998) (both answering yes). How unpredictable does the employee's schedule have to be? In Griffin v. Wake County, 142 F.3d 712, 715 (4th Cir.1998), although the county's "emergency medical technicians" (EMTs) worked a schedule that fluctuated in a predictable manner, the court held that the regulations do not require an unpredictable schedule, only "a schedule that fluctuates * * *."

b. *"Comp Time" in Lieu of Overtime Pay.* Currently, compensatory time off in lieu of overtime pay is available only to state and local government employees. 29 U.S.C. § 207(*o*)(1). Compensatory time off may be provided at a rate not less than 1 1/2 hours for each hour of employment for up to 240 hours of compensatory time (or 480 hours for employees engaged in public safety, emergency response or seasonal activities). Employees must be permitted to use accrued compensatory time "within a reasonable time of making the request if the use * * * does not unduly disrupt the operations of the public agency." Id. § 207(*o*)(5). Upon termination of employment, the employee must be paid "for the unused compensatory time at a rate of compensation" not less than average regular rate during previous three years of employment, or the employee's final regular rate, whichever is higher. Id. § 207(*o*)(4).

Can a public employer limit the accrual of compensatory time off? In Christensen v. Harris County, 529 U.S. 576, 120 S.Ct. 1655, 146 L.Ed.2d 621 (2000), the Court held that nothing in the FLSA or its implementing regulations prohibits public employers from compelling the use of compensatory time. In that case, the employer issued a policy requiring its employees to schedule time off in order to reduce the amount of accrued time and, absent voluntary steps by the employees to effect such reductions, compelling the use of compensatory time at specified times.

5. *FLSA Reform?* Republicans have sponsored FLSA reform legislation that would, inter alia, allow employer policies/agreements providing (i) for compensatory time off in lieu of overtime in private-sector employment for up to 240 hours; and (ii) biweekly work programs whereby employees could be required to work no more than 80 hours over a 2–week period "in which more than 40 hours of the work requirement may occur in a week of the period," with only work in excess of the 80 hours triggering the overtime premium. These arrangements would require the consent of the employee (or labor union in represented workplaces), and employers would be prohibited from coercing employees for the purpose of "interfering with the rights of the employee * * * to request or not request compensatory time off" or to participate in the biweekly program. See S.4, 86th Cong., 1st Sess. (intro-

duced Jan. 21, 1997). What arguments might be made against this proposed legislation?

2. *FLSA Exemptions*

a. *"Salary Basis" Test*

AUER v. ROBBINS

Supreme Court of the United States, 1997.
519 U.S. 452, 117 S.Ct. 905, 137 L.Ed.2d 79.

JUSTICE SCALIA delivered the opinion of the Court.

I

Petitioners are sergeants and a lieutenant employed by the St. Louis Police Department. They brought suit in 1988 against respondents, members of the St. Louis Board of Police Commissioners, seeking payment of overtime pay that they claimed was owed under § 7(a)(1) of the FLSA, 29 U.S.C. § 207(a)(1). Respondents argued that petitioners were not entitled to such pay because they came within the exemption provided by § 213(a)(1) for "bona fide executive, administrative, or professional" employees.

Under regulations promulgated by the Secretary, one requirement for exempt status under § 213(a)(1) is that the employee earn a specified minimum amount on a "salary basis." 29 CFR §§ 541.1(f), 541.2(e), 541.3(e) (1996). According to the regulations, "an employee will be considered to be paid 'on a salary basis' * * * if under his employment agreement he regularly receives each pay period on a weekly, or less frequent basis, a predetermined amount constituting all or part of his compensation, which amount is not subject to reduction because of variations in the quality or quantity of the work performed." § 541.118(a). Petitioners contended that the salary-basis test was not met in their case because, under the terms of the St. Louis Metropolitan Police Department Manual, their compensation could be reduced for a variety of disciplinary infractions related to the "quality or quantity" of work performed. Petitioners also claimed that they did not meet the other requirement for exempt status under § 213(a)(1): that their duties be of an executive, administrative, or professional nature. See §§ 541.1(a)–(e), 541.2(a)–(d), 541.3(a)–(d).

The District Court found that petitioners were paid on a salary basis and that most, though not all, also satisfied the duties criterion. The Court of Appeals affirmed in part and reversed in part, holding that both the salary-basis test and the duties test were satisfied as to all petitioners. * * *

II

The FLSA grants the Secretary broad authority to "define and delimit" the scope of the exemption for executive, administrative, and professional employees. § 213(a)(1). Under the Secretary's chosen approach, exempt status requires that the employee be paid on a salary basis, which in turn requires that his compensation not be subject to reduction because of variations in the "quality or quantity of the work performed," 29 CFR § 541.118(a) (1996). Because the regulation goes on to carve out an exception from this rule for "penalties imposed * * * for infractions of safety rules of major significance," § 541.118(a)(5), it is clear that the rule embraces reductions in pay for disciplinary violations. The Secretary is of the view that employees whose pay is adjusted for disciplinary reasons do not deserve exempt status because as a general matter true "executive, administrative, or professional" employees are not "disciplined" by piecemeal deductions from their pay, but are terminated, demoted, or given restricted assignments.

The FLSA did not apply to state and local employees when the salary-basis test was adopted in 1940. See 29 U.S.C. § 203(d) (1940 ed.); 5 Fed. Reg. 4077 (1940) (salary-basis test). In 1974 Congress extended FLSA coverage to virtually all public-sector employees, Pub. L. 93–259, § 6, 88 Stat. 58–62, and in 1985 we held that this exercise of power was consistent with the Tenth Amendment, *Garcia v. San Antonio Metropolitan Transit Authority,* 469 U.S. 528, 83 L.Ed. 2d 1016, 105 S.Ct. 1005 (1985) (over-ruling *National League of Cities v. Usery,* 426 U.S. 833, 49 L.Ed.2d 245, 96 S.Ct. 2465 (1976)). The salary-basis test has existed largely in its present form since 1954, see 19 Fed. Reg. 4405 (1954), and is expressly applicable to public-sector employees, see 29 CFR §§ 553.2(b), 553.32(c) (1996).

Respondents * * * contend * * * that the "no disciplinary deductions" element of the salary-basis test is invalid for public-sector employees because as applied to them it reflects an unreasonable interpretation of the statutory exemption. That is so, they say, because the ability to adjust public-sector employees' pay—even executive, administrative or professional employees' pay—as a means of enforcing compliance with work rules is a necessary component of effective government. In the public-sector context, they contend, fewer disciplinary alternatives to deductions in pay are available.

Because Congress has not "directly spoken to the precise question at issue," we must sustain the Secretary's approach so long as it is "based on a permissible construction of the statute." *Chevron U.S.A. Inc.* v. *Natural Resources Defense Council, Inc.,* 467 U.S. 837, 842–843, 81 L.Ed.2d 694, 104 S.Ct. 2778 (1984). While respondents' objections would perhaps support a different application of the salary-basis test for public employees, we cannot conclude that they compel it. The Secretary's view that public employers are not so differently situated with regard to disciplining their employees as to require wholesale revision of his time-tested rule simply cannot be said to be unreasonable. * * *

Respondents appeal to the "quasi military" nature of law enforcement agencies such as the St. Louis Police Department. The ability to use the full range of disciplinary tools against even relatively senior law enforcement personnel is essential, they say, to maintaining control and discipline in organizations in which human lives are on the line daily. It is far from clear, however, that only a pay deduction, and not some other form of discipline—for example, placing the offending officer on restricted duties—will have the necessary effect. Because the FLSA entrusts matters of judgment such as this to the Secretary, not the federal courts, we cannot say that the disciplinary-deduction rule is invalid as applied to law enforcement personnel. * * *

III

A primary issue in the litigation unleashed by application of the salary-basis test to public-sector employees has been whether, under that test, an employee's pay is "subject to" disciplinary or other deductions whenever there exists a theoretical possibility of such deductions, or rather only when there is something more to suggest that the employee is actually vulnerable to having his pay reduced. Petitioners in effect argue for something close to the former view; they contend that because the police manual nominally subjects all department employees to a range of disciplinary sanctions that includes disciplinary deductions in pay, and because a single sergeant was actually subjected to a disciplinary deduction, they are "subject to" such deductions and hence nonexempt under the FLSA.

The Court of Appeals rejected petitioners' approach, saying that "the mere possibility of an improper deduction in pay does not defeat an employee's salaried status" if no practice of making deductions exists. * * * In the Court of Appeals' view, a "one-time incident" in which a disciplinary deduction is taken under "unique circumstances" does not defeat the salaried status of employees. * * * (In this case the sergeant in question, who had violated a residency rule, agreed to a reduction in pay as an alternative to termination of his employment.) * * *

The Secretary of Labor, in an amicus brief filed at the request of the Court, interprets the salary-basis test to deny exempt status when employees are covered by a policy that permits disciplinary or other deductions in pay "as a practical matter." That standard is met, the Secretary says, if there is either an actual practice of making such deductions or an employment policy that creates a "significant likelihood" of such deductions. The Secretary's approach rejects a wooden requirement of actual deductions, but in their absence it requires a clear and particularized policy—one which "effectively communicates" that deductions will be made in specified circumstances. This avoids the imposition of massive and unanticipated overtime liability (including the possibility of substantial liquidated damages * * *) in situations in which a vague or broadly worded policy is nominally applicable to a whole range of personnel but is not "significantly likely" to be invoked against salaried employees.

Because the salary-basis test is a creature of the Secretary's own regulations, his interpretation of it is, under our jurisprudence, controlling unless " 'plainly erroneous or inconsistent with the regulation.' " *Robertson v. Methow Valley Citizens Council*, 490 U.S. 332, 359, 104 L.Ed.2d 351, 109 S.Ct. 1835 (1989) * * *. That deferential standard is easily met here. The critical phrase "subject to" comfortably bears the meaning the Secretary assigns. See American Heritage Dictionary 1788 (3d ed. 1992) (def. 2: defining "subject to" to mean "prone; disposed"; giving as an example "a child who is subject to colds"). * * *

The Secretary's approach is usefully illustrated by reference to this case. The policy on which petitioners rely is contained in a section of the police manual that lists a total of 58 possible rule violations and specifies the range of penalties associated with each. All department employees are nominally covered by the manual, and some of the specified penalties involve disciplinary deductions in pay. Under the Secretary's view, that is not enough to render petitioners' pay "subject to" disciplinary deductions within the meaning of the salary-basis test. This is so because the manual does not "effectively communicate" that pay deductions are an anticipated form of punishment for employees in petitioners' category, since it is perfectly possible to give full effect to every aspect of the manual without drawing any inference of that sort. If the statement of available penalties applied solely to petitioners, matters would be different; but since it applies both to petitioners and to employees who are unquestionably not paid on a salary basis, the expressed availability of disciplinary deductions may have reference only to the latter. No clear inference can be drawn as to the likelihood of a sanction's being applied to employees such as petitioners. Nor, under the Secretary's approach, is such a likelihood established by the one-time deduction in a sergeant's pay, under unusual circumstances. * * *

IV

One small issue remains unresolved: the effect upon the exempt status of Sergeant Guzy, the officer who violated the residency requirement, of the one-time reduction in his pay. The Secretary's regulations provide that if deductions which are inconsistent with the salary-basis test—such as the deduction from Guzy's pay—are made in circumstances indicating that "there was no intention to pay the employee on a salary basis," the exemption from the FLSA is "[not] applicable to him during the entire period when such deductions were being made." 29 CFR § 541.118(a)(6) (1996). Conversely, "where a deduction not permitted by [the salary-basis test] is inadvertent, or is made for reasons other than lack of work, the exemption will not be considered to have been lost if the employer reimburses the employee for such deductions and promises to comply in the future." *Ibid.*

Petitioners contend that the initial condition in the latter provision (which enables the employer to take corrective action) is not satisfied here because the deduction from Guzy's pay was not inadvertent. That it was not inadvertent is true enough, but the plain language of the regulation sets out "inadvertence" and "made for reasons other than lack of work" as alternative grounds permitting corrective action. Petitioners also contend that the corrective provision is unavailable to respondents because Guzy has yet to be reimbursed for the residency-based deduction; in petitioners' view, reimbursement must be made immediately upon the discovery that an improper deduction was made. The language of the regulation, however, does not address the timing of reimbursement, and the Secretary's amicus brief informs us that he does not interpret it to require immediate payment. Respondents are entitled to preserve Guzy's exempt status by complying with the corrective provision in § 541.118(a)(6). * * *

Notes and Questions

1. *Rationale for "Salary Basis" Test.* Why do the Labor Department's regulations require that exempt employees be paid on a salary basis? Is such payment (i) evidence of duties the value of which cannot be measured in hours, and therefore should not be compensated by wages (reflecting hours in a workweek); or (ii) an indication that the employer views the employees as like-positioned to management and worthy of empathic treatment not requiring overtime regulations? Is the fact that an employee is subject to partial-day deductions inconsistent with either? See note 3 below.

2. *Exceptions to the "Salary Basis" Rule.* Consider the following exceptions to the salary-basis rule:

   a. deductions for absences from work "for one or more full days for personal reasons, other than sickness or disability" (29 C.F.R. § 541.602(b)(1));

   b. deductions for absences "of a day or more occasioned by sickness or disability" in accordance with a bona-fide plan or policy (§ 541.602(b)(2));

   c. "[p]enalties imposed in good faith for infractions of safety rules of major significance," i.e., "those relating to the prevention of serious danger in the workplace or to other employees" (§ 541.602(b)(4));

   d. employees "need not be paid for any workweek in which they perform no work" (§ 541.602(a));

   e. full workweek or multiple-period suspensions for violations of non-safety-related work rule, see Hackett v. Lane County, 91 F.3d 1289 (9th Cir.1996);

   f. charging partial-day absences against accrued leave time, provided no salary deductions occur if accrued leave is exhausted, see Aaron v. City of Wichita, 54 F.3d 652 (10th Cir.1995); and

   g. partial-day deductions for intermittent or reduced-schedule leaves pursuant to the Family and Medical Leave Act (29 U.S.C. § 825.206(a)).

In In re Wal-Mart Stores, 395 F.3d 1177, 1184 (10th Cir. 2005), the court held that prospective salary reductions do not violate the salary basis test: "[A]n employer may prospectively reduce salary to accommodate the employer's business needs unless it is done with such frequency that the salary is the functional equivalent of an hourly wage.... [W]e would read the regulation as prohibiting only reductions in pay made in response to certain events in a period for which the pay had been set, not salary reductions to take effect in future pay periods."

3. *"Compensation" for Purposes of the Salary–Basis Test?* Do an employee's fringe benefits, such as accrued leave time or business expense reimbursement accounts, constitute "compensation" under the salary-basis test? What if the accrued time, if unused, is subject to a cash pay-out? A few courts have taken the view that deductions from an employee's leave account should be construed as "deductions in pay" to the extent any lump sum cash pay-out might be reduced accordingly at time of termination of employment. See Yourman v. Dinkins, 826 F.Supp. 736 (S.D.N.Y.1993), affirmed, 84 F.3d 655 (2d Cir.1996), vacated & remanded on other grounds sub nom. Giuliani v. Yourman, 519 U.S. 1145, 117 S.Ct. 1078, 137 L.Ed.2d 213 (1997); Carpenter v. City & County of Denver, 82 F.3d 353, 360 n. 6 (10th Cir.1996), vacated & remanded on other grounds, 519 U.S. 1145, 117 S.Ct. 1078, 137 L.Ed.2d 213, op. on remand, 115 F.3d 765 (10th Cir.1997). Do these rulings make sense? Are they consistent with the thrust of *Auer*?

4. *Additional or Variable Payments.* Is the salary-basis test violated where an otherwise exempt employee receives additional compensation or compensatory time off for hours exceeding a normal workweek? The regulations state that

> An employer may provide an exempt employee with additional compensation without losing the exemption or violating the salary basis requirement, if the employment arrangement also includes a guarantee of at least the minimum weekly-required amount paid on a salary basis.

29 C.F.R. § 541.604(a). Compare Boykin v. Boeing Co., 128 F.3d 1279 (9th Cir.1997) (employer's provision of overtime pay for unscheduled "spot" overtime held consistent with salary basis), with Brock v. Claridge Hotel and Casino, 846 F.2d 180 (3d Cir.1988) (policy paid exempt employees weekly salary of $250 and wages in excess of that amount for additional hours beyond normal workweek; held that Labor Department regulations permitting "additional compensation" refer only to commissions and profit-bonuses, but not this type of pay structure).

5. *"Significant Likelihood" of Partial–Day Deductions.* In Ahern v. County of Nassau, 118 F.3d 118 (2d Cir.1997), plaintiffs argued they were nonexempt employees because the Police Department rules provided that the Commissioner had the power to impose discipline by reprimand, fine or suspension for violations of department rules. In plaintiffs' view, this policy made their salary "subject to reduction" even in the absence of a major safety rule violation. The court held that the "significant likelihood" standard in *Auer* requires the existence of a policy which states that deductions will be made in certain circumstances; here, deductions were only possible, not certain. As the Second Circuit stated in Kelly v. City of Mount Vernon, 162 F.3d 765 (2d Cir.1998):

> [T]he employees must be able to "point to [a] rule that state(s) that if they commit[ ] a specified infraction, their pay [will] be docked."

Id. at 768 (quoting *Auer* and *Ahern*). Is this a correct reading of *Auer*? At what point should a "significant likelihood" be found?

6. *"Window of Correction" Defense.* The regulations provide a "window of correction" defense:

> Improper deductions that are either isolated or inadvertent will not result in loss of the exemption for any employees subject to such improper deductions, if the employer reimburses the employees for such improper deductions.

29 C.F.R. § 541.604(c). Is this defense available where the employer has engaged in a "pattern" of improper deductions? Compare Hoffmann v. Sbarro, Inc., 982 F.Supp. 249, 256 (S.D.N.Y.1997) (deferring to DOL appellate counsel's statement of agency policy that this defense is not "available in cases of multiple or recurring improper deductions or a longstanding policy permitting such deductions"), with Moore v. Hannon Food Serv., Inc., 317 F.3d 489 (5th Cir. 2003) (exempt status of fast food restaurant managers retained despite deducting cash register shortfalls from their paychecks for four months because employer repaid improper deductions and dropped the practice).

The Department of Labor's regulations adopt the position of the *Sbarro* court: "An actual current practice of making improper deductions demonstrates that the employer did not intend to pay employees on a salary basis." 29 C.F.R. § 541.603(a).

b.   The "Duties" Test

DALHEIM v. KDFW–TV

U.S. Court of Appeals for the Fifth Circuit, 1990.
918 F.2d 1220.

Rubin, J.

A television station appeals a judgment of the district court holding it liable for violations of the Fair Labor Standards Act (FLSA) by failing to compensate its general-assignment reporters, news producers, directors, and assignment editors for overtime work. * * *

I

A.   Facts and Procedural History

* * *

Plaintiffs are nineteen present and former general-assignment reporters, producers, directors, and assignment editors employed in the news and programming departments of television station KDFW–TV (KDFW). As its call letters imply, KDFW serves the Dallas–Fort Worth area which, with approximately 3.5 million viewers, is the eighth largest television market in the nation. The news and programming departments are responsible for producing KDFW's local news broadcasts and its public affairs programming.

KDFW's general-assignment reporters usually receive a new coverage assignment each day. The assignment manager or an assignment editor tells the reporter the story to be covered, what she is expected to "shoot," and the intended angle or focus of the story. After the reporter interviews the persons that she or another KDFW employee has arranged to interview, she obtains pertinent video footage, and then writes and records the text of the story, subject to review by the producer. Some reporters help assemble the video and text narration; others rely on a video editor to put the final package together. General-assignment reporters are only infrequently assigned to do a series of reports focusing on a single topic or related topics. Successful reporters usually have a pleasant physical appearance and a strong and appealing voice, and are able to present themselves as credible and knowledgeable.

Producers are responsible for determining the content of the ten-to-twelve minute news portion of KDFW's thirty-minute newscast. They participate in meetings to decide which stories and story angles will be covered; they also decide the amount of time to be given a particular story, the sequence in which stories will be aired, and when to take commercial breaks. Producers have the authority to revise reporters' stories. All of the producers' actions are subject to approval by the executive producer.

Directors review the script for the newscast in order to prepare technical instructions for "calling" the show. The director decides which camera to use and on which machine to run videotaped segments or preproduction graphics. During the broadcast, the director cues the various technical personnel, telling them precisely when to perform their assigned tasks. The overall appearance of KDFW's newscasts, however, is prescribed by station management. The director therefore has no discretion concerning lighting, camera-shot blocking, closing-shot style, or the sequence of opening and closing graphics. KDFW's directors also direct some public affairs programming, which have no prescribed format but involve only simple camera work and a basic set. In addition, KDFW's directors screen commercials to be aired by the station to ensure that they meet the standards set by KDFW's parent, Times Mirror Corporation.

Assignment editors are primarily responsible for pairing reporters with both photographers and videotape editors. They also monitor the wire services, police and fire department scanners, newspapers, and press releases for story ideas that conform to KDFW's general guidelines. Assignment editors have no authority to decide the stories to be covered, but they may reassign reporters if they learn of a story requiring immediate action. Assignment editors operate under the supervision of the assignment manager.

Plaintiffs brought this suit in May, 1985, alleging that KDFW's reporters, producers, directors, and assignment editors were required to work more than forty hours per week without overtime pay, in willful violation of § 7 of the FLSA, and seeking to recover back wages from May, 1982 to the present. After an eight-day bench trial, the district court concluded that none of the plaintiffs was exempt from § 7 as a bona fide executive, administrative, or professional employee under

§ 13(a)(1) and that KDFW had violated the FLSA by failing to pay overtime. The court further concluded, however, that KDFW's violation was not willful, and that KDFW therefore was not liable for damages outside the FLSA's two-year statute of limitations for nonwillful violations.

B. THE FLSA AND THE § 13(A)(1) EXEMPTIONS

* * *

The short test for the executive exemption requires that an employee's "primary duty" consist of the "management of the enterprise" in which she is employed "or a customarily recognized subdivision thereof." In addition, the executive employee's work must include "the customary and regular direction of the work" of two or more employees.[8] The regulations define an exempt administrative employee as one whose "primary duty" consists of "office or nonmanual work directly related to management policies or general business operations" that "includes work requiring the exercise of discretion and independent judgment."[9] The exemption for creative professionals requires that the employee's "primary duty" consist of work that is "original and creative in character in a recognized field of artistic endeavor," the result of which depends "primarily on the invention, imagination, or talent of the employee."[10]

* * *

III

Each of the three exemptions claimed by KDFW requires the district court to infer from its findings of historical fact what constitutes the employees' "primary duty." KDFW claims that the district court in this case misconstrued the concept of "primary duty" as used in the regulations to mean duties that occupy "a major part, or over fifty percent, of an employee's time." If the district court did indeed misconstrue "primary duty," then its inferences of fact were made with the wrong legal standard in mind, and it erred as a matter of law.

* * *

We cannot agree * * * with KDFW's contention that the district court misconstrued the concept of primary duty. * * * After examining the district court's opinion and reviewing the record, we are convinced that the district court did not base its decision solely on the amount of time KDFW's employees spend at various tasks. Instead, the district court's opinion evidences a careful assessment of the nature of each of the job classifications that KDFW claims is exempt. In determining the employees' primary duties, the district court did not act as a judicial punch clock. The district court painstakingly catalogued the tasks per-

---

8. 29 C.F.R. § 541.1(f).   **10.** *Id.* § 541.3(a)(2).

9. *Id.* § 541.2(e)(2).

formed by each type of employee, and related how each task contributes to producing a KDFW newscast. Accordingly, we find no error.

IV

A.   KDFW's General-Assignment Reporters

KDFW argues that its general-assignment reporters are exempt artistic professionals. Under the regulations, KDFW must prove that the reporter's "primary duty" consists of work that is "original and creative in character in a recognized field of artistic endeavor," the result of which depends "primarily on the invention, imagination, or talent of the employee."

The regulations and interpretations at issue here, §§ 541.3(a)(2) and 541.303(e) and (f), have not changed in any material respect since 1949, long before broadcast journalism evolved into its modern form. * * *

KDFW argues that the district court gave the [Labor Department's] interpretation undue weight, thus blinding itself to the realities of modern broadcast journalism. Rather than focusing on the "essential nature" of reporters' duties, KDFW contends, the district court "pigeonholed" reporters according to standards that are decades out of date. * * *

The interpretations are not binding authority, for they are not statements of law, but are only "a body of experience and informed judgment to which courts and litigants may properly resort for guidance." * * *

* * * To the extent that a district court finds in the interpretations an analogy useful in deciding the case before it, it may rely on the interpretations as persuasive evidence of both Congress's legislative and the Secretary's regulatory intent. At the same time, should a district court find the concepts expressed inapposite to the facts before it, the court is free to engage in its own application of § 13(a)(1) and the pertinent regulations. * * *

* * * KDFW makes much of the recognition in § 541.303(e) that a television announcer's "presence"—that "inherent special ability or talent which, while difficult to define, is nevertheless real"—is an important consideration in determining her exempt status. KDFW claims that it is this intangible element, along with the reporter's daily responsibility for melding language and visual images into an informative and memorable presentation, that gives reporters' work its essential creative character.

* * *

The Secretary's interpretations make it abundantly clear that § 541.3(a)(2) was intended to distinguish between those persons whose work is creative in nature from those who work in a medium capable of bearing creative expression, but whose duties are nevertheless functional in nature. The factual inquiry in this case was directed precisely at determining on which side of that line KDFW's reporters stand. The district court found that, at KDFW, the emphasis was on "good reporting, in the aggregate," and not on individual reporters with the "presence" to draw an audience. The district court found that the process by which reporters meld sound and pictures relies not upon the reporter's creativity, but upon her skill, diligence, and intelligence. More importantly, the district court found that "reporters are told the story that the station intends they cover, what they are expected to shoot, and the intended angle or focus of the story."

In essence, the district court found that KDFW failed to prove that the work constituting its reporters' primary duty is original or creative in character. * * *

B. KDFW's News Producers

KDFW argues that its news producers are exempt either as creative professionals, administrators, executives, or a combination thereof. We address each argument in turn.

1.   Producers as Creative Professionals.—KDFW does not press this argument much, for good reason. The district court found that KDFW failed to prove that what the work producers do in rewriting reporters' copy and in formatting the newscast are products of their "invention, imagination, and talent." Rather, producers perform their work within a well-defined framework of management policies and editorial convention. To the extent that they exercise discretion, it is governed more by skill and experience than by originality and creativity. Because the district court's findings are supported by the record, we find no error.

2.   Producers as Administrators.—The argument KDFW pursues most vigorously with respect to producers is that they are exempt administrative employees. Section 541.2 of the regulations requires that an exempt administrator perform (1) office or nonmanual work (2) that is directly related to the employer's management policies or general business operations and (3) involves the exercise of discretion and independent judgment. The Secretary's interpretation, § 541.205(a), defines the "directly related" prong by distinguishing between what it calls "the administrative operations of a business" and "production." Administrative operations include such duties as "advising the management, planning, negotiating, representing the company, purchasing, promoting sales, and business research and control."[50] Work may also be "directly related" if it is of "substantial importance" to the business operations of the enterprise in that it involves "major assignments in conducting the operations of the business, or * * * affects business operations to a substantial degree."[51] * * *

KDFW first asserts that the district court erroneously applied the distinction between "administrative work" and "production" drawn in § 541.205(a) to the work of producers. The concept of "production,"

---

50.   29 C.F.R. § 541.205(b).   **51.**   *Id.* § 541.205(c).

claims KDFW, applies only to "blue collar manufacturing employees." White collar employees such as producers cannot be involved in production; therefore, their work is directly related to general business operations.

That argument makes little sense. Section 541.205(a) is not concerned with distinguishing between white collar and blue collar employees, or between service industries and manufacturing industries. The distinction § 541.205(a) draws is between those employees whose primary duty is administering the business affairs of the enterprise from those whose primary duty is producing the commodity or commodities, whether goods or services, that the enterprise exists to produce and market. * * *

KDFW claims that applying the § 541.205 distinction between production and administration in the white-collar setting would be contrary to the decisions in previous cases in which employees involved in what would be "production" under our definition were nevertheless held to be exempt administrators. Those cases fail to support KDFW's position. *Cobb v. Finest Foods, Inc.*, [755 F.2d 1148 (5th Cir.1985) (per curiam),] which KDFW claims involved a chef whose primary duty was "producing" food, actually involved a chef whose primary duty was managing the hot food section of a contract food service operation. In contrast to the producers at KDFW, the chef had no direct on-the-job supervision; had a great deal of discretion in setting his own work schedule; trained, supervised, and set the work schedules for a number of employees; and planned the menus. In both *Adams v. St. Johns River Shipbuilding Co.* [, 69 F.Supp. 989 (S.D.Fl.), rev'd on other grounds, 164 F.2d 1012 (5th Cir.1947),] and *Donovan v. Reno Builders Exchange, Inc.*, [100 Lab.Cas. (CCH) para. 34,516, 1984 WL 3149 (D.Nev.1984),] which KDFW claims involved editors whose primary duties were "producing" periodicals, actually involved editors who were in charge of editing and publishing his or her respective periodical. * * * The courts accordingly found that their duties were "directly related to management policies or general business operations," as each was primarily responsible for the success or failure of the venture.

That is not the case with KDFW's news producers. Their responsibilities begin and end with the ten-to-twelve minute portion of the newscast they are working on. They are not responsible for setting business policy, planning the long- or short-term objectives of the news department, promoting the newscast, negotiating salary or benefits with other department personnel, or any of the other types of "administrative" tasks noted in § 541.205(b). The district court determined, based on the facts before it, that "the duties of a producer clearly relate to the production of a KDFW news department product and not to defendant's administrative operations." That determination was not erroneous.

KDFW next asserts that the district court erred in holding that producers' work does not consist of carrying out "major assignments" of "substantial importance" to KDFW's business. * * * The "importance" of producers' work we are left to infer is that, if a producer performs poorly, KDFW's bottom line might suffer.

As a matter of law, that is insufficient to establish the direct relationship required by § 541.2 by virtue of the "substantial importance" contemplated by § 541.205(c). The Secretary's interpretations specifically recognize that the fact that a worker's poor performance may have a significant profit-and-loss impact is not enough to make that worker an exempt administrator. "An employee's job can even be 'indispensable' and still not be of the necessary 'substantial importance' to meet the 'directly related' element."[58] In assessing whether an employee's work is of substantial importance, it is necessary yet again to look to "the nature of the work, not its ultimate consequence." The nature of producers' work, the district court found, is the application of "techniques, procedures, repetitious experience, and specific standards" to the formatting of a newscast. * * * [T]he evidence shows that the work one would think of as being "substantially important"—such as setting news department policy and designing the uniform "look" of the newscast—is done by employees who seem clearly to be exempt administrators: the executive producer and the news director, for example. * * *

3. Producers as Executives.—On appeal, KDFW argues that producers are exempt executives only in the context of arguing for a combination exemption. We address the issue briefly here as a prelude to the discussion of combination exemptions below.

To qualify for an executive exemption under the short test, an employee's primary duty must consist of the "management of the enterprise" in which she is employed "or a customarily recognized subdivision thereof." In addition, the employee must customarily and regularly direct the work of two or more employees. The district court found that management was not the producers' primary duty, and that producers do not customarily direct the work of two or more employees.

We agree with the district court. The evidence establishes that, while the producer plays an important role in coordinating and formatting a portion of the newscast, the other members of the ensemble—that is, the reporters, technicians, assignment editors, and so on—are actually supervised by other management personnel. Producers perform none of the executive duties contemplated by the regulations, such as training, supervising, disciplining, and evaluating employees.[63] . . .

4. The Combination Exemption.—KDFW argues that the district court erred as a matter of law by failing to consider whether producers qualify for a combination exemption under § 541.600. Section 541.600 allows the "tacking" of exemptions only where (1) an employee performs more than one type of work that would be exempt except that (2) neither type of work alone can be termed the employee's primary duty, but (3) all of the putatively exempt work taken together constitutes the employee's primary duty. That is not the case here. The district court found

58. * * * 29 C.F.R. § 541.205(c)(2)   **63.** See *id.* § 541.102(b).
* * *.

that the producers at KDFW do no exempt work. This is not a case in which the producers do some administrative work and some executive work. Producers do neither administrative work nor executive work. Only the reporters do some exempt work, though that work is not their primary duty. * * *

C. KDFW's DIRECTORS AND ASSIGNMENT EDITORS

For the same reasons it asserts with respect to its producers, KDFW claims that the district court erred in concluding that its directors and assignment editors are not exempt either as executives or administrators or a combination thereof. KDFW's arguments with respect to directors and assignment editors thus fail for the reasons set out above. First, the evidence wholly fails to establish that the work of either directors or assignment editors is "directly related" to management policies or business operations, as required by § 541.2. Second, the evidence does not demonstrate that either directors or assignment editors "manage" anything, as required by § 541.1. KDFW's directors are, as the district court found, highly skilled coordinators, but they are not managers. Assignment editors have no real authority, and participate in no decisions of consequence. Finally, because neither directors nor assignment editors do any exempt work, the district court did not err in failing to consider a combination exemption under § 541.600.

Notes and Questions

1. *Rationale for the "Duties" Test.* Why are the exemptions at issue in *Dalheim* cast in terms of the duties performed by exempt personnel rather than, say, keyed to compensation level or "white collar" status? For the argument that class-status considerations motivated the exemption for "upper level" jobs, see Deborah C. Malamud, Engineering the Middle Classes: Class Line–Drawing in New Deal Hours Legislation, 96 Mich. L. Rev. 2212 (1998).

2. *Interpretations vs. Regulations.* In reviewing the Labor Department's pronouncements on the white-collar exemptions, keep in mind the distinction between the "regulations" promulgated as binding rules, pursuant to Administrative Procedure Act requirements, 5 U.S.C. § 553, to which courts must defer unless they are not authorized by the FLSA, and its "interpretations" (also contained in the Code of Federal Regulations, Title 29), which typically are not subjected to the rulemaking process and receive less deference from reviewing courts. Note the discussion in *Dalheim* as to whether the trial judge had impermissibly treated 29 U.S.C. § 541.303 as a binding regulation rather than simply persuasive authority. See also Freeman v. National Broadcasting Company, Inc., 80 F.3d 78, 84 (2d Cir.1996) (rejecting reliance on "out-of-date" and "nonbinding" interpretation in § 541.302 concerning professional exemption). Did the Court in Appeals in *Dalheim* consistently treat the Department's interpretations as merely persuasive authority? Current DOL regulations eliminate this distinction between "regulations" and "interpretations" in place of a unitary set of regulations.

3. *Executive Exemption*: *Management as a "Primary Duty"*. Prior agency regulations concerning the executive exemption contained no express requirement that the manager exercise independent judgment and discretion; it required only that the "employee's primary duty consists of the management of the enterprise" and that the manager engages in "the customary and regular direction" of at least two employees. 29 C.F.R. § 541.119(a). This led to criticism that the exemption was overinclusive.

In 2003, the DOL revised its formulation of the duties test for executive employees, which includes any employee:

(2) Whose primary duty is management of the enterprise in which the employee is employed or of a customarily recognized department or subdivision thereof;

(3) Who customarily and regularly directs the work of two or more employees; and

(4) Who has the authority to hire or fire other employees or whose suggestions and recommendations as to the hiring, firing, advancement, promotion or any other change of status of other employees are given particular weight.

29 C.F.R. § 541.100(a). The Department claimed that decisions like Donovan v. Burger King Corp., 672 F.2d 221 (1st Cir.1982); Donovan v. Burger King Corp., 675 F.2d 516 (2d Cir.1982) required a de-emphasis on discretionary authority and some latitude for allowing exempt executives to perform some nonexempt work. See 68 Fed. Reg. 15565.

4. *Administrative Exemption*: *Administrative vs. Production Dichotomy*. Under the current DOL regulations, an administrative employee is any employee:

(2) Whose primary duty is the performance of office or non-manual work directly related to the management or general business operations of the employer or the employer's customers; and

(3) Whose primary duty includes the exercise of discretion and independent judgment with respect to matters of significance.

29 C.F.R. § 541.200(a).

The agency's regulations previously employed an administrative vs. production dichotomy, which is also relied upon in *Dalheim*. The dichotomy was first articulated by the Labor Department in the 1940s with the manufacturing industry as its paradigm. To what extent does this dichotomy fit well white-collar positions that are not directly involved in production or sales activities?

In addition to the principal reading, consider Reich v. John Alden Life Ins. Co., 126 F.3d 1 (1st Cir.1997), where the court held that defendant insurance company's marketing representatives were not directly involved in product design, generation, or sales, and hence should be considered administrative employees. The company relied on independent insurance agents to deal directly with customers of its insurance products. The primary duty of the marketing representatives was "to cultivate this independent sales force," by keeping assigned agents abreast of the company's product line and changes in its pricing policy. The *John Alden* court observed:

[A]pplying the administrative-production dichotomy is not as simple as drawing the line between white-collar and blue-collar workers. On the contrary non-manufacturing employees can be considered "production" employees * * * where their job is to generate (i.e., "produce") the very product or service that the employer's business offers to the public. * * *

* * * John Alden is in the business of designing, creating, and selling insurance policies to the public. * * * [T]he "products" generated by John Alden are these insurance policies themselves. As the marketing representatives are in no way involved in the design or generation of insurance policies, the very product "that the enterprise exists to produce and market," *Dalheim*, 918 F.2d at 1230, they cannot be considered production employees.

* * *

* * * [T]he Secretary contends that, in addition to the production of insurance policies, John Alden also produces sales, and that any employee engaged in the generation of sales should be deemed non-exempt. * * * [However, in] the instant case, the activities of the marketing representatives are clearly ancillary to John Alden's principal production activity—the creation of insurance policies—and therefore could be considered administrative "servicing" within the meaning of section 541.205(b).

[T]he day-to-day activities of the marketing representatives are more in the nature of "representing the company" and "promoting sales" of John Alden products, two examples of exempt administrative work provided by [the agency's] interpretations.

126 F.3d at 9–10. To what extent is the administrative vs. production dichotomy providing any analytic support for the court's conclusion?

The DOL's 2003 updating of its regulation no longer relies expressly on the administrative vs. production distinction. The agency's intent was to

reduce the emphasis on the so-called "production versus staff" dichotomy distinguishing between exempt and non-exempt workers, while retaining the concept that an exempt administrative employee must be engaged in work related to the management or general business operations of the employer or of the employer's customers.

68 Fed.Reg. 15566. The Labor Department notes, however, that to meet the "related to management or general business operations" prong, an employee "must perform work related to assisting with the running or servicing of the business, as distinguished, for example, from working on a manufacturing production line or selling a product in a retail or service establishment." 29 C.F.R. § 541.201(a). Examples given of exempt administrative employees include—

- insurance claims adjusters if their work includes interviewing insureds and witnesses, determining liability, negotiating settlements, and making recommendations regarding litigation (§ 541.203(a));
- "[a]n employee who leads a team of other employees assigned to complete major projects for the employer (such as purchasing, selling or closing all or part of a business * * * or designing and implementing productivity improvements) * * * even if the employee does not

have direct supervisory responsibility over the other employees on the team" (§ 541.203(c)); and

- purchasing agents "with authority to bind the company on significant purchases * * * even if they must consult with top management officials when making a purchase commitment for raw materials in excess of the contemplated plant needs." (§ 541.203(f)).

5. *Professional Exemption: Creative vs. Functional Dichotomy. Dalheim* relies on the creative vs. functional dichotomy, now found at § 541.302, in rejecting KDFW's defense that its general-assignment reporters were exempt professional employees. Under the DOL's current regulations, journalists are exempt creative professionals "if their primary duty is work requiring invention, imagination or talent, as opposed to work which depends primarily on intelligence, diligence and accuracy." Id. § 541.302(d). Moreover, they "do not qualify as exempt creative professionals if their work product is subject to substantial control by the employer." Id.

6. *FLSA Reform.* Consider the following suggestions for amending the FLSA:

a. *Exemption for "Knowledge Workers"?* According to a 1999 GAO study, employers believe that a new exemption should be crafted for "knowledge workers":

> Employers believe that the current exemptions leave a gap by not including workers who are not engaged in traditional manual labor but who follow detailed procedures to perform their jobs. Because these workers can be both highly skilled and well paid, employers think that they should be classified similarly to exempt professionals. This would allow both the worker and management more flexibility in scheduling and offer the worker what employers consider prestigious jobs in management positions.

> Employee representatives argue against the expansion of the exemptions to include technical workers. They believe that today's computer-assisted technicians are the modern equivalents of traditional factory workers. * * * They assert that while everyone would like more flexibility in the work place, in reality, exempt status means that employees work longer hours for less pay. * * * Finally, they told us that discretion and independent judgment remain the key indicators of professional and managerial status—rote work, however well paid, shows that a worker is only a "cog in the wheel," not a key managerial employee.

Government Acct. Office, Report to the Subcomm. on Workforce Reductions, House Comm. on Educ. and the Workforce, Fair Labor Standards Act: White–Collar Exemptions in the Modern Workplace (GAO/HLHS–99–164, Sept. 1999), pp. 22–23.

In evaluating this proposal, consider as a model for FLSA reform the manner in which Congress in 1996 exempted certain employees in the computer industry on a basis that specified particular skill and (if paid on an hourly basis) compensation criteria:

> The provisions [concerning minimum wage and maximum hours] shall not apply with regard to: (17) any employee who is a computer systems analyst, computer programmer, software engineer, or other similarly skilled worker, whose primary duty is (A) the application of systems analysis techniques and procedures, including consulting with users, to

determine hardware, software, or system functional specifications; (B) the design, development, documentation, analysis, creation, testing, or modification of computer systems or programs, including prototypes, based on and related to user or system design specifications; (C) the design, documentation, testing, creation, or modification of computer programs related to machine operating systems; or (D) a combination of duties described in subparagraphs (A), (B), and (C) the performance of which requires the same level of skills; and who, in the case of an employee who is compensated on an hourly basis, is compensated at a rate of not less than $27.63 an hour.

Pub. L. 104–188, § 2105(a) (1996), codified at 29 U.S.C. § 213(a)(17).

b. *Abolition of the Duties Test?* Why not simply abolish the duties test and make any exemption rest exclusively on the employee's salary (which, as in the above example, could be set at an appropriate multiple of the minimum wage)? Such a change would reduce administrative costs and promote compliance by simplifying this area of the law? What would be lost? Can an amendment be crafted that would not sweep into the exempt category traditional hourly workers who work considerable amounts of regularly scheduled overtime?

c. Employer dissatisfaction with these exemptions is catalogued in GAO Study, White–Collar Exemptions, supra, 16 ff. For a proposal from the employers' perspective to reform FLSA exemptions, see Michael Faillace, Automatic Exemption of Highly–Paid Employees and Other Proposed Amendments to the White–Collar Exemptions: Bringing the Fair Labor Standards Act into the Twenty–First Century, 15 Lab. Lawy. 357 (2000).

D. STATE WAGE PAYMENT LAWS

TRUELOVE v. NORTHEAST CAPITAL & ADVISORY, INC.

Court of Appeals of New York, 2000.
95 N.Y.2d 220, 738 N.E.2d 770, 715 N.Y.S.2d 366.

LEVINE, J.

Plaintiff William B. Truelove, Jr. brought this action against his former employer, defendant Northeast Capital & Advisory, Inc., under article 6 of the Labor Law to recover the unpaid balance of a bonus he was awarded in December 1997, payable in quarterly installments through the following year. His complaint alleges that his bonus constituted "wages" within the meaning of Labor Law § 190(1) and that, following his resignation after the first bonus payment, defendant violated Labor Law § 193 by enforcing an express condition in the bonus plan predicating payment of each quarterly installment on continued employment. We agree with Supreme Court and the Appellate Division that plaintiff's bonus does not fall within the definition of wages protected by Labor Law article 6.

Defendant, a small investment banking firm, hired plaintiff in June 1996 as a financial analyst in a non-revenue generating position. Plaintiff elected a compensation plan under which he was to receive an annual salary of $40,000 and be eligible to participate in a bonus/profit sharing pool. Plaintiff's offer of employment stated that a "bonus, if paid, would reflect a combination of the individual's performance and Northeast Capital's performance."

The terms of the bonus plan were further clarified in two memoranda by defendant's Chief Executive Officer. The memoranda explained that a bonus/profit sharing pool would be established only if the firm generated a certain stated minimum of revenues and that the pool, once established, would be calculated pursuant to a graduated percentage schedule of firm revenues. The memoranda further stipulated that bonus/profit sharing distributions would be allocated in the CEO's sole discretion and would be paid in quarterly installments, with each payment contingent upon the recipient's continued employment at the firm. Employees were required to have an "acceptable" performance rating to participate in the bonus/profit sharing pool.

At the end of 1997, defendant established a bonus/profit sharing pool of $240,000 based upon firm revenues of approximately $1.6 million for that year. Defendant's CEO allocated $160,000 of that pool to plaintiff. Defendant paid plaintiff an initial bonus installment of $40,000, but refused to make any further payments after plaintiff's resignation.

Plaintiff brought this suit under Labor Law article 6, alleging that his bonus fell within the definition of wages set forth in Labor Law § 190(1). Plaintiff claimed that defendant's failure to pay him the three remaining bonus installment payments for 1997 violated Labor Law § 193, which provides that "no employer shall make any deduction from the wages of an employee, except" under certain limited circumstances not relevant here. Supreme Court granted summary judgment to defendant on the ground that plaintiff's bonus did not constitute wages within the meaning of Labor Law article 6. The Appellate Division affirmed. * * *

Article 6 of the Labor Law sets forth a comprehensive set of statutory provisions enacted to strengthen and clarify the rights of employees to the payment of wages. * * * An employer who violates the requirements of Labor Law article 6 is subject to civil liability and criminal penalties (see, Labor Law §§ 198 and 198–a). The dispositive issue in this case is whether plaintiff's bonus constitutes "wages" within the meaning of the Labor Law.

Although New York has provided statutory protection for workers' wages for more than a century * * *, the Legislature first defined the term "wages" in the 1966 enactment of Labor Law article 6 (L 1996, ch 548). Labor Law § 190(1) defines "wages" as "the earnings of an employee for labor or services rendered, regardless of whether the amount of earnings is determined on a time, piece, commission or other basis". Courts have construed this statutory definition as excluding certain forms of "incentive compensation" that are more in the nature of a profit-sharing arrangement and are both contingent and dependent, at least in part, on the financial success of the business enterprise (see, *International Paper Co. v. Suwyn*, 978 F.Supp. 506, 514; *Tischmann v. ITT/Sheraton Corp.*, 882 F.Supp. 1358, 1370; see also, *Magness v. Human Resource Servs., Inc.*, 161 A.D.2d 418, 419, 555 N.Y.S.2d 347). We arrive at the same conclusion with respect to plaintiff's bonus compensation arrangement.

The terms of defendant's bonus compensation plan did not predicate bonus payments upon plaintiff's own personal productivity nor give plaintiff a contractual right to bonus payments based upon his productivity. To the contrary, the declaration of a bonus pool was dependent solely upon his employer's overall financial success. In addition, plaintiff's share in the bonus pool was entirely discretionary and subject to the non-reviewable determination of his employer. These factors, we believe, take plaintiff's bonus payments out of the statutory definition of wages.

Unlike in other areas where the Legislature chose to define broadly the term "wages" to include every form of compensation paid to an employee, including bonuses (see Unemployment Insurance Law §§ 517, 518), the Legislature elected not to define that term in Labor Law § 190(1) so expansively as to cover all forms of employee remuneration. We therefore agree with those courts that have concluded that the more restrictive statutory definition of "wages," as "earnings for labor or services rendered," excludes incentive compensation "based on factors falling outside the scope of the employee's actual work" * * *. In our view, the wording of the statute, in expressly linking earnings to an employee's labor or services personally rendered, contemplates a more direct relationship between an employee's own performance and the compensation to which that employee is entitled. Discretionary additional remuneration, as a share in a reward to all employees for the success of the employer's entrepreneurship, falls outside the protection of the statute.

* * *

Finally, we reject plaintiff's argument that he had a vested right to the bonus payments once defendant declared that a bonus would be paid and calculated the amount of that bonus. In *Hall v. United Parcel Serv.* (76 N.Y.2d 27, 36, 556 N.Y.S.2d 21, 555 N.E.2d 273), we held that an "employee's entitlement to a bonus is governed by the terms of the employer's bonus plan." Here, the bonus plan explicitly predicated the continuation of bonus payments upon the recipient's continued employment status. Because plaintiff resigned shortly after he received his first quarterly payment, he was not entitled to receive the remaining three payments.

Notes and Questions

1. *Rationale for Wage Payment Laws.* Why do many states like New York not permit employers to set off against wages due any debts owed by the employee? Is it the fear that employers will overreach by asserting

doubtful obligations and engaging in a form of self-help through deductions from wages, thereby forcing the employee to undertake the costs of bringing suit to recover the withheld amounts? Is it likely that employees will continue to work for employers that engage in such behavior? If so, under what circumstances?

Should set-offs be permitted where the obligations owed by the employee are related to the work of the employee? What if a supermarket establishes a policy that tellers are responsible for any cash shortages at the close of a business day, and that deductions for such shortages will be taken out of weekly pay? Are such deductions permitted by § 193? What about situations where employers seek to recoup from wages due previous erroneous overpayment of wages? See Feinberg v. Board of Education, 74 Misc.2d 371, 344 N.Y.S.2d 618 (Sup. Ct. Kings. Co. 1973). Should § 193 be amended to allow employees expressly to waive the protections of § 193 for such "related" obligations? To authorize employees represented by exclusive bargaining agents to authorize such individual waiver agreements?

Some states do allow set-offs in some circumstances. For example, under Colorado's statute, "an employer is permitted to set off 'any lawful charges or indebtedness' owed by the employee to the employer against the unpaid wages or compensation to be paid to the employee at the time employment is severed. * * * If the employer refuses to pay wages or compensation without a good faith legal justification when it terminates an employment relationship, the employer becomes liable for a penalty in the amount of fifty percent of the amount due." Jet Courier Service, Inc. v. Mulei, 771 P.2d 486, 501 (1989) (quoting § 8–4–104, 3B C.R.S. (1986)). Does the Colorado law provide a better resolution of the competing interests?

2. *"Discretionary" Bonuses?* In Reilly v. Natwest Markets Group Inc., 181 F.3d 253 (2d Cir.1999), the court held that the plaintiff was entitled to his incentive bonus and his employer was subject to a liquidated damages penalty under New York Labor Law § 198 (1–a) of 25% of the amount due:

> Here, Reilly's pay was guaranteed under the Percentage Bonus formula to be a percentage of the revenues he generated, and was not left to NatWest's discretion. The jury found that NatWest owed Reilly $2.054 million under his contract, but that it willfully withheld $1.054 million from that amount. * * * Reilly was clearly entitled to the $1.054 million as earned and vested compensation. * * * As such, Reilly's Percentage Bonus falls within the definition of a "commission" that is expressly included within the Labor Law's definition of "wages."

181 F.3d at 265. Is this decision still good law after *Truelove*? What factors should go into the determination of whether bonuses are part of "wages"? Is an employer's insistence that the bonus is "discretionary" determinative if bonuses are closely tied to revenues generated by the employee and have been consistently awarded every year that the firm generated profits, but not in bad years?

3. *Employees Exercising Managerial Discretion.* Review the structure of New York Labor Law §§ 160–169a. Does the exclusion from the definition of "[c]ommission salesman" in § 190, subd. 6 of "an employee whose principal activity is of a supervisory, managerial, executive or administrative

nature", mean that such individuals are also excluded from the protection afforded "employee[s]" in § 193?

In Pachter v. Bernard Hodes Group, Inc., 505 F.3d 129 (2d Cir. 2007), the Second Circuit certified this issue to the New York Court of Appeals.

4. *When are Commissions "Earned"?* The *Pachter* court also certified the question of when commissions are "earned" for purposes of the New York wage payment law:

> When a commission becomes "earned" so that an employee has a "vested right" to these moneys usually depends on the terms of an agreement providing for the commission. Once "earned," it is clear that deductions other than those set forth in section 193 are improper. In this case, no written agreement exists. However, under common law, in the absence of a written agreement, a commission is deemed earned "upon sale."
>
> This rule applies to "conventional" brokerage relationships. * * * Pachter arguably brokered the sale of advertising space between Hodes and its clients. Though the caselaw is somewhat ambiguous, under the common law, her commission could be considered "earned" either when: (1) payment is advanced by Hodes to the media company; (2) a client is presented a bill that includes Hodes' fee; or (3) she initially secures the client's commitment. * * * However, [the New York appellate courts have not] definitively addressed the applicability of this common law rule to section 193 and the definition of "wages" in Article 6.

Id. at 134–35 (citations omitted). The court's certified question is predicated on "the absence of a governing written agreement" in this case. Id. at 134.

5. *"Wages" vs. "Company Funds"?* Consider the following situation, as set forth In the Matter of John F. Hudacs v. Frito–Lay, Inc., 90 N.Y.2d 342, 344–45, 660 N.Y.S.2d 700, 683 N.E.2d 322 (1997):

> Respondent Frito–Lay, Inc. manufactures and distributes snack foods. As part of its distribution process, it employs route salespeople who pick up the snack food from the company's wholesale distribution warehouses, deliver them to retailers and collect payments from those stores on behalf of the company. * * *
>
> When a salesperson picks up the product each morning from the Frito–Lay warehouse, the amount taken and the cost is verified by both the salesperson and a warehouse employee. The salesperson then delivers the product to various retail markets, and collects payment from the retailer for the product delivered. For the most part, retailers pay the salespeople through either "charge tickets," a form of credit, or checks written directly to Frito–Lay. However, those retailers that the company does not consider sufficiently creditworthy are required to pay cash. * * * The company requires cash receipts to be converted into either checks or money orders, which are then mailed directly to Frito–Lay along with checks from retailers and charge tickets. The company reimburses employees for the costs of money orders; however, the checks forwarded by employees come directly from their personal checking accounts.

Every 20 business days, the company issues an accounting report to each employee. * * * The reports shows any discrepancies between the amount of product taken by a salesperson, and the amount of money remitted to Frito–Lay. The salespeople are required to reimburse the company for any deficit shown on the report. * * * Frito–Lay provides the employees an opportunity to demonstrate that the deficit is the result of such things as damaged or stale product, bounced checks, or third-party theft of either product or cash. Frito–Lay does not attempt to recoup those types of losses from its employees. Moreover, wages are paid regardless of any outstanding account deficiencies existing at the time of payment, although the company does impose other sanctions [including discipline] for the failure to make up account deficits.

Has Frito–Lay violated New York Labor Law § 193? Is the case distinguishable from that of more typical service workers such as supermarket cashiers or waiters whom the New York Legislature presumably intended to protect from payback schemes?

6. *Are Stock Options "Wages"?* In IBM v. Bajorek, 191 F.3d 1033 (9th Cir.1999), the court held that a forfeiture provision in a stock option plan that was triggered when an optionee went to work for a competitor did not violate California Labor Code § 221, which makes it unlawful (with limited exceptions) "for any employer to collect or receive from an employee any part of wages theretofore paid by said employer to said employee." Noting the law's definition of "wages" in § 201 ("all amounts for labor performed by employees of every description, whether the amount is fixed or ascertained by the standard of time, task, piece, commission basis, or other method of calculation"), the *Bajorek* court concluded that stock options are not "amounts" but contractual rights to buy shares of stock the value of which depend on the vagaries of the stock market and hence are not "fixed or ascertained" by any method of calculation when the agreements were made or exercised.

7. *Deductions "For the Benefit of the Employee"?* Law firms often provide their employees with vouchers with which they can call car services to take them home when working late. Can a law firm lawfully require its employees under § 193, subd. 1(b) to authorize deductions from pay for use of vouchers to go to restaurants, theaters, or other unauthorized purposes?

Deductions from pay for fringe benefits may violate the state payment law if not within the allowed exceptions for deductions. See, e.g., Ressler v. Jones Motor Co., 337 Pa.Super. 602, 487 A.2d 424 (1985).

8. *Reimbursement of Expenses?* Is an employer's obligation to reimburse employees for expenses incurred on its behalf a form of "wages" covered by laws like New York's? What if some of the items for which reimbursement is sought are disputed by the employer because the employee failed to follow its reimbursement procedures?

9. *Withholding the Final Paycheck?* Can an employer lawfully withhold delivery of its final paycheck to departing employees until they return their uniforms, keys to their locker, access keys to company offices, and computers provided for business use at home?

10. *Deductions Authorized by Collective Bargaining Agreements.* California Labor Code § 222 provides that "[i]t shall be unlawful, in case of any

wage agreement arrived at through collective bargaining, either wilfully or unlawfully or with intent to defraud an employee, a competitor, or any other person, to withhold from said employee any part of the wage agreed upon." However, § 224 exempts from this prohibition deductions that are (i) "expressly authorized in writing by the employee" and (ii) do not amount to "a rebate or deduction from the standard wage arrived at collective bargaining or pursuant to a wage agreement or statute * * *." Can an employer lawfully solicit individual employees to sign written agreements that their employer-paid meal allowance may be credited toward their minimum wage? Does it matter whether the union simply acquiesces in this practice or has agreed to language in the collective agreement authorizing the practice? Cf. Division of Labor Standards Enforcement v. Williams, 121 Cal.App.3d 302, 175 Cal.Rptr. 347 (Cal.App.1981). How would the case come out under New York law?

11. *Wage Payment Laws and Independent Contractors.* In Bynog v. Cipriani Group, 1 N.Y.3d 193, 770 N.Y.S.2d 692, 802 N.E.2d 1090 (2003), professional banquet managers sued under N.Y. Labor Law § 196–d to recover certain payments, alleged to be gratuities, as part of their catering contracts. The New York Court of Appeals held that the managers were not employees of the restaurant under the common law "right of control" test, see discussion in chapter 1, and therefore could not sue the restaurant under the wage payment law.

12. *FLSA as a Wage Payment Law.* The FLSA creates a private cause of action to recover "unpaid minimum wages, * * * unpaid overtime compensation, * * * and * * * an additional equal amount as liquidated damages." Where prohibited retaliation has occurred, the plaintiff may recover "such legal and equitable relief as may be appropriate * * *, including without limitation * * * the payment of wages lost and an additional equal amount as liquidated damages." 29 U.S.C. § 216(b). Can otherwise exempt managerial employees who complain of a breach of contract resulting in their receiving no compensation, maintain a FLSA action to recover minimum wages? See Nicholson v. World Business Network, Inc., 105 F.3d 1361, 1365 (11th Cir.1997) (holding that FLSA-exempt employees cannot convert contract actions into FLSA suits, and that the appropriate analysis is "what an employee was owed, not what he actually received").

Consider also the claim in Hoffmann v. Sbarro, Inc., 982 F.Supp. 249 (S.D.N.Y.1997), that the salary-basis test for exempt employees was not met due to an employer's policy of requiring its restaurant managers to authorize deductions from their pay for cash and inventory shortages and other losses occurring during their supervision.

13. *ERISA Preemption?* Are state wage payment laws preempted by ERISA to the extent they affect employee benefit plans? See, e.g., Beckwith v. United Parcel Service, Inc., 889 F.2d 344 (1st Cir.1989) (no preemption of Maine statute prohibiting employers from satisfying employee obligations through payroll deductions required as a condition of employment); see generally pp. 1172–97 infra.

14. *Predispute Arbitration Agreements.* In Perry v. Thomas, 482 U.S. 483, 107 S.Ct. 2520, 96 L.Ed.2d 426 (1987), the Supreme Court held that wage payment claims under Calif. Labor Code § 229 are arbitrable under the Federal Arbitration Act, 9 U.S.C. §§ 1 et seq., despite a state statutory policy against arbitration of such claims. See generally pp. 1132–57 infra.

Chapter Sixteen

REGULATION OF EMPLOYEE BENEFITS

A. OVERVIEW

In 1974 Congress enacted the Employee Retirement Income Security Act (ERISA), Pub.L. No. 93–406, 88 Stat. 829, codified at various places in the Internal Revenue Code (Code) and at 29 U.S.C. §§ 1000 et seq. Congress entered the retirement benefits area because of the perception that state laws governing contracts and pension trusts had proven incapable of protecting the pension benefits of workers who lost their jobs prior to retirement age or who learned upon retirement that their employer lacked sufficient assets to satisfy its pension obligations. See generally Richard A. Ippolito, Pensions, Economics, and Public Policy (1986); Altman & Marmar, ERISA and the American Retirement Income System, 7 Am.J. of Tax Policy 31 (1988). Although ERISA does not mandate that employers either offer a pension or specify a particular level of retirement benefit, it requires employers to meet a number of rules on pension and welfare benefit plans as a condition of tax-advantaged treatment.

There are two basic types of ERISA pension plans: "defined contribution" plans that provide for an individual account for each participant and for benefits based solely upon the amount contributed to that account plus any income or other gain (earned by the contributions); and "defined benefit" plans which are defined as any other pension plan but generally involve plans where the employer promises to pay a specific or definitely determinable benefit. In addition to "employee pension benefit" plans, ERISA also covers "employee welfare benefit" plans, defined in 29 U.S.C. § 1002(1), which can cover such non-retirement benefits as health insurance, disability insurance and severance pay.

ERISA regulations fall into three basic categories: (i) minimum standards designed to promote nonforfeitable pension rights, such as vesting (initially, after 10 years of service, now reduced to 5 years' "cliff" vesting or 3–7 years' phased vesting as a result of 1986 tax reform legislation), benefit accrual, and minimum age and service conditions; (ii) plan funding requirements to ensure that defined-benefit pension plans will have adequate assets to meet promised benefits; and (iii) fiduciary standards and reporting and disclosure obligations. Whereas many pension benefit plans are subject to all three, welfare benefit plans are subject only to fiduciary and reporting and disclosure obligations.

The Department of Labor is charged with the responsibility of interpreting and enforcing the labor provisions of ERISA. However, the statute authorizes private rights of action. Participants or beneficiaries may bring a civil action in federal court for any violation of the statute, including breach of fiduciary duties. 29 U.S.C. § 1132(a)(3). In addition, individuals challenging a retaliatory discharge have a remedy under § 510 of ERISA, 29 U.S.C. § 1140. Section 510 issues are treated below at pp. 1039–1050.

Aside from ERISA, there are a few other federal laws that regulate employee benefits. Recent examples are the Family and Medical Leave Act (FMLA) of 1993, 29 U.S.C. §§ 2601 et seq., and the Workers Adjustment and Retraining Notification Act (WARN) of 1988, 29 U.S.C. §§ 2101–2109, the federal plant-closing law. In addition, the Consolidated Omnibus Budget Reconciliation Act (COBRA), 29 U.S.C. §§ 1161 et seq., requires employee health care benefits plans to provide for continuation coverage for 18 months (in some situations, 36 months), at the departing employee's expense; and the Health Insurance Portability and Accountability Act of 1996 (HIPAA), 29 U.S.C. § 1181, limits exclusions for preexisting medical conditions and posits other rules to enable departing employees to qualify under the health care plans of their new employer. State laws dealing with employee benefits (other than insurance regulation) are generally preempted by ERISA (see pp. 1172–97 infra), although there are a few areas, where federal law expressly permits states to enact higher levels of worker protection.

Notes and Questions

1. *Why Do Employers Provide Pensions?* In view of the fact that neither federal nor state laws mandate pension benefits for employees, why do employers voluntarily provide such benefits? One important reason is that pension and other benefits, such as health care plans, can be "purchased" by the employee with pre-tax dollars; in a sense, the government subsidizes compensation in the form of employee benefits by allowing employers to deduct from their income contributions to benefit plans and by not requiring employees to pay income tax on the "receipt" of such contributions (and in the case of pensions, not realizing any gains for tax purposes until retirement benefits are paid). These tax consequences, however, do not tell the entire story. It is also often in the employer's interest to promote long-term commitment on the part of its workforce because employees willing to make such a commitment may be higher-quality workers or workers willing to invest in job-specific skills (i.e., skills that, while helpful to the particular employer, do not increase the employee's value in the general labor market, and hence are not portable). Pension benefits, especially defined-benefit plans which often take the form of "backloading" higher benefits with longer periods of service, help further this "bonding" of the employee to the particular employer. Indeed, until relatively recently, pension benefits often did not "vest" (i.e., become non-forfeitable) until the

employee became eligible to retire under the terms of the pension plan. One effect of ERISA regulation has been progressively to reduce this vesting period—thus making pension benefits more portable among jobs. As noted above, as a result of 1986 tax reform legislation, the vesting period for defined-benefit pension plans is now 5 years' "cliff" vesting (or 3–7 years on a phased schedule).

In recent years, many employers have become less concerned with promoting long-term commitment to the firm, or put differently, have become increasingly interested in attracting and retaining (for a time) high-mobility employees not likely to remain with a firm over their careers. For this reason, and perhaps to avoid burdensome ERISA regulations that apply only to defined-benefit plans, these employers have shifted to defined-contributions plans. Benefits under these plans are portable since vesting typically occurs contemporaneously with the making of the employer's contribution; they also contain no "backloaded" future rewards for long-term employment. The downside, from the employees' standpoint, is that the risk of investment loss is borne entirely by employees, whereas in defined-benefit plans the risk is borne entirely by the plan. The recent emergence of "cash balance" plans is an attempt to capture some of the portability of defined-contribution plans without shifting investment risk to employees. See note 3 & "Note on Conversion to 'Cash Balance' Plans," below.

2. *Why Regulate?* Why did the federal government choose to regulate employee benefit plans in 1974 in a manner that does not mandate the creation of plans or the provision of particular benefits but does impose fiduciary, financing, reporting and disclosure duties for pension benefit plans? Consider the following rationales:

a. *Uniformity.* One justification for federal law is to achieve the efficiency gains of a uniform set of rules for what are likely to be firm-wide benefit plans for multistate companies. ERISA preemption principles seek to advance this interest in uniformity.

b. *Shoring up the Credibility of Pension Promises.* Pension promises are not simple contracts:

> On its face, the pension contract is tenuous. In exchange for lower cash wages, the firm promises workers pension payments many years in the future. Yet it can either terminate the plan at any time or fire workers prior to retirement; in either case, the firm can impose large capital losses on workers. Because of the complexity of the contract and its long-term nature, informational problems would appear to abound. And, the contract is largely implicit, making it unenforceable in the courts. Moreover, there is a potential for a lemons market; if some firms perpetrate fraud, the expected "quality" of all pensions is reduced. Pensions appear to offer a classic example of a product that could not survive in an unfettered competitive market, one that would require at least some governmental regulation to survive.

Richard A. Ippolito, The Implicit Pension Contract: Development and New Directions, 22 J. Human Resources 441, 459–60 (no. 3, summer 1987).

ERISA seeks to "enforce" pension promises by (i) requiring plan administrators or anyone with discretionary authority over plan assets to adhere to the terms of existing plans and to act as fiduciaries with respect to plan assets; (ii) reducing the service period for vesting and prohibiting strategic terminations for the purpose of defeating well-established pension benefit expectations; (iii) establishing minimum-funding requirements for defined-benefit plans; (iv) placing some restrictions on plan terminations; and (v) creating an insurer of last resort, the Pension Benefit Guarantee Corporation (PBGC), to ensure partial benefit payments to plan beneficiaries in the event of termination of an underfunded plan.

Note that this rationale applies principally to defined-benefit plans, and not to defined-contribution plans where the employer "performs" its obligation by making the promised contributions. Moreover, it may be questioned, as an initial matter, why reputational sanctions are not sufficient to curb opportunistic employer behavior: employers who act to defeat expectations of plan beneficiaries may have difficulty encouraging employees to make these sorts of investments in the future.

c. *Correcting for Informational Failures.* In view of the preceding observation, ERISA may also depend on a judgment that employees will not be able, on their own, to make intelligent choices about pension plan benefits. This explains the statute's disclosure provisions. It may also explain its rules on vesting:

> We believe a stronger argument for mandatory vesting is to encourage greater pension savings than would otherwise occur among workers who regularly switch employers. One would expect a five-year cliff vesting provision to be associated with low quit rates just prior to five years of tenure, followed by a spike in quits. We are not aware of strong evidence for a vesting spike in quits, suggesting that young workers are not well informed about pension rules or that they highly discount the accrued pension benefits. Either explanation would lend support to a mandated vesting rule, although not necessarily at five years.

John T. Addison & Barry T. Hirsch, The Economic Effects of Employment Regulation: What Are the Limits?, ch. 4 in Government Regulation of the Employment Relationship 152 (Bruce E. Kaufman ed., 1997).

d. *Mandatory Insurance.* The mandatory insurance feature of ERISA may be explained as an effort to encourage pension savings by ensuring that the "lemons" (defaulting employer-sponsors) do not drive down the willingness to invest in pensions:

> Why mandatory federal pension insurance? Prior to the mandate, private markets did not develop because of adverse selection (firms in poor financial shape are most likely to insure), asymmetric information (companies have better knowledge than insurers), and moral hazard (insured companies may underfund absent minimum financing requirements). Federal insurance pooling across risk classes overcomes some of these difficulties and might be warranted on grounds of imperfect worker knowledge and a reduction in externalities resulting from terminated pension plans. * * *
>
> That being said, federal insurance is not without its own set of problems; in particular, adverse selection. Many firms have dropped out of the PBGC pool by phasing out their [defined-benefit (DB)] plans,

instead making [defined-contribution (DC)] plans available to workers. Plans remaining with the PBGC then become more risky and require higher premiums, in turn accelerating the movement out of DB plans. * * *

Id.

3. *Implications of the Shift to Defined–Contribution Plans.* Defined-benefit plan coverage is on the decline, from 89% of medium and large firm employees in 1985 to 50% in 1997. See Olivia S. Mitchell, New Trends in Pension Benefit and Retirement Provisions, NBER Working Paper Series 7381 (Oct. 1999), p. 19; also Living with Defined Contribution Plans (Olivia S. Mitchell & Sylvester Schieber eds., 1998). This shift suggests that the productivity-enhancing incentive effects stressed by writers like Richard A. Ippolito may not be as strong as suggested or that the strength of these effects has declined. But cf. Richard A. Ippolito, Pension Plans and Employee Performance: Evidence, Analysis, and Policy (1998) (arguing that defined-contribution plans also influence productivity and turnover). The move to defined-contribution plans empowers employees to make investment decisions but, as some have argued, a tendency to risk adverseness may lead to underinvestment in equity due to feared volatility of equity returns. See Jeffrey N. Gordon, Employees, Pensions, and the New Economic Order, 97 Colum. L. Rev. 1519, 1562–66 (1997) (advocating a new capital market instrument, a "pension equity collar," that would provide a guarantee of a minimum return close to the long-term average equity return in exchange for giving up or sharing returns that exceed the long-term average).

Is the more likely danger that employee-participants, until they do experience directly stock market downturns, may overinvest in equity? If so, should the law restrict investment options for defined-contribution plan participants? Under current law, fiduciary obligations apply when the plan "limit[s] or designat[es] investment options which are intended to constitute all or part of the investment universe" for the participant. See Final Regulation Regarding Participant Directed Individual Retirement Accounts (ERISA Section 404(c) Plans) (Preamble), 57 Fed.Reg. 46,906, 46,924 n.27 (1982), quoted in Gordon, supra, at 1565 n.148; see, e.g., In re Unisys Savings Plan Litigation, 173 F.3d 145 (3d Cir.1999) (plan trustees acted prudently in their choice of investment options). The general issues are usefully explored in Symposium: Getting Ready for Individually Managed Pensions: A Global Perspective, 64 Bklyn. L. Rev. 739 ff. (no. 3, Fall 1998). See also "Note on Fiduciary Duties in Participant–Directed Defined–Contribution Plans," pp. 1038–39 infra.

4. *ESOPs and ERISA's Diversification Requirement.* Plan fiduciaries that have discretionary authority to invest plan assets have a duty to diversify their holdings, § 404(a)(1)(C) of ERISA; moreover, § 407(a) prohibits defined-benefit plans from holding more than 10 percent of the plan assets in the stock of the sponsor-employers. 29 U.S.C. § 1107(a). Employee stock ownership plans (ESOPs) are a type of defined-contribution plan under ERISA intended to encourage employee ownership, and such plans are exempted from the diversification requirement and 10% cap on ownership of employer stock. A common criticism of ESOPs is that, whatever their merits as employee motivators, they exacerbate employee risk by making both

compensation and retirement benefits dependent on the employer's continued solvency. See Deborah M. Weiss, Worker Ownership and Retirement Security, ch. 26 in Employee Representation in the Emerging Workplace: Alternatives/Supplements to Collective Bargaining 627–41 (Samuel Estreicher, ed. 1998). Some countries take a different view of the merits of diversification. In Germany, for example, companies may fund pensions by creating book reserves against their own retained earnings; in essence, pension promises are entirely unfunded liabilities. Pension security is provided in the form of a mandatory pension termination insurance funded by German employers and insurance carriers. The German system assumes that German managers will do a better job of investing the assets allocated to pension promises than would outside investors. See James H. Smalhout, The Uncertain Retirement: Securing Pension Promises in a World of Risk 223–30 (1996); Lothar Schruff, Pensions and Post–Retirement Benefits by Employers in Germany, 64 Bklyn. L. Rev. 795 (1998). See generally The Economics of Pensions: Principles, Policies and International Experience (Salvador Valdes–Prieto ed. 1997).

5. *Stock Option Plans.* A considerable portion of compensation for U.S. managers, and increasingly for nonmanagerial personnel as well, takes the form of stock options. See David Lebow, Louise Sheiner, Larry Slifman & Martha Starr–McCluer, Recent Trends in Compensation Practices (July 15, 1999). A stock option gives the holder the right (but not the obligation) to purchase a specified number of shares of company stock at a price that is fixed at the date of the grant of the option. Stock option plans are not currently regulated by ERISA or comprehensively regulated by the federal securities laws. See In re Cendant Corporation Securities Litigation, 76 F.Supp. 2d 539 (D.N.J.1999). The *Cendant* court dismissed any transactional fraud claim under § 10(b) of the Securities Exchange Act of 1934, 15 U.S.C. § 78j(b), because no "purchase or sale" of a security occurs where plaintiff acquired her options, at no direct cost to herself, "when she was already employed by Cendant under a plan that offered the options not to her as an individual, but as a member of an employee group"; compulsory, noncontributory stock options plans do not require an employee "to make an affirmative investment decision * * *." As for the ERISA claim, the court noted that optionholders merely have an expectancy interest, "a contractual right to purchase an equitable interest in a corporation at some later date." Whatever discretionary authority the company's Compensation Committee had over the stock option plan, the court held, did not implicate ERISA because stock option plans do not fit within the statute's definitional framework. See generally Matthew T. Bodie, Aligning Incentives with Equity: Employee Stock Options and Rule 10b–5, 88 Iowa L. Rev. 539 (2003); Susan J. Stabile, Another Look at 401(k) Plan Investments in Employer Securities, 35 John Marshall L. Rev. 539 (2002); and her earlier article, Motivating Executives: Does Performance–Based Compensation Positively Affect Managerial Performance?, 2 U.Pa. J. Lab. & Employ. L. 227 (1999). See also the Ninth Circuit's *Vizcaino* ruling at p. 1001 below (discussing a non-ERISA employee stock purchase plan).

6. *Other Non–ERISA Benefit Plans.* The Department of Labor has stated that payroll deduction plans for individual retirement accounts are not ERISA plans, provided (i) no employer contributions are made; (ii)

employee participation is voluntary; (iii) the employer permits but does not sponsor the program; and (iv) the employer receives no consideration (other than reasonable compensation for services rendered in connection with the payroll deduction process). See DOL Bull. 99–1, discussed in Interpretive Bulletin Assures Employer Payroll Deduction IRAs Are Not ERISA Plans, (BNA) Daily Labor Rep., No. 117, June 18, 1999, p. A–2; see also Judy C. Bauserman, Allowing Employees to Choose Transportation Fringe Benefits, 24 Employee Rels. L.J. 123 (no. 4, Spring 1999).

Note on Conversion to "Cash Balance" Plans

Traditional "final average pay" defined-benefit plans favor long-service workers because the retirement benefit is keyed to compensation received during the last few years of employment. This feature served employer objectives to encourage long-term service. In recent years, however, greater labor market mobility has led to concerns that "final average pay" plans are not suited to employees who are unlikely to remain with the employer over the course of their careers. Presumably, in order to attract and retain high-mobility, early-career employees, some companies have converted to "cash balance" plans. Such plans are defined-benefit plans, but participant benefits are determined by reference to a hypothetical account balance that appears to operate much like a defined-contribution plan. A hypothetical account is established for each participant-employee, and contributions and interest are credited to the individual's hypothetical account in much the same way actual contributions and earnings would be allocated to the participant's account in a defined-contribution plan. However, unlike a defined-contribution plan, contributions and interest allocated to the participant's hypothetical account are specified by the plan document and do not depend on actual plan earnings. Thus, like a defined-benefit plan, the employer bears the investment risk in a cash balance plan, whereas individuals bear that risk in a defined-contribution plan. See Alvin D. Lurie, Cash Balance Plans: Enigma Variations, 85 Tax Notes 503, Oct. 25, 1999, at 507–08.

For participant-employees beginning employment or still in their early years of service with the particular employer, the transfer to a cash-balance plan is beneficial because once the vesting period is met, the individuals enjoy fully mobile pension benefits without the "lock in" effect of "final average pay" plans. Moreover, benefits are likely to be larger for these workers because benefits are no longer keyed to late-career earnings. However, for participant-employees in the middle of their careers or approaching retirement, the transfer to a cash-balance plan usually will be experienced as a lowering of their expected pension benefit. In September 1999, IBM's attempt to move to the cash-balance formula ignited a near-revolt of its middle-aged employees, even sparking some unionization efforts (an unprecedented development for this company). IBM felt compelled to promise employees 40 or older with at least 10 years of service that they could remain in the old plan. See Boomer Backlash: Controversy Besetting New Pension Plan Rise with IBM's Retreat, Wall St. J., Sept. 20, 1999, p. A1, col. 1. In its November 1999 report to the Secretary of Labor, a working group of the ERISA Advisory Council issued calls for improved disclosure to plan participants and other rules to ease transition difficulties during conversions to cash-balance plans. See ERISA Advisory Council Approves Cash Balance Plan Recommendations, 68 U.S.L.W. (Legal News), Nov. 23, 1999, p. 2296.

Legal challenges to cash-balance plans involve claims of violations of ERISA and age discrimination rules. First, it might be argued that "front-loaded" cash-balance plans violate § 411(b)(1)(H) of the Internal Revenue Code, which prohibits the rate of "benefit accrual" under a defined-benefit plan from decreasing with the age of the participant. For example, a cash balance plan using a typical level percent of pay credit (such as 4% of pay) has a rate of benefit accrual that decreases with the age of the participant. Employers would respond that the "benefit accrual" is simply measured by the pay credit, and would rely on IRS and Treasury positions taken in 1991 rejecting the § 411(b)(1)(H) argument. Second, opponents might argue that the Age Discrimination in Employment Act of 1967 (ADEA), 29 U.S.C. §§ 621 et seq., is violated because older workers will have a lower age 65 benefit than if the traditional defined-benefit formula had continued and, in many cases, will have a benefit that is lower than younger workers will have if the cash-balance formula continues into the future. The responses here may be that the cash-balance formula is age neutral (a level pay credit), that employers should not be penalized for previously having established a plan that favored the long-service, typically older worker, and that disparate-impact challenges are not (or should not be) available under ADEA. Presumably, even if ADEA is held to authorize the disparate-impact approach in some situations, it does not offer a basis for challenging benefits plans that provide for equal contributions irrespective of age. See § 4(f)(2)(B) of ADEA, 29 U.S.C. § 623(f)(2)(B).

The first court of appeals to address squarely the status of cash-balance plans under ERISA § 204(b)(1)(H)(i) found no violation. In Cooper v. IBM Personal Pension Plan, 457 F.3d 636, 639 (7th Cir.2006), the Seventh Circuit reasoned that (i) the "rate of an employee's benefit accrual" is not reduced on account of age when employees receive the same pay credit and the same interest credit each year irrespective of their age; (ii) the provision requires that "benefit accrual," rather than the "accrued benefit," not decrease on account of age, and "the phrase benefit accrual reads most naturally as a reference to what the employer puts in (either in absolute terms or as a rate of change) while the [statutorily] defined phrase accrued benefit refers to outputs after compounding [of interest]"; and (iii) the fact that the present value of the contributions to a younger employee's account is greater than the present value of the same contributions to an older worker is simply a function of the time value of money rather than age.

The controversy over cash balance plans is likely to be resolved by the Pension Protection Act of 2006, Pub. L. 109–280, 120 Stat. 780, which amends ERISA to make clear that a DB plan does not discriminate on the basis of age if a participant's accrued benefit under a DB is not less than the accrued benefit of any "similarly situated" employee, defined to mean identical in every respect other than age.

Accounting obligations presented by cash-balance plans are the subject of a pending rulemaking by the Financial Accounting Standards Board. See FASB Gives Tentative Nod to Direction of Staff Proposal on Cash Balance Plans, (BNA) Daily Lab. Rep., No. 14, Jan. 23, 2004, p. A-4.

B. ERISA–COVERED "PLANS"

WILLIAMS v. WRIGHT
U.S. Court of Appeals for the Eleventh Circuit, 1991.
927 F.2d 1540.

ANDERSON, J.

This appeal raises issues involving the Employee Retirement Income Security Act of 1974 ("ERISA"), 29 U.S.C. §§ 1001–1461, and state contract law. Appellant James T. Williams ("Williams") brought an action under § 502 of ERISA, 29 U.S.C. § 1132, against appellees Fred P. Wright ("Wright") and Wright Pest Control Co. ("WPCC"), alleging violations of ERISA. Williams also included a state law claim for breach of a retirement contract. The district court eventually granted summary judgment in favor of appellees on all counts. * * *

I. FACTS

James T. Williams began working for WPCC in 1947. In October of 1981, Williams and Fred P. Wright, Jr., president of WPCC, discussed the possibility and terms of Williams' retirement. Although these talks were inconclusive, on October 23, 1981, Wright presented to Williams the letter set out in the [Appendix below] (the "1981 letter").

Williams received benefits in accordance with this letter until September,1984. On September 7, 1984, "Wright informed [Williams] that for business reasons it would be necessary 'to slow the gravy train down from a race to a crawl.' " Subsequently, WPCC reduced the country club, telephone, and automobile expenses, but continued the monthly payments of $500.00 and the insurance benefits.

On September 1, 1985, Wright informed Williams that WPCC's dissolution and imminent asset sale to Terminex Service, Inc. necessitated termination of Williams' retirement benefits. Accordingly, after the asset sale and dissolution occurred, in December, 1985, WPCC terminated Williams' benefits. Wright did transfer title to the company car that Williams had been using to Williams and forgive $1,906.63 in personal debt owed to WPCC by Williams. This lawsuit followed.

II. DISCUSSION

A. *The ERISA Claim.* * * *

ERISA recognizes two types of plans, "employee welfare benefit plans"[4] and "employee pension benefit plans."[5] In order for appellant to

---

4. 29 U.S.C. § 1002(1) provides:

The terms "employee welfare benefit plan" and "welfare plan" mean any plan, fund, or program which was heretofore or is hereafter established or maintained by an employer or by an employee organization, or by both, to the extent that such plan, fund, or program was established or

is maintained for the purpose of providing for its participants or their beneficiaries, through the purchase of insurance or otherwise, (A) medical, surgical, or hospital care or benefits, or benefits in the event of sickness, accident, disability, death or unemployment, or vacation benefits, apprenticeship or other training

invoke ERISA's substantive provisions covering either type, appellant must prevail on the threshold question of whether the benefits arrangement set out in the 1981 letter is a "plan, fund, or program" covered by ERISA. *Donovan v. Dillingham*, 688 F.2d 1367 (11th Cir.1982) (en banc); 29 U.S.C. §§ 1002(1) and (2)(A). Although the definition of these terms has proved to be elusive at best, *Donovan* at 1372, this court has prescribed general guidelines for resolving the threshold question: "[A] 'plan, fund, or program' under ERISA is established if from the surrounding circumstances a reasonable person can ascertain the intended benefits,[7] a class of beneficiaries, the source of financing, and procedures for receiving benefits." Id. at 1373. * * *

The district court applied the *Donovan* analysis and concluded that the retirement arrangement at issue was not covered by ERISA. The district court was troubled by the fact that the only ascertainable source of financing for Williams' benefits was the general assets of the corporation rather than any separate fund or trust, that the class of beneficiaries was limited to Williams and his wife, and that, in the court's view, there were no procedures for receiving benefits. The district court also viewed the arrangement as, at best, "an individual employment contract which included post-retirement compensation" rather than an ERISA "plan, fund, or program." * * * [W]e conclude that the district court erred in holding that the letter from Wright to Williams did not establish a plan covered by ERISA.

1.   The Donovan Analysis

a.   Source of Financing

Although noting that the source of financing for the benefits at issue was the general assets of WPCC, the district court found no ascertainable source of financing under *Donovan*. Although, with some exceptions, it is true that the assets of employee benefit plans are required to be held in trust, see 29 U.S.C. § 1103, it is equally true that an employer's failure to meet an ERISA requirement does not exempt the plan from ERISA coverage. *Scott v. Gulf Oil Corp.*, 754 F.2d 1499, 1503 (9th

---

programs, or day care centers, scholarship funds, or prepaid legal services, or (B) any benefit described in section 186(c) of this title (other than pensions on retirement or death, and insurance to provide such pensions).

5.   29 U.S.C. Sec. 1002(2)(A) provides:

Except as provided in subparagraph (B), the terms "employee pension benefit plan" and "pension plan" mean any plan, fund, or program which was heretofore or is hereafter established or maintained by an employer or by an employee organization, or by both, to the extent that by its express terms or as a result of surrounding circumstances such plan, fund, or program—

> (i) provides retirement income to employees, or

(ii) results in a deferral of income by employees for periods extending to the termination of covered employment or beyond, regardless of the method of calculating the contributions made to the plan, the method of calculating the benefits under the plan or the method of distributing benefits from the plan.

7.   With regard to this first prong of *Donovan*, we can easily ascertain the benefits intended by Wright's October 23, 1981 letter. The promise of monthly payments of $500.00 and group health and life insurance coverage is certainly not ambiguous.

Cir.1985). "An employer * * * should not be able to evade the requirements of the statute merely by paying * * * benefits out of general assets." *Fort Halifax Packing Co., Inc. v. Coyne*, 482 U.S. 1, 18, 107 S.Ct. 2211, 2221, 96 L.Ed.2d 1 (1987). Therefore, we conclude that the payment of benefits out of an employer's general assets does not affect the threshold question of ERISA coverage. See also U.S. Dept. of Labor Opinion Letters 78–18 (Sept. 20, 1978) and 79–75 (Oct. 29, 1979) (finding ERISA coverage where benefit payments were made from general assets of employer and other requirements satisfied).

b. Procedures for Receiving Benefits

Relying in part on *Fort Halifax*, supra, the district court held that the instant case lacked the administrative program or procedures characteristic of ERISA plans. However, *Fort Halifax* does not support the conclusion that the retirement arrangement at issue is not covered by ERISA for this reason. Although the procedures for receiving benefits provided by the 1981 letter are simple, they are sufficiently ascertainable under the Donovan analysis.

In *Fort Halifax*, after the employer closed its poultry packaging and processing plant, the state of Maine sued to enforce a state statute requiring the employer to provide a one-time severance payment to certain employees. The employer argued, inter alia, that the state statute was preempted by ERISA and therefore unenforceable. The Supreme Court held that ERISA was inapplicable because a one-time payment did not require the sort of ongoing administrative scheme characteristic of an ERISA plan. The Court reasoned that a purpose of ERISA preemption, "to afford employers the advantages of a uniform set of administrative procedures governed by a single set of regulations," *Fort Halifax* at 11, 107 S. Ct. at 2217, was not compromised where "the employer assumes no responsibility to pay benefits on a regular basis." *Id.* at 12, 107 S.Ct. at 2218. The Court concluded that "the theoretical possibility of a one-time obligation in the future simply creates no need for an ongoing administrative program for processing claims and paying benefits." *Id.*

The situation in *Fort Halifax* is easily distinguishable from the instant case which does involve a continuing obligation necessitating ongoing, though simple, procedures. The letter of October 23, 1981 expressly provides that the company "will issue you a check * * * each month * * * until your death or when you have no use for [the benefits]." In addition the letter provides that in the event that the arrangement does not "fill all needs as anticipated," revisions will be considered after April 1, 1982. Therefore, we conclude that the 1981 letter provides for sufficiently ascertainable procedures or receiving benefits under *Donovan*.

c. The Class of Beneficiaries

The requirement of an ascertainable class of beneficiaries is perhaps more troublesome. However, we do not interpret *Donovan*'s use of the word "class" as an absolute requirement of more than one beneficiary or that a plan tailored to the needs of a single employee can not be within ERISA. Rather, Donovan referred only to the fact that most pension plans falling within ERISA involve identical treatment of a group of employees.

Furthermore, we find nothing in the ERISA legislation pointing to the exclusion of plans covering only a single employee. In fact, ERISA's predecessor statute, the Welfare and Pension Plans Disclosure Act, Pub.L. No. 85–836, § 4(b)(4), 72 Stat. 998–999 (1958), expressly excluded plans covering less than 25 employees. Congress was aware of this limitation in the prior legislation but apparently decided not to include it in ERISA. See S.Rep. No. 127, 93d Cong., 1st Sess., at 6 (1973).

It is also significant that Department of Labor regulations refer to a plan covering one or more employees as within ERISA. See, e.g., 29 C.F.R. § 2510.3–3(b) (1988) ("[A] Keogh plan under which one or more common law employees, in addition to the self-employed individuals, are participants covered under the plan, will be covered under Title I [of ERISA].") (emphasis added). See also 29 C.F.R. § 2510.3–2(d) (under some circumstances, individual retirement accounts or annuities are covered by ERISA).

* * *

2. *The Employment Contract Cases*

Aside from the *Donovan* analysis, further support for our conclusion that the 1981 letter establishes an ERISA plan or program is found in the cases that appellee cites for the opposite conclusion. For example, in *Jervis* v. *Elerding*, 504 F. Supp. 606 (C.D.Cal.1980), an owner of apartment buildings, Elerding, entered into an employment contract with his apartment manager, Jervis, agreeing to provide Jervis with an apartment upon her retirement or termination after at least ten years in his employ. After Jervis terminated her employment, Elerding refused to provide the apartment as agreed. The court held that "a contract between an employer and an individual employee providing for post-retirement or post-termination in-kind compensation is not a 'plan, fund, or program' within the definitional framework of ERISA." *Id.* at 608. The court based this holding on its observation that the agreement to provide the apartment "was part of the present compensation arrangement, inserted as consideration for plaintiff's continued services to defendant, rather than as part of a 'plan' providing for retirement income or deferral of income." *Id.* at 609 (emphasis added). Also, the court noted that the employer's promise of a rent-free apartment was not conditioned on the employee's retirement and that "the parties merely memorialized their employee-employer relationship; they did not enter into an agreement for a separate and specific retirement plan." *Id.* (emphasis added).

Similarly, other cases cited by appellee and relied on by the district court generally involve the promise of post-retirement payments offered only incidentally to a present individual employment agreement. * * *

The distinction between payments after retirement or termination pursuant to a current employment contract and a plan to specifically provide for an employee's retirement was perhaps made most clearly in *Murphy v. Inexco Oil Co.*, 611 F.2d 570 (5th Cir.1980). In *Murphy*, Murphy, the president of Inexco, was one of a number of employees given a bonus in the form of royalties from the company's drilling projects. Murphy eventually sued the company, alleging various violations of ERISA. The court did not address the substantive ERISA violations because it concluded that the bonus program was not a pension plan covered by ERISA. * * *

* * * The court's rationale for excluding the bonus program from ERISA was expressed in the following language: "[The bonus program] was evidently designed to provide current rather than retirement income to Inexco's employees." *Murphy*, 611 F.2d at 575–76 (emphasis added). The court interpreted "the words 'provides retirement income' [in 29 U.S.C. § 1002(2)(A)(i) as referring] only to plans designed for the purpose of paying retirement income whether as a result of their express terms or surrounding circumstances." Id. at 575 (emphasis added). The *Murphy* analysis would not include within ERISA payments that incidentally might be made after retirement but were not designed for retirement purposes. Id. at 574–75. * * *

The facts of this case reveal that the letter presented to Williams by Wright on October 23, 1981 contemplated Williams immediate retirement. We initially note that the letter itself expressly changed Williams' status at WPCC as of October 26, 1981, just three days after the date of the letter. Furthermore, although the letter states that "in exchange for these payments and benefits, you will be expected to function for the company in the manner of consultant and advisor on pest control matters * * *," the record shows that Williams performed only minimal, if any, consulting services after October 26, 1981 * * * In fact, Wright stated that he typed and presented the letter to Williams specifically for the purpose of procuring Williams' retirement, or, as Wright put it, Williams' termination. * * * In addition, in a letter dated April 3, 1987, Wright stated that "the money paid by Wright Pest Control to James Williams was retirement pay and not salary." * * * Finally, in defense of appellant's contract claims, appellees stated in the joint proposed pretrial order that the letter was "a gratuitous promise to pay retirement income * * *."

Therefore, it is clear that the 1981 letter's arrangement primarily constituted payment of retirement income and was not an employment contract outside the scope of ERISA.

4. Conclusion

Although ERISA does not mandate the establishment of employee benefit plans, a primary purpose of the legislation is to protect employees once a plan is established and certain other requirements are met. In light of this purpose, we conclude that the district court erred in ruling that the 1981 letter did not establish a "plan" or "program" within ERISA. * * *

[*Eds.* The *Wright* court's discussion of ERISA preemption is omitted.]

Appendix

The letter reads [in relevant part] as follows:

* * *

Dear Jim:

This letter is to formalize our earlier conversations regarding your compensation as General Manager of Wright Pest Control as of January 1, 1982 and your duties thereafter.

After consultation with attorneys and accountants, I have arrived at the following plan, which will provide for an uninterrupted continuation of cash as you gradually alter your work schedule to a retirement status.

Your current net pay is $1200.00 per month, plus or minus $50.00. I understand that you have applied for social security benefits beginning January 1, 1982, and that these benefits will net you approximately $700.00 per month.

As of January 1, 1982, you are permitted to earn up to $6000.00 per year without any effect on your social security benefits. The company will issue you a check in the amount of $500.00 each month, on the first of each month. This amount will completely take care of your allowed earned income under social security regulations.

The total of your social security benefits, plus this monthly amount[,] should equal the $1200.00 target amount, plus or minus $50.00. In addition, we will also:

Pay all dues and fees at the Augusta Country Club, including meal tickets when appropriate receipts are executed.

Furnish you with a vehicle, equal or better than that which has been furnished you in the past. All expenses are to be paid, including gasoline. A radio will also be furnished for communication with the company. The vehicle is to be returned to the company should you ever become unable to drive.

Pay all premiums for yourself and Mrs. Williams on the company's group medical insurance plan, and the maximum available term life insurance available through the plan for your age group.

These benefits will continue until your death or when you have no use for them. It is understood that your country club membership will be made available to me personally when you no longer have use for it.

In exchange for these payments and benefits, you will be expected to function for the company in the manner of consultant and advisor on pest control matters, and various activities of a social nature related to sales activity or general public relations. You will not have any operational authority or duties except in a life or death situation, such as when observing an unsafe act by a company employee.

Your office and desk will be maintained as per your wishes, until an acute need for space in the office should dictate otherwise. Your desk will be kept locked, but for security reasons we ask that all company documents of a confidential or sensitive nature be destroyed. This will include any past profit and loss statements, personnel records, etc. In a like manner we can not be responsible for any personal items of a confidential or sensitive nature.

As this program is as we agreed, but in fact may not fill all needs as anticipated, future revisions are to be expected, but no changes will be considered until a sufficient amount of time has passed. April 1, 1982 will be the earliest date that revisions will be considered. * * *

Sincerely,

Fred P. Wright, Jr., President

Notes and Questions

1. *Plaintiffs and ERISA Preemption.* It is unusual for a plaintiff, as in *Wright*, to argue that his benefits are governed by an ERISA plan, because a typical consequence of finding an ERISA plan is preemption of state-law claims, as the court held and as discussed at pp. 1172–85 infra. The opinion does not reveal why Wright's lawyer made the ERISA argument; perhaps the lawyer was seeking the benefit of ERISA-authorized attorney's fees. Employers will almost always make this argument, as they face little disincentive in asserting that the benefits are covered by an ERISA plan because, as *Wright* illustrates, the absence of a separate trust fund or violations of the disclosure and reporting requirements of ERISA do not negate the preemptive force of ERISA.

2. *Why Regulate Welfare Benefit Plans?* Welfare benefits, such as severance pay and health insurance, are nonvested benefits and do not require advance funding by the employer-sponsor. Because of gaps in ERISA and its preemption of state law, courts have developed an "ERISA common law" as a gap-filler. See, e.g., Noorily v. Thomas & Betts Corp., 188 F.3d 153 (3d Cir.1999) (employer initially announced that employees choosing not to relocate would receive severance payments from unfunded benefit plan, but changed policy when it became clear that most of its product managers and engineers would not be relocating; plaintiffs, after this policy change, declined to transfer and sued unsuccessfully to recover once-promised severance pay). Consider the justifications for ERISA regulation set out at p. ___, note 2. To what extent do they apply to welfare benefits? What would be lost by amending ERISA to cover only pension benefit plans?

3. *"Mixed" Severance Agreements: Compensation vs. ERISA Benefits.* Ronald Dranchak, while vice-president for Human Resources of Akzo America, Inc., negotiated improvements in his own severance and retirement package with Jadel, president of Akzo, at a time when Dranchak was

negotiating for the company a severance agreement for the departing Jadel. When the Akzo board learned of this, Dranchak was sacked, and Dranchak then sued to collect on the promises Jadel had made and for age discrimination. A jury awarded him $3 million, but the district court set aside the contract claim on grounds of ERISA preemption. The Seventh Circuit in Dranchak v. Akzo Nobel Inc., 88 F.3d 457, 459–60 (1996) affirmed:

> * * * Dranchak * * * insists that the letter agreements [he negotiated on his own behalf with the outgoing Jadel] do not affect Akzo's plans. ERISA does not regulate executives' pay and bonuses, and it is possible to draft severance agreements that are unrelated to a "plan" and therefore fall outside of ERISA's scope. *Nagy* v. *Riblet Products Corp.*, 79 F.3d 572, 574 (7th Cir.1996). Dranchak observes that the letter agreements do not set any plan's level of benefits or rules for payment; they simply afford him extra years of pension credit and extended medical coverage. It is as if Jadel said to the pension plan's administrator: "Calculate what Dranchak is due under the terms of the plan, then pay him twice that amount." But that is precisely why the letter agreements are covered by ERISA rather than state law. * * * They instruct the plan's administrator how much to disburse from the pension and welfare trusts.

> * * * Portions of the letter agreements that promise the continuation of wages, favorable recommendations, and so on, cannot sensibly be divorced from the portions that deal with pension and welfare benefits; if one portion is valid (because Jadel had the necessary authority), everything is valid. The letter agreements affect ERISA plans, state law enforcing the letter agreements would relate to the plans, and the promises they contain therefore must stand or fall together under federal common law.

4.   On the requirement of an "ongoing and administrative scheme," as stated in First Halifax Packing Co., Inc. v. Coyne, see pp. 1172–81 infra.

C. ELIGIBLE "PARTICIPANTS"

As is true of virtually all employment regulations, and as we have seen in connection with the *Darden* decision, p. ___ supra, ERISA's protections extend only to "employees". Federal law does not require an employer to provide all undisputed common-law employees with pension or welfare benefits, but the language used in plan documents and ERISA regulations may make it difficult for employers to limit plans to particular employees while excluding others who are similarly situated. The *Microsoft* litigation provides a vivid illustration of this issue.

VIZCAINO v. MICROSOFT CORPORATION

U.S. Court of Appeals for the Ninth Circuit (en banc), 1997.
120 F.3d 1006.

FERNANDEZ, J.

Donna Vizcaino, Jon R. Waite, Mark Stout, Geoffrey Culbert, Lesley Stuart, Thomas Morgan, Elizabeth Spokoiny, and Larry Spokoiny brought this action on behalf of themselves and a court-certified class (all are hereafter collectively referred to as "the Workers"). They sued Microsoft Corporation and its various pension and welfare plans, including its Savings Plus Plan (SPP), and sought a determination that they were entitled to participate in the plan benefits because those benefits were available to Microsoft's common law employees. The district court granted summary judgment against the Workers, and they appealed the determinations that they were not entitled to participate in the SPP or in the Employee Stock Purchase Plan (ESPP). We reversed the district court because we decided that the Workers were common law employees who were not properly excluded from participation in those plans. See *Vizcaino v. Microsoft Corp.*, 97 F.3d 1187 (9th Cir.1996) (*Vizcaino I*). However, we then decided to rehear the matter en banc, and we now agree with much of the panel's conclusion and reverse the district court.

BACKGROUND

At various times before 1990, Microsoft hired the Workers to perform services for it. They did perform those services over a continuous period, often exceeding two years. They were hired to work on specific projects and performed a number of different functions, such as production editing, proofreading, formatting, indexing, and testing. "Microsoft fully integrated [the Workers] into its workforce: they often worked on teams along with regular employees, sharing the same supervisors, performing identical functions, and working the same core hours. Because Microsoft required that they work on site, they received admittance card keys, office equipment and supplies from the company." Id. at 1190. However, they were not paid for their services through the payroll department, but rather submitted invoices to and were paid through the accounts payable department.

Microsoft did not withhold income or Federal Insurance Contribution Act [(FICA)] taxes from the Workers' wages, and did not pay the employer's share of the FICA taxes. Moreover, Microsoft did not allow the Workers to participate in the SPP or the ESPP. The Workers did not complain about those arrangements at that time.

However, in 1989 and 1990 the Internal Revenue Service examined Microsoft's records and decided that it should have been withholding and paying over taxes because, as a matter of law, the Workers were employees rather than independent contractors. It made that determination by applying common law principles. Microsoft agreed with the IRS and made the necessary corrections for the past by issuing W–2 forms to the Workers and by paying the employer's share of FICA taxes to the government.

Microsoft also realized that, because the Workers were employees, at least for tax purposes, it had to change its system. It made no sense to have employees paid through the accounts payable department, so those who remained in essentially the same relationship as before were tendered offers to become acknowledged employees. Others had to discontinue working for Microsoft, but did have the opportunity to go to work for a temporary employment agency, which could then supply temporary Workers to Microsoft on an as-needed basis. Some took advantage of that opportunity, some—like Vizcaino—did not.

The Workers then asserted that they were employees of Microsoft and should have had the opportunity of participating in the SPP and the ESPP because those plans were available to all employees who met certain other participation qualifications, which are not relevant to the issues before us. Microsoft disagreed, and the Workers asked the SPP plan administrator to exercise his authority to declare that they were eligible for the benefits. A panel was convened; it ruled that the Workers were not entitled to any benefits from ERISA plans—for example, the SPP—or, for that matter, from non-ERISA plans—for example, the ESPP. That, the administrative panel seemed to say, was because the Workers had agreed that they were independent contractors and because they had waived the right to participate in benefit plans. This action followed * * *.

DISCUSSION

Although the Workers challenge both their exclusion from the SPP and their exclusion from the ESPP, the two plans are subject to rather different legal regimes. The former is a 26 U.S.C. § 401(k) plan, which is governed by ERISA; the latter is a 26 U.S.C. § 423 plan, which is not governed by ERISA. It, instead, is governed, at least in large part, by principles arising out of the law of the State of Washington. Nevertheless, certain issues, perhaps the most critical ones, cut across both regimes, and we will address them first.

I. GENERAL CONSIDERATIONS

A. *The Workers' Status*

It is important to recognize that there is no longer any question that the Workers were employees of Microsoft, and not independent contractors. The IRS clearly determined that they were. In theory one could argue that what the IRS said was fine for withholding and FICA purposes, but that is as far as it goes.

* * *

That question is obviated here for * * * both Microsoft and the SPP have conceded for purposes of this appeal that the Workers were common law employees. * * *

B. *The Employment Agreements*

* * * Microsoft also entered into special agreements with the Workers, and it is those which complicate matters to some extent. Each of the Workers and Microsoft signed agreements which stated, among other things not relevant here, that the worker was "an Independent Contractor for [Microsoft]," and nothing in the agreement should be construed as creating an "employer-employee relationship." As a result, the worker agreed "to be responsible for all of [his] federal and state taxes, with-

holding, social security, insurance, and other benefits." At the same time, Microsoft had the Workers sign an information form, which explained: "As an Independent Contractor to Microsoft, you are self employed and are responsible to pay all your own insurance and benefits. * * * Microsoft * * * will not subject your payments to any withholding. * * * You are not either an employee of Microsoft, or a temporary employee of Microsoft." We now know beyond peradventure that most of this was not, in fact, true because the Workers actually were employees rather than independent contractors. What are we to make of that?

We now know that as a matter of law Microsoft hired the Workers to perform their services as employees and that the Workers performed those services. Yet we are also obligated to construe the agreements. * * * In doing so, we could take either a negative or a positive view of Microsoft's intent and motives. We could decide that Microsoft knew that the Workers were employees, but chose to paste the independent contractor label upon them after making a rather amazing series of decisions to violate the law. Or we could decide that Microsoft mistakenly thought that the Workers were independent contractors and that all else simply seemed to flow from that status.

* * *

* * * Viewed in the proper light, it can be seen that the Workers were indeed hired by Microsoft to perform services for it. We know that their services were rendered in their capacities as employees. The contracts indicate, however, that they are independent contractors, which they were not. The other terms of the contracts do not add or subtract from their status or, indeed, impose separate agreements upon them. In effect, the other terms merely warn the Workers about what happens to them if they are independent contractors. Again, those are simply results which hinge on the status determination itself; they are not separate freestanding agreements. Therefore, the Workers were employees, who did not give up or waive their rights to be treated like all other employees under the plans. The Workers performed services for Microsoft under conditions which made them employees. They did sign agreements, which declared that they were independent contractors, but at best that declaration was due to a mutual mistake, and we know that even Microsoft does not now seek to assert that the label made them independent contractors.

* * *

II.   THE PLANS

A.   *The SPP*

The SPP is an ERISA plan. See 29 U.S.C. § 1002(2)(A)(ii); * * * *In re Dunn*, 988 F.2d 45, 46 (7th Cir.1993). The Workers seek enforcement of the terms of that plan. That is, they seek to have us review the determination of the plan administrator and to require that the plan make its benefits available to them. See 29 U.S.C. § 1132(a)(1)(B). As we have already pointed out, the administrative panel of the SPP determined that the Workers are not entitled to benefits. The reasons appear to have been that the Workers were independent contractors and that they waived the benefits. We must review those determinations to see if they were arbitrary or capricious. * * * Based upon what we have already said, it is pellucid that they were. To the extent that the decision was based upon the supposed independent contractor status of the Workers, the plan conceded that the decision was wrong when it conceded that the Workers were, in fact, employees. To the extent that the decision was based upon a supposed waiver of benefits, the plan administrator purported to construe the agreements rather than the plan itself. But, as we have pointed out, our construction is the opposite. We, therefore, determine that the reasons given for denying benefits were arbitrary and capricious because they were based upon legal errors which "misconstrued the Plan and applied a wrong standard to a benefits determination." * * *

* * *

We are asked to decide what is meant by the SPP's restriction of benefits to common law employees who are "on the United States payroll of the employer." The [Ninth Circuit] panel explored some of the reasonably possible meanings of that phrase and construed the apparent ambiguity in favor of the Workers. See [97 F.3d] at 1193–96. No doubt the plan administrator should pay careful attention to what was said there. We have also pointed out that we are dubious about the proposition that Microsoft would manipulate plan coverage by assigning recognized common law employees to its accounts payable department or to its payroll department, as it saw fit. We have our doubts that it could properly do so. But it is the terms of the SPP which control, and the plan is separate from Microsoft itself. Thus, we cannot, and will not, predict how the plan administrator, who has the primary duty of construction, will construe the terms of the SPP.

* * *

B. The ESPP

The ESPP was a plan adopted for the purpose of taking advantage of the benefits conferred under 26 U.S.C. § 423. It was approved by the board of directors and by the shareholders of Microsoft. Their action was an offer to employees, as that term is defined in § 423. As we have already suggested, we doubt that the corporate officers set out to withdraw the offer from some employees, even if they could have done that. The Workers knew about the fact of that offer, even if they were not aware of its precise terms. Under the law of the State of Washington, which all agree applies here, a contract can be accepted, even when the employee does not know its precise terms. See *Dorward* v. *ILWU-PMA Pension Plan*, 75 Wash. 2d 478, 452 P.2d 258 (1969). * * *

The ESPP was created and offered to all employees, the Workers knew of it, even if they were not aware of its precise terms, and their labor gave them a right to participate in it. Of course, Microsoft's officers would not allow that participation because they were under the misapprehension that the board and the shareholders had not extended the offer to the Workers. That error on the officers' part does not change the fact that there was an offer, which was accepted by the Workers' labor. Of course, the ESPP provides for a somewhat unusual benefit. An employee, who chooses to participate, must pay for any purchase of stock, and the Workers never did that. We, however, leave the determination of an appropriate remedy to the district court.

[*Eds.* The opinion of Judge Fletcher, with whom Chief Judge Hug and Judges Pregerson, Hawkins and Thomas joined, concurring in part and dissenting in part, is omitted.]

O'SCANNLAIN, J., joined by HALL, and T.G. NELSON, JJ., concurring in part and dissenting in part.

I respectfully dissent from all but Part II–A of the court's opinion because Microsoft and the plaintiffs never formed a valid contract under Washington law for the benefits now claimed. I concur in the result of Part II–A of the court's opinion but not in its analysis.

* * *

II

As I see it, this is a simple contracts case. The Washington law of contracts governs the freelancers' claim of entitlement to benefits under the Employee Stock Purchase Plan ("ESPP"). No law, state or federal, mandates that Microsoft provide such benefits even to its employees. Plaintiffs are eligible to participate in the ESPP only to the extent that they entered into a valid contract with Microsoft for such participation.

Offer, acceptance, and consideration are requisites to contract formation under Washington law. * * * In order to be entitled to benefits under the ESPP, therefore, Microsoft must have offered the benefits to the freelancers, and the freelancers must have accepted that offer.

The court claims that Microsoft's board of directors offered ESPP benefits to the freelancers when they promulgated the ESPP, reasoning that an offer of benefits in a pension plan extends to and may be accepted by employees who do not know its precise terms, as long as they generally know of its existence, citing *Dorward* v. *ILWU-PMA Pension Plan*, 75 Wash. 2d 478, 452 P.2d 258, 261 (Wash. 1969). The ESPP is not a pension plan, however, and, therefore, standard principles of contract law govern. Even so, as a matter of contract law, *Dorward* might have supported the result in this case if Microsoft's board had merely promulgated the ESPP and the freelancers, knowing of its existence, satisfied the ESPP's eligibility requirements. But in a line of general employment law cases apparently ignored by the court's opinion, Washington courts have held that an employer revokes a generally promulgated offer when it enters into a specific agreement with an employee which is inconsistent with the offer. *Thompson* v. *St. Regis Paper Co.*, 102 Wash. 2d 219, 685 P.2d 1081, 1087 (Wash. 1984). * * *

Exactly such a revocation occurred here. Microsoft's board offered the ESPP to employees generally, and then Microsoft told the freelancers: "We aren't offering the ESPP to you; ESPP benefits are not included in your contract." Knowing that they wouldn't get ESPP benefits, the freelancers nevertheless agreed to work for Microsoft. Their contract therefore does not include ESPP benefits because the offer of those benefits was revoked.

* * *

If this is not enough, the court's alleged contract suffers from another defect: a lack of consideration. There was no detrimental reliance on the ESPP by the freelancers—they did not think they would get ESPP benefits, and they still chose to work for Microsoft on Microsoft's terms. Indeed, it is hard to imagine what consideration the freelancers could have given for the ESPP benefits since they chose to work for Microsoft for several years without benefits. If anything, the freelancers received consideration (a higher hourly rate) for their agreement that they would not get ESPP benefits.

* * *

III

The freelancers also claim that Microsoft should have allowed them to participate in its Savings Plus Plan ("SPP"), which is governed by ERISA. The SPP provides that "each employee who is 18 years of age or older and who has been employed for six months shall be eligible to participate in this Plan." It then defines "employee" as "any common law employee who receives remuneration for personal services rendered to the employer and who is on the United States payroll of the employer." The freelancers argue that they fit this definition of employee; Microsoft retorts that the freelancers were not "on the United States payroll of the employer." Our first task, therefore, is ascertaining what that phrase means.

We cannot immediately set about this task, however, because the SPP grants discretion to the plan administrator to construe the plan. The Supreme Court has instructed us that when the plan vests discretion in the administrator, principles of trust law require that we leave the plan administrator's interpretation undisturbed if reasonable. *Firestone Tire & Rubber Co.* v. *Bruch*, 489 U.S. 101, 111, 103 L.Ed.2d 80, 109 S.Ct. 948 (1989). * * *

In order for this rule protecting a plan administrator's discretion to be meaningful, however, the administrator must be given an opportunity to interpret the meaning of plan provisions before the court rules. In this case, the plan administrator did not overtly construe the phrase "on the United States payroll of the employer," at least so far as I can tell from the record. * * *

I write separately to clarify that I do not concur in the court's analysis of the meaning and implications of "on the United States payroll of the employer," and, as dicta, the court's statements do not bind the plan administrator in any way. In my view, that phrase is a term of art with significance within the Microsoft community. * * *

Notes and Questions

1. *The Court's Holding?* Did the court in *Vizcaino* hold that the misclassified "freelancers" were entitled to participate in Microsoft's pension and stock purchase plans, or did it hold this was an issue to be determined by the plan administrators in the first instance? If the administrators rule that the "freelancers" were not eligible, what basis will there be to find such a ruling "arbitrary and capricious"? If the decision ultimately is for the plan administrators, why did the majority set out, and evaluate, various conceptions of what Microsoft may have had in mind in purporting to exclude the "freelancers". Does the decision in any way stand for the proposition that workers misclassified as "independent contractors" must be included in broad-based ERISA-covered pension plans?

2. *Agreements Acknowledging Nonemployee Status.* What effect should be given to agreements between companies and freelancers acknowledging that the latter are not employees of the company? Should they be given any weight?

3. *State Contract Law.* Consider the proposition of Washington law relied upon by the majority in the portion of its ruling dealing with the non-ERISA employee stock purchase plan. Is it clear that the Washington courts would hold that employees are bound by the terms of a benefit plan even if they were not made aware of its terms? Even where the plan contemplates employee contributions, as it did in the instant case? Review the materials on state contract law and unilateral employer modification/rescission of employee-handbook promises, in Chapter 12.

4. *"Leased" Employees and IRS "Nondiscrimination" Testing.* Although the *Microsoft* court relied on the language of the plan documents, a few district courts have relied on the Internal Revenue Code's definition of a "leased" employee to require companies to include "common law employees", though on the payroll of a "leasing organization", in their pension benefit plans.

One way to avoid directly hiring a person is for a company to enter into a contract with a third party (the "leasing organization"), whereby the latter entity places the person on the premises of the organization that needs the services (the "recipient organization"). The leasing organization purports to be the "employer," and may even provide the "leased" employee with pension and welfare benefits. This organization retains the formal authority to hire, fire, discipline and promote the "leased" employee, although as a practical matter the recipient organization exercises day-to-day control over the employee. Under 1992 amendments to the Internal Revenue Code, see Tax Equity and Fiscal Responsibility Act of 1982, Pub.L. No. 97–248, § 248(a), 96 Stat. 324, § 414(n) of the Code requires the sponsor of a qualified plan that uses the services of "leased" employees to treat that person "as an employee of the recipient" for certain testing purposes. The purpose of this provision is to ensure that employer-sponsors do not evade the "nondiscrimination" requirements applicable to qualified plans by using "leased" employees to perform services traditionally performed by employees who would have qualified for plan participation. In other words, the Code requires that a certain percentage of the workforce be plan-eligible (including, for this computation, "leased" employees) for a pension plan to be a "qualified" plan.

Section 414(n) provides in relevant part:

> (1) In general.—For purposes of the requirements listed in paragraph (3), with respect to any person (hereinafter in this subsection referred to as the "recipient") for whom a leased employee performs services—

>> (A) the leased employee shall be treated as an employee of the recipient, but

>> (B) contributions or benefits provided by the leasing organization which are attributable to services performed for the recipient shall be treated as provided by the recipient.

> (2) Leased employee.—For purposes of paragraph (1), the term "leased employee" means any person who is not an employee of the recipient and who provides services to the recipient if—

>> (A) such services are provided pursuant to an agreement between the recipient and any other person (in this subsection referred to as the "leasing organization"),

>> (B) such person has performed such services for the recipient (or for the recipient and related persons) on a substantially full-time basis for a period of at least 1 year, and

>> (C) such services are performed under primary direction or control by the recipient.

26 U.S.C. § 414(n). The third criterion, § 414(n)(2)(C), had been amended in 1996 to replace what had been a "historically performed" test with the "primary direction or control" test now in the Code.

Does a finding of "leased employee" status under § 414(n) have any bearing on substantive entitlement to employee benefits? The text of the Code would suggest a negative answer. The definition of "leased employee" refers expressly to "nondiscrimination" testing requirements listed in § 414(n)(3). Moreover, the ERISA coverage tests in Code § 410(b)(2)(A) "look to the percentage of employees required to be covered as opposed to mandating coverage of all employees whose exclusion is not permitted under § 410(b)(3)." Howard Pianko, *Microsoft* and Its Legacy—Employers Confront "Contingent" Worker Benefit Issues, 5 ERISA and Benefits L.J. 249, 257 n.21 (1999). See also Micah Berul, Courts' Treatment of ERISA Claims Brought by Nonstandard Workers, 29 Employee Rels. L.J. 70 (Fall 2003).

A few district courts have held that workers falling within the § 414(n) definition of "leased employees" must be treated as employee-participants in the benefit plans of the recipient organization. See Renda v. Adam Meldrum & Anderson Co., 806 F.Supp. 1071, 1079–80, 1082 (W.D.N.Y.1992); Bronk v.

Mountain States Tel. & Tel., Inc., 943 F.Supp. 1317 (D.Colo.1996), reversed, 140 F.3d 1335 (10th Cir.1998). This view has not, however, been adopted by the courts of appeals that have ruled on the question. In *Bronk*, for example, the Tenth Circuit stated:

> It is well established that ERISA does not prohibit an employer from distinguishing between groups or categories of employees, providing benefits for some but not for others. * * * It simply may not make such distinctions based upon age or length of service. Accordingly, an employer need not include in its pension plans all employees who meet the test of common law employees. * * *

> * * *

> The *Renda* court, and in turn the district court below, held that certain provisions of the Internal Revenue Code and Treasury Department regulations were effectively incorporated into ERISA's substantive requirements. * * * We read the function of the Treasury regulations more narrowly. The regulations purport to do no more than determine whether a plan is a qualified tax plan. Failure to meet the requirements of those regulations results in the loss of a beneficial tax status; it does not permit a court to rewrite the plan to include additional employees. * * *

> Accordingly, neither 26 U.S.C. § 410 nor § 414 * * * compel the interpretation of ERISA adopted by the district court. Indeed, they highlight the error in that interpretation. Section 410(b) requires a tax-qualified retirement plan to benefit a certain percentage of an employer's non-highly compensated employees who participate in the plan. For that purpose, employees who do not meet a plan's prescribed minimum age and service requirements are disregarded as employees under that section. 26 U.S.C. § 410(b)(4). That section would be pointless if, as the district court held in this case, all employees who satisfy ERISA's minimum participation requirement and meet the definition of common law employees must be included within a plan. No employees could ever be excluded under that section.

> * * * [I]t is irrelevant that, for certain purposes, the Code treats leased employees as employees of the entity to whom the leased employee provides services. * * * Even those Code provisions do not require ERISA plans to include leased employees; they merely require employers to take leased employees into account in showing that their plans meet the nondiscriminatory coverage requirements of the Code. * * *

140 F.3d at 1338–39. Accord, MacLachlan v. ExxonMobil Corp., 350 F.3d 472 (5th Cir. 2003); Clark v. E.I. Dupont De Nemours & Co., 105 F.3d 646 (4th Cir.1997); Trombetta v. Cragin Fed. Bank for Sav. Employee Stock Ownership Plan, 102 F.3d 1435 (7th Cir.1996); Abraham v. Exxon Corp., 85 F.3d 1126 (5th Cir. 1996).

5. *"Colorable Claim"*? Even where courts have rejected the approach in *Renda*, holding that the "leased employee" provision does not require employer-plan sponsors to include all common-law employees in their benefit plans, plaintiffs may be able to establish a "colorable claim" to benefits based on the plan documents. If so, plan administrators must determine

their eligibility—a determination that will be subject to limited (in *Vizcaino*, somewhat more heightened) judicial review. In the Abraham v. Exxon litigation, for example, the Fifth Circuit held:

> * * * Abraham was a "participant" under ERISA because he had a colorable claim that he would prevail in this suit. ERISA's definition of "participant" includes anyone with a colorable claim that he will prevail in a suit for benefits * * *. * * * Abraham was a participant under this standard and has standing to seek penalties under ERISA because the administrator failed to provide him with information.
>
> We recognize that this result may appear harsh: We conclude that the plan unambiguously excludes the employees, yet we find that the administrator may be liable for failing to provide them with plan information. * * * [However, s]tatus as a participant is simply a threshold requirement a plaintiff must meet before he can request penalties. The district court has the discretion to grant or deny such a request.

85 F.3d at 1132.

6. *"Injury to the Plan":* Time Warner *Litigation.* Since 1984, Time Warner's publishing group had classified new workers for payroll purposes as "regular," "project," "supplementary," or "temporary" employees; others were treated as independent contractors. Most of the Time Warner plans exclude temporary employees and independent contractors from participating. In 1998, the Department of Labor sued Time Warner and its plans for misclassifying temporary employees and independent contractors and thus depriving them of eligibility to participate in the plans. During the relevant period, a single committee (the "Administrative Committee") administered all of the plans in question. The Government argued that Time Warner and the members of the Administrative Committee violated ERISA, by (1) failing to act solely in the interest of the plan participants and beneficiaries (ERISA § 404(a)(1)(A)); (2) failing to act in accordance with plan documents (ERISA § 404(a)(1)(D)); and (3) failing to provide required documents and information to the allegedly misclassified workers (ERISA §§ 101(a), 102(a)(1), 104(b)(1) and 3, and 105(c)). The district court denied defendants' motion to dismiss:

> * * * First, as a technical matter, the government has sufficiently alleged that the Administrative Committee and Time Warner breached their fiduciary duties under ERISA * * * primarily by failing to identify workers who were indeed eligible to participate in the plans but who were misclassified by the hiring managers as temporary employees and independent contractors. The government contends that as a consequence defendants failed to comply with ERISA's mandatory disclosure requirements (as defendants could not provide information to unidentified employees) and with plan documents (as the misclassified employees were excluded from participation). * * *
>
> Second, from a broader perspective, if the allegations of the complaint are true, governmental action is appropriate here. * * *
>
> Defendants' contention that the government's breach of fiduciary duty claim is in reality an impermissible claim for benefits is rejected. That the misclassified employees might have been deprived of benefits

does not mean that the plans themselves could not have been injured as well. The government * * * contends, for example, that employees who should have been included in the plans were not and that as a consequence the plans suffered losses. The government seeks relief on behalf of the plans, including, for example, removal of fiduciaries pursuant to ERISA § 409 and recoupment of damages alleged suffered by the plans.
* * *

Herman v. Time Warner, Inc., 56 F.Supp. 2d 411, 417–18 (S.D.N.Y.1999). See also Time Warner, Inc. v. Biscardi, 2000 WL 1721168 (S.D.N.Y.2000) (independent contractors found to be properly excluded).

7. *Working Owners.* In Yates v. Hendon, 541 U.S. 1, 124 S.Ct. 1330, 158 L.Ed.2d 40 (2004), the Court held that a working owner (here, the sole shareholder and president of a professional corporation) could qualify as a "participant" in an ERISA plan where the plan covers one or more employees in addition to the owner.

8. See generally Pianko, *Microsoft* and Its Legacy, supra; Mark Berger, The Contingent Employee Benefits Problem, 32 Ind., L. Rev. 301 (1999) and his Unjust Dismissal and the Contingent Worker: Restructuring Doctrine for the Restructured Employee, 16 Yale L. & Pol'y Rev. 1 (1997); Kenneth A. Jenero & Eric E. Mennel, New Risks for Employers: Misclassified "Independent Contractors" May Be Entitled to Costly Employee Benefits, 22 Employee Rels. L.J. 5 (no. 4, Spring 1997).

D. DISCLOSURE OBLIGATIONS

HUGHES SALARIED RETIREES ACTION COMMITTEE v. ADMINISTRATOR
U.S. Court of Appeals for the Ninth Circuit (en banc), 1995.
72 F.3d 686.

NORRIS, J.

I

BACKGROUND

Plaintiffs are three retirees (the "Retirees") who receive defined pension benefits from the Hughes Non–Bargaining Retirement Plan (the "Plan"). They are members of a self-appointed committee called the Hughes Salaried Retirees Action Committee, an organization that is also a named plaintiff. The Plan has some 60,000 participants, of whom some 10,000 are retirees.

The Retirees brought this action under ERISA to compel the Plan administrator (the "Administrator") to furnish them with a list of the names and addresses of all retired participants of the Plan so the Retirees can "communicate with them about matters of concern to all retired participants regarding their pensions. * * * *" In particular, the Retirees say they want to communicate with other retirees about Hughes's allegedly "unlawful use of excess Plan assets for the sole purpose of meeting Hughes' funding obligations" and "to gain support for their efforts to obtain increased benefits through negotiation or if required, litigation, as well as to monitor the Plan." * * *

The district court dismissed the complaint under Federal Rule of Civil Procedure 12(b)(6) for failure to state a claim. A three-judge panel of our court reversed.

II
ERISA § 104(B)(4)

We first consider the Retirees' claim that the Administrator must furnish them with the names and addresses of retired Plan participants because this information is an "instrument[ ] under which the plan is established or operated" within the meaning of ERISA § 104(b)(4). * * * Section 104(b)(4) provides:

> The administrator shall, upon written request of any participant or beneficiary, furnish a copy of the latest updated summary plan description, plan description, and the latest annual report, any terminal report, the bargaining agreement, trust agreement, con- tract, or other instruments under which the plan is established or operated. The administrator may make reasonable charge to cover the cost of furnishing such complete copies.

29 U.S.C. § 1024(b)(4) (emphasis added). According to the Retirees, the requested list of names and addresses falls within the statute because the Plan could not operate without it.

* * *

We agree with the district court that the Retirees' interpretation of § 104(b)(4) would "strain the meaning" of the section. The district court reasoned:

> * * * [A] list of plan participants cannot possibly be considered an instrument "under which the plan is established or operated." The plain language of the statute limits the universe of documents falling within that phrase to documents similar in nature to those specifically identified, which describe the terms and conditions of the plan, as well as its administration and financial status. While this Court need not define precisely those documents falling under that provision, it is clear that a list of plan participants does not. Obtaining such a list provides participants with absolutely no infor- mation whatsoever about the plan, and therefore ERISA neither requires nor contemplates its disclosure. * * *

* * * The relevant documents are those documents that provide individual participants with information about the plan and benefits. As the legislative history bears out, the documents contemplated by 104(b)(4) are those that allow "the individual participant [to] know[] exactly where he stands with respect to the plan—what benefits he may be entitled to, what circumstances may preclude him from obtaining benefits, what procedures he must follow to obtain benefits, and who are the persons to whom the management and investment of his plan funds

have been entrusted." S. Rep. No. 127, 93d Cong., 2d Sess. (1974), reprinted in 1974 U.S.C.C.A.N. 4838, 4863.

Unlike the documents specifically listed in § 104(b)(4)—plan descriptions, annual and terminal reports, and bargaining and trust agreements—participants' names and addresses provide no information about the plan or benefits. * * *

* * *

[U]nder the original [Ninth Circuit] panel's interpretation of § 104(b)(4), a plan administrator would be required to disclose virtually everything in its plan files upon request. The panel reasoned that the language "other instruments" is not limited to documents similar to the documents specifically listed in § 104(b)(4) because the statutory language "contains no such limitation, and we have found no other authority for limiting the statutory language this way." In other words, according to the panel, § 104(b)(4) creates a generalized disclosure obligation subject only to articulated limits. * * * Such a broad disclosure requirement, however, is not supported by either the language of the statute or its legislative history. * * * [Section] 104(b)(4) requires the disclosure of only the documents described with particularity and "other instruments" similar in nature.

* * *

III

ERISA § 404(a)(1)(A)

Retirees claim in the alternative that even if § 104(b)(4) does not require the Administrator to disclose the names and addresses, ERISA's general fiduciary duty provision does. See ERISA § 404(a)(1)(A), 29 U.S.C. § 1104(a)(1)(A). Section 404(a) is a general standard of care provision that requires an ERISA plan fiduciary to "(1) * * * discharge his duties * * * solely in the interest of the participants and beneficiaries and (A) for the exclusive purpose of (i) providing benefits * * * and (ii) defraying reasonable expenses * * *."

* * *

* * * In their amended complaint, the Retirees alleged that § 404(a)(1)(A) encompasses a duty to provide the participant list when sought "for purposes of communicating with the participants and beneficiaries of the Plan about matters concerning the provision of benefits and the administration of the plan." * * * They further alleged that the dispute at issue—whether ERISA requires the Plan to distribute all or part of the allegedly "surplus" assets to the beneficiaries in the form of increased pension benefits—"is a matter concerning the provision of benefits and administration of the Plan which entitles the plaintiffs to a copy of the list of Plan participants." * * *

[S]ince a participant list will not provide the Retirees with any information about the Plan, we fail to see how the list, or the access to other participants that it would facilitate, will aid in monitoring the Plan's management. The Retirees' argument that "unless retirees can communicate with one another and organize to protect their rights under ERISA and under the plan, they will not be able to raise the support needed to enforce their rights against a well-funded pension plan," is unavailing. As this argument makes clear, the Retirees want to use the list to solicit financial support for future litigation. Congress has provided for recovery of costs and attorneys' fees under ERISA § 502(g), 29 U.S.C. § 1132(g), and we find nothing in ERISA suggesting that Congress intended to help plan participants amass a litigation war chest by soliciting donations from other plan participants and beneficiaries.

[*Eds.* The dissenting opinion of Judge Pregerson, joined in by Judges Hug, Fletcher and Reinhardt, is omitted.]

FIRESTONE TIRE & RUBBER CO. v. BRUCH

Supreme Court of the United States, 1989.
489 U.S. 101, 109 S.Ct. 948, 103 L.Ed.2d 80.

JUSTICE O'CONNOR delivered the opinion of the Court.

I

Late in 1980, petitioner Firestone Tire and Rubber Company (Firestone) sold, as going concerns, the five plants composing its Plastics Division to Occidental Petroleum Company (Occidental). Most of the approximately 500 salaried employees at the five plants were rehired by Occidental and continued in their same positions without interruption and at the same rates of pay. At the time of the sale, Firestone maintained three pension and welfare benefit plans for its employees: a termination pay plan, a retirement plan, and a stock purchase plan. Firestone was the sole source of funding for the plans and had not established separate trust funds out of which to pay the benefits from the plans. All three of the plans were either "employee welfare benefit plans" or "employee pension benefit plans" governed (albeit in different ways) by ERISA. By operation of law, Firestone itself was the administrator, 29 U.S.C. § 1002(16)(A)(ii), and fiduciary, § 1002(21)(A), of each of these "unfunded" plans. At the time of the sale of its Plastics Division, Firestone was not aware that the termination pay plan was governed by ERISA, and therefore had not set up a claims procedure, § 1133, nor complied with ERISA's reporting and disclosure obligations, §§ 1021–1031, with respect to that plan.

Respondents, six Firestone employees who were rehired by Occidental, sought severance benefits from Firestone under the termination pay plan. In relevant part, that plan provides as follows:

> "If your service is discontinued prior to the time you are eligible for pension benefits, you will be given termination pay if released because of a reduction in work force or if you become physically or mentally unable to perform your job.

"The amount of termination pay you will receive will depend on your period of credited company service."

Several of the respondents also sought information from Firestone regarding their benefits under all three of the plans pursuant to certain ERISA disclosure provisions. See §§ 1024(b)(4), 1025(a). Firestone denied respondents severance benefits on the ground that the sale of the Plastics Division to Occidental did not constitute a "reduction in work force" within the meaning of the termination pay plan. In addition, Firestone denied the requests for information concerning benefits under the three plans. Firestone concluded that respondents were not entitled to the information because they were no longer "participants" in the plans.

Respondents then filed a class action on behalf of "former, salaried, non-union employees who worked in the five plants that comprised the Plastics Division of Firestone." * * * The action was based on § 1132(a)(1), which provides that a "civil action may be brought * * * by a participant or beneficiary [of a covered plan] * * * (A) for the relief provided for in [§ 1132(c)], [and] (B) to recover benefits due to him under the terms of his plan." In Count I of their complaint, respondents alleged that they were entitled to severance benefits because Firestone's sale of the Plastics Division to Occidental constituted a "reduction in work force" within the meaning of the termination pay plan. * * *

The District Court granted Firestone's motion for summary judgment. * * *

The Court of Appeals reversed the District Court's grant of summary judgment on Counts I and VII. * * * With respect to Count I, the Court of Appeals acknowledged that most federal courts have reviewed the denial of benefits by ERISA fiduciaries and administrators under the arbitrary and capricious standard. * * * It noted, however, that the arbitrary and capricious standard had been softened in cases where fiduciaries and administrators had some bias or adverse interest. * * * The Court of Appeals held that where an employer is itself the fiduciary and administrator of an unfunded benefit plan, its decision to deny benefits should be subject to de novo judicial review. It reasoned that in such situations deference is unwarranted given the lack of assurance of impartiality on the part of the employer. * * * With respect to Count VII, the Court of Appeals held that the right to request and receive information about an employee benefit plan "most sensibly extend[s] both to people who are in fact entitled to a benefit under the plan and to those who claim to be but in fact are not." * * * Because the District Court had applied different legal standards in granting summary judgment in favor of Firestone on Counts I and VII, the Court of Appeals remanded the case for further proceedings consistent with its opinion. [*Eds.*—The Court's discussion of the Ninth Circuit's treatment of Count I is presented at p. 1020 infra.]

* * *

III

Respondents unsuccessfully sought plan information from Firestone pursuant to 29 U.S.C. § 1024(b)(4), one of ERISA's disclosure provisions. That provision reads as follows:

> "The administrator shall, upon written request of any participant or beneficiary, furnish a copy of the latest updated summary plan description, plan description, and the latest annual report, any terminal report, the bargaining agreement, trust agreement, contract, or other instruments under which the plan is established or operated. The administrator may make a reasonable charge to cover the cost of furnishing such complete copies. The Secretary [of Labor] may by regulation prescribe the maximum amount which will constitute a reasonable charge under the preceding sentence."

When Firestone did not comply with their request for information, respondents sought damages under 29 U.S C. § 1132(c)(1)(B) (1982 ed., Supp. IV), which provides that "[a]ny administrator * * * who fails or refuses to comply with a request for any information which such administrator is required by this subchapter to furnish to a participant or beneficiary * * * may in the court's discretion be personally liable to such participant or beneficiary in the amount of up to $100 a day." Respondents have not alleged that they are "beneficiaries" as defined in § 1002(8). * * *

The dispute in this case therefore centers on the definition of the term "participant," which is found in § 1002(7):

> "The term 'participant' means any employee or former employee of an employer, or any member or former member of an employee organization, who is or may become eligible to receive a benefit of any type from an employee benefit plan which covers employees of such employer or members of such organization, or whose beneficiaries may be eligible to receive any such benefit."

The Court of Appeals noted that § 1132(a)(1) allows suits for benefits "by a participant or beneficiary." Finding that it would be illogical to say that a person could only bring a claim for benefits if he or she was entitled to benefits, the Court of Appeals reasoned that § 1132(a)(1) should be read to mean that " 'a civil action may be brought by someone who claims to be a participant or beneficiary.' " * * * It went on to conclude that the same interpretation should apply with respect to § 1024(b)(4): "A provision such as that one, entitling people to information on the extent of their benefits, would most sensibly extend both to people who are in fact entitled to a benefit under the plan and to those who claim to be but in fact are not." * * *

The Court of Appeals "concede[d] that it is expensive and inefficient to provide people with information about benefits—and to permit them to obtain damages if information is withheld—if they are clearly not entitled to the benefits about which they are informed." It tried to solve this dilemma by suggesting that courts use discretion and not award damages if the employee's claim for benefits was not colorable or if the employer did not act in bad faith. There is, however, a more fundamental problem with the Court of Appeals' interpretation of the term "participant": it strays far from the statutory language. Congress did not say that all "claimants" could receive information about benefit plans. To say that a "participant" is any person who claims to be one begs the question of who is a "participant" and renders the definition set forth in § 1002(7) superfluous. Indeed, respondents admitted at oral argument that "the words point against [them]." * * *

In our view, the term "participant" is naturally read to mean either "employees in, or reasonably expected to be in, currently covered employment," *Saladino* v. *I.L.G.W.U. National Retirement Fund*, 754 F. 2d 473, 476 (C.A.2 1985), or former employees who "have * * * a reasonable expectation of returning to covered employment" or who have "a colorable claim" to vested benefits, *Kuntz* v. *Reese*, 785 F. 2d 1410, 1411 (CA 9) (per curiam), cert. denied, 479 U.S. 916 (1986). In order to establish that he or she "may become eligible" for benefits, a claimant must have a colorable claim that (1) he or she will prevail in a suit for benefits, or that (2) eligibility requirements will be fulfilled in the future. "This view attributes conventional meanings to the statutory language since all employees in covered employment and former employees with a colorable claim to vested benefits 'may become eligible.' A former employee who has neither a reasonable expectation of returning to covered employment nor a colorable claim to vested benefits, however, simply does not fit within the [phrase] 'may become eligible.' " *Saladino* * * *, at 476.

We do not think Congress' purpose in enacting the ERISA disclosure provisions—ensuring that "the individual participant knows exactly where he stands with respect to the plan," H. R. Rep. No. 93–533, p. 11 (1973)—will be thwarted by a natural reading of the term "participant." Faced with the possibility of $100 a day in penalties under § 1132(c)(1)(B), a rational plan administrator or fiduciary would likely opt to provide a claimant with the information requested if there is any doubt as to whether the claimant is a "participant," especially when the reasonable costs of producing the information can be recovered. See 29 CFR § 2520.104b–30(b) (1987) (the "charge assessed by the plan administrator to cover the costs of furnishing documents is reasonable if it is equal to the actual cost per page to the plan for the least expensive means of acceptable reproduction, but in no event may such charge exceed 25 cents per page").

The Court of Appeals did not attempt to determine whether respondents were "participants" under § 1002(7). We likewise express no views as to whether respondents were "participants" with respect to the benefit plans about which they sought information. Those questions are best left to the Court of Appeals on remand.

Notes and Questions

1. *Information and Collective–Action Problems of Participants?* Did the Ninth Circuit in the *Hughes* decision give adequate weight to the organizational problems confronting participants who suspect a violation of their ERISA rights? Note that unions, who might be expected to pursue such claims on behalf of participants, represent less than 10 percent of the private-sector workforce. The problem is exacerbated for participants who are retirees because even where unions bargain on behalf of active employees, they have no right to insist on bargaining on behalf of retirees. See Allied Chem. & Alkali Workers v. Pittsburgh Plate Glass Co., 404 U.S. 157, 92 S.Ct. 383, 30 L.Ed.2d 341 (1971) (retirees are neither "employees" under the National Labor Relations Act, 29 U.S.C. §§ 151 et seq., nor bargaining-unit members, and benefits for retirees are not a mandatory subject of collective bargaining); see also Schneider Moving & Storage Co. v. Robbins, 466 U.S. 364, 376 n. 22, 104 S.Ct. 1844, 80 L.Ed.2d 366 (1984) (suggesting that unions owe no duty of fair representation to retirees). Is the underlying problem here one of agency—that, at least in the absence of a union representative, there is no basis for assuming that the participant requesting the information sought in *Hughes* has any authority to act on behalf of other participants? Are there ways of solving (or mitigating) this problem? Consider the special procedures for termination/modification of retiree welfare-benefits in bankruptcy reorganizations, see § 1114 of the Bankruptcy Code, 11 U.S.C. § 1114.

2. *Information Rights of Benefit Claimants.* What was the Supreme Court's disagreement in *Firestone* with the Court of Appeals' disposition of the § 1024(b)(4) information claim? Which court had the better of the argument?

3. *Welfare and Pension Plan Disclosure Act Experience.* Congress, in enacting ERISA, was mindful of the limited disclosure requirements of the Welfare and Pension Plan Disclosure Act, Pub. L. No. 85–836, 29 U.S.C. §§ 301–309, which was repealed by ERISA:

> Changes are * * * required to increase the information and data required in the reports both in scope and detail. Experience has also demonstrated a need for a more particularized form of reporting so that the individual participant knows where he stands with respect to the plan—what benefits he may be entitled to, what circumstances may preclude him from obtaining benefits, what procedures he must follow to obtain benefits, and who are the persons to whom management and investment of his plan funds have been entrusted. At the same time, the safeguarding effect of the fiduciary responsibility section will operate efficiently only if fiduciaries are aware that the details of their dealings will be open to inspection, and that individual participants and beneficiaries will be armed with enough information to enforce their own rights as well as the obligations owed by the fiduciary to the plan in general.

H.R. Rep. N. 533, 93d Cong., 1st Sess. 11 (1974).

4. *Summary Plan Description*. An important piece of the disclosure regime erected by ERISA is the "summary plan description" (SPD) a written summary of an employee benefit plan written in a manner to be understood by the average plan participant and sufficiently accurate and comprehensive to advise participants and beneficiaries of their rights under the plan. See ERISA § 102, 29 U.S.C. § 1022; 29 C.F.R. § 2520.102. Deficient SPDs may give rise to benefit claims inconsistent with plan documents. See, e.g., Burke v. Kodak Retirement Income Plan, 336 F.3d 103 (2d Cir. 2003). For a useful account of the full extent of ERISA disclosure requirements. See ABA Section of Labor and Employment Law, Employee Benefits Law ch. 3 (1991 & as supplemented).

E. FIDUCIARY OBLIGATIONS

1. Plan Administrator Decisions

FIRESTONE TIRE & RUBBER CO. v. BRUCH

Supreme Court of the United States, 1989.
489 U.S. 101, 109 S.Ct. 948, 103 L.Ed.2d 80.

[*Eds.* For prior excerpt from this case, see pp. 1015–18 supra.]

JUSTICE O'CONNOR delivered the opinion of the Court.

II

ERISA provides "a panoply of remedial devices" for participants and beneficiaries of benefit plans. *Massachusetts Mutual Life Ins. Co.* v. *Russell*, 473 U.S. 134, 146 (1985). Respondents' action asserting that they were entitled to benefits because the sale of Firestone's Plastics Division constituted a "reduction in work force" within the meaning of the termination pay plan was based on the authority of § 1132(a)(1)(B). That provision allows a suit to recover benefits due under the plan, to enforce rights under the terms of the plan, and to obtain a declaratory judgment of future entitlement to benefits under the provisions of the plan contract. The discussion which follows is limited to the appropriate standard of review in § 1132(a)(1)(B) actions challenging denials of benefits based on plan interpretations. We express no view as to the appropriate standard of review for actions under other remedial provisions of ERISA.

A

Although it is a "comprehensive and reticulated statute," *Nachman Corp.* v. *Pension Benefit Guaranty Corp.*, 446 U.S. 359, 361 (1980), ERISA does not set out the appropriate standard of review for actions under § 1132(a)(1)(B) challenging benefit eligibility determinations. To fill this gap, federal courts have adopted the arbitrary and capricious standard developed under 61 Stat. 157, 29 U.S.C. § 186(c), a provision of the Labor Management (LMRA). * * * A comparison of the LMRA and ERISA, however, shows that the wholesale importation of the arbitrary and capricious standard into ERISA is unwarranted. In relevant part, 29

U.S.C. § 186(c) authorizes unions and employers to set up pension plans jointly and provides that contributions to such plans be made "for the sole and exclusive benefit of the employees * * * and their families and dependents." The LMRA does not provide for judicial review of the decisions of LMRA trustees. Federal courts adopted the arbitrary and capricious standard both as a standard of review and, more importantly, as a means of asserting jurisdiction over suits under § 186(c) by beneficiaries of LMRA plans who were denied benefits by trustees. * * * Unlike the LMRA, ERISA explicitly authorizes suits against fiduciaries and plan administrators to remedy statutory violations, including breaches of fiduciary duty and lack of compliance with benefit plans. See 29 U.S.C. §§ 1132(a), 1132(f). See generally *Pilot Life Ins. Co. v. Dedeaux*, 481 U.S. 41, 52–57 (1987) (describing scope of § 1132(a)). Thus, the raison d'etre for the LMRA arbitrary and capricious standard—the need for a jurisdictional basis in suits against trustees—is not present in ERISA. * * * Without this jurisdictional analogy, LMRA principles offer no support for the adoption of the arbitrary and capricious standard insofar as § 1132(a)(1)(B) is concerned.

B

ERISA abounds with the language and terminology of trust law. See, e.g., 29 U.S.C. §§ 1002(7) ("participant"), 1002(8) ("beneficiary"), 1002(21)(A) ("fiduciary"), 1103(a) ("trustee"), 1104 ("fiduciary duties"). ERISA's legislative history confirms that the Act's fiduciary responsibility provisions, 29 U.S.C. §§ 1101–1114, "codif[y] and mak[e] applicable to [ERISA] fiduciaries certain principles developed in the evolution of the law of trusts." H. R. Rep. No. 93–533, p. 11 (1973). Given this language and history, we have held that courts are to develop a "federal common law of rights and obligations under ERISA-regulated plans." *Pilot Life Ins. Co. v. Dedeaux*, supra, at 56. See also *Franchise Tax Board v. Construction Laborers Vacation Trust*, 463 U.S. 1, 24, n. 26 (1983) (" '[A] body of Federal substantive law will be developed by the courts to deal with issues involving rights and obligations under private welfare and pension plans' ") (quoting 129 Cong. Rec. 29942 (1974) (remarks of Sen. Javits)). In determining the appropriate standard of review for actions under § 1132(a)(1)(B), we are guided by principles of trust law. *Central States, Southeast and Southwest Areas Pension Fund v. Central Transport, Inc.*, 472 U.S. 559, 570 (1985). Trust principles make a deferential standard of review appropriate when a trustee exercises discretionary powers. See Restatement (Second) of Trusts 187 (1959) ("Where discretion is conferred upon the trustee with respect to the exercise of a power, its exercise is not subject to control by the court except to prevent an abuse by the trustee of his discretion"). * * * Firestone can seek no shelter in these principles of trust law, however, for there is no evidence that under Firestone's termination pay plan the administrator has the power to construe uncertain terms or that eligibility determinations are to be given deference. * * *

Finding no support in the language of its termination pay plan for the arbitrary and capricious standard, Firestone argues that as a matter of trust law the interpretation of the terms of a plan is an inherently discretionary function. But other settled principles of trust law, which point to de novo review of benefit eligibility determinations based on plan interpretations, belie this contention. As they do with contractual provisions, courts construe terms in trust agreements without deferring to either party's interpretation. "The extent of the duties and powers of a trustee is determined by the rules of law that are applicable to the situation, and not the rules that the trustee or his attorney believes to be applicable, and by the terms of the trust as the court may interpret them, and not as they may be interpreted by the trustee himself or by his attorney." 3 W. Fratcher, Scott on Trusts § 201, at 221 (emphasis added). A trustee who is in doubt as to the interpretation of the instrument can protect himself by obtaining instructions from the court. * * * Restatement (Second) of Trusts § 201, Comment b (1959). * * * The terms of trusts created by written instruments are "determined by the provisions of the instrument as interpreted in light of all the circumstances and such other evidence of the intention of the settlor with respect to the trust as is not inadmissible." Restatement (Second) of Trusts § 4, Comment d (1959). The trust law de novo standard of review is consistent with the judicial interpretation of employee benefit plans prior to the enactment of ERISA. Actions challenging an employer's denial of benefits before the enactment of ERISA were governed by principles of contract law. If the plan did not give the employer or administrator discretionary or final authority to construe uncertain terms, the court reviewed the employee's claim as it would have any other contract claim—by looking to the terms of the plan and other manifestations of the parties' intent. * * *

* * * Neither general principles of trust law nor a concern for impartial decisionmaking, however, forecloses parties from agreeing upon a narrower standard of review. Moreover, as to both funded and unfunded plans, the threat of increased litigation is not sufficient to outweigh the reasons for a de novo standard that we have already explained. As this case aptly demonstrates, the validity of a claim to benefits under an ERISA plan is likely to turn on the interpretation of terms in the plan at issue. Consistent with established principles of trust law, we hold that a denial of benefits challenged under § 1132(a)(1)(B) is to be reviewed under a de novo standard unless the benefit plan gives the administrator or fiduciary discretionary authority to determine eligibility for benefits or to construe the terms of the plan. Because we do not rest our decision on the concern for impartiality that guided the Court of Appeals, * * * we need not distinguish between types of plans or focus on the motivations of plan administrators and fiduciaries. Thus, for purposes of actions under § 1132(a)(1)(B), the de novo standard of review applies regardless of whether the plan at issue is funded or unfunded and regardless of whether the administrator or fiduciary is operating under a possible or actual conflict of interest. Of course, if a

benefit plan gives discretion to an administrator or fiduciary who is operating under a conflict of interest, that conflict must be weighed as a "facto[r] in determining whether there is an abuse of discretion." Restatement (Second) of Trusts § 187, Comment d (1959).

[*Eds.* Justice Scalia's opinion, concurring in part and concurring in the judgment, is omitted.]

Notes and Questions

1. *Pyrrhic Victory?* Is it likely that post-*Firestone* plans will be amended to make clear that plan administrators exercise authority to construe ambiguous terms, in order to ensure applicability of the deferential "arbitrary and capricious" or "abuse of discretion" standard of judicial review? In rulings soon after *Firestone* issued, two Courts of Appeals adopted the deferential standard, finding that the plan documents lodged interpretive authority with plan administrators. See Lowry v. Bankers Life & Casualty Retirement Plan, 871 F.2d 522 (5th Cir.1989) (on rehearing); Lakey v. Remington Arms Co., 874 F.2d 541 (8th Cir.1989).

2. *Agents for the Employer–Sponsor?* In most single-employer plans, plan administrators are managerial employees of the employer-sponsor. Even though plan administrators are supposed to act as fiduciaries for participants and beneficiaries, isn't an inevitable conflict of interest present, thus warranting application of a less deferential standard of judicial review? Is this the Third Circuit's position rejected by the Court? Note that in *Firestone*, the benefits were paid from an unfunded plan so that money spent to pay for severance benefits was money spent by Firestone. For a ruling stating that heightened judicial review is required when the plan administrator both administers the plans and pays the benefits, see Torres v. Pittston Co., 346 F.3d 1324 (11th Cir. 2003). Is this ruling reconcilable with *Firestone*?

3. *Contract-Law Analogy?* Is deferential review consistent with the general law of contracts? Consider a company that established an internal grievance resolution system for resolving contractual claims for compensation and non-ERISA benefits. Would the courts ordinarily defer to interpretations by company officials of the system's governing documents in deciding breach of contract claims? Is the ERISA context different because, as a formal matter, plan administrators are fiduciaries? Would participants and beneficiaries be better off with de novo review of their claims in the courts, and without the formal fiduciary rule? Or would this discourage employers from establishing ERISA benefit plans?

4. *When Is De Novo Review Appropriate?* In what situations is a less deferential standard of review appropriate after *Firestone*? Review the *Vizcaino* decision. On remand, what standard of review should the courts use in reviewing the decision of plan administrators adjudicating the benefit claims of the freelancers? Consider also *Torres*, note 2 supra.

5. *"Reasonable" Claims Procedure.* Employee benefit plans covered by ERISA are required to notify participants or beneficiaries of the denial of their claims, and provide an opportunity to seek review of the decisions denying claims. See ERISA § 503, 29 U.S.C. § 1133. The requirements for a

"reasonable claims procedure" are set out in 29 C.F.R. § 2560.503–1 (claims procedure). Although an exhaustion requirement is not specified in the statute, the courts have held that, in general, a participant or beneficiary may not bring an action under § 502(a)(1)(B) for claims under the plan unless he has first exhausted the plan's internal claims procedure, including appeals. See, e.g., Barrowclough v. Kidder, Peabody & Co., 752 F.2d 923 (3d Cir.1985). Exhaustion of plan procedures is not required where such resort would be futile or the claimant has been wrongfully denied meaningful access to the claims procedures. See, e.g., Carter v. Signode Indus., Inc., 688 F.Supp. 1283, later proceeding, 694 F.Supp. 493 (N.D. Ill. 1988).

6. *Taft-Hartley Plans.* Note the *Firestone* Court's treatment of the principles developed under the Labor–Management Relations Act (or Taft–Hartley Act) of 1947. Prior to 1947, employee benefit plans sponsored or initiated by labor unions for their members were often informally administered by the union or its officers. Perceived abuses led Congress to enact a general ban on employer payments to labor unions, subject to specified exceptions. Under § 302(c)(5) of the Taft–Hartley Act, 29 U.S.C. § 186(c)(5), employers may submit payments to an employee benefits plan administered in part by a labor union, provided (i) the payments are made to a separate trust fund established for specified purposes; (ii) payments are held in trust for the sole and exclusive benefit of employees and their dependents; (iii) the detailed basis for making payments is specified in a written agreement; (iv) the employees and employers are equally represented in the administration of such fund, together with jointly-designated neutral persons to break a deadlock; and (v) an annual audit of the fund's assets is conducted by an independent accountant. The Taft–Hartley provision does not apply to plans administered exclusively by employers or to plans administered exclusively by unions without use of any employer funds.

Jointly administered plans were the primary focus of the Multiemployer Pension Plan Amendments Act of 1980 (MPPAA), Pub.L. No. 96–364, 94 Stat. 1208 (Sept. 26, 1980), which amended ERISA to impose withdrawal liability on these plans for unfunded vested benefits, to enhance the ability of plans to collect delinquent employer contributions, to revise the PBGC guarantee program, and to regulate transfers of assets between plans.

Despite the formal guarantee of joint administration, is it likely that employer trustees are truly independent in multiemployer plans involving a single, dominant union and a series of small, widely dispersed employers? See also NLRB v. Amax Coal Co., 453 U.S. 322, 101 S.Ct. 2789, 69 L.Ed.2d 672 (1981) (union insistence that management appoint or retain particular trustees for a § 302(c)(5) trust does not violate § 8(b)(1)(B) of the Taft–Hartley Act, which protects employers in their selection of bargaining representatives, because trustees are fiduciaries, not agents of the appointing party):

> The management-appointed and union-appointed trustees do not bargain with each other to set the terms of the employer-employee contract; they can neither require employer contributions not required by the original collectively-bargained contract, nor compromise the claims of the union or the employer with regard to the latter's contributions.

Id. at 336.

2. *Plan Amendments*

LOCKHEED CORPORATION v. SPINK

Supreme Court of the United States, 1996.
517 U.S. 882, 116 S.Ct. 1783, 135 L.Ed.2d 153.

JUSTICE THOMAS delivered the opinion of the Court.

I

Respondent Paul Spink was employed by petitioner Lockheed Corporation from 1939 until 1950, when he left to work for one of Lockheed's competitors. In 1979, Lockheed persuaded Spink to return. Spink was 61 years old when he resumed employment with Lockheed. At that time, the terms of the Lockheed Retirement Plan for Certain Salaried Individuals (Plan), a defined benefit plan, excluded from participation employees who were over the age of 60 when hired. This was expressly permitted by ERISA. See 29 U.S.C. § 1052(a)(2)(B) (1982 ed.).

Congress subsequently passed the Omnibus Budget Reconciliation Act of 1986 (OBRA), Pub. L. 99–509, 100 Stat. 1874. Section 9203(a)(1) of OBRA, 100 Stat. 1979, repealed the age-based exclusion provision of ERISA, and the statute now flatly mandates that "no pension plan may exclude from participation (on the basis of age) employees who have attained a specified age." 29 U.S.C. § 1052(a)(2). Sections 9201 and 9202 of OBRA, 100 Stat. 1973–1978, amended ERISA and the ADEA to prohibit age-based cessations of benefit accruals and age-based reductions in benefit accrual rates. See 29 U.S.C. §§ 1054(b)(1)(H)(i), 623(i)(1).

In an effort to comply with these new laws, Lockheed ceased its prior practice of age-based exclusion from the Plan, effective December 25, 1988. As of that date, all employees, including Spink, who had previously been ineligible to participate in the Plan due to their age at the time of hiring became members of the Plan. Lockheed made clear, however, that it would not credit those employees for years of service rendered before they became members.

When later faced with the need to streamline its operations, Lockheed amended the Plan to provide financial incentives for certain employees to retire early. Lockheed established two programs, both of which offered increased pension benefits to employees who would retire early, payable out of the Plan's surplus assets. Both programs required as a condition of the receipt of benefits that participants release any employment-related claims they might have against Lockheed. Though Spink was eligible for one of the programs, he declined to participate because he did not wish to waive any ADEA or ERISA claims. He then retired, without earning any extra benefits for doing so.

Spink brought this suit, in his individual capacity and on behalf of others similarly situated, against Lockheed and several of its directors and officers. Among other things, the complaint alleged that Lockheed and the members of the board of directors violated ERISA's duty of care and prohibited transaction provisions, 29 U.S.C. §§ 1104(a), 1106(a), by amending the Plan to create the retirement programs. Relatedly, the complaint alleged that the members of Lockheed's Retirement Committee, who implemented the Plan as amended by the board, violated those same parts of ERISA. The complaint also asserted that the OBRA amendments to ERISA and the ADEA required Lockheed to count Spink's pre–1988 service years toward his accrued pension benefits. For these alleged ERISA violations, Spink sought monetary, declaratory, and injunctive relief pursuant to § 502(a)(2) and (3) of ERISA's civil enforcement provisions, 29 U.S.C. § 1132(a)(2), (3). Lockheed moved to dismiss the complaint for failure to state a claim, and the District Court granted the motion.

The Court of Appeals for the Ninth Circuit reversed in relevant part. The Court of Appeals held that the amendments to the Plan were unlawful under ERISA § 406(a)(1)(D), 29 U.S.C. § 1106(a)(1)(D), which prohibits a fiduciary from causing a plan to engage in a transaction that transfers plan assets to a party in interest or involves the use of plan assets for the benefit of a party in interest. The court reasoned that because the amendments offered increased benefits in exchange for a release of employment claims, they constituted a use of Plan assets to "purchase" a significant benefit for Lockheed. Though the court found a violation of § 406(a)(1)(D), it decided that there was no need to address Lockheed's status as a fiduciary. In addition, the Court of Appeals agreed with Spink that Lockheed had violated the OBRA amendments by refusing to include Spink's service years prior to 1988 in determining his benefits. In so holding, the court found that the OBRA amendments apply retroactively. * * *

II

Nothing in ERISA requires employers to establish employee benefits plans. Nor does ERISA mandate what kind of benefits employers must provide if they choose to have such a plan. *Shaw v. Delta Air Lines, Inc.*, 463 U.S. 85, 91, 77 L.Ed.2d 490, 103 S.Ct. 2890 (1983); *Alessi v. Raybestos-Manhattan, Inc.*, 451 U.S. 504, 511, 68 L.Ed.2d 402, 101 S.Ct. 1895 (1981). ERISA does, however, seek to ensure that employees will not be left emptyhanded once employers have guaranteed them certain benefits. As we said in *Nachman Corp. v. Pension Benefit Guaranty Corporation*, 446 U.S. 359, 64 L.Ed. 2d 354, 100 S.Ct. 1723 (1980), when Congress enacted ERISA it "wanted to * * * mak[e] sure that if a worker has been promised a defined pension benefit upon retirement— and if he has fulfilled whatever conditions are required to obtain a vested benefit—he actually will receive it." *Id.*, at 375. Accordingly, ERISA tries to "make as certain as possible that pension fund assets [will] be adequate" to meet expected benefits payments. * * * To increase the chances that employers will be able to honor their benefits commitments—that is, to guard against the possibility of bankrupt pension funds—Congress incorporated several key measures into ERISA. Section

302 of ERISA sets minimum annual funding levels for all covered plans, see 29 U.S.C. §§ 1082(a), 1082(b), and creates tax liens in favor of such plans when those funding levels are not met, see § 1082(f). Sections 404 and 409 of ERISA impose respectively a duty of care with respect to the management of existing trust funds, along with liability for breach of that duty, upon plan fiduciaries. See §§ 1104(a), 1109(a). Finally, § 406 of ERISA prohibits fiduciaries from involving the plan and its assets in certain kinds of business deals. See § 1106. It is this last feature of ERISA that is at issue today. Congress enacted § 406 "to bar categorically a transaction that [is] likely to injure the pension plan." *Commissioner* v. *Keystone Consolidated Industries, Inc.*, 508 U.S. 152, 160, 124 L.Ed. 2d 71, 113 S.Ct. 2006 (1993). That section mandates, in relevant part, that "[a] fiduciary with respect to a plan shall not cause the plan to engage in a transaction, if he knows or should know that such transaction constitutes a direct or indirect * * * transfer to, or use by or for the benefit of a party in interest, of any assets of the plan." 29 U.S.C. § 1106(a)(1)(D). The question here is whether this provision of ERISA prevents an employer from conditioning the receipt of early retirement benefits upon the participants' waiver of employment claims. For the following reasons, we hold that it does not.

III

Section 406(a)(1) regulates the conduct of plan fiduciaries, placing certain transactions outside the scope of their lawful authority. When a fiduciary violates the rules set forth in § 406(a)(1), § 409 of ERISA renders him personally liable for any losses incurred by the plan, any ill-gotten profits, and other equitable and remedial relief deemed appropriate by the court. See 29 U.S.C. § 1109(a). But in order to sustain an alleged transgression of § 406(a), a plaintiff must show that a fiduciary caused the plan to engage in the allegedly unlawful transaction. Unless a plaintiff can make that showing, there can be no violation of § 406(a)(1) to warrant relief under the enforcement provisions. * * * The Court of Appeals erred by not asking whether fiduciary status existed in this case before it found a violation of § 406(a)(1)(D).

A

We first address the allegation in Spink's complaint that Lockheed and the board of directors breached their fiduciary duties when they adopted the amendments establishing the early retirement programs. Plan sponsors who alter the terms of a plan do not fall into the category of fiduciaries. As we said with respect to the amendment of welfare benefit plans in *Curtiss-Wright Corp. v. Schoonejongen*, 514 U.S. 73, 131 L.Ed.2d 94, 115 S.Ct. 1223 (1995), "employers or other plan sponsors are generally free under ERISA, for any reason at any time, to adopt, modify, or terminate welfare plans." *Id.*, at 78 * * *. When employers undertake those actions, they do not act as fiduciaries, 514 U.S. at 78, but are analogous to the settlors of a trust, see *Johnson* v. *Georgia-Pacific Corp.*, 19 F.3d 1184, 1188 (C.A.7 1994).

This rule is rooted in the text of ERISA's definition of fiduciary. See 29 U.S.C. § 1002(21)(A). * * * As the Second Circuit has observed, "only when fulfilling certain defined functions, including the exercise of discretionary authority or control over plan management or administration," does a person become a fiduciary under § 3(21)(A). *Siskind v. Sperry Retirement Program, Unisys*, 47 F.3d 498, 505 (1995). "Because [the] defined functions [in the definition of fiduciary] do not include plan design, an employer may decide to amend an employee benefit plan without being subject to fiduciary review." *Ibid.* We recently recognized this very point, noting that "it may be true that amending or terminating a plan * * * cannot be an act of plan 'management' or 'administration.'" *Varity Corp. v. Howe*, 516 U.S. 489, 505, 134 L.Ed.2d 130, 116 S.Ct. 1065 (1996). As noted above, we in fact said as much in *Curtiss-Wright*, see 514 U.S. at 78, at least with respect to welfare benefit plans.

We see no reason why the rule of *Curtiss-Wright* should not be extended to pension benefit plans. Indeed, there are compelling reasons to apply the same rule to cases involving both kinds of plans, as most courts of appeals have done. The definition of fiduciary makes no distinction between persons exercising authority over welfare benefit plans and those exercising authority over pension plans. It speaks simply of a "fiduciary with respect to a plan," 29 U.S.C. § 1002(21)(A), and of "management" and "administration" of "such plan," ibid. And ERISA defines a "plan" as being either a welfare or pension plan, or both. See § 1002(3). Likewise, the fiduciary duty provisions of ERISA are phrased in general terms and apply with equal force to welfare and pension plans. See, e. g., § 1104(a) (specifying duties of a "fiduciary * * * with respect to a plan"). * * * Given ERISA's definition of fiduciary and the applicability of the duties that attend that status, we think that the rules regarding fiduciary capacity—including the settlor-fiduciary distinction—should apply to pension and welfare plans alike.

Lockheed acted not as a fiduciary but as a settlor when it amended the terms of the Plan to include the retirement programs. Thus, § 406(a)'s requirement of fiduciary status is not met. While other portions of ERISA govern plan amendments, see, e.g., 29 U.S.C. § 1054(g) (amendment generally may not decrease accrued benefits); § 1085b (if adoption of an amendment results in underfunding of a defined benefit plan, the sponsor must post security for the amount of the deficiency), the act of amending a pension plan does not trigger ERISA's fiduciary provisions.

B

Spink also alleged that the members of Lockheed's Retirement Committee who implemented the amended Plan violated § 406(a)(1)(D). As with the question whether Lockheed and the board members can be held liable under ERISA's fiduciary rules, the Court of Appeals erred in holding that the Retirement Committee members violated the prohibited transaction section of ERISA without making the requisite finding of fiduciary status. It is not necessary for us to decide the question whether the Retirement Committee members acted as fiduciaries when they paid out benefits according to the terms of the amended Plan, however, because we do not think that they engaged in any conduct prohibited by § 406(a)(1)(D).

The "transaction" in which fiduciaries may not cause a plan to engage is one that "constitutes a direct or indirect * * * transfer to, or use by or for the benefit of a party in interest, of any assets of the plan." 29 U.S.C. § 1106(a)(1)(D). Spink reads § 406(a)(1)(D) to apply in cases where the benefit received by the party in interest—in this case, the employer—is not merely a "natural inciden[t] of the administration of pension plans." * * * Lockheed, on the other hand, maintains that a plan administrator's payment of benefits to plan participants and beneficiaries pursuant to the terms of an otherwise lawful plan[5] is wholly outside the scope of 406(a)(1)(D). * * * We agree with Lockheed.

Section 406(a)(1)(D) does not in direct terms include the payment of benefits by a plan administrator. And the surrounding provisions suggest that the payment of benefits is in fact not a "transaction" in the sense that Congress used that term in § 406(a). Section 406(a) forbids fiduciaries from engaging the plan in the "sale," "exchange," or "leasing" of property, 29 U.S.C. § 1106(a)(1)(A); the "lending of money" or "extension of credit," § 1106(a)(1)(B); the "furnishing of goods, services, or facilities," § 1106(a)(1)(C); and the "acquisition * * * of any employer security or employer real property," § 1106(a)(1)(E), with a party in interest. See also § 1108(b) (listing similar types of "transactions"). These are commercial bargains that present a special risk of plan underfunding because they are struck with plan insiders, presumably not at arm's length. * * * What the "transactions" identified in § 406(a) thus have in common is that they generally involve uses of plan assets that are potentially harmful to the plan. * * * The payment of benefits conditioned on performance by plan participants cannot reasonably be said to share that characteristic.

According to Spink and the Court of Appeals, however, Lockheed's early retirement programs were prohibited transactions within the meaning of § 406(a)(1)(D) because the required release of employment-related claims by participants created a "significant benefit" for Lockheed. * * * Spink concedes, however, that among the "incidental" and thus legitimate benefits that a plan sponsor may receive from the operation of a pension plan are attracting and retaining employees, paying deferred compensation, settling or avoiding strikes, providing increased compensation without increasing wages, increasing employee turnover, and reducing the likelihood of lawsuits by encouraging employees who would otherwise have been laid off to depart voluntarily. * * *

We do not see how obtaining waivers of employment-related claims can meaningfully be distinguished from these admittedly permissible

---

5. [T]here is no claim in this case that the amendments resulted in any violation of the participation, funding, or vesting requirements of ERISA. See 29 U.S.C. §§ 1051–1061 (participation and vesting); §§ 1081–1086 (funding).

objectives. Each involves, at bottom, a quid pro quo between the plan sponsor and the participant: that is, the employer promises to pay increased benefits in exchange for the performance of some condition by the employee. By Spink's admission, the employer can ask the employee to continue to work for the employer, to cross a picket line, or to retire early. The execution of a release of claims against the employer is functionally no different; like these other conditions, it is an act that the employee performs for the employer in return for benefits. Certainly, there is no basis in § 406(a)(1)(D) for distinguishing a valid from an invalid quid pro quo. Section 406(a)(1)(D) simply does not address what an employer can and cannot ask an employee to do in return for benefits. See generally *Alessi* v. *Raybestos-Manhattan, Inc.*, 451 U.S. at 511 (ERISA "leaves th[e] question" of the content of benefits "to the private parties creating the plan. * * * The private parties, not the Government, control the level of benefits").[6] Furthermore, if an employer can avoid litigation that might result from laying off an employee by enticing him to retire early, as Spink concedes, it stands to reason that the employer can also protect itself from suits arising out of that retirement by asking the employee to release any employment-related claims he may have.

In short, whatever the precise boundaries of the prohibition in § 406(a)(1)(D), there is one use of plan assets that it cannot logically encompass: a quid pro quo between the employer and plan participants in which the plan pays out benefits to the participants pursuant to its terms. When § 406(a)(1)(D) is read in the context of the other prohibited transaction provisions, it becomes clear that the payment of benefits in exchange for the performance of some condition by the employee is not a "transaction" within the meaning of § 406(a)(1). A standard that allows some benefits agreements but not others, as Spink suggests, lacks a basis in § 406(a)(1)(D); it also would provide little guidance to lower courts and those who must comply with ERISA. We thus hold that the payment of benefits pursuant to an amended plan, regardless of what the plan requires of the employee in return for those benefits, does not constitute a prohibited transaction.[8]

IV

[*Eds.* The Court's discussion finding that the OBRA amendments do not apply retroactively is omitted.]

6. Indeed, federal law expressly approves the use of early retirement incentives conditioned upon the release of claims. The Older Workers Benefit Protection Act, Pub. L. 101–433, 104 Stat. 983 (1990), establishes requirements for the enforceability of employee waivers of ADEA claims made in exchange for early retirement benefits. See 29 U.S.C. § 626(f). Of course, the enforceability of a particular waiver under this and other applicable laws, including state law, is a separate issue from the question whether such an arrangement violates ERISA's prohibited transaction rules. But absent clearer indication than what we have in § 406(a)(1)(D), we would be reluctant to infer that ERISA bars conduct affirmatively sanctioned by other federal statutes.

8. If the benefits payment were merely a sham transaction, meant to disguise an otherwise unlawful transfer of assets to a party in interest, or involved a kickback scheme, that might present a different question from the one before us. Spink does not suggest that Lockheed's payment was a cover for an illegal scheme, only that payment of the benefits conditioned on the release was itself violative of § 406(a)(1)(D).

JUSTICE BREYER, with whom JUSTICE SOUTER joins, concurring in part and dissenting in part.

I join the Court's opinion except for its conclusion in Part III–B that "the payment of benefits pursuant to an amended plan, regardless of what the plan requires of the employee in return for those benefits, does not constitute a prohibited transaction." * * * The legal question addressed in Part III–B is a difficult one, which we need not here answer and which would benefit from further development in the lower courts, where interested parties who are experienced in these highly technical, important matters could present their views.

Notes and Questions

1. *"Dual Hat" Problems: Settlor vs. Fiduciary.* The Supreme Court in *Spink* and other cases has insisted that a sharp line be drawn between "settlor" and "fiduciary" roles, holding that when the employer amends or terminates a plan it acts as a "settlor" under trust law and should not be held to the standard of a "fiduciary". This premise works best in the area of defined-benefit plans where ERISA funding requirements presumably protect the expectations of plan participants and beneficiaries. Does it apply equally well to ERISA-covered welfare benefit plans, where employers do not advance funding and a separate trust fund is not required? Even in the context of defined-benefit plans, much will depend on whether adequate reserves are set aside in the pension trust to meet obligations. The issue has arisen with particular saliency in the "reducing plan benefit accruals" cases, see, e.g., Stamper v. Total Petroleum, Inc. Retirement Plan, 188 F.3d 1233 (10th Cir.1999), and fund "spinoff" cases, see, e.g., Systems Council EM–3 v. AT&T Corp., 159 F.3d 1376 (D.C.Cir.1998), where employer-settlors in essence withdraw assets from "overfunded" defined-benefit pension plans. See generally Charles C. Shulman, Qualified Plans in Mergers and Acquisitions, 5 ERISA and Benefits L.J. 297 (Spring 1999); Henry Talavera, ERISA Plans at Risk: How to Take Control of Control Group Rules, 12 Benefits L.J. 67 (no. 2, Summer 1999).

2. Spink *and Contributory Plans.* Does *Spink* apply to "contributory" pension plans, where employees are required to make contributions in addition to employer contributions? The Supreme Court answered in the affirmative in Hughes Aircraft Company v. Jacobson, 525 U.S. 432, 119 S.Ct. 755, 142 L.Ed.2d 881 (1999). In that case, because the plan was overfunded, Hughes suspended its contributions in 1987, and two years later amended the plan to provided that new participants could not contribute to the plan and would receive fewer benefits. However, existing participants could continue to contribute or opt to be treated as new participants who would not be required to make contributions. The Court held that the amendment did not affect the rights of pre-existing plan participants and that Hughes' use of the plan surplus to fund the noncontributory portion of the plan did not violate the ERISA provision barring plan assets from "inur[ing]" to the benefit of any employer * * *. 29 U.S.C. § 1103(c)(1) ("anti-inurement provision"):

To understand why respondents have no interest in the Plan's surplus, it is essential to recognize the difference between defined contributions plans and defined benefit plans, such as Hughes'. [Under defined-contribution plans,] "there can never be an insufficiency of funds in the plan to cover plan benefits" since each beneficiary is entitled to whatever assets are dedicated to his individual account. A defined benefit plan, on the other hand, consists of a general pool of assets rather than individual dedicated accounts. * * * The asset pool may be funded by employer or employee contributions, or a combination of both. * * * But the employer typically bears the entire investment risk and—short of the consequences of plan termination—must cover any underfunding as the result of a shortfall that may occur from the plan's investments. * * * Conversely, if the defined benefit plan is overfunded, the employer may reduce or suspend his contributions. * * * Given the employer's obligation to make up any shortfall, no plan member has a claim to any particular asset that composes a part of the plan's general asset pool. Instead, members have a right to a certain defined level of benefits, known as "accrued benefits." * * * In order to prevent a subsequent downward adjustment in benefits below a member's contribution amount, a defined benefit plan participant has a nonforfeitable right to the greater of (1) the benefits provided under the plan, or (2) an amount derived from the employee's accumulated contributions, determined using an interest rate fixed by statute. See § 204(c)(2)(B); 29 U.S.C. § 1054 (c)(2)(B). * * * Given this accumulated contribution floor, plan members have a nonforfeitable right only to their "accrued benefit," so that a plan's actual investment experience does not affect their statutory entitlement. Since a decline in the value of a plan's assets does not alter accrued benefits, members similarly have no entitlement to share in a plan's surplus—even if it is partially attributable to the investment growth of their contributions.

Therefore, Hughes could not have violated ERISA's vesting requirements by using assets from the surplus attributable to the employees' contributions to fund the noncontributory structure. * * * Hughes never deprived respondents of their accrued benefits. Indeed, when it implemented the noncontributory structure, Hughes permitted the Plan's existing participants to switch into the new structure. * * *

Respondents further contend that, even if they have no interest in the Plan's assets, the creation of the new contributory structure permitted Hughes to use assets from the surplus attributable to employer and employee contributions for its sole and exclusive benefit, in violation of ERISA's anti-inurement provision. * * *

As the language of [the anti-inurement provision] makes clear, the section focuses exclusively on whether fund assets were used to pay pension benefits to plan participants, without distinguishing either between benefits for new and old employees under one or more benefit structures of the same plan, or between assets that make up a plan's surplus as opposed to those needed to fund the plan's benefits. * * * [A]t all times, Hughes satisfied its continuing obligations under the provisions of the Plan and ERISA to ensure that the Plan was adequately funded. * * * Hughes did not act impermissibly by using surplus assets from the contributory structure to add the noncontributory structure of the Plan. The act of amending a pre-existing plan cannot as a matter of law create two de facto plans if the obligations (both preamendment and postamendment) continue to draw from the same single, unsegregated pool or fund of assets. * * * Because only one plan exists and respondents do not allege that Hughes used any of the assets for a purpose other than to pay its obligations to the Plan's beneficiaries, Hughes could not have violated the anti-inurement provision under ERISA § 403(c)(1).

Each of respondents' fiduciary duty claims must fail because ERISA's fiduciary provisions are inapplicable to the amendments. This conclusion follows from our decision in *Spink*. * * *

* * * Our conclusion [in *Spink*] applies with equal force to persons exercising authority over a contributory plan, a noncontributory plan, or any other type of plan. Our holding did not turn, as the Court of Appeals below thought, on the type of plan being amended. * * * Rather, it turned on whether the employer's act of amending its plan constituted an exercise of fiduciary duty. In *Spink*, we concluded it did not. * * *

119 S.Ct. at 761–63 (citations omitted).

3. *Non-Solicitation Covenants in Severance Benefit Plans?* Under *Spink*, can a plan administrator condition enhanced severance benefits on the employee's agreement to an otherwise lawful no-solicitation covenant? Compare, e.g., Friz v. J & H Marsh & McLennan, Inc., 2 Fed. Appx. 277 (4th Cir. 2001), with Cirulis v. UNUM Corp., 321 F.3d 1010 (10th Cir. 2003).

4. *"Party in Interest"?* In footnote 3 of *Spink* (not reprinted above), the Court limited the scope of § 406(a)'s prohibition on transactions with "a party in interest":

* * * [T]he Court of Appeals found that Lockheed was a "party in interest" under § 3(14)(C), and asserted that "a party in interest who benefitted from an impermissible transaction can be held liable under ERISA." 60 F.3d 616, 623 (C.A.9 1995). For that same proposition, several Courts of Appeals have relied on statements in *Mertens v. Hewitt Associates*, 508 U.S. 248, 113 S.Ct. 2063, 124 L.Ed.2d 161 (1993), that "ERISA contains various provisions that can be read as imposing obligations upon nonfiduciaries," id., at 253–254; see also id., at 254, n. 4 (citing 406(a)), and that "professional service providers * * * must disgorge assets and profits obtained through participation as parties-in-interest in transactions prohibited by § 406," id., at 262. * * * Insofar as they apply to § 406(a), these statements in *Mertens* (which were in any event dicta, since § 406(a) was not at issue) suggest liability for parties in interest only when a violation of § 406(a) has been established—which, as we have discussed, requires a showing that a fiduciary caused the plan to engage in the transaction in question. The Court of Appeals thus was not necessarily wrong in saying that "a party in interest who benefitted from an impermissible transaction can be held liable under ERISA" (emphasis added); but the only transactions rendered impermissible by § 406(a) are transactions caused by fiduciaries.

5. *"Sham" Transaction?* Consider footnote 8 of *Spink*, and its later treatment in *Hughes*:

> Respondents attempt to circumvent [the] conclusion [in *Spink*] by arguing that the amendments amounted to a sham transaction. Specifically, respondents argue that Hughes—by effectively increasing certain employees' wages through either providing increased retirement incentives or including those employees in the Plan's noncontributory structure—reduced its labor costs by spending down the Plan's surplus to cover its own obligations. * * * Even assuming that a sham transaction may implicate a fiduciary duty, the incidental benefits conferred upon Hughes when it amended the Plan are not impermissible under the statute. It is irrelevant whether Hughes received lower labor costs or other such incidental benefits * * *
>
> * * * Receipt of these types of benefits no more constitutes a breach of the fiduciary duties than they would constitute improper inurement or otherwise violate ERISA. To find that such benefits somehow violated the statute would forestall employers' efforts to implement a pension plan. ERISA, by and large, is concerned with "ensuring that employees will not be left emptyhanded once employers have guaranteed them certain benefits," * * * not with depriving employers of benefits incidental thereto. * * *

119 S.Ct. at 763–64. What might constitute a sham transaction? Would a sham transaction necessarily implicate a fiduciary duty?

6. *Employer Misrepresentations as Fiduciary Acts.* In Varity Corp. v. Howe, 516 U.S. 489, 502–503, 116 S.Ct. 1065, 134 L.Ed.2d 130 (1996), the Court held that Varity was acting as an ERISA "fiduciary" when it deliberately misled its employees into persuading them to work for a separately incorporated subsidiary, Massey Combines, by conveying the impression that employees' benefits would remain secure when they transferred to the subsidiary, despite Varity's awareness that Massey Combines was insolvent from the day it was created:

> To decide whether Varity's action fall within the statutory definition of "fiduciary" acts, we must interpret the statutory terms which limit the scope of fiduciary activity to discretionary acts of plan "management" and "administration." ERISA § 3(21)(A). * * * The ordinary trust law understanding of fiduciary "administration" of a trust is that to act as an administrator is to perform the duties imposed, or exercise the powers conferred by the trust documents. See Restatement (Second) of Trusts § 164 (1957). * * * The law of trusts also understands a trust document to implicitly confer "such powers as are necessary or appropriate for the carrying out of the purposes" of the trust. 3 A. Scott & W. Fratcher, Law of Trusts § 186, p.6 (4th ed. 1988). * * * Conveying information about the likely future of plan benefits, thereby permitting beneficiaries to make an informed choice about continued participation, would seem to be an exercise of a power "appropriate" to carrying out an important plan purpose. After all, ERISA itself specifically requires administrators to give beneficiaries certain information about the plan. See, e.g., ERISA §§ 102, 104(b)(1), 105(a). And administrators, as part of their administrative responsibilities, frequently offer beneficiaries

more than the minimum information that the statute requires–for example, answering beneficiaries' questions about the meaning of the terms of a plan so that those beneficiaries can more easily obtain the plan's benefits. * * *

Moreover, [the information at a critical meeting with Varity employees] came from those within the firm who had authority to communicate as fiduciaries with plan beneficiaries. Varity does not claim that it authorized only special individuals, not connected with [the documents distributed at the meeting], to speak as plan administrators. See § 402(b)(2) (a plan may describe a "procedure under the plan for the allocation of responsibilities for the operation and administration of the plan").

Finally, reasonable employees, in the circumstances found by the District Court, could have thought that Varity was communicating with them both in its capacity as employer and its capacity as plan administrator. Reasonable employees might not have distinguished consciously between the two roles. But they would have known that the employer was their plan's administrator and had expert knowledge about how their plans worked. The central conclusion ("your benefits are secure") could well have drawn strength from their awareness of that expertise, and one could reasonably believe that the employer, aware of the importance of the matter, so intended.

For advice to employers on how to limit liability under *Varity*, picking up on the Court's reference to § 402(b)(2), see Howard Pianko, To Limit ERISA Liability Exposure[:] Adopt a "PAPA" ("Process and Procedure Approach"), 1 ERISA Panel Counsel 1 (no. 1, Summer 1996).

7. *Enron Litigation*. The collapse of the Enron and Global Crossing companies spawned significant ERISA litigation. On September 30, 2003, the district court in In re Enron Corp. Securities, Derivative & ERISA Litigation (Tittle v. Enron Corp.), 284 F.Supp.2d 511 (S.D. Tex. 2003) found that former Enron employees had stated a claim that Enron and its officers and directors breached their ERISA fiduciary duties by, inter alia, (i) initiating a "lockdown" in October 2001 that prevented employees from moving their pension assets out of Enron at a time when Enron's stock price was plummeting; and (ii) heavily promoting Enron stock and encouraging employees to invest their retirement funds in company stock, despite knowledge that Enron stock was an imprudent investment choice. See generally Susan J. Stabile, Enron, Global Crossing, and Beyond: Implications for Workers, 76 St. John's L. Rev. 815 (2002). The Enron litigation also raised the issue whether ERISA fiduciaries have a duty to disclose nonpublic information to plan participants. See also Rankin v. Rots, 278 F.Supp.2d 853 (E.D. Mich. 2003).

8. *Communicating Proposals Under "Serious Consideration" to Offer Early Retirement Incentives*. Does the employer-plan administrator, as an ERISA fiduciary, have a duty to tell its employees that it is seriously considering a proposal to offer eligible employees early-retirement incentives? See, e.g., Bins v. Exxon Company U.S.A., 189 F.3d 929 (9th Cir.1999) ("once [the employer] began serious consideration of a proposal to offer more advantageous severance benefits, information about that proposal was mate-

rial to the retirement decisions of employees."); Fischer v. Philadelphia Elec. Co., 96 F.3d 1533, 1539 (3d Cir.1996) ("serious consideration" takes place when "(1) a specific proposal (2) is being discussed for the purpose of implementation (3) by senior management with the authority to implement the change.").

9. *Retiree Health Care Benefits.* In part because of changing accounting rules that require companies to report the anticipated cost of postretirement medical expenses and other non-pension benefits, see Employers' Accounting for Postretirement Benefits Other than Pensions, Financial Accounting Standard No. 106 (Fin. Accounting Standards Bd., 1990), many employers have terminated or substantially reduced programs that had provided for retiree health care benefits. See Marilyn J. Ward Ford, Broken Promises: Implementation of Financial Accounting Standards Board Rule 106, ERISA, and Legal Challenges to Modification and Termination of Postretirement Health Care Benefit Plans, 68 St. John's L. Rev. 427 (1994). Challenges to these employer-sponsor decisions are difficult to mount because retiree health care benefits are "welfare benefits" not subject to the vesting requirement applicable to pension benefits. Contract-based claims are possible where employers have made unqualified promises of postretirement benefits. These claims are adjudicated under a "federal common law" that has developed pursuant to ERISA, not state contract law. Compare, e.g., UAW v. Yard–Man, Inc., 716 F.2d 1476, 1482 (6th Cir.1983) ("retiree benefits are in a sense 'status' benefits which, as such, carry with them an inference that they continue so long as the prerequisite status is maintained"), with UAW v. Skinner Engine Co., 188 F.3d 130, 140–41 (3d Cir.1999) ("We cannot agree with *Yard-Man* and its progeny that there exists a presumption of lifetime benefits in the context of employee welfare benefits"; "*Yard-Man's* inference may be contrary to Congress' intent in choosing specifically not to provide for the vesting of employee welfare benefits"); United Paperworkers International Union v. Champion International Corp., 908 F.2d 1252 (5th Cir.1990); Anderson v. Alpha Portland Industries, Inc., 836 F.2d 1512, 1517 (8th Cir.1988).

In Curtiss–Wright Corp. v. Schoonejongen, 514 U.S. 73, 78–79, 115 S.Ct. 1223, 131 L.Ed.2d 94 (1995), the company amended its employee benefit plan to provide that postretirement health care coverage would cease for retirees upon the termination of business operations in the facility from which they retired. The lower courts held that Curtiss–Wright had not reserved the authority to amend the plan because the plan's reservation clause—which stated that "[t]he Company reserves the right * * * to modify or amend" the plan—was too vague to be a valid amendment procedure under § 402(b)(3) of ERISA, 29 U.S.C. § 1102(b)(3). The Supreme Court unanimously reversed:

> The text of § 402(b)(3) actually requires *two* things: a "procedure for amending (the) plan" *and* "(a procedure) for identifying the persons who have authority to amend the plan." With respect to the second requirement, the general "Definitions" section of ERISA makes quite clear that the term "person," wherever it appears in the statute, includes companies. See 29 U.S.C. § 1002(9). * * *

The text of § 402(b)(3) speaks, somewhat awkwardly, of requiring a *procedure* for identifying the persons with amendment authority, rather than requiring identification of those persons outright. Be that as it may, a plan that simply identifies the persons outright necessarily indicates a procedure for identifying the persons as well. With respect to the Curtiss–Wright plan, for example, to identify "(t)he Company" as the person with amendment authority is to say, in effect, that the procedure for identifying the person with amendment authority is to look always to the "(t)he Company." * * *

Curtiss-Wright appears not to have dampened litigation over termination of retiree health care plans. *Yardman* is still alive, at least in the Sixth Circuit. See Golden v. Kelsey–Hayes Co., 73 F.3d 648 (6th Cir.1996). Despite clear language in the reservation clause, plaintiffs have been able in some cases successfully to argue that such language was essentially negated by representations in summary plan descriptions to the effect that medical benefits would "be continued for the rest of your life." See, e.g., Unisys Corp. Retiree Medical Benefit "ERISA" Litigation, 57 F.3d 1255, 1266 (3d Cir.1995) (claim for breach of fiduciary duty under § 502(a)(3)(B) of ERISA, 29 U.S.C. § 1132(a)(3)(B), may be maintained in such circumstances for failing to disclose to employees that they did not have a lifetime medical benefit before they retired):

> [W]e hold that the district court did not err as a matter of law in concluding that the duty to convey complete and accurate information that was material to its employees' circumstance arose from these facts since the trustees had to know that their silence might cause harm. The district court's findings that the company actively misinformed its employees by affirmatively representing to them that their medical benefits were guaranteed once they retired, when in fact the company knew that this was not true and that employees were making important retirement decisions relying upon this information, clearly support a claim for breach of fiduciary duty under ERISA.

Under this court's reasoning, if employees retire after the employer amends its summary plan descriptions and other materials to correct this misinformation, will they be entitled to lifetime medical benefits?

11. *"Social Investing"*. Is it consistent with ERISA fiduciary standards for pension funds to engage in "economically targeted investments" (ETIs) as a means of promoting, say, labor relations objectives of existing plan members (who may or may not be ultimate plan beneficiaries)? The Labor Department in 1994 offered some qualified encouragement for investment of plan investments in an ETI, "if the ETI has an expected rate of return that is commensurate to rates of return of alternative investments with similar risk characteristics that are available to the plan, and if the ETI is otherwise an appropriate investment for the plan in terms of such factors as diversification and the investment policy of the plan." See DOL Interpretive Bull. 94–1 on Economically Targeted Investments, 59 Fed. Reg. 32,606 (June 23, 1994). For a defense of the "social investing" approach, see Teresa Ghilarducci, Employee Investment on Pension Investment Boards: An Economic Model of the Pension Contract, in Employee Representation in the Emerging Workplace, supra, at 703–24; Jayne Elizabeth Zanglein, High Performance

Investing: Harnessing the Power of Pension Funds to Promote Economic Growth and Workplace Integrity, 11 Labor Lawyer 59 (1995). For a critique, see Geoffrey P. Miller, On the Advantages of Defined–Contribution Plans: Commentary on Ghilarducci, in Employee Representation in the Emerging Workplace, supra, at 725–34. On the related phenomenon of shareholder activism by pension funds, see Stewart J. Schwab & Randall S. Thomas, Realigning Corporate Governance: Shareholder Activism by Labor Unions, 96 Mich. L.Rev. 1018 (1998).

Note on Fiduciary Duties in Participant–Directed Defined–Contribution Plans

As discussed above, employers increasingly have moved away from defined-benefit plans in favor of defined-contribution plans. The latter offer employers certain administrative efficiencies, shift the burden of market risk to participants, and pursuant to ERISA § 404 (c) can remove a good deal of fiduciary responsibility when such plans take the form of "participant directed" plans. Because of a claimed financial illiteracy on the part of most participants, these plans have come under criticism as poorly designed retirement vehicles. See Lorraine Schmall, Defined Contribution Plans After Enron, 41 Brandeis L.J. 891 (2003); Susan J. Stabile, Paternalism Isn't Always a Dirty Word: Can the Law Better Protect Defined Contribution Plan Participants?, 5 Employee Rts. & Emp. Pol'y J. 491 (2001) ; Colleen E. Medill, The Individual Responsibility Model of Retirement Plans Today: Conforming ERISA Policy to Reality, 49 Emory L.J. 1 (2000).

The Department of Labor (DOL) has tried to create some incentives for employers to provide essential financial information. Its 1992 regulations provide that a plan will not be deemed to meet § 404(c)'s participant-control requirement unless the participant is provided with "an opportunity to choose, from a broad range of investment alternatives, the manner in which some or all of the investments in his account are invested," 29 C.F.R. § 2550.404(c)–1(b)(1)(ii), and the participant "is provided or has the opportunity to obtain sufficient information to make informed decisions with regard to the investment alternatives available under the plan," id. § 2550.404(c)–1(b)(2)(i)(B). "Sufficient information" must include a "description of the investment alternatives available under the plan, and, with respect to each designated investment alternative, a general description of the investment objectives and risk and return characteristics of each alternative, including information relating to the type and diversification of assets comprising the portfolio of the designated investment alternative." Id. § 2550.404(c)–1(b)(2)(i)(B)(ii). To address concerns of employers and financial institutions that any provision of information might trigger fiduciary status, DOL issued a 1996 bulletin specifying a range of financial information that will not be presumed to constitute investment advice possibly triggering fiduciary duties, including descriptions of "hypothetical" portfolio recommendations not tailored to the objectives of particular participants. See 29 C.F.R. § 2509.96–1.

DOL has also experimented under its ERISA § 408 authority in granting administrative exceptions to the prohibited-transaction rules of § 406 as a means of broadening the availability of financial information. For example, on December 14, 2001, the agency issued an advisory opinion endorsing SunAmerica's request for § 408 relief. SunAmerica proposed to hire an independent contractor to collect investment goals and risk tolerance information from participants, and then send the information to an independent financial consultant who would produce computer-generated portfolio recommendations for each individual. The participant could then choose either the "Discretionary Asset Allocation" option, in which the computer-generated recommendations would be automatically implemented, or the "Recommended Asset Allocation Service," where the participant would be provided with a suggested portfolio which he could choose to implement or disregard. SunAmerica would collect all usual fees from the purchase and holding of its mutual funds by the plan participants. The Department reasoned that although SunAmerica would be acting as a financial advisor, and thus an ERISA fiduciary, it would not be using its fiduciary authority to cause the plan to pay additional fees to SunAmerica because the participants' investment decisions would be guided not by SunAmerica's advice, but by the recommendations of an independent consultant. See Advisory Opinion Letter 2001–09A from Louis Campagna, Chief Division of Fiduciary Interpretations, Pension & Welfare Benefits Admin. to William A. Schmid & Eric Berger, Kirkpatrick & Lockhart, LLP (U.S. Dept. of Labor, Dec. 14, 2001), available at http://www.dol.gov/ebsa/regs/AOs/ao2001-09a.html

F. § 510: NON–"INTERFERENCE" OBLIGATIONS

Section 510 prohibits an employer from discharging an employee "for the purpose of interfering with the attainment of any right to which [an employee] may become entitled" under an employee pension or welfare benefit plan. Although the principal purpose of § 510 was to ensure the integrity of the vesting rules by preventing discharges strategically timed to prevent vesting from occurring, the courts have held that even employees who are fully qualified for benefits may state a § 510 claim. As the following decision makes clear, such an action may also lie for discharges allegedly motivated by a desire to stop paying welfare benefits which are not vested under ERISA. The Supreme Court has held that ERISA preempts state wrongful termination suits based on allegations that the employee was discharged in order to prevent his attainment of benefits under an ERISA-covered plan. See Ingersoll–Rand Co. v. McClendon, 498 U.S. 133, 111 S.Ct. 478, 112 L.Ed.2d 474 (1990), discussed also at page 1185, n.8 infra.

1. *"Fundamental Business Decisions"*

INTER-MODAL RAIL EMPLOYEES ASSN. v. ATCHISON, TOPEKA AND SANTA FE RAILWAY CO.

Supreme Court of the United States, 1997.
520 U.S. 510, 117 S.Ct. 1513, 137 L.Ed.2d 763.

JUSTICE O'CONNOR delivered the opinion of the Court.

Section 510 of the Employee Retirement Income Security Act of 1974 (ERISA), 88 Stat. 895, makes it unlawful to "discharge, fine, suspend, expel, discipline, or discriminate against a participant or beneficiary [of an employee benefit plan] * * * for the purpose of interfering with the attainment of any right to which such participant may become entitled under the plan." 29 U.S.C. § 1140. The Court of Appeals for the Ninth Circuit held that § 510 only prohibits interference with the attainment of rights that are capable of "vesting," as that term is defined in ERISA. We disagree.

I

The individual petitioners are former employees of respondent Santa Fe Terminal Services, Inc. (SFTS), a wholly owned subsidiary of respondent, the Atchison, Topeka and Santa Fe Railway Co. (ATSF), which was responsible for transferring cargo between railcars and trucks at ATSF's Hobart Yard in Los Angeles, California. While petitioners were employed by SFTS, they were entitled to retirement benefits under the Railroad Retirement Act of 1974, 88 Stat. 1312, as amended, 45 U.S.C. § 231 et seq., and to pension, health, and welfare benefits under collective bargaining agreements involving SFTS and the Teamsters Union. SFTS provided its workers with pension, health, and welfare benefits through employee benefit plans subject to ERISA's comprehensive regulations.

In January 1990, ATSF entered into a formal "Service Agreement" with SFTS to have SFTS do the same "inter-modal" work it had done at the Hobart Yard for the previous 15 years without a contract. Seven weeks later, ATSF exercised its right to terminate the newly formed Agreement and opened up the Hobart Yard work for competitive bidding. Respondent In–Terminal Services (ITS) was the successful bidder, and SFTS employees who declined to continue employment with ITS were terminated. ITS, unlike SFTS, was not obligated to make contributions to the Railroad Retirement Account under the Railroad Retirement Act. ITS also provided fewer pension and welfare benefits under its collective bargaining agreement with the Teamsters Union than had SFTS. Workers who continued their employment with ITS "lost their Railroad Retirement Act benefits" and "suffered a substantial reduction in Teamsters benefits." * * *

Petitioners sued respondents SFTS, ATSF, and ITS in the United States District Court for the Central District of California, alleging that respondents had violated § 510 of ERISA by "discharging" petitioners "for the purpose of interfering with the attainment of * * * rights to which" they would have "become entitled" under the ERISA pension and welfare plans adopted pursuant to the SFTS–Teamsters collective bargaining agreement. Had SFTS remained their employer, petitioners contended, they would have been entitled to assert claims for benefits under the SFTS–Teamsters benefits plans, at least until the collective bargaining agreement that gave rise to those plans expired. The substitution of ITS for SFTS, however, precluded them from asserting those claims and relegated them to asserting claims under the less generous ITS–Teamsters benefits plans. According to petitioners, the substitution "interfered with the attainment" of their "right" to assert those claims and violated § 510. Respondents moved to dismiss these § 510 claims, and the District Court granted the motion.

The Court of Appeals for the Ninth Circuit affirmed in part and reversed in part. * * * The court reinstated petitioners' claim under § 510 for interference with their pension benefits, concluding that § 510 " 'protects plan participants from termination motivated by an employer's desire to prevent a pension from vesting.' " * * * But the Court of Appeals affirmed the dismissal of petitioners' claim for interference with their welfare benefits. "Unlike pension benefits," the Court of Appeals observed, "welfare benefits do not vest." * * * As a result, the Court of Appeals noted, "employers remain free to unilaterally amend or eliminate [welfare] plans," and "employees have no present 'right' to future, anticipated welfare benefits." * * * Because the "existence of a present 'right' is [a] prerequisite to section 510 relief," the Court of Appeals concluded that § 510 did not state a cause of action for interference with welfare benefits. * * *

II

The Court of Appeals' holding that § 510 bars interference only with vested rights is contradicted by the plain language of § 510. As noted above, that section makes it unlawful to "discharge * * * a [plan] participant or beneficiary * * * for the purpose of interfering with the attainment of any right to which such participant may become entitled under the plan." 29 U.S.C. § 1140 (emphasis added). ERISA defines a "plan" to include both "an employee welfare benefit plan [and] an employee pension benefit plan," § 1002(3), and specifically exempts "employee welfare benefit plans" from its stringent vesting requirements, see § 1051(1). Because a "plan" includes an "employee welfare benefit plan," and because welfare plans offer benefits that do not "vest" (at least insofar as ERISA is concerned), Congress' use of the word "plan" in § 510 all but forecloses the argument that § 510's interference clause applies only to "vested" rights. Had Congress intended to confine § 510's protection to "vested" rights, it could have easily substituted the term "pension plan," see 29 U.S.C. § 1002(2), for "plan," or the term "nonforfeitable" right, see § 1002(19), for "any right." But § 510 draws no distinction between those rights that "vest" under ERISA and those that do not.

The right that an employer or plan sponsor may enjoy in some circumstances to unilaterally amend or eliminate its welfare benefit plan does not, as the Court of Appeals apparently thought, justify a departure from § 510's plain language. * * *

The flexibility an employer enjoys to amend or eliminate its welfare plan is not an accident; Congress recognized that "requiring the vesting of these ancillary benefits would seriously complicate the administration and increase the cost of plans." S. Rep.No. 93–383, p. 51 (1973). Giving employers this flexibility also encourages them to offer more generous benefits at the outset, since they are free to reduce benefits should economic conditions sour. If employers were locked into the plans they initially offered, "they would err initially on the side of omission." *Heath v. Varity Corp.*, 256, 71 F.3d 256, 258 (C.A.7, 1995). Section 510 counterbalances this flexibility by ensuring that employers do not "circumvent the provision of promised benefits." *Ingersoll-Rand Co.* [v. *McClendon*], 498 U.S. [133,] 143 (1990) (citing S. Rep. No. 93–127, pp. 35–36 (1973); H. R. Rep. No. 93–533, p. 17 (1973)). In short, "§ 510 helps to make promises credible." *Heath*, supra, at 258. An employer may, of course, retain the unfettered right to alter its promises, but to do so it must follow the formal procedures set forth in the plan. See 29 U.S.C. § 1102(b)(3) (requiring plan to "provide a procedure for amending such plan"); [*Curtiss-Wright Corp.* v.] *Schoonejongen*, [514 U.S.73, 78, 131 L.Ed.2d 94, 115 S.Ct. 1223 (1995)] (observing that the "cognizable claim [under ERISA] is that the company did not [amend its welfare benefit plan] in a permissible manner"). Adherence to these formal procedures "increases the likelihood that proposed plan amendments, which are fairly serious events, are recognized as such and given the special consideration they deserve." *Schoonejongen*, supra, at 82. The formal amendment process would be undermined if § 510 did not apply because employers could "informally" amend their plans one participant at a time. Thus, the power to amend or abolish a welfare benefit plan does not include the power to "discharge, fine, suspend, expel, discipline, or discriminate against" the plan's participants and beneficiaries "for the purpose of interfering with [their] attainment of * * * rights * * * under the plan." To be sure, when an employer acts without this purpose, as could be the case when making fundamental business decisions, such actions are not barred by § 510. But in the case where an employer acts with a purpose that triggers the protection of § 510, any tension that might exist between an employer's power to amend the plan and a participant's rights under § 510 is the product of a careful balance of competing interests, and is most surely not the type of "absurd or glaringly unjust" result, *Ingalls Shipbuilding Inc. v. Director, Office of Workers' Compensation Programs*, 519 U.S. 248, 261 (1997), that would warrant departure from the plain language of § 510.

Respondents argue that the Court of Appeals' decision must nevertheless be affirmed because § 510, when applied to benefits that do not "vest," only protects an employee's right to cross the "threshold of eligibility" for welfare benefits. * * * In other words, argue respondents, an employee who is eligible to receive benefits under an ERISA welfare benefits plan has already "attained" her "rights" under the plan, so that any subsequent actions taken by an employer cannot, by definition, "interfere" with the "attainment of * * * rights" under the plan. According to respondents, petitioners were eligible to receive welfare benefits under the SFTS–Teamsters plan at the time they were discharged, so they cannot state a claim under § 510. The Court of Appeals' approach precluded it from evaluating this argument, and others presented to us, and we see no reason not to allow it the first opportunity to consider these matters on remand.

Notes and Questions

1. *Post-Attainment Claims*. How should the court below rule on the question left open by the Court's last paragraph? Would adoption of the employer's argument blunt the thrust of the Court's analysis in its penultimate paragraph?

2. *A Rule Barring Ad Hoc Departures from Existing Plans?* The *Intermodal* Court holds that § 510 applies to nonvested benefits, but what does this mean in practice? Is it simply a guarantee that employers must abide by the terms of existing plans until they are properly amended? See, e.g., Heath v. Varity Corp., 71 F.3d 256, 258–59 (7th Cir.1995), where Judge Easterbrook writes:

> * * * Suppose the supervisor who fired Heath had purported to amend the plan to strip him of access to the early retirement package. Consider two possibilities: (i) the amendment reads "The early retirement program is hereby abolished," or (ii) the amendment retains the program but adds "Notwithstanding the criteria ordinarily used to award early retirement benefits, Alan T. Heath is ineligible." The first possibility is open until the date Heath retires, but only if Massey Ferguson uses the amendment procedure laid out in the plan. * * * The decision to fire Heath did not follow the procedures appropriate to amending a plan, and it was not made by the persons authorized to change the plan. As for the second possibility * * * [t]he statutory distinction between an unbridled power to control the terms of the plan and the fiduciary duty to implement an existing plan in employees' interest supposes that the plan will contain certain rules of general applicability. We need not consider what would happen if the employee were a legitimate class of one (for example, the president of the firm). * * * The 1998 amendment grouped Heath with other persons still eligible for "30 and out" benefits. When an employer's board of directors makes such a decision, ERISA does not allow supervisors to override it, one employee at a time.

3. *Section 510's Applicability to Organizational Decisions?* What role, if any, does § 510 play in cases where "fundamental business decisions," like the sale of a business, essentially wipe away long-expected eligibility for nonvested welfare benefits? Does *Intermodal* leave intact decisions in the courts of appeals broadly suggesting that § 510 has no meaningful applicability to organizational decisions? Consider, e.g., Andes v. Ford Motor Co., 70 F.3d 1332, 1337–38 (D.C.Cir.1995). In *Andes*, Ford saved $18.5 million in expected pension benefit costs by selling its subsidiary DCS, which provided computer services to Ford dealers, to Universal Computer Services (UCS). Former DCS employees were given the option of losing their jobs or working for UCS, which had announced plans to reduce the workforce after an initial evaluation period. Ford had rejected proposals from its personnel department to allow former DCS employees to "grow into" early retirement benefits under Ford's plan by crediting service with UCS for this purpose, or to keep these individuals on Ford's payroll and simply lease them to UCS. UCS made clear that it would not duplicate Ford retirement benefits, but would replicate Ford's severance benefits for one year and provide a periodic

cash bonus equal to a portion of the total value of the benefits that the former DCS employees lost. As part of the sale, UCS also agreed to allow Ford some continuing influence over UCS prices and technological developments. The D.C. Circuit agreed with the trial courts that these facts did not establish a § 510 claim:

> Examining the language of § 510 closely, one notes the word "discharge" is included along with the words "fine, suspend, expel, discipline, or discriminate," all words that connote actions aimed directly at individuals. * * * In this case, it seems rather clear to us that * * * an employer's decision to sell or close down an operation would not normally implicate § 510 merely because the action caused the termination of employees. If Congress had wished for § 510 to apply routinely to such decisions, which are virtually always based, at least in part, on labor costs, it would surely have included the terms "layoff" and "termination."
>
> The legislative history supports this interpretation. * * * The Senate report on the provision that eventually became § 510 states:
>
>> These provisions were added * * * in the face of evidence that in some plans a worker's pension rights or the expectations of those rights were interfered with by the use of economic sanctions or violent reprisals. Although the instances of these occurrences are relatively small in number, the Committee has concluded that safeguards are required to preclude this type of abuse. * * *
>
> S. Rep. No. 93–127, 93d Cong., 2d Sess., reprinted in 1974 U.S. Code Cong. & Admin. News 4838, 4872 (1974). Selling a subsidiary is not an "economic sanction" or a "violent reprisal," nor are such actions "relatively small in number." * * *
>
> This is not to say that § 510 could never be implicated in a company's basic organizational decisions. If, for example, a plaintiff produced evidence that a particular company determined that 20 of its employees were soon to become eligible for a rich benefits package and noted that 19 of those employees were conveniently located in one subdivision with perhaps only a few other employees—a company shutdown might be only an indirect method of discharging those high benefit employees. In such a situation, the organization's decision merely masks a determination to interfere with the employees' attainment of benefit plan rights.
>
> * * *
>
> Of course, even after an organizational decision, determinations as to which individuals, if any, are to be retained by the selling company might implicate § 510. In this case, however, since Ford was selling a going business to UCS, Ford naturally wished all of the existing employees to go with the business; otherwise its value to the purchaser would be less.

Id. at 1337–39

4. *"Specific Intent" Requirement.* Cases like *Andes* explain why some courts have engrafted a "specific intent" requirement onto § 510. To estab-

lish a § 510 violation, plaintiff must show that "an employer was at least in part motivated by the specific intent to engage in activity prohibited by Sec. 510"; "mere cost savings and proximity to benefits are [not] sufficient *per se* to create a genuine issue of fact requiring a trial." Dister v. The Continental Group, 859 F.2d 1108, & n. 1 (2d Cir.1988); Gavalik v. Continental Can Co., 812 F.2d 834, 851–52 (3d Cir.1987). In *Gavalik*, the company employed a "liability avoidance" scheme to minimize benefit costs by "shift[ing] business to plants that either had low unfunded pension liability or plants that needed the work in order to retain employees with vested 70/75 benefits." 812 F.2d at 853. *Gavalik* is cited with qualified approval in the *Andes* decision, 70 F.3d at 1338, as a case where the Third Circuit determined that pension eligibility was the "determinative" factor in each of Continental's challenged actions. See also Gitlitz v. Compagnie Nationale Air France, 129 F.3d 554 (11th Cir.1997) (questioning employer's motivation for converting outside sales employees to independent-contractor status).

Is the requisite "specific intent" shown by an employer's consideration of the level of pension and welfare benefits and other labor costs associated with a particular facility or department in deciding to close down that facility or department? Does it make sense to bar employers from considering benefit costs, provided they do not act strategically to deprive employees of vested benefits on the eve of entitlement? Compare McLendon v. Continental Can Co., 908 F.2d 1171 (3d Cir.1990) (sustaining nationwide injunction against company's use of computerized system for identifying high-cost employees who had not yet qualified for pension benefits as possible targets for layoff, while requiring trial on a plant-by-plant basis of company's defense that layoffs at particular plants would have occurred because of legitimate economic factors irrespective of the computerized targeting scheme), with Colizza v. United States Steel Corp., 116 F.R.D. 653 (W.D.Pa. 1987) (the fact that plaintiffs' termination was a few months shy of qualification for enhanced pension benefits was "a mere consequence of a termination of employment due to a total restructuring of USX'[s] steel operations" rather than the "motivating factor" behind the decision). See also McGann v. H & H Music Company below.

5. *Relationship to Age Discrimination Claims?* In Hazen Paper Co. v. Biggins, 507 U.S. 604, 113 S.Ct. 1701, 123 L.Ed.2d 338 (1993), the Supreme Court held that an allegation that an employer engineered the discharge of an employee in order to prevent vesting of a pension benefit did not state a claim of intentional age discrimination in violation of ADEA, because reliance on a factor merely correlated with age—here, length of service—could not be equated with reliance on age. The *Hazen* Court suggested, however, that the plaintiff in that case may have stated a claim under § 510 of ERISA. The Court also intimated that where eligibility for pension benefits was based on a combination of age and length of service, a similarly motivated discharge might also violate ADEA. See pp. 457–62 supra.

6. *Relationship to Implied Covenant of Good Faith and Fair Dealing?* Compare also the facts in a case like *Gavalik* with the situation that confronted the Massachusetts court in *Fortune*, p. 774 supra. The implied-covenant approach may be available in cases involving compensation or non-ERISA benefits.

2. *Targeted Benefit Plan Changes*

McGANN v. H & H MUSIC COMPANY

United States Court of Appeals for the Fifth Circuit, 1991.
946 F.2d 401.

GARWOOD, J.

Plaintiff-appellant John McGann (McGann) filed this suit under section 510 of the Employee Retirement Income Security Act of 1974, Pub. L. No. 93–406, 88 Stat. 832 (29 U.S.C. §§ 1001–1461) (ERISA), against defendants-appellees H & H Music Company (H & H Music), Brook Mays Music Company (Brook Mays) and General American Life Insurance Company (General American) (collectively defendants) claiming that they discriminated against McGann, an employee of H & H Music, by reducing benefits available to H & H Music's group medical plan beneficiaries for treatment for acquired immune deficiency syndrome (AIDS) and related illnesses. The district court granted defendants' motion for summary judgment on the ground that an employer has an absolute right to alter the terms of medical coverage available to plan beneficiaries. * * * We affirm.

FACTS AND PROCEEDINGS BELOW

McGann, an employee of H & H Music, discovered that he was afflicted with AIDS in December 1987. Soon thereafter, McGann submitted his first claims for reimbursement under H & H Music's group medical plan, provided through Brook Mays, the plan administrator, and issued by General American, the plan insurer, and informed his employer that he had AIDS. McGann met with officials of H & H Music in March 1988, at which time they discussed McGann's illness. Before the change in the terms of the plan, it provided for lifetime medical benefits of up to $1,000,000 to all employees.

In July 1988, H & H Music informed its employees that, effective August 1, 1988, changes would be made in their medical coverage. These changes included, but were not limited to, limitation of benefits payable for AIDS-related claims to a lifetime maximum of $5,000.[9] No limitation was placed on any other catastrophic illness. H & H Music became self-insured under the new plan and General American became the plan's administrator. By January 1990, McGann had exhausted the $5,000 limit on coverage for his illness.

In August 1989, McGann sued H & H Music, Brook Mays and General American under section 510 of ERISA * * *.

McGann claimed that defendants discriminated against him in violation of both prohibitions of section 510. He claimed that the provision limiting coverage for AIDS-related expenses was directed specifically at

---

9. Other changes included increased individual and family deductibles, elimination of coverage for chemical dependency treatment, adoption of a preferred provider plan and increased contribution requirements.

him in retaliation for exercising his rights under the medical plan and for the purpose of interfering with his attainment of a right to which he may become entitled under the plan.

* * *

McGann contends that defendants violated both clauses of section 510 by discriminating against him for two purposes: (1) "for exercising any right to which [the beneficiary] is entitled," and (2) "for the purpose of interfering with the attainment of any right to which such participant may become entitled." * * * At trial, McGann would bear the burden of proving the existence of defendants' specific discriminatory intent as an essential element of either of his claims. * * * Thus, in order to survive summary judgment McGann must make a showing sufficient to establish that a genuine issue exists as to defendants' specific intent to retaliate against McGann for filing claims for AIDS-related treatment or to interfere with McGann's attainment of any right to which he may have become entitled.

Although we assume there was a connection between the benefits reduction and either McGann's filing of claims or his revelations about his illness, there is nothing in the record to suggest that defendants' motivation was other than as they asserted, namely to avoid the expense of paying for AIDS treatment (if not, indeed, also for other treatment), no more for McGann than for any other present or future plan beneficiary who might suffer from AIDS. McGann concedes that the reduction in AIDS benefits will apply equally to all employees filing AIDS-related claims and that the effect of the reduction will not necessarily be felt only by him. He fails to allege that the coverage reduction was otherwise specifically intended to deny him particularly medical coverage except "in effect." He does not challenge defendants' assertion that their purpose in reducing AIDS benefits was to reduce costs.

Furthermore, McGann has failed to adduce evidence of the existence of "any right to which [he] may become entitled under the plan." The right referred to in the second clause of section 510 is not simply any right to which an employee may conceivably become entitled, but rather any right to which an employee may become entitled pursuant to an existing, enforceable obligation assumed by the employer. * * *

McGann's allegations show no promised benefit, for there is nothing to indicate that defendants ever promised that the $1,000,000 coverage limit was permanent. The H & H Music plan expressly provides: "Termination or Amendment of Plan: The Plan Sponsor may terminate or amend the Plan at any time or terminate any benefit under the Plan at any time." There is no allegation or evidence that any oral or written representations were made to McGann that the $1,000,000 coverage limit would never be lowered. Defendants broke no promise to McGann. The continued availability of the $1,000,000 limit was not a right to which McGann may have become entitled for the purposes of section

510.[10] To adopt McGann's contrary construction of this portion of section 510 would mean that an employer could not effectively reserve the right to amend a medical plan to reduce benefits respecting subsequently incurred medical expenses, as H & H Music did here, because such an amendment would obviously have as a purpose preventing participants from attaining the right to such future benefits as they otherwise might do under the existing plan absent the amendment. But this is plainly not the law, and ERISA does not require such "vesting" of the right to a continued level of the same medical benefits once those are ever included in a welfare plan. See *Moore* v. *Metropolitan Life Insurance Co.*, 856 F.2d 488, 492 (2d Cir.1988).

McGann appears to contend that the reduction in AIDS benefits alone supports an inference of specific intent to retaliate against him or to interfere with his future exercise of rights under the plan. McGann characterizes as evidence of an individualized intent to discriminate the fact that AIDS was the only catastrophic illness to which the $5,000 limit was applied and the fact that McGann was the only employee known to have AIDS. He contends that if defendants reduced AIDS coverage because they learned of McGann's illness through his exercising of his rights under the plan by filing claims, the coverage reduction therefore could be "retaliation" for McGann's filing of the claims.[11] Under McGann's theory, any reduction in employee benefits would be impermissibly discriminatory if motivated by a desire to avoid the anticipated costs of continuing to provide coverage for a particular beneficiary. McGann would find an implied promise not to discriminate for this purpose; it is the breaking of this promise that McGann appears to contend constitutes interference with a future entitlement.

* * *

McGann's claim cannot be reconciled with the well-settled principle that Congress did not intend that ERISA circumscribe employers' control over the content of benefits plans they offered to their employees. McGann interprets section 510 to prevent an employer from reducing or eliminating coverage for a particular illness in response to the escalating costs of covering an employee suffering from that illness. Such an interpretation would, in effect, change the terms of H & H Music's plan. Instead of making the $1,000,000 limit available for medical expenses on an as-incurred basis only as long as the limit remained in effect, the policy would make the limit permanently available for all medical expenses as they might thereafter be incurred because of a single event, such as the contracting of AIDS. Under McGann's theory, defendants would be effectively proscribed from reducing coverage for AIDS once

10. McGann does not claim that he was not fully reimbursed for all claimed medical expenses incurred on or prior to August 1, 1988; or that the full $5,000 has not been made available to him in respect to AIDS related medical expenses incurred by him on or after July 1, 1988.

11. We assume that discovery of McGann's condition—and realization of the attendant, long-term costs of caring for McGann—did in fact prompt defendants to reconsider the $1,000,000 limit with respect to AIDS-related expenses and to reduce the limit for future such expenses to $5,000.

McGann had contracted that illness and filed claims for AIDS-related expenses. If a federal court could prevent an employer from reducing an employee's coverage limits for AIDS treatment once that employee contracted AIDS, the boundaries of judicial involvement in the creation, alteration or termination of ERISA plans would be sorely tested.

* * *

* * * ERISA does not broadly prevent an employer from "discriminating" in the creation, alteration or termination of employee benefits plans; thus, evidence of such intentional discrimination cannot alone sustain a claim under section 510. That section does not prohibit welfare plan discrimination between or among categories of diseases. Section 510 does not mandate that if some, or most, or virtually all catastrophic illnesses are covered, AIDS (or any other particular catastrophic illness) must be among them. It does not prohibit an employer from electing not to cover or continue to cover AIDS, while covering or continuing to cover other catastrophic illnesses, even though the employer's decision in this respect may stem from some "prejudice" against AIDS or its victims generally. The same, of course, is true of any other disease and its victims. That sort of "discrimination" is simply not addressed by section 510. Under section 510, the asserted discrimination is illegal only if it is motivated by a desire to retaliate against an employee or to deprive an employee of an existing right to which he may become entitled. The district court's decision to grant summary judgment to defendants therefore was proper.

Notes and Questions

1. *Lawful "Benefit Consciousness"?* As we have seen in connection with the Third Circuit's decision in *Gavalik*, p. 1044, note 4, if an employer is specifically motivated by benefit-cost considerations in making a personnel decision, "specific intent" for § 510 purposes would seem to be established. Yet, in *McGann* such "benefit consciousness" did not establish the requisite "specific intent". Is this because employers when designing benefit plans— whether establishing, modifying or withdrawing benefits—must be given wide latitude so as not to deter them from providing benefits in the first place? Are we not equally worried about deterring economically necessary layoff decisions, as in *Gavalik*, or conversion to independent-contractor status, as in *Gitlitz*, p. 1044, note 4?

2. *Ad Hoc or Discriminatory Benefit Consciousness?* The *McGann* court makes clear that the selective or discriminatory character of the employer's benefit design—targeting only one particular disease for disfavored treatment—does not implicate § 510. This sort of targeted decision, however, might raise questions under § 501(c) of the Americans with Disabilities Act of 1990, 42 U.S.C. § 12201(c). See discussion at pp. 580–84 supra.

3. *Taking Benefits Into Account in Setting Wages?* Prior to 1994, Ms. Garratt had been paid $10 an hour. Starting in January 1994 she was paid a monthly wage of $2000. Dr. Walker, her employer, had been contributing 15% of his wages to a "Simplified Employee Pension" (SEP) on his own

behalf. An SEP, authorized by § 408(k) of the Code, is a form of independent retirement account funded by employer contributions. After increasing Garratt's salary to $2000 a month, Dr. Walker focused on the fact that an annual SEP contribution of 15% might be required for Garrett if Walker wanted to obtain the 15% contribution he had been accustomed to, for § 408(k) requires that all employees meeting certain service and compensation requirements be eligible to participate in a SEP. Dr. Walker ultimately gave Garratt two choices: She could take a salary cut to $21,000 with a 15% contribution to the SEP, or maintain her salary with no SEP contribution. The latter option was not, however, legally available without disqualifying the SEP entirely. Assume Garratt accepts the salary cut and then quits. Has Dr. Walker violated § 510? See Garratt v. Walker, 164 F.3d 1249 (10th Cir.1998) (en banc) (reversing panel and finding violation). Does a finding of a § 510 violation here elevate form over substance? Does it have implications for commonplace employer decisions to take benefit costs into account when setting wage levels?

4. *Section 510 and ERISA Preemption.* Some courts may be reluctant to find that § 510 applies in order to avoid ERISA preemption of a state law cause of action for wrongful discharge. See, e.g., King v. Marriott Int'l, Inc., 337 F.3d 421 (4th Cir. 2003) (holding that intra-company complaints does not qualify as an "inquiry or proceeding" under § 510, and thus allowing state law claim to proceed). On retaliation issues, see Chapter 10 supra; on ERISA preemption, see 1172–85 infra.

Part Six

ISSUES OF PROCEDURAL
DESIGN

Chapter Seventeen

PROCEDURAL AND REMEDIAL ISSUES

A. INTRODUCTION

Lawyers representing plaintiffs in employment cases must consider which laws will form the basis of their claims, in which courts or other fora to assert their claims, whether to bring a case on behalf of individual claimants or, rather, that of a larger group, and what will be the range of relief open to them if they prove a violation. Defense counsel also must be prepared to evaluate and possibly challenge the choices made by plaintiff counsel.

Note on Range of Procedural Choice

Designing a regulatory scheme requires making difficult policy choices in the resolution of procedural, as well as substantive, issues.

1. Private Suit or Agency Enforcement?

Perhaps the most important procedural design decision is the choice of enforcement vehicle: whether to rely exclusively on the private suit or on a specialized administrative agency, or to utilize some mixture of both.

The private-suit model of enforcement offers several distinct advantages. First, because private suits draw from the general resources of the court system, regulatory norms can be promulgated without special allocation of scarce budgetary resources for enforcement. Second, at least where legal assistance is available, claimants enjoy direct access to the remedial scheme. Third, where courts are receptive to the substantive claims, they may be quite vigorous enforcement agents; where jury trials are afforded, there also may be a distinctly pro-claimant tilt.

Each of these advantages, however, has its corresponding disadvantages. First, congestion in the courts may lead to multiple-year delay in the redress of wrongs. Second, even where attorney's fees are recoverable by successful claimants, the availability of legal counsel may be problematic. Third, courts may not be very good at coherent development of the subsidiary policy decisions that have to be made under any statutory scheme. Judicial agreement on particular issues also may be long in coming. Moreover, private suits usually turn not on legal issues of general importance but on fact-specific disputes. Judges who have too steady a diet of such cases may develop undesirable predispositions toward them. This in turn may lead to distortions in the actual development of the statutory scheme. Also, even judges free of such predispositions do not generally have any expertise with most regulatory statutes; their answers to novel, difficult questions may resolve a particular dispute, but often without a full appreciation of competing considerations or of the effect of their ruling on the statute as a whole.

These difficulties can generally be avoided by administrative enforcement—if the administrative agency is given sufficient resources, develops a good esprit de corps, is relatively free from political influences, and commands respect in the courts by the quality of its work. This ideal is, however, not always achieved. Reliance on agencies can result in underenforcement of the statute, either because of budgetary cutbacks, poor internal management, or the hostility of new administrations to the goals of the statutory scheme. It can also result in overenforcement, when political criteria rather than fidelity to the statutory design explain staffing and enforcement decisions.

Examples of exclusive reliance on private suits include the state-law private tort and contract actions and suits under 42 U.S.C.§ 1981 and 1983. For the private tort/contract claimant or § 1981 plaintiff, there are no administrative exhaustion requirements; access to the courts requires only the securing of counsel. The action is often one for damages, and there is a right to a jury trial for disputed issues of fact. Broad-based, systemic litigation is possible with the advent of the modern class action. Judicial opinions elaborate regulatory norms in the course of litigation of private wrongs.

The National Labor Relations Act of 1935 presents a good example of exclusive reliance on an administrative agency. A worker seeking union representation or complaining of an unfair labor practice must secure the assistance of the NLRB. Representation proceedings take place solely on the administrative level; a decision of the director of a regional office of the NLRB on matters of representation unit determination or voter eligibility may be reviewed by the five-member Board in Washington, D.C., but there is no direct recourse to the courts. See Michael C. Harper, The Case for Limiting Judicial Review of Labor Board Certification Decisions, 55 Geo. Wash.L.Rev. 262 (1987). Unfair labor practice proceedings occur only upon the issuance of a complaint by the General Counsel; with the exception of secondary boycott violations, there is no private right of action to secure relief from an alleged unfair labor practice. Once a complaint issues, an adjudicatory proceeding occurs before an administrative law judge. At this proceeding, an agent of the NLRB represents the Government; private charging parties may only intervene to supplement the Board's presentation. The decision of the administrative law judge may be reviewed by the Board in Washington, D.C. Persons aggrieved by the Board's order may also secure judicial review in the Courts of Appeals. That review is, however, of an appellate nature; the statute and administrative law principles require deference to agency findings of fact and policy decisions.

The nondiscrimination and affirmative action obligations under government contracts, particularly in connection with Executive Order 11246 and § 503 of the Rehabilitation Act, are also enforced through the agency model. Here, exclusive enforcement responsibility is lodged with the Office of Federal Contract Compliance Programs (OFCCP) of the Department of Labor. There is no private right of action, see, e.g., Cohen v. Illinois Institute of Technology, 524 F.2d 818 (7th Cir.1975) (Executive Order 11246); Simpson v. Reynolds Metals Co., 629 F.2d 1226 (7th Cir.1980) (§ 503), although some courts have permitted private parties to sue, in the nature of mandamus, to compel OFCCP enforcement of nondiscretionary duties, see, e.g., Legal Aid Soc'y of Alameda County v. Brennan, 608 F.2d 1319 (9th Cir.1979), and as third-party beneficiaries of affirmative action agreements, see, e.g., Jones v. Local 520, International Union of Operating Engineers, 603 F.2d 664 (7th Cir.1979).

Title VII, ADEA, ADA (§ 107 of the latter incorporates Title VII procedures), by contrast, are "hybrid regulatory systems," borrowing features from both the private suit and administrative enforcement models. Claimants ultimately have a private right of action in state or federal courts, and the courts have been the principal formulators of the substantive policy choices left open by the statutes. Unlike the pure private-suit model, however, Title VII, ADEA and ADA also give administrative processes a prominent role. Claimants must first file charges with the EEOC. (Charges under ADEA were processed by the Department of Labor until July 1, 1979, when the EEOC was given compliance responsibility under Reorganization Plan No. 1 of 1978, 43 Fed.Reg. 19,807.) The purpose of such filings is to take advantage of the agency's investigative capacity and to permit an opportunity for informal conciliation. Prior to the 1972 amendments to Title VII, the EEOC did not have authority to file suit, although the Justice Department could institute "pattern and practice" litigation under § 707 of Title VII. Now, the EEOC can file suits on behalf of individuals under § 706 and systemic actions under § 707. It enjoys comparable authority under ADEA and ADA; the Justice Department retains authority for "pattern and practice" suits against state and local government employers. Issues arising under both private-and EEOC-initiated litigation are discussed below in this chapter.

Yet another approach is suggested by statutes like the FLSA, which authorize a private cause of action without any requirement of resort to administrative remedies, but provide that a government enforcement suit in the courts, once it has been filed, displaces the opportunity to bring a private suit.

2. *Nature of the Adjudicative Tribunal*

In addition to the choice of enforcement vehicle, there are several other important procedural design questions. One is the nature of the adjudicative tribunal. Policymakers have to decide, first, whether to utilize the general court system or some other process. Typically, use of the private-suit model entails reliance on the civil courts. This need not always be so. The European countries which have enacted "unjust dismissal" legislation have also provided for special labor courts to adjudicate privately-initiated and privately-prosecuted claims. In our country, unemployment compensation and workers' compensation claims are initiated by private claimants but processed in an administrative adjudication. Many state civil rights laws, unlike Title VII, ADEA and ADA, provide a choice between private suit in the courts and an administrative adjudication before a civil rights commission.

Even if the civil courts are used, policymakers have to decide whether judges or juries will be the trier of fact. Jury trials are common in actions seeking damages under the various contract and tort theories explored earlier in this book. Under the 1991 Civil Rights Act, jury trials are available for claims for compensatory or punitive damages resulting from intentional discrimination in violation of Title VII, ADA and the Rehabilitation Act of 1973. Generally, the lower courts have held that a jury trial is available for actions seeking compensatory damages under § 1981.

The ADEA and the Equal Pay Act differ from Title VII (and ADA) because these statutes incorporate (to some extent) the FLSA's enforcement provisions. In Lorillard v. Pons, 434 U.S. 575, 98 S.Ct. 866, 55 L.Ed.2d 40 (1978), the Supreme Court held that Congress's decision to utilize FLSA procedures required that a private action for unpaid wages under ADEA be treated the same as a jury-tried action for unpaid wages under § 16(b) of FLSA. Congress in 1978 amended § 7(c) of ADEA, 29 U.S.C. § 626(c)(2), to expressly provide for a right to a jury trial in private suits "regardless of whether equitable relief is sought by any party in such action." A private EPA action for unpaid wages is similarly likened to a FLSA § 16(b) action. Although EEOC actions under FLSA § 17 are viewed as bench-tried actions to redress a public offense even where unpaid wages are sought in addition to equitable relief, see *Lorillard,* 434 U.S. at 580 n. 7, 98 S.Ct. at 870 n. 7, it remains unresolved whether EEOC-maintained ADEA or EPA actions on behalf of individuals under FLSA § 16(c) are triable before a jury.

Jury trials are not available for Title VII disparate-impact claims or failure of reasonable-accommodation claims under the ADA or § 501 of the Rehabilitation Act (where a good faith effort to accommodate has been made). However, claimants may append jury-triable claims under Title VII, ADA, ADEA, EPA, § 1981 or state laws, in order to obtain a jury trial over issues of fact common to the non-jury Title VII (or ADA) claim. See also Lytle v. Household Mfg., Inc., 494 U.S. 545, 110 S.Ct. 1331, 108 L.Ed.2d 504 (1990) (plaintiffs securing a reversal on appeal of an erroneous dismissal of their § 1981 claim have a right to a jury trial on that claim free of any issue preclusive effect inhering in the adjudication of their Title VII claim before an appeal could be taken).

3. *Remedies*

a. *Reinstatement and Backpay*

Although the matter is rarely litigated, reinstatement is generally not awarded for violations of state contract and tort law; the relief typically sought is damages. By contrast, statutory schemes typically provide for reinstatement and backpay. The Supreme Court has made clear that in Title VII cases successful plaintiffs are normally entitled to reinstatement, backpay, and restoration of lost seniority and benefits. Such "make whole" relief is presumptively available and may be denied only on grounds which, if generally applied, would not undermine the statute. See Franks v. Bowman Transp. Co., 424 U.S. 747, 96 S.Ct. 1251, 47 L.Ed.2d 444 (1976); Albemarle Paper Co. v. Moody, 422 U.S. 405, 95 S.Ct. 2362, 45 L.Ed.2d 280 (1975). Title VII courts have awarded a partnership in a major accounting firm, see Hopkins v. Price Waterhouse, 920 F.2d 967 (D.C.Cir.1990); Ezold v. Wolf, Block, etc., 758 F.Supp. 303 (E.D.Pa.1991), and have sometimes "bumped" an innocent incumbent in a unique high-level government position, even in the absence of employer recalcitrance, see Lander v. Lujan, 888 F.2d 153 (D.C.Cir.1989).

Given its make-whole rationale, relief under Title VII usually has included all compensation, including fringe benefits, the employee would have received in the absence of discrimination. See, e.g., Neiman–Marcus Group v. Dworkin, 919 F.2d 368 (5th Cir.1990) (sustaining $800,000 award despite higher pay with new employer because jury could assign such value to lost nonsalary benefits with old employer). Plaintiff has a duty to mitigate under Title VII, but need not accept a significant demotion or change of salary. See, e.g., Carrero v. N.Y.C. Housing Authority, 668 F.Supp. 196, 204 (S.D.N.Y.1987), affirmed in part & reversed on other grounds, 890 F.2d 569, 580 (2d Cir.1989). "A wrongfully discharged employee is required to make only a reasonable effort to obtain interim employment, and is not held to the highest standard of diligence." NLRB v. IBEW, Local Union 112, 992 F.2d 990 (9th Cir.1993). The defendant, moreover, has the burden of proving a failure to mitigate. See, e.g., Padilla v. Metro–North Commuter R.R., 92 F.3d 117 (2d Cir.1996). See also Chris Erath, Two Myths Exposed: Why Losses Don't Go On Forever and Why Plaintiffs Should Find Employment (National Econ. Res. Associates, Oct. 12, 1995).

Backpay terminates when a plaintiff begins new employment at a salary he or she would have earned in the previous job. See EEOC v. Delight Wholesale Co., 973 F.2d 664, 670 (8th Cir.1992) (termination from subsequent employment does not toll backpay period if discharge is due to unreasonable working conditions). Under Ford Motor Co. v. EEOC, 458 U.S. 219, 102 S.Ct. 3057, 73 L.Ed.2d 721 (1982), only unconditional offers of reinstatement toll backpay liability. See, e.g., Lesko v. Clark Publr. Servs., 904 F.Supp. 415 (M.D. Pa. 1995).

b. "Frontpay"

Although Title VII and ADEA awards normally include reinstatement, in some cases this remedy may be impracticable because there is no vacancy or because of frictions resulting from the litigation. In such cases, courts will award "front pay" in lieu of reinstatement. See, e.g., McNeil v. Economics Laboratory, Inc., 800 F.2d 111 (7th Cir.1986).

In Pollard v. E.I. du Pont de Nemours & Co., 532 U.S. 843, 121 S.Ct. 1946, 150 L.Ed.2d 62 (2001), the Court held that front pay is an instance of equitable relief authorized by § 706(g), and is not an element of compensatory damages under § 1981a and hence not subject to the damages "caps" in § 1981a(b)(3) of the 1991 Civil Rights Act. The Court did not expressly address whether the front pay determination is made by a judge or jury, but the clear implication is that equitable relief would be bench tried; a jury convened to hear damages questions could sit in an advisory capacity on front pay. For this issue in the ADEA context, see Chace v. Champion Spark Plug Co., 725 F.Supp. 868 (D.Md.1989) (collecting authorities).

How far into the future may the "frontpay" award extend? At what point does the award become impermissibly speculative? See, e.g., *Padilla, supra,* at 126 (sustaining award to plaintiff in his 40s, "in the amount of the difference between his salary as a train dispatcher and the salary paid to the superintendent of train operations until he reaches the age of 67"); Kelley v. Airborne Freight Corp., 140 F.3d 335, 355–56 (1st Cir.1998) (sustaining $1 million award because plaintiff was six years away from becoming fully vested in pension plan). Can courts assume that plaintiffs would have retired at the "normal" retirement age of 65? See Curtis v. Electronics & Space Corp., 113 F.3d 1498, 1503 (8th Cir.1997) (plaintiff's testimony that she would have worked until 70 and that she had few resources left when her husband died, held sufficient).

c. Pre- and Postjudgment Interest

The lower courts have held that an award of prejudgment interest, although routinely made, is discretionary. See, e.g., Hunter v. Allis–Chalmers Corp., 797 F.2d 1417 (7th Cir.1986)—a position endorsed (in dicta) in Loeffler v. Frank, 486 U.S. 549, 108 S.Ct. 1965, 100 L.Ed.2d 549 (1988), and codified at 42 U.S.C. § 2000e–16(d) ("the same interest to compensate for delay in payment shall be available as in cases involving nonpublic parties"). Some courts have referred to analogous practice under the federal labor laws, see Florida Steel Corp., 231 N.L.R.B. 651 (1977); New Horizons for the Retarded, Inc., 283 N.L.R.B. No. 181 (1987), in employing IRS rates for underpayment of taxes. See, e.g., EEOC v. Guardian Pools, Inc., 828 F.2d 1507, 1512 (11th Cir.1987). Postjudgment interest must be granted under 28 U.S.C. § 1961, on the assumption that a backpay award is a "money judgment," and is also available against federal sector employers (as a result of the 1991 amendments). Prejudgment interest also raises questions of sovereign immunity in suits against federal sector employers, see Library of Congress v. Shaw, 478 U.S. 310, 106 S.Ct. 2957, 92 L.Ed.2d 250 (1986), overruled at 42 U.S.C. § 2000e–16(d).

Some decisions hold that in ADEA cases prejudgment interest on backpay awards is not available because the cost of delay is already accounted for in the provision of liquidated damages. See Shea v. Galaxie Lumber & Construction Co., Ltd., 152 F.3d 729, 733–34 (7th Cir.1998); McCann v. Texas City Refining, Inc., 984 F.2d 667 (5th Cir. 1993); Linn v. Andover Newton Theological School, Inc., 874 F.2d 1 (1st Cir.1989); but see Starceski v. Westinghouse Electric Corp., 54 F.3d 1089, 1099–1100 (3d Cir.1995) (liquidated damages are "punitive" under Trans World Airlines, Inc. v. Thurston, 469 U.S. 111, 105 S.Ct. 613, 83 L.Ed.2d 523 (1985), and do not foreclose prejudgment interest).

d. Compensatory Damages

One important question is whether the statute provides for recovery of compensatory damages to redress injuries such as mental distress, humiliation, deprivation of a civil right or out-of-pocket expenses. The availability of such damages will have a bearing not only on whether there is a jury trial, but also on the practical availability of private counsel under contingency-fee arrangements. Such damages are routinely awarded for state law tort claims.

Most lower courts have held that such awards are not available under ADEA, even in a retaliation case. See, e.g., Flamand v. American International Group, 876 F.Supp. 356 (D.P.R.1994). The Seventh Circuit takes the view that a 1977 amendment to the FLSA authorizes damages awards in FLSA and EPA retaliation cases. See Shea v. Galaxie Lumber & Constr. Co., 152 F.3d 729 (7th Cir.1998); Avitia v. Metropolitan Club of Chicago, Inc., 49 F.3d 1219, 1226 n. 2 (7th Cir.1995).

The 1991 amendments to Title VII authorize recovery of compensatory damages for future pecuniary and nonpecuniary losses (other than "front pay") as well as punitive damages, all of which are subject to certain aggregate monetary limits or "caps" (that are not to be revealed to the jury); these caps, as discussed, do not affect § 706(g) equitable relief. Uncapped compensatory damages are available, however, in most state tort actions, and for § 1981 and § 1983 claims. See Sullivan v. Little Hunting Park, Inc., 396 U.S. 229, 90 S.Ct. 400, 24 L.Ed.2d 386 (1969) (damages under 42 U.S.C. § 1982, which has a common origin with § 1981 in the Civil Rights Act of 1866); Carey v. Piphus, 435 U.S. 247, 98 S.Ct. 1042, 55 L.Ed.2d 252 (1978) (damages for due process violation under § 1983).

Under Commissioner v. Schleier, 515 U.S. 323, 115 S.Ct. 2159, 132 L.Ed.2d 294 (1995), monies received in settlement of an ADEA liquidated-damages claim are taxable. See Gray v. Commissioner of Internal Revenue, 104 F.3d 1226 (10th Cir.1997) (back- and front-pay awards are not excludable from gross income). This result is not likely to change for compensatory damages awards under Title VII, for § 104(a) of the Internal Revenue Code (IRC) provides that "emotional distress shall not be treated as a physical injury or physical sickness" for purposes of the IRC exclusion from income of damages "on account of personal physical injuries or physical sickness," 26 U.S.C. § 104(a).

e. *Punitive Damages*

Another important question is whether the statute permits recovery of punitive damages or other remedies of a predominantly deterrent rather than compensatory nature. Such awards are generally available under state tort law and for claims under §§ 1981 and 1983. See Johnson v. Railway Express Agency, Inc., 421 U.S. 454, 460, 95 S.Ct. 1716, 1720, 44 L.Ed.2d 295 (1975) (punitive damages are available for § 1981 violations "under certain circumstances"); Smith v. Wade, 461 U.S. 30, 56, 103 S.Ct. 1625, 1640, 75 L.Ed.2d 632 (1983) (punitive damages for § 1983 violations require a showing of "evil motive or intent, or * * * reckless or callous indifference to the [plaintiff's] federally protected rights" and that such conduct warrants a punitive award).

Although punitive damages are not available in ADEA actions, the statute authorizes an award of liquidated damages (doubling the unpaid wages due) for "willful" violations. The Supreme Court in Trans World Airlines v. Thurston, 469 U.S. 111, 126, 105 S.Ct. 613, 624, 83 L.Ed.2d 523 (1985), held that such an award serves a punitive purpose and is available only where the employer "knew or showed reckless disregard ... whether its conduct was prohibited by the ADEA." FLSA and EPA claimants may seek liquidated damages under § 16 of the FLSA, subject to an employer's good-faith defense under the Portal-to-Portal Act, as incorporated into the FLSA,

29 U.S.C. § 260. As noted, "capped" punitive damages are now available for intentional discrimination claims under Title VII, ADA and the Rehabilitation Act.

On the issue of employer liability for punitive damages under the 1991 Civil Rights Act, see Kolstad v. American Dental Assn., 527 U.S. 526, 119 S.Ct. 2118, 144 L.Ed.2d 494 (1999), pp. 378–85 supra; the analogous issue under state law is discussed in note 6, p. 387 supra.

B. THE ROLE OF THE ADMINISTRATIVE AGENCY

1. *Nature of Delegated Administrative Authority*

GENERAL ELECTRIC CO. v. GILBERT
Supreme Court of the United States, 1976.
429 U.S. 125, 97 S.Ct. 401, 50 L.Ed.2d 343.

JUSTICE REHNQUIST delivered the opinion for the Court.

We are told, however, that [our] this analysis of the congressional purpose underlying Title VII is inconsistent with the guidelines of the EEOC, which, it is asserted, are entitled to "great deference" in the construction of the Act, *Griggs* [*v. Duke Power Co.*, 401 U.S. 424, 433–34, 91 S.Ct. 849, 854–55, 28 L.Ed.2d 158 (1 971)]; *Phillips v. Martin Marietta Corp.*, 400 U.S. 542, 545, 91 S.Ct. 496, 498, 27 L.Ed.2d 613 (1971) (Marshall, J., concurring). * * *

In evaluating this contention it should first be noted that Congress, in enacting Title VII, did not confer upon the EEOC authority to promulgate rules or regulations pursuant to that Title. *Albemarle Paper Co. v. Moody,* 422 U.S. 405, 431, 95 S.Ct. 2362, 2378, 45 L.Ed.2d 280 (1975).[20] This does not mean that EEOC guidelines are not entitled to consideration in determining legislative intent, see *Albemarle, supra; Griggs v. Duke Power Co., supra,* 401 U.S., at 433–434, 91 S.Ct., at 854–855; *Espinoza v. Farah Mfg. Co.,* 414 U.S. 86, 94, 94 S.Ct. 334, 339, 38 L.Ed.2d 287 (1973). But it does mean that courts properly may accord less weight to such guidelines than to administrative regulations which Congress has declared shall have the force of law, see *Standard Oil Co. v. Johnson,* 316 U.S. 481, 484, 62 S.Ct. 1168, 1169–1170, 86 L.Ed. 1611 (1942), or to regulations which under the enabling statute may themselves supply the basis for imposition of liability, see, e.g., § 23(a). Securities Exchange Act of 1934, 15 U.S.C. § 78w(a). The most comprehensive statement of the role of interpretative rulings such as the EEOC guidelines is found in *Skidmore v. Swift & Co.,* 323 U.S. 134, 140, 65 S.Ct. 161, 164, 89 L.Ed. 124 (1944), where the Court said:

> "We consider that the rulings, interpretations and opinions of the Administrator under this Act, while not controlling upon the

---

20. The EEOC has been given "authority from time to time to issue * * * suitable procedural regulations to carry out the provisions of this subchapter," § 713(a), 42 U.S.C. § 2000e–12(a). No one contends, however, that the above-quoted regulation is procedural in nature or in effect.

courts by reason of their authority, do constitute a body of experience and informed judgment to which courts and litigants may
properly resort for guidance. The weight of such a judgment in a
particular case will depend upon the thoroughness evident in its
consideration, the validity of its reasoning, its consistency with
earlier and later pronouncements, and all those factors which give it
power to persuade, if lacking power to control."

The EEOC guideline in question does not fare well under these
standards. It is not a contemporaneous interpretation of Title VII, since
it was first promulgated eight years after the enactment of that Title.
More importantly, the 1972 guideline flatly contradicts the position
which the agency had enunciated at an earlier date, closer to the
enactment of the governing statute.

Notes and Questions

1. Chevron *Deference* vs. Skidmore *Respect.* Eight years after the
Gilbert decision, the Supreme Court in Chevron U.S.A., Inc. v. Natural
Resources Defense Council, Inc., 467 U.S. 837, 842–43, 104 S.Ct. 2778, 81
L.Ed.2d 694 (1984), announced a strong rule of deference to an agency's
interpretation of its governing statute:

> Where a court reviews an agency's construction of the statute which it
> administers, it is confronted with two questions. First, always, is the
> question whether Congress has directly spoken to the precise question
> at issue. If the intent of Congress is clear, that is the end of the matter,
> for the court, as well as the agency, must give effect to the unambigu-
> ously expressed intent of Congress. If, however, the court determines
> Congress has not directly addressed the precise question at issue, the
> court does not simply impose its own construction on the statute. * * *
> Rather, if the statute is silent or ambiguous with respect to the specific
> issue, the question for the court is whether the agency's answer is based
> on a permissible construction of the statute.

In more recent cases, the Court has indicated that deference to agency
views, in the strong sense used in *Chevron,* is owed only where the agency
itself has exercised Congressionally delegated authority to fashion policy or
law. Where the agency has merely interpreted the statute, the lower level of
deference, or respect, delineated in *Skidmore,* as cited in *Gilbert,* is appropriate. See United States v. Mead Corp., 533 U.S. 218, 121 S.Ct. 2164, 150
L.Ed.2d 292 (2001); Christensen v. Harris County, 529 U.S. 576, 120 S.Ct.
1655, 146 L.Ed.2d 621 (2000); but cf. e.g., Auer v. Robbins, 519 U.S. 452, 117
S.Ct. 905, 137 L.Ed.2d 79 (1997), p. 962 supra (deferring to Department of
Labor interpretative regulations).

In contrast to the Department of Labor, which has substantive rulemaking authority under the FLSA, ERISA and OSHA, but does not always use it,
see, e.g., Freeman v. National Broadcasting Co., 80 F.3d 78 (2d Cir.1996),
the EEOC does not have the authority to issue substantive regulations under
Title VII. It does, however, have such authority with respect to Title I of the
ADA, see Sutton v. United Air Lines, 527 U.S. 471, 119 S.Ct. 2139, 144
L.Ed.2d 450 (1999), supra p. 507, and to ADEA, see Smith v. City of Jackson,

544 U.S. 228, 243, 125 S.Ct. 1536, 161 L.Ed.2d 410 (2005) (Scalia, J., concurring), supra p. 467. In practice, however, the EEOC may receive considerable deference even for its interpretative guidance. The Uniform Guidelines on Employee Selection Procedures, 29 C.F.R. §§ 1607.1–.7, offer an example of a carefully developed set of interpretations jointly promulgated by all of the federal agencies with EEO responsibility, that have significantly influenced judicial decisions, despite the absence of formal substantive rulemaking authority.

2. *Implications of Rejection of NLRA Exclusive Agency Enforcement Model*. In enacting Title VII, Congress deliberately rejected an agency enforcement model patterned after the NLRB. Indeed, until the 1972 amendments, the EEOC lacked authority to bring enforcement actions. Would the Title VII scheme have evolved differently if, like the NLRB, (i) the EEOC enjoyed exclusive enforcement authority; (ii) the agency could determine in the first instance in an administrative proceeding whether the statute had been violated and what the appropriate remedy should be; (iii) its administrative determinations were reviewed by the courts of appeals under a "substantial evidence" standard for findings of fact and a "rational basis" standard for policy determinations; and (iv) its regulations were treated as legislative rather than interpretive rules? Would such a scheme have promoted better public acceptance of Title VII objectives? Would it have led to greater judicial deference to EEOC views? What benefits obtainable under current arrangements would have been lost?

3. *Deference and Distrust*. *Gilbert* reflects an instance in which the Supreme Court refused to pay deference to EEOC views. In other cases, the Court has accepted the agency's position. See, e.g., Clackamas, p. ___ supra; Meritor Savings Bank, FSB v. Vinson, 477 U.S. 57, 106 S.Ct. 2399, 91 L.Ed.2d 49 (1986) (approving for the most part the agency's sexual harassment guidelines, 29 C.F.R. § 1604.11). What factors explain the uneven pattern of judicial deference to EEOC interpretations? What could the agency do to improve this record? Should it, for example, always use the notice-and-public-comment procedures of the APA? Consider also the regulations dealing with employee waiver of ADEA rights, see 29 C.F.R. § 1625.22, where the EEOC engaged in a form of "negotiated" rulemaking with plaintiff and employer groups. See generally Melissa Hart, Skepticism and Expertise: The Supreme Court and the EEOC, 74 Ford. L. Rev. 1937 (2006).

4. *Agency "Safe Harbor" Rules*. Would you recommend that the EEOC make greater use of its "safe harbor" authority under § 713(b)? See Alfred Blumrosen, The Binding Effect of Affirmative Action Guidelines, 1 Labor Lawy. 261 (Spring 1985):

> In Section 713(b), Congress authorized the EEOC to advise employers that if they follow a certain course of action, they will be immune from liability under Title VII. This means that the EEOC can provide employers with defenses which are not spelled out in the statute, even if the EEOC's view of the law is later found to be incorrect. This power, therefore, includes the ability to affect the substantive rights of individuals, employers, and unions. It seems almost self-evident that this is a grant of authority to make "substantive rules." The guidelines must be considered to have the "force of law" in order to implement the

congressional policy of protecting reliance on agency interpretations. This grant of power to the EEOC is limited to defenses. Beyond the Section 713(b) area, the EEOC's authority is limited to issuance of interpretations which receive "deference" but do not have the force of law.

In what particular areas might "safe harbor" guidelines be useful? Recall the Labor Department's use of its administrative exemption authority to encourage employer-sponsors of self-directed defined-contribution plans to provide financial information to plan participants.

5. *Agency Review of Waiver/Settlement Agreements.* Another role for the administrative agency is to ensure that private resolutions do not undermine statutory goals. The Supreme Court has held, for example, that otherwise valid private arbitration agreements do not preclude an EEOC suit on behalf of individuals who themselves were bound to pursue arbitration. EEOC v. Waffle House, Inc., 534 U.S. 279, 122 S.Ct. 754, 151 L.Ed.2d 755 (2002). In the FLSA context, early decisions of the Court held that individual claimants' post-dispute waiver agreements require Department of Labor supervision. See discussion in Runyan v. National Cash Register Corp., 787 F.2d 1039 (6th Cir. 1986).

2. Administrative Filing Requirements

State contract and tort actions can be brought directly without exhausting administrative procedures. State antidiscrimination laws tend to follow the approach of the FLSA in providing an administrative investigation and possible enforcement proceeding as an optional alternative to a private suit. See, e.g., N.Y. Human Rts. L., N.Y. Executive L., § 297. Federal government employees can exercise a somewhat similar choice. See Title VII, 42 U.S.C. § 2000e–16; ADEA, 29 U.S.C. § 633a(b)–(c). By contrast, for employees of private employers and state and local government, the administrative filing requirements of Title VII, ADEA and ADA are prerequisites to bringing a lawsuit.

Note on Administrative Filing Requirements Under Federal Antidiscrimination Laws

1. *De Facto 300–Day Filing Period?*

Although Title VII, ADEA and ADA in terms provide a 180–day period for filing a charge with the EEOC, as a practical matter most claimants have 300 days from the occurrence of the unlawful employment decision to make such a filing. In EEOC v. Commercial Office Products Co., 486 U.S. 107, 108 S.Ct. 1666, 100 L.Ed.2d 96 (1988), the Court effectively extended the filing period to 300 days for claimants living in states with civil rights agencies approved as § 706 deferral agencies. The Court there approved "worksharing" agreements between the EEOC and the state agency whereby charges "filed" with the state agency can be "terminated" for § 706(c) purposes without sacrificing the state agency's authority later to reactivate those charges under state law. In Love v. Pullman Co., 404 U.S. 522, 92 S.Ct. 616, 30 L.Ed.2d 679 (1972), the Court upheld the EEOC's deferral procedure, under which the EEOC itself refers a charge to an appropriate state deferral agency, and then begins its own processing of the charge 60 days later or on termination of the state agency proceeding, whichever occurs first. By treating the EEOC filing as being in a state of "suspended animation" until the expiration of the deferral period, the Court enabled Title VII claimants, who are often unrepresented by counsel, to avoid having to make an independent filing with the state agency.

2. *Judicial Treatment of Statutory Prerequisites to Suit*

a. *Conciliation.* Although one of the EEOC's responsibilities is to attempt informal conciliation with respondents named in an EEOC charge, the lower courts have held that private actions are not blocked by the EEOC's failure to serve notice of the charge on the respondents, see, e.g., Watson v. Gulf & Western Ind., 650 F.2d 990 (9th Cir.1981), or by its failure to attempt informal conciliation, see, e.g., Dent v. St. Louis–San Francisco Ry., 406 F.2d 399 (5th Cir.1969). Courts typically will not dismiss the action but stay proceedings to give the EEOC an opportunity to pursue conciliation. But see EEOC v. Asplundh Tree Expert Company, 340 F.3d 1256 (11th Cir. 2003) (sustaining district court's exercise of discretion to dismiss action and award costs and fees for agency's failure to engage in good faith conciliation by not giving employer notice over 32–month investigation of agency's intent to sue and then "in a flurry of action" issuing a Letter Determination followed by a proposed nationwide Conciliation Agreement, without being open to further discussions once employer retained counsel); EEOC v. Sears, Roebuck & Co., 650 F.2d 14 (2d Cir.1981) (affirming dismissal where EEOC insisted on nationwide conciliation of all of the employer's facilities); cf. Brennan v. Ace Hardware, 495 F.2d 368 (8th Cir.1974) (sustaining dismissal of Secretary's failure to inform employer that case was being referred for review and possible legal action).

Some courts also have declined to allow the EEOC to issue right-to-sue letters prior to expiration of the 180–day period in § 706(f)(1), which may reflect a desire to prod the agency to pursue conciliation. Compare, e.g., Martini v. Federal National Mortgage Assn., 178 F.3d 1336 (D.C. Cir. 1999), with Sims v. Trus Joist MacMillan, 22 F.3d 1059 (11th Cir. 1994).

b. *EEOC "Cause" Determination.* The EEOC plays no screening function. Whereas it must under § 706(b) find "reasonable cause" before it can bring a lawsuit, such a finding is not required for the issuance of a right-to-sue letter authorizing a private suit. See McDonnell Douglas Corp. v. Green, 411 U.S. 792, 798–99, 93 S.Ct. 1817, 1822–23, 36 L.Ed.2d 668 (1973).

In EEOC v. Caterpillar, Inc., 409 F.3d 831 (2005), the Seventh Circuit held that courts do not have authority to review an EEOC's investigation or its probable cause determination. The case involved a challenge to plant-wide sex discrimination at Caterpillar's Aurora, Illinois facility. As Chief Judge Posner explained: "If courts may not limit a suit by the EEOC to claims made in the administrative charge, they likewise have no business limiting that suit to claims that the court finds to be supported by the evidence obtained in the Commission's investigation. The existence of probable cause to sue is generally and in this instance not judicially reviewable." Id. at 833.

c. *Scope of Charge vs. Scope of Suit.* As the quote from *Caterpillar* suggests, the scope of a Title VII–ADA–ADEA lawsuit is only loosely determined by the scope of the charge filed with the EEOC. Although additional parties cannot be named in the suit unless they were the subject of conciliation, and a serious divergence between the scope of the court action and the scope of the agency's investigation will be frowned upon, the scope of the charge itself is not determinative. An influential liberal standard can be found in Sanchez v. Standard Brands, Inc., 431 F.2d 455, 466 (5th Cir.1970):

> [T]he allegations in a judicial complaint filed pursuant to Title VII "may encompass any kind of discrimination like or related to allegations contained in a charge and growing out of such allegation during the pendency of the case before the Commission".... In other words, the "scope" of the judicial complaint is limited to the "scope" of the EEOC investigation which can reasonably be expected to grow out of the charge of discrimination.

In *Sanchez,* the suit added a new basis of discrimination (national origin) and a new incident (discharge) not recited in the charge. Should claimants be able to add entirely new theories of discrimination not recited in their charge? Although many Title VII claimants proceed *pro se,* some are represented by counsel even when filing a charge. Should this liberal approach be available to the counseled claimant? To cases initiated by a Commissioner's charge?

In Edelman v. Lynchburg College, 535 U.S. 106, 122 S.Ct. 1145, 152 L.Ed.2d 188 (2002), the Court upheld an EEOC interpretation that deemed the requirement in § 706(b) that a charge of discrimination be "under oath or affirmation" to be satisfied by a later oath that had been omitted from what otherwise would have been a timely filing under § 706(e)(1).

3. *Tolling of the 180/300 Day Charge–Filing Period*

The Court in McDonnell Douglas v. Green, supra, used the term "jurisdictional prerequisite" in referring to the 180/300 day filing requirements in § 706(c). However, in Zipes v. Trans World Airlines, Inc., 455 U.S. 385, 393, 102 S.Ct. 1127, 1132, 71 L.Ed.2d 234 (1982), the Court stated that the requirement of filing a timely charge "is subject to waiver, estoppel and equitable tolling." The issue in that case was whether a defendant waived its right to object to an untimely filing by failing to plead untimeliness.

Although the Court generally has given little guidance as to the kinds of situations in which tolling should be recognized, it has established at least two rules. First, recourse to the grievance procedure of a collective bargaining agreement will not toll the 180/300 day filing period. Electrical Workers (IUE) Local 790 v. Robbins & Myers, Inc., 429 U.S. 229, 97 S.Ct. 441, 50 L.Ed.2d 427 (1976). Is this decision consistent with the solicitude for lay claimants expressed in *Commercial Office Products* and the Congressional emphasis on informal conciliation? Is it explainable as a means of preserving the independence of the Title VII cause of action, a concept which the Court has developed on other occasions to the advantage of claimants? See Alexander v. Gardner–Denver, 415 U.S. 36, 94 S.Ct. 1011, 39 L.Ed.2d 147 (1974) (resort to grievance machinery in collective bargaining agreement does not foreclose Title VII action), p. 1132 infra; Johnson v. Railway Express, 421 U.S. 454, 95 S.Ct. 1716, 44 L.Ed.2d 295 (1975) (administrative filing requirements do not apply to § 1981 action), p. 1123 infra.

Second, the filing of a class action will toll the filing period for members of the class, so that if the class is not certified, particular class members "may choose to file their own suits or to intervene as plaintiffs in the pending action." Crown, Cork & Seal Co. v. Parker, 462 U.S. 345, 354, 103 S.Ct. 2392, 2398, 76 L.Ed.2d 628 (1983) (addressing requirement to file suit within 90 days of receipt of EEOC "right to sue" letter). See also Tolliver v. Xerox Corp., 918 F.2d 1052 (2d Cir.1990) (approving "single filing" ruling for ADEA representative action, thus permitting separate ADEA suits after decertification of representative action without requiring filing of separate, individually timely administrative charges). At what point does the tolling effect of a class action filing cease: (i) the entry of an order denying class certification or (ii) completion of an appeal from the order denying certification? See Armstrong v. Martin Marietta Corp., 138 F.3d 1374 (11th Cir.1998) (en banc) (adopting the former position).

Does the notion that Title VII filing periods are subject to "waiver, estoppel and equitable tolling" provide some allowance for erroneous filings with other federal agencies? See, e.g., Bethel v. Jefferson, 589 F.2d 631 (D.C.Cir.1978) (filing with OFCCP); but see Stafford v. Muscogee County Bd. of Educ., 688 F.2d 1383 (11th Cir.1982).

4. *90–Day Period for Filing Court Action*

Part of the Court's rationale in *Zipes* was that the administrative filing requirement was not contained in § 706(f)(1), the provision authorizing the private civil action. Section 706(f)(1) does, however, require suit by a person aggrieved within 90 days of receipt of the Commission's "right to sue" letter—a requirement that the Court in *McDonnell Douglas* also termed a "jurisdictional prerequisite." Does the placement of the 90–day period in § 706(f)(1) suggest that this requirement is truly "jurisdictional" and hence not subject to "waiver, estoppel and equitable tolling"? Cf. Irwin v. Department of Veterans Affairs, 498 U.S. 89, 111 S.Ct. 453, 112 L.Ed.2d 435 (1990). Note also that *Crown Cork* recognized tolling of the 90–day period by the filing of a class action.

5. *Statutory Cap on Backpay Liability*

The timing of the filing of a charge will also determine the scope of liability. Under § 706(g) "[b]ack pay liability shall not accrue from a date more than two years prior to the filing of a charge with the Commission." There is no similar provision under the ADEA or the Rehabilitation Act.

Note on EEOC Litigation

The 1972 amendments to Title VII transformed the EEOC from a predominantly investigative and conciliation body to an agency with substantial independent litigation authority. Responsibility for "pattern or practice" litigation under § 707, see, e.g., International Brotherhood of Teamsters v. United States, 431 U.S. 324, 97 S.Ct. 1843, 1865, 52 L.Ed.2d 396 (1977), was transferred from the Justice Department to the Commission. In addition, the EEOC was expressly given the authority to sue on behalf of charging parties under § 706(f)(1). EEOC § 706 actions can be brought on behalf of both individuals and classes. The Supreme Court has held that an EEOC action seeking classwide relief is in the nature of a public action not governed by Rule 23 of the Federal Rules of Civil Procedure, and hence findings rejecting liability will not have binding effects on individual employees. See General Telephone Co. v. EEOC, 446 U.S. 318, 100 S.Ct. 1698, 64 L.Ed.2d 319 (1980). The Court also has ruled that the EEOC may seek both prospective and victim-specific relief on behalf of individual employees who have entered into otherwise valid arbitration agreements that would require arbitration of their individual claims were they to bring suit on their own. See EEOC v. Waffle House, Inc., 534 U.S. 279, 122 S.Ct. 754, 151 L.Ed.2d 755 (2002). Moreover, the lower courts have held that settlements with individual charging parties do not moot the EEOC's right of action to seek injunctive relief. See, e.g., EEOC v. United Parcel Service, 860 F.2d 372 (10th Cir.1988); EEOC v. Goodyear Aerospace Corp., 813 F.2d 1539 (9th Cir.1987).

Under § 706(b), members of the Commission may file charges that form the basis of an EEOC suit under § 706(f)(1) or § 707. In EEOC v. Shell Oil Co., 466 U.S. 54, 104 S.Ct. 1621, 80 L.Ed.2d 41 (1984), the Court sustained an EEOC subpoena issued in connection with a Commissioner's "pattern or practice" charge that did not identify victims of discrimination or the precise manner in which they were injured. The Court did require that—

> Insofar as he is able, the Commissioner should identify the groups of persons that he has reason to believe have been discriminated against, the categories of employment positions from which they have been excluded, the methods by which the discrimination may have been effected, and the periods of time in which he suspects the discriminations to have been practiced.

Id. at 73, 104 S.Ct. at 1633.

Under § 706(f)(1), an EEOC suit against a respondent named in a charge cuts off the charging party's right to bring an action, but the charging party has a statutory right to intervene. Similarly, an EEOC suit on behalf of a charging party under § 7(c)(1) of ADEA "terminates" the charging party's right of action. See also EEOC v. United States Steel Corp., 921 F.2d 489 (3d Cir.1990) (discussion of doctrine of "representative claim preclusion"). Can the EEOC file an independent ADEA action on behalf of an individual who has already brought suit? See EEOC v. Wackenhut Corp., 939 F.2d 241 (5th Cir.1991).

EEOC subpoena authority can also help private charging parties effectively obtain far-reaching discovery of firm practices. See EEOC v. Morgan Stanley & Co., Inc., 1999 WL 756206, Civ. Action M 18–304 (DLC) (S.D.N.Y. 1999).

C. STATUTES OF LIMITATIONS

1. *Range of Limitations Periods*

Congress has not provided a traditional statute of limitations for claims under Title VII, ADA or ADEA. A suit must be brought within 90 days of the EEOC's issuance of a right-to-sue letter, but otherwise there is no requirement that a suit be brought within a certain period of time from the occurrence of the violation. In the context of EEOC suits, the Supreme Court held in Occidental Life Insurance Co. v. EEOC, 432 U.S. 355, 97 S.Ct. 2447, 53 L.Ed.2d 402 (1977), that while the agency is free of any federal or state statute of limitations, it is subject to the unreasonable-delay and prejudice restraints of the doctrine of laches. Compare, e.g., EEOC v. Alioto Fish Co., 623 F.2d 86 (9th Cir. 1980) (finding prejudice in 62–month delay where key witnesses for the employer had retired or were deceased), with EEOC v. Great Atlantic & Pacific Tea Co., 735 F.2d 69 (3d Cir.1984) (nine-year delay held excusable).

Under § 706(f)(1), a Title VII claimant may request a right-to-sue letter from the EEOC 180 days after filing a charge. Should a claimant who awaits the completion of a multi-year EEOC investigation and conciliation, before making such a request, ever be barred from suit by laches? See, e.g., Cleveland Newspaper Guild, Local 1 v. Plain Dealer Publishing Co., 839 F.2d 1147 (6th Cir.1988) (en banc).

Congress has provided a statute of limitations for FLSA claims: a two-year period for filing suit, extended for an additional year for "willful" violations by § 6 of the 1947 Portal-to-Portal Act, 29 U.S.C. § 255(a). See McLaughlin v. Richland Shoe Co., 486 U.S. 128, 108 S.Ct. 1677, 100 L.Ed.2d 115 (1988). In addition, some state wage-and-hour laws, like New York's provide a limitations period as long as six years, see N.Y. Labor L. § 663.

Initially, Congress utilized the FLSA limitations system for ADEA claims. Because of EEOC backlogs during the 1980s, ADEA claimants awaiting the outcome of the administrative process risked having their civil actions time-barred by the limitations period. The 1991 Civil Rights Act (§ 115) discarded the FLSA-based limitations period, and ADEA claimants, like Title VII (and ADA) claimants, face only the 180/300 day filing requirements and the same 90–day period (from receipt of the EEOC's right-to-sue letter) within which to file suit. However, unlike Title VII (and ADA) claimants, individuals with ADEA claims are not expressly subject to the same 2–year limit on pre-charge backpay liability.

In 1990 Congress enacted a default four-year statute of limitations for actions arising under federal statutes enacted after December 1, 1990. See 28 U.S.C. § 1658(a). This statute posed a special issue for § 1981, which like § 1983, does not contain a statute of limitations, but whose scope was expanded by amendments included in the Civil Rights Act of 1991. In Goodman v. Lukens Steel Co., 482 U.S. 656, 107 S.Ct. 2617, 96 L.Ed.2d 572 (1987), before the passage of § 1658, the Court had held that the courts should apply "the most appropriate or analogous state statute of limitations" to claims based on alleged violations of § 1981. In Jones v. R.R. Donnelley & Sons Co., 541 U.S. 369, 124 S.Ct. 1836, 158 L.Ed.2d 645 (2004), however, the Court held that § 1658's four-year statute of limitations governs any § 1981 cause of action, such as those against racial harassment, made possible by the 1991 amendments' expansion of § 1981's scope.

For other federal statutes affecting the employment area, the Court has heeded the general directive of 42 U.S.C. § 1988, which requires resort to "not inconsistent" state laws to fill in gaps in the federal scheme. The Court in Wilson v. Garcia, 471 U.S. 261, 105 S.Ct. 1938, 85 L.Ed.2d 254 (1985), held that the appropriate state statute of limitations for § 1983 claims was the statute for personal injury actions. In states having statutes of limitations for enumerated intentional torts and a residual statute for all other personal injury actions, the residual or general personal injury statute applies. See Owens v. Okure, 488 U.S. 235, 109 S.Ct. 573, 102 L.Ed.2d 594 (1989). The residual statute at issue in *Owens* provided for a three-year period. The Court left open whether a residual statute providing a shorter period would be "inconsistent with federal interests." 109 S.Ct. at 582 n. 13.

2. *Timing of Violation*

Perhaps the most important question in applying a statute of limitations or administrative filing requirement is determining when a violation has commenced. The two decisions that follow deal expressly with the running of the charge-filing period under Title VII, but the principles developed therein have general applicability to the timing of violations triggering the running of statutes of limitations.

NATIONAL R.R. PASSENGER CORP. v. MORGAN

Supreme Court of the United States, 2002.
536 U.S. 101, 122 S.Ct. 2061, 153 L.Ed.2d 106.

Justice Thomas delivered the opinion of the Court

Respondent Abner Morgan, Jr., sued petitioner National Railroad Passenger Corporation (Amtrak) under Title VII of the Civil Rights Act of 1964, 78 Stat. 253, as amended, 42 U.S.C. §§ 2000e et seq. (1994 ed. and Supp.V), alleging that he had been subjected to discrete discriminatory and retaliatory acts and had experienced a racially hostile work environment throughout his employment. Section 2000e–5(e)(1) (1994 ed.) requires that a Title VII plaintiff file a charge with the Equal Employment Opportunity Commission (EEOC) either 180 or 300 days "after the alleged unlawful employment practice occurred." We consider whether, and under what circumstances, a Title VII plaintiff may file suit on events that fall outside this statutory time period.

* * *

I

On February 27, 1995, Abner J. Morgan, Jr., a black male, filed a charge of discrimination and retaliation against Amtrak with the EEOC and cross-filed with the California Department of Fair Employment and Housing. Morgan alleged that during the time period that he worked for Amtrak he was "consistently harassed and disciplined more harshly than other employees on account of his race." The EEOC issued a "Notice of Right to Sue" on July 3, 1996, and Morgan filed this lawsuit on October 2, 1996. While some of the allegedly discriminatory acts about which Morgan complained occurred within 300 days of the time that he filed his charge with the EEOC, many took place prior to that time period.

Amtrak filed a motion, arguing, among other things, that it was entitled to summary judgment on all incidents that occurred more than 300 days before the filing of Morgan's EEOC charge. The District Court granted summary judgment in part to Amtrak, holding that the company could not be liable for conduct occurring before May 3, 1994, because that conduct fell outside of the 300–day filing period. * * *

Morgan appealed. The United States Court of Appeals for the Ninth Circuit reversed, relying on its previous articulation of the continuing violation doctrine, which "allows courts to consider conduct that would ordinarily be time barred 'as long as the untimely incidents represent an ongoing unlawful employment practice.' " * * *

II

* * *

[*Eds.* The Court discusses its prior decisions in Delaware State College v. Ricks, 449 U.S. 250, 101 S.Ct. 498, 66 L.Ed.2d 431 (1980), and United Air Lines, Inc. v. Evans, 431 U.S. 553, 97 S.Ct. 1885, 52 L.Ed.2d 571 (1977).] We derive several principles from these cases. First, discrete discriminatory acts are not actionable if time barred, even when they are related to acts alleged in timely filed charges. Each discrete discriminatory act starts a new clock for filing charges alleging that act. The charge, therefore, must be filed within the 180– or 300–day time period after the discrete discriminatory act occurred. The existence of past acts and the employee's prior knowledge of their occurrence, however, does not bar employees from filing charges about related discrete acts so long as the acts are independently discriminatory and charges addressing those acts are themselves timely filed. Nor does the statute bar an employee from using the prior acts as background evidence in support of a timely claim.

* * *

Discrete acts such as termination, failure to promote, denial of transfer, or refusal to hire are easy to identify. Each incident of discrimination and each retaliatory adverse employment decision constitutes a separate actionable "unlawful employment practice." Morgan can only file a charge to cover discrete acts that "occurred" within the appropriate time period.[7] While Morgan alleged that he suffered from numerous discriminatory and retaliatory acts from the date that he was hired through March 3, 1995, the date that he was fired, only incidents that took place within the timely filing period are actionable. Because Morgan first filed his charge with an appropriate state agency, only those acts that occurred 300 days before February 27, 1995, the day that Morgan filed his charge, are actionable. During that time period, Morgan contends that he was wrongfully suspended and charged with a violation of

---

7. * * * There may be circumstances where it will be difficult to determine when the time period should begin to run. One issue that may arise in such circumstances is whether the time begins to run when the injury occurs as opposed to when the injury reasonably should have been discovered. But this case presents no occasion to resolve that issue.

Amtrak's "Rule L" for insubordination while failing to complete work assigned to him, denied training, and falsely accused of threatening a manager. All prior discrete discriminatory acts are untimely filed and no longer actionable. [9]

B

Hostile environment claims are different in kind from discrete acts. Their very nature involves repeated conduct. See 1 B. Lindemann & P. Grossman, Employment Discrimination Law 348–349 (3d ed. 1996) (hereinafter Lindemann) ("The repeated nature of the harassment or its intensity constitutes evidence that management knew or should have known of its existence"). The "unlawful employment practice" therefore cannot be said to occur on any particular day. It occurs over a series of days or perhaps years and, in direct contrast to discrete acts, a single act of harassment may not be actionable on its own. See *Harris v. Forklift Systems, Inc.*, 510 U.S. 17, 21, 126 L.Ed.2d 295, 114 S.Ct. 367 (1993) ("As we pointed out in *Meritor* [*Savings Bank, FSB v. Vinson*, 477 U.S. 57, 67, 91 L.Ed. 2d 49, 106 S.Ct. 2399 (1986)], 'mere utterance of an . . . epithet which engenders offensive feelings in a employee,' ibid. (internal quotation marks omitted) does not sufficiently affect the conditions of employment to implicate Title VII"). Such claims are based on the cumulative affect of individual acts.

In determining whether an actionable hostile work environment claim exists, we look to "all the circumstances," including "the frequency of the discriminatory conduct; its severity; whether it is physically threatening or humiliating, or a mere offensive utterance; and whether it unreasonably interferes with an employee's work performance." *Id.*, at 23. To assess whether a court may, for the purposes of determining liability, review all such conduct, including those acts that occur outside the filing period, we again look to the statute. It provides that a charge must be filed within 180 or 300 days "after the alleged unlawful employment practice occurred." A hostile work environment claim is comprised of a series of separate acts that collectively constitute one "unlawful employment practice." 42 U.S.C. § 2000e–5(e)(1). The timely filing provision only requires that a Title VII plaintiff file a charge within a certain number of days after the unlawful practice happened. It does not matter, for purposes of the statute, that some of the component acts of the hostile work environment fall outside the statutory time period. Provided that an act contributing to the claim occurs within the filing period, the entire time period of the hostile environment may be considered by a court for the purposes of determining liability.

That act need not, however, be the last act. As long as the employer has engaged in enough activity to make out an actionable hostile environment claim, an unlawful employment practice has "occurred," even if it is still occurring. Subsequent events, however, may still be part

---

9. We have no occasion here to consider the timely filing question with respect to "pattern-or-practice" claims brought by private litigants as none are at issue here.

of the one hostile work environment claim and a charge may be filed at a later date and still encompass the whole.

It is precisely because the entire hostile work environment encompasses a single unlawful employment practice that we do not hold, as have some of the Circuits, that the plaintiff may not base a suit on individual acts that occurred outside the statute of limitations unless it would have been unreasonable to expect the plaintiff to sue before the statute ran on such conduct. The statute does not separate individual acts that are part of the hostile environment claim from the whole for the purposes of timely filing and liability. And the statute does not contain a requirement that the employee file a charge prior to 180 or 300 days "after" the single unlawful practice "occurred." Given, therefore, that the incidents comprising a hostile work environment are part of one unlawful employment practice, the employer may be liable for all acts that are part of this single claim. In order for the charge to be timely, the employee need only file a charge within 180 or 300 days of any act that is part of the hostile work environment.

The following scenarios illustrate our point: (1) Acts on days 1–400 create a hostile work environment. The employee files the charge on day 401. Can the employee recover for that part of the hostile work environment that occurred in the first 100 days? (2) Acts contribute to a hostile environment on days 1–100 and on day 401, but there are no acts between days 101–400. Can the act occurring on day 401 pull the other acts in for the purposes of liability? In truth, all other things being equal, there is little difference between the two scenarios as a hostile environment constitutes one "unlawful employment practice" and it does not matter whether nothing occurred within the intervening 301 days so long as each act is part of the whole. Nor, if sufficient activity occurred by day 100 to make out a claim, does it matter that the employee knows on that day that an actionable claim happened; on day 401 all incidents are still part of the same claim. On the other hand, if an act on day 401 had no relation to the acts between days 1–100, or for some other reason, such as certain intervening action by the employer, was no longer part of the same hostile environment claim, then the employee can not recover for the previous acts, at least not by reference to the day 401 act.

* * *

With respect to Morgan's hostile environment claim, the Court of Appeals concluded that "the pre- and post-limitations period incidents involved the same type of employment actions, occurred relatively frequently, and were perpetrated by the same managers." To support his claims of a hostile environment, Morgan presented evidence from a number of other employees that managers made racial jokes, performed racially derogatory acts, made negative comments regarding the capacity of blacks to be supervisors, and used various racial epithets. Although many of the acts upon which his claim depends occurred outside the 300 day filing period, we cannot say that they are not part of the same actionable hostile environment claim. On this point, we affirm.

C

Our holding does not leave employers defenseless against employees who bring hostile work environment claims that extend over long periods of time. Employers have recourse when a plaintiff unreasonably delays filing a charge. As noted in *Zipes v. Trans World Airlines, Inc.*, 455 U.S. 385 (1982), the filing period is not a jurisdictional prerequisite to filing a Title VII suit. Rather, it is a requirement subject to waiver, estoppel, and equitable tolling "when equity so requires." *Id.*, at 398. These equitable doctrines allow us to honor Title VII's remedial purpose "without negating the particular purpose of the filing requirement, to give prompt notice to the employer." *Ibid.*

* * *

In addition to other equitable defenses, . . . an employer may raise a laches defense, which bars a plaintiff from maintaining a suit if he unreasonably delays in filing a suit and as a result harms the defendant. This defense " 'requires proof of (1) lack of diligence by the party against whom the defense is asserted, and (2) prejudice to the party asserting the defense.' " *Kansas v. Colorado*, 514 U.S. 673, 687, 131 L.Ed.2d 759, 115 S.Ct. 1733 (1995) * * *.

[*Eds.* The partial dissent of Justice O'Connor, joined in different parts by Chief Justice Rehnquist and Justices Scalia, Kennedy and Breyer, is omitted.]

Notes and Questions

1. *Reach of* Morgan's *Holding*? Why did the Court hold that Morgan's hostile environment claim was timely as long as a single act contributing to the hostile environment occurred during the 180/300 day period? Why did the Court go on to hold that not only was Morgan's charge timely filed but that his employer would be liable for "the entire time period of the hostile environment"? Did the Court believe that a hostile environment entails unusual cumulative offenses warranting special treatment, or does *Morgan* auger a more receptive approach generally to a "continuing violations" doctrine?

Why did the Court distinguish challenges to "discrete acts" of discrimination? Consider the Court's examples of such "discrete acts." Are they the same as the "tangible" employment decisions for which an employer is automatically liable under the doctrine pronounced in *Faragher* and *Ellerth*, pp. 360–78 supra?

Does the ruling in *Morgan* promote or undermine the incentives developed by the Supreme Court in *Faragher* and *Ellerth* for employers to establish training and internal complaint processes, and for victims to give prompt notice of their complaints? How do you read the Court's suggestion that "certain intervening action" by the employer may indicate that prior conduct is "no longer part of the same hostile environment claim"? What role, if any, might the doctrine of laches play in hostile environment litigation?

2. *Challenges to Discriminatory Systems*: *Viability of "Continuing Violations" Theory*? Consider footnote 9 in *Morgan*. Prior to *Morgan* and an earlier decision, Lorance v. AT&T Technologies, 490 U.S. 900, 109 S.Ct. 2261, 104 L.Ed.2d 961 (1989), lower courts had invoked a "continuing violations" doctrine to find timely challenges to patterns or systems of discrimination that commenced, but did not cease, before the start of the limitations period. See, e.g., Cox v. United States Gypsum Co., 409 F.2d 289 (7th Cir.1969); Reed v. Lockheed Aircraft Corp., 613 F.2d 757 (9th Cir.1980). In some cases like *Reed,* plaintiffs did not even allege specific incidents of discrimination within the filing period because they attacked an ongoing "system" of discrimination. Are these rulings still good law?

Consider the following explanation from Douglas Laycock, Continuing Violations, Disparate Impact in Compensation, and Other Title VII Issues, 49 L. & Contem.Prob. 53, 59–60 (1986):

> Some refusals to hire are similar to discharges for limitations purposes; some are different. Limitations should run from the date a plaintiff was rejected if he were arguably rejected because of an individualized decision about him or about circumstances at the time of the event. The result should sometimes be different, however, when the plaintiff reapplies later and gets rejected again. If the employer makes a new and independent decision to reject him, there is no reason not to start the limitations period running again. * * * If, instead, the employer rejects a reapplying plaintiff on 'res judicata' grounds, it is certainly plausible to conclude that the plaintiff should not be allowed to renew the old dispute * * *.

> However, if the plaintiff were rejected because of an openly stated and continuing policy, there is strong reason to conclude that the employer committed a new act of discrimination each time he applied that policy. The issue will be the legality of the fixed policy, not the employer's one-time motive * * *. Indeed, I think the violation continues whether or not the plaintiff reapplies * * *.

> Now consider another variation: job assignment claims. A claim that plaintiff was hired as an administrative secretary when she was qualified to be a management trainee looks very much like a claim that her application to be a management trainee was rejected * * *. But a discriminatory job assignment is more than just a refusal to hire. It is equally plausible to find a new violation every day. Every day, she reports to work with the skills to be a management trainee * * *. She is continuously underutilized and underpaid because of her sex.

Is this analysis still viable after *Morgan*?

3. *Congressional Support for "Continuing Violations" Theory*? There is some indication of congressional support for the "continuing violation" theory. The Conference Report to the 1972 amendments to Title VII expressly approved "existing case law which has determined that certain violations are continuing in nature, thereby measuring the running of the required

time period from the last occurrence of the discrimination and not from the first experience." 118 Cong.Rec. 7166, 7167 (1972). Moreover, § 706(g), expressly relied upon by the *Morgan* Court, states that back pay can be recovered for up to two years prior to filing a charge with the EEOC, a period that reaches back more than a year before the start of the 180/300 day filing period. But see Laycock, supra, at 58 (arguing that the two-year back pay clause was not a response to "continuing violation" theory and can be made effective by application to cases in which commencement of the filing period is tolled).

LEDBETTER v. GOODYEAR TIRE & RUBBER CO.

Supreme Court of the United States, 2007.
127 S.Ct. 2162, 167 L.Ed.2d 982.

JUSTICE ALITO delivered the opinion of the Court.

This case calls upon us to apply established precedent in a slightly different context. We have previously held that the time for filing a charge of employment discrimination with the Equal Employment Opportunity Commission (EEOC) begins when the discriminatory act occurs. We have explained that this rule applies to any "discrete act" of discrimination, including discrimination in "termination, failure to promote, denial of transfer, [and] refusal to hire." National Railroad Passenger Corporation v. Morgan, 536 U.S. 101, 114, 122 S. Ct. 2061, 153 L. Ed. 2d 106 (2002). Because a pay-setting decision is a "discrete act," it follows that the period for filing an EEOC charge begins when the act occurs. Petitioner, having abandoned her claim under the Equal Pay Act, asks us to deviate from our prior decisions in order to permit her to assert her claim under Title VII. Petitioner also contends that discrimination in pay is different from other types of employment discrimination and thus should be governed by a different rule. But because a pay-setting decision is a discrete act that occurs at a particular point in time, these arguments must be rejected. We therefore affirm the judgment of the Court of Appeals.

I

Petitioner Lilly Ledbetter (Ledbetter) worked for respondent (Goodyear) at its Gadsden, Alabama, plant from 1979 until 1998. During much of this time, salaried employees at the plant were given or denied raises based on their supervisors' evaluation of their performance. In March 1998, Ledbetter submitted a questionnaire to the EEOC alleging certain acts of sex discrimination, and in July of that year she filed a formal EEOC charge. After taking early retirement in November 1998, Ledbetter commenced this action, in which she asserted, among other claims, a Title VII pay discrimination claim and a claim under the Equal Pay Act of 1963 (EPA), 29 U.S.C. § 206(d).

The District Court granted summary judgment in favor of Goodyear on several of Ledbetter's claims, including her Equal Pay Act claim, but allowed others, including her Title VII pay discrimination claim, to proceed to trial. In support of this latter claim, Ledbetter introduced evidence that during the course of her employment several supervisors had given her poor evaluations because of her sex, that as a result of these evaluations her pay was not increased as much as it would have been if she had been evaluated fairly, and that these past pay decisions continued to affect the amount of her pay throughout her employment. Toward the end of her time with Goodyear, she was being paid significantly less than any of her male colleagues. Goodyear maintained that the evaluations had been nondiscriminatory, but the jury found for Ledbetter and awarded her backpay and damages.

On appeal, Goodyear contended that Ledbetter's pay discrimination claim was time barred with respect to all pay decisions made prior to September 26, 1997—that is, 180 days before the filing of her EEOC questionnaire. And Goodyear argued that no discriminatory act relating to Ledbetter's pay occurred after that date.

The Court of Appeals for the Eleventh Circuit reversed, holding that a Title VII pay discrimination claim cannot be based on any pay decision that occurred prior to the last pay decision that affected the employee's pay during the EEOC charging period. 421 F.3d 1169, 1182–1183 (2005). The Court of Appeals then concluded that there was insufficient evidence to prove that Goodyear had acted with discriminatory intent in making the only two pay decisions that occurred within that time span, namely, a decision made in 1997 to deny Ledbetter a raise and a similar decision made in 1998. Id., at 1186–1187.

* * *

II

* * *

In addressing the issue whether an EEOC charge was filed on time, we have stressed the need to identify with care the specific employment practice that is at issue. *Morgan*, 536 U.S., at 110–111, 122 S. Ct. 2061, 153 L. Ed. 2d 106. Ledbetter points to two different employment practices as possible candidates. Primarily, she urges us to focus on the paychecks that were issued to her during the EEOC charging period (the 180-day period preceding the filing of her EEOC questionnaire), each of which, she contends, was a separate act of discrimination. Alternatively, Ledbetter directs us to the 1998 decision denying her a raise, and she argues that this decision was "unlawful because it carried forward intentionally discriminatory disparities from prior years." Both of these arguments fail because they would require us in effect to jettison the defining element of the legal claim on which her Title VII recovery was based.

Ledbetter asserted disparate treatment, the central element of which is discriminatory intent. * * * However, Ledbetter does not assert that the relevant Goodyear decisionmakers acted with actual discriminatory intent either when they issued her checks during the EEOC charging period or when they denied her a raise in 1998. Rather, she argues that the paychecks were unlawful because they would have been larger if she had been evaluated in a nondiscriminatory manner prior to the EEOC charging period. Similarly, she maintains that the 1998 decision was unlawful because it "carried forward" the effects of prior, uncharged discrimination decisions. In essence, she suggests that it is sufficient that discriminatory acts that occurred prior to the charging period had continuing effects during that period. * * * This argument is squarely foreclosed by our precedents.

In United Air Lines, Inc. v. Evans, 431 U.S. 553, 97 S. Ct. 1885, 52 L. Ed. 2d 571 (1977), we rejected an argument that is basically the same as Ledbetter's. Evans was forced to resign because the airline refused to employ married flight attendants, but she did not file an EEOC charge regarding her termination. Some years later, the airline rehired her but treated her as a new employee for seniority purposes. Id., at 554–555, 97 S. Ct. 1885, 52 L. Ed. 2d 571. Evans then sued, arguing that, while any suit based on the original discrimination was time barred, the airline's refusal to give her credit for her prior service gave "present effect to [its] past illegal act and thereby perpetuated the consequences of forbidden discrimination." Id., at 557, 97 S. Ct. 1885, 52 L. Ed. 2d 571.

We agreed with Evans that the airline's "seniority system [did] indeed have a continuing impact on her pay and fringe benefits," id., at 558, 97 S. Ct. 1885, 52 L. Ed. 2d 571, but we noted that "the critical question [was] whether any present violation existed." Ibid. (emphasis in original). We concluded that the continuing effects of the precharging period discrimination did not make out a present violation. As JUSTICE STEVENS wrote for the Court:

> "United was entitled to treat [Evans' termination] as lawful after respondent failed to file a charge of discrimination within the 90 days then allowed by § 706(d). A discriminatory act which is not made the basis for a timely charge ... is merely an unfortunate event in history which has no present legal consequences." Ibid.

It would be difficult to speak to the point more directly.

Equally instructive is Delaware State College v. Ricks, 449 U.S. 250, 101 S. Ct. 498, 66 L. Ed. 2d 431 (1980), which concerned a college librarian, Ricks, who alleged that he had been discharged because of race. In March 1974, Ricks was denied tenure, but he was given a final, nonrenewable one-year contract that expired on June 30, 1975. Id., at 252–253, 101 S. Ct. 498, 66 L. Ed. 2d 431. Ricks delayed filing a charge with the EEOC until April 1975, id., at 254, 101 S. Ct. 498, 66 L. Ed. 2d 431, but he argued that the EEOC charging period ran from the date of his actual termination rather than from the date when tenure was denied. In rejecting this argument, we recognized that "one of the effects of the denial of tenure," namely, his ultimate termination, "did not occur until later." Id., at 258, 101 S. Ct. 498, 66 L. Ed. 2d 431 (emphasis in original). But because Ricks failed to identify any specific discriminatory act "that continued until, or occurred at the time of, the actual termination of his employment," id., at 257, 101 S. Ct. 498, 66 L. Ed. 2d 431, we held that the EEOC charging period ran from "the time the tenure decision was made and communicated to Ricks," id., at 258, 101 S. Ct. 498, 66 L. Ed. 2d 431.

This same approach dictated the outcome in Lorance v. AT&T Technologies, Inc., 490 U.S. 900, 109 S. Ct. 2261, 104 L. Ed. 2d 961 (1989), which grew out of a change in the way in which seniority was calculated under a collective-bargaining agreement. Before 1979, all employees at the plant in question accrued seniority based simply on years of employment at the plant. In 1979, a new agreement made seniority for workers in the more highly paid (and traditionally male) position of "tester" depend on time spent in that position alone and not in other positions in the plant. Several years later, when female testers were laid off due to low seniority as calculated under the new provision, they filed an EEOC charge alleging that the 1979 scheme had been adopted with discriminatory intent, namely, to protect incumbent male testers when women with substantial plant seniority began to move into the traditionally male tester positions. Id., at 902–903, 109 S. Ct. 2261, 104 L. Ed. 2d 961.

We held that the plaintiffs' EEOC charge was not timely because it was not filed within the specified period after the adoption in 1979 of the new seniority rule. We noted that the plaintiffs had not alleged that the new seniority rule treated men and women differently or that the rule had been applied in a discriminatory manner. Rather, their complaint was that the rule was adopted originally with discriminatory intent. Id., at 905, 109 S. Ct. 2261, 104 L. Ed. 2d 961. And as in *Evans* and *Ricks,* we held that the EEOC charging period ran from the time when the discrete act of alleged intentional discrimination occurred, not from the date when the effects of this practice were felt. 490 U.S., at 907–908, 109 S. Ct. 2261, 104 L. Ed. 2d 961. We stated:

> "Because the claimed invalidity of the facially nondiscriminatory and neutrally applied tester seniority system is wholly dependent on the alleged illegality of signing the underlying agreement, it is the date of that signing which governs the limitations period." Id., at 911, 109 S. Ct. 2261, 104 L. Ed. 2d 961.[2]

Our most recent decision in this area confirms this understanding. In *Morgan*, we explained that the statutory term "employment practice" generally refers to "a discrete act or single 'occurrence'" that takes place at a particular point in time. 536 U.S., at 110–111, 122 S. Ct. 2061, 153 L. Ed. 2d 106. We pointed to "termination, failure to promote, denial

---

2. After *Lorance*, Congress amended Title VII to cover the specific situation involved in that case. See 42 U.S.C. § 2000e–5(e)(2) (allowing for Title VII liability arising from an intentionally discriminatory seniority system both at the time of its adoption and at the time of its application). * * * For present purposes, what is most important about the amendment in ques- tion is that it applied only to the adoption of a discriminatory seniority system, not to other types of employment discrimination. *Evans* and *Ricks*, upon which Lorance relied, 490 U.S., at 906–908, 109 S. Ct. 2261, 104 L. Ed. 2d 961, and which employed identical reasoning, were left in place, and these decisions are more than sufficient to support our holding today.

of transfer, [and] refusal to hire" as examples of such "discrete" acts, and we held that a Title VII plaintiff "can only file a charge to cover discrete acts that 'occurred' within the appropriate time period." Id., at 114, 122 S. Ct. 2061, 153 L. Ed. 2d 106.

* * *

Ledbetter's arguments here—that the paychecks that she received during the charging period and the 1998 raise denial each violated Title VII and triggered a new EEOC charging period—cannot be reconciled with *Evans*, *Ricks*, *Lorance*, and *Morgan*. Ledbetter, as noted, makes no claim that intentionally discriminatory conduct occurred during the charging period or that discriminatory decisions that occurred prior to that period were not communicated to her. Instead, she argues simply that Goodyear's conduct during the charging period gave present effect to discriminatory conduct outside of that period. But current effects alone cannot breathe life into prior, uncharged discrimination; as we held in *Evans*, such effects in themselves have "no present legal consequences." 431 U.S., at 558, 97 S. Ct. 1885, 52 L. Ed. 2d 571. Ledbetter should have filed an EEOC charge within 180 days after each allegedly discriminatory pay decision was made and communicated to her. She did not do so, and the paychecks that were issued to her during the 180 days prior to the filing of her EEOC charge do not provide a basis for overcoming that prior failure.

In an effort to circumvent the need to prove discriminatory intent during the charging period, Ledbetter relies on the intent associated with other decisions made by other persons at other times. Reply Brief for Petitioner 6 ("Intentional discrimination ... occurs when ... differential treatment takes place, even if the intent to engage in that conduct for a discriminatory purpose was made previously").

Ledbetter's attempt to take the intent associated with the prior pay decisions and shift it to the 1998 pay decision is unsound. It would shift intent from one act (the act that consummates the discriminatory employment practice) to a later act that was not performed with bias or discriminatory motive. The effect of this shift would be to impose liability in the absence of the requisite intent.

* * *

A disparate-treatment claim comprises two elements: an employment practice, and discriminatory intent. Nothing in Title VII supports treating the intent element of Ledbetter's claim any differently from the employment practice element.[3] If anything, concerns regarding stale

---

3. Of course, there may be instances where the elements forming a cause of action span more than 180 days. Say, for instance, an employer forms an illegal discriminatory intent towards an employee but does not act on it until 181 days later. The charging period would not begin to run until the employment practice was executed on day 181 because until that point the employee had no cause of action. The act and intent had not yet been joined. Here, by contrast, Ledbetter's cause of action was fully formed and present at the time that the discriminatory employment actions were taken against her, at which point she could have, and should have, sued.

claims weigh more heavily with respect to proof of the intent associated with employment practices than with the practices themselves. For example, in a case such as this in which the plaintiff's claim concerns the denial of raises, the employer's challenged acts (the decisions not to increase the employee's pay at the times in question) will almost always be documented and will typically not even be in dispute. By contrast, the employer's intent is almost always disputed, and evidence relating to intent may fade quickly with time. * * *[4]

III

A

In advancing her two theories Ledbetter * * * argues that our decision in Bazemore v. Friday, 478 U.S. 385, 106 S. Ct. 3000, 92 L. Ed. 2d 315 (1986) (per curiam), requires different treatment of her claim because it relates to pay. Ledbetter focuses specifically on our statement that "each week's paycheck that delivers less to a black than to a similarly situated white is a wrong actionable under Title VII." Id., at 395, 106 S. Ct. 3000, 92 L. Ed. 2d 315. She argues that in *Bazemore* we adopted a "paycheck accrual rule" under which each paycheck, even if not accompanied by discriminatory intent, triggers a new EEOC charging period during which the complainant may properly challenge any prior discriminatory conduct that impacted the amount of that paycheck, no matter how long ago the discrimination occurred. On this reading, *Bazemore* dispensed with the need to prove actual discriminatory intent in pay cases and, without giving any hint that it was doing so, repudiated the very different approach taken previously in *Evans* and *Ricks*. Ledbetter's interpretation is unsound.

Bazemore concerned a disparate-treatment pay claim brought against the North Carolina Agricultural Extension Service (Service). 478 U.S., at 389–390, 106 S. Ct. 3000, 92 L. Ed. 2d 315. Service employees were originally segregated into "a white branch" and "a Negro branch," with the latter receiving less pay, but in 1965 the two branches were merged. Id., at 390–391, 106 S. Ct. 3000, 92 L. Ed. 2d 315. After Title VII was extended to public employees in 1972, black employees brought suit claiming that pay disparities attributable to the old dual pay scale persisted. Id., at 391, 106 S. Ct. 3000, 92 L. Ed. 2d 315. The Court of Appeals rejected this claim, which it interpreted to be that the "discriminatory difference in salaries should have been affirmatively eliminated." Id., at 395.

---

4. [T]his case illustrates the problems created by tardy lawsuits. Ledbetter's claims of sex discrimination turned principally on the misconduct of a single Goodyear supervisor, who, Ledbetter testified, retaliated against her when she rejected his sexual advances during the early 1980's, and did so again in the mid-1990's when he falsified deficiency reports about her work. His misconduct, Ledbetter argues, was "a principal basis for [her] performance evaluation in 1997." Brief for Petitioner 6; see also id., at 5–6, 8, 11 (stressing the same supervisor's misconduct). Yet, by the time of trial, this supervisor had died and therefore could not testify. A timely charge might have permitted his evidence to be weighed contemporaneously.

This Court reversed in a per curiam opinion, 478 U.S., at 386–388, 106 S. Ct. 3000, 92 L. Ed. 2d 315, but all of the Members of the Court joined Justice Brennan's separate opinion, see id., at 388, 106 S. Ct. 3000, 92 L. Ed. 2d 315 (opinion concurring in part). Justice Brennan wrote:

"The error of the Court of Appeals with respect to salary disparities created prior to 1972 and perpetuated thereafter is too obvious to warrant extended discussion: that the Extension Service discriminated with respect to salaries prior to the time it was covered by Title VII does not excuse perpetuating that discrimination after the Extension Service became covered by Title VII. To hold otherwise would have the effect of exempting from liability those employers who were historically the greatest offenders of the rights of blacks. A pattern or practice that would have constituted a violation of Title VII, but for the fact that the statute had not yet become effective, became a violation upon Title VII's effective date, and to the extent an employer continued to engage in that act or practice, it is liable under that statute. While recovery may not be permitted for pre-1972 acts of discrimination, to the extent that this discrimination was perpetuated after 1972, liability may be imposed." Id., at 395, 106 S. Ct. 3000, 92 L. Ed. 2d 315 (emphasis in original).

Far from adopting the approach that Ledbetter advances here, this passage made a point that was "too obvious to warrant extended discussion," ibid.; namely, that when an employer adopts a facially discriminatory pay structure that puts some employees on a lower scale because of race, the employer engages in intentional discrimination whenever it issues a check to one of these disfavored employees. An employer that adopts and intentionally retains such a pay structure can surely be regarded as intending to discriminate on the basis of race as long as the structure is used.

Bazemore thus is entirely consistent with our prior precedents, as Justice Brennan's opinion took care to point out. Noting that *Evans* turned on whether "any present violation existed," Justice Brennan stated that the *Bazemore* plaintiffs were alleging that the defendants "had not from the date of the Act forward made all their employment decisions in a wholly nondiscriminatory way," 478 U.S., at 396–397, n. 6, 106 S. Ct. 3000, 92 L. Ed. 2d 315 (emphasis in original; internal quotation marks and brackets omitted)—which is to say that they had engaged in fresh discrimination. Justice Brennan added that the Court's "holding in no sense gave legal effect to the pre-1972 actions, but, consistent with *Evans* ... focused on the present salary structure, which is illegal if it is a mere continuation of the pre-1965 discriminatory pay structure." Id., at 397, n. 6, 106 S. Ct. 3000, 92 L. Ed. 2d 315 (emphasis added).

The sentence in Justice Brennan's opinion on which Ledbetter chiefly relies comes directly after the passage quoted above, and makes a similarly obvious point:

"Each week's paycheck that delivers less to a black than to a similarly situated white is a wrong actionable under Title VII, regardless of the fact that this pattern was begun prior to the effective date of Title VII." Id., at 395, 106 S. Ct. 3000, 92 L. Ed. 2d 315.

In other words, a freestanding violation may always be charged within its own charging period regardless of its connection to other violations. We repeated this same point more recently in *Morgan:* "The existence of past acts and the employee's prior knowledge of their occurrence ... does not bar employees from filing charges about related discrete acts so long as the acts are independently discriminatory and charges addressing those acts are themselves timely filed." 536 U.S., at 113, 122 S. Ct. 2061, 153 L. Ed. 2d 106. Neither of these opinions stands for the proposition that an action not comprising an employment practice and alleged discriminatory intent is separately chargeable, just because it is related to some past act of discrimination.

* * *

Bazemore stands for the proposition that an employer violates Title VII and triggers a new EEOC charging period whenever the employer issues paychecks using a discriminatory pay structure. But a new Title VII violation does not occur and a new charging period is not triggered when an employer issues paychecks pursuant to a system that is "facially nondiscriminatory and neutrally applied." *Lorance*, 490 U.S., at 911, 109 S. Ct. 2261, 104 L. Ed. 2d 961. The fact that precharging period discrimination adversely affects the calculation of a neutral factor (like seniority) that is used in determining future pay does not mean that each new paycheck constitutes a new violation and restarts the EEOC charging period.

Because Ledbetter has not adduced evidence that Goodyear initially adopted its performance-based pay system in order to discriminate on the basis of sex or that it later applied this system to her within the charging period with any discriminatory animus, *Bazemore* is of no help to her. Rather, all Ledbetter has alleged is that Goodyear's agents discriminated against her individually in the past and that this discrimination reduced the amount of later paychecks. Because Ledbetter did not file timely EEOC charges relating to her employer's discriminatory pay decisions in the past, she cannot maintain a suit based on that past discrimination at this time.

B

The dissent also argues that pay claims are different. Its principal argument is that a pay discrimination claim is like a hostile work environment claim because both types of claims are "based on the cumulative effect of individual acts," but this analogy overlooks the critical conceptual distinction between these two types of claims. And although the dissent relies heavily on *Morgan*, the dissent's argument is fundamentally inconsistent with *Morgan*'s reasoning.

Morgan distinguished between "discrete" acts of discrimination and a hostile work environment. A discrete act of discrimination is an act that in itself "constitutes a separate actionable 'unlawful employment practice'" and that is temporally distinct. *Morgan*, 536 U.S., at 114, 117, 122 S. Ct. 2061, 153 L. Ed. 2d 106. As examples we identified "termination, failure to promote, denial of transfer, or refusal to hire." Id., at 114, 122 S. Ct. 2061, 153 L. Ed. 2d 106. A hostile work environment, on the other hand, typically comprises a succession of harassing acts, each of which "may not be actionable on its own." In addition, a hostile work environment claim "cannot be said to occur on any particular day." Id., at 115–116, 122 S. Ct. 2061, 153 L. Ed. 2d 106. In other words, the actionable wrong is the environment, not the individual acts that, taken together, create the environment.

Contrary to the dissent's assertion, what Ledbetter alleged was not a single wrong consisting of a succession of acts. Instead, she alleged a series of discrete discriminatory acts, see Brief for Petitioner 13, 15 (arguing that payment of each paycheck constituted a separate violation of Title VII), each of which was independently identifiable and actionable, and Morgan is perfectly clear that when an employee alleges "serial violations," i.e., a series of actionable wrongs, a timely EEOC charge must be filed with respect to each discrete alleged violation. 536 U.S., at 113, 122 S. Ct. 2061, 153 L. Ed. 2d 106.

* * *

If, as seems likely, the dissent would apply the same rule in all pay cases, then, if a single discriminatory pay decision made 20 years ago continued to affect an employee's pay today, the dissent would presumably hold that the employee could file a timely EEOC charge today. And the dissent would presumably allow this even if the employee had full knowledge of all the circumstances relating to the 20-year-old decision at the time it was made. The dissent, it appears, proposes that we adopt a special rule for pay cases based on the particular characteristics of one case that is certainly not representative of all pay cases and may not even be typical. We refuse to take that approach.

IV

In addition to the arguments previously discussed, Ledbetter relies largely on analogies to other statutory regimes and on extrastatutory policy arguments to support her "paycheck accrual rule."

A

Ledbetter places significant weight on the EPA, which was enacted contemporaneously with Title VII and prohibits paying unequal wages for equal work because of sex. 29 U.S.C. § 206(d). Stating that "the lower courts routinely hear [EPA] claims challenging pay disparities that first arose outside the limitations period," Ledbetter suggests that we should hold that Title VII is violated each time an employee receives a paycheck that reflects past discrimination.

The simple answer to this argument is that the EPA and Title VII are not the same. In particular, the EPA does not require the filing of a charge with the EEOC or proof of intentional discrimination. See § 206(d)(1) (asking only whether the alleged inequality resulted from "any other factor other than sex"). Ledbetter originally asserted an EPA claim, but that claim was dismissed by the District Court and is not before us. If Ledbetter had pursued her EPA claim, she would not face the Title VII obstacles that she now confronts.

* * *

B

Ledbetter, finally, makes a variety of policy arguments in favor of giving the alleged victims of pay discrimination more time before they are required to file a charge with the EEOC. Among other things, she claims that pay discrimination is harder to detect than other forms of employment discrimination.[10]

We are not in a position to evaluate Ledbetter's policy arguments, and it is not our prerogative to change the way in which Title VII balances the interests of aggrieved employees against the interest in encouraging the "prompt processing of all charges of employment discrimination," Mohasco, 447 U.S., at 825, 100 S. Ct. 2486, 65 L. Ed. 2d 532, and the interest in repose.

Ledbetter's policy arguments for giving special treatment to pay claims find no support in the statute and are inconsistent with our precedents. We apply the statute as written, and this means that any unlawful employment practice, including those involving compensation, must be presented to the EEOC within the period prescribed by statute.

JUSTICE GINSBURG, with whom JUSTICES STEVENS, SOUTER and BREYER join, dissenting.

The Court's insistence on immediate contest overlooks common characteristics of pay discrimination. Pay disparities often occur, as they did in Ledbetter's case, in small increments; cause to suspect that discrimination is at work develops only over time. Comparative pay information, moreover, is often hidden from the employee's view. Employers may keep under wraps the pay differentials maintained among supervisors, no less the reasons for those differentials. Small initial discrepancies may not be seen as meet for a federal case, particularly when the employee, trying to succeed in a nontraditional environment, is averse to making waves.

Pay disparities are thus significantly different from adverse actions "such as termination, failure to promote, ... or refusal to hire," all involving fully communicated discrete acts, "easy to identify" as discrim-

---

10. We have previously declined to address whether Title VII suits are amenable to a discovery rule. National Railroad Passenger Corporation v. Morgan, 536 U.S. 101, 114, n. 7, 122 S. Ct. 2061, 153 L. Ed. 2d 106 (2002). Because Ledbetter does not argue that such a rule would change the outcome in her case, we have no occasion to address this issue.

inatory. See National Railroad Passenger Corporation v. Morgan, 536 U.S. 101, 114, 122 S. Ct. 2061, 153 L. Ed. 2d 106 (2002). It is only when the disparity becomes apparent and sizable, e.g., through future raises calculated as a percentage of current salaries, that an employee in Ledbetter's situation is likely to comprehend her plight and, therefore, to complain. Her initial readiness to give her employer the benefit of the doubt should not preclude her from later challenging the then current and continuing payment of a wage depressed on account of her sex.

* * *

Ledbetter's petition presents a question important to the sound application of Title VII: What activity qualifies as an unlawful employment practice in cases of discrimination with respect to compensation. One answer identifies the pay-setting decision, and that decision alone, as the unlawful practice. Under this view, each particular salary-setting decision is discrete from prior and subsequent decisions, and must be challenged within 180 days on pain of forfeiture. Another response counts both the pay-setting decision and the actual payment of a discriminatory wage as unlawful practices. Under this approach, each payment of a wage or salary infected by sex-based discrimination constitutes an unlawful employment practice; prior decisions, outside the 180-day charge-filing period, are not themselves actionable, but they are relevant in determining the lawfulness of conduct within the period. The Court adopts the first view, but the second is more faithful to precedent, more in tune with the realities of the workplace, and more respectful of Title VII's remedial purpose.

In *Bazemore*, we unanimously held that an employer, the North Carolina Agricultural Extension Service, committed an unlawful employment practice each time it paid black employees less than similarly situated white employees. 478 U.S., at 395, 106 S. Ct. 3000, 92 L. Ed. 2d 315 (opinion of Brennan, J.). Before 1965, the Extension Service was divided into two branches: a white branch and a "Negro branch." Id., at 390, 106 S. Ct. 3000, 92 L. Ed. 2d 315. Employees in the "Negro branch" were paid less than their white counterparts. In response to the Civil Rights Act of 1964, which included Title VII, the State merged the two branches into a single organization, made adjustments to reduce the salary disparity, and began giving annual raises based on nondiscriminatory factors. Id., at 390–391, 394–395, 106 S. Ct. 3000, 92 L. Ed. 2d 315. Nonetheless, "some pre-existing salary disparities continued to linger on." Id., at 394, 106 S. Ct. 3000, 92 L. Ed. 2d 315 (internal quotation marks omitted). We rejected the Court of Appeals' conclusion that the plaintiffs could not prevail because the lingering disparities were simply a continuing effect of a decision lawfully made prior to the effective date of Title VII. See id., at 395–396, 106 S. Ct. 3000, 92 L. Ed. 2d 315. Rather, we reasoned, "each week's paycheck that delivers less to a black than to a similarly situated white is a wrong actionable under Title VII." Id., at 395, 106 S. Ct. 3000, 92 L. Ed. 2d 315. Paychecks perpetuating past discrimination, we thus recognized, are actionable not simply because they are "related" to a decision made outside the charge-filing period, cf. *ante*, at 17, but because they discriminate anew each time they issue, see *Bazemore*, 478 U.S., at 395–396, 106 S. Ct. 3000, 92 L. Ed. 2d 315, and n. 6; *Morgan*, 536 U.S., at 111–112, 122 S. Ct. 2061, 153 L. Ed. 2d 106.

Subsequently, in *Morgan,* we set apart, for purposes of Title VII's timely filing requirement, unlawful employment actions of two kinds: "discrete acts" that are "easy to identify" as discriminatory, and acts that recur and are cumulative in impact. See *id.*, at 110, 113–115, 122 S. Ct. 2061, 153 L. Ed. 2d 106. "[A] discrete act such as termination, failure to promote, denial of transfer, or refusal to hire," *id.*, at 114, 122 S. Ct. 2061, 153 L. Ed. 2d 106, we explained, " 'occurs' on the day that it 'happens'. A party, therefore, must file a charge within … 180 … days of the date of the act or lose the ability to recover for it." *Id.*, at 110, 122 S. Ct. 2061, 153 L. Ed. 2d 106; see *id.*, at 113, 122 S. Ct. 2061, 153 L. Ed. 2d 106 ("Discrete discriminatory acts are not actionable if time barred, even when they are related to acts alleged in timely filed charges. Each discrete discriminatory act starts a new clock for filing charges alleging that act.").

* * *

Pay disparities, of the kind Ledbetter experienced, have a closer kinship to hostile work environment claims than to charges of a single episode of discrimination. Ledbetter's claim, resembling Morgan's, rested not on one particular paycheck, but on "the cumulative effect of individual acts." Initially in line with the salaries of men performing substantially the same work, Ledbetter's salary fell 15 to 40 percent behind her male counterparts only after successive evaluations and percentage-based pay adjustments. Over time, she alleged and proved, the repetition of pay decisions undervaluing her work gave rise to the current discrimination of which she complained. Though component acts fell outside the charge-filing period, with each new paycheck, Goodyear contributed incrementally to the accumulating harm. See *Morgan*, 536 U.S., at 117, 122 S. Ct. 2061, 153 L. Ed. 2d 106; *Bazemore*, 478 U.S., at 395–396, 106 S. Ct. 3000, 92 L. Ed. 2d 315; cf. Hanover Shoe, Inc. v. United Shoe Machinery Corp., 392 U.S. 481, 502, n. 15, 88 S. Ct. 2224, 20 L. Ed. 2d 1231 (1968).

The realities of the workplace reveal why the discrimination with respect to compensation that Ledbetter suffered does not fit within the category of singular discrete acts "easy to identify." A worker knows immediately if she is denied a promotion or transfer, if she is fired or refused employment. And promotions, transfers, hirings, and firings are generally public events, known to co-workers. When an employer makes a decision of such open and definitive character, an employee can immediately seek out an explanation and evaluate it for pretext. Compensation disparities, in contrast, are often hidden from sight. It is not unusual, decisions in point illustrate, for management to decline to publish employee pay levels, or for employees to keep private their own salaries. See, e.g., Goodwin v. General Motors Corp., 275 F.3d 1005, 1008–1009 (CA10 2002) (plaintiff did not know what her colleagues earned until a printout listing of salaries appeared on her desk, seven years after her starting salary was set lower than her co-workers' salaries); McMillan v. Massachusetts Soc. for the Prevention of Cruelty to Animals, 140 F.3d 288, 296 (CA1 1998) (plaintiff worked for employer for years before learning of salary disparity published in a newspaper).[3] Tellingly, as the record in this case bears out, Goodyear kept salaries confidential; employees had only limited access to information regarding their colleagues' earnings.

The problem of concealed pay discrimination is particularly acute where the disparity arises not because the female employee is flatly denied a raise but because male counterparts are given larger raises. Having received a pay increase, the female employee is unlikely to discern at once that she has experienced an adverse employment decision. She may have little reason even to suspect discrimination until a pattern develops incrementally and she ultimately becomes aware of the disparity. Even if an employee suspects that the reason for a comparatively low raise is not performance but sex (or another protected ground), the amount involved may seem too small, or the employer's intent too ambiguous, to make the issue immediately actionable—or winnable.

* * *

The Court asserts that treating pay discrimination as a discrete act, limited to each particular pay-setting decision, is necessary to "protect employers from the burden of defending claims arising from employment decisions that are long past." * * * But the discrimination of which Ledbetter complained is not long past. As she alleged, and as the jury found, Goodyear continued to treat Ledbetter differently because of sex each pay period, with mounting harm. Allowing employees to challenge discrimination "that extends over long periods of time," into the charge-filing period, we have previously explained, "does not leave employers defenseless" against unreasonable or prejudicial delay. Morgan, 536 U.S., at 121, 122 S. Ct. 2061, 153 L. Ed. 2d 106. Employers disadvantaged by such delay may raise various defenses. Id., at 122, 122 S. Ct. 2061, 153 L. Ed. 2d 106. Doctrines such as "waiver, estoppel, and equitable tolling" "allow us to honor Title VII's remedial purpose without negating the particular purpose of the filing requirement, to give prompt notice to the employer." Id., at 121, 122 S. Ct. 2061, 153 L. Ed. 2d 106 (quoting Zipes v. Trans World Airlines, Inc., 455 U.S. 385, 398, 102 S. Ct. 1127, 71 L. Ed. 2d 234 (1982)); see 536 U.S., at 121, 122 S. Ct. 2061, 153 L. Ed. 2d 106 (defense of laches may be invoked to block an employee's suit "if he unreasonably delays in filing [charges] and as a

---

3. See also Bierman & Gely, "Love, Sex and Politics? Sure. Salary? No Way": Workplace Social Norms and the Law, 25 Berkeley J. Emp. & Lab. L. 167, 168, 171 (2004) (one-third of private sector employers have adopted specific rules prohibiting employees from discussing their wages with co-workers; only one in ten employers has adopted a pay openness policy).

result harms the defendant"); EEOC Brief 15 ("If Ledbetter unreasonably delayed challenging an earlier decision, and that delay significantly impaired Goodyear's ability to defend itself ... Goodyear can raise a defense of laches....").

In a last-ditch argument, the Court asserts that this dissent would allow a plaintiff to sue on a single decision made 20 years ago "even if the employee had full knowledge of all the circumstances relating to the ... decision at the time it was made." Ante, at 20. It suffices to point out that the defenses just noted would make such a suit foolhardy. No sensible judge would tolerate such inexcusable neglect. See *Morgan*, 536 U.S., at 121, 122 S. Ct. 2061, 153 L. Ed. 2d 106 ("In such cases, the federal courts have the discretionary power ... to locate a just result in light of the circumstances peculiar to the case." (internal quotation marks omitted)).

Ledbetter, the Court observes, dropped an alternative remedy she could have pursued: Had she persisted in pressing her claim under the Equal Pay Act of 1963 (EPA), 29 U.S.C. § 206(d), she would not have encountered a time bar. See ante, at 21 ("If Ledbetter had pursued her EPA claim, she would not face the Title VII obstacles that she now confronts."); cf. Corning Glass Works v. Brennan, 417 U.S. 188, 208–210, 94 S. Ct. 2223, 41 L. Ed. 2d 1 (1974). Notably, the EPA provides no relief when the pay discrimination charged is based on race, religion, national origin, age, or disability. Thus, in truncating the Title VII rule this Court announced in *Bazemore,* the Court does not disarm female workers from achieving redress for unequal pay, but it does impede racial and other minorities from gaining similar relief.[9]

Notes and Questions

1. *A Discrete Employment Decision?* Does the majority or the dissent have the better of the argument whether discriminatory pay decisions are fully completed within the time period or whether, as with hostile environments in *Morgan,* they are almost always cumulative?

2. *Discovery Exception?* The Court leaves open in footnote 10 the question whether the charge-filing period begins only when the plaintiff knows or should know that his or her pay has been discriminatorily set. Should such a rule be adopted? Would it adequately address the problems raised by the dissent?

The Court earlier reserved decision on whether a "discovery" rule was appropriate for the Title VII filing period in Mohasco Corp. v. Silver, 447 U.S. 807, 818 n. 22, 100 S.Ct. 2486, 2493 n. 22, 65 L.Ed.2d 532 (1980). In

---

9. For example, under today's decision, if a black supervisor initially received the same salary as his white colleagues, but annually received smaller raises, there would be no right to sue under Title VII outside the 180-day window following each annual salary change, however strong the cumulative evidence of discrimination might be. The Court would thus force plaintiffs, in many cases, to sue too soon to prevail, while cutting them off as time barred once the pay differential is large enough to enable them to mount a winnable case.

Reeb v. Economic Opportunity Atlanta, Inc., 516 F.2d 924 (5th Cir.1975), the plaintiff had been terminated on grounds of "limitations of funds" but subsequently learned that her previous position had been filled by a presumably less qualified male employee; the court held that the filing period began with the subsequent discovery. Does *Reeb* provide support for a general "discovery" rule or is it an instance of equitable tolling because of defendant's concealment of the true facts? See Kale v. Combined Insurance Co. of America, 861 F.2d 746 (1st Cir.1988) (recognizing tolling because of "equitable estoppel" due to employer misrepresentations). Do the holdings in *Reeb* or *Kale* survive *Lorance*?

For post-*Lorance* authority, compare Rhodes v. Guiberson Oil Tools Div., 927 F.2d 876 (5th Cir.1991) (equitable-estoppel doctrine applies to toll limitations period for filing EEOC charge; employee was told he was being terminated because of a reduction-in-force and therefore was "precluded from evaluating his legal options until he discovered that he had been misled by the misrepresentations"), with Hamilton v. 1st Source Bank, 928 F.2d 86 (4th Cir.1990) (en banc) (rejecting "discovery" rule for tolling 180–day charge filing period for ADEA pay-discrimination claim).

3. *Employee Opportunism?* Was the holding in *Ledbetter* necessary to avoid employees not calling attention to correctable pay disparity until the problem becomes much more expensive for the employer to evaluate and resolve? Is such opportunism likely given the statute's two-year limitation on back-pay liability?

D. CLASS ACTIONS

GENERAL TELEPHONE COMPANY OF THE SOUTHWEST v. FALCON

Supreme Court of the United States, 1982.
457 U.S. 147, 102 S.Ct. 2364, 72 L.Ed.2d 740.

JUSTICE STEVENS delivered the opinion of the Court.

The question presented is whether respondent Falcon, who complained that petitioner did not promote him because he is a Mexican–American, was properly permitted to maintain a class action on behalf of Mexican–American applicants for employment whom petitioner did not hire.

I

In 1969 petitioner initiated a special recruitment and training program for minorities. Through that program, respondent Falcon was hired in July 1969 as a groundman, and within a year he was twice promoted, first to lineman and then to lineman-in-charge. He subsequently refused a promotion to installer-repairman. In October 1972 he applied for the job of field inspector; his application was denied even though the promotion was granted several white employees with less seniority.

Falcon thereupon filed a charge with the Equal Employment Opportunity Commission stating his belief that he had been passed over for promotion because of his national origin and that petitioner's promotion policy operated against Mexican–Americans as a class. In due course he received a right-to-sue letter from the Commission and, in April 1975, he commenced this action under Title VII of the Civil Rights Act of 1964, 78 Stat. 253, as amended, 42 U.S.C. § 2000e *et seq.* (1976 ed. and Supp. IV), in the United States District Court for the Northern District of Texas. His complaint alleged that petitioner maintained "a policy, practice, custom, or usage of: (a) discriminating against [Mexican–Americans] because of national origin and with respect to compensation, terms, conditions, and privileges of employment, and (b) * * * subjecting [Mexican–Americans] to continuous employment discrimination." Respondent claimed that as a result of this policy whites with less qualification and experience and lower evaluation scores than respondent had been promoted more rapidly. The complaint contained no factual allegations concerning petitioner's hiring practices.

Respondent brought the action "on his own behalf and on behalf of other persons similarly situated, pursuant to Rule 23(b)(2) of the Federal Rules of Civil Procedure." The class identified in the complaint was "composed of Mexican–American persons who are employed, or who might be employed, by GENERAL TELEPHONE COMPANY at its place of business located in Irving, Texas, who have been and who continue to be or might be adversely affected by the practices complained of herein."

After responding to petitioner's written interrogatories, respondent filed a memorandum in favor of certification of "the employees who have been employed, are employed, or may in the future be employed and all those Mexican–Americans who have applied or would have applied for employment had the Defendant not practiced racial discrimination in its employment practices." His position was supported by the ruling of the United States Court of Appeals for the Fifth Circuit in *Johnson v. Georgia Highway Express, Inc.,* 417 F.2d 1122 (1969), that any victim of racial discrimination in employment may maintain an "across the board" attack on all unequal employment practices alleged to have been committed by the employer pursuant to a policy of racial discrimination. Without conducting an evidentiary hearing, the District Court certified a class including Mexican–American employees and Mexican–American applicants for employment who had not been hired.

Following trial of the liability issues, the District Court entered separate findings of fact and conclusions of law with respect first to respondent and then to the class. The District Court found that petitioner had not discriminated against respondent in hiring, but that it did discriminate against him in its promotion practices. The court reached converse conclusions about the class, finding no discrimination in promotion practices, but concluding that petitioner had discriminated against Mexican–Americans at its Irving facility in its hiring practices.

* * *

Both parties appealed. The Court of Appeals rejected respondent's contention that the class should have encompassed all of petitioner's operations in Texas, New Mexico, Oklahoma, and Arkansas. On the other hand, the court also rejected petitioner's argument that the class had been defined too broadly. For, under the Fifth Circuit's across-the-board rule, it is permissible for "an employee complaining of one employment practice to represent another complaining of another practice, if the plaintiff and the members of the class suffer from essentially the same injury. In this case, all of the claims are based on discrimination because of national origin."

* * *

II

* * *

We have repeatedly held that "a class representative must be part of the class and 'possess the same interest and suffer the same injury' as the class members." *East Texas Motor Freight System, Inc. v. Rodriguez,* 431 U.S. 395, 403, 97 S.Ct. 1891, 1896, 52 L.Ed.2d 453 (quoting *Schlesinger v. Reservists Committee to Stop the War,* 418 U.S. 208, 216, 94 S.Ct. 2925, 2929–2930, 41 L.Ed.2d 706.) In *East Texas Motor Freight,* a Title VII action brought by three Mexican–American city drivers, the Fifth Circuit certified a class consisting of the trucking company's black and Mexican–American city drivers allegedly denied on racial or ethnic grounds transfers to more desirable line-driver jobs. We held that the Court of Appeals had "plainly erred in declaring a class action." 431 U.S., at 403, 97 S.Ct., at 1896. Because at the time the class was certified it was clear that the named plaintiffs were not qualified for line-driver positions, "they could have suffered no injury as a result of the allegedly discriminatory practices, and they were, therefore, simply not eligible to represent a class of persons who did allegedly suffer injury." *Id.,* at 403–404, 97 S.Ct., at 1897.

* * *

We cannot disagree with the proposition underlying the across-the-board rule—that racial discrimination is by definition class discrimination. But the allegation that such discrimination has occurred neither determines whether a class action may be maintained in accordance with Rule 23 nor defines the class that may be certified. Conceptually, there is a wide gap between (a) an individual's claim that he has been denied a promotion on discriminatory grounds, and his otherwise unsupported allegation that the company has a policy of discrimination, and (b) the existence of a class of persons who have suffered the same injury as that individual, such that the individual's claim and the class claims will share common questions of law or fact and that the individual's claim will be typical of the class claims. For respondent to bridge that gap, he must prove much more than the validity of his own claim. Even though evidence that he was passed over for promotion when several less deserving whites were advanced may support the conclusion that respondent was denied the promotion because of his national origin, such evidence would not necessarily justify the additional inferences (1) that this discriminatory treatment is typical of petitioner's promotion practices, (2) that petitioner's promotion practices are motivated by a policy of ethnic discrimination that pervades petitioner's Irving division, or (3) that this policy of ethnic discrimination is reflected in petitioner's other employment practices, such as hiring, in the same way it is manifested in the promotion practices. These additional inferences demonstrate the tenuous character of any presumption that the class claims are "fairly encompassed" within respondent's claim.

* * * Without any specific presentation identifying the questions of law or fact that were common to the claims of respondent and of the members of the class he sought to represent, it was error for the District Court to presume that respondent's claim was typical of other claims against petitioner by Mexican–American employees and applicants. If one allegation of specific discriminatory treatment were sufficient to support an across-the-board attack, every Title VII case would be a potential companywide class action. We find nothing in the statute to indicate that Congress intended to authorize such a wholesale expansion of class-action litigation.

The trial of this class action followed a predictable course. Instead of raising common questions of law or fact, respondent's evidentiary approaches to the individual and class claims were entirely different. He attempted to sustain his individual claim by proving intentional discrimination. He tried to prove the class claims through statistical evidence of disparate impact. Ironically, the District Court rejected the class claim of promotion discrimination, which conceptually might have borne a closer typicality and commonality relationship with respondent's individual claim, but sustained the class claim of hiring discrimination. As the District Court's bifurcated findings on liability demonstrate, the individual and class claims might as well have been tried separately. It is clear that the maintenance of respondent's action as a class action did not advance "the efficiency and economy of litigation which is a principal purpose of the procedure." *American Pipe & Construction Co. v. Utah*, 414 U.S. 538, 553, 94 S.Ct. 756, 766, 38 L.Ed.2d 713.

Notes and Questions

1. *Advantages of Class Actions.* Class actions have been important to antidiscrimination and wage-and-hour litigation because they enable individual claimants and advocacy organizations to mount systemic, high-impact challenges to employer decisionmaking. Class actions enable large numbers of victims of discrimination to obtain relief from the outcome of a single disparate impact or systemic disparate treatment suit. The filing of such actions offers other advantages to claimants. The Court held in Albemarle Paper Co. v. Moody, p. 151 supra, that a class action may be brought on behalf of individuals who have not themselves filed charges with the EEOC; and in Crown, Cork and Seal Co. v. Parker, p. 1065 supra, it held that the filing of such an action tolls Title VII filing periods for members of the class with viable claims at the time of filing who might wish to initiate or join in

an individual suit if the class is not certified. Moreover, once a class action has been certified, it acquires a life of its own, surviving the death or resolution of the individual claims of the representative parties. See Sosna v. Iowa, 419 U.S. 393, 95 S.Ct. 553, 42 L.Ed.2d 532 (1975). A denial of class certification may be reviewed on appeal despite the fact that the representative party's claim has become moot. See Parole Comm'n v. Geraghty, 445 U.S. 388, 100 S.Ct. 1202, 63 L.Ed.2d 479 (1980); Deposit Guaranty National Bank v. Roper, 445 U.S. 326, 100 S.Ct. 1166, 63 L.Ed.2d 427 (1980).

2. *"Across the Board" Certification?* Why did the Court in *Falcon* reject the Fifth Circuit's "across the board" approach to Title VII certifications? Is this an instance of meaningless formalism, or is the Court concerned about potential conflicts of interest between incumbent employees and disappointed applicants, or between past employees and current employees? Should *potential* conflicts be relevant when the court is charged with an ongoing monitoring of the adequacy of representation by the representative parties and will review the adequacy of any settlements under Rule 23(e) of the F.R.Civ.P.? For an insightful discussion, see George Rutherglen, Notice, Scope, and Preclusion in Title VII Class Actions, 69 Va.L.Rev. 11 (1983). Is *Falcon* explainable in part by the fact that the charges filed by representative parties will determine both the scope of the lawsuit and the duration of the liability period (because the back pay period will be measured from the date of the charges filed by such parties)?

3. *"Across the Board" Certifications After* Falcon? In light of *Falcon* what must Title VII plaintiffs establish in order to satisfy the typicality and commonality requirements of Rule 23? Does *Falcon* rule out all "across the board" actions which allege discriminatory treatment of both applicants and incumbent employees? What about challenges to discriminatory systems? Consider footnote 15 of the decision in *Falcon*:

> If petitioner used a biased testing procedure to evaluate both applicants for employment and incumbent employees, a class action on behalf of every applicant or employee who might have been prejudiced by the test clearly would satisfy the commonality and typicality requirements of Rule 23(a). Significant proof that an employer operated under a general policy of discrimination conceivably could justify a class of both applicants and employees if the discrimination manifested itself in hiring and promotion practices in the same general fashion, such as through entirely subjective decisionmaking processes.

For an application of this suggestion, see Rossini v. Ogilvy & Mather, Inc., 798 F.2d 590, 596, 598 (2d Cir.1986) ("Zukofsky did not ask the district court to presume that she was a proper class representative of a class asserting claims of discrimination in promotion and training. Rather, she attempted to prove that O & M had denied women opportunities to advance themselves, either as she sought to do, by transfer, or as other class members sought, by training or promotion, through its use of a subjective evaluation system without formal job descriptions, objective experience or education requirements, posting of job openings or listing of employees seeking better positions. Moreover, evidence was offered to show that many of the decisions affecting employees' opportunities for transfer, training and promotion were made by the same, central group of people within O & M.").

4. *Notice and "Opt Out" Rights in Discrimination Class Actions?* Class actions of the Rule 23 variety purport to have binding effect on the members of the class; if the class loses, individual suits by class members generally cannot be brought. This raises concerns because many class actions are brought under Rule 23(b)(2) of the F.R.Civ.P. which, unlike Rule 23(b)(3), does not by its terms require that notice and an opportunity to opt out be furnished to class members. Is it consistent with due process, or even simple fairness, to bind persons to the outcome of someone else's lawsuit without those persons ever having been given notice of the pendency of the suit? The Court mitigated somewhat the harshness of this rule in Cooper v. Federal Reserve Bank, 467 U.S. 867, 104 S.Ct. 2794, 81 L.Ed.2d 718 (1984), by confining the binding effect of a class action to the issues actually litigated therein, and holding that a court's rejection of a systemic disparate treatment case does not necessarily foreclose individual discrimination claims. The dilemma nevertheless remains to the extent the class action purports to resolve individual claims or will have that effect as a practical matter. Some courts have required notice to class members before foreclosure of their individual claims may occur. See, e.g., Johnson v. General Motors Corp., 598 F.2d 432 (5th Cir.1979). Professor Rutherglen faults *Johnson* for exposing defendants to multiple and inconsistent litigation. His proposal is to treat Title VII class suits as hybrids: (b)(2) actions as to classwide injunctive and declaratory relief, and (b)(3) actions requiring individual notice and opt-out rights as to claims for compensatory relief. Rutherglen, supra, at 33–34. See also Eubanks v. Billington, 110 F.3d 87 (D.C.Cir.1997) (district court has discretion to grant opt-out rights to members of (b)(1) and (b)(2) classes). Even under Rutherglen's approach, issues determined in the (b)(2) phase would bind those opting out during the (b)(3) phase. See also Allison v. Citgo Petr. Corp., infra.

5. *Class Action Settlements.* How should settlements of Rule 23(b)(2) class actions be treated? Rule 23(e) requires notice to class members and the holding of a "fairness" hearing by the district court before approval of a settlement. At the hearing, class members opposed to the settlement may seek to intervene or simply voice their objections. Should opponents of the settlement also be allowed to opt out? Would this complicate the process of settling class actions because defendants will often insist on foreclosure of all claims before agreeing to a settlement? Are opt outs likely except in instances of grossly unfair agreements? The Fifth and Eleventh Circuits have held that while there is no absolute opt-out right, the trial court must be assured of the continuing homogeneity of interests between class representatives and passive class members at the settlement stage. See Cox v. American Cast Iron Pipe Co., 784 F.2d 1546 (11th Cir.1986); Holmes v. Continental Can Co., 706 F.2d 1144 (11th Cir.1983); Penson v. Terminal Transport Co., 634 F.2d 989 (5th Cir.1981).

6. *"Opt–In" Collective Actions Under FLSA, EPA and ADEA.* Representative actions differ under ADEA and EPA. These statutes utilize the enforcement procedures of the FLSA, rather than Rule 23, and thus permit only "opt-in" collective actions; individuals can only be bound to the extent they have affirmatively consented to representation. See 29 U.S.C. § 216(b). ADEA group actions are relatively rare in part because of the difficulty lawyers have faced in soliciting consents, and judicial reluctance to engage in

what was deemed a nonjudicial task of sending notices to claimants. See, e.g., McKenna v. Champion Int'l Corp., 747 F.2d 1211 (8th Cir.1984); see generally Elizabeth K. Spahn, Resurrecting the Spurious Class: Opting–In to the Age Discrimination in Employment Act and the Equal Pay Act through the Fair Labor Standards Act, 71 Geo.L.J. 119 (1982). However, in Hoffman–La Roche, Inc. v. Sperling, 493 U.S. 165, 110 S.Ct. 482, 107 L.Ed.2d 480 (1989), the Court held that district courts may facilitate notice of ADEA representative actions to potential plaintiffs by allowing discovery of names and addresses of similarly situated employees, provided the appearance of judicial endorsement of the merits of the action is avoided.

a. *"Single Filing" Rule.* Most courts accept the "single filing" rule under which an opt-in plaintiff may join the ADEA action after the limitations period for that individual has expired if the representative plaintiff's action was timely filed and indicated its representative nature. The leading case is the lower-court decision in the *Sperling* litigation, 24 F.3d 463, 471–72 (3d Cir.1994) (Congress in ADEA selectively incorporated § 6 of the Portal-to-Portal Act, 29 U.S.C. § 255, but did not incorporate § 7, id. § 256 (opt-in plaintiffs must file consents within statute of limitations)). But see Grayson v. K Mart Corp., 79 F.3d 1086, 1105 (11th Cir.1996).

b. *"Similarly Situated".* FLSA-model collective actions may be brought only on behalf of employees who are "similarly situated" to the named plaintiffs. See 29 U.S.C. § 216(b). Some courts take the view that the "similarly situated" standard is "considerably less stringent than the requirement of Fed.R.Civ.P. 23(b)(3) that common questions 'predominate.'" In re Food Lion, Inc., 151 F.3d 1029 (4th Cir. 1998) (unpublished); Hoffmann v. Sbarro, Inc., 982 F.Supp. 249, 261 (S.D.N.Y.1997) ("plaintiffs can meet this burden by making a modest factual showing sufficient to demonstrate that they and potential plaintiffs together were victims of a common policy or plan"); see also Federal Judicial Center, Manual for Complex Litigation Third § 33.52, at 351 (1995) ("the possibility of varied defenses does not vitiate a collective action"). For examples of rulings restricting discovery requests to "similarly situated" employees, see, e.g., Nelson v. Telecable of Overland Park, 70 FEP Cas. 859, 861, 1996 WL 111250 (D.Kan.1996); Hicks v. Arthur, 159 F.R.D. 468, 470 (E.D.Pa.1995). See also Lusardi v. Lechner, 855 F.2d 1062 (3d Cir.1988).

c. *Two-Stage "Certification".* A court has two opportunities to decide whether to permit the collective action to proceed. First, upon the plaintiffs' request to send a notice to the prospective class, it may "conditionally certify" a class using the fairly lenient approach to the "similarly situated" standard stated above. After discovery has been completed, the court may use a more demanding version of the "similarly situated" standard. See, e.g., Thiessen v. General Electric Capital Corp., 996 F.Supp. 1071, 1080 n. 13 (D.Kan.1998); Vaszlavik v. Storage Tech. Corp., 175 F.R.D. 672, 678–79 (D.Colo.1997).

7. *Plaintiff Communications with Current and Former Employees.*

a. *Present Employees.* Lawyers bringing class actions often claim a need to communicate with class members or, prior to certification, potential class members. Based in part on ABA Model Rule of Professional Conduct 4.2 & DR 7–104(A)(1) of the ABA Model Code of Professional Responsibility, many jurisdictions prohibit ex parte contacts between plaintiffs' attorney and present employees of a represented party (i) who have managerial responsibility, (ii) whose acts may be imputed to the organization for purposes of liability assessments, or (iii) whose statements might constitute an admission on the part of the organization. See, e.g., McCallum v. CSX Transportation, Inc., 149 F.R.D. 104 (M.D.N.C.1993). A few courts have imposed a blanket prohibition on ex parte contact with all present employees. See Public Serv. Elec. & Gas v. Associated Elec. & Gas Ins. Servs., 745 F.Supp. 1037 (D.N.J.1990); Cagguila v. Wyeth Laboratories, Inc., 127 F.R.D. 653 (E.D.Pa.1989). A blanket prohibition on all communications, in the absence of specific findings of abuse, may undermine legitimate interests in communicating legal advice and information under Gulf Oil Co. v. Bernard, 452 U.S. 89, 101 S.Ct. 2193, 68 L.Ed.2d 693 (1981). See EEOC v. Mitsubishi Motor Mfg., 960 F.Supp. 164 (N.D.Ill.1997) (extending *Bernard* to governmental litigation).

b. *Former Employees.* Most courts do not bar ex parte contacts with former employees, presumably because the latter do not speak for, and cannot bind, the organization. See, e.g., Polycast Technology Corp. v. Uniroyal, Inc., 129 F.R.D. 621, 629 (S.D.N.Y.1990). Some courts insist that such contacts are permitted as long as none of the information so obtained is imputed to the organization. See, e.g., Curley v. Cumberland Farms, Inc., 134 F.R.D. 77, 82–83 (D.N.J.1991). The ABA's standing committee takes the view that Rule 4.2 does not apply to former employees. See ABA Comm. on Ethics and Professional Responsibility, Formal Op. 91–359 (1991) & Formal Op. 95–396 (1995).

c. *Employer Communications with Absent Class Members.* Some jurisdictions prohibit or limit communications between the employer and absent class members, other than what would transpire in the conduct of the business. Generally employers may communicate with putative class members to gather evidence after a class action has been filed, as long as they do not make misleading statements or dissuade employees from participating in the class action. See Manual on Complex Litigation (Third) § 30.24 (1995). After the class has been certified, however, ex parte communications become problematical, unless they are communications in the ordinary course of business. See, e.g., High v. Braniff Airways, Inc., 20 Fed. R. Serv.2d 439 (W.D.Tex. 1975). See generally Vincent R. Johnson, The Ethics of Communicating with Putative Class Members, 17 Rev. of Litig. 497 (1998); Charles S, Mishkind & Yvonne R. Haddad, Class Action Litigation: Communicating with the Public and Class Members, 23 Employee Rels. L.J. 83 (no. 3, Winter 1997).

ALLISON v. CITGO PETROLEUM CORP.

U.S. Court of Appeals for the Fifth Circuit, 1998.

151 F.3d 402, per cur. op. denying reh'g en banc, 151 F.3d 434.

JOLLY, J.

I

* * *

In September 1993, the plaintiffs filed a motion for the certification of a class estimated to contain more than 1000 potential members. The class was identified as "all African–American employees and applicants of Citgo Petroleum Corporation (Citgo) from April 11, 1979 until the present." Its members are current and former employees and unsuccessful applicants for employment in "hourly" positions at Citgo's Lake Charles complex. They are spread across two separate facilities. They are represented by six different unions, come from five different skill groups, and work in seven different functional areas at the complex. Nevertheless, the plaintiffs maintain that a class action is appropriate because they are challenging general hiring, training, and promotional policies applied uniformly throughout the complex.

* * *

The district court referred the plaintiffs' motion for class certification to a magistrate judge, who conducted an evidentiary hearing and subsequently entered a report and recommendation denying class certification. The magistrate judge determined that, although the proposed class met the requirements of Rule 23(a) of the Federal Rules of Civil Procedure, it could not be certified under any of the alternatives provided in 23(b). * * *

* * *

The district court adopted the report and recommendation in its entirety and denied class certification. * * *

V

A

We consider first whether the district court erred in determining that the primary limitation on a Rule 23(b)(2) class action is the requirement that injunctive or declaratory relief be the predominant relief sought for the class. Naturally, we begin by looking at the plain language of the rule. Rule 23(b)(2) permits cases meeting the requirements of Rule 23(a) to be certified as class actions if:

> the party opposing the class has acted or refused to act on grounds generally applicable to the class, thereby making appropriate final injunctive relief or corresponding declaratory relief with respect to the class as a whole.

The rule is clear that claims seeking injunctive or declaratory relief are appropriate for (b)(2) class certification. Thus, if the plaintiffs sought only injunctive and declaratory relief, this case could readily be certified as a class action under Rule 23(b)(2).

The plaintiffs, however, also seek monetary relief. Rule 23(b)(2) is silent as to whether monetary remedies may be sought in conjunction with injunctive or declaratory relief. The Advisory Committee Notes on Rule 23 state that class certification under (b)(2) "does not extend to cases in which the appropriate final relief relates exclusively or predominantly to money damages." Fed. R. Civ. P. 23 (advisory committee notes) * * *. This commentary implies that the drafters of Rule 23 believed that at least some form or amount of monetary relief would be permissible in a (b)(2) class action. See *Pettway v. American Cast Iron Pipe Co.*, 494 F.2d 211, 257 (5th Cir.1974).

In addressing what monetary relief is permissible in a (b)(2) class action, this circuit has chosen an intermediate approach, neither allowing certification without regard to the monetary remedies being sought, nor restricting certification to classes seeking exclusively injunctive or declaratory relief. See *Johnson v. General Motors Corp.*, 598 F.2d 432, 437 (5th Cir.1979). We, like nearly every other circuit, have adopted the position taken by the advisory committee that monetary relief may be obtained in a (b)(2) class action so long as the predominant relief sought is injunctive or declaratory. * * *

B

* * *

Under Rule 23, the different categories of class actions, with their different requirements, represent a balance struck in each case between the need and efficiency of a class action and the interests of class members to pursue their claims separately or not at all. See *Amchem Prod., Inc. v. Windsor*, 138 L.Ed.2d 689, 117 S.Ct. 2231, 2246 (1997); *United States Parole Comm'n v. Geraghty*, 445 U.S. 388, 402–03, 63 L.Ed. 2d 479, 100 S.Ct. 1202 (1980); Rutherglen, Title VII Class Actions, 47 U. Chi. L. Rev. 688, 697–98 (1980) (citing Kaplan, Continuing Work of the Civil Committee: 1966 Amendments of the Federal Rules of Civil Procedure, 81 Harv. L. Rev. 356, 387–92 (1967)). * * *

First, different presumptions with respect to the cohesiveness and homogeneity of interests among members of (b)(1), (b)(2), and (b)(3) classes are reflected in the different procedural safeguards provided for each potential class. * * * For example, the drafters of Rule 23 found it unnecessary to provide (b)(1) and (b)(2) class members with the absolute right to notice or to opt-out of the class—procedural safeguards made mandatory under (b)(3) for class members who might wish to pursue their claims for money damages in individual lawsuits and to not be bound by membership in a class action. See Fed. R. Civ. P. 23(c)(2). Providing these rights exclusively to (b)(3) classes demonstrates concern for the effect of monetary claims on class cohesiveness. See Fed. R. Civ. P. 23 (advisory committee notes) ("in the degree there is cohesiveness or unity in the class and the representation is effective, the need for notice to the class will tend toward a minimum"). Monetary remedies are more often related directly to the disparate merits of individual claims. * * *

In contrast, because of the group nature of the harm alleged and the broad character of the relief sought, the (b)(2) class is, by its very nature, assumed to be a homogenous and cohesive group with few conflicting interests among its members. * * *

We know * * * that monetary relief "predominates" under Rule 23(b)(2) when its presence in the litigation suggests that the procedural safeguards of notice and opt-out are necessary, that is, when the monetary relief being sought is less of a group remedy and instead depends more on the varying circumstances and merits of each potential class member's case. * * * Because it automatically provides the right of notice and opt-out to individuals who do not want their monetary claims decided in a class action, Rule 23(b)(3) is the appropriate means of class certification when monetary relief is the predominant form of relief sought and the monetary interests of class members require enhanced procedural safeguards.

* * *

Consistent with this analysis, we reach the following holding: monetary relief predominates in (b)(2) class actions unless it is incidental to requested injunctive or declaratory relief. * * * By incidental, we mean damages that flow directly from liability to the class as a whole on the claims forming the basis of the injunctive or declaratory relief. See Fed. R. Civ. P. 23(b)(2) (referring only to relief appropriate "with respect to the class as a whole"). Ideally, incidental damages should be only those to which class members automatically would be entitled once liability to the class (or subclass) as a whole is established. See Manual for Complex Litigation, supra, at 348 (citing *Simer* v. *Rios*, 661 F.2d 655 (7th Cir.1981)); see also, e.g., *Arnold* v. *United Artists Theatre Circuit, Inc.*, 158 F.R.D. 439 (N.D.Cal.1994) (defendant's liability entitled class to a statutorily mandated damage award). That is, the recovery of incidental damages should typically be concomitant with, not merely consequential to, class-wide injunctive or declaratory relief. Moreover, such damages should at least be capable of computation by means of objective standards and not dependent in any significant way on the intangible, subjective differences of each class member's circumstances. Liability for incidental damages should not require additional hearings to resolve the disparate merits of each individual's case; it should neither introduce new and substantial legal or factual issues, nor entail complex individualized determinations. Thus, incidental damages will, by definition, be more in the nature of a group remedy, consistent with the forms of relief intended for (b)(2) class actions.

Our holding in this respect is not inconsistent with our cases permitting back pay under Title VII in (b)(2) class actions. In *Pettway*, for example, we noted that Rule 23(b)(2), by its own terms, does not preclude all claims for monetary relief. See 494 F.2d at 257. We construed (b)(2) to permit monetary relief when it was an equitable remedy, and the defendant's conduct made equitable remedies appropriate. See *id.* Back pay, of course, had long been recognized as an equitable remedy under Title VII. See *Johnson* v. *Georgia Highway Express, Inc.*, 417 F.2d 1122, 1125 (5th Cir.1969) ("[a] demand for back pay is not in the nature of damages, but rather is an integral part of the statutory equitable remedy"). * * * In short, *Pettway* held that back pay could be sought in a (b)(2) class action because, as an equitable remedy similar to other forms of affirmative injunctive relief permitted in (b)(2) class actions, it was an integral component of Title VII's "make whole" remedial scheme. See *id.* at 252, 257. If the instant case involved only claims for equitable monetary relief, *Pettway* would control. *Pettway*, however, did not address the availability in (b)(2) class actions of other forms of monetary relief, such as compensatory and punitive damages, nor did it have any occasion to do so.

* * *

C

We have little trouble affirming the district court's finding that the plaintiffs' claims for compensatory and punitive damages are not sufficiently incidental to the injunctive and declaratory relief being sought to permit them in a (b)(2) class action. We start with the premise that, in this circuit, compensatory damages for emotional distress and other forms of intangible injury will not be presumed from mere violation of constitutional or statutory rights. See *Patterson v. P.H.P Healthcare Corp.*, 90 F.3d 927, 938–40 (5th Cir.1996). Specific individualized proof is necessary, and testimony from the plaintiff alone is not ordinarily sufficient. See 90 F.3d at 940; *Price v. City of Charlotte, N.C.*, 93 F.3d 1241, 1250–54 (4th Cir.1996). Compensatory damages may be awarded only if the plaintiff submits proof of actual injury, often in the form of psychological or medical evidence, or other corroborating testimony from a third party. See *Patterson*, 90 F.3d at 940 (citing *Carey v. Piphus*, 435 U.S. 247, 264, 55 L.Ed.2d 252, 98 S.Ct. 1042 (1978)) * * *. The very nature of these damages, compensating plaintiffs for emotional and other intangible injuries, necessarily implicates the subjective differences of each plaintiff's circumstances; they are an individual, not class-wide, remedy. * * *

The plaintiffs' claims for punitive damages are similarly non-incidental. Although the plain language of the Civil Rights Act of 1991 could be interpreted to preclude class-wide punitive damages awards in any case without individualized proof of injury, see 42 U.S.C. § 1981a(b)(1) (punitive damages available if employer acted with malice or reckless indifference to rights of "aggrieved individual"), we need not determine today whether it is so limiting. Assuming punitive damages may be awarded on a class-wide basis, without individualized proof of injury, where the entire class or subclass is subjected to the same discriminatory act or series of acts, no such discrimination is alleged in this case. The plaintiffs challenge broad policies and practices, but they do not contend that each plaintiff was affected by these policies and practices in the same way. Indeed, the plaintiffs seek to certify a class of a thousand potential plaintiffs spread across two separate facilities, represented by six different unions, working in seven different departments, challenging various policies and practices over a period of nearly twenty years. Some plaintiffs may have been subjected to more [virulent] discrimination than others: with greater public humiliation, for longer periods of time, or based on more unjustifiable practices, for example. Particular discriminatory practices may have been gradually ameliorated year by year over the twenty-year period. Some discriminatory policies may have been implemented more—or less—harshly depending on the department or facility involved.

Punitive damages cannot be assessed merely upon a finding that the defendant engaged in a pattern or practice of discrimination. Such a finding establishes only that there has been general harm to the group and that injunctive relief is appropriate. See *Price Waterhouse v. Hopkins*, 490 U.S. 228, 266, 104 L.Ed.2d 268, 109 S.Ct. 1775 (1989) (O'Connor, J., concurring in the judgment). Actual liability to individual class members, and their entitlement to monetary relief, are not determined until the second stage of the trial. See *id.*; *Dillon v. Coles*, 746 F.2d 998, 1004 (3d Cir.1984). And because punitive damages must be reasonably related to the reprehensibility of the defendant's conduct and to the compensatory damages awarded to the plaintiffs, see *Patterson*, 90 F.3d at 943–44 (citing *BMW v. Gore*, 517 U.S. 559, 116 S.Ct.1589, 1598–99, 134 L.Ed.2d 809 (1996)), recovery of punitive damages must necessarily turn on the recovery of compensatory damages. Thus, punitive damages must be determined after proof of liability to individual plaintiffs at the second stage of a pattern or practice case, not upon the mere finding of general liability to the class at the first stage. Moreover, being dependent on non-incidental compensatory damages, punitive damages are also non-incidental—requiring proof of how discrimination was inflicted on each plaintiff, introducing new and substantial legal and factual issues, and not being capable of computation by reference to objective standards.

Given the degree to which recovery of compensatory and punitive damages requires individualized proof and determinations, they clearly do not qualify as incidental damages in this case. * * *

VI

A

* * * [W]e next consider the plaintiffs' argument that the district court erred in refusing to certify a "hybrid" class action, whereby the plaintiffs' claims for compensatory and punitive damages would be certified under Rule 23(b)(3), and the rest of the class action certified under Rule 23(b)(2). * * * The plaintiffs * * * contend that the (b)(3) predominance standard focuses on the issue of liability, and if the liability issues are common to the class, common questions predominate over individual ones * * *. The plaintiffs insist further that, here, a class action is plainly superior to hundreds of individual lawsuits.

* * *

B

In assessing whether the district court abused its discretion in refusing to certify a (b)(3) class action, we begin with this circuit's most recent case on Rule 23(b)(3) analysis, *Castano v. American Tobacco Co.*, 84 F.3d 734 (5th Cir.1996). *Castano* makes clear that deciding whether common issues predominate and whether the class action is a superior method to resolve the controversy requires an understanding of the relevant claims, defenses, facts, and substantive law presented in the case. *Id.* at 744. As we have discussed previously, *Patterson* holds that the recovery of compensatory and punitive damages in Title VII cases requires individualized and independent proof of injury to, and the means by which discrimination was inflicted upon, each class member. * * * The plaintiffs' claims for compensatory and punitive damages must therefore focus almost entirely on facts and issues specific to individuals rather than the class as a whole: what kind of discrimination was each plaintiff subjected to; how did it affect each plaintiff emotionally and physically, at work and at home; what medical treatment did each plaintiff receive and at what expense; and so on and so on. Under such circumstances, an action conducted nominally as a class action would "degenerate in practice into multiple lawsuits separately tried." *Castano*, 84 F.3d at 745 n.19 (citing Fed. R. Civ. P. 23 (advisory committee notes)).

The predominance of individual-specific issues relating to the plaintiffs' claims for compensatory and punitive damages in turn detracts from the superiority of the class action device in resolving these claims. * * * These manageability problems are exacerbated by the fact that this action must be tried to a jury and involves more than a thousand potential plaintiffs spread across two separate facilities, represented by six different unions, working in seven different departments, and alleging discrimination over a period of nearly twenty years. * * * In order to manage the case, the district court faced the likelihood of bifurcated proceedings before multiple juries. This result in turn increased the probability that successive juries would pass on issues decided by prior ones, introducing potential Seventh Amendment problems and further decreasing the superiority of the class action device. See *Castano*, 84 F.3d at 750–51; *In re Rhone–Poulenc Rorer, Inc.*, 51 F.3d 1293, 1302–03 (7th Cir.1995). Finally, the "most compelling rationale for finding superiority in a class action—the existence of a negative value suit," is missing in this case. *Castano*, 84 F.3d at 748; see also *Amchem*, 117 S.Ct. at 2246. The relatively substantial value of these claims (for the statutory maximum of $300,000 per plaintiff) and the availability of attorneys' fees eliminate financial barriers that might make individual lawsuits unlikely or infeasible. See *Castano*, 84 F.3d at 748. Thus, the principles underlying the (b)(3) class action counsel against (b)(3) certification in this case.

* * *

VII

Finally, the plaintiffs argue that, in the event their claims for compensatory and punitive damages cannot be certified in a class action at this initial stage of the litigation, they are entitled to have some part of this case certified now and tried as a class action to whatever extent permissible under Rule 23. More specifically, as we understand the plaintiffs' argument, they suggest that the court should certify a class action on the disparate impact claim and the first stage of the pattern or practice claim—under Rule 23(b)(2) or 23(b)(3)—and reserve judgment on whether to certify under 23(b)(3) the other claims—including the claims for compensatory and punitive damages—until these initial issues have been resolved. * * *

A

We should make clear from the outset that in asserting this partial certification argument, the plaintiffs have not agreed to drop their claims for compensatory and punitive damages as a class action issue. In making their argument for a tentative, "partial certification," the plaintiffs are relying presumably on the possibility that class-wide discovery and the resolution of the disparate impact claim and first stage of the pattern or practice claim may narrow the issues in the case, which in turn may make later certification of the remaining claims in a (b)(3) class action appropriate. * * *

* * * [W]e fail to see how certifying the first stage of the pattern or practice claim significantly increases the likelihood that later certification of the second stage of the pattern or practice claim, including the claims for compensatory and punitive damages, would be possible. The second stage of a pattern or practice claim is essentially a series of individual lawsuits, except that there is a shift of the burden of proof in the plaintiff's favor. As the Supreme Court has made clear, there are no common issues between the first stage of a pattern or practice claim and an individual discrimination lawsuit. See *Cooper v. Federal Reserve Bank*, 467 U.S. 867, 877–80, 81 L. Ed. 2d 718, 104 S. Ct. 2794 (1984). As a result, we see no legal basis for the district court to certify a class action on the first stage of the plaintiffs' pattern or practice claim when there is no foreseeable likelihood that the claims for compensatory and punitive damages could be certified in the class action sought by the plaintiffs. * * *

[I]n the context of the plaintiffs' partial certification argument, we will consider the possibility of certifying a class action on the disparate impact claim, with the district court reserving judgment on whether to certify the pattern or practice claim under Rule 23(b)(3) until the disparate impact claim has been resolved.

The standards of Rule 23, however, are not the only limitations on the availability of a class action in this case. As the district court recognized, the right to a jury trial provided by the Civil Rights Act of 1991, and demanded by the plaintiffs, implicates the Seventh Amendment. We therefore consider whether Seventh Amendment concerns preclude a class action on the plaintiffs' disparate impact claim, severed from their pattern or practice claim.

B

* * *

Because the statute expressly provides that compensatory and punitive damages are not available in disparate impact claims, see § 1981a(a)(1), the right to a jury trial under Title VII extends only to the plaintiffs' pattern or practice claim, see § 1981a(c). Once the right to a jury trial attaches to a claim, however, it extends to all factual issues necessary to resolving that claim. See *Beacon Theatres, Inc. v. Westover*, 359 U.S. 500, 510–11, 3 L. Ed. 2d 988, 79 S. Ct. 948 (1959). Thus, under section 1981a, the right to a jury trial extends to all factual issues necessary to determine liability on the plaintiffs' pattern or practice claim and the recovery of compensatory and punitive damages.

* * *

Resolution of the disparate impact claim and of equitable remedies must * * * take into account the Seventh Amendment. When claims involving both legal and equitable rights are properly joined in a single case, the Seventh Amendment requires that all factual issues common to these claims be submitted to a jury for decision on the legal claims before final court determination of the equitable claims. *Roscello v. Southwest Airlines Co.*, 726 F.2d 217, 221 (5th Cir.1984) (citing *Dairy Queen, Inc. v. Wood*, 369 U.S. 469, 479, 8 L. Ed. 2d 44, 82 S. Ct. 894 (1962)) * * *. In this case, both parties have a Seventh Amendment right to have a jury determine all factual issues necessary to establish the plaintiffs' pattern or practice claim, a claim for legal damages that they have properly joined in the same action with a disparate impact claim for equitable relief. As a result, each factual issue common to these claims, if any, must be decided by the jury before the district court considers the merits of the disparate impact claim and whether the plaintiffs are entitled to any equitable relief. * * *

C

In deciding whether the district court should have temporarily severed the disparate impact claim for class treatment, we must ascertain whether this claim shares any factual issues with the pattern or practice claim, which both parties are entitled to have decided first by a jury.

Because the same employment policies and practices are challenged under both claims, it is clear that there are overlapping issues. First and foremost, an essential factual element of both claims is a finding that the challenged employment practice caused each individual class member to suffer an adverse employment action (e.g., whether each individual class member failed a challenged employment test and was not hired because of that failure). Indeed, in resolving either claim, the trier of fact must determine whether each class member was even in a position to be affected by the challenged employment practice (e.g., whether each class member applied for an open job). * * *

Similarly, the business necessity defense to disparate impact claims and the legitimate nondiscriminatory reason defense to disparate treatment claims are not "so distinct and separable" from one another that they may be considered separately by multiple factfinders without violating the Seventh Amendment. See *Gasoline Prod. Co. v. Champlin Refining Co.*, 283 U.S. 494, 500, 75 L.Ed. 1188, 51 S.Ct. 513 (1931). To rebut the plaintiffs' claim that any one of Citgo's challenged employment practices resulted in a disparate impact, Citgo would have to establish that the "challenged practice is job-related for the position in question and consistent with business necessity." 42 U.S.C. § 2000e–2(k)(1)(A)(i). It is the rare case indeed in which a challenged practice is job-related and a business necessity, yet not a legitimate nondiscriminatory reason for an adverse employment action taken pursuant to that practice. Thus, a finding that a challenged practice is job related and a business necessity in response to a disparate impact claim strongly, if not wholly, implicates a finding that the same practice is a legitimate nondiscriminatory reason for the employer's actions in a pattern or practice claim. These issues are questions of fact, see, e.g., *St. Mary's Honor Ctr. v. Hicks*, 509 U.S. 502, 524, 125 L.Ed.2d 407, 113 S.Ct. 2742 (1993); *Wards Cove Packing Co. v. Atonio*, 490 U.S. 642, 660, 104 L.Ed.2d 733, 109 S.Ct. 2115 (1989), common to the plaintiffs' disparate impact and pattern or practice claims.

In sum, the existence of factual issues common between the plaintiffs' disparate impact and pattern or practice claims precludes trial of the disparate impact claim in a class action severed from the remaining nonequitable claims in the case. The claims for injunctive relief, declaratory relief, and any equitable or incidental monetary relief cannot be litigated in a class action bench trial (in the same case prior to certification of any aspects of the pattern or practice claim) without running afoul of the Seventh Amendment. See *Roscello*, 726 F.2d at 221. Nor may they be advanced in a subsequent class action without being barred by res judicata and collateral estoppel, see *Montana v. United States*, 440 U.S. 147, 153, 59 L.Ed.2d 210, 99 S.Ct. 970 (1979); *Nilsen v. City of Moss Point*, 701 F.2d 556, 559–64 (5th Cir.1983) (en banc), because all of the common factual issues will already have been decided, or could have been decided, in the prior litigation. The district court, therefore, did not abuse its discretion in denying partial certification in a temporarily severed class action nor in denying class certification on any or all aspects of this case.

[*Eds.* The dissenting opinion of Judge Dennis is omitted.]

Notes and Questions

1. *Holding of the Court?* In explaining the denial of rehearing, the *Allison* majority stated:

> The trial court utilized consolidation under rule 42 rather than class certification under rule 23 to manage this case. We review that decision for abuse of discretion and we find no abuse in this case. We are not

called upon to decide whether the district court would have abused its discretion if it had elected to bifurcate liability issues that are common to the class and to certify for class determination those discrete liability issues. Judge Dennis dissents from the denial of panel rehearing.

(5th Cir., Oct. 2, 1998). What is left of the panel majority's ruling?

2. *Backpay vs. Damages as "Incidental" Relief?* The *Allison* court purports to distinguish a host of rulings, typified by the Fifth Circuit's *Pettway* decision, that allow (b)(2) class actions to be certified even though backpay and other individualized relief are sought. How is backpay distinguishable for damages for these purposes? Consider the following:

    a.   "Backpay has a different historical pedigree, for it developed as a form of injunctive relief. Damages have always been treated as legal, not equitable, relief."

    b.   "In most cases, the entitlement to payback will flow automatically from the finding of classwide discrimination, and at most will involve mechanical computational issues, such as how long the affected employees have been on the payroll. Compensation for personal injury is inherently individualized, even if in many cases plaintiffs will have suffered the same type of harm."

    c.   "If the (b)(1) requirements of typicality and adequate representation are satisfied, backpay claims pose no serious risk of divergence of interest within a no-opt out class."

3. *Punitive Damages and Consideration of Individual Plaintiff Circumstances?* Does the *Kolstad* decision, p. 378 supra, call into question the assumption of the *Allison* court that punitive damages claims always, or even often, require determinations of how individual employees were treated? If Citgo had adopted discriminatory policies with an awareness of their illegality, might it be liable for punitive damages regardless of the circumstances of individual members of the class?

In Dukes v. Wal–Mart, 474 F.3d 1214 (9th Cir. 2007), the appeals court sustained certification under F.R.Civ.P. 23(b)(2) of a nationwide class action of current and former employees complaining of sexual discrimination in pay and promotions. Plaintiffs did not seek compensatory damages but sought punitive damages and backpay relief. The court reasoned:

> While Plaintiffs do not ask for compensatory damages in this case, they do seek punitive damages to punish Wal–Mart for its allegedly "reckless disregard of the rights of its women employees to equal employment opportunity, and to deter similar misconduct by Wal–Mart and other large retailers in the future." Wal–Mart contends that Plaintiffs' request for punitive damages is "wholly inconsistent" with Rule 23(b)(2) certification. This view, however, has not been adopted by this circuit. * * * As mentioned above, Plaintiffs stated that their primary intention in bringing this case was to obtain injunctive and declaratory relief—not money damages—and Wal–Mart has failed to effectively rebut Plaintiffs' statements or cast doubt on their reliability. Therefore, we find that the district court acted within its discretion when it concluded that Plain-

tiffs' claims for punitive damages do not predominate over claims for injunctive and declaratory relief.

* * *

In addition, the district court's order contains a provision to allow Plaintiffs to opt-out of claims for punitive damages. * * * Although there is no absolute right of opt-out in a rule 23(b)(2) class, "even where monetary relief is sought and made available," other courts have recognized that district courts should consider the possibility of opt-out rights. In re Monumental Life Ins. Co., 365 F.3d 408, 417 (5th Cir. 2004); Jefferson v. Ingersoll Int'l, Inc., 195 F.3d 894, 898 (7th Cir. 1999); see also Ticor Title Ins. Co. v. Brown, 511 U.S. 117, 121, 114 S.Ct. 1359, 128 L.Ed.2d 33 (1994) (suggesting that provisions allowing plaintiffs to opt-out of damages claims may be appropriate where plaintiffs move to certify a class bringing a claim for punitive damages).

4. *"Split–Certification" Option?* Why did the *Allison* majority appear to reject the split-certification approach: certifying the claims for classwide injury ("pattern or practice" and disparate-impact claims) under (b)(2), and the claims for individualized relief (compensatory damages) under (b)(3)? Consider the Seventh Circuit's decision in Jefferson v. Ingersoll International, Inc., 195 F.3d 894, 897–99 (7th Cir.1999):

* * * When substantial damages have been sought, the most appropriate approach is that of Rule 23(b)(3), because it allows notice and an opportunity to opt out.

Divided certification also is worth consideration. It is possible to certify the injunctive aspects of the suit under Rule 23(b)(2) and the damages aspects under Rule 23(b)(3), achieving both consistent treatment of class-wide equitable relief and an opportunity for each affected person to exercise control over the damages aspects. *Beacon Theatres, Inc.* v. *Westover*, 359 U.S. 500, 79 S.Ct. 948, 3 L.Ed.2d 988 (1959), and *Dairy Queen, Inc.* v. *Wood*, 369 U.S. 469, 82 S.Ct. 894, 8 L.Ed.2d 44 (1962), would require the district judge to try the damages claims first, to preserve the right to jury trial, a step that would complicate the management of separate classes—and mean, as a practical matter, that the damages claims and the Rule 23(b)(3) class would dominate the litigation—but the damages-first principle holds even when there is a single class under a single subdivision of Rule 23. That the seventh amendment gives damages the dominant role just strengthens the conclusion that Rule 23(b)(3) must be employed. Instead of divided certification—perhaps equivalently to it—the judge could treat a Rule 23(b)(2) class as if it were under Rule 23(b)(3), giving notice and an opportunity to opt out on the authority of Rule 23(d)(2). See *Williams* v. *Burlington Northern, Inc.*, 832 F.2d 100, 103 (7th Cir.1987).

If Rule 23(b)(2) ever may be used when the plaintiff class demands compensatory or punitive damages, that step would be permissible only when monetary relief is incidental to the equitable remedy—so tangential that the principle of *Beacon Theatres* and *Dairy Queen* does not apply, and that the due process clause does not require notice. On this subject we agree with the fifth circuit's principal holding in *Allison*, 151 F.3d at 411–16.

5. *"Injunction–Only Certification" and Later Use of Burden of Proof Shifting*? If plaintiffs in *Allison* had asked for class certification only to seek an injunction against continuation of a "pattern or practice" of discrimination, would they have succeeded? Could members of the plaintiff class then have used any finding of such a pattern or practice in individual litigation to obtain damages? Such a finding might accomplish the same reversal of the burden of persuasion as authorized in *Teamsters*, p. 90 supra, and *Franks*, p. 209 supra, both pre-1991 Act rulings. Does this approach also avoid the seventh amendment difficulties raised by the *Allison* majority?

6. *Examples of Class Certifications After the 1991 Act.* A number of courts continue to certify Title VII class actions despite inclusion of compensatory-damages claims and defense arguments that found a receptive audience in the *Allison* majority. For instance, the court in Robinson v. Metro–North Commuter R.R., 267 F.3d 147 (2d Cir. 2001), expressly rejected the the *Allison* court's approach. *Robinson* involved both systemic disparate treatment and disparate impact challenges to company policies that delegated to department supervisors, allegedly without sufficient oversight, authority to make discipline and promotion decisions. In the court's view, Rule 23(b)(2) certification is appropriate if "(1) the positive weight or value of the injunctive or declaratory relief sought is predominant even though compensatory or punitive damages are also claimed, and (2) class treatment would be efficient and manageable, thereby achieving an appreciable measure of judicial economy." Id. at 164.

See also, e.g., Gaines v. Boston Herald, Inc., 998 F.Supp. 91 (D.Mass., 1998) (class of black and Hispanic applicants for unskilled positions challenging employer's nepotistic hiring practices); Butler v. Home Depot, 70 FEP Cas. 51 (N.D.Cal.1996) (class of female employees and former employees in employer's Western Division as well as female applicants for sales and assistant manager positions; action bifurcated into stages: the first stage, which would have covered classwide liability and relief as well as punitive damages, was certified under (b)(2); the certification of the second stage, which would deal with individual relief, was deferred); cf. EEOC v. Mitsubishi Motor Mfg. of America, Inc., 990 F.Supp. 1059 (C.D.Ill.1998) (approving "pattern or practice" challenge to hostile work environment at assembly plant).

7. *Consolidation.* Consider the *Allison* majority's endorsement of consolidation of individual actions, under F.R.Civ. P. 42(a), as an alternative to class certification? What are the benefits of this approach? The costs?

8. *Violation of Jury Trial Right?* Is the *Allison* court correct in its assertion that a two-stage procedure, in which disparate-impact claims were certified and severed from "pattern or practice" claims, created a substantial risk that successive juries would pass on issues decided by prior juries, in violation of the seventh amendment's reexamination clause ("no fact tried by a jury shall be otherwise reexamined in any Court of the United States, than according to the rules of the common law")? See generally Keith R. Fentonmiller, Reconciling the Seventh Amendment with the "Pattern or

Practice" Class Action, 24 Employee Rels. L.J. 55, 66–68 (no. 3, Winter 1998).

9. *Waiver of Jury Trial?* If you are a plaintiff counsel seeking certification of a Title VII class action in a district court within the Fifth Circuit, should you consider not demanding a jury trial? Is the defendant likely to demand one?

E. ATTORNEY'S FEES

Plaintiffs pursuing state law contract and tort claims ordinarily cannot recover attorney's fees even if they prevail. The so-called "American Rule" on attorney's fees requires each party to pay its own lawyer costs. In addition to awards for bad-faith filings, a limited exception has been recognized in cases where plaintiffs by their litigation create a "common fund" for enriching themselves and others in the class action; plaintiffs' attorney's fees would be assessable against this fund. See discussion in Hall v. Cole, 412 U.S. 1, 93 S.Ct. 1943, 36 L.Ed.2d 702 (1973).

However, employment statutes, such as federal or state antidiscrimination laws or state "whistleblower" laws, often expressly authorize the award of attorney's fees to a prevailing plaintiff; such awards are quite common.

The provision for attorney's fees for "prevailing parties" under Title VII, ADEA, ADA, and FLSA reflects these statutes' reliance on the private suit as a principal enforcement vehicle. Absent such a provision, the complexity of litigation and the relatively small recoveries in individual cases would make it very difficult to attract private counsel. Attorney's fees are also available for other federal civil rights actions by virtue of 42 U.S.C. § 1988.

CHRISTIANSBURG GARMENT CO. v. EEOC

Supreme Court of the United States, 1978.

434 U.S. 412, 98 S.Ct. 694, 54 L.Ed.2d 648.

MR. JUSTICE STEWART delivered the opinion of the Court.

Section 706(k) of Title VII of the Civil Rights Act of 1964 provides:

"In any action or proceeding under this title the court in its discretion, may allow the prevailing party * * * a reasonable attorney's fee * * *."

The question in this case is under what circumstances an attorney's fee should be allowed when the defendant is the prevailing party in a Title VII action—a question about which the federal courts have expressed divergent views.

* * *

In *Newman v. Piggie Park Enterprises,* 390 U.S. 400, 88 S.Ct. 964, 19 L.Ed.2d 1263, the Court considered a substantially identical statute authorizing the award of attorney's fees under Title II of the Civil Rights

Act of 1964. In that case the plaintiffs had prevailed, and the Court of Appeals had held that they should be awarded their attorney's fees "only to the extent that the respondents' defenses had been advanced 'for purposes of delay and not in good faith.' " *Id.,* at 401, 88 S.Ct. at 966. We ruled that this "subjective standard" did not properly effectuate the purposes of the counsel-fee provision of Title II. Relying primarily on the intent of Congress to cast a Title II plaintiff in the role of "a 'private attorney general,' vindicating a policy that Congress considered of the highest priority," we held that a prevailing plaintiff under Title II "should ordinarily recover an attorney's fee unless special circumstances would render such an award unjust." *Id.,* at 402, 88 S.Ct. at 966. * * *

In *Albemarle Paper Co. v. Moody,* 422 U.S. 405, 95 S.Ct. 2362, 45 L.Ed.2d 280, the Court made clear that the *Piggie Park* standard of awarding attorney's fees to a successful plaintiff is equally applicable in an action under Title VII of the Civil Rights Act. * * *

The question in the case before us is what standard should inform a district court's discretion in deciding whether to award attorney's fees to a successful *defendant* in a Title VII action. * * *

* * *

Relying on what it terms "the plain meaning of the statute," the company argues that the language of § 706(k) admits of only one interpretation: "A prevailing defendant is entitled to an award of attorney's fees on the same basis as a prevailing plaintiff." But the permissive and discretionary language of the statute does not even invite, let alone require, such a mechanical construction. The terms of § 706(k) provide no indication whatever of the circumstances under which either a plaintiff *or* a defendant should be entitled to attorney's fees. And a moment's reflection reveals that there are at least two strong equitable considerations counseling an attorney's fee award to a prevailing Title VII plaintiff that are wholly absent in the case of a prevailing Title VII defendant.

First, as emphasized so forcefully in *Piggie Park,* the plaintiff is the chosen instrument of Congress to vindicate "a policy that Congress considered of the highest priority." 390 U.S., at 402, 88 S.Ct. at 966. Second, when a district court awards counsel fees to a prevailing plaintiff, it is awarding them against a violator of federal law. As the Court of Appeals clearly perceived, "these policy considerations which support the award of fees to a prevailing plaintiff are not present in the case of a prevailing defendant." A successful defendant seeking counsel fees under § 706(k) must rely on quite different equitable considerations.

But if the company's position is untenable, the Commission's argument also misses the mark. It seems clear, in short, that in enacting § 706(k) Congress did not intend to permit the award of attorney's fees to a prevailing defendant only in a situation where the plaintiff was motivated by bad faith in bringing the action. As pointed out in *Piggie Park,* if that had been the intent of Congress, no statutory provision would have been necessary, for it has long been established that even under the American common-law rule attorney's fees may be awarded against a party who has proceeded in bad faith.

Furthermore, while it was certainly the policy of Congress that Title VII plaintiffs should vindicate "a policy that Congress considered of the highest priority," *Piggie Park,* 390 U.S., at 402, 88 S.Ct., at 966, it is equally certain that Congress entrusted the ultimate effectuation of that policy to the adversary judicial process, *Occidental Life Ins. Co. v. EEOC,* 432 U.S. 355, 97 S.Ct. 2447, 53 L.Ed.2d 402. A fair adversary process presupposes both a vigorous prosecution and a vigorous defense. It cannot be lightly assumed that in enacting § 706(k), Congress intended to distort that process by giving the private plaintiff substantial incentives to sue, while foreclosing to the defendant the possibility of recovering his expenses in resisting even a groundless action unless he can show that it was brought in bad faith.

* * *

The first federal appellate court to consider what criteria should govern the award of attorney's fees to a prevailing Title VII defendant was the Court of Appeals for the Third Circuit in *United States Steel Corp. v. United States,* 519 F.2d 359. There a District Court had denied a fee award to a defendant that had successfully resisted a Commission demand for documents, the court finding that the Commission's action had not been " 'unfounded, meritless, frivolous or vexatiously brought.' " *Id.,* at 363. The Court of Appeals concluded that the District Court had not abused its discretion in denying the award. *Id.,* at 365. A similar standard was adopted by the Court of Appeals for the Second Circuit in *Carrion v. Yeshiva University,* 535 F.2d 722. In upholding an attorney's fee award to a successful defendant, that court stated that such awards should be permitted "not routinely, not simply because he succeeds, but only where the action brought is found to be unreasonable, frivolous, meritless or vexatious." *Id.,* at 727.

To the extent that abstract words can deal with concrete cases, we think that the concept embodied in the language adopted by these two Courts of Appeals is correct. We would qualify their words only by pointing out that the term "meritless" is to be understood as meaning groundless or without foundation, rather than simply that the plaintiff has ultimately lost his case, and that the term "vexatious" in no way implies that the plaintiff's subjective bad faith is a necessary prerequisite to a fee award against him. In sum, a district court may in its discretion award attorney's fees to a prevailing defendant in a Title VII case upon a finding that the plaintiff's action was frivolous, unreasonable, or without foundation, even though not brought in subjective bad faith.

* * *

That § 706(k) allows fee awards only to *prevailing* private plaintiffs should assure that this statutory provision will not in itself operate as an incentive to the bringing of claims that have little chance of success. To take the further step of assessing attorney's fees against plaintiffs simply because they do not finally prevail would substantially add to the risks inhering in most litigation and would undercut the efforts of Congress to promote the vigorous enforcement of the provisions of Title VII. Hence, a plaintiff should not be assessed his opponent's attorney's fees unless a court finds that his claim was frivolous, unreasonable, or groundless, or that the plaintiff continued to litigate after it clearly became so. And, needless to say, if a plaintiff is found to have brought or continued such a claim in *bad faith,* there will be an even stronger basis for charging him with the attorney's fees incurred by the defense.

PENNSYLVANIA v. DELAWARE VALLEY CITIZENS' COUNCIL

Supreme Court of the United States, 1987.
483 U.S. 711, 107 S.Ct. 3078, 97 L.Ed.2d 585.

JUSTICE WHITE announced the judgment of the Court and delivered an opinion, Parts I, II, and III–A of which represent the views of the Court, and Parts III–B, IV, and V of which are joined by THE CHIEF JUSTICE, AND JUSTICES POWELL and SCALIA.

This case involves the award of an attorney's fee to the prevailing party pursuant to § 304(d) of the Clean Air Act, 42 U.S.C. § 7604(d). [*Eds.* The Court explained that attorney's fees under § 304(d) "should follow the principles and case law governing the award of such fees under 42 U.S.C. § 1988, which provide * * * 'the court, in its discretion, may allow the prevailing party, other than the United States, a reasonable attorney''s fee as part of the costs.' "]

* * *

II

* * * The issue before us is whether, when a plaintiff prevails, its attorney should or may be awarded separate compensation for assuming the risk of not being paid. That risk is measured by the risk of losing rather than winning and depends on how unsettled the applicable law is with respect to the issues posed by the case and by how likely it is that the facts could be decided against the complainant. Looked at in this way, there are various factors that have little or no bearing on the question before us.

First is the matter of delay. When plaintiffs' entitlement to attorney's fees depends on success, their lawyers are not paid until a favorable decision finally eventuates, which may be years later, as in this case. Meanwhile, their expenses of doing business continue and must be met. In setting fees for prevailing counsel, the courts have regularly recognized the delay factor, either by basing the award on current rates or by adjusting the fee based on historical rates to reflect its present value. See, *e.g., Sierra Club v. Environmental Protection Agency,* 248 U.S.App. D.C. 107, 120–121, 769 F.2d 796, 809–810 (1985); *Louisville Black Police*

Officers Organization, Inc. v. City of Louisville, 700 F.2d 268, 276, 281 (C.A.6 1983). Although delay and the risk of nonpayment are often mentioned in the same breath, adjusting for the former is a distinct issue that is not involved in this case. We do not suggest, however, that adjustments for delay are inconsistent with the typical fee-shifting statute.

Second, that a case involves an issue of public importance, that the plaintiff's position is unpopular in the community, or that defendant is difficult or obstreperous does not enter into assessing the risk of loss or determining whether that risk should be compensated. Neither does the chance that the court will find unnecessary and not compensate some of the time and effort spent on prosecuting the case.

Third, when the plaintiff has agreed to pay its attorney, win or lose, the attorney has not assumed the risk of nonpayment and there is no occasion to adjust the lodestar fee because the case was a risky one. See, *e.g., Jones v. Central Soya Co.,* 748 F.2d 586, 593 (C.A.11 1984) where the court said that "[a] lawyer may not preserve a right of recourse against his client for fees and still expect to be compensated as if he had sacrificed completely his right to payment in the event of an unsuccessful outcome."

[*Eds.* In Part III–A, Justice White recounted developments in the lower courts; in Part III–B, he surveyed prior decisions of the Court as a prelude to concluding that the judgment below must be reversed.]

IV

We are impressed with the view of the Court of Appeals for the District of Columbia Circuit that enhancing fees for risk of loss forces losing defendants to compensate plaintiff's lawyers for not prevailing against defendants in other cases. This result is not consistent with Congress' decision to adopt the rule that only prevailing parties are entitled to fees. If risk multipliers or enhancement are viewed as no more than compensating attorneys for their willingness to take the risk of loss and of nonpayment, we are nevertheless not at all sure that Congress intended that fees be denied when a plaintiff loses, but authorized payment for assuming the risk of an uncompensated loss. Such enhancement also penalizes the defendants who have the strongest case; and in theory, at least, would authorize the highest fees in cases least likely to be won and hence encourage the bringing of more risky cases, especially by lawyers whose time is not fully occupied with other work. Because it is difficult ever to be completely sure that a case will be won, enhancing fees for the assumption of the risk of nonpayment would justify some degree of enhancement in almost every case.

Weighing all of these considerations, we are unconvinced that Congress intended the risk of losing a lawsuit to be an independent basis for increasing the amount of any otherwise reasonable fee for the time and effort expended in prevailing. * * *

The contrary argument is that without the promise of multipliers or enhancement for risk-taking, attorneys will not take cases for clients who cannot pay, and the fee-shifting statutes will therefore not serve their purpose. We agree that a fundamental aim of such statutes is to make it possible for those who cannot pay a lawyer for his time and effort to obtain competent counsel, this by providing lawyers with reasonable fees to be paid by the losing defendants. But it does not follow that fee enhancement for risk is necessary or allowable. Surely that is not the case where plaintiffs can afford to pay and have agreed to pay, win or lose. The same is true where any plaintiff, impecunious or otherwise, has a damages case that competent lawyers would take in the absence of fee-shifting statutes. Nor is it true in those cases where plaintiffs secure help from organizations whose very purpose is to provide legal help through salaried counsel to those who themselves cannot afford to pay a lawyer. It is also unlikely to be true in any market where there are competent lawyers whose time is not fully occupied by other matters.

* * *

It may be that without the promise of risk enhancement some lawyers will decline to take cases; but we doubt that the bar in general will so often be unable to respond that the goal of the fee-shifting statutes will not be achieved. In any event, risk enhancement involves difficulties in administration and possible inequities to those who must pay attorney's fees; and in the absence of further legislative guidance, we conclude that multipliers or other enhancement of a reasonable lodestar fee to compensate for assuming the risk of loss is impermissible under the usual fee-shifting statutes.

Even if § 304(d) and other typical fee-shifting statutes are construed to permit supplementing the lodestar in appropriate cases by paying counsel for assuming the risk of nonpayment, for the reasons set out below, it was error to do so in this case.

V

* * * [I]f it be assumed that this is one of the exceptional cases in which enhancement for assuming the risk of nonpayment is justified, we conclude that doubling the lodestar for certain phases of the work was excessive. We have alluded to the uncertainties involved in determining the risk of not prevailing and the burdensome nature of fee litigation. We deem it desirable and an appropriate application of the statute to hold that if the trial court specifically finds that there was a real risk of not prevailing on an issue in the case, an upward adjustment of the lodestar may be made, but, as a general rule, in an amount no more than 1/3 of the lodestar. Any additional adjustment would require the most exacting justification. This limitation will at once protect against windfalls for attorneys and act as some deterrence against bringing suits in which the attorney believes there is less than a 50–50 chance of prevailing. Riskier suits may be brought, and if won, a reasonable lodestar may

be awarded, but risk enhancement will be limited to 1/3 of the lodestar, if awarded at all. Here, even assuming an adjustment for risk was justified, the multiplier employed was excessive.

* * * Whatever the risk of winning or losing in a specific case might be, a fee award should be informed by the statutory purpose of making it possible for poor clients with good claims to secure competent help. Before adjusting for risk assumption, there should be evidence in the record, and the trial court should so find, that without risk-enhancement plaintiff would have faced substantial difficulties in finding counsel in the local or other relevant market. Here, there were no such findings.

JUSTICE O'CONNOR, concurring in part and concurring in the judgment.

For the reasons explained by the dissent I conclude that Congress did not intend to foreclose consideration of contingency in setting a reasonable fee under fee-shifting provisions such as that of the Clean Air Act, 42 U.S.C. § 7604(d), and the Civil Rights Attorney's Fees Awards Act, 42 U.S.C. § 1988. I also agree that compensation for contingency must be based on the difference in market treatment of contingent fee cases *as a class*, rather than on an assessment of the "riskiness" of any particular case. But in my view the plurality is also correct in holding that the "novelty and difficulty of the issues presented, and * * * the potential for protracted litigation," are factors adequately reflected in the lodestar, and that the District Court erred in employing a risk multiplier in the circumstances of this case.

* * *

To be "reasonable," the method for calculating a fee award must be not merely justifiable in theory but also objective and nonarbitrary in practice. Moreover, if the concept of treating contingency cases as a class is to be more than symbolic, a court's determination of how the market in a community compensates for contingency should not vary significantly from one case to the next. I agree with the plurality that without guidance as to the trial court's exercise of discretion, adjustment for risk could result in "severe difficulties and possible inequities." In my view, certain constraints on a court's discretion in setting attorney's fees are appropriate.

First, District Courts and Courts of Appeals should treat a determination of how a particular market compensates for contingency as controlling future cases involving the same market. Haphazard and widely divergent compensation for risk can be avoided only if contingency cases are treated as a class; and contingency cases can be treated as a class only if courts strive for consistency from one fee determination to the next. Determinations involving different markets should also comport with each other. Thus, if a fee applicant attempts to prove that the relevant market provides greater compensation for contingency than the markets involved in previous cases, the applicant should be able to point to differences in the markets that would justify the different rates of compensation.

Second, at all times the fee applicant bears the burden of proving the degree to which the relevant market compensates for contingency. * * *

Finally, a court should not award any enhancement based on "legal" risks or risks peculiar to the case. The lodestar—"the product of reasonable hours times a reasonable rate," *Hensley v. Eckerhart*, [461 U.S. 424, 434, 103 S.Ct. 1933, 1940, 76 L.Ed.2d 40 (1983)]—is flexible enough to account for great variation in the nature of the work performed in, and the challenges presented by, different cases. * * * Thus it is presumed that when counsel demonstrates considerable ability in overcoming unusual difficulties that have arisen in a case, counsel will be compensated for those accomplishments by means of an appropriate hourly rate multiplied by the hours expended.

JUSTICE BLACKMUN, with whom JUSTICES BRENNAN, MARSHALL and STEVENS join, dissenting.

* * *

In view of Congress' desire that statutory fees be competitive with the private market, the plurality needs a compelling reason in order to reject the market approach for determining what constitutes a reasonable fee. Although the plurality suggests some reasons, its objections are all based on a fundamental mischaracterization of the enhancement for contingency in awarding attorney's fees. * * *

* * *

The underlying flaw is that the appropriate enhancement for risk does not depend, in the first instance, on the *degree* of risk presented by a particular case. Enhancement for risk is not designed to equalize the prospective returns among contingent cases with different degrees of merit. Rather, it is designed simply to place contingent employment *as a whole* on roughly the same economic footing as noncontingent practice, in order that such cases receive the equal representation intended by Congress. Enhancement compensates attorneys for the risk of nonpayment associated with contingent employment, a risk that does not exist in noncontingent cases. As discussed above, without the possibility of enhancement for contingency, an attorney, from a simple economic point of view, would prefer noncontingent employment to contingent employment. This is because even contingent cases with the best merit may sometimes fail, because delay in payment is inherent in any contingent arrangement, and because other economic risks may be aggravated by the contingency in payment. Thus, contrary to the plurality's vision of an enhancement that radically increases as a case's chance of success decreases, an enhancement for contingency in ordinary cases will not be based on the relative likelihood of success of a particular case.

Once it is recognized that it is the fact of contingency, not the likelihood of success in any particular case, that mandates an increase in an attorney's fee, the frightening difficulties envisioned by the plurality disappear. There is no reason to assume that, in most cases, a court will have to delve into the strengths and weaknesses of a particular case, that potential conflict of interests will arise between attorneys and clients, or that large enhancements disproportionate to the success of a case will be granted. Rather, a court's job simply will be to determine whether a case was taken on a contingent basis, whether the attorney was able to mitigate the risk of nonpayment in any way, and whether other economic risks were aggravated by the contingency of payment.

* * *

The basic objective for courts to keep in mind in awarding enhancements for risk is that a "reasonable attorney's fee" should aim to be competitive with the private market, even if it is not possible to reflect that market perfectly. Thus, an enhancement for contingency, whether calculated as an increase in the reasonable hourly rate used to arrive at the lodestar or added to the lodestar as a bonus or a multiplier, is not designed to be a "windfall" for the attorney of the prevailing party. Rather, it is designed to ensure that lawyers who take cases on contingent bases are properly compensated for the risks inherent in such cases.

Notes and Questions

1. *Screening Mechanism to Discourage Frivolous Suits?* Does the *Christiansburg* Court's construction of the "prevailing party" language in § 706(k) adequately discourage frivolous suits? Note that whereas the NLRB's General Counsel screens all NLRA unfair labor practice charges, the EEOC has no power to block any private suits that it deems frivolous; its failure to find "reasonable cause" that a charge is "true," see § 706(b), provides no justification for refusing to issue a right-to-sue letter. Should the EEOC have some screening power? Alternatively, the 1983 amendments to Rule 11 of the F.R.Civ.P. may help deter frivolous actions by requiring attorneys to certify that a suit reflects a good-faith factual investigation and a good-faith basis in existing law or its reasonable extension. A filing not in good faith may result in the plaintiff or plaintiff's attorney having to pay the defendant's attorney's fees. For a critical perspective, see Lawrence M. Grosberg, Illusion and Reality in Regulating Lawyer Performance: Rethinking Rule 11, 32 Vill.L.Rev. 575 (1987).

Distinguishing *Christiansburg* as a civil-rights case, the Court in Fogerty v. Fantasy, Inc., 510 U.S. 517, 114 S.Ct. 1023, 127 L.Ed.2d 455 (1994), held that the "prevailing party" language in the Copyright Act's attorney's fees provision should be read in an "evenhanded" manner that treats prevailing plaintiffs and prevailing defendants in a similar fashion. Does this case signal a new approach on the Court's part to similarly worded statutes other than Title VII, such as the ADA and the Workers Adjustment and Retraining Notification Act (WARN) of 1988, 29 U.S.C. §§ 2101–2109, the federal plant-closing law?

2. *Comparative Note.* Compare the British "loser pays" system, which is commonly thought to deter both low-probability-of-success suits and risk-averse claimants. But cf. A. Mitchell Polinsky & Daniel L. Rubinfeld, Does the English Rule Discourage Low-Probability-of-Prevailing Plaintiffs?, 17 J. Leg. Stud. 519 (1998) (when settlement process is taken into account, "English rule" results in more low-probability plaintiffs going to trial than does U.S. system).

3. *"Lodestar" Method.* The *Delaware Valley* decision reaffirms the Supreme Court's adoption in Hensley v. Eckerhart, 461 U.S. 424, 103 S.Ct. 1933, 76 L.Ed.2d 40 (1983), and Blum v. Stenson, 465 U.S. 886, 104 S.Ct. 1541, 79 L.Ed.2d 891 (1984), of the "lodestar" method of calculating attorney's fees. Under this method, the "initial estimate of a reasonable attorney's fee is properly calculated by multiplying the number of hours reasonably expended on the litigation times a reasonable hourly rate." 465 U.S. at 888, 104 S.Ct. at 1543. In these cases, the Court suggested that the reasonableness of an hourly rate and of the hours expended may turn on a range of factors, encompassing several first suggested by an early influential Fifth Circuit case, Johnson v. Georgia Highway Express, Inc., 488 F.2d 714 (5th Cir.1974). The *Johnson* factors include, in addition to time expended and contingency: "the novelty and difficulty of the questions"; "the skill requisite to perform the legal service properly"; "the preclusion of employment * * * due to acceptance of the case"; "the customary fee"; "time limitations imposed by the client or the case"; "the amount involved and the results obtained"; "the experience, reputation, and ability of the attorneys"; "the 'undesirability' of the case"; "the nature and length of the professional relationship with the client"; and "awards in similar cases". In *Blum,* the Court held that an upward adjustment of the lodestar is appropriate only in "the rare case," 465 U.S. at 901, 902 n. 18, 104 S.Ct. at 1550, 1551 n. 18, and indicated that factors such as these normally should only be relevant when calculating the lodestar and should not be counted again in a multiplier of that lodestar. *Id.* at 898–901, 104 S.Ct. at 1548–50. The lodestar method of calculating fees in a civil rights case was also approved by the Court in a case in which this method yielded a fee that was many times greater than the monetary recovery achieved. City of Riverside v. Rivera, 477 U.S. 561, 106 S.Ct. 2686, 91 L.Ed.2d 466 (1986) (rejecting argument that it was beyond the discretion of trial court to find reasonable the expenditure of $245,456 of attorney time for recovery of $33,350 in a civil rights case).

4. Delaware Valley*'s Holding?* What exactly is the holding of the *Delaware Valley* case concerning when a court may appropriately multiply the lodestar by a contingency or risk factor? Does the holding turn on Justice O'Connor's concurring opinion, given the alignment of the Court? Compare Lattimore v. Oman Const., 868 F.2d 437, 439 (11th Cir.1989) (100% upward adjustment in the lodestar is appropriate on a finding of a "dearth" of attorneys willing to accept employment discrimination cases on a contingency basis in a given area), with King v. Palmer, 950 F.2d 771 (D.C.Cir.1991) (en banc) (reasonable lodestar fee may not be enhanced to compensate prevailing plaintiff for initial risk of loss).

5. *Merits of Contingency Multiplier?* Is the *Delaware Valley* plurality or dissent right about whether multiplying by a contingency factor is consistent with congressional intent to allow only prevailing plaintiffs to recover fees?

Who has the better of the argument on whether multiplying by a risk factor will normally be necessary to ensure adequate representation for plaintiffs? Does it matter whether the goal is representation equal to that available to defendants that pay on a non-contingent basis, or merely minimal or adequate representation? Why would a lawyer sufficiently accomplished to have a choice ever prefer to represent plaintiffs, working hours that might or might not be compensated at a rate that would be assured for hours spent representing institutional defendants? See generally Thomas D. Rowe, Jr., The Legal Theory of Attorney Fee Shifting: A Critical Overview, 1982 Duke L.J. 651.

6. *Guidance to the Lower Courts?* Justice O'Connor expresses concern about giving lower courts adequate guidance to choose an appropriate contingency multiplier. Could the Court have crafted a per se contingency factor applicable in all cases?

7. *Accounting for Time Value of Money?* Does *Delaware Valley* foreclose courts from taking into account the time value of money and the effects of inflation by awarding compensation at current rather than historic rates? See Gaines v. Dougherty Board of Education, 775 F.2d 1565, 1572 n. 14 (11th Cir.1985).

8. *"Changing the Legal Relationship": Fees Despite Partial Success.* Should a fee award be reduced to the extent a claimant does not prevail on certain claims or legal theories? Might such a rule have a discouraging effect on lawyers' willingness to press creative arguments requiring an extension of existing law? On the other hand, does it make sense to award attorney's fees when plaintiffs prevail on a relatively minor issue?

In Hensley v. Eckerhart, supra, the Court held that a prevailing plaintiff may recover fees for legal services expended on unsuccessful claims if those claims were not "distinct in all respects from his successful claims"; but "where the plaintiff achieved only limited success, the district court should award only that amount of fees that is reasonable in relation to the results obtained." 461 U.S. at 440, 103 S.Ct. at 1943. In Texas State Teachers Assn. v. Garland Independent School Dist., 489 U.S. 782, 109 S.Ct. 1486, 103 L.Ed.2d 866 (1989), the Court unanimously rejected the doctrine in the Fifth Circuit that a party does not "prevail" within the meaning of § 1988 unless it succeeds on the "central issue" in the litigation and achieves the "primary relief sought." *Garland* holds that once the plaintiff is "able to point to a resolution of the dispute which changes the legal relationship between itself and the defendant," the prevailing-party threshold is met; the degree of success goes to the reasonableness of the award rather than to the availability of a fee award altogether.

In Farrar v. Hobby, 506 U.S. 103, 115, 113 S.Ct. 566, 575, 121 L.Ed.2d 494 (1992), a § 1983 case, the Court held that a plaintiff who recovers only nominal damages is a "prevailing party" for § 1988 purposes, but that the extent of recovery should influence the size of the attorney's fee award. In actions principally seeking money damages, a nominal award "highlights the plaintiff's failure to prove actual, compensable injury." Some courts have read *Farrar* as not establishing a per se rule against fees awards in such cases. See, e.g., Brandau v. Kansas, 168 F.3d 1179 (10th Cir.1999).

To be a "prevailing" plaintiff, is a formal judgment required? Some courts had adopted a "catalyst" theory whereby a formal judgment is not required if the plaintiff accomplishes the original objectives of the lawsuit, see, e.g., Baumgartner v. Harrisburg Housing Auth., 21 F.3d 541 (3d Cir.1994); but cf. S–1 v. State Board of Educ. of N.C., 21 F.3d 49 (4th Cir.1994) (formal judgment, consent decree or settlement is required). The "catalyst theory" was rejected in Buckhannon Board and Care Home, Inc. v. West Virginia. Dept. of Health and Hum. Res., 532 U.S. 598, 121 S.Ct. 1835, 149 L.Ed.2d 855 (2001), where the Court held that a "prevailing party" must secure on "alteration in the legal relationship of the parties", under the Fair Housing Amendments of 1988, 42 U.S.C. § 3613(c)(2) and the ADA, 42 U.S.C. § 12205. In Graham v. Daimler-Chrysler Corp., 34 Cal.4th 553, 21 Cal.Rptr.3d 331, 101 P.3d 140 (2004), the California high court held that state law authorized attorney's fees awards to prevailing plaintiffs on the "catalyst" theory rejected as a matter of federal law in Buckhannon Board & Care Home, Inc. v. West Virginia Dept. of Health & Human Res., 532 U.S. 598, 121 S.Ct. 1835, 149 L.Ed.2d 855 (2001). The plaintiff must show the suit was a catalyst motivating defendant to provide the primary relief sought, had merit, and achieved its catalytic effect "by threat of victory, not by dint of nuisance and threat of expense," and that a reasonable attempt at pre-litigation settlement was made.

9. *"Market Rate" for Nonprofit Lawyers?* Blum v. Stenson, supra, is also significant for its holding that the "prevailing market rate" determines attorney's fees awards even where claimants are represented by nonprofit organizations that pay their attorneys at lower than market rates. See also Blanchard v. Bergeron, 489 U.S. 87, 109 S.Ct. 939, 103 L.Ed.2d 67 (1989) (attorney's fees are not limited to the amount provided in the plaintiff's contingent-fee arrangement with private counsel). How should a market rate be determined for a plaintiff's bar for the disadvantaged? Is it appropriate to draw analogies to comparable plaintiffs' actions in such potentially lucrative areas as antitrust and securities? See Norman v. Housing Authority of the City of Montgomery, 836 F.2d 1292, 1300 (11th Cir.1988). In Missouri v. Jenkins, 491 U.S. 274, 109 S.Ct. 2463, 105 L.Ed.2d 229 (1989), the Court held that the work of paralegals, law clerks, and recent law graduates could be compensated at the market rates for their services, rather than at the reduced costs paid by their attorney-employers. Section 113 of the 1991 Civil Rights Act authorizes inclusion of expert fees as part of the attorney's fee.

10. *"Mixed Motive" Cases.* In Title VII cases where defendants are able to show they would have made the same decision but for their discriminatory motive, the court under § 706(g) "may grant * * * attorney's fees and costs demonstrated to be directly attributable only to the pursuit of a claim under section 703(m) * * *." Some courts have held that, in view of the use of the word "may" in § 706(g), they have broad discretion even to disallow attorney's fees altogether where plaintiffs have achieved only limited success. Compare Sheppard v. Riverview Nursing Center, 88 F.3d 1332 (4th Cir.1996), with Gudenkauf v. Stauffer Communications, Inc., 158 F.3d 1074, 1081 (10th Cir.1998) (fees may be awarded when a plaintiff prevails "on a significant issue that furthers a public goal"). See also Nancy L. Lane, After *Price Waterhouse* and the Civil Rights Act of 1991: Providing Attorney's Fees

to Plaintiffs in Mixed Motive Age Discrimination Cases, 3 Elder L.J. 341 (1995).

11. *Pro-Settlement Policy?* In some cases, the Court has cited a pro-settlement policy in considering attorney's fees-related issues. See Marek v. Chesny, 473 U.S. 1, 105 S.Ct. 3012, 87 L.Ed.2d 1 (1985) (under Rule 68 of F.R.Civ.P., plaintiff cannot recover attorney's fees for services rendered after rejection of an offer of settlement that is greater than the judgment ultimately recovered and must pay defendant's post-offer "costs" defined to include attorney's fees, even where the offer does not separate the amount for attorney's fees from the amount offered for damages—ruling under § 1988 and perhaps other statutes that define "costs" to include attorney's fees); Evans v. Jeff D., 475 U.S. 717, 106 S.Ct. 1531, 89 L.Ed.2d 747 (1986) (district courts have discretion to uphold proposed settlements of class claims that waive attorney's fees). Do such decisions further settlement at the cost of reducing the supply of attorneys able to look only to statutory attorney's fees provisions for their compensation? Do such decisions also benefit defendants more than they encourage settlement by driving downward the relevant settlement range?

Is *Buckhannon*, see note 8 above, consistent with a pro-settlement policy? The Court there distinguished between negotiated settlements and the "voluntary cessation" of challenged activity by the defendant. See 532 U.S. at 609.

Rule 68 has had limited use in Title VII cases, in part because the defendants are reluctant to make an "offer of judgment" that may have collateral estoppel and negative publicity consequences for them. Also, where the underlying statute does not define "costs" to include attorney's fees, as in Title VII, the defendant's offer of judgment, even if accepted by the plaintiff, does not foreclose an award of attorney's fees.

For a discussion of Rule 68 issues, see Lucian Arye Bebchuk & Howard F. Chang, The Effect of Offer-of-Settlement Rules on the Terms of Settlement, 28 J.Leg.Stud. 489 (1999); Geoffrey P. Miller, An Economic Analysis of Rule 68, 15 J.Leg.Stud. 93 (1986). Post–*Jeff D.* developments are criticized in Note, Fee as the Wind Blows: Waivers of Attorney's Fees in Individual Civil Rights Actions Since *Evans v. Jeff D.*, 102 Harv.L.Rev. 1278 (1989).

12. *Fees for Related Administrative Proceedings?* Should a Title VII claimant receive attorney's fees for legal representation in administrative proceedings before a state deferral agency? See New York Gaslight Club, Inc. v. Carey, 447 U.S. 54, 100 S.Ct. 2024, 64 L.Ed.2d 723 (1980). Should ADEA claimants? See, e.g., Reichman v. Bonsignore, 818 F.2d 278 (2d Cir.1987).

Section 1988 authorizes a fee award for any "proceeding to enforce" § 1983. Should a § 1983 claimant receive fees for successful representation in an administrative proceeding that obviated the need to file suit? See Webb v. County Board of Educ., 471 U.S. 234, 105 S.Ct. 1923, 85 L.Ed.2d 233 (1985). What about representation resulting in an out-of-court settlement before any charges are filed or proceedings of any sort are commenced? Does the pro-settlement policy informing the *Marek* and *Jeff D.* rulings argue for creating incentives here to settle rather than sue?

13. *Fees For and Against Intervenors?* Is a union that intervenes to defend the seniority rights of its members in a suit brought against the employer liable for attorney's fees to prevailing plaintiffs? Should awards against unsuccessful intervenors be governed by the same standards that would be applied for awards against unsuccessful plaintiffs who challenge a settlement in a collateral suit? See Independent Federation of Flight Attendants v. Zipes, 491 U.S. 754, 109 S.Ct. 2732, 105 L.Ed.2d 639 (1989) (holding that fees may be assessed only if intervenors' claims are frivolous, unreasonable or without foundation).

14. *Fees Against the Government: Sovereign Immunity Considerations?* The eleventh amendment does not prohibit the grant of attorney's fees as part of an award of prospective relief against a state. Hutto v. Finney, 437 U.S. 678, 98 S.Ct. 2565, 57 L.Ed.2d 522 (1978). It also does not preclude enhancement of a fee award against a state to compensate for delay in payment. Missouri v. Jenkins, supra. Section 114 of the 1991 Civil Rights Act authorizes the court to award against federal sector employers "the same interest to compensate for delay in payment * * * as in cases involving nonpublic parties." But cf. Social Security Admin. v. Federal Labor Relations Auth., 201 F.3d 465 (D.C.Cir.2000) (Back Pay Act does not waive U.S.'s sovereign immunity from liability on postjudgment interest on FLSA liquidated-damages awards because such awards are not "pay, allowances, or differentials" and failure timely to pay such damages is not a "withdrawal or reduction" of compensation within the meaning of the statute, 5 U.S.C. § 5596(b)(1)).

15. *Court Appointment of Title VII Counsel.* In addition to the attorney's fees provision in § 706(k) of Title VII, § 706(f)(1) authorizes the district court to appoint counsel in appropriate circumstances and authorizes commencement of an action "without payment of fees, costs, or security." Should § 706(f)(1) be limited to indigent claimants?

16. *Tax Consequences of Fee Awards*: In Commissioner v. Banks, 543 U.S. 426, 125 S.Ct. 826, 160 L.Ed.2d 859 (2005), the Court held that a discrimination plaintiff whose recovery constitutes income must report as gross income the contingent free paid to his attorney. The "sting" of the ruling is somewhat mitigated because under the Civil Rights Tax Relief Act, part of the American Jobs Creation Act of 2004, 26 U.S.C. § 62(a)(19), attorney's fees paid by or on behalf of the taxpayer in connection with discrimination claims will be treated as an above the line item not subject to the limitation on itemized deductions.

Chapter Eighteen

PROBLEMS OF COORDINATION, DEFERRAL AND PREEMPTION

A. INTRODUCTION

This chapter considers a special set of interesting and complicated procedural problems presented by the regulation of employment in America. The problems concern the relationships between the multiple and sometimes overlapping causes of action available to employees to challenge a particular personnel decision.

Rational policymakers might have good reason to want to minimize overlapping, multiple regulation. Both efficiency and fairness would seem to be furthered by allowing complainants or public authorities to mount only a single proceeding against employers, or unions, on a particular complex of facts. Multiple proceedings in multiple fora of course create the potential for compounded litigation costs, inconsistent determinations, and prolongation of disputes. In addition, it may not seem fair that an employer or union in order to escape liability should have to successfully defend a particular course of action in numerous tribunals, while a complainant can be victorious by winning in only one.

Yet, there may be several advantages to a system that provides multiple points of regulation of a particular employment decision. First, specialized enforcement structures permit legislators to intervene in labor markets in a manner tailored to the particular problems thought to require regulation. For instance, different administrative structures offering different remedies may seem more appropriate for the regulation of status discrimination than for the protection of employee whistleblowing. Second, enforcement structures that do not claim comprehensive regulation allow room for the private resolution of disputes, especially through collective bargaining and the grievance arbitration system that almost invariably emerge from such bargaining. There may be an interest in keeping separate private dispute resolution systems from any external regulatory system based on public law. Third, federalism values may be served. The division of authority between different levels of government, it is thought, helps preserve liberty by diffusing governmental authority. It also facilitates more direct citizen involvement in public decisionmaking processes, and permits the states to function as a laboratory for regulatory innovation.

Such arguments may justify multiple sources of regulation without necessarily justifying giving employee grievants multiple opportunities to contest a given personnel decision. Exposing employers to multiple actions, however, might be defended as a way to ensure more complete eradication of particular employment practices. If a challenged personnel decision can be reviewed through multiple regulatory lenses, the error costs of failing to discover illegality can be minimized. For some, certain employment practices may be sufficiently undesirable to justify not only the costs of multiple litigation, but also over-enforcement against innocent employers.

None of these arguments, of course, necessarily establishes the desirability of multiple regulation or litigation. The benefits of particular schemes must be weighed against the attendant costs. Policymakers must think carefully about how various regulatory structures should relate to each other in order to insure the most effective and efficient achievement of their regulatory goals. The cases in this chapter reflect the complicated choices that Congress, state legislatures, and the courts have been making in defining the relationships among American employment laws.

B.   RELATIONSHIPS AMONG FEDERAL SYSTEMS

1.   *The Civil Rights Statutes, the Constitution and Modern Administrative Systems*

JOHNSON v. RAILWAY EXPRESS AGENCY, INC.

Supreme Court of the United States, 1975.
421 U.S. 454, 95 S.Ct. 1716, 44 L.Ed.2d 295.

MR. JUSTICE BLACKMUN delivered the opinion of the Court.

This case presents the issue whether the timely filing of a charge of employment discrimination with the Equal Employment Opportunity Commission (EEOC), pursuant to § 706 of Title VII of the Civil Rights Act of 1964, 78 Stat. 259, 42 U.S.C. § 2000e–5, tolls the running of the period of limitation applicable to an action based on the same facts, instituted under 42 U.S.C. § 1981.

* * *

Despite Title VII's range and its design as a comprehensive solution for the problem of invidious discrimination in employment, the aggrieved individual clearly is not deprived of other remedies he possesses and is not limited to Title VII in his search for relief. "[T]he legislative history of Title VII manifests a congressional intent to allow an individual to pursue independently his rights under both Title VII and other applicable state and federal statutes." *Alexander v. Gardner–Denver Co.*, 415 U.S. [36, 94 S.Ct. 1011, 39 L.Ed.2d 147 (1974)], at 48, 94 S.Ct., at 1019. In particular, Congress noted "that the remedies available to the individual under Title VII are co-extensive with the indiv(i)dual's right to sue under the provisions of the Civil Rights Act of 1866, 42 U.S.C. § 1981, and that the two procedures augment each other and are not mutually exclusive." H.R.Rep. No. 92–238, p. 19 (1971), U.S.Code Cong. & Admin.News, 1972, pp. 2137, 2154. See also S.Rep. No. 92–415, p. 24 (1971). Later, in considering the Equal Employment Opportunity Act of 1972, the Senate rejected an amendment that would have deprived a claimant of any right to sue under § 1981. 118 Cong.Rec. 3371–3373 (1972).

Title 42 U.S.C. § 1981, being the present codification of § 16 of the century-old Civil Rights Act of 1870, 16 Stat. 144, on the other hand, on its face relates primarily to racial discrimination in the making and enforcement of contracts. Although this Court has not specifically so held, it is well settled among the federal Courts of Appeals—and we now join them—that § 1981 affords a federal remedy against discrimination in private employment on the basis of race. An individual who establishes a cause of action under § 1981 is entitled to both equitable and legal relief, including compensatory and, under certain circumstances, punitive damages. * * * And a backpay award under § 1981 is not restricted to the two years specified for backpay recovery under Title VII.

Section 1981 is not coextensive in its coverage with Title VII. The latter is made inapplicable to certain employers. 42 U.S.C. § 2000e(b) (1970 ed., Supp. III). Also, Title VII offers assistance in investigation, conciliation, counsel, waiver of court costs, and attorneys' fees, items that are unavailable at least under the specific terms of § 1981.

* * *

We are satisfied * * * that Congress did not expect that a § 1981 court action usually would be resorted to only upon completion of Title VII procedures and the Commission's efforts to obtain voluntary compliance. Conciliation and persuasion through the administrative process, to be sure, often constitute a desirable approach to settlement of disputes based on sensitive and emotional charges of invidious employment discrimination. We recognize, too, that the filing of a lawsuit might tend to deter efforts at conciliation, that lack of success in the legal action could weaken the Commission's efforts to induce voluntary compliance, and that a suit is privately oriented and narrow, rather than broad, in application, as successful conciliation tends to be. But these are the natural effects of the choice Congress has made available to the claimant by its conferring upon him independent administrative and judicial remedies. The choice is a valuable one. Under some circumstances, the administrative route may be highly preferred over the litigatory; under others the reverse may be true. We are disinclined, in the face of congressional emphasis upon the existence and independence of the two remedies, to infer any positive preference for one over the other, without a more definite expression in the legislation Congress has enacted, as, for example, a proscription of a § 1981 action while an EEOC claim is pending.

We generally conclude, therefore, that the remedies available under Title VII and under § 1981, although related, and although directed to most of the same ends, are separate, distinct, and independent. With this base established, we turn to the limitation issue.

* * *

Since there is no specifically stated or otherwise relevant federal statute of limitations for a cause of action under § 1981, the controlling period would ordinarily be the most appropriate one provided by state law.

* * *

Petitioner argues that a failure to toll the limitation period in this case will conflict seriously with the broad remedial and humane purposes of Title VII. Specifically, he urges that Title VII embodies a strong federal policy in support of conciliation and voluntary compliance as a means of achieving the statutory mandate of equal employment opportunity. He suggests that failure to toll the statute on a § 1981 claim during the pendency of an administrative complaint in the EEOC would force a plaintiff into premature and expensive litigation that would destroy all chances for administrative conciliation and voluntary compliance.

We have noted this possibility above and, indeed, it is conceivable, and perhaps almost to be expected, that failure to toll will have the effect of pressing a civil rights complainant who values his § 1981 claim into court before the EEOC has completed its administrative proceeding. One answer to this, although perhaps not a highly satisfactory one, is that the plaintiff in his § 1981 suit may ask the court to stay proceedings until the administrative efforts at conciliation and voluntary compliance have been completed. But the fundamental answer to petitioner's argument lies in the fact—presumably a happy one for the civil rights claimant—that Congress clearly has retained § 1981 as a remedy against private employment discrimination separate from and independent of the more elaborate and time-consuming procedures of Title VII. Petitioner freely concedes that he could have filed his § 1981 action at any time after his cause of action accrued; in fact, we understand him to claim an unfettered right so to do. Thus, in a very real sense, petitioner has slept on his § 1981 rights. The fact that his slumber may have been induced by faith in the adequacy of his Title VII remedy is of little relevance inasmuch as the two remedies are truly independent. * * * We find no policy reason that excuses petitioner's failure to take the minimal steps necessary to preserve each claim independently.

GREAT AMERICAN FEDERAL SAVINGS
& LOAN ASSN. v. NOVOTNY

Supreme Court of the United States, 1979.
442 U.S. 366, 99 S.Ct. 2345, 60 L.Ed.2d 957.

Mr. Justice Stewart delivered the opinion of the Court.

* * * In the case now before us, we consider the scope of 42 U.S.C. § 1985(3) (1976 ed., Supp. II), the surviving version of § 2 of the Civil Rights Act of 1871.[1]

I

The respondent, John R. Novotny, began his career with the Great American Federal Savings and Loan Association (hereinafter Association) in Allegheny County, Pa., in 1950. By 1975, he was secretary of the Association, a member of its board of directors, and a loan officer. According to the allegations of the complaint in this case the Association "intentionally and deliberately embarked upon and pursued a course of conduct the effect of which was to deny to female employees equal employment opportunity * * *." When Novotny expressed support for the female employees at a meeting of the board of directors, his connection with the Association abruptly ended. He was not re-elected as secretary; he was not re-elected to the board; and he was fired. His support for the Association's female employees, he alleges, was the cause of the termination of his employment.

Novotny filed a complaint with the Equal Employment Opportunity Commission under Title VII of the Civil Rights Act of 1964. After receiving a right-to-sue letter, he brought this lawsuit against the Association and its directors in the District Court for the Western District of Pennsylvania. He claimed damages under 42 U.S.C. § 1985(3) (1976 ed., Supp. II), contending that he had been injured as the result of a conspiracy to deprive him of equal protection of and equal privileges and immunities under the laws.[4] The District Court granted the defendants' motion to dismiss. It held that § 1985(3) could not be invoked because the directors of a single corporation could not, as a matter of law and fact, engage in a conspiracy.[5]

1. Title 42 U.S.C. § 1985(c) [42 USCS § 1985(3)], Rev.Stat. § 1980, provides:

"If two or more persons in any State or Territory conspire or go in disguise on the highway or on the premises of another, for the purpose of depriving, either directly or indirectly, any person or class of persons of the equal protection of the laws; or of equal privileges and immunities under the laws; * * * in any case of conspiracy set forth in this section, if one or more persons engaged therein do, or cause to be done, any act in furtherance of the object of such conspiracy, whereby another is injured in his person or property, or deprived of having and exercising any right or privilege of a citizen of the United States, the party so injured or deprived may have an action for the recovery of damages occasioned by such injury or deprivation, against any one or more of the conspirators."

4. His complaint also alleged, as a second cause of action, that his discharge was in retaliation for his efforts on behalf of equal employment opportunity, and thus violated § 704(a) of Title VII of the Civil Rights Act of 1964. * * *

5. As to the Title VII claim, the District Court held that Novotny was not a proper plaintiff under § 704(a).

Novotny appealed. After oral argument before a three-judge panel, the case was reargued before the en banc Court of Appeals for the Third Circuit, which unanimously reversed the District Court's judgment. The Court of Appeals ruled that Novotny had stated a cause of action under § 1985(3). It held that conspiracies motivated by an invidious animus against women fall within § 1985(3), and that Novotny, a male allegedly injured as a result of such a conspiracy, had standing to bring suit under that statutory provision. It ruled that Title VII could be the source of a right asserted in an action under § 1985(3), and that intracorporate conspiracies come within the intendment of the section. Finally, the court concluded that its construction of § 1985(3) did not present any serious constitutional problem.[6]

* * *

Section 1985(3) provides no substantive rights itself; it merely provides a remedy for violation of the rights it designates. The primary question in the present case, therefore, is whether a person injured by a conspiracy to violate § 704(a) of Title VII of the Civil Rights Act of 1964 is deprived of "the equal protection of the laws, or of equal privileges and immunities under the laws" within the meaning of § 1985(3).

* * *

If a violation of Title VII could be asserted through § 1985(3), a complainant could avoid most if not all of [the] detailed and specific provisions of [Title VII]. Section 1985(3) expressly authorizes compensatory damages; punitive damages might well follow. The plaintiff or defendant might demand a jury trial. The short and precise time limitations of Title VII would be grossly altered. Perhaps most importantly, the complaint could completely bypass the administrative process, which plays such a crucial role in the scheme established by Congress in Title VII.

The problem in this case is closely akin to that in *Brown v. GSA,* 425 U.S. 820, 96 S.Ct. 1961, 48 L.Ed.2d 402. There, we held that § 717 of Title VII provides the exclusive remedy for employment discrimination claims of those federal employees that it covers. Our conclusion was based on the proposition that

"[t]he balance, completeness, and structural integrity of § 717 are inconsistent with the petitioner's contention that the judicial reme-

---

6. The Court of Appeals ruled that Novotny had also stated a valid cause of action under Title VII. It held that § 704(a) applies to retaliation for both formal and informal actions taken to advance the purposes of the Act. That holding is not now before this Court.

We note the relative narrowness of the specific issue before the Court. It is unnecessary for us to consider whether a plaintiff would have a cause of action under § 1985(3) where the defendant was not subject to suit under Title VII or a comparable statute. Cf. *United States v. Johnson,* 390 U.S. 563, 88 S.Ct. 1231, 20 L.Ed.2d 132. Nor do we think it necessary to consider whether § 1985(3) creates a remedy for statutory rights other than those fundamental rights derived from the Constitution. Cf. *Griffin v. Breckenridge,* 403 U.S. 88, 91 S.Ct. 1790, 29 L.Ed.2d 338

dy afforded by § 717(c) was designed merely to supplement other putative judicial relief." 425 U.S., at 832, 96 S.Ct. at 1968.

Here, the case is even more compelling. In *Brown,* the Court concluded that § 717 displaced other causes of action arguably available to assert substantive rights similar to those granted by § 717. Section 1985(3), by contrast, *creates* no rights. It is a purely remedial statute, providing a civil cause of action when some otherwise defined federal right—to equal protection of the laws or equal privileges and immunities under the laws—is breached by a conspiracy in the manner defined by the section. Thus, we are not faced in this case with a question of implied repeal. The right Novotny claims under § 704(a) did not even arguably exist before the passage of Title VII. The only question here, therefore, is whether the rights created by Title VII may be asserted within the *remedial* framework of § 1985(3).

This case thus differs markedly from the cases recently decided by this Court that have related the substantive provisions of last century's Civil Rights Acts to contemporary legislation conferring similar substantive rights. In those cases we have held that substantive rights conferred in the 19th century were not withdrawn, *sub silentio,* by the subsequent passage of the modern statutes. * * * [The Court cited here its previous decisions in *Johnson* and *Runyon v. McCrary,* 427 U.S. 160, 96 S.Ct. 2586, 49 L.Ed.2d 415 (1976)].

* * *

This case, by contrast, does not involve two "independent" rights, and for the same basic reasons that underlay the Court's decision in *Brown v. GSA, supra,* reinforced by the other considerations discussed in this opinion, we conclude that § 1985(3) may not be invoked to redress violations of Title VII. It is true that a § 1985(3) remedy would not be coextensive with Title VII, since a plaintiff in an action under § 1985(3) must prove both a conspiracy and a group animus that Title VII does not require. While this incomplete congruity would limit the damage that would be done to Title VII, it would not eliminate it. Unimpaired effectiveness can be given to the plan put together by Congress in Title VII only by holding that deprivation of a right created by Title VII cannot be the basis for a cause of action under § 1985(3).

[*Eds.* The concurring opinion of Justice Stevens and the dissenting opinion of Justice White, joined in by Justices Brennan and Marshall, are omitted.]

Notes and Questions

1. *Section 1981 and Private Employment Discrimination.* Note that the *Johnson* Court's assertion that § 1981 "affords a federal remedy against discrimination in private employment on the basis of race" was confirmed by § 101 of the Civil Rights Act of 1991.

2. *Judicial Power to Reconcile Statutes?* Before the Court's 1968 ruling in Jones v. Alfred H. Mayer Co., 392 U.S. 409, 88 S.Ct. 2186, 20 L.Ed.2d

1189 (1968), the Civil Rights Act of 1866, of which § 1981 is a part, was not thought to apply to private action. When Congress enacted Title VII in 1964, it did so without awareness that there might be another federal statute covering private employment. How should courts go about reconciling the long dormant post-Civil War legislation with provisions of later legislation that focus specifically on employment discrimination? Do the two stand as entirely separate enactments irrespective of particularized policy judgments in the latter such as those found in § 703(h), or must such judgments be read into the earlier enactment in order to render coherent the body of federal employment discrimination law? Is there an implied judicial power to integrate statutes passed by different Congresses without any specific legislative statement concerning their reconciliation? See Samuel Estreicher, Note, Federal Power to Regulate Private Discrimination: The Revival of the Enforcement Clauses of the Reconstruction Era Amendments, 74 Colum.L.Rev. 449, 473–500 (1974).

3. Johnson's *Rationale.* Does the very availability of an independent § 1981 cause of action complicate the conciliation and settlement of a Title VII race discrimination claim? If so, is there any reason why Congress would want to encourage the initiation of independent actions before the completion of the EEOC conciliation process? Which, if any, policies underlying statutes of limitation might support the holding in *Johnson* concerning tolling of § 1981 limitation periods? Does *Johnson* in fact repudiate the accommodation process suggested in the preceding note? But cf. notes 8 and 9 below.

4. *Are* Johnson *and* Novotny *Consistent?* Can the *Johnson* Court's acknowledgment that there is an independent § 1981 cause of action for employment discrimination after Title VII be reconciled with the decision in *Novotny* not to allow § 1985(3) actions that would circumvent the Title VII administrative scheme? Should it matter that the § 1981 cause of action asserted in *Johnson*, unlike the § 1985(3) action in *Novotny*, would exist in the absence of Title VII?

5. *Does § 1985(3) Provide Only Remedies?* The *Novotny* Court is surely correct to view § 1985(3) as being dependent on other rights-creating statutory or constitutional provisions, but is it also correct to assert that § 1985(3) is only a remedial provision? As § 704 of Title VII establishes a different right than that secured by § 703, does § 1985(3) also add an additional guarantee—the right to be free of injuries due to conspiracies to deprive others of their independent federal substantive rights? In his dissent not reproduced here, Justice White suggests that § 1985(3) would protect individuals who are not themselves protected from retaliation by § 704(a) of Title VII, such as a nonemployee director or customer, but who are penalized by firms for coming to the aid of employees denied rights under Title VII. Is this suggestion now foreclosed by the reasoning of the majority opinion?

6. *Use of § 1985(3) in Employment Discrimination Litigation Based on the Constitution.* Does *Novotny* leave any role for § 1985(3) in employment discrimination litigation? Does it preclude § 1985(3) actions against conspiracies to deprive a constitutional right, as well as a Title VII right, whenever those actions are based on the same set of facts that could have supported a Title VII action? The lower courts are split. Compare, e.g., Roybal v.

Albuquerque, 653 F.Supp. 102, 105–06 (D.N.M.1986) (*Novotny* does not preclude action against conspiracy to deny equal protection of laws), with Polisoto v. Weinberger, 638 F.Supp. 1353, 1368–69 (W.D.Tex.1986) (§ 1985(3) claim based on equal protection precluded because it could have been brought under Title VII).

Even if *Novotny* does not preclude most § 1985(3) employment discrimination actions based on the deprivation of constitutional rights, such actions face other hurdles. Justice Stevens in his concurring opinion not produced here states that § 1985(3) would provide a cause of action for wholly private conspiracies to deny blacks the right to be free of the badges of slavery protected by the thirteenth amendment, see Griffin v. Breckenridge, 403 U.S. 88, 91 S.Ct. 1790, 29 L.Ed.2d 338 (1971). However, Stevens explains, because the fourteenth amendment's right to equal protection is secured only against state action, only conspiracies to deny an individual some governmental benefit or opportunity, such as a public sector job, could be covered by § 1985(3) through the equal protection clause. This last position was sustained by a majority of the Court in United Bhd. of Carpenters v. Scott, 463 U.S. 825, 103 S.Ct. 3352, 77 L.Ed.2d 1049 (1983). Moreover, the *Scott* Court also held that § 1985(3) does not reach conspiracies against economic groups, and suggested (contrary to *Griffin*'s broader "class-based" prejudice formulation) that it may only reach private conspiracies motivated by racial bias.

In Bray v. Alexandria Women's Health Clinic, 506 U.S. 263, 113 S.Ct. 753, 122 L.Ed.2d 34 (1993), the Court confirmed that § 1985(3) requires proof of animus against a class, like blacks, defined by status. The Court reserved judgment on whether animus against women in general would be sufficient, but held that animus against women who engage in a particular activity is not sufficient, even if the activity, such as abortions, is one in which only women can engage. The *Bray* Court also confirmed that § 1985(3) reaches private conspiracies only against those few rights, notably interstate travel and freedom from slavery, protected by the Constitution from private impairment. Since *Bray* a number of circuits have held that women are a protected class under § 1985(3). See, e.g., Lyes v. City of Riviera Beach, 166 F.3d 1332 (11th Cir.1999) (en banc); Libertad v. Welch, 53 F.3d 428, 448–49 (1st Cir. 1995); but see, e.g., Deubert v. Gulf Fed. Sav. Bank, 820 F.2d 754, 757 (5th Cir.1987) (dicta).

7. *Intracorporate Conspiracies Under § 1985(3).* Novotny might not have prevailed on his § 1985(3) claim in any event. It has been held that the conspiracy requirement in § 1985(3) cannot be satisfied by the participation in a discriminatory decision by two or more individuals acting as agents of the same employer. See, e.g., Dombrowski v. Dowling, 459 F.2d 190, 196 (7th Cir.1972); but cf., e.g., Hodgin v. Jefferson, 447 F.Supp. 804, 807 (D.Md. 1978) (unauthorized acts of individuals employed by same corporation may constitute a § 1985(3) violation).

8. *Implications of* Novotny *for Use of § 1983 to Reach Government Employment Decisions that Violate Title VII Rights?* The holding in *Novotny* raises questions concerning when nonconstitutionally based employment discrimination claims can be brought under § 1983, the other surviving descendant of the Civil Rights Act of 1871. Section 1983, like § 1985(3),

creates no substantive rights independent of those created by other statutes or the constitution. See also Chapman v. Houston Welfare Rights Org., 441 U.S. 600, 99 S.Ct. 1905, 60 L.Ed.2d 508 (1979). In Maine v. Thiboutot, 448 U.S. 1, 100 S.Ct. 2502, 65 L.Ed.2d 555 (1980), the Court held that § 1983 provides a cause of action to remedy the deprivation of federal statutory as well as constitutional rights. However, a year later in Middlesex County Sewerage Authority v. National Sea Clammers Ass'n, 453 U.S. 1, 20, 101 S.Ct. 2615, 2626, 69 L.Ed.2d 435 (1981), the Court narrowed *Thiboutot* by holding that the inclusion of a comprehensive remedial scheme in a statute "may suffice to demonstrate congressional intent to preclude the remedy of suits under § 1983" for violations of that statute. The Court's effort in *Novotny,* as well as in Brown v. GSA, on which it in part relied, to protect the policy judgments embodied in the Title VII remedial scheme strongly suggests that the Court, following the lead of the lower courts, would find congressional intent to preclude use of § 1983 to remedy the deprivation of Title VII rights by public sector employers. See, e.g., Foster v. Wyrick, 823 F.2d 218, 221–22 (8th Cir.1987).

9. *Use of § 1983 to Reach Government Employment Decisions that Violate Constitutional Rights?* A more difficult question is whether Title VII should be read to preclude § 1983 causes of action based on a public employer's alleged discrimination in violation of the equal protection clause of the fourteenth amendment. In Smith v. Robinson, 468 U.S. 992, 104 S.Ct. 3457, 82 L.Ed.2d 746 (1984), the Supreme Court held that a comprehensive federal regulatory scheme established by the Education of the Handicapped Act, 84 Stat. 175, precluded a disabled plaintiff's equal protection claim to a publicly financed special education. Although *Smith* was overturned on its facts by Congress, see 20 U.S.C. § 1415(f), some district courts relied on its reasoning to hold that Title VII provides an exclusive remedy unless the plaintiff alleges a factual basis for the constitutional claim that could not support a Title VII claim. See, e.g., Reiter v. Center Consolidated School District, 618 F.Supp. 1458 (D.Colo.1985). See also Marrero–Rivera v. Department of Justice, 800 F.Supp. 1024, 1029–30 (D.P.R.1992) (reading Civil Rights Act of 1991 to provide a more comprehensive remedial system that preempts § 1983). A number of court of appeals decisions, relying on the 1972 Title VII legislative history, however, have held that § 1983 constitutional claims against public employers are not precluded. See, e.g., Southard v. Texas Board of Criminal Justice, 114 F.3d 539 (5th Cir.1997); Bradley v. Pittsburgh Bd. of Educ., 913 F.2d 1064, 1079 (3d Cir.1990); Keller v. Prince George's County, 827 F.2d 952 (4th Cir.1987); Trigg v. Fort Wayne Community Schools, 766 F.2d 299 (7th Cir.1985); Day v. Wayne County Board of Auditors, 749 F.2d 1199 (6th Cir.1984). Is it relevant that the Supreme Court has held that § 1983 plaintiffs need not exhaust even adequate and appropriate state administrative remedies because § 1983 provides a direct right of action to the federal courts for the vindication of constitutional rights? See Patsy v. Florida Board of Regents, 457 U.S. 496, 102 S.Ct. 2557, 73 L.Ed.2d 172 (1982). If the availability of Title VII does not preclude use of § 1983 for constitutional claims, should the availability of the ADEA bar § 1983 constitutional claims? Compare Zombro v. Baltimore City Police Dept., 868 F.2d 1364, 1370–71 n. 5 (4th Cir.1989) (unlike Title VII, there is "no comparable evidence of congressional intent to support § 1983 equal

protection challenges concurrent * * * with the comprehensive remedial framework of the ADEA"), with Mummelthie v. City of Mason City, Iowa, 873 F.Supp. 1293 (N.D.Iowa 1995) (since Congress did not amend § 1983 by implication when establishing ADEA remedial scheme, independent constitutional actions should be allowed).

2. *Private Grievance Arbitration and Federal Statutory Claims*

ALEXANDER v. GARDNER–DENVER COMPANY

Supreme Court of the United States, 1974.

415 U.S. 36, 94 S.Ct. 1011, 39 L.Ed.2d 147.

MR. JUSTICE POWELL delivered the opinion of the Court.

This case concerns the proper relationship between federal courts and the grievance-arbitration machinery of collective-bargaining agreements in the resolution and enforcement of an individual's rights to equal employment opportunities under Title VII of the Civil Rights Act of 1964, 78 Stat. 253, 42 U.S.C. § 2000e et seq. Specifically, we must decide under what circumstances, if any, an employee's statutory right to a trial *de novo* under Title VII may be foreclosed by prior submission of his claim to final arbitration under the nondiscrimination clause of a collective-bargaining agreement.

In May 1966, petitioner Harrell Alexander, Sr., a black, was hired by respondent Gardner–Denver Co. (the company) to perform maintenance work at the company's plant in Denver, Colorado. In June 1968, petitioner was awarded a trainee position as a drill operator. He remained at that job until his discharge from employment on September 29, 1969. The company informed petitioner that he was being discharged for producing too many defective or unusable parts that had to be scrapped.

On October 1, 1969, petitioner filed a grievance under the collective-bargaining agreement in force between the company and petitioner's union, Local No. 3029 of the United Steelworkers of America (the union). The grievance stated: "I feel I have been unjustly discharged and ask that I be reinstated with full seniority and pay." No explicit claim of racial discrimination was made.

Under Art. 4 of the collective-bargaining agreement, the company retained "the right to hire, suspend or discharge [employees] for proper cause." Article 5, § 2, provided, however, that "there shall be no discrimination against any employee on account of race, color, religion, sex, national origin, or ancestry," and Art. 23, § 6(a), stated that "[n]o employee will be discharged, suspended or given a written warning notice except for just cause." The agreement also contained a broad arbitration clause covering "differences aris[ing] between the Company and the Union as to the meaning and application of the provisions of this Agreement" and "any trouble aris[ing] in the plant."

* * * In the final pre-arbitration step, petitioner raised, apparently for the first time, the claim that his discharge resulted from racial

discrimination. The company rejected all of petitioner's claims, and the grievance proceeded to arbitration. Prior to the arbitration hearing, however, petitioner filed a charge of racial discrimination with the Colorado Civil Rights Commission, which referred the complaint to the Equal Employment Opportunity Commission on November 5, 1969.

At the arbitration hearing on November 20, 1969, petitioner testified that his discharge was the result of racial discrimination and informed the arbitrator that he had filed a charge with the Colorado Commission because he "could not rely on the union." The union introduced a letter in which petitioner stated that he was "knowledgeable that in the same plant others have scrapped an equal amount and sometimes in excess, but by all logical reasoning I * * * have been the target of preferential discriminatory treatment." The union representative also testified that the company's usual practice was to transfer unsatisfactory trainee drill operators back to their former positions.

On December 30, 1969, the arbitrator ruled that petitioner had been "discharged for just cause." He made no reference to petitioner's claim of racial discrimination. The arbitrator stated that the union had failed to produce evidence of a practice of transferring rather than discharging trainee drill operators who accumulated excessive scrap, but he suggested that the company and the union confer on whether such an arrangement was feasible in the present case.

On July 25, 1970, the Equal Employment Opportunity Commission determined that there was not reasonable cause to believe that a violation of Title VII of the Civil Rights Act of 1964, 42 U.S.C. § 2000e et seq., had occurred. The Commission later notified petitioner of his right to institute a civil action in federal court within 30 days. Petitioner then filed the present action in the United States District Court for the District of Colorado, alleging that his discharge resulted from a racially discriminatory employment practice in violation of § 703(a)(1) of the Act, 42 U.S.C. § 2000e–2(a)(1).

The District Court granted respondent's motion for summary judgment and dismissed the action. The court found that the claim of racial discrimination had been submitted to the arbitrator and resolved adversely to petitioner. It then held that petitioner, having voluntarily elected to pursue his grievance to final arbitration under the nondiscrimination clause of the collective-bargaining agreement, was bound by the arbitral decision and thereby precluded from suing his employer under Title VII. The Court of Appeals for the Tenth Circuit affirmed *per curiam* on the basis of the District Court's opinion.

* * *

III

Title VII does not speak expressly to the relationship between federal courts and the grievance-arbitration machinery of collective-bargaining agreements. It does, however, vest federal courts with plenary powers to enforce the statutory requirements; and it specifies with precision the jurisdictional prerequisites that an individual must satisfy before he is entitled to institute a lawsuit. In the present case, these prerequisites were met when petitioner (1) filed timely a charge of employment discrimination with the Commission, and (2) received and acted upon the Commission's statutory notice of the right to sue. 42 U.S.C. § 2000e–5(b), (e), and (f). * * * There is no suggestion in the statutory scheme that a prior arbitral decision either forecloses an individual's right to sue or divests federal courts of jurisdiction.

In addition, legislative enactments in this area have long evinced a general intent to accord parallel or overlapping remedies against discrimination. * * * Moreover, the legislative history of Title VII manifests a congressional intent to allow an individual to pursue independently his rights under both Title VII and other applicable state and federal statutes. The clear inference is that Title VII was designed to supplement, rather than supplant, existing laws and institutions relating to employment discrimination. In sum, Title VII's purpose and procedures strongly suggest that an individual does not forfeit his private cause of action if he first pursues his grievance to final arbitration under the nondiscrimination clause of a collective-bargaining agreement.

In reaching the opposite conclusion, the District Court relied in part on the doctrine of election of remedies. That doctrine, which refers to situations where an individual pursues remedies that are legally or factually inconsistent, has no application in the present context. In submitting his grievance to arbitration, an employee seeks to vindicate his contractual right under a collective-bargaining agreement. By contrast, in filing a lawsuit under Title VII, an employee asserts independent statutory rights accorded by Congress. The distinctly separate nature of these contractual and statutory rights is not vitiated merely because both were violated as a result of the same factual occurrence. And certainly no inconsistency results from permitting both rights to be enforced in their respectively appropriate forums. * * *

We are also unable to accept the proposition that petitioner waived his cause of action under Title VII. To begin, we think it clear that there can be no prospective waiver of an employee's rights under Title VII. It is true, of course, that a union may waive certain statutory rights related to collective activity, such as the right to strike. *Mastro Plastics Corp. v. NLRB*, 350 U.S. 270, 76 S.Ct. 349, 100 L.Ed. 309 (1956); *Boys Markets, Inc. v. Retail Clerk's Union*, 398 U.S. 235, 90 S.Ct. 1583, 26 L.Ed.2d 199 (1970). These rights are conferred on employees collectively to foster the processes of bargaining and properly may be exercised or relinquished by the union as collective-bargaining agent to obtain economic benefits for union members. Title VII, on the other hand, stands on plainly different ground; it concerns not majoritarian processes, but an individual's right to equal employment opportunities. Title VII's strictures are absolute and represent a congressional command that each employee be free from discriminatory practices. Of necessity, the rights conferred can form no part of the collective-bargaining process since waiver of these rights would defeat the paramount congressional purpose behind Title VII. In these circumstances, an employee's rights under Title VII are not susceptible of prospective waiver. See *Wilko v. Swan*, 346 U.S. 427, 74 S.Ct. 182, 98 L.Ed. 168 (1953).

The actual submission of petitioner's grievance to arbitration in the present case does not alter the situation. Although presumably an employee may waive his cause of action under Title VII as part of a voluntary settlement,[15] mere resort to the arbitral forum to enforce contractual rights constitutes no such waiver. Since an employee's rights under Title VII may not be waived prospectively, existing contractual rights and remedies against discrimination must result from other concessions already made by the union as part of the economic bargain struck with the employer. It is settled law that no additional concession may be exacted from any employee as the price for enforcing those rights. *J.I. Case Co. v. NLRB*, 321 U.S. 332, 338–339, 64 S.Ct. 576, 580– 581, 88 L.Ed. 762 (1944).

Moreover, a contractual right to submit a claim to arbitration is not displaced simply because Congress also has provided a statutory right against discrimination. Both rights have legally independent origins and are equally available to the aggrieved employee. This point becomes apparent through consideration of the role of the arbitrator in the system of industrial self-government. As the proctor of the bargain, the arbitrator's task is to effectuate the intent of the parties. His source of authority is the collective-bargaining agreement, and he must interpret and apply that agreement in accordance with the "industrial common law of the shop" and the various needs and desires of the parties. The arbitrator, however, has no general authority to invoke public laws that conflict with the bargain between the parties: * * *. Thus the arbitrator has authority to resolve only questions of contractual rights, and this authority remains regardless of whether certain contractual rights are similar to, or duplicative of, the substantive rights secured by Title VII.

IV

The District Court and the Court of Appeals reasoned that to permit an employee to have his claim considered in both the arbitral and judicial forums would be unfair since this would mean that the employer, but not the employee, was bound by the arbitral award. * * * But in instituting an action under Title VII, the employee is not seeking review of the arbitrator's decision. Rather, he is asserting a statutory right independent of the arbitration process. An employer does not have "two strings to his bow" with respect to an arbitral decision for the simple reason that Title VII does not provide employers with a cause of action

---

15. In this case petitioner and respondent did not enter into a voluntary settlement expressly conditioned on a waiver of petitioner's cause of action under Title VII. In determining the effectiveness of any such waiver, a court would have to determine at the outset that the employee's con- sent to the settlement was voluntary and knowing. In no event can the submission to arbitration of a claim under the nondiscrimination clause of a collective-bargaining agreement constitute a binding waiver with respect to an employee's rights under Title VII.

against employees. An employer cannot be the victim of discriminatory employment practices. * * *

V

Respondent contends that even if a preclusion rule is not adopted, federal courts should defer to arbitral decisions on discrimination claims where: (i) the claim was before the arbitrator; (ii) the collective-bargaining agreement prohibited the form of discrimination charged in the suit under Title VII; and (iii) the arbitrator has authority to rule on the claim and to fashion a remedy. Under respondent's proposed rule, a court would grant summary judgment and dismiss the employee's action if the above conditions were met. The rule's obvious consequence in the present case would be to deprive the petitioner of his statutory right to attempt to establish his claim in a federal court.

At the outset, it is apparent that a deferral rule would be subject to many of the objections applicable to a preclusion rule. The purpose and procedures of Title VII indicate that Congress intended federal courts to exercise final responsibility for enforcement of Title VII; deferral to arbitral decisions would be inconsistent with that goal. Furthermore, we have long recognized that "the choice of forums inevitably affects the scope of the substantive right to be vindicated." *U.S. Bulk Carriers v. Arguelles*, 400 U.S. 351, 359–360, 91 S.Ct. 409, 413–414, 27 L.Ed.2d 456 (1971) (Harlan, J., concurring). Respondent's deferral rule is necessarily premised on the assumption that arbitral processes are commensurate with judicial processes and that Congress impliedly intended federal courts to defer to arbitral decisions on Title VII issues. We deem this supposition unlikely.

Arbitral procedures, while well suited to the resolution of contractual disputes, make arbitration a comparatively inappropriate forum for the final resolution of rights created by Title VII. This conclusion rests first on the special role of the arbitrator, whose task is to effectuate the intent of the parties rather than the requirements of enacted legislation. Where the collective-bargaining agreement conflicts with Title VII, the arbitrator must follow the agreement. To be sure, the tension between contractual and statutory objectives may be mitigated where a collective-bargaining agreement contains provisions facially similar to those of Title VII. But other facts may still render arbitral processes comparatively inferior to judicial processes in the protection of Title VII rights. Among these is the fact that the specialized competence of arbitrators pertains primarily to the law of the shop, not the law of the land. *United Steelworkers of America v. Warrior & Gulf Navigation Co.*, 363 U.S. 574, 581–583, 80 S.Ct. 1347, 1352–1353, 4 L.Ed.2d 1409 (1960). Parties usually choose an arbitrator because they trust his knowledge and judgment concerning the demands and norms of industrial relations. On the other hand, the resolution of statutory or constitutional issues is a primary responsibility of courts, and judicial construction has proved especially necessary with respect to Title VII, whose broad language frequently can be given meaning only by reference to public law concepts.

Moreover, the factfinding process in arbitration usually is not equivalent to judicial factfinding. The record of the arbitration proceedings is not as complete; the usual rules of evidence do not apply; and rights and procedures common to civil trials, such as discovery, compulsory process, cross-examination, and testimony under oath, are often severely limited or unavailable. See *Bernhardt v. Polygraphic Co.*, 350 U.S. 198, 203, 76 S.Ct. 273, 276, 100 L.Ed. 199 (1956); *Wilko v. Swan*, 346 U.S., at 435–437, 74 S.Ct., at 186–188. And as this Court has recognized, "[a]rbitrators have no obligation to the court to give their reasons for an award." *United Steelworkers of America v. Enterprise Wheel & Car Corp.*, 363 U.S. [593], at 598, 80 S.Ct. [1358], at 1361 [(1960)]. Indeed, it is the informality of arbitral procedure that enables it to function as an efficient, inexpensive, and expeditious means for dispute resolution. This same characteristic, however, makes arbitration a less appropriate forum for final resolution of Title VII issues than the federal courts.[19]

* * *

A deferral rule also might adversely affect the arbitration system as well as the enforcement scheme of Title VII. Fearing that the arbitral forum cannot adequately protect their rights under Title VII, some employees may elect to bypass arbitration and institute a lawsuit. The possibility of voluntary compliance or settlement of Title VII claims would thus be reduced, and the result could well be more litigation, not less.

We think, therefore, that the federal policy favoring arbitration of labor disputes and the federal policy against discriminatory employment practices can best be accommodated by permitting an employee to pursue fully both his remedy under the grievance-arbitration clause of a collective-bargaining agreement and his cause of action under Title VII. The federal court should consider the employee's claim *de novo*. The arbitral decision may be admitted as evidence and accorded such weight as the court deems appropriate.[21]

19. A further concern is the union's exclusive control over the manner and extent to which an individual grievance is presented. See *Vaca v. Sipes*, 386 U.S. 171, 87 S.Ct. 903, 17 L.Ed.2d 842 (1967); *Republic Steel Corp. v. Maddox*, 379 U.S. 650, 85 S.Ct. 614, 13 L.Ed.2d 580 (1965). * * *

21. We adopt no standards as to the weight to be accorded an arbitral decision, since this must be determined in the court's discretion with regard to the facts and circumstances of each case. Relevant factors include the existence of provisions in the collective-bargaining agreement that conform substantially with Title VII, the degree of procedural fairness in the arbitral forum, adequacy of the record with respect to the issue of discrimination, and the special competence of particular arbitrators. Where an arbitral determination gives full consideration to an employee's Title VII rights, a court may properly accord it great weight. This is especially true where the issue is solely one of fact, specifically addressed by the parties and decided by the arbitrator on the basis of an adequate record. But courts should ever be mindful that Congress, in enacting Title VII, thought it necessary to provide a judicial forum for the ultimate resolution of discriminatory employment claims. It is the duty of courts to assure the full availability of this forum.

Notes and Questions

1. *Should a Prior Arbitral Decision on a Discrimination Claim Fore-close a Title VII Action on the Same Issue?* The *Alexander* Court rejects the argument that Title VII should be construed to preclude a grievant having more than one chance to prove that an employer discriminated, at least when the first chance is a hearing before a labor arbitrator. What are the important elements of the Court's reasoning?

2. *What Weight Should Title VII Courts Give to Prior Arbitral Decisions?* Is footnote 21 and the textual sentence to which it is attached consistent with the rest of the *Alexander* opinion? For what type of issues should an arbitrator's opinion be given substantial weight by a Title VII court? Issues of statutory interpretation? Issues of contractual interpretation? Issues of fact? Many post-*Alexander* decisions have given considerable, though ostensibly not conclusive, weight to arbitrators' findings of fact. See, e.g., Wilmington v. J.I. Case Co., 793 F.2d 909 (8th Cir.1986) (trial court could refuse to admit text of arbitrator's decision into evidence so that jury could make independent judgment of credibility); Becton v. Detroit Terminal Consol. Freightways, 687 F.2d 140 (6th Cir.1982) (arbitration award can be cited by employer to articulate legitimate reason, but Title VII court may reconsider evidence rejected by arbitrator). But see Collins v. New York City Transit Authority, 305 F.3d 113 (2d Cir. 2002) (To survive a summary judgment motion, the employee "must present strong evidence that the decision was wrong as a matter of fact—e.g., new evidence not before the tribunal—or the impartiality of the proceeding was somehow compromised.").

3. *Implications of* Alexander *for Grievant Who Obtains a Favorable Decision from the Arbitrator?* Can a grievant proceed to a Title VII court if the arbitrator does not award all the relief that the grievant might obtain in court? What weight should the court give the arbitrator's finding of discrimination under the labor contract? Compare Swint v. Pullman–Standard, 11 FEP Cas. 943, 959 n. 55 (N.D.Ala.1974), affirmed in part & vacated in part, 539 F.2d 77 (5th Cir.1976), with Strozier v. General Motors Corp., 635 F.2d 424 (5th Cir., Unit B 1981).

4. *Maintenance of Nondiscrimination Clauses in Collective Agreements.* The *Alexander* decision has not resulted in the exclusion of nondiscrimination clauses from collective bargaining agreements. Almost all agreements include some guarantees against discrimination, and many include commitments to comply with all federal and state laws prohibiting discrimination. See Bureau of National Affairs, Inc., Basic Patterns in Union Contracts 126–28 (14th ed. 1995). Why might employers want discrimination complaints to be subject to arbitration even if the complainants can later sue on their Title VII claim? How likely is it that most individuals who lose before an arbitrator will be able to find a lawyer to take their case to court? How difficult might it be for an employer to bargain for the deletion of a nondiscrimination clause from a predecessor contract? Might such a bargaining demand, or the union's acceding to it, lead to difficulties under § 703 of Title VII, in light of Goodman v. Lukens Steel Corp., 482 U.S. 656, 107 S.Ct.

2617, 96 L.Ed.2d 572 (1987) (potential union liability for declining to raise race bias issues in the processing of grievances under collective agreement).

5. *Arbitral Foreclosure of Other Claims?* The Supreme Court followed *Alexander* with three decisions holding that private grievance arbitration under a collective bargaining agreement does not result in relinquishment of an employee's independent statutory claims. See Barrentine v. Arkansas–Best Freight System, 450 U.S. 728, 101 S.Ct. 1437, 67 L.Ed.2d 641 (1981) (minimum wage claim under the FLSA); McDonald v. City of West Branch, 466 U.S. 284, 104 S.Ct. 1799, 80 L.Ed.2d 302 (1984) (claimed deprivation of first amendment rights under § 1983); Atchison, Topeka and Santa Fe Ry. v. Buell, 480 U.S. 557, 107 S.Ct. 1410, 94 L.Ed.2d 563 (1987) (a personal injury damage action under the Federal Employers Liability Act). In these decisions, as in *Alexander,* the Court stressed, inter alia, the independence of statutory rights from the labor contracts that arbitrators are charged with enforcing.

Note on Alexander v. Gardner–Denver and the Waiver of Title VII Rights in Collective Agreements

Perhaps the most significant part of the Alexander v. Gardner–Denver decision for future planning and litigation is the Court's treatment of the employer's argument that the negotiation or at least invocation of the arbitration system waived the plaintiff's Title VII cause of action. The Court initially states that the union's predispute negotiation of the system did not relinquish the cause of action because "there can be no prospective waiver of an employee's rights under Title VII." It then adds (in footnote 15) that the actual post-dispute submission of a grievance to arbitration in that case also could not constitute an effective waiver, because even post-dispute settlements or waivers must be "voluntary and knowing."

The *Alexander* decision, however, does not make fully clear whether there could be effective, "voluntary and knowing" waivers of the right to go to court to enforce statutory claims in other cases. In *Alexander* the text of the labor agreement did not provide, and hence there was no basis for asserting that either the plaintiff or the union manifested any understanding, that submitting a case to arbitration would sacrifice Title VII remedies. In another case might an employer negotiate an agreement that did manifest such an understanding? More specifically, would Title VII prevent the implementation of a clause in a collective bargaining agreement that rendered nonarbitrable under the labor agreement any discrimination claim that had been lodged with a public authority like the EEOC? Compare Board of Higher Educ. v. Professional Staff Congress/CUNY, 80 Misc.2d 297, 362 N.Y.S.2d 985 (1975) (enforcing such a clause), with EEOC v. Board of Governors of State Colleges & Univ., 957 F.2d 424 (7th Cir.1992) (finding such a clause to be illegal retaliation for filling claim under the ADEA). Cf. Weaver v. Florida Power & Light, 966 F.Supp. 1157 (S.D.Fla. 1997) (litigation of Title VII and ADA claims to judgment precludes arbitration on same allegations under implied waiver and res judicata theories), reversed, 172 F.3d 771 (11th Cir.1999) (waiver and preclusion claims should be made to arbitrator).

Might an employer instead negotiate a clause in a collective bargaining agreement that conditioned arbitration of discrimination claims on the employee grievant's waiver of any statutory cause of action on the claim? Should such a clause, because it seems to induce employees to waive Title VII remedies before initiating arbitration, be treated differently than the provision described in the last paragraph, or are the two types of clauses functionally the same? Might the negotiation of a prearbitration-waiver clause expose a union to a Title VII suit under the *Goodman* decision because of its special treatment of discrimination grievances? See Johnson v. Palma, 931 F.2d 203 (2d Cir.1991). Is the viability of such a clause in any event addressed by Justice Powell's statements in *Alexander* that "existing contractual rights and remedies against discrimination must result from other concessions [than the waiver of Title VII rights] already made by the union" and "that no additional concession may be exacted from any employee as the price for enforcing those rights"? Or do these statements mean only that any qualification of access to the contractual arbitration system must be negotiated by the union as part of the system, rather than levied in an ad hoc manner on individual employees?

Even more difficult issues presumably would be presented by clauses in collective agreements that purport expressly to waive Title VII judicial actions prospectively as consideration either for the opportunity to use the contractual arbitration system to press a discrimination complaint or for other employer concessions in the labor agreement. Was the *Alexander* Court's statement that "there can be no prospective waiver of an employee's rights under Title VII" meant to render any such prospective waiver nugatory? Or should this statement be read only to cover substantive employee rights and thus not applicable to a case where the collective agreement offers arbitration as an alternative procedure for direct consideration of the statutory claim, rather than (as in *Alexander*) only consideration of an analogous contractual claim? For further discussion, see "Note on Wright v. Universal Maritime Service and the Continuing Viability of Alexander v. Gardner–Denver", p. 1156 infra.

What if the employee himself negotiates a trade of his Title VII judicial rights of action for adjudication of such claims under a private arbitration system? Is *Alexander* best understood as an expression of judicial disquiet only with a union's purported waiver of an individual employee's independent statutory claims? Consider the following decision.

GILMER v. INTERSTATE/JOHNSON LANE CORP.

Supreme Court of the United States, 1991.
500 U.S. 20, 111 S.Ct. 1647, 114 L.Ed.2d 26.

JUSTICE WHITE delivered the opinion of the Court.

Respondent Interstate/Johnson Lane Corporation (Interstate) hired petitioner Robert Gilmer as a Manager of Financial Services in May 1981. As required by his employment, Gilmer registered as a securities representative with several stock exchanges, including the New York Stock Exchange (NYSE). His registration application, entitled "Uniform

Application for Securities Industry Registration or Transfer," provided, among other things, that Gilmer "agreed to arbitrate any dispute, claim or controversy" arising between him and Interstate "that is required to be arbitrated under the rules, constitutions or by-laws of the organizations with which I register." Of relevance to this case, NYSE Rule 347 provides for arbitration of "any controversy between a registered representative and any member or member organization arising out of the employment or termination of employment of such registered representative."

* * *

Interstate terminated Gilmer's employment in 1987, at which time Gilmer was 62 years of age. After first filing an age discrimination charge with the Equal Employment Opportunity Commission (EEOC), Gilmer subsequently brought suit in the United States District Court for the Western District of North Carolina, alleging that Interstate had discharged him because of his age, in violation of the ADEA. In response to Gilmer's complaint, Interstate filed in the District Court a motion to compel arbitration of the ADEA claim. In its motion, Interstate relied upon the arbitration agreement in Gilmer's registration application, as well as the Federal Arbitration Act (FAA), 9 U.S.C. § 1 *et seq.* The District Court denied Interstate's motion, based on this Court's decision in *Alexander v. Gardner–Denver Co.,* 415 U.S. 36, 94 S.Ct. 1011, 39 L.Ed.2d 147 (1974), and because it concluded that "Congress intended to protect ADEA claimants from the waiver of a judicial forum." The United States Court of Appeals for the Fourth Circuit reversed.

* * *

The FAA was originally enacted in 1925, 43 Stat. 883, and then reenacted and codified in 1947 as Title 9 of the United States Code. Its purpose was to reverse the longstanding judicial hostility to arbitration agreements that had existed at English common law and had been adopted by American courts, and to place arbitration agreements upon the same footing as other contracts. *Dean Witter Reynolds, Inc. v. Byrd,* 470 U.S. 213, 219–220, and n. 6, 105 S.Ct. 1238, 1241–1242, and n. 6, 84 L.Ed.2d 158 (1985); *Scherk v. Alberto–Culver Co.,* 417 U.S. 506, 510, n. 4, 94 S.Ct. 2449, 2453, n. 4, 41 L.Ed.2d 270 (1974). Its primary substantive provision states that "[a] written provision in any maritime transaction or a contract evidencing a transaction involving commerce to settle by arbitration a controversy thereafter arising out of such contract or transaction * * * shall be valid, irrevocable, and enforceable, save upon such grounds as exist at law or in equity for the revocation of any contract." 9 U.S.C. § 2. The FAA also provides for stays of proceedings in federal district courts when an issue in the proceeding is referable to arbitration, § 3, and for orders compelling arbitration when one party has failed, neglected, or refused to comply with an arbitration agreement, § 4. These provisions manifest a "liberal federal policy favoring arbitration agreements." *Moses H. Cone Memorial Hospital v. Mercury*

Construction Corp., 460 U.S. 1, 24, 103 S.Ct. 927, 941, 74 L.Ed.2d 765 (1983).[2]

It is by now clear that statutory claims may be the subject of an arbitration agreement, enforceable pursuant to the FAA. Indeed, in recent years we have held enforceable arbitration agreements relating to claims arising under the Sherman Act, 15 U.S.C. §§ 1–7; §§ 10(b) of the Securities Exchange Act of 1934, 15 U.S.C. § 78j(b); the civil provisions of the Racketeer Influenced and Corrupt Organizations Act (RICO), 18 U.S.C. § 1961 *et seq.;* and § 12(2) of the Securities Act of 1933, 15 U.S.C. § 771(2). See *Mitsubishi Motors Corp. v. Soler Chrysler–Plymouth, Inc.,* 473 U.S. 614, 105 S.Ct. 3346, 87 L.Ed.2d 444 (1985); *Shearson/American Express Inc. v. McMahon,* 482 U.S. 220, 107 S.Ct. 2332, 96 L.Ed.2d 185 (1987); *Rodriguez de Quijas v. Shearson/American Express, Inc.,* 490 U.S. 477, 109 S.Ct. 1917, 104 L.Ed.2d 526 (1989). In these cases we recognized that "by agreeing to arbitrate a statutory claim, a party does not forgo the substantive rights afforded by the statute; it only submits to their resolution in an arbitral, rather than a judicial, forum." *Mitsubishi, supra,* at 628, 105 S.Ct., at 3354.

Although all statutory claims may not be appropriate for arbitration, "having made the bargain to arbitrate, the party should be held to it unless Congress itself has evinced an intention to preclude a waiver of judicial remedies for the statutory rights at issue." *Ibid.* In this regard, we note that the burden is on Gilmer to show that Congress intended to preclude a waiver of a judicial forum for ADEA claims. See *McMahon,* 482 U.S., at 227, 107 S.Ct., at 2337–2338. If such an intention exists, it will be discoverable in the text of the ADEA, its legislative history, or an "inherent conflict" between arbitration and the ADEA's underlying purposes. See *ibid.* Throughout such an inquiry, it should be kept in mind that "questions of arbitrability must be addressed with a healthy regard for the federal policy favoring arbitration." *Moses H. Cone,* 460 U.S., at 24, 103 S.Ct., at 941.

* * *

As Gilmer contends, the ADEA is designed not only to address individual grievances, but also to further important social policies. See, e.g., *EEOC v. Wyoming,* 460 U.S. 226, 231, 103 S.Ct. 1054, 1057–1058,

---

2. Section 1 of the FAA provides that "nothing herein contained shall apply to contracts of employment of seamen, railroad employees, or any other class of workers engaged in foreign or interstate commerce." 9 U.S.C. Sec. 1. Several *amici curiae* in support of Gilmer argue that that section excludes from the coverage of the FAA all "contracts of employment." Gilmer, however, did not raise the issue in the courts below, it was not addressed there, and it was not among the questions presented in the petition for certiorari. In any event, it would be inappropriate to address the scope of the Sec. 1 exclusion be- cause the arbitration clause being enforced here is not contained in a contract of employment. The FAA requires that the arbitration clause being enforced be in writing. See 9 U.S.C. Secs. 2, 3. The record before us does not show, and the parties do not contend, that Gilmer's employment agreement with Interstate contained a written arbitration clause. Rather, the arbitration clause at issue is in Gilmer's securities registration application, which is a contract with the securities exchanges, not with Interstate. * * * Consequently, we leave for another day the issue raised by *amici curiae.*

75 L.Ed.2d 18 (1983). We do not perceive any inherent inconsistency between those policies, however, and enforcing agreements to arbitrate age discrimination claims. It is true that arbitration focuses on specific disputes between the parties involved. The same can be said, however, of judicial resolution of claims. Both of these dispute resolution mechanisms nevertheless also can further broader social purposes. The Sherman Act, the Securities Exchange Act of 1934, RICO, and the Securities Act of 1933 all are designed to advance important public policies, but, as noted above, claims under those statutes are appropriate for arbitration. "So long as the prospective litigant effectively may vindicate [his or her] statutory cause of action in the arbitral forum, the statute will continue to serve both its remedial and deterrent function." *Mitsubishi, supra,* at 637, 105 S.Ct., at 3359.

We also are unpersuaded by the argument that arbitration will undermine the role of the EEOC in enforcing the ADEA. An individual ADEA claimant subject to an arbitration agreement will still be free to file a charge with the EEOC, even though the claimant is not able to institute a private judicial action. Indeed, Gilmer filed a charge with the EEOC in this case. In any event, the EEOC's role in combating age discrimination is not dependent on the filing of a charge; the agency may receive information concerning alleged violations of the ADEA "from any source," and it has independent authority to investigate age discrimination. See 29 CFR §§ 1626.4, 1626.13 (1990). Moreover, nothing in the ADEA indicates that Congress intended that the EEOC be involved in all employment disputes. Such disputes can be settled, for example, without any EEOC involvement. See, e.g., *Coventry v. United States Steel Corp.,* 856 F.2d 514, 522 (C.A.3 1988); *Moore v. McGraw Edison Co.,* 804 F.2d 1026, 1033 (C.A.8 1986); *Runyan v. National Cash Register Corp.,* 787 F.2d 1039, 1045 (CA6), cert. denied, 479 U.S. 850, 107 S.Ct. 178, 93 L.Ed.2d 114 (1986).[3] * * *

* * *

Gilmer also argues that compulsory arbitration is improper because it deprives claimants of the judicial forum provided for by the ADEA. Congress, however, did not explicitly preclude arbitration or other nonjudicial resolution of claims, even in its recent amendments to the ADEA. * * * Moreover, Gilmer's argument ignores the ADEA's flexible approach to resolution of claims. The EEOC, for example, is directed to pursue "informal methods of conciliation, conference, and persuasion," 29 U.S.C. § 626(b), which suggests that out-of-court dispute resolution, such as arbitration, is consistent with the statutory scheme established by Congress. In addition, arbitration is consistent with Congress' grant of concurrent jurisdiction over ADEA claims to state and federal courts, see 29 U.S.C. § 626(c)(1) (allowing suits to be brought "in any court of

---

3. In the recently enacted Older Workers Benefit Protection Act, Pub.L. 101–433, 104 Stat. 978, Congress amended the ADEA to provide that "an individual may not waive any right or claim under this Act unless the waiver is knowing and voluntary." See Sec. 201. Congress also specified certain conditions that must be met in order for a waiver to be knowing and voluntary. *Ibid.*

competent jurisdiction"), because arbitration agreements, "like the provision for concurrent jurisdiction, serve to advance the objective of allowing [claimants] a broader right to select the forum for resolving disputes, whether it be judicial or otherwise." *Rodriguez de Quijas,* 490 U.S., at 483, 109 S.Ct., at 1921.

* * *

In arguing that arbitration is inconsistent with the ADEA, Gilmer also raises a host of challenges to the adequacy of arbitration procedures. * * *

Gilmer first speculates that arbitration panels will be biased. However, "we decline to indulge the presumption that the parties and arbitral body conducting a proceeding will be unable or unwilling to retain competent, conscientious and impartial arbitrators." *Mitsubishi, supra,* at 634. In any event, we note that the NYSE arbitration rules, which are applicable to the dispute in this case, provide protections against biased panels. The rules require, for example, that the parties be informed of the employment histories of the arbitrators, and that they be allowed to make further inquiries into the arbitrators' backgrounds. In addition, each party is allowed one peremptory challenge and unlimited challenges for cause. Moreover, the arbitrators are required to disclose "any circumstances which might preclude [them] from rendering an objective and impartial determination." The FAA also protects against bias, by providing that courts may overturn arbitration decisions "where there was evident partiality or corruption in the arbitrators." 9 U.S.C. § 10(b). There has been no showing in this case that those provisions are inadequate to guard against potential bias.

Gilmer also complains that the discovery allowed in arbitration is more limited than in the federal courts, which he contends will make it difficult to prove discrimination. It is unlikely, however, that age discrimination claims require more extensive discovery than other claims that we have found to be arbitrable, such as RICO and antitrust claims. Moreover, there has been no showing in this case that the NYSE discovery provisions, which allow for document production, information requests, depositions, and subpoenas, will prove insufficient to allow ADEA claimants such as Gilmer a fair opportunity to present their claims. Although those procedures might not be as extensive as in the federal courts, by agreeing to arbitrate, a party "trades the procedures and opportunity for review of the courtroom for the simplicity, informality, and expedition of arbitration." *Mitsubishi, supra,* at 628, 105 S.Ct., at 3354. Indeed, an important counterweight to the reduced discovery in NYSE arbitration is that arbitrators are not bound by the rules of evidence.

A further alleged deficiency of arbitration is that arbitrators often will not issue written opinions, resulting, Gilmer contends, in a lack of public knowledge of employers' discriminatory policies, an inability to obtain effective appellate review, and a stifling of the development of the law. The NYSE rules, however, do require that all arbitration awards be in writing, and that the awards contain the names of the parties, a summary of the issues in controversy, and a description of the award issued. In addition, the award decisions are made available to the public. Furthermore, judicial decisions addressing ADEA claims will continue to be issued because it is unlikely that all or even most ADEA claimants will be subject to arbitration agreements. Finally, Gilmer's concerns apply equally to settlements of ADEA claims, which, as noted above, are clearly allowed.[4]

It is also argued that arbitration procedures cannot adequately further the purposes of the ADEA because they do not provide for broad equitable relief and class actions. As the court below noted, however, arbitrators do have the power to fashion equitable relief. Indeed, the NYSE rules applicable here do not restrict the types of relief an arbitrator may award, but merely refer to "damages and/or other relief." The NYSE rules also provide for collective proceedings. * * * Finally, it should be remembered that arbitration agreements will not preclude the EEOC from bringing actions seeking class-wide and equitable relief.

* * *

An additional reason advanced by Gilmer for refusing to enforce arbitration agreements relating to ADEA claims is his contention that there often will be unequal bargaining power between employers and employees. Mere inequality in bargaining power, however, is not a sufficient reason to hold that arbitration agreements are never enforceable in the employment context. Relationships between securities dealers and investors, for example, may involve unequal bargaining power, but we nevertheless held in *Rodriguez de Quijas* and *McMahon* that agreements to arbitrate in that context are enforceable. See 490 U.S., at 484, 109 S.Ct., at 1921–1922; 482 U.S., at 230, 107 S.Ct., at 2339–2340. As discussed above, the FAA's purpose was to place arbitration agreements on the same footing as other contracts. Thus, arbitration agreements are enforceable "save upon such grounds as exist at law or in equity for the revocation of any contract." 9 U.S.C. § 2. "Of course, courts should remain attuned to well-supported claims that the agreement to arbitrate resulted from the sort of fraud or overwhelming economic power that would provide grounds 'for the revocation of any contract.'" *Mitsubishi,* 473 U.S., at 627, 105 S.Ct., at 3354. There is no indication in this case, however, that Gilmer, an experienced businessman, was coerced or defrauded into agreeing to the arbitration clause in his registration application. As with the claimed procedural inadequacies discussed above, this claim of unequal bargaining power is best left for resolution in specific cases.

* * *

---

4. Gilmer also contends that judicial review of arbitration decisions is too limited. We have stated, however, that "although judicial scrutiny of arbitration awards necessarily is limited, such review is sufficient to ensure that arbitrators comply with the requirements of the statute" at issue. *Shearson American Express Inc. v. McMahon,* 482 U.S. 220, 232, 107 S.Ct. 2332, 2340, 96 L.Ed.2d 185 (1987).

In addition to the arguments discussed above, Gilmer vigorously asserts that our decision in *Alexander v. Gardner–Denver Co.,* 415 U.S. 36, 94 S.Ct. 1011, 39 L.Ed.2d 147 (1974), and its progeny—*Barrentine v. Arkansas–Best Freight System, Inc.,* 450 U.S. 728, 101 S.Ct. 1437, 67 L.Ed.2d 641 (1981), and *McDonald v. City of West Branch,* 466 U.S. 284, 104 S.Ct. 1799, 80 L.Ed.2d 302 (1984)—preclude arbitration of employment discrimination claims. Gilmer's reliance on these cases, however, is misplaced.

* * *

There are several important distinctions between the *Gardner–Denver* line of cases and the case before us. First, those cases did not involve the issue of the enforceability of an agreement to arbitrate statutory claims. Rather, they involved the quite different issue whether arbitration of contract-based claims precluded subsequent judicial resolution of statutory claims. Since the employees there had not agreed to arbitrate their statutory claims, and the labor arbitrators were not authorized to resolve such claims, the arbitration in those cases understandably was held not to preclude subsequent statutory actions. Second, because the arbitration in those cases occurred in the context of a collective-bargaining agreement, the claimants there were represented by their unions in the arbitration proceedings. An important concern therefore was the tension between collective representation and individual statutory rights, a concern not applicable to the present case. Finally, those cases were not decided under the FAA, which, as discussed above, reflects a "liberal federal policy favoring arbitration agreements." *Mitsubishi,* 473 U.S., at 625, 105 S.Ct., at 3353. Therefore, those cases provide no basis for refusing to enforce Gilmer's agreement to arbitrate his ADEA claim.

JUSTICE STEVENS, with whom JUSTICE MARSHALL joins, dissenting.

Section 1 of the Federal Arbitration Act (FAA) states:

"[N]othing herein contained shall apply to contracts of employment of seamen, railroad employees, or any other class of workers engaged in foreign or interstate commerce." 9 U.S.C. § 1.

The Court today, in holding that the FAA compels enforcement of arbitration clauses even when claims of age discrimination are at issue, skirts the antecedent question of whether the coverage of the Act even extends to arbitration clauses contained in employment contracts, regardless of the subject matter of the claim at issue.

* * *

There is little dispute that the primary concern animating the FAA was the perceived need by the business community to overturn the common-law rule that denied specific enforcement of agreements to arbitrate in contracts between business entities. The Act was drafted by a committee of the American Bar Association (ABA), acting upon instructions from the ABA to consider and report upon "the further extension of the principle of commercial arbitration." Report of the Forty-third Annual Meeting of the ABA, 45 A.B.A.Rep. 75 (1920). At the Senate Judiciary Subcommittee hearings on the proposed bill, the chairman of the ABA committee responsible for drafting the bill assured the Senators that the bill "is not intended [to] be an act referring to labor disputes, at all. It is purely an act to give the merchants the right or the privilege of sitting down and agreeing with each other as to what their damages are, if they want to do it. Now that is all there is in this." Hearing on S. 4213 and S. 4214 before a Subcommittee of the Senate Committee on the Judiciary, 67th Cong., 4th Sess., 9 (1923). At the same hearing, Senator Walsh stated:

> "The trouble about the matter is that a great many of these contracts that are entered into are really not [voluntary] things at all. Take an insurance policy; there is a blank in it. You can take that or you can leave it. The agent has no power at all to decide it. Either you can make that contract or you can not make any contract. It is the same with a good many contracts of employment. A man says, 'These are our terms. All right, take it or leave it.' Well, there is nothing for the man to do except to sign it; and then he surrenders his right to have his case tried by the court, and has to have it tried before a tribunal in which he has no confidence at all." *Ibid.*

Given that the FAA specifically was intended to exclude arbitration agreements between employees and employers, I see no reason to limit this exclusion from coverage to arbitration clauses contained in agreements entitled "Contract of Employment." In this case, the parties conceded at oral argument that Gilmer had no "contract of employment" as such with respondent. Gilmer was, however, required as a condition of his employment to become a registered representative of several stock exchanges, including the New York Stock Exchange (NYSE).

* * *

Not only would I find that the FAA does not apply to employment-related disputes between employers and employees in general, but also I would hold that compulsory arbitration conflicts with the congressional purpose animating the ADEA, in particular. As this Court previously has noted, authorizing the courts to issue broad injunctive relief is the cornerstone to eliminating discrimination in society. *Albemarle Paper Co. v. Moody,* 422 U.S. 405, 415, 95 S.Ct. 2362, 2370, 45 L.Ed.2d 280 (1975). The ADEA, like Title VII, authorizes courts to award broad, class-based injunctive relief to achieve the purposes of the Act. 29 U.S.C. § 626(b). Because commercial arbitration is typically limited to a specific dispute between the particular parties and because the available remedies in arbitral forums generally do not provide for class-wide injunctive relief, see Shell, ERISA and Other Federal Employment Statutes: When is Commercial Arbitration an "Adequate Substitute" for the Courts?, 68 Texas L.Rev. 509, 568 (1990), I would conclude that an essential purpose of the ADEA is frustrated by compulsory arbitration of employment discrimination claims. * * * The Court's holding today clearly eviscerates the important role played by an independent judiciary in eradicating employment discrimination.

When the FAA was passed in 1925, I doubt that any legislator who voted for it expected it to apply to statutory claims, to form contracts between parties of unequal bargaining power, or to the arbitration of disputes arising out of the employment relationship. In recent years, however, the Court "has effectively rewritten the statute", and abandoned its earlier view that statutory claims were not appropriate subjects for arbitration.

Notes and Questions

1. *Predispute Waivers of a Judicial Forum for ADEA Claims.* The principal holding of *Gilmer* seems to be that predispute agreements to resolve ADEA claims through arbitration, rather than through litigation in court, may be enforceable. This holding follows from the Court's premise that statutory employment claims, like agreements to arbitrate other statutory claims, are enforceable under the FAA "unless Congress itself has evinced an intention to preclude a waiver of judicial remedies for the statutory rights at issues." Do you agree with the Court's premise? Why should Gilmer have had the "burden" of showing "that Congress intended to preclude a waiver of a judicial forum for ADEA claims?" Is it because the FAA is read to establish a general presumption or "default" rule favoring arbitration? Do you also agree with the Court's application of its approach to the ADEA? How does the Court respond to Gilmer's arguments that there is an "inherent conflict" between compelling arbitration in a case like his and "the ADEA's underlying purposes"?

Because of the date of the agreement and dispute, the *Gilmer* Court notes but does not consider the possible relevance of the amendments to the ADEA in Title II of the OWBPA of 1990. Should the amended § 7(f)(1)(C) of ADEA be read to evince a Congressional intention to preclude predispute waiver of the right to a judicial forum and jury trial for ADEA claims? Or does this section only protect from predispute waiver "substantive" rights to be free of discrimination, rather than "procedural" rights to press claims of substantive violations in court? See Rosenberg v. Merrill Lynch, Pierce, Fenner & Smith, 170 F.3d 1, 12–14 (1st Cir.1999); Seus v. John Nuveen & Co., 146 F.3d 175, 181–82 (3d Cir.1998); Williams v. Cigna Fin. Advisors, Inc., 56 F.3d 656, 660–61 (5th Cir.1995) (all interpreting OWBPA not to affect *Gilmer* holding).

For the story behind the *Gilmer* decision, see Samuel Estreicher, The Story of Gilmer v. Interstate/Johnson Lane Corp.: The Emergence of Employment Arbitration, in Employment Law Stories, ch. 7 (Samuel Estreicher & Gillian Lester eds., 2007).

2. *Does the FAA Apply to All Contracts of Employment?* Note that the Court in footnote 2 of *Gilmer*, in its treatment of Gilmer's securities representative registration application, avoids interpreting the scope of the exclusion in § 1 of the FAA. A broad reading of this exclusion to cover all

employment contracts over which Congress has power under the foreign and interstate commerce clause could limit *Gilmer*'s impact to a few industries, like the securities industry, where there is some form of private regulation by a bona fide third party. See also Horne v. New England Patriots Football Club, Inc., 489 F.Supp. 465 (D.Mass.1980) (football league arbitration presided over by league commissioner). However, in Circuit City Stores, Inc. v. Adams, 532 U.S. 105, 121 S.Ct. 1302, 149 L.Ed.2d 234 (2001), the Court adopted a transportation-worker-only interpretation of the FAA § 1 exclusion, exempting only contracts of employment of seamen, railroad employees and any other class of workers similarly directly engaged in foreign or interstate commerce. For pre-*Circuit City* commentary, compare, e.g., Samuel Estreicher, Predispute Agreements to Arbitrate Statutory Employment Claims, 72 N.Y.U. L.Rev. 1344, 1369–71 (1997), with Robert Covington, Employment Arbitration After *Gilmer*: Have Labor Courts Come to the United States?, 15 Hofstra Lab. & Emp. L.J. 345, 364 (1998); Richard Epstein, Fidelity Without Translation, 1 Green Bag 2d 21, 27–29 (1997); and Matthew Finkin, "Workers' Contracts" Under the United States Arbitration Act: An Essay in Historical Clarification, 17 Berkeley J.Emp. & Lab.L. 282, 298 (1996).

3. *Predispute Waivers of a Judicial Forum for Claims Under Title VII and Other Federal Antidiscrimination Statutes?* Notwithstanding the resistance of the EEOC, see EEOC Notice No. 915.002 (July 10, 1997), the courts of appeals have found the analysis of *Gilmer* to be equally applicable to Title VII claims. See *Rosenberg, supra*, 170 F.3d, at 10 (collecting citations). Only the Ninth Circuit for a time dissented from this view. See Duffield v. Robertson Stephens & Co., 144 F.3d 1182 (9th Cir.1998) (holding that the amendments to Title VII in the Civil Rights Act of 1991 evince a congressional intent to preclude enforcement of a predispute arbitration agreement, or at least one which is imposed as a condition of employment as in *Gilmer*). The *Duffield* court stressed that the 1991 Act was intended to provide strengthened remedies and procedures, including the right to jury trials, for the protection of Title VII rights and relied on legislative history to find congressional approval of only fully voluntary arbitration in § 118 of the 1991 Act which encourages "[w]here appropriate and to the extent authorized by law, the use of alternative means of dispute resolution, including * * * arbitration." See also Joseph R. Grodin, Arbitration of Employment Discrimination Claims: Doctrine and Policy in the Wake of *Gilmer*, 14 Hofstra Lab.L.J. 1, 30–35 (1996). However, in EEOC v. Luce, Forward, Hamilton & Scripps, 345 F.3d 742 (9th Cir. 2003), the Ninth Circuit, sitting en banc, overruled *Duffield*—finding no ambiguity in Title VII's text (including § 118) warranting resort to legislative history.

4. *FAA Preemption of State Laws.* Can a state law bar the enforcement of predispute arbitration agreements for claims made under its own law? The lower courts, e.g., Great Western Mortgage Corp. v. Peacock, 110 F.3d 222 (3d Cir. 1997); Topf v. Warnaco, Inc., 942 F.Supp. 762 (D.Conn.1996), have held that any such bar would be preempted by the FAA under controlling Supreme Court precedent. See, e.g., Southland Corp. v. Keating, 465 U.S. 1, 104 S.Ct. 852, 79 L.Ed.2d 1 (1984) (holding preempted a California law requiring claims brought under it to have judicial consideration); Perry v. Thomas, 482 U.S. 483, 107 S.Ct. 2520, 96 L.Ed.2d 426 (1987)

(holding preempted private employees' wage payment claims despite the state's declared policy that such actions "may be pursued without regard to private arbitration agreements"); Allied–Bruce Terminix Cos. v. Dobson, 513 U.S. 265, 115 S.Ct. 834, 130 L.Ed.2d 753 (1995) (confirming the *Southland* Court's holding that "state courts cannot apply state statutes that invalidate arbitration agreements") See generally Christopher R. Drahozal, Federal Arbitration Act Preemption, 79 Ind. L.J. 393 (2002).

5. *FAA § 2 Review.* The FAA (§ 2) declares that arbitration agreements "shall be valid, irrevocable, and enforceable, save upon such grounds as exist at law or in equity for the revocation of any contract." 9 U.S.C. § 2. This provision authorizes review of such agreements under generally applicable contract law, but does not permit courts to craft special rules for arbitration agreements. See Preston v. Ferrer, 552 U.S. ___, 128 S.Ct. 978 (2008); Doctor's Associates, Inc. v. Casarotto, 517 U.S. 681, 687, 116 S.Ct. 1652, 134 L.Ed.2d 902 (1996). Purportedly acting under their § 2 authority, courts have begun to identify certain limits on the enforceability of arbitration agreements.

a. *Knowing, Voluntary Waiver of Right of Access to Judicial Forum?* The Court in *Gilmer* holds that a "take-it-or-leave-it employment" agreement like that which Gilmer signed is sufficiently *voluntary* to be an effective waiver. Might a court still find an employee's agreement to an arbitration system to be defective because it does not reflect a "knowing waiver"? In a series of cases the Ninth Circuit has held that "[a]ny bargain to waive the right to a judicial forum for civil rights claims * * * in exchange for employment or continued employment must at the least be express: The choice must be explicitly presented to the employee and the employee must explicitly agree to waive the specific right in question." Nelson v. Cyprus Bagdad Copper Corp., 119 F.3d 756, 762 (9th Cir.1997). See Kummetz v. Tech Mold, Inc., 152 F.3d 1153, 1155 (9th Cir.1998); Prudential Insurance Co. v. Lai, 42 F.3d 1299 (9th Cir.1994).

Are these Ninth Circuit decisions consistent with *Gilmer*? With the FAA requirement that courts may apply only generally applicable principles for contract revocation in declining to enforce arbitration agreements? In both *Nelson* and *Kunmetz* the employer had included a description of the arbitration system and the waiver of rights to a judicial forum in an employee handbook wherein each employer also attempted to preserve the at-will status of its employees. In Campbell v. General Dynamics Government Systems Corp., 407 F.3d 546 (1st Cir. 2005), the court refused to compel arbitration of an ADA claim because the arbitration program had been distributed to employees by email without sufficiently alerting them to the fact that they were asked to agree to a waiver of judicial remedies. Links were provided to the full text of the arbitration program but the cover email was held not to contain sufficiently clear notice, nor were employees asked to acknowledge receipt or take some other affirmative step that might have provided a basis for establishing notice. Is this ruling problematic?

b. *Consideration?* Can an employer impose an otherwise valid arbitration program on existing employees by telling them that continued employment is conditioned on their agreement to arbitrate all future claims pursuant to the program? Is independent consideration required? Must there be at least some express form of employee assent other than simply continuing employment? Compare, e.g., In re Halliburton, 80 S.W.3d 566 (Tex. 2002), with Bailey v. Federal National Mortgage Assn., 209 F.3d 740 (D.C. Cir. 2000).

c. *Unconscionability*? Perhaps the most significant area for recognizing limits on arbitration agreements is unconscionability doctrine under state law. As articulated by the California Supreme Court in Armendariz v. Foundation Health Psychcare Services, Inc., 24 Cal.4th 83, 99 Cal.Rptr.2d 745, 6 P.3d 669 (2000), the doctrine requires a showing of both procedural and substantive unconscionability, although a strong showing on one prong may allow a modest showing on the other prong. The *Armendariz* court further stated that procedural unconscionability is ordinarily found where employees are presented with an agreement on a "take it or leave it" basis; and that substantive unconscionability may be found where employers do not undertake obligations parallel to those required of employees in the arbitration agreement. Similarly, in West Virginia ex rel. Saylor v. Wilkes, 216 W.Va. 766, 613 S.E.2d 914 (2005), the West Virginia high court held that a former waitress was not bound to a mandatory arbitration agreement she signed when applying for a job with Ryan's Family Steakhouse, finding the agreement to be unconscionable and not backed by consideration: "Since Ryan's had not promised to submit its employment-related claims to arbitration, the only possible basis to assert that Ryan's action constituted adequate consideration was that Ryan's promised to review a candidate's application for employment if the applicant promised to arbitrate employment disputes."

6. *May Courts Require Particular Minimum Procedures As a Condition of Enforcing Agreements to Arbitrate?* Does *Gilmer* require the courts to enforce any "knowing and voluntary" predispute agreement to arbitrate—regardless of the arbitral system—ADEA (and, by extension, Title VII) claims arising out of any employment relationship under the FAA's coverage? Or does a court have authority to refuse to compel arbitration if dissatisfied with the essential fairness of the arbitration's procedures?

Without clear articulation of the source of their authority, lower courts since *Gilmer* have been prepared to judge the adequacy of arbitration systems before compelling arbitration. Arbitration agreements that provide for lesser remedies than would be available in court for statutory violations would seem to contravene the Supreme Court's insistence that arbitration involves the waiver of a judicial forum, not the waiver of any substantive right. See, e.g. Paladino v. Avnet Computer Technologies, Inc., 134 F.3d 1054 (11th Cir.1998) (arbitration clause that does not permit relief equivalent to judicial remedies is not enforceable); Graham Oil Co. v. ARCO Prods. Co., 43 F.3d 1244, 1248–49 (9th Cir.1994) (arbitration agreement that denied statutory remedies and shortened statutory statute of limitations periods is unenforceable). But see, e.g., *Great Western Mortgage,* supra, (compelling arbitration though punitive damages not available). A failure to provide for joint selection of the arbitrator from a broad panel of potential arbiters is also problematic. See, e.g., Hooters of America v. Phillips, 173 F.3d 933, 938–40 (4th Cir.1999) (Hooters promulgated egregiously unfair arbitration rules, including selection procedures ensuring company control of membership of arbitration panel). Some of the more difficult issues are surveyed in notes 9–10 below.

7. *"Due Process Protocol" for the Arbitration of Statutory Disputes?* Can courts use the authority asserted in the cases in the last note to require in all cases a particular set of defined procedures before enforcing agreements to arbitrate? A "Due Process Protocol for Arbitration of Statutory Disputes" has been developed and endorsed by the Labor & Employment Law Section of the American Bar Association as well as by major arbitration associations. See Disp. Resol. J. Oct.-Dec. 1995, at 37. The protocol posits seven minimum standards: (1) a jointly selected arbitrator who knows the applicable law; (2) simple but adequate discovery; (3) some cost-sharing between the parties to ensure arbitrator neutrality and to deter frivolous claims, though the employer should pay a higher percentage; (4) employee selection of own representative; (5) availability of all remedies provided by law; (6) opinion and award with reasoning from arbitrator; and (7) judicial review of legal issues. See also Commission on the Future of Worker–Management Relations, Report and Recommendations 30–31 (1994). Do courts have authority to require this protocol? Does the EEOC? See Samuel Estreicher, Arbitration of Employment Disputes without Unions, 66 Chi.-Kent L. Rev. 753, 790 (1990): In deciding "whether to bring an enforcement action, the EEOC could consider the nature of the arbitration forum (including the quality of the hearing procedures) provided in the employment contract. The agency could also issue regulations setting forth minimum procedural safeguards."

8. *Permissibility of Cost–Sharing Provisions?* As Due Process Protocol standard (3) indicates, "cost-sharing" can be viewed as a means of ensuring arbitrator neutrality, but the costs of arbitration–both the fees of the arbitration organization and the fees charged by the arbitrator–can erect a prohibitive barrier for claimants of average income. See, e.g., Cole v. Burns Int'l Sec. Serv., 105 F.3d 1465, 1483–85 (D.C.Cir.1997) (an agreement that obligated the employee to pay all or part of the arbitrators' fees would undermine substantive rights by creating costly barrier to assertion of claims). The question is whether the courts may refuse to enforce arbitration agreements that impose costs on claimants higher than the nominal filing fees assessed in commencing a suit in the courts. In Green Tree Financial Corp. v. Randolph, 531 U.S. 79, 90–92, 121 S.Ct. 513, 148 L.Ed.2d 373 (2000), involving a consumer dispute under the Truth in Lending Act, 15 U.S.C. § 1601 *et seq.*, the Court reversed a lower court's refusal to order arbitration:

> It may well be that the existence of large arbitration costs could preclude a litigant such as Randolph from effectively vindicating her federal statutory rights in the arbitral forum. But the record does not show that Randolph will bear such costs if she goes to arbitration. Indeed, it contains hardly any information on the matter. As the Court of Appeals recognized, "we lack ... information about how claimants fare under Green Tree's arbitration clause." The record reveals only arbitration agreement's silence on the subject, and that fact alone is plainly insufficient to render it unenforceable. The "risk" that Randolph will be saddled with prohibitive costs is too speculative to justify the invalidation of an arbitration agreement.

* * * We have held that the party seeking to avoid arbitration bears the burden of establishing that Congress intended to preclude arbitration of the statutory claims at issue. See *Gilmer, supra*; * * *. Similarly, we believe that where, as here, a party seeks to invalidate an arbitration agreement on the ground that arbitration would be prohibitively expensive, that party bears the burden of showing the likelihood of incurring such costs. Randolph did not meet that burden. How detailed the showing of prohibitive expense must be before the party seeking arbitration must come forward with contrary evidence is a matter we need not discuss; for in this case neither during discovery nor when the case was presented on the merits was any timely showing at all on the point. The Court of Appeals therefore erred in deciding that the arbitration agreement's silence with respect to costs and fees rendered it unenforceable.

See generally Michael H. LeRoy & Peter Feuille, When is Cost an Unlawful Barrier to Alternative Dispute Resolution? The Evergreen Tree of Mandatory Employment Arbitration, 50 U.C.L.A. L. Rev. 143 (2002).

9. *Availability of Class Actions?* The Court has yet to decide whether an employee who has signed an otherwise valid predispute arbitration agreement can serve as a named representative, or share in the recovery obtained, in a class action asserting statutory employment rights. It has ruled, however, that a state court lacks authority to compel classwide arbitration of claims where the underlying arbitration agreement is silent on the question; rather the availability of classwide arbitration is an issue for the arbitrator to decide. See Green Tree Financial Corp. v. Bazzle, 539 U.S. 444, 123 S.Ct. 2402, 156 L.Ed.2d 414 (2003).

Some employers responded to *Bazzle* by inserting provisions waiving class actions or the consolidation of claims. The California Supreme Court in Discover Bank v. Superior Court, 36 Cal.4th 148, 30 Cal.Rptr.3d 76, 113 P.3d 1100 (2005), held that an express class action waiver in an arbitration agreement dealing with consumer credit card claims was unconscionable under state law because, in the context of small consumer claims, ruling out a class action or class-wide arbitration effected a substantive waiver of rights. The court did not hold that "all class action waivers are necessarily unconscionable".

In Gentry v. Circuit City Stores, Inc., 42 Cal.4th 443, 64 Cal.Rptr.3d 773, 165 P.3d 556 (2007), the California high court (4–3) remanded to the lower court the question whether the class action waiver in Circuit City's arbitration program was substantively unconscionable because it did not provide as effective a mechanism for advancing statutory wage-hour claims as would class-wide arbitration. The court also rejected Circuit City's argument that the program was not procedurally unconscionable because employees could if they wish have opted out of the arbitration requirement.

10. *Standards of Judicial Review of Awards.* Note Due Process Protocol standard (7), requiring judicial review of legal issues. The FAA itself authorizes a number of grounds for vacating arbitration awards. See 9 U.S.C. § 10(a). In addition to these statutory grounds, the Supreme Court also has confirmed in a modern FAA decision that arbitration awards can be vacated for being in "manifest disregard" of the law. First Options of

Chicago Inc. v. Kaplan, 514 U.S. 938, 942, 115 S.Ct. 1920, 131 L.Ed.2d 985 (1995) (citing Wilko v. Swan, 346 U.S. 427, 436–37, 74 S.Ct. 182, 98 L.Ed. 168 (1953)). Although this "manifest disregard" standard has not been applied consistently by the federal courts, it generally has not been the basis for de novo review of the law. See, e.g., Merrill Lynch, Pierce, Fenner & Smith, Inc. v. Jaros, 70 F.3d 418, 421 (6th Cir.1995) ("applicable legal principle [must be] clearly defined and not subject to reasonable debate"). Some courts have also ruled that arbitrators' failure to follow even a clearly applicable legal principle does not warrant reversal if the arbitrators are not informed of the principle. Compare DiRussa v. Dean Witter Reynolds Inc., 121 F.3d 818, 821 (2d Cir.1997), with DeGaetano v. Smith Barney, Inc., 983 F.Supp. 459 (S.D.N.Y.1997).

Does the rationale of *Gilmer* support applying the "manifest disregard" standard more strictly in cases dealing with statutory rather than contractual claims, especially where arbitration has been imposed as a condition of employment? See *Cole,* supra, 105 F.3d at 1487("judicial review [must be] sufficiently rigorous to ensure that arbitrators have properly interpreted and applied statutory law"). Does the rationale also support review of facts under a "clearly erroneous" standard? See Halligan v. Piper Jaffray, Inc., 148 F.3d 197 (2d Cir.1998) (arbitration award finding no violation of ADEA vacated because of "overwhelming" evidence of age discrimination). Does judicial review also require the arbitrator to issue some explanatory opinion? Although not requiring an opinion in every case, the *Halligan* court stated that "when a reviewing court is inclined to hold that an arbitration panel manifestly disregarded the law, the failure of the arbitrators to explain the award can be taken into account." Id. at 204. See also Estreicher, Arbitration of Employment Disputes, 66 Chi.-Kent L. Rev. at 791 ("The court should review the award for conformity with applicable legal standards and to ensure that findings of fact are not clearly erroneous. In order to permit meaningful review by the court, a transcript of the hearings should be kept and the award should be accompanied by an opinion containing findings of fact and reasons for the manner of disposition of the statutory claim."); Martin Malin, Arbitrating Statutory Employment Claims in the Aftermath of *Gilmer*, 40 St. Louis U. L.J. 77, 105 (1996) ("arbitral interpretations of statutory law must be subject to *de novo* review"); Calvin William Sharpe, Integrity Review of Statutory Arbitration Awards, 54 Hast. L.J. 311 (2003) (appropriate level of judicial scrutiny for "substantive integrity" requires written opinion). See generally Aleta G. Estreicher, Judicial Review of Arbitration Awards Resolving Statutory Claims, in Alternative Dispute Resolution in the Employment Arena: Proc. NYU 53d Ann. Conf. on Labor (S. Estreicher & D. Sherwyn eds., 2004).

In a non-employment case, the Supreme Court has held that under the FAA judicial review of arbitration awards is limited to the grounds for vacatur set forth in 9 U.S.C. §§ 10–11, but left open the possibility of enhanced review under state law. See Hall Street Assoc. v. Mattel, 128 S.Ct. 1396 (2008).

11. *Predispute vs. Postdispute Arbitration Agreements?* Do arguments about the advantages of arbitration to employees only support its encouragement post-dispute, rather than its acceptance as a condition of employment? Or is there good reason to think that employers who would have entered into a general predispute agreement to arbitrate to avoid the uncertainty of jury awards will not agree post-dispute to arbitrate, rather than litigate, the more common claim that does not threaten such awards? Is the plaintiff's bar

likely to agree post-dispute to arbitrate the cases they have chosen to take on, or would such agreement weaken the bargaining leverage of their clients? See David Sherwyn, Because It Takes Two: Why Post–Dispute Voluntary Arbitration Programs Will Fail to Fix the Problems Associated with Employment Discrimination Law Adjudication, 24 Berk. J. Emp. & Lab. L. 1 (2003).

12. *Do* Gilmer *and Its Progeny Compromise Employee Statutory Rights?* Gilmer and its progeny have been the object of strong attacks from some academics and employee advocates. See, e.g., David S. Schwartz, Enforcing Small Print to Protect Big Business: Employee and Consumer Rights Claims in an Age of Compelled Arbitration, 1997 Wis.L.Rev. 33; Katherine Stone, Mandatory Arbitration of Individual Employment Rights: The Yellow Dog Contract of the 1990's, 73 Denv.U.L.Rev. 1017 (1996). The critics have argued that employees' substantive rights to be free of discrimination are inevitably compromised by the loss of the right to a jury trial and by other qualifications of formal judicial processes. The critics also contend that independent arbitrators will tend to favor employers as "repeat players" who, unlike grieving employees not represented by unions, will return again and again to select arbitrators in future cases. The EEOC has also argued that mandatory employment arbitration slows the development of the law through precedent and otherwise impedes the EEOC's enforcement efforts by discouraging the filing of complaints. See EEOC Notice No., 915.002 (July 10, 1997), reprinted at BNA Daily Labor Rep. No. 133, July 11, 1997, p. E–4.

Do you agree? Can the integrity of legal doctrine be adequately protected by judicial review and published arbitration opinions? Is the EEOC's ability to bring an independent action regardless of private arbitration agreements between employers and employees an important part of the balance? See EEOC v. Waffle House, Inc., 534 U.S. 279, 122 S.Ct. 754, 151 L.Ed.2d 755 (2002). Can the EEOC's access to information about discriminatory practices be assured without the incentive of private actions in court after EEOC investigations? Can the "repeat player" problem be addressed by the development of a sophisticated plaintiff's bar and published arbitration awards? Do jury trials really offer promise to most workers who do not have substantial monetary claims? Might the greater speed and privacy and the reduced costs of arbitration actually be in the best interests of many employees, especially those in lower-wage positions? See generally Samuel Estreicher, Saturns for Rickshaws: The Stakes in the Debate Over Predispute Arbitration Agreements, 16 Ohio St. J. Disp. Res. 559 (2001).

A lively debate flourishes in the empirical literature about employment arbitration. Compare, e.g., Lisa B. Bingham & Denise R. Chachere, Dispute Resolution in Employment: The Need for Research, in Employment Dispute Resolution and Worker Rights in the Changing Workplace 95 (Adrienne E. Eaton & Jeffrey H. Keefe eds., 1999): Lisa B. Bingham, Employment Arbitration: The Repeat Player Effect, 1 Employee Rts. & Emp. Pol'y J. 189 (1997), with Richard Bales & Jason N.W. Plowman, Compulsory Arbitration as Part of a Broader Employment Dispute Resolution Process: The Annheuser–Busch Example (unpub., 2008, available at ssrn.org); David Sherwyn, Samuel Estreicher & Michael Heise, Assessing the Case for Employment Arbitration: A New Path for Empirical Research, 57 Stan. L. Rev. 1557 (2005); Theodore Eisenberg & Elizabeth Hill, Arbitration and Litigation: An Empirical Comparison, Disp. Res. J., Nov. 2003/Jan. 2004, p. 44; Michael

Delikat & Morris M. Kleiner, An Empirical Study of Dispute Resolution Mechanism: Where Do Plaintiffs Better Vindicate Their Rights?, Disp. Res. J., Nov. 2003/Jan. 2004, p. 56; Elizabeth Hill, Due Process at Low Cost: An Empirical Evaluation of Employment Arbitration Under the Auspices of the American Arbitration Association, 18 Ohio St. J. Disp. Res. 777 (2003).

Note on Wright v. Universal Maritime Service and the Continuing Viability of Alexander v. Gardner–Denver

Does *Gilmer* suggest that unions may effect predispute waivers of represented employees' rights to a judicial forum for statutory claims of employment discrimination? To what extent does *Gilmer* limit the holding of *Alexander*? Note the three grounds on which the Court in *Gilmer* distinguished *Alexander*. Did the Court intend each ground to be sufficient alone? Does a clause in a collective agreement that assigns statutory claims to arbitration bar a represented employee from asserting such a claim in court?

In Wright v. Universal Maritime Service Corp., 525 U.S. 70, 119 S.Ct. 391, 142 L.Ed.2d 361 (1998), the Court rejected any presumption of arbitrability under collective agreements for statutory rather than contractual claims. It read *Alexander* to "at least stand[] for the proposition that the right to a federal judicial forum is of sufficient importance to be protected against less-than-explicit union waiver." 119 S.Ct. At 396. The Court thus held that general arbitration clauses in collective agreements covering "[m]atters under dispute", as in *Wright*, do not meet the "clear and unmistakable" standard that is the minimum hurdle for union waiver. The Court expressly declined to "reach the question whether such a waiver would be enforceable" even if it met this standard.

What will constitute an effective union waiver after *Wright*? The Fourth Circuit, the only court of appeals that had held after *Gilmer* but before *Wright* that generally worded arbitration clauses in collective agreements effectively waive rights to a judicial forum, see Austin v. Owens–Brockway Glass Container, Inc., 78 F.3d 875 (4th Cir.1996), has held after *Wright* that it will continue to find effective waivers under two kinds of collective agreements: (1) agreements containing arbitration clauses that expressly waive the right of individual employees to a judicial forum for statutory claims; and (2) agreements containing both generally worded arbitration clauses (e.g., covering "all disputes") and also clauses expressly incorporating "statutory antidiscrimination requirements" into the agreement. See Carson v. Giant Food, Inc., 175 F.3d 325 (4th Cir.1999). See also Brown v. ABF Freight Systems, Inc., 183 F.3d 319 (4th Cir.1999) (no effective waiver because anti-discrimination clause did not make it "unmistakably clear" that it incorporated federal statutory employment discrimination law). Before *Wright* other circuit courts had found that under *Alexander* and *Gilmer* a waiver of a right to a judicial forum for statutory employment discrimination claims could not be effective without the individual agreement of the grieving employee or employees. See, e.g., Brisentine v. Stone & Webster Engineering Corp., 117 F.3d 519 (11th Cir.1997); Harrison v. Eddy Potash,

Inc., 112 F.3d 1437 (10th Cir.1997); Pryner v. Tractor Supply Co., 109 F.3d 354 (7th Cir.1997); Varner v. National Super Markets, Inc., 94 F.3d 1209 (8th Cir.1996).

The Supreme Court will decide the issue left open in *Wright* in 14 Penn Plaza, LLC v. Pyett, No. 07–581. Does it make sense to give effect to an individual employee's waiver of access to a judicial forum in a "take-it-or-leave-it" employment agreement, but not to give the same effect to an individual employee's decision to work in a bargaining unit covered by a collective agreement that has expressly waived such access? Will employees represented by experienced "repeat player" unions in a collectively bargained arbitration system be more assured of due process than employees in an arbitration system unilaterally designed by an employer? On the other hand, should effective union waiver of judicial access at least turn on whether the collective agreement authorizes the individual employee to insist on arbitration of any unresolved statutory claim? See *Brisentine, supra,* 117 F.3d at 526–27, (arguing that this, in addition to express agreement of affected individual employees, should be a condition of waiver). Generally, collective agreements are read to grant the union, and not individual employees, authority to control access to arbitration; and the labor laws only require unions to exercise this authority without being "arbitrary, discriminatory, or in bad faith." See Vaca v. Sipes, 386 U.S. 171, 87 S.Ct. 903, 17 L.Ed.2d 842 (1967). However, is it clear that a union can refuse to take a claim of discrimination to arbitration that could not be brought to court because of a waiver to which it agreed in negotiations?

If "clear and unmistakable" union waivers are accepted, should the Fourth Circuit's approach in *Carson* be adopted by the other circuits? Does the Fourth Circuit approach assure that any waiver be "clear and unmistakable?" Does that depend on whether the *Carson* court's second option, as well as its first option, require that the arbitrator expressly be granted full authority, including full remedial authority, to apply the incorporated statutory requirements? See David Feller, Compulsory Arbitration of Statutory Discrimination Claims Under a Collective Bargaining Agreement, 16 Hofstra Lab. & Employment L.J. 53, 75–77 (1998) (courts should not find effective waiver without express grant of full statutory authority to arbitrator).

If union waivers, even if clear, are not accepted because unions as collective bargaining agents do not have authority over the individual rights granted by the employment discrimination laws, then can employers instead obtain agreements to arbitrate statutory claims directly from individual employees who are represented by unions? See ALPA v. Northwest Airlines Inc., 199 F.3d 477 (D.C.Cir.1999) (holding that *Gilmer* arbitration agreements are "permissive" bargaining subjects that need not be negotiated with collective bargaining agent), judg. and op. reinstated as judg. and op. of court sitting en banc, 211 F.3d 1312 (2000). See Ann C. Hodges, Arbitration of Statutory Claims in the Unionized Workplace: Is Bargaining with the Union Required?, 16 Ohio St. J. Disp. Res. 513 (2001).

C. RELATIONSHIPS AMONG FEDERAL AND STATE SYSTEMS

1. *Effect of State Adjudication on Federal Actions*

KREMER v. CHEMICAL CONSTRUCTION CORP.

Supreme Court of the United States, 1982.
456 U.S. 461, 102 S.Ct. 1883, 72 L.Ed.2d 262.

JUSTICE WHITE delivered the opinion of the Court.

As one of its first acts, Congress directed that all United States courts afford the same full faith and credit to state court judgments that would apply in the State's own courts. Act of May 26, 1790, ch. 11, 1 Stat. 122, 28 U.S.C. § 1738. * * * The principal question presented by this case is whether Congress intended Title VII to supersede the principles of comity and repose embodied in § 1738. Specifically, we decide whether a federal court in a Title VII case should give preclusive effect to a decision of a state court upholding a state administrative agency's rejection of an employment discrimination claim as meritless when the state court's decision would be res judicata in the State's own courts.

I

Petitioner Rubin Kremer emigrated from Poland in 1970 and was hired in 1973 by respondent Chemical Construction Corp. (Chemico) as an engineer. Two years later he was laid off, along with a number of other employees. Some of these employees were later rehired, but Kremer was not although he made several applications. In May 1976, Kremer filed a discrimination charge with the Equal Employment Opportunity Commission (EEOC), asserting that his discharge and failure to be rehired were due to his national origin and Jewish faith. Because the EEOC may not consider a claim until a state agency having jurisdiction over employment discrimination complaints has had at least 60 days to resolve the matter, § 706(c), 42 U.S.C. § 2000e–5(c), the Commission referred Kremer's charge to the New York State Division of Human Rights (NYHRD), the agency charged with enforcing the New York law prohibiting employment discrimination. N.Y.Exec.Law §§ 295(6), 296(1)(a) (McKinney 1972 and Supp.1981–1982).

After investigating Kremer's complaint, the NYHRD concluded that there was no probable cause to believe that Chemico had engaged in the discriminatory practices complained of. The NYHRD explicitly based its determination on the findings that Kremer was not rehired because one employee who was rehired had greater seniority, that another employee who was rehired filled a lesser position than that previously held by Kremer, and that neither Kremer's creed nor age was a factor considered in Chemico's failure to rehire him. The NYHRD's determination was upheld by its Appeal Board as "not arbitrary, capricious or an abuse of discretion." Kremer again brought his complaint to the attention of the

EEOC and also filed, on December 6, 1977, a petition with the Appellate Division of the New York Supreme Court to set aside the adverse administrative determination. On February 27, 1978, five justices of the Appellate Division unanimously affirmed the Appeal Board's order. Kremer could have sought, but did not seek, review by the New York Court of Appeals.

Subsequently, a District Director of the EEOC ruled that there was no reasonable cause to believe that the charge of discrimination was true and issued a right-to-sue notice. The District Director refused a request for reconsideration, noting that he had reviewed the case files and considered the EEOC's disposition as "appropriate and correct in all respects." [*Eds.* Kremer then brought a Title VII action in a federal district court claiming national origin and religious discrimination. The district court dismissed the action on grounds of res judicata and the court of appeals affirmed.]

* * *

II

Section 1738 requires federal courts to give the same preclusive effect to state court judgments that those judgments would be given in the courts of the State from which the judgments emerged. Here the Appellate Division of the New York Supreme Court has issued a judgment affirming the decision of the NYHRD Appeals Board that the discharge and failure to rehire Kremer were not the product of the discrimination that he had alleged. There is no question that this judicial determination precludes Kremer from bringing "any other action, civil or criminal, based upon the same grievance" in the New York courts. N.Y.Exec.Law § 300 (McKinney 1972). By its terms, therefore, § 1738 would appear to preclude Kremer from relitigating the same question in federal court.

Kremer offers two principal reasons why § 1738 does not bar this action. First, he suggests that in Title VII cases Congress intended that federal courts be relieved of their usual obligation to grant finality to state court decisions. Second, he urges that the New York administrative and judicial proceedings in this case were so deficient that they are not entitled to preclusive effect in federal courts and, in any event, the rejection of a state employment discrimination claim cannot by definition bar a Title VII action. * * *

Allen v. McCurry, 449 U.S. 90, 99, 101 S.Ct. 411, 417, 66 L.Ed.2d 308 (1980), made clear that an exception to § 1738 will not be recognized unless a later statute contains an express or implied partial repeal. There is no claim here that Title VII expressly repealed § 1738; if there has been a partial repeal, it must be implied. "It is, of course, a cardinal principle of statutory construction that repeals by implication are not favored," *Radzanower v. Touche Ross & Co.,* 426 U.S. 148, 154, 96 S.Ct. 1989, 1993, 48 L.Ed.2d 540 (1976); *United States v. United Continental Tuna Corp.,* 425 U.S. 164, 168, 96 S.Ct. 1319, 1322, 47 L.Ed.2d 653

(1976), and whenever possible, statutes should be read consistently.
* * *

* * *

No provision of Title VII requires claimants to pursue in state court an unfavorable state administrative action, nor does the Act specify the weight a federal court should afford a final judgment by a state court if such a remedy is sought. While we have interpreted the "civil action" authorized to follow consideration by federal and state administrative *agencies* to be a "trial *de novo*," *Chandler v. Roudebush*, 425 U.S. 840, 844–845, 96 S.Ct. 1949, 1951–52, 48 L.Ed.2d 416 (1976); *Alexander v. Gardner–Denver Co.*, [415 U.S. 36,] 38, 94 S.Ct. [1011,] 1015; *McDonnell Douglas Corp. v. Green*, [411 U.S. 792,] 798–799, 93 S.Ct. [1817,] 1822–1823, neither the statute nor our decisions indicate that the final judgment of a state *court* is subject to redetermination at such a trial. Similarly, the congressional directive that the EEOC should give "substantial weight" to findings made in state proceedings, § 706(b), 42 U.S.C. § 2000e–5(b), indicates only the minimum level of deference the EEOC must afford all state determinations; it does not bar affording the greater preclusive effect which may be required by § 1738 if judicial action is involved.[7] To suggest otherwise, to say that either the opportunity to bring a "civil action" or the "substantial weight" requirement implicitly repeals § 1738, is to prove far too much. For if that is so, even a full trial on the merits in state court would not bar a trial *de novo* in federal court and would not be entitled to more than "substantial weight" before the EEOC. The state courts would be placed on a one-way street; the finality of their decisions would depend on which side prevailed in a given case.

* * *

Nothing in the legislative history of the 1964 Act suggests that Congress considered it necessary or desirable to provide an absolute right to relitigate in federal court an issue resolved by a state court. While striving to craft an optimal niche for the States in the overall enforcement scheme, the legislators did not envision full litigation of a single claim in both state and federal forums. Indeed, the requirement of a trial *de novo* in federal district court following EEOC proceedings was

---

7. EEOC review of discrimination charges previously rejected by state agencies would be pointless if the federal courts were bound by such agency decisions. *Batiste v. Furnco Constr. Corp.*, 503 F.2d 447, 450, n. 1 (C.A.7 1974), cert. denied, 420 U.S. 928, 95 S.Ct. 1127, 43 L.Ed.2d 399 (1975). Nor is it plausible to suggest that Congress intended federal courts to be bound further by state administrative decisions than by decisions of the EEOC. Since it is settled that decisions by the EEOC do not preclude a trial *de novo* in federal court,

it is clear that unreviewed administrative determinations by state agencies also should not preclude such review even if such a decision were to be afforded preclusive effect in a State's own courts. *Garner v. Giarrusso*, 571 F.2d 1330 (C.A.5 1978); *Batiste v. Furnco Constr. Corp., supra; Cooper v. Phillip Morris, Inc.*, 464 F.2d 9 (C.A.6 1972); *Voutsis v. Union Carbide Corp.*, 452 F.2d 889 (C.A.2 1971), cert. denied, 406 U.S. 918, 92 S.Ct. 1768, 32 L.Ed.2d 117 (1972).

added primarily to protect employers from overzealous enforcement by the EEOC.

* * *

It is sufficiently clear that Congress, both in 1964 and 1972, though wary of assuming the adequacy of state employment discrimination remedies, did not intend to supplant such laws. We conclude that neither the statutory language nor the congressional debates suffice to repeal § 1738's long-standing directive to federal courts.

* * *

Finally, the comity and federalism interests embodied in § 1738 are not compromised by the application of res judicata and collateral estoppel in Title VII cases. Petitioner maintains that the decision of the Court of Appeals will deter claimants from seeking state court review of their claims ultimately leading to a deterioration in the quality of the state administrative process. On the contrary, stripping state court judgments of finality would be far more destructive to the quality of adjudication by lessening the incentive for full participation by the parties and for searching review by state officials. Depriving state judgments of finality not only would violate basic tenets of comity and federalism, *Board of Regents v. Tomanio,* 446 U.S. 478, 488, 491–492, 100 S.Ct. 1790, 1797, 1798–99, 64 L.Ed.2d 440 (1980), but also would reduce the incentive for States to work towards effective and meaningful antidiscrimination systems.

III

The petitioner nevertheless contends that the judgment should not bar his Title VII action because the New York courts did not resolve the issue that the District Court must hear under Title VII—whether Kremer had suffered discriminatory treatment—and because the procedures provided were inadequate. Neither contention is persuasive. Although the claims presented to the NYHRD and subsequently reviewed by the Appellate Division were necessarily based on New York law, the alleged discriminatory acts are prohibited by both federal and state laws. The elements of a successful employment discrimination claim are virtually identical; petitioner could not succeed on a Title VII claim consistently with the judgment of the NYHRD that there is no reason to believe he was terminated or not rehired because of age or religion. The Appellate Division's affirmance of the NYHRD's dismissal necessarily decided that petitioner's claim under New York law was meritless, and thus it also decided that a Title VII claim arising from the same events would be equally meritless.

The more serious contention is that even though administrative proceedings and judicial review are legally sufficient to be given preclusive effect in New York, they should be deemed so fundamentally flawed as to be denied recognition under § 1738. We have previously recognized that the judicially created doctrine of collateral estoppel does not apply when the party against whom the earlier decision is asserted did not have a "full and fair opportunity" to litigate the claim or issue. * * *

Our previous decisions have not specified the source or defined the content of the requirement that the first adjudication offer a full and fair opportunity to litigate. But for present purposes, where we are bound by the statutory directive of § 1738, state proceedings need do no more than satisfy the minimum procedural requirements of the Fourteenth Amendment's Due Process Clause in order to qualify for the full faith and credit guaranteed by federal law. It has long been established that § 1738 does not allow federal courts to employ their own rules of res judicata in determining the effect of state judgments. Rather, it goes beyond the common law and commands a federal court to accept the rules chosen by the State from which the judgment is taken.

* * *

We have little doubt that Kremer received all the process that was constitutionally required in rejecting his claim that he had been discriminatorily discharged contrary to the statute. * * * Under New York law, a claim of employment discrimination requires the NYHRD to investigate whether there is "probable cause" to believe that the complaint is true. Before this determination of probable cause is made, the claimant is entitled to a "full opportunity to present on the record, though informally, his charges against his employer or other respondent, including the right to submit all exhibits which he wishes to present and testimony of witnesses in addition to his own testimony." *State Div. of Human Rights v. New York State Drug Abuse Comm'n,* 59 A.D.2d 332, 336, 399 N.Y.S.2d 541, 544 (1977). The complainant also is entitled to an opportunity "to rebut evidence submitted by or obtained from the respondent." 9 N.Y.C.R.R. § 465.6 (1977). He may have an attorney assist him and may ask the division to issue subpoenas. 9 N.Y.C.R.R. § 465.12(c) (1977).

If the investigation discloses probable cause and efforts at conciliation fail, the NYHRD must conduct a public hearing to determine the merits of the complaint. N.Y.Exec.Law § 297(4)(a) (McKinney Supp. 1981–1982). A public hearing must also be held if the Human Rights Appeal Board finds "there has not been a full investigation and opportunity for the complainant to present his contentions and evidence, with a full record." *State Div. of Human Rights v. New York State Drug Abuse Comm'n, supra,* at 337, 399 N.Y.S.2d, at 542–543. Finally, judicial review in the Appellate Division is available to assure that a claimant is not denied any of the procedural rights to which he was entitled and that the NYHRD's determination was not arbitrary and capricious.

We have no hesitation in concluding that this panoply of procedures, complemented by administrative as well as judicial review, is sufficient under the Due Process Clause.

JUSTICE BLACKMUN, with whom JUSTICES BRENNAN and MARSHALL join, dissenting.

The Court purports to give preclusive effect to the New York court's decision. But the Appellate Division made no finding one way or the other concerning the *merits* of petitioner's discrimination claim. The NYHRD, not the New York court, dismissed petitioner's complaint for lack of probable cause. In affirming, the court merely found that the *agency's* decision was not arbitrary or capricious. Thus, although it claims to grant a state *court* decision preclusive effect, in fact the Court bars petitioner's suit based on the state *agency's* decision of no probable cause. The Court thereby disregards the express provisions of Title VII, for, as the Court acknowledges, Congress has decided that an adverse state agency decision will not prevent a complainant's subsequent Title VII suit.

* * *

* * * The lesson of the Court's ruling is: *An unsuccessful state discrimination complainant should not seek state judicial review.* If a discrimination complainant pursues state judicial review and loses—a likely result given the deferential standard of review in state court—he forfeits his right to seek redress in a federal court. If, however, he simply bypasses the state courts, he can proceed to the EEOC and ultimately to federal court. Instead of a deferential review of an agency record, he will receive in federal court a *de novo* hearing accompanied by procedural aids such as broad discovery rules and the ability to subpoena witnesses. Thus, paradoxically, the Court effectively has eliminated state reviewing courts from the fight against discrimination in an entire class of cases. Consequently, the state courts will not have a chance to correct state agency errors when the agencies rule against discrimination victims, and the quality of state agency decisionmaking can only deteriorate. It is a perverse sort of comity that eliminates the reviewing function of state courts in the name of giving their decisions due respect.

JUSTICE STEVENS, dissenting.

Both the text of Title VII and its legislative history indicate that Congress intended the claimant to have at least one opportunity to prove his case in a *de novo* trial in court. Thus, while I agree with the Court that Title VII did not impliedly repeal § 1738, I cannot accept the Court's construction of § 1738 in this case. In New York, as Justice Blackmun demonstrates, the judicial review is simply a part of the "proceedings" that are entitled to "substantial weight" under Title VII.

Notes and Questions

1. *Collateral Estoppel or Res Judicata?* Conventionally understood, the doctrine of collateral estoppel, or issue preclusion, requires that (i) the issue sought to be precluded in the later action is the same as the issue litigated in the prior action; (ii) the issue in the prior action was actually litigated in that action; (iii) the determination of the issue in the prior action was necessary to the judgment in that action; and (iv) an identity of parties in both actions (although in many jurisdictions, the party asserting preclusion in the second action need not have been a party to the prior action). The related doctrine of res judicata, or claim preclusion, applies where (i) the

claim sued upon in the second action is the same as in the first; (ii) the first action involved an adjudication on the merits; and (iii) there is an identity of parties. The latter doctrine differs from the former in its preclusive effect on an entire claim whether or not a particular issue or legal theory was actually litigated in the first action. See Restatement (Second) of Judgments §§ 18–19 & 27 (1982). Is it clear which of the two doctrines was applied in *Kremer?*

2. *Section 1738 and State Claim Preclusion Law?* If the *Kremer* decision involved only issue preclusion, is there reason to think that its holding that Title VII claims are not exempt from § 1738 does not apply to state claim preclusion law as well? Assume, for instance, that Kremer had appealed to state court only the New York agency's rejection of his religion discrimination claim, without also appealing its rejection of his national origin discrimination claim. Assume further that under New York res judicata law Kremer then would have been precluded from later pressing a charge of national origin discrimination in state court. The Supreme Court two years after *Kremer* held that under § 1738 the doctrine of res judicata, or claim preclusion, applies to bar a § 1983 claim that could have been litigated in an earlier state court proceeding. See Migra v. Warren City School Dist. Bd. of Educ., 465 U.S. 75, 104 S.Ct. 892, 79 L.Ed.2d 56 (1984).

3. *Plaintiff's Dilemma.* As argued by Justice Blackmun, under *Kremer* Title VII claimants might be wise to forgo the opportunity to seek state judicial review of an unfavorable state agency determination on the merits of their charge. Seeking such review might result in the sacrifice of any opportunity to have their Title VII claims adjudicated in court, as the type of state appellate review involved in that case might not include authority to exercise the state's concurrent jurisdiction (as recognized in Yellow Freight System, Inc. v. Donnelly, 494 U.S. 820, 110 S.Ct. 1566, 108 L.Ed.2d 834 (1990) to try Title VII claims. On the other hand, a direct action in a federal court, which presumably would lack authority to review the state agency determination, also might not seem fully satisfactory to claimants who lack access to private counsel and would prefer, at least initially, to convince the state agency to prosecute their claims. See also note 7 below.

4. *Does "Due Process" Provide the Only Limit on the Impact of State Preclusion Law in Federal Court?* The *Kremer* Court holds that "state proceedings need do no more than satisfy the minimum procedural requirements of the Fourteenth Amendment's Due Process Clause in order to qualify for the full faith and credit guaranteed by federal law." Does this mean that so long as state administrative proceedings satisfy due process standards and are given some level of review in state court, those proceedings preclude litigation of Title VII claims in federal court if state law would preclude litigation in state court? Could a state court's dismissal for lack of timeliness of a plaintiff's appeal of an adverse administrative ruling preclude a timely Title VII action in federal court? See Bray v. New York Life Ins., 851 F.2d 60 (2d Cir.1988) (federal court action precluded where state res judicata law would preclude state action after untimely filing).

5. *Defendant Appeals to State Courts?* In *Kremer* the Title VII claimant initiated the state court's review of the state administrative findings. As the Court confirmed in University of Tennessee v. Elliott, 478 U.S. 788, 106 S.Ct. 3220, 92 L.Ed.2d 635 (1986) (see note 7 below), Title VII complainants

who are unsuccessful in state administrative proceedings can bypass their state judicial remedies and proceed directly to federal court to obtain a de novo trial. It is likely that in light of *Kremer* most such complainants will choose this bypass, at least where state law does not offer de novo state court review. Consider, moreover, a case in which the *defendant*, before the plaintiff has had an opportunity to file in federal court, has successfully moved a state court to overturn a state administrative decision favorable to the plaintiff. If this reversal would bar consideration of a parallel Title VII claim in the state's courts, given *Kremer*'s reasoning, is there any basis for not precluding consideration of the claim in federal courts as well? The lower courts have found none. See, e.g., Trujillo v. County of Santa Clara, 775 F.2d 1359 (9th Cir.1985); Gonsalves v. Alpine Country Club, 727 F.2d 27 (1st Cir.1984); Davis v. United States Steel Supply Co., 688 F.2d 166 (3d Cir.1982). Does *Kremer*, as so interpreted, also encourage discrimination complainants to take steps to avoid an appealable final state administrative decision before they can proceed to a full trial in federal court? Would Congress have wanted to encourage such pro forma treatment of the system of deferral to state administrative remedies it crafted in Title VII?

6. *Preclusive Effect of Judicially Reviewed Arbitration Awards?* Does the holding in *Kremer* that Title VII does not effect an implied repeal of § 1738 mean that the review of an arbitration award in state court could preclude Title VII litigation of the same issue in federal as well as state courts? Under *Kremer* if state preclusion law would bar a Title VII action in state courts, can a federal court proceed to consider a Title VII claim, regardless of the limited scope of state court review of the arbitration decision on the parallel discrimination grievance? Can the federal court avoid preclusion only by finding a denial of due process in the arbitration? Cf. Caldeira v. County of Kauai, 866 F.2d 1175 (9th Cir.1989) (finding preclusion in § 1983 action). Should it matter whether the arbitrator applied Title VII doctrine to the discrimination grievance when the state's res judicata law would prevent any state court consideration of a statutory discrimination claim on the same facts? Compare Rider v. Commonwealth of Pennsylvania, 850 F.2d 982, 991 (3d Cir.1988) (finding preclusion because both arbitrator and state court "grafted classic Title VII BFOQ analysis onto their respective interpretations of the agreement"), with Jalil v. Avdel Corp., 873 F.2d 701 (3d Cir.1989) (no preclusion; issue before state court of whether arbitrator had contractual authority for award did not require consideration of Title VII issue). What are the implications for the *Alexander-Gilmer* line of cases of permitting state court review of arbitration decisions to preclude Title VII actions?

7. *A Federal Common Law of Preclusion Based on Unreviewed State Administrative Proceedings.* In University of Tennessee v. Elliott, cited in note 5 above, the Court held that unreviewed state administrative proceedings do not have a preclusive effect on Title VII claims. The Court stressed that § 1738 does not by its terms apply to administrative proceedings, and that § 706(b) of Title VII makes clear that Congress did not intend that unreviewed state agency determinations would receive preclusive effect either in EEOC proceedings or in federal court. However, the *Elliott* Court also held, as a matter of federal common law, that issues determined in a

state trial-type agency proceeding could be given preclusive effect in a later § 1983 action in federal court. The Court pronounced a general principle that in the absence of contrary congressional intent, as was the case with respect to Title VII, "when a state agency 'acting in a judicial capacity * * * resolves disputed issues of fact properly before it which the parties have had an adequate opportunity to litigate,' * * * federal courts must give the agency's factfinding the same preclusive effect to which it would be entitled in the State's courts." 478 U.S. at 799, 106 S.Ct. at 3227. Does *Elliott* discourage use of state administrative remedies? Or do plaintiffs' lawyers in any event (and regardless of *Elliot*) want to press any case of merit to court without inviting an administrative adjudication? Presumably, *Elliot* does not affect cases where the state administrative agency merely investigates but does not engage in any adjudicatory process.

The *Elliott* decision leaves open a series of questions:

a. Are actions under other modern status discrimination laws precluded by unreviewed state administrative adjudications? In Astoria Federal Savings and Loan Ass'n v. Solimino, 501 U.S. 104, 111 S.Ct. 2166, 115 L.Ed.2d 96 (1991), the Court held that unreviewed state administrative adjudications of ADEA claims do not have a preclusive effect on suits in federal court.

b. If the state would not attach preclusive effect to the administrative proceeding, is it correct to assume that federal common law principles under *Elliott* do not require that such effect be given in the federal action? See Marrese v. American Acad. of Ortho. Surgeons, 470 U.S. 373, 105 S.Ct. 1327, 84 L.Ed.2d 274 (1985) (leaving question open); Frazier v. King, 873 F.2d 820, 825 (5th Cir.1989) (§ 1983 claim not precluded where state law does not recognize collateral estoppel doctrine).

c. What constitutes an "adequate opportunity to litigate" a claim of discrimination in state administrative proceedings? Some courts have held that there should be no preclusion where the issues before the state administrative body were different, see Kelley v. TYK Refractories Co., 860 F.2d 1188, 1198 (3d Cir.1988), or where the state administrative body could not provide the same remedies, see Frazier v. King, supra, at 824–25. Should adjudications by state agencies other than fair employment practice agencies ever be adequate? The courts have found the procedures in certain types of state agencies to be deficient. See Hill v. Coca Cola Bottling Co., 786 F.2d 550 (2d Cir.1986) (action not precluded by findings of unemployment compensation board); Heller v. Ebb Auto Co., 308 Or. 1, 774 P.2d 1089 (1989) (same); Pizzuto v. Perdue Inc., 623 F.Supp. 1167 (D.Del.1985) (court not bound by findings of state industrial accident board). Can there be any preclusion of the federal claim if the administrative agency lacked authority under state law to entertain a discrimination claim? See Carpenter v. Reed, 757 F.2d 218 (10th Cir.1985) (record unclear whether board had authority under state law to consider discrimination claim). What if the state agency could not award federal statutory remedies? Note that the findings reached in the state administrative proceeding may not always receive preclusive effect under state law.

d. Are grievants who could have raised discrimination claims in state administrative proceedings, but did not do so, precluded from raising the claim in federal court actions? Although the Court has held that claim preclusive effect may attach to a state *judicial* proceeding under § 1738, see Migra v. Warren City School Dist. Bd. of Educ., supra, are there reasons for not construing the federal common law of preclusion to attach claim preclusive effect to unreviewed state *administrative* proceedings?

2. *Preemption of State Law by Title VII*

CALIFORNIA FEDERAL SAVINGS
AND LOAN ASSN. v. GUERRA

Supreme Court of the United States, 1987.
479 U.S. 272, 107 S.Ct. 683, 93 L.Ed.2d 613.

JUSTICE MARSHALL delivered the opinion of the Court.

The question presented is whether Title VII of the Civil Rights Act of 1964, as amended by the Pregnancy Discrimination Act of 1978, preempts a state statute that requires employers to provide leave and reinstatement to employees disabled by pregnancy.

I

California's Fair Employment and Housing Act (FEHA), Cal.Gov't Code Ann. § 12900 *et seq.* (West 1980 and Supp.1986), is a comprehensive statute that prohibits discrimination in employment and housing. In September 1978, California amended the FEHA to proscribe certain forms of employment discrimination on the basis of pregnancy. See Cal.Labor Code Ann. § 1420.35, 1978 Cal.Stats. ch. 1321, § 1, p. 4320–4322, now codified at Cal.Gov't Code Ann. § 12945(b)(2) (West 1980).[1] Subdivision (b)(2)—the provision at issue here—is the only portion of the statute that applies to employers subject to Title VII. See § 12945(e). It requires these employers to provide female employees an unpaid pregnancy disability leave of up to four months. Respondent Fair Employment and Housing Commission, the state agency authorized to interpret the FEHA, has construed § 12945(b)(2) to require California employers to reinstate an employee returning from such pregnancy leave to the job she previously held, unless it is no longer available due to business

---

1. Section 12945(b)(2) provides, in relevant part:

"It shall be an unlawful employment practice unless based upon a bona fide occupational qualification:

* * *

"(b) For any employer to refuse to allow a female employee affected by pregnancy, childbirth, or related medical conditions * * *."

* * *

"(2) To take a leave on account of pregnancy for a reasonable period of time; provided, such period shall not exceed four months. * * * Reasonable period of time means that period during which the female employee is disabled on account of pregnancy, childbirth, or related medical conditions * * *."

"An employer may require any employee who plans to take a leave pursuant to this section to give reasonable notice of the date such leave shall commence and the estimated duration of such leave."

necessity. In the latter case, the employer must make a reasonable, good faith effort to place the employee in a substantially similar job. The statute does not compel employers to provide *paid* leave to pregnant employees. Accordingly, the only benefit pregnant workers actually derive from § 12945(b)(2) is a qualified right to reinstatement.

* * *

III

A

In determining whether a state statute is pre-empted by federal law and therefore invalid under the Supremacy Clause of the Constitution, our sole task is to ascertain the intent of Congress. See *Shaw v. Delta Air Lines, Inc.,* 463 U.S. 85, 95, 103 S.Ct. 2890, 2898, 77 L.Ed.2d 490 (1983); *Malone v. White Motor Corp.,* 435 U.S. 497, 504, 98 S.Ct. 1185, 1189, 55 L.Ed.2d 443 (1978). Federal law may supersede state law in several different ways. First, when acting within constitutional limits, Congress is empowered to pre-empt state law by so stating in express terms. *E.g., Jones v. Rath Packing Co.,* 430 U.S. 519, 525, 97 S.Ct. 1305, 1309, 51 L.Ed.2d 604 (1977). Second, congressional intent to pre-empt state law in a particular area may be inferred where the scheme of federal regulation is sufficiently comprehensive to make reasonable the inference that Congress "left no room" for supplementary state regulation. *Rice v. Santa Fe Elevator Corp.,* 331 U.S. 218, 230, 67 S.Ct. 1146, 1152, 91 L.Ed. 1447 (1947). Neither of these bases for pre-emption exists in this case. Congress has explicitly disclaimed any intent categorically to pre-empt state law or to "occupy the field" of employment discrimination law. See 42 U.S.C. §§ 2000e–7 and 2000h–4.

As a third alternative, in those areas where Congress has not completely displaced state regulation, federal law may nonetheless pre-empt state law to the extent it actually conflicts with federal law. Such a conflict occurs either because "compliance with both federal and state regulations is a physical impossibility," *Florida Lime & Avocado Growers, Inc. v. Paul,* 373 U.S. 132, 142–143, 83 S.Ct. 1210, 1217, 10 L.Ed.2d 248 (1963), or because the state law stands "as an obstacle to the accomplishment and execution of the full purposes and objectives of Congress." *Hines v. Davidowitz,* 312 U.S. 52, 67, 61 S.Ct. 399, 404, 85 L.Ed. 581 (1941). * * *

This third basis for pre-emption is at issue in this case. In two sections of the 1964 Civil Rights Act, §§ 708 and 1104, Congress had indicated that state laws will be pre-empted only if they actually conflict with federal law. Section 708 of Title VII provides:

"Nothing in this title shall be deemed to exempt or relieve any person from any liability, duty, penalty, or punishment provided by any present or future law of any State or political subdivision of a State, other than any such law which purports to require or permit the doing of any act which would be an unlawful employment practice under this title." § 2000e–7.

Section 1104 of Title XI, applicable to all titles of the Civil Rights Act, establishes the following standard for pre-emption:

"Nothing contained in any title of this Act shall be construed as indicating an intent on the part of Congress to occupy the field in which any such title operates to the exclusion of State laws on the same subject matter, nor shall any provision of this Act be construed as invalidating any provision of State law unless such provision is inconsistent with any of the purposes of this Act, or any provision thereof." § 2000h–4.

Accordingly, there is no need to infer congressional intent to pre-empt state laws from the substantive provisions of Title VII; these two sections provide a "reliable indicium of congressional intent with respect to state authority" to regulate employment practice. *Malone v. White Motor Corp., supra,* 435 U.S. at 505, 98 S.Ct., at 1190.

Sections 708 and 1104 severely limit Title VII's pre-emptive effect. Instead of pre-empting state fair employment laws, § 708 " 'simply left them where they were before the enactment of title VII.' " *Shaw v. Delta Air Lines, Inc., supra,* 463 U.S., at 103, n. 24, 103 S.Ct., at 2903, n. 24. Similarly, § 1104 was intended primarily to "assert the intention of Congress to preserve existing civil rights laws." 110 Cong.Rec. 2788 (1964) (remarks of Rep. Meader). See also H.R.Rep. No. 914, 88th Cong., 1st Sess., 59 (1963), U.S.Code Cong. & Admin.News 1964, pp. 2355 (additional views of Rep. Meader). The narrow scope of preemption available under §§ 708 and 1104 reflects the importance Congress attached to state antidiscrimination laws in achieving Title VII's goal of equal employment opportunity. * * *

In order to decide whether the California statute requires or permits employers to violate Title VII, as amended by the PDA, or is inconsistent with the purposes of the statute, we must determine whether the PDA prohibits the States from requiring employers to provide reinstatement to pregnant workers, regardless of their policy for disabled workers generally.

B

Petitioners * * * contend that the second clause of the PDA forbids an employer to treat pregnant employees any differently than other disabled employees. * * *

It is well established that the PDA was passed in reaction to this Court's decision in *General Electric Co. v. Gilbert,* 429 U.S. 125, 97 S.Ct. 401, 50 L.Ed.2d 343 (1976). * * * By adding pregnancy to the definition of sex discrimination prohibited by Title VII, the first clause of the PDA reflects Congress' disapproval of the reasoning in *Gilbert. Newport News [v. EEOC,]* [462 U.S. 669] at 678–679, 103 S.Ct. [2622], at 2628, and n. 17 [(1983)] (citing legislative history). Rather than imposing a limitation on the remedial purpose of the PDA, we believe that the second clause was intended to overrule the holding in *Gilbert* and to illustrate how discrimination against pregnancy is to be remedied. Cf. 462 U.S., at 678,

n. 14, 103 S.Ct., at 2628, n. 14 ("The meaning of the first clause is not limited by the specific language in the second clause, which explains the application of the general principle to women employees"); see also *id.,* at 688, 103 S.Ct., at 2633 (Rehnquist, J., dissenting). Accordingly, subject to certain limitations, we agree with the Court of Appeals' conclusion that Congress intended the PDA to be "a floor beneath which pregnancy disability benefits may not drop—not a ceiling above which they may not rise."

The context in which Congress considered the issue of pregnancy discrimination supports this view of the PDA. * * * In contrast to the thorough account of discrimination against pregnant workers, the legislative history is devoid of any discussion of preferential treatment of pregnancy, beyond acknowledgments of the existence of state statutes providing for such preferential treatment.

* * *

We also find it significant that Congress was aware of state laws similar to California's but apparently did not consider them inconsistent with the PDA. In the debates and reports on the bill, Congress repeatedly acknowledged the existence of state antidiscrimination laws that prohibit sex discrimination on the basis of pregnancy. * * *

* * *

We emphasize the limited nature of the benefits § 12945(b)(2) provides. The statute is narrowly drawn to cover only the period of *actual physical disability* on account of pregnancy, childbirth, or related medical conditions. Accordingly, unlike the protective labor legislation prevalent earlier in this century, § 12945(b)(2) does not reflect archaic or stereotypical notions about pregnancy and the abilities of pregnant workers. A statute based on such stereotypical assumptions would, of course, be inconsistent with Title VII's goal of equal employment opportunity. See, *e.g., Los Angeles Dept. of Water and Power v. Manhart,* 435 U.S. 702, 709, 98 S.Ct. 1370, 1375, 55 L.Ed.2d 657 (1978); *Phillips v. Martin Marietta Corp.,* 400 U.S. 542, 545, 91 S.Ct. 496, 498, 27 L.Ed.2d 613 (1971) (Marshall, J., concurring).

C

Moreover, even if we agreed with petitioners' construction of the PDA, we would nonetheless reject their argument that the California statute requires employers to violate Title VII. Section 12945(b)(2) does not prevent employers from complying with both the federal law (as petitioners construe it) and the state law. This is not a case where "compliance with both federal and state regulations is a physical impossibility," *Florida Lime & Avocado Growers, Inc. v. Paul,* 373 U.S. 132, 142–143, 83 S.Ct. 1210, 1217, 10 L.Ed.2d 248 (1963), or where there is an "inevitable collision between the two schemes of regulation." *Id.,* at 143, 83 S.Ct., at 1217. Section 12945(b)(2) does not compel California employers to treat pregnant workers *better* than other disabled employees; it merely establishes benefits that employers must, at a minimum, provide to pregnant workers. Employers are free to give comparable benefits to other disabled employees, thereby treating "women affected by pregnancy" no better than "other persons not so affected but similar in their ability or inability to work." Indeed, at oral argument, petitioners conceded that compliance with both statutes "is theoretically possible."

* * *

JUSTICE WHITE, with whom THE CHIEF JUSTICE and JUSTICE POWELL join, dissenting.

The second clause [of the PDA] could not be clearer: it mandates that pregnant employees "shall be treated the same for all employment-related purposes" as non-pregnant employees similarly situated with respect to their ability or inability to work. This language leaves no room for preferential treatment of pregnant workers. * * *

Contrary to the mandate of the PDA, California law requires every employer to have a disability leave policy for pregnancy even if it has none for any other disability. An employer complies with California law if it has a leave policy for pregnancy but denies it for every other disability. On its face, § 12945(b)(2) is in square conflict with the PDA and is therefore pre-empted. Because the California law permits employers to single out pregnancy for preferential treatment and therefore to violate Title VII, it is not saved by § 708 which limits pre-emption of state laws to those that require or permit an employer to commit an unfair employment practice.[1]

Notes and Questions

1. *Rationales for Limited Preemption.* Note the narrow preemptive force of Title VII on state law as confirmed by the *Guerra* Court. The Court stresses that "Congress has explicitly disclaimed any intent categorically to pre-empt state law or to "occupy the field" of employment discrimination law." Why would Congress want to preserve state regulatory power in this area? Is it to expand the resources and tools to be used against discrimination? To encourage diverse and innovative approaches in antidiscrimination law? Or simply to preserve some measure of greater local control over this kind of regulation? Are your answers relevant to any of the issues raised by the *Kremer* case?

2. *An Interpretation of § 708, As Well As of the PDA?* In a separate concurrence (not reprinted above), Justice Scalia argues that § 12945(b)(2) of the California Act is protected from preemption by § 708 of Title VII,

---

1. The same clear language preventing preferential treatment based on pregnancy forecloses respondents' argument that the California provision can be upheld as a legislative response to leave policies that have a disparate impact on pregnant workers. Whatever remedies Title VII would otherwise provide for victims of disparate impact, Congress expressly ordered pregnancy to be treated in the same manner as other disabilities.

regardless of whether the PDA would allow preferential treatment, because the California Act, while it does not prohibit, also does not require or authorize, any refusal to accord to other disabled employees the same leave and reinstatement rights it requires be accorded to those disabled by pregnancy. On what basis does Justice White disagree? Does the majority share Justice Scalia's interpretation of § 708?

3. *Application to Maternity Leave.* Given the rationale of the Court in *Guerra,* might Title VII preempt a state statute requiring employers to provide 90 days of maternity leave to all women after childbirth? Could such a statute be challenged through equal protection law? What if the statute required both maternity and paternity leave?

3. Preemption of State Law by ERISA

FORT HALIFAX PACKING CO., INC. v. COYNE

Supreme Court of the United States, 1987.
482 U.S. 1, 107 S.Ct. 2211, 96 L.Ed.2d 1.

JUSTICE BRENNAN delivered the opinion of the Court.

In this case we must decide whether a Maine statute requiring employers to provide a one-time severance payment to employees in the event of a plant closing, Me.Rev.Stat.Ann., Tit. 26, § 625–B (Supp.1986–1987),[1] is pre-empted by either the Employee Retirement Income Security Act of 1974, 88 Stat. 832, as amended, 29 U.S.C. §§ 1001–1381 (ERISA), or the National Labor Relations Act, 49 Stat. 452, as amended, 29 U.S.C. §§ 157–158 (NLRA).

* * *

II

Appellant's basic argument is that any state law pertaining to a type of employee benefit listed in ERISA necessarily regulates an employee benefit plan, and therefore must be pre-empted. Because severance benefits are included in ERISA, see 29 U.S.C. § 1002(1)(B), appellant

---

1. The statute provides in pertinent part:

"2. Severance pay. Any employer who relocates or terminates a covered establishment shall be liable to his employees for severance pay at the rate of one week's pay for each year of employment by the employee in that establishment. The severance pay to eligible employees shall be in addition to any final wage payment to the employee and shall be paid within one regular pay period after the employee's last full day of work, notwithstanding any other provisions of law.

"3. Mitigation of severance pay liability. There shall be no liability for severance pay to an eligible employee if:

"A. Relocation or termination of a covered establishment

is necessitated by a physical calamity;

"B. The employee is covered by an express contract providing for severance pay;

"C. That employee accepts employment at the new location; or

"D. That employee has been employed by the employer for less than 3 years."

§ 625–B(1)(A) defines "covered establishment" as a facility that employs 100 or more persons, while § 625–B(1)(F) defines "relocation" as the removal of all or substantially all operations at least 100 miles away from their original location.

argues that ERISA pre-empts the Maine statute.[5] In effect, appellant argues that ERISA forecloses virtually all state legislation regarding employee benefits. This contention fails, however, in light of the plain language of ERISA's pre-emption provision, the underlying purpose of that provision, and the overall objectives of ERISA itself.

A

The first answer to appellant's argument is found in the express language of the statute. ERISA's pre-emption provision does not refer to state laws relating to "employee benefits," but to state laws relating to "employee benefit *plans*":

> "[T]he provisions of this subchapter * * * shall supersede any and all State laws insofar as they may now or hereafter relate to any *employee benefit plan* described in § 1003(a) of this title and not exempt under § 1003(b) of this title." 29 U.S.C. § 1144(a) (emphasis added).

We have held that the words "relate to" should be construed expansively: "[a] law 'relates to' an employee benefit plan, in the normal sense of the phrase, if it has a connection with or reference to such a plan." *Shaw v. Delta Air Lines, Inc.,* 463 U.S. 85, 96–97, 103 S.Ct. 2890, 2900, 77 L.Ed.2d 490 (1983). Nothing in our case law, however, supports appellant's position that the word "plan" should in effect be read out of the statute.

* * *

B

The second answer to appellant's argument is that pre-emption of the Maine statute would not further the purpose of ERISA pre-emption. * * *

Statements by ERISA's sponsors in the House and Senate clearly disclose the problem that the pre-emption provision was intended to address. In the House, Representative Dent stated that "with the pre-emption of the field [of employee benefit plans], we round out the protection afforded participants by eliminating the threat of conflicting and inconsistent State and local regulation." 120 Cong.Rec. 29197 (1974). Similarly, Senator Williams declared, "It should be stressed that with the narrow exceptions specified in the bill, the substantive and enforcement provisions of the conference substitute are intended to preempt the field for Federal regulations, thus eliminating the threat of

---

5. Section 1002(1)(B) defines an employee welfare benefit plan as a plan that pays, *inter alia,* benefits described in 29 U.S.C. § 186(c). The latter section includes, *inter alia,* money paid by an employer to a trust fund to pay for severance benefits. Section 1002(1)(B) has been construed to include severance benefits paid out of general assets, as well as out of a trust fund. See *Holland v. Burlington Industries, Inc.,* 772 F.2d 1140 (C.A.4 1985), summarily aff'd, 477 U.S. 901, 106 S.Ct. 3267, 91 L.Ed.2d 559 (1986); *Gilbert v. Burlington Industries, Inc.,* 765 F.2d 320 (C.A.2 1985), summarily aff'd, 477 U.S. 901, 106 S.Ct. 3267, 91 L.Ed.2d 558 (1986); *Scott v. Gulf Oil Corp.,* 754 F.2d 1499 (C.A.9 1985); 29 CFR § 2510.3–1(a)(3) (1986).

conflicting or inconsistent State and local regulation of employee benefit plans." *Id.*, at 29933.

* * *

It is thus clear that ERISA's pre-emption provision was prompted by recognition that employers establishing and maintaining employee benefit plans are faced with the task of coordinating complex administrative activities. A patchwork scheme of regulation would introduce considerable inefficiencies in benefit program operation, which might lead those employers with existing plans to reduce benefits, and those without such plans to refrain from adopting them. Pre-emption ensures that the administrative practices of a benefit plan will be governed by only a single set of regulations.

* * *

The Maine statute neither establishes, nor requires an employer to maintain, an employee benefit *plan*. The requirement of a one-time lump-sum payment triggered by a single event requires no administrative scheme whatsoever to meet the employer's obligation. The employer assumes no responsibility to pay benefits on a regular basis, and thus faces no periodic demands on its assets that create a need for financial coordination and control. Rather, the employer's obligation is predicated on the occurrence of a single contingency that may never materialize. The employer may well *never* have to pay the severance benefits. To the extent that the obligation to do so arises, satisfaction of that duty involves only making a single set of payments to employees at the time the plant closes. To do little more than write a check hardly constitutes the operation of a benefit plan. Once this single event is over, the employer has no further responsibility. The theoretical possibility of a one-time obligation in the future simply creates no need for an ongoing administrative program for processing claims and paying benefits.

This point is underscored by comparing the consequences of the Maine statute with those produced by a state statute requiring the establishment of a benefit plan. In *Standard Oil of California v. Agsalud,* 633 F.2d 760 (C.A.9 1980), summarily aff'd, 454 U.S. 801, 102 S.Ct. 79, 70 L.Ed.2d 75 (1981), for instance, Hawaii had required that employers provide employees with a comprehensive health care plan. The Hawaii law was struck down, for it posed two types of problems. First, the employer in that case already had in place a health care plan governed by ERISA, which did not comply in all respects with the Hawaii Act. If the employer sought to achieve administrative efficiencies by integrating the Hawaii plan into its existing plan, different components of its single plan would be subject to different requirements. If it established a separate plan to administer the program directed by Hawaii, it would lose the benefits of maintaining a single administrative scheme. Second, if Hawaii could demand the operation of a particular benefit plan, so could other States, which would require that the employer coordinate perhaps dozens of programs. *Agsalud* thus illustrates that whether a State requires an existing plan to pay certain benefits, or whether it requires the establishment of a separate plan where none existed before, the problem is the same. Faced with the difficulty or impossibility of structuring administrative practices according to a set of uniform guidelines, an employer may decide to reduce benefits or simply not to pay them at all.

By contrast, the Maine law does not put the employer to the choice of either: (1) integrating a state-mandated ongoing benefit plan with an existing plan or (2) establishing a separate plan to process and pay benefits under the plan required by the State. This is because there is no State-mandated benefit plan to administer. In this case, for instance, Fort Halifax found no need to respond to passage of the Maine statute by setting up an administrative scheme to meet its contingent statutory obligation, any more than it would find it necessary to set up an ongoing scheme to deal with the obligations it might face in the event that some day it might go bankrupt. The company makes no contention that its statutory duty has in any way hindered its ability to operate its retirement plan in uniform fashion, a plan that pays retirement, death, and permanent and total disability benefits on an ongoing basis. The obligation imposed by the Maine statute thus differs radically in impact from a requirement that an employer pay ongoing benefits on a continuous basis.

* * *

C

* * * [T]he Maine statute not only fails to implicate the concerns of ERISA's pre-emption provision, it fails to implicate the regulatory concerns of ERISA itself. The Congressional declaration of policy, codified at 29 U.S.C. § 1001, states that ERISA was enacted because Congress found it desirable that "disclosure be made and safeguards be provided with respect to the establishment, operation, and administration of [employee benefit] plans." § 1001(a). Representative Dent, the House sponsor of the legislation, represented that ERISA's fiduciary standards "will prevent abuses of the special responsibilities borne by those dealing with plans." 120 Cong.Rec. 29197 (1974). Senator Williams, the Senate sponsor, stated that these standards would safeguard employees from "such abuses as self-dealing, imprudent investing, and misappropriation of plan funds." *Id.,* at 29932. The focus of the statute thus is on the administrative integrity of benefit plans—which presumes that some type of administrative activity is taking place. * * *

The foregoing makes clear both why ERISA is concerned with regulating benefit "plans," and why the Maine statute does not establish one. Only "plans" involve administrative activity potentially subject to employer abuse. The obligation imposed by Maine generates no such activity. There is no occasion to determine whether a "plan" is "operated" in the interest of its beneficiaries, because nothing is "operated." No financial transactions take place that would be listed in an annual report, and no further information regarding the terms of the severance pay obligation is needed because the statute itself makes these terms clear. It would make no sense for pre-emption to clear the way for exclusive federal regulation, for there would be nothing to regulate. Under such circumstances, pre-emption would in no way serve the overall purpose of ERISA.

D

* * *

Appellant also argues that its contention that the severance obligation under the Maine statute is an ERISA plan is supported by *Holland v. Burlington Industries, Inc.,* 772 F.2d 1140 (C.A.4 1985), summarily aff'd, 477 U.S. 901, 106 S.Ct. 3267, 91 L.Ed.2d 559 (1986), and *Gilbert v. Burlington Industries, Inc.,* 765 F.2d 320 (C.A.2 1985), summarily aff'd, 477 U.S. 901, 106 S.Ct. 3267, 91 L.Ed.2d 558 (1986). We disagree. Those cases hold that a plan that pays severance benefits out of general assets is an ERISA plan. That holding is completely consistent with our analysis above. There was no question in the *Burlington* cases, as there is in this case, whether the employer had a "plan";[10] there was a "plan" and the only issue was whether the type of benefits paid by that plan are among those covered by ERISA. The precise question was simply whether severance benefits paid by a plan out of general assets, rather than out of a trust fund, should be regarded as employee welfare benefits under 29 U.S.C. § 1002.

The courts' conclusion that they should be so regarded took into account ERISA's central focus on administrative integrity: if an employer has an administrative scheme for paying benefits, it should not be able to evade the requirements of the statute merely by paying those benefits out of general assets. Some severance benefit obligations by their nature necessitate an ongoing administrative scheme, but others do not. Those that do not, such as the obligation imposed in this case, simply do not involve a state law that "relate[s] to" an employee benefit "plan." 29 U.S.C. § 1144(a).[12] The *Burlington* cases therefore do not support appellant's argument.

10. The employer had made a commitment to pay severance benefits to employees as each person left employment. This commitment created the need for an administrative scheme to pay these benefits on an ongoing basis, and the company had distributed both a Policy Manual and Employees' Handbook that provided details on matters such as eligibility, benefit levels, and payment schedules. * * * The fact that the employer had not complied with the requirements of ERISA in operating this scheme therefore does not, * * * mean that no such program for paying benefits was in existence.

12. Thus, if a State required a benefit whose regularity of payment necessarily required an ongoing benefit program, it could not evade pre-emption by the simple expedient of somehow formally characterizing the obligation as a one-time lump-sum payment triggered by the occurrence of a certain contingency. It is therefore not the case, * * * that a State could dictate the payment of numerous employee benefits "by simply characterizing them as non-'administrative'."

Justice White, with whom The Chief Justice, Justice O'Connor, and Justice Scalia join, dissenting.

* * * By making pre-emption turn on the existence of an "administrative scheme," the Court creates a loophole in ERISA's pre-emption statute, 29 U.S.C. § 1144, which will undermine Congress' decision to make employee-benefit plans a matter of exclusive federal regulation. The Court's rule requiring an established "administrative scheme" as a prerequisite for ERISA pre-emption will allow States to effectively dictate a wide array of employee benefits that must be provided by employers by simply characterizing them as non-"administrative."

FMC CORPORATION v. HOLLIDAY

Supreme Court of the United States, 1990.
498 U.S. 52, 111 S.Ct. 403, 112 L.Ed.2d 356.

Justice O'Connor delivered the opinion of the Court.

This case calls upon the Court to decide whether the Employee Retirement Income Security Act of 1974 (ERISA) as amended pre-empts a Pennsylvania law precluding employee welfare benefit plans from exercising subrogation rights on a claimant's tort recovery.

* * *

Petitioner, FMC Corporation (FMC), operates the FMC Salaried Health Care Plan (Plan), an employee welfare benefit plan within the meaning of ERISA that provides health benefits to FMC employees and their dependents. The Plan is self-funded; it does not purchase an insurance policy from any insurance company in order to satisfy its obligations to its participants. Among its provisions is a subrogation clause under which a Plan member agrees to reimburse the Plan for benefits paid if the member recovers on a claim in a liability action against a third party.

* * *

* * * Three provisions of ERISA speak expressly to the question of pre-emption:

"Except as provided in subsection (b) of this section [the saving clause], the provisions of this subchapter and subchapter III of this chapter shall supersede any and all State laws insofar as they may now or hereafter relate to any employee benefit plan." § 514(a), as set forth in 29 U.S.C. § 1144(a) (pre-emption clause).

"Except as provided in subparagraph (B) [the deemer clause], nothing in this subchapter shall be construed to exempt or relieve any person from any law of any State which regulates insurance, banking, or securities." § 514(b)(2)(A), as set forth in 29 U.S.C. § 1144(b)(2)(A) (saving clause).

"Neither an employee benefit plan * * * nor any trust established under such a plan, shall be deemed to be an insurance company or other insurer, bank, trust company, or investment company or to be engaged in the business of insurance or banking for purposes of any law of any State purporting to regulate insurance companies, insurance contracts, banks, trust companies, or investment companies." § 514(b)(2)(B), as set forth in 29 U.S.C. § 1144(b)(2)(B) (deemer clause).

We indicated in *Metropolitan Life Ins. Co. v. Massachusetts,* 471 U.S. 724, 105 S.Ct. 2380, 85 L.Ed.2d 728 (1985), that these provisions "are not a model of legislative drafting." Id., at 739, 105 S.Ct., at 2389. Their operation is nevertheless discernible. The pre-emption clause is conspicuous for its breadth. It establishes as an area of exclusive federal concern the subject of every state law that "relates to" an employee benefit plan governed by ERISA. The saving clause returns to the States the power to enforce those state laws that "regulate insurance," except as provided in the deemer clause. Under the deemer clause, an employee benefit plan governed by ERISA shall not be "deemed" an insurance company, an insurer, or engaged in the business of insurance for purposes of state laws "purporting to regulate" insurance companies or insurance contracts.

* * *

Pennsylvania's antisubrogation law "relates to" an employee benefit plan. We made clear in *Shaw v. Delta Air Lines* [463 U.S. 85, 103 S.Ct. 2890, 77 L.Ed.2d 490 (1983)], that a law relates to an employee welfare plan if it has "a connection with or reference to such a plan." *Id.,* at 96–97, 103 S.Ct., at 2899–2900 (footnote omitted). We based our reading in part on the plain language of the statute. Congress used the words " 'relate to' in § 514(a) [the pre-emption clause] in their broad sense." *Id.,* at 98, 103 S.Ct., at 2900. It did not mean to pre-empt only state laws specifically designed to affect employee benefit plans. That interpretation would have made it unnecessary for Congress to enact ERISA § 514(b)(4), which exempts from pre-emption "generally" applicable criminal laws of a State. We also emphasized that to interpret the pre-emption clause to apply only to state laws dealing with the subject matters covered by ERISA, such as reporting, disclosure, and fiduciary duties, would be incompatible with the provision's legislative history because the House and Senate versions of the bill that became ERISA contained limited pre-emption clauses, applicable only to state laws relating to specific subjects covered by ERISA. These were rejected in favor of the present language in the Act, "indicating that the section's pre-emptive scope was as broad as its language." [*Shaw v. Delta Air Lines,* 463 U.S.] at 98, 103 S.Ct., at 2901.

Pennsylvania's antisubrogation law has a "reference" to benefit plans governed by ERISA. The statute states that "in actions arising out of the maintenance or use of a motor vehicle, there shall be no right of subrogation or reimbursement from a claimant's tort recovery with respect to * * * benefits * * * paid or payable under section 1719." 75 Pa. Cons.Stat. § 1720 (1987). Section 1719 refers to "any program, group contract or other arrangement for payment of benefits." These terms "include, but [are] not limited to, benefits payable by a hospital plan corporation or a professional health service corporation." § 1719.

The Pennsylvania statute also has a "connection" to ERISA benefit plans. In the past, we have not hesitated to apply ERISA's pre-emption clause to state laws that risk subjecting plan administrators to conflicting state regulations. See, e.g., *Shaw v. Delta Air Lines,* supra, at 95–100, 103 S.Ct., at 2898–2902 (state laws making unlawful plan provisions that discriminate on the basis of pregnancy and requiring plans to provide specific benefits "relate to" benefit plans); *Alessi v. Raybestos-Manhattan, Inc.,* 451 U.S. 504, 523–526, 101 S.Ct. 1895, 1906–1908, 68 L.Ed.2d 402 (1981) (state law prohibiting plans from reducing benefits by amount of workers' compensation awards "relates to" employee benefit plan). To require plan providers to design their programs in an environment of differing State regulations would complicate the administration of nationwide plans, producing inefficiencies that employers might offset with decreased benefits. See *Fort Halifax Packing Co. v. Coyne,* 482 U.S. 1, 10, 107 S.Ct. 2211, 2216, 96 L.Ed.2d 1 (1987). Thus, where a "patchwork scheme of regulation would introduce considerable inefficiencies in benefit program operation," we have applied the pre-emption clause to ensure that benefit plans will be governed by only a single set of regulations. *Id.,* at 11, 107 S.Ct., at 2217.

There is no dispute that the Pennsylvania law falls within ERISA's insurance saving clause. * * * Section 1720 directly controls the terms of insurance contracts by invalidating any subrogation provisions that they contain. See *Metropolitan Life,* 471 U.S., at 740–741, 105 S.Ct., at 2389–2390. It does not merely have an impact on the insurance industry; it is aimed at it. See *Pilot Life Ins. Co. v. Dedeaux,* 481 U.S. 41, 50, 107 S.Ct. 1549, 1554, 95 L.Ed.2d 39 (1987). This returns the matter of subrogation to state law. Unless the statute is excluded from the reach of the saving clause by virtue of the deemer clause, therefore, it is not pre-empted.

We read the deemer clause to exempt self-funded ERISA plans from state laws that "regulate insurance" within the meaning of the saving clause. By forbidding States to deem employee benefit plans "to be an insurance company or other insurer * * * or to be engaged in the business of insurance," the deemer clause relieves plans from state laws "purporting to regulate insurance." As a result, self-funded ERISA plans are exempt from state regulation insofar as that regulation "relates to" the plans. State laws directed toward the plans are pre-empted because they relate to an employee benefit plan but are not "saved" because they do not regulate insurance. State laws that directly regulate insurance are "saved" but do not reach self-funded employee benefit plans because the plans may not be deemed to be insurance companies, other insurers, or engaged in the business of insurance for purposes of such state laws. On the other hand, employee benefit plans that are insured are subject to indirect state insurance regulation. An insurance company that insures a plan remains an insurer for purposes of state laws "purporting to regulate insurance" after application of the deemer clause. The insurance company is therefore not relieved from state insurance regulation. The ERISA plan is consequently bound by state insurance regulations insofar as they apply to the plan's insurer.

* * *

Congress intended by ERISA to "establish pension plan regulation as exclusively a federal concern." *Alessi v. Raybestos–Manhattan, Inc.,* 451 U.S., at 523, 101 S.Ct., at 1906 (footnote omitted). Our interpretation of the deemer clause makes clear that if a plan is insured, a State may regulate it indirectly through regulation of its insurer and its insurer's insurance contracts; if the plan is uninsured, the State may not regulate it. As a result, employers will not face " 'conflicting or inconsistent State and local regulation of employee benefit plans.' " *Shaw v. Delta Air Lines, Inc.,* 463 U.S., at 99, 103 S.Ct., at 2901 (quoting remarks of Sen. Williams). A construction of the deemer clause that exempts employee benefit plans from only those state regulations that encroach upon core ERISA concerns or that apply to insurance as a business would be fraught with administrative difficulties, necessitating definition of core ERISA concerns and of what constitutes business activity. It would therefore undermine Congress' desire to avoid "endless litigation over the validity of State action," see 120 Cong.Rec. 29942 (1974) (remarks of Sen. Javits), and instead lead to employee benefit plans' expenditure of funds in such litigation.

JUSTICE STEVENS, dissenting.

The Court's construction of the statute draws a broad and illogical distinction between benefit plans that are funded by the employer (self-insured plans) and those that are insured by regulated insurance companies (insured plans). Had Congress intended this result, it could have stated simply that "all State laws are pre-empted insofar as they relate to any self-insured employee plan." There would then have been no need for the "saving clause" to exempt state insurance laws from the pre-emption clause, or the "deemer clause," which the Court today reads as merely reinjecting into the scope of ERISA's pre-emption clause those same exempted state laws insofar as they relate to self-insured plans.

From the standpoint of the beneficiaries of ERISA plans—who after all are the primary beneficiaries of the entire statutory program—there is no apparent reason for treating self-insured plans differently from insured plans. Why should a self-insured plan have a right to enforce a subrogation clause against an injured employee while an insured plan may not? The notion that this disparate treatment of similarly situated beneficiaries is somehow supported by an interest in uniformity is singularly unpersuasive. If Congress had intended such an irrational result, surely it would have expressed it in straightforward English.
* * *

* * *

If one accepts the Court's broad reading of the "relate to" language in the basic pre-emption clause, the answer to the question whether petitioner must comply with state laws regulating entities including but not limited to insurance companies depends on the scope of the saving clause. In this case, I am prepared to accept the Court's broad reading of that clause but it is of critical importance to me that the category of state laws described in the saving clause is broader than the category described in the deemer clause. A state law "which regulates insurance," and is therefore exempted from ERISA's pre-emption provision by operation of the saving clause, does not necessarily have as its purported subject of regulation an "insurance company" or an activity that is engaged in by persons who are insurance companies. Rather, such a law may aim to regulate another matter altogether, but also have the effect of regulating insurance. The deemer clause, by contrast, reinjects into the scope of ERISA pre-emption only those state laws that "purport to" regulate insurance companies or contracts—laws such as those which set forth the licensing and capitalization requirements for insurance companies or the minimum required provisions in insurance contracts. While the saving clause thus exempts from the pre-emption clause all state laws that have the broad effect of regulating insurance, the deemer clause simply allows pre-emption of those state laws that expressly regulate insurance and that would therefore be applicable to ERISA plans only if States were allowed to deem such plans to be insurance companies.

Notes and Questions

1. *General Purposes of ERISA Preemption?* Why might Congress have wanted to displace some state laws when passing the ERISA? Congress clearly would have wanted to preempt any state laws that directly conflict with some provision in ERISA. In order to avoid indirect conflicts and insure consistency, Congress also might have intended that ERISA provide the only source of regulation for those issues that it addresses. Might Congress also have wanted to displace other state law in order to encourage employers to grant employees additional benefits without worrying about the costs of special requirements in various states? Might Congress simply have wanted to reduce the costs of state regulation of employers? What evidence of legislative purpose is marshaled in the *Fort Halifax* and *Holliday* decisions?

2. *The Meaning of "Plan"?* Are you persuaded that the line drawn between benefits and benefit plans by the majority opinion in *Fort Halifax* reflects congressional intent? Is the line purely formal or does it provide a workable standard that is grounded in the policy of the statute? Do you agree with Justice White's dissent?

How should the *Fort Halifax* decision be applied to a state law that requires severance payments to be made to employees not discharged for cause, but terminated within two years of a change in corporate control? See Simas v. Quaker Fabric Corp., 6 F.3d 849 (1st Cir.1993).

3. *Does ERISA Coverage (and Preemption) Depend on Creation and Use of a Special Trust Fund Rather than General Assets to Finance Benefits?* Does the analysis in part II C of the *Fort Halifax* opinion suggest that as long as an employer pays benefits out of its general assets without use of

some separate accumulated fund there is no plan regulated by ERISA? Is any such suggestion necessarily negated by part II D of the opinion? In Massachusetts v. Morash, 490 U.S. 107, 109 S.Ct. 1668, 104 L.Ed.2d 98 (1989), the Court held that state criminal prosecution of a corporate officer for failing to pay discharged employees their unused vacation time is not preempted by ERISA. The Court sustained U.S.Department of Labor regulations excluding from the sphere of ERISA preemption, types of regular compensation and "payroll practices," including the payment of vacation benefits from an employer's general assets. The Court explained that in ERISA "Congress' primary concern was with the mismanagement of funds accumulated to finance benefits and the failure to pay employees benefits from accumulated funds * * *. Because ordinary vacation payments are typically fixed, due at known times, and do not depend on contingencies outside the employee's control, they present none of the risks that ERISA is intended to address." 490 U.S. at 115, 109 S.Ct. at 1673. The Court confirmed this approach in California Div. of Labor Standards Enforcement v. Dillingham Construction, N.A., Inc., 519 U.S. 316, 117 S.Ct. 832, 136 L.Ed.2d 791, 805 (1997). Is this relevant to the hypothetical case raised in note 2? See also discussion of state wage payment laws at 979–85 supra.

4. *Does ERISA Preclude State Minimum Benefit Regulation?* ERISA defines an employee welfare benefit plan as "any plan * * * which * * * is hereafter established or maintained * * * for the purpose of providing for its participants or their beneficiaries * * * medical, surgical, or hospital care or benefits, or benefits in the event of sickness, accident, disability, death or unemployment, or vacation benefits, apprenticeship or other training programs, or day care centers, scholarship funds, or prepaid legal services * * *." 29 U.S.C. § 1002(1). Does § 514(a) of ERISA, as interpreted in *Fort Halifax* and *Holliday*, prevent states from requiring employers to grant certain minimum benefits to their employees? Can California, for example, require employers either to offer a minimum level of health care coverage or pay a fee to a state-run health insurance found (S.B.2, enacted in 2003)?

Could § 514(a) have been interpreted more narrowly? Could it have been read to preempt only state laws relating to plan administration, or to any particular regulatory issue actually addressed in ERISA, rather than state laws relating to benefit levels? ERISA aims to protect employees by compelling employer disclosures and imposing fiduciary responsibilities on those with discretionary authority over plan assets, but it does not require provision of substantive benefits. Note that ERISA makes no provision for the vesting of welfare benefits. Such benefits are typically created by agreement; but in the absence of federal stipulation of benefit levels, why should the states be ousted from their traditional role of requiring minimum terms and conditions of employment, including a minimum level of welfare benefits? Would the Court have interpreted § 514 more narrowly had it simply applied its traditional "field" and "conflict" preemption analysis (see the discussion in the *Guerra* case on page 317). Cf. California Div. of Labor Standards Enforcement v. Dillingham Construction, N.A., Inc., supra, 519 U.S. at 334 (Scalia, J., concurring: interpreting "relate to" to contemplate only field and conflict preemption analysis). Should Congress amend ERISA so as to nullify the Court's broader interpretation of § 514(a)? Or are the qualifications on ERISA preemption discussed in the following notes adequate to preserve an appropriate domain for state regulation?

5. *Insulation of Self–Insured Plans: A Competitive Advantage for Large Employers?* Does the *Holliday* Court's interpretation of the saving and deemer clauses make sensible social policy? Why would Congress want to permit much greater state regulation of insured benefit plans than of self-insured plans? Is this distinction necessary to protect general state regulation of insurance? Will the distinction encourage some employers to change to self-funding? Will it give possible competitive advantages to larger employers better able to fund benefit plans without insurance? Is there a reasonable interpretation of the wording of the clauses that could have avoided the insulation of self-insured plans from state regulation? Is Justice Stevens's interpretation plausible?

6. *Does the Insurance "Saving" Clause in § 514(b)(2)(B) Salvage State Regulation?* Does the *Holliday* Court's interpretation of the saving clause enable states, through regulation of insurers rather than employers, to achieve the goals of most state minimum benefit laws that could be preempted by ERISA? See also Metropolitan Life Ins. Co. v. Massachusetts, 471 U.S. 724, 105 S.Ct. 2380, 85 L.Ed.2d 728 (1985) (saving clause allows state to require insurers to offer specified minimum mental health benefits in employee health-care plans covering hospital expenses). Or does the Court's interpretation of the deemer clause in § 514(b)(2)(B) allow employers to escape state regulation of most benefit plans through self-funding of benefit plans? Cf. American Medical Security, Inc. v. Bartlett, 111 F.3d 358 (4th Cir.1997) (finding preempted a state statute that sought to limit self-funded plans' reinsurance of their losses by preventing regulated insurers from agreeing to low stop-loss trigger points). See also discussion of § 501(c) of the ADA at pp. 580–84 supra.

The Court has stated that it will apply the saving clause only to state laws that both are "aimed at" insurance, as stated in *Holliday*, and also regulate the "business of insurance," as that phrase is defined in cases interpreting the act protecting state insurance law, the McCarran–Ferguson Act, 59 Stat. 33, as amended, 15 U.S.C. § 1011 et seq. See UNUM Life Insurance Co. of Amer. v. Ward, 526 U.S. 358, 119 S.Ct. 1380, 143 L.Ed.2d 462 (1999) (saving clause protects state law banning insurer from denying benefits based on insured giving untimely notice that is not shown to have prejudiced insurer); Metropolitan Life Ins. Co. v. Massachusetts, supra, 471 U.S. at 743. The Court has found McCarran–Ferguson Act cases to weigh three factors: (1) whether the regulated practice has the effect of transferring or spreading a policyholder's risk; (2) whether the practice is an integral part of the policy relationship between insurer and insured; and (3) whether it is limited to entities within the insurance industry.

For an example of state regulation of disability classifications in disability insurance policies, see In the Matter of the Application of Charlene Polan, 3 A.D.3d 30, 768 N.Y.S.2d 441 (1st Dept. 2003).

7. *State Regulation of HMOs.* The Court arguably has allowed state regulation of health maintenance organizations as insurers. In Rush Prudential HMO, Inc. v. Moran, 536 U.S. 355, 122 S.Ct. 2151, 153 L.Ed.2d 375 (2002), the Court held that ERISA did not preempt a state law providing for

an independent medical review of an HMO's denial of a claim for benefits; the law regulated an "integral part of the policy relationship between the insurer and the insured," Union Labor Life Ins. Co. v. Pireno, 458 U.S. 119, 129, 102 S.Ct. 3002, 73 L.Ed.2d 647 (1982), and hence came within the saving clause for insurance-industry regulation. On similar grounds, in Kentucky Assn. of Health Plans, Inc. v. Miller, 538 U.S. 329, 123 S.Ct. 1471, 155 L.Ed.2d 468 (2003), the Court rejected an ERISA preemption challenge to a state law requiring HMOs to include "any willing provider" within their provider network. But see Aetna Health Inc. v. Davila, 542 U.S. 200, 124 S.Ct. 2488, 159 L.Ed.2d 312 (2004) (finding preempted a state tort action against an HMO for denying a benefit; any state law "will be pre-empted if it provides a separate vehicle to assert a claim for benefits outside of, or in addition to, ERISA's remedial scheme.")

8. *Other Special Exemptions from § 514 Preemption.* State laws "regulating insurance, banking, or securities" are not the only state laws that "relate to" ERISA regulated plans that are nonetheless exempted from ERISA preemption. Section 514 contains other limited exemptions, including "any generally applicable criminal law of a state", 29 U.S.C. § 1144(b)(4). Furthermore, § 514(d) provides that the preemption provision shall not "be construed to alter, amend, modify, invalidate, impair, or supersede any law of the United States * * *." The latter provision was interpreted in Shaw v. Delta Air Lines, Inc., 463 U.S. 85, 103 S.Ct. 2890, 77 L.Ed.2d 490 (1983), to exempt from preemption state antidiscrimination laws that assist the Title VII enforcement scheme by prohibiting practices that are unlawful under Title VII, but not to exempt state anti-discrimination laws relating to ERISA benefit plans that prohibit practices that are lawful under Title VII.

The *Shaw* Court also interpreted another important limitation on the scope of ERISA preemption. Section 514(a) is not applicable to state laws that relate to benefit plans that are exempt from ERISA regulation, including plans that are "maintained solely for the purpose of complying with applicable workmen's compensation laws or unemployment compensation or disability insurance laws." 29 U.S.C. § 1003(b)(3). The *Shaw* Court held that only "separately administered * * * plans maintained solely to comply" with the kinds of state laws covered by § 1003(b)(3) are exempt from ERISA coverage, but that states may require employers to maintain separate plans to make possible the enforcement of their disability insurance (or presumably workers' compensation or unemployment compensation) laws. Does *Shaw* mean that a state, through a disability insurance law rather than through a "human rights" law, could require employers who do not provide disability insurance generally to provide such insurance for pregnancy disability?

9. *Section 502 and ERISA Preemption.* Section 514(a) is not the only provision of ERISA that bears on preemption. In Pilot Life Insurance Co. v. Dedeaux, 481 U.S. 41, 107 S.Ct. 1549, 95 L.Ed.2d 39 (1987), the Supreme Court held preempted tort and breach of contract claims for an employer's failure to pay benefits under an ERISA-regulated disability benefits plan. Although the Court relied on § 514, it also stressed that under § 502 of ERISA a plan participant or beneficiary may sue to recover or clarify rights to benefits. It then concluded that Congress intended § 502 to be "the

exclusive vehicle for * * * asserting improper processing of a claim for benefits * * *." 481 U.S. at 52.

In Ingersoll–Rand Co. v. McClendon, 498 U.S. 133, 111 S.Ct. 478, 112 L.Ed.2d 474 (1990), the Court held preempted by ERISA a state common law claim that an employee was unlawfully discharged to prevent his attainment of pension benefits. All members of the Court agreed that *Dedeaux* stands for the proposition that § 502 of ERISA provides the exclusive remedy for rights guaranteed under the substantive provisions of ERISA, including § 510—which makes it unlawful to discriminate against a benefit plan participant "for the purpose of interfering with the attainment of any right to which such participant may become entitled under the plan". The preemptive force of § 502 is not limited to state actions seeking recovery of benefits; it extends to state actions providing remedies not afforded by § 510. (A majority of the Court also held that the cause of action asserted in *McClendon* was preempted under § 514(a) because "the existence of a pension plan was a critical factor in establishing liability under the State's wrongful discharge law." 498 U.S. at 139–40.)

In 1999, however, in UNUM Life Insurance Co. of America v. Ward, 526 U.S. 358, 119 S.Ct. 1380, 143 L.Ed.2d 462 (1999), the Court held that *Dedeaux* does not bar a participant from invoking in a § 502 action to recover benefits from an ERISA plan a state common law rule that prevents an insurer from asserting a defense of untimely notice unless it can prove prejudice. The *Ward* Court held that this state law is not preempted under § 514 because it is saved as a law that regulates insurance. The Court therefore concluded that the state law can be asserted in an action brought under § 502, as the latter provision preempts only independent common law actions. The *Ward* Court reserved judgment on the Solicitor General's argument that a state law that is exempted from preemption by the saving clause also could provide a cause of action independent of § 502.

10. *Time For Reform?* Beginning with its first case on ERISA preemption in 1981, the Supreme Court has issued nearly two dozen decisions on the topic. There have been literally thousands more in the lower courts. Is the law that has been engendered by this judicial effort coherent, clear, and well grounded in the policies of the statute? If you think not, how would you draft an amendment to the statute to achieve these goals?

4. *Preemption of State Law by LMRA**

LINGLE v. NORGE DIVISION OF MAGIC CHEF, INC.

Supreme Court of the United States, 1988.
486 U.S. 399, 108 S.Ct. 1877, 100 L.Ed.2d 410.

JUSTICE STEVENS delivered the opinion of the Court.

* [*Eds.*—The basic federal law governing labor relations in all industries other than rail or air transportation is the National Labor Relations Act (NLRA) of 1935. The Labor Management Relations Act (LMRA) of 1947 included amendments to the NLRA and other provisions regulating the collective bargaining process. Section 301 of the LMRA, 29 U.S.C. § 185, establishes federal jurisdiction to hear claims for breach of collective bargaining agreements.]

In Illinois an employee who is discharged for filing a worker's compensation claim may recover compensatory and punitive damages from her employer. The question presented in this case is whether an employee covered by a collective-bargaining agreement that provides her with a contractual remedy for discharge without just cause may enforce her state law remedy for retaliatory discharge. The Court of Appeals held that the application of the state tort remedy was pre-empted by § 301 of the Labor Management Relations Act of 1947, 61 Stat. 156, 29 U.S.C. § 185. We disagree.

I

Petitioner was employed in respondent's manufacturing plant in Herrin, Illinois. On December 5, 1984, she notified respondent that she had been injured in the course of her employment and requested compensation for her medical expenses pursuant to the Illinois Workers' Compensation Act. On December 11, 1984, respondent discharged her for filing a "false worker's compensation claim."

The union representing petitioner promptly filed a grievance pursuant to the collective-bargaining agreement that covered all production and maintenance employees in the Herrin plant. The agreement protected those employees, including petitioner, from discharge except for "proper" or "just" cause, and established a procedure for the arbitration of grievances. The term grievance was broadly defined to encompass "any dispute between * * * the Employer and any employee, concerning the effect, interpretation, application, claim of breach or violation of this Agreement." Ultimately, an arbitrator ruled in petitioner's favor and ordered respondent to reinstate her with full back pay.

Meanwhile, on July 9, 1985, petitioner commenced this action against respondent by filing a complaint in the Illinois Circuit Court for Williamson County, alleging that she had been discharged for exercising her rights under the Illinois worker's compensation laws. [S]ee *Kelsay v. Motorola, Inc.,* 74 Ill.2d 172, 23 Ill.Dec. 559, 384 N.E.2d 353 (1978); *Midgett v. Sackett–Chicago, Inc.,* 105 Ill.2d 143, 85 Ill.Dec. 475, 473 N.E.2d 1280 (1984); see also Ill.Rev.Stat., ch. 48, ¶ 138.4(h) (1987). Respondent removed the case to the Federal District Court on the basis of diversity of citizenship, and then filed a motion praying that the Court either dismiss the case on preemption grounds or stay further proceedings pending the completion of the arbitration. Relying on our decision in *Allis–Chalmers Corp. v. Lueck,* 471 U.S. 202, 105 S.Ct. 1904, 85 L.Ed.2d 206 (1985), the District Court dismissed the complaint. * * *

The Court of Appeals agreed that the state-law claim was preempted by § 301. * * *

II

Section 301(a) of the Labor Management Relations Act of 1947, 61 Stat. 156, 29 U.S.C. § 185(a), provides:

"Suits for violation of contracts between an employer and a labor organization representing employees in an industry affecting commerce as defined in this Act, or between any such labor organizations, may be brought in any district court of the United States having jurisdiction of the parties, without respect to the amount in controversy or without regard to the citizenship of the parties."

In *Textile Workers v. Lincoln Mills,* 353 U.S. 448, 77 S.Ct. 912, 1 L.Ed.2d 972 (1957), we held that § 301 not only provides federal-court jurisdiction over controversies involving collective-bargaining agreements, but also "authorizes federal courts to fashion a body of federal law for the enforcement of these collective bargaining agreements." *Id.,* at 451, 77 S.Ct., at 915.

In *Teamsters v. Lucas Flour Co.,* 369 U.S. 95, 82 S.Ct. 571, 7 L.Ed.2d 593 (1962), we were confronted with a straightforward question of contract interpretation: whether a collective-bargaining agreement implicitly prohibited a strike that had been called by the union. The Washington Supreme Court had answered that question by applying state-law rules of contract interpretation. We rejected that approach, and held that § 301 mandated resort to federal rules of law in order to ensure uniform interpretation of collective-bargaining agreements, and thus to promote the peaceable, consistent resolution of labor-management disputes.

In *Allis–Chalmers Corp. v. Lueck,* 471 U.S. 202, 105 S.Ct. 1904, 85 L.Ed.2d 206 (1985), we considered whether the Wisconsin tort remedy for bad-faith handling of an insurance claim could be applied to the handling of a claim for disability benefits that were authorized by a collective-bargaining agreement. We began by examining the collective-bargaining agreement, and determined that it provided the basis not only for the benefits, but also for the right to have payments made in a timely manner. *Id.,* at 213–216, 105 S.Ct., at 1912–1914. We then analyzed the Wisconsin tort remedy, explaining that it "exists for breach of a 'duty devolv[ed] upon the insurer by reasonable implication from the express terms of the contract,' the scope of which, crucially, is 'ascertained from a consideration of the contract itself.' " *Id.,* at 216, 105 S.Ct., at 1914 (quoting *Hilker v. Western Automobile Ins. Co.,* 204 Wis. 1, 16, 235 N.W. 413, 415 (1931)). Since the "parties' agreement as to the manner in which a benefit claim would be handled [would] necessarily [have been] relevant to any allegation that the claim was handled in a dilatory manner," 471 U.S., at 218, 105 S.Ct., at 1915, we concluded that § 301 pre-empted the application of the Wisconsin tort remedy in this setting.

Thus, *Lueck* faithfully applied the principle of § 301 preemption developed in *Lucas Flour.* If the resolution of a state-law claim depends upon the meaning of a collective-bargaining agreement, the application of state law (which might lead to inconsistent results since there could be as many state-law principles as there are States) is pre-empted and federal labor-law principles—necessarily uniform throughout the nation—must be employed to resolve the dispute.

III

Illinois courts have recognized the tort of retaliatory discharge for filing a worker's compensation claim, *Kelsay v. Motorola, Inc.,* 74 Ill.2d 172, 23 Ill.Dec. 559, 384 N.E.2d 353 (1978), and have held that it is applicable to employees covered by union contracts, *Midgett v. Sackett–Chicago, Inc.,* 105 Ill.2d 143, 85 Ill.Dec. 475, 473 N.E.2d 1280 (1984), cert. denied, 474 U.S. 909, 106 S.Ct. 278, 88 L.Ed.2d 243 (1985). "[T]o show retaliatory discharge, the plaintiff must set forth sufficient facts from which it can be inferred that (1) he was discharged or threatened with discharge and (2) the employer's motive in discharging or threatening to discharge him was to deter him from exercising his rights under the Act or to interfere with his exercise of those rights." *Horton v. Miller Chemical Co.,* 776 F.2d 1351, 1356 (C.A.7 1985) (summarizing Illinois state court decisions), cert. denied, 475 U.S. 1122, 106 S.Ct. 1641, 90 L.Ed.2d 186 (1986); see *Gonzalez v. Prestress Engineering Corp.,* 115 Ill.2d 1, 104 Ill.Dec. 751, 503 N.E.2d 308 (1986). Each of these purely factual questions pertains to the conduct of the employee and the conduct and motivation of the employer. Neither of the elements requires a court to interpret any term of a collective-bargaining agreement. To defend against a retaliatory discharge claim, an employer must show that it had a nonretaliatory reason for the discharge, cf. *Loyola University of Chicago v. Illinois Human Rights Comm'n,* 149 Ill.App.3d 8, 102 Ill.Dec. 746, 500 N.E.2d 639 (1986); this purely factual inquiry likewise does not turn on the meaning of any provision of a collective-bargaining agreement. Thus, the state-law remedy in this case is "independent" of the collective-bargaining agreement in the sense of "independent" that matters for § 301 pre-emption purposes: resolution of the state-law claim does not require construing the collective-bargaining agreement.

The Court of Appeals seems to have relied upon a different way in which a state-law claim may be considered "independent" of a collective-bargaining agreement. The court wrote that "the just cause provision in the collective-bargaining agreement may well prohibit such retaliatory discharge," and went on to say that if the state law cause of action could go forward, "a state court would be deciding precisely the *same issue* as would an arbitrator: whether there was 'just cause' to discharge the worker." The Court concluded, "the state tort of retaliatory discharge is inextricably intertwined with the collective-bargaining agreements here, because it implicates the *same analysis of the facts* as would an inquiry under the just cause provisions of the agreements." We agree with the Court's explanation that the state-law analysis might well involve attention to the same factual considerations as the contractual determination of whether Lingle was fired for just cause. But we disagree with the Court's conclusion that such parallelism renders the state-law analysis dependent upon the contractual analysis. For while there may be instances in which the National Labor Relations Act pre-empts state law on the basis of the subject matter of the law in question, § 301 pre-emption merely ensures that federal law will be the basis for interpreting collective-bargaining agreements, and says nothing about the substantive rights a State may provide to workers when adjudication of those rights does not depend upon the interpretation of such agreements.[9] In other words, even if dispute resolution pursuant to a collective-bargaining agreement, on the one hand, and state law, on the other, would require addressing precisely the same set of facts, as long as the state-law claim can be resolved without interpreting the agreement itself, the claim is "independent" of the agreement for § 301 pre-emption purposes.[10]

IV

The result we reach today is consistent both with the policy of fostering uniform, certain adjudication of disputes over the meaning of collective-bargaining agreements and with cases that have permitted separate fonts of substantive rights to remain unpre-empted by other federal labor-law statutes.

First, as we explained in *Lueck*, "[t]he need to preserve the effectiveness of arbitration was one of the central reasons that underlay the Court's holding in *Lucas Flour*." 471 U.S., at 219, 105 S.Ct., at 1915. "A rule that permitted an individual to sidestep available grievance procedures would cause arbitration to lose most of its effectiveness, * * * as well as eviscerate a central tenet of federal labor contract law under § 301 that it is the arbitrator, not the court, who has the responsibility

---

9. Whether a union may *waive* its members' individual, nonpre-empted state-law rights, is, likewise, a question distinct from that of whether a claim is pre-empted under § 301, and is another issue we need not resolve today. We note that under Illinois law, the parties to a collective-bargaining agreement may not waive the prohibition against retaliatory discharge nor may they alter a worker's rights under the state worker's compensation scheme. *Byrd v. Aetna Casualty & Surety Co.*, 152 Ill.App.3d 292, 298, 105 Ill.Dec. 347, 352, 504 N.E.2d 216, 221, app. denied, 115 Ill.2d 539, 110 Ill.Dec. 454, 511 N.E.2d 426 (1987). Before deciding whether such a state law bar to waiver could be pre-empted under federal law by the parties to a collective-bargaining agreement, we would require "clear and unmistakable" evidence, see *Metropolitan Edison Co. v. NLRB*, 460 U.S. 693, 708, 103 S.Ct. 1467, 1477, 75 L.Ed.2d 387 (1983), in order to conclude that such a waiver had been intended. No such evidence is available in this case.

10. Thus, what we said in *Caterpillar Inc. v. Williams*, 482 U.S. 386, 394–395, 107 S.Ct. 2425, 2430–31, 96 L.Ed.2d 318 (1987) (emphasis in original), is relevant here:

"Caterpillar asserts that respondents' state-law contract claims are in reality completely pre-empted § 301 claims, which therefore arise under federal law. We disagree. Section 301 governs claims founded directly on rights created by collective-bargaining agreements, and also claims 'substantially dependent on analysis of a collective-bargaining agreement.' *Electrical Workers v. Hechler*, 481 U.S. 851, 859, n. 3 [107 S.Ct. 2161, 2166–2167, n. 3, 95 L.Ed.2d 791] (1987); see also *Allis–Chalmers Corp. v. Lueck*, 471 U.S., at 220 [105 S.Ct., at 1916]. Respondents allege that Caterpillar has entered into and breached *individual* employment contracts with them. Section 301 says nothing about the content or validity of individual employment contracts. It is true that respondents, bargaining unit members at the time of the plant closing, possessed substantial rights under the collective agreement, and could have brought suit under § 301. As masters of the complaint, however, they chose not to do so." * * *

to interpret the labor contract in the first instance." *Id.*, at 220, 105 S.Ct., at 1916. See *Paperworkers v. Misco, Inc.*, 484 U.S. 29, 108 S.Ct. 364, 98 L.Ed.2d 286 (1987); *Steelworkers v. Enterprise Wheel & Car Corp.*, 363 U.S. 593, 80 S.Ct. 1358, 4 L.Ed.2d 1424 (1960). Today's decision should make clear that interpretation of collective-bargaining agreements remain firmly in the arbitral realm; judges can determine questions of state law involving labor-management relations only if such questions do not require construing collective-bargaining agreements.

Second, there is nothing novel about recognizing that substantive rights in the labor relations context can exist without interpreting collective-bargaining agreements.

This Court has, on numerous occasions, declined to hold that individual employees are, because of the availability of arbitration, barred from bringing claims under federal statutes. See, *e.g.*, *McDonald v. West Branch*, 466 U.S. 284 [104 S.Ct. 1799, 80 L.Ed.2d 302] (1984); *Barrentine v. Arkansas–Best Freight System, Inc.*, 450 U.S. 728 [101 S.Ct. 1437, 67 L.Ed.2d 641] (1981); *Alexander v. Gardner–Denver Co.*, 415 U.S. 36 [94 S.Ct. 1011, 39 L.Ed.2d 147] (1974). Although the analysis of the question under each statute is quite distinct, the theory running through these cases is that notwithstanding the strong policies encouraging arbitration, "different considerations apply where the employee's claim is based on rights arising out of a statute designed to provide minimum substantive guarantees to individual workers." *Barrentine, supra*, 450 U.S., at 737 [101 S.Ct. at 1443]." *Atchison, T. & S.F.R. Co. v. Buell*, 480 U.S. 557, 564–565, 107 S.Ct. 1410, 1415, 94 L.Ed.2d 563 (1987) (emphasis added).

Although our comments in *Buell*, construing the scope of Railway Labor Act pre-emption, referred to independent *federal* statutory rights, we subsequently rejected a claim that federal labor law pre-empted a *state* statute providing a one-time severance benefit to employees in the event of a plant closing. In *Fort Halifax Packing Co. v. Coyne*, 482 U.S. 1, 21, 107 S.Ct. 2211, 2222, 96 L.Ed.2d 1 (1987), we emphasized that "pre-emption should not be lightly inferred in this area, since the establishment of labor standards falls within the traditional police power of the State." We specifically held that the Maine law in question was not pre-empted by the NLRA, "since its establishment of a minimum labor standard does not impermissibly intrude upon the collective-bargaining process." *Id.*, at 23, 107 S.Ct., at 2223.

The Court of Appeals "recognize[d] that § 301 does not pre-empt state anti-discrimination laws, even though a suit under these laws, like a suit alleging retaliatory discharge, requires a state court to determine whether just cause existed to justify the discharge." The court distinguished those laws because Congress has affirmatively endorsed state antidiscrimination remedies in Title VII of the Civil Rights Act of 1964, 78 Stat. 241, see 42 U.S.C. §§ 2000e–5(c) and 2000e–7, whereas there is no such explicit endorsement of state worker's compensation laws. As should be plain from our discussion in Part III, *supra*, this distinction is unnecessary for determining whether § 301 preempts the state law in question. The operation of the anti-discrimination laws does, however, illustrate the relevant point for § 301 pre-emption analysis that the mere fact that a broad contractual protection against discriminatory—or retaliatory—discharge may provide a remedy for conduct that coincidentally violates state law does not make the existence or the contours of the state law violation dependent upon the terms of the private contract. For even if an arbitrator should conclude that the contract does not prohibit a particular discriminatory or retaliatory discharge, that conclusion might or might not be consistent with a proper interpretation of state law. In the typical case a state tribunal could resolve either a discriminatory or retaliatory discharge claim without interpreting the "just cause" language of a collective-bargaining agreement.[12]

Notes and Questions

1. *Should the* Lingle *Court Have Attempted To Promote Arbitration As Well As Uniform Federal Law?* The logic of the *Lingle* opinion seems straightforward: Only state causes of action that depend upon the meaning of a collective bargaining agreement threaten the uniform interpretation of collective agreements under federal labor law principles, and hence are preempted by § 301 of the LMRA. Since resolution of Lingle's state law cause of action for tortious retaliatory discharge did not depend upon an interpretation of the collective agreement that governed her workplace, the action was not preempted by § 301.

The *Lingle* Court, however, appears to emphasize the proceduralist consideration of ensuring a uniform body of law for interpreting collective agreements without acknowledging that state causes of action, even if not dependent in any way on such agreements, might undermine the primary substantive goal that this uniform law has been fashioned to achieve—the resolution of labor-management disputes through a private system of collective bargaining and grievance arbitration. Would a formulation of § 301 preemption to maximize use of arbitration have required a different result in *Lingle*? Would it have suggested that the states may not stipulate minimum substantive rights for employees covered by collective agreements because such rights might also be treated in such agreements? See Jane Byeff Korn, Collective Rights and Individual Remedies, 41 Hastings L.J. 1149, 1170–73 (1990); Rebecca H. White, Section 301's Preemption of State Law, 41 Ala.L.Rev. 377, 386–88(1990). See also discussion of Metropolitan Life Ins.

---

12. A collective-bargaining agreement may, of course, contain information such as rate of pay and other economic benefits that might be helpful in determining the damages to which a worker prevailing in a state law suit is entitled. See *Baldracchi v. Pratt & Whitney Aircraft Div., United Technologies Corp.,* 814 F.2d 102, 106 (C.A.2 1987). Although federal law would govern the interpretation of the agreement to determine the proper damages, the underlying state law claim, not otherwise pre-empted, would stand. Thus, as a general proposition,

a state law claim may depend for its resolution upon both the interpretation of a collective-bargaining agreement and a separate state law analysis that does not turn on the agreement. In such a case, federal law would govern the interpretation of the agreement, but the separate state law analysis would not be thereby pre-empted. As we said in *Allis–Chalmers Corp. v. Lueck,* 471 U.S., at 211, 105 S.Ct., at 1911, "not every dispute * * * tangentially involving a provision of a collective-bargaining agreement is pre-empted by § 301 * * *."

Co. v. Massachusetts, at p. ___ infra. Should it matter to the wisdom of such broader preemption that § 301 law has encouraged arbitration as an alternative to work stoppages, rather than as an alternative to judicial consideration of state law's provision of minimum benefits? See Michael C. Harper, Limiting Section 301 Preemption: Three Cheers for the *Trilogy*, Only One for *Lingle* and *Lueck*, 66 Chi.-Kent L.Rev. 685, 702–05 (1990).

2. *Can States Protect Minimum Rights From Union Waiver?* A key feature of the private dispute resolution process contemplated by § 301 is the exclusive authority of the collective bargaining agent to negotiate the terms and conditions of employment in the labor agreement. See J.I. Case Co. v. NLRB, 321 U.S. 332, 64 S.Ct. 576, 88 L.Ed. 762 (1944). To what extent does a union have the power to waive the state law rights of the employees whom it represents in bargaining?

Note that the *Lingle* Court in footnote 9 reserves judgment on whether a state law barring union waiver of a nonpreempted state law right itself might be preempted by the LMRA. Would the preemption of such state law bars to union waiver be consistent with the thrust of the *Lingle* opinion? Preemption of such bars would preclude states from preventing unions from trading state law rights for some other benefit. If individual rights are subject to negotiation in the collective bargaining process, in what sense do they remain individual rights?

Would preemption of state law bars to waiver be consistent with the protection given Title VII rights by the *Alexander* Court? Note also the citation to Metropolitan Edison Co. v. NLRB, 460 U.S. 693, 103 S.Ct. 1467, 75 L.Ed.2d 387 (1983), in footnote 9 of the *Lingle* decision. That case concerned the waiver of rights secured by the National Labor Relations Act, a statute framed to encourage collective bargaining processes, rather than to secure minimum individual substantive rights. See also "Note on *Wright v. Universal Maritime Service* and the Continuing Viability of *Alexander v. Gardner–Denver*," pp. 1156–57 supra.

3. *Application to Employee Privacy Rights Secured by State Law.* In cases involving challenges to private employers' drug testing programs, a number of circuits have held that union-represented employees' privacy rights under state law, whether founded in statutory or constitutional provisions, are preempted by § 301 of the LMRA. The courts have reasoned that such rights were not intended to be absolute and that interpretation of the collective agreement is unavoidable because the reasonableness of an employee's privacy expectations in the workplace

> depend[s] to a great extent upon the concessions the union made regarding working conditions during collective bargaining. If the Agreement allowed L–Corp, as part of the "required" medical examination, to demand that workers assent to the additional laboratory analysis of urine specimens, and L–Corp did nothing more than exercise this contractual prerogative, then the rationality of Jackson's asserted expectation of urologic privacy would be diminished accordingly.

Jackson v. Liquid Carbonic Corp., 863 F.2d 111, 119 (1st Cir.1988) (state statutory privacy right); accord, Clark v. Newport News Shipbuilding & Dry Dock Co., 937 F.2d 934 (4th Cir.1991); Strachan v. Union Oil Co., 768 F.2d 703 (5th Cir.1985). But see Cramer v. Consolidated Freightways, Inc., 255

F.3d 683 (9th Cir. 2001) (en banc) (no preemption where privacy right is not negotiable, or where no clear waiver in the collective agreement).

Are the *Liquid Carbonic* line of cases decided correctly? Is it likely that a state would want an individual's right to privacy to be subject to modification by a collective representative? If not, should the state's judgment be subject to § 301 preemption? See also Harper, supra, at 709–10 (arguing that these cases deny employees causes of action that would be available to them if they were not represented by union, only because court decides union *could* have modified cause of action, regardless of whether union actually did so).

4. *Independent of Collective Agreement vs. Requiring Interpretation of Collective Agreement?* The cases cited in the last note also raise the question whether the need to interpret the collective agreement in order to assess an employer's *defense* should be a basis for § 301 preemption even where the employee's state law claim would exist independently of the agreement. Cf. also Martin v. Shaw's Supermarkets, 105 F.3d 40 (1st Cir.1997) (preemption because state statute creating rights upon which action was based expressly stated that collective agreement could abrogate the rights); Miller v. AT & T Network Systems, 850 F.2d 543 (9th Cir. 1988) (preemption of intentional infliction of emotional distress claim because state law would permit union to modify what was socially tolerable). Should § 301 preemption turn on the question of whether the state cause of action would exist independently of the collective bargaining agreement, rather than on whether the collective agreement must be interpreted to consider the state cause of action? Cf. Caterpillar Inc. v. Williams, 482 U.S. 386, 398–99, 107 S.Ct. 2425, 96 L.Ed.2d 318 (1987) ("the presence of a federal question, even a § 301 question, in a defensive argument does not overcome the paramount policies embodied in the well-pleaded complaint rule—that the plaintiff may, by eschewing claims based on federal law, choose to have the cause heard in state court"). For an argument that preemption should turn on the independence of the state cause of action, because only causes of action that are dependent on the existence of a collective agreement are likely to disrupt the collective bargaining process, see Harper, supra, at 714–31.

In two 1994 cases the Supreme Court may have supported the suggestion in *Williams* that the independence *vel non* of the state law cause of action should be the critical consideration in § 301 preemption analysis. In Hawaiian Airlines, Inc. v. Norris, 512 U.S. 246, 114 S.Ct. 2239, 129 L.Ed.2d 203 (1994), the Court held that an employee's claims under Hawaii's wrongful-discharge common law and its Whistleblower Protection Act, Haw. Rev. Stat. §§ 378–61 to 378–69 (1988), were not preempted by the requirement of the Railway Labor Act (RLA) that "minor" disputes, which grow "out of grievances or out of the interpretation and application" of collective bargaining agreements, are subject to the Act's mandatory arbitration mechanism. The Court found the RLA preemption standard to turn on whether the state-law cause of action "involves rights and obligations that exist independent of the collective bargaining agreement." The Court then found this standard to be "virtually identical" to the preemption standard under § 301.

In Livadas v. Bradshaw, 512 U.S. 107, 114 S.Ct. 2068, 129 L.Ed.2d 93 (1994), the Court held that an employee's right under California law to receive a penalty payment from an employer who failed to pay her promised wages promptly was not preempted under § 301 even though the penalty was based on the level of wages set in a collective bargaining agreement. Relying on footnote 12 in *Lingle*, the Court stated that "the bare fact that a collective-bargaining agreement will be consulted in the course of state-law litigation plainly does not require the claim to be extinguished." Id. at 124. Nonetheless, the *Livadas* Court expressly declined to decide whether causes of action that exist in the absence of any collective agreement might still be preempted in some cases that require the interpretation of the agreement.

5. *State Tort Law Actions.* Regardless of whether a "need-to-interpret-agreement" standard or a "dependent-on-agreement" standard is used, do *Lingle* and *Norris* suggest that there should not be preemption of most actions based on rights created for all individuals by a state's statutory law or common law of torts? See also, e.g., Peterson v. BMI Refractories, 132 F.3d 1405 (11th Cir.1998) (no preemption of assault and battery or of intentional infliction of emotional distress claim); Martin Marietta v. Maryland Commission on Human Relations, 38 F.3d 1392 (4th Cir.1994) (state law handicap discrimination claim not dependent on collective agreement not preempted); Jarvis v. Nobel/Sysco Food Services Co., 985 F.2d 1419 (10th Cir.1993) (retaliatory discharge claim not preempted).

Some common law torts, however, may be subject to § 301 preemption because they depend on some commitment made in a contract such as a collective agreement. Note, for instance, the *Lingle* Court's reaffirmation of Allis–Chalmers Corp. v. Lueck, a case involving a tort claim for bad faith in handling of a disability benefit claim. The *Lueck* Court held that the claim was preempted because state law predicated tort liability on the existence of an underlying contractual duty and the "parties' agreement as to the manner in which a benefit claim would be handled [would] necessarily [have been] relevant to any allegation that the claim was handled in a dilatory manner." 471 U.S. at 218, 105 S.Ct. at 1915. *Lueck* thus indicates that tort actions that are dependent upon some commitment in a collective agreement are preempted by § 301. See also, e.g., St. John v. International Ass'n of Machinists and Aerospace Workers, 139 F.3d 1214 (8th Cir.1998) (preemption of emotional distress claim that depends on extreme departure from terms of collective agreement): Stone v. Writer's Guild of America West, Inc., 101 F.3d 1312 (9th Cir.1996) (preemption of claim for emotional distress from consequences of violation of collective agreement); Terwilliger v. Greyhound Lines, Inc., 882 F.2d 1033 (6th Cir.1989) (preempting claim for bad faith processing of a reinstatement request pursuant to a right to reinstatement secured by collective agreement).

How then should the courts treat actions for defamation and emotional distress caused by false accusations made by an employer during the processing of a grievance? Do such actions require interpretation of a collective agreement? Do they in some way depend on rights created by such an agreement? See Scott v. Machinists Automotive Trades Dist. Lodge 190, 827 F.2d 589 (9th Cir.1987); Hull v. Central Transp., Inc., 628 F.Supp. 784 (N.D.Ind.1986). Would the threat of such actions inhibit an employer's acceptance of private arbitration? A supervisor's willingness to give candid testimony in the arbitration hearing? Could the Court fashion a qualified privilege for statements made during the investigation and processing of a grievance without totally preempting such causes of action under § 301?

6. *State Contract Law Actions.* Section 301 would seem to preempt any state law cause of action claiming a breach of a commitment made in a collective agreement. See, e.g., Smith v. Ameritech, 129 F.3d 857, 868 (6th Cir.1997) (preemption of state law claim that employer breached collective agreement by termination without just cause); Greenslade v. Chicago Sun–Times, Inc., 112 F.3d 853 (7th Cir.1997) (preemption of breach of contract claim based on alleged denial of procedures promised in collective agreement). Does *Lueck* also suggest that § 301 preempts a state cause of action asserted by a union-represented employee for violation of an implied-in-law covenant of good faith and fair dealing? See, e.g., Newberry v. Pacific Racing Assn., 854 F.2d 1142 (9th Cir.1988) (finding preemption).

What if the state law action, however, is based on written or oral or implied contracts or promises made by the employer with individual employees either before or during the term of a collective agreement covering the employees? Consider the *Lingle* Court's quotations from Caterpillar Inc. v. Williams, supra note 4, in footnote 10. In that case, the Court held improper the removal to federal court of claims based on alleged individual employment contracts because these claims were not "completely pre-empted" by § 301. The *Williams* Court explained:

> Caterpillar next relies on this Court's decision in *J.I. Case Co. v. NLRB*, 321 U.S. 332, 64 S.Ct. 576, 88 L.Ed. 762 (1944), arguing that when respondents returned to the collective-bargaining unit, their individual employment agreements were subsumed into, or eliminated by, the collective-bargaining agreement. Thus, Caterpillar contends, respondents' claims under their individual contracts actually *are* claims under the collective agreement and pre-empted by § 301.

> Caterpillar is mistaken. First, *J.I. Case* does not stand for the proposition that all individual employment contracts are subsumed into, or eliminated by, the collective-bargaining agreement. In fact, the Court there held:

>> "Individual contracts cannot subtract from collective ones, and whether under some circumstances they may add to them in matters covered by the collective bargain, we leave to be determined by appropriate forums under the law of contracts applicable, and to the Labor Board if they constitute unfair labor practices." 321 U.S., at 339, 64 S.Ct., at 581.

> Thus, individual employment contracts are not inevitably superseded by any subsequent collective agreement covering an individual employee, and claims based upon them may arise under state law. Caterpillar's basic error is its failure to recognize that a plaintiff covered by a collective-bargaining agreement is permitted to assert legal rights *independent* of that agreement, including state-law contract rights, so long as the contract relied upon is *not* a collective-bargaining agreement. *See Allis–Chalmers, supra.*

482 U.S. at 395, 107 S.Ct. at 2431. See also, e.g., Foy v. Pratt & Whitney Group, 127 F.3d 229 (2d Cir.1997) (no preemption of claims based on employer's promise to individual employees of further employment opportunities if they did not transfer); Trans Penn Wax Corp. v. McCandless, 50 F.3d 217 (3d Cir. 1995) (no preemption of claims based on promises of job security made to individual employees on eve of union decertification election). But see, e.g., Beals v. Kiewit Pacific Co., Inc., 114 F.3d 892 (9th Cir.1997) (distinguishing *Williams* as involving individual contracts for positions not covered by collective agreement); Darden v. United States Steel Corp., 830 F.2d 1116 (11th Cir.1987) (preemption of action based on promises made to plaintiffs while they were covered by collective agreement).

7. *Can the States Provide Union–Represented Employees an Alternative Procedural System for Consideration of Wrongful Discharge Claims?* Does the above quotation from the *Williams* opinion suggest that states could apply wrongful termination legislation to union-represented employees without regard to the provisions of a particular collective agreement? Could the states also provide their own enforcement mechanism—say, a system of industrial tribunals—for union-represented environments? These may be "minimum" employment rights that are "independent" of the labor agreement, but might their coexistence with such agreements effectively abrogate the union's exclusive role as contract maker and contract enforcer? On the other hand, need collective bargaining be undermined as long as the union maintains control of contractual benefits, including access to the grievance system established by the collective agreement?

Indeed, might the denial to union-represented employees of employment rights, including rights to invoke procedures otherwise generally available, threaten unions even more than a state's provision of alternative dispute resolution mechanisms? In *Livadas*, supra note 4, the Court also held that the NLRA preempted the California Commissioner of Labor's interpretation of California law to bar relief for the denial of promised wages to employees whose employment terms are set in a collective bargaining agreement containing an arbitration clause. The Court held that states cannot withhold benefits to employees who engage in conduct, like collective bargaining, that is protected and encouraged by the NLRA. Does *Livadas* mean that the states would have to offer union-represented employees the same procedures offered to other employees?

Note on Machinists Preemption

Footnote 8 in the *Lingle* opinion (not reprinted above) alluded to an additional labor law preemption doctrine, for which Machinists v. Wisconsin Employment Relations Comm'n, 427 U.S. 132, 96 S.Ct. 2548, 49 L.Ed.2d 396 (1976), is now cited as the leading case. In *Machinists,* the Court held that when fashioning the NLRA Congress intended to leave unregulated and "controlled by the free play of economic forces" certain employer and employee conduct, such as the partial work stoppages involved in that case. Id. at 140, 96 S.Ct. at 2552. The NLRA establishes a comprehensive system to define the types of economic weapons that labor and management can employ to achieve their often conflicting goals. State regulation of this economic conflict thus could "upset the balance of power between labor and management" expressed in federal law. Teamsters v. Morton, 377 U.S. 252, 259, 84 S.Ct. 1253, 1258, 12 L.Ed.2d 280 (1964) (holding Ohio cannot prohibit a type of secondary boycott neither protected nor prohibited by NLRA). See also Barnes v. Stone Container Corp., 942 F.2d 689 (9th Cir.1991) (claim under Montana wrongful discharge law was preempted by *Machinists* doctrine because employee was fired for unprotected activity during negotiation of a new collective agreement).

Most state law developments providing employees protection from unjust dismissals would not seem to threaten the NLRA's balance of power between labor and management, however. They guarantee employees certain minimum substantive rights rather than providing further protection for employees' efforts to extract better benefits from their employers. Of course, the state's grant of any desirable substantive right to employees makes bargaining easier for their collective representatives because it obviates extracting that particular benefit from employers. A pre-*Machinists* Supreme Court opinion, Teamsters v. Oliver, 358 U.S. 283, 79 S.Ct. 297, 3 L.Ed.2d 312 (1959), moreover, held that Ohio's antitrust law could not "prevent the contracting parties from carrying out their agreement upon a subject matter as to which federal law directs them to bargain." Id. at 295, 79 S.Ct. at 304. However, this language from *Oliver*—which could have substantially reduced the role of state employment regulation in the union-represented sector— was never developed by the Court in subsequent cases. See, e.g., Malone v. White Motor Corp., 435 U.S. 497, 98 S.Ct. 1185, 55 L.Ed.2d 443 (1978); Metropolitan Life Ins. Co. v. Massachusetts, 471 U.S. 724, 105 S.Ct. 2380, 85 L.Ed.2d 728 (1985). In *Metropolitan Life,* the Court held that a state could guarantee all employees within its jurisdiction minimum substantive benefits that would be subject to mandatory bargaining under the NLRA. The *Metropolitan Life* Court also challenged the *Oliver* dicta by declaring that it would not significantly advance the NLRA "to allow unions and employers to bargain for terms of employment that state law forbids employers to establish unilaterally." Id. at 755, 105 S.Ct. at 2397.

Do *Metropolitan Life, Fort Halifax,* and *Lingle* together represent a firm decision by the Court to permit states to choose the minimum substantive rights model of employment regulation, and thus set a "floor," however high, for collective bargaining? See Paige v. Henry J. Kaiser Co., 826 F.2d 857 (9th Cir.1987) (*Metropolitan Life* and *Fort Halifax* make clear that antiretaliation claims implied from state safety and health statute are not preempted by NLRA). Does *Livadas* suggest that the "floor" must be the same as that provided nonrepresented employees? See generally Arthur Herman, Wrongful Discharge Actions After *Lueck* and *Metropolitan Life Insurance:* The Erosion of Individual Rights and Collective Strength?, 9 Ind.Rel.L.J. 596 (1987).

Even if these cases preclude *Machinists* preemption of actions based on state laws providing minimum rights for all employees, do they necessarily preclude *Machinists* preemption of state law claims based on individual contracts inconsistent with collective agreements? The *Williams* Court expressly reserved this issue, noting that in state court "[t]he employer may argue that the individual employment contract has been pre-empted due to the principle of exclusive representation. * * *" 482 U.S. at 397. But see Harper, supra, at 740–43, for an argument against *Machinists* preemption of actions based on individual employment contracts.

†